THE OXFORD HANDBOOK OF

SENTENCING AND CORRECTIONS

THE OXFORD HANDBOOKS IN CRIMINOLOGY AND CRIMINAL JUSTICE

General Editor: Michael Tonry, University of Minnesota

THE OXFORD HANDBOOKS IN CRIMINOLOGY AND CRIMINAL JUSTICE offer authoritative, comprehensive, and critical overviews of the state of the art of criminology and criminal justice. Each volume focuses on a major area of each discipline, is edited by a distinguished group of specialists, and contains specially commissioned, original essays from leading international scholars in their respective fields. Guided by the general editorship of Michael Tonry, the series will provide an invaluable reference for scholars, students, and policy makers seeking to understand a wide range of research and policies in criminology and criminal justice.

OTHER TITLES IN THIS SERIES:

Crime and Criminal Justice
Michael Tonry

Crime Prevention
Brandon C. Welsh & David P. Farrington

Sentencing and Corrections
Joan Petersilia & Kevin R. Reitz

Crime and Public Policy
Michael Tonry

THE OXFORD HANDBOOK OF

SENTENCING AND CORRECTIONS

Edited by

JOAN PETERSILIA

KEVIN R. REITZ

OXFORD
UNIVERSITY PRESS

OXFORD
UNIVERSITY PRESS

Oxford University Press, Inc., publishes works that further
Oxford University's objective of excellence
in research, scholarship, and education.

Oxford   New York
Auckland   Cape Town   Dar es Salaam   Hong Kong   Karachi
Kuala Lumpur   Madrid   Melbourne   Mexico City   Nairobi
New Delhi   Shanghai   Taipei   Toronto

With offices in
Argentina   Austria   Brazil   Chile   Czech Republic   France   Greece
Guatemala   Hungary   Italy   Japan   Poland   Portugal   Singapore
South Korea   Switzerland   Thailand   Turkey   Ukraine   Vietnam

Published by Oxford University Press, Inc.
198 Madison Avenue, New York, New York 10016

www.oup.com

Oxford is a registered trademark of Oxford University Press

Library of Congress Cataloging-in-Publication Data
The Oxford handbook of sentencing and corrections / edited by Joan Petersilia, Kevin R. Reitz.
p.   cm.
Includes bibliographical references and index.
ISBN 978-0-19-973014-8 (cloth : alk. paper)
1. Prison sentences—United States. 2. Corrections—United States.
3. Criminal justice, Administration of—United States.
I. Petersilia, Joan. II. Reitz, Kevin R.
HV8708.O94   2011
364.60973—dc22   2011016855

1 3 5 7 9 8 6 4 2

Printed in the United States of America
on acid-free paper

Contents

....

Contributors

STEVEN BELENKO, Professor of Criminal Justice, Temple University

THOMAS G. BLOMBERG, Professor of Criminology, The Florida State University

GEORGE M. CAMP, Co-President, Criminal Justice Institute, Inc.

LT. GARY F. CORNELIUS, (retired) Fairfax Country (VA) Office of the Sheriff, Adjunct Faculty George Mason University

ANTHONY N. DOOB, Professor of Criminology, University of Toronto

ALEC EWALD, Associate Professor, Department of Political Science, University of Vermont

RICHARD S. FRASE, Benjamin N. Berger Professor of Criminal Law, University of Minnesota Law School

CRAIG HANEY, Professor of Psychology, University of California, Santa Cruz

RICHARD W. HARDING, Emeritus Professor, Crime Research Centre, University of Western Australia

KIMBERLY A. HOUSER, Research Associate, Department of Criminal Justice, Temple University

DAVID T. JOHNSON, Professor of Sociology, University of Hawaii

NANCY J. KING, Lee S. and Charles A. Speir Professor of Law, Vanderbilt Law School

THOMAS P. LEBEL, Associate Professor, Department of Criminal Justice, University of Wisconsin-Milwaukee

ROXANNE LIEB, Associate Director, Washington State Institute for Public Policy, Olympia, WA

KAROL LUCKEN, Associate Professor, Department of Criminal Justice, University of Central Florida

DORIS LAYTON MACKENZIE, Professor of Crime, Law and Justice, The Pennsylvania State University

SHADD MARUNA, Director, Institute of Criminology and Criminal Justice, Queen's University

JAMES L. NOLAN, JR., Professor of Sociology, Williams College

JOAN PETERSILIA, Adelbert H. Sweet Professor of Law, Stanford Law School

JILLIAN K. PETERSON, Graduate Student, Department of Psychology and Social Behavior, University of California, Irvine

KEVIN R. REITZ, James Annenberg La Vea Professor of Criminal Procedure, University of Minnesota Law School

EDWARD E. RHINE, Deputy Director, Office of Offender Reentry, Ohio Department of Rehabilitation and Correction

BETH RICHIE, Professor of African American Studies and Criminology, University of Illinois at Chicago

JULIAN V. ROBERTS, Professor of Criminology, University of Oxford

MICHAEL G. SANTOS, Prison Reform Spokesman, MichaelSantos.net

LAWRENCE W. SHERMAN, Wolfson Professor of Criminology, Director of the Jerry Lee Centre for Experimental Criminology, Director of the Police Executive Programme, University of Cambridge

JONATHAN SIMON, Adrian A. Kragen Professor of Law, Berkeley Law, University of California

JENNIFER L. SKEEM, Professor of Psychology and Social Behavior, University of California, Irvine

CHRISTOPHER SLOBOGIN, Milton R. Underwood Chair in Law, Professor of Psychiatry, Director, Criminal Justice Program, Vanderbilt Law School

CAROL S. STEIKER, Henry J. Friendly Professor of Law, Special Advisor for Public Service, Harvard Law School

JORDAN M. STEIKER, Judge Robert M. Parker Endowed Chair in Law, University of Texas School of Law

HEATHER STRANG, Deputy Director, Jerry Lee Centre for Experimental Criminology, Deputy Director, Police Executive Programme, University of Cambridge; Associate Professor and Director of Centre for Restorative Justice, Australian National University

FAYE S. TAXMAN, University Professor, Criminology, Law & Society, George Mason University

MICHAEL TONRY, Russell M. and Elizabeth M. Bennett Chair in Excellence, Director, Robina Institute of Criminal Law and Criminal Justice, University of Minnesota Law School

JEREMY TRAVIS, President, John Jay College of Criminal Justice

LATOSHA TRAYLOR, Doctoral Student, Department of Criminology, Law, and Justice, University of Illinois at Chicago

CHRISTOPHER UGGEN, Distinguished McKnight Professor, Chair, Department of Sociology, University of Minnesota

BERT USEEM, Professor of Sociology, Purdue University

CHRISTY A. VISHER, Professor of Sociology and Criminal Justice, University of Delaware

CHERYL MARIE WEBSTER, Associate Professor, Department of Criminology, University of Ottawa

ROBERT WEISBERG, Edwin E. Huddleson, Jr. Professor of Law, Faculty Co-Director, Stanford Criminal Justice Center, Stanford Law School

WAYNE WELSH, Professor of Criminal Justice, Temple University

RONALD F. WRIGHT, Professor of Law, Wake Forest University School of Law

FRANKLIN E. ZIMRING, William G. Simon Professor of Law and Wolfen Distinguished Scholar, Berkeley Law, University of California

THE OXFORD HANDBOOK OF

SENTENCING AND CORRECTIONS

SENTENCING AND CORRECTIONS: OVERLAPPING AND INSEPARABLE SUBJECTS

JOAN PETERSILIA AND KEVIN R. REITZ

THE volume that you hold in your hands is the comprehensive, multidisciplinary *Oxford Handbook of Sentencing and Corrections.* "Sentencing," defined narrowly, is the legal process by which criminal sanctions are authorized and imposed in individual cases following criminal convictions. "Corrections," also conceived narrowly, deals with the implementation, administration, and evaluation of criminal sentences after they are handed down. It is a mistake to insist upon myopic distinctions between the two fields, however. From a policy viewpoint, the two subject areas are inseparable. Sentencing judges have reason to hope, if not expect, that the theories and policies behind their sentencing decisions will be pursued during the corrections phase. A judicial sentence is a mere abstraction until given effect in the correctional context. Continuity across the two stages cannot merely be assumed, but requires coordinating effort. From a wide angle spanning both sentencing and corrections, it is evident that the determination of penalty in an individual case is almost never concluded in the courtroom. The sentence as experienced by an offender will depend on many later decisions, the availability and quality of correctional and treatment resources, the conditions of life and governance strategies of individual prisons and jails, and the tilt between enforcement and support philosophies in probation and parole. Spreading our vision more broadly still, sentencing and corrections are subject matters that live on even after criminal penalties are fully executed in individual cases, and offenders are released from the jurisdiction of the state. From a societal perspective, the downstream effects of sentences are what matter most to the public, including crime avoidance, victim and community restoration, and public confidence that the justice system acts with fairness, consistency, and proportionality when it punishes individual human beings.

This handbook examines the intertwined and multilayered fields of American sentencing and corrections from global and historical viewpoints, from theoretical and policy perspectives, and with close attention to many problem-specific arenas. The goals throughout are to present state-of-the art knowledge in specific subject areas, to investigate current practices, and to explore the implications of differing approaches wherever possible. All of our contributors have aspired to bridge the gap between research and policy—and were chosen because of their distinguished track records in doing so in their past scholarship. Individual chapters reflect expertise and source materials from multiple fields including criminology, law, sociology, psychology, public policy, economics, political science, history, and cultural theory. One narrative thread of the handbook is that problems of sentencing and corrections, writ large, cannot be addressed effectively with the toolbox of any one discipline.

The need for rigor and ambition in these fields has never been greater. It is now axiomatic to say that America's sentencing and corrections systems are in crisis. The weakening of the "rehabilitative ideal" and the shift toward more punitive practices in the 1970s through the 1990s led to an expansion of America's corrections populations unprecedented in this country, other parts of the world, or any historical time period. When the prison population count was released for year-end 2009, it revealed that the total number of Americans behind bars increased for the 37th consecutive year, touching off a fresh round of grim editorializing and national soul searching. America's prisons and jails now confine more than 2.3 million individuals on any given day—roughly one in every 100 adults—giving the United States the highest incarceration rate of any nation in the world. As a proportion of its population, the United States incarcerates five times more people than Britain, nine times more than Germany, and 12 times more than Japan (Bureau of Justice Statistics 2010; Walmsey 2009).

Prison and jail statistics are almost always recited in terms of snapshot, one-day counts. This conventional way of thinking misses the reality that the essential attribute of confinement as a criminal sanction is its *duration*—its reliance upon the dimension of time as a means to achieve punitive or consequential effect. Thoreau wrote that "the cost of a thing is the amount of . . . life which is required to be exchanged for it" (1854, 31). Pursuing this insight, figure 0.1 estimates the number of "person-years" of confinement meted out by decade in U.S. prison and jails since the 1960s (each unit is one year served by one inmate). The figure ends with a projection of the number of person-years that will be served across the decade 2010–2019, on the assumption that nationwide incarceration rates will remain stable at 2009 levels.

One thing that figure 0.1 demonstrates is that zero incarceration growth (were it to be achieved) upon the base of 2009 prison and jail populations is hardly the

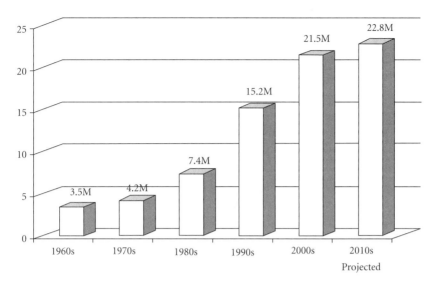

Figure 0.1. Person-Years of Incarceration by Decade in Millions. 1960s– (Projected).
Sources: Sourcebook of Criminal Justice Statistics Online, Adults on Probation, in Jail or Prison, and on Parole, United States, 1980–2009, Table 6.1.2009 (2011), http://www.albany.edu/sourcebook/csv/t612009.csv (prison and jail counts for 1980 through 2009); Margaret Werner Cahalan, Bureau of Justice Statistics, Historical Corrections Statistics in the United States, 1850–1984, at 76, table 4–l (1986).

stuff of pendulum swings. Social scientists and armchair statisticians alike are wont to view the absence of change as a non-event. But the persistence of historically high incarceration rates is an aggressive policy to import into the future. As the sixth bar in figure 0.1 reveals, 2010–2019 will be the most punitive decade in U.S. history— unless incarceration populations fall into decline. Without dramatic decreases, the current decade would still enjoy the distinction of being the *second* most punitive decade in American history.

Concern over mass confinement is inextricably bound up in questions of distributive justice. Racial and ethnic disparities in U.S. incarcerated populations are severe. Figure 0.2 compares white male and black male prison rates from 1880 to 2009. It is evident from these data that there has never been a meaningful civil rights movement in American prison policy. Since Reconstruction, black-white disparities in prison rates have always been pronounced, and they have generally grown over the past 130 years.[1] In 2009, an estimated 65 percent of all inmates in America's prisons and jails were either African American or Hispanic. Compared with a white male incarceration rate of 487 per 100,000 nationwide, the black male rate was 3,119 and the Hispanic male rate was 1,193 (Bureau of Justice Statistics 2010: app. table 14). This translates into a "disparity ratio" for black and white males of 6.4 to one, and a ratio of 2.4 to one for Hispanic and white males.

For the various dates shown on the chart, where reasonably reliable prison counts are available, the black-white disparity ratio went from 2.8:1 (1880), to 3.2:1 (1890), to 3.9:1 (1910), to 4.3:1 (1923), to 4.8:1 (1950), to 5.2:1 (1960), to 5.7:1 (1970), to 6.9:1 (1980), to 7:1 (1990), to 7.7:1 (2000), and a decline to 6.4:1 in 2009. While the recent decline in the disparity ratio is somewhat heartening, it is partly due to a

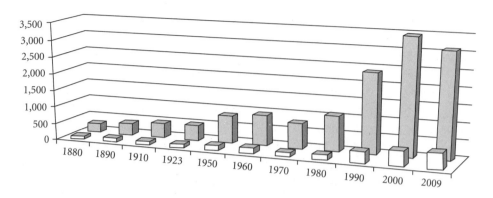

Figure 0.2. Prison Rates, White and Black Males, 1880 to 2009.

Sources: Bureau of Justice Statistics, Prisoners in 2009 (2010), p. 28, appendix table 14; BJS, Prisoners in 2000 (2001), p. 11, table 15; Bureau of Justice Statistics, Correctional Populations in the United States, 1995 (1997), p. 8, tables 1.8 and 1.9 (for 1990); Margaret Werner Cahalan, Historical Corrections Statistics in the United States, 1850–1984 (Washington, DC: GPO, 1986), p. 34, table 3–6; p. 65, table 3–31; Margaret Werner Cahalan, "Trends in Incarceration in the United States since 1880: A Summary of Reported Rates and the Distribution of Offenses," Crime and Delinquency 25 (1979), p. 40, table 11; U.S. Census Bureau, Census of Population (various years).

change in the way Hispanics and African Americans are counted in the national statistics, and likely overstates the change for the better (Tonry 2011, 32).

Yet to focus on disparity ratios misses most of the painful truth. The generally increasing ratios, worrisome as they are, grossly understate the impact of incarceration upon African American communitites. Not only has the black share of the imprisonment pie been going up over most decades, but, as noted in figure 0.1, the entire pie has been expanding even faster. Even if we accept that black-male-white-male disparities fell off from 2000 to 2009, the absolute black male imprisonment rate remains at nearly an all-time high—and roughly three times the rate of 1980.

Although there is much tragedy in the history of American criminal justice, and a sense that the lessons of the past are too often ignored, the most recent prison census signaled a possible turning point: the population of the nation's *state* prisons (excluding the federal system), which house more than 90 percent of all convicted felony offenders, decreased by nearly 3,000 inmates (down 0.2 percent). This was the first decline in the state prison population since 1972. In California, which has the nation's largest state prison system, with nearly 170,000 men and women incarcerated, the prison population fell for the first time in 38 years, and the Supreme Court in 2011 upheld an order for further significant reductions (*Brown v. Plata*). Texas, also historically an incarceration powerhouse, has likewise seen prison population declines, and has even had the novel experience of closing one of its prisons (Fabelo 2010; Ward 2011). The national prison population—including those held in federal facilities—grew at the slowest rate (0.2 percent) in the last decade (Bureau of Justice Statistics 2010). Some observers believe that we may be witnessing the beginning of the end of America's long commitment to what some critics call "mass incarceration" (American Civil Liberties Union 2011; Simon, chapter 1 of this volume).

A large part of the downturn is the fact that cash-strapped states are looking for ways to save money, and reducing the number of prisoners has a positive effect on the bottom line (e.g., Vera Institute of Justice 2010). Prisons are overcrowded and corrections absorbs increasing and significant resources—more than $60 billion in 2009. Second only to Medicaid, corrections has become the fastest growing general fund expenditure in the United States (Pew Center on the States 2009). The high cost to taxpayers is unsustainable, especially during times of economic instability. And despite the vast and increasing investment, the national recidivism rate remains high and virtually unchanged, with about half of released prisoners returning to jail or prison within three years (Bureau of Justice Statistics 2002). No one is surprised that most ex-prisoners reoffend. After all, most of those released from prison have serious social, medical, or mental-illness problems, and most of their needs will have gone unaddressed while they were in prison. Prisoners remain largely uneducated, unskilled, and usually without solid family support—and now they have the added stigma of a prison record and the distrust and fear that it inevitably elicits (Petersilia 2003).

The exceptional severity of American criminal justice is no longer an exclusively "liberal" issue. As the conservative editors of *The Economist* magazine declared, "No other rich country is nearly as punitive as the Land of the Free" (2010, 13). Prominent Republicans Newt Gingrich and Pat Nolan, on behalf of a coalition called "Right on Crime," have come to the view that, "There is an urgent need to address the astronomical growth in the prison population, with its huge costs in dollars and lost human potential" (Gingrich and Nolan 2011).

Budget cutters may leap at the chance to reduce corrections budgets, and liberal critics of "mass incarceration" may approve of any move that brings prison populations down, but all of the current flux will prove counterproductive if we act without giving serious thought to how we deal with the offenders who are convicted, sentenced, and eventually released. Progress in the short term is easily lost. Until recently, for example, Kansas appeared to be making great strides in innovative prison policy. In 2007, the state legislature increased funding to a range of reentry programs, including education, drug treatment, and subsidized housing. The approach appeared to work: the number of ex-offenders returning to prison dropped by 16 percent between 2007 and 2009. But then came the economic crisis and cutbacks in effective programming. According to Pat Colloton, a Republican member of the state's House of Representatives, recidivism rates quickly spiked. Kansas is back where it started from in 2007 (Yoder 2010).

To avoid throwing away much of the progress we have made in reducing crime, it is more imperative than ever to pursue alternatives to prison and new ways to ease inmates' reentry into civilian life. The good news is that after decades of false starts, researchers have finally begun to identify the things that can make a difference in at least some cases. Advances in the science of behavior change, the development of more accurate risk assessments, public support for prison alternatives, advances in supervision technology, strengthening of community supervision and reentry programs, and rethinking the application of the death penalty are all leading to some lessening of the earlier political demagoguery around crime policy. We have also recently begun to see that the public is less passionately in favor of prison and long sentences as solutions to the crime problem, especially because we now have less of a crime problem.

So how do we move forward? We have assembled the most gifted and accomplished scholars working in the fields of sentencing and corrections today, and their chapters discuss the large contextual issues of American punishment policy, the applied theories put to work in real-world settings, the institutional and procedural frameworks for penalty decisions, corrections agency operations and sanctions, the characteristics and needs of correctional populations, and the scientific literature identifying effective programs. Some of the authors have also written about their firsthand experiences of incarceration and release. The contributors provide a rich array of scholarly and practitioner insights into the potential and challenges of reforming American sentencing and corrections.

The first several chapters deal with macro-scale realities of American sentencing and corrections in the twenty-first century, including the nation's vast investment in prisons and jails, the appalling racial and ethnic disparities in criminal punishment, the proliferation of non-criminal or "collateral" consequences of contact with the justice system, and the rising importance of crime victims in the determination of sentences and the lengths of prison terms. Jonathan Simon opens this section with an examination of "mass incarceration," perhaps the most salient feature of American criminal justice policy in the late twentieth and early twenty-first centuries. He argues that the spatial and temporal borderlines of mass incarceration are still poorly understood, and its causes will be disputed for years to come. He sees the prison explosion as a uniquely American phenomenon, albeit with many regional, state, and local differences in its particulars. In Professor Simon's telling, the unbroken period of U.S. prison and jail expansion dating back to 1972 has reached its end in the 2010s, rendering mass confinement a "problem" to be solved—no longer anyone's ongoing policy or political objective. He cautions, however, that high incarceration rates will probably not fall dramatically in the near future, and that "the era has begun in which policy discussion seems likely to focus on managing the pathological processes unleashed by mass incarceration."

Alongside the sheer scale of imprisonment, the overrepresentation of racial and ethnic minorities in correctional populations is the most significant—and deplorable—reality of American criminal justice. One hundred years in the future, the twin dynamics of scale and disparity in punishment are likely to trouble historians of American criminal justice greatly—and together these subjects will pose profound questions about the moral compass of our era. Michael Tonry presents a fact-intensive indictment of the realities of race, crime, and punishment in the United States, with emphasis on the damage inflicted on African Americans by the "War on Drugs" started in the mid-1980s. Among Professor Tonry's prescriptions, none is more important than reducing the overall size of prison populations, which would provide far greater relief to minority communities than any other measure that might realistically be placed on the table. He also proposes a number of ways to attack the disparate treatment of African Americans, including a reconsideration of punitive drug enforcement strategies, attacks on "racial profiling" by the police, a searching reexamination of common sentencing factors that correlate with race, and the introduction of "racial disparity impact projections . . . as a routine element of consideration of proposed sentencing legislation."

An essential dimension of the expanding punitiveness of American law, but one that often goes under-noticed, is the gross accumulation of "collateral," or non-criminal, consequences that follow convictions—and sometimes are triggered by arrests or charges that do not result in convictions. These include such things as occupational and licensing bans, exclusion from public housing, termination of parental rights, ineligibility for student loans, voter disenfranchisement, and deportation. Alec Ewald and Christopher Uggen survey the broad and thorny field of "invisible punishments," including both legal consequences and practical impacts upon individuals, families, and communities. The combined effects of these collateral harms exceed that of the formal criminal sentence in many cases, and often endure for many years after a sentence has been served. Professors Ewald and Uggen observe that the cumulative weight of collateral consequences hinder the reentry of ex-offenders into the law-abiding community, and thus "fly in the face of theory and research on desistance from crime."

Seasoned criminal justice professionals often observe that the increased participation of crime victims in all stages of the criminal justice process has been one of the cardinal developments of the last 30 years. Yet a balanced jurisprudence of crime victims' role in public law has been slow to develop. Julian Roberts examines the legal settings for victims' inputs into both the judicial sentencing and parole release processes in the United States and other common law jurisdictions. He also surveys the empirical evidence of the effects of this participation, including enhanced victim satisfaction and—perhaps—changes in official penalty decisions to respond to victim preferences. While Roberts sees both a defensible rationale and some positive outcomes associated with victims' contributions to sentencing proceedings, he is far more critical of the commonplace practice of inviting or allowing victim input at the prison release stage. He writes that, "victim input has been shown to have an important effect on parole authorities and—if unrelated to the criteria for release—may threaten the integrity of parole decision making."

The next several chapters deal with the underlying theories of sentencing and corrections, not as philosophical abstractions, but with a close eye toward their actual application in contemporary criminal justice systems. Richard Frase begins the sequence with an in-depth discussion of sentencing "proportionality," or the problem of "making the punishment fit the crime." Proportionality constraints are regularly disregarded in many U.S. jurisdictions, where drug offenders can receive harsher penalties than murderers, and "three strikes" laws can mete out 50-year prison terms (with no good time or parole) for the theft of six videotapes (*Lockyer v. Andrade* 2003). Professor Frase argues that proportionality can supply meaningful limits upon punitive severity, but the concept must be fleshed out in both retributive and utilitarian terms. His utilitarian "ends-benefit" and "alternative-means" forms of proportionality are original and important contributions to the field of sentencing theory—but are also developed to capture how real-world decision makers think about actual cases. Professor Frase surveys existing systems that exemplify the "hybrid proportionality model" he recommends, including the much-lauded Minnesota sentencing guidelines system, concluding that "[t]he application of . . . these proportionality constraints has allowed Minnesota to retain one of the lowest per-capita incarceration rates in the nation."

The subject of rehabilitation theory in action is taken up by James Nolan, who evaluates the success of "therapeutic jurisprudence" in the setting of problem-solving courts such as drug courts, mental health courts, domestic violence courts, and community courts. He reviews the development of these specialty courts in the United States and other countries, and finds many fundamental differences in approach. He contrasts the enthusiasm and high utilitarian expectations (even "boosterism") in the United States with the restraint and modest harm-reduction goals often seen in other countries. Professor Nolan cautions that, as in the high rehabilitation period of the 1960s, U.S. advocates may be overselling the successes of problem-solving courts while worrying too little about the procedural sacrifices required of defendants, and the prospects of unintended net-widening. He notes more generally that American policy makers are unfailingly eager to export their own programs and ideas, but are not equally inclined to draw upon the experience of other nations. He urges that, "Americans could perhaps do well to learn about, and perhaps follow the example of, some of the legal-cultural qualities of the other countries considered here."

Next, Cheryl Webster and Anthony Doob mount a frontal attack on one of the mainstays of deterrence theory: that increased severity of punishments will yield greater general deterrence of criminal acts (the "deterrence through severity" or DTS thesis). DTS would seem an inarguable truth from the economic view of human behavior, because it is a raising of costs relative to benefits—and intuitive faith in DTS drives criminal justice policies in force today in a number of countries, notably the United States and Canada. Professors Webster and Doob meticulously canvass the empirical evidence, with closest attention to studies since 1990, and find a "repeated lack of support for DTS policies" demonstrated across multiple methodologies, units of analysis, types of sentencing laws, and objects of study. They urge that the same critical scrutiny applied to rehabilitation theory in the 1970s should now be brought to bear on deterrence, and write that "the continued centrality of [DTS] as a sentencing objective constitutes a false promise, contributing to a waste of resources and a reduction in the public's confidence in the criminal justice system, while encouraging policy makers to ignore more effective crime control strategies."

The grail of "selective incapacitation" has been part of the debate of prison policy for several decades, but became tarnished in the 1980s due to demonstrated weaknesses in prediction technology, especially when attempted in the roughshod environment of real criminal courthouses. In recent years, however, substantial improvements in the actuarial tools used to predict serious criminal behavior have once again thrust the subject forward to the cutting edge of policy discussions. As

Christopher Slobogin observes of today's practices, "about half the states make some use of formal risk assessment instruments in the sentencing or post-sentence process." This number will almost certainly grow in the coming years. Professor Slobogin performs a close and skeptical examination of available risk assessment methodologies, the empirical research into their validity, and the legal and ethical issues surrounding their use. He ends in ambivalence: "Risk assessment is only likely to be sufficiently and knowably accurate if it is based on actuarial instruments, but it is only likely to avoid constitutional, justice, and fairness objections if it relies on demonstrably less accurate unstructured clinical judgment that eschews use of demographic information and other immutable traits." He proposes several policy alternatives, including the use of risk assessment only as a prison-diversion tool (as it is currently used in Virginia), or the elimination of the consideration of risk from sentencing and corrections decisions altogether.

The most fully realized new framework for criminal sanctions to arise in the past 30 years is the restorative justice theory (or RJ), which posits that the goal of criminal sentences should be to repair the damage done to victims, families, and communities by criminal acts, and to restore the offender to a productive life. RJ seeks to engage the positive effects of personal accountability (literally in person, when offenders engage with their victims), remorse, empathy, and forgiveness. While it is an optimistic theory of human psychology and emotion, Lawrence Sherman and Heather Strang argue that RJ has been subjected to rigorous empirical testing beyond that applied to the more traditional sentencing purposes. Their survey of the relevant research (including their own famous studies) shows positive outcomes for both offenders and victims in a number of settings, and suggests that—contrary to conventional wisdom—RJ innovations may be at their most effective when used in cases of serious offending. Along with a close consideration of RJ, this chapter presents a compelling exegesis on the meaning and implementation of an "evidence-based" sensibility in sentencing and corrections.

The next four chapters focus on the processes and institutional structures for sentencing decisions in America, spanning topics from courtroom rules of procedure to the institutional design of entire sentencing systems. The pressing questions include: Who holds decisional power (or "sentencing discretion") in a given jurisdiction, and subject to what constraints? Ronald Wright opens this section with an examination of claims that prosecutorial charging and plea-bargaining discretion is a form of sentencing power—and, indeed, that de facto prosecutorial authority eclipses that of judges to fix penalties in some sentencing systems. Professor Wright finds these assertions largely true of American legal systems, and increasingly true elsewhere in the world. Criminal case processing in the United States, he writes, has come to rely on "the methods of modern administrative government." He complicates the picture, however, by insisting that defendants must be included as independent agents in any model of plea bargaining in action, because they possess substantial bargaining power vis-à-vis the government. He also concludes that sentencing guidelines systems tend to enlarge prosecutors' power, but that "judicial discretion still has an important effect on the sentences imposed and served, even after a system adopts guidelines." On the future policy horizon, Professor Wright argues that attempts to create external legal controls on prosecutorial discretion have proven inadequate, and that greater emphasis should be placed on the development of "internal control mechanisms," such as "office structures that require more collaborative decisions, periodic review of the prosecutor's work, regular training of prosecutors to enhance skills and promote consistency, and articulated office policies."

Next, Kevin Reitz focuses upon the traditional American "indeterminate" sentencing systems, still used in roughly half the states, in which parole boards hold the lion's share of authority over the lengths of most prison terms. While prosecutorial power is exerted at the "front end" of the case-processing chronology, parole-release discretion is concentrated at the "back end." Professor Reitz argues that the traditional indeterminate systems have been under-studied in the last 30 years, when most researchers of systemic design have turned their attention to various sentencing "reforms," including sentencing guidelines and "determinate" systems (that remove the parole board's power over prison release). He finds that the traditional structures are far more diverse and complex than commonly supposed. He outlines what we currently know about these systems, and documents some of the differences across systems, but concludes that we have no basis upon which to form policy judgments of "worse" or "best" practices. He argues that a new field of "indeterminate sentencing studies" is needed to understand how best to design and administer indeterminate sentencing structures, and to inform the question of whether indeterminacy ought to remain a viable policy option for American governments.

In the late twentieth century, the sentencing guidelines model, with guidelines created by a nonpartisan sentencing commission, emerged as the major systemic alternative to the traditional U.S. indeterminate sentencing scheme. Robert Weisberg traces this movement from the seminal work of Marvin Frankel (who first proposed the sentencing commission) to the present, when roughly half of the states and the federal system now work with sentencing commissions, judicial sentencing guidelines, or both. Ironically, as Professor Weisberg points out, the federal system has been the most visible commission-guidelines system on the American scene—but also the least successful and most derided of those systems. Federal policy makers work with unique national and symbolic politics, a disorganized criminal code, and—most importantly—the absence of tight budgetary pressure on corrections that is felt by every state. By most measures, the state commission-guidelines systems have been far more successful, and certainly less controversial, than the anomalous federal system. Professor Weisberg argues that a "consensus system" among lawmakers and academics has developed at the state level over the past 30 years, and explores this theme with reference to specific systems in Minnesota, Missouri, North Carolina, Pennsylvania, Utah, and Virginia. He offers criteria for evaluation of guidelines reforms, including reductions in crime and recidivism, lowering incarceration rates, reducing racial and ethnic disparities, increasing the system's cost-efficiency, and promoting evidence-based sentencing practices. Overall, Professor Weisberg concludes that the commission model "represents legislators' commitment to restrain their own tendencies to generate politically charged and often wasteful sentencing policies and instead to treat sentencing as a regulatory matter that warrants cost-benefit rationality in the first place."

Nancy King closes the section on legal architecture with a disturbing examination of the procedural rules that attend judicial sentencing decisions across the United States. She observes that there is a near void of constitutional law applied to criminal sentencing (other than the death penalty). Due process safeguards that the Supreme Court has recognized for criminal trials, and the constitutional requirements for capital sentencing proceedings, have seldom been extended to noncapital sentencings. For example, proof beyond a reasonable doubt is not mandated at the vast majority of sentencings—nor is any particular evidentiary standard, and the burden may even be placed on the defendant for some kinds of sentencing factors; formal rules of evidence are not in force; defendants have no right to confront witnesses against them; discovery rights are undeveloped; double jeopardy protections simply evaporate; exclusionary rules for unconstitutionally obtained evidence are inapplicable; sentencing judges need not state the reasons for their decisions; and most jurisdictions make no provision for meaningful sentence appeals. Most striking of all, perhaps, the Supreme Court has ruled that sentences in most U.S. courtrooms may be based on uncharged offenses and even crimes of which defendant has been acquitted. Professor King analyzes the relatively new constitutional holdings of *Blakely v. Washington* and *United States v. Booker*, based on the Due Process Clause and Sixth Amendment jury trial guarantee, and concludes that these cases affect only a narrow subset of the nation's sentencing cases. The general absence of constitutional regulation, in Professor King's telling, has had a number of important effects. Most fundamentally, sentencing process is almost entirely a sub-constitutional domain for legislatures and rule-makers. Second, great pressure has been placed on the "trial-sentencing distinction," because legislatures may shift fact-finding from trial to sentencing in order to relieve prosecutors of the burdens affixed to guilt determinations. Third, even the weak procedural protections that exist at sentencing may be bargained away by the parties. For example, federal prosecutors routinely require defendants to waive their rights to appeal sentence in order to obtain plea agreements.

Next, the handbook offers a series of chapters on community sanctions, jails, and prisons, followed by focused discussions of assessment efforts across the correctional landscape. Professors Karol Lucken and Thomas G. Blomberg present an overview of America's corrections system, tracing its unique history and offering observations on what led to the massive prison buildup. Interestingly, incarceration of lawbreakers was meant to be a humane alternative to the two options used at the end of the eighteenth century—corporal and capital punishment. Through work and penitence, offenders in prison would be rehabilitated and returned to society. But now, 200 years later, Lucken and Blomberg conclude, "What appeared to be true on paper was not always true in practice." The system tried to adapt, and an assortment of prison alternatives were invented, including work release, halfway houses, home confinement, sex offender civil commitment, and other variously named sanctions. Today, America's correctional system reveals a complex of strategies and mostly failed interventions, or according to the authors, "reform without change." Lucken and Blomberg believe that the core of the problem are the inconsistencies in ideology and practice, which create a system that is not only volatile and contradictory but "regressive and oscillatory." The burgeoning corrections system will not be controlled until these underlying systematic issues are addressed and balance is brought back to sentencing. The authors suggest that a well-balanced justice system can be achieved by better utilizing scientific and criminological knowledge.

Professor Faye Taxman's chapter comprehensively reviews what we know about community-based correctional supervision, that subfield of corrections in which offenders are supervised and provided services outside jail and prison. Offenders on probation and parole outnumber those in prison by nearly three to one, those in jail by over seven to one. More than 7 million Americans are under some form of correctional control, and four-fifths of them are not in prison or jail; they are on probation or parole or in another community-based program. Surveying topics that are often misunderstood and neglected, Professor Taxman reviews the history, supervision conditions, programs, and recidivism rates of persons on probation and other intermediate sanctions. Here, too, the story is one of unfocused mission, ever-changing goals, and system overcrowding. Community supervision has been characterized by an increasing number of supervision conditions being placed on probationers, accompanied by greater monitoring of those conditions. Yet, the research reviewed by Taxman suggests that the value of added conditions during supervision does not seem to have a deterrent effect. And, given that increased conditions tend to result in more technical violations, the consequences for prison overcrowding have been significant. Taxman identifies a set of core principles, which if implemented correctly, *can* reduce recidivism. She believes that such evidence could shift the current preference for punitive policies, arguing that, "The gains from punishment are limited, whereas the gains from evidence-based community corrections systems are unlimited."

Lieutenant Gary F. Cornelius brings a practitioner's perspective to the wholly important and understudied subject of America's jails. Lieutenant Cornelius, retired from the Fairfax County (Virginia) Office of the Sheriff after serving as an administrator for over 27 years in the Fairfax County Adult Detention Center, describes how local jails were developed, how they are managed in today's overcrowded environment, and how they are struggling to deliver programming to inmates and public safety. Crowding in jails has created the same pressure-cooker effect as it does in prisons, and Lieutenant Cornelius discusses how the system has been impacted and has coped. Topics include the evolution of the mega jail, the changing nature of the inmate population and its implication for jail security, the growing importance of privatization, and how prison crowding has reduced the ability to deliver programming. Lieutenant Cornelius suggests that, due to successful litigation and national standards, jails—once the stepchild of the American corrections system—are entering a new frontier characterized by greater professionalism and leadership.

As the number of inmates has grown, so too has the need for strong leaders to oversee programs and regulate jail and prison conditions. George M. Camp, a seasoned correctional manager, and Professor Bert Useem, a nationally recognized scholar on prison management, write about the complex challenges of operating safe institutions. They note the importance of public support in the funding, mission, and regulation of America's prisons, and discuss how crowding has exacerbated prison challenges. Contrary to expectations, expanding prison populations have not caused more riots. In fact, there has been a steep drop in the number of prison riots. The authors attribute the decline in prison disturbances to a more professionalized workforce, accreditation of facilities, and judicial intervention.

One domain in which many America governments fall short, and where worldwide experience may supply salutary models for reform, is the maintenance of humane conditions of life within massive prison and jail systems, and the provision of opportunities for rehabilitation to those incarcerated. Richard Harding's chapter examines in detail the "patchwork" of mechanisms used to regulate prison conditions, comparing those in the United States and elsewhere in the world. He stresses that "the U.S. regulatory framework is almost entirely disconnected from international standards." Instead, it relies on the relatively weak (and arguably weakening) regulatory tools of "judicial intervention on grounds of constitutional law, and prison accreditation by a private organization of corrections professionals." In contrast, Professor Harding reports on the more rigorous prison inspectorate systems used in the United Kingdom and Western Australia, and the inspection regimes promoted by the European Committee for the Prevention of Torture and Inhuman or Degrading Treatment or Punishment (the CPT), and the United Nation's Optional Protocol to the Convention against Torture and other Cruel, Inhuman or Degrading Treatment or Punishment (OPCAT). While acknowledging that each society must find its own solutions, Professor Harding concludes that "international comparisons establish beyond dispute that autonomous visits-based inspections of prisons and other closed institutions comprise an essential tool in any package of mechanisms for regulating prison conditions."

Does the U.S. corrections system rehabilitate criminals? Does it provide education, vocational education, or substance abuse programming that helps people become more productive members of society? This is perhaps the most challenging question in corrections, and the next two chapters address it. Steven Belenko, Kimberly Houser, and Wayne Welsh review the evidence on the effectiveness of drug and alcohol treatment, and Doris MacKenzie reviews the evidence on vocational, educational, and work programs. Both chapters identify and discuss the emergence of a body of literature identifying evidence-based treatment practices and principles. If these principles are used with the right client group (selected through risk and needs assessments), recidivism can be reduced. The reductions in recidivism aren't huge (on the order of 5 to 15 percent), but they are cost-beneficial and result in public safety gains that are worth the investment. Both chapters also end with a recommendation for continued rigorous program evaluations, and they also urge caution, noting that successfully implementing and sustaining effective treatment require careful attention to the systems, organizations, and staff factors that affect implementation.

One of the major themes running throughout the Belenko et al. and the MacKenzie chapters is that not all offenders are alike, and effective treatments must match the "right program with the right offender. " As corrections populations have risen, so too has the prevalence of three groups of offenders who present unique challenges: persons with mental illnesses, females, and sex offenders. Jennifer L. Skeem and Jillian K. Peterson vividly describe how persons with mental illness increasingly find themselves caught up in the corrections system, and how their unique (usually unmet) needs translate into significant management problems for corrections agencies. As Skeem and Peterson discuss, the deinstitutionalization movement of the 1970s served to move the mentally ill out of state hospitals and into the community. The hope was that a community-based approach, with programs, medication, and the necessary supports, would replace institutionalization. But these supports never materialized, and former patients often failed to take their medications. Many persons with mental illness become unemployed and homeless, and abuse alcohol and drugs—and many are eventually recycled in and out of corrections. But Skeem and Peterson write that we know a great deal about how to identify and effectively treat persons with mental illness, and the public seems increasingly sympathetic to providing services to the nonviolent mentally ill who can be supported in the community.

We then reserve a number of chapters for consideration of specific offender populations and sets of experiences, including sex offenders, female offenders, juveniles, and the most serious violent offenders. Roxanne Lieb, one of the nation's foremost experts on sex offenders, traces the evolution of punishment policies toward sex offenders, and notes the difficulty of devising management and treatment and surveillance strategies when sex offenders define such a broad group. Her review of the treatment literature is not particularly promising for more serious sex offenders, as the interventions tried so far have not reduced reoffending, although they seem to reassure the public. LaTosha Traylor and Beth Richie write about the ever-increasing number of females in corrections and the need for gender-based programs, both inside prisons and on the outside. Drug offenses seem to account for the great increase of women in corrections, and their prior life experiences (often characterized by physical and sexual abuse) make treatment more challenging. Nonetheless, Traylor and Richie describe several innovative programs addressing the needs of imprisoned females, particularly mothers and their children.

Of course, corrections is more than the sum of its programs (or lack thereof). State prisoners will spend, on average, about two and a half years in confinement. That period might be beneficial to some inmates, who choose to participate in programs or use the time for personal reflection and growth. But for others, the pains of imprisonment take a horrendous personal and psychological toll. These inmates will return to society more socially isolated, embittered, and unable to successfully reintegrate. The next two chapters discuss these issues in detail. No one knows the pains of prison more completely than Michael G. Santos, a federal prisoner who wrote his chapter from behind prison walls. Mr. Santos has been confined in federal prison since 1987 due to a cocaine conviction, his first offense. His chapter provides a graphic description of life inside prison and illustrates how American prisons perpetuate a cycle of failure. Professor Craig Haney, an expert on the psychological impact of prison confinement, would agree with Mr. Santos. His chapter argues that our justice system suffers from structural and legal flaws that causes pain to the imprisoned and ultimately increase crime. Adapting to prison means exposure to overcrowding, violence, and sexual assault, which ultimately cause personal and social problems that prevent successful reintegration. Mr. Santos and Professor Haney make clear that what happens in our prisons eventually spills out into our communities.

Next, the handbook turns to the critical problems of the reintegration or reentry of ex-offenders into the community. In 2010 alone, more than 700,000 people will leave prison and return home. The next three chapters focus on prisoner reentry: the process of leaving prison and returning to free society. Edward E. Rhine, a scholar and respected correctional administrator, traces the dramatic changes that have occurred in parole release and supervision over the past 25 years. The majority of prisoners are now released "mandatorily," without appearing before a parole board with discretion to set their dates of release. How parole boards make these decisions, and the implications those decisions have for parole agents, the culture of supervision, and public safety, are clearly articulated. Thomas P. LeBel and Shadd Maruna describe the increasingly difficult realities of transitioning from prison to the community. Using narratives from people who have struggled with the transition, LeBel and Maruna highlight the importance of creating and supporting programs that promote family and community bonding. People need to be given an opportunity to redeem themselves and start over. Christy A. Visher and Jeremy Travis have spent the last decade studying the needs of prisoners returning home, and they show once again that rehabilitation is not dead. Communities around the country have implemented prisoner reentry programs over the past decade, and the knowledge is now strong enough to identify principles of effective programs. The authors urge the research community to engage in interdisciplinary, longitudinal studies of prisoner reintegration, using multiple outcome measures, so that we may better understand the full effects of recent social policies.

The final two chapters focus on the nation's ultimate penalty, death, which has been falling into decline, and its near equal in severity: the ever-more-popular sanction of life without parole (or LWOP). Carol S. Steiker and Jordan M. Steiker examine the long and unsuccessful project of regulating the death penalty through constitutional law (denounced, late in their careers, by Justices Powell, Blackmun, and Stevens, and for decades by Justices Marshall and Brennan). The constitutional jurisprudence has been beset since the 1970s by the incompatible aims of individualized sentencing and the quest for consistency in the legal standards used for selection of those defendants to be put to death. The Professors Steiker call into question whether capital-punishment regimes, in place in three-fourths of the U.S. states, are ever likely to meet basic concerns of fairness in process and outcome.

They report that enormous problems of politicization, racial discrimination, jury confusion, underfunded defense services, erroneous convictions of the innocent, and inadequate enforcement of federal rights have proven impervious to reform. They conclude that, "The basic preconditions for an adequately administered regime of capital punishment do not currently exist in the United States and cannot reasonably be expected to be achieved."

The death penalty is not an isolated phenomenon, unattached to other legal practices. Franklin E. Zimring and David T. Johnson observe that, while state execution is a tiny numerical part of the American sentencing landscape, it nonetheless "casts long shadows over the principles and practice of criminal justice generally." They argue that the availability of the death penalty has contributed to distortions in the substantive law of homicide and the "penal inflation" of extraordinarily severe non-capital punishments in the United States—particularly the increased use of prison terms of life without parole. Indeed, many death penalty abolitionists have embraced the use of LWOP sentences in efforts to displace capital punishment, but this has resulted in an unintended explosion in the use of LWOP—far out of proportion to any moderating effect on the use of the death penalty. Professors Zimring and Johnson argue that this trade-off has "provided moral camouflage for a penalty . . . which is almost as brutal as state killing." More generally, the long-running controversy over capital punishment has drained enormous energy, attention, and resources that otherwise might have been focused on reforms elsewhere in the system. Professors Zimring and Johnson observe that "In any developed nation there are only a limited number of lawyers with the political values and special skills required to defend against governmental excess in the prohibition of conduct and the punishment of crime. . . . [W]hen most of these fine lawyers are concentrating on the 3,500 capital defendants on death row in the United States, the result is a shortage of resources to monitor state authority in a nation with more than 2 million persons behind bars."

On one level, each chapter in the handbook paints a portrait of a sentencing and corrections system in crisis, with programs and policies often driven by politics rather than evidence about whether they work. Individuals cycle in and out of an increasingly expensive system with most of their needs left unmet. The challenges of reintegration can appear insurmountable. Yet each chapter also draws upon emerging scientific and experiential knowledge pointing to a better way. One perverse "advantage" exists for criminal justice reformers of the twenty-first century: Because the system has become so overgrown, and is dysfunctional in so many ways, there are myriad opportunities to make changes that will improve the lives of thousands of individuals. Even incremental deflections of how things are done in American sentencing and corrections, if in a beneficial direction, can have outsize rewards in how human lives are lived and how our communities cohere. We hope that readers will study these chapters closely and will consider their recommendations because, as a whole, they build the foundation for a sentencing and corrections system that is more humane, less expensive, and ultimately more effective than the one we now have.

NOTE

....

1. The prison rates reported for 2000 and 2009 do not correct for changes in the way that the U.S. Department of Justice counts blacks, whites, and Hispanics, instituted in the mid-1990s (Frase 2009; Tonry 2011). The changes had the effect of reducing the reported black and white imprisonment rates because Hispanic prisoners were for the first time disaggregated from both the black and white totals.

REFERENCES

....

Cases

Brown v. Plata, 131 S. Ct. 1910 (2011).
Lockyer v. Andrade, 538 U.S. 63 (2003).

Other Sources

American Civil Liberties Union. 2011. *Smart Reform is Possible: States Reducing Incarceration Rates and Costs While Protecting Comunities*. New York: American Civil Liberties Union.

Bureau of Justice Statistics. 2002. *Recidivism of Prisoners Released in 1994*. Washington, DC: U.S. Department of Justice.

Bureau of Justice Statistics. 2010. *Prisoners in 2009*. Washington, DC: U.S. Department of Justice.

Fabelo, Tony. 2010. "Texas Justice Reinvestment: Be More Like Texas?" *Justice Research and Policy* 12: 113-131.

Frase, Richard S. 2009. "What Explains Persistent Racial Disproportionality in Minnesota's Prison and Jail Populations?" In *Crime and Justice: A Review of Research*, ed. Michael Tonry, Vol. 38: 201–280.

Gingrich, Newt, and Pat Nolan. 2011. "Prison Reform: A Smart Way for States to Save Money and Lives." *The Washington Post*, January 7, 2011.

Petersilia, Joan. 2003. *When Prisoners Come Home: Parole and Prisoner Reentry*. New York: Oxford University Press.

Pew Center on the States. 2009. *One in 31: The Long Reach of American Corrections*. Washington, DC: The Pew Charitable Trusts.

The Economist. 2010. "Rough Justice: America Locks Up Too Many People, Some for Acts That Should Not Even Be Criminal." *The Economist* (July 24, 2010): 13.

Thoreau, Henry David. 1854. *Walden*. 1971 ed., J. Lyndon Shanley, ed. Princeton: Princeton University Press.

Tonry, Michael. 2011. *Punishing Race: A Continuing Dilemma*. New York: Oxford University Press.

Vera Institute of Justice. 2010. *The Continuing Fiscal Crisis in Correction: Setting a New Course*. New York: Vera Institute of Justice.

Walmsey, Roy. 2009. *World Prison Population List*, 8th ed. London: International Centre
    for Prison Studies.
Ward, Mike. 2011. "As Prison Closes, Could Others Be Next?" *American Statesman*, August
    11, 2011. Available at: http://www.statesman.com/news/texas-politics/as-prison-closes-
    could-others-be-next-1730178.html.
Yoder, Steve. 2010. "Crime and the Governors." *The Crime Report*, October 27, 2010.
    Available at: http://www.thecrimereport.org/archive/crime-and-the-governors/.

PART I

SENTENCING AND
CORRECTIONS:
HISTORY AND
PRESENT
CONTEXT

CHAPTER 1

....

MASS INCARCERATION: FROM SOCIAL POLICY TO SOCIAL PROBLEM

....

JONATHAN SIMON[1]

INTRODUCTION: THE BIRTH OF A SOCIAL PROBLEM

....

In the winter of 2004–2005, as Arnold Schwarzenegger took over as governor of California following the recall of the previous governor, he pronounced the state's mammoth, litigation-strapped, and catastrophically overcrowded prison system to be in a state of crisis, denounced its penal philosophy of "warehousing" inmates, and declared the parole system that had long returned the vast majority of its charges to prison "broken." By the time you read these words, such statements may not seem unusual; indeed, they may be on their way to becoming a new "common sense" of high crime societies (Garland 2001a). But in California, they were words that had not been spoken by anyone in leadership for more than a quarter century. Like other states, California participated in a remarkable expansion of imprisonment by the states and federal government, resulting in current populations on average more than four times the relative portion of the population imprisoned at the end of the 1970s. Sustained by periodic upswings in reported crime, and by non-stop media and political attention to the threat posed by criminals, America became the global leader of what has come to be called (primarily by its critics) "mass incarceration." By calling the system "broken" and by admitting that warehousing felons could not create public safety for California communities, Governor Schwarzenegger, in effect, declared the era of "mass incarceration" over.

From the early 1980s, California governors, and most serious aspirants for the office of both parties, uniformly embraced expanding imprisonment to more categories of crimes and for longer sentences. It was an exercise in which the entire political establishment participated with at least eighty "substantive increases in sentencing" since the enactment of the state's Determinate Sentencing Law in 1976 (Little Hoover 2007, Appendix F, p. 68).[2] While California's imprisonment rate today places it slightly below the national average, that status belies the significance of the change since 1980 and the role of Southern states with their racially marked and historically high imprisonment rates in setting the national average. Looked at as its own region, California in 1980 was just slightly higher in imprisonment rate than the Northeast, below that of the next most lenient Midwest, and at just 50 percent of the high Southern imprisonment rate. In 2005 California was significantly higher than either than the Northeast or the Midwest and at 84 percent of the Southern norm (Sourcebook of Criminal Justice Statistics Online 2008, Table 6.29.2008). In other words, between 1980 and 2005, at least as a penal state, California went from being a progressive Midwestern state, say Michigan or Minnesota, to being a Southern state.

This transformation was led from the top by California governors. Moreover, these governors embraced incarceration in terms that would come to epitomize the excesses of "mass incarceration," not as a targeted strategy to rehabilitate or incapacitate individuals, but as deliberate strategy to raise imprisonment rates a quantum level by mandating imprisonment for entire categories of crimes.[3] No one better articulated this philosophy than Governor George Deukmejian (1983–1989). In his concluding State of the State address in 1990, the conservative Republican pointed with pride to his enormous expansion of prisons:

> In 1983, California had just 12 state prisons to house dangerous criminals. Since then, we have built 14 new prison facilities. That has enabled us to remove an additional 52,000 convicted felons from neighborhoods to send them to state prison. (Simon 2007, 158)

The intent of mass incarceration as a policy is wonderfully transparent here. The state has "removed" people from "neighborhoods" and sent them to "state prison"—end of story. There is no pretense that this will effectuate change among those imprisoned; it will only provide security through removal and custody in prison.

The logic of mass incarceration also typified the 22 new prisons that California built between 1983 and 2000 (Gilmore 2008). Penal complexes more than prisons, the new prisons typically held more than 1,500 prisoners in a variety of custody levels. All of them were located far from the large cities where most prisoners come from (and where most treatment professionals reside). Most were designed with housing as the major priority, without workshops or much space designed for educational or rehabilitative programming. More shockingly, as recent court cases have documented, these prisons were designed without providing even minimally adequate space for the delivery of medical care. This shocking record of failing to imagine the prison as anything but a site of punitive segregation has produced an equally alarming projected cost of $7 billion to bring prison health care facilities up to a minimal constitutional standard (Rothfeld 2008). It is this fiscal pressure that is bringing mass incarceration to a day of reckoning in California.

While California's prisons remain unsustainably overcrowded, and the legal machinery that has kept filling prisons remains largely intact, no California governor after Schwarzenegger will be able to treat building and filling prisons as a generic and promising solution to the ubiquitous social problems facing California communities (from urban blight to teen pregnancy). Instead, in a surprising but now undeniable way, mass incarceration has become itself, like crime a generation ago, a serious social problem.

There are a number of signs indicating that the impending end of the era of mass incarceration is a broader phenomenon, extending well beyond the State of California:

1. After decades of being an issue largely invisible outside criminological circles, mass incarceration and its consequences (especially racial disproportionate incarceration rates) have begun to be identified as a major problem that needs solving by a growing number of foundations (see, e.g., Pew 2008), civil society organizations, and even some members of the United States Congress. In 2009, Senator Jim Webb, a former Republican turned independent minded Democrat, representing Virginia, one of the most punitive states in the nation, started a subcommittee on the disproportionate impact of incarceration (Webb 2007).
2. The Great Recession that began in 2008 has seen state legislatures across the country considering ways to responsibly trim correctional budgets and lessen the impact of future sentencing on state budgets (PEW 2009).
3. After a period of relative neglect, the number of academic and trade books devoted to over-incarceration has soared.
4. State prison populations have begun to decline for the first time since 1972 (Pew 2010).

The closing of the era of mass incarceration does not necessarily suggest a rapid reduction in state or federal prison populations. While the political expectations necessary to continue expanding incarceration seem to be weakening, the forms of identity and routine action that have been framed around the problem of violent crime during the ramping-up period of mass incarceration (1975–1995) are likely to be with us for some time, easily mobilized to check efforts at reform in the name of protecting potential victims. It does, however, provide an appropriate vantage point to begin looking back and taking stock of just what mass incarceration was, what produced it, and what it means to us going forward.

Scholars have debated whether mass incarceration was more of a policy (Blumstein 2000), or more a kind of politics, albeit democratic or pathological (Zimring

2000; Stuntz 2002). The answer is that it was surely both, and perhaps more importantly, it was a "political rationality" (Foucault 1977; Rose, O'Malley, and Valverde 2006), that is, a way of for a whole generation or two of politicians and citizens to imagine the conditions of public safety, and to act strategically on people, institutions, and practices for the purpose of protecting the public from violent crime (Simon 2007).

Was mass incarceration ever a policy, as such? As David Garland (2001b) pointed out, no actual politician ever campaigned on growing the prison population many times over. Fewer still would accept the notion that incarceration as practiced has been indiscriminate.[4] But while no one advocated the level of expansion that we have at present, there were of course both academic and political exponents of expanding imprisonment (more prisons for more people) beginning in the 1970s and reaching broad political support in the 1980s and 1990s (Wilson 1975; Bennett et al. 1996). From the perspective of that period, say 1975 to 1980, U.S. imprisonment rates remained rather modest by historical standards, while violent crime levels remained well above the (possibly inaccurate) norms of the early 1960s.

Perhaps the most famous and influential policy accounts in favor of more incarceration were Gary Becker's (1968) article on the economics of crime, and James Q. Wilson's (1975) book, *Thinking About Crime*. Both made the case that high crime rates proved that the "price" of crime, that is, punishment, was too low, and that better crime prevention was likely to be produced by raising the cost of crime. Both Becker and Wilson argued that raising the costs of crime could be achieved either by raising the punitive price for the crime (the sentence length) or raising the certainty of being caught and convicted (integral to the real "price" of the crime in economists' terms). For a variety of reasons, Wilson, an expert on police, advocated longer prison sentences as the better way to raise prices.[5]

In the remaining sections of this chapter we examine the journey of mass incarceration from policy to problem through a variety of dimensions:

- First we will consider what might be called the "analytics" of mass incarceration: How should we understand its temporal and spatial dimensions? Temporally speaking, is mass incarceration a singular unitary project that began in the late 1970s (when the familiar chart of American imprisonment rates begins to noticeably rise) and continued through the 1990s (Garland 2001a; Simon 2007; Wacquant 2009)? Or is better seen as a multistage development in which quite different governmental projects launched by quite different elements of government aggregated toward a common end (or high incarceration rates) (Zimring 2000; 2005). When we seek to explain this development (however conceptualized), should our explanations look primarily to the developments of the 1970s and 1980s that occurred proximately to the rise in rates? Or do the origins of mass incarceration lay farther back in history? If in history, should we look back to the 1960s (Simon 2007), or part of a longer running relationship between American governance and crime control that dates back at least the problem of lynching in the late nineteenth century (Gottschalk 2006)?

- The spatial distribution of mass incarceration has also been an important issue. Is mass incarceration to be seen as primarily a U.S. phenomenon, determined by its distinctive national political and social factors? Or, is mass incarceration a global phenomenon emerging from the political economic factors shaping many countries around the world, and some, for example, the United Kingdom and the United States, in particular? In contrast, is even a national story of mass incarceration too macro and abstract, since most prisoners in the United States are subject to state laws and penal policies, so that the vital transformations necessary to a change in the scale of imprisonment must be tracked down at the state or possibly even the county level (Lynch 2009a)?
- A third analytic dimension is institutional. Which specific practices and or organizational factors were critical in producing mass incarceration? Presidents and national politicians and their role in signaling the political productivity of crime have been the focus of many of the first studies (Beckett 1997; Gottschalk 2006). Later accounts often add a focus on the state level, and the role of governors and legislatures, law enforcement agencies, prosecutors, and correctional unions in shaping the legislation that actually authorizes greater numbers of prisoners to be held for longer terms (Simon 2007; Lynch 2009b; Schoenfeld 2010; Page 2011). Other accounts have stressed the importance of local actors, especially county-level prose- cutors who have seen an unremitting expansion of their authority over the last several decades (Simon 2007; Weiman and Weiss 2009).
- Having attempted to assess the nature of the phenomenon for which we are seeking an explanation, we will next review macro- and medium-range accounts of mass incarceration that emphasize competing (or possibly complicit) factors, including the cultural sensibilities of high crime, neolib- eral economic and political adjustments, the war on drugs, correctional Keynsianism and a correctional industrial complex, a backlash to the victories of the civil rights movement, a response to the increasing sense of moral fragmentation in society, fear of crime, and crisis of legitimacy and trust in government.
- In conclusion, the chapter considers signs of an emerging policy/politics field around the problem of mass incarceration.

CONCEPT OF MASS INCARCERATION

The phrase "mass imprisonment" was coined by David Garland (2001b) in 2000 to describe the distinctive expansion of imprisonment in the United States between 1975 and the late 1990s. To Garland, mass imprisonment constituted a new regime

of penality that differed along two dimensions from varying policies of imprisonment in use by modern societies since the end of the eighteenth century. First, U.S.
imprisonment rates in the late 1990s marked a substantial departure from historic
norms for the scale of imprisonment during the twentieth century by several
magnitudes (Zimring and Hawkins 1991). Second, in contrast to a history of using
imprisonment against individuals based on crime and criminal history, contemporary mass imprisonment reflected a "systematic imprisonment of whole groups
of the population" (Garland 2001b, 2; Feeley and Simon 1992).

The conceptualization of mass imprisonment has been adopted by many other
contemporary criminologists (Western 2006; Clear 2008). It has also been criticized
on a number of grounds. For some, the term is inherently political rather than scientific, embodying a normative perspective on the social value of contemporary imprisonment. For others, the concept falsely implies that the risk of incarceration is evenly
distributed in society, while it is clear that some demographic categories, particularly
African American and Latino males, especially those without high school graduation, are incarcerated at dramatically higher rates than similarly situated whites
(Wacquant 2009). Loic Wacquant has argued that the term "hyper incarceration"
could better capture the dramatic change in the scale of imprisonment without im-
plying a false equality of incarceration risk. However, the term "mass imprisonment"
need not be misleading, and it captures an important degree to which incarceration
risk has been generalized. While African American and Latino males may be incarcerated at rates many times the level of their white peers, the latter face incarceration
rates unprecedented historically or in other countries. Other institutions that have
been described as "mass," including the military or higher education, also have distinctive demographic patterns of stratification.

A more telling criticism might be that mass imprisonment is not as new as
criminologists have sometimes described it. The imprisonment of African Americans by Southern states after the Civil War, in what has come to be known as the
"convict lease system," involved historically high rates of imprisonment (for African
Americans) along with a concentration of the sanction on a specific group (African
Americans) (Ayers 1985; Lichtenstein 1996).

In this chapter, I adopt the term, modified to "mass incarceration." The distinction between imprisonment and incarceration is that the latter includes pre-trial
detainees and shorter-term inmates held in jails (what would be called "remand"
prisoners in Europe). In order to facilitate cross-national comparison, I use "incarceration" to indicate the wider expansion of state custody in response to crime
(except where I am referring to the experience of U.S. states and have imprisonment
specifically in mind).

This new penality, in additional to its categoric and gigantic scale, has largely
abandoned the focus on rehabilitation in favor of punitive segregation intended to
achieve deterrence and, more reliably, incapacitative effects. In addition, the form of
imprisonment that has become common in many states is far more heavily securi-
tized than ever (Zedner 2009). Prisons, naturally, have always been concerned with
security, but the current regime places security not only above but in place of most

other considerations, including rehabilitation but also sanitation, medical hygiene, and mental health (non-trivial inputs to security). In many states, classification, once the central technology of penal modernist hopes for individualized treatment, has become exclusively concerned with security. One distinctive marker of this approach is the "super-max," or security housing unit, style of prison building and control regime in which inmates are typically subjected to 23-hour-a-day lockdown inside technologically controlled isolation cells (Shalev 2009; Reiter 2010).

TEMPORALITY

Most of the theoretical discussion of mass incarceration in the United States (Garland 2001a; Gottschalk 2006; Simon 2007; Wacquant 2009) and even some of the more empirical examinations (Western 2006) have tended to treat the rise of incarceration rates from 1975 to the present in the United States as a rather continuous phenomenon, even as they may disagree on the relevant temporal sequence factors giving rise to the growth of imprisonment. Franklin Zimring has been the leading analyst arguing for important discontinuities, not simply between states but in the overall driving factors of penal growth across the states (Zimring 2000; 2005).

Zimring identifies three distinctive phases. The first, from the late 1970s through the mid-1980s, was driven by local prosecutors who began to use existing sentencing laws and the plentiful prosecutorial discretion already available under existing law to send more and more marginal felons to state prison rather than jail or probation. The second phase, from the late 1980s through the mid-1990s, saw the fulcrum of increasing imprisonment turn to drug offenders, who were the focus of increasing action by Congress (this was the moment of the infamous five-year minimum mandatory sentence for possession of five grams or more of crack cocaine, compared to more than 500 grams of powder cocaine) and state legislatures to give prosecutors yet more discretion to seek longer prison sentences, and stripping courts of the power to exercise leniency by setting mandatory minimums. The third phase, beginning in the late 1990s, driven largely by Congress with acquiescence from state legislatures, consisted of laws locking long sentences in place by eliminating or reducing the scope of early release mechanisms allowing subsequent shortening of prison sentences beyond minor amounts, or permitting very substantial sentence enhancements for offenders with previous felonies (most notoriously California's "three strikes" law) (Zimring, Hawkins, and Kamen 2003). As Zimring points out, the first two phases were not driven by secularly increasing crime, but at least required the persons to be convicted of new crimes before becoming subject to new, enhanced prison sentences. In the third phase, existing laws were made to bite more punitively against existing crimes and criminal records. As a result, prison populations and imprisonment rates continued to rise throughout the 1990s, despite a nationwide crime decline that was among the most robust in U.S. history (Zimring 2007).

In addition to the temporality of the penal boom itself, scholars of mass incarceration have differed over the temporal sequence of causation. Some approaches focus most intensively on the 1960s and 1970s, as a period in which the place of punishment within the larger political and bureaucratic field was reshaped by the larger crisis of postwar liberalism that played out most visibly in the 1980s (Garland 2001a; Simon 2007; Wacquant 2009). Others have argued that it is myopic to place so much emphasis on the immediate context of the penal turn. They argue that the nineteenth-century past, a time when a politicization of crime and law enforcement became part of American political culture (Gottschalk 2006), laid the groundwork for periodic efforts to govern through crime, of which the current era of mass incarceration is only the most extensive.

SPATIAL DIMENSIONS

Initial analyses tended to treat the United States as a singular unit and to speak largely in terms of the growing imprisonment rate of Americans as if the prison system were a unified legal and administrative unit, instead of a compilation of 52 distinctive systems (Zimring and Hawkins 1991). More recently, however, studies of mass incarceration have distinguished between different states, regions, and in some cases have treated mass incarceration more broadly as a spatial phenomenon in which not only the number or size of prisons is interpreted, but where they are, where their inmates come from, and which sorts of spatially specific interests are served by mass incarceration (Gilmore 2007; Lynch 2009a; Schoenfeld 2010; Page 2011).

State and Regional Variation Within the United States

Research on interstate differences has pointed to a number of factors that may drive that variation (to be discussed below), but more recent work has stressed specific patterns among states and regions. One spatially variable dimension that has been recently studied is political culture. Vanessa Barker (2009) studied the construction of penal policy in three states, California, Washington, and New York, representative of high, low, and medium states in terms of incarceration growth. Barker argued that distinctive forms of political participation in each state was a key factor in determining how much the state participated in building mass incarceration. Barker attributes Washington's relatively low growth in imprisonment rates to the state's traditions of intense public participation in the form of commissions, grand juries, and other local vehicles of self-government. New York, which during the years Barker studied experienced growing incarceration, though not as radically as states like California, has a highly centralized structure of decision making and some tradition of a more insulated and expert-based approach to penal policy (albeit with significant gestures toward punitiveness). California, which Barker profiles as an example of high imprisonment growth, is a populist regime in which there is little trust in government, but participation is limited to the plebiscite form of ballot initiatives.

Mona Lynch's recent study of Arizona's journey into mass incarceration (2009a) suggests that the "Sunbelt" states from Florida through Arizona and Nevada, which have experienced high levels of internal migration since the 1950s based on climate, lifestyle, and economic growth related to tourism and real estate, share a distinctive path into the punitive turn. Unlike the pattern depicted in David Garland's (2001a) now classic account of the change in which a highly politicized and punitive penal field emerges out of a crisis of confidence in the peno-correctional modernist approach that had dominated penology, Arizona had no lengthy embrace of rehabilitation and not even a correctional administration of any bureaucratic heft. Indeed, the state's brief experiment with rehabilitation in the 1970s, which produced a Department of Corrections, helped to move the state away from a commitment to low-cost, punitive, but parsimonious and cheap penal justice. After a prolonged struggle with the federal courts and prisoners' rights lawyers over conditions inside Arizona prisons, the state's political class committed itself to a rapid expansion of prison space that would transform Arizona into one of the most punitive states in the nation, with one of the highest rates of incarceration.

Globalization

Although the U.S. imprisonment rate increase between the late 1970s and the 2000s remains the defining example of mass incarceration, there is less agreement on its status as a global policy. In the *Culture of Control*, David Garland (2001a) focused on the United States and the United Kingdom but suggested that the same turn in penal policy might follow in other countries as they experienced the same social and economic conditions of late modernity (especially the loss of state capacity to manage economic risk). Critics of Garland pointed to the huge gulf between U.S. and UK incarceration rates (Zimring 2001), yet most analysts agree that the United Kingdom is closer than any other European nation to mass incarceration and that its incarceration rate has grown markedly since the late 1990s.

Cavadino and Dignan (2006) extend Garland's analysis, suggesting that the United States and the United Kingdom represent a broader pattern of neoliberal governance, which they associate with mass incarceration. Other countries that retain distinctive political economies (when contrasted with the pro-market approach of the English-speaking countries) follow different and distinct patterns—including the "Nordic socialist" path of Sweden and Norway, the "conservative corporatist" path of Germany and France, and the "oriental corporatist" approach of Japan—seem likely to avoid mass incarceration.

Loic Wacquant (2009) suggests that mass incarceration is part of a tool kit of neoliberal governmental techniques for managing populations rendered marginal and superfluous by economic change that is actively marketed around the globe by a class of carceral entrepreneurs who have also pushed policies like "zero tolerance" policing that complement and feed mass incarceration. Tim Newburn and Trevor Jones (2007) studied the U.S./UK relationship to see if something like "policy transfer" had taken place. Their qualitative analysis of UK policies and decision makers suggested that U.S. models were important, but only in terms of their fit with values that British elites were independently anxious to push—sometimes, as in the case of private prisons, resulting in a very different pattern from that of the United States (where private prisons remain a much smaller portion of overall imprisonment).

INSTITUTIONS

Mass incarceration at its core requires an enormous expansion of prison space and the legal authority and political will to send a far higher proportion of criminal suspects to prison than in the past. When it comes to exploring which institutions are responsible for mass incarceration, for example, legislatures, prosecutors, or crime victims' advocacy groups, there are two dimensions of causation that should be explored: which institutions carried the flag for expanding incarceration; and which institutions might have been expected to resist mass incarceration, or at least diffuse, delay, and diminish it (Roche 2007). As Franklin Zimring notes about "tough on crime" legislation (a frequent suspect):

> [E]ven when legislation providing for large change becomes law, the usual pattern
> is for the substantial discretion of executive and legislative branch agents to
> moderate the extent to which mandated changes happen. (Ziming 2005, 328)

Studies of the punitive turn in the United States and a growing body of studies based on Europe point to a wide range of institutional features of legal and political systems that may render it more or less prone (either positively through affirmative efforts, or negatively, through the absence of robust opposition or veto). Michael Tonry's (2007) metaphor of risk factors is an apt one. The presence of one or two may mean little, and even the concentration of a great number of them may mean little in the absence of significant social factors like rising violent crime rates or high levels of immigration.

Knowledge and Power in Penal Decision Making

One of the most influential comparative studies of mass incarceration identified the overall degree of institutional insulation of penal decisions (both at the systemic and individual level) from actors subject to political pressure and potential penal populism. Savelsberg's (1994) "Knowledge, Domination and Criminal Punishment," compared the United States, the advanced country in the mid-1990s that had experienced the most incarceration growth in the world, with Germany, the advanced country with one of the most stable and low incarceration rates. Savelsberg pointed to the flow of knowledge and power around penal decisions, identifying Germany as a country where penal decisions were generally highly insulated from public attention and intervention by politically accountable actors. The United States, in contrast, generally permits penal decisions to be made by elected local officials with full exposure to the general public and the media. This insulation allows German penal decision makers to use expert criteria to remain focused on modern correctional objectives like reintegration. Its absence in the United States means that populist concerns tend to infiltrate penal decisions, and the overall objectives of the system have taken on a punitiveness that has a populist rather than rationalistic quality (indeed, it has been usefully described as "populist punitiveness" (Bottoms 1995).

In the United States, this decision maker is almost everywhere a local elected official who represents a territorial community in the exercise of the power to punish. As David Garland and others have argued, the populist character of the U.S. administration of justice is extended by the fact that so many other elected officials can claim to have some role in setting policy on the toughness of punishment, including legislators, governors, attorney generals, as well as mayors, and at the national level, the president, the attorney general of the United States, and all of the members of Congress. This can set up a dynamic of competition between prosecutors and politicians over who is more committed to public safety and punitive justice (Simon 2007).

Savelsberg's study raises the question of whether these institutional factors matter as much as the presence or absence of a public mobilized around crime, which the United States had in the decades leading up to the 1990s but which Germany lacked, at least at the time of Savelsberg's study. It is possible that institutional insulation would "burn off" rapidly in the face of "hot" public sentiments around crime (Loader and Sparks 2010). Recent studies of European national experiences with penal policy and politics suggest that most retain a considerable degree of insulation that has, in fact, allowed them to avoid mass incarceration despite the emergence of a stronger level of crime fear politics. In Belgium, for example, a very significant victims' rights movement developed in the 1990s through public outrage over numerous law enforcement errors showcased in the trials of a serial killer who raped and murdered girls and women while on parole for another violent crime. Despite that movement, imprisonment rates have stayed rather stable because a consensus-oriented government among the mainstream parties has targeted some increases in imprisonment at violent crime and sex offenses, while balancing the population effects through efforts to reduce imprisonment for other crimes (Snacken 2007; Roche 2007).

Right-wing Party Domination and Party Competition

Another risk factor emphasized by political scientists is partisan competition. This should be distinguished from (both empirically and in theory building) the degree to which "conservative" or "right-wing" parties predominate in a state or nation's legislative or executive branches. Where party competition is routinely intense, we would expect that competition over the relative "toughness" of incarceration policy might produce legislation driving mass incarceration (especially when harnessed to ready prosecutors). In contrast, the right-wing theory suggests that where right-wing parties dominate, they will find in crime an effective lever to appeal to voters whose interests would otherwise not find resonance in right-wing platforms. Empirical work on American states finds a significant effect on imprisonment for partisan competition, especially in the context of executive elections (for state governor). Right-wing domination is also positively associated with increased imprisonment (Jacobs and Helms 2001; Smith 2004).

Qualitative work on Europe highlights the degree to which patterns of party competition can modify and mediate the potential for politics to generate populist pressure for punitive expansions of imprisonment. In Belgium (Snacken 2007), centrist parties coalesced around moderate increases in punishment to take the crime issue away from an excluded right-wing party. In the Netherlands (Downes 2007), however, party competition went along with a policy choice to significantly expand imprisonment.

Others have argued that mass incarceration is more of a compromise between right-wing and left-wing parties in the United States (Simon 2007). Right-wing parties may have benefited more conspicuously from the narrative terrain of crime and punishment (or law and order) than left-wing ones, but the crisis of liberalism that coincided with the war on crime in the United States presented enormous opportunities for conservatives to gain the narrative upper hand in American politics, and it is far from clear that crime was the most advantageous of them. Moreover, crime as a social problem can be mobilized by both Right and Left to support their policy preferences. The fact that mass incarceration resulted from the war on crime, rather than, say, a tremendous expansion of police and police powers, is not clearly linked to right-wing ideologies, which often have problems with growing large state institutions (Lynch 2009a).

Proximity of Government to the Reality of Crime

While the analysis of knowledge and power might predict that national control over penal policy would provide a buffer against populist pressures for penal severity that would be felt more strongly if undertaken at the local level (cities and counties), an important line of empirical work suggests that the contrary may be true (Scheingold 1992; Miller 2008). Political science research on the formation of policy suggests that decision makers are more likely to demonize around crime where they are at a distant remove from the on-the-ground reality of high-crime neighborhoods (Scheingold 1992). In the United States, both federal and state lawmakers tend to hear nearly exclusively from professional law enforcement (and a few professional defense organizations) (Miller 2009). Only at the local city or county level do lawmakers tend to hear from people representing high-crime communities (Miller 2009). This may be related as well to the finding that states with higher levels of participation in their political culture may be less prone to mass incarceration (Barker 2009).

Prosecutorial Discretion

The United States has historically been distinctive in the power accorded locally elected executives to determine the extent of punishment to which a criminal defendant is exposed, limited primarily by the discretion of juries, judges, and post-sentencing administrative release procedures (parole). Logically we might expect the rise of imprisonment to be linked to increases in the degree of prosecutorial discretion to determine who is likely to go to prison and for how long, or decreases in countervailing institutional checks on that discretion. Both trends have been true in varying degree across U.S. penal systems. Mandatory minimum sentences laws that became popular for drug and other offenses in the 1980s and 1990s removed discretion from judges to set a lower sentence or probation. Other statutes aimed at juveniles charged with violent crimes, mostly adopted in the 1990s, gave prosecutors discretion to file charges in adult court for juveniles charged with certain violent crimes, instead of having to seek a judicial "waiver" (Feld 1999). The plummeting of parole release rates in some states and the abolition of discretionary parole release in others have choked off the capacity of state governments to release prisoners earlier than their maximum sentence (Rhine, chapter 26 of this volume).

Talk of prosecutorial discretion, however, may risk normalizing what has actually been an important shift in the incentive structure of risks and rewards in which penal decisions are made. The rise of the prosecutor has been underwritten by legislators who are able to reap electoral rewards for laws that promise to solve broad social problems by handing more powers to prosecutors (Stuntz 2001). Those laws inadvertently give to county-level elected officials the power to fill state institutions, and spend state dollars for which they are in no way accountable (Zimring and Hawkins 1991).

Sentencing and Parole

Many observers have pointed to changes in law and policy concerning sentencing and release from prison (the latter is often called parole in the United States) as a likely culprit behind mass incarceration (Parenti 2000; Mauer 1999). There are a number of plausible features to this relationship. Sentencing reform was indeed a major topic of legislative discussion and sometimes action in the period proximate to and during the buildup of imprisonment (Feeley 1983). The formal features of some sentencing reforms, including a variety of "determinate sentence" systems, as well as "guidelines" systems, seem to fit the logic of mass incarceration with their shift away from individualized sentencing toward the more categoric application of the law. Likewise, some of the states undergoing sentencing reform explicitly rejected rehabilitation as a dominant objective of prison, either replacing it with "punishment" (as California famously did) or reducing it down to one among a laundry list of penal purposes. In at least one widely publicized example, the reform of the Federal sentencing system, a rehabilitative system based on an administrative system of release within long sentence ranges based on prospects for rehabilitation was replaced by a system of fixed sentences set through the application of complex guidelines with the intentional result that the federal prison population began a rapid rise. But research on sentencing guidelines in states suggests that there is no necessary relationship here, with some states that utilize guidelines, like North Carolina, Minnesota, and Washington, being among those with the least significant increase in imprisonment during the relevant period (Reitz 1998). The U.S. Sentencing Commission, which drafted the first set of federal guidelines and regularly revises them, expressly acknowledged that the first edition of the guidelines would result in a substantial increase in imprisonment, an outcome the Commission took to be substantively beneficial (Tonry 1993).

California's 1976 Determinate Sentence Law is another good example of how complex the relationship between sentencing and prison population trends can be. The law expressly embraced "punishment" as the purpose of prison, but largely to limit the overreach that rehabilitation seemed to permit the state (Messinger in Zimring and Frase 1980). The initial sentence ranges established were remarkably lenient by contemporary standards. They were intended to maintain rough stability in the length of actual time served in prison while removing the uncertainties unleashed by the indeterminate sentence and its complex game of parole release (Rothman 1980). Prison population in California rose precipitously during the years when sentences remained historically lenient as prosecutors sent marginal felons to prison rather than probation (Zimring 2005). Determinate sentencing, as in California (which lacks a sentencing commission), permits the highly politicized legislature to make all sentence range decisions directly. Over time, new sentences were revised upward as a new legislative politics of penal severity took over, which added to growth of imprisonment, and the inflexible nature of the determinate sentencing system made it impossible for administrative mechanisms to be used to moderate prison population growth (Danksy 2009).

The abolition of parole is often pointed to as a singular cause of growth. In tone and direction, it seems consistent with mass incarceration. However, comparative study across the states has not shown a strong relationship with parole release abolition and prison growth (Sorensen and Stemen 2002). In California, which did abolish parole release for most prisoners (lifers aside) in the Determinate Sentence Law of 1976, mass incarceration did follow, but until recently, when parole policies have had an impact on the prison population through the buildup of long-serving lifers, the most important consequence of the California approach to parole was not the elimination of discretionary release but the fact that parole supervision continued as a requirement for virtually all released prisoners. This policy exposed tens of thousands of former prisoners to the risk of being returned to prison for minor crimes or technical violations of parole (Simon 1993; Petersilia 2003). The California parole approach, combined with a political policy of proactively incapacitating felons, led to the nation's highest recidivism rate and is the primary institutional problem identified by experts and judges in the intense litigation over California's prison overcrowding.

Criminology

One factor that may cut against the development of mass incarceration as either policy or politics is the existence of a robust community of criminological experts who play a role in establishing penal policy. The latter part of that description seems particularly significant because no contemporary nation has a more developed scientific criminology sector than the United States, and no contemporary nation has pursued mass incarceration with a similar vigor. Yet U.S. criminology has had a largely subordinate role to politically established crime policy (Zimring, Hawkins, and Kamin 2003). In the United Kingdom, the Netherlands, and Germany, criminological influence over penal policy through the central government might appear over the long run to have had a moderating influence on imprisonment.[6] Yet other European nations with relatively stable prison populations have developed criminological expertise late or not at all (e.g., Belgium, France) (Roche 2007; Snacken 2007).

BROADER EXPLANATIONS

While Tonry's risk factors approach is extremely attractive and offers a good framework for comparative penological work across nations and histories, a variety of more comprehensive efforts have tried to make sense of the emergence of mass incarceration as policy and/or politics, mostly in respect to the United States, in some cases as a more global development. These accounts, especially those that have emerged since 2001, include considerable overlap, but with different emphases. One way to observe these overlaps and differences is to array the various explanations of mass incarceration from explanations grounded primarily in the social or cultural to those grounded primarily in the political. In between are accounts that focus on the emergence of neoliberalism as a political-economic order. These perspectives might also be arrayed in terms of their theoretical axis, with social and cultural explanations drawing explicitly or implicitly on Emile Durkheim's (1997) account of punishment and social solidarity; the political accounts drawing on Michel Foucault's account of punishment as a political technology (1977); and the economic accounts drawing on Marxist theories of punishment and labor markets (Rusche and Kirchheimer 1939). Once again, almost all of these major accounts address culture as well as political economy, and draw on the rich theoretical legacy of social theory on punishment (Garland 1990).

High Anxiety Societies

The legal scholar Francis Allen (1981) may have been the first to tie the shifting logics of punishment in the United States to a declining level of confidence in social values and solidarity. In his pathbreaking book *The Culture of Control* (2001), David

Garland developed a much broader and more complex picture of transformations in the life world of the middle class from the 1970s on, especially the growing need for two incomes and the suburbanization of the middle class, which broke up traditional familial and community resources for overseeing children. The significant and visible increases in violent crime experienced in the United States, the United Kingdom, and elsewhere around the world during these years helped galvanize and frame a "common sense" of social threat.

Garland does not argue that this anxiety alone, or mixed with real or imagined crime increases, was enough to uproot more than half a century of penal modernism and stable prison populations. Instead, he suggests that the crisis of public confidence associated with the growing anxiety confronted a state increasingly disabled from using its major mid-century tools of welfare and regulation by the demands for deregulation and tax cutting coming from resurgent global capitalism. Meanwhile, Garland shows that the demoralization of liberal elites both in the penal field and in the broader bureaucratic and political fields left the major principles of correctional modernism undefended. It is this combination—public anxiety, a state whose sovereignty can no longer be effectively deployed through social welfare mechanisms, and a demoralized penological community—that made penal welfarism so vulnerable to the rhetoric of "tough on crime" and the reality of more and harsher prison sentences.

Thus, while we have mentioned Garland here as the exemplar of a cultural sensibility–based theory of mass imprisonment, his broad account includes all three perspectives, including the political-economy constraints that neoliberalism places on the post-industrial state, and the role of a new politics built around crime fear, outrage, and demands for tough exclusionary sanctions.

Other social theorists have also emphasized the role of the new anxieties associated with the last quarter of the twentieth century and the experience broadly of globalization and postmodernity (Young 1999; Bauman 2000). In the face of profound disturbances in societal consensus values, mass incarceration may serve as a way to symbolically manage risks that can no longer really be managed by the modern infrastructure of governance. Others have argued that the cultural change is more of a cyclical swing between control and freedom (Tonry 2004)

Racialized Threat and Animus

Many observers have noted the proximity between the apparent triumph of the civil rights movement in the late 1960s and the rise of "law and order" politics and rhetoric. The disproportionate incarceration of minorities has in many respects nullified the legal equalities achieved by federal legislation in areas like voting and equal employment opportunity (Uggen and Manza 2002; Pager 2009). In 1968, for example, the Civil Rights movement reached its modern peak with the adoption of the Civil Rights Act of 1968, the last of the great federal civil rights statutes adopted in the 1960s, but also enactment of the Omnibus Crime Control and Safe Streets Act of 1968, which kicked off the modern war on crime (Simon 2007). Was the national mobilization around crime some kind of backlash or at least a response to the pro-found changes in social order and values marked by the legislative triumph of civil rights? Has the sustained commitment to expanding imprisonment since the 1970s reflected an ongoing unease by white residents (and voters) with the absence of visible markers of racial subordination in law or social custom, an unease exacerbated in many respects with the rise of non-white immigration to the United States since the 1970s (De Giorgi 2006; Tyler and Boeckmann 1997)?

As we will discuss below, there is also a political analysis of how civil rights and crime reconfigured the political order, but the backlash/response account emphasized here is distinctly Durkheimian insofar as it views punishment as a response to the perception that the social order is being challenged, not simply by crime, but by the absence of barriers to racial equality or to immigration. This reaction to racial change may reflect two distinct but related dynamics, both of which have found support in somewhat different literatures. One well-known account that has received strong empirical support is the "racial threat" (Jacobs and Helms 2001; Crawford, Chiricos, and Kleck 1998) or the "racial animus" (Unnever and Cullen 2010), which holds that the majority (which still means white everywhere but perhaps California), as well as criminal justice decision makers responding to voters, support policies that are identified with their group racial interests, or oppose policies that are seen as favorable to others (regardless of their personal self-interest). This theory suggests that policies are useful ways to signal government protection of majority (white) interests vis-à-vis minorities. From this perspective, tough punishment, especially directed against minority members, is a signal to whites and is demanded in some proportion to the "threat" of racial equality. This yields the prediction that mass imprisonment (a result of tough and categoric penal sanctions) ought to be greatest in those states where the minority population(s) are largest and thus pose the greatest presumptive threat to achieve political power. This prediction has received substantial support in empirical studies, even when controlling for factors associated with other potential triggers of demand for imprisonment (Unnever and Cullen 2010; Smith 2004; Greenberg and West 2001), although the quantitative evidence seems to suggest that the relationship is significant only where the target minority is African American (Greenberg and West 2001).[7]

While it is easy to associate the penal salience of race with racial animus, it leads to some paradoxical implications. The racial threat or animus hypothesis is generally studied either spatially (looking at the association between minority population and incarceration rate) or in terms of public opinion (Do people who hold racially intolerant views also tend to support more punitive sanctions?). While this association may hold up in snapshot form, it seems peculiar when considered historically. While most evidence suggests that racial animus has declined over the last 40 years (Omi and Winant 1994, 157), incarceration has increased markedly. It is possible that racial animus/threat helped to determine which states would initiative the legislative policies necessary for mass incarceration during the 1980s, and that those policies have carried on through political inertia in the 1990s and 2000s, despite some improvement in the climate of racial tolerance.

Neoliberalism

The rise of mass incarceration took place during a long decline in Marxist analyses of penality.[8] The emergence of mass incarceration as a social problem, however, has fortuitously corresponded with the renewal of this vital tradition of penal theory. Recent work in the tradition of Rusche and Kirchheimer suggests that the rise of mass incarceration was a response by the state to new conditions for the organization of labor and the investment of capital, both in the United States (Parenti 2000; Gilmore 2007) and in the United Kingdom. In Europe, relatively modest growth of incarceration, compared to the United States, has been paralleled by increases in the detention and deportation of immigrants, including asylum seekers (De Giorgi 2006; Calavita 2005).

The most economically deterministic versions of this account view the threat and reality of harsh prison sentences as powerful tools to discipline labor during a period when intense global competition has made wage growth and other concessions to labor unaffordable (Parenti 2000). This disciplinary side of mass incarceration is coupled to a more positive economic function, which has been variably described as "carceral Keynsianism" (Davis 1990) and the "prison industrial complex" (Gilmore 2007). On this account, building and filling prisons provides a stream of revenue for certain providers of state goods and services and, just as importantly, a form of public investment into which private capital can safely be poured at a time when the forms of spending and investment stimulated by the social welfare and military dimensions of the state were waning (Gilmore 2007).

The same economic conditions that have crippled the ability of the state to manage economic risk for the population also make the forms of corporate and public welfare formerly used to manage the conditions of the working poor less sustainable. Punishment becomes one of the few available tools for the state to assist capital in making labor docile and useful (De Giorgi 2006; Wacquant 2009). Mass incarceration, on this account, might be called the "penal state," and represents a new form of political-economic government (rather than a simple tool of market regulation), one that has significantly replaced the welfare state as the major framework for governing the poor (Beckett and Western 2001; Wacquant 2009). This framework offers several "advantages" for both state and some segments of capital, providing a narrative of social fortune consistent with the uplifting promise of success for those with discipline and the infamy of prison punishment for those who engage in wrongdoing (Melossi 2009).

Most of these accounts share the view that mass incarceration is part of a broader realignment of the state in line with the reliberalization of capitalism. From the end of World War II through the 1960s, tight labor markets in both Europe and the United States, and surging state revenues (and commitments) went along with strong unions and electoral power by the working classes, creating a climate of historic affluence. Despite the fact that crime began to grow in both Europe and the United States during the 1960s, incarceration rates in general remained stable or trended down. In this era, often described as "Fordism" (De Giorgi 2006) or social welfarism, the prison was a minor tool of government, and one best managed in line with the larger welfarist strategy of governance, with its tool kit of clinical methods, normalizing objectives, and individualized judgments. Since the 1970s, the post-Fordist or neoliberal era in the United States and at least some parts of Europe, prison and other tools of law enforcement and immigration control have become central to the strategy of government, with a tool kit oriented toward punishment, exclusion, and categoric judgments. While the United States is taken as the extreme example of this neoliberal logic, other states, particularly in Europe, are also headed in the same directions, with variation in terms of how much they have abandoned social welfarist tools of governance in adherence to liberal political economic principles. Mass incarceration, along with harsh immigration enforcement (De Giorgi 2006), zero tolerance policing (Wacquant 2009) and other manifestations of a warlike approach to crime control, are expected to migrate along with the spread of neoliberal government.

The neoliberal thesis appears to fit relatively well the timing and distribution of incarceration growth internationally. U.S. imprisonment rates began to grow visibly in the 1980s as the national political agenda was being recast by President Ronald Reagan, and imprisonment rates continued to grow throughout the 1990s as Bill Clinton gave a bipartisan stamp to policies of reduced welfare and heightened deregulation. In the United Kingdom, Margaret Thatcher's parallel movement of public policy toward economic liberalism, however, did not go along with any significant departure in penal trends (Newburn 2007).

In a comparison of imprisonment rates among advanced post-industrial economies (Europe, Australia, Japan, Canada, South Africa, and the U.S.) countries categorized as neoliberal (U.S., UK, Australia, and South Africa) have higher incarceration rates than other categories, with those countries with the most welfarist governance approaches (the Nordic countries) having the lowest incarceration rates (Cavadino and Dignan 2006). But this association has not been tested using more control variables. It is not clear how coherent these categories really are. The United States appears to many to be the most "neoliberal" country. But if that is supposed to indicate a swing away from social welfarism and a reassertion of liberalism, the U.S. experience is far from extreme, since American public policy has never veered far from orthodox liberalism. Moreover, the U.S. incarceration rate is so much higher than those of the other "neoliberal" countries that the difference is greater than the difference between all the categories themselves. The United Kingdom leads Europe in incarceration today, but it did so as well in the 1960s, when social welfarism was at its height.

Nor is it clear that growth in incarceration always means "mass incarceration." Most of the countries of Europe have grown their prison population and capacity beyond population growth between the 1970s and the 1990s. In some cases, such as the Netherlands, the shift in scale matches that of the United States (and the Netherlands has been one of the European countries trending toward liberalism in political economy), but from a remarkably low starting point (Downes 2007). But nowhere in Europe is there strong evidence of the full combination of (1) a dramatic change in scale of incarceration, (2) a shift toward categoric utilization of incarceration, and (3) the emergence of warehouse imprisonment aimed at nothing but custody and security.

Perhaps the greatest challenge facing the neoliberalism thesis is the degree to which any cause at that level of abstraction must under-determine the specificities observed. Thus, proponents of the neoliberalism thesis tend to treat mass incarceration as just one of a whole family of exclusionary policies toward the poor that span both the penal and the welfare state (Wacquant 2009), though in the United States it has predominated far beyond other policies. Thus, zero tolerance practices in schools and in policing have received a fair amount of publicity in the United States (partially because they do ensnare middle-class people as well), but with relatively little actual implementation. While public spending on prisons went up more than 400 percent between 1970 and 2000, public spending on police went up only 20 percent (McCrary 2010). What explains the importance of prisons over police? Indeed, why did the same states decimate their mental health systems, also largely coercive and custodial institutions for society's marginal members, and which once held tens of thousands of "patients" in the same period (Harcourt 2005).

Focused on specific national and regional economies, such as Italy (De Giorgi 2006) and California (Gilmore 2007), the political economy approach helps integrate social and political precursors to mass incarceration. In California, for example, a vibrant home owner–based anti-tax movement long gave the state the appearance of being a vanguard of neoliberalism, even though its economy was highly tied to public spending, and remained so during the growth years of incarceration. While Reagan was rhetorically associated with shrinking government, he aggressively grew the military aspect of government spending, much of it in California. Thus, the growth of incarceration in California took place in the 1980s amidst an expansion of military industrial jobs, and continued in the 1990s as that expansion was reversed. Throughout this period, however, downward trends in the use of rural land, urban populations, and state (as opposed to federal) public borrowing made building prisons a consistently successful policy for absorbing surpluses in all these sectors (Gilmore 2007).

What remains clear is that the Marxist tool kit for analyzing punishment in its relationship to labor markets and to the construction of an exclusionary normative order is more vital than ever (or at least in the more than three-quarters of a century since the end of the last period of relatively unfettered global capitalism in the 1930s.

The Politics of Crime Control

In an undeniable sense, mass incarceration is a product of politics. A quantum leap in prison populations in the United States (and to the degree that it has been partially replicated in certain European countries) required changes in the administration and legislation of punishment. In a democracy, that process can be accelerated, challenged, or checked by popular politics. As we have seen, both the cultural and the economic accounts take this seriously and describe a "culture of control" and a penalization of the political field in which the possibilities of governing are reshaped around the determinate constraints of either a new common sense of "high crime societies" (Garland 2001a, 11), or the place of the urban poor under neoliberalism (Wacquant 2009). What has distinguished the political school from Scheingold (1992) or (Zimring, Hawkins, and Kamin 2001; Gottschalk 2006; Simon 2007) is viewing the political field itself—as well as the political formations, factions, and actors making it up—as the primary location of the shifts determining mass incarceration. Crime policy, in this analysis, is determined less by its fit with cultural values (Durkheim), or by the political-economy of labor, than by its value in constituting politically useful "publics" behind a politics of "tough on crime."

Mass incarceration and capital punishment (Gottschalk 2006; Sarat 2002) have been the most distinctive tools of this kind of public built around the (often very selective) image of the crime victim as an idealized citizen-subject or everyman-woman (Simon 2007; Gottschalk 2006; Garland 2001a).

The salience of crime as a kind of "trickster medium" that can convert political capital in the U.S. experience has been explained in two primary ways. One focuses on the civil rights movement, and the importance of crime control as a policy field into which retreating defenders of the old white supremacist politics in the U.S. South could take up a strong and righteous stand while still signaling their racial animus (Weaver 2007; Western 2006). The policy shift allowed politicians laden with potentially toxic policy positions to convert themselves into strong advocates of a popular position in which their primary former adversaries (African Americans and their leaders) were on the defensive (Weaver 2008). The other approach emphasizes race as just one, albeit a central and constitutive one, of several historical legacies driving this politicization of crime. Crime as a field of potential contestation between state and federal governments made it a politically charged area from the start of the Republic, and race, the driving force of political change for most of the nineteenth century (if not the twentieth) was often the explicit focus of the controversy, for example over proposed federal anti-lynching legislation (Gottschalk 2006).

As noted above, the racial animus hypothesis has been found one of the strongest predictors of support of harsh punishments in national opinion survey analyses. Likewise, racial threat seems to be a potent driver of policies, including "tough on crime" policies, that are racially identified and are served up to reassure majority white voters in states (and potentially, national units in Europe, with the primary example being tough immigration measures). The racial politics analysis of mass incarceration is a bit different, placing the central emphasis on either the strategies of political elites (Southern white Democrats, Nixon's "Southern" strategy) as they attempted to pivot from losing battles over segregation and national employment discrimination to new terrains on which they would have advantages to defend their traditional interests and flout those of the triumphant civil rights movement (Beckett 1997; Weaver 2007).

Weaver usefully distinguishes crime as a policy "frontlash," from a more traditional "backlash" in which conservative voters push back on the civil rights front

directly. A frontlash shifts grounds to a new policy field. Crime allowed segrega-
tionists to recast their fears of black integration and to demand slowdowns in
housing and school desegregation. But it also means that as the crime policy issue
creates its own policy feedback and generates new possibilities for political identity
in crime victim status, it can play out in new ways fundamentally unconnected from
the conservative racial agenda that helped initially fuel its takeoff. Thus feminists
could find in crime victim status and "tough on crime" policies a new front for contestation and collaboration with state and federal authorities (Gottschalk 2006),
and even African American politicians can present "tough on crime" policies as a
benefit to the community without fear of being read as appealing to racists (including Barak Obama, who refused to be outdone by John McCain in support for
tough crime policies during the 2008 election cycle).

Another productive way of framing the relationship between race and mass
incarceration is to view heavy imprisonment as the new axis of racial ordering for
a post–civil rights era America in which the traditional urban ghetto has been
rendered unnecessary by deindustrialization and less viable due to greater housing
opportunity for middle-class African Americans (Wacquant 2001). From this perspective, the criminal justice system itself need not be racially discriminatory in
either the motives of its agents or its managers. Its goal is to replace the no longer
acceptable rule of Jim Crow and ghetto norms with a new formally egalitarian and
race-blind court system.

The power of the race politics interpretation of "tough on crime" policies in the
1960s, 1970s, and 1980s is formidable. Less clear is how well this interpretation can
explain the continuing productivity of crime policy as a central platform for governing during the 1990s and 2000s, when mass incarceration grew and then consolidated its hold on an American political landscape increasingly transformed by
globalization, immigration, and internal migration to the Sunbelt (of all races).

An alternative is to view U.S. race conflict as only one, albeit a very central one,
of the features of U.S. history conditioning mass incarceration as a preferred policy
for American politicians in the period 1980–2000. From this perspective, it is features of U.S. constitutional structure (especially federalism and strong state powers
over criminal justice), many of them rooted in slavery, that made crime an effective
pathway for governance at various times in American history, especially those times
of fear and mistrust of government (Gottschalk 2006; Simon 2007; Miller 2008).

The specific conjunctural features of the 1960s that led to a far greater expansion in scope and scale of crime as a defining problem for government and mass
incarceration as a central public policy may not lend themselves to a sweeping
cause like racial backlash or neoliberalism, but involve those and other factors.
Many of them are highly contingent and not predictable elements of a particular
racial or economic order. One of these was the remarkable battle over capital punishment, which put the state's power to punish on the political agenda at a moment
of very high homicide rates and national alarm about law and order (Gottschalk
2006). You can look at this as an outgrowth of the civil rights movement, but hardly
the kind of strategic response assumed by backlash theories. Likewise, a litigation

MASS INCARCERATION 45

battle over prisoners' rights, coming out of the same civil rights movement, put prison construction on the table at a time when populist punitive politics were taking root in states like Florida, Arizona, and California (Lynch 2009a; Schoenfeld 2010). Another factor that receives little attention from those who see mass incarceration as a strategy of racial control or neoliberalism is the role of second wave feminism in constituting the crime victim (gendered female for certain purposes) as an idealized citizen (Gottschalk 2006). Thus, while racial conflict over civil rights—and the political realignments to which it led—may be the most important singular "cause" in pushing the United States toward mass incarceration, these other factors help explain why it could become a sustainable citizenship project with broad support from all segments of American society. Indeed, the specific form of mass incarceration (of all the ways that a "war on crime" may have played out) may be best understood as a kind of unintended compromise or strategic balance between the forces of racial backlash and realignment, and the civil rights movement itself (or at least its legal extension).

The political accounts of mass incarceration are, somewhat more than the cultural and economic accounts, rooted in the specificities of U.S. history and are not easily generalized to other countries. On the other hand, as thick descriptions of how many of the "risk factors" discussed above have played out in the country with the most distinctive experience with mass incarceration, this account can be a resource for similarly grounded accounts of nations outside the United States and of sub-state units.

CONCLUSION

Beginning in the 1970s, the United States began a precipitous increase in prison populations that 30 years later saw an increase of more than 400 percent in the rate of imprisonment. With considerable variation from state to state, a profile has emerged of American incarceration that includes: (1) a quantum shift in the scale of imprisonment; (2) a categorical approach to using prison on entire categories of offenders in place of prison as an individual option; and (3) the reshaping of the practice of imprisonment around a model of punitive segregation with little emphasis on education, labor, or rehabilitation. At the end of the twentieth century, this mass incarceration system had moved prisons from the margins of the modern state to near the center, as toward an overarching hegemony over the lives of urban poor.

The era of mass incarceration as a public policy is over; its history as a social problem has begun. This does not mean that prison populations will return to historic norms or practices to traditional logics. We may be at the beginning of a long new equilibrium in which prisons remain a central site of control for a large portion of the urban poor already marked by its touch through the generations. However, mass incarceration is clearly over as a public policy, and the era has begun in which policy discussion seems likely to focus on managing the pathological processes unleashed by mass incarceration.

Some broader theories of mass incarceration suggest that mass incarceration should be on the rise in other nations undergoing neoliberal transformation (Cavadino and Dignan 2006; Wacquant 2009). Once we look beyond the United States, it is hard to find substantial evidence that mass incarceration is becoming anything like a global norm. Western Europe has experienced significant growth in the rate of imprisonment since the 1970s (with considerable variation), but even in the nations with the most rapid growth and the most decisive policy election of imprisonment, for example, the United Kingdom (Newburn 2007), and the Netherlands (Downes 2007), where one can find elements of securitization as well, it is hard to find the categoric approach to imprisonment that has become the U.S. style. In the developing world, there is little if any evidence that states are turning to mass incarceration with its extraordinarily high direct and indirect costs. What one can find is the politics of crime fear almost everywhere, but in most cases, specific institutional factors, such as centralized control over penal decision making or the force of regional human rights norms, have produced substantial resistance to full-fledged mass incarceration.

Historians and social scientists will continue to argue over the precise causes of U.S. mass incarceration, a debate that stands imminently to be enriched by new studies of subnational and non-U.S. national experiences (see Lynch 2010; Schoenfeld 2010; Kilcommins et al. 2004). But much of the research agenda is rightly shifting to documenting the extraordinary social, economic, and political consequences of this 30-year effort in areas like the voter disenfranchisement (Uggen and Manza 2002), inequality (Western 2006; 2006; Wakefield and Uggen 2010), families and children (Hagan and Dinovitzer 1999; Comfort 2009), and public safety (Clear 2008).

NOTES

1. The Adrian Kragen Professor of Law, UC Berkeley.
2. According to the researchers who prepared this appendix, their search represented only a fraction of laws that may have enhanced the length of prison sentences in California since the 1970s (Little Hoover 2007, 68).
3. Mass incarceration is defined by sociologists as a penal regime, that is, the policies and practices behind raising incarceration rates a quantum scale and applying it to entire categories of people (rather than individually) (Garland 2001b, 1–2; Western 2006, 12).
4. For example, when the Arizona legislature held hearings recently on the costs of incarceration, the state's association of prosecuting attorneys filed a descriptive statistical report on Arizona prisoners, showing that the vast majority were either guilty of a serious, violent, or repeat offense (Arizona House of Representatives 2010).
5. Research in the 1970s was largely unable to document effective crime-reduction results from improved policy deployment strategies. The empirical record appears quite different today (Zimring 2007)

6. This is difficult to assess, since in the case of the UK and the Netherlands, prison populations have been growing rapidly as politicians seem to have taken more direct control over penal policy (Downes 2007; Newburn 2007).

7. This may reflect difficulties in measuring Latinos. Qualitative work on Arizona suggests that state's very significant leap in incarceration after the 1970s paralleled growing Anglo concern about growing Mexican immigration; see Lynch 2009a and 2009b.

8. Ironically, the Marxist studies of penality crested just as the U.S. incarceration rate was reaching its nadir, leading to expectations of decarceration (Scull 1979).

REFERENCES

Allen, Francis. 1981. *Decline of the Rehabilitative Ideal-Penal Policy and Social Purpose*. New Haven: Yale University Press.

American Law Institute. 2011. *Model Penal Code: Sentencing, Tentative Draft No. 2*. Philadelphia: American Law Institute.

Arizona House of Representatives. 2010. House Study Commission on Sentencing: Minutes of Meeting, Friday, May 14, 2010. Available at: http://cecilash.com/uploads/MINUTES_Sentencing_Committee_May_14_2010.doc.

Ayers, Edward L. 1985. *Vengeance and Justice: Crime and Punishment in the 19th Century South*. New York: Oxford University Press.

Barker, Vanessa. 2006. "The Politics of Punishing: Building a State Governance Theory of American Imprisonment Variation." *Punishment and Society* 8: 5–33.

Barker, Vanessa. 2009. *The Politics of Imprisonment: How the Democratic Process Shapes the Way America Punishes Offenders*. New York: Oxford University Press.

Baumann, Zygmaunt. 2000. "Social Issues of Law and Order." *The British Journal of Criminology* 40: 205–221.

Becker, Gary. 1968. "Crime and Punishment: An Economic Approach." *Journal of Political Economy* 76: 169.

Beckett, Katherine. 1997. *Making Crime Pay: Law and Order in Contemporary American Politics*. New York: Oxford University Press.

Beckett, Katherine, and Bruce Western. 2001. "Governing Social Marginality: Welfare, Incarceration, and the Transformation of State Policy." *Punishment and Society* 3: 43–59.

Bennett, William J., John J. Diulio, Jr., and John P. Walters. 1996. *Body Count: Moral Poverty . . . And How to Win America's War Against Crime and Drugs*. New York: Simon and Schuster.

Blumstein, Alfred. 1988. "Prison Populations: A System Out of Control?" *Crime and Justice* 10: 231–266.

Blumstein, Alfred, Jacqueline Cohen, and William Gooding. 1983. "The Influence of Capacity on Prison Population: A Critical Review of Some Recent Evidence." *Crime and Delinquency* 29(1): 1–51.

Bottoms, Anthony. 1995. "The Philosophy and Politics of Punishment and Sentencing," in *The Politics of Sentencing Reform*, eds. C. Clarkson and R. Morgan, pp. 17–50. Oxford: Clarendon Press.

Calavita, Kitty. 2005. *Migrants at the Margins: Law, Race, and Exclusion in Southern Europe*. Cambridge: Cambridge University Press.

Caplow, Theodore, and Jonathan Simon. 1999. "Understanding Prison Policy and Population Trends." *Crime and Justice* 26: 63–120.

Cavadino, Michael, and James Dignan. 2006. *Penal Systems: A Comparative Approach.* London: Polity.

Clear, Todd. 2008. *Imprisoning Communities: How Mass Incarceration Makes Disadvantaged Neighborhoods Worse.* New York: Oxford University Press.

Comfort, Megan. 2009. *Doing Time Together: Love and Family in the Shadow of the Prison.* Chicago: University of Chicago Press.

Crawford, Charles, Ted Chiricos, and Gary Kleck. 1998. "Race, Racial Threat and Sentencing of Habitual Offenders." *Criminology* 36(3): 481–512.

Dansky, Kara. 2009. "Understanding California Sentencing." *University of San Francisco Law Review* 43: 42–86.

Davis, Mike. 1990. *City of Quartz: Excavating the Future in LA.* London: Verso.

De Giorgi, Alessandro. 2006. *Re-thinking the Political Economy of Punishment: Perspectives on Post-Fordism and Penal Politics.* Burlington, VT: Ashgate Publishing.

Didion, Joan. 2003. *Where I Was From.* New York: Knopf.

Downes, David. 2007. "Visions of Penal Control in the Netherlands." *Crime and Justice* 36.

Durkheim, Emile. 1997. *The Division of Labor in Society.* New York: Simon and Schuster.

Feeley, Malcolm. 1983. *Court Reform on Trial: Why Simple Solutions Fail.* New York: Basic Books.

Feeley, Malcolm, and Jonathan Simon. 1992. "The New Penology: Notes on the Emerging Strategy of Corrections and its Implications." *Criminology* 30: 449–474.

Foucault, Michel. 1977. *Discipline and Punishment: The Birth of the Prison.* New York: Pantheon.

Garland, David. 1987. *Punishment and Welfare: A History of Penal Strategies.* Surrey, UK: Ashgate Publishing.

Garland, David. 1990. *Punishment and Modern Society: A Study in Social Theory.* Chicago: University of Chicago Press.

Garland, David. 2001a. *The Culture of Control: Crime and Social Order in Contemporary Society.* Chicago: University of Chicago Press.

Garland, David. 2001b. *Mass Imprisonment.* London: Sage.

Gilmore, Ruth W. 2007. *Golden Gulag: Prisons, Surplus, Crisis, and Opposition in Globalizing California.* Berkeley: University of California Press.

Goffman, Erving. 1961. *Asylums: Essays on the Social Situation of Mental Patients and Other Inmates.* New York: Anchor Books.

Gottschalk, Marie. 2006. *The Prison and the Gallows: The Politics of Mass Incarceration in America.* Cambridge: Cambridge University Press.

Greenberg, David, and Valerie West. 2001. "State Prison Populations and Their Growth, 1971–1991." *Criminology* 39: 615–653.

Hagan, John, and Ronit Dinovitzer. 1999. "Children of the Prison Generation: Collateral Consequences of Imprisonment for Children and Communities." *Crime and Justice* 26: 121–162.

Haney, Craig. 1998. "Riding the Punishment Wave: On the Origins of Our Devolving Standards of Decency." *Hastings Women's Law Journal* 9: 27–78.

Harcourt, Bernard. 2005. "From the Asylum to the Prison: Rethinking the Incarceration Revolution." *Texas Law Review* 84: 1751.

Harcourt, Bernard. 2007. *Against Prediction: Punishing and Policing in an Actuarial Age.* Chicago: University of Chicago Press.

Jacobs, David, and Jason T. Carmichael. 2001. "The Politics of Punishment across Time and Space: A Pooled Time Series Analysis of Imprisonment Rates." *Social Forces* 80: 61–91.

Jacobs, David, and Ronald Helms. 2001. "Toward a Political Sociology of Punishment: Politics and Changes in the Incarcerated Population." *Social Science Research* 30(2): 171–194.

Jacobs, James B. 1983. "The Politics of Prison Expansion." *New York University Review of Law and Social Change* 12: 209–241.

Kilcommins, Sean. Ian O'Donnell, Eoin O'Sullivan, and Barry Vaughan. 2004. *Crime, Punishment and the Search for Order in Ireland*. Dublin: Institute of Public Administration.

Langan, Patrick. 1991. "America's Soaring Prison Populaiton." *Science* 251(5001): 1568–1573.

Liazos, Alexander. 1974. "Class Oppression: the Functions of Juvenile Justice." *Critical Sociology* 5: 2–24.

Lichtenstein, Alex. 1996. *Twice the Work of Free Labor: The Political Economy of Convict Labor in the New South*. London: Verso.

Little Hoover Commission. 2007. *Solving California's Corrections Crisis: Time Is Running Out*. State of California: Little Hoover Commission.

Loader, Ian, and Richard Sparks. 2010. *Public Criminology*. London: Routledge.

Lynch, Mona. 2009a. *Sunbelt Justice: Arizona and the Transformation of American Punishment*. Stanford, CA: Stanford University Press.

Lynch, Mona. 2009b. "Punishment, Purpose and Place: A Case Study of Arizona's Prison Siting Decisions." *Studies in Law, Politics, and Society* 50: 105–137.

Mauer, Marc. 1999. *Race to Incarcerate*. New York: The New Press

Mauer, Marc, and Meda Chesney-Lind, eds. 2002. *Invisible Punishment: The Collateral Consequences of Mass Imprisonment*. New York: The New Press.

McCrary, Justin. 2010. "Dynamic Perspectives on Crime," in *Handbook on the Economics of Crime*, eds. Bruce Benson and Paul Zimmerman. North Hampton, MA: Edward Elgar.

Melossi, Dario. 2009. *Controlling Crime, Controlling Society: Thinking about Crime in Europe and America*. Cambridge: Polity Press.

Messinger, Sheldon. 1980. In *Criminal Justice*, eds. Franklin Zimring and Richard Frase. Boston: Little, Brown.

Miller, Lisa. 2008. *The Perils of Federalism: Race, Poverty, and the Politics of Crime Control*. New York: Oxford University Press.

Newburn, Tim. 2007. "'Tough on Crime': Penal Policy in England and Wales." *Crime and Justice* 36: 425.

Newburn, Tim, and Trevor Jones. 2007. *Policy Transfer and Criminal Justice: Exploring US Influence over British Crime Policy*. Maindenhead, UK: Open University Press.

Omi, Michael, and Howard Winant. 1994. *Racial Formation in the United States: From the 1960s to the 1990s*. New York: Routledge.

Page, Joshua. 2011. *The Toughest Beat: Politics, Punishment, and the Prison Officers Union*. New York: Oxford University Press.

Pager, Devah. 2009. *Marked: Race, Crime, and Finding Work in an Era of Mass Incarceration*. Chicago: University of Chicago Press.

Parenti, Christian. 2000. *Lockdown America: Police and Prisons in the Age of Crisis*. London: Verso.

Perkinson, Robert. 2008. *Texas Tough: The Rise of America's Prison Empire*. New York: Metropolitan Books.

Petersilia, Joan. 2003. *When Prisoners Come Home: Parole and Prisoner Reentry*. New York: Oxford University Press.

PEW Center on the States. 2008. "One in 100: Behind Bars in America 2008." Available at: http://www.pewcenteronthestates.org/uploadedFiles/8015PCTS_Prison08_FINAL_2-1-1_FORWEB.pdf.

PEW Center on the States. 2009. "The Fiscal Crisis in Corrections: Rethinking Policies and Practices." Available at: http://www.pewcenteronthestates.org/report_detail. aspx?id=54384.

PEW Center on the States. 2010. "Prison Count 2010: State Population Declines for the First Time in 38 Years." Available at: http://www.pewcenteronthestates.org/uploaded-Files/Prison_Count_2010.pdf?n=880.

Platt, Anthony. 1969. *The Child Savers: The Invention of Delinquency.* Chicago: University of Chicago Press.

Pratt, John, David Brown, Simon Hallsworth, Mark Brown, and Wayne Morrison, eds. 2005. *The New Punitiveness: Current Trends, Theories, Perspectives.* Devon, UK: Willan Publishing.

Reiter, Keramet. 2010. "Parole, Snitch, or Die: California's Supermax Prisons & Prisoners, 1987–2007." ISSC Fellows Working Papers, Institute for the Study of Social Change, UC Berkeley. Available at: http://escholarship.org/uc/item/04w6556f.

Reitz, Kevin. 1998. "The Disassembly and Reassembly of US Sentencing Practices," in *Sentencing and Sanctions in Western Countries,* eds. Michael H. Tonry, Richard S. Frase. New York: Oxford University Press.

Roche, Sebastian. 2007. "Criminal Justice Policy in France: Illusions of Severity." *Crime and Justice* 36: 471.

Rose, Nikolas, Pat O'Malley, and Mariana Valverde. 2006. "Governmentality." *Annual Review of Law and Social Science* 2: 83–104.

Rothfeld, Michael. 2008. "Healthcare for Prisons: $7 Billion." *Los Angeles Times,* April 12, 2008. Available at: http://articles.latimes.com/2008/apr/12/local/me-prisons12.

Rothman, David. 1971. *Discovery of the Asylum.* Boston: Little, Brown.

Rothman, David. 1980. *Conscience and Convenience: The Asylum and its Alternatives in Progressive America.* Boston: Little, Brown.

Rusche, Georg, and Otto Kirchheimer. 1939. *Punishment and Social Structure.* New York: Columbia University Press.

Sarat, Austin. 2002. *When the State Kills: Capital Punishment and the American Condition.* Princeton, NJ: Princeton University Press.

Savelsberg, Joachim. 1994. "Knowledge, Domination, and Criminal Punishment." *American Journal of Sociology* 99: 911.

Savelsberg, Joachim. 2004. "Religion, Historical Contingencies, and Criminal Punishment: The German Case and Beyond." *Law and Social Inquiry* 29(2): 373–401.

Scheingold, Stuart. 1992. *The Politics of Street Crime: Criminal Process and Cultural Obsession.* Philadelphia: Temple University Press.

Schoenfeld, Heather. 2010. "Mass Incarceration and the Paradox of Prison Conditions Litigation." *Law & Society Review* 44(3/4): 731–768.

Scull, Andrew. 1977. "Madness and Segregative Control: The Rise of the Insane Asylum." *Social Problems* 24(3): 337–351.

Scull, Andrew. 1979. *Museums of Madness: The Social Organisation of Insanity in Nineteenth-Century England.* London: Palgrave Macmillan.

Shalev, Sharon. 2009. *Supermax: Controlling Risk Through Solitary Confinement.* London: Willan.

Simon, Jonathan. 1993. *Poor Discipline: Parole and the Social Underclass, 1890–1990.* Chicago: University of Chicago Press.

Simon, Jonathan. 2007. *Governing Through Crime: How the War on Crime Transformed American Democracy and Created a Culture of Fear.* New York: Oxford University Press.

Smith, Kevin. 2004. "The Politics of Punishment: Evaluating Political Explanations of Incarceration Rates." *The Journal of Politics* 66: 925–938.

Snacken, Sonja. 2007. "Penal Policy and Practice in Belgium." *Crime and Justice* 36: 127.

Sorensen, Jon, and Don Stemen. 2002. "The Effect of State Sentencing Policy on Incarceration Rates." *Crime & Delinquency* 48: 456–475.

Sourcebook of Criminal Justice Statistics Online. 2008. Available at: http://www.albany.edu/sourcebook/pdf/t6292008.pdf.

Stuntz, William. 2001. "The Pathological Politics of Criminal Law." *The Michigan Law Review* 100: 505ff.

Tonry, Michael. 1993. "The Success of Judge Frankel's Sentencing Commission." *University of Colorado Law Review* 64: 713ff.

Tonry, Michael. 1996. *Malign Neglect: Race, Crime, and Punishment in America*. New York: Oxford University Press.

Tonry, Michael. 2004. *Thinking about Crime: Sense and Sensibility in American Penal Culture*. New York: Oxford University Press.

Tonry, Michael. 2007. "Determinants of Penal Policies." *Crime and Justice* 36: 1ff.

Tyler, Tom, and Robert Boeckman. 1997. "Three Strikes and You Are Out, but Why? The Psychology of Public Support for Punishing Rule Breakers." *Law and Society Review* 31: 237–265.

Uggen, Chris, and Jeffrey Manza. 2002. "Democratic Contraction? The Political Consequences of Felon Disenfranchisement in the United States." *American Soiological Review* 67: 777–803.

Unnever, James D., and Francis T. Cullen. 2010. "The Social Sources of Americans' Punitiveness: A Test of Three Competing Models." *Criminology* 48: 99ff.

Useem, Bert, and Anne Piehl. 2008. *Prison State: The Challenge of Mass Incarceration*. New York: Cambridge University Press.

Wacquant, Loic. 2001. "Deadly Symbiosis: When Ghetto and Prison Meet and Mesh." *Punishment & Society* 3: 95–133a.

Wacquant, Loic. 2009. *Punishing the Poor: The Neoliberal Governance of Insecurity*. London: Polity.

Wakefield, Sara, and Chris Uggen. 2010. "Incarceration and Stratification." *Annual Review of Sociology*.

Weaver, Vesla. 2007. "Frontlash: Race the Development of Punitive Crime Policy." *Studies in American Political Development* 21: 230–265.

Webb, Jim. 2007. "Opening Statement of Senator Jim Webb: Mass Incarceration in the United States: At What Cost?" Available at: http://webb.senate.gov/newsroom/pressreleases/2007-10-04-01.cfm.

Weiman, David F., and Christopher C. Weiss. 2009. "The Origins of Mass Incarceration in New York State: The Rockefeller Drug Laws and the Local War on Drugs." In *Do Prisons Make Us Safer: The Benefits and Costs of the Prison Boom*, eds. Steven Raphael and Michael A. Stoll. New York: Russell Sage Foundation.

Western, Bruce. 2002. "The Impact of Incarceration on Wage Mobility and Inequality." *American Sociological Review* 67(4): 526–546.

Western, Bruce. 2006. *Punishment and Inequality in America*. New York: Russell Sage Foundation.

Western, Bruce, and Katheirne Beckett. 1999. "How Unregulated is the U.S. Labor Market? The Penal System as a Labor Market Institution." *American Journal of Sociology* 104: 1030–1060.

Whitman, James. 2003. *Harsh Justice: Criminal Policy and the Widening Divide Between America and Europe*. New York: Oxford University Press.

Wilson, James Q. 1975. *Thinking about Crime*. New York: Basic Books.

Wright, David. 1997. "Getting Out of the Asylum: Understanding the Confinement of the Insane in the Nineteenth Century." *Social History of Medicine* 10(1): 137–155.

Zedner, Lucia. 2009. *Security*. London: Routledge.

Zimring, Franklin. 2000. "Incarceration Patterns," in *Mass Incarceration: Perspectives on U.S. Imprisonment, University of Chicago Law School Roundtable, A Journal of Interdisciplinary Legal Studies*, Volume 7. Chicago: University of Chicago Press.

Zimring, Franklin. 2001. "Review of David Garland, The Culture of Control: Crime and Social Order in Contemporary Society," *Criminal Justice* 1: 465.

Zimring, Franklin. 2005. "Penal Policy and Penal Legislation: Recent American Experience." *Stanford Law Review* 58: 323–338.

Zimring, Franklin. 2007. *The Great American Crime Decline*. New York: Oxford University Press.

Zimring, Franklin, and Gordon Hawkins. 1991. *The Scale of Imprisonment*. Chicago: University of Chicago Press.

Zimring, Franklin, Gordon Hawkins, and Sam Kamin. 2003. *Democracy and Punishment: Three Strikes and You're Out in California*. New York: Oxford University Press.

CHAPTER 2

RACE, ETHNICITY, AND PUNISHMENT

MICHAEL TONRY

BLACK men in the United States have for a quarter century been five to seven times more likely than white men to be in prison, are much more likely to receive decades-long sentences or to be sentenced to life without the possibility of parole, and are much likelier to be on death row. Disparities in imprisonment and punishment also exist between black and white women, but the racial differences are much less and the absolute levels of imprisonment are far lower. Hispanic men and women also are more likely than non-Hispanic whites to be in prison, but the differences are far less than those between whites and blacks.

In 2008, for example, 3,161 per 100,000 non-Hispanic black men were confined in state or federal prisons, compared with 487 per 100,000 non-Hispanic white men and 1,200 per 100,000 Hispanic men. Put differently, nearly one in every 33 black male Americans, children and the elderly included, was in prison. For white male Americans, less than one in 200 was locked up. Among women, the rates were far lower and the differences were less. The female rates were 50 per 100,000 for non-Hispanic whites, 149 for non-Hispanic blacks, and 75 for Hispanics (Sabol, West, and Cooper 2009, table 2).

The differences between non-Hispanic whites and Hispanics largely, but not completely, disappear when account is taken of differences in the age composition of the two groups. The kinds of violent and drug-related crimes that commonly result in prison sentences are heavily disproportionately committed by teenagers and young adults. The Hispanic population is much younger than the non-Hispanic white population. In 2008, nearly 44 percent of American Hispanics were younger than 25, compared with 30 percent of non-Hispanic whites (U.S. Department of Commerce 2010, table 10).[1] Many more Hispanics than whites are thus in their high-crime ages. As a result, comparatively more Hispanics than whites would be expected to be arrested and imprisoned solely because of age differences.

Figure 2.1 shows the Hispanic percentage of the total U.S. population since 1990, the percentages of Hispanics and non-Hispanic whites and blacks aged 24 and under, and the Hispanic percentages among jail and prison inmates. The percentage of Hispanics in the total population increased by two-thirds in 18 years (from 8.9 percent in 1990 to 15.4 percent in 2008). Higher percentages of Hispanics than of the other groups are under age 25, and the percentages of Hispanics among jail and prison inmates have grown accordingly.

Figure 2.2 shows Hispanic and non-Hispanic black and white percentages of federal and state prisoners since 1990. Before 1999 such data were published only for selected years; beginning in 1999, they were published every year. The table presents the available data. The broad pattern since 2000, disregarding minor fluctuations, is that the Hispanic percentage has increased significantly in absolute terms, but not when compared with the increasing Hispanic share of the total population. White percentages have fallen since 2000 and black percentages have changed little.[2]

The fundamental problem with racial disparities in punishment thus primarily affects black Americans, especially black men. The primary emphases of this article

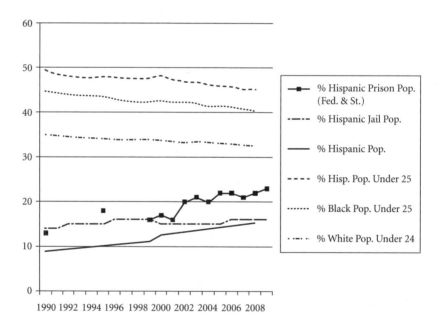

Figure 2.1. Hispanic Percentage of Total Population; Percentages of Hispanic and Non-Hispanic Black and White Populations Ages 25 and Under; Hispanic Percentages of Jail and Prison Inmates, 1990–2008.

Sources: Bureau of Justice Statistics. Various Years. "Correctional Populations in the United States [various years 1990–2009]." Washington, DC: Bureau of Justice Statistics, U.S. Department of Justice; U.S. Department of Commerce. Various Years. Statistical Abstract of the United States: [various years]. Washington, DC: Bernan Press.

accordingly are on documenting and explaining the overrepresentation of black Americans in U.S. prisons and jails and on death rows.[3]

Stark disparities in imprisonment and entanglement in the criminal justice system affecting black Americans result partly from racial differences in offending. Arrest rates for violent crimes have long been higher for blacks than for whites, but the differences have been diminishing since the 1980s. We know why this is: black Americans much more often than whites are affected by the conditions—being raised in poverty-level, single-parent households; living in disadvantaged, socially disorganized neighborhoods; being educated in substandard schools; having limited employment prospects; lacking positive role models—that are correlated with higher levels of crime and victimization by crime (e.g., Lauritsen 2003; McNulty and Bellair 2003). To a major extent, disparities also result from the adoption in the 1980s and 1990s of drug and crime control policies that place much heavier burdens on black Americans than on whites (Tonry 2011, chaps. 2 and 3). To a lesser extent, disparities result from practitioners' conscious biases and unconscious stereotypes (ibid., chap. 4).

Sentencing decisions by judges are not a major contributor to racial disparities. Most studies of disparities in sentencing conclude that, once the offense for which an offender is sentenced and his or her prior criminal record are taken into account, blacks are not significantly more likely than whites to be sentenced to imprisonment for violent crimes, though they are more likely to receive prison sentences for drug and property crimes (Demuth and Steffensmeier 2004). The latter differences

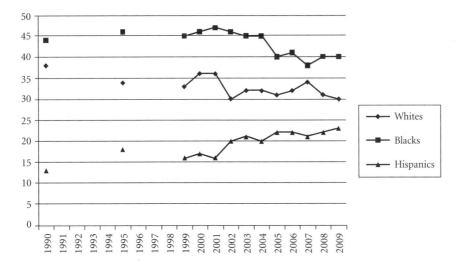

Figure 2.2. Percentages of Hispanic and Non-Hispanic Black and White Inmates in State and Federal Prisons, 1990–2008.

Sources: Bureau of Justice Statistics. Various Years. "Correctional Populations in the United States [various years 1990–2009]." Washington, DC: Bureau of Justice Statistics, U.S. Department of Justice.

exist in substantial part because police arrest many more blacks than whites for drug trafficking offenses (although fewer blacks than whites sell drugs) and because black defendants are more likely than whites to have prior arrests and convictions. Black defendants sentenced to imprisonment typically receive somewhat longer terms (Spohn 2011).

The police are a different matter. Police decisions to target drug law enforcement on disadvantaged minority neighborhoods in large cities generate drug arrest rates for blacks three to six times higher than those for whites (King 2008; Fellner 2009). This happens despite consistent findings from national surveys on drug use that show that comparatively fewer blacks than whites use most drugs (e.g., cocaine powder, heroin, marijuana, amphetamines, alcohol); for drugs that blacks do use more often than whites (e.g., crack cocaine), the differences are small (Office of Applied Studies 2010). Other national surveys show that blacks do not sell drugs more often than whites, but that they are much more likely to sell them in places where they are easy to arrest (Tonry 2011, chap. 3).

Racial profiling by the police also makes a big difference. Blacks are much more likely than whites to be stopped by the police without legally adequate cause in cars or on the street. Although smaller percentages of blacks than whites are typically found to possess drugs, guns, or other contraband, they are more likely to be arrested and to be treated abusively. A study released by the Center for Constitutional Rights (2009) on racial profiling in New York City showed, for example, that nearly 1,600,000 people were stopped by the police in a 42-month period. Ten percent of those stopped were non-Hispanic whites, though they made up 44 percent of the population. Half of those stopped were non-Hispanic blacks, though they made up only a quarter of the population. Hispanics constituted 28 percent of the population and 30 percent of those stopped.

The litany of ways in which drug and crime control policies disproportionately affect black Americans is depressing, but so familiar as to surprise no one with even nodding acquaintance with the subject. Blacks in 2005 constituted 12.8 percent of the general population but nearly half of prison inmates and 42 percent of death row residents. About a third of young black men aged 20 to 29 were in prison or jail or on probation or parole on an average day in 2005. The Bureau of Justice Statistics estimated in 2003 that 32 percent of black baby boys born in 2001 would spend some part of their lives in a state or federal prison. That is a substantial underestimate of imprisonment of black Americans; it does not take account of confinement in local jails, which is much more common than time in prison. By 2004 a third of adult black men had a felony conviction and half had been convicted of a felony or a misdemeanor (Bonczar 2003; Bureau of Justice Statistics 2007, tables 6.33.2005, 6.17.2006, 6.80.2007; Pager 2007, p. 157; Uggen, Manza, and Thompson 2006).

What is most striking about these patterns of racial disparity is not that they exist, but that they are well-known, have long been well-known, and have changed little in recent decades. Few people except academics, liberal law reformers, and offenders and their loved ones much notice or care. Strangely, even civil rights organizations give the subject little emphasis (Alexander 2010).

The classic example of a law that unfairly and disproportionately affects blacks was a 1986 federal law generally referred to as the "100-to-1 law." It punished sales of crack cocaine, mostly by blacks, as severely as sales a hundred times larger, mostly by whites, of cocaine powder. The two substances are pharmacologically indistinguishable. The sale of five grams of crack, a typical low-level street transaction, was punished as severely as the sale of a half-kilogram of powder, an amount typical of high-level distributors. Not surprisingly, federal prisons filled up with convicted black crack dealers.[4] Many other statutes—most conspicuously, mandatory minimum sentence and three-strikes-and-you're-out laws—enacted in the 1980s and 1990s worked in the same way. They targeted offenses for which blacks were especially likely to be arrested, and they worsened racial disparities in imprisonment.

The racial disparities caused by the federal 100-to-1 law were foreseeable when the law was passed (Tonry 1995, pp. 4–6) and were irrefutably documented long ago (McDonald and Carlson 1993). The same is true of racial profiling by the police and of the effects more generally of the wars on crime and drugs: their effects have long been well-known.

This article explains what happened. Section I discusses increases in racial disparities in imprisonment over the past 50 years and presents data that show what happened. Section II more briefly discusses the role of drug law enforcement in causing and exacerbating disparities. Section III discusses ways in which the effects of current disparities can be ameliorated and how laws, institutions, and practices can be changed so that they produce fewer disparities in the future.

I. Crime and Punishment

The massive imprisonment of black men in twenty-first-century America did not happen overnight; it happened in the years since 1973. In 1960 blacks made up 36 percent of the prison population. The black imprisonment rate was 661 per 100,000. Part of the long-standing racial disparity in prison resulted from racial bias, stereotyping, and insensitivity, and part from the greater involvement of blacks in the kinds of crimes, mostly violent, that commonly resulted in prison sentences.

Disparities in imprisonment grew steadily worse after the 1960s. Overall, the imprisonment rate in the United States increased from 161 per 100,000 population in 1970 to 780 in 2010. That increase, enormous though it is, dwarfs what happened to black Americans. The black imprisonment rate increased from 593 per 100,000 in 1970 to 2,661 in 2006. The percentage of prisoners who were black reached 50 percent in the mid-1980s, a level at which it remained for a decade and from which it has since fallen only slightly.

Problems of excessive and disproportionate imprisonment of black Americans are of long standing and are not getting better. In a 1995 book, *Malign Neglect: Race,*

Crime, and Punishment in America, I surveyed what was known about racial disparities and their causes. Here is how things then stood. For a century before the 1960s, black people had been more likely to be held in prison than whites. Racial disparities began to rise in the 1960s and then shot up to all-time highs in the 1980s, during the Reagan administration: blacks by then accounted for half of American prisoners, though they were only 12 percent of the U.S. population. A black American was seven times more likely to be in prison on any given day than a white American.

A large part of the explanation for the historical pattern was that blacks were more likely than whites to be arrested for robbery, rape, aggravated assault, and homicide, offenses that have long resulted in prison sentences. Victims' descriptions of assailants and police data on victim-offender relationships in homicides indicated that the racial offending patterns shown in arrest data were not far off from reality, at least for serious crimes. Critically, however, there had been no significant shifts in racial patterns in arrests for decades, and increased involvement by black people in serious violent crime could not explain why imprisonment rates shot up after the 1960s. A primary cause of the increase in the 1980s was disproportionate arrest and imprisonment of black people for drug offenses (Blumstein and Beck 1999).

Little in the preceding two paragraphs needs to be changed to describe conditions in 2011, with three important exceptions. First, overall imprisonment rates were much higher in 2011 than in 1993. With their increase, the lifetime probability of imprisonment for black men and the percentage of young black men in prison increased substantially. Second, the absolute number of blacks in prison was substantially higher in 2011. Third, however, blacks' involvement in violent crimes had declined substantially. If prison were used primarily as a punishment for serious violent crimes, as it is in most other countries, racial disparities should have been falling for at least fifteen years.

The black fractions of the prison, jail, and death row populations did not change much between 1993 and 2010. Nor did the ratio of black to white imprisonment rates: black men remain five to seven times more likely than white men to be inmates. Police arrest policies for drug offenses continue to be a primary cause of racial disparities. Racial profiling by the police plays an increasingly large role. Other important causes include mandatory minimum sentence, three-strikes, and life-without-the-possibility-of-parole laws that mandate decades-long and life sentences, and the elimination of parole release and other devices that enabled officials in earlier times to shorten unduly long sentences.

Black Americans have borne the brunt of this tougher sentencing. Arrest rates for black people for drug crimes are far higher—in recent years, three to four times higher—than for whites and bear no relationship to levels of black Americans' drug use or involvement in drug trafficking (Fellner 2009). Black Americans are less likely to use most drugs than are whites, and there is no credible evidence that they sell drugs more often. High arrest rates for drug crimes result from police policy decisions to focus on substances that blacks more often sell and places where they sell them. High imprisonment rates for drug crimes result partly from skewed arrest patterns and partly from legislative decisions, exemplified by the 100-to-1 law, to mandate the longest sentences for drug offenses for which blacks are more often arrested.

Black people are also disproportionately damaged by tougher sentencing policies for violent crimes. Partly this is because black people more often commit violent crimes and are arrested for them, even though their relative over-involvement has been declining. In absolute numbers, violent crimes by black people have plummeted as part of the national decline in crime since 1991, and constitute smaller percentages of absolute numbers that are about half what they were 20 years ago. The murder rate in 1980, for example, was 10.2 per 100,000 inhabitants of the United States. In 2008 it was 5.4. The robbery rape in 1980 was 251.1 per 100,000. In 2008 it was 145.3.

Imprisonment Rates

Figure 2.3 shows black and white percentages of state and federal prisoners (including Hispanics) from 1950 to 2008. Blacks were about a third of prisoners in 1960 and under 40 percent in 1970. The black percentage rose continuously to the mid-forties through 1980, rising slowly thereafter until the early 1990s and reaching a plateau at about 50 percent. If comparisons exclude Hispanics, in every year since 1990 the absolute number of non-Hispanic black prisoners has exceeded the absolute number of non-Hispanic whites. In 2008, for example, 34 percent of sentenced state and federal prisoners were non-Hispanic whites; 38 percent were non-Hispanic blacks (Sabol, West, and Cooper 2009, table 5).

Calculation of trend data has been complicated by a U.S. Bureau of Justice Statistics decision in the late 1990s to report separate figures for blacks, whites, and Hispanics. In earlier years, Hispanics were included within racial categories and sometimes were also reported separately. The change had the misleading effect of reducing "black" imprisonment rates. Skin color and "racial" identity, however, have been more salient social characteristics in recent decades in the United States than has the difference between being Hispanic or non-Hispanic. Insofar as racial bias, stereotypes, and attributions have influenced officials' decisions, skin color is much more likely than a Hispanic surname or ancestry to influence decisions in individual cases. Accordingly, in figure 2.3 (and most other figures) Bureau of Justice Statistics prison population data have been adjusted to take account of the estimated black and white fractions among Hispanics.

The jail story is much the same. Jails hold people before trial and hold convicted offenders who receive short custodial sentences, usually of less than one year. Figure 2.4 shows black and white percentages of local jail inmates from 1950 to 2008. About a third of jail inmates in 1950 and in 1960 were black and about 40 percent in 1970, a level around which the black percentage oscillated until the mid-1980s. For a decade after that, coinciding with the most aggressive years of the war on drugs, blacks were 45 to 48 percent of inmates, after which the percentage declined somewhat.

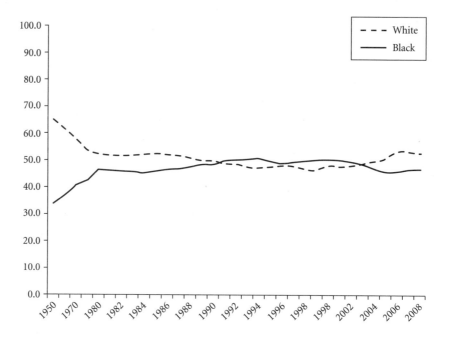

Figure 2.3. Percentages of State and Federal Prisoners, by Race, 1950–2008.
Sources: for 1950–1980, Cahalan (1986); for 1980–2008, Bureau of Justice Statistics. Until the late 1990s, race was broken down into three categories for all statistics: white, black, and other. In recent years, the Bureau of Justice Statistics has added Hispanic as a racial category to various statistics, thus complicating linear representations of the data. In 1999 the Bureau added Hispanic as a racial category to combined state and federal prison statistics. The Hispanic category has been removed and redistributed for each year since 1999. For earlier years, data without the Hispanic separation were used. The category "two or more races" has been redistributed evenly between blacks and whites.

Because these two figures are expressed in black and white percentages, they do not reflect the true magnitude of racial differences in imprisonment rates. It would be natural for someone new to the subject to compare the black percentage of the general population (12–13) to the black percentage of the combined jail and prison populations (46–50) and conclude that blacks are four times more likely to be confined than should be expected.

That would be incorrect, and misleading. Calculating the difference that way understates the extent of racial disparity. That is because whites, relative to their presence in the general population, are underrepresented in prison. The correct way to calculate racial disparities in imprisonment is to compare the black imprisonment rate per 100,000 black people with the white imprisonment rate per 100,000 white people.

For the past two decades, that comparison has shown that total imprisonment rates for blacks have been five to seven times those for whites. The differential is greater for men than for women. In 2000, for example, the total imprisonment rate for non-Hispanic black men for jail and prison combined was 3,457 per 100,000,

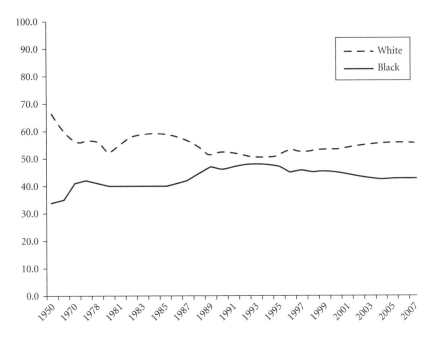

Figure 2.4. Percentages of Local Jail Inmates, by Race, 1950–2008.
Sources: For 1950–1983: Cahalan (1986); BJS (1984, 1990); for 1983–1989: BJS, "Jail Inmates," various years; for 1990–1995: Gilliard and Beck (1996); for 1996–2008: BJS, "Prison and Jail Inmates at Midyear," various years. BJS began using a separate Hispanics category much earlier in reporting jail data than in reporting prisoner data. For every year starting in 1990, the Hispanic category has been removed and redistributed, estimating that one-fourth of Hispanics were previously counted as black and three-quarters were counted as white.

and the rate for non-Hispanic white men was 449 per 100,000 (the corresponding rates for non-Hispanic black and white women were 205 and 34). The black male rate was seven times that for whites. The black female rate was six times higher. In 2008, the disparity among men was about the same. The difference in female rates had fallen to three (Sabol, West, and Cooper 2009, table 6).

In recent years the number of people serving life sentences has exploded. There were 70,000 in 1992. In 2008, despite more than 15 years of declining crime rates, nearly 141,000 people were serving life sentences. That means that the life sentence imprisonment rate for the United States was nearly 50 per 100,000, not much below the total rates for all prisoners, including people being held before trial, in the Scandinavian countries (Nellis and King 2009; Sabol, West, and Cooper 2009).

Disparities affecting black people serving life sentences are even greater than prison disparities generally. As table 2.1 shows, 38 percent of sentenced federal and state prisoners in 2008 were non-Hispanic blacks, 34 percent were non-Hispanic whites, and 20 percent were Hispanics. However, among people serving life sentences, 64.7 percent of those in federal prisons were non-Hispanic blacks, and in all prisons 48.3 percent were. Among the 41,000 people serving sentences of life without

Table 2.1. Life Sentences in the United States, 2008, Black, White, Hispanic Percentages

Population	Black	White	Hispanic
Sentenced state and federal prisoners, Total	38	34	20
Life sentences, federal	64.7	17.8	13.7
Life sentences, state and federal combined	48.3 ($N = 66,918$)	33.4 ($N = 47,032$)	14.4 ($N = 20,309$)
LWOPs, federal	66.8	15.6	14.7
LWOPs, state and federal combined	56.4 ($N = 23,181$)	33.5 ($N = 13,751$)	7.4 ($N = 3,052$)

Note: LWOP is the sentence of life without the possibility of parole.

Source: Nellis and King (2009), tables 3, 5.

Table 2.2. Life Sentences in the United States, 2008, Black, White, Hispanic Juvenile Percentages

Population	Black	White	Hispanic
Life sentences, federal	53.9	22.9	17.1
Life sentences, state and federal combined	47.3 ($N = 3,219$)	22.7 ($N = 1,547$)	23.7 ($N = 1,615$)
LWOPs, federal	54.3	25.7	17.1
LWOPs, state and federal combined	56.1 ($N = 984$)	28.3 ($N = 497$)	11.7 ($N = 205$)

Note: LWOP is the sentence of life without the possibility of parole.

Source: Nellis and King (2009), tables 8, 9.

the possibility of parole (LWOP) in federal or state prisons, the racial skewing is even greater: 56.4 percent were non-Hispanic blacks.

Table 2.2 shows similar patterns for juveniles. In most developed countries, few or no people are serving time in adult prisons for crimes they committed as children. In the United States, nearly 7,000 people were serving life sentences in 2008 for crimes committed as juveniles; 47.3 percent were non-Hispanic blacks. Of the nearly 1,800 serving LWOP sentences, 56.1 percent were non-Hispanic blacks. If Hispanics had been apportioned among black and white prisoners in this table and in table 2.1, the black percentages and numbers would be even higher.

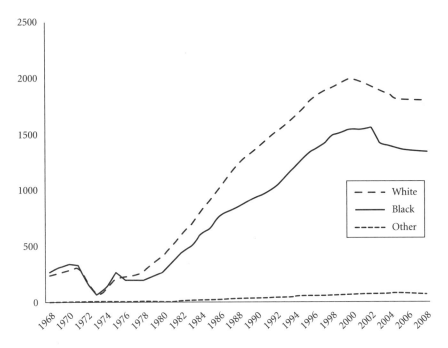

Figure 2.5. Prisoners under Sentence of Death, by Race, 1968–2008.

Source: Snell (2009).

Death, finally, is not different. Racial disparities on death row parallel those for imprisonment generally. Figure 2.5 shows absolute numbers of blacks and whites on death row. The black share has not changed significantly for 25 years, despite the huge and disproportionate increase in blacks serving LWOPs, and significant declines in the numbers of blacks arrested for homicide. Among residents of death row on July 23, 2010, 41.6 percent were non-Hispanic blacks (Death Penalty Information Center 2010).

There are at least five reasons why the disproportionate presence of blacks in American prisons and jails has not changed substantially since 1980. The two most important are that the "War on Drugs" and racial profiling by police unfairly target black people, and that enormous increases in prison sentence lengths for violent and drug crimes have disproportionately affected black offenders. The other reasons, less important empirically but as or more important morally, are racial bias, the influence of unconscious bias and stereotypes, and that black Americans engage in violent crime at higher rates than whites do.[5]

Crime Rates

Thirty years ago, possible explanations for why the prison population was nearly half black were contentious and hotly disputed. The belief was widespread that criminal justice officials were racially biased and too much influenced by racial stereotypes (e.g., American Friends Service Committee 1971). During the 1980s, however, a consensus view emerged that, though bias and stereotyping existed, they were not the primary causes of racial disparities. For serious violent crimes, racial differences in offending were a significant factor: blacks committed homicides, rapes, robberies, and serious assaults at higher rates than whites did. Much violent offending is intra-racial, so failure to take black offenders' violent crimes seriously would constitute indifference to the experiences of black victims. Few people would want to do that. Racial disparities preponderantly based on differences in rates of violent offending are difficult to challenge on normative grounds.

There are two important caveats to the observation that racial offending differences account for a significant portion of imprisonment differences. First, it applied mostly to serious violent offenses; for less serious offenses, offending explained much less of imprisonment disparities. For the most serious crimes, the crime itself appeared to be the primary factor explaining sentencing decisions, leaving comparatively little room for bias or stereotyping to operate. Less serious crimes allowed more room for discretionary decision making, and the crime itself explained less. Second, for some crimes, arrest differences have no necessary link to offending differences; drug arrests are the most important example. Police can arrest inner-city street-level drug dealers almost at will, meaning that arrests measure police activity, not criminality. Disparities in arrests for drug offenses occur because police choose to arrest more black people.

The preceding paragraphs summarize analyses catalyzed by a landmark article by Alfred Blumstein (1982) that compared racial differences in arrests to racial differences in imprisonment, by offense and overall. It prompted additional, more refined analyses by others (e.g., Langan 1985; Tonry 1995). Blumstein's basic conclusions held up and were broadly confirmed by research on sentencing disparities (e.g., Blumstein et al. 1983; Harrington and Spohn 2007; Spohn 2011).

Matthew Melewski and I replicated Blumstein's analysis using arrest and prison population data for 2004 (Tonry and Melewski 2008; Tonry 2011, chap. 2). A much smaller part of racial disparities in imprisonment can be explained by arrest patterns in 2004 than Blumstein found for 1979. In Blumstein's analysis, arrests explained all but 2.8 percent of imprisonment disparities in homicide imprisonment; 11.6 percent remained unexplained in 2004. For robbery in 1979, 15.6 percent of imprisonment disparities went unexplained; in 2004, 37.2 percent. Overall, Blumstein's 1979 analysis left 20.5 percent of imprisonment disparities unexplained; the 2004 analysis left 38.9 percent unexplained. That is a staggering difference. Racial disparities in imprisonment in the United States have been getting worse over the past quarter century.

Pulling things together to this point: black people are arrested for violent crimes at significantly higher rates than whites, but that difference has been declining over time. Racial disparities in imprisonment have, however, not appreciably declined since they reached historic highs during the Reagan administration in the 1980s. Blacks are to an enormous extent disproportionately affected by prison sentences generally, life sentences, LWOPs, and death sentences.

Police and Courts

Why are so many blacks in prison, compared with whites, despite both absolute and relative reductions in violent crimes committed by black people? Sentencing policies for violent and drug crimes and police drug law enforcement practices are a major part of the explanation. So is racial profiling by the police. Biased judges are not.

Sentencing Policies

Black Americans have borne the brunt of tougher sentencing policies. For drug crimes, police arrest blacks at rates that are way out of proportion to their drug use or involvement in drug trafficking. For understandable reasons of social disadvantage and limited life chances, blacks have long been more involved than whites in violent crime, but that difference is becoming less. Laws that increase sentences for drug and violent crimes inevitably exacerbate racial disparities.

The National Corrections Reporting Program of the Bureau of Justice Statistics, for example, reports new state prison commitments by conviction offense and race. In 2003, among whites 53.7 percent were committed for violent, drug, or gun crimes, compared with 69.4 percent of black offenders (in both cases including Hispanic same-race offenders). The racial skew is even greater when the focus is narrowed to robbery, drugs, and guns (52.1 percent of black prisoners, 32.3 percent of white). The effects of police policies concerning drug arrests explain much of the difference. Among black prisoners, 37.5 percent were committed for drug crimes; among white prisoners, 25.5 percent were (Bureau of Justice Statistics 2010).

Biased Sentencing

The sentencing literature documents relatively small racial differences in sentences for black and white offenders convicted of the same crime. Black defendants, all else being equal, are no more likely than whites to be sentenced to confinement for violent crimes, but, among those incarcerated, they receive somewhat longer sentences (Spohn 2011). Blacks are more likely to be sentenced to imprisonment for drug and property crimes. Overall, when statistical controls are used to take account of offense characteristics, prior criminal records, and personal characteristics, black defendants are on average sentenced somewhat but not substantially more severely than whites. Overall, there is no credible evidence that biased decision making by judges is a major cause of sentencing disparities.

The sentencing literature, however, misses a major point. Researchers compare punishments received by black and white offenders for the same offense and attempt to control for other individual characteristics, notably differences in prior criminal records. Such comparisons overlook the larger reality that black defendants are much more likely than white to be convicted of drug and violent offenses for which American laws authorize or mandate sentences measured in decades and lifetimes. In 2008, for example, 79.8 percent of offenders sentenced in federal courts for crack cocaine offenses were black; 10.4 percent were white (U.S. Sentencing Commission 2009, table 34). That there were not major differences in the sentences received by black and white crack defendants is much less consequential than that the prison sentences that crack offenders, mostly black, received were vastly longer than the sentences that powder cocaine offenders received for offenses involving comparable amounts of drugs. Judges may not impose substantially longer sentences on blacks than on whites when they are convicted of the same offense, but the federal 100-to-1 rule resulted in much longer sentences for black defendants and for many more blacks in prison. The 18-to-1 rule that replaced it in 2010 will reduce the difference but only slightly. Three-strikes laws, "dangerous offender" laws, and mandatory minimum sentences for violent and drug crimes work the same way. Vastly higher imprisonment rates for black Americans are attributable primarily not to bad and biased judges but to bad and biased laws.

Racial Profiling

No one doubts that racial profiling by the police takes place or that it results in many more arrests of black people than would otherwise occur. The fundamental questions concerning racial profiling are whether police stop blacks at higher rates than they do whites (yes, they do) and whether police have valid bases for stopping blacks much more often than whites (no, they do not). Answers to the second question are usually sought in evidence about the outcomes of the stops. If blacks are stopped at twice the rate of whites but drugs, guns, and other contraband are found in the same or a higher percentage of cases, that implicitly demonstrates that police had valid reasons more often to be suspicious of blacks. However, the reverse is true. Research on profiling generally concludes that police stop blacks disproportionately often on sidewalks and streets and generally find contraband at lower rates for blacks than for whites (e.g., Engel and Calnon 2004).

An especially comprehensive analysis of police stop-and-frisk practices documenting these patterns was released early in 2009 (Center for Constitutional Rights 2009). I mentioned it above. The data, on police practices in New York City for 42 months ending in mid-2008, were compiled by the New York City Police Department under a federal district court order relating to a lawsuit on racial profiling. There were nearly 1,600,000 police stops of citizens in those 42 months. Half of those stopped were non-Hispanic blacks, 30 percent were Hispanic, and 10 percent were non-Hispanic whites. Those three groups constituted respectively 25, 44, and 28 percent of the population. Blacks were heavily overrepresented. Whites were heavily underrepresented.

Arrest rates were about the same for the three groups, but the arrests of blacks were more intrusive and less productive. Once stopped, blacks were much more likely than whites to be frisked (28 percent of whites in 2006 and 41 percent in 2008, compared with 46 percent of blacks in 2006 and 56 percent in 2008). Only in one percent of cases were weapons found, but at higher rates among whites than among blacks and Hispanics. Overall and in each year separately, whites were more likely than blacks and Hispanics to be in possession of drugs or other contraband. Over the four years, 15 to 18 percent of whites stopped were the victims of police use of force, compared with 21 to 26 percent of blacks and Hispanics.

This massive data set on the operations of the largest police department in the United States thus strongly corroborates the findings of scholarly research. Blacks are stopped much more often than whites, and are much more likely when stopped to be frisked and to have force used against them. They are, however, no more likely to be arrested. That last point warrants elaboration lest an important reality be ignored. Because so many more blacks than whites are stopped, the same or a somewhat lower arrest rate produces vastly larger numbers of black than white people taken into police custody.

Black Americans suffer from imprisonment rates five to seven times higher than whites primarily for two reasons. First, American sentencing laws and policies specify punishments that are both absolutely and relatively severe for violent, drug, and gun crimes, for which blacks are more likely than whites to be arrested and prosecuted. The effects of racial profiling exacerbate those differences. Second, as the following section shows, police arrest policies for drugs target a type of drug trafficking (street-level transactions in inner-city areas) in which blacks are disproportionately involved, even though overall they are less likely than whites to use drugs and no more likely to sell drugs.

II. Drugs

The War on Drugs produced massive racial disparities in arrest, conviction, and imprisonment. In 2008 the arrest rate of blacks for drug crimes was 3.5 times higher than that for whites. In 2006, the last year for which national data from state courts are available, 49 percent of defendants in urban courts charged with drug crimes were non-Hispanic blacks and 26 percent were non-Hispanic whites. For trafficking the racial imbalance is greater: 59 percent black, 16 percent white (Kyckelhahn and Cohen 2010, table A2). In 2003, 37.5 percent of black people committed to state prisons had been convicted of drug crimes; among whites newly committed to prison, 25.5 percent were (Bureau of Justice Statistics 2010). Among those held in state prisons for drug offenses in 2006, 45 percent (117,600) were non-Hispanic blacks and 27 percent (72,100) were non-Hispanic whites (Sabol, West, and Cooper 2009, table A15).

These differences do not occur because black Americans are more involved with drugs than whites. Black Americans do not use drugs as much or as often as white Americans. Drug selling is at least as frequent among whites as among blacks. Racial disparities are a product of how the drug wars have been fought.

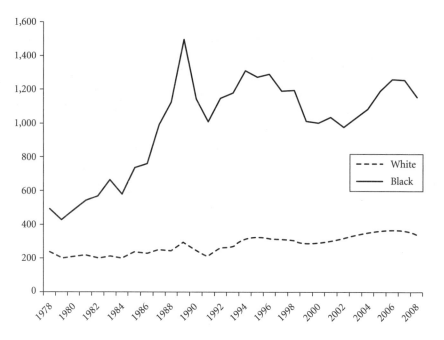

Figure 2.6. Total arrests for Drug Offenses, by Race, 1978–2008.
Sources: BJS *Sourcebook of Criminal Justice Statistics* (http://www.albany.edu/sourcebook/), various years.

To be imprisoned, people first must be arrested. Figure 2.6 shows black and white drug arrest rates per 100,000 population from 1978 to 2008. The black rate in 1978 was approximately twice the white rate. By the mid-1980s the black rate was three times higher. Startlingly, in the late 1980s the black arrest rate for drug crimes was nearly six times the white rate. Since then the arrest rate disparity has usually been at Reagan administration levels, with the black rate between three and four times higher.

Why are blacks so much more often arrested and imprisoned for drug crimes? There are four possible answers: blacks use drugs at higher rates than whites; blacks sell drugs at higher rates than whites; police arrest blacks for drug offenses in numbers disproportionate to their involvement in drug dealing; and black drug offenders receive harsher sentences than white offenders. The first two explanations do not withstand scrutiny: blacks neither use nor sell drugs at higher rates than whites. The second two explain what has been happening: police focus substantially greater attention on drug sales by blacks, and once blacks are arrested they are dealt with more severely.

Racial Patterns in Drug Use

The explanation for high black rates of drug arrests is not that more blacks than whites use drugs. National surveys carried out for the federal government have tracked self-reported drug use since the 1970s. The National Survey on Drug Use and Health is an annual representative survey among persons 12 years and older (Office of Applied Studies 2010). The survey shows percentages of blacks and whites who reported in 2007 and 2008 using alcohol, any other drugs, and five specific illicit substances ever, in the past year, and in the past month.[6]

For everything but crack, the percentages of whites reporting that they had ever used particular substances were higher than the black percentages. For hallucinogens and inhalants, the white percentages were two to three times higher. For cocaine, the white percentages were 50 percent higher. For alcohol, the white percentages were 15 percent higher; for marijuana they were 10 percent higher. Only for crack, for which use levels are far lower than for powder cocaine, are the black percentages higher.

Even though lower percentages of whites than blacks, for example, report having used crack ever in their lives or in the preceding year or month, the absolute numbers of white crack users are far higher. In 2007, nearly 5.8 million whites were estimated ever to have used crack, compared with 1.5 million blacks. Among whites, 938,000 were estimated to have used crack in the preceding year compared with 385,000 blacks. The use estimates for the preceding month were 399,000 for whites and 155,000 for blacks (Office of Applied Studies 2010, table 1.34A). One conclusion is clear: blacks are not arrested or imprisoned so much more often than whites for drug crimes because black people use drugs much more extensively than whites. They don't.

Racial Patterns in Drug Sales

The second possible reason that blacks might more often be arrested for drug crimes is that they are much more extensively involved in drug trafficking. Several sources suggest that this is not true. The best sources are the national drug use surveys based on representative samples of the U.S. population. Figure 2.7 shows self-reported drug selling by 12-to-17-year-old blacks and whites for the years 2001 to 2008. Three to 4 percent of each group typically reported selling drugs at least once during the preceding year, and one percent of each group reported selling drugs ten or more times. The black and white rates are nearly identical. However, on average for the entire period and for most years, self-reported rates of drug selling by whites were slightly higher than rates for blacks.

The reason that so many more blacks than whites are arrested for drug crimes is well-known and long recognized. As figure 2.8 shows, they are much easier to arrest. Much white drug trafficking occurs behind closed doors and in private. Much black drug dealing occurs in public or semi-public, on the streets, and in open-air drug markets. And much black drug dealing occurs between strangers.

The importance of that difference should not be underestimated. Purchasing drugs is a much riskier activity for young black people than for young whites. Only one in ten whites bought marijuana from someone they did not already know. The chances that they were purchasing from an undercover police officer who might arrest them were low. Conversely, the chances that sellers to white buyers were

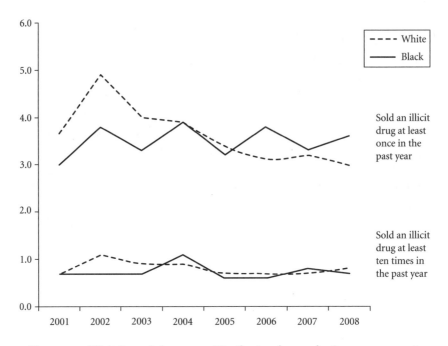

Figure 2.7. Illicit Drug Sales among Youths Aged 12–17, by Race, 2001–2008.
Source: Office of Applied Studies, *National Survey on Drug Use and Health*, various years.

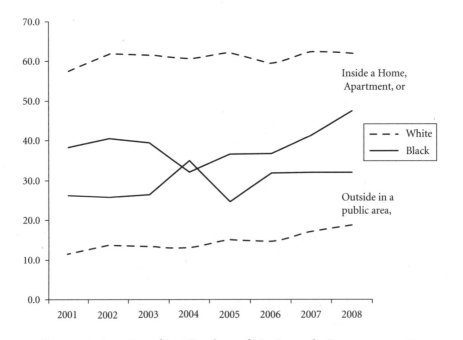

Figure 2.8. Location of Last Purchase of Marijuana, by Race, 2001–2008.
Source: Office of Applied Studies, *National Survey on Drug Use and Health*, various years. Categories do not account for 100 percent of purchases because the following response categories were excluded: inside a public building, such as a store or restaurant; inside a school building; outside on school property; and some other place.

selling to an undercover police officer were also low. For blacks, the transactions were far riskier for buyers and sellers alike. Especially for the black seller: a much larger proportion of sales are to strangers.

The most extensive and fine-grained studies of street-level drug markets and police arrest policies were carried out in Seattle. Overall, only 8.4 percent of Seattle's residents in 2000 were black, but in a 28-month period during 1999–2001, 51.1 percent of those arrested for drug offenses were black (Beckett et al. 2005, 424). A majority of people who shared, sold, or transferred drugs were white, but 64 percent of people arrested for trafficking offenses were black. Among outdoor drug transactions, a third involved crack, a third involved heroin, and a fourth involved powder cocaine. Among arrests for outdoor drug dealing, 79 percent were for crack, 17 percent involved heroin, and 3 percent involved powder cocaine (Beckett, Nyrop, and Pfingst 2006, figure 1).

The researchers concluded that the disparity was the result of the police department's emphasis on the outdoor drug market in the racially diverse downtown, its lack of attention to other outdoor markets that were predominantly white, its relative disinterest in heroin sellers (who were predominantly white), and its emphasis on crack cocaine:

> In over two-thirds of buy-bust operations (in which undercover enforcement officers solicit drugs from suspected drug dealers), officers requested crack cocaine. We even came across records of cases in which undercover officers were offered heroin and powder cocaine by street dealers (both black and white) and refused to purchase those substances, saying they only wanted crack. (Beckett et al. 2005, 429)

Racial Patterns in Drug Arrests

Undercover drug agents can relatively easily penetrate black urban drug markets in socially disorganized areas and make arrests almost at will. An undercover police officer can purchase drugs on the street from strangers. Even with street-level dealers who are more cautious, a minority officer working undercover can within hours or days become a familiar local figure. Most white drug dealing, by contrast, occurs within existing social networks in which people know one another and in private places—homes, locker rooms in factories, local bars—to which strangers cannot easily gain admission. Undercover agents have to invest much more time in establishing their bona fides. A stranger in a bar asking "Who here will sell me some coke?" is unlikely to find a willing seller. Getting into private homes or factories to buy drugs is even harder.

Sociologist John Hagedorn conducted ethnographic studies of black and white drug markets in Milwaukee. Black drug sales generally occurred openly in the inner city, on the streets, and often to strangers. In white suburban communities, where "nearly all drug transactions were at places of employment or at after-work leisure activities," the picture was different and more insular:

Drugs are sold mainly by "word-of-mouth" means in the suburbs and to white youth. There are no stable, neighborhood, drug-selling locales like [in the African American neighborhoods studied]. . . . White youth and suburban drug dealers hire very few employees, and drug dealing is more part of a "partying" lifestyle than a job. Drugs are sold to whites through contacts at work, at taverns and athletic leagues, and at alternative cultural events. . . . These methods are more hidden from law enforcement than neighborhood-based sales. (Hagedorn 1998, 1–2)

The arrest yield from a fixed amount of time or effort is much lower when pursuing white than when pursuing black sellers. In a city in which drug arrests are emphasized, an individual officer's productivity in a given amount of time is much greater when black dealers are targeted. If the department wants to maximize arrests, the individual officer will also.

Black arrest rates for drug crimes are high for two reasons. First, police invest more energy and effort in arresting people in inner cities and on the streets, circumstances that disproportionately target drug transactions involving blacks. Second, racial profiling in police stops of citizens identifies disproportionate numbers of black people possessing drugs who can be arrested. There is therefore no mystery as to why blacks are so much more often arrested for drug crimes than whites, even though they use drugs less often and sell drugs no more. It results from the ways the police choose to enforce drug laws.

Racial Patterns in Conviction and Imprisonment for Drug Crimes

Once the arrests are made, the machinery of the criminal justice system is set in motion. Racial disparities in imprisonment for drug crimes are vastly greater than can be explained by reference even to racially disparate patterns of arrest.

Blacks' much higher drug arrest rates lead to even greater disparities in imprisonment, as a series of Bureau of Justice Statistics reports on state court operations shows for 2006. Two-thirds of drug felony charges resulted in convictions, and two-thirds of drug felony convictions resulted in imprisonment. Although blacks constituted about a third of drug arrestees, they constituted 49 percent of drug felony defendants in 2006. Among people convicted of drug felonies, 71 percent of blacks were sentenced to confinement, compared with 63 percent of whites (Cohen and Kyckelhahn 2010).

A compounding is going on: blacks are arrested for drug crimes much more often than their participation in drug use or trafficking would justify, but then, in addition, they are sent to prison in numbers much greater than their arrests for drug offenses would justify.

Table 2.3 shows that blacks were much more heavily overrepresented among felony drug defendants in 2006 in state courts than their 35 percent share among arrestees appears to justify: 49 percent of felony drug defendants were non-Hispanic blacks, 26 percent were non-Hispanic whites, and 24 percent were Hispanic. Fifty-nine percent of those prosecuted for trafficking were non-Hispanic blacks. That

Table 2.3. Race and Hispanic Origin of Defendants, Drug Felonies, Percentages, State Courts, 2006

Offense	Black, non-Hispanic	White, non-Hispanic	Hispanic	Other
Total	49	26	24	1
Trafficking	59	16	23	2
Other drugs	43	33	24	1

Source: Cohen and Kyckelhahn (2010), table A2.

Table 2.4. Racial Characteristics of Persons Convicted of Drug Felonies, State Courts, 2006

Drug Offense	Black*	White*	Other
All drugs	44	55	1
Possession	36	62	2
Trafficking	49	50	1

Source: Durose, Farole, and Rosenmerkel (2009), table 3.2.

racial breakdown is used in the original source. If Hispanics were allocated between the racial groups, the black percentage would be even higher.

Table 2.4 points up the disproportionate black presence among people convicted of drug offenses in 2006. Forty-four percent of people convicted of any drug offense were non-Hispanic blacks, as were 49 percent of those convicted for drug trafficking. Here, as always, if Hispanics were included within racial categories, the black percentages would be higher.

Blacks convicted of drug offenses receive harsher sentences than whites. This is primarily because many more black than white offenders are arrested and convicted for crack cocaine offenses and because more blacks are affected by mandatory minimum sentence laws.

Table 2.5 shows the types of sentences received following drug felony convictions by black and white drug offenders in state courts in 2006. The general pattern is that blacks more often receive prison sentences and that whites more often receive jail and non-incapacitative sentences. The first two columns show that 70 percent of black drug felons receive incarcerative sentences, compared with 61 percent of white drug felons. The last two columns show that 39 percent of whites receive non-incarcerative sentences compared with 30 percent of blacks. The intermediate columns show that slightly more whites receive (by definition, short) jail sentences. Blacks are much more likely to be sentenced to state prisons.

So there it is. When all the relevant data are pulled together, it is clear that black people bear most of the brunt of the War on Drugs. It is also clear that racial disparities among people imprisoned for drug offenses arise primarily from racial profiling by the police, deliberate police policies to focus drug law enforcement on

Table 2.5. Type of Sentence, Drug Felonies in Urban Counties, By Race, 2006, Percentages

Offense	Total Incarceration Black / White	Prison Black / White	Jail Black / White	Non-incarceration Black / White
All drug	70 / 61	43 / 31	27 / 30	30 / 39
Trafficking	70 / 59	46 / 33	25 / 26	30 / 41
Possession	71 / 63	38 / 28	33 / 35	29 / 37

Source: Rosenmerkel, Durose, and Farole (2009), table 3.4.

inner-city drug markets, and deliberate legislative decisions to attach the longest prison sentences to drug offenses for which blacks are disproportionately arrested.

III. Doing Less Damage to Black Americans

Much of the damage done to disadvantaged black Americans and their loved ones in the name of crime control and drug law enforcement was, and is, avoidable. Two approaches are corrective: radical reduction in the use of prison sentences and abandonment of policies and laws that do unnecessary damage. Two others are preventive: reduction of bias and stereotyping and creation of devices that make future adoption of policies that cause unjustifiable racial disparities less likely.

Reduced Use of Imprisonment

The only way to reduce the massive damage that current policies do to black Americans is to reduce the prison population substantially, as is illustrated in table 2.6, using data for 2006. Prison disparities do not result primarily from biased or unconsciously stereotyped decisions. The top row of Part A shows black and white imprisonment rates per 100,000 population for jail and prison combined in 2006.[7] The second row shows what would happen if black rates were decreased by 10 percent—a high estimate of the degree to which bias and stereotyping enhance disparities—while white rates were left unchanged. The black imprisonment rate would fall from approximately 2,661 per 100,000 to 2,395 and the ratio of black-to-white imprisonment rates would fall from 5.5 to 1 to 5.0 to 1. The number of black people locked up would fall by about 100,000.

If instead, as Part B shows, the prison population were cut by half across the board, disparities would not be reduced, but the black imprisonment rate would fall from 2,661 to 1,330. Or if, as Part C shows, imprisonment rates were cut to 1980 levels, disparities would not be reduced; the black imprisonment rate would be 827 per 100,000.

Table 2.6. Hypothetical Reduction in Incarceration Rates

	Black	White	Ratio
	A. Disparity Reduced 10%		
Imprisonment rate, 2006	2,661	483	5.5:1
10% less disparity	2,395	483	5.0:1
Reduction in prison per 100,000	266	0	
Reduction in black prisoners	101,000		
	B. Use of Imprisonment Halved		
Imprisonment rate, 2006	2,661	483	5.5:1
Imprisonment halved	1,330	241	5.5:1
Reduction in prison per 100,000	1,330	241	
Reduction in black prisoners	505,400		
	C. Return to 1980 Imprisonment Rates		
Imprisonment rate, 1980	827	134	6.2:1
Reduction in prison per 100,000	1,834	349	
Reduction in black prisoners	697,000		

Source: Tonry and Melewski (2008), table 5.

The differing effects of these alternative approaches are enormous. The U.S. Census estimated that 38.34 million U.S. residents in 2006 were black. If the number of people in prison were halved, but nothing else changed, the black imprisonment rate would fall from 26,613 per million to 13,306. Over 500,000 fewer black Americans would be in prison or jail. Returning to the 1980 level would mean 700,000 fewer black Americans behind bars.

Only radical reduction in the scale of imprisonment in America can make a big difference. Devices need to be created for reducing the lengths of current prison sentences and releasing hundreds of thousands of people serving unnecessarily long terms. Sentencing laws and guidelines need to be changed to reduce the use of imprisonment and to shorten prison sentences. New programs need to be created to divert many people from prison or jail into community correctional programs. New systems of parole, pardon, and commutation need to be developed. So do new programs of social welfare and support to ease ex-prisoners' transition back into the free community. None of these changes need be focused on black offenders or on black prisoners. Black imprisonment rates are so high partly for the reasons set out here, but also because American imprisonment rates are so high.

Changes in Drug Policy

The enormous increase in the size of the prison population over the past 30 years is to a significant extent the product of the police and sentencing policies associated with the War on Drugs. The clear weight of the evidence, however, and the conclusions of most leading drug policy scholars concur: arresting hundreds of thousands of inner-city street-level drug dealers and sending them to prison for long periods has had little or no effect on the availability of drugs in the United States. A single measure—street prices of drugs—shows this. Federal drug enforcement agencies for 40 years have regularly purchased drugs from street-level dealers in order to monitor drug prices and availability. If massive arrests and severe penalties were making drugs less available, simple economic theory instructs that prices should be rising. Instead, they have fallen steadily since the early 1980s.

Data from the Office of National Drug Control Policy show that the street price of one gram of pure crack fell from about $650 in 1982 to about $200 in 1992 (both in 2007 constant dollars) and has continued to fall since then. The principal reason for this is that street-level drug dealers who are arrested are quickly replaced. Other disadvantaged young people are willing to accept substantial risks for what—mistakenly—they believe to be prospects of better earnings than are otherwise available to them (MacCoun and Martin 2009; Caulkins and Reuter 2010; Caulkins and Kleiman 2011).

Targeting the Causes of Racial Disparities

A wide range of contemporary criminal justice policies do unnecessary damage to black Americans. Some can be addressed by the police. Others require administrative or legislative changes.

Racial Profiling

Under current American law, racial profiling is legal as long as police offer another, pretextual reason for stopping someone. Michelle Alexander (2010) and Kevin R. Johnson (2010) have shown, through a careful analysis of U.S. Supreme Court decisions over four decades, that the court has systematically dismantled constitutional procedural protections that in earlier times would have made racial profiling difficult to impossible. Under current law, police can stop people *because* they are black or Hispanic or are members of other ethnic groups, as long as the police provide some additional reason for doing so. This reason can be no more than a hunch, or a statement that "my experience led me to believe. . . . " Subjective considerations such as those are impossible for courts to second guess.

Racial profiling is per se unfair. It alienates many minority citizens and makes them distrust the police and the criminal justice system. It also puts black people at greater risk than whites of being arrested for reasons that would otherwise not come to the attention of the police. It should stop. When an arrest results from an unlawful search or seizure, the criminal charges are tossed out. Criminal charges resulting from arrests based on racial profiling should be dealt with in the same way. Police incentives would change substantially if, after the fact, every arrest arguably resulting from profiling were subject to the same degree of judicial scrutiny that warrants before the fact are supposed to receive.

Drug Arrests

Drug arrests are the second source of disparity that is within the power of police executives to alter. Police targeting of inner-city drug markets has produced racial disparities between blacks and whites for drug arrests as high as six to one in some years. Retargeting to focus equally on white drug dealers would make an important symbolic statement about racial fairness, would reduce racial disparities, and would pursue the aims of drug law enforcement no less effectively. As a practical matter, police efforts to target whites and blacks equally would reduce arrests overall. It takes much more time to apprehend whites selling drugs behind closed doors than to arrest black sellers in open-air street markets. Greatly increased emphasis on drug dealing by whites would most likely produce a political backlash that would lead to a reconsideration of drug enforcement policy, as happened with marijuana in the 1970s. I don't really want the police to arrest more whites for drug crimes; great harm to many individuals would result, and for no good reason, given the proven ineffectiveness of the War on Drugs. Similar considerations dictate—as a moral matter—that many fewer blacks should be arrested.

Criminal Records

The United States is unique among Western countries in giving very great weight to prior convictions in setting sentences for new crimes. In most countries, the effect of an offender having one or more prior convictions is to increase sentences for new crimes by a few months. In the United States, the "recidivist premium" often doubles or triples the sentence. Because black offenders are arrested more often and at younger ages than whites, they are more often affected by prior record increments. Richard Frase (2009) has shown that two-thirds of the difference in prison sentences received by blacks and whites in Minnesota result from racial differences in prior records. Ways need to be devised to change that. Exactly how is not so important. What is important is recognition that current practices and policies greatly worsen racial disparities in imprisonment, to no good end, and that means must be found to lessen the damage they do.

Lengthy Prison Sentences

Mandatory minimum, life without the possibility of parole, and truth-in-sentencing laws mostly affect drug and violent criminals, often require sentences measured in decades, and are a major contributor to racial disparities. They should be repealed and no new ones should be enacted. American jurisdictions need to establish principled new systems of sentencing guidelines, coupled with new mechanisms for shortening unduly, disparately, or disproportionately long prison sentences. Parole release systems long performed that function, among others, but many have been abolished. They need to be reestablished. Parole boards that survived became much too cautious and in doing so increased both lengths of sentences served and prison populations. They need to rethink their policies. New sentencing guidelines will need to call for proportionate sentences measured mostly in months for many crimes, in single-digit years for most serious crimes, and in longer periods only for very serious crimes and very dangerous offenders.

Reduce Racial Bias and Stereotyping

Many states have created racial equity task forces in their court systems. Continuing education programs attempt to sensitize judges and court and correctional personnel about the ubiquity and perniciousness of unconscious stereotyping and attribution. These are important programs and they need to continue and to be expanded.

U.S. federal and state governments should in addition require that racial disparity impact projections be prepared as a routine element of consideration of proposed sentencing legislation, and that operating agencies conduct racial disparity audits. Both should be relatively uncontroversial. Most legislatures now require that fiscal impact assessments accompany proposed legislation. Every American jurisdiction requires development of environmental impact projections before new buildings are built or existing ones are altered in sensitive environments. Racial disparity audits examine current practices to see, in the first instance, whether they affect members of different groups differently. When disparities are documented, the next question is whether they can be justified. Disparity impact projections are similar, except that they focus on proposed changes in policy and practice in order to identify foreseeable disparities and to determine whether they can be justified. If disparities cannot be justified, the policies should be abandoned.

Proposals for disparity audits and impact assessments are not novel. Iowa enacted a law requiring use of racial impact assessment. The Minnesota Sentencing Guidelines Commission regularly conducts disparity audits and impact assessments, as do many other criminal justice agencies. The second edition of the *Model Penal Code* (American Law Institute 2007) requires them.

Proposals for major reductions in America's prison population, repeal of punitive legislation, and requirement of race and ethnicity impact assessments may strike some readers as fanciful. But if racial disparities and the damage they have unarguably done to millions of individual black Americans and their families, and to black Americans as a group, are pressing social problems, then strong measures are called for.

NOTES

1. Usually in this article, unless otherwise indicated, data on black and white populations include Hispanics. Since the late 1990s, the U.S. Bureau of Justice Statistics (BJS) has reported prison and jail data separately for Hispanics and non-Hispanic blacks and whites, departing from an earlier practice of reporting data for blacks and whites including Hispanics among them. To maintain continuity in data sources, Hispanics have been redistributed among black and white populations for the years since BJS changed its practice.

2. The discussion in the text is in general terms. Much finer-grained analyses could be carried out that compare Hispanic percentages among prisoners and jail inmates with year-to-year changes in the size and the age and gender composition of the Hispanic population. Even the simple calculations described in the text, however, make it clear that much of the rise in numbers of black and Hispanic prisoners results from population increases and group differences in age composition. Morin (2008) and Oboler (2009) are recent comprehensive examinations of Hispanics' experiences in the criminal justice system. Demuth and Steffensmeier (2004), one of the most exhaustive studies of sentencing disparities affecting Hispanics compared with blacks and whites, concludes that blacks are sentenced more severely than whites, and that Hispanics are sentenced more like blacks than like whites.

3. There is in any case only a small, and not very rigorous, literature on Hispanics' experience in the criminal justice system. A Recent relatively comprehensive overview can be found in Oboler (2009). Disparity analyses are especially difficult because the FBI's Uniform Crime Reports do not include a separate Hispanic category for arrestees.

4. Change occurred only in August 2010 when President Obama signed the Fair Sentencing Act of 2010. It modestly amended the 100-to-1 law, but removed neither its fundamental unfairness nor its foreseeable disparate effects on black offenders. It became an 18-to-1 law. A mandatory minimum five-year prison sentence awaits any low-level dealer convicted of selling 28 grams of crack. A powder cocaine dealer must sell a half-kilogram to face such a destiny.

5. Large recent literatures on colorism (light-skinned blacks are sentenced like whites; middle- and dark-skinned blacks are sentenced more severely), Afro-American feature bias (blacks with distinctly African American features, including thick lips, broad noses, and dark skins, are punished more severely), and implicit bias (almost all Americans associate black people with crime) document the influence of conscious and unconscious stereotypes. These literatures are summarized in Tonry (2011, chap. 4).

6. These results are presented and discussed at greater length in Tonry (2011), chapter 3.

7. The black/white ratio is not higher than 5.5 to 1 because the table uses BJS data that exclude Hispanics of all races and because it contains combined data on men and women. The disparity ratio, so calculated, for women in 2006 was significantly lower (3.8 to 1) than that for men (6.3 to 1) (Sabol, Minton, and Harrison 2007, table 14).

REFERENCES

Alexander, Michelle. 2010. *The New Jim Crow: Mass Incarceration in the Age of Colorblind-edness*. New York: New Press.

American Friends Service Committee. 1971. *Struggle for Justice*. New York: Hill & Wang.

American Law Institute. 2007. *Model Penal Code: Sentencing*. Tentative draft no. 1 (April 9, 2007). Philadelphia: American Law Institute.

Beckett, Katherine, Kris Nyrop, and Lori Pfingst. 2006. "Race, Drugs, and Policing: Understanding Disparities in Drug Delivery Arrests." *Criminology* 44(1): 105–137.

Beckett, Katherine, Kris Nyrop, Lori Pfingst, and Melissa Bowell. 2005. "Drug Use, Drug Possession Arrests, and the Question of Race." *Social Problems* 52(3): 419–441.

Blumstein, Alfred. 1982. "On Racial Disproportionality of the United States' Prison Populations." *Journal of Criminal Law and Criminology* 73: 1259–1281.

Blumstein, Alfred, and Allen Beck. 1999. "Population Growth in U.S. Prisons, 1980–1996." In *Prisons*, eds. Michael Tonry and Joan Petersilia. Vol. 26 of *Crime and Justice: A Review of Research*, ed. Michael Tonry. Chicago: University of Chicago Press.

Blumstein, Alfred, Jacqueline Cohen, Susan Martin, and Michael Tonry, eds. 1983. *Research on Sentencing: The Search for Reform*. Washington, DC: National Academy Press.

Bonczar, Thomas P. 2003. *Prevalence of Imprisonment in the U.S. Population, 1974–2001*. Washington, DC: Bureau of Justice Statistics, U.S. Department of Justice.

Bureau of Justice Statistics. 2007. "Prison and Jail Inmates at Mid-Year 2006." Washington, DC: Bureau of Justice Statistics, U.S. Department of Justice.

Bureau of Justice Statistics. 2010. "National Corrections Reporting Program." Available at: http://bjs.ojp.usdoj.gov/index.cfm?ty=dcdetail&iid=268.

Caulkins, Jonathan P., and Mark A. R. Kleiman. 2011. "Drugs and Crime." In *The Oxford Handbook of Crime and Criminal Justice*. New York: Oxford University Press.

Caulkins, Jonathan P., and Peter Reuter. 2010. "How Drug Enforcement Affects Drug Prices." In *Crime and Justice: A Review of Research*, vol. 39, ed. Michael Tonry. Chicago: University of Chicago Press.

Center for Constitutional Rights. 2009. *Racial Disparity in NYPD Stops-and-Frisks*. New York: Center for Constitutional Rights. Available at: www.CCRJustice.org.

Coase, Ronald. 1978. "Economics and Contiguous Disciplines." *Journal of Legal Studies* 7: 210–211.

Cohen, Thomas H., and Tracey Kyckelhahn. 2010. *Felony Defendants in Large Urban Counties, 2006*. Washington, DC: Bureau of Justice Statistics, U.S. Department of Justice.

Death Penalty Information Center. 2010. "National Statistics on the Death Penalty and Race; Death Row Populations by Race." Available at: http://www.deathpenaltyinfo.org/race-death-row-inmates-executed-1976#inmaterace (accessed July 29, 2010).

Demuth, Stephen, and Darrell Steffensmeier. 2004. "Ethnicity Effects on Sentence Outcomes in Large Urban Courts: Comparisons Among White, Black and Hispanic Defendants." *Social Science Quarterly* 85(4): 994–1011.

Engel, Robin Shepard, and Jennifer M. Calnon. 2004. "Examining the Influence of Drivers' Characteristics During Traffic Stops with Police: Results from a National Survey." *Justice Quarterly* 21(1): 49–90.

Fellner, Jamie. 2009. "Race, Drugs, and Law Enforcement in the United States." *Stanford Law and Policy Review* 20: 257–291.

Frase, Richard. 2009. "What Explains Persistent Racial Disproportionality in Minnesota's Prison and Jail Populations?" In *Crime and Justice: A Review of Research*, vol. 38, ed. Michael Tonry. Chicago: Chicago University Press.

Hagedorn, John. 1998. "The Business of Drug Dealing in Milwaukee." Milwaukee: Wisconsin Policy Research Institute. Available at: http://www.csdp.org/research/drugdeal.pdf.

Harrington, Michael P., and Cassia Spohn. 2007. "Defining Sentence Type: Further Evidence Against Use of the Total Incarceration Variable." *Journal of Research in Crime and Delinquency* 44(1): 36–63.

International Centre for Prison Studies. 2010. *World Prison Brief*. Kings College London. Available at: www.kcl.ac.uk/depsta/law/research/icps/worldbrief/wpb_stats.php (consulted July 20, 2010).

Johnson, Kevin R. 2010. "How Racial Profiling in America Became the Law of the Land." *Georgetown Law Review* 98(4): 1005–1077.

King, Ryan S. 2008. *Disparity by Geography: The War on Drugs in America's Cities*. Washington. DC: The Sentencing Project.

Kyckelhahn, Tracey, and Thomas H. Cohen. 2008. *Felony Defendants in Large Urban Counties, 2004*. NCJ 221152. Washington, DC: Bureau of Justice Statistics, U.S. Department of Justice.

Langan, Patrick. 1985. "Racism on Trial: New Evidence to Explain the Racial Composition of Prisons in the United States." *Journal of Criminal Law and Criminology* 76: 666–683.

Lauritsen, Janet L. 2003. "How Families and Communities Influence Youth Victimization." *OJJDP Juvenile Justice Bulletin*. Washington, DC: U.S. Department of Justice, Office of Juvenile Justice and Delinquency Prevention.

MacCoun, Robert, and Karin D. Martin. 2009. "Drugs." In *Handbook on Crime and Public Policy*, ed. Michael Tonry. New York: Oxford University Press.

McDonald, Douglas C., and Kenneth C. Carlson. 1993. *Sentencing in the Federal Courts: Does Race Matter?* Washington, DC: Bureau of Justice Statistics, U.S. Department of Justice.

McNulty, Thomas, and Paul E. Bellair. 2003. "Explaining Racial and Ethnic Differences in Serious Adolescent Violent Behavior." *Criminology* 41: 709–748.

Morin, Jose Luis. 2008. "Latinas/os and US Prisons: Trends and Challenges." *Latino Studies* 6: 11–34.

Nellis, Ashley, and Ryan S. King. 2009. *No Exit: The Expanding Use of Life Sentences in America*. Washington, DC: The Sentencing Project.

Oboler, Suzanne, ed. 2009. *Behind Bars: Latino/as and Prison in the United States*. New York: Palgrave Macmillan.

Office of Applied Studies. 2010. Results from the 2008 *National Survey on Drug Use and Health: National Findings*. Rockville, MD: Substance Abuse and Mental Health Services Administration. Available at: http://www.oas.samhsa.gov/ NSDUH/2K8NSDUH/tabs/toc.htm (consulted August 6, 2010).

Pager, Devah. 2007. *Marked: Race, Crime, and Finding Work in an Era of Mass Incarceration*. Chicago: University of Chicago.

Sabol, William J., Todd D. Minton, and Paige M. Harrison. 2007. "Prison and Jail Inmates at Midyear 2006." Washington, DC: Bureau of Justice Statistics, U.S. Department of Justice Report.

Sabol, William J., Heather C. West, and Matthew Cooper. 2009. *Prisoners in 2008*. (Revised April 1, 2010). Washington, DC: Bureau of Justice Statistics, U.S. Department of Justice.

Spohn, Cassia. 2011. "Race, Ethnicity, and Criminal Justice." In *The Oxford Handbook of Crime and Criminal Justice*, ed. Michael Tonry. New York: Oxford University Press.

Tonry, Michael. 1995. *Malign Neglect: Race, Crime, and Punishment in America*. New York: Oxford University Press.

Tonry, Michael. 2011. *Punishing Race: An American Dilemma Continues*. New York: Oxford University Press.

Tonry, Michael, and Matthew Melewski. 2008. "The Malign Effects of Drugs and Crime Control Policies on Black Americans." In *Crime and Justice: A Review of Research*, vol. 37, ed. Michael Tonry. Chicago: University of Chicago Press.

Uggen, Christopher, Jeff Manza, and Melissa Thompson. 2006. "Citizenship, Democracy, and the Civic Reintegration of Criminal Offenders." *Annals of the American Academy of Political and Social Science* 605(1): 281–310.

U.S. Department of Commerce. 2010. *Statistical Abstract of the United States: 2010*. Washington, DC: Bernan Press.

U.S. Sentencing Commission. 2009. *2008 Sourcebook of Federal Sentencing Statistics*. Washington, DC: U.S. Sentencing Commission.

CHAPTER 3

THE COLLATERAL EFFECTS OF IMPRISONMENT ON PRISONERS, THEIR FAMILIES, AND COMMUNITIES

ALEC EWALD AND CHRISTOPHER UGGEN

THE term "collateral" connotes a variety of phenomena, ranging from specific legal restrictions imposed on people caught up in the criminal-justice process—but not included in the formal terms of their sentence—to the broader impacts of incarceration on children, families, specific communities, and democratic institutions. This chapter examines both types of collateral effects. With the rapid growth in U.S. criminal punishment over the past four decades, such effects have taken on greater meaning for socio-legal scholars, practitioners, policy makers, and, most importantly, people convicted of criminal offenses.

Over the last decade in particular, there has been a dramatic increase in public, academic, and governmental interest in sanctions imposed on individuals and the collateral effects of imprisonment. A spate of articles in the national media, major publications from organizations such as the American Bar Association and the Uniform Law Commission, federal legislation such as the Second Chance Act of 2007[1] and public hearings all foreground concepts such as reentry and reintegration—and the barriers posed by the formal and informal collateral consequences of incarceration. Despite this growing attention and interest, how-ever, it is still the case that "not just offenders, but many participants in the crim-inal justice system remain wholly unaware of these consequences" (Pinard and Thompson 2006, 590), and there are still considerable gaps in what we know about the collateral impacts of the ongoing American experiment in mass incarceration. While evidence is accumulating on the direct effects of restrictions on former prisoners, we are only beginning to understand how these consequences ripple outward to affect families and communities.

This chapter will thus introduce and describe the landscape of "invisible pun-ishment," as collateral consequences are often called (Travis 2002). The first section briefly identifies significant legal consequences of involvement with the criminal-justice system—restrictions attaching to a conviction or even to mere allegations of illegal conduct, but usually not a formal part of the sentence. The second section assays the impact of incarceration and criminal-justice contact on the convicted person—including their prospects for employment, desistance from crime, and social integration—as well as on families. The third section examines this topic from a broader social vantage, describing research on how specific communities and democracy itself are impacted by mass incarceration. The chapter concludes by sketching some of the more promising reform proposals in this area.

I. LEGAL CONSEQUENCES

Scope and Definition

A long list of federal and state-specific restrictions related to political, economic, social, and domestic activities are imposed on people who have been convicted of crime, or in some cases, merely arrested or charged. Because they are most often located outside the penal code, implemented by non–criminal justice institutions, and interpreted by the courts as civil regulations rather than criminal penalties, these restrictions are called "collateral consequences" or "collateral sanctions."[2] Some such restrictions are quite old, but many have either been altered in recent years or are new altogether; both the American Bar Association (ABA) and the National Confer-ence of Commissioners on Uniform State Laws (NCCUSL) conclude that federal and state collateral sanctions have expanded in the United States in the last 20 years (ABA 2004; NCCUSL 2010). Many restrictions are not lifted automatically and can indeed be quite difficult to remove: one expert writes that existing state relief mech-anisms are "generally inaccessible, or ineffective, or both" (Love 2003, 101). The result is that collateral consequences often persist long after a sentence has been served.

The alliterative term "collateral consequences of criminal convictions" is com-monly used in discussion of these laws (see, e.g., U.S. House of Representatives,

Committee on the Judiciary 2010), and indeed some restrictions are triggered by a conviction. Yet it is vital to understand that several of the most serious collateral consequences may befall people at stages well short of a felony conviction. Eviction from private or public housing in New York City, for example, may follow the mere issuance of a search warrant, if the relevant district attorney believes that narcotics activity is present; *most* of those evicted from their Manhattan homes under this policy in a recent period never went to trial (Levy 2008, 544, 554).[3] Some employers suspend an employee without pay for an indefinite period following a criminal charge, whether or not any trial or conviction follows. Children may be taken from their parents' custody immediately after police find narcotics in the home. For legal residents who are not citizens, a great many misdemeanors and even petty "non-criminal offenses" may lead to deportation. Although researchers have begun to catalog and explicate the full range of such collateral consequences, we must emphasize the great disparities in their imposition, driven in part by vagaries in the laws themselves as well as by local variation in norms among police, prosecutors, the defense bar, and other institutions.

Certainly, these policies influence the lives of vast numbers of people who may never have seen the inside of a prison cell. The Department of Justice estimates that as of 2008, about 100 million people in the United States had criminal records of some sort (U.S. Department of Justice 2009: 3). A more conservative recent tally, discounting for individuals with multiple records and other factors, settles on 65 million – still amounting to about one-third of the country's adult population (Rodriguez and Emsellem 2011: 27). One study estimated the U.S. ex-felon population—those subject to the widest array of formal collateral consequences—at about 11.7 million, representing 5 percent of adults, 9 percent of adult males, and almost one-fourth of all African American adult males (Uggen, Manza, and Thompson 2006). When combined with the current population of felons supervised in prisons, jails, probation, and parole, this produces a "felon class" of more than 16 million people either now serving a felony sentence or living with a felony conviction, representing 7.5 percent of the adult population—and a full one-third of the African American adult male population.

Legally, a formal sentence is understood as a "direct" consequence of a criminal conviction, while collateral restrictions that may be imposed by non-judicial entities are generally called "indirect." That means that judges are not legally compelled to advise a defendant of the collateral consequences that may accompany a guilty plea. As the scope, severity, and reach of collateral sanctions have expanded, this doctrinal distinction between direct and indirect consequences has come under increasing pressure (J. Roberts 2008), and with its landmark 2010 ruling in *Padilla v. Kentucky*, the U.S. Supreme Court has cast new doubt on its future. In *Padilla*, the Court held that a lawyer's failure to advise his client of the deportation consequences of a conviction constituted ineffective counsel in violation of the Sixth Amendment. The Court observed that with deportation now "virtually inevitable" for many non-citizens convicted of crime, deportation is now "an integral part—indeed, sometimes the most integral part—of the penalty."[4]

The Court declined to draw a new line "between direct and collateral conse-quences" for Sixth Amendment purposes, concluding that deportation is "uniquely difficult to classify as either a direct or a collateral consequence."[5] Only future cases can determine *Padilla*'s impact on the place of other such restrictions in Sixth Amendment jurisprudence and defense practice. But in his concurring opinion in *Padilla*, Justice Samuel Alito predicted that the Court's attempt at elevating depor-tation alone—while leaving the law relating to all other collateral consequences unchanged—was doomed to fail, and already some prominent interpreters have concluded that Alito was likely right (Love and Chin 2010). Sex-offender restric-tions may pose the most logical target for expansion of the *Padilla* principle: already, a Pennsylvania court hearing an ineffective-counsel claim applied *Padilla*'s logic to a law stripping pension benefits from a man convicted of indecent assault, and the Eleventh Circuit Court of Appeals cited *Padilla* in allowing a habeas petition to go forward in a civil commitment case (*Commonwealth of Pennsylvania v. Abraham* 2010; *Bauder v. Department of Corrections* 2010).

Federal and State Restrictions

The ABA recently tallied more than one hundred federal statutes that include re-strictions on the rights and privileges of people convicted of criminal offenses (American Bar Association 2009). Regardless of whether the *Padilla* Court was right in calling deportation "uniquely" burdensome, there is no question that for many people—including non-citizen legal residents—deportation is a severe conse-quence indeed. The number of immigrants deported by virtue of a criminal offense has risen sharply in recent years. In 2004, for example, "criminal violation" (e.g., as opposed to overstaying a visa) was the basis for approximately 43,000 deportations, which constituted 21 percent of all deportations that year (U.S. Department of Homeland Security 2005, table 40). This represents an immense increase from the 391 criminals deported in 1980, which constituted fewer than 3 percent of all depor-tees. Notably, many misdemeanor offenses as well as nonviolent felonies can bring about removal from the United States, and some infractions defined as misde-meanors under state law may be classified as aggravated felonies under federal law.

Three federal restrictions are imposed on virtually everyone convicted of a felony. Federal law bans the sale of firearms to people convicted of felonies (Legal Community Against Violence 2008), and federal grand and petit juries are closed to them as well (Kalt 2003). All felons lose the ability to serve in the military (Office of the Pardon Attorney 2001), though as we have seen during the Iraq and Afghan wars, that restriction may be lifted by the secretary of a given branch of the armed forces. Aside from these relatively straightforward restrictions, federal collateral-consequence laws are shot through with complexity and ambiguity. In some areas, that character comes from detailed laws that address a given consequence only to certain offenses; other wrinkles are provided by discretion granted to sentencing courts or implementing officials, or by uncertain expiration dates or relief proce-dures; in others, the American federal system introduces variation.

Many federal occupational-licensure statutes restrict access to a range of professions for people guilty of specified offenses. These occupational and licensing bans vary in their means of imposition (automatic or at the discretion of the sentencing court or a licensing agency, for example) and possibilities for relief, if any (Office of the Pardon Attorney 2001; American Bar Association 2009). Several statutes enacted in the last 20 years withdraw federal benefits from people with criminal convictions, either automatically or at the discretion of the sentencing court. Diverse statutes now deprive those convicted of misdemeanor and felony drug offenses of access to federal student loans, work assistance, educational tax credits, some health care benefits, and community-service work (Page 2004; Wacquant 2005; American Bar Association 2009; Cassidy 2010).

Federal law also limits the possession of driver's licenses and the provision of public assistance and food stamps for people with drug convictions. In both areas, federal law establishes a default policy of exclusion, while allowing states to opt out if they choose to do so. Under a statute enacted in 1992, for example, states must either suspend for six months the driver's licenses of people convicted of drug offenses or decline—by both legislative and gubernatorial action—to do so. Although about half the states have opted out, one study concludes that over one million people have nevertheless been affected by this policy (Marcus 2004). Similarly, welfare-reform legislation enacted in 1996 denies benefits and food stamps to anyone convicted of a drug felony.[6] Here, too, federal law excludes people convicted of drug crimes unless states choose not to do so. State-by-state variation in this area is more complex, though most states have either wholly or partly opted out of the ban (Allard 2002; Legal Action Center 2009; Mauer 2010).

Several other important federally imposed collateral restrictions build in a measure of discretion for state or local officials. Those convicted of certain sex and narcotics crimes must be evicted and permanently barred from federally funded housing, but other statutes enable housing authorities to determine which crimes bring eviction and exclusion, as well as whether arrests not leading to conviction merit removal; as noted above, in some localities prosecutors may seek eviction based on a mere search warrant. Local housing authorities are empowered by statute to "establish standards that prohibit admission" of anyone the authority believes "may interfere with the health, safety, or right to peaceful enjoyment of the premises by other residents."[7] Importantly, eviction can be a collective sanction: the alleged criminal's family members may also be evicted, even if they commit no crime (Mukamal and Samuels 2003; Levy 2008). These judicially-approved restrictions have led some housing authorities "to exclude virtually all of those coming back from prison" (Thompson 2008: 186). Such policies make securing stable housing "one of the most confounding of obstacles that the ex-offender will encounter when he or she leaves prison," despite the enormous practical and emotional importance to reentry of having a home and a fixed address (Thompson 2008: 69).

Biological parents involved in the criminal-justice process as well as those hoping to engage in volitional parenting—that is, to adopt a child or serve as a foster parent—face different restrictions and procedures in each state (Child Welfare

Information Gateway 2009). However, such variation has been considerably narrowed by recent federal statutes. The Adoption and Safe Families Act of 1997 authorized states to begin termination of parental rights proceedings against biological parents when a child has been in foster care for 15 months in a 22-month period—a common consequence of having an incarcerated parent. The law also required states to perform background checks on would-be adoptive and foster parents if their households were to receive Social Security payments, and recommended that states permanently bar those convicted of some crimes from being foster or adoptive parents and restrict others for five years. The Adam Walsh Child Protection and Safety Act of 2006 limited states' ability to opt out of these policies. Federal restrictions now apply to *every* foster care arrangement, not just those seeking Social Security support; states are required to bar those convicted of certain offenses from volitional parenting altogether; and states were required to impose uniform registration requirements. However, five years after the law's enactment, only seven states had met the Walsh Act's requirements (Klopott 2011).

Though these federal restrictions are considerable, they are far exceeded by the number of state laws limiting the rights and privileges of those with a criminal record. Forty-eight states deprive incarcerated felons of the right to vote, some only during their confinement, others for the full duration of their sentences, and some for waiting periods or indefinitely thereafter. Voting is both a deeply symbolic activity in American citizenship and historically a deeply contested one, and disenfranchisement law has received a good deal of scrutiny from scholars and advocates in recent years. As many as 5.4 million Americans, or one in 40 U.S. adults, are unable to vote as a result of a felony conviction; rates are far higher in some states than others, however, and in some states as many as one in four African American men are disenfranchised because of a felony conviction (Manza and Uggen 2006). With increased recognition of these and other startling statistics, many states have moved to reform their disenfranchisement laws and practices in the last decade (King 2008; Ewald 2009).

Disenfranchisement, however, is just the tip of the proverbial iceberg. To date no state has compiled an official tally of all its collateral-sanctions laws, so that even a person eager to understand and comply with every restriction upon her activities could not find them listed and explained in one place. Combined with considerable interstate variation and official ignorance of policies in many areas, this situation leads inevitably to purely accidental violations, particularly by those whose offenses occurred years or decades ago.

In those states where legal researchers have sought to compile all of a given state's collateral-sanctions policies, they have produced lists hundreds of items long (Cassidy 2010). In addition to voting, these restrictions reach core political activities such as the right to hold office (many states allow only eligible voters to win election), own firearms (virtually every state mirrors or extends the federal ban, in part so that states may prosecute offenders on their own), and hold employment. State restrictions influence the administration of justice itself, given that about half of the states bar felons from juries for life (Kalt 2003; Love 2009), altering the size and character of jury pools. Owing to racial disparities in convictions, African Americans are less likely than whites to qualify for jury service, and African American defendants are correspondingly less likely to be judged by a jury of their peers (Wheelock 2006).

Many states specifically bar people with criminal records from large numbers of occupations. As one critic observes, these jobs can include everything from "barber, boxer, [to] bingo operator" (Smyth 2005, 482). In addition to explicit restrictions, states require licensure of workers in hundreds of occupations, and usually instruct licensing boards to consider the "character" of an applicant. This leads to the exclusion of people with criminal records from many jobs (Thompson 2008). About half of U.S. states have put in place some statutory or regulatory directive related to employment of those with criminal backgrounds. As Love's research (2006, 2009) shows, however, these laws typically provide vague language and only limited protection—for example, applying only to government jobs, or requiring that an infraction be "substantially related" to the job in question in order to serve as grounds for rejection. A handful of states' laws go further—requiring licensing boards to consider evidence of rehabilitation, for example—but even these laws are difficult or impossible to enforce (Love 2006, 2009). Meanwhile, the expansion of criminal-records databases adds to the challenges facing job seekers, including those whose offenses are now years or decades behind them but who often find that acknowledging possession of a criminal record on a job application eliminates them from consideration (Rodriguez and Emsellem 2011; Goode 2011; Legal Action Center 2009). Few states limit the content or use of such databases; in some states, for example, even arrests not leading to convictions are included and may legally serve as grounds for refusal to hire.[8]

Unlike some peer nations, the United States has no statutory law protecting people with criminal records against discrimination against them on that basis, whether in the employment setting or elsewhere. The U.S. Equal Employment Opportunity Commission has ruled that absolute bars to employment based on a conviction record alone violate Title VII of the Civil Rights Act of 1964, but this applies only to the most extreme policies and has proven relatively difficult to enforce.[9] A handful of challenges to policies explicitly banning former offenders from certain professions have succeeded in court, but people with criminal records do not hold "suspect class" status in American law, so restrictions on their rights and privileges have no claim to heightened judicial scrutiny (Aukerman 2005; Geiger 2006).

We lack reliable contemporary international data, but American policies are likely among the most restrictive in the world. Research conducted some 40 years ago concluded that while many European nations did impose some political and civil constraints on people convicted of crime, "the sweeping penalty of loss of civil rights seems to be slowly passing to the museum of judicial antiquities" (Damaska 1968b, 567). Disenfranchisement law, an area in which some comparative research has been conducted, suggests that Damaska was correct about Europe, and that most industrialized democracies operate from a far more integrative approach to life after the sentence. In most European countries, prisoner voting is not only allowed but facilitated; a handful of countries do disqualify people convicted of select crimes from voting, but these restrictions typically apply to extremely few individuals (Ewald and Rottinghaus 2009; Demleitner 1999; Ispahani 2009; Uggen, Van Brakle, and McLaughlin 2009).[10]

As the Supreme Court's analysis of deportation in the *Padilla* case suggests, the term "collateral" itself can be misleading. In terms of their impact on affected individuals, these formally "non-penal" consequences "may in fact dwarf the criminal sanction" (J. Roberts 2008). As noted above, a person may lose her children, job, or home well before trial for a criminal offense, even when the potential charges are relatively minor. Or consider, for example, a person whose sentence extends only to a few years' probation, but who may face indefinite restrictions related to employment, firearms ownership, military service, parenting, voting, jury service, federal benefits, and access to federal housing. Such scenarios led the president of the National District Attorneys Association to describe collateral consequences as "simply a new form of mandated sentences" (Johnson 2001, 33), whose imposition, according to some authorities, "has become an increasingly central purpose of the modern criminal process" (Chin and Holmes 2002, 699) and "the real point of achieving a conviction" (NCCUSL 2010). In practice, many defense attorneys believe they must now treat collateral sanctions as part of the potential punishment their clients face (Pinard 2004; Smyth 2005), regardless of whether courts define them that way. Despite their formal "invisibility," then, collateral sanctions do sometimes surface in the American courtroom (Ewald and Smith 2008).

II. Effects on Inmates and Families

In the past four decades, as the rate of U.S. criminal punishment rose to historically unprecedented levels, the prison emerged as an increasingly powerful force for reproducing and reinforcing social inequalities. As the prevalence of incarceration has increased, so too has research on the consequences of punishment. Social scientists today recognize incarceration as a powerful "engine of social inequality" (Western 2006, 198). A new wave of research has documented how punishment affects the individual life course, the family as a basic unit of social organization, and the structure and process of social stratification.

Although many incarcerated men and women have experienced some degree of conventional success, most people enter prison with little human capital in the form of education and work history. To the extent that prisons fail to address these deficits—and there is little reason to believe that they are currently effective in doing so—incarceration reinforces and steps up existing disadvantages, to the detriment of inmates and the communities to which they return.

People convicted of crime face not only the legal restrictions described above, but also considerable social costs. Chief Justice Earl Warren observed in 1960 that a felony conviction "seriously affects [one's] reputation and economic opportunities" in the United States (*Parker v. Ellis*, 362 U.S. at 594). Certainly that is no less true today, given the prevailing view among policy makers that criminals are to be labeled, separated from society, and stigmatized in the interest of public safety.

Employment, Health, and Well-being

As von Hirsch and Wasik put it, "The more that convicted persons are restricted by law from pursuing legitimate occupations, the fewer opportunities they will have for remaining law abiding" (1997, 605). President George W. Bush recognized this fact in his 2004 State of the Union address, observing that if people released from prison "can't find work, or a home, or help, they are much more likely to commit crime and return to prison." With regard to labor market inequalities, large-scale incarceration removes potential workers from the labor force (Western and Beckett 1999), erodes the already shaky job skills of the incarcerated (Travis and Visher 2005), and confers a stigma that hinders employability (Pager 2003). Both experimental (Pager 2003) and observational (Western 2006) studies have established that incarceration sharply reduces employment prospects. Moreover, incarceration can mask inequality by artificially reducing unemployment rates among more disadvantaged groups in the non-incarcerated population (Western and Beckett 1999, Pager 2007).

How big is the prison effect on employment and earnings? Estimates of the wage penalty of incarceration range from 10 percent to 30 percent (Geller et al. 2006; Pettit and Lyons 2007; Waldfogel 1994; Western 2006), although the duration of incarceration does not appear to exert a strong effect on wages (Kling 2006). With regard to unemployment, Pager's experimental audit studies (2003, 2007) show significant labor market discrimination against former inmates. As with research on wage penalties, her results also reveal a greater penalty of incarceration for African American ex-inmates relative to white ex-inmates. In her Milwaukee experiment (Pager 2003), approximately 34 percent of white men without criminal records received positive responses (or callbacks) from employers, relative to 17 percent of white men with records. For African Americans, however, the corresponding percentages were only 14 percent and 5 percent.

As noted above, there are legal as well as social barriers to employment for ex-prisoners, with many states barring former felons from working in health care and other occupations, for example (Mukamal and Samuels 2003). Norms in hiring practices erect more widespread barriers. The proportion of employers conducting criminal background checks on potential employees is rising rapidly, such that 45 percent of employers in a recent California study were routinely checking the criminal backgrounds of applicants (Holzer, Raphael, and Stoll 2007). A 2009 survey of Human Resource Management professionals found that 92 percent of their members were conducting criminal background checks for some or all jobs—almost twice the percentage doing so 13 years earlier (Society for Human Resource Management 2010). Reasons for the increase include technological advances that make it cheap and easy to conduct such checks, employer fears of liability, confusion over legal responsibility to check records (Bushway, Stoll, and Weiman 2007), a desire to avoid high monitoring costs and negligent hiring suits (Finlay 2008), and simple distrust of those with criminal backgrounds (Bushway, Briggs, Taxman, Thanner, and Van Brakle 2007). Such background checks ensure that former inmates put their "worst foot forward" when applying for jobs (see Chiricos et al. 2007).

In the face of these daunting barriers to employment, numerous organizations have arisen to help former prisoners find work. In addition to many locally oriented groups, the Legal Action Center's H.I.R.E. Network serves as a national resource center for efforts to change policies, practices, and public opinion related to employing people with criminal records. Meanwhile, the speedy growth of this population has led to the publication of several self-help books aimed directly at former offenders seeking to join or rejoin the workforce (Krannich 2008; Jackson 2008).

Just as inmates bring poor work histories and educational deficits into the prison, they also bring substantial health problems and may become less healthy while doing time. Imprisonment results in short-term health improvement, but these gains quickly dissipate and are wholly absent upon release (Schnittker and John 2007). In the few long-term studies that have been conducted, incarceration is strongly related to later health problems (Massoglia 2008a; Schnittker and John 2007). Perhaps unsurprisingly, given the conditions and overcrowding common in today's prisons, the strongest effects involve infectious diseases (Massoglia 2008b; Schnittker and John 2007).

Families

Although incarcerated persons are often treated as social isolates, they are in fact embedded in every facet of social life—as neighbors, as partners, and as parents (see, e.g., Comfort 2008). Most notably, most incarcerated adults are parents of minor children (Travis et al. 2005; Uggen, Wakefield, and Western 2005). About 52 percent of state prison inmates and 63 percent of federal inmates are parents, and almost one in four inmates have three or more children (Glaze and Maruschak 2008). Incarceration clearly alters the existing family relationships of these inmates (Braman 2002; Comfort 2008; Edin et al. 2004; Lopoo and Western 2005; Wildeman 2009), while diminishing future marital prospects among those who have yet to marry or have children (Edin 2000). Moreover, debts and child support orders often continue to accrue during spells of incarceration, leaving inmates little real opportunity to contribute materially to families left behind (Cancian et al. 2011).

Children often benefit when an abusive or otherwise unsuitable parent is removed from the home. On balance, however, the best longitudinal studies consistently show that that paternal incarceration worsens the mental and behavioral health of inmates' children (Foster and Hagan 2009; Wakefield 2007; Wildeman

2009). More specifically, the imprisonment of a parent may increase children's aggression and delinquency (Murray and Farrington 2008; Hagan and Palloni 1990; Wakefield 2007; Wildeman 2010), diminish their educational attainment (Foster and Hagan 2009), and drive them into the foster care system (Johnson and Waldfogel 2002).

III. Impact on Communities and Democracy

Beyond these effects on individuals and families, mass incarceration—accompanied by collateral sanctions—is changing specific communities and may be altering fundamental aspects of American democracy itself. Petersilia (2003) and Clear (2007), among others, describe the spatial concentration of incarceration in predominately poor and African American communities. This concentration has brought public attention to Eric Cadora's conception of "million dollar blocks"—criminal justice expenditures in excess of $1 million just to incarcerate the residents of single city blocks in New York (see, e.g., Gonnerman 2004). In these communities, heavy incarceration may reduce crime by temporarily incapacitating would-be offenders, but it also erodes neighborhood stability. In high-incarceration neighborhoods, as many as 15 percent of adult males are cycling back and forth to prison, a process Clear (2007) describes as "coercive mobility" (p. 73). Clear and others suggest that this excessive residential mobility inhibits the formation of interpersonal trust and social capital, which in turn can lead to increases in crime.

Housing restrictions further alter neighborhood social and civic life. Beckett and Herbert (2010) document a new form of banishment, in the form of contemporary applications of trespass law, off-limits orders, spatial exclusion from parks and other areas, and similar housing and public order restrictions. As we have seen elsewhere, such policies are based in civil and administrative law, yet have indisputably punitive effects. The heavy application of such community-based collateral sanctions adds a significant degree of political, economic, and social alienation to the psychological separation and stigma already experienced by former prisoners.

Less effective law enforcement is among the social harms that may follow; after all, a society "can control effectively only those who perceive themselves to be members of it," as Leslie Wilkins put it (Young 1971, 39). The existence of post-sentence legal restrictions likely "hardens the resentment offenders commonly feel toward society in general" as the National Advisory Commission on Criminal Justice Standards and Goals said in 1973 (see Uggen, Manza, and Thompson 2006, 297). Recalling that parental engagement in politics is among the best predictors of a child's electoral participation, it is possible that disenfranchisement may contribute to geometric growth in some communities in the number of people who cannot or do not vote (Preuhs 2001, 746). Indeed, at least one Tennessee politician grimly acknowledges that he cannot afford to campaign in his poorest precincts, because disenfranchisement and alienation together mean that virtually no one living there votes (Abramsky 2006, 162). Such problems likely exacerbate the already deep racial fractures in American society.

From the broader social vantage, policies restricting the rights and privileges of people convicted of crime appear to be distorting some of the United States' most fundamental social measurements. The Census's practice of counting inmates as residents of the prison town skews basic demographics, causing problems for state and local apportionment (Lotke and Wagner 2004; S. Roberts 2008; Prison Policy Initiative 2010). Voter-turnout figures need to be calibrated based on the voting-*eligible* population, because the old voting-*age* denominator now includes so many people ineligible to vote because of a criminal conviction (McDonald and Popkin 2001). The disenfranchisement of current and former felons has also likely altered the outcome of numerous state and national elections, including numerous pivotal U.S. Senate races and the 2000 presidential election (Manza and Uggen 2006). And unemployment figures in the United States and Europe cannot be compared without factoring in the large number of working-age Americans who are unable to seek employment because they are incarcerated (Western 2006, 105).

Collateral sanctions are thus changing, in a piecemeal, incremental, and largely unexamined fashion, the nature and content of American citizenship itself. People who are under no form of criminal supervision but cannot by law serve in the military, vote, own a firearm, sit on a jury, drive a car, receive governmental benefits, or work in numerous professions are no longer full citizens, despite what their passports may say. Those with criminal histories live in a condition that Nora Demleitner first identified as "internal exile" (Demleitner 1999; American Bar Association 2009), and which others have called "second-class citizenship" (Geiger 2006, 1198) or likened to a caste-like state (Uggen, Manza, and Thompson 2006). These "gradations of citizenship" (Gottschalk 2006) are not clearly articulated in the law, resting as they do on diverse and often-uncertain state policies, the discretion of numerous authorities within and outside the criminal justice system, and a legal doctrine unable to identify them as the punishments they are.

IV. Conclusion

In the past 20 years, life course criminologists have made tremendous progress in understanding the changing life conditions associated with leaving or desisting from crime. A steady job, stable family relationships, and secure housing are among the strongest predictors of leaving crime (Laub and Sampson 2003; Maruna 2001; Massoglia and Uggen 2010; Sampson and Laub 1993; Uggen 2000). Influenced by that research, academic, advocacy, and governmental efforts to diminish the costly collateral effects of punishment now place the idea of effective reentry and reintegration at the center of the inquiry (Travis 2000; Thompson 2008).

Many of the collateral sanctions discussed in this chapter thus fly in the face of theory and research on desistance from crime. The proliferation of such policies has also confounded conventional understandings of where, when, and by whom punishment is imposed. Today, American punishment features a wide array of social-control mechanisms enforced by institutions and actors scattered throughout civil society. In effect, with little fanfare or public scrutiny, a massive diffusion of the work of punishment has taken place. Well beyond the precinct house, the courtroom, the prison, and the probation office, governmental and nongovernmental officials in a wide array of capacities are imposing significant restrictions on people accused or convicted of crime, often long after their formal sentence has expired.

The most common element of contemporary collateral-consequence reform proposals is simply to exhume and expose these policies, compiling all the collateral consequences of a given jurisdiction in a single place. The American Bar Association is currently working to create and publish a list of all federal and state collateral consequences, having received a grant from the National Institutes of Justice to support such research; in 2011, a "demonstration" version of the database was posted online.[11] The NCCUSL has offered model legislation by which each state could do the same (Cassidy 2010).[12] A second aspect of such proposals, not surprisingly, is an emphasis on the need to apprise defendants and those leaving criminal supervision of the sanctions to which they are—or may be—subject. Third is the idea of "reentry courts," tribunals with the authority to lift some or all sanctions; under current law, it is often unclear whether a given judge (or indeed any judge at all) has the authority to restore specific rights or privileges, and even formal pardons do not all have the same force (American Bar Association 2004; Cassidy 2010). Numerous reform organizations go further, urging the abolition of some restrictions and at least a close scrutiny of the costs and benefits of others (Legal Action Center 2009; Wood and Budnitz 2010).

Defense attorneys are already engaged in a kind of street-level reform, as some have gained favorable dispositions by alerting prosecutors and judges to the considerable collateral consequences that clients would face if convicted of charges against them. As one practitioner writes, public defenders engaged in what is now called "holistic defense" have won favorable pleas and even outright dismissals "when they [were] able to educate prosecutors and judges on the draconian hidden consequences for the clients and their families" (Smyth 2005, 494). A broader understanding of those consequences, paired with increasing emphasis on the human and social value of effective reentry, is sorely needed.

NOTES

....

1. H.R. 1593, Second Chance Act of 2007: Community Safety Through Recidivism Prevention, P.L. 110–199, 122 Stat. 657 (April 9, 2008).

2. A recent effort at terminological clarification came with the Court Security Improvement Act of 2007. Adopting terms initially suggested by the American Bar Association, the Act defines collateral "sanctions" as restrictions imposed *automatically* upon conviction, while "disqualifications" are those penalties that a court, agency, or official is authorized but *not* required to impose. H.R. 660, the Court Security Improvement Act of 2007, P.L. 110–177, 121 Stat. 2534 (January 6, 2008), Section 503(b) (1)-(3). This chapter will use these terms interchangeably, in part because lawmakers, attorneys, and scholars are only now sorting out clearly which restrictions fall into which categories.

3. Notably, the city's Narcotics Eviction Program rests on civil law, such as nuisance-abatement and civil-forfeiture statutes, rather than the criminal law, so those subject to this severe sanction lack the protections afforded them in criminal procedure.

4. *José Padilla v. Kentucky*, 130 S.Ct. 1473, 1480 (2010).

5. Id., 1481, 1482.

6. Senate debate on the measure lasted a mere two minutes (Rubinstein and Mukamal 2002).

7. 42 U.S.C. § 13661, "Screening of Applicants for Federally Assisted Housing" (2003).

8. Because criminal-records databases sometimes include everything a person was *charged* with, someone who many years ago pleaded to only a very minor infraction such as disorderly conduct, for example, may find himself turned away by a potential employer years later because his rap sheet lists a more serious offense for which he was never tried or found guilty.

9. Guidelines published by the Equal Employment Opportunity Commission (EEOC) has have stated that because an "absolute measure" preventing all individuals with conviction records from being hired could disproportionately exclude African Americans and Latinos, such blanket hiring bans run afoul of Title VII. Such guidelines have been issued on several occasions. See, for example, EEOC Notice 915.061, "Policy Guidance on the Consideration of Arrest Records in Employment Decisions under Title VII of the Civil Rights Act of 1964," September 7, 1990. Current guidance is in "Prohibited Practices: Pre-Employment Inquiries and Arrest & Conviction," available at EEOC.gov/laws/practices/inquiries_arrest_conviction.cfm (accessed January 26, 2011); for a discussion of EEOC policies in a recent lawsuit, see *Douglas El v. SEPTA*, 479 F.3d 232 (U.S.C.A. 3rd Cir., 2007).

10. In the last 15 years, constitutional courts in Israel, South Africa, Canada, and Australia, as well as the European Court of Human Rights, have either struck down or seriously limited their country's disenfranchisement laws. See generally Ewald and Rottinghaus 2009.

11. See http://isrweb.isr.temple.edu/projects/accproject/.

12. The current reform wave is not the first time that attorneys, academics, and policy makers have collaborated to propose changes in the scope and imposition of collateral consequences in the United States. Half a century ago, the National Conference on Parole called such civil and political restrictions "an archaic holdover from early times," and urged their abolition (National Probation and Parole Association 1957, 136, quoted in Love 2003, 104). Over the next 30 years, other public and nongovernmental groups would call for

other reforms, such as streamlined expungement procedures and laws empowering sentencing courts to discharge or relieve collateral penalties once a sentence was served (Love 2003, 107–112). Though some reforms were adopted in individual states, by the mid-1980s U.S. policy makers had adopted a more harshly punitive approach toward offenders, and thereafter state and federal collateral penalties would expand.

REFERENCES

Abramsky, Sasha. 2006. *Conned: How Millions Went to Prison, Lost the Vote, and Helped Send George W. Bush to the White House*. New York: The New Press.

Allard, Patricia. 2002. "Life Sentences: Denying Welfare Benefits to Women Convicted of Drug Offenses." Available at: http://www.sentencingproject.org/tmp/File/Women%20in%20CJ/women_lifesentences.pdf (accessed Aug. 30, 2011).

American Bar Association, Criminal Justice Standards Committee. 2004. *ABA Standards for Criminal Justice*, 3rd ed., *Collateral Sanctions and Discretionary Disqualification of Convicted Persons*. Chicago: American Bar Association.

American Bar Association Commission on Effective Criminal Sanctions. 2009. "Internal Exile: Collateral Consequences of Conviction in Federal Laws and Regulations." Available at: http://www.abanet.org/cecs/internalexile.pdf (accessed August 30, 2011).

Aukerman, Miriam. 2005. "The Somewhat Suspect Class: Toward a Constitutional Framework for Evaluating Occupational Restrictions Affecting People with Criminal Records." *Journal of Law in Society* 7: 18–87.

Bauder v. Department of Corrections, State of Florida, 619 F.3d 1272 (2010).

Beckett, Katherine, and Steve Herbert. 2010. *Banished: The New Social Control in Urban America*. New York: Oxford University Press.

Bushway, Shawn, Michael Stoll, and David Weiman. 2007. *Barriers to Reentry? The Labor Market for Released Prisoners in Post-Industrial America*. New York: Russell Sage Foundation.

Bushway, Shawn, Shauna Briggs, Faye Taxman, Meredith Thanner, and Mischelle Van Brakle. 2007. "Private Providers of Criminal History Records: Do You Get What You Pay For?" In *Barriers to Reentry?: The Labor Market for Released Prisoners in Post-Industrial America*, eds. Shawn Bushway, Michael Stoll, and David Weiman. New York: Russell Sage Foundation.

Braman, Donald. 2002. "Families and Incarceration." In *Invisible Punishment: The Collateral Consequences of Mass Imprisonment*, eds. M. Mauer, M. Chesney-Lind, pp. 117–135. New York: The New Press.

Cancian, Maria, Daniel R. Meyer, and Eunhee Han. 2011. "Child Support: Responsible Fatherhood and the Quid Pro Quo." *Annals Am. Acad. Pol. Soc. Sci.* 635: 140–162.

Cassidy, Richard T. 2010. Prepared Testimony, United States House of Representatives, Committee on the Judiciary, Subcommittee on Crime, Terrorism, and Homeland Security: "Collateral Consequences of Criminal Convictions: Barriers to Reentry for the Formerly Incarcerated." June 9, 2010.

Child Welfare Information Gateway. 2009. "Major Federal Legislation Concerned with Child Protection, Child Welfare, and Adoption." Available at: http://www.childwelfare.gov/pubs/otherpubs/majorfedlegis.pdf (accessed August 30, 2011).

Chin, Gabriel J., and Richard W. Holmes, Jr. 2002. "Effective Assistance of Counsel and the Consequences of Guilty Pleas." *Cornell Law Review* 87: 697.

Chin, Gabriel J. 2002. "Race, the War on Drugs, and the Collateral Consequences of Criminal Conviction." *Journal of Gender, Race and Justice* 6: 253.

Chiricos, Ted, Kelle Barrick, William Bales, and Stephanie Bontrager. 2007. "The Labeling of Convicted Felons and Its Consequences for Recidivism." *Criminology* 45(3): 547–581.

Clear, Todd R. 2007. *Imprisoning Communities: How Mass Incarceration Makes Disadvantaged Neighborhoods Worse*. New York: Oxford University Press.

Comfort, Megan. 2008. *Doing Time Together: Love and Family in the Shadow of the Prison*. Chicago: University of Chicago Press.

Commonwealth of Pennsylvania v. Abraham, 996 A.2d 1090 (2010).

Damaska, Mirjan. 1968a. "Adverse Legal Consequences of Conviction and Their Removal: A Comparative Study." *Journal of Criminal Law, Criminology and Police Science* 59(3): 347–360.

Damaska, Mirjan. 1968b. "Adverse Legal Consequences of Conviction and Their Removal: A Comparative Study (Part 2)." *Journal of Criminal Law, Criminology and Police Science* 59(4): 542–568.

Demleitner, Nora V. 1999. "Preventing Internal Exile: The Need for Restrictions on Collateral Consequences." *Stanford Law and Policy Review* 11: 153.

Edin, Kathryn. 2000. "Few Good Men: Why Low-Income Single Mothers Don't Get Married." *The American Prospect* 11(4): 26–31.

Edin, Kathryn, Timothy J. Nelson, and Rechelle Paranal. 2004. "Fatherhood and Incarceration as Potential Turning Points in the Criminal Careers of Unskilled Men." In *Imprisoning America: The Social Effects of Mass Incarceration*, eds. Mary Pattillo, David Weiman, and Bruce Western, pp. 46–75. New York: Russell Sage Foundation.

Ewald, Alec C., and Marnie Smith. 2008. "Collateral Consequences of Criminal Convictions in American Courts: The View from the State Bench." *Justice System Journal* 29(2): 145–165.

Ewald, Alec C., and Brandon Rottinghaus. 2009. *Criminal Disenfranchisement in an International Perspective*. New York: Cambridge University Press.

Ewald, Alec C. 2009. "Criminal Disenfranchisement and the Challenge of American Federalism." *Publius: The Journal of Federalism* 39(3): 527–556.

Finlay, Keith. 2008. "Effect of Employer Access to Criminal History Data on the Labor Market Outcomes of Ex-Offenders and Non-Offenders." *NBER Working Papers 13935*, National Bureau of Economic Research.

Finzen, Margaret F. (2005). "Systems of Oppression: The Collateral Consequences of Incarceration and Their Effects on Black Communities," *Georgetown Journal on Poverty Law and Policy* 12: 299.

Foster, Holly, and John Hagan. 2009. The Mass Incarceration of Parents in America: Issues of Race/Ethnicity, Collateral Damage to Children, and Prisoner Reentry. *Annals Am. Acad. Pol. Soc. Sci.* 623: 179–194.

Garland, David. 1990. *Punishment and Modern Society: A Study in Social Theory*. Chicago: University of Chicago Press.

Geiger, Ben. 2006. "The Case for Treating Ex-Offenders as a Suspect Class." *California Law Review* 94: 1191.

Geller, Amanda, Irwin Garfinkel, and Bruce Western. 2006. "The Effects of Incarceration on Employment and Wages: An Analysis of the Fragile Families Survey." Work. Pap. 2006-01-FF., Cent. Res. Child Well-Being.

Glaze, Lauren E. and Laura M. Maruschak. 2008. *Parents in Prison and Their Minor Children*. United States Department of Justice. Washington, DC: U.S. Government Printing Office.

Goode, Erica. 2011. "Internet Lets a Criminal Past Catch Up Quicker." *New York Times*, April 28, 2011.

Gonnerman, Jennifer. 2004. "Million-Dollar Blocks: The Neighborhood Costs of America's Prison Boom." *The Village Voice*, November 16, 2004.

Gottschalk, Marie. 2006. *The Prison and the Gallows: The Politics of Mass Incarceration in America*. New York: Cambridge University Press.

Hagan, John, and Alberto Palloni. 1990. "The Social Reproduction of a Criminal Class in Working Class London, circa 1950–1980." *American Journal of Sociology* 96(2): 265–299

Holzer, Harry J., Steven Raphael, and Michael A. Stoll. 2007. "The Effect of an Applicant's Criminal History on Employer Hiring Decisions and Screening Practices: Evidence from Los Angeles." In *Barriers to Reentry?: The Labor Market for Released Prisoners in Post-Industrial America,*. eds. Shawn Bushway, Michael Stoll, and David Weiman, New York: Russell Sage Foundation.

Ispahani, Laleh. 2009. "Voting Rights and Human Rights: A Comparative Analysis of Criminal Disenfranchisement Laws." In *Criminal Disenfranchisement in an International Perspective*, eds. Alec C. Ewald and Brandon Rottinghaus, New York: Cambridge University Press.

Jackson, Michael B. 2008. *How to Do Good after Prison: A Handbook for Successful Reentry*. Willingboro, NJ: Joint FX Press.

Johnson, Robert M.A. 2001. "Collateral Consequences," *Criminal Justice* 16, p. 33.

Johnson, Elizabeth I., and Jane Waldfogel. 2002. "Parental Incarceration: Recent Trends and Implications for Child Welfare." *Social Service Review* 76(3): 460–479.

Kalt, Brian C. 2003. "The Exclusion of Felons from Jury Service." *American University Law Review* 53: 65–188.

Kanstroom, Daniel. 2007. *Deportation Nation: Outsiders in American History*. Cambridge, MA: Harvard University Press.

Keyssar, Alexander. 2000. *The Right to Vote: The Contested History of Democracy in the United States*. New York: Basic Books.

King, Ryan. 2008. "Expanding the Vote: State Felony Disenfranchisement Reform, 1997–2008." Washington: DC: The Sentencing Project.

Kling, Jeffrey R. 2006. "Incarceration Length, Employment, and Earnings." *American Economic Review* 96(3): 863–876.

Klopott, Freeman. 2011. "Trouble from the Start with Walsh Act." *Washington Examiner*, June 12, 2011.

Krannich, Ron. 2008. *Best Jobs for Ex-Offenders: 101 Opportunities to Jump-Start Your New Life*. Manassas Park, VA: Impact Publications.

Laub, John H., and Robert J. Sampson. 2003. *Shared Beginnings, Divergent Lives: Delinquent Boys to Age 70*. Cambridge, MA: Harvard University Press.

Legal Action Center. 2009. "After Prison: Roadblocks to Reentry." Available at: http://www.lac.org/roadblocks-to-reentry/ (accessed August 30, 2011).

Legal Community Against Violence. 2008. "Regulating Guns in America." Available at: http://www.lcav.org/publications-briefs/reports_analyses/RegGuns.entire.report.pdf (accessed August 30, 2011).

Levy, Scott Duffield. 2008. "The Collateral Consequences of Seeking Order Through Disorder: New York's Narcotics Eviction Program." *Harvard Civil Rights—Civil Liberties Law Review* 43(2): 539–580.

Lopoo, Leonard M., and Bruce Western. 2005. "Incarceration and the Formation and Stability of Marital Unions." *Journal of Marriage and Family* 67(3): 721–734.

Lotke, Eric and Peter Wagner. 2004. "Prisoners of the Census: Electoral and Financial Consequences of Counting Prisoners Where They Go, Not Where They Come From." *Pace Law Review* 24: 587–607.

Love, Margaret Colgate. 2003. "Starting Over with a Clean Slate: In Praise of a Forgotten Section of the Model Penal Code." *Fordham Law Journal* 30(1): 101–136.

Love, Margaret Colgate. 2006. *Relief from the Collateral Consequences of a Criminal Conviction: A State-by-State Resource Guide.* Buffalo: William S. Hein.

Love, Margaret Colgate. 2009. "Relief from the Collateral Consequences of a Criminal Conviction: A State-By-State Resource Guide." Available at: http://www.sentencing-project.org/detail/publication.cfm?publication_id=115 (accessed August 30, 2011).

Love, Margaret Colgate, and Gabriel J. Chin. 2010. "*Padilla* v. *Kentucky*: The Right to Counsel and the Collateral Consequences of Conviction." *The Champion* 34(18) (May 2010): 18–24.

Manza, Jeff, and Christopher Uggen. 2006. *Locked Out: Felon Disenfranchisement and American Democracy.* New York: Oxford University Press.

Marcus, Aaron J. 2004. "Are the Roads a Safer Place Because Drug Offenders Aren't on Them?: An Analysis of Punishing Drug Offenders with License Suspensions." *Kansas Journal of Law & Public Policy* 13: 557.

Maruna, Shadd. 2001. *Making Good. How Ex-Convicts Reform and Rebuild Their Lives.* Washington, DC: American Psychological Association.

Massoglia, Michael. 2008a. "Incarceration, Health, and Racial Health Disparities." *Law & Society Review* 42(2): 275–306.

Massoglia, Michael. 2008b. "Incarceration as Exposure: The Prison, Infectious Disease, and Other Stress-Related Illnesses." *Journal of Health & Social Behavior* 49(1): 56–71.

Massoglia, Michael, and Christopher Uggen. 2010. "Settling Down and Aging Out: Toward an Interactionist Theory of Desistance and the Transition to Adulthood." *American Journal of Sociology* 116 (2): 543–582.

Mauer, Marc. 2010. Prepared Testimony, United States House of Representatives, Committee on the Judiciary, Subcommittee on Crime, Terrorism, and Homeland Security: "Collateral Consequences of Criminal Convictions: Barriers to Reentry for the Formerly Incarcerated." June 9, 2010.

McDonald, Michael P., and Samuel L. Popkin. 2001. "The Myth of the Vanishing Voter." *American Political Science Review* 95: 963.

Mukamal, Debbie, and Paul Samuels. 2003. "Statutory Limitations on Civil Rights of People with Criminal Records." *Fordham Urban Law Journal* 30: 1501–1518.

Murray, Joseph, and David P. Farrington. 2008. "Parental Imprisonment: Long-Lasting Effects on Boys Internalizing Problems Through the Life-Course." *Development and Psychopathology* 20: 273–290.

National Conference of Commissioners on Uniform State Laws (NCCUSL). 2010. "Draft, Amendments to Uniform Collateral Sanctions and Disqualifications Act." Available at: http://www.law.upenn.edu/bll/archives/ulc/ucsada/2010am_draft.htm (accessed August 30, 2011).

Office of the Pardon Attorney, U.S. Department of Justice. 2001. "Federal Statutes Imposing Collateral Sanctions Upon Conviction." Available at: http://www.usdoj.gov/pardon/collateral_consequences.pdf (accessed August 30, 2011).

[José] *Padilla v. Kentucky*, 130 S.Ct. 1473 (2010), 1473–1497.

Page, Joshua A. 2004. "Eliminating the Enemy: The Import of Denying Prisoners Access to Higher Education in Clinton's America." *Punishment and Society* 6: 357–378.

Pager, Devah. 2003. "The Mark of a Criminal Record." *American Journal of Sociology* 108: 937–975.

Pager, Devah. 2007. *Marked: Race, Crime, and Finding Work in an Era of Mass Incarceration.* Chicago: University Of Chicago Press.

Petersilia, Joan. 2003. *When Prisoners Come Home: Parole and Prisoner Reentry.* New York: Oxford University Press.

Pettit, Becky, and Christopher J. Lyons. 2007. "Status and the Stigma of Incarceration: The Labor Market Effects of Incarceration by Race, Class, and Criminal Involvement." In *The Labor Market for Released Prisoners in Post-Industrial America*, eds. S. Bushway, M. A. Stoll, D. F. Weiman, pp. 203–226. New York: Russell Sage Foundation.

Pinard, Michael M. 2004. "Broadening the Holistic Mindset: Incorporating Collateral Consequences and Reentry into Criminal Defense Lawyering." *Fordham Urban Law Journal* 31: 1067–1097.

Pinard, Michael, and Anthony C. Thompson. 2006. "Offender Reentry and the Collateral Consequences of Criminal Convictions: An Introduction." *New York University Review of Law and Social Change* 30: 585–620.

Preuhs, Robert R. 2001. "State Felon Disenfranchisement Policy." *Social Science Quarterly* 82(4): 734–748.

Prison Policy Initiative. 2010. "Prisoners of the Census: The Problem." Available at: http://www.prisonersofthecensus.org/impact.html (accessed June 22, 2010).

Roberts, Jenny. 2008. "The Mythical Divide Between Collateral and Direct Consequences of Criminal Convictions: Involuntary Commitment of 'Sexually Violent Predators.'" *Minnesota Law Review* 93: 670–740.

Roberts, Sam. 2008. "Census Bureau's Counting of Prisoners Benefits Some Rural Voting Districts." *New York Times*, October 23, 2008.

Rodriguez, Michelle Natividad, and Maurice Emsellem. 2011. "65 Million 'Need Not Apply:' The Case for Reforming Criminal Background Checks for Employment." Available at: http://www.nelp.org/page/-/65_Million_Need_Not_Apply.pdf?nocdn=1 (accessed May 26, 2011).

Rubinstein, Gwen, and Debbie Mukamal. 2002. "Welfare and Housing-Denial of Benefits to Drug Offenders." In *Invisible Punishment: The Collateral Consequences of Mass Imprisonment*, pp. 37–49. New York: The New Press.

Sampson, Robert J., and John H. Laub. 1993. *Crime in the Making: Pathways and Turning Points Through Life.* Cambridge, MA: Harvard University Press.

Schnittker, Jason, and Andrea John. 2007. "Enduring Stigma: The Long-Term Effects of Incarceration on Health." *Journal of Health & Social Behavior* 48(2): 115–130.

Simon, Jonathan. 2000. "Megan's Law: Crime and Democracy in Late Modern America." *Law & Social Inquiry* 25: 1111–1150.

Smyth, McGregor. 2005. "Holistic Is Not a Bad Word: A Criminal Defense Attorney's Guide to Using Invisible Punishments as an Advocacy Strategy." *University of Toledo Law Review* 36: 479–504.

Society for Human Resource Management. 2010. "Background Checking: Conducting Criminal Background Checks." January 22, 2010. Available at: http://www.shrm.org/Research/SurveyFindings/Articles/Pages/BackgroundCheckCriminalChecks.aspx (accessed August 30, 2011).

Thompson, Anthony C. 2008. *Releasing Prisoners, Redeeming Communities.* New York: New York University Press.

Tonry, Michael, and Joan Petersilia. 2000. *Crime and Justice*, Volume 26: *Prisons*, 2nd ed. Chicago: University of Chicago Press Journals.

Travis, Jeremy. 2000. "New Challenges in Evaluating Our Sentencing Policy: Exploring the Public Safety Nexus." *Corrections Compendium*. Address delivered June 1, at the National Workshop on Sentencing and Corrections in Hilton Head, South Carolina.

Travis, Jeremy. 2002. "Invisible Punishment: An Instrument of Social Exclusion." In *Invisible Punishment: The Collateral Consequences of Mass Imprisonment*, eds. M. Mauer and M. Chesney-Lind, pp. 15–36. New York: The New Press.

Travis, Jeremy. 2005. *But They All Come Back: Facing the Challenges of Prisoner Reentry*. Washington, DC: Urban Institute Press.

Travis, Jeremy, Elizabeth C. McBride, and Amy L. Solomon. 2005. *Families Left Behind: The Hidden Costs of Incarceration and Reentry*. Washington, DC: Urban Institute.

Travis, Jeremy, and Christy Visher, eds. 2005. *Prisoner Reentry and Crime in America; Prisoner Reentry and Crime in America*. Cambridge: Cambridge University Press.

Uggen, Christopher. 2000. "Work as a Turning Point in the Life Course of Criminals: A Duration Model of Age, Employment, and Recidivism." *American Sociological Review* 65: 529–546.

Uggen, Christopher, Jeff Manza, and Melissa Thompson. 2006. "Citizenship, Democracy, and the Civic Reintegration of Criminal Offenders." *Annals of the American Academy of Political and Social Science* 605: 281–310.

Uggen, Christopher, Sara Wakefield, and Bruce Western. 2005. "Work and Family Perspectives on Reentry." In *Prisoner Reentry and Crime in America*, eds. Jeremy Travis and Christy Visher, pp. 209–243. Cambridge, UK: Cambridge University Press.

Uggen, Christopher, Mischelle Van Brakle, and Heather McLaughlin. 2009. "Punishment and Social Exclusion: National Differences in Prisoner Disenfranchisement." In *Criminal Disenfranchisement in an International Perspective*, eds. Alec C. Ewald and Brandon Rottinghaus, New York: Cambridge University Press.

U.S. Department of Homeland Security. Office of Immigration Statistics. 2005. *2005 Yearbook of Immigration Statistics*. Available at: http://www.dhs.gov/xlibrary/assets/statistics/yearbook/2005/OIS_2005_Yearbook.pdf (accessed June 27, 2010).

U.S. Department of Justice, Bureau of Justice Statistics. 2009. Survey of State Criminal History Information Systems, 2008. NCJ 228661.

U.S. House of Representatives, Committee on the Judiciary. Subcommittee on Crime, Terrorism, and Homeland Security. Hearing on Collateral Consequences of Criminal Convictions: Barriers to Reentry for the Formerly Incarcerated. June 9, 2010.

Von Hirsch, Andrew, and Martin Wasik. 1997. "Civil Disqualifications Attending Conviction: A Suggested Conceptual Framework." *Cambridge Law Journal* 56(3): 600.

Wacquant, Loic. 2005. "Race as Civic Felony." *International Social Science Journal* 183: 130.

Wakefield, Sara. 2009. *Parental Loss of Another Sort? Parental Incarceration and Children's Mental Health*. Working Paper, University of California-Irvine.

Wakefield, Sara. 2007. "The Consequences of Incarceration for Parents and Children." Doctoral Dissertation, University of Minnesota.

Waldfogel, Joel. 1994. "The Effect of Criminal Conviction on Income and the Trust "Reposed in the Workmen." *Journal of Human Resources* 29(1): 62–81.

Western, Bruce. 2006. *Punishment and Inequality in America*. New York: Russell Sage Foundation.

Western, Bruce, and Katherine Beckett. 1999. "How Unregulated is the U.S. Labor Market? The Penal System as a Labor Market Institution." *American Journal of Sociology* 104: 1030–1060.

Wheelock, Darren. 2006. "A Jury of 'Peers': Felon Jury Exclusion, Racial Threat, and Racial Inequality in United States Criminal Courts." Ph.D. dissertation, University of Minnesota, Department of Sociology.

Wildeman, Christopher. 2009. "Parental Imprisonment, the Prison Boom, and the Concentration of Childhood Advantage." *Demography* 46(2): 265–280.

Wildeman, Christopher. 2010. "Paternal Incarceration and Children's Physically Aggressive Behaviors: Evidence from the Fragile Families and Child Wellbeing Study." *Social Forces* 89(1): 285–309.

Wood, Erika, and Liz Budnitz. 2010. *Jim Crow in New York*. New York: Brennan Center for Justice at New York University. Available at: http://brennan.3cdn. net/50080b21f7f0197339_z7m6i2oud.pdf (accessed August 30, 2011).

Young, Jock. 1971. *The Drugtakers: The Social Meaning of Drug Use*. London: MacGibbon and Kee.

CHAPTER 4

··

CRIME VICTIMS, SENTENCING, AND RELEASE FROM PRISON

··

JULIAN V. ROBERTS[1]

CRIME victims have become increasingly important players in the criminal process
in recent years. This is true across the United States and at the federal level, where the
Crime Victims' Rights Act (CVRA) of 2004 accords victims a wide range of rights,
including being notified of all public proceedings in criminal cases, and the right to
participate in many of those proceedings (see Bierschbach 2006). Victims' rights
statutes are found in other Common Law jurisdictions such as England and Wales,
Scotland, Canada, and Australia (see Hoyle and Zedner 2007; Bottoms and Roberts
2010). Finally, Article 68 of the Rome Statute of the International Criminal Court
(ICC) recognizes the security interests and participatory rights of victims.

The role of the victim has evolved throughout the common law world to a
greater degree than the continental justice systems in Europe, where the victim has
always enjoyed greater participatory rights (see Kool and Moerings 2004; Henham
and Mannozzi 2003). For example, in France and Germany, victims have standing as
parties to the proceedings (see Brienen and Hoegen 2000). In France, the *partie
civile* can attach her civil claim to obtain reparations onto an existing criminal trial
and has the right to fully participate as a party in the hearing as well as to benefit
from legal representation. She can provide her own evidence and expertise, which is
considered supplementary to the prosecutor's case (see Lopez 2007).[2] However, it is
in the United States that crime victims now exercise the greatest influence over criminal proceedings. In light of the victims' interest in sentencing and parole, it is not
surprising that victim advocates have focused on these stages of the justice system.

Much of the concern and controversy about victim input has focused on sentencing and early release from prison. A number of factors explain the increased victim involvement in the imposition and administration of sentences. Victims' rights groups and advocates have been particularly successful in attracting political support. In addition, the public shares the view that crime victims have traditionally been poorly treated by the criminal justice system. The public has long supported the creation of more rights for victims in the criminal justice system. For example, one poll found that nine out of ten Americans would support amendments to state constitutions to promote victims' rights (National Victim Center 1991).

CHAPTER OVERVIEW

This chapter reviews the role of the victim at sentencing and parole release proceedings in the United States and other common law jurisdictions.[3] The scholarly literature on victim impact evidence has been accumulating for years, and is now vast. Accordingly, this essay restricts itself to addressing a number of critical questions (see Roberts 2009 for a more comprehensive review of research findings and Cassell 2009 for a recent discussion of the use of impact statements). It is hard to make firm generalizations about the nature and effects of victim impact evidence since victim impact statement regimes vary widely. This variation naturally affects victim participation rates, as well as the degree to which victim impact evidence influences decision making in the criminal justice system.

The chapter makes a conceptual distinction between sentencing and parole, which has important consequences for crime victims. At sentencing, courts follow a principle of proportionality—between the seriousness of the crime and the severity of the imposed punishment (von Hirsch and Ashworth 2005). This principle functions either as a primary consideration in the setting of penalties, or as a constraint upon the permissible severity of punishment. Proportionality is most often understood in light of the harm inflicted and the offender's level of culpability for the offense (see von Hirsch and Ashworth 2005; Roberts 2008; chapter 5 by Frase, this volume). The victim is a primary source of information about the harm created by the crime. Victim input emerges from testimony at trial, through submissions by the prosecution, or as a result of a victim impact statement deposed for the purposes of sentencing. In addition, by providing information about the effects of the crime, victims help to communicate a message to offenders—who might otherwise fail to appreciate the full consequences of their actions. In this sense, the crime victim serves a communicative function at the sentencing hearing (Roberts and Erez 2004). In short, there is a compelling argument for victim participation at sentencing.

Discretionary release from prison (on parole) raises a different set of issues. Parole boards have no mandate to ensure proportionality but are required to evaluate the offender's risk of re-offending, along with the likelihood that he will benefit from release into the community (see chapter 26 by Rhine, this volume). Absent exceptional circumstances, the victim is unlikely to have information relevant to either determination. In cases of serious violence, when the offender has been sentenced to a long period of custody, the victim and the offender have probably had no contact for years. Nor is there any expressive or communicative role for the crime victim at parole (although, as noted, there may have been at sentencing). For these reasons, although parole boards need to consider victim interests to a degree—for example, by ensuring that the prisoner released on parole does not end up living on the same street as his victim, or does not communicate with the victim unless the victim so desires—the role of the victim at parole should arguably be limited.

SUMMARY

This chapter makes the following points:

- Across all common law jurisdictions, crime victims have become increasingly active participants at sentencing and parole.
- An important distinction is made between allowing victims to describe the effect of the crime, and allowing them to recommend a specific sentence or oppose release of the offender on parole.
- The research evidence reveals that most—but by no means all—victims benefit from deposing victim impact statements at sentencing.
- There are also benefits to the sentencing process of allowing information from the victim to be placed before the court. For example, impact statements allow courts to make a more accurate calibration of the harm inflicted upon the crime victim.
- Parole decisions have traditionally reflected the offender's risk of reoffending and the likelihood of benefiting from release on parole. It is harder to see the relevance of the impact of the crime upon these considerations, and this may make victim input problematic.
- Due process safeguards are often weaker at parole, where crime victims in many jurisdictions may offer opinions on the release of the prisoner in the absence of any opportunity for rebuttal.
- There is little research evidence to suggest that victim input results in more punitive sentencing, but several studies have shown an effect at parole hearings; prisoners are less likely to be granted parole when their release is opposed by the victim.

I. Victim Input at Sentencing

The primary vehicle for permitting input at sentencing around the common law world is a victim impact statement (VIS). Since their creation over 30 years ago, a number of different purposes have been ascribed to impact statements at sentencing, including the following (for discussion in Katz 2010; Giannini 2008; Roberts 2003; Edwards 2004; Erez 1999):

- to provide a sentencing court with information about the seriousness of the crime, and the culpability of the offender;
- to provide the court with a direct source of information about the victim's needs—this may assist in the determination of more appropriate reparative sanctions;
- to provide victims with a public forum in which to make a statement reflecting the harm caused by the offense;
- to provide the court with an opportunity to acknowledge that victims have been wronged, and not just harmed;
- to enable the victim to communicate the effects of the crime to the offender;
- to promote the idea that although crimes are committed against the state, many crimes are committed against individual victims, and thereby to enhance the perceived legitimacy of the sentencing and release systems.

A number of arguments have been offered to oppose victim participation at sentencing (see also Ashworth 1993; Hall 1991).

- Victim impact statements add no probative information to the sentencing decision and are therefore redundant.
- Victim input may be very emotional and this will prejudice the court against the defendant.
- Victims are not, within the adversarial model, parties to proceedings involving the state and the defendant.
- Reactions to victimization vary considerably. Some victims may be very upset, and demand imposition of the maximum penalty; a few may be surprisingly forgiving, while others will fall between these extremes. Allowing victims to provide input will therefore lead to inconsistent sentencing.
- Victims often have inaccurate perceptions of sentencing patterns, and for this reason may request unrealistic sentences, close to the maximum penalties.
- Allowing victims to depose impact evidence without letting them also recommend sentence may further increase victims' dissatisfaction with the sentencing process.

Victim Status as an Influential Element at Sentencing

Another argument offered to oppose victim participation at sentencing is the danger that judges may take into consideration the victim's status when imposing a sentence. In the United States—particularly in capital cases—victim status has been influential in sentencing. Phillips (2009) found that victim social status is a factor that influences the outcome in death penalty cases. Thus in his study in Texas, the death penalty was more likely to be sought and imposed on behalf of high-status victims. Further, according to a study conducted in Ohio, the victim's race and gender also had effects: homicides involving white female victims were significantly more likely to result in a death sentence than homicides with other victim characteristics (see Williams and Holcomb 2004).

Victim Statement as a Source of Mitigation and Aggravation at Sentencing

Many U.S. jurisdictions allow victims to make sentence recommendations or to take a position regarding a sentencing proposal. For example, in Minnesota, crime victims have a right to submit a statement that may include their "reaction to the proposed sentence" (Minnesota Statutes, § 611A.038). Sentencing scholars (e.g., Ashworth 1993) generally oppose this practice, arguing that, in the interests of consistency and fairness, the court alone should determine sentence. For this reason, victims in common law jurisdictions outside the United States are not allowed to recommend any specific sentence. Victim impact forms often (but not always) make this exclusion clear. For example, the victim impact statement (VIS) form used in Alberta, Canada, explicitly states the following: "Do NOT include your recommendation as to the type of sentence or the severity of punishment the accused should receive" (Alberta Solicitor General 2008).

Under an adversarial model of justice, in which the two parties are the State and the offender, it may be problematic to allow a third party—the crime victim—to influence the sentence imposed. However, there are three ways in which victim impact evidence can legitimately influence the severity of sentence imposed, even under this model.

First, the statement may reveal that the crime was unusual in some way—less or more serious than most other instances of the offense. If this is the case, it may justify a court imposing a less or more severe sanction, or imposing a "departure" sentence in jurisdictions in which courts are obliged to follow sentencing guidelines. Second, the statement may reveal circumstances in which the imposition of a particular sentence—usually custody—would create disproportionate hardship for the victim or other third parties, such as dependents of the victim or offender. We may call this *collateral harm*. For example, in a case of domestic violence, the court may be reluctant to incarcerate the offender if he is the only source of income for the victim and her children. If he were imprisoned for a lengthy period, this would mean that the crime victim—and her dependents—would be materially disadvantaged. Having suffered criminal victimization, the victim's life would now be made even worse by the criminal justice system. In cases such as this, in which the imposition of a "deserved" sentence would result in additional victimization, courts sometimes mitigate or change the sentence in order to avoid creating further hardship for the victim (see Ashworth 2010).

A victim's statement may also affect sentence if it documents harm to victims other than the direct victim. We may call this latter circumstance *ancillary harm* (see discussion in Roberts and Manikis 2010). For example, consider a case of murder in which the offender kills his intimate partner who was raising three young children. In this case, the harm of the crime is not restricted to the single murder victim; other lives—those of secondary victims—are irreparably affected. The offender should be held accountable for this additional harm, which was reasonably foreseeable. When ancillary injuries are involved, arguably the total harm occasioned to victims is over and above the harm implicit in the nature of the offense itself. On retributive grounds, this justifies enhanced punishment, especially when there is reason to believe that the additional harm was intended or knowingly risked by the offender.

At this point I will review the research upon victim impact statements in common law jurisdictions to address a number of critical issues.

Frequency of Impact Statements at Sentencing

It is the prerogative of the victim to decide whether or not to submit a statement, and many victims have sound reasons for not wishing to participate in the sentencing process in this way. Participation statistics vary. However, it seems clear that only a minority of crime victims submit an impact statement. Early surveys in the United States found that VIS were prepared in only a minority of felony actions. McLeod (1987) reported that impact statements were prepared in less than half of all felony actions, while Hall cites a smaller scale survey in New York City which found that approximately one-quarter of victims submitted a statement. There is little reason to believe participation rates have increased since these reviews were published.

Studies in other countries have also asked victims whether they had submitted an impact statement for the purposes of sentencing. For example, a survey of victims in England and Wales found that only 21 percent recalled having submitted an impact statement (Roberts and Manikis 2011; see also Moore and Blakeborough 2008). In Scotland, Chalmers, Duff, and Leverick (2007) monitored the responses of victims who had been sent victim impact statement packs for the purposes of submitting an impact statement and found that only 15 percent of the victims ultimately submitted a statement. Some studies have focused on specific categories of victims—those more likely to submit a statement. Tapley (2005) found that 42 percent of a sample composed primarily of personal injury victims in England had completed a victim statement. Other general victim statement participation rates include 23 percent in Canada (Roberts 2003) and 14 percent in New Zealand (Church et al. 1995). Finally, Yun, Johnson, and Kercher (2006) report that in Texas in 2004, approximately 100,000 victim statements were given to victims, but only 22 percent were submitted to district attorneys' offices. These relatively modest participation rates are confirmed by practitioners. For example, a sample of Canadian judges reported seeing victim impact statements in only one sentencing hearing in ten (Roberts and Edgar 2005).

Reasons for Submitting an Impact Statement

Victims participate at sentencing for a variety of reasons, some instrumental—in order to influence the sentence imposed—while others are purely expressive. Sentencing regimes vary with respect to whether victims are allowed to recommend sentence; it is not surprising therefore that research demonstrates more support for the instrumental perspective in some locations. Since victims' opinions on this issue are generally solicited *after* they have been given information about the approach in their jurisdiction, their views may reflect the "official" objectives described in materials provided to them. For example, Erez and Tontodonato's research with crime victims in Ohio in the mid-1980s found that approximately half the sample expected to influence the sentence imposed.

In other jurisdictions, there appears to be more support for the expressive rather than the instrumental function. This presumably explains the prohibition on victim sentence recommendations in these countries. Thus Chalmers et al. (2007) found that the most frequently cited reason for submitting a statement in Scotland was expressive rather than instrumental. Indeed, this study provides strong support for the expressive function of victim input. Fully half the participants who had submitted a statement acknowledged that they did not know whether the court had considered their statement, yet were still intending to submit a statement in the future (in the event of further victimization). A survey of victims in South Australia also found that communicating with the offender was the most frequent reason offered by victims for completing a victim impact statement (Justice Strategy Unit, 2000). Similarly, over half of the English victims interviewed by Hoyle et al. (1998) cited expressive reasons for submitting a statement.

Victims' Understanding of the Role of VIS in Sentencing

It is hardly surprising that some victims want to influence the sentencing decision; indeed, it is a natural reaction, reflecting widespread public confusion over the role of the victim in the sentencing process, and the nature of a criminal proceeding under the adversarial model of justice. But victims may well accept a limited role at sentencing if it is explained thoroughly by the appropriate authority. A clear danger associated with VIS concerns the problem of unfulfilled expectations. If victims expect their statement to affect sentence outcome, and then perceive that their input had no discernible impact, what is their reaction likely to be? This question has been addressed in a number of studies. Erez and Tontodonato (1992) for example, report that victims in Ohio who expected to influence the outcome but who thought that their input had not affected the sentence were less satisfied. This negative reaction generalized to the criminal justice system as a whole; victims who had expected their statement to affect sentencing held more negative opinions of the system. Herein lies the danger of arousing—and then failing to fulfill—crime victims' expectations. In this way, a reform designed to promote victim satisfaction may actually result in lower levels of satisfaction. This finding demonstrates the importance of clarifying for victims the true nature and purpose of a VIS.

Contents of Impact Statements: Prejudicial or Legally Relevant Information?

One criticism of victim impact statements is that they are redundant, containing only material that is already available in the police report or in submissions on sentence made by the prosecution. There are two ways of determining whether the VIS contains legally relevant information that is unavailable through other means. The contents of statements can be compared to the description of the crime in the police reports, and criminal justice professionals such as prosecutors and judges can be asked whether they encounter new (and legally relevant) information in the victim impact statement. Although few studies have adopted the content analysis approach, it seems that victim impact statements do contain additional information of use to a sentencing court. Surveys of judges in Canada and Australia found that courts perceived that VIS contained legally relevant information unavailable from other sources (Roberts and Edgar 2005; O'Connell 2009).

Reactions of Criminal Justice Professionals

Recent surveys of criminal justice professionals reveal a positive picture with respect to practitioners' reactions to victim input. Leverick et al. (2007) interviewed legal professionals in Scotland and found very few objections to the impact statement scheme. Similarly, Morgan and Sanders note that the small number of sentencers they interviewed in England were "broadly in favour of a [victim impact statement] system" (1999, p. 22). A multi-site Canadian study found that even defense counsel—who might be expected to hold negative views of victim impact statements—appear untroubled by the introduction of impact statements, as long as they have the right to cross-examine the victim on the contents of the statement (Prairie Research Associates 2005a). Defense counsel interviewed by Leverick et al. (2007) were unopposed to the expansion of the victim statement scheme in Scotland and agreed that courts were well able to disregard irrelevant information contained in the statements (see also Erez and Rogers 1999). Positive reactions from criminal justice professionals also emerge from research in Minnesota (Schuster and Propen 2007); South Australia (O'Connell 2009); and Holland (see Kool and Moerings 2004).[4]

Effect of Victim Impact Statements on Sentencing Practices

Much of the research in the area has addressed the question of whether the introduction of victim impact statements changes sentencing practices. The answer is critical to advocates and critics alike. Advocates of the instrumental approach to

VIS assert that if they do not affect sentencing practices, victims will become disillusioned. Critics respond that if sentencing practices do change as a result of the introduction of victim impact statements, the principle of parity in sentencing will be undermined. Indeed, apprehension of the effect of VIS on sentencing patterns drives much of the opposition toward the role of the victim in sentencing. VIS are therefore criticized from both directions: if they affect the sentence of the court, they will be criticized for undermining equity in sentencing; if they have no impact, they will be faulted for having raised (and then subsequently dashed) victims' expectations.

Tests of the "impact" hypothesis have been conducted in a number of jurisdictions, and have generally found little effect on sentencing patterns. For example, Erez and Tontodonato (1990) found that victim input did not influence sentencing decisions in Ohio. Erez et al. (1994) report the results of an analysis of aggregate sentencing patterns in South Australia before and after the introduction of victim impact statements (in 1989). The results were clear: sentencing patterns did not become more severe in the post-reform phase (see also Erez and Roeger 1995). The researchers also concluded that the introduction of the VIS did not have any significant impact on the length of sentences of imprisonment. The same pattern has been replicated in other studies (e.g., Davis and Smith 1994). In Canada, the introduction of victim impact statements had no discernible effect on the overall custody rate (Roberts 2009). Finally, interviews with legal professionals confirm the findings from empirical research. Erez et al. (1997) found agreement among legal professionals in South Australia that victim input had not increased sentence severity. This conclusion also applies to surveys of criminal justice professionals in other jurisdictions.

There are several explanations for the lack of effect of victim impact statements on sentencing patterns. First, as noted, these statements appear in a small percentage of all cases appearing for sentencing, insufficient to affect the overall severity of sentencing patterns. Second, as Elias (1993) and others have suggested, the proliferation of mandatory and presumptive sentencing laws has restricted the influence of variables such as victim impact statements. The most likely reason that victim impact statements have little effect upon sentencing outcomes is that criminal justice professionals are able to protect the sentencing process from the influence of "extralegal" material. Prosecutors often exercise editorial control over the statements by excising material designed to enhance the severity of the statement, including allegations of prior misconduct by the defendant or appeals for a specific (and punitive) sanction. Judges—who are trained to ignore evidence with no probative value—appear unaffected by any appeals for severity from the crime victim. This conclusion is supported by surveys and interviews with prosecutors, defense counsel, and judges (e.g., Leverick et al. 2007).

At this point I turn to the domain of prison-release decisions, where, as noted in the introduction, the mandate of the criminal justice system is rather different from judicial sentencing.

II. VICTIMS AND RELEASE FROM PRISON

The United States was the first country to allow victim input into the release process. By 1987, victims were authorized to submit statements to parole authorities in 38 states. Kinnevy and Caplan (2008) note that input from victims is allowed by 94 percent of releasing authorities, making the victim the most frequent participant other than the prisoner, with in-person victim input permissible in 87 percent of jurisdictions. Other jurisdictions, including England and Wales, Canada, and New Zealand, have recently enhanced the role of the victim in the domain of corrections (see Reeves and Dunn 2010). Victims in all jurisdictions have the right to submit an impact statement and to attend parole hearings. As with sentencing, most jurisdictions preclude victims from simply expressing an opinion against the release of the prisoner, although in a number of U.S. states they do enjoy this as a right.

Dissemination of Information Relating to Prisoners

Most correctional systems provide, upon application, information to the crime victim about developments relating to the offender. Victims in Michigan may receive, on request, a copy of the prisoner's parole eligibility report, which contains the individual's misconduct record, work and educational records, and other such information related to his time in custody (Michigan Judicial Institute 2009). Similarly, in New Zealand victims can request a list of any correctional programs that the prisoner may have attended since admission to custody, the prisoner's security classification at any given time, as well as any misconduct infractions that he may have accumulated in prison (New Zealand Parole Board 2007). Victims enjoy a comparable level of access to information in Western Australia as a result of the Victims of Crime Rights and Services Act (2006).

An important distinction may be made between providing victims with information about the offender's time in prison and allowing input into the early release decision. A number of scholars have expressed reservations about giving victims the right to participate in parole hearings. For example, Ranish and Shichor concluded that: "It seems clear that the victim's participation in the [parole] hearing is designed to put pressure on the board" (1985, p. 55). Allowing victims to influence the decision to release the offender creates a clear anomaly in jurisdictions in which victims are prevented from recommending a specific sentence. Having been silenced with respect to the question of whether the offender should be incarcerated, the victim is now allowed to express a view on the question of whether he should be released from custody. Thus a victim's right denied at one stage of the criminal process is inexplicably accorded at a later stage.[5]

Criteria for Release

The decision to grant parole usually depends upon the response of parole authorities to two principal questions: Does the prisoner represent a significant risk to the community, and will his release on conditions promote his rehabilitation? For example, in Arkansas, in order to reach a decision, the Parole Board is guided by two legislative criteria: the risk posed to the community by the potential to reoffend as well as the rehabilitation and reintegration of the offender back into the community (see Arkansas Parole Board 2010). The New Jersey Parole Act of 1979 creates a presumption that an adult inmate shall be released at parole eligibility, unless it is demonstrated "by a preponderance of the evidence that the inmate will commit a crime under the laws of the State if released" (New Jersey Parole Board 2002, 1). In England and Wales the criteria are found in the practice directions governed by s. 239(6) of the Criminal Justice Act (2003): ". . . . The Parole Board shall consider primarily the risk to the public of a further offense being committed at a time when the prisoner would otherwise be in prison." Similar criteria are identified by the Corrections and Conditional Release Act in Canada. From sentencing to parole, the justice system therefore changes from one concerned with retribution to one preoccupied primarily with risk and the rehabilitation of the offender. This raises questions about the relevance of information derived from the victim.

Victim Input into Parole Decision-Making

Some victims express an interest in developments occurring after the offender is admitted to custody, particularly with respect to an impending release. A survey in the United States found that victims assigned high importance to being informed of the date of release from custody (Kilpatrick et al. 1998, 4). Victims may well have legitimate security concerns that need to be communicated to the releasing authority. In addition, parole authorities may wish to review the neighborhood in which the prisoner will be serving his sentence in the community, in case it is close to the victim's residence. This seems reasonable; it surely would be inappropriate for parole authorities to release the prisoner to live in close proximity to his or her victim. In this sense, the victim provides input with respect to one specific element of the release plan—but not an opinion regarding the timing of parole, or the nature of conditions imposed upon the parolee.

Victim Input Regimes at Parole

As with sentencing, victim input arrangements vary considerably across different jurisdictions. An important distinction exists between those that permit victims to oppose the offender's release and those that restrict the victim's input to submissions about the conditions that might be imposed if parole is granted. In Maryland, victims may submit a written statement to the Parole Commission, meet with a Parole Commissioner, as well as speak at the parole hearing (Maryland Department of Public Safety and Correctional Services 2010). In Missouri, crime victims may attend and provide input into parole hearings, and may also specifically request that the board deny parole to the offender in their case (Attorney General of Missouri 2008, 20). Similarly, in Montana, the Board of Pardons and Parole permits victims to present a statement including "the victim's opinion regarding whether the prisoner should be paroled" (Montana Board of Pardons and Parole 2010, 2).

In contrast, in England and Wales, as a result of the Code of Practice for Victims of Crime, releasing authorities are required to consult the victim with respect to the conditions of release, but not the decision to grant or deny parole (see Code of Practice for Victims of Crime, section 12.2). A similar arrangement exists in Canada, where victims should provide in their victim impact statements relevant information related only to the risk the offender may pose (see National Parole Board 2009). There is little consistency across Australian jurisdictions regarding victim input at parole hearings (see Black 2003).

Permissible and Prohibited Content

Some parole boards provide direction about the appropriate contents of the impact statement. For example, victims in New Jersey are encouraged to include material about any continuing effects of the crime upon their lives, the extent of any loss of earnings, but also to provide "any other information that would help the State Parole Board to determine the likelihood of the inmate committing a new crime" (State of New Jersey Parole Board 2008, 1). This information could include threats issued by the offender directly or indirectly to the crime victim. Directions such as these focus the victim's attention on providing information of clear relevance to the parole decision. Generally speaking, however, victims are encouraged to adopt an expansive approach to the contents of their statement.

According to the Virginia Parole Board guidelines, crime victims and their relatives may provide the Board with such information as "they consider necessary or helpful to the board to make a decision" (Virginia Parole Board Policy Manual 2006). In Georgia, victims wishing to submit an impact statement to the Board of Pardons and Paroles are told: " [The statement] allows you the opportunity to voice your opinion about the possible parole of the inmate. . . . Include *all information and concerns you want taken into consideration by the Parole Board*" (Georgia State Board of Pardons and Paroles 2008, emphasis added). Similarly, the National Parole Board of Canada encourages crime victims to "send any new or additional information that he/she thinks is relevant for the NPB to consider" (National Parole Board 2009). Such directions will be interpreted in a wide variety of ways by crime victims. Moreover, relevance is defined by the victim rather than the decision-making authority, and this may well be problematic.

Impact of the Crime versus Impact of the Criminal Justice Outcome

An important difference between victim input at sentencing and parole concerns the subject matter of the impact statement. Impact schemes at sentencing do not canvass the victim's opinion of the impact that the *sentence* will have upon their lives. At parole, however, victims are often asked to express a view on whether the prisoner should be granted parole, and to state how they will feel if parole is granted. The Tasmanian Parole Board is directed to consider "any statement provided by a victim." The directions to victims note the following three issues: how the crime has affected and continues to affect them, how they would feel about the prisoner being released from prison, and the kinds of conditions they would like to see included in the parole order (Tasmania Department of Justice, undated). A similar arrangement exists in New South Wales where the Crimes (Administration of Sentences) Act (1999) stipulates that this Board must consider "the likely effect on the victim and the victim's family of the offender being released." Victims in the state are provided with the following directions regarding their impact statement: "The submission should state how you, as the victim, feel about the impending release of the offender."

Victims who submit a victim personal statement (VPS) to the Parole Board of England and Wales are expressly prevented from offering an opinion on whether the offender should or should not be released. The reason cited for this is that the Parole Board's decision to release "must be based solely upon the potential risk presented by the offender" and not, presumably, on the opinions of the victim (National Probation Service 2007, 4). Yet the VPS may consist of an updated statement of the impact of the crime as well as a statement about "the likely impact of the offender's release on the victim, or those with close emotional ties to the victim's family" (National Probation Service 2007). This kind of language may confuse victims. Are they supposed to provide an opinion about the likelihood that the offender will target them again, or to describe the impact that knowing he is living in the community will have upon them?[6]

An evolution has therefore taken place from sentencing to parole. At sentencing the victim describes the effect of the crime, whereas at parole she describes the impact that a parole decision may have upon her life—a very different matter. The adjudicating authority has therefore moved from considering the consequences of the offense to the impact of its own decisions on the victim. The determination of release conditions placed upon prisoners granted parole should reflect any statutory conditions as well as restrictions and requirements designed to minimize risk of reoffending and to promote rehabilitation and reintegration. But they should not be constructed to offer solace to the crime victim. Even when the mandate of the releasing authority directs parole boards to consider risk and not retribution, research suggests that both will enter the equation. Thus, in Canada, when members of the National Parole Board were asked how they consider victim input, "measuring the impact of the crime" was one of the ways cited (Prairie Research Associates 2005b).

Finally, there are questions about whether information about the impact of the crime should be placed before the releasing authority. The impact of the crime on the victim prior to conviction has been reflected in the sentence imposed, and need not be repeated. Parole boards will usually have a copy of any victim impact statement at sentencing. What about crime impacts occurring—or continuing—*after* sentencing? Many victims of serious violent crimes continue to suffer physically and mentally long after the offender leaves the court to begin serving his sentence in prison (e.g., Shapland 1984). However, it is unclear why—under current releasing criteria—the protracted suffering of the crime victim should be a consideration for the authority charged with evaluating risk of reoffending and offender rehabilitation.

Taking either the pre-or post-sentencing suffering into account in determining whether the offender should be granted parole reflects a logic that either the court underestimated the seriousness of the crime (and imposed an inappropriately lenient sentence), or the court was not in a position to anticipate the longer-term consequences, an error that can now be rectified by the releasing authority. Of course, the criteria for parole release could be expanded to include a "recalibration" of the harm inflicted. This might require reevaluating the impact on the victim to reflect additional suffering in the time since sentencing. If this were done, the relevance of the victim's input would be much clearer. However, such a proposal would amount to resentencing the offender, and would be problematic if this adjustment of the "retributive value" of the crime were undertaken by a non-judicial authority without the clear guidelines available at sentencing.

Due Process Concerns Arising from Victim Input at Parole Hearings

Aside from the substantive question of whether a parole board should consider victim impact evidence, a number of important procedural issues arise. If parole boards are required to consider impact evidence, careful attention needs to be paid to ensure procedural fairness. At sentencing, due process concerns arising from the use of victim impact statements are addressed by disclosure requirements, by swearing the witness with respect to the evidence, and by allowing cross-examination of the victim's testimony.

Parole hearings are generally not subject to the procedural safeguards of a sentencing proceeding; indeed, some jurisdictions take steps to protect the victim's evidence from any kind of adversarial scrutiny.

Victims in New Jersey, for example, may testify before the state parole board during a confidential hearing, or they may submit written comments regarding the possible release of the prisoner; neither the testimony nor the comments are shared with the parole applicant (see State of New Jersey Parole Board 2008). Elsewhere, including Virginia and New Jersey, the inmate is not informed as to whether any victim chose to provide testimony (see Virginia Department of Corrections 2010; State of New Jersey Parole Board 2008). A prisoner will not know: whether a victim has submitted a statement; anything about the contents of any statement; or whether board members were influenced by the statement. In Rhode Island, victims are allowed to meet with parole board members prior to any meeting with the prisoner, and neither the prisoner nor his attorney is allowed to be present at this meeting (State of Rhode Island Parole Board and Sex Offender Community Notification Unit, undated).

Across the United States, disclosure to the inmate of any victim impact statement has historically been the exception rather than the norm (McLeod 1989; Bernat et al. 1994). In Florida release hearings, representations on behalf of the prisoner will be made first at the hearing, followed by the victim impact statement. Since the

Commission does not allow rebuttal of any testimony, not only will victims have the last word, but there is no opportunity for the offender's representative to respond to the victim's submissions. The offender is denied attendance at the hearing (Florida Parole Commission 2008).[7]

In contrast, the Utah parole board is required to provide the offender with copies of all documents reviewed by the board when considering parole, except where confidentiality is "absolutely required," and this includes the victim impact statement. If confidentiality is deemed necessary, the board at least provides a summary of the original document (State of Utah Board of Pardons and Parole 2010). The threat to the liberty interests of restricting access to the victim's submissions is demonstrated by research. Smith, Watkins, and Morgan (1997) found that the prisoner's chances of being granted parole diminished significantly if the victim attended the hearing in his absence.

Victims in some states are allowed to bring supporters to the parole hearing. In Arkansas, victims are allowed to bring "as many people as they would like" to the impact hearing, and with prior approval of the board are also allowed to bring members of the press or news media (Arkansas Board of Parole 2008). Crime victims in New Zealand may be accompanied by a lawyer and up to three supporters (New Zealand Parole Board 2007). The presence of these individuals may undermine the integrity of the parole process by creating pressure on parole board members to accede to the victim's wishes. Indeed, research by Smith et al. (1997) found that the number of victims participating was inversely related to the probability of the prisoner being granted parole. Similarly, a survey of releasing authorities across the United States found that the number of victims was a more important factor affecting release decisions than the offender's institutional conduct (Kinnevy and Caplan 2008).

Effect of Victim Input on Parole Outcomes

As noted (above), only a minority of victims submit an impact statement at sentencing. Although there is less research on parole than sentencing, it appears that an even smaller proportion of victims submit impact evidence or make representations at parole hearings. As with sentencing, the data on victim participation at parole hearings across the United States are rather dated now. Rhine et al. (1991) noted that victim input was "seldom received . . . in most states" (p. 75). Another survey found that victim testimony was present in 10 percent of parole reviews in Pennsylvania (Parsonage, Bernat, and Helfgott 1992). As with sentencing, then, an important research question concerns the effect of victim participation on parole hearing outcomes.

The first published evaluation suggested that victim input at parole influences the outcome of hearings. Parsonage et al. (1992) found a significant association between the presence of victim statements and a negative parole decision in hearings in Pennsylvania. Similarly, Smith et al. (1997) demonstrated that in Alabama, victim participation was a significant predictor of parole outcome. Morgan and

Smith (2005) examined parole outcomes in cases in which an inmate had had a hearing and in which victims had been notified of the impending hearing. These researchers found that victim influence—but not the offender's institutional behavior or program participation—was a significant predictor of parole outcome. When the victim submitted impact evidence, the prisoner was less likely to be granted parole—independent of the influence of other factors related to the parole decision.

The most recent research on the question was reported by Caplan (2010a, b), who studied the effect of victim impact evidence at parole hearings in the state of New Jersey. Caplan found that victim input was *not* a significant predictor of parole release. One explanation for the discrepancy between this study and the previous tests of the "victim effect" at parole may involve the nature of the input allowed. Instructions to victims in New Jersey make it clear that the input should include "information that would help the State Parole Board determine the likelihood of the inmate committing a new crime" (State of New Jersey Parole Board 2008). By focusing the victim's attention on the issue of primary concern, the directions may restrict or eliminate the introduction of prejudicial material that may have otherwise influenced the Board's decision making. If this is the case, it suggests that the effect of victims' representations is mediated by factors such as the nature of the input allowed and other variables relating to the prisoner's application. Clearly, further research is needed to clarify the ways in which victim input into parole decisions benefits crime victims, as well as the ways in which this input can promote better releasing decisions.

Finally, parole board members appear to recognize the influence of victims at parole hearings. Interviews conducted by McLeod (1989) in the United States and Polowek (2005) in Canada found that board members acknowledged the effect of victim input on decisions taken. More recently, a survey of releasing authorities found that 40 percent of participants acknowledged that victim input was "very influential" in their decisions to grant or deny parole (Kinnevy and Caplan 2008).

Explaining the Influence of Victim Input at Parole

Why might victim input have a greater effect at parole than sentencing, if indeed it does? Several explanations may be offered. First, as noted, fewer victims participate at parole compared to sentencing, and those who do participate may well be particularly affected by the crime and therefore strongly motivated to oppose the prisoner release. Victims appearing at sentencing may have one of several different motives—to secure some compensation as part of the sentence, to communicate a message to the offender, to receive some official recognition of their suffering from a court of law, and so forth. At parole, the primary motive is more likely to be opposing parole, or securing tight restrictions on the prisoner in the event that he is granted release from prison. For example, in the research reported by Caplan (2010a), 18 victims submitted input in favor of release, compared to 120 who opposed granting of parole.

Second, victims are more likely to attend in person to depose their impact statements at parole—and their submissions may therefore be harder to ignore. Research suggests that personal statements are more moving than written statements or victim impact forms. At sentencing, victim impact statements are usually submitted by means of a VIS form, and few victims provide oral testimony (McLeod 1989; Roberts and Edgar 2005). Third, the restrictions on victim input are clearly more relaxed at parole, and this increases the likelihood that the parole board will hear emotional and moving appeals for a particular outcome—most likely to deny parole. Fourth, at sentencing the decision maker is a legal professional (judge) trained to distinguish probative from prejudicial material, and to act upon the former, not the latter. Parole board members are seldom legally trained, and therefore may be more likely to be influenced by victim appeals. Finally, parole boards in a number of jurisdictions specifically reserve places for victims' representatives, and this must make them more likely to accede to victims' wishes than a sentencing court.

Conclusion

The days when victims played a peripheral role as witnesses for the prosecution and were excluded from decisions made at sentencing and parole are long over. Today, victims in common law jurisdictions participate actively at both stages of the criminal process—usually by submitting victim impact statements or by appearing at sentencing and parole hearings. Research has demonstrated that although only a minority of victims participate, those who do report benefiting from participation. Victims appear to appreciate being part of the sentencing (or parole process), and derive satisfaction from communicating directly with the offender. In addition, this participation does not appear to have had adverse effects on the sentencing system, where the relevance of victim input evidence is relatively clear.

In the domain of corrections, victims have important interests in being kept informed on the offender's release and can provide decision-makers with useful information regarding their safety concerns. Contrary to sentencing, victim input has been shown to have an important effect on parole authorities and—if unrelated to the criteria for release—may threaten the integrity of parole decision-making. At this stage, since the offender's freedom remains at stake, justified and principled decision-making based on relevant criteria should continue to govern the system. Finally, in many jurisdictions there appear to be important procedural imbalances favoring victims while depriving offenders with minimal fundamental safeguards. These important concerns regarding the process should be addressed to avoid any detrimental effects on the parole system's legitimacy.

NOTES

1. I am grateful to Marie Manikis for research assistance, and the editors for helpful feedback on an earlier draft.

2. A similar process exists in Germany and is known as *nebenklage*. For certain offenses, victims can become a secondary prosecutor with legal representation and full participation in criminal proceedings.

3. The essay does not deal with the use of victim impact statements in capital punishment proceedings in the United States (see Bandes 1999; 2008).

4. Judges in juvenile courts were significantly more likely to agree than disagree with the statement that "Victims should have input into sanctioning and dispositional decisions of the court" (Bazemore and Leip 2000).

5. Moreover, if victims have a right to express an opinion on whether the prisoner is released, should they not be allowed input into the decision of whether he is recalled to prison in the event of an alleged breach of conditions, or whether he is allowed to transfer from a maximum to a less restrictive category?

6. Reevaluating the sentence in light of the seriousness of the offense is not part of the board's mandate, however. If they assume this role, it may undermine sound correctional practices. Indeed, parole board members interviewed by Polowek (2005) expressed concern that the presence of the victim undermined the ability of the board to conduct an adequate risk assessment.

7. Even in England and Wales, where reports and submissions to the parole board are potentially disclosable to the prisoner, victims may request that certain information remains confidential. The probation service circular that deals with victim statements at parole notes that information from victims is frequently withheld from the prisoner (National Probation Service 2007). If the information is deemed non-disclosable, the prisoner will be informed of the existence of such information but not its specific contents; he or she will not be aware of what it is or who has submitted it (National Probation Service 2007).

REFERENCES

Alberta Solicitor General, Victims Programs. 2008. *Victim Impact Statement*. Online. Available at: http://www.reddeerruralvictimassistance.com/images/VIS_brochue.pdf.

Arkansas Board of Parole. 2008. *What Crime Victims Need to Know about the Parole Process*. Little Rock: Arkansas Board of Parole.

Arkansas Parole Board. 2010. *About Us*. Online. Available at: http://www.arbop.org/about.html.

Ashworth, Andrew. 1993. "Victim Impact Statements and Sentencing." *The Criminal Law Review* (July): 498–509.

Ashworth, Andrew. 2010. *Sentencing and Criminal Justice*. 5th ed. Cambridge: Cambridge University Press.

Attorney General of Missouri. 2008. *Crime Victims' Rights*. Jefferson City: Attorney General of Missouri.

Bandes, Susan. 1999. "Reply to Paul Cassell: What We Know about Victim Impact Statements." *Utah Law Review* 2: 545–552.

Bandes, Susan. 2009. "Victim Closure and the Sociology of Emotion." *Law and Contemporary Problems* 72 (Spring): 1–26.

Bazemore, Gordon, and Leslie Leip. 2000. "Victim Participation in the New Juvenile Court: Tracking Judicial Attitudes Towards Restorative Justice Reforms." *The Justice System Journal* 21: 199–226.

Bernat, Francis P., William H. Parsonage, and Jacqueline Helfgott. 1994. "Victim Impact Laws and the Parole Process in the United States: Balancing Victim and Inmate Rights and Interests." *International Review of Victimology* 3: 121–140.

Bierschbach, Richard. 2006. "Allocution and the Purposes of Victim Participation under the CVRA." *Federal Sentencing Reporter* 19: 44–48.

Black, Matt. 2003. "Victim Submissions to Parole Boards: The Agenda for Research." *Trends and Issues in Criminal Justice* 251. Canberra: Australian Institute of Criminology.

Bottoms, Anthony, and Julian V. Roberts, eds. 2010. *Hearing the Victim: Adversarial Justice, Crime Victims, and the State*. Cullompton: Willan Publishing.

Brienen Mario, E. I., and E. H. Hoegen. 2000. *Victims of Crime in 22 European Criminal Justice Systems: The Implementation of Recommendation (85) 11 of the Council of Europe on the Position of the Victim in the Framework of Criminal Law and Procedure.* Nijmegen: Wolf Legal Productions.

Caplan, Joel. 2010a. "Parole Release Decisions: Impact of Victim Input on a Representative Sample of Inmates." *Journal of Criminal Justice* 38: 291–300.

Caplan, Joel. 2010b. "Parole Release Decisions: Impact of Positive and Negative Victim and Nonvictim Input on a Representative Sample of Parole-Eligible Inmates." *Violence and Victims* 25: 224–242.

Cassell, Paul. 2009. "In Defense of Victim Impact Statements." *Ohio State Journal of Criminal Law* 6: 611–648.

Chalmers, James, Peter Duff, and Fiona Leverick. 2007. "Victim Impact Statements: Can Work, Do Work (or Those Who Bother to Make Them)." *Criminal Law Review* (May): 360–379.

Church, Alison, et al. 1995. *Victims' Court Assistance: An Evaluation of the Pilot Scheme.* Wellington: New Zealand Department of Justice.

Davis, Robert, and Barbara Smith. 1994a. "The Effects of Victim Impact Statements on Sentencing Decisions: A Test in an Urban Setting." *Justice Quarterly* 11: 453–512.

Davis, Robert, and Barbara Smith. 1994b. "Victim Impact Statements and Victim Satisfaction: an Unfulfilled Promise?" *Journal of Criminal Justice* 22: 1–12.

Edwards, Ian. 2004. "An Ambiguous Participant: The Crime Victim and Criminal Justice Decision-Making." *British Journal of Criminology* 44: 967–982.

Elias, Robert. 1993. *Victims Still: The Political Manipulation of Crime Victims*. London: Sage Publications.

Erez, Edna. 1999. "Who's Afraid of the Big Bad Victim? Victim Impact Statements as Victim Empowerment and Enhancement of Justice." *The Criminal Law Review* (July): 545–556.

Erez, Edna, and Leigh Roeger. 1995. "The Effect of Victim Impact Statements on Sentencing Patterns and Outcomes: The Australian Experience." *Journal of Criminal Justice* 23: 363–375.

Erez, Edna, Leigh Roeger, and Frank Morgan. 1994. *Victim Impact Statements in South Australia: An Evaluation*. Office of Crime Statistics, South Australian Attorney General's Department, Adelaide, Australia Series C No. 6.

Erez, Edna, Leigh Roeger, and Frank Morgan. 1997. "Victim Harm, Impact Statements and Victim Satisfaction with Justice: An Australian Experience." *International Review of Criminology* 5: 37–60.

Erez, Edna, and Linda Rogers. 1999. "Victim Impact Statements and Sentencing Outcomes and Processes." *British Journal of Criminology* 2(39): 216–239.

Erez, Edna, and Pamela Tontodonato. 1990. "The Effect of Victim Participation in Sentencing on Sentence Outcome." *Criminology* 28: 451–474.

Erez, Edna, and Pamela Tontodonato. 1992. "Victim Participation in Sentencing and Satisfaction with Justice." *Justice Quarterly* 9: 393–417.

Florida Parole Commission. 2008. *Victims' Rights.* Available at: https://fpc.fl.us/Victims.htm.

Georgia State Board of Pardons and Paroles. 2008. *Victim Impact Statement.* Online. Available: http://oldweb.pap.state.ga.us/victim.nsf/fVIS2?openform.

Giannini, Mary. 2008. "Equal Rights for Equal Rites?: Victim Allocution, Defendant Allocution, and the Crime Victims' Rights Act." *Yale Law and Policy Review* 26: 431–484.

Hall, Donald. 1991. "Victims' Voices in Criminal Court: The Need for Restraint." *American Criminal Law Review* 28: 233–266.

Henham, Ralph, and Grazia Mannozzi. 2003. "Victim Participation and Sentencing in England and Italy: A Legal and Policy Analysis." *European Journal of Crime, Criminal Law and Criminal Justice* 11: 278–313.

Hoyle, Carolyn, Ed Cape, Rod Morgan, and Andrew Sanders. 1998. *Evaluation of the "One Stop Shop" and Victim Statement Pilot Projects.* London: Home Office, Research Development and Statistics Directorate.

Hoyle, Carolyn, and Lucia Zedner. 2007. "Victims, Victimization and Criminal Justice." In *The Oxford Handbook of Criminology*, eds. Mike Maguire and Robert Reiner. 4th ed. New York: Oxford University Press.

Justice Strategy Unit. 2000. *Victims of Crime Review. Report Two: Survey of Victims of Crime.* Online. Available at: www.voc.sa.gov.au/Publications/Reports/victimsofcrimesurvey.

Katz, Karen. 2010. "Opposing Scales of Justice: Victims' Voices in the Sentencing Process." *Canadian Criminal Law Review* 14: 181–230.

Kilpatrick, Dean, David Beatty, and Susan Howley. 1998. *The Rights of Crime Victims—Does Legal Protection Make a Difference?* Research in Brief. Washington, DC: National Institute of Justice.

Kinnevy, Susan, and Joel Caplan. 2008. *Findings from the APAI International Survey of Releasing Authorities.* Philadelphia: Center for Research on Youth and Policy.

Kool, Renée, and Martin Moerings. 2004. "The Victim Has the Floor." *European Journal of Crime, Criminal Law and Criminal Justice* 12: 46–60.

Leverick, Fiona, James Chalmers, and Peter Duff. 2007. *An Evaluation of the Pilot Victim Statement Schemes in Scotland.* Edinburgh: Scottish Executive Social Research. Online. Available at: www.scotland.gov.uk/publications.

Lopez, Gérard. 2007. *Les droits des victimes: droits, auditions, expertise, clinique.* 2nd ed. Paris: Dalloz.

Maryland Department of Public Safety and Correctional Services. 2010. *Victim Services.* Online. Available at: www.dpscs.state.md.us.

McLeod, Maureen. 1987. "An Examination of the Victim's Role at Sentencing: Results of a Survey of Probation Administrators." *Judicature* 71(3): 162–168.

McLeod, Maureen. 1989. "Getting Free: Victim Participation in Parole Board Decisions". *Criminal Justice* 4: 13–15, 41–43.

Meredith, Colin, and Chantal Paquette. 2001. *Report on Victim Impact Statement Focus Groups: Victims of Crime and Research Series.* Ottawa: Department of Justice Canada.

Michigan Judicial Institute. 2009. *Crime Victim Rights Manual*. Rev. ed. Online. Available
    at: http://courts.michigan.gov/mji/resources/cvr/CVRM_2009-2010_December.pdf.
Montana Board of Pardons and Parole. 2010. *Victim information for the Board of Pardons
    and Parole*. Available at: http://mt.gov/bopp/victim_information.asp.
Moore, Louise, and Laura Blakeborough. 2008. *Early Findings from WAVES: Information
    and Service Provision*. London: Office for Criminal Justice Reform.
Morgan, Kathryn, and Brent Smith. 2005. "Victims, Punishment, and Parole:
    The Effect of Victim Participation on Parole Hearings." *Crime and Public Policy*
    4: 333–360.
Morgan, Rod, and Andrew Sanders. 1999. *The Uses of Victim Statements*. London: Home
    Office, Research Development and Statistics Directorate.
National Parole Board. 2009. *Guidelines for Writing Victims Statements to be Presented at
    the National Parole Board Hearings*. Online. Available at: http://www.npb-cnlc.gc.ca/
    victims/guidelines-eng.shtml.
National Parole Board. 2009. *Victims—Providing Information*. Online. Available at:
    http://www.npb-cnlc.gc.ca/infocntr/factsh/provid-eng.shtml.
National Probation Service. 2007. *Victim Representation at Parole Board Hearings. Proba-
    tion Circular*. London: National Offender Management Service.
National Victim Center. 1991. *America Speaks Out: Citizens' Attitudes about Victims' Rights*.
    New York: National Victim Center.
New Jersey State Parole Board. 2002. *A Brief Overview of the Parole Process in New Jersey*.
    Available at: www.state.nj.us/parole.
New South Wales Victims of Crime Bureau and Department of Corrective Services. 2001.
    Submissions. Sydney: New South Wales.
New Zealand Parole Board. 2007. *Information for Victims*. Wellington: New Zealand Parole
    Board.
O'Connell, Michael. 2009. "Victims in the Sentencing Process—South Australia's Judges
    and Magistrates Give Their Verdict." *International Perspectives in Victimology*
    4: 50–57.
Padfield, Nicola, and Julian V. Roberts. 2010. "Victims and Parole: Probative or Prejudi-
    cial?" In *Hearing the Victim: Adversarial Justice, Crime Victims, and the State*.
    Cullompton: Willan Publishing.
Parsonage, William, Frances Bernat, and Jacqueline Helfgott. 1992. "Victim Impact
    Testimony and Pennsylvania's Parole Decision-Making Process: A Pilot Study."
    Criminal Justice Policy Review 6: 187–206.
Phillips, Scott. 2009. "Status Disparities in the Capital of Capital Punishment." *Law &
    Society Review* 43(4): 807–838.
Polowek, Kim. 2005. "Victim Participatory Rights in Parole: Their role and the dynamics of
    victim influence as seen by board members." Ph.D. dissertation, Burnaby, BC: School
    of Criminology, Simon Fraser University.
Prairie Research Associates. 2005a. *Multi-Site Survey of Victims of Crime
    and Criminal Justice Professionals Across Canada: Summary of Defence
    Counsel Respondents*. Ottawa: Department of Justice, Policy Centre for
    Victim Issues.
Prairie Research Associates. 2005b. *Multi-site Survey of Victims of Crime and Criminal
    Justice Professionals across Canada: Summary of Probation Officer, Corrections, and
    Parole Board Respondents*. Ottawa: Policy Centre for Victim Issues, Department of
    Justice Canada.

Ranish, Donald, and David Shichor. 1985. "The Victim's Role in the Penal Process: Recent Developments in California." *Federal Probation* 49: 50–57.

Reeves, Helen, and Peter Dunn. 2010. "The Status of Crime Victims and Witnesses in the Twenty-first Century." In *Hearing the Victim: Adversarial Justice, Crime Victims, and the State*, eds. A. Bottoms and J. V. Roberts. Cullompton: Willan Publishing.

Rhine, Edward, William Smith, and Ronald Jackson. 1991. *Paroling Authorities: Recent History and Current Practice*. Laurel, MD: American Correctional Association,.

Roberts, Julian V. 2003. "Victim Impact Statements and the Sentencing Process: Enhancing communication in the courtroom". *Criminal Law Quarterly* 47(3): 365–396.

Roberts, Julian V. 2008. *Punishing Persistent Offenders: Exploring Community and Offender Perspectives*. Oxford: Oxford University Press.

Roberts, Julian V. 2009. "Listening to the Crime Victim: Evaluating Victim Input at Sentencing and Parole." In *Crime and Justice*, ed. M. Tonry. Chicago: University of Chicago Press.

Roberts, Julian V., and A. Edgar. 2005. *Judicial Attitudes to Victim Impact Statements: Findings from a Survey in Three Jurisdictions*. Ottawa: Policy Centre for Victim Issues, Department of Justice Canada.

Roberts, Julian V., and Edna Erez. 2004. "Communication in Sentencing: Exploring the Expressive and the Impact Model of Victim Impact Statements." *International Review of Victimology* 10: 223–244.

Roberts, Julian V., and Marie Manikis. 2010. "Victim Impact Statements at Sentencing: Exploring the Relevance of Ancillary Harm." *Canadian Criminal Law Review* 15: 1–26.

Roberts, Julian V., and Marie Manikis. 2011. *Victim Impact Statements at Sentencing: A Review of Empirical Research Findings*. London: Commissioner for Victims and Witnesses.

Schuster, Mary, and Amy Propen. 2007. *2006 WATCH Victim Impact Study*. Minneapolis: University of Minnesota, Department of Rhetoric.

Shapland, Joanna. 1984. "Victims, the Criminal Justice System and Compensation." *British Journal of Criminology* 24: 131–149.

Shapland, Joanna. 2009. "Victims and Criminal Justice in Europe." In *The International Handbook of Victimology*, eds. Paul Knepper and Shlomo Shoham. London: Francis and Taylor.

Smith, Brent, Erin Watkins, and Kathryn Morgan. 1997. "The Effect of Victim Participation on Parole Decisions: Results from a Southeastern State." *Criminal Justice Policy Review* 8: 7–74.

State of New Jersey Parole Board. 2008. *Victim Services*. Online. Available at: www.state.nj.us/parole/victim.html.

State of Rhode Island Parole Board and Sex Offender Community Notification Unit. Undated. Online: Available at: http://www.paroleboard.ri.gov/parole/.

State of Utah Board of Pardons and Parole. 2010. Information for Victims. *Information for Victims*. Available at: http://bop.utah.gov/victims.html.

Tapley, Jacki. 2005. "Political Rhetoric and the Reality of Victims' Experiences." *Prison Service Journal* 158: 45–52.

Tasmania Department of Justice. Undated. *Having Your Say*. Available at: http://www.justice.tas.gov.au/victims/victimsregister/parole/having_your_say.

Texas Department of Criminal Justice. 1997. *It's Your Turn: A Victims' and Survivors' Handbook to Victim Impact Information*. Dallas: Texas Department of Criminal Justice, Victim Services Division.

Virginia Department of Corrections. 2010. *Victim Input Program*. Online. Available at: http://www.vadoc.state.va.us/victim/input-program.shtm.

Virginia Parole Board Policy Manual. 2006. Available at: http://www.vadoc.state.va.us/vpb/manuals/pb-policymanual-1006.pdf.

von Hirsch, Andrew, and Andrew Ashworth. 2005. *Proportionate Sentencing*. Oxford: Oxford University Press.

Williams, Marian, and Jefferson Holcomb. 2004. "The Interactive Effects of Victim Race and Gender on Death Sentence Disparity Findings." *Homicide Studies* 8(4): 350–376.

Yun, Ihlung, Johnson, Mathew and Kercher, Glen. (2006) *Victim Impact Statements. What Victims have to Say*. Huntsville, TX: Crime Victims' Institute.

PART II

SENTENCING

Section A
Sentencing Theories and Their Application

....

CHAPTER 5

THEORIES OF PROPORTIONALITY AND DESERT

....

RICHARD S. FRASE

SENTENCING proportionality—"making the punishment fit the crime"—is a widely shared goal. Although this concept is most often associated with retributive theories, proportionality principles also play a role in several non-retributive accounts of the purposes of punishment.

There are several versions of retributive proportionality theory. The strictest "positive" versions seek to closely tie punishment severity to the offender's degree of blameworthiness or moral "desert." Several looser "negative" versions of retributive proportionality, known variously as "limiting" retributivism or "modified just deserts," do not seek to achieve such precise matching of punishment severity and desert; instead, these theories use retributive proportionality principles to set outer limits (especially: upper limits) on punishment severity.

There are also several non-retributive proportionality concepts. Utilitarian sentencing philosophers have long argued that punishment should be proportionate to the harm caused or threatened by different crimes; this ensures that the costs and burdens of each sentence will be not outweigh the benefits, and also achieves other practical effects. This concept will be referred to as "ends-benefits" proportionality. A second utilitarian proportionality principle—often seen as a question of "necessity" or "narrow-tailoring," rather than proportionality—prohibits severe punishment when the alternative of a lesser penalty would achieve substantially the same benefits. This will be referred to as "alternative-means" proportionality.

The remainder of this chapter is organized as follows. Section I examines retributive proportionality principles in general, the two varieties of retributive theory, and the ways in which non-retributive theories have incorporated elements of retributive proportionality. Section II discusses the two utilitarian proportionality principles, and the ways in which these principles have been applied. Section III examines hybrid theories incorporating both retributive and non-retributive proportionality principles, and identifies examples of such hybrids in modern sentencing systems.

Here are the main conclusions of this chapter:

- Proportionality is most often associated with retributive theories of punishment, although these theories differ in how strictly proportionality principles are applied;
- Retributive proportionality principles are also explicitly embodied in some non-retributive theories of punishment;
- The goal of uniformity or equality in sentencing often explicitly or implicitly employs retributive principles as criteria for determining which offenders are "similarly situated" and thus entitled to equality of treatment;
- In all of the theories just mentioned, retributive proportionality principles can be applied strictly (closely matching punishment severity to the offender's blameworthiness) or more loosely ("limiting retributivism" or "modified just deserts," in which desert only sets outer limits on punishment severity);
- Proportionality is also an important component of utilitarian punishment philosophy, but there are two very different utilitarian proportionality principles: ends-benefits proportionality (a version of cost-benefit analysis), and alternative-means proportionality (the requirement of necessity, or narrow tailoring);
- The limiting retributive and utilitarian proportionality principles can be combined into a single, hybrid theory in which the two utilitarian principles operate within a limiting retributive range. Some American sentencing guidelines systems are explicitly based on a version of this approach and looser, implicit versions are found in most other modern sentencing systems.

I. Retributive Proportionality

Punishment as state-imposed retribution—the idea that people are punished because their criminal acts render them morally blameworthy and deserving of punishment—can serve as a either a positive goal and sufficient rationale for punishment, or as a negative principle that limits the severity of penalties imposed to achieve other purposes. Retributive principles have also been explicitly or implicitly incorporated in other punishment theories that are not primarily retributive. But the leading theories agree on the essential nature of retributive values, and on the

THEORIES OF PROPORTIONALITY AND DESERT   133

principles that render some criminal acts more blameworthy than others. These common assumptions are examined in the first subsection below. The second subsection discusses positive and negative versions of retributive theory, and the third subsection looks at the ways in which positive or negative retributive values have been incorporated into non-retributive punishment theories.

Common Features of Retributive Punishment Theories

There is an extensive English-language literature on retributive punishment theories (see, e.g., Dressler 2009; Feinberg 1970; Moore 1997; Robinson and Darley 1995; von Hirsch 1976, 1993). For present purposes, the most important and widely accepted principles of these theories are the following:

- Retributive (or "just deserts") theory is concerned only with calibrating the offender's punishment according to his past criminal acts; unlike utilitarian or other "consequentialist" theories, it does not consider the crime control or other practical effects that punishment might have in the future.
- Retribution examines the offender's degree of blameworthiness for his or her past criminal acts, focusing primarily on the offense(s) now being sentenced. Some retributive scholars believe that the current offense is the only relevant consideration, and that any crimes for which the offender has already been sentenced are irrelevant; other scholars accept that prior convictions modestly increase an offender's blameworthiness (Roberts and von Hirsch 2010). Some sentencing guidelines reforms which purport to adopt a retributive model go even further, permitting substantial sentence enhancements based on prior convictions.
- The offender's blameworthiness for an offense is generally assessed according to two kinds of elements: the nature and seriousness of the harm caused or threatened by the crime, and the offender's degree of culpability in committing the crime (in particular, his or her degree of intent (mens rea), good or bad motives, role in the offense, and mental illness or other forms of diminished capacity).

Retribution as a Positive or Negative Punishment Criterion

There are two very different theories about the role that retributive values should play in sentencing. These two approaches have sometimes been referred to as positive or "defining" and negative or "limiting" retributivism (Morris 1982). According to the first theory, principles of just deserts should define the degree of punishment severity as precisely as possible; offenders should receive their just deserts, no more and no less, and offenders of differing blameworthiness should be punished in direct proportion to their relative desert. This theory, as elaborated by writers such as Andrew von Hirsch (1993), permits crime-control, budgetary, or other non-retributive values to affect both the overall scale of punishment severity (absolute amounts, as determined by the most and least severe penalties) and the choice among penalties deemed to be equal in severity, but it insists on fairly strict "ordinal" retributive proportionality in the relative severity of penalties imposed on different offenders.

The other approach, negative or "limiting" retributivism, places desert-based limits both on who may be punished (only those who are blameworthy), and how hard they may be punished. One theory, elaborated in the writings of Norval Morris, posits a range of "not-undeserved" penalties that would be widely viewed as neither unfairly severe or unduly lenient (Morris 1974; Morris and Tonry 1990; Morris's theory is examined at length in Frase 1997, 2004). Morris viewed retributive assessments as imprecise; he argued that, while there might be widespread agreement in any given case that certain penalties are clearly more severe or clearly more lenient than the offender deserves, there is little consensus among persons of varying philosophical and political views as to that offender's precise deserts, given the number and complexity of morally-relevant factors. Morris's not-undeserved range was stricter at the top than at the bottom; he opposed all mandatory minimum penalties, and suggested that lower, desert-based limits on punishment severity might only be required for serious offenses.

Other writers have supported limiting retributivism on different grounds, emphasizing the special importance of avoiding unfairly severe penalties. For example, the philosopher K. G. Armstrong (1969, 155) wrote that justice grants

> the *right* to punish offenders up to some limit, but one is not necessarily and invariably *obliged* to punish to the limit of justice. . . . For a variety of reasons (amongst them the hope of reforming the criminal) the appropriate authority may choose to punish a man less than [that authority] is entitled to, but it is never just to punish a man more than he deserves [emphasis in original].

Similarly, H. L. A. Hart (1968, 237) noted that "many self-styled retributivists treat appropriateness to the crime as setting a *maximum* within which penalties [are chosen on crime-control grounds]" (emphasis in original). Numerous other authors and model codes likewise advocate an "asymmetric" approach emphasizing strict desert limits on maximum severity, with looser or no desert-based requirements of minimum severity (Frase 2004). In practice, however, some minimum degree of punishment severity will usually still be required to achieve one or more *non-retributive* sentencing purposes, in particular, incapacitation of dangerous offenders and goals related to various expressive theories (moral-education, norm-reinforcement, denunciation) that seek to avoid a penalty so lenient that it would "depreciate the seriousness" of the offense (American Law Institute 1962, Sec. 7.01(1)(c)).

State guidelines systems based on the limiting retributive model (discussed more fully in Section III) appear to have adopted a blend of the Morris and asymmetric approaches. They provide a range of allowable penalties based on desert, but the upper desert limits are relatively strict and also quite specific, while the lower limits are more flexible. Moreover, the allowable ranges, especially in practice, often seem too wide to be justified by an imprecise-desert theory.

A more precise conception of the upper limits of desert has several practical advantages—it provides a more defensible basis for constructing specific numeric sentencing ranges than does Morris's imprecise-desert theory; it better serves important expressive sentencing goals (offenders and the public are told "this is how bad the offense was," rather than "we're not sure how bad this offense was, but we think its relative severity could be as high as X, or as low as Y"); and it provides more guidance and restraint when dealing with persistent, politically motivated pressures to escalate the severity of criminal penalties. The asymmetric theory's more flexible lower limits are also consistent with the reality of prosecutorial screening discretion and plea bargaining—minimum-sentence rules are likely to be enforced sporadically, at best.

Another advantage of the precise-asymmetric approach is that it is more consistent with constitutional sentence-proportionality standards (which always apply asymmetrically), and it is less likely to undercut those standards. When an imprecise-desert theory is used to define sub-constitutional proportionality standards, this invites courts to conclude that constitutional limits are weak or even nonexistent, since those limits are assumed to be less constraining due to the inherent limitations of constitutional judicial review.

As a matter of sentencing policy, whether one prefers Morris's "not-undeserved" range or some version of the asymmetric approach, there are compelling practical arguments in favor of limiting retributivism and against an approach that insists on strict matching of punishment severity to the offender's desert. The latter model seems unworkable, given three pervasive needs in all modern criminal justice systems: 1) the need to encourage and reward defendant cooperation; 2) the need for flexibility in responding to lack of cooperation and/or new evidence of offender risk; and 3) the need to economize and set priorities in the use of scarce correctional resources. Before and at trial, resource limits require that defendants be given leniency to induce and reward guilty pleas, jury trial waivers, and testimony against other defendants. At sentencing, the court must initially give defendants less than they deserve (or less than the maximum "not-undeserved" penalty) to reward the defendant's cooperation up to that point and induce further cooperation in making restitution, accepting treatment and supervision, obtaining and holding employment, and supporting dependents, while also leaving room for subsequent tightening of sanctions (up to and including probation revocation and incarceration) if the defendant appears to be unable or unwilling to cooperate, or if he presents risks that require tightening of sanctions. Finally, at all stages of the process resource limits require that additional charge and sanction severity, even if deserved, be withheld if it does have tangible, crime-control or other practical value; spending scarce resources to bring additional charges or impose additional punishments solely because they are deserved cannot be justified given other pressing needs for these resources within and outside of the criminal justice system.

Most strict (positive) desert theorists have ignored these important practical problems (Moore 1997; Robinson 2008). Other theorists have recognized the need for "backup sanctions" (Duff 2001; von Hirsch 1992; von Hirsch, Wasik, and Greene 1989), but have not explained how that need can be reconciled with a strict-desert model. Although some forms of cooperation might be seen as reducing the defendant's "deserts," at least under a very broad definition of that term, and some forms of non-cooperation arguably increase desert, many forms of cooperation and non-cooperation have little bearing on desert; society often needs to reward cooperation, or respond to evidence of heightened risk, whether or not these sentence adjustments are deserved. Thus, in practice, modern systems of law enforcement and punishment must either routinely ignore desert or function according to a limiting retributive model in which most offenders initially receive at least partial remission of their full just deserts, conditioned on their cooperation.

Despite the theoretical and practical arguments above, many sentencing theorists reject the limiting retributive model. For example, Andrew von Hirsch argues that Morris's imprecise-desert theory yields unfair results (equally culpable offenders receive different penalties); is too lax to prevent major escalations in punishment severity; and provides no standards for determining how the desert ranges are calculated (see Frase 1997, comparing the Morris and von Hirsch theories). Paul Robinson (2008) has criticized Morris's theory, and by implication also the precise-but-asymmetric version of limiting retributivism favored by writers such as Armstrong and H. L. A. Hart, on the additional ground that the public strongly supports penalties closely tied to relative desert, and that if penalties fail to respect these views the public will lose respect for, and be less likely to comply with, criminal prohibitions. Finally, some critics of limiting retributivism accept Morris's view of the imprecision of desert judgments, but go further and seem to reject any desert-based theory, viewing desert concepts as too elastic, opaque, and non-falsifiable by empirical data to provide meaningful limits on punishment (see, e.g., Ristroph 2006; Zimring and Hawkins 1995).

These critiques are strongest when applied to the earliest versions of Morris's imprecise-desert theory, in which the "not-undeserved" range was potentially quite broad; the critiques lose much of their force under the more restrictive version that Morris endorsed in his later writings, and especially under the precise-asymmetric approach adopted under sentencing guidelines (see further discussion in Section III). Under such guidelines, sentencing ranges are substantially narrowed, thus reducing unfairness and the potential for excessive severity. Furthermore, the precise ranges are determined by the Sentencing Commission in a deliberative process that assesses the relative seriousness of different crimes, and the fiscal impact of any selective or overall increases in sentencing severity (Frase 2005c, 2005d). Commissions have generally made such relative-desert judgments themselves, but it would certainly be possible for the commission to collect and take into account data on public attitudes (Frase 1997).

Of course, such guidelines still permit equally culpable offenders to receive sanctions of differing severity, at least conditionally (for example: a less risky offender may have his or her deserved prison sentence suspended, subject to satisfactory compliance with probation conditions). But any such unfairness and lack of proportionality has not prevented guidelines in Minnesota and other states from earning and maintaining public support. This is probably because the public cares not only about matching punishment to desert, but also about achieving effective crime control in a cost-effective manner (see further discussion, in Sections II and III below, of efficiency-promoting utilitarian proportionality principles that can be embodied in a guidelines system based on a limiting retributive model, but not in a system based strictly on desert). Citizens and their elected leaders may also recognize that guidelines increase retributive proportionality relative to more discretionary pre-guidelines sentencing procedures.

It is certainly true that sentencing commissions can and sometimes do decide to escalate certain penalties, and that supposed maximum-desert limits and even warnings of substantial fiscal impact cannot totally prevent such escalation. But the same or greater risk arises in the application of non-retributive (crime-control) sentencing goals. Moreover, the uncontrolled sentencing and correctional discretion required to pursue such goals precludes the kinds of severity-restraining, fiscal-impact assessments that have become feasible with the greater predictability of desert-based guidelines. The available evidence confirms that states with Minnesota-style guidelines have had slower rates of growth in their prison populations (Stemen, Rengifo, and Wilson 2005).

Non-Retributive Theories Incorporating Elements of Retributive Proportionality

Several punishment theories that emphasize non-retributive goals also incorporate, expressly or implicitly, the general principles of retributive theory summarized previously. For example, Antony Duff's "communicative" theory (2001) views punishment as designed to convey society's censure of criminals, and to foster a two-way dialogue encouraging offender remorse, apology, and penance. Similarly, Herbert Morris's "paternalistic" theory (1981) views punishment as furthering several intrinsic "goods"—that offenders appreciate the wrongfulness of their acts, feel guilt, repent, desire to make amends, commit themselves to avoid doing wrong in the future, and emerge with a reinforced sense of being a moral person. Both of these theories expressly incorporate retributive principles, viewing the offender's blameworthiness as determining the degree of censure and repentance appropriate in a given case.

Unlike the two theories described above, the sentencing goal of uniformity—equal treatment of "similarly situated" offenders and the avoidance of "disparity"—does not necessarily incorporate retributive principles; uniformity, per se, does not presuppose any particular criteria for determining which offenders are "similar" and which are not. Nevertheless, in recent years appeals to uniformity have often implicitly assumed retributive values as the underlying normative framework—equally blameworthy offenders should receive equal punishment (or at least, roughly equal punishment). Sentencing uniformity can also have utilitarian value (discussed in Section II below), but the non-utilitarian version of this goal is, like retributive theory itself, based at least in part on notions of the intrinsic value of fairness—if two equally blameworthy offenders receive (very) different punishment severity, the offender with the more severe penalty has been treated unfairly; there may also be unfairness to the victim(s) of the offender punished less severely. Unlike retributive theory, however, the uniformity goal does not provide any guidance when deciding how to punish two offenders of differing blameworthiness.

II. Utilitarian Proportionality Principles

Non-retributive (utilitarian or consequentialist) purposes of punishment focus on the future—what effect will the proposed sentence have on the offender, on other would-be offenders, and/or on society, and at what cost? (see generally Dressler 2009; Frase 2005b). The traditional non-retributive purposes focus on the prevention of future crimes, and achieve this in several ways: through special (or individual, or specific) deterrence, incapacitation, and/or rehabilitation of offenders who are thought likely to commit further crimes; by general deterrence of other would-be violators who fear receiving similar punishment; and by general prevention resulting from the moral-education or norm-reinforcing effects that penalties have on views about the relative harmfulness and wrongness of different crimes (Greenawalt 2001; Robinson and Darley 1997).

In light of these non-retributive punishment goals, a penalty can be disproportionate in two distinct and independent ways:

1. A penalty may be disproportionately severe because its costs and burdens outweigh the likely benefits produced by the penalty (or because the added costs and burdens, compared to a lesser penalty, outweigh the added benefits). Alternatively, a penalty may be disproportionately lenient because it is less effective than a more severe (but still cost-effective) penalty would be. This concept will be referred to as "ends-benefits" (or "ends") proportionality.

2. A penalty may be disproportionately severe because such severity is unnecessary when compared to other, less costly or burdensome means of achieving the same goals. This concept will be referred to as "alternative-means" (or "means") proportionality.

Each of these utilitarian proportionality principles has ancient roots, as discussed more fully below. The ends-benefits proportionality principle is, of course, quite similar to "cost-benefit" and similar principles that are found throughout American law; similarly, there are many examples of principles akin to alternative-means proportionality, requiring government measures to be necessary, narrowly tailored, or the "least restrictive means" (Sullivan and Frase 2009).

Ends-Benefits Proportionality

The mid-eighteenth century philosopher Cesare Beccaria (1764) argued in favor of criminal penalties proportional to the seriousness of the offense, as measured by the harm done to society. Similarly, in his Commentaries on the Law of England, William Blackstone (1769) cited Beccaria's work and stated that English common law had already adopted the general principle that "the greater and more exalted the object of injury is, the more care should be taken to prevent that injury, and [therefore] the punishment should be more severe."

In the early nineteenth century, Jeremy Bentham (1802) further developed these utilitarian arguments, and proposed several specific reasons that punishments should be proportional to the seriousness of the offense. From the point of view of public resource allocation, "the greater an offence is, the greater reason there is to hazard a severe punishment for the chance of preventing it." Similarly, from the point of view of the suffering imposed on the offender, Bentham argued that "the evil of the punishment [should not exceed] the evil of the offence." But Bentham also argued that penalties can be too lenient: "[A]n insufficient punishment is an evil thrown away. No good comes from it, either to the public who are left exposed to like offenses, or to the offender, whom it makes no better." Bentham further pointed out the marginal deterrent value of penalties proportionate to offense severity: offenders should "have a motive to stop at the lesser" crime. Beccaria (1764) may have had the same idea in mind when he wrote that "If an equal punishment be ordained for two crimes that do not equally injure society, men will not be any more deterred from committing the greater crime, if they find a greater advantage associated with it." Similarly, Blackstone (1769) implicitly made this argument by noting that in England and China highway robbers rarely murdered their victims because of the more severe penalty if they did, whereas in France robbers often murdered since the penalty was no greater.

In addition to the problem of lost marginal deterrence noted above, here are some sample cases illustrating other ways in which a sentence can violate ends-benefits proportionality: (1) a lengthy prison term given to a minor property offender, especially one whose criminal career is declining or soon will; (2) a prison term whose deterrent or short-term incapacitation effects are outweighed by its costs and collateral consequences, in particular, the likelihood that the prison experience will make the offender worse (less employable, more likely to escalate to more serious and/or more frequent crimes); (3) imprisonment of a drug seller who will be immediately replaced on the street, thus canceling any incapacitation effect and suggesting very weak general deterrent effects.

The utilitarian ends-benefits proportionality principle has some elements in common with retributive proportionality—in particular, both principles require proportionality relative to offense severity. But the two theories operate quite differently, in at least three ways:

1. Retributive theory considers the harm caused or threatened by the defendant's crimes, and considers punishment in proportion to that harm to be intrinsically good; utilitarian theory also argues for punishment in proportion to the harm of defendant's crimes, but only when this will prevent future similar crimes by this offender (through special deterrence, incapacitation, and/or rehabilitation) or will prevent such crimes by others (through general deterrence and norm-reinforcement). Moreover, utilitarian theory considers not only the harm associated with a particular act similar to the defendant's, but also the aggregate harm caused by all such actions, and the difficulty of detecting and deterring such actions (Wheeler 1972).
2. Retributive theory punishes in direct proportion not just to the actual or threatened harms associated with the offender's crime(s) but also to his culpability (intent, motive, role in the offense, diminished capacity, etc.). For utilitarians, such culpability factors are only relevant to the extent that they are related to the likely future benefits of punishment (e.g., the dangerousness and deterrability of this offender or others).
3. Utilitarian theory considers not only the actual crime-control or other benefits produced by sanctions, but also, as an offset against those benefits, any undesirable collateral consequences of the sanction (Radin 1978). One example previously cited is loss of marginal deterrence, or even *reverse* deterrence: a severe penalty (e.g., in a "three strikes" habitual offender law) might encourage felons to kill victims, other potential witnesses, or arresting officers. Other possible undesirable consequences of penalties that are grossly or frequently disproportionate to the conviction offense include undermining the public's sense of the relative gravity of different crimes, and public loss of respect for, and willingness to obey and cooperate with, criminal justice authorities. As the philosopher H. L. A. Hart (1968) said,

> [If] the relative severity of penalties diverges sharply from this rough scale [of proportionality], there is a risk of either confusing common morality or flouting it and bringing the law into contempt.

Robinson and Darley (1997) cite this reason and other utilitarian arguments against penalties disproportionate to crime seriousness. Unlike Hart, however, these authors explicitly invoke retributive principles to measure crime seriousness.

Alternative-Means Proportionality

This principle recognizes basic utilitarian efficiency values: among equally effective means to achieve a given end, those that are less costly or burdensome should be preferred. Cesare Beccaria (1764) argued that punishment must not only be proportionate to the crime but also "necessary, the least possible in the circumstances." William Blackstone (1769) stated that "punishment ought always to be proportioned to the particular purpose it is meant to serve, and by no means exceed it." Jeremy Bentham (1802) held that "punishment itself is an evil and should be used as sparingly as possible"; a measure should not be used if "the same end may be obtained by means more mild."

Numerous modern authors have endorsed the alternative-means proportionality principle. Norval Morris (1974) called it the principle of parsimony, and gave it a key role in his theory (discussed below). Support for the principle has also been expressed by Radin (1978); Singer (1972); Tonry (1998); and Zimring, Hawkins, and Kamin (2001). In addition, the original Model Penal Code and all three editions of the American Bar Association sentencing standards explicitly or implicitly recognized the principle of parsimony (Frase 2004), and the principle has been recently endorsed in the revised Model Penal Code sentencing provisions (American Law Institute 2007). Limitations on unnecessarily excessive punishments are also found in numerous state statutes and court opinions (Sullivan and Frase 2009).

Here are two examples of sentences that violate alternative-means proportionality: (1) a lengthy prison term given to an addict who commits crimes solely to support his drug use, and whose addiction could have been safely and less expensively controlled by drug treatment in a community-based sentence (or during a shorter custodial term); (2) an unnecessarily severe mandatory-minimum sentence (unnecessary severity is *inevitable*, under mandatory-minimum laws—in at least some (and perhaps many) of the cases subject to the law, the court is forced to impose a more severe punishment than would be required to achieve all utilitarian sentencing purposes).

Differences Between Public Policy and Constitutional Proportionality Analysis

The utilitarian proportionality principles described above have application in the setting of constitutional punishment standards as well as in subconstitutional policy making, but the principles apply differently in each of these legal contexts. Constitutional proportionality limits operate in an entirely asymmetric fashion, setting upper but no lower limits on sanction severity; in the public policy context, retributive and ends-benefits proportionality principles sometimes require a minimum or increased sentence.

Another important distinction, in the application of utilitarian proportionality principles, has to do with which kinds of costs and burdens of a government measure are weighed against the expected benefits, or against alternative means. For public officials and policy makers, the public costs of a measure are very important elements in proportionality analysis—measures should not cost (including privately borne as well as public costs) more than the benefits they are expected to produce, or more than effective alternative measures. But when defining a defendant's constitutional right not to be subjected to an excessive sentence, the crime control and other benefits of the sentence should probably be weighed only against the burdens that the sentence imposes on the defendant (ends proportionality), and alternative measures should be examined only in terms of their relative burdens on the defendant (means proportionality). The constitutional argument is that it is fundamentally unfair to impose severe burdens that greatly outweigh the expected public benefits, or to impose such burdens when effective alternative measures are much less burdensome. It may be unwise, but is probably not unconstitutional, to impose a sentence that costs taxpayers more than its benefits are worth, or more than an effective alternative.

A further difference between public policy and constitutional proportionality analysis relates to the inherent limits of constitutional limit-setting. Public policy strives for as close a fit as possible between costs and benefits, and as efficient a choice as possible among alternative means. But when courts seek to enforce constitutional proportionality limits on sentencing, they should only intervene if the burdens on the defendant are clearly excessive relative to the benefits, or if equally effective alternative sanctions or other measures are clearly less burdensome. These inherent limits on judicial review decisions are reflected in the Supreme Court's requirements of "gross disproportionality," under the Eighth Amendment. But in reviewing lengthy prison terms the Court has, unfortunately, carried this principle of deference too far; its decisions amount to a near-total abdication of judicial responsibility to protect defendants from abuse of governmental power (Frase 2005a).

III. Hybrid Approaches Incorporating Retributive and Non-retributive Proportionality Principles

Numerous writers have argued that punishment systems may pursue both retributive and utilitarian purposes (see, e.g., Hart 1968; Packer 1968), but have not specifically recognized that both types of purposes can embody proportionality principles. Similarly, most modern sentencing systems are hybrids, seeking to achieve both types of purposes without articulating the role of proportionality. But some writers and systems have expressly endorsed both retributive and utilitarian proportionality principles.

Hybrid Proportionality Theories

One of the earliest elaborations of an approach explicitly combining retributive and utilitarian proportionality was by Norval Morris (1974). As noted previously, and as discussed more fully in this author's previous writings (Frase 1997, 2004), Morris viewed desert assessments as imprecise, and thus gave retributive values only a negative or limiting role. For similar reasons, he also viewed considerations of uniformity—the goal of treating "like cases alike"—as only a "guiding" principle, requiring at most rough equality in the treatment of equally culpable offenders. Within the range of "not-undeserved" and not-too-unequal penalties, Morris would permit courts to pursue most of the traditionally recognized crime-control and other utilitarian purposes of punishment, subject to a general principle of alternative-means proportionality, which Morris called "parsimony"—within the desert range, penalties should be no more severe than necessary to achieve all utilitarian sentencing goals applicable to the case. Morris also implicitly recognized the application of the ends-benefits proportionality principle, within his not-undeserved range, when he condemned several examples of sentences violating that principle—expensive, over-incarceration of minor offenders, and custody sentencing that severs the offender's crime-preventive social ties (Morris 1974).

The flexibility inherent in Morris's "range" model was further enhanced by his proposal for a system of intermediate punishments that can be substituted for custody (Morris and Tonry 1990). Each type of punishment would receive a given exchange-rate or punishment equivalency value per unit (for example: two days of home detention, or one day in jail, equals one punishment severity unit); judges could then maintain rough retributive proportionality and uniformity, while giving each offender a sanction or package of sanctions tailored to the particular crime control and individual needs of that offender.

The idea of interchangeable sanction types has also been endorsed by proponents of a stricter (non-range) desert-based model (von Hirsch, Wasik, and Greene 1989; Robinson 2008). This approach thus provides another kind of hybrid blend of desert and non-desert principles, but it gives much less emphasis to utilitarian proportionality. Von Hirsch (1993) did recognize alternative-means proportionality (Morris's parsimony principle), but gave it the very limited role of determining the maximum and minimum authorized sanctions (what von Hirsch calls the "anchoring points" of the penalty scale), which in turn determine the absolute magnitude of punishment severity. Other hybrid theories seem to exclude any consideration of utilitarian proportionality; retributive proportionality is the primary goal, but exceptions are made to achieve selected utilitarian or other goals—for example, avoiding or reducing deserved incarceration to permit restorative justice measures such as community service or restitution, or imposing an above-desert custodial penalty to prevent serious harms (Robinson 1987).

Real-World Examples of Hybrid Proportionality Models

It does not appear that any modern jurisdiction has ever implemented a punishment system based entirely on retributive proportionality, but such considerations have never been entirely ignored either. Instead, virtually all modern systems have adopted some version of limiting retributivism, and a few systems have expressly recognized alternative-means proportionality (parsimony) as a criterion operating within the range of deserved punishment. Ends-benefit proportionality principles have not been expressly recognized (they should be), but it seems likely that in practice judges often make such commonsense, cost-benefit assessments when choosing a sentence within the authorized range.

There is a wide variety of more-or-less limiting retributive systems, which can be ranged along a continuum, from those giving desert a very minor role, to those in which desert is seen as the "primary" sentencing goal, and the desert range is (at least formally) quite narrow. At one end of the continuum we find traditional indeterminate sentencing systems—still the most common approach, among American states (Reitz 2001). In these systems the statutory maximum sentence, and occasional mandatory minimum requirements, set upper and lower limits on sanction severity based solely on the offense of conviction (and, in the case of repeat-offender laws, prior convictions). Within these wide ranges, judges and parole boards may tailor the sentence to reflect crime-control purposes. However, these systems lack an explicit desert rationale for the statutory maxima and minima, or for the choice of sentence within the statutory range. They also lack any procedural commitment to sentencing proportionality and uniformity (e.g., via required reasons or appellate review), and they do not recognize the principle of parsimony. The design of traditional systems was originally attributable to the emphasis in almost all jurisdictions on rehabilitation goals, which were seen as requiring a high degree of judicial and parole discretion. The survival of so many indeterminate sentencing regimes, despite the widespread loss of faith in the "rehabilitative ideal" (Allen 1981), is probably due both to institutional inertia and vested interests, and to the continued popularity of sentencing based on offender risk assessments. But at least part of the durability of these regimes, despite decades of sustained criticism, may be due to the widespread support for a hybrid approach—one that grants substantial scope for case-level application of crime-control purposes, but which also recognizes that the maximum (and sometimes the minimum) allowable sanction severity must be limited by the seriousness of the conviction offense (and thus, by the implicit retributive proportionality considerations that underlie offense-severity rankings).

Outside the United States, virtually all sentencing regimes are essentially based on the indeterminate limiting-retributive model; many of these systems expressly recognize retributive proportionality, and some of them also recognize alternative-means proportionality (Frase 2001). In some systems, retributive values define a range of allowable severity and available forms of punishment (e.g., custody, community service, or fines); in choosing the particular form and amount of punishment, courts consider offender characteristics, crime-control goals, and other non-retributive factors. Many foreign systems place a high priority on avoiding disproportionately severe sentences, while granting courts greater flexibility in mitigating penalties and choosing among sanction types of roughly equal severity; some countries take an entirely asymmetric approach, with upper but no lower desert-based limits on sanction severity. A limiting retributive model is also implicit in the frequent use in many countries of conditional prison sentences—the defendant is spared the full measure of his deserved penalty (as measured by the duration of his suspended prison term), provided that he complies with the court's conditions.

American sentencing guidelines systems lie at the other end of the continuum of more-or-less limiting retributive systems. In Minnesota and Washington state, desert was adopted as the primary sentencing goal, and many of the desert ranges were (at least formally, and in the initial set of guidelines) quite narrow. The Minnesota and federal guidelines expressly recognize principles akin to alternative-means proportionality (parsimony). Other American guidelines systems lack a primary sentencing purpose, and in many of these systems, sentencing severity is only loosely constrained, in one or more of the following respects—the guidelines are voluntary (not subject to sentence appeals or other enforcement measures); they prescribe very wide sentencing ranges; and/or they retain broad parole release discretion (Frase 2005d). Nevertheless, sentencing ranges in these systems are usually much narrower than the previous statutory ranges. And because the ranges reflect the severity of the offender's conviction offense and prior conviction record, they are consistent with retributive proportionality (although the impact of prior record on recommended sentence severity seems much greater than could be justified solely on retributive grounds; Frase 2010).

In all guidelines systems, plea bargaining concessions are largely or completely unregulated, which allows considerable scope for sentence mitigation on practical and other non-desert grounds. Many of these systems also allow and make frequent use of suspended prison sentences, the duration of which is scaled to offense severity. The suspension may be revoked for non-desert-based reasons, but usually is not; hence, these offenders do not receive their full deserts. The design and operation of American guidelines systems is thus more consistent with the "precise-asymmetric" version of limiting retributivism—maximum desert is defined quite specifically, but the lower limits of deserved punishment severity are loose or nonexistent.

The Minnesota Sentencing Guidelines, in effect since 1980, provide a particularly strong example of a successful guidelines system based on a limiting retributive model (Frase 1997, 2004, 2005b). Minnesota's desert-based limits are precise but asymmetric, especially in practice—the upper limits are relatively strict, but lower limits are often not present and, when present, are much more flexible. The resulting effective sentencing ranges, particularly for offenders with recommended suspended-prison sentences (about 70 percent of all cases), are more consistent with a precise-asymmetric model than with Morris's imprecise desert theory.

The Guidelines expressly endorse an alternative-means proportionality limit akin to Morris's parsimony principle, and sentencing practices suggest that judges and other practitioners are applying the principle—75 to 80 percent of offenders receive a sentence of probation; judges generally sentence in the lower half of the recommended sentencing range; downward departures from the Guidelines far outnumber upward departures; and many additional downward departures are achieved, de facto, by charging discretion. Overall, Minnesota sentencing is more parsimonious than almost any other American jurisdiction; since 1983 the state's per capita incarceration rate has consistently been the lowest or second-lowest of any state, notwithstanding the emergence of "law-and-order" politics and other pressures to escalate sentencing severity (Frase 2005c).

Minnesota has implicitly recognized the ends-benefits proportionality principle in a line of cases authorizing departure from a recommended executed prison term for a defendant who would be victimized or made worse in prison. And the state's remarkably low incarceration rate may be due in part to judges frequently applying this commonsense principle within the broad effective sentencing ranges provided to them.

Minnesota's sentencing guidelines were not explicitly based on a "limiting retributive" model; instead, reformers in Minnesota called their approach "modified just deserts." Nevertheless, Minnesota's approach in practice, and especially over time, has come to closely resemble the precise-asymmetric limiting retributive model. The 30-year survival of Minnesota's guidelines, and the success of similar guidelines in other states, has led to the adoption of limiting retributivism as the theoretical model and guidelines as the structural framework for the revised Model Penal Code sentencing provisions (American Law Institute 2007).

CONCLUSION

All modern punishment systems respect retributive proportionality principles at least to some degree, and some also recognize one or more utilitarian proportionality principles, especially alternative-means proportionality (parsimony, necessity, narrow tailoring). Some theorists argue that punishment severity should be precisely proportional to the offender's desert, but such a strict version of retributivism is impractical, and no modern system has adopted it. Instead, virtually all modern systems follow some version of limiting retributivism: desert sets upper and occasionally lower proportionality limits on punishment severity; within these limits, crime control and other utilitarian purposes are pursued to the extent that the benefits of the sentence outweigh the costs and negative collateral consequence (ends-benefits proportionality), and cannot be achieved by less severe sanctions (alternative-means proportionality, or parsimony). Sentencing guideline systems such as those in Minnesota and several other states provide working examples of sentencing based on a precise-asymmetric limiting retributive model: upper limits on sanction severity, based on retributive proportionality, are relatively strict and precise; lower limits are looser or absent; within the broad effective sentencing ranges provided, crime-control goals are pursued subject to requirements of alternative-means proportionality (parsimony) and ends-benefits proportionality (in particular: avoiding a prison term that would make the offender more crime-prone). The application of all three of these proportionality constraints has allowed Minnesota to retain one of the lowest per-capita incarceration rates in the nation.

REFERENCES

Allen, Francis A. 1981. *The Decline of the Rehabilitative Ideal: Penal Policy and Social Purpose*. New Haven, CT: Yale University Press.

American Law Institute. 1962. *Model Penal Code, Proposed Official Draft*. Philadelphia: American Law Institute.

American Law Institute. 2007. *Model Penal Code: Sentencing, Tentative Draft No. 1* (approved May 16, 2007). Philadelphia: American Law Institute.

Armstrong, K. G. 1969. "The Retributivist Hits Back." In *The Philosophy of Punishment*, ed. Harry B. Acton. London: St. Martin's Press.

Beccaria, Cesare. 1764. *On Crimes and Punishments*, trans. Henry Paolucci. Indianapolis: Bobbs-Merill [1963].

Bentham, Jeremy. 1802. *The Theory of Legislation*, ed. C. K. Ogden. New York: Harcourt, Brace, & Co. [1931].

Blackstone, Sir William. 1769. *Commentaries on the Laws of England*. Chicago: University of Chicago Press [1979].

Duff, Antony. 2001. *Punishment, Communication, and Community*. New York: Oxford University Press.

Dressler, Joshua. 2009. *Understanding Criminal Law*. 5th ed. Newark, NJ: LexisNexis Matthew Bender.

Feinberg, Joel. 1970. *Doing and Deserving: Essays in the Theory of Responsibility*. Princeton, NJ: Princeton University Press.

Fletcher, George P. 1978. *Rethinking Criminal Law*. Boston: Little, Brown & Co.

Frase, Richard S. 1997. "Sentencing Principles in Theory and Practice." *Crime and Justice: A Review of Research*, ed. Michael Tonry, 22: 363–433.

Frase, Richard S. 2001. "International Perspectives on Sentencing Policy and Research." In *Sentencing and Sanctions in Western Countries*, eds. Michael Tonry and Richard S. Frase. New York: Oxford University Press.

Frase, Richard S. 2004. "Limiting Retributivism." In *The Future of Imprisonment*, ed. Michael Tonry. New York: Oxford University Press.

Frase, Richard S. 2005a. "Excessive Prison Sentences, Punishment Goals, and the Eighth Amendment: 'Proportionality' Relative to What?" *Minnesota Law Review* 89: 571–651.

Frase, Richard S. 2005b. "Punishment Purposes." In *Symposium, A More Perfect System: Twenty-five Years of Guideline Sentencing Reform, Stanford Law Review* 58: 67–83.

Frase, Richard S. 2005c. "Sentencing Guidelines in Minnesota, 1978–2003." *Crime and Justice: A Review of Research*, ed. Michael Tonry, 32: 131–219.

Frase, Richard S. 2005d. "State Sentencing Guidelines: Diversity, Consensus, and Unre-
    solved Policy Issues." In *Symposium, Sentencing: What's at Stake for the States?
    Columbia Law Review* 105: 1190.

Frase, Richard S. 2010. "Prior-Conviction Sentencing Enhancements: Rationales and
    Limits Based on Retributive and Utilitarian Proportionality Principles, and on Social
    Equality Goals." In *Previous Convictions at Sentencing: Theoretical and Applied
    Perspectives*, eds. Julian V. Roberts and Andrew von Hirsch. Oxford: Hart Publishing.

Greenawalt, Kent. 2001. "Punishment." In 3 *Encyclopedia of Crime and Justice*, 2nd ed., ed.
    Joshua Dressler. New York: Macmillan Reference USA.

Hart, H. L. A. 1968. *Punishment and Responsibility: Essays in the Philosophy of Law*. Oxford:
    Oxford University Press.

Moore, Michael S. 1997. *Placing Blame: A Theory of Criminal Law*. Oxford: Clarendon
    Press.

Morris, Herbert. 1981. "A Paternalistic Theory of Punishment." *American Philosophical
    Quarterly* 18: 263–271.

Morris, Norval. 1974. *The Future of Imprisonment*. Chicago: University of Chicago Press.

Morris, Norval. 1982. *Madness and the Criminal Law*. Chicago: University of Chicago Press.

Morris, Norval, and Michael Tonry. 1990. *Between Prison and Probation: Intermediate
    Punishments in a Rational Sentencing System*. New York: Oxford University Press.

Packer, Herbert L. 1968. *The Limits of the Criminal Sanction*. Stanford, CA: Stanford
    University Press.

Radin, Margaret J. 1978. "The Jurisprudence of Death: Evolving Standards for the Cruel and
    Unusual Punishments Clause." *University of Pennsylvania Law Review* 126: 989–1064.

Reitz, Kevin R. 2001."The Disassembly and Reassembly of U.S. Sentencing Practices." In
    Sentencing and Sanctions in Western Countries, eds. Michael Tonry and Richard S.
    Frase. New York: Oxford University Press.

Ristroph, Alice. 2006. "Desert, Democracy, and Sentencing Reform." *Journal of Criminal
    Law and Criminology* 96: 1293–1352.

Roberts, Julian V., and Andrew von Hirsch, eds. 2010. *Previous Convictions at Sentencing:
    Theoretical and Applied Perspectives*. Oxford: Hart Publishing.

Robinson, Paul H. 1987. "Hybrid Principles for the Distribution of Criminal Sanctions,"
    Northwestern University Law Review 82: 19–42.

Robinson, Paul H. 2008. *Distributive Principles of Criminal Law*. New York: Oxford
    University Press.

Robinson, Paul H., and John M. Darley. 1995. *Justice, Liability and Blame: Community
    Views and the Criminal Law*. Boulder, CO: Westview Press.

Robinson, Paul H., and John M. Darley. 1997. "The Utility of Desert." *Northwestern
    University Law Review* 91: 453–499.

Singer, Richard G. 1972. "Sending Men To Prison: Constitutional Aspects of the Burden of
    Proof and the Doctrine of the Least Drastic Alternative as Applied to Sentencing
    Determinations." *Cornell Law Review* 58: 51–89.

Stemen, Don, Andres F. Rengifo, and James A. Wilson. 2005. *Of Fragmentation and
    Ferment: The Impact of State Sentencing Policies on Incarceration Rates, 1975–2002*.
    Available at: http://www.vera.org/download?file=415/Of%2BFragmentation%2Band%2
    BFerment.pdf.

Sullivan, E. Thomas, and Richard S. Frase. 2009. *Proportionality Principles in American
    Law: Controlling Excessive Government Actions*. New York: Oxford University Press.

Tonry, Michael. 1998. "Parsimony and Desert in Sentencing." In *Principled Sentencing: Readings on Theory and Policy*, 2nd ed., eds. Andrew von Hirsch and Andrew Ashworth.Oxford: Hart Publishing.

Tonry, Michael, and Richard S. Frase, eds. 2001. *Sentencing and Sanctions in Western Countries*. New York: Oxford University Press.

von Hirsch, Andrew. 1976. *Doing Justice: The Choice of Punishments*. New York: Hill & Wang.

von Hirsch, Andrew. 1992. "Proportionality in the Philosophy of Punishment." *Crime and Justice: A Review of Research*, ed. Michael Tonry, 16: 55–98.

von Hirsch, Andrew. 1993. *Censure and Sanctions*. Oxford: Clarendon Press.

von Hirsch, Andrew, Martin Wasik, and Judith Greene. 1989. "Punishments in the Community and the Principles of Desert." *Rutgers Law Journal* 20: 595–618.

Wheeler, Malcolm E. 1972. "Toward a Theory of Limited Punishment: An Examination of the Eighth Amendment." *Stanford Law Review* 24: 838–873.

Zimring, Franklin E., and Gordon Hawkins. 1995. *Incapacitation: Penal Confinement and the Restraint of Crime*. New York: Oxford University Press.

Zimring, Franklin E., Gordon Hawkins, and Sam Kamin. 2001. *Punishment and Democracy: Three Strikes and You're Out in California*. New York: Oxford University Press.

CHAPTER 6

......

PROBLEM-SOLVING COURTS: AN INTERNATIONAL COMPARISON

......

JAMES L. NOLAN, JR.

PROBLEM-SOLVING courts represent a fundamentally new form of adjudicating mostly low-level criminal offenders. Though the movement began in the United States in the late 1980s, problem-solving courts are no longer an exclusively American phenomenon. A number of other countries around the world—including England, Australia, South Africa, Norway, and Canada—have introduced problem-solving courts based on the U.S. model. The international movement is instructive in several respects. First, it provides an interesting example of the processes of globalization. In this instance, as in other examples of America's global influence, American ideals and practices are openly denounced even while, paradoxically, they are at the same time eagerly embraced—demonstrating a sort of ambivalence that is characteristic of international attitudes toward the United States more generally.[1] Second, a comparison of the development of problem-solving courts in the United States and in other countries—at least in the early years of the movement—reveals a clear difference between the U.S. version of problem-solving courts and their counterparts in the countries where the movement is most advanced.

These differences, and the interpretation of them by the legal actors in the receiving countries, offer cautionary lessons both to Americans and to international importers of problem-solving courts, as they concern the processes of legal borrowing and changing understandings of the meaning of justice. The differences are of interest to legal comparativists in that they provide a compelling example of the inextricable link between law and culture. That is, the particular styles and forms of problem-solving courts, as compared internationally, tell an interesting story about cultural differences. The story of the international borrowing of problem-solving courts—which is still very much in the process of unfolding—also reveals at least some evidence that these differences may be waning, a development that portends a significant transformation in international understandings of the meaning and practice of justice. The analysis of this important international movement, covered in this chapter, addresses the following summary points:

- Since 1989 problem-solving courts have spread dramatically in the United States.
- Over the past decade, problem-solving courts have been exported from the United States to a number of countries around the world.
- At least in the early years of the international movement, the differences between courts in the United States and in the receiving countries were pronounced.
- Initially, the U.S. dimension of the movement was characterized by enthusiasm, boldness, and pragmatism; the non-U.S. problem-solving courts were characterized by moderation, deliberation, and restraint.
- There is some evidence that these differences have begun to dissipate, a development that portends important changes in international understandings of the meaning and practice of justice.

The Development of Problem-Solving Courts in the United States

The problem-solving court movement started in the United States with the establishment of the Dade County drug court in Miami, Florida, in 1989. The crack epidemic of the 1980s—and the ensuing conditions of overcrowded jails, overloaded court dockets, and judicial frustration with the revolving door of repeat offenders—led judicial officers to introduce a new kind of criminal court. In the Miami drug court, first presided over by Judge Stanley Goldstein, offenders are offered court-monitored treatment as an alternative to the normal adjudication process. In drug court, clients (as they are often called in this setting) participate in a variety of treatment modalities, including Alcoholics Anonymous (AA), Narcotics Anonymous (NA), group therapy, acupuncture treatment, regular urinalysis testing, and individual counseling. Drug court clients may also be encouraged to take classes toward a general equivalency degree (GED), perform community service, and/or secure some form of employment. If clients do not comply with court-mandated treatment requirements, judges have the power to impose short stints in jail, what one judge has referred to as "motivational jail."[2] The drug court program is typically advertised to last one year; often it lasts much longer.

Drug courts can be either pre-adjudicative or post-adjudicative in format. In the former, defendants are not required to enter a plea and are offered, as an incentive for participation, the expungement of their arrest or the dismissal of their charge should they successfully complete the program. The pre-adjudicative model has presented some legal quandaries, especially for defense lawyers, in that clients may have to spend time in jail, even though they have not pled to (or been found guilty of) a charge. In the post-adjudicative model, clients may actually be mandated into the program, sometimes as a condition of a probation order. In this scenario, the problem of incarceration (absent the admission of guilt) is avoided. However, this format contradicts the common public assertion that these courts are voluntary. Inasmuch as the program is a mandatory condition of probation, it is, of course, anything but voluntary. Even in pre-adjudicative courts, it is not clear that participation is always entirely voluntary. Some judges (and lawyers) are not shy about persuading clients to participate in the programs and even openly endorse coerced treatment on the grounds that it is just as effective as voluntary treatment.[3]

The most important and innovative feature of the drug court is the redefined role of the judge. Rather than simply adjudicating an offender in the traditional, passive role of the classical common law judge, the drug court judge plays an active and ongoing role in the rehabilitation of the offender. In drug court, the client regularly returns to the courtroom, where the judge engages him or her directly and monitors the client's progress in the prescribed treatment program. Thus, the main dialogue in the courtroom is between the client and the judge (instead of between the prosecutor and the defense lawyer), and tends of be personal and expressive in nature. Lawyers play reduced roles and often are not even present during the regular court review sessions. The court sessions are characterized by tearful testimonies, applause, handshakes, and hugs between judge and client, and elaborate graduation ceremonies for those who complete the program. Successful compliance with court mandates is often rewarded with prizes, including certificates, tickets to professional sports events, fresh donuts, coffee mugs, candy, and pens.

In some cases, the theatrical aspects of the programs are such that they resemble American daytime talk shows. A Washington, D.C., drug court judge roams the courtroom with microphone in hand interviewing clients and discussing recently viewed court-sponsored films. A Kentucky judge sheds his black robe (to appear more personal and familiar) and sometimes attends court sessions with acupuncture needles in his ears (in order to advertise this part of the treatment program). A North Carolina judge promises to do cartwheels for clients who successfully attend 90 treatment sessions in 90 days. A California judge brings a balloon to court to celebrate a drug court client's birthday. While these particular examples may represent outliers of a sort, they are indicative of the informal, innovative, and demonstrative flavor of American drug courts more generally.

The drug court model quickly spread to other American cities. Programs in Oakland, Las Vegas, Baltimore, Fort Lauderdale, Phoenix, and Portland were among the first generation of drug courts in the United States. Today, every state has a least one drug court, and there are more than 2,300 drug courts throughout the country.[4] In addition to the remarkable expansion of drug courts in the United States, a number of other specialty courts, based on the drug court model, have been initiated in the American criminal justice system. Among these are community courts, the first of which was established in 1993 in midtown Manhattan in New York City. Community courts focus on so-called "quality of life" crimes, such as illegal vending, prostitution, loitering, and subway turnstile jumping, in order to address the sort of low-level offending that undermines the quality of life in a local community, and that, if not addressed, will lead to more serious criminal activity and further degradation of the neighborhood.[5]

Community courts impose a range of sanctions and offer a variety of services to clients in the program, including quality of life groups, GED classes, community service, and (in instances of noncompliance with program requirements) time in jail. Restitution is applied in community courts more than in any other type of problem-solving court. In this regard, someone caught vandalizing may be required to paint over graffiti, or another caught stealing in New York's fashion district may be required to distribute donated clothing through the Salvation Army. As with drug courts, the community court model has continued to expand in recent years. In 1998, the Midtown community court was the only community court in the United States. Today there are several dozen community courts and, as Julius Lang at the Center for Court Innovation observed, soon "most big cities in the United States and many smaller cities will have one or more community courts."[6]

After drug courts and community courts, specialty domestic violence courts and mental health courts are among the most advanced types of problem-solving courts in the United States. Domestic violence courts offer a range of interventions— including victim and witness support services and, for offenders, anger management classes and batterer intervention programs. Domestic violence courts differ from other problem-solving courts in that there is a clearly identifiable victim. Because of this, some domestic violence courts play down the therapeutic qualities of the court program, and emphasize instead holding the offender responsible for his or her behavior. When possible, however, courts do attempt therapeutic intervention for both victims and offenders.[7] The first domestic violence court was started in Dade County, Florida, in 1992. Today there are over 300 domestic violence courts throughout the United States.

Mental health courts have also expanded in recent years. The first mental health court was established in Broward County, Florida, in 1997. Today there are more than 180 mental health courts nationwide. Offenders in mental health courts are offered (or subjected to) many of the same types of interventions found in other problem-solving courts, including ongoing judicial monitoring and jail for noncompliance with program requirements. Among the activities that the judge monitors in a mental health court is a client's use of prescribed medications, obviously a unique role for a judge, and one that sets mental health courts apart from other problem-solving courts. Some see the need for mental health courts as a direct consequence of the deinstitutionalization of mental health facilities that occurred in the 1960s and 1970s.[8] Critics argue, in light of this, that money directed to problem-solving courts should instead be directed to the restoration and strengthening of other social institutions.[9]

In addition to drug courts, community courts, domestic violence courts, and mental health courts, a range of other specialty courts have been developed in recent years, including prostitution courts, homeless courts, driving under the influence (DUI) courts, tobacco courts, teen courts, gambling courts, veterans courts, and reentry courts (programs that provide judicial oversight to recently released prisoners). In all, there are more than 3,200 problem-solving courts in the United States.[10] While these vary considerably from place to place, problem-solving courts, at least in the United States, typically share the following five traits: (1) ongoing judicial monitoring; (2) a multidisciplinary or team-oriented approach; (3) a therapeutic or treatment orientation; (4) the altering of the traditional roles in the adjudication process; and (5) a focus on solving the underlying problems of offenders, hence the umbrella term that has been used to describe these courts—*problem-solving courts*.

Even beyond these specialty courts, advocates argue in favor of taking problem-solving justice "to scale." That is, they wish to advance the problem-solving approach within the criminal justice system more broadly; or, as Francis Hartman, at Harvard's Kennedy School, explains, "Going to scale is importing some of the values and operations from problem-solving courts into the court system as a whole."[11] Along these lines, Greg Berman and John Feinblatt, from the Center for Court Innovation, ambitiously wish to transform the entire criminal court system to reflect a problem-solving mentality: "We must figure out how to 'go to scale' with problem-solving justice, altering the DNA of state court systems so that problem solving becomes part of the practice of every courtroom."[12]

The distinctively therapeutic or treatment orientation of American problem-solving courts has been fostered, in part, by its association with therapeutic jurisprudence (TJ), a new legal theory first developed by legal scholars David Wexler and Bruce Winick. Emerging on the scene at approximately the same time as did the first wave of problem-solving courts, therapeutic jurisprudence has provided a theoretical underpinning for these innovative courts. The theory is rather straightforward, if not also intentionally vague and open to various interpretations. As TJ advocates repeatedly assert, law has both therapeutic and anti-therapeutic consequences. The goal of therapeutic jurisprudence is to assess legal rules, programs, and processes in order to determine their therapeutic and anti-therapeutic effects. Once these effects are ostensibly determined, TJ aims to encourage therapeutic legal outcomes and discourage anti-therapeutic legal outcomes.[13]

Arguably, therapeutic jurisprudence, like problem-solving courts themselves, is a product of a particular cultural context, a social reality that those working within the TJ milieu neither seem to recognize nor acknowledge. Elsewhere, however, the therapeutic tendencies in American culture have been widely documented, beginning in 1966 with Philip Rieff's seminal work, *The Triumph of the Therapeutic*.[14] From the cultural understanding advanced by Rieff and others, one can view both problem-solving courts and therapeutic jurisprudence as derived from the same generative source (or "vector," to use Susan Daicoff's term): an influential and pervasive therapeutic culture. While TJ is popular among problem-solving court practitioners in the United States, it has not always been enthusiastically embraced in the borrowing countries (particularly in England, Scotland, and Ireland), which is itself an indication of important cultural differences.[15]

International Transplantation

Approximately a decade after the start of America's first drug court, actors in other countries began to introduce variations of the model in their own jurisdictions. The first drug court outside the United States was the Toronto drug court, started in 1998 and initially presided over by Judge Paul Bentley. A year later, England launched two drug courts in West Yorkshire County, which were influenced directly by exposure to Judge Stanley Goldstein and the Dade County drug court. Shortly thereafter, England and Scotland initiated Drug Treatment and Testing Orders (DTTOs), which were also inspired by the American drug court model. Australia's first drug court was started in Sydney in 1999. Instituted through the legislative directives of the New South Wales Parliament, Judge Gay Murrell served as Australia's first drug court judge. Drug courts have also spread to Ireland, Scotland, Bermuda, and Norway.

A similar type of transplantation has occurred in the case of community courts. Brooklyn, New York's Red Hook Community Justice Center, which started in 2000, has become the role model for the transference of community courts internationally. The Red Hook community court was initiated partly in response to the tragic shooting of a popular public school principal in 1998 in Red Hook. Motivated by this unfortunate event and the wish to end rampant crime in Red Hook, officials purchased and renovated an old parochial school building to house the new community court. Thus, the court is situated in the very center of the Red Hook community and offers its services—including assistance with housing, education, and drug counseling—to the community. The services are available both to those who find themselves in the criminal justice system and those who do not. Officials from around the world have visited Red Hook and have used the court, led by the friendly and charismatic judge Alex Calabrese, as a template to develop community courts in their own countries.

The first community court transplant was the Liverpool Community Justice Centre in Liverpool, England. The court so closely approximates the Red Hook court that it is also situated in a renovated Catholic school building and is run by an active and energetic judge, David Fletcher, who behaves in many ways very similar to Judge Calabrese. Since the start of the Liverpool court in 2004, community courts have been launched in Melbourne, Australia (also in a building that once housed an educational institution), Vancouver, Canada, and in a number of towns in South Africa. In every case, officials visited Red Hook and other problem-solving courts in the United States before starting their community courts. The same story of legal transference can be found with other problem-solving courts, including mental health courts and domestic violence courts.

COMPARATIVE DIFFERENCES

Though officials have looked to the United States as the model and inspiration for the development of problem-solving courts abroad, importers have consistently maintained that the programs must be adapted and modified to suit the needs of their own local situation. These efforts to indigenize make evident some of the clear differences between the style and scope of problem-solving courts in the various regions. What one finds, in this regard, is a pronounced distinction between the legal accent of the American courts and the legal accent of the problem-solving courts in the non-U.S. countries.[16] Specifically, a comparison of problem-solving courts in the United States, England, Ireland, Scotland, Australia, and Canada reveals a conspicuous expression of American exceptionalism. That is, in the United States, the courts are characterized by enthusiasm, boldness, and pragmatism; whereas, in the five other countries, the contrasting disposition is one of moderation, deliberation, and restraint.[17]

With respect to the American version of problem-solving courts, one typically finds problem-solving court judges and other advocates to be very enthusiastic about the movement. They are "true believers" who see problem-solving courts as a revolutionary innovation that promises to radically transform or "reinvent" the American criminal justice system. The court innovations are viewed as an exciting and promising alternative to a failing court system whose very legitimacy is somehow in question. So enthusiastic are problem-solving court practitioners that they sometimes come across as salespersons or religious zealots in their promotion of these courts. Greg Berman, for example, encourages advocates to look "for every possible opportunity—PSAs [public service announcements], op-eds, public events—to spread the gospel of problem-solving justice." Laurie Robinson, former assistant attorney general in the U.S. Department of Justice, even argues that enthusiasm is a feature of the movement that should be fostered. "The energy, enthusiasm, and optimism embedded in the burgeoning problem-solving courts movement," says Robinson, "is a significant asset right now for the nation's beleaguered justice system, one that should be . . . nurtured."[18]

Along with this quality of enthusiasm, American problem-solving court judges are also bold in the sense that they are willing to transgress the normal conventions of their judicial role. As noted above, many problem-solving court judges were frustrated by their traditional roles. They felt like "computers on the bench," hampered by mandatory sentencing rules, and unable to help the troubled individuals repeatedly passing through their courtrooms. Problem-solving courts afford judges more flexibility and power. As one problem-solving court judge put it, "We are the judges who get to color outside the lines." This boldness finds expression both inside and outside the courtroom. Inside the courtroom, judges directly engage the defendants who come before their benches. They speak openly and personally, offering words of encouragement when clients are doing well and admonishing and chastising them when they are not. Because of the ongoing nature of judicial oversight, a sort of relationship develops between judge and client; it is a relationship that is seen as a defining and positive attribute of the program. Judges enjoy this informal style of relating (as well as the greater flexibility and power the format affords) and report higher levels of job satisfaction than do judges in conventional criminal courts.[19]

Judges are also activist judges outside the courtroom. Community court judges, for example, regularly meet with residents of the community in order to better respond to community concerns and address specific areas of criminal activity. Drug court and other problem-solving court judges likewise engage in a range of extracurricular activities, including lobbying Congress for support, talking to the media, coordinating and soliciting help from the various agencies working with the court, contacting clients at their places of work, and even fund-raising for their local program. This last activity is one that officials in other countries find particularly worrying.

Finally, American problem-solving courts are characterized by a distinctive quality of pragmatism. Advocates repeatedly defend the programs (including such practices as coerced treatment) on the grounds of program efficacy. That is, they argue that problem-solving courts work, are better than "business as usual," and will help to restore confidence in the criminal justice system—a system, they argue, that suffers from a crisis of legitimacy. Problem-solving courts are not nearly as effective as many movement activists claim.[20] Local court programs often boast of radically reduced recidivism rates.[21] However, these studies are commonly fraught with a number of methodological limitations, including problematic experimental designs, the lack of long-term follow-up assessments, and the absence of appropriate comparison groups.[22] External evaluations, such as those conducted by the American Bar Association, the Rand Corporation, and the U.S. General Accounting Office (GAO), on the other hand, reveal that the claims of problem-solving court advocates have often been significantly overstated.[23]

A comprehensive analysis of 20 drug court evaluations, for example, issued by the GAO in 1997, concluded that it could "not reach definitive conclusions concerning the overall impact of drug courts," mainly because of a number of methodological problems in the various studies. Only 6 of the 20 studies were determined to have proper comparison groups, and among these were evaluations that revealed no reductions in (or even higher levels of) recidivism among drug court participants.[24] Eight years later, the GAO issued another assessment of drug court evaluations and again found that many studies lacked appropriate evaluation designs and comparison groups. Of the 117 evaluations considered, only 27 were determined to be "methodologically sound" in their assessment of recidivism rates and other factors.[25] And while most of these more "relatively rigorous" studies showed statistically significant reductions in rearrest rates among drug court participants, the GAO still concluded that "evidence about the effectiveness of drug court programs in reducing participants' substance abuse is limited and mixed."[26] Moreover, the GAO report was unable to determine from these evaluations which features of the programs positively impacted recidivism rates.[27]

However, to engage the debate over efficacy is to ignore a larger issue. A preoccupation with efficiency is itself a peculiarly American predilection. Italy represents an instructive counterexample in this regard. As David Nelken and other comparativists have observed, Italy's criminal justice system is not nearly so focused on issues of efficiency. Instead, there is a greater concern with taking the necessary time to achieve just outcomes. As a consequence, in Italy there is a notable dearth of studies on recidivism rates and a tendency for unusually long criminal trials.[28] From an Italian perspective, at least in principle, concerns with program efficacy should not override concerns with preserving formal and open justice; or, as Timothy Cases puts it, efficiency "should only be considered as ancillary to the primary objective of providing a fair and neutral method of resolving disputes."[29] Thus, whether or not these courts are as effective as advocates claim, there is no denying that they are repeatedly defended on the grounds of program efficacy.

In contrast to the American qualities of boldness, enthusiasm, and pragmatism, courts in the other countries are characterized by moderation, deliberation, and restraint. International importers of problem-solving courts are more moderate with respect to how they behave in the courtroom and are openly dismissive of the theatrical and demonstrative behavior of American judges. They are also more moderate in terms of what they claim that these courts can actually achieve. In the early years of the movement, notably in Australia and Canada, some even used different nomenclature to describe these court innovations, preferring the term "problem-oriented" courts over "problem-solving" courts, viewing the former as "less hubristic" and more "pessimistic" than the latter.[30] Unlike in the United States, legal actors in other countries do not view problem-solving courts as a revolutionary panacea that will resolve deeply entrenched and intractable social problems. Rather, the courts are viewed as one type of program among others that may be worth trying on a limited basis and that may prove helpful for a certain type of defendant.

Practitioners in other countries are also more moderate in the sense that they commonly embrace a "harm reduction" or "harm minimization" philosophy that stands in contrast to the American emphasis, in the case of drug courts, on "total abstinence," or what others have referred to as a "demand reduction" approach.[31] The harm reduction philosophy finds expression in a number of ways. In non-U.S. drug courts, methadone maintenance is a more common treatment modality, whereas, in the United States, methadone maintenance is viewed more critically; and in some drug court programs it is actually prohibited.[32] Additionally, programs abroad are more tolerant of some drug and alcohol use and do not typically require the achievement of total abstinence from clients in order to graduate from the program. Another example of the harm reduction philosophy in practice is needle exchange programs, common in both Australia and Canada but rejected in the United States.

One of the more interesting applications of a harm reduction mentality is found in Melbourne, Australia, where Magistrate Jelena Popovic runs a prostitution court (or "Tuesday afternoon list," as it is euphemistically called). In Melbourne, Popovic explains, there are three types of prostitutes: the high-end "call girls," the women in Melbourne's brothels, and those who work the streets. The women in the last category commonly have drug addiction problems and are the ones who most often find themselves before Magistrate Popovic's prostitution court. One of the goals of the court, according to Popovic, is to get the women off the streets and into the brothels. Such an effort does not represent an endorsement of brothels, only a realization that on the streets women face greater dangers with respect to health and safety. Thus, by getting them into the brothels, the court is helping to minimize potential harm.

Deliberation, a second feature of non-U.S. problem-solving courts, refers most importantly to the processes by which these programs are established. In the United States, problem-solving courts have been primarily a grassroots movement. Industrious and entrepreneurial judges initiate courts at the local level, often without any legislative direction or guidance.[33] Outside the United States, problem-solving courts have more typically been generated in a top-down fashion, and usually find their birth through legislation. Thus, courts are necessarily an outcome of parliamentary debate and deliberation. Moreover, when developing problem-solving courts, officials commonly establish a working group comprising representatives from the various agencies (social work, treatment, probation, education, etc.) that will be working with the court. The working groups engage in comprehensive studies of other problem-solving courts (both in their own country and abroad) and deliberate over what type of model they think would best suit their local jurisdiction.

Deliberative exercises continue even after the launching of the various courts. It is a common practice outside the United States to establish pilot programs for a limited period of time, in order to assess whether specific problem-solving courts are suitable and effective. Moreover, even after establishing pilot programs, courts have, in a number of instances, had to wait for legislative approval in order to institute sought-after features of the court, such as the power to impose a short jail term for noncompliance with court mandates. In general, outside the United States, there is much greater judicial deference to the other branches of government. To provide just one example, the Sydney drug court would not start until the New South Wales Parliament passed enabling legislation. Even after the court commenced, court officials repeatedly referred back to the legislation; and several amendments were added over time to give additional guidance and direction to the court. Relatedly, outside the United States, there is more evidence of critical self-reflection about the courts after they have been established, and a willingness to change, adjust, and even stop practices that are seen to challenge more traditional understandings of formal and open justice.[34]

Finally, the legal accent of problem-solving courts in countries outside the United States is characterized by a clear sense of restraint. As has already been noted, judges exercise restraint in deference to statutory law and legislative authority. They are also restrained structurally by the peculiarities of their court systems. For example, in England the magistrate system prevents magistrates from having the sort of flexibility and power exercised by judges in the American version of problem-solving courts.[35] In addition to these interpretive and structural forms of restraint, non-U.S. judges also exercise notable personal restraint. That is, they recognize that the more informal and flexible format of problem-solving courts establishes a courtroom environment whereby judges can act in a manner that may violate the traditional protections of individual freedoms and due process rights. In a number of instances, most notably in Scotland and Australia, judges personally choose not to exercise certain powers, even when they have been given the legal authority to do so; and they restrain themselves out of a consideration for protecting due process rights and maintaining the dignity and decorum of the court.

Australian criminologist Arie Freiberg is cognizant of some of these differences in his comparative assessments of criminal justice practices in the United States and Australia more generally. As he puts it, "Where the United States treads boldly, rapidly, and sometimes foolishly, Australia tiptoes carefully, slowly, and most times reluctantly."[36] In the case of problem-solving courts, the latter description applies not only to Australia, but to England, Ireland, Scotland, and Canada as well. Consequently, courts outside the United States are more likely to preserve what have long been regarded as essential qualities of formal and open justice; whereas, in the United States, the bold and enthusiastic embrace of programs informed by therapeutic and pragmatic cultural sensibilities may lead court officials into practices that undermine, if only unwittingly, classical understandings of justice.

LADY JUSTICE AND THE CHANGING FACE OF JUSTICE

Like the previously discredited practices of the rehabilitative era, American problem-solving courts have resulted in processes that some find troubling.[37] Among these concerns, the distinction between treatment and punishment becomes blurred, resulting in practices that are sometimes more punitive than a client would receive in a normal criminal court.[38] Therapeutic nomenclature cloaks the essentially punitive nature of certain sanctions. However, a "therapeutic remand" or "motivational jail" is still, at the end of the day, time spent in jail.[39] As Richard Boldt observes, "From the point of view of the defendant . . . problem-solving courts may be 'more difficult to complete, more onerous and far more intrusive on liberty' than traditional criminal court dispositions."[40] The therapeutic intent behind problem-solving courts can also lead to indeterminate periods of involvement in the criminal justice system. Again, cases of indeterminacy are often justified in deference to the prevailing therapeutic idiom. The goal, it is argued, is not the fulfillment of a sentence that is proportional to the crime committed, but is getting the client well or healed, however long that may take. Measured against traditional standards of justice, however, multiple stints in jail and long-term court-monitoring programs can result in sanctions that are clearly disproportional to the original offense.

Programs have also resulted in unanticipated net-widening, both with respect to the type and number of criminal activities overseen by the courts as well as the nature and extent of judicial involvement in defendants' personal lives. Moreover, in American problem-solving courts, offenders are sometimes asked to waive constitutional rights in order to participate in problem-solving courts and, as noted above, the "voluntary" nature of their involvement is sometimes questionable. Problem-solving court officials sidestep these legal issues by asserting the preeminence of a therapeutic perspective. TJ scholars like Wexler and Winick often assert that therapeutic principles should not trump traditional justice principles; however, in the enthusiasm to act therapeutically, concern about the preservation of traditional court processes and due process rights fade into the background. Such tendencies have been less pronounced—at least in the early years of the international movement—in the countries outside the United States, due in no small measure to the contrasting legal accents discussed above.

A helpful illustration of this difference is found in a 2004 exchange between American and British officials on the topic of community courts and community justice. The exchange, set up in London by the Center for Court Innovation, addressed, among other issues, the establishment of England's first community court in Liverpool. Judge David Fletcher was among those who participated in the forum. In the course of the day's discussion, one participant defined community justice as "removing the blindfolds from Lady Justice."[41] The image of Lady Justice—situated as she is above many courtrooms throughout the United States and Europe—represents several themes central to classical understandings of justice. Her scales convey notions of fairness and proportionality; her sword, the power of the court to impose a punishment and to act decisively; and her blindfold, the ideas of neutrality and impartiality and the absence of prejudice and bias. In community courts, as noted above, the judge is actively engaged with—and directly receives input from—the community. The judge (in the U.S., anyway) also meets regularly with team members in pre-court sessions to discuss in detail the lives of defendants participating in the court program. In this sense, the community court judge is decidedly not blind to a considerable amount of information—information that he or she would not normally be privy to in a conventional criminal court. Lady Justice without her blindfold, therefore, is a fitting iconic representation of community courts (and other problem-solving courts).

During the 2004 meeting in London, not all British officials agreed with this revised image of justice: "Several participants stated concerns that offering community input in sentencing could ultimately erode the traditional British legal protection of due process and encourage community 'vengeance.'"[42] Such resistance is not surprising, given the important quality of restraint exercised by judges in the non-U.S. countries. Robert Cover, in fact, sees in Lady Justice's blindfold an element of self-restraint. "The blindfold (as opposed to blindness) suggests an act of self-restraint," he posits. "She could act otherwise and there is, thus, an everpresent element of choice in assuming this posture."[43] Even when the structure of specialty courts allows for increased judicial activism, judges and magistrates outside the United States still restrain themselves in a manner consistent with this understanding of the blindfold's import.

Judge Fletcher, for example, unlike his American counterparts, does not attend pre-court meetings in the Liverpool community court. Sheriffs, in the new Scottish youth courts, though encouraged to relate to defendants in a more personal and interactive manner, have resisted, based on the view that it is not "really part of a judge's job to get too close to the accused." Judge Murrell of the Sydney drug court thinks that this sort of self-restraint is imperative in the context of drug court, precisely because the format gives the judge so much flexibility and power. As she puts it:

> It is quite important to be a little bit restrained, because the judge does have such enormous power—not just in terms of things like sanctions or sentences, but in terms of emotional abuse of the person, if you'd like, in throwing their weight around generally. And I think the whole boundaries in which the judge operates [in this kind of court] are so blurred as compared to a traditional judicial setting that you've got to try to be aware of those boundaries. To that extent, restraint helps you not to transgress those boundaries.[44]

Creeping Americanization

While the differences highlighted here were certainly evident in the early years of the movement, over time, at least in some cases, they have dissipated. Consider an example from a recent iteration of drug courts in the United Kingdom. In 2005, England launched the West London drug court, a court that looks more like the American model than any previous version of drug court in the United Kingdom. As with earlier manifestations of drug courts in England, this court was directly inspired by the American model. Judge Justin Philips, the first drug court judge in the West London court, explains how he "started reading about the American model." He notes specifically his "online research of the American courts" and his discovery of the "donut court in Florida," presumably referring to the Fort Lauderdale drug court, where successful clients are rewarded in court with fresh donuts. Holding up the American innovation as the model, he laments that "the UK is ten-plus years behind the U.S.A."[45]

Judge Philips has moved his court even closer to—or, some might say, beyond—the kind of expressivism typical of American drug courts, representing a notable departure from the more staid and cautious style of British and other non-U.S. problem-solving courts. For review hearings, he will literally change clothes to look more informal. He makes clients sit near him, on his level. That is, clients stand not before an elevated bench, but side by side, just a few feet from the judge. Philips speaks in familiar terms, often calling clients by their first names, and is not afraid to make physical contact. Consider his own description of his behavior in the courtroom:

> I do my reviews in a completely and utterly informal way. I pick a shirt or T-shirt or football shirt or whatever it is, and the most revolting socks. . . . And it breaks down the ice. And I call them by their first names, and if they come in and call me Justin, I actually say, "As long as you give me negative [urinalysis] tests, I don't mind." . . . And the language I use—well . . . I'm correctly quoted as saying to one guy, "If you give me another positive [urinalysis test], I'll kick you out on the ass." And this is my way of doing things.[46]

Magistrates involved in the early British drug courts and DTTO programs were explicitly disapproving of the American proclivity for physical contact with clients. Judge Philips has no such misgivings. In fact, he regularly shakes hands with and/or hugs drug court participants. As Philips puts it, "I've got no problem, if someone's done well, whether it's a woman or a man, in giving them a hug and a kiss. Because I think it is absolutely essential that we show them 1) we're human, 2) we care, and 3) if they've done well, they've got to be told".[47]

As Judge Philips' court suggests, some of the cultural restraints that once limited the style and scope of British drug courts have, at least in some instances, been relaxed.[48] Only time will tell whether and to what extent these cultural infiltrations—be they welcomed or regretted—will result in further homogenization or some kind of subtle yet transformative legal irritation of Britain's legal culture.[49] While there are certainly examples of at least limited and initial resistance, there are other signs, as is evident in Judge Philips' court, of fuller Americanization in the receiving legal systems.

One way to explain the emerging Americanization of the problem-solving courts in the United Kingdom and other places is to appreciate the extent to which these programs, borrowed as they are from the United States, are themselves significant reflections of American culture. Therapeutic jurisprudence has been largely dismissed as a relevant judicial philosophy in England.[50] However, as noted above, U.S.-bred problem-solving courts are a product of American therapeutic culture, just as is therapeutic jurisprudence. The imported programs are not easily disentangled from their cultural roots. Thus, importers may be bringing on board more of American culture than they realize or want. As is glaringly displayed in Judge Philips' court, some features of the American courts, once openly disparaged, have over time come to fruition.

Importing countries, therefore, wishing to maintain such qualities as deliberation, moderation, and restraint in their local legal cultures do well to recognize the

difficulty of disentangling law from its cultural roots. Embedded in problem-
solving courts (even in the nomenclature used to label them) are the very features
of American culture that many say they do not like. To import problem-solving
courts is to import elements of the particular culture out of which the programs first
emerged—and from which they are not easily extricated. A fuller appreciation of
the culturally embedded nature of law, as such, might prevent borrowers from
losing the valued and defining features of their local legal culture.

LESSONS FROM ABROAD

Thus, the lesson for practitioners outside the United States may be the need to be
more careful about what they import. As Jonathan Freedland observes, regarding
indiscriminate borrowing from the United States more generally, Brits need to be
more discerning about "what to let in and what to keep out."[51] He fears that, too
often, the British "are shipping in junk and leaving behind gold" and thinks that a
more critical selection process is possible.[52] Concerning Australia's ability to selectively borrow, Arie Freiberg is less optimistic: "Resistance may not be useless," says
Freiberg, "but it is difficult." He seems to suggest that a full Americanization of Australian legal culture is almost inevitable: "From baseball to boot camps, from Macy's
to macing, the process of Coca-colonizing Australian criminal justice, while not a
fait accompli, has more than a little commenced. In the new Australian fashion, we
could say, it has just got to first base!"[53] If importers of problem-solving courts may
be cautioned to be more discerning about their importation of culturally determined legal products, the lesson for Americans may be to pay more attention to the
legal accents of those who are borrowing from them. As noted above, the common
practice in other countries is to proceed through a rather lengthy process of deliberation before establishing a new problem-solving court. This typically involves a
thorough study and examination of practices in other countries. In contrast, the
United States does not often look to other countries to inform its legal decisions or
the development of legal programs. This is a tendency that one finds at the level of
the U.S. Supreme Court as well, where justices have been scolded for making even
oblique references to foreign law.[54] Justice Ruth Bader Ginsburg observes that, in
contrast to the practices of judges abroad, the "same readiness to look beyond one's
own shores has not marked the decisions of the court on which I serve."[55]

In the case of problem-solving courts, one does encounter references by Americans to legal developments overseas, not so much for the purposes of informing
practices in the United States, but as a way of demonstrating the movement's success
and growing influence. Robert Wolf, from the Center for Court Innovation, argues
that one way to determine an idea's success is "to measure how far the concept
travels."[56] He highlights the Center's work internationally to illustrate how, according to this measure, problem-solving courts have been "highly successful."[57]

Another report from the Center for Court Innovation observes that between 1996 and 2006, visitors from over 50 countries have toured such projects as the Red Hook and Midtown community courts. According to the Center, "the impacts of these visits can be seen across the globe."[58] The Center also boasts that it has "counseled jurisdictions around the world in the development of groundbreaking justice experiments."[59] This international influence thus contributes to the movement's own legacy and standing, and helps to solidify its "reputation as an international leader in justice reform."[60] Again, focus on work in other countries serves not as a way for Americans to learn about—much less from—other societies and cultures, but as a kind of "feather in the cap," underscoring the significance and genius of their own innovations. Thus the Center sees as its "most lasting legacy" the notion that it "sits at the fulcrum of an international movement."[61]

Visits by U.S. officials to other countries for the purposes of observing and learning, as opposed to instructing and spreading "the gospel of problem-solving justice," have been comparatively rare. An official from Scotland's first problem-solving court says that her court has had a number of international visitors, including representatives from Ireland, Norway, Russia, and Macedonia, but no visits from any U.S. officials or practitioners. Moreover, when the Scottish have presented as a panel at annual National Association of Drug Court Professionals (NADCP) conferences, they do not typically get much interest from U.S. conferees wanting to learn about the Scottish experience. Instead, among the few who attended their sessions were those "planning a vacation to Scotland and wanted to get tips from the panel." A Scottish sheriff (judge) observes a lack of interest in things foreign among Americans in a more general sense. He notes that some Americans "are completely unaware of what is going on in the rest of the world. I mean not only are they unaware, but they don't care. They're not interested."[62]

This observation parallels findings from the 2007 Pew Global Attitudes survey, in particular the results from a question about foreign policy. In this survey, respondents were asked if they thought the United States takes into account the interests of other countries in making international policy decisions. Significantly, respondents in Canada and western European countries overwhelmingly felt that the United States did not take into account the interests of other countries.[63] The survey reports that 83 percent of Canadians, 74 percent of the British, 89 percent of the French, and 91 percent of the Swedish hold such a view.[64] One could argue that this question has more to do with recent foreign policy initiatives than it does with the borrowing of local court innovations. In both cases, though, what one finds is a perceived lack of concern on the part of the United States in learning about the interests, practices, and cultures of other places, and a preoccupation among Americans with spreading their own ideas and programs.[65] Thus, the contrasting cultural dispositions revealed in the case of problem-solving courts may be evident in the international transference (or attempted transference) of other American exports. One finds in these efforts—whether it be the transplantation of problem-solving courts or the forced exportation of American-style democracy—pronounced and particular features of national character.

As such, Americans could perhaps do well to learn about, and perhaps follow the example of, some of the legal-cultural qualities of the other countries considered here. In so doing, they may better avoid the potential violations of open and formal justice that their culturally inspired legal accent sometimes appears to encourage. Put another way, as long as Americans have removed the metaphorical blindfold from Lady Justice, they may wish to look more carefully at the criminal justice practices of other countries. In so doing, they might not only learn something about the values that animate other legal cultures but may also gain some insights into why people around the world perceive the United States as they do.

NOTES

1. See Pew Global Attitudes Project, *Global Unease with Major World Powers* (June 27, 2007), 6. Here the 2007 survey report offers the following paradoxical conclusion: while "large proportions in most countries think it is bad that American ideas and customs are spreading to their countries," there is also "near universal admiration for U.S. technology and a strong appetite for its cultural exports in most parts of the world."

2. See James L. Nolan, Jr., *Reinventing Justice: The American Drug Court Movement* (Princeton University Press, 2001), 40.

3. See Peggy Fulton Hora, William G. Schma, and John T. A. Rosenthal, "Therapeutic Jurisprudence and the Drug Treatment Court Movement: Revolutionizing the Criminal Justice System's Response to Drug Abuse and Crime in America," *Notre Dame Law Review* 74, 2 (January 1999): 526. For a comprehensive discussion of the efficacy of coerced treatment, see Sally Satel, *Drug Treatment: The Case for Coercion* (Washington, DC: AEI Press, 1999). For other discussions of the issue, see Satel, "Observational Study of Courtroom Dynamics in Selected Drug Courts," 53; William McColl, "Baltimore City's Drug Treatment Court: Theory and Practice in an Emerging Field," *Maryland Law Review* 55 (1996): 476. Another document on drug courts reports that, "Research indicates that a person coerced to enter treatment by the criminal justice system is likely to do as well as one who volunteers" in "Defining Drug Courts: The Key Components," Drug Courts Program Office, Office of Justice Programs, U.S. Dept. of Justice (January 1997): 9, citing R. Hubbard, M. Marsden, J. Rachal, H. Harwood, E. Cavanaugh, and H. Ginzburg, *Drug Abuse Treatment: A National Study of Effectiveness* (Chapel Hill: University of North Carolina Press, 1989). For further discussion of this point, see also, Nolan, *Reinventing Justice*, 199–200.

4. Mae C. Quinn, "The Modern Problem-Solving Court Movement: Domination of Discourse and Untold Stories of Criminal Justice Reform," *Journal of Law and Policy* 31 (2009): 60.

5. Such a focus is informed, in part, by the "broken windows" theory made famous by the article by James Q. Wilson and George L. Kelling. According to this theory, "street crime flourishes in areas where disorderly behavior goes unchecked" (James Q. Wilson and George L. Kelling, "Broken Windows," *The Atlantic Monthly* [March 1982]: 34).

6. Quintin Johnstone, "The Hartford Community Court: An Experiment That Has Succeeded," 124.

7. See Angela R. Gover, "Domestic Violence Courts: A Judicial Response to Intimate Partner Violence," in *Problem Solving Courts: Justice for the Twenty-First Century*, ed.

Mitchell B. Mackinem and Paul Higgins (Santa Barbara, CA: Praeger, 2009), 121–122, 126. See also James L. Nolan, Jr., *Legal Accents, Legal Borrowing: The International Problem-Solving Court Movement* (Princeton: Princeton University Press, 2009), 14–16.

8. See John S. Goldkamp and Cheryl Irons-Guynn, "Emerging Judicial Strategies for the Mentally Ill in the Criminal Caseload: Mental Health Courts in Fort Lauderdale, Seattle, San Bernardino, and Anchorage," Bureau of Justice Assistance, Office of Justice Programs, U.S. Department of Justice (April 2000): xiv; and Richard Schneider, Hy Bloom, and Mark Heerema, *Mental Health Courts: Decriminalizing the Mentally Ill* (Toronto: Irwin Law, 2007).

9. Richard Boldt identifies this as one of the primary concerns raised by critics of problem-solving courts: "that problem-solving courts too often cause a misallocation of scarce social services resources" (Richard Boldt, "A Circumspect Look at Problem-Solving Courts," in *Problem-Solving Courts: Justice for the Twenty-First Century?*" eds. Paul Higgins and Mitchell B. Mackinem [Santa Barbara, CA: Praeger, 2009]: 14). On this point, see also Victoria Malkin, "Community Courts and the Process of Accountability: Consensus and Conflict at the Red Hook Community Justice Center," *American Criminal Law Review* 40, no. 4 (Fall 2003): 1590; Betsy Tsai, "The Trend Toward Specialized Domestic Violence Courts: Improvements of an Effective Innovation," *Fordham Law Review* 68 (2000): 1314; and Victoria Malkin, "Problem-Solving in Community Courts: Who Decides the Problem?" *Problem-Solving Courts: Justice for the Twenty-First Century?*, eds. Paul Higgins and Mitchell B. Mackinem (Santa Barbara, CA: Praeger, 2009): 155.

10. *Problem-Solving Courts: Justice for the Twenty-First Century?*, eds. Paul Higgins and Mitchell B. Mackinem (Santa Barbara, CA: Praeger, 2009): ix.

11. John Feinblatt and Derek Denckla, eds., "Prosecutors, Defenders, and Problem-Solving Courts," *Judicature* 84, no. 4 (January–February 2001): 214.

12. Greg Berman and John Feinblatt, *Good Courts: The Case for Problem-Solving Justice* (New York: The New Press, 2005), 190.

13. *Law in a Therapeutic Key: Developments in Therapeutic Jurisprudence*, eds. David B. Wexler and Bruce J. Winick (Durham, NC: Carolina Academic Press, 1996); *Judging in a Therapeutic Key: Therapeutic Jurisprudence and the Courts*, eds. Bruce J. Winick and David B. Wexler (Durham, NC: Carolina Academic Press, 2003).

14. Philip Rieff, *The Triumph of the Therapeutic* (Chicago: University of Chicago Press, 1966). For more recent discussions of the therapeutic culture, see Jonathan B. Imber, ed., *Therapeutic Culture: Triumph and Defeat* (New Brunswick: Transaction, 2004); Eva Illouz, *Saving the Modern Soul: Therapy, Emotions, and the Culture of Self-Help* (Berkeley: University of California Press, 2008); Frank Furedi, *Therapy Culture: Cultivating Vulnerability in an Uncertain Age* (New York: Routledge, 2004); and James L. Nolan, Jr., *The Therapeutic State: Justifying Government at Century's End* (New York: New York University Press, 1998).

15. See Nolan, *Legal Accents, Legal Borrowing*, 35.

16. The notion of legal accent is inspired by Clifford Geertz's discussion of law and local knowledge. Geertz observes that law is "local not just to place, time, class, and variety of issue, but as to accent" (Clifford Geertz, *Local Knowledge: Further Essays in Interpretive Anthropology* [New York: Basic Books, 1983], 123).

17. For a fuller discussion of these differences see Chapter 6 of Nolan, *Legal Accents, Legal Borrowing*.

18. Laurie O. Robinson, "Commentary on Candace McCoy," *American Criminal Law Review* 40, no. 4 (Fall 2003): 1539.

19. Peggy Fulton Hora and Deborah J. Chase, "Judicial Satisfaction When Judging in a Therapeutic Key," *Contemporary Issues in Law* 7, no. 1 (2003–2004): 18.

168 SENTENCING THEORIES AND THEIR APPLICATION

20. For a recent challenge to these common claims, see Mae Quinn, "The Modern Problem-Solving Court Movement: Domination of Discourse and Untold Stories of Criminal Justice Reform," *Journal of Law and Policy* 31 (2009): 57–82. Quinn observes, "Their proponents [of problem-solving courts] assert that such courts cure addiction, address intimate violence, prevent recidivism, reduce costs, and even save lies. But this success story . . . is misleading. . . . Questions remain about the efficacy and propriety of problem-solving courts. It is not at all clear that specialized courts offer a superior alternative to the traditional case-processing model in preventing recidivism or that they resolve the underlying social problems they are created to address. In addition, there has been insufficient study of the real economic costs of such courts, or the extent to which defendants' legal rights and our system of justice may be undermined by the informal procedures that such institutions use," 58, 63.

21. There is a strong incentive to do this—as Timothy Casey points out, "many studies suffer internal bias as they are self-reported and linked to the continuation of grant money" (Timothy Casey, "When Good Intentions Are Not Enough: Problem-Solving Courts and the Impending Crisis of Legitimacy," *SMU Law Review* 57 [Fall 2004]: 1484).

22. See Nolan, *Reinventing Justice*, 127–132.

23. In his assessment of a range of drug court evaluations, Morris Hoffman concludes that, of the dozens of drug court impact studies conducted, only a handful have used the proper comparison groups, and that "the recidivism results in those handful of studies are substantially less promising than the wild claims regularly made in informal surveys" (Morris B. Hoffman, "The Drug Court Scandal," *North Carolina Law Review*, 78 [June 2000]: 1491). For a fuller discussion of these sorts of discrepancies, see Nolan, *The Therapeutic State: Justifying Government at Century's End* (New York: New York University Press), 103–111.

24. "Drug Courts: Overview and Growth, Characteristics, and Results" (United States General Accounting Office, July 1997).

25. "Adult Drug Courts: Evidence Indicates Recidivism Reductions and Mixed Results for Other Outcomes," (United States General Accounting Office, February 2005), 10.

26. Ibid., 6.

27. Ibid., 7. Evaluations of other problem-solving courts have been equally underwhelming. As Mae Quinn observes, "Even less impressive than drug courts are the batterer intervention programs touted by many domestic violence court advocates as a revolutionary approach to abuse between intimates. The data demonstrate that such programs are ineffectual as a method of treatment—they simply do not work to deter violence" (Quinn, "The Modern Problem-Solving Court Movement," 68). A recent evaluation of an Australian community court found that recidivism rates among participants were actually higher than the reoffending rates of non-participants. For a report on this study see: http://au.news.yahoo.com/thewest/a/-/newshome/7038746/aboriginal-court-trial-flops.

28. David Nelken, "Using the Concept of Legal Culture," *Australian Journal of Legal Philosophy* 29 (2004): 21. For an example of the absence of studies on recidivism in Italy, see A. Stevens, D. Berto, W. Heckmann, V. Kerschl, K. Oeuvray, M. van Ooyen, E. Steffan, and A. Uchtenhagen, "Quasi-Compulsory Treatment of Drug Dependant Offenders: An International Literature Review," *Substance Use and Misuse* 40 (2005): 269–283.

29. Timothy Casey, "When Good Intentions Are Not Enough," 1502.

30. Arie Freiberg, "Problem-Oriented Courts: Innovative Solutions to Intractable Problems?" *Journal of Judicial Adminstration* 11, no. 1 (August 2001): 25, fn. 5. Australian criminologist John Braithwaite has also used the term "problem-oriented," (John Braithwaite, "Restorative Justice and Therapeutic Jurisprudence," *Criminal Law Bulletin* 38,

no. 2 [March–April 2002]: 246), as has Susan Eley in her analysis of the Toronto K Court; she only qualifies this by noting that "problem-solving" is the nomenclature used "in the American literature" (Susan Eley, "Changing Practices: The Specialised Domestic Violence Court Process," 113).

31. Dan Small, Ernest Drucker, an Editorial for *Harm Reduction Journal*, "Policy Makers Ignoring Science and Scientists Ignoring Policy: The Medical Ethical Challenges of Heroin Treatment", *Harm Reduction Journal* 3, no. 16 (May 2, 2006): 9

32. Caroline S. Cooper, Shanie R. Bartlett, Michelle A. Shaw, and Kayla K. Yang, "Drug Courts: 1997 Overview of Operational Characteristics and Implementation Issues, Part Six: Drug Court Treatment Services" (May 1997): 83.

33. Timothy Casey, "When Good Intentions Are Not Enough: Problem-Solving Courts and the Impending Crisis of Legitimacy," *Southern Methodist University Law Review* 57 (2004): 1459–1519.

34. Nolan, *Legal Accents, Legal Borrowing*, 150–151.

35. Lay magistrates typically sit as a panel of three. They are not legally trained (though they are assisted by a legally trained court clerk) and must contend with a stronger probation service than exists in the United States. British lay magistrates do not have the power to impose short stints in jail, as often occurs in American problem-solving courts. Even outside the problem-solving courts, they can only sentence up to six months for a single offense and 12 months for multiple offenses. Moreover, because they participate in the courts on a rotating basis, the sort of rapport and continuity achieved in relationships between clients and judges in American problem-solving courts is difficult to achieve. For a fuller discussion of the structural restraints of the lay magistracy, see Nolan, *Legal Accents, Legal Borrowing*, 47–50.

36. Arie Freiberg, "Three Strikes and You're Out—It's Not Cricket: Colonization and Resistance in Australian Sentencing," in *Sentencing and Sanctions in Western Countries*, eds. Michael Tonry and Richard S. Frase (Oxford: Oxford University Press, 2001), 53.

37. See Mae Quinn, "An RSVP to Professor Wexler's Warm Invitation to the Criminal Defense Bar: Unable to Join You, Already (Somewhat Similarly) Engaged," *Boston College Law Review* 48 (2007): 539–595; Timothy Casey, "When Good Intentions Are Not Enough: Problem-Solving Courts and the Impending Crisis of Legitimacy," *Southern Methodist University Law Review* 57 (2004): 1459–1519; Eric Miller, "Embracing Addiction: Drug Courts and the False Promise of Judicial Interventionism," *Ohio State Law Journal* 65 (2004): 1479–1576; Morris B. Hoffman, "Therapeutic Jurisprudence, Neo-Rehabilitationism, and Judicial Collectivism: The Least Dangerous Branch Becomes the Most Dangerous," *Fordham Urban Law Journal* 29 (June, 2002): 2063–2098; Richard Boldt, "A Circumspect Look at Problem-Solving Courts," in *Problem-Solving Courts: Justice for the Twenty-First Century?*" eds. Paul Higgins and Mitchell B. Mackinem (Santa Barbara, CA: Praeger, 2009): 13–32; and Mae C. Quinn, "The Modern Problem-Solving Court Movement: Domination of Discourse and Untold Stories of Criminal Justice Reform," *Journal of Law and Policy* 31 (2009): 57–82.

38. As Quinn notes, "These defendants often are sent to prison for faltering in their treatment efforts—sometimes for longer periods than they would have served had they forgone the problem-solving court option" (Mae Quinn, "The Modern Problem-Solving Court Movement," 65). Victoria Malkin notes the same in her discussion of the Red Hook community court: "In Red Hook, defendants with minor violations that might have merited a 'time served' in the downtown court (after spending 48 hours in a cell waiting to go to court) were assessed and monitored by the court . . . and in many cases kept under supervision for long periods of time" (Victoria Malkin, "Problem-Solving in Community

Courts: Who Decides the Problem?" *Problem-Solving Courts: Justice for the Twenty-First Century?*, eds. Paul Higgins and Mitchell B. Mackinem [Santa Barbara, CA: Praeger, 2009]: 148).

39. Dawn Moore, for example, has written about the manner in which practices in the Canadian drug courts "have concerning implications for questions of due process and the ethical treatment of court clients." She observes that procedures in Canadian drug courts "explicitly erase fundamental protections against abuse of power in the realms of both therapy and justice." In particular, Moore highlights the way in which punitive practices, including incarceration, are given therapeutic classifications. "In the treatment court, the notion of punishment is translated into the therapeutic goal of motivation." Yet, such sanctions as "increasing surveillance and the possibility of arrest and incarceration" are still, at the end of the day, "decidedly punitive" (Dawn Moore, "Translating Justice and Therapy: The Drug Treatment Court Networks," *British Journal of Criminology* 47 [2007]: 44–50.

40. Richard Boldt, "A Circumspect Look at Problem-Solving Courts," 17.

41. "Community Justice: A US-UK Exchange," a summary report of a meeting convened by the Center for Court Innovation and the Office for Public Management at the latter's London headquarters on 22 October 2004, available at: www.opm.co.uk/download/papers/CCI_UK_OPM_report.doc.

42. Ibid.

43. As cited in Dennis E. Curtis and Judith Resnick, "Images of Justice," *The Yale Law Journal* 96 (1987): 1728.

44. Nolan, *Legal Accents, Legal Borrowing*, 92.

45. The Lord Chief Justice of England and Wales, Nicholas Phillips (no relation), who attended the December 2005 opening of the West London Drugs Court, complimented the "inspiring leadership" of Judge Justin Philips and also noted the manner in which the judge and the court are "following the American model."

46. The quote to which Judge Philips refers in this interview was cited in the following article: Ben Leapman, "In Session: London's First Drugs-Only Court," *Evening Standard* (23 December 2005). Judge Philips was speaking to Rodney, "a van driver who lost his job due to crack addiction." Leapman quotes Judge Philips as having said to Rodney, "If I see any positive test results next time you come here, I'm going to kick your arse."

47. Nolan, *Legal Accents, Legal Borrowing*, 57.

48. Likewise, British domestic violence courts, though initially resistant to a rehabilitative orientation toward the accused and concomitant review sessions for defendants, have begun to experiment with judicial reviews of offenders in some instances. Even Scottish sheriffs, once openly averse to open expressions of emotions, show some signs of engaging defendants in a more personal, informal manner. See Nolan, *Legal Accents, Legal Borrowing*, 62–63, 173–176.

49. For a fuller discussion of the notion of legal irritation, see Gunther Teubner, "Legal Irritants: How Unifying Law Ends up in New Divergences," in *Varieties of Capitalism*, eds. Peter A. Hall and David Soskice (Oxford: Oxford University Press, 2001). As applied to international problem-solving court movement, see Nolan, *Legal Accents, Legal Borrowing*, 30–41, 172–174.

50. See Nolan, *Legal Accents, Legal Borrowing*, 72–73.

51. Jonathan Freedland, *Bring Home the Revolution: The Case for a British Republic* (London: Fourth Estate, 1998), 10.

52. Ibid., 12–14.

53. Ibid., 56

54. See, for example, *Atkins v. Virginia*—a 2002 case in which the court ruled that it was cruel and unusual punishment to execute mentally retarded criminals—Justice John Paul Stevens observed in a footnote that such a punishment was "overwhelmingly disapproved" of "within the world community" and specifically cited a brief for the European Union in support of this observation. In his dissenting opinion, Justice Antonin Scalia responded indignantly: "[I]rrelevant are the practices of the 'world community,' whose notions of justice are (thankfully) not always those of our people" (*Atkins v. Virginia*, 536 U.S. 304, 347–348 [Scalia, dissenting]).

55. Anne-Marie Slaughter, *A New World Order* (Princeton University Press, 2004): 76–77.

56. Robert V. Wolf, "Community Justice Around the Globe: An International Overview," *Crime and Justice* 22, no. 93 (July/August 2006): 4.

57. Ibid.

58. Center for Court Innovation, White Paper, "A Decade of Change: The First 10 Years of the Center for Court Innovation" (2006): 10; available at: http://www.courtinnovation.org/_uploads/documents/10th_Anniversary1.pdf.

59. Ibid., 16.

60. Ibid., 4.

61. Ibid., 15.

62. See Jeffrey Toobin, "Swing Shift," *The New Yorker* (September 12, 2005): 42–48. Justice Anthony Kennedy observes that European judges are "concerned" and "feel demeaned" that American judges don't "cite their decisions with more regularity." Kennedy, moreover, thinks American ideas would be more welcomed overseas if the U.S. posture included "listening as well as lecturing," 47.

63. Pew Global Attitudes Project, *Global Unease with Major World Powers* (June 27, 2007), 97.

64. Ibid.

65. In the 2007 Pew Global Attitudes Survey, 67 percent of Americans said the spread of American ideas and customs was a good thing. Only one other country had a higher percentage on this survey question: the Ivory Coast at 79 percent. See *Global Unease with Major World Powers* (2007), 99.

REFERENCES

Berman, Greg, and John Feinblatt. 2005. *Good Courts: The Case for Problem-Solving Justice.* New York: The New Press.

Boldt, Richard. "A Circumspect Look at Problem-Solving Courts." 2009. In *Problem-Solving Courts: Justice for the Twenty-First Century?*, eds. Paul Higgins and Mitchell B. Mackinem, 13–32. Santa Barbara, CA: Praeger.

Casey, Timothy. 2004. "When Good Intentions Are Not Enough: Problem-Solving Courts and the Impending Crisis of Legitimacy." *Southern Methodist University Law Review* 57 (Fall): 1459–1519.

Daicoff, Susan. 2000. "The Role of Therapeutic Jurisprudence Within the Comprehensive Law Movement." *Practicing Therapeutic Jurisprudence: Law as Helping Profession*, eds. Dennis P. Stolle, David B. Wexler, and Bruce J. Winick. Durham, NC: Carolina Academic Press.

Freedland, Jonathan. 1998. *Bring Home the Revolution: The Case for a British Republic*. London: Fourth Estate.

Freiberg, Arie. 2001. "Problem-Oriented Courts: Innovative Solutions to Intractable Problems?" *Journal of Judicial Adminstration* 11(1): 8–27.

Freiberg, Arie. 2001. "Three Strikes and You're Out—It's Not Cricket: Colonization and Resistance in Australian Sentencing." *Sentencing and Sanctions in Western Countries*, eds. Michael Tonry and Richard S. Frase. Oxford: Oxford University Press.

Furedi, Frank. 2004. *Therapy Culture: Cultivating Vulnerability in an Uncertain Age*. New York: Routledge.

Geertz, Clifford. 1983. *Local Knowledge: Further Essays in Interpretive Anthropology*. New York: Basic Books.

Higgins, Paul, and Mitchell B. Mackinem, eds. 2009. *Problem Solving Courts: Justice for the Twenty-First Century*. Santa Barbara, CA: Praeger.

Hora, Peggy Fulton, William G. Schma, and John T. A. Rosenthal. 1999. "Therapeutic Jurisprudence and the Drug Treatment Court Movement: Revolutionizing the Criminal Justice System's Response to Drug Abuse and Crime in America." *Notre Dame Law Review* 74(2): 439–538.

Illouz, Eva. 2008. *Saving the Modern Soul: Therapy, Emotions, and the Culture of Self-Help*. Berkeley: University of California Press.

Imber, Jonathan B., ed. 2004. *Therapeutic Culture: Triumph and Defeat*. New Brunswick: Transaction.

Malkin, Victoria. 2009. "Problem-Solving in Community Courts: Who Decides the Problem?" *Problem-Solving Courts: Justice for the Twenty-First Century?*, eds. Paul Higgins and Mitchell B. Mackinem, 139–159. Santa Barbara, CA: Praeger.

Nelken, David. 2004. "Using the Concept of Legal Culture," *Australian Journal of Legal Philosophy* 29: 1–26.

Nolan, James L, Jr. 1998. *The Therapeutic State: Justifying Government at Century's End*. New York: New York University Press.

Nolan, James L., Jr. 2001. *Reinventing Justice: The American Drug Court Movement*. Princeton: Princeton University Press.

Nolan, James L., Jr., ed. 2002. *Drug Courts: In Theory and in Practice*. New York: Aldine de Gruyter.

Nolan, James L., Jr. 2009. *Legal Accents, Legal Borrowing: The International Problem-Solving Court Movement*. Princeton: Princeton University Press.

Quinn, Mae C. 2009. "The Modern Problem-Solving Court Movement: Domination of Discourse and Untold Stories of Criminal Justice Reform." *Journal of Law and Policy* 31: 57–82.

Rieff, Philip. 1996. *The Triumph of the Therapeutic*. Chicago: University of Chicago Press.

Robinson, Laurie O. 2003. "Commentary on Candace McCoy Paper." *American Criminal Law Review* 40(4): 1535–1539.

Wexler, David B., and Bruce Winick. 1996. *Law in a Therapeutic Key: Developments in Therapeutic Jurisprudence*. Durham, NC: Carolina Academic Press.

Winick, Bruce J., and David B. Wexler. 2003. *Judging in a Therapeutic Key: Therapeutic Jurisprudence and the Courts*. Durham, NC: Carolina Academic Press.

CHAPTER 7

SEARCHING FOR SASQUATCH: DETERRENCE OF CRIME THROUGH SENTENCE SEVERITY

CHERYL MARIE WEBSTER AND
ANTHONY N. DOOB

. . . many go on in search of the allusive man-beast, unde-terred in their quest for cryptozoological truth.

—Gary Popella (2010)

(Sasquatch filmmaker)

[The marginal deterrent effect of harsher sentences on crime] . . . is predicted by the economic model of crime but has proven elusive empirically.

—Kessler and Levitt (1999)

INTRODUCTION

Prison-growth policies have frequently been justified as means of crime reduction through two different criminal justice strategies. On the one hand, deterrence-based theories argue that offenders are dissuaded from committing criminal acts through the threat of harsher punishment. On the other hand, incapacitation-based approaches reduce the opportunity to commit crime by incarcerating offenders for longer periods of time (Pratt, Cullen, Blevins, Daigle and Madensen 2006; Bushway and Paternoster, 2009; Donohue 2009; Bennet, DiIulio, and Walters 1996; Wilson 1975).

This chapter examines the deterrence perspective. Specifically, it focuses exclusively on the marginal deterrent impact of increased sentence severity. We investigate the hypothesis that, through a mechanism of general deterrence, decreases in crime may be achieved through increases in the severity of punishments—a theory which we abbreviate as "deterrence through severity" or DTS.

Within this context, the chapter highlights one of the most striking paradoxes in the field of sentencing. On the one hand, commitment to the DTS perspective continues to be widespread, even constituting a pillar of criminal justice policy in some jurisdictions. On the other hand, the effectiveness of this sentencing objective in reducing crime is almost entirely lacking in empirical verification. Despite enormous research efforts, no credible and consistent body of evidence has been found to support the conclusion that harsher sentences (within ranges conceivable in Western democracies) achieve marginal deterrent effects on crime.

In brief, this chapter examines this sharp disjuncture between research and policy. To this end:

- Section I will review the empirical evidence examining the effectiveness of DTS policies. Our focus will be on the multiple reviews of the deterrence literature as well as the most recent studies conducted during the last several decades, which arguably constitute the most sophisticated tests of marginal deterrent effects.
- Section II will show that, despite this body of evidence, DTS remains a prominent sentencing goal in many jurisdictions.
- Section III will explore several possible explanations for the coexistence of widespread belief in DTS and its lack of empirical foundation.
- The final section of this chapter will discuss the ramifications of our continuing invocation of the DTS objective despite the compelling lack of empirical support of its effectiveness.

The chapter does not address the effectiveness of incapacitation policies in reducing crime. However, this does not suggest that these two criminal justice approaches are unrelated. In fact, there are obvious intersections between them, as harsher sanctions may not only deter potential offenders (as the benefits of criminal activity may no longer outweigh the costs) but also keep those still choosing to commit crime behind bars for longer.

Further, this article does not directly address issues surrounding the other cornerstone of deterrence theories—the (perception of) certainty of apprehension—and its effectiveness in reducing crime (on this sentencing objective, see, for example, Apel and Nagin 2010; Pratt, Cullen, Blevins, Daigle, and Madensen 2006). While "certainty" of punishment is unrelated to sentencing per se, our selective focus on the severity of punishment does not imply that these two deterrence-based strategies are not entwined. Indeed, increased sentence severity can affect police activity and consequently alter the actual likelihood of apprehension. Conversely, harsher sanctions (or simply increased public discussion about them) can temporarily alter the perceived likelihood of apprehension.

I. Empirical Evidence

Since 1978, numerous reviews have been published on the research literature examining the marginal deterrent effect of increased sentence severity on crime. The most prominent examples are listed in table 7.1. The virtues of examining these comprehensive summaries are twofold: they amass a large number of studies, permitting us to draw general conclusions about the deterrent effects of variations in sentence severity and they allow us to discern trends over time, providing insights into the stability of results.

Table 7.1. Reviews of the Deterrence Literature (1975–2010)

- Blumstein, Cohen, and Nagin (1978) U.S. National Academy of Sciences (1978)
- Cook (1980) *Crime and Justice*
- Lewis (1986) British Journal of Criminology
- Canadian Sentencing Commission (1987)
- Cavanagh (1993) for U.S. Office of National Drug Control Policy
- Nagin (1998) *Crime and Justice*
- Tonry (1998) *Handbook of Crime and Justice* (1998)
- Sentencing project (1996)
- Greenwood et al. (1996) *Three Strikes: You're Out!*
- Cambridge, Institute of Criminology (von Hirsch et al., 1999)
- Levitt (2002) *Crime: Public Policies for Crime Control*
- Doob and Webster (2003) *Crime and Justice*
- Pratt, Cullen, Blevins, Daigle, and Madensen (2006) *Taking Stock*
- Tonry (2008) *Crime and Justice*
- Bushway and Paternoster (2009) *Do Prisons Make us Safer?*
- Tonry (2009) *Crime and Justice*
- Apel and Nagin (2010) *Crime*

Most notably, the vast majority of these comprehensive summaries found no convincing evidence suggesting that harsher sentences deter. In fact, only two of them (Lewis and Levitt) claim that harsher sanctions reduce crime. Further, these latter reviews provide only weak evidence in support of a DTS effect, as neither of them purport to be comprehensive, failing to address most of the relevant research literature. In addition, they are based on a highly selected group of papers of questionable value. Specifically, Lewis's summary (1986) was based on a small and selective set of studies, largely used a single methodology, and presented evidence that was not entirely consistent with the conclusions drawn by the original authors. Levitt's review of deterrence generally (2002) only dedicated approximately three of 16 pages to the deterrent impact of harsh sentences other than execution. Moreover, the bulk of his discussion focused on three of his own studies (one of which he suggests is only marginally relevant since its effects could be explained without invoking deterrence).

Equally notable, the other 15 reviews generally become bolder in their rejection of the DTS theory over time. Certainly until the turn of the century, most deterrence scholars were reluctant to conclude that variation in the severity of sentences (within ranges that are plausible in Western countries) does *not* have an impact on crime. Instead, the majority suggested that more evidence was needed before a firm conclusion could be drawn. More recently, stronger statements have emerged, likely reflecting both the sheer accumulation of studies over the past 40 years that continue to show no credible or consistent support for the DTS theory, as well as the increasingly more sophisticated methodologies available to test this effect. Drawing potentially the boldest conclusions, Doob and Webster (2003, 143)—with agreement from Tonry (2008, 2009)—affirm simply that "it is time to accept the null hypothesis [that] variation in the severity of sanctions is unrelated to levels of crime." However, even those who continue to advocate additional research acknowledge that the deterrent perspective "falls well short of being a theory that should continue to enjoy the allegiance of criminologists" (Pratt et al. 2006, 385). Bushway and Paternoster (2009, 144) sum up the problem: "We . . . have evidence of countless criminal-justice policies (such as laws that provide for enhanced punishments for gun crimes), with no evidence that such laws effectively prevent crime (McDowall, Loftin and Wiersema 1995)."

Doob and Webster (2003) critically reviewed a number of individual studies which are held as evidence that harsher sentences deter crime. Two important observations emerged. First, these studies frequently suffer from one or more methodological, statistical, or conceptual problems that undermine the validity of their conclusions. Even with more sophisticated research, any identified marginal deterrent effects of sentence severity on crime are generally statistically non-significant and too weak to be of substantive significance (Pratt et al. 2006, 385).

Second, this literature has generally been unable to meet the conventional burden of proof in order to accept the DTS hypothesis. Specifically, researchers—like responsible policy makers—contextualize individual studies within the broader literature in order to look for consistency or robustness. A particular finding of a marginal deterrent effect that has not been replicated across comparable people, offenses, and settings lends little persuasive support to the DTS theory. Indeed, it is likely that the effect is the result of other (non-deterrent) factors that have not been controlled. In fact, Pratt et al. (2006, 384) found in their meta-analysis that "the effect sizes of the deterrence variables are substantially reduced—often to zero—in multivariate models." Further, consistent theoretical justifications have been lacking that might explain the existence of a deterrent effect in one study but not in others of a similar nature (for a useful illustration, see McDowall et al. 1992). Without an explanation of the particular deterrent mechanism at work, it becomes impossible to predict when and in which situations one can expect to find a marginal deterrent effect (see also Tonry 2009).

In striking contrast is the much larger body of research that fails to find support for DTS. Illustratively, Doob and Webster (2003) focused their examination on those individual studies that assessed the impact of changes in sentencing laws that occurred since the early 1990s in the United States. This recent body of literature is impressive in its scope and volume and constitutes some of the most methodologically sophisticated tests of the DTS theory. Despite almost ideal circumstances for finding a deterrent effect (e.g., widespread publicity surrounding the sudden and dramatic changes in sentencing severity; actual implementation of the new laws), no consistent support was found. Similarly, the only consistency that Tonry (2009) identified in his review of 15 studies of three-strikes legislation was the repeated lack of support for DTS policies. This finding has been demonstrated across multiple methodologies (e.g., cross-sectional comparisons, longitudinal studies), units of analysis (e.g., states, counties, cities, etc.), types of sentencing laws (e.g., "three strikes" legislation, mandatory minimum penalties, habitual offender laws) and objects of study (e.g., legislative changes, offenders' thought processes) (Doob and Webster, 2003).

II. CONTINUING PROMINENCE OF THE DTS THEORY AS A SENTENCING OBJECTIVE

Given the significant body of deterrence literature that has amassed over the last 30 to 40 years and the consistency of its findings over time, place, measures, and methods, it is no coincidence that sentencing systems that do not subscribe to DTS—in part or in whole—already exist in several Western nations. For instance, the Canadian Parliament enacted new youth criminal justice legislation in 2003 that clearly distanced itself from traditional utilitarian purposes of sentencing, instead establishing a proportionality model of official response to crime. More importantly for our current purposes, it completely removed deterrence from its sentencing principles (Webster and Doob 2007).

Equally notable, several European countries have largely (if not entirely) abandoned the traditional theory of general deterrence whereby crime is reduced through the threat or fear of harsher sanctions. It has been superseded in Germany and Portugal by a variant of this utilitarian sentencing objective, referred to as affirmative or positive general prevention. Accordingly, the primary purpose of criminal sanctions is the public reaffirmation of the validity of basic social norms that have been violated by the offender's flagrant norm violation (Weigend 2001, 209; Figueiredo Dias 1993, 72–73). In Finland, a similar justification of punishment—designated as general prevention—has been adopted. Paralleling, to a large extent, notions of denunciation, this sentencing theory argues in favor of the "moral-creating and value-shaping effect of punishment" whereby people refrain from illegal behavior because "the norms of criminal law and the value they reflect are internalized" such that crime is regarded as morally blameworthy (Lappi-Seppälä 2000, 28).

However, 40 years of empirical research on the DTS hypothesis appears to have had little effect on the commitment of a number of other Western democratic countries to harsher sanctions, particularly in the English-speaking world. In the United States, the theoretical gap created by the decline in rehabilitation-based indeterminate sentencing in the 1970s was largely filled by deterrence (Wilson 1975; Ruth and Reitz 2003; Gottschalk 2006). Indeed, such legislative policies as the introduction or escalation of mandatory minimum sentences, "three strikes" laws, or habitual offender legislation have been mobilized in numerous American states—most notably Florida and California—in pursuit of increased marginal deterrence (Tonry 1996; Zimring, Hawkins, and Kamin 2003).

Glimpses of the continuing role played by the DTS hypothesis can also be seen in England. Illustratively, despite the intention of the 1990 White Paper to give primacy to sentencing based on proportionality, this legislation was "reinterpreted" by the Court of Appeal to include deterrence as a primary sentencing objective. In speculating about the reasoning behind such guidance for the lower courts, Ashworth (2001, 78) suggests that it was likely part of the wider struggle for power between the judiciary and Parliament whereby "judges were announcing 'business as usual, despite the small inconvenience of a statutory intrusion.'" Although the same Court of Appeal subsequently criticized the government's belief in the marginal deterrent effects of harsher sanctions (Taylor 1996, cited in Ashworth 2001, 78).), the very need to call attention to the limitations of DTS policy underlines its continued invocation.

Similar commitment to the DTS theory can be found in Canada. While sentencing provisions in the Criminal Code of Canada have historically stipulated a smorgasbord of purposes from which trial judges can choose, the Canadian Sentencing Commission (1987) reported that deterrence was the utilitarian goal of sentencing most frequently invoked by sentencing judges. Equally relevant would be the complete disregard by legislators of this commission's recommendation—based on its evaluation of the deterrence literature—that "deterrence cannot be used, with empirical justification, to guide the impositions of sentences" (Report of the Canadian Sentencing Commission 1987, 8). In a similar vein, although general deterrence was written out of the law governing young offending in 2003, some judges refused to believe that this sentencing objective could be eliminated and attempted to write it in. As a result, the Supreme Court of Canada was forced to remind them that clearly written laws should be interpreted as they are written (*R v. P (B.W.)* 2006).

Even for those judges who have been compelled by the arguments/research highlighting the limitations of handing down more severe sentences as a means of deterring potential offenders, their rejection of general deterrence as a sentencing objective may arguably be more abstract or theoretical (than practical) in nature. Specifically, it is reasonable to assume that judges—in the actual day-to-day process of sentencing convicted criminals—are focused on the pragmatic issues of sentencing. In the absence of comprehensive sentencing theories to guide their sentences—which is clearly the case in Canada (Doob and Brodeur 1995)—judges are encouraged to think on a case-by-case basis in which the question of sentence severity is decontextualized and determined by intuitions relating to the particular offender being sentenced. Although harsher sanctions may not deter most offenders, judges may believe that in particular instances, with specific types of offenders, an increase in sentence severity may be effective in deterring others. Indeed, it would not seem unreasonable to expect context-specific or offense-specific deterrent effects of harsher sanctions. Unfortunately, the empirical research to-date has generally only found modest—if any—support (see, for example, Pratt et al. 2006 on white-collar/organizational offending).

The political realm has arguably also become a forum for support for DTS policies. Particularly with the "democratization of crime" and the ensuing increase in public concern (Garland 2001), the political salience of sentencing has exploded in many nations. In Canada, starting in 2006, a Conservative government has repeatedly used DTS theory as a justification for a number of apparently popular "crime" bills (Webster and Doob 2007). Parallel political platforms can easily be found in the United States ("Senate's Rule for Its Anti-Crime Bill: The Tougher the Provisions, the Better," cited in Tonry 1996, 146) and England ("If you don't want to do the time, don't do the crime," cited in Doob and Webster 2006, 350).

This message has resonated with the public as well. Whether they have assimilated the frequently repeated messages from politicians and the media that increased sentence severity will make them safer, or these messages are simply consistent with their own beliefs, deterrence as a principal sentencing objective has received wide support. Illustratively, when asked to indicate the importance of each of the "standard" sentencing objectives (deterrence, incapacitation, rehabilitation, compensation, denunciation), a sample of Canadians gave the highest average rating to deterrence for both adult and youth offenders (Doob, Sprott, Marinos, and Varma 1998). Indeed, whether one looks to political, popular, or judicial culture, the belief in the crime-reductive effect of increased sentence severity continues to be firmly rooted and widespread.

III. Explanations for the Disjuncture

The continued commitment to DTS policies is—at the least—perplexing. One could arguably explain the disjuncture between research and actual practice as yet another example of the frequent disregard of empirical research or a general distrust of academics. Indeed, the policy arena is filled with examples, humorously spoofed by *The Onion* in its news report of the mass resignation of 240,000 of America's foremost experts "citing years of frustration over their advice being misunderstood, misrepresented or simply ignored" (*The Onion*, June 16, 1999). However, we suggest that the explanations are more complex, albeit not entirely unrelated to those commonly put forth in similar circumstances.

The Intuitive Nature of General Deterrence

Perhaps the greatest challenge to the empirical evidence in persuading people that harsher sentences are not an effective deterrent to crime resides in the fundamentally intuitive nature of this sentencing objective. It seems natural to assume that changes in disincentives to criminal activity would affect the behavior of a potential offender. Indeed, the notion that people will not engage in prohibited behavior if they know that they will receive a harsh penalty seems so intuitively obvious that one might wonder why it is even necessary to carry out research on the topic.

This intuitive assumption is vividly illustrated by Nobel Laureate (Economics) Ronald Coase when he affirmed that "An economist will not debate whether increased punishment will reduce crime; he will merely try to answer the question, by how much?" (1978, 210). For many economists, the fundamental beliefs in the notions that a higher price lowers the demand and that human beings are rational decision-makers naturally translate—in the language of criminal activity—into the marginal deterrent effect of increased penalties. Empirical evidence is unnecessary because such a relationship constitutes a natural law or truth.

In fact, in an attempt to explain why economists—in contrast with most criminologists—conclude that research on general deterrence demonstrates that variations in sentence severity affect levels of crime, Tonry (2008) proposes that their allegiance to deterrence may be a conscious or unconscious product of ideological commitment. As price theory and the model of rational self-interested behavior constitute two of the cornerstones of economic theories and, more broadly, their view of all social systems, it makes it very difficult—if not impossible—for this discipline to accept (or permit) that criminal behavior represents an "exception" to the "laws" governing human behavior. Rather, these deeply held moral intuitions are affirmed as "simple valuable truths which economics has to offer [to other practitioners]" (Coase 1978, 210).

For the general public, the intuitive nature of the DTS theory may reside fundamentally in the extrapolations from their own "criminal" opportunities and corresponding thought processes to the common offender. When evaluating DTS policies, most individuals are likely thinking of ordinary minor circumstances in which they, themselves, make cost calculations in order to determine whether to commit the offense. In these situations of relatively minor forms of prohibited behavior (e.g., littering), the perceived increase in the severity of sanctions may, in fact, influence the ordinary person's decision to engage in it, in part because he/she perceives a relatively high likelihood of apprehension. A common example would be an increase in the penalty for illegal parking from a small fine to the towing of one's car. From those circumstances, they naturally assume that the process of decision-making involved in engaging in other—more serious—crimes would be the same.

However, the generalization of a deterrent response to the mass of ordinary (property, violence, drugs, prostitution, gambling, etc.) crimes is problematic. As Tonry (2008) notes, these types of criminal behavior are fundamentally different from those in which common citizens might engage. Most ordinary crimes are not highly calculated but are, instead, more impulsive in nature, being committed "under the influence of drugs, alcohol, peer influences, powerful emotions, or situational pressures" (p. 2). Further, the vast majority of them are unambiguously wrong—most people would not commit them under any circumstances. Finally, most of these crimes are committed by individuals "who are deeply socialized into deviant values and lifestyles" (p. 2). While it is natural for the public—as well as judges, for that matter—to over-generalize from their own "deterrent-sensitive" reactions to substantial increases in the severity of penalties for such matters as driving offenses to those of unusual, hypothetical offenders who were already willing to commit more serious crimes for a lesser penalty, this intuitive generalization is faulty.

Indeed, there is a complex sequence of conditions that must be met in order that variation in sentence severity can potentially affect levels of crime (von Hirsch et al. 1999, 7). While people's pro-DTS intuitions assume a simple "if-then" mental construct (that is, *if* a harsher sanction is attached to a particular criminal act, *then* a potential offender will be deterred from committing it), there are at least four pre-conditions for the success of the DTS program. Further, none of these logical steps has received compelling empirical support. It is precisely by unpacking these prerequisites that one can show that the DTS theory is hardly an intuitive "slam dunk." In fact, it becomes clear that it is empirically implausible.

First, for a harsher sanction to have a deterrent impact, individuals must be aware that the punishment has changed in order for harsher sentences to deter. Consequences that are unknown to potential offenders cannot affect their behavior. However, public opinion studies have found repeatedly that most citizens are unable to correctly identify the maximum sanction for most offenses (Roberts and Stalans 1997). Roberts (2003) also reports that people are generally unaware of those crimes for which mandatory minimum sentences are assigned. Similarly, Kleck, Sever, Li, and Gertz (2005) found that those individuals living in more punitive locations did not perceive their locations to be more punitive than those of people living in less punitive areas—a critical link in DTS theory. This result is consistent with other research (see, for example, Doob and Roberts 1982) demonstrating that people are largely ignorant of punishment levels in their communities.

Second, potential offenders must rationally weigh the consequences of their actions before engaging in criminal activity—an assumption also lacking empirical support. Many offenses—particularly those of a violent nature—tend to be committed in the heat of the moment. For instance, a Canadian study on homeless male youth in Edmonton by Baron and Kennedy (1998) suggested that serious crimes committed on the street "are guided more by impulse and the sway of emotion than by reflection or rational judgement, or premeditation" (p. 48). More broadly, research conducted in three Canadian penitentiaries (Benaquisto, 1997) found that when describing their "crime story," only 13 percent of inmates explicitly spoke of their actions in terms of costs and benefits.

Indeed, DTS strategies assume that potential offenders conduct sophisticated analyses of the relative costs of various penalties. In order for harsher sentences to be an effective deterrent, individuals must be willing to commit a crime for which they think that there is a reasonable likelihood of serving the current sanction (for instance, 4 years in prison—the minimum sentence in Canada introduced in 1996 for certain gun-related offenses) but would not do so if they thought that the penalty would be harsher (e.g., a 5-year mandatory minimum sentence for one of these offenses, legislated in 2008). Within this context, it is notable that most of the active and persistent burglars interviewed by Wright and Decker (1994) never even considered the possible consequences of their actions, much less distinguished fine gradations between them.

Third, this criminal justice strategy is dependent on the potential offender perceiving the actual increased penalty as costly or punitive. DTS policies are ultimately perceptual in nature, whereby an individual's assessment of the criminal justice costs associated with illicit activity may not correspond to those projected by legislation (Doob and Webster 2003). Corroborating this premise, research conducted on street youth (Baron and Kennedy 1998) concluded that "[h]arsher penalties would not deter those most at risk for criminal behaviour, [precisely] because [this population is] involved in a lifestyle that reduces the perceptions of risk and provides an environment [in which] criminal behaviour is required and rewarded" (p. 52). In other words, punishment—less or more severe—is frequently seen simply as a rite of passage or part of the "normal" course of life events. Similarly, Foglia (1997) found in her study of the perceived likelihood of arrest on the behavior of inner-city teenagers in a large U.S. northeastern city that " . . . the threat of formal sanctions means little to young people from economically depressed urban neighbourhoods. . . . The irrelevance of arrest is understandable considering these young people have less to lose if arrested" (p. 433).

Fourth, individuals must also believe that there is a reasonable likelihood that they will be apprehended for the offense and receive the punishment that is imposed by a court in order for harsher sanctions to deter crime. In fact, potential offenders rarely even think about getting caught, and when they do, they generally assume that the likelihood of being apprehended is low. In one study (Tunnel 1996), 87 percent of serious offenders reported in interviews that they never thought that they would be caught. Further, a panel study by Pogarsky, Kim, and Paternoster (2005) found that the number of times that the respondent was arrested between the two interviews was unrelated to the respondent's estimate of the change in the perceived certainty of apprehension—a finding that contradicts one of the central tenets of deterrence theory. Specifically, "punished individuals should be less apt to recidivate at least partly because they increase their estimate of the certainty of punishment" (p. 20).

And, in fact, the actual likelihood of apprehension is not more encouraging for those who see crime as controllable through deterrence mechanisms. For example, fewer than half (46 percent) of the robberies committed against adults in 1999 in Canada were reported to the police (Besserer and Trainor 2000). Further, the police were only able to apprehend suspects in approximately 30 percent of these reported cases (Canadian Centre for Justice Statistics 2000). Taken together, the likelihood of a robber being caught and charged with the offense was only 14 percent. A similar reality is found elsewhere. For instance, it is estimated (from victimization surveys) that there were 501,820 robberies in the United States in 2004, of which 61 percent (306,110) were reported to the police. There were 83,710 adults arrested for robbery, of whom 38,850 were convicted. Those convicted, therefore, constitute about 13 percent of the number reported to the police and about 8 percent of those robberies reported by victims (Bureau of Justice Statistics 2010).

Clearly, the number of intervening processes that must take place between (a) the change in penalties for a crime and (b) the possible impact of that alteration on the population of potential offenders is large. Further, the empirical evidence supporting these necessary pre-conditions is generally lacking at best. When viewed from this strictly rational perspective, the very logic upon which the DTS theory rests quickly breaks down. By extension, the lack of evidence in favor of a deterrent effect for variation in sentence severity may gain its own intuitive appeal.

Indistinguishability of Bad and Good Science

It is easy to find "evidence" supportive of the DTS theory, if one's definition of "evidence" is sufficiently relaxed. Certainly in our current era of "tough on crime" approaches to crime and criminals, politicians often use methodologically flawed research—if not blatantly junk science—as a means of either justifying or gaining support for new (generally harsher) criminal justice legislation rooted in a deterrence-based strategy. Given the sheer frequency of this message, it is only natural that people believe what they hear, particularly when the message coincides with their own intuitive beliefs.

Clearly, the challenge is not to locate evidence purporting to show that harsher sentences deter crime. Instead, it is to assess the validity of these findings—that is, to determine the degree of confidence which we can have that the conclusions are accurately drawn. The problem—for most people—is that we lack the expertise needed to critically assess these inferences, particularly from a methodological standpoint. As such, we are simply left with little choice but to accept the findings at face value.

The danger of this approach is that bad science becomes indistinguishable from good science and conclusions with little or no scientific merit are accepted as empirical evidence of the truth. As an illustrative example crossing the U.S.-Canadian border, the Canadian Parliament debated a bill in 2005 that mandated a new set of harsh mandatory minimum sentences based on a Florida law referred to as the "10–20-Life Law." The bill was designed to reduce the use of firearms during the commission of serious offenses. The Parliamentary Committee examining the bill heard from a Florida prosecutor who suggested that:

> Starting in about 1999, the State of Florida implemented several tough-on-crime types of measures, 10–20-Life probably being the most public or having the most notoriety. . . . [In] the 10–20-Life period, violent crime is down 30%. The staggering thing about that is that 10,567 fewer people were robbed, 380 fewer people were killed, and I think the thing that makes those numbers more staggering is that in that same period, the state of Florida's population increased 2.5 million, or 16.8%. I'm a prosecutor. I'm in the courtroom every day. These laws are good; these laws work. (38th Parliament, 1st session, Standing Committee on Justice, Human Rights, Public Safety and Emergency Preparedness. Tuesday, November 22, 2005)

These findings were echoed on the State of Florida's web site which was even more enthusiastic about the deterrent effect of the law. The State's web site declared that:

- In only five years, from 1998–2003, 10–20-Life has helped drive down violent gun crime rates 28 percent statewide.
- During the 10–20-Life era, compared to 1998 statistics, 8,134 fewer people were robbed by armed criminals.

At face value, the findings are impressive. Most ordinary citizens could not help but accept the existence of a marginal deterrent effect of the harsher sanctions. However, this assessment is most likely based on the assumption that levels of crime are stable over time. As such, any change in these rates is automatically attributed to external factors such as the 10–20-Life law. Figure 7.1—a graphical depiction of the trend in Florida's violent crime index from 1989 to 2004—challenges this assumption, giving the careful reader cause for concern.

The problem is one of preexisting trends in violent crime in Florida. Specifically, Piquero (2005) demonstrated that crime generally, and violent crime in particular, had already been decreasing in Florida since about 1990–six years before implementation of the 10–20-Life law. In fact, the rate of decrease appeared higher before the change in the law than afterward. Using sophisticated statistical analyses, Piquero showed that there was no real evidence of a decrease associated with the timing of the change in the law. Rather, other factors occurring simultaneously (e.g., changes in the age structure of the community or the introduction of new crime prevention programs) are likely to have led to the drop in crime.

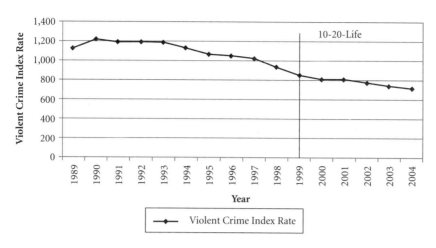

Figure 7.1. Florida's Violent Crime Index Rate, 1989–2004 (from Piquero 2005).

A similar danger is demonstrated by a study by Kessler and Levitt (1999) which examines the impact of California's 1982 Proposition 8—a sentencing enhancement for repeat offenders for a number of eligible crimes in California. Because of the extensive publicity that this new legislation received (increasing the likelihood that potential offenders were aware of the change in the law), the particular harshness of the sanctions (increasing the deterrent impact, if one exists) and the ability of the study to examine the deterrent impact of the law separately from the incapacitative impact (by looking only at the immediate effects of the new legislation that would not be contaminated by any incapacitation effect because the criminal would have been sentenced to prison even without the law change), this study is arguably a powerful test of the marginal deterrent effect of sentence severity on crime rates. Not surprisingly, it is commonly cited as evidence supporting the notion that harsh sentences deter crime.

Kessler and Levitt demonstrate that immediately following the introduction of this new legislation, California experienced a drop in the crime rates of those offenses falling under Proposition 8. Further, this effect is shown to be independent of other state or national changes occurring during this period that may have also affected the crime rates of the eligible offenses. Indeed, this study uses a number of comparison groups in an attempt to rule out other factors that may have affected crime rates in California during the study period. Specifically, the trends in crime rates for those offenses falling under Proposition 8 were compared with those of a number of other offenses not covered by the new law, both within California and for the "rest of the United States."

Once again, the findings are very compelling—at least at first glance. In contrast with the above-mentioned Florida study, the sudden decrease in crime for the eligible offenses coincides almost perfectly with the change in the new law. Figure 7.2 presents graphic illustrations of the crime trends for two eligible

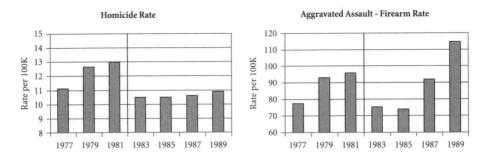

Figure 7.2. Rates of Homicide and Aggravated Assault with a Firearm in California (1977–1989) (from Kessler and Levitt 1999).

offenses. In both cases, crime is increasing until the introduction of Proposition 8 (indicated by the vertical line) and then falls dramatically immediately following the new legislation. The other eligible offenses (not shown) display the same pattern.

However, these findings fail to withstand more careful scrutiny. Webster, Doob, and Zimring (2006) note that Kessler and Levitt conducted their analyses based exclusively on odd-numbered years. When more complete and more detailed crime data were examined, the prima facie support for a deterrent effect is significantly called into question. Figure 7.3 illustrates the problem.

One quickly sees that the crime drop in California actually began before, rather than after, the passing into law of Proposition 8. But equally important, the rise in crime prior to the change in the law was typically higher in California than elsewhere and was typically sharper than was the rise for the other non-eligible offenses (see also Raphael 2006). Simply said, the "controls" or comparison groups used in the study to rule out other possible explanations for the drop in crime were not adequate. It is equally plausible—for example—that the crime rates of the eligible offenses were unusually high at the time of the introduction of Proposition 8 and simply reverted back to their previous levels—a phenomenon (referred to as "regression to the mean") that would have occurred independent of the new law.

As one final illustration of the dangers of uncritical acceptance of study findings, Shepherd (2005) examined the deterrent impact of executions (as the harshest sanction available) on murder rates in the 27 states in the United States that had at least one execution during the period 1977–1999. The findings of this study were mixed. Specifically, Shepherd—an economist—found that following an execution, there was no change in the murder rates in 8 states, an increase in murders in 13 states, and a decrease in murders (a deterrent effect) in 6 states. Based on these findings, she suggests that the states in which murders increased following executions might have experienced a net "brutalization" effect from small numbers of executions. The post hoc argument that she makes is essentially that not enough of a good thing (executions) leads to bad outcomes (murders), but in the case that a

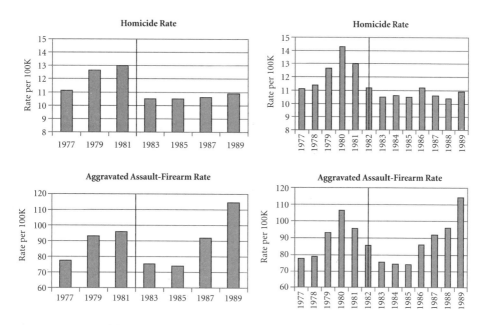

Figure 7.3. Partial (Kessler and Levitt 1999) and Full Data (Webster et al. 2006) for Two Offenses.

substantial number of people are executed (as in South Carolina, Florida, and Texas), a deterrent impact will be shown.

Zimring (2008) is especially critical of this conclusion, pointing out that with only 6 out of 27 states (22 percent) showing a "marginal deterrent effect" of executions on murder rates and 13 showing effects in the opposite direction, her conclusion supporting general deterrence might best be termed a creative leap of faith. The lack of consistency of her findings—even across the 27 states under study—renders her conclusions suspect, since the opposite conclusion could be drawn with a similar degree of empirical support.

From a methodological perspective, Shepherd's findings are not dramatically different from those of Kovandzic, Sloan, and Vieraitis (2004) on the deterrent impact of state-level "three strikes" laws on crime in 188 U.S. cities. They conclude that "[f]or every crime type, the number of states experiencing statistically significant decreases in crime rates over time [after the implementation of 'three strikes' laws] was roughly equivalent to the number of states experiencing significant increases" (p. 229). The difference between these two studies resides in the conclusions. While Shepherd affirms support for the DTS theory, Kovandzic et al. conclude that their study "finds no credible statistical evidence that passage of three strikes laws reduces crime by deterring potential criminals or incapacitating repeat offenders" (p. 234). Without any theoretical basis to justify a deterrent effect in some states but not others or with some offenses and not others, this type of finding simply underlines the meaninglessness of isolated support for deterrence.

Conflation

Conflation constitutes the final element in our trilogy of explanations for the continued primacy of DTS. Specifically, we may be unconsciously blurring or blending this concept with other (different) notions that have, in fact, received empirical support. For example, most people naturally associate sanctions with the criminal justice system more broadly. In other words, ordinary citizens confound the mere criminalization of certain behavior and the knowledge that an array of sanctions is imposed with the marginal deterrent effect of sentence severity. Criminologists (e.g., Apel and Nagin 2010) note that criminalizing certain behavior dissuades most people from engaging in it. A lay-person's statement that "I wouldn't commit crime X if I thought that I would be punished that severely" may simply be a recognition that the criminal justice system as a whole inhibits or deters ordinary people from committing crime but says nothing about the impact of an incremental increase in criminal sanctions.

Another form of potential conflation is rooted in the other cornerstone of deterrence-based approaches to crime control—the issue of certainty. When potential offenders are thinking about committing a crime, their decisions may actually be based on a combination of severity and certainty. For instance, publicity surrounding sanctions (or changes in sanctions) for such offenses as impaired driving may increase the perceived likelihood of apprehension for the crime (e.g., Ross 1982). Certainly in the case that "talk" about penalties makes those penalties seem to be more likely to be imposed, it is not surprising that people will think that (more) severe sanctions will be more likely to deter.

Finally, it is also plausible that judges—and perhaps ordinary people—conflate general deterrence with other sentencing objectives. Most obviously, judges may implicitly merge deterrence-based theories with the Durkheimian notion of norm clarification. That is, sentencing judges may feel that it is important in some fundamental way to "send a message" without recognizing or understanding that the two putative processes are different. Harsher sanctions may be handed down by judges primarily as a means of providing moral education (by underscoring basic social norms through the attachment of consequences) rather than sending an effective threat to potential offenders. In fact, Canadian judges will often justify harsh sentences with the combined invocation of "deterrence and denunciation" without explaining (or perhaps considering) the different mechanisms necessary to achieve these two sentencing objectives. The distinction for judges may not be important because they appear to believe that harsher sentences will increase the likelihood that either goal will be accomplished.

IV. Ramifications of our Continued Belief in DTS Policies

Principled arguments against sentencing according to deterrence principles have been made by others (e.g. von Hirsch 1985). It is not our purpose to review those arguments here. We would simply suggest that in addition to those more theoretically based discussions, serious consideration should be given to those of a more practical or pragmatic nature.

On the one hand, criminological research has identified a number of acute problems accompanying the most extreme examples of severity-enhancing laws that are often supported on DTS grounds. First, they can disrupt the efficient functioning of the courts. Harris and Jesilow (2000) found that in four of five Californian counties implementing "three strikes" laws, the prediction of case outcomes was difficult, significantly hampering plea bargaining and the encouragement of guilty pleas. Further, defendants facing long prison terms were unlikely to agree to plead guilty, increasing the trial rate and, by extension, case-processing times and ulti-mately public expense (see, also, Austin, Clark, Hardyman, and Henry 1999; Merritt, Fain, and Turner 2006).

Second, inconsistencies in the application of the law and the outcome of crim-inal cases occur. Most obviously, both judges and prosecutors have been shown to circumvent laws in cases which they feel are in conflict with standard criminal law principles (Morgan 2000; Harris and Jesilow 2000; Freiberg 2000). Further, the balance of powers in the courtroom is disrupted, whereby the discretionary powers (and hence sentencing powers) of the prosecutor are enlarged at the expense of the judge (Austin et al. 1999; Merritt et al. 2006).

Third, the inflexibility of many of the more draconian laws sometimes results in the imposition of sanctions in individual cases that are unjustly severe (Tonry 1996; Austin et al. 1999). By extension, prison populations (and their high financial burden on the state) have increased, though not necessarily as dramatically as might be projected from a model that assumes complete compliance with the law (Austin et al. 1999). Further, Vitiello (1997) reported that with the introduction of the "three strikes" legislation in California, "adjustments" had to be made whereby the "time served" for non–"three strikes" offenders has had to be reduced dramati-cally in order to make room for "three strikes" offenders. Vitiello (1997) (as well as Tonry 1996) also noted that because these laws often include drug offenses, they are particularly harsh on African Americans.

On the other hand, the negative ramifications of DTS policies extend well beyond the more draconian severity-enhancing laws. In fact, an uncritical accep-tance of this sentencing objective as applied to any offense produces system-wide deleterious effects. Specifically, the act of basing sentencing decisions on the DTS theory encourages people to believe that it is possible to address serious crime problems through the wave of a judge's—or legislature's—arm. By accepting that harsher sentences will act as a general deterrent, legislatures, politicians, and social scientists give members of the public false hope that crime can be easily "cured." Once we believe that the solution to crime resides in the criminal justice system, it becomes a slippery slope toward crises of public confidence and wasted resources.

Indeed, the criminal justice system is very poorly placed to dramatically affect the rates or patterns of criminal activity (Webster 2004). While it continues to play a fundamental role—as a whole—in inhibiting or deterring most people from com-mitting crime through the criminalization and sanctioning of certain behaviors, its ability to achieve additional crime reduction above and beyond this overall effect is substantially limited, particularly through tougher sentencing practices and policies. A persistent belief in DTS theory ensures that the courts—and particularly judges—continue to be "evaluated" according to utilitarian concerns, which are largely beyond their reach, rather than the more realistic task of handing down sentences that are just and fair.

Further, as long as the public believes that crime can be deterred by legislatures or judges through harsh sentences, there is no perceived need to consider other approaches to crime reduction. Indeed, the problem with a focus on general deterrence is that effective crime-reduction strategies are ignored (more broadly, see the discussion on opportunity costs by Donohue 2009). Criminologists (for example, Olds et al. 1998; Tremblay and Japle 2003; Visher and Travis 2003) have identified a number of strategies that have proven to be effective in reducing criminal activity. Moreover, Pratt et al. (2006) note that the size of the impact of *any* of the deterrence strategies is small compared to other crime reduction strategies. It is only with an increasing awareness of the modest effects of the criminal justice system on patterns of crime that we can begin to focus on broad-based prevention rather than limited responses to crime after the fact.

CONCLUSIONS

In the 1970s, the accumulated weight of research on rehabilitative programming brought about a sea change in the practice and orthodoxy of criminal justice policy. The vast majority of methodologically sound studies found that treatment-based sanctions had little positive effect, and some programs were even (unintentionally) criminogenic (Martinson 1974; Sechrest et al. 1979). This message resonated widely across criminal justice systems, academia, and public perceptions.

From the 1980s to the present, the corpus of empirical studies testing the DTS hypothesis is even more damning than the earlier case against rehabilitation theory. Yet, DTS policies still thrive as a powerful determinant of sentencing policy. We would argue that it is past time to encourage policy makers and the public to ask "What works?" in the realm of general deterrence.

Indeed, in discussing their findings, Kessler and Levitt (1999) make a telling statement: "Our results suggest that criminals respond to the severity and not just the certainty of sentences, a result that is predicted by the economic model of crime *but has proven elusive empirically*" (p. 359, italics added). Based on the large body of literature on the marginal deterrent effect of harsher sentences on crime that has accumulated over the past 40 years, "elusive" would necessarily have to be interpreted as "very unlikely." Much like the continuing and unsuccessful search for Sasquatch (a.k.a. Bigfoot), harsh sentencing practices have simply not been shown to be effective in reducing crime, despite a number of isolated sightings.

Strictly speaking, one cannot logically "prove" that harsher sentences do not deter. The proof may exist somewhere, and research may have simply not yet identified where this is. However, the problems with this continuing "search for Sasquatch" approach to understanding the impact of variation in harsher sanctions on levels of crime are multiple in nature and dangerous in their ramifications. Most obviously, it implicitly assumes that evidence that is non-supportive of the DTS hypothesis is—more or less—irrelevant, just as the failure to find Sasquatch behind a given tree tells us little about whether he might be behind another tree. However, with no adequate theories to predict when and where to expect a "deterrent effect," this approach is seriously flawed.

While one must always reserve judgment for the possibility that—in the future—someone may discover persons, offenses, or situations in which the relative severity of sentences does, in fact, have a credible and robust impact on crime, it would seem that the responsible approach until such time is to conclude that currently in Western countries, with the methods and measures presently available, variation in sentence severity does not affect the levels of crime in society. In more practical terms, DTS should no longer be a basis of determining sentence severity. Indeed, the continued centrality of this deterrence theory as a sentencing objective constitutes a false promise, contributing to a waste of resources and a reduction in the public's confidence in the criminal justice system, while encouraging policy makers to ignore more effective crime control strategies.

REFERENCES

Apel, Robert, and Daniel S. Nagin. 2010. "Deterrence." In *Crime*, 4th ed., eds. James Q. Wilson and Joan Petersilia. Oxford: Oxford University Press.

Ashworth, Andrew. 2001. "The Decline of English Sentencing and Other Stories." In *Sentencing and Sanctions in Western Countries*, eds. Michael Tonry and Richard S. Frase, 62–91. Oxford: Oxford University Press.

Austin, James, John Clark, Patricia Hardyman, and D. Alan Henry. 1999. "The Impact of 'Three Strikes and You're Out.'" *Punishment and Society* 1: 131–162.

Baron, Stephen W., and Leslie W. Kennedy. 1998. "Deterrence and Homeless Male Street Youths." *Canadian Journal of Criminology* 40(1): 27–60.

Benaquisto, Lucia. 1997. "The Non-Calculating Criminal: Inattention to Consequences in Decisions to Commit Crime." Unpublished paper. Montreal: Department of Sociology, McGill University.

Bennett, William J., John J. Diulio, Jr., and John P. Walters. 1996. *Body Count: Moral Poverty . . . And How to Win America's War Against Crime and Drugs*. New York: Simon and Schuster.

Besserer, Sandra, and Catherine Trainor. 2000. *Criminal Victimization in Canada, 1999*. Ottawa: Statistics Canada, Canadian Centre for Justice Statistics.

Blumstein, Alfred, Jacqueline Cohen, and Daniel Nagin, eds. 1978. *Deterrence and Incapacitation: Estimating the Effects of Criminal Sanctions on Crime Rates*. Washington, DC: National Academy of Sciences.

Bureau of Justice Statistics. 2010. *Sourcebook for Criminal Justice Statistics*. Available at: http://www.albany.edu/sourcebook/ (accessed September 26, 2010).

Bushway, S., and R. Paternoster. 2009. "The Impact of Prison on Crime." In *Do Prisons Make Us Safer?*, eds. Stephen Raphael and Michael A. Stoll, 119–150. New York: Russell Sage Foundation.

Canadian Centre for Justice Statistics. 2000. Canadian Crime Statistics. *Catalogue no. 85–205-XPE*. Ottawa: Statistics Canada.

Canadian Sentencing Commission. 1987. *Sentencing Reform: A Canadian Approach*. Ottawa: Minister of Supply and Services, Canada.

Cavanagh, David P. 1993. "Relations Between Increases in the Certainty, Severity, and Celerity of Punishment for Drug Crimes and Reductions in the Level of Crime, Drug Crime, and the Effects of Drug Abuse." Report conducted by Botec Analysis Corporation for the Office of National Drug Control Policy.

Coase, Ronald. 1978. "Economics and Contiguous Disciplines." *Journal of Legal Studies* 7: 210–211.

Cook, Philip J. 1980. "Research in Criminal Deterrence: Laying the Groundwork for the Second Decade." In *Crime and Justice: An Annual Review of Research*, vol. 2, eds. Norval Morris and Michael Tonry. Chicago: University of Chicago Press.

Donohue, John J. 2009. "Assessing the Relative Benefits of Incarceration: The Overall Change over the Previous Decades and the Benefits on the Margin." In *Do Prisons Make Us Safer? The Benefits and Costs of the Prison Boom*, eds. Steven Raphael and Michael Stoll. New York: Russell Sage Foundation.

Doob, Anthony N., and Jean-Paul Brodeur. 1995. "Achieving Accountability in Sentencing." In *Accountability for Criminal Justice: Selected Essays*, ed. Philip Stenning, 376–396. Toronto: University of Toronto Press.

Doob, Anthony, and Julian Roberts. 1982. *Crime and the Official Response to Crime: The View of the Canadian Public*. Ottawa: Department of Justice, Canada.

Doob, Anthony N., Jane B. Sprott, Voula Marinos, and Kimberly N. Varma. 1998. *An Exploration of Ontario Residents' Views of Crime and the Criminal Justice System*. Toronto: University of Toronto, Centre of Criminology.

Doob, Anthony N., and Cheryl Marie Webster. 2003. "Sentence Severity and Crime: Accepting the Null Hypothesis." *Crime and Justice: A Review of Research*, vol. 30, ed. Michael Tonry, 143–195. Chicago: University of Chicago Press.

Figueiredo Dias, Jorge de. 1993. "Direito Penal Português. Parte Geral II: *As Consequências Jurídicas do Crime*." Lisbon: Aequitas Editorial Notícias.

Foglia, Wanda D. 1997. "Perceptual Deterrence and the Mediating Effect of Internalized Normals among Inner-City Teenagers." *Journal of Research in Crime and Delinquency* 34: 414–442.

Freiberg, Arie. 2000. "Affective versus Effective Justice: Instrumentalism and Emotionalism in Criminal Justice." *Punishment and Society* 65: 547–559.

Garland, David. 2001. *The Culture of Control: Crime and Social Order in Contemporary Society*. Chicago: University of Chicago Press.

Gottschalk, Marie. 2006. *The Prison and the Gallows: The Politics of Mass Incarceration in America*. Cambridge: Cambridge University Press.

Greenwood, Peter, C. Peter Rydell, Allan F. Abrahamse, Jonathan P. Caulkins, James Chiesa, Karyn E. Model, and Stephen P. Klein. 1996. "Estimated Benefits and Costs of California's New Mandatory-Sentencing Law." In *Three Strikes and You're Out: Vengeance as Public Policy*, eds. David Shichor and Dale K. Sechrest. Thousand Oaks, CA: Sage.

Harris, John C., and Paul Jesilow. 2000. "It's Not the Old Ball Game: Three Strikes and the Courtroom Workgroup." *Justice Quarterly* 17: 185–203.

Kessler, Daniel, and Steven D. Levitt. 1999. "Using Sentence Enhancements to Distinguish Between Deterrence and Incapacitation." *Journal of Law and Economics* 42: 343–363.

Kleck, Gary, Brion Sever, Spencer Li, and Mac Gertz. 2005. "The Missing Link in General Deterrence Research." *Criminology* 43(3): 623–659.

Klepper, Steven, and Daniel Nagin. 1989. "Tax Compliance and Perceptions of the Risks of Detection and Criminal Prosecution." *Law and Society Review* 23: 209–240.

Kovandzic, Thomislav V., John J. Sloan, III, and Lynne M. Vieraitis. 2004. "Striking Out as Crime Reduction Policy: The Impact of 'Three Strikes' Laws on Crime Rates in U.S. Cities." *Justice Quarterly* 21(2): 207–239.

Lappi-Seppälä, Tapio. 2000. "The Fall in the Finnish Prison Population." *Journal of Scandinavian Studies in Criminology and Crime Prevention* 1: 27–40.

Levitt, Steven D. 1996. "The Effect of Prison Population Size on Crime Rates: Evidence from Prison Overcrowding Litigation." *Quarterly Journal of Economics* 111: 319–351.

Levitt, Steven D. 1998. "Juvenile Crime and Punishment." *Journal of Political Economy* 106: 1156–1185.

Levitt, Steven D. 2002. "Deterrence." In *Crime: Public Policies for Crime Control*, eds.James Q. Wilson and Joan Petersilia. Oakland, CA: Institute for Contemporary Studies Press.

Lewis, Donald E. 1986. "The General Deterrent Effect of Longer Sentences." *British Journal of Criminology* 26: 47–62.

Martinson, R. 1974. "What Works? Questions and Answers about Prison Reform." *The Public Interest* 35: 22–54.

Mauer, Marc, and Malcolm C. Young. 1996. *Truths, Half-Truths, and Lies: Myths and Realities about Crime and Punishment*. Washington, DC: Sentencing Project.

McDowall, David, Colin Loftin, and Brian Wiersema. 1995. "Easing Concealed Firearm Laws: Effects on Homicide in Three States." *Journal of Criminal Law and Criminology* 86: 193–206.

McDowall, David, Colin Loftin, and Brian Wiersema. 1992. "A Comparative Study of the Preventive Effects of Mandatory Sentencing Laws for Gun Crimes." *Journal of Criminal Law and Criminology* 83: 378–394.

Merritt, Nancy, Terry Fain, and Susan Turner. 2006. "Oregon's Get Tough Sentencing Reform: A Lesson in Justice System Adaptation." *Criminology and Public Policy* 5(1): 5–36.

Morgon, N. 2000. "Mandatory Sentencing in Australia: Where We Have Been and Where We Are Going." *Criminal Law Journal* 24: 164–182.

Nagin, Daniel S. 1998. "Criminal Deterrence Research at the Outset of the Twenty-First Century." In *Crime and Justice: A Review of Research*, vol. 23, ed. Michael Tonry. Chicago: University of Chicago Press.

Newburn, Tim. 2002. "Atlantic Crossings: 'Policy Transfer' and Crime Control in the USA and Britain." *Punishment and Society* 4: 165–194.

Olds, David, Charles R. Henderson Jr., Robert Cole, John Eckenrode, Harriet Kitzman, Dennis Luckey, Lisa Pettitt, Kimberly Sidora, Pamela Morris, and Jane Powers. 1998. "Long-term Effects of Nurse Home Visitation on Children's Criminal and Antisocial Behaviour." *Journal of the American Medical Association* 280: 1238–1244.

Onion (The), June 16, 1999. "Nation's Experts Give Up." Available at: http://www.theonion.com/articles (accessed September 26, 2010).

Piquero, Alex R. 2005. "Reliable Information and Rational Policy Decisions: Does Gun Research Fit the Bill?" *Criminology and Public Policy* 4(4): 779–798.

Popella, Gary. 2010, February 2. "Big Foot Filmmaker Sets Sights on Humboldt."Available
at: http://www.ghosttheory.com/2010/02/02/big-foot-filmmaker-sets-sights-on-
humboldt (accessed September 26, 2010).

Pogarsky, Greg, KiDeuk Kim, and Ray Paternoster. 2005. "Perceptual Change in the
National Youth Survey: Lessons for Deterrence Theory and Offender Decision-Making." *Justice Quarterly* 22(1): 1–29.

Pratt, T. C., F. T. Cullen, K. R. Blevins, L. E. Daigle, and T. D. Madensen. 2006. "The
Empirical Status of Deterrence Theory: A Meta-Analysis." In *Taking Stock: The Status
of Criminological Theory*, eds. F. T. Cullen, J. P. Wright, and K. R. Blevins. Piscataway,
NJ: Transaction Publishers/Rutgers University Press.

Raphael, Steven. 2006. "The Deterrent Effects of California's Proposition 8: Weighing the
Evidence." *Criminology and Public Policy* 5(3): 471–478.

Roberts, Julian V. 2003. "Public Opinion and Mandatory Sentencing." *Criminal Justice and
Behavior* 30: 483–508.

Roberts, Julian V., and Loretta J. Stalans. 1997. *Public Opinion, Crime, and Criminal Justice.*
Boulder: Westview Press.

Ross, H. Laurence. 1982. *Deterring the Drinking Driver: Legal Policy and Social Control.*
Lexington, MA: Lexington Books.

Ruth, Henry, and Kevin R. Reitz. 2003. *The Challenge of Crime: Rethinking Our Response.*
Cambridge, MA: Harvard University Press.

Sechrest, L., S. G. West, M. A. Phillips, R. Redner, and W. Yeaton. 1979. "Some Neglected
Problems in Evaluation Research: Strength and Integrity of Treatments." In *Evaluation
Studies Review Annual*, Vol. 4., eds. L. Sechrest, S. G. West, M. A. Phillips, R. Redner,
and W. Yeaton, 15–35. Beverly Hills, CA: Sage.

Shepherd, Joanna M. 2005. "Deterrence versus Brutalization: Punishment's Differing
Impacts among States." *Michigan Law Review* 104: 203–255.

Tonry, Michael. 1996. *Sentencing Matters.* New York: Oxford University Press.

Tonry, Michael. 1998. *The Handbook of Crime and Justice.* Oxford: Oxford University Press.

Tonry, Michael. 2008. "Learning from the Limits of Deterrence Research." In *Crime and
Justice: A Review of Research*, vol. 37, ed. Michael Tonry, 279–312. Chicago: University
of Chicago Press.

Tonry, Michael. 2009. "The Mostly Unintended Effects of Mandatory Penalties: Two
Centuries of Consistent Findings." In *Crime and Justice: A Review of Research*, ed.
Michael Tonry. Chicago: University of Chicago Press.

Tremblay, Richard E., and Christa Japel. 2003. "Prevention During Pregnancy, Infancy, and
the Preschool Years." In *Early Prevention of Adult Antisocial Behaviour*, eds. David P.
Farrington and Jeremy W. Coid. Cambridge: Cambridge University Press.

Tunnell, Kenneth D. 1996. "Choosing Crime: Close Your Eyes and Take Your Chances." In
Criminal Justice in America: Theory, Practice, and Policy, eds. Barry W. Hancock and
Paul M. Sharp. Upper Saddle River, NJ: Prentice-Hall.

Visher, Christy A., and Jeremy Travis. 2003. "Transitions from Prison to Community:
Understanding Individual Pathways." *Annual Review of Sociology* 29: 89–113.

Vitiello, Michael. 1997. "Three Strikes: Can We Return to Rationality?" *The Journal of
Criminal Law and Criminology* 87(2): 395–481.

Von Hirsch, Andrew. 1985. *Past or Future Crimes: Deservedness and Dangerousness in the
Sentencing of Criminals.* New Brunswick, NJ: Rutgers University Press.

Von Hirsch, Andrew, Anthony E. Bottoms, Elizabeth Burney, and Per-Olof Wikström.
1999. *Criminal Deterrence and Sentence Severity: An Analysis of Recent Research.*
Oxford: Hart.

Webster, Cheryl Marie. 2004. "Limits of Justice: The Role of the Criminal Justice System in Addressing the Problem of Crime." In *From Enforcement and Prevention to Civic Engagement: Research on Community Safety*, eds. Bruce Kidd and Jim Phillips, 96–121. Toronto: Centre of Criminology.

Webster, Cheryl Marie, and Anthony N. Doob. 2007. "Punitive Trends and Stable Imprisonment Rates in Canada." In *Crime and Justice: A Review of Research*, vol. 36, ed. Michael Tonry, 297–369. Chicago: University of Chicago Press.

Webster, Cheryl Marie, Anthony N. Doob and Franklin E. Zimring. 2006. "Proposition 8 and Crime Rates in California: The Case of the Disappearing Deterrent." *Criminology and Public Policy* 5(3): 417–447.

Weigend, T. 2001. "Sentencing and Punishment in Germany." In *Sentencing and Sanctions in Western Countries*, eds. M. Tonry and R. S. Frase. New York: Oxford University Press.

Wilson, James Q. 1975. *Thinking about Crime*. New York: Basic Books.

Wright, R. T., and S. H. Decker. 1994. *Burglars on the Job: Streetlife and Residential Break-Ins*. Boston: Northeastern University Press.

Zimring, Franklin E. 2008. "Criminology and Its Discontents: The American Society of Criminology 2007 Sutherland Address." *Criminology* 46(2): 255–266.

Zimring, Franklin E., Gordon Hawkins, and Sam Kamin. 2003. *Punishment and Democracy: Three Strikes and You're Out in California*. New York: Oxford University Press.

Cases Cited

R v. P (B.W.), 209 CCC(3d) 97 (2006).

Statutes Cited

Criminal Code, R.S.C. 1985, Chapter C-46 (as amended).

CHAPTER 8

RISK ASSESSMENT

CHRISTOPHER SLOBOGIN[1]

RISK assessment is the identification of "risk" factors and "protective" factors that make involvement in crime more or less likely. Risk and protective factors can be either static or dynamic. Static factors are phenomena that cannot be changed through human intervention; dynamic risk factors are those that can be. Typical static factors include gender, age, and prior criminal history, while typical dynamic factors include psychoactive substance use, family support, and motivation to alter behavior. Risk assessment is usually a precursor to or coincident with needs assessment and risk management, which are efforts to identify and implement the best methods of curtailing dynamic risk factors and of enhancing dynamic protective factors (Redding 2009, 3–4, 14).

Risk assessment is often equated with assessment of dangerousness, and needs assessment and risk management are often associated with rehabilitation. These concepts are best kept distinct, however. "Dangerousness" determinations are usually meant to address the binary issue of whether the person will reoffend, while risk assessments are designed to identify the circumstances under which a person is most likely and least likely to offend, the probability that reoffending will occur, and the type of offending that is risked (Heilbrun 2009, 129–30). Rehabilitation is often broadly construed to encompass interventions aimed at making an offender a socially productive individual, while risk management and needs assessment are focused on reducing recidivism. This chapter will use the terms "risk assessment" and "risk management," on the ground that they more accurately describe the type of information that sentencers need to have to make effective decisions.

The central conclusions of the chapter are as follows:

- Initially relegated to parole decision-making, formal risk assessment is playing an increasingly larger role in the initial sentencing decisions that determine which offenders to divert out of the prison system and which offenders to subject to longer sentences.

- Modern risk assessment techniques—particularly actuarial and structured professional judgment instruments—produce error rates below 50 percent, sometimes well below, and the predictions they generate are significantly superior to random selection.
- Nonetheless, the ability of risk evaluators to make precise individualized predictions is compromised by their reliance on risk factors derived from dissimilar validation samples, small variable sets, and data about recidivism based on tangentially relevant outcome measures.
- Because most risk assessment techniques rely in part on demographic variables and other immutable or relatively static personal characteristics, they raise constitutional and normative concerns about whether they can coexist in a system of criminal justice predominantly aimed at punishing individuals based on desert.

THE RELEVANCE OF RISK ASSESSMENT TO SENTENCING

The relevance of risk assessment to sentencing depends on a number of variables, including the type of sentencing regime in place, prison capacity, and attitudes about the efficacy of rehabilitation and incapacitation. In an indeterminate sentencing regime, risk assessment often plays a significant role at both the front and back ends of the process. The sentence range initially imposed by the sentencing body may be reduced or enhanced by perceptions of risk. More significantly, the back-end release decision, usually made by parole boards, is often based entirely on assessments of risk (Chanenson 2005; Rhine, chapter 26 of this volume).

In a determinate sentencing regime, in contrast, parole boards are abolished or at least seriously circumscribed in power (Chanenson 2005). In some of these jurisdictions, consideration of risk may be prohibited at the front end as well as the back end (Frase 2005, 1202–1203). In many other jurisdictions, however, risk can modulate the sentence within the sentencing range dictated by retributive considerations, an approach sometimes called "limiting retributivism" (Morris 1974; Morris and Miller 1985). In most of these latter regimes, the sentence is usually still determinate, because the risk assessment dictates sentence length at the time of sentencing (Harcourt 2007, 96–100).

Many state systems, regardless of sentencing philosophy in the typical case, also divert offenders from prison if they are found to pose a low risk. These diversion programs are designed primarily to free up prison beds for more serious offenders. But they may also be motivated by a belief that risk management in the community through traditional intermediate sanctions or specialized mechanisms such as drug courts can reduce recidivism, both directly through treatment and by avoiding the criminogenic effects of prison (Wolff 2008; Nolan, chapter 6 of this volume).

Finally, in both indeterminate and determinate sentencing jurisdictions, risk assessments can lead to sentence enhancements beyond the usual term. In most states that have the death penalty, "dangerousness" is a statutory aggravator in capital cases; if proven beyond a reasonable doubt, it can justify imposition of the death penalty rather than life without parole (Dorland and Krauss 2005, nn. 5 and 12). A large number of states also have enacted dangerous offender statutes that permit extension of confinement in non-capital cases. For instance, over 20 states authorize confinement of sex offenders for an additional indeterminate period beyond the sentence imposed for their crime if they are found to have a mental abnormality that predisposes them to commit further crimes of sexual violence (Davey and Goodnough 2007).

Types of Risk Assessment

Current risk assessment techniques can be divided into three types: unstructured clinical assessment, actuarial assessment, and structured professional judgment (Hart 2009). Unstructured clinical risk assessment depends upon the evaluator to determine the relevant risk and protective factors and how they should influence the ultimate determination, with the result that neither the information gathered nor the way in which it is analyzed is consistent across evaluators or even, perhaps, across evaluations by the same individual. A variant of clinical risk assessment is anamnestic in orientation, meaning that the evaluator focuses on the precise risk and protective factors that are associated with previous antisocial behavior by the individual in question. This type of evaluation is somewhat more structured, but because it relies on the nuances of the offender's crimes it cannot be called standardized.

Dissatisfied with the unscientific nature of unstructured clinical risk assessment, researchers over the past several decades have developed actuarial prediction devices that rely on empirical discovery of factors associated with recidivism, which are then weighted and combined according to an algorithm that produces recidivism probability estimates. An example of an actuarial device is the Violence Risk Appraisal Guide (VRAG), a 12-item instrument developed on a sample of 685 Canadian offenders. The item accorded the most weight on the VRAG—the score on the Psychopathy Checklist-Revised (PCL-R)—measures theoretically changeable traits, such as glibness, grandiosity, callousness, and other variables associated with psychopathy. But most of the remaining risk factors on the VRAG are static: elementary school misconduct; diagnosis; age at time of triggering offense; absence of one or both parents before 16 other than through death; failure on conditional release;

nonviolent offenses; marital status; victim injury; history of alcohol abuse; and victim gender. Each item is associated with a score that reflects its relative weight (for example, points for the PCL-R rating can total 12, failure on conditional release 3 points, and unmarried status 1 point). The individual item scores are then added and compared to actuarial tables, which categorize individuals within one of nine "bins." A score of 0 through 6 is associated with at least a 35 percent probability of "violent recidivism" within seven years, and a score of 21 through 27 is associated with at least a 76 percent risk of such recidivism over that period (Quinsey et al. 2005).

Perhaps the most widely used actuarial risk assessment device in the sentencing context is the Level of Service instrument, which focuses on numerous dynamic as well as static factors and is used in needs assessment as well. The Level of Service Inventory-Revised requires a 54-item survey of domains such as criminal history, education and employment, financial means, family and marital status, companions, alcohol and drug problems, emotional and personal traits, and attitude and orientation. Most items are scored either 0 (absent) or 1 (present), although some are rated on a 4-point scale. Researchers have also developed other versions of the Level of Service instrument, designed to assist with case management, gauge risk-need-responsivity, and screen offenders to determine who needs further evaluation (Andrews, Bonta, and Wormith 2010).

The third type of risk assessment technique, structured professional judgment, is clinical rather than actuarial in nature, but much more structured than traditional clinical techniques. For instance, the HCR-20 directs the evaluator to consider 20 static and dynamic variables derived from the risk literature, relating to history (e.g., previous violence), clinical features (e.g., negative attitudes), and risk (e.g., lack of personal support). Each of these items can be scored from 0–2 but, in contrast to the actuarial approach, neither the individual nor the combined score is meant to be associated with a particular probability estimate, and factors other than those on the HCR-20 may be considered. The primary goal of this type of instrument is to provide information relevant to needs assessment and a risk management plan rather than to predict antisocial behavior (Douglas and Reeves 2010). A variation of this approach, called adjusted actuarial risk assessment, is to use an actuarial device such as the VRAG to establish a base rate but then to adjust the probability estimate through consideration of other variables. Because these adjustments are not part of the algorithm associated with the actuarial instrument, the resulting judgment cannot be called actuarial (Meehl 2005, 435).

Structured professional judgment tools can be used like actuarial devices, however. For instance, the scores on the HCR-20 can be added and correlated with recidivism rates through follow-up research. Studies examining the accuracy of HCR-20, some of which have included correctional populations, have found that violent acts have subsequently been committed by 54 to 86 percent of the individuals whom HCR-20 evaluators considered high risk, 8 to 59 percent of individuals assigned to a moderate risk category, and 0 to 19 percent of those assigned to the low risk category (Douglas and Reeves 2010, 170). These numbers might provide ballpark probability estimates for offenders who receive similar risk ratings on the HCR-20. The scores on

another structured professional judgment device—the PCL-R—have also been correlated with recidivism rates, and indeed are used in precisely that way on the VRAG.

A final, still nascent form of risk assessment relies on brain imaging. For instance,
evidence from functional magnetic resonance imaging (fMRI) research indicates
that psychopathy is associated with activity in certain areas of the brain when particular stimuli occur. Psychopathy in turn is highly correlated with antisocial behavior.
Thus, in theory, fMRI could assist in assessing risk (Greely 2009, 689–693; Kiehl et
al. 2001). However, fMRI technology is at present too imprecise, and its results too
open to different interpretations, to permit a definitive diagnosis of psychopathy
(Hughes 2010). Even if such a diagnostic procedure were possible, virtually nothing
is yet known about the degree of risk posed by psychopathy when measured neuro-
logically (Baskin, Edersheim, and Price 2007, 264–265; Blair 2003). The most likely
use of such information in the near future is to provide corroboration of risk assessments made through other means and perhaps also to identify individuals who
could benefit from biological or other types of therapy (Greely 2008).

ACCURACY OF RISK ASSESSMENT

Risk assessment methodologies have become increasingly sophisticated, but they
still can result in significant error when used to predict reoffending. Traditionally,
the accuracy of risk assessment has been measured in terms of true positives (persons predicted to recidivate who in fact do reoffend) and true negatives (persons
predicted to be non-dangerous who avoid reoffending) and their opposites, false
positives and false negatives. In practice, false positive rates generally far exceed
false negative rates, both because the relatively lower base rate for reoffending makes
true positives harder to identify and because evaluators have more incentives to err
in the direction of confinement rather than release.

Early studies of risk assessment, usually measuring the accuracy of unstructured
evaluation techniques, produced false positive rates of well over 50 percent (Monahan
1981, 44–49). More recent studies, often measuring the accuracy of actuarial or structured professional judgments of people in presumptively high-risk populations, tend
to produce much lower false positive rates, usually between 15 and 50 percent (Douglas and Reeves 2010, 170; Slobogin 2007, 106–109; Monahan 2006, 408–12). Moreover,
the false positive rates in these studies are probably exaggerated, for two reasons.
First, once a person is predicted to be high risk, he or she is usually confined or
treated, which reduces the likelihood that the predicted outcome (offending) will
occur. Second, the usual outcome measure of recidivism is either conviction or arrest,
both of which significantly underestimate the actual rate of offending if offender self-
reports are to be believed (Farrington 2003; Bremer 1992; Greenwood 1982, 19–26).

Of course, even false positive rates much lower than 50 percent are a concern.
Each false positive can lead to an unjustified sentence enhancement or an erroneous

failure to divert an individual out of the criminal justice system. Yet any attempt to reduce false positives by raising the threshold for enhancement or intervention is likely to raise false negative rates, thus increasing the threat to public safety.

A second method of measuring accuracy that more clearly demarcates this trade-off between false positives and false negatives involves computation of the Receiver Operating Characteristic Curve, which plots true positive rates over false positive rates. The area under this curve (AUC) provides a measure of the extent to which a given cut-off score provides information that is superior to mere chance. An AUC value below .5 means that the evaluation technique produces results worse than chance, while an AUC value of 1 indicates perfect accuracy.

One meta-review found that unstructured clinical risk assessment is associated with AUC values of around .67, while more structured risk assessment techniques produce AUC values ranging from .71 to .78 (Mossman 1994). Other reviews of the accuracy of actuarial and structured professional judgment instruments have calculated AUC values between .62 and .88 (Heilbrun, Yasuhara, and Shah, 2010, 8–13; Rice, Harris and Hilton 2010, 104–105). To understand the practical usefulness of these numbers, consider that, armed with an actuarial method associated with an AUC of .78, evaluators can assign a cut-off score that produces a 30 percent false positive rate and a 20 percent false negative rate or, alternatively, a cut-off score that produces a 20 percent false positive rate and a 40 percent false negative rate.

This discussion should make clear the speciousness of the argument that risk assessment is less accurate than flipping a coin—a contention that appeared, among other places, in the dissenting opinion to the Supreme Court's decision in *Barefoot v. Estelle* (1983, 931; see also Ennis and Litwack 1974). Even a risk assessment technique that produces false positive rates *higher* than 50 percent only compares unfavorably to flipping a coin when the base rate for recidivism in the population of interest is 50 percent or higher. Typically the base rate for recidivism among the relevant populations is much lower, in the 20 to 40 percent range (Rice, Harris and Hilton 2010, 104). That means that modern risk assessment techniques, which produce true positive rates of 50 to 85 percent, obtain results much better than chance. It should also be noted, however, that the risk assessment techniques used in sentencing today do not always perform as well as instruments such as the VRAG and the HCR-20.

Illustrative Uses of Formal Risk Assessment in Sentencing

Until the mid-twentieth century, any risk assessment that took place at sentencing or parole hearings was unstructured. By the late 1950s, however, a few states had begun relying on actuarial prediction for parole decision-making purposes (Harcourt 2007, 69). By the end of the 1980s, the sentencing guidelines adopted by the federal government and a number of states had also incorporated a primitive form of structured risk assessment—consisting entirely of prior criminal history—into front-end sentencing (Harcourt 2007, 84).

In the past decade, states have adopted more sophisticated risk and needs assessment schemes, in what has recently come to be called "evidence-based sentencing." An early example of this trend is Virginia, which after experimenting with the idea in the late 1990s, began statewide use of a risk assessment tool in 2002 for the purpose of deciding which offenders should be diverted from prison. Ironically, the state established this diversion program because of its passage of "truth-in-sentencing" legislation that abolished parole and required that all felons serve at least 85 percent of their sentences. To relieve the prison overcrowding caused by this move toward determinate sentencing, the legislature directed that 25 percent of the nonviolent offenders who would normally receive a prison sentence instead be given alternative punishments (Virginia Code §17–235, 1994). Since 2002, the selection of offenders to be diverted has been based in part on an actuarial instrument validated on a study of released Virginia prisoners and composed of nine factors (type of offense, gender, age, employment status, marital status, and four factors related to criminal record) (Virginia Commission 2001, 83).

As of 2007, this program had reduced the proportion of nonviolent offenders in Virginia's prisons to approximately 20 percent, compared to 75 percent of federal prisoners (Virginia Commission 2007, 18). Even so, many of those offenders judged to be low risk on the basis of the actuarial instrument ended up in prison, because judges in Virginia retain sentencing discretion and frequently exercise it to prevent diversion; in 2009, for instance, 59 percent of eligible nonviolent offenders who were considered low risk according to the instrument still received a prison sentence of at least one year (Virginia Commission 2009, 36). With respect to those offenders who *are* diverted, a 2002 study found that, of 555 offenders diverted from prison using the initial version of the actuarial instrument, 36 (6.6 percent) were convicted of a new felony within an average of two years, while 95 (17.1 percent) were arrested for a new felony and 159 (or 28.6 percent) were arrested for a new felony or misdemeanor during that time period (NCSC 2001, 120). These figures do not reveal how many false positives the instrument generated, but do elucidate its trade-off in terms of false negatives.

Virginia also enhances sentences for sex offenders based on an actuarial risk assessment instrument similar to the VRAG but normed on a Virginia sex offender population (Virginia Commission 2001, 55–58). Under sentencing guidelines promulgated in 2001, the maximum guidelines range for offenders scoring 28 points or more on this instrument is increased substantially, by 50 percent if the score is 28 through 33 (Level 1), by 100 percent if the score is 34 through 43 (Level 2), and by 300 percent if the score is 44 or higher (Level 3). Again, however, Virginia judges have frequently exercised their sentencing discretion, and in 2009 they only used their extended guidelines range authority in 14 percent, 28 percent, and 11 percent of Levels 1, 2, and 3 cases, respectively (Virginia Commission 2009, 39–40).

A few other states have developed similar risk assessment programs. Missouri relies on an instrument with 11 factors (6 relating to prior criminal history, as well as age, escape history, employment status, education, and substance abuse) to place offenders within one of five risk groups, which in turn are used by judges to decide between prison and community placement as well as to assist in determining the duration of an offender's prison sentence (Wolff 2006, 113–114). At least one jurisdiction in Oregon uses a form of risk assessment that relies on data about which prison or community dispositions are most likely to reduce recidivism by particular types of offenders, described in terms of offense, gender, age, and race, among other characteristics (Marcus 2005).

In those states that have retained parole, formal risk assessment continues to play a significant role. The Georgia Parole Board has developed an actuarial risk assessment instrument that automatically updates risk on a daily basis for the state's 21,000 parolees (Warren 2009, 604). California also recently instituted a risk assessment regime for parole violators, based on what it calls the Parole Violation Decision Making Instrument (PVDMI). The PVDMI begins with an actuarial risk assessment that relies on 22 static risk indicators primarily focusing on criminal history (but also including age and gender) to determine the likelihood that an offender will be arrested for a felony within a three-year period. The parole severity score that results helps to determine the intensity of response to a parole violation, ranging from reimprisonment to outright release. However, parole officials can modify this response if, in their opinion, the offender exhibits "stabilizing" factors such as solid social support, job stability, and positive performance history, or "destabilizing" factors such as an unstable home situation, escalating drug or alcohol addiction, or a chronic pattern of violations while under supervision. This adjusted actuarial approach is subject to several layers of review, including a possible hearing in front of the Board of Parole Hearings (California Regulations 2009).

Finally, in states that authorize post-sentence commitment of sex offenders, risk assessments are routine. The most popular actuarial instrument in this context is the Static-99, which produces four types of probability estimates (low, moderate-low, moderate-high, and high) based on ten factors: age, live-in relationships, three items relating to the victim, and five items pertaining to prior offenses (Anderson and Hanson 2010). A structured professional judgment device that is widely used in connection with evaluations of sex offenders is the Sexual Violence Risk-20, which looks at 20 factors in the domains of psychosocial adjustment, history of sexual offenses, and future plans (Hart and Boer 2010).

In short, today risk assessment is a major aspect of sentencing and related practices. A 2006 survey found that about half the states make some use of formal risk assessment instruments in the sentencing or post-sentence process (Warren 2009, 603).

CONSTITUTIONAL/NORMATIVE ISSUES

Risk assessment implicates at least three constitutional provisions. The first is the Sixth Amendment's right to jury trial. In a line of cases driven by *Apprendi v. New Jersey* (2000), the U.S. Supreme Court has established that facts other than prior convictions that lead to a term longer than the normal maximum sentence must be found by a jury beyond a reasonable doubt (see also *Blakely v. Washington* 2004; *United States v. Booker* 2005). As a result of *Apprendi*, to the extent a punishment based on risk assessment extends beyond the statutory maximum, or beyond the guidelines maximum in a system in which guidelines are presumptive, the ultimate conclusion about risk must come from a jury. By analogy to the requirement that each element of a crime be proven to the jury, *Apprendi* might also require a jury finding beyond a reasonable doubt with respect to each *individual* risk factor (other than prior convictions), whether they are prior arrests, employment status, or "negative attitude."

The impact of *Apprendi* jurisprudence on risk-based sentencing is minimal, however. The right to a jury determination probably does apply when dangerousness is an aggravating factor in a capital case (*Ring v. Arizona* 2002). But because most non-capital sentences based on risk stay within statutory and guideline ranges, this type of constitutional challenge will otherwise be rare. Even in Virginia, where guideline ranges for sex offenders are explicitly extended based on risk, the Sixth Amendment is not applicable because Virginia's guidelines are voluntary rather than mandatory (cf. *Luttrell v. Commonwealth* 2004). Only if the sex offender's sentence were raised above the statutory maximum would *Apprendi* be implicated. Dangerous- and sex-offender statutes that permit post-sentence commitment also avoid running afoul of the Sixth Amendment, because confinement that is focused entirely on incapacitation and rehabilitation is, according to the Supreme Court, a "civil" measure rather than "punishment" (*Kansas v. Hendricks* 1997).

A second constitutional provision possibly implicated by risk assessment is the Equal Protection Clause of the Fourteenth Amendment, which could form the basis for a challenge that certain risk factors illegitimately discriminate between offenders. Under traditional Fourteenth Amendment analysis, use of race, ethnicity, and religious beliefs as risk factors should require a compelling justification, rather than merely a rational one, and use of factors such as gender, age, and alienage to determine risk should or could trigger intermediate scrutiny of the government's justification (*United States v. Virginia* 1996, 530–534). The government's goal of protecting the public is undoubtedly compelling. But because the first three factors (race, ethnicity, and religious beliefs) are considered highly suspect classifications, traditional Fourteenth Amendment analysis would also require the government to show that their use as risk factors is crucial to achieving that objective. Such a showing is unlikely, given the less-than-robust correlation between these characteristics and risk, as well as the large number of other risk factors available to the government. In any event, most courts have accepted the proposition that race may not be considered in determining dangerousness (see *United States v. Taveras* 2008, 336; *Gonzalez v. Quarterman* 2006, 389).[2]

In contrast, age and gender play a significant, if not crucial, role in many actuarial risk assessments, and under the Equal Protection Clause the government justification for using these quasi-suspect classifications need not be as strong. Thus, reliance on these types of risk factors is less open to constitutional challenge

(Monahan 2006; *Brooks v. Commonwealth* 2004). A more complicated question is whether risk factors that might serve as a proxy for one of these classifications are legitimate. For instance, employment and education status could be statistical stand-ins for both race and age. Under current equal protection law, however, unless the intent behind using these types of factors is race- or age-motivated, such a claim is likely to fail (Cf. *San Antonio v. Rodriguez* 1973, 24–29; *McCleskey v. Kemp* 1987).

A closely related concern about risk assessment is that it is fundamentally at odds with the purposes of criminal punishment. Enhancing the punishment of an offender because of gender, age, or any other immutable characteristic strikes some as grossly unfair: men do not "deserve" more time in prison than women; youthful, single offenders are not more culpable than older, married ones; a person whose father leaves home (a risk factor on the VRAG) is not more blameworthy than a person with an intact family (Goodman 1987; Netter 2007). Others have expanded this criticism to include sentences based on any trait or characteristic, such as diagnosis or employment status, that is not directly related to commission of a criminal act (Monahan 2006). Only risk factors to which moral blame can be attributed, it is argued, are legitimately considered in a system of punishment.

The Supreme Court, however, does not believe that risk assessment is antithetical to criminal justice. It has even approved death sentences based on dangerousness determinations (*Jurek v. Texas* 1976, 275–276). If sentences can be enhanced in response to risk, then neither society's nor the offender's interests are advanced by prohibiting consideration of factors that might aggravate or mitigate that risk simply because they consist of immutable characteristics. In any event, risk-based sentences are ultimately based on a prediction of what a person will do, not what he is; immutable risk factors are merely *evidence* of future conduct, in the same way that various pieces of circumstantial evidence that are not blameworthy in themselves (e.g., presence near the scene of the crime; possession of a weapon) can lead to a finding of guilt (cf. *Malenchik v. State*, 2010, 573–575).

Even if risk assessment can be defended as a matter of theory, however, its increasing influence could alter the nature of criminal justice in undesirable ways (Feeley and Simon 1992; Garland 2001). Hollywood's images of regimes in which prisoners are selected according to genetic makeup or brain chemistry are discomfiting to many (Erickson 2010). The difference between bio-prediction of this sort and a VRAG score, which relies largely on static or congenital factors, is one of degree, not kind.

Linked with this existential concern are the negative consequences of unfair stigmatization that risk assessment might generate. For instance, under the Virginia risk assessment diversion measure, no young, unmarried, and unemployed male offender who has any other aggravating factor (e.g., a prior crime) is eligible for diversion (NCSC Report 2002, 48). While young males who are jobless and single may, all else being equal, be more likely to reoffend, official use of these characteristics in computing sentences may disproportionately taint this group in the eyes of parole officers who make risk assessments, police officers who make arrests, and the public at large. It may even contribute to more crime, if offenders convince themselves that the stereotype is accurate and act accordingly, or if those who don't fit the stereotype think they have a free ride or are ignored by law enforcement authorities pursuing those who fit the risk assessment profile (Harcourt 2007).

Unfair treatment can also result from heavy reliance on static risk factors, an obvious attribute of many actuarial risk assessment instruments, but also implicitly a common aspect of less structured evaluation approaches. To the extent that risk assessments are based on static factors pre-dating the triggering offense, meeting the relevant release criteria may be impossible (unless, for instance, the state is forced to meet increasingly higher levels of proof to continue confinement). This dynamic may explain why so few offenders confined under post-sentence sex offender commitment statutes have been released (Morris 2002, 561; Janus 1996, 206). To avoid this type of legal paralysis, risk assessment must, at the least, be combined with needs assessment and a risk management plan.

A final constitutional challenge to the use of risk assessment, based in due process, is that it is not sufficiently accurate to form the basis for a deprivation of life or liberty. But the Supreme Court rejected this type of argument in *Barefoot v. Estelle* (1983), stating that a contrary holding would be akin to "disinventing the wheel" and would ignore the ability of legal fact-finders, aided by the adversary process, to "separate the wheat from the chaff" (pp. 896, 900). Because *Barefoot* involved government reliance on unstructured clinical testimony in a death penalty proceeding, its generous approach to prediction expertise presumably applies to all other types of risk assessment and in all other sentencing and post-sentence proceedings, at least when they are adversarial in nature.

Barefoot only sets the constitutional floor, however. Jurisdictions are free to impose greater limitations on the admissibility of prediction testimony under their rules of evidence. The Supreme Court's decisions in *Daubert v. Merrell Dow Pharmaceuticals* (1993) and *Kumho Tire v. Carmichael* (1999) and the ensuing changes to the federal rules of evidence require that the basis of all expert testimony be subject to some sort of verification process—ideally involving scientific testing and the production of error rates—that assures it is "reliable" (Federal Rule of Evidence 702, 2010). Expert testimony based on methodologies that produce false positive rates of up to 50 percent and not insubstantial false negative rates might be said to be "unreliable."

Most courts, however, have held that prediction evidence—whether it is clinical or actuarial—is admissible at sentencing proceedings (for summary, see *United States v. Diaz* 2007, *7, *23–24; Slobogin 2007, 108–109). Many of these decisions simply declare that the rules of evidence do not apply in sentencing and post-sentencing contexts (*United States v. Fields* 2007, 342). Others state that, even if *Daubert* or some variant of it applies, that decision allows the judge flexibility in deciding which evidence is admissible (*United States v. Shields* 2008). Evaluating the relative worth of these positions requires delving more deeply into the methodology of risk assessment instruments.

Methodological and Evidentiary Concerns

Each risk assessment technique—unstructured clinical, structured clinical, and actuarial—presents its own methodological challenges. Unstructured clinical prediction is most problematic, for reasons that have already been suggested. First, research has firmly established that predictions based on the clinical method, while typically better than chance, are less valid than actuarial predictions, by a significant magnitude (Janus and Prentky 2003, 1455–1458). Second, clinical predictions are hard to assess in terms of error rates, since the clinical method varies from evaluator to evaluator. Third, experts relying on clinical prediction can at most make general statements about an offender's propensities, such as "the offender poses a higher than average risk." These latter types of statements can mean different things to different evaluators, and in any event are not susceptible to verification. Finally, laboratory research and evidence from actual cases indicates that, despite its more questionable reliability, clinical prediction testimony presented by the government is extremely influential with judges and juries, much more so than actuarial prediction (Krauss et al. 2004; Krauss and Sales 2003; Slobogin 2006). Clinical testimony that a person is likely to be violent is difficult to rebut even with effective cross-examination and opposing witnesses (Diamond, 1996). Fact finders may attribute too much weight to this type of testimony precisely because it is so vague.

Structured clinical judgment, to the extent that it is not linked to probability estimates, shares some of the same drawbacks. An assessment based on an instrument like the HCR-20 is more trustworthy than one based on unstructured clinical judgment because the evaluator is committed to looking at the same 20 factors in each evaluation, all of which the literature has shown are related to risk. However, a conclusion derived from the HCR-20 that an offender is "high risk" is not based on statistical comparison but on the evaluator's sense that a person with a particular HCR-20 profile or score is more likely to reoffend than a person whom the evaluator would designate moderate or low risk. If, as the HCR-20 protocol permits (and as occurs in states like Virginia and California), the evaluator considers other factors besides the 20 designated in the instrument, the evaluation becomes even more like unstructured professional judgment.

Actuarial risk assessment largely avoids all of these deficiencies. It provides error rate information and permits comparison of one offender to another in terms of risk, because it is based on statistical analysis of large groups of offenders. Even when, as often occurs, group error rates are high, they are useful because they provide the fact-finder with information about how much weight to give the evidence (Saks 2003, 1168).

Precisely because of its nomothetic nature, however, actuarial prediction suffers from three other problems. First, the population on which the actuarial device is validated may be quite different from the population to which it is applied; recall that the VRAG was developed in Canada, using a predominantly white group of offenders. This inadequacy can be minimized through cross-validation on other samples, as has occurred with the VRAG (Rice, Harris and Hilton 2010), or by validating the instrument on a local population, as in Virginia. Even in the latter situation, however, evaluators must remain sensitive to the fact that an instrument designed to evaluate the risk of one type of offender may be misleading (i.e., lack generalizability) when applied to another offender type (Bartosh et al. 2003). Evaluators must also ensure that the instrument has in fact been validated; critics of the actuarial instrument underlying California's PVDMI, for instance, note that empirical support for its scales, which have changed several times, is virtually nonexistent (Skeem and Louden 2007).

A closely related problem is that, because actuarial devices do not permit consideration of risk factors other than those in the instrument and in fact often include only a narrow subset of such factors, they may fail to reflect salient risk or protective variables, and will rarely provide the basis for a comprehensive needs assessment. Some of the sentencing instruments in use today—consisting of only five or six factors, most of which are related to prior criminal history—suffer significantly from this problem. But even actuarial instruments that incorporate numerous factors are flawed to some extent in this respect, because no validation sample is large enough to include statistically useful cohorts relevant to every possible risk variable.

Third, an actuarial device, at bottom, merely allows the evaluator to say that a person with a particular risk score has characteristics similar or identical to a group of people, x percent of whom reoffended during a specified follow-up period. This fact has led some to argue that actuarial risk assessment should never be the sole determinant of a specific individual's risk. Stephen Hart has gone so far as to state that "[i]t is impossible to directly measure (using some technology) or calculate (using some natural law) the specific probability or absolute likelihood that a particular offender will commit . . . violence, and even impossible to estimate this risk with any reasonable degree of scientific or professional certainty" (Hart 2009, 164).

Others have vigorously disputed this claim (Hanson and Howard 2010). In any event, no other risk assessment technique is demonstrably more accurate than actuarial prediction. Furthermore, even clinical judgment rests on stereotypes, derived either from the same risk literature that informs actuarial judgments (in the case of structured judgment) or from personal experience (in the case of unstructured judgment). Thus, the nomothetic nature of prediction can only be mitigated, not avoided.

A final methodological problem that afflicts the accuracy of any risk assessment technique is the definition of the outcome measure. The VRAG, for instance, was validated on the commission of a "violent" act, defined as virtually any crime against person—including assault that does not involve bodily harm—within a seven-year period (Rice, Harris, and Hilton 2010, 102). Arguably, an offender who is at risk for committing a simple assault within seven years, even if the risk is high, should be handled very differently from an offender who is at risk for aggravated assault, rape or homicide, or an offender who is at risk of committing assault within seven weeks. The VRAG assessment is incapable of addressing these nuances, while clinical judgment, even if it is anamnestic in orientation, can do so only in a vaguely empirical way.

CONCLUSION

Risk assessment in sentencing raises numerous concerns, which can be expressed in terms of one significant conundrum: risk assessment is only likely to be sufficiently and knowably accurate if it is based on actuarial instruments, but it is only likely to avoid constitutional, justice, and fairness objections if it relies on demonstrably less accurate unstructured clinical judgment that eschews use of demographic information and other immutable traits. Compromise approaches such as structured professional judgment and adjusted actuarial risk assessment can mitigate this tension but not eliminate it, while creating accuracy and efficacy problems of their own.

Given these difficulties, some commentators have suggested that risk assessment should only be used to divert an offender from prison or to mitigate a prison sentence (Gottfredson and Gottfredson 1985). An additional reason for adopting this practice is that the relationship between recidivism and sentence length—short of a term that pushes the offender into old age—may well be a positive one (Lipsey and Cullen 2008, 302–306; Wolff 2006, 1394). If so, then using risk assessment to enhance sentences will often not make sense from a public safety perspective.

Two other alternatives envision a somewhat larger sentencing role for risk assessment. One option, advanced by the Council of Europe, is to establish that "factors such as unemployment, cultural or social conditions of the offender should not influence the sentence to discriminate against the offender" (Wandall 2008, 31). This principle would prohibit increased restrictions on liberty based on an offender's employment, educational, or socioeconomic status, but would allow enhanced dispositions based on prior criminal acts. Another approach is to place limitations not on risk factors but on the dispositional consequences of a risk assessment. The revisions to the Model Penal Code's sentencing provisions permit "sufficiently reliable" risk assessment to inform both diversion and sentence enhancements, as long as the dispositions are within the range dictated by retributive principles (Model Penal Code Council Draft, § 6B.09(1), 62). Of course, if only past crimes can enhance the sentence (as with the Council of Europe proposal), then important risk factors will not be acknowledged and prior criminal history—which is entirely static—may assume an exaggerated importance. If the risk assessment takes place at the front end and results in a determinate sentence (as occurs under the MPC's provisions), then the effects of aging and risk management will not be taken into account.

A final option is to eliminate risk assessment as a consideration at sentencing, and instead rely entirely on desert or deterrence theories within the criminal justice system. As other chapters in this book make clear, these latter approaches also have their drawbacks (Frase, chapter 5 of this volume; Reitz, chapter 11 of this volume).[3] In particular, desert-based punishment, like modern risk assessment, is usually focused on a very narrow subset of factors, despite the huge number of variables that might be related to culpability. Furthermore, these factors—consisting primarily of antisocial conduct and the accompanying mental states and circumstances—can result from the same status-like traits that inform risk assessment. Most importantly, assessments of blameworthiness are rife with uncertainty; a desert-based system of punishment makes large sentencing differentials dependent on provably unreliable decisions about whether a crime was premeditated, reckless, or negligent; a mistake was reasonable or unreasonable; or provocation was understandable (Slobogin 2006, 109–111). The case against risk assessment must also consider the case against other reasons to punish.

NOTES

1. Milton Underwood Professor of Law, Vanderbilt University Law School.
2. But see *United States v. Barnette* 2000, p. 816, where the court held that reliance on race, age and poverty in a capital proceeding is permissible because the expert "utilized several other bases for his diagnosis of psychopathy and future dangerousness".
3. One author has proposed that sentencing be based entirely on desert but that the post-sentence regime currently focused on sex offenders be expanded to include all offenders (Robinson 2001). Because it takes place outside the criminal justice system, this regime could more easily rely on immutable risk factors. But it may be unconstitutional to the extent that post-sentence commitment applies to offenders who are not "dangerous beyond their control" (*Kansas v. Hendricks* 1997, p. 358), or the desert-based sentence fails to give an offender "some meaningful opportunity to obtain release based on demonstrated maturity and rehabilitation" (*Graham v. Florida* 2010, p. 2030).

REFERENCES

Anderson, Dana, and R. Karl Hanson. 2010. "Static-99." In *Handbook of Violence Risk Assessment*, eds. Randy K. Otto and Kevin S. Douglas, 251–267. New York: Routledge.
Andrews, D. A., James Bonta, and J. Stephen Wormith. 2010. "The Level of Service (LS) Assessment of Adults and Older Adolescents." In *Handbook of Violence Risk Assessment*, eds. Randy K. Otto and Kevin S. Douglas, 199–225. New York: Routledge.
Apprendi v. New Jersey, 530 U.S. 466 (2000).
Barefoot v. Estelle, 463 U.S. 880 (1983).
Bartosh, Darcy L., Tina Garvey, Deborah Lewis, and Steve Gray. 2003. "Differences in the Predictive Validity of Actuarial Risk Assessments in Relation to Sex Offender Type." *International Journal of Offender Therapy and Comparative Criminology* 47: 422–437.

Baskin, Joseph, Judith Edersheim, and Bruce Price. 2007. "Is a Picture Worth a Thousand Words?: Neuroimaging in the Courtroom." *American Journal of Law and Medicine* 33: 239–269.

Blair, James R. 2003. "Neurological Basis of Psychopathy." *British Journal of Psychiatry* 182: 5–7.

Blakely v. Washington, 542 U.S. 296 (2004).

Bremer, Janis F. 1992. "Serious Juvenile Sex Offenders: Treatment and Long-Term Followup." *Psychiatric Annals* 22: 326–332.

Brooks v. Commonwealth of Virginia, Record No. 2540-02-3 (Va. Ct. App. Jan. 28, 2004).

California Regulations on the CSRA and PVDMI Risk Assessment Instruments. Online. Available at: http://www.oal.ca.gov/res/docs/pdf/emergency_postings/2009-1218-01EON.pdf, 2009.

Chanenson, Steven L. 2005. "The Next Era of Sentencing Reform." *Emory Law Journal* 54: 377–460.

Daubert v. Merrell Dow Pharmaceuticals, 509 U.S. 579 (1993).

Davey, Monica, and Abby Goodnough. 2007. "Doubts Rise as States Hold Sex Offenders after Prison." *New York Times* (March 4, 2007): sec. 1, 1.

Diamond, Shari S., Jonathan Casper, Cami Heiert, and Anna-Marie Marshall. 1996. "Juror Reactions to Attorneys at Trial." *Journal of Criminal Law & Criminology* 97: 17–47.

Dorland, Mitzi, and Daniel Krauss. 2005. "The Danger of Dangerousness in Capital Sentencing: Exacerbating the Problem of Arbitrary and Capricious Decision Making." *Law & Psychology Review* 29: 63–104.

Douglas, Evin S., and Kim A. Reeves. 2010. "Historical-Clinical-Risk Mangagment-20 (HCR-20) Violence Risk Assessment Scheme: Rationale, Application, and Empirical Overview." In *Handbook of Violence Risk Assessment*, eds. Randy K. Otto and Kevin S. Douglas, 157–185. New York: Routledge.

Ennis, Bruce, and David Litwak. 1974. "Psychiatry and the Presumption of Expertise: Flipping Coins in the Courtroom." *California Law Review* 62: 671–692.

Erickson, Steven K. 2010. "Blaming the Brain." *Minnesota Journal Law, Science & Technology* 11: 27–77.

Farrington, David P., et al. 2003. "Comparing Delinquency Careers in Court Records and Self-Reports." *Criminology* 41: 933–958.

Federal Rules of Evidence. Washington, DC. Available at: http://federalevidence.com/rules-of-evidence.

Feeley, Malcolm, and Jonathan Simon. 1992. "The New Penology: Notes on the Emerging Strategy of Corrections and Its Implications." *Criminology* 30: 449–480.

Frase, Richard. 2005. "State Sentencing Guidelines: Diversity, Consensus and Unresolved Policy Issues." *Columbia law Review* 105: 1190–1232.

Garland, David. 2001. *The Culture of Control: Crime and Social Order in Contemporary Society*. Chicago: University of Chicago Press.

Gonzalez v. Quarterman, 458 F.3d 384 (5th Cir. 2006).

Goodman, Daniel S. 1987. "Demographic Evidence in Capital Sentencing." *Stanford Law Review* 39: 499–543.

Gottfredson, Stephen D., and Don M. Gottfredson. 1985. "Selective Incapacitation?" *Annals of the American Academy of Political and Social Science* 478: 135–149.

Graham v. Florida, 130 S.Ct. 2011 (2010).

Greenwood, Peter W. 1982. *Selective Incapacitation*. Santa Monica, CA: Rand, 1982.

Greely, Henry T. 2008. "Neuroscience and Criminal Justice: Not Responsibility but Treatment." *Kansas Law Review* 56: 1103–1138.

Greely, Henry T. 2009. "Law and the Revolution in Neuroscience: An Early Look at the Field." *Akron Law Review* 41: 687–708.

Hanson, R. Karl, and Phil D. Howard. 2010. "Individual Confidence Intervals Do Not Inform Decision-makers about the Accuracy of Risk Assessment Evaluations." *Law and Human Behavior* 34: 275–281.

Harcourt, Bernard. 2007. *Against Prediction: Profiling, Policing and Punishing in an Actuarial Age.* Chicago: University of Chicago Press.

Hart, Stephen. 2009. "Evidence-Based Assessment of Risk for Sexual Violence." *Chapman Journal of Criminal Justice* 1: 143–166.

Hart, Stephen, and Douglas P. Boer. 2010. "Structured Professional Judgment Guidelines for Sexual Violence Risk Assessment". In *Handbook of Violence Risk Assessment*, eds. Randy K. Otto and Kevin S. Douglas, 269–294. New York: Routledge.

Heilbrun, Kirk, Kento Yasuhara, and Sanjay Shah. 2010. "Violence Risk Assessment Tools: Overview and Critical Analysis." In *Handbook of Violence Risk Assessment*, eds. Randy K. Otto and Kevin S. Douglas, 1–17. New York: Routledge.

Heilbrun, Kirk. 2009. "Risk Assessment in Evidence-Based Sentencing: Context and Promising Uses." *Chapman Journal of Criminal Justice* 1: 127–142.

Hughes, Virginia. 2010. "Head Case." *Nature* (March 18, 2010): 340–342.

Janus, Eric S. 1996. "Preventing Sexual Violence: Setting Principles Constitutional Boundaries on Sex Offender Commitments." *Indiana Law Journal* 72: 157–213.

Janus, Eric S., and Robert A. Prentky. 2003. "Forensic Use of Actuarial Risk Assessment with Sex Offenders: Accuracy, Admissibility and Accountability." *American Criminal Law Review* 40: 1433–1499.

Jurek v. Texas, 428 U.S. 262 (1976).

Kiehl, Kent A., A. M. Smith, and Robert D. Hare. 2001. "Limbic Abnormalities in Affective Processing by Criminal Psychopaths as Revealed by Functional Magnetic Resonance Imaging." *Biological Psychiatry* 50: 677–684.

Kansas v. Hendricks, 521 U.S. 346 (1997).

Krauss, Daniel et al. 2004. "The Effects of Rational and Experiential Information Processing of Expert Testimony in Death Penalty Cases." *Behavioral Science and Law* 22: 801–822.

Krauss, Daniel, and Bruce D. Sales. 2003. "The Effects of Clinical and Scientific Expert Testimony on Juror Decision Making in Capital Cases". *Psychology, Public Policy & Law* 7: 267–310.

Kumho Tire v. Carmichael, 527 U.S. 137 (1999).

Lipsey, Mark W., and Francis T. Cullen. 2008. "The Effectiveness of Correctional Rehabilitation: A Review of Systematic Reviews." *Annual Review of Law & Social Science* 3: 297–320.

Luttrell v. Commonwealth, Record No. 2092–02–4 (Va. Ct. App. Feb. 17, 2004).

Malenchik v. State, 928 N.E.2d 564 (Ind. 2010).

Marcus, Michael. 2005. "Justitia's Bandage: Blind Sentencing." *International Journal of Punishment and Sentencing* 1: 1–35.

McKlesky v. Kemp, 481 U.S. 279 (1987).

Meehl, Paul E. 2005. "The Power of Quantitative Reasoning." In *A Paul Meehl Reader: Essays on the Practice of Scientific Psychology*, eds. Niels G. Waller et al., 433–44. New York: Routledge.

Model Penal Code: Sentencing (Council Draft No. 2, 2008).

Monahan, John. 2006. "A Jurisprudence of Risk: Forecasting Harm Among Prisoners, Predators and Patients". *Virginia Law Review* 92: 391–435.

Monahan, John. 1981. *Predicting Violent Behavior: An Assessment of Clinical Techniques.* Washington, DC: National Institute of Mental Health.

Morris, Grant. 2002. "Punishing the Unpunishable—The Abuse of Psychiatry to Confine Those We Love to Hate." *Journal of American Academy of Psychiatry & Law* 30: 556–562.

Morris, Norval. 1974. *The Future of Imprisonment.* Chicago: University of Chicago Press.

Morris, Norval, and Marc Miller. 1985. "Predictions of Dangerousness." In *Crime and Justice: An Annual Review of Research*, eds. Michael Tonry and Norval Morris, Vol. 6, 1–50. Chicago: University of Chicago.

Mossman, Douglas. 1994. "Assessing Predictions of Violence: Being Accurate about Accuracy." *Journal of Consulting and Clinical Psychology* 62: 783–792.

National Center for State Courts. 2002. *Offender Risk Assessment in Virginia: A Three Stage Evaluation.* Online. Available at: http://www.vcsc.state.va.us/risk_off_rpt.pdf.

Netter, Brian. 2007. "Using Group Statistics to Sentence Individual Criminals: An Ethical and Statistical Critique of the Virginia Risk Program." *Journal of Criminal Law & Criminology* 97: 699–729.

Quinsey, Vernon, Grant T. Harris, Marnie E. Rice, and Catherine A. Cormier. 2005. *Violent Offenders: Appraising and Managing Risk* (2d ed.). Washington, D.C.: American Psychological Association Press.

Redding, Richard E. 2009. "Evidence-Based Sentencing: The Science of Sentencing Policy and Practice." *Chapman Journal of Criminal Justice* 1: 1–19.

Rice, Marnie E, Grant T. Harris, and N. Zoe Hilton. 2010. "The Violence Risk Appraisal Guide and Sex Offender Risk Appraisal Guide for Violence Risk Assessment." In *Handbook of Violence Risk Assessment*, eds. Randy K. Otto and Kevin S. Douglas, 99–119. New York: Routledge.

Ring v. Arizona, 536 U.S. 584 (2002).

Robinson, Paul. 2001. "Punishing Dangerousness: Cloaking Preventive Detention as Criminal Justice." *Harvard Law Review* 114: 1429–1456.

Saks, Michael J. 2003. "The Legal and Scientific Evaluation of Forensic Science (Especially Fingerprint Expert Testimony)." *Seton Hall Law Review* 33: 1167–1187.

San Antonio v. Rodriguez, 411 U.S. 1 (1973).

Skeem, Jennifer L., and Jennifer Eno Louden. "Assessment of the Evidence on the Quality of the COMPAS." Online. Available at: http://www.nicic.org/Library/023770.

Slobogin, Christopher. 2007. *Proving the Unprovable: The Role of Law, Science and Specula-tion in Adjudi-cating Culpability and Dangerousness.* New York: Oxford University Press.

Slobogin, Christopher. 2006. *Minding Justice: Laws that Deprive People with Mental Disability of Life and Liberty.* Cambridge, Massachusetts: Harvard University Press.

United States v. Barnette, 221 F.3d 803 (2000).

United States v. Booker, 543 U.S. 220 (2005).

United States v. Diaz, 2007 WL 656831 (N.D. Cal.).

United States v. Fields, 483 F.3d 313 (5th Cir. 2007).

United States v. Shields, 2008 WL 544940, at *1 (D. Mass, 2008).

United States v. Taveras, 585 F.Supp. 327 (2008).

United States v. Virginia, 518 U.S. 515 (1996).

Virginia Criminal Sentencing Commission. *Annual Reports 2001–2009.* Online. Available at: http://www.vcsc.state.va.us/reports.htm.

Virginia Criminal Sentencing Commission. *Assessing Risk Among Sex Offenders in Virginia.* Online. Available at: http://www.vcsc.state.va.us/reports.htm, 2001.

Wandall, Rasmus H. 2008. *Decisions to Imprison: Court Decision-Making Inside and Outside the Law*. Burlington, VT: Ashgate.

Warren, Roger K. 2009. "Evidence-Based Sentencing: The Application of Principles of Evidence-Based Practice to State Sentencing Practice and Policy." *University of San Francisco Law Review* 43: 585–634.

Wolff, Michael A. 2006. "Missouri's Information-Based Discretionary Sentencing System." *Ohio State Journal of Criminal Law* 4: 95–120.

Wolff, Michael A. 2008. "Evidence-based Judicial Discretion: Promoting Public Safety Through State Sentencing Reform." *New York University Law Review* 83: 1389–1419.

CHAPTER 9

....

RESTORATIVE JUSTICE AS EVIDENCE-BASED SENTENCING

....

LAWRENCE W. SHERMAN
AND HEATHER STRANG

THE idea that justice should repair harm, and not just inflict it, has waxed and waned for thousands of years. In the past two decades, that idea—now called restorative justice—has enjoyed a resurgence of discussion and experimentation, especially in the common law countries of British heritage. The operational impact of those developments on sentencing and corrections has been relatively marginal so far. Yet a growing body of systematic evidence has stockpiled ample fuel to power a restorative justice (RJ) movement, if ever a sudden political "tipping point" could set it on fire. With rising awareness of the cost of imprisonment, an economic recession has added more heat to the most incendiary question of all: whether RJ could produce greater public benefit for less money than current practices, especially mass incarceration and probation.

Our conclusion is that RJ can reduce both reoffending and costs, as well as harm to crime victims, in a wide range of applications to existing criminal justice systems. Whether it can reduce imprisonment without increasing crime is a *causal* question that requires further testing, but the evidence so far is encouraging. Whether RJ *should* reduce imprisonment is a *moral* question that cannot be resolved by causal research, given the moral opposition to the utilitarian principle of what "works" found on one side of that debate. Most criticisms of restorative justice are moral rather than causal, despite morally driven attempts to portray RJ as "impractical" for causal reasons. Debates over RJ would be more transparent if each side would distinguish their moral and causal theories of justice, as this chapter attempts to do. Yet we conclude that all decisions about justice are ultimately framed by emotions (Sherman 2003; Sherman and Strang 2011). Any attempt to reform justice must therefore be as emotionally intelligent as it is "evidence-based."

This chapter reviews the conclusions from two decades of RJ innovations as they stand in early 2011. Our primary focus is on the most rigorously evaluated form of RJ: the face-to-face *restorative justice conference* (RJC) that brings together offenders, their victims, and their respective kin and communities, in order to decide what the offender should do to repair the harm that a crime has caused. This method of dispensing justice has been applied in criminal cases on at least three continents, in six major ways:

a. RJ Conferences instead of prosecution, with cautions or no criminal records;
b. RJ Conferences after a guilty plea but before sentencing, as "mitigation";
c. RJ Conferences as the process for making sentencing decisions, with court review;
d. RJ Conferences imposed by a sentence as part of probation or imprisonment;
e. RJ Conferences that precede reentry after prison;
f. RJ Conferences and Life or Death Sentences.

This chapter assesses the evidence for the comparative effectiveness of justice with and without RJ conferences in most of these applications. It sets the stage for that assessment with several building blocks. Section I examines the history and theories of restorative justice, including the definitions of the many varieties that RJ has taken. The history includes primordial and traditional systems of justice, many of which have continued uninterrupted for over 5,000 years. Our discussion of moral theories explains why some of them support RJ while others attack it. Our review of causal theories highlights only some of the many hypotheses about human behavior that fit the facts of restorative justice research. It concludes by showing how research has helped to reformulate theories, in keeping with the scientific method.

Section II summarizes the logic of evaluation research on RJ, which is a comparison of results. The question of whether RJ "works" is inherently comparative, requiring that one must first answer the logical pre-cursor question: *as compared to what?* Increasingly, the question of whether RJ "works" must be framed in terms of cost-effectiveness for government, and in terms of emotions for politics. Running through all these issues is the logic and methods of randomized controlled trials (RCTs), in contrast to more biased methods of making comparisons. We therefore exclude a large body of research on RJ that is potentially biased in favor of it, not by the researchers themselves but by the nature of their research methods.

Section III reports the available research on the six comparisons listed in points a–f above. Much of this research was conducted or designed by the authors, but with an independent evaluator assessing the outcomes in the UK tests, and independent authors designing and conducting the U.S. experiment. The research suggests that the greatest cost-effectiveness of RJ is found with some of the most frequent, serious, and persistent offenders. This conclusion sharply contradicts conventional wisdom among criminal justice policy makers that RJ is more appropriate for minor criminals than for major ones.

Section IV briefly reviews the global social movement promoting wider use of RJ. Led primarily by present or former public servants, this movement has attracted the attention of legislatures from Australia to Indiana. With the exception of New Zealand, however, the movement has failed so far to reshape sentencing and corrections. The key organizations and opportunities are identified, with Gladwell's (2006) description of a "tipping point" presented as the key question for the future of the movement.

Section V presents the eight major conclusions:

1. RJ conferencing is now the most evidence-based strategy in corrections.
2. That evidence is more than sufficient to implement it widely, even while doing more research to answer further questions about it.
3. RJ conferencing is especially cost-effective with some of the more serious criminals, yet
4. Any reduction in prison populations must insure incapacitation of the "worst" offenders.
5. The prospects of expanding RJ depend upon evidence that a person committing a notorious crime would not escape imprisonment by agreeing to an RJ conference.
6. RJ may need the added evidence of statistical risk assessments in determining which offenders and offenses would be eligible for RJCs that would be used instead of prison, rather than in addition to it.
7. Whether or not their offenders are imprisoned, victims can benefit from RJCs in ways that no conventional court process appears able to provide without an RJ conference.
8. Direct benefits of RJC to victims can justify its possible mitigation of retribution and general deterrence, eliminating most legal theory against its use.

I. History and Theories

The history of justice among primates, including chimpanzees and monkeys, is replete with restorative practices. That fact alone offers no logical basis for preferring restoration, since the history of primate justice is also replete with revenge. This section begins by reviewing the long history, which merely describes the larger biohistorical context in which several varieties of RJ may be defined. These definitions allow us to limit our review of current debates to one form of RJ, the RJ Conference (RJC). Those debates embrace both *moral* and *causal* theories of behavior.

History

In the twenty-first century, "restorative justice" is a broadly defined term. Ranging from compulsory financial payments (restitution) to voluntary apologies (remorse) and compulsory community service in marked jackets by "chain gang"–style work groups (called "payback justice" in the UK), "restorative justice" has become almost anything that someone thinks is a pathway to offenders' redemption.

A definition this broad is far too heterogeneous for meaningful policy assessments in sentencing and corrections. It also leaves out values and processes that are intrinsic to the concept (Braithwaite and Strang 2001). Yet that breadth is a useful starting point for surveying the long history of group responses to harms by their members. That survey then allows us to focus on one very specific modern version of the broad idea: restorative justice conferences (RJCs).

The broad concept of rebuilding social ties after aggression encompasses primate behavior that is millions of years old. Primatologist Frans de Waal (2009) describes monkeys who respond to fights between other monkeys by encouraging them to "make up" after the fight. The peacemaker monkeys encourage the winners to "groom" the losers (picking insects out of each other's fur), and vice versa, as an expression of mutual support. De Waal's equally clear descriptions of well-planned acts of group revenge on abusive group members shows that restoration is far from the only response to conflict. Yet the evolutionary advantage of membership in a group large enough to defend itself appears to support ongoing efforts to maintain group harmony. Even self-sacrifice during efforts to save the lives of other group members—such as those who may drown after falling into water—support the limitation on punishment in many species.

Other primate species besides humans practice banishment and even homicide, as well as intergroup warfare. Yet any effort to characterize vengeance as the overriding, genetically driven social response to harm (e.g., Diamond 2008) misses the equally compelling bio-social evidence for forgiveness and reconciliation (Sherman and Strang 2011; McCullough 2008). This is true whether we consider all primates, or only humans—whose capacity for speech broadens the range of possibility for restorative practices.

For millennia, humans have used speech extensively in repairing the harm of crimes. These practices still survive among indigenous people from New Zealand to Canada and the United States to the Middle East, Africa, and South Asia (Braithwaite 1998, 2002). The most common process is the template for the modern RJC. Communities that have suffered crimes assemble a substantial group of people to confer on what should be done. The composition of the group varies across cultures, subject at times to the exclusion of women, offenders, or anyone besides village elders. The conference group may span tribal or familial divisions, and sometimes even languages (Huxley 1939). Yet they all use talk to express emotions, consider evidence about damages, consider precedents, and (usually) agree upon a fair means to repair the harm.

European tribes in the first century C.E. (A.D.) developed highly standardized tariffs for compensation of damages. The systems of *bot* and *wergeld* ("man-price") in Anglo-Saxon law, for example, provided for standard sums in coins for each kind of injury to a man or woman: so much for the loss of an arm, an eye, an ear, or a life—a system that arguably persisted well into Tudor England (Musson 2009). African tribes did the same, using goats or oxen as currency (Huxley 1939). There seems to have been no question of punishing an offender by death or disfigurement in these systems unless the agreement was not kept. A healthy offender was necessary to provide the restorative payments, which even in eighteenth-century Scotland included lifetime support for widows (Braithwaite 2002). This system resembles what is today described as "civil" law, but in its context it was a complete system of "penal" law, with no other penalties imposed. Only the coming of strong nation-states and kings seems to have displaced this community-based system with the idea of crime as an offense against the "King's peace," rather than the victim (Christie 1977).

Definitions

Three key concepts must be defined in modern restorative justice: mediation, restitution, and restorative justice conferencing.

Mediation

Since the 1960s, many innovations in criminal justice have tested diversion of cases from prosecution by the state. One of the most widely used practices is *mediation*, which we define as an out-of-court agreement between a victim and an offender about what the offender should do for the victim (usually, but not always, a cash payment). This process is usually managed face-to-face (or in "shuttle diplomacy") by a single trained professional called a "mediator," whose work is modeled on civil and labor disputes. There is no formal interaction ritual (Collins 2004) that unleashes emotions. Nor are members of the family or friends of either the victim or offender (usually) allowed to be present. Use of the process is widely seen as a means of avoiding imprisonment, yet there is only weak evidence from comparing like-with-like cases treated by mediation or prosecution.

Restitution

Results similar to those from mediation can be imposed after prosecution by a judge as *restitution*. This decision will usually be imposed without direct contact between offender and victim. As in fines paid to the state, restitution for the victim is imposed on the offender with the threat of imprisonment for failure to pay (Schneider 1986). This does not deter millions of American offenders annually from failing to pay, with many going to prison as a result. Nor does it guarantee that victims receive the money, even when it is paid. Over $10 million in restitution payments to crime victims in Philadelphia remains in the hands of the courts, for example, due to their inability to locate the victims (Malvestuto 2009).

Restorative Justice Conferencing (RJC)

This third method of RJ, about which the best and most research is available, differs substantially from both mediation and restitution. Sometimes called "family group conferencing" (in New Zealand and Australia) or "youth conferencing" (in Northern Ireland), RJC is defined by three elements:

1. The presence in one room at the same time of one or more victims, the victims' offender(s) who accept(s) responsibility (if not legal guilt) for a crime, the respective friends or families of victims and offenders present, and a facilitator to guide their discussion;
2. The provision of enough time for everyone present (including the offender) to express their emotions about the crime and the harm it has caused, as well as to suggest what should be done about it;
3. The facilitator's effort to reach a conclusion of the conference that expresses a group consensus about what the offender should do.

There are many other procedures described as "restorative justice" that may look like RJC, but which lack one of the three defining elements. Victims who visit prisons to talk to groups of prisoners, as in the Sycamore Tree Program, do not create an RJC because the victims' own offenders are not present. Youth justice panels (Sherman and Strang 2007), in which juvenile delinquents appear before a group of community residents and criminal justice officials, fail to meet the RJC definition on three grounds: victims are not usually present, offenders are rarely allowed or encouraged to say very much, and stakeholders to the crime are excluded from the decisions made.

As noted above, *the rest of this chapter focuses solely on RJCs*, for several reasons. One is that RJCs are the modern equivalent of the most widely practiced form of restorative justice in human history. Another is that RJCs have been subjected to more rigorous testing than any other variety of restorative justice. A third is that RJCs have been used in six different ways across the criminal justice process, a far broader reach than any other form of RJ. Fourth, and most important, is that RJCs are the version of RJ that is closest to a "tipping point" of mainstream adoption in developed, common law nations.

Moral Theories

Two major moral theories dominate the policy debate on RJCs in sentencing and corrections. One is *utilitarianism*. The other is *deontologism*, or non-consequentialism. These theories both arose during the eighteenth-century Enlightenment, with the Italian philosopher Cesare Beccaria (1764) the original exponent of utilitarianism in sentencing and the German philosopher Immanuel Kant (1785) the exponent of non-consequentialism (but see Murphy 1987). Libraries are filled with the interpretation and debates about these competing perspectives. Space limits us to one paragraph to summarize these ideas, with another to apply them to RJC.

Utilitarians seek decisions that cause the greatest good for the greatest number. Deontologists seek decisions based on moral principles such as culpability and desert, regardless of the consequences of those principles in any given case (Moore 1987). Utilitarianism is the philosophy of empirical cost-benefit analysis, and may be "bounded" by such principles as the human right of offenders not to be tortured, and not to be imprisoned without a fair trial (Frase, chapter 5 of this volume). Deontologism is a philosophy of consistency in both how and what decisions are made, with equality of both procedural and distributive justice (von Hirsch 1976). This preference for consistency led Kant to reject mercy as unfairly inconsistent, a problem that directly affects restorative justice (Mason 2002; Ashworth 2002).

Broadly speaking, utilitarians support RJC *if and only if* it leads to less harm than not using RJC. Deontologists oppose it. Utilitarians therefore reject RJC where it causes more harm, but support RJC wherever it reduces harm to victims, offenders and communities, taking all stakeholders together in the calculation. But the inconsistency across cases that utilitarians allow is unacceptable to "just desert" deontologists, who refuse to use offenders (or victims) as a means to the end of less total harm. Desert theory prefers an exact tariff looking backward, not forward, with the goal of minimizing inequalities in punishment severity from one human being to the next (von Hirsch and Ashworth 2005). Deontologism, in its strong form, privileges moral judgments over possible facts, such as that this approach could cause more crime (or punishment) than utilitarianism, inflict more harm on offenders overall, or deprive children of health care because of high imprisonment costs. Such consequences are arguably not relevant to a principled Kantian analysis of fairness in sentencing. That is why the rest of this chapter is relevant only to a bounded utilitarian framework for sentencing policy (e.g., Dignan 2003). Pure Kantians (but see Murphy 1987) can stop right here.

Causal Theories

The effects of RJC on victims and crime embrace a wide range of theories. One theory about why *victims* benefit from RJC is that it reduces their post-traumatic stress symptoms. By discussing the memory of the crime in a safe place, especially with the criminal present, RJC may fit the hypothesis of desensitizing the victim's conditioned response of anxiety whenever recalling the crime (Foa et al. 1991). Another theory about why victims benefit is procedural justice theory (Tyler 1990), which holds that people find the legal system more legitimate if they are treated with equality and respect by legal authorities. Because victims are widely reported to feel anger at being silenced by common law adversarial procedures (Strang 2002), the experience of being heard by the offender and others may heal that anger in ways that a courtroom would never allow.

A third theory predicts the effect of RJC on both victims and offenders, as well as others present at the RJC. Collins (2004) hypothesizes that meetings like RJCs bring people together in a way that lifts their energy and their commitment to shared norms. Thus an RJ conference could help both victims and offenders to become more positive about their own lives, as well as to be more morally committed to obeying the law.

The central question raised by policy makers is the effect of RJC on repeat offending. Answers to this question embrace numerous criminological theories (Sherman 2003): reintegrative shaming (Braithwaite 1989), life-course "turning points" of desistance from crime (Laub and Sampson 2003), and even specific deterrence from the enormous trauma offenders can suffer from undergoing an RJC (see Woolf 2008).

The effect of RJC on crime rates in a community or society is the single issue that may appear to lack theoretical clarity. Yet clarity can be found easily in certain kinds of facts. These facts require comparisons of entire communities with and without RJC in widespread use. While this may appear difficult in a Western context, it might be easily achieved where community-level units of analysis are available in large samples. Using police stations in India, for example, would encompass huge populations in each station. There are about 100,000 such stations. Experiments assigning some stations to RJC would offer evidence on the three key components of general deterrence theory: community-level perceptions of certainty, severity, and speed of punishment.

General deterrence would predict that RJC *increases* crime if it reduces the certainty, severity, or speed of punishment. Yet RJC could just as easily *reduce* crime by increasing *certainty* and *speed* of sanctions (Sherman and Strang 2007) even if the *severity* appears to be less than in conventional justice (CJ). Moreover, a public perception that RJC constitutes a harsh enough punitive experience for rational offenders to avoid it could allow RJC to satisfy general deterrence doctrine. Consistent with de Waal's (2009) argument that all primates experience empathy for other people's pain, RJC may create traumatic stress for the offender, who must listen to a victim's tears and pain for hours. As one delinquent in Northern Ireland said after stealing an elderly woman's car, it was so painful to see her crying that he decided not to commit crimes against people any more (BBC Radio 4, 2010). This kind of specific deterrent effect can contribute to a general deterrent effect by word-of-mouth (Zimring and Hawkins 1973), especially if it is coupled with a high certainty of apprehension and speedy sanctioning in this way (Durlauf and Nagin, 2011).

II. COMPARING RESULTS

Far too few innovations in criminal justice—let alone long-standing practices—have been evaluated using rigorous methods. In that respect, RJC stands out as one of the most rigorously tested innovations in sentencing and corrections (Ruth and Reitz 2003, 56–66). The main reason for this distinction is the use of *randomized controlled trials*, or RCTs, which provide the strongest method possible for an unbiased test of the effects of RJC on victims, criminals, recidivism, and crime rates. While the central questions of corrections and sentencing have been almost devoid of such rigorous testing, RJC has now been subjected to 12 high-integrity experiments with a total of 3,000 cases, spread over three continents. We are unable to find another aspect of sentencing that has been subjected to an equal level of scrutiny, in which the exact same protocol has been used by personnel with identical training from the same trainer—which is exactly how the RJC evidence was developed.

This section briefly reviews the concepts needed to understand and assess the claim that RJC is supported by the best evidence available. Rather than RJC having "mixed evidence," as a senior official of the UK Ministry of Justice recently described it, the truth is that prison itself has far less evidence supporting its use than RJC (Durlauf and Nagin 2011). The central reason for the lack of evidence on most forms of sentencing is the absence of the most reliable method for testing causal theories: experimentation. Experiments differ from other kinds of research in their use of *manipulation* of the factors of interest, in addition to *observation* of behavior over time.

One purist adage holds that we can infer "no causation without experimentation." Others would argue that we can come close to inferring causes without manipulating key factors, especially with factors causing very large effects—such as effects of smoking on cancer. Yet when it comes to sentencing, the experimental evidence to date suggests no large effects. Hence progress in sentencing will arguably require a substantial investment in experiments that detect small to moderate effects. Given the millions of people sentenced annually, even small differences in sentencing practices can cause large numbers of crimes to occur (or not), with differences in savings or spending of billions of dollars.

RJC is an excellent example of this claim. Even though the effects of RJC on crime are small to moderate, they can produce enormous cost savings. Few policy makers may understand, however, *why* the evidence of small effects is so compelling, and so important. The answer depends on four key concepts: unbiased comparisons, statistical power, replication, and cost-effectiveness. Once the reader grasps these concepts, it is an easy step to multiply small differences across huge populations to conclude that RJC can create enormous benefits.

Unbiased Comparisons

Public policy debates constantly cite comparisons as evidence supporting a policy choice. Yet the rhetoric of such comparisons rarely acknowledges their flaw. Most such comparisons suffer from a *statistical* bias, or prejudice. Like racial and religious prejudice, statistical bias is a false claim made with much self-assurance, based on flawed empirical premises. Yet statistical bias is harder to spot. It is found wherever someone implies that a comparison is fair, when it is in fact biased in favor of one side over another. The best way to detect such bias is to ask the key question: *Are there any other factors that might explain the difference between two groups besides the one being cited?*

Racial bias itself is a good example of statistical bias. When someone cites the comparison of murder rates between white and black people in the United States, they may imply that black people are more violent than whites because of their race.

Such a claim obviously fails to consider differences between the races in the age structure of their populations (younger people are more violent than older people), their respective household structures (married men are less violent than single men), and the historic discrimination in education and employment that has reduced the "marriageability" of black men compared to white men. The list of other differences between blacks and whites, other than race, is almost endless. Hence to identify one and only one difference associated with different murder rates is a sort of statistical lie, or at least a statement that is indifferent to the truth about the number of competing explanations that are equally plausible.

The same is true when comparisons are made about sentencing. It is often claimed that as the imprisonment rate in the United States increased, the crime rates declined. This claim is actually incorrect, since in many states crime rates and prison populations have declined together. But to the extent that any general claim can be made about crime going down when imprisonment went up, it necessarily disregards hundreds of other factors that changed at the same time: the age structure of the population, the economy, immigration by low-crime populations (especially into high-poverty areas), and many more. To disregard these competing explanations is to make a claim that is *biased* in favor of one theory over others.

Even proponents of restorative justice are guilty of such bias. Many evaluations of RJ and RJC make comparisons between people who have volunteered for RJ and those who have not. These comparisons show that offenders who have been through RJ have lower rates of repeat offending than "similar" offenders who have not. But the "similarity" of the offenders is gravely in doubt unless they were both offered RJC and were willing to undertake it. Offenders who refuse RJC are by definition different from those who agree to it. A refusal to meet a victim could well predict a higher rate of offending. Hence the correlation may be backward: it is not that RJC causes less recidivism, but that people who are less likely to recidivate are also more likely to agree to RJC.

A "spurious" explanation may be defined as the explanation of a correlation between two facts (doing RJC and having low recidivism) by an underlying *third* factor common to both. Spuriousness is simply one kind of statistical bias. It is also the most important reason that RJC cannot be evaluated by comparing cases that "naturally" get RJC to those that do not. It also explains that *historical* comparisons between RJC cases this year to similar cases last year that were not offered RJC are biased: such comparisons usually leave out the people who refused it this year, but include likely refusers in the historical sample. Finally, spuriousness plagues the comparison of *completers* of a treatment to a sample of people similar to those like the *starters* of any treatment. Since completing the program may be caused by the same third factor that causes low recidivism, the comparison to completers only is biased in favor of showing that the program works.

Our insistence on accepting these brute facts of causal inference is often seen as an insult to the many hard-working evaluators who eke out the best evidence they can from innovative and courageous programs. We certainly mean them no disrespect. Our position is to praise the innovators, as well as the evaluators, for adding to the knowledge base of experience and evidence. But as Iain Chalmers (2003), a founder of the movement for evidence-based medicine, has observed, the main concern should not be people who are running or evaluating treatments. The primary duty for all interventions is to insure that they do less harm than good. Our duty to offenders and victims is to become as certain as possible about the likely effects of RJC, and then to make it clear to policy makers why such evidence is far less "mixed" than the highly biased claims they accept about prison and other untested policies.

The reason that the evidence is not "mixed" is that in 12 independent experiments called "randomized controlled trials," the average effect of restorative justice was a statistically significant *pattern* of reducing repeat offending among offenders willing to meet with their victims. These offenders were compared to almost identical offenders who were also willing to meet with their victims, but who were (by lottery) *not* assigned to do so. These experiments were undertaken at different points of the criminal justice system, and the samples were not identical across the 12 tests. Yet that is all the more reason to conclude from the evidence that RJC is likely to reduce repeat offending wherever it is used. That reason derives almost entirely from the lack of bias used in this kind of experiment (an RCT, or randomized controlled trial).

Statisticians generally consider comparisons in well-executed RCTs to be *unbiased* in relation to the program being tested. The reason that they are unbiased is that they usually rule out all other possible explanations. By using a lottery method of equal chances for each unit to be chosen for one treatment or another, RCTs make comparisons between groups that are close to identical in their distributions of all other factors that could explain a difference in results—except for the difference that is intentionally assigned to them. One group had RJC; the other did not. The difference in repeat offending between those two groups is unlikely to be caused by any other factor. As long as the difference is not due to chance, that is, it is "statistically significant," then that difference is likely to be due to RJC. That is what statisticians say in general, as long as the RCTs are well-executed.

Not all of the RCTs of RJC have been equally well-executed. Yet all of them arguably have less bias than any other evaluations of RJC that do not use random assignment as the basis for comparing offenders who did or did not participate in an RJC. That bias stems from creating a more level playing field at the outset of a comparison than used in study designs other than RCTs.

Unfortunately, by the high standard of the frequency rate of repeat convictions (as opposed to arrests), all of the *individual* results have been statistically "insignificant." Fortunately, the *combined pattern* of all the results taken together is clearly significant, or unlikely to be due to chance. This is true for both an independent evaluation of seven RCTs in the UK (Shapland et al. 2008) and for our own review of all 12 RCTs ever reported (Strang and Sherman, forthcoming). Understanding why the pattern can be significant while the individual tests are not requires that we address the concept of statistical power, as well as the concept of replication.

Statistical Power

Policy makers are often unduly impressed with the idea of "statistical significance." This view comes, of course, from researchers themselves, who have often used the idea of "significance" as a simplistic formula for passing judgments on programs. One example of misuse of the concept, seen in hindsight, is the Report to the U.S. Congress by Sherman and his colleagues (1997) that required at least two "significant" results to conclude that a crime prevention program is effective.

What is wrong with this approach? One answer is that it confuses *certainty* of a result with the magnitude of a result, or how large the effect size is (Weisburd et al. 2003, 2001). Another answer is that emphasizing *significance* may blind the debate to the equally important emphasis on *power*, or the capacity of a test to detect a true effect as "significant." Many results that are "statistically insignificant" may be unable to detect effects that are large enough to save millions of lives, or to prevent millions of crimes. The lack of adequate power for a test is increasingly recognized as another form of bias, one that can easily mislead policy makers into thinking a strategy is ineffective when it is actually very beneficial.

The three key elements of statistical power are complicated but important. The most obvious element is *sample size*. A small sample, other things equal, is less likely to detect a true effect than a larger sample. But other things are not usually equal, and other things matter. The two other factors in power are *effect size* and sample *heterogeneity* (Cohen 1988). The idea of effect size describes how big an effect is, such as heating a pot of water on a gas stove with a low flame (small effect) or a high flame (larger effect, heating the same amount of water more quickly). More complex is the idea of sample heterogeneity, which underlies such statistical concepts as variance and standard deviation.

A *heterogeneous sample* is comprised of units that are different from each other in characteristics that may affect the results of an experiment for each member of the sample. All samples have some such differences, but some samples are far more heterogeneous than others. Imagine a sample of first offenders in which all are white, female, and between the ages of 16 and 17. Compare that sample to a second one in which the offenders have anywhere from 0 to 50 previous criminal convictions, half are white, half are male, and the age range varies from 12 to 83. The first sample is far more homogeneous than the second. Other things equal (like sample size and effect size), the chances of a statistically significant result are far lower with the second sample than with the first (Weisburd 1993).

Taken together, sample size, effect size, and heterogeneity can bias a test toward or against a "statistically significant" result. In very large sample sizes, often found in medical research, tiny differences in rates can lead to changes in medical treatments of millions of people (Haas et al. 2004). Yet such results are only statistically significant because governments spent large sums of money on the medical research needed to obtain the sample size needed to detect the difference. Since governments rarely spend on RCTs in crime prevention even one-tenth of what they spend on medical RCTs, it can be said that government funding is biased against finding statistically significant results in crime prevention. This bias is entirely due to a lack of statistical power.

Criminologists have generally failed to educate policy makers, and even each other, about statistical power. Yet it is impossible to evaluate the evidence on RJC without grasping the essence of this idea. The fact that a series of randomized trials might be unable to obtain large enough samples (from change-resistant criminal justice agencies) to be *statistically powerful* in each test should not prejudice policy makers against the benefits of small to moderate effects of RJC. It is arguably more important to consider the overall pattern of results, using the greater statistical power generated by the combined analysis of repeated replications of the tests.

Replications

The goal of similar results from repeated experiments is often cited as a test of scientific truth. This test is known as "replication," whereby independent researchers undertaking the same experiment can get the same result, over and over again. The image of an apple falling on Isaac Newton's head suggests how often the experiment of dropping something has tested the gravity hypothesis. Never mind the fact that replication has become increasingly problematic in a wide range of sciences, for reasons that are not at all clear (Lehrer 2010). The fact is that RJC experiments undertaken by different researchers, in different countries, and in different parts of the criminal justice system, have generally obtained similar results. Thus we can conclude that this evidence has passed at least one test of replication: the test of identical methods under different conditions.

A second test of replication has not, as yet, been attempted: one that uses identical methods under the same conditions but with different samples (see, e.g., Sherman 1992). This could be an important addition to evidence-based policy. We know, for example, that in Australia the effects of RJC on Aboriginal offenders was the opposite of its effect on white offenders, even within the same experiments with the same police officers delivering the RJC (Sherman 2006). Each society that undertakes RJC may have alienated minority groups who might react differently to RJC's attempt to create a shared morality about obeying the law. Thus separate tests of RJC on majority and minority samples could be a vitally important kind of replication.

A more general problem of replication is to learn whether what works in one community (or nation) will work in another. Relatively few social interventions have been tested in the same way across a wide range of communities, let alone with different legal systems and languages.

The most fundamental purpose of replication remains to test whether a finding reflects a general pattern or a "fluke" result from an unusual set of conditions. These conditions could include the people leading the experiment, the people administering the treatment, the victims or offenders in the sample, or the communities in which the offenders may be committing repeat offenses. The more often a finding is repeated, the less likely it is that the finding was due to chance. The greater the proportion of all tests with the same results, the same conclusion can be reached. If 10 out of 12 tests reach positive results, then the risk of positive results being due to chance is greatly diminished over having just one test result.

Just as these facts of replication strengthen the general findings about RJC, they also weaken the specific findings about using RJC at different stages of the criminal justice system. There are 12 independent tests of RJC in RCTs, but only one test of RJC with drinking-driving violations. There are four RCTs of violent crime, but only two RCTs with an all-adult (over-18) sample. For each subgroup, the uncertainty about RJC effects for only that subgroup is greater than the uncertainty about RJC in general.

These and other caveats are required to prevent any bias in our presentation of results. It is also necessary for those biased against RJC to compare the evidence base that we discuss with the evidence for other sentencing and corrections practices. All evidence is relative. In an absolute sense, there is far more evidence to be gained about all aspects of life, let alone criminology. In a relative sense, the evidence for RJC is far in front of the evidence for any other new initiative that attempts to serve both victims and offenders.

Whether crime victims are important, however, is something that many civil servants in the United Kingdom would dispute, at least in private. While they might accept the unequivocal evidence that victims who consent to RJC are far more satisfied by experiencing it than if they do not (Strang 2002; Sherman et al. 2005), they might discount it because it does not matter to their budgets. Such issues show how important it is to reveal the definitions of cost-effectiveness, and to make them central to the policy analysis.

Cost-Effectiveness

How is the cost-effectiveness of sentencing and corrections to be defined? The United Kingdom is far ahead of the United States or Australia in even thinking about this question. The United Kingdom's answers pose a clear moral and political dilemma. While the cost of crime can be estimated from the kind of detailed studies that have been done on both sides of the Atlantic, the biggest cost of crime is to the victims of crime (see, e.g., Shapland et al. 2008). Reducing the cost of crime will therefore help victims far more than it will help governments to balance their budgets.

In consultations with UK civil servants—the permanent officials who run the government at the direction of a succession of Members of Parliament who direct the officials—advocates for RJC have been told that reducing crime costs to victims does not matter. In the view of these officials, all that should drive government policy is saving money for taxpayers in general, not for those who have become crime victims. That is, unless RJC can reduce the costs of policing, prosecution, sentencing, probation and imprisonment, *relative to the cost of providing RJC*, then it cannot be considered to be cost-effective.

This position can be argued morally but not technically. Yet even on its own terms, the question posed can be answered in the affirmative. Does RJC save the government money? According to calculations by Shapland et al. (2008), it does in some tests, if not all. Moreover, it can save so much money in some tests that the average effect of RJC across all tests in the United Kingdom is to save money for the government.

The simple formula for reaching these conclusions requires a complex menu. The menu assigns two prices to each type of crime. One is the overall cost of that type of crime, based on surveys of crime victims, their employers, the health care system, and welfare benefits drawn. The other is the cost of crime just to the government, which is currently calculated as just criminal justice system costs (arguably an error, since taxpayers pay for most health and welfare costs). For each crime of which an offender is convicted, the two prices can be applied from the menu. The price of all the crimes is then summed across each offender's history for two years after random assignment to RJC or not. Then the average costs of crime for all offenders in the RJC group is subtracted from the average cost of crime for all offenders in the non-RJC control group. This difference is defined as the "benefit" of RJC, either in total costs or criminal justice costs.

The average cost of producing each RJC is then computed across all RJC cases in the experiment. This includes largely the salaries and expenses of the people delivering RJ services, usually police officers. This cost includes meetings with offenders and victims who refuse to consent to RJC, which happened in over half of all cases in the UK tests. The average cost of all activities needed to produce the number of RJC cases in the experiment is defined as the cost. By dividing the cost into the benefit, as calculated above, the cost-benefit of RJC can be calculated in two ways—one for each definition of the benefit. The results of these calculations are presented below in figure 9.3, just for the seven UK experiments, after the following section presents descriptions of the applications for which the calculations were done.

III. Applications

The major applications of RJC have been spread across six basic stages of the criminal justice process under the common law systems of the Australia, the United Kingdom, and the United States. These applications take two basic forms: diversion from prosecution as an *alternative* to criminal justice, and in addition to prosecution as a *supplement* to criminal justice. Using a systematic review process to identify all RCTs of RJC using random assignment *after* asking victims and offenders for their consent to participate in RJC,[1] Strang and Sherman (forthcoming) have compiled the results of 12 RCTs with almost 3,000 cases. This section reports on the evidence from that review. That evidence is first presented across all the different points of criminal justice en masse, and then again on a stage-by-stage basis.

The overall evidence is presented in figures 9.1 and 9.2. Figure 9.1 displays a brief description and sample size of each of the RCTs, arranged roughly in the chronological order in which the experiments were conducted. Figure 9.2 displays the

	Offender N
1. Australia RISE Canberra <30 years violence	121
2. Australia RISE Canberra juvenile personal property	248
3. Australia RISE Canberra juvenile shoplifting	142
4. Australia RISE Canberra Driving Under influence	897
5. US Indianapolis juvenile property/violence	782
6. UK Northumbria juvenile property/violence	208
7. UK Northumbria adult property	63
8. UK Northumbria adult assault	44
9. UK London robbery pre-sentence	88
10. UK London burglary pre-sentence	167
11. UK Thames Valley violence - probation	64
12. UK Thames Valley violence - prison before re-entry	94
Total offender N =	2,918

Figure 9.1. Description: 12 RCTs of Restorative Justice Conferencing.

results of each of the RCTs, arranged in the order of their effect sizes using a standardized mean difference [data not displayed] called Cohen's D (Cohen 1988). Rather than explaining the complexities of this statistic, the chapter presents the much more accessible calculation of the percentage differences in each experiment.

For each RCT, figure 9.2 displays the percentage difference in the frequency of convictions over a two-year period after the random assignment. The comparison shows first the average number of convictions (crimes) per offender per year in that period among consenting offenders assigned to RJC. It then shows the same average for the consenting group *not* assigned to RJC. In the column on the far right, figure 9.2 shows the percentage difference in the frequency of convictions between the two groups.

The offenders did not always experience the treatment to which they were assigned. Some of the offenders assigned to RJC never completed it, for a variety of reasons. Almost all offenders assigned not to get RJC remained in that condition. The evidence therefore may understate the potential benefit of RJC, since so many cases without RJC were included in the group randomly assigned to it. This "intent-to-treat" approach is considered by statisticians as the least worst way to analyze experiments with relatively small sample sizes (Peto et al. 1976).

Figure 9.2 shows that the frequency of post-random-assignment convictions was lower for the offenders assigned to RJC than for those not assigned in 10 out of 12 RCTs. It also shows that the average of the differences between RJC and non-RJC assigned groups was 22 percent fewer convictions for those randomly assigned to RJC than for those assigned not to have RJC. While this method of analysis is not preferred by statisticians, it is preferred by policy makers for ease of communication to a wide range of audiences.

By displaying the raw averages of criminal convictions per offender in each group, figure 9.2 allows anyone to calculate the percentage differences on their own. They can also estimate the number of crimes prevented in each test, which varies according to the frequency of offending in each sample, independent of whether RJC was used. The latter can be estimated by simply inspecting the non-RJC conviction

Experiment	Mean Crimes Per Offender After RJC- Assignment	Mean Crimes Per Offender After No RJC- Assignment	Percent Difference: Mean of RJC Compared to Mean of No-RJC
Canberra Drink-Driving	0.09	0.06	+50%
Canberra Juvenile Property	1.02	0.69	+48%
London Robbery	1.85	2.01	−8%
London Burglary	2.88	3.41	−16%
Thames Valley Prison	1.39	2.06	−33%
Canberra Juvenile Shoplifting	0.57	0.82	−30%
Northumbria Magistrates' Property	3.03	3.97	−24%
Indianapolis Juvenile	1.29	1.67	−23%
Thames Valley Probation	0.59	1.32	−55%
Northumbria Juvenile Warnings	0.41	0.79	−48%
Canberra Youth Violence (under 30)	0.42	0.88	−52%
Northumbria Magistrates' Assault	0.82	2.08	−61%
Average of Average Differences of Treatment Groups	NA	NA	−22%

Figure 9.2. Results: 12 RCTs of Restorative Justice Conferencing.

rates, which vary from .09 convictions per offender per year in the drinking-driving experiment to 3.03 convictions per year in the Northumbria Magistrates' Court property crime experiment.

The preferred method for synthesizing these results is called a "meta-analysis," in which a more complex calculation gives each experiment a different weight based upon the number of cases it contains. While this procedure has important advantages, it has one large disadvantage: the sample size of each experiment bears an unknown relationship to the proportions of cases for which RJC may be used. In these 12 RCTs, for example, almost one-third of all the cases come from a drinking-driving experiment in Canberra. Given the negative effect of RJC in causing more offending (but at a very low rate), it is unlikely that RJC will be used for drinking-driving cases in the future. It certainly has not been used in Canberra since the results of the experiment were announced. Yet the preferred method gives substantial weight to a type of crime now deemed irrelevant.

Displaying the raw data for each experiment, figure 9.2 still omits important information for statisticians, including the heterogeneity of each sample, as well as the overall statistical power of each test. Yet it still provides a reasonable basis for

SITE	RJ COST	CJ Benefit**	Total Benefit	Cost: Benefit	
				CJ Ratio	Total Ratio
London	598,848	1,817,426	8,261,028	1:3	1:14
Northumbria	275,411	70,420	320,125	1:0.26	1:1.2
Thames Valley	222,463	101,520	461,455	1:0.46	1:2
Total	1,096,722	1,989,734	9,042,608	1:1.8	1:8

Figure 9.3.* Cost: Benefit.
* Computed from Shapland et al, 2008. All amounts expressed in Pounds Sterling. **CJ benefit estimated at an average 22 percent of total costs of crime.

non-statisticians to assess the results of these experiments, individually and overall. It is especially important to see it this way in order to assess the cost-effectiveness of RJC, as in the data from the seven UK experiments across three sites presented in figure 9.3.

Figure 9.3 shows that across all seven UK experiments, RJC saved eight times as much money as it cost to deliver, earning that payback in just two years. That calculation is based on total costs of crime, including costs to victims. But even when we examine only the costs saved to the criminal justice system, the payback is still "profitable." RJC saved 1.8 times as much money in the costs of crime to the criminal justice system.

What figure 9.3 also shows is that for two of the sites, the cost of RJC was greater than the costs saved just to criminal justice. In Thames Valley and Northumbria, the experiments still saved money in total costs of crime. But delivering RJC to anyone other than the highly serious and active criminals pleading guilty in the London Crown Courts did not, on average, save the criminal justice system money. This finding is all the more striking because the percentage reductions in crime frequency were so much larger in Thames Valley correctional cases and in Northumbria non-prisonable court cases than in the London Crown Courts robbery and burglary cases, almost all of which entailed a prison sentence. What this means is that when the London offenders got out of prison, they committed less costly crimes to the taxpayer, as well as to victims of crime.

The data in figure 9.3 emphasize the importance of using a crime harm index (CHI) to evaluate sentencing and corrections, rather than simply counting crimes or convictions (Sherman 2011). A CHI approach abandons the myth that each crime causes equal harm to society, and that mere counts of crime have any meaningful role in policy analysis. By contrasting the count results of figure 9.3 with the cost results of figure 9.2, the reader can see stark evidence of the difference between assuming that "all crimes are created equal" and the more accurate premise that they are not. For the time being, however, it is almost impossible to discuss sentencing options without accepting raw counts of undifferentiated types of crime as the primary criterion for success or failure.

RJ Conferences Instead of Prosecution

The evidence from these 12 RCTs includes five experiments that diverted offenders from criminal convictions as a part of RJ. Two of these, however, were juvenile experiments in which diversion with RJC was compared to diversion without RJC (Northumbria and Indianapolis). These two experiments provide little basis for a more pressing policy question in an era of cost-cutting: Could RJC provide a low-cost alternative to prosecution of adults, without increasing crime?

The only answer to this question so far for adult offenders is a clear but equivocal statement: it depends. Both diversion experiments were conducted in Canberra, Australia, a jurisdiction with historically low rates of imprisonment. Almost no cases in the control group (prosecution) were sentenced to prison. That said, it is striking that the violence cases assigned to prosecution did so much worse than the cases diverted to RJC, especially for adults over 18; there was virtually no effect of RJC for the under-18s, thereby making the overall estimate dependent on the adult subgroup [data not displayed]. Since the adult subgroup is too small for adequate statistical power, we cannot make too much of this finding without replication. Unfortunately, no such replication was allowed by the central government in the UK experiments.

At the same time, the victimless RJC conferences in Canberra did worse than prosecution in relation to the low base rate of repeat offending. Technically, we could exclude the drinking-driving diversion to RJC from the analysis altogether, on the grounds that there was never a personal victim of crime present in the conferences to make offenders feel ashamed. But because we conducted the experiment, transparency requires that we include it the reporting and discussion.

If one concludes that the drinking-driving experiment is irrelevant, then there is a good case to replicate the diversion from prosecution to RJC for adult offenders in minor assaults. The large effect of adding RJC to such cases in Northumbria (figure 9.2) combined with the Canberra findings yields an average of 56 percent fewer reconvictions with RJC over the two experiments. Since neither the Northumbria nor Canberra control group received imprisonment, the case is even stronger for reducing reconvictions. Whether it would save money is a different question.

RJ Conferences Before Sentencing

Figure 9.2 shows four tests of using RJC after guilty pleas but before sentencing. In all four cases, RJC yielded fewer reconvictions. But it is not clear whether RJC was cost-effective in all four cases, measured only by criminal justice costs. Shapland and her colleagues (2008) did not separately report the cost of crime effects of each experiment in each site, so we simply do not know whether the results for RJC before sentencing are consistently cost-effective. Yet there is clearly a strong case for replications, and for a policy rollout in the serious burglary and robbery cases of the kind that we tested in London—where prison sentences are longest and most costly to a government presently trying to reduce the prison population.

RJ Conferences as Sentencing Decisions

A third application of RJC has virtually no unbiased evidence about its effects. There is not a single RCT on the use of RJC to decide what the sentence should be, including prison versus no prison. Yet that is exactly what is done in thousands of cases in New Zealand, Canada, Australia, and elsewhere. For that reason alone, we offer the following discussion, with no conclusions on the cost-effectiveness of this application.

While the RJ paradigm embraces very different values and processes from those of formal justice, maximizing the use of RJ for the benefit of both offenders and their victims requires them to intersect in a fashion that preserves the conventions of both. Only then can RJ be used for serious offences for which diversion alone would not generally be acceptable. Positioning RJ within the court system allows it to be used either in addition to formal justice processes—as a referral from court, or in conjunction with it—as in Canadian sentencing circles (Green 1997). Most often, RJ tends to be restricted to juvenile offenders, but increasingly courts are using it for adults as well. It is certainly restricted to cases in which the offender has admitted responsibility for the harm suffered by the victim. RJC is not a forum for adjudication of guilt but a means of deciding in a consensual way what can be done to repair an acknowledged harm.

RJ as a Referral from Court

Over the past two decades, Australia and New Zealand have allowed cases to be referred to RJ by the courts. In South Australia and the Australian Capital Territory, for example, where police have the discretion to divert cases from the court to RJ themselves, judges may also decide that cases coming before them would more appropriately be dealt with by RJC alone. Judges can then divert these case completely out of the court system. This is often a response to the tendency of police to err on the side of caution. Rather than diverting cases to RJC themselves, police may prefer judicial direction about what kinds of cases ought to be dealt with in court.

More often than diverting cases, however, Antipodean courts treat RJC as a sentencing option for offenders before them. In some jurisdictions this is now obligatory. Since 2002 in New Zealand, for instance, RJC language has been incorporated into its sentencing provisions. Courts are now required to consider the results of RJC and to take into account "offer, agreement, response or measure to make amends" (New Zealand Sentencing Act 2002, No. 9, S10). In deciding whether and to what extent to take these into account, the court must decide whether the offer was genuine and feasible and whether it has been accepted by the victim as expiation or in mitigation of the wrong.

New Zealand uses the provisions of this act in both juvenile and adult cases. In a serious case of aggravated robbery committed by a 17-year-old youth, for example, the judge in the case noted that the circumstances of the offence would normally require a four-year sentence of imprisonment. In light of the outcome of the RJ conference, however, a custodial sentence of ten months was imposed (*Crown v. Makatuu Folaumoeloa* 2004).

While New Zealand, like other countries, has used RJ mainly in juvenile cases, it has been at the forefront in piloting the use of RJ for adults. Indeed, the introduction of the 2002 act may have been strongly influenced by a signal case involving a very serious assault by an adult, *R. v. Clotworthy* (unreported, T971545, Auckland District Court, 24 April 1998). Mr. Clotworthy was drunk when he stabbed his victim six times, an assault for which he could give no explanation. The victim wanted cosmetic surgery for the ugly scarring that he suffered. He was reported in court as saying "The deed is done and I would now like it undone." The judge suggested an RJ conference where the offender's apology was accepted and the offender agreed to pay for the surgery. The victim was definite that he did not want Mr. Clotworthy to go to prison, in part because he knew that the loan involved to pay the reparation could only be obtained if Mr. Clotworthy kept his job. The judge ordered the necessary reparation, substantial community service, and a two-year suspended sentence.

The court's judgment, however, was then appealed. The appeals court agreed that the offending was too serious for such a short sentence. It then required the offender to serve time in prison, even though the court agreed that Mr. Clotworthy was unlikely to offend again. His custodial sentence meant that the victim was unable to receive the funds necessary for the surgery he wanted, a factor that may have contributed to the victim's suicide several years later. It is unlikely that this appeal and prison sentence would have been successful after the introduction of the 2002 legislation.

While rigorous evaluations have been carried out for some of these RJ practices, more commonly RJ has been introduced as policy without testing its effects. In New Zealand, for example, RJ for youths became policy overnight with the introduction of the governing legislation in 1989, leaving no opportunity for assessing its consequences.

RJ Conferences Imposed by a Sentence

Figure 9.2 reports on one RCT that imposed an RJC conference as part of a probation sentence, subject to whether the probation officers randomly assigned the case to undertake such a conference. The experiment was limited to cases in which the victim was willing, and the offender was risk-assessed as being not unduly resistant to the idea. While the sample size was not large and the statistical power was not adequate for a statistically significant result, the RJC-assigned offenders had 55 percent fewer reconvictions than the offenders who were not assigned to RJC. This is a striking result that strongly merits attempts at replication.

RJ Conferences and Re-Entry after Prison

Figure 9.2 also reports on one RCT with prisoners sentenced for violent crimes who were within six months of scheduled release back to the community. The 94 cases in this experiment produced a result that showed 33 percent fewer reconvictions for the RJC group than for the group not assigned to RJC. All of these comparisons from figure 9.2 are at some risk of being based on preexisting differences in frequency rates of convictions, especially for the smaller samples. Random assignment is less reliable at controlling for preexisting differences with small samples than it is with larger samples, and a before-after comparison would have been better for eliminating the theory that the large difference was merely a preexisting condition rather than a result of RJC. Yet it is the best evidence available, and better evidence than from non-randomized designs.

RJ Conferences and Life or Death Sentences

A brief word is required on RJC for life sentences and execution cases. The benefits for victims, which we have not presented in detail here, can potentially justify substantial investments in homicide cases to assist the survivors of these crimes. In a number of cases, RJC has been conducted with the family of murder victims. Qualitative reports from these conferences are generally favorable, with victims reporting feelings of forgiveness that allow them to release their anger (Umbreit and Vos 2000). Whether these feelings can promote better physical health and longevity is a reasonable question for research. As long as the United States continues to execute 30 or more people per annum, this question remains relevant to public policy. Even in Europe, where the death penalty is considered a violation of human rights, there are many murder survivors who could benefit from RJC. Given the public health care systems in these countries, RJC may even be cost-effective at reducing medical costs from post-traumatic stress symptoms among families of murder victims.

IV. RJ AS A SOCIAL MOVEMENT

The research reported above shows strong evidence that using an RJC is comparatively more effective than conventional justice without using an RJC, across a wide range of stages and decisions in sentencing and corrections. Yet evidence alone is not enough. The history of innovations suggests that widespread adoption of new practices is driven more by social movements than by the rational evidence for the changes the movements advocate. This conclusion emerges from the history of many major reforms, from the abolition of slavery (Hochschild 2005) and the creation of juvenile justice (Platt 1969) to the criminalization of alcohol consumption (Gusfield 1986) and increased punishment for drunken driving (Fell and Voas 2006).

Reforms that did not happen quickly, in contrast, have included those for which the technical evidence was very strong, but no social movement arose to promote them. The first U.S. state to require automobile users to wear seat belts, New York, passed its law in 1983. This law was enacted 82 years after the first mass production of automobiles, and 24 years after the invention of the shoulder belt by Volvo's first safety engineer, Nils Bohlin, during which countless people died preventable deaths in auto accidents. In another famous example, the value of limes and lemons to prevent scurvy on British navy ships was first demonstrated by a naval surgeon 42 years before the Navy finally agreed to supply its sailors with citrus fruits (Chalmers 2003).

By some accounts, restorative justice already has the kind of social movement that eluded lime juice and seat belts. The *Wikipedia* (2010) entry on restorative justice, for example, claims that restorative justice is a "a growing social movement to institutionalize peaceful approaches to harm." Yet there is little evidence that the use of RJCs in response to criminal charges has been growing in sentencing and corrections. By the standards of over 3 million members (Hamilton 2000) of the Mothers Against Drunk Driving (MADD)—about one in every 100 Americans—or the one million members of the Royal Society for the Protection of Birds (2010)—about one in every 60 Britons—there is no large membership organization to promote the use of RJC in sentencing and corrections in either the United States or the United Kingdom.

Yet the political conditions for advancing restorative justice remain fertile. Despite the lack of movement, the rhetoric in support of victims remains strong. As one Canadian reporter notes (McKnight 2010):

> . . . it's curious that RJ hasn't gone mainstream, since it aims to do exactly what politicians and others claim they want from the justice system. Rarely a day goes by that we don't hear politicians stressing the importance of meeting victims' needs or of ensuring offenders take responsibility, yet the system, focused as it is on punishment, has never been very good at doing either. Restorative justice, on the other hand, aims to make this rhetoric a reality.

The UK election of a coalition government in 2010 led immediately to similar statements of priorities on meeting victims' needs, but with a key difference. The new government explicitly promised to deliver more restorative justice. Whether and how that promise is kept is an important question for the future of RJ internationally. If it succeeds, it will not be without the active campaigning of civil society groups outside of political parties.

Civil Society Organizations for Restorative Justice

At least three civil society organizations, however, have become established to promote restorative justice conferences. The most global is the Prison Fellowship, which hosts a web site at www.restorativejustice.org. The home page displays the picture of a globe under the title "RJ Around the World." Under the globe are links to click for each continent, including "the Pacific." Each continent has further links to reports from specific countries. These reports suggest, once again, more intellectual interest in RJ than grassroots organizing. The Prison Fellowship itself is a Christian charity founded in the United States by Charles Colson, who served prison time on charges related to the 1972 Watergate burglary. It operates a wide array of programs, including rehabilitation services under contracts from governments. One such service is the Sycamore Tree Program, which does not feature face-to-face meetings between specific victims and their offenders, but does entail real crime victims coming into prisons to talk with groups of offenders. Its primacy in holding and operating the main Internet name for restorative justice (since 1996) suggests its early interest in RJ. It also may suggest the absence of a global victim-centric organization of comparable resources.

A national victim-centric organization was established in the United Kingdom in 2008 by crime victims (and at least one offender) who had participated in the Home Office–funded randomized trials that the authors led in 2002–2005. "Why Me?" is found at www.Why-Me.org, where its subtitle is identified as "Victims for Restorative Justice." The organization was launched in a bookstore at the launch of a book (Woolf 2008) by the offender who had attacked one of the founders, Will Riley—the royalties of which he is donating to the charity. The group has been supported by an older, more government-oriented UK charity, which had been founded in 1997 as the Restorative Justice Consortium (RJC). With the advent of "Why Me?" the RJC decided to emphasize the establishment of standards, training and education for professional practice in restorative justice generally, including what this chapter calls "RJCs" (restorative justice conferences).

In addition to what might be called the advocacy organizations, there are also training and consulting services provided to a wide range of clients in the United States, the United Kingdom, and Australia. Examples include Restorative Solutions (www.RestorativeSolutions.org.uk); the International Institute of Restorative Practices, based in Pennsylvania (www.iirp.org); and Proactive Resolutions (www.proactive-resolutions.com), the Australian company affiliated with the former New South Wales police trainer John McDonald, who trained all of the police officers who participated in the randomized trials of restorative justice reviewed above (figure 9.2). Each of these organizations teaches and leads RJ conferences, rather than organizing members. None can be described as a "corporate interest" attempting to lobby governments to increase the volume of RJ services paid for by tax dollars.

In many ways, these organizations can be said to suffer from an excess of altruism, and a lack of selfish passions. In contrast to medical charities or MADD, there is a distinct absence of trauma-motivated volunteerism. With the exception of "Why Me?" there is no visible victim associated with the social movement. The founder of MADD was motivated by drunk driving that caused the death of her daughter (Fell and Voas 2006). The March of Dimes was strongly supported by polio victim Franklin Roosevelt (Smith 1990). Yet RJ groups are largely staffed by former officials of national governments or local criminal justice agencies. Their leadership is committed but not visibly emotional. They neither comprise nor supply the kind of "heroic victim" that has been identified in campaigns to increase punishment (Zaffaroni 2009). Yet they could still succeed in creating a tipping point to expand RJ.

Elements of a Tipping Point

In speculating about the antecedents of a geometric increase in the rate of change he calls a "tipping point," Malcolm Gladwell (2006) identifies three key concepts: leadership, stickiness, and context. Without elaborating on these ideas here, let us simply observe that a Gandhi-like leader of great national fame could make a big difference, perhaps a family member of a victim of a tragic and highly publicized murder. The use of a "sticky" or memorable slogan would also empower such a movement, as long as it tapped deeply felt emotions.

Most important, however, may be the social context of a social movement. The context that could matter most might be the economy. The impact of the global recession on changing the context is evident in both the United States and the United Kingdom. In the United States, many states facing bankruptcy also bear the burden of an increasing prison population. In the United Kingdom, a plan to build more prisons for a rising prison population was abandoned after the 2010 election put a new government into power. In the latter context, a new criminal justice minister offered these comments in his first public address in that role (Herbert 2010): "There are two kinds of people: those who really get it about the importance of crime victims, and those who don't." As long as it is both financially prudent and morally right to help victims as RJC does, then the context may be ripe for a social movement to advance restorative justice.

V. Conclusion

This chapter has shown strong evidence that RJ conferencing is the now most evidence-based strategy in corrections, given a consistent method across a wide range of settings. That evidence is more than sufficient to justify implementing it widely and immediately, even while doing more research to answer further questions about it. The defense that "more research is needed" is not something we would support, especially after our 15 years of research on the topic. While more research would always be helpful, it is not "needed" to be sure enough that RJC will work in the same settings in which it has been tested and shown to be successful. At the very least, offering RJC to victims of burglary and robbery in English Crown Courts, the location of our London research, is about as evidence-based a decision as any sentencing policy has ever enjoyed.

What is hardest to communicate is the idea that RJC works best—and most cost-effectively—for the most serious crimes and criminals. Shapland et al. (2008) in their independent evaluation of our UK research showed that the greatest savings were for the criminals with the most serious records—those in Crown Court. Yet officials in the United Kingdom and elsewhere remain biased in seeing RJC as appropriate for "kid stuff," or trivial crimes. Several have told us that it is completely "inappropriate" for serious crime, regardless of the evidence. This view can be interpreted kindly as deontologism, for which no amount of evidence will be enough. Yet the same officials may contend that "more evidence is needed." Most recently, we can cite Woods's (2009) analysis of the Canberra results for all three juvenile RCTs, showing that RJC had the biggest effect on the offenders with the longest criminal careers and the highest frequency of convictions. How much more evidence is required?

Any reduction in prison populations, by any means, must insure incapacitation of the "worst" or most dangerous offenders. Some opposition to RJC may be based on a fear that it could be used instead of incapacitation in such cases. Developing risk assessment tools based on large sample sizes (Berk et al. 2009), using a crime harm index (Sherman 2011), can help to reduce the risk of using RJC with very dangerous people. But the risk has always been small, given the requirement that police conduct risk assessments before declaring offenders or defendants eligible for RJCs.

The most important point is that whether or not their offenders are imprisoned, victims can benefit from RJCs in ways that no conventional court process appears able to provide without an RJ conference. Direct benefits of RJC to victims can justify its possible mitigation of retribution and general deterrence, eliminating most legal theory against its use. Even easier is to limit RJC to use as a supplement to prison, rather than as an alternative. After years or decades of using RJC in addition to prison, it could be much easier to test the idea of using RJC as an alternative.

Many criminal justice reforms have been seized by activists and implemented without adequate testing. In this case we have just the opposite. Criminologists have tested RJC repeatedly for over 15 years. We do not believe that more research is needed. What we believe is that more action is needed.

NOTE

1. McCold and Wachtel's (1998) Bethlehem, PA, restorative police experiment was excluded from this review on the grounds that random assignment was conducted before victims and offenders were asked to consent to be randomly assigned, resulting in a very high level of non-compliance with random assignment. This non-compliance reduced the integrity of the experiment as a test of RJC to an unacceptably low level, which conforms with the expectation that post-random assignment consent will fail to provide an unbiased estimate of the effect of RJC when consent is requested in advance under non-experimental conditions.

REFERENCES

Ashworth, Andrew. 2002. "Responsibilities, Rights and Restorative Justice." *British Journal of Criminology* 42: 578–595.

BBC Radio 4. Today Show Interview. July 16, 2010.

Beccaria, Cesare. 1764 [1986]. *On Crimes and Punishments: Milan*, trans. David Young. Indianapolis, IN: Hackett Publishing.

Berk, Richard, Lawrence Sherman, Geoffrey Barnes, Ellen Kurtz, and Lindsay Ahlman. 2009. "Forecasting Murder Within a Population of Probationers and Parolees: A High Stakes Application of Statistical Learning." *Journal of the Royal Statistical Society: Series A (Statistics in Society)* 172: 191–211.

Braithwaite, John. 1989. *Crime, Shame and Reintegration*. Cambridge: Cambridge University Press.

Braithwaite, John. 1998. "Restorative Justice." In *The Handbook of Crime and Punishment*, ed. Michael Tonry, 323–344. New York: Oxford University Press.

Braithwaite, John. 2002. *Restorative Justice and Responsive Regulation*. New York: Oxford University Press.

Braithwaite, John, and Heather Strang. 2001. "Introduction: Restorative Justice and Civil Society." In *Restorative Justice and Civil Society*, eds. Heather Strang and John Braithwaite, 1–14. Cambridge: Cambridge University Press.

Chalmers, Iain. 2003. "The James Lind Initiative." *Journal of the Royal Society of Medicine* 96: 575–576.

Christie, Nils. 1977. "Conflicts as Property." *British Journal of Criminology* 17(1): 1–15.

Cohen, Jacob. 1988. *Statistical Power Analysis for the Behavioral Sciences*, 2nd ed. Hillsdale, NJ: Lawrence Erlbaum Associates.

Collins, Randall. 2004. *Interaction Ritual Chains*. Princeton: Princeton University Press.

Crown v. Makatuu Folaumoeloa. 2004.

de Waal, Frans. 2009. *The Age of Empathy*. New York: Random House.

Diamond, Jared. 2008. "Vengeance Is Ours." *The New Yorker*, 21 April 2008.

Dignan, James. 2003. "Towards a Systemic Model of Restoratve Justice: Reflections on the Concept, Its Context and the Need for Clear Constaints." In *Restorative Justice and Criminal Justice*, eds. A. von Hirsch, A. Roberts and A Bottoms, 135–156, Oxford, Hart Publishing.

Durlauf, Steven F., and Daniel Nagin. 2011. "Imprisonment and Crime: Can Both Be Reduced?" *Criminology and Public Policy* 10: 13–62.

Durlauf, Steven F., and Daniel S. Nagin. 2011. "The Deterrent Effect of Imprisonment." In *Controlling Crime: Strategies and Tradeoffs*, eds. Philip J. Cook, Jens Ludwig, and Justin McCrary. Chicago: University of Chicago Press.

Fell, James C., and Robert Voas. 2006. "Mothers Against Drunk Driving (MADD): The First 25 Years." *Traffic Injury Prevention* 7: 195–212.

Foa, Edna, Barbara Rothbaum, and David Riggs. 1991. "Treatment of Post-Traumatic Stress Disorder in Rape Victims: A Comparison Between Cognitive-Behavioral Procedures and Counseling." *Journal of Consulting and Clinical Psychology* 59(5): 715–723.

Gladwell, Malcolm. 2006. *The Tipping Point*. Boston: Little, Brown.

Green, Ross. 1997. "Aboriginal Community Sentencing and Mediation: Within and Without the Circle." *Manitoba Law Review* 25: 77–126.

Gusfield, Joseph. 1963 [1986]. *Symbolic Crusade: Status Politics and the American Temperance Movement*. Chicago: University of Illinois Press.

Hamilton, Wendy J. 2000. "Mothers Against Drunk Driving—MADD in the USA." *Injury Prevention* 6: 90–91.

Haas, Jennifer, Celia P. Kaplan, Eric P. Gerstenberger, and Karla Kerlikowske. 2004. "Changes in the Use of Postmenopausal Hormone Therapy after the Publication of Clinical Trial Results." *Annals of Internal Medicine* 140: 184–188.

Herbert, Nick. 2010. Speech Presented to the Policy Exchange, 23 June 2010 (spoken, not published, version).

Hochschild, Adam. 2005. *Bury The Chains*. Boston: Houghton Mifflin.

Huxley, Elspeth. 1939 [1999]. *Red Strangers*. London: Penguin Classics.

Kant, Immanuel. 1785 [2005]. *Groundwork of the Metaphysics of Morals*. London, Routledge Classics.

Laub, John, and Robert Sampson. 2003. *Shared Beginnings, Divergent Lives: Delinquent Boys to Age 70*. Cambridge, MA: Harvard University Press.

Lehrer, Jonah. 2010. "The Truth Wears Off." *The New Yorker*, December 13.

McCullough, Michael. 2008. *Beyond Revenge: The Evolution of the Forgiveness Instinct*. San Francisco: Jossey-Bass.

McKnight, Peter. 2010. "Help for the Victims of Crime—and the Offenders." *Vancouver Sun*, July 10, 2010. Online. http://www.vancouversun.com/news/Help+victims+crime+offenders/3260197/story.html#ixzz0tOSMOTFK (accessed July 11, 2010).

Malvestuto, Robert. 2009. Personal communication with the Chief Probation Officer, Adult Probation and Parole Department, First Judicial District of Pennsylvania.

Mason, Anthony. 2001. "Restorative Justice: Courts and Civil Society." In *Restorative Justice: From Philosophy to Practice*, eds. Heather Strang and John Braithwaite. Aldershot, Hants: Ashgate.

Moore, Michael. 1987. "The Moral Worth of Retribution." In *Responsibility, Character, and the Emotions: New Essays in Moral Psychology*, ed. Ferdinand Schoeman, 179–218. New York and Cambridge: Cambridge University Press.

Murphy, Jeffrie. 1987. "Does Kant Have a Theory of Punishment?" *Columbia Law Review* 87: 509–532.

Musson, Anthony. 2009. "Wergeld: Crime and the Compensation Culture in Medieval England." Gresham College Lecture at the Museum of London, 10 May. Available at: http://www.gresham.ac.uk/event.asp?PageId=45&EventId=951 (accessed January 17, 2011).

New Zealand Sentencing Act 2002, No. 9, S10

Peto, Richard, M. Pike, P. Armitage, et al. 1976. "Design and Analysis of Randomised Clinical Trials Requiring Prolonged Observation of Each Patient, Part 1—Introduction and Design." *British Journal of Cancer* 34: 585–612.

Platt, Anthony. 1969. *The Child Savers: The Invention of Delinquency*. Chicago: University of Chicago Press.

R. v. Clotworthy (unreported, T971545, Auckland District Court, 24 April 1998.

Royal Society for Protection of Birds, 2010. Online. Available at: www.rspb.org.uk/abouts/facts.asp (accessed June 27, 2010).

Ruth, Henry, and Kevin Reitz. 2003. *The Challenge of Crime: Rethinking Our Response*. Cambridge, MA: Harvard University Press.

Shapland, Joanna, Anne Atkinson, Helen Atkinson, James Dignan, Lucy Edwards, Jeremy Hibbert, Marie Howes, Jennifer Johnstone, Gwen Robinson, and Angela Sorsby. 2008. *Does Restorative Justice Affect Reconviction? The Fourth Report from the Evaluation of Three Schemes*. London: Ministry of Justice.

Schneider, Anne. 1986. "Restitution and Recidivism Rates of Juvenile Offenders: Results from Four Experimental Studies." *Criminology* 24(3): 533–552.

Sherman, Lawrence. 1992. *Policing Domestic Violence*: Experiments and Dilemmas. NY: Free Press.

Sherman, Lawrence. 2003. "Reason for Emotion: Reinventing Justice with Theories, Innovations and Research—the American Society of Criminology Presidential Address." *Criminology* 41(1): 1–38.

Sherman, Lawrence 2006. "Criminogenic vs. Preventive Effects of Restorative Justice by Offender Race: Findings and Next Steps." Paper presented at the annual meeting of the American Society of Criminology, November 2006.

Sherman, Lawrence. 2011. "Al Capone, the Sword of Damocles, and the Police—Corrections Budget Ratio: Afterword to the Special Issue" *Criminology and Public Policy* 10: 195–202.

Sherman, Lawrence, Denise Gottfredson, Doris MacKenzie, John Eck, Peter Reuter, and
    Shawn D. Bushway. 1997. *Preventing Crime: What Works, What Doesn't, What's
    Promising*. Washington, DC: US Department of Justice, Office of Justice Programs.
Sherman, Lawrence W., Heather Strang, Caroline Angel, Daniel Woods, Meredith Rossner,
    Geoffrey C. Barnes, Sarah Bennett, and Nova Inkpen. 2005. "Effects of Face-to-Face
    Restorative Justice on Victims of Crime in Four Randomized, Controlled Trials."
    Journal of Experimental Criminology 1(3): 367–395.
Sherman, Lawrence, and Heather Strang. 2007. *Restorative Justice: The Evidence*. London:
    Smith Institute. Available at: www.smith-institute.org.uk/publications.htm.
Sherman, Lawrence, and Heather Strang. 2011. "Empathy for the Devil." In *Emotions, Crime
    and Justice*, eds. Susanne Karstedt, Ian Loader and Heather Strang. Oxford: Hart
    Publishing.
Smith, Jane. 1990. *Patenting the Sun: Polio and the Salk Vaccine*. New York: Anchor Books.
Strang, Heather. 2002. *Repair or Revenge: Victims and Restorative Justice*. Oxford: Claren-
    don Press.
Strang, Heather, and Lawrence Sherman. Forthcoming. *Systematic Review of Effects of
    Restorative Justice Conferencing on Victims and Repeat Offending*. Campbell Collabora-
    tion.
Tyler, Tom. 1990. *Why People Obey the Law*. New Haven: Yale University Press.
Umbreit, Mark, and Betty Vos. 2000. " Homicide Survivors Meet the Offender Prior to
    Execution: Restorative Justice Through Dialogue." *Homicide Studies* 4(1): 63–87.
von Hirsch, Andrew. 1976. *Doing Justice: The Choice of Punishments*. New York: Farrar,
    Strauss and Giroux.
von Hirsch, Andrew, and Andrew Ashworth. 2005. *Proportionate Sentencing: Exploring the
    Principles*. New York and Oxford: Oxford University Press.
Weisburd, David. 1993. "Design Sensitivity in Criminal Justice Experiments." *Crime and
    Justice* 17: 337–379.
Weisburd, David, Cynthia Lum, and Sue-Ming Yang. 2003. "When Can We Conclude That
    Treatments or Programs 'Don't Work'?" *The ANNALS of the American Academy of
    Political and Social Science* 587: 31–48,
Woods, Daniel. 2009. "Unpacking the Impact of Restorative Justice in the RISE Experi-
    ments: Facilitators, Offenders, and Conference Non-Delivery." Ph.D. dissertation,
    University of Pennsylvania.
Woolf, Peter. 2008. *The Damage Done*. London: Bantam Press.
Zaffaroni, Raul. 2009. "Can Criminal Law Really Contribute to the Prevention of Crimes
    Against Humanity?" *Journal of Scandinavian Studies in Criminology and Crime
    Prevention* 10: 2–25.
Zimring, Frank, and Gordon Hawkins. 1973. *Deterrence: The Legal Threat in Crime Control*.
    Chicago: University of Chicago Press.

Section B
Sentencing Systems

CHAPTER 10

CHARGING AND PLEA BARGAINING AS FORMS OF SENTENCING DISCRETION

RONALD F. WRIGHT

INTRODUCTION

The common law tradition places the judge at the center of the action in setting a criminal sentence. In this view, sentencing at the individual case level is primarily a judicial function (Stith and Cabranes 1998). At the same time, the adversarial ideal of the common law tradition offers a modest vision of the judge and depends instead on the parties—the prosecutor and the defense attorney—to shape the charges, the available evidence, and the remedial options. Thus, the judge's purportedly central role at sentencing creates something of an anomaly in the common law world.

It is not surprising, then, that in reality, judges in the United States share sentencing authority with the parties. This shared authority over the sentence to be imposed in a particular case operates in both the federal and the state systems, including jurisdictions that rely on sentencing guidelines and those that do not.

The parties influence the sentencing outcome in various ways. To begin with, the prosecutor dominates the original selection of the criminal charges. Particularly in jurisdictions that use sentencing guidelines and other forms of structured sentences, the charge of conviction has a powerful effect on the sentence imposed and the actual sentence served.

The parties also influence the sentencing outcome through their plea negotiations. Defendants can offer to the prosecution the convenience and certainty of conviction—and the finality of that conviction through a waiver of trial rights, appeal, and collateral review rights. Defendants also commonly cooperate in the collection of evidence for additional criminal investigations. In exchange, the prosecution can offer to revise charges, to stipulate to the presence or absence of facts that might affect the sentence, to refrain from filing allegations that trigger sentencing enhancements, or to recommend to the judge a reduced sentence within the legally permitted boundaries.

While these practices shift sentencing authority away from the judge toward the parties, they do not empower the prosecution and the defense equally. The prosecutor has accumulated enough influence over sentence outcomes in the great majority of cases that it is most accurate to characterize the state and federal sentencing systems as administrative rather than adversarial (Lynch 1998). The prosecutor does not merely present legal and factual arguments to the judge on an equal footing with the defense attorney; instead, the prosecutor hears arguments from the defense and makes choices about charges and proof that determine much about the sentence. The judge, in effect, reviews these decisions for possible error in exceptional cases.

New sentencing regimes change the available terms of negotiation between the parties. Several effects flow from laws that shift authority from the judge to the parties:

- The adoption of sentencing guidelines and other legal mechanisms that assert control over judicial sentencing discretion allow the prosecution and the defense to predict with more assurance the sentences that judges will impose; this reduces the chances that the parties will predict different sentencing outcomes after a conviction at trial, and thus increases the odds that the parties will reach a plea agreement based on their shared prediction.
- Legal rules that attach sentencing consequences to the finding of particular "sentencing factors" interact with criminal codes that offer a wide range of charging options to prosecutors; in combination, these laws increase the power of prosecutors to introduce evidence that controls the final sentencing outcome, an effect that is most pronounced in the federal system.
- In such systems, the benefits available to defendants who plead guilty (or the penalties that face defendants who go to trial) grow larger, increasing system volume and raising questions about the accuracy of the convictions that the system produces.
- External limits on the terms of negotiation between prosecution and defense are available in some systems, but are still unusual and have shown only limited practical effects.
- Internal limits on bargaining practices imposed within the bureaucratic hierarchy of the prosecutor's office are still the most common limits on individual sentencing discretion of a prosecuting attorney; these are probably the most effective mechanisms for controlling prosecutorial discretion, and the most promising techniques for future development.

This chapter begins with an account of the methods that the prosecutor and the defense attorney use to influence the sentencing outcomes in criminal cases. It then discusses the systemic effects of those party negotiations, the objectives of prosecutors in their exercise of discretion, the external and internal controls that a system might use to structure prosecutorial discretion, and the impact of those controls.

COLLECTION OF EVIDENCE AND INITIAL SELECTION OF CHARGES

The prosecutor can influence the sentence in a criminal case from the earliest moments of the investigation. Prosecutors in many countries exercise significant control over the work of law enforcement officers as they assemble the evidence of alleged crimes (Jehle and Wade 2006; Johnson 2002). In the United States, however, the prosecutor typically does not control the investigative work of law enforcement agencies, at least not directly. The police develop the case file according to their own lights and present it to the prosecutor—in some states after the initial filing of charges in the courts, and in other states before any filing takes place. In many jurisdictions, the relationship between the local prosecutor and law enforcement agencies is politically fraught because prosecutors do not prioritize the crimes that the police present to them, or perhaps because they fault the quality of the investigation as a reason for refusing to file charges (Uviller 1988; Forst et al. 1982).

In some circumstances, however, the prosecutor and police investigators interact on more positive terms, giving the prosecutor some control over the facts that might support criminal charges. Such interaction is especially prevalent in complex investigations by federal agents (Richman 2003). This control over facts can lead directly to increases in the sentence, as when investigators purchase additional amounts of illegal narcotics from a seller in an effort to trigger more serious criminal sanctions that depend on the total weight of the drugs sold. While courts have recognized a possible defense of "sentencing entrapment" or "sentencing manipulation," judicial regulation of this practice is more theoretical than real (Fisher 1996).

The police choose a crime that forms the basis for an arrest, and in some jurisdictions the police selection becomes the initial complaint in a criminal proceeding against the defendant. Whatever the precise legal status of the police decision, a prosecutor evaluates the case within a matter of days and selects charges that are supportable under the facts as they initially appear (Zeisel 1981).

The prosecutor chooses the initial charge without input from judges, who declare that the selection of criminal charges is a quintessential executive function, and must remain free from judicial scrutiny under the separation of powers doctrine (*United States v. Caceres*, 440 U.S. 741 [1979]). The defense attorney is not normally involved in the case at this point, although in some specialized settings (for instance, white-collar crime investigations in the federal system), some pre-charge negotiations take place (Taha 2001).

Criminal codes in both the federal and state systems give prosecutors a generous menu of options; many common fact scenarios could support criminal charges under multiple sections of the criminal code, each leading to different potential sentencing outcomes. The depth of available charges in criminal codes appears to be increasing over time. Indeed, legislators have the institutional incentives to delegate more and more authority to the prosecutor, because the voters credit their legislators for adding to the government's crime-fighting arsenal, but will not attribute any delayed negative effects—such as prison costs or overzealous enforcement—to the legislature (Stuntz 2001,2004). In some areas involving defendants capable of organizing to influence the legislature, one can find examples of decriminalization (Brown 2007). On the whole, however, prosecutors can normally expect to choose among several available code sections that could apply to a set of alleged facts.

Negotiation Terms: Government Concessions

After the government files charges and the defendant is informed of the charges at an initial judicial hearing, defense attorneys typically enter the case. Most often, the court appoints the defense attorney because the defendant is indigent. With both negotiation partners in place, the government and the defense enter discussions about whether the case will go to trial.

The prosecution can offer to the defendant concessions of three major types. First, under a "charge bargain," the prosecutor agrees to reduce the total number of counts in the indictment or information (also known as a "horizontal" charge bargain), or to reduce the most serious charge to some lesser offense (a "vertical" charge bargain). The effect of this amendment of the charges is to reduce the potential exposure of the defendant to more severe sentence outcomes.

Second, under a "sentence bargain," the prosecutor agrees to recommend to the judge a sentence below the maximum available, without amending the charges. In a common variation on this type of agreement, the prosecuting attorney promises to "stand silent" at the sentencing hearing, making no objection when the defendant requests a lesser sentence.

Third, under a "fact bargain," the prosecution and defense agree to represent to the court that certain facts were either present or absent in a case. Under the sentencing rules of some jurisdictions, these facts trigger specific sentencing consequences. In addition to such non-binding factual representations to the court, the government sometimes agrees *not* to file a binding request for a sentencing enhancement based on some potential aggravating factor.

We will now review each of these types of government concessions in more detail.

Sentence Bargains

In jurisdictions that leave broad discretion to judges in the selection of a sentence, the parties still influence that judicial discretion. In particular, the sentence recommendation of the parties carries great weight with the sentencing judge. The parties develop the most detailed knowledge about the facts of the case, the wishes of the victims, the strength of the evidence, the most likely outcomes of any legal issues presented, and the normal sentences imposed in similar cases. The judge, meanwhile, faces the administrative pressures of a crowded criminal docket, and has not become as familiar as the parties with the specifics of the crime and the offender's background. Under such circumstances, when the parties declare together that a given sentence is appropriate, and if that recommendation falls roughly into a range of sentences normally imposed for this crime of conviction, committed by an offender with a criminal history comparable to this defendant, the judge has every reason to accept the recommendation (Scott and Stuntz 1992).

The ability to influence the judge through a sentencing recommendation is especially valuable in jurisdictions that limit judicial involvement in plea negotiations. Some jurisdictions, including the federal system, completely bar the judge from participating in guilty plea negotiations with the parties. In those systems, the parties cannot be certain that the judge will accept their proposal, but a joint recommendation still makes the judge's decision easier to predict (Alschuler 1976). In a smaller number of jurisdictions, the rules of procedure and common law decisions allow the judge to participate in plea negotiations; some of these jurisdictions only allow the judge to review a proposed settlement and to indicate whether the judge finds it acceptable (American Bar Association 1997). Such judicial involvement in plea negotiations makes sentencing recommendations marginally less important to the parties.

Sometimes the parties want a level of certainty about the sentencing outcome that is not possible based on sentencing recommendations alone. The criminal procedure rules and common practice in some jurisdictions allow the defendant to enter a plea of guilty conditioned on the judge's acceptance of the agreed-upon sentence. For instance, under Federal Rule of Criminal Procedure 11(c)(1)(C), a plea agreement may specify that the prosecutor will "agree that a specific sentence or sentencing range is the appropriate disposition of the case," and the defendant may withdraw the plea of guilty if the court later rejects the specified sentence.

Some scholars consider non-binding sentence bargains to be the most desirable form of plea agreement, because they retain more substantial input for the judge in the selection of the sentence (Alschuler 1976; Wright and Miller 2002).

Charge Bargains

Although judges in most jurisdictions must approve dismissal of charges after they are filed, it is difficult to convince judges in a high-volume system to interfere with a prosecutor's amendment of the initial charges. Similarly, while state legislatures have enacted laws regulating judicial discretion in sentencing, they have been reluctant to impose similar constraints on prosecutors. Thus, prosecutorial discretion in amending charges is unilateral for all practical purposes.

Prosecutorial power over charging takes on even greater importance in the context of more highly structured sentencing systems. Sentencing laws that structure or reduce judicial discretion, including mandatory minimum sentences and presumptive sentencing guidelines, make the charge of conviction a more important predictor of the sentence. Because a structured sentencing environment makes visible the sentencing consequences of charging decisions, it becomes possible to isolate the impact of a charge reduction and to compare it with other factors that influence the sentence.

Mandatory minimum sentencing laws offer the most closely studied context for the interplay of prosecutorial charging practices and sentencing outcomes. These laws create "cliff effects" that dramatically affect the potential sentence, depending on whether the prosecutor chooses the charge subject to a mandatory sentence versus a similar crime with no mandatory penalty attached (Schulhofer 1993). Mandatory penalties give prosecutors the means to coerce guilty pleas from defendants, and could lead to wholesale increases in sentence severity. Several empirical studies and abundant anecdotal evidence indicate, however, that prosecutors selectively mitigate the impact of specific mandatory sentencing laws by dismissing or reducing charges in some cases (Bjerk 2005; Farrell 2003).

Presumptive sentencing guidelines tie sentencing options to the charge of conviction, much like mandatory minimum sentencing laws do. In states that have adopted guidelines, the charge of conviction determines the seriousness of the offense conduct: these are known as "charge offense" systems. In the federal system, the offense of conviction creates a starting point for guideline calculations, which can be adjusted up or down based on the "real offense" conduct of the defendant: this system is known as a "modified real offense" system. The relationship between the charge of conviction and proof of other unconvicted offenses at sentencing is discussed further in chapter 13 of this volume (see also Reitz 1993).

Systems that link the charge of conviction to a narrow range of sentence outcomes empower the prosecutor, who controls both the filing of charges and the proof of the defendant's conduct. A few empirical studies have examined what prosecutors in guideline jurisdictions actually do about charge reductions. Among the earliest empirical analyses of prosecutorial discretion under guidelines dealt with sentencing practices in Minnesota, one of the first states to adopt presumptive sentencing guidelines (Miethe 1987; Miethe and Moore 1985; Frase 2005). These studies found only small shifts from sentence bargains to charge bargains in the aggregate. Apparently, busy prosecutors in high-volume systems do not change their customary negotiation practices across the board to take full advantage of new laws that create theoretical bargaining advantages.

Charge bargains increased more markedly, however, in more serious cases. Whenever conviction on the original charge would have resulted in a presumed prison sentence, and conviction on a lesser charge would have allowed probation or a shorter jail sentence, charge bargains happened more often after the arrival of sentencing guidelines. Parties shifted their negotiation practices from sentence bargains to charge bargains because the conversion gave the parties a larger, more meaningful change in the sentencing outcome.

Research in other state systems confirms that charge bargains powerfully influence the outcomes in sentencing guidelines jurisdictions. A study of North Carolina found that sentencing charge reductions were common, occurring in roughly half of all felony cases that resulted in conviction, and that the prosecutor's decision to reduce criminal charges made a large impact on average sentence severity. These effects did not apply equally, however, to all crimes. Groups of related crimes that offered "deeper" charging options (that is, a larger number of charges that might apply to a given set of facts) produced charge reductions most often. The "distance" between charges also mattered. Large gaps between the sentences that attached to the original charge and the sentences attached to the next lowest charging option made it less likely that the prosecution and defense would agree on a particular charge reduction, because a charge reduction in that setting became more costly for the government (Wright and Engen 2006). Thus, the structure of the criminal code made some charge reductions more acceptable to both parties, and therefore more common.

Research on the charging practices of federal prosecutors under the federal sentencing guidelines also suggests that prosecutors frequently exercise their charging discretion to reduce sentences, often to avoid the imposition of mandatory minimum sentences, particularly in drug and weapon possession cases. A multi-district study of federal sentences during the first few years of guideline sentencing showed that prosecutors "circumvented" the guidelines in 25 percent to 35 percent of cases (Nagel and Schulhofer 1992; Schulhofer and Nagel 1997).

Taken together, the empirical evidence suggests that sentencing guideline systems make charge bargains somewhat more attractive than they are in discretionary sentencing regimes. The parties use charge reductions to influence sentences in precisely those categories of cases where the charge makes the clearest difference in the sentence.

Fact Bargains

The parties must prove the facts necessary to move the sentence up or down. Often those facts amount to elements of a crime, which the prosecutor must prove beyond a reasonable doubt. Other facts, however, are not elements of the offense and yet are relevant to the sentence.

Such non-element facts are especially prevalent in the federal system, which uses the offense of conviction only as a starting point in determining the seriousness of the offense for sentencing purposes. For instance, a defendant who plays a "minor role" or "minimal role" in a group offense receives a lower sentence. A defendant who accepts responsibility for the offense earns a discount. If a defendant offers "substantial assistance" to the government in proving a criminal case, the court can reduce the sentence—and the government's motion alleging substantial assistance is a prerequisite for this mitigation. Larger weights of drugs and larger amounts of losses from fraud or other financial crimes will increase a sentence. Use of a weapon or injury to a crime victim will also aggravate the sentence (U.S. Sentencing Guidelines, §§ 3B1.2, 3E1.1, 5K1.1, 2D1.1, 2B1.1). Other examples from the federal system are too numerous to mention.

The presence or absence of non-element facts does not have such an obvious impact on sentences in state guideline systems or in unstructured sentencing systems. In state guideline systems, the crime of conviction (and thus, the elements of the crime) drives the sentence. As a result, fact bargaining is not typically as important in state courts as it is in federal court. Nevertheless, negotiations do occur in state court over some factors relevant to sentencing. For instance, the criminal codes in some states treat the use of a weapon during a crime as an aggravating sentencing factor, even though it does not amount to an element of the offense. The parties in state criminal proceedings sometimes negotiate over whether the government will allege and prove the presence of a weapon under this type of provision.

Facts other than the elements of the offense have always been relevant to criminal sentences in the United States. Even under a discretionary sentencing system, facts other than elements of the crime can influence the judge's choice of sentence. Such sentencing factors surely include an offender's prior criminal record or cooperation with the government. Yet in a traditional discretionary system, each of these factors mingles with others to influence the final outcome, making it difficult to track the impact of each factor (Reitz 1993). With the arrival of sentencing guidelines in many jurisdictions, the separate influence of distinct sentencing factors on the judge is now easier to quantify.

Given this opportunity to control changes in the available sentence, the parties naturally turn to negotiations about the proof of these non-element facts, and agree in some cases to represent to the judge that the fact is present or absent from the case. The parties cannot compel the judge to make the factual finding that forms the basis for their agreement, but the parties do exercise serious practical influence over judicial fact-finding when they present a united front to the judge. Agreements between the parties on some key drivers of the sentence also streamline the necessary fact-finding at the sentence hearing.

A study of federal drug prosecutions in the 1990s shows the interaction of fact bargains with charge bargains and sentence bargains to deflate sentencing outcomes, reflecting the intuitions of the veteran courtroom actors about appropriate sentencing levels in such cases. Federal prosecutors and judges used a variety of features in the sentencing guidelines to reduce the sentences imposed in drug cases during the decade. Prosecutors became more willing to agree that defendants had "accepted responsibility" for their crimes. They also filed fewer requests for enhanced sentences based on the use of a handgun. These and numerous other techniques allowed judges to reduce the offense levels in drug cases (Bowman and Heise 2001).

The prosecutor plays a strong gatekeeper role for some non-element facts, exercising control beyond that of a party submitting proof to the court. In the federal system (and in some states), the offender is eligible for a sentence discount for cooperating in the government's investigation of further crimes only if the government requests the discount for "substantial assistance" (U.S. Sentencing Guidelines 5K1.1). The government's willingness to file such a motion is often the subject of plea negotiations, and represents one of the important bargaining chips available to the prosecutor. Some states give the prosecutor a similar gatekeeper function over certain sentencing enhancement facts, such as the proximity of a narcotics sale to school grounds or the fact that a defendant's prior record makes him or her a "habitual felon" (*State v. Brimage*, 706 A.2d 1096 [N.J. 1998]). The willingness of the prosecutor to forego the filing of such automatic sentence enhancements figures into many plea negotiations.

Negotiation Terms: Defense Concessions

Just as the prosecutor brings a range of possible concessions to the bargaining table, the defense attorney also holds certain chips to bargain. A common thread runs through the defendant's concessions: the power to remove procedural hurdles from the prosecutor's path.

The defendant's power to smooth the path for the government begins with the investigation. If the defendant cooperates in an ongoing investigation, the government might be able to reach additional defendants. This form of assistance can reduce the sentence for a defendant in any system, whether discretionary or more structured. It tends not be used often in state court, since prosecutors and law enforcement officers operate on a more reactive basis in those systems; volume constraints do not normally leave much room for investigators to seek evidence of crimes not yet reported (Wright and Miller 2002). The defendant's cooperation, however, is crucial in the federal system. The large discounts available for "substantial assistance" lead to some difficult anomalies in the sentences among defendants engaged in group crimes, with some discounts awarded to the most blameworthy organizers of the criminal enterprise, because they also can offer background knowledge about their crimes (Maxfield and Kramer 1998).

The sentencing guidelines that apply to corporate entities as criminal defendants in the federal system make cooperation by the corporation a central determinant of the sentence. A corporation that discovers wrongdoing by its officers or other agents can reduce the eventual criminal sentence imposed if it volunteers its investigative findings to the government and provides access to its documents and employees as government agents assemble the necessary proof (U.S. Sentencing Guidelines 8B2.1). The high value of cooperation in this setting, combined with the involvement of corporate counsel in the investigation, creates some conflicts with the defendant's attorney-client and work product privileges. The Department of Justice, in a series of memoranda dating back to the Clinton administration, attempted to reconcile this conflict by insisting on disclosure of evidence of wrongdoing, while recognizing a theoretical right to withhold privileged information without increasing the sentence for the corporation (McNulty 2006).

Another procedural hurdle that the defendant can remove for the prosecution is discovery and disclosure. While the prosecution has a legal duty to disclose all material exculpatory information in its possession (*Brady v. Maryland*, 373 U.S. 83 [1963]), and to respond to the discovery requests allowed by statute or by the rules of procedure in the jurisdiction, the defendant can remove most of those obligations from the prosecution. The U.S. Supreme Court has ruled that a waiver of the right to see impeachment material relevant to prosecution witnesses does not deprive a defendant of the effective assistance of counsel (*United States v. Ruiz*, 536 U.S. 622 [2002]). Apart from constitutional doctrine, waiver of discovery is still disfavored in practice. Because discovery rights give the defense attorney the factual basis for evaluating all other aspects of the proposed plea agreement, many defense attorneys are more reluctant to waive these rights than any others.

The most valuable concessions that defendants make in plea negotiations are waivers of pre-trial hearings and the trial itself. These waivers might extend to all the procedural rights at trial, including the right to a jury, confrontation of adverse witnesses, counsel, and so forth. In some jurisdictions, defendants can obtain some benefits by offering to waive the jury trial in favor of a bench trial (Schulhofer 1984). In addition to waiving the proof of every crime element beyond a reasonable doubt, the defendant can waive the right to force the government to prove sentencing factors, either at trial or at the sentencing hearing.

The defendant can also offer the government certainty and finality of outcomes by waiving the right to appeal or to file post-conviction collateral attacks on the conviction. Most state and federal courts have concluded that a defendant may explicitly waive the right to appeal a conviction as part of a plea agreement (*People v. Seaberg*, 541 N.E.2d 1022 [N.Y. 1989]). One empirical study of federal cases found that nearly two-thirds of the cases settled by plea agreement included a waiver of appeal rights, and three-quarters of the defendants who waived appeal also waived collateral review (King and O'Neill 2005).

Some courts insist that a few legal challenges to a conviction cannot be waived. Courts have taken this position on speedy trial rights (*People v. Callahan*, 604 N.E.2d 108 [N.Y. 1992]); some courts (but not all) say that the parties may not agree to a sentence outside the statutorily authorized range (*Ex parte Johnson*, 669 So. 2d 205 [Ala. 1995]; *Patterson v. State*, 660 So. 2d 966 [Miss. 1995]). The range of non-waivable rights appears to be shrinking over time (King 1999).

NEGOTIATION EFFECTS

The concessions that the prosecutor and the defense attorney can offer during nego-tiations produce results: plea agreements account for the overwhelming majority of convictions in every jurisdiction in the United States. The proportion of negotiated pleas does not remain constant over time, nor does it remain the same across dif-ferent systems. Negotiated outcomes were not at all common in the mid-nineteenth century in state systems (Fisher 2003). In the federal system, fewer than two-thirds of convictions were obtained through guilty pleas in the early 1970s; that number rose inexorably through the decades to reach the current level, above 95 percent (Wright 2005a).

The United States is unusual in an international context in its heavy reliance on party negotiations to resolve criminal proceedings, and the tight connection that it promotes between plea negotiations and sentencing outcomes. Only a generation ago, Germany was known as the "land without plea bargaining" (Langbein 1979), and other nations such as Japan also produced high conviction rates without overt bargaining between the parties. Over time, however, many European nations have faced a higher volume of cases in their criminal justice systems; crowded dockets have led to various methods of allowing the prosecutor to designate some cases for summary treatment. While the levels of plea bargaining in most systems have not reached the high rates found in the United States, party negotiations explain a siz-able group of cases in some countries. For instance, current estimates state that about 20 to 30 percent of all convictions in Germany result from plea negotiations (Dubber 1997), compared to 95 percent in the state and federal courts in the United States. Parties not only negotiate guilty pleas, but also dismissals and diversion into alternative punishment or restitution programs (Jehle and Wade 2006).

The heavy use of negotiated guilty pleas in the United States has produced some distinctive sentencing effects, with some potentially troubling implications.

Size of Trial Penalty

Established constitutional doctrine declares that the courts may not punish a crim-inal defendant simply for exercising the constitutional right to a trial (*Jennings v. State*, 664 A.2d 903 [Md. 1995]). This statement, however, is widely recognized to be out of step with reality. It is clear that defendants receive more severe sentences after being convicted at trial than they would receive if they were to enter a plea of guilty: one might call it a "guilty plea discount" or a "trial penalty," but it is an enormous and unescapable reality (Brereton and Casper 1981).

The exact size of the trial penalty is difficult to measure. In gross terms, the mean sentence in state felony cases in 2004 was 34 months for guilty pleas and 88 months for felony defendants convicted after a jury trial, which amounts to a 159 percent trial penalty (Bureau of Justice Statistics 2007). More nuanced studies of the trial penalty that attempt to control for the seriousness of the offense and other variables also find a substantial gap between post-trial sentences and post-plea sentences. One study found a wide range of differences—between 13 percent and 461 percent—depending on the crime and the jurisdiction involved (King et al. 2005). A study of pre-guidelines sentences in the federal system led to an estimate of the trial penalty at 30 to 40 percent (U.S. Sentencing Commission 1987).

Questions about Accuracy and Effectiveness

When defendants face such a large trial penalty, concerns start to mount that some defendants with valid defenses nevertheless plead guilty. Although there is a reasonable prospect that such defendants would be acquitted at trial, they dare not risk the large increase in the sentence that happens after a conviction at trial (Bar-Gill and Ayal 2006). Behavioral economics offers some reasons to believe that defendants will undervalue the long-term impact of a felony conviction, leading defendants to accept a guilty plea too easily (Bibas 2004). Moreover, a defendant who experiences plea negotiations as coercive may not prove amenable to the restorative effects of apology and genuine expressions of remorse (Bibas and Bierschbach 2004).

While the risk of coercing innocent defendants into pleading guilty is inherent in any system that tolerates a trial penalty, the risk is acute at this time in the United States. The structure of the typical criminal code contributes to the risk of inaccurate outcomes. Legislatures that increase the depth of charging options for a prosecutor to apply to a recurring factual situation make it possible for the prosecutor to make a plausible threat of high punishment after conviction after trial. Likewise, they make it possible for the prosecutor to offer a substantial reduction in the charge, or to calibrate the charge reduction to the amount of concessions that the defendant offers. Criminal codes that offer more bargaining options to the prosecutor make it possible to increase the trial penalty, and to pressure some defendants into waiving potentially effective defenses.

The same holds true for increased sentence severity. When the law of a jurisdiction authorizes higher maximum sentences for a wide range of offenses and retains low potential sentences for lesser-included offenses and other related offenses, defendants face an enormous range of risk. Particularly in those states with sentencing guidelines or other limits on judicial sentencing discretion, the defendant can control some of that risk through a charge bargain.

This is not to say that sentencing guidelines lead directly to more inaccurate convictions. They can, however, contribute to a coercive environment for defendants. If the introduction of major code revisions or an overhaul of sentencing laws leads to increases in the percentage of guilty pleas and pronounced decreases in the rates of acquittals and dismissals, there are reasons to inquire closely about the accuracy of the outcomes in that system. One study interprets the long-term increase in federal guilty plea rates over the last few decades, coupled with decreases in acquittals, as indications that federal sentencing law has produced larger trial penalties. As a result, more innocent defendants are likely pleading guilty (Wright 2005a).

Finally, the structure of criminal justice institutions increases the risk of coercive and inaccurate guilty pleas. The public does not invest in enough judges, courtrooms, prosecutors, and public defenders to try a substantial proportion of the cases filed each year. The public defenders cannot press for a trial for one client without compromising the interests of other clients. The "working group" dynamic that develops in most courtrooms places the highest value on agreements that will move cases more quickly through the system (Nardulli, Flemming, and Eisenstein 1985). On this theory, overcoming the objections of the defendant becomes a central priority of all the regular courtroom actors (Dixon 1995).

Balance of Power among Sentencing Actors

Sentencing guidelines and other structured sentencing laws that began to proliferate in the 1970s were designed to regulate judicial discretion in sentencing. As a result, some critics of these laws expressed concern that the reforms would transfer power from judges to prosecutors. Compared to traditional indeterminate sentencing schemes, the more structured systems would concentrate sentence authority in one branch rather than allowing one institution to check and balance the other (Alschuler 1991).

Structured sentencing laws do appear to increase the power of prosecutors relative to judges at the level of individual sentences (Freed 1992). As we have seen, studies of guideline systems confirm that charge bargains become more common for at least some crimes, and charge reductions determine an important component of the sentence actually served (Frase 2005; Wright and Engen 2006; Schulhofer and Nagel 1997). In particular, the federal sentencing guidelines appear to have upset customary checks and balances in criminal sentencing (Bowman 2005; Miller 2004).

Nevertheless, fears that prosecutors would *entirely* usurp the judge's sentencing authority in presumptive guideline jurisdictions may have been overstated. For one thing, judges in an indeterminate sentencing system announce a sentence that the offender might not actually serve, since parole authorities could later modify the sentence. Under sentencing guidelines, the judge's selection of available sentences is more limited, but the time actually served corresponds far more closely to the sentence that the judge announced (Knapp 1993).

It is also true that presumptive sentencing guidelines leave important zones of discretion available to judges in the selection of sentences (Reitz 1998). Under state guideline systems in particular, the difference between the lowest and highest sentences authorized within a single cell of the sentencing grid gives the judge authority to determine many months or years of an offender's freedom. Voluntary sentencing guidelines offer judges additional discretion to individualize a sentence, while continuing to reduce variation in the system as a whole (Pfaff 2006).

At least one study has attempted to quantify the impact of prosecutorial discretion and judicial discretion on sentences in a state court operating under voluntary guidelines. The researchers measured the impact of prosecutorial charge reductions by finding the difference between the midpoint of the sentencing range of the most serious original charge and the midpoint of the sentencing range for the most serious charge of conviction. They estimated judicial discretion by calculating the difference between the midpoint of the guideline range for the most serious charge of conviction and the sentence actually imposed (Miller and Sloan 1994). Based on these definitions, prosecutorial charge reductions resulted in an average of 46-month reductions in sentences, while judicial discretion reduced the sentence imposed by over 100 months. This study does not demonstrate the precise impact of sentencing guidelines on the balance of power between prosecutors and judges. But it does suggest that judicial discretion still has an important effect on the sentences imposed and served, even after a system adopts guidelines.

Objectives of Prosecutorial Discretion

Given the influence that prosecutors exercise over sentences, it is worth asking what objectives prosecutors hope to achieve through their selection and amendment of charges and their sentencing recommendations. There are many candidates.

The prosecutor might simply aim for a criminal punishment that is proportional to the offense. She also might attempt to promote public safety through incapacitation of the most dangerous offenders, or through general deterrence, or rehabilitation of offenders. The criminal charge, conviction, and sentence might express and reinforce public values. In short, the prosecutor might select any of the classic purposes of the criminal law. Very likely, a single purpose would not do the job for most prosecutors, and they would emphasize distinct purposes when dealing with different categories of crimes and offenders (Miller 1992).

Prosecutors also invoke several secondary values as means to support their pursuit of those primary criminal law purposes (Tonry 2005). The secondary values include, most prominently, efficient use of limited prosecutorial and correctional resources. Economic models of prosecutor behavior sometimes posit that an individual prosecutor strives to maximize the amount of punishment imposed after the expenditure of the available public funds (Easterbrook 1983).

The equal treatment of offenders is another aspiration of prosecutors that supports their larger objectives. This equality objective includes consistency across time and consistency from prosecutor to prosecutor in the same office. Finally, individual prosecutors might pursue self-interested and illegitimate objectives, such as their own career development, as they decide how to charge and dispose of cases (Glaeser et al. 2000).

It is plausible to believe that each of these primary and secondary purposes operate to some extent in the real world of criminal prosecution. There is remarkably little evidence, however, on the actual prevalence of each objective. Prosecutorial bureaucracies in the United States usually do not require line prosecutors to record their reasons—at the time of decision—for selecting a charge or disposing of a case.

We are left, then, with sporadic surveys of prosecutors, asking them in general terms which objectives they pursue and which they value most highly. One such survey compared the objectives of prosecutors in the United States and Japan (Johnson 2002). Prosecutors in the United States placed the highest value on "protecting the public." Close behind that leading objective were two others: "discovering the truth" and "respecting the rights of suspects." The remaining top objectives included "proper charge decisions," "giving offenders the punishment they deserve," and "treating like cases alike." Note that at least four of these six common statements mostly relate to the primary objectives of prosecutors discussed above rather than any of the secondary or supporting functions. Japanese prosecutors responding to the same survey placed less emphasis on respecting the rights of suspects, and put far more weight on objectives such as "invoking remorse in offenders" and "rehabilitating and reintegrating offenders."

One other feature of prosecutors' objectives bears emphasis. Chief prosecutors in the United States are elected officials, for the most part. As a result, prosecutors do not emphasize their own deliberations about the proper objectives of criminal punishment, as a sentencing judge might. Instead, prosecutors often highlight their obligation to follow public priorities and values in the enforcement of criminal law. Those values might be embodied in statutes that list several purposes of criminal punishment (Wash. Rev. Code § 9.94A.010), or they might draw on surveys or more informal methods of public input to reveal current local priorities and values.

LIMITS ON PROSECUTORIAL DISCRETION

The negotiations between prosecutors and defense attorneys do not simply determine the fate of an individual defendant; they also implicate public corrections resources and apply public values. What controls does the public place on the exercise of prosecutorial discretion in the selection and resolution of criminal charges? Those constraints might originate from outside the office of the prosecutor, or they might derive from the internal workings of a local prosecutor's office.

External Constraints

The most immediate source of public control over the work of the prosecutor comes from a parsimonious criminal code. If the legislature defines crimes narrowly and sets penalties at modest levels, it confines the power of the prosecutor to misuse the criminal sanction. Less power available means less power to abuse. As we have seen, however, this technique does not flourish in the American political climate. Voters expect prosecutors to take the lead in addressing crime, and they expect legislators to give them the legal tools to do the job (Cahill and Robinson 2005).

Although legislators do not seriously constrain prosecutors through the terms of the substantive criminal law, they sometimes hold them accountable through other techniques. The state budget might include line items that fund extra prosecutors to pursue designated crimes, such as child sex offenses, that the legislature hopes to give a higher priority. In a few exceptional areas, the legislature presses the prosecutor to file more charges. For example, some jurisdictions have laws that encourage or mandate charges for domestic violence crimes (Wisconsin Statutes §968.075). Statutes in a few jurisdictions also limit the timing of plea negotiations or limit the size of the charge reduction that a prosecutor can offer to dispose of a case (California Penal Code § 1192.7; New York Criminal Procedure Law § 220.10).

While these legislative directives can be meaningful, their current impact is small. When the legislature designates funds to beef up certain types of enforcement, the prosecutor can redirect some other generic funds formerly devoted to that type of case. "Mandatory charge" or "no drop" laws still leave it to the prosecutor to determine whether the minimum factual basis for the charge is provable in a given case (Schulhofer 1993). Limits on the timing of negotiations simply push plea bargains into earlier phases of the proceedings (McCoy 1993). On the whole, then, legislatures in the United States do not effectively control the exercise of power by prosecutors.

Judges also refuse, for the most part, to monitor and control the selection of charges and the negotiation of guilty pleas. When defendants invite judges to override prosecutor choices about the selection or pre-trial disposition of charges, judges view those requests through the lens of the separation of powers doctrine. The judge only insists that the charges have some factual support in the available evidence—support that can be minimal at the pretrial stage. (*Tooley v. District Court*, 549 P.2d 772 [Colo. 1976]; *United States v. Batchelder*, 442 U.S. 114 [1979]). The judge does not evaluate the prosecutor's decision to decline prosecution and has nothing to say at all about relative priorities among the cases that a prosecutor files.

Constitutional doctrine does authorize courts to overturn a conviction if the prosecutor selected the defendant on the basis of race or some other constitutionally suspect class. The defendant must prove, however, that the prosecutor intentionally discriminated, making this doctrine irrelevant to criminal defendants as a practical matter (Davis 2007).

Granted, judges hold the power to accept or reject guilty pleas, along with the plea agreements that the parties present to them. These judicial powers, however, operate within a system of mass justice. The caseload would become overwhelming if judges balked regularly at proposals to remove a case from the trial docket, or even took the time regularly to investigate this possibility. The exigencies of high-volume criminal courts block judges from becoming an important limit on prosecutorial discretion.

The rules of professional responsibility as enforced by state licensing authorities are also a potential source of limits on the choices of prosecutors. Again, however, we get limited accountability from these regulators. State bar authorities rarely discipline prosecutors, and the penalties are usually not severe (Zacharias 2001; Green 2003).

Although institutions external to the prosecutor's office do not exert much power over the discretion of line prosecutors, the chief prosecutor is directly accountability to the voters. Prosecutors in the United States are normally elected (Perry 2006). In theory, elections keep the local prosecutor in line with local priorities and values in the enforcement of the criminal law. The influence of voters over the policies and priorities of the prosecutor's office, however, is quite limited. The heavy advantage of incumbents in prosecutorial elections and the lack of challengers in election campaigns make this an imperfect accountability mechanism (Wright 2009).

Recent experiments with "community prosecution" hold some promise for giving the chief prosecutor meaningful feedback about community values and priorities. The notion of community prosecution draws on the lessons and philosophy of the decades-old community policing movement (Levine 2005). The community prosecution philosophy calls on prosecutors to build partnerships with communities by incorporating the priorities of citizens into their mission, engaging in crime prevention along with prosecutions for past crimes, and treating the residents' quality of life as the essential objective of the system. This sometimes means a physical dispersion of the line prosecutors into field offices around the jurisdiction. It also sometimes entails surveys, regular discussion with community groups, and other techniques to keep the chief prosecutor informed about public values and priorities for the enforcement of criminal law (Nugent and Rainville 2001). These ongoing forms of public input have the potential to give the prosecutor more detailed information than one might glean from a political campaign once every four years.

Internal Constraints

While legal institutions outside the prosecutor's office do not fully meet the need for checks and balances, internal regulation has a substantial constraining effect. Forces within the prosecutor's office can produce decisions that remain true to declared sources of law, in keeping with current public priorities in the enforcement of that law, applied with reasonable consistency across cases (Bibas 2009; Miller and Wright 2008).

The internal control mechanisms include office structures that require more collaborative decisions, periodic review of the prosecutor's work, regular training of prosecutors to enhance skills and promote consistency, and articulated office policies. Each of these internal controls merit attention.

First, the managers in a prosecutor's office sometimes arrange the flow of cases in the office to encourage line attorneys to interact during their case processing decisions. This might involve the use of "horizontal" prosecution for some crimes, with different attorneys or units in the office making decisions as a file moves up through the system. It is also common, particularly in larger offices, to require supervisor review and approval for some decisions of a line prosecutor. In some offices, for instance, a supervisor must approve any dismissal of charges in a domestic violence case; for the most serious crimes such as rape and homicide, supervisors might conduct periodic reviews to ensure proper discovery and preparation for trial (Wright and Miller 2002).

Second, the formal training of prosecutors is an opportunity that chief prosecutors in the United States have only begun to tap. Line prosecutors do, of course, receive training. The instruction, however, is more haphazard and more focused on trial techniques than the comprehensive early-career training that new attorneys routinely receive in the prosecutorial services in some other countries (Frase 1990).

Finally, chief prosecutors can promote consistency and fidelity to public values among their line attorneys by articulating guidelines for charging and disposition of cases. Written guidelines are relatively common, particularly in larger offices, where it is difficult for the chief prosecutor to monitor the work of the office informally (Mayer 1996; James 1995). The *United States Attorney's Manual* is one such resource. The guidelines typically declare that they do not carry the force of law and are not enforceable in judicial proceedings, but they nevertheless exert some control over the behavior of prosecutors (Abrams 1971).

The written guidelines tend to deal with crimes that carry an especially high priority for the elected district attorney: for instance, office policy might prohibit the line prosecutors from reducing armed robbery charges to simple robbery if there is credible evidence of the use of a weapon (Worden 1990; Blum 1996). Prosecutors have from time to time banned the use of plea bargains for certain classes of cases, although such guidelines require serious monitoring and enforcement to remain effective (Berger 1976; Kuh 1975; Weninger 1987). For instance, statewide limits on the use of plea bargains in Alaska had an impact for a few years, but practices eventually returned to normal (Carns and Kruse 1992).

The chief prosecutor usually adopts office guidelines voluntarily, in an effort to manage so many line attorneys in a large bureaucracy. In rare circumstances, courts have ordered prosecutors in a jurisdiction to develop their own guidelines, to promote consistency in charging decisions that have a direct impact on the sentences available to the judge. For example, state courts in New Jersey ruled that individual prosecutor decisions to file for mandatory sentencing enhancements amounted to a constitutional infringement on the judicial role in sentence. To remedy this violation, the court ordered the prosecutors in the state to issue guidelines on the use of such sentencing enhancements (*State v. Vasquez*, 609 A.2d 29 [N.J. 1992]). In response, the prosecutors issued what are known as *Brimage* guidelines. (New Jersey Attorney General 2004). This technique for prompting prosecutors to create internal guidance holds some promise, and draws on established traditions from the realm of administrative law (Davis 1969). The arrangement respects the expertise of prosecutors while promoting the value of consistency.

Proponents of sentencing commissions have suggested that guidelines for prosecutorial charging might become a future topic for commission regulation (Tonry 1993). Some states have authorized their sentencing commissions to consider guidelines for prosecutors, but thus far the commissions have not waded into these waters (*Kan. Stat. Ann.* § 74–9101(b)(10); *Wash. Rev. Code Ann.* § 9.94A.850(2)(b)). While sentencing commissions might face serious questions about their constitutional authority and expertise when crafting prosecutor guidelines, perhaps commissions could prompt prosecutors to develop their own charging guidelines (Wright 2005b).

While there is much promise in the power of chief prosecutors to hold their line prosecutors accountable, the system also depends on professional tradition and individual conscience to achieve just results. At the end of the day, each prosecutor must remain individually committed to the ideal of responsible prosecution.

Conclusion

In jurisdictions that strengthen the connection between the sentence imposed and the charge of conviction or the proof of sentencing enhancement facts, the parties gain more power to influence and predict the sentence. Because the prosecutor holds the power to decline charges or to refuse to seek sentencing enhancements, the executive branch becomes the key decision point for many sentencing questions. The judge still participates, but performs a more limited review function. In this sense, the sentencing process depends less heavily than the traditional criminal trial on adversarial testing of evidence. This reliance on the methods of modern administrative government is understandable in the high-volume context of criminal courts in the United States. It means, however, that input from multiple institutions (the ideal embodied in the constitutional checks and balances) occurs mostly at the policy-making level, and is less relevant at the case level of sentencing.

References

Abrams, Norman. 1971. "Internal Policy: Guiding the Exercise of Prosecutorial Discretion." *UCLA Law Review* 19: 1–58.

Alschuler, Albert W. 1976. "The Trial Judge's Role in Plea Bargaining (pt. 1)." *Columbia Law Review* 76: 1059–1154.

Alschuler, Albert W. 1991. "The Failure of Sentencing Guidelines: A Plea for Less Aggregation." *University of Chicago Law Review* 58: 901–951.

American Bar Association. 1997. "Pleas of Guilty." In *Standards for Criminal Justice*, 14–3.3.

Bar-Gill, Oren, and Oren Gazal Ayal. 2006. "Plea Bargains Only for the Guilty." *Journal of Law and Economics* 49: 353–364.

Berger, Moise. 1976. "The Case Against Plea Bargaining." *American Bar Association Journal* 62: 621–624.

Bibas, Stephanos. 2004. "Plea Bargaining Outside the Shadow of Trial." *Harvard Law Review* 117: 2463–2547.

Bibas, Stephanos. 2009. "Prosecutorial Regulation Versus Prosecutorial Accountability." *University of Pennsylvania Law Review* 157: 959–1016.

Bibas, Stephanos, and Richard A. Bierschbach. 2004. "Integrating Remorse and Apology into Criminal Procedure." *Yale Law Journal* 114: 85–148.

Bjerk, David. 2005. "Making the Crime Fit the Penalty: The Role of Prosecutorial Discretion under Mandatory Minimum Sentencing." *Journal of Law and Economics* 48: 591–625.

Blum, Andrew. 1996. "No Plea Policies Sprout Across the U.S.: Prosecutors Reject Revolving-Door Justice, But Risk Bigger Backlogs." *National Law Journal*, Sept. 9.

Bowman, Frank O., III. 2005. "Mr. Madison Meets a Time Machine: The Political Science of Federal Sentencing Reform." *Stanford Law Review* 58: 235–265.

Bowman, Frank O., III and Michael Heise. 2001. "Quiet Rebellion? Explaining Nearly a Decade of Declining Federal Drug Sentences." *Iowa Law Review* 86: 1043–1136.

Brereton, David, and Jonathan Casper. 1981. "Does It Pay to Plead Guilty? Differential Sentencing and the Functioning of Criminal Courts." *Law and Society Review* 16: 45–70.

Brown, Darryl K. 2007. "Democracy and Decriminalization." *Texas Law Review* 86: 223–276.

Bureau of Justice Statistics. *State Court Sentencing of Convicted Felons 2004—Statistical Tables*, table 4.4. Washington, DC. Available at: http://bjs.ojp.usdoj.gov/content/pub/html/scscf04/tables/scs04404tab.cfm.

Cahill, Michael T., and Paul H. Robinson. 2005. "The Accelerating Degradation of American Criminal Codes." *Hastings Law Journal* 56: 633–655.

Carns, Teresa White, and John A. Kruse. 1992. "Alaska's Ban on Plea Bargaining Reevaluated." *Judicature* 75: 310–317.

Davis, Angela J. 2007. *Arbitrary Justice: The Power of the American Prosecutor*. New York: Oxford University Press.

Davis, Kenneth Culp. 1969. *Discretionary Justice: A Preliminary Inquiry*. Baton Rouge: Louisiana State University Press.

Dixon, Jo. 1995. "The Organizational Context of Criminal Sentencing." *American Journal of Sociology* 100: 1157–1198.

Dubber, Markus. 1997. "American Plea Bargains, German Lay Judges, and the Crisis of Criminal Procedure." *Stanford Law Review* 49: 547–605.

Easterbrook, Frank H. 1983. "Criminal Procedure as a Market System." *Journal of Legal Studies* 12: 289–332.

Farrell, Jill. 2003. "Mandatory Minimum Firearm Penalties: A Source of Sentencing Disparity?" *Justice Research and Policy* 5: 95–116.

Fisher, George. 2003. *Plea Bargaining's Triumph: A History of Plea Bargaining in America*. Palo Alto: Stanford University Press.

Fisher, Jeffrey L. 1996. "When Discretion Leads to Distortion: Recognizing Pre-Arrest Sentence-Manipulation Claims Under the Federal Sentencing Guidelines." *Michigan Law Review* 94: 2385–2421.

Forst, Brian, et al. 1982. *Arrest Convictability as a Measure of Police Performance*. Washington, DC: U.S. Department of Justice, National Institute of Justice.

Frase, Richard S. 2005. "Sentencing Guidelines in Minnesota, 1978–2003." In *Crime and Justice: A Review of Research* 32: 131–219.

Frase, Richard S. 1990. "Comparative Criminal Justice as a Guide to American Law Reform: How Do the French Do it, How Can We Find Out, and Why Should We Care?" *California Law Review* 78: 539–683.

Freed, Daniel J. 1992. "Federal Sentencing in the Wake of Guidelines: Unacceptable Limits on the Discretion of Sentencers." *Yale Law Journal* 101: 1681–1754.

Glaeser, Edward L., Daniel P. Kessler, and Anne Morrison Piehl. 2000. "What Do Prosecutors Maximize? An Analysis of the Federalization of Drug Crimes." *American Law and Economics Review* 2: 259–290.

Green, Bruce A. 2003. "Prosecutorial Ethics as Usual." *University of Illinois Law Review* 2003: 1573–1604.

James, David C. 1995. "The Prosecutor's Discretionary Screening and Charging Authority." *The Prosecutor* (March/April): 22–29.

Jehle, Jorg-Martin, and Marianne Wade, eds. 2006. *Coping with Overloaded Criminal Justice Systems: The Rise of Prosecutorial Power Across Europe.* Berlin: Springer.

Johnson, David T. 2002. *The Japanese Way of Justice: Prosecuting Crime in Japan.* New York: Oxford University Press.

King, Nancy J. 1999. "Priceless Process: Nonnegotiable Features of Criminal Litigation." *UCLA Law Review* 47: 113–181.

King, Nancy J., and Michael O'Neill. 2005. "Appeal Waivers and the Future of Sentencing Policy." *Duke Law Journal* 55: 209–261.

King, Nancy J., David A. Soule, Sara Steen, and Robert R. Weidner. 2005. "When Process Affects Punishment: Differences in Sentences after Guilty Plea, Bench Trial, and Jury Trial in Five Guidelines States." *Columbia Law Review* 105: 959–1009.

Knapp, Kay A. 1993. "Allocation of Discretion and Accountability Within Sentencing Structures." *University of Colorado Law Review* 64: 679–705.

Kuh, Richard H. 1975. "Plea Bargaining: Guidelines for the Manhattan District Attorney's Office." *Criminal Law Bulletin* 11: 48–61.

Langbein, John H. 1979. "Land Without Plea Bargaining: How the Germans Do It." *Michigan Law Review* 78: 204–225.

Levine, Kay L. 2005. "The New Prosecution." *Wake Forest Law Review* 40: 1125–1214.

Lynch, Gerard E. 1998. "Our Administrative System of Criminal Justice." *Fordham Law Review* 66: 2117–2151.

Maxfield, Linda Drazga, and John H. Kramer. 1998. *Substantial Assistance: An Empirical Yardstick Gauging Equity in Current Federal Policy and Practice.* Washington, DC: United States Sentencing Commission.

Mayer, Kim Banks. 1996. "Applying Open Records Policy to Wisconsin District Attorneys: Can Charging Guidelines Promote Public Awareness?" *Wisconsin Law Review* 1996: 295–344.

McCoy, Candace. 1993. *Politics and Plea Bargaining: Victims' Rights in California.* Philadelphia: University of Pennsylvania Press.

McNulty, Paul J. 2006. *Principles of Federal Prosecution of Business Organizations.* Available at: http://www.justice.gov/dag/speeches/2006/mcnulty_memo.pdf, Dec. 12.

Miethe, Terance D. 1987. "Charging and Plea Bargaining Practices Under Determinate Sentencing: An Investigation of the Hydraulic Displacement of Discretion." *Journal of Criminal Law and Criminology* 78: 155–176.

Miethe, Terance D., and Charles A. Moore. 1985. "Socioeconomic Disparities under Determinate Sentencing Systems: A Comparison of Preguideline and Postguideline Practices in Minnesota." *Criminology* 23: 337–363.

Miller, J. Langley, and John J. Sloan, III. 1994. "A Study of Criminal Justice Discretion." *Journal of Criminal Justice* 22: 107–123.

Miller, Marc L. 2004. "Domination and Dissatisfaction: Prosecutors as Sentencers." *Stanford Law Review* 56: 1211–1269.

Miller, Marc L. 1992. "Purposes At Sentencing." *Southern California Law Review* 66: 413–481.

Miller, Marc L., and Ronald F. Wright. 2008. "The Black Box." *Iowa Law Review* 94: 125–196.

Nagel, Ilene H., and Stephen J. Schulhofer. 1992. "A Tale of Three Cities: An Empirical Study of Charging and Bargaining Practices Under the Federal Sentencing Guidelines." *Southern California Law Review* 66: 501–561.

Nardulli, Peter F., Roy B. Flemming, and James Eisenstein. 1985. "Criminal Courts and Bureaucratic Justice: Concessions and Consensus in the Guilty Plea Process." *Journal of Criminal Law and Criminology* 76: 1103–1131.

New Jersey Attorney General. Available at: http://www.acpo.org/guidelines/brimage.pdf.

Nugent, Elaine, and Gerard A. Rainville. 2001. "State of Community Prosecution: Results of a National Survey." *The Prosecutor* 35(2): 26–33.

Pfaff, John. 2006. "The Continued Vitality of Structured Sentencing Following Blakely: The Effectiveness of Voluntary Guidelines." *UCLA Law Review* 54: 235–307.

Perry, Steven W. 2006. *Prosecutors in State Courts, 2005.* Washington, DC: Bureau of Justice Statistics.

Reitz, Kevin R. 1993. "Sentencing Facts: Travesties of Real-Offense Sentencing." *Stanford Law Review* 45: 523–573.

Reitz, Kevin R. 1998. "Modeling Sentencing Discretion in American Sentencing Systems." *Law and Policy* 20: 389–428.

Richman, Daniel. 2003. "Prosecutors and Their Agents, Agents and Their Prosecutors." *Columbia Law Review* 103: 749–832.

Schulhofer, Stephen J. 1993. "Rethinking Mandatory Minimum Sentences." *Wake Forest Law Review* 28: 199–222.

Schulhofer, Stephen J. 1984. "Is Plea Bargaining Inevitable?" *Harvard Law Review* 97: 1037–1107.

Schulhofer, Stephen J., and Ilene H. Nagel. 1997. "Plea Negotiations under the Federal Sentencing Guidelines: Guideline Circumvention and Its Dynamics in the Post-*Mistretta* Period." *Northwestern University Law Review* 91: 1284–1316.

Scott, Robert E., and William J. Stuntz. 1992. "Plea Bargaining as Contract." *Yale Law Journal* 101: 1909–1968.

Stith, Kate, and Jose A. Cabranes. 1998. *Fear of Judging: Sentencing Guidelines in the Federal Courts.* Chicago: University of Chicago Press.

Stuntz, William J. 2004. "Plea Bargaining and Criminal Law's Disappearing Shadow." *Harvard Law Review* 117: 2548–2569.

Stuntz, William J. 2001. "The Pathological Politics of Criminal Law." *Michigan Law Review* 100: 505–600.

Taha, Ahmed E. 2001. "The Equilibrium Effect of Legal Rule Changes: Are the Federal Sentencing Guidelines Being Circumvented?" *International Review of Law and Economics* 21: 251–269.

Tonry, Michael. 2005. "Functions of Sentencing and Sentencing Reform." *Stanford Law Review* 58: 37–66.

Tonry, Michael. 1993. "The Success of Judge Frankel's Sentencing Commission." *University of Colorado Law Review* 64: 713–722.

United States Sentencing Commission. 1987. *Supplemental Report on the Initial Sentencing Guidelines and Policy Statements.* Washington, DC: U.S. Department of Justice.

Uviller, H. Richard. 1988. *Tempered Zeal: A Columbia Professor's Year on the Streets with New York City Police.* Chicago: Contemporary Books.

Weninger, Robert A. 1987. "The Abolition of Plea Bargaining: A Case Study of El Paso County, Texas." *UCLA Law Review* 35: 265–313.

Worden, Alissa Pollitz. 1990. "Policymaking by Prosecutors: The Uses of Discretion in Regulating Plea Bargaining." *Judicature* 73: 335–340.

Wright, Ronald F. 2005a. "Trial Distortion and the End of Innocence in Federal Criminal Justice." *University of Pennsylvania Law Review* 154: 79–156.

Wright, Ronald F. 2005b. "Sentencing Commissions as Provocateurs of Prosecutorial Self-Regulation." *Columbia Law Review* 105: 1010–1047.

Wright, Ronald F. 2009. "How Prosecutor Elections Fail Us." *Ohio State Journal of Criminal Law* 6: 581–610.

Wright, Ronald F., and Rodney Engen. 2006. "The Charging and Sentencing Effects of Depth and Distance in a Criminal Code." *North Carolina Law Review* 84: 1935–1982.

Wright, Ronald F., and Marc L. Miller. 2002. "The Screening/Bargaining Tradeoff." *Stanford Law Review* 55: 29–118.

Zacharias, Fred C. 2001. "The Professional Discipline of Prosecutors." *North Carolina Law Review* 79: 725–743.

Zeisel, Hans. 1981. "The Disposition of Felony Arrests." *American Bar Foundation Research Journal* 6: 407–462.

CHAPTER 11

THE "TRADITIONAL" INDETERMINATE SENTENCING MODEL

KEVIN R. REITZ[*]

"It was a fine idea having only the defect that it did not work."
—Norval Morris on indeterminate sentencing (1974, 47)

"[A]s a matter of political judgment, I find it hard to imagine a scenario under which discretionary release through parole boards can be revived in this country."

—Jeremy Travis (2002, 2)

INTRODUCTION

As recently as the early 1970s, every jurisdiction in the United States operated with a traditional *indeterminate* sentencing structure, in which judges had broad and unregulated discretion to select criminal sentences constrained only by maximum statutory penalties (normally much higher than any sentence a judge was likely to impose). In prison cases, parole boards held broad and unregulated authority to determine actual time served within a wide range of possibilities between the minimum and maximum terms set for each prisoner according to state law (Frankel 1973, 86–102; Tonry 1996, 6–7). Half of the American states continue to use such systems today, at least for the majority of felony cases (see Petersilia 2003, 66-67).[1]

Starting in the mid-1970s, the other half of the states, the District of Columbia, and the federal government have moved away from the traditional indeterminate framework through the elimination of the parole board's release discretion, the adoption of judicial sentencing guidelines, or both (Rhine, chapter 26 of this volume; Weisberg, chapter 12 of this volume). These changes, more successful in some jurisdictions than in others, have all sailed under the banner of "sentencing reform" (American Bar Association 1994; Tonry 1996; Stith and Cabranes 1998; Frase 2005; Barkow and O'Neill 2006; American Law Institute 2007).

For the past 30 years, most of the empirical research and policy analysis of U.S. sentencing systems has focused on the "reform" jurisdictions, and scant attention has been devoted to the many holdover states that persist in the traditional setup. To the extent that systems-builders have paid attention to the indeterminate states, it has been to categorically disapprove of them in favor of the determinate framework (e.g., American Bar Association 1994; American Law Institute 2011, App. B), while ignoring the question of how parole-release structures might be made better. This has left an enormous range of law and policy questions neglected, including: Which among the current indeterminate systems are the best (to be emulated) and the worst (to be models of what not to do)? Have there been *past* indeterminate systems that, in hindsight, may have been more successful than believed at the time?[2] What are the building-block legal and institutional elements of the most effective systems? What practical advice, based on proven experience elsewhere, can be given to policymakers in an indeterminate state experiencing some form of acute crisis, such as prison overcrowding?

To approach these questions, what is needed is nothing less than a new field of "indeterminate sentencing studies" that compares whole systems one to another, explores how specific legal and institutional elements are working within different structural and political contexts, and develops criteria for systemwide performance evaluation. The largely unstudied mass of traditional systems adds up to about half the country, including populous states like New York and Texas, and most of the nation's highest-incarceration-rate jurisdictions.

This chapter comments on what we know, or can readily find out, today about U.S. indeterminate sentencing systems.[3] Its major observations will be:

- The standard definitions of "indeterminacy" and "determinacy" are less airtight than is commonly understood.
- Indeterminate sentencing systems differ from one another in many visible ways, both large and small, but our knowledge base is too thin for comparative policy judgments.
- Nearly all American parole release agencies have adopted incapacitation through actuarial risk assessment as a major component of their decision-making process. This is a low-visibility policy built on imperfect risk-prediction technology that is not subject to meaningful challenge by prisoners in their own cases.

- Legislatures and parole boards have no coherent vision of the functions of parole-release decisions. In most indeterminate states, the parole board is permitted to reappraise virtually any aspect of the judge's original sentence.
- There is conflicting evidence on the question of whether discretionary release fosters lower recidivism rates among ex-prisoners, and none of the evidence is terribly credible. If there is such an effect, it is impossible to know whether it is due to prisoner rehabilitation, risk predictions at the release stage, or a combination of the two.
- Parole boards generally work within an abysmal procedural and institutional framework for the delivery of fair and rational release decisions.
- Although many people in the United States associate parole release with leniency, it has not acted as an inhibitor upon prison population growth. Indeterminate sentencing states have higher incarceration rates, and have experienced greater prison growth in the last 30 years, than states making use of other systems. States with both determinate systems and sentencing guidelines have experienced the least amount of prison growth since 1980 when compared with other system types.

Categorizing Sentencing Systems

The conventional terminologies used to describe different sentencing systems over the past 40 years are outmoded. They no longer tell us what we need to know about the important differences among systems. Sometimes the accepted usages are merely uninformative, but they can also be seriously misleading.[4] This chapter will not try to create a new lexicon of American sentencing systems, however. That is a big job. Instead, the chapter will build on the standard definitions, with frequent caveats about the complexities hidden beneath them.

As a matter of conventional understanding, *indeterminate sentencing systems* are those that empower a parole-release agency to rule on the actual lengths of prison terms (Frankel 1973, 86; Rothman 1980, 44; Wool and Stemen 2004, 2). What I will refer to as the *traditional* indeterminate systems—a subgroup of the whole—are those that make little or no effort to structure the judge's sentencing discretion at the front end of the sentencing timeline, while also featuring parole-release discretion at the back end.[5]

By historical use, the word "indeterminate" is meant to denote that, on the day a prison sentence is handed down in court, no one—including the judge—can estimate with any certainty how long the defendant will actually be confined (von Hirsch and Hanrahan 1979, 27). The true severity of an indeterminate sentence is unknowable, sometimes for many years.

In American indeterminate jurisdictions, the most powerful decision maker in prison cases is the parole board at the back end of the system. The board decides whether individual prisoners will be released at their first parole-eligibility dates, will be held to serve their full maximum terms, or will be freed at some point between. Typically, parole eligibility occurs long before expiration of the maximum term. Thus, for an indeterminate sentence of two-to-ten years, parole-release discretion controls the last eight years of the possible ten-year prison stay (American Law Institute 1985a, § 6.06).

Release does not hinge solely on parole boards, however. Most prisoners may also earn credits against their terms for good behavior, participation in programs, and the like. This adds a further back-end adjustment to the judicial sentence, typically administered by departments of correction. Good-time allowances are usually a smaller part of the overall confinement equation than parole-release discretion. In some indeterminate jurisdictions they are applied only to maximum terms, and not to parole-eligibility dates. They generally affect fewer weeks and months of prison terms than parole-release discretion, and the grounds for loss of credits are supposed to be narrow, limited to disciplinary violations. While arbitrary or vindictive forfeitures no doubt occur, and can work serious injustices in individual cases, good-time credits seem to be granted routinely—even perfunctorily—to the majority of prisoners (Schriro 2009; Demleitner 2009; Jacobs 1982).

Determinate sentencing systems, by conventional definition, are those that have abolished the release discretion of the parole board (Wool and Stemen 2004). Although the terminology is misleading,[6] release under determinate laws is often described as "mandatory," while indeterminate systems are said to employ "discretionary" release. Determinate prison sentences hold a predictable relationship to the term imposed in court, enough so that they have sometimes been advertised as "truth in sentencing" (Knapp 1993, 684–685; Marvell and Moody 1996, 108). In determinate systems—similar to their indeterminate counterparts—prisoners may earn good-time credits that shorten their prison stays (American Law Institute 2011, § 305.1; Jacobs 1982). The existence of a good-time program, however, is not thought to give rise to an indeterminate structure according to the conventional classification scheme. On the day of judicial sentencing, the length of term that most defendants will actually serve is reasonably calculable so long as one makes a mental correction for the expected good-time discount. If good-time credits are in fact routinely granted in most instances, punishment severity is predominantly fixed by judges.

Sentencing guidelines are laws or rules or recommendations, usually created by a sentencing commission, that are addressed to trial judges for use in the courtroom sentencing process (Weisberg, chapter 12 of this volume).[7] Such guidelines limit or inform the vast front-end discretion that exists in traditional indeterminate systems, and are therefore an important step away from the traditional program. They do not speak to back-end discretion, however. Some states have adopted judicial sentencing guidelines while retaining the parole board's prison-release discretion; other guidelines jurisdictions have eliminated parole release. The 20 guidelines jurisdictions in the United States today are roughly split down the middle on this issue (American Law Institute 2011, § 6.06; Frase 2005).

Considering these major design elements together (indeterminacy versus determinacy; guidelines versus no guidelines), we can identify four broad categories of sentencing system types in America: (1) the "traditional" indeterminate systems with parole release and no guidelines; (2) indeterminate systems modified by the introduction of guidelines, but retaining parole release; (3) determinate systems that have eliminated parole release but have not adopted judicial sentencing guidelines; and (4) determinate guidelines systems.

Within each of the four major headings, there are many important—and sometimes vast—differences across jurisdictions. One theme of this chapter is that we need more knowledge of intra-system-type variations—especially among the type (1) "traditional" indeterminate sentencing structures.

Degrees of Indeterminacy

Even when traditional indeterminacy reigned supreme in American law, there were many permutations in the implementation of the program. One key design feature is the formula for calculation of the minimum term that a prisoner must serve before the parole board's discretion is activated. In many systems of the 1970s, parole-release eligibility was triggered at 25 or 33 or 50 percent of an inmate's maximum prison stay, or by some alternative mathematical or offense-specific requirement. In a number of states, however, parole eligibility was statutorily defined so that it sprang to life on the very first day of a prison term—with no minimum to limit the release discretion of the parole board. In a minority of states, sentencing judges were given discretion to set both minimum and maximum prison terms, although an available range for each was usually dictated by statute (American Law Institute 1985a, 139–152). In a handful of states, including California and Washington, common felonies were assigned extraordinarily high maximum prison terms, including life imprisonment, with the date of release (in practice, usually a small fraction of the maximum) wholly in the hands of the parole board (Messinger and Johnson 1977, 953–954; Boerner and Lieb 2001, 73).

Wide diversity continues across present-day indeterminate states, although all have cut back on the use of indeterminate sentences for selected categories of cases. For example, the sanction of life without parole was little used circa 1970, but has greatly increased nationwide in the last 40 years (Nellis and King 2009; Harvard Law Review 2006, 1840). It is also common to exclude from parole eligibility prisoners convicted of designated violent and sex offenses, or prisoners convicted under "three strikes" or other habitual offender laws (see, e.g., Ala. Code § 15–22–27.1; Conn. Gen. Stat. § 54–125a(b)(1); Fla. Stat. § 775.084(4)(k)(2),(3); Ga. Code § 17–10–6.1 & 17–10–7(c); N.J.

Stat. § 30:4–123.51). Still, for the bulk of prison cases in traditional systems, release eligibility is set according to familiar formulas such as one-quarter or one-third or one-half of the maximum term (Ala. Code § 15–22–28(e); Ga. Code § 42–9–45(b); Mo. Code of State Regulations, Title 14, § 80–2.010(1)(A)-(F); Colo. Rev. Stat. § 17–22.5–403(1); Conn. Gen. Stat. § 54–125; Laws of R.I., § 13–8–10), or, in some states, immediately upon admission to prison, with no minimum stay other than determined by the parole board (Hawaii Rev. Stat. § 706–669(1); Iowa Admin. Code § 205–8.6(906)8.6(1)).

It is hard to say whether any one approach is superior to any other. For instance, should an enlightened policy maker prefer eligibility dates that occur very soon in a prison term, or only after a significant portion of the maximum is served, and on what grounds? While the "early" approach may seem more lenient, and some may gravitate toward it on this basis alone, the appearance could be deceiving. A 10-year sentence with a 25 percent eligibility date is a harsher penalty than a 5-year sentence with a 50 percent eligibility date—*much* more so if we imagine a risk-averse parole board reluctant to release prisoners far short of their maximum term.

If we look more deeply into system design, the picture only becomes more complex. For example, most state laws vest the parole board with discretion to release or refuse each prisoner that comes before it, in light of decisional criteria of one kind or another (see the following section). In some other states, however, the board is instructed to release an eligible prisoner *unless* certain statutorily defined conditions are found to exist (See N.J. Stat. § 30:4–123.53(a); American Law Institute 1985b, § 305.6). We have no way of knowing, however, whether the legal presumption affects parole board decisions in any way. No jurisdiction has created an effective review mechanism for parole release decisions, so board members are free to give no weight to a statutory presumption, or to administer it inconsistently.

Nor should the policy inquiry focus only on the parole board and its workings. It is probably a mistake to continue to think of indeterminacy as solely a function of parole release. All American criminal justice systems include an additional hodge-podge of official actors—with decisional authority exercised later in time than courtroom proceedings—who may contribute to the indefiniteness of judicial sentences.[8]

The most important of these are departments of corrections, which typically have jurisdiction to administer good-time or earned-time credits, and these credits sometimes come in multiple sizes and shapes in a single jurisdiction. In some systems, this power is substantial. For example, under current New Jersey law, a prisoner sentenced to a maximum prison term of 10 years becomes parole eligible at 3 years and 4 months (one-third the maximum) (see N.J. Stat. § 30:4–123.51(a)), yet eligibility is further subject to an array of "commutation" and "work" and "minimum custody" credits, so that the actual "earliest eligibility date" for a 10-year maximum is 1 year, 11 months, and 5 days (N.J. State Parole Board 2010, 35; see also American Law Institute 2003, 20–26).

There are numerous additional sources of indeterminacy in U.S. sentencing systems, usually affecting small numbers of cases, and with no expectation of routine application (Love 2009). These include mechanisms such as compassionate release or "medical parole," mainly available to inmates with disabling or terminal illnesses, and the executive's clemency powers, which in most jurisdictions are used only sporadically (American Law Institute 2011, § 305.7; Barkow 2009; Love 2009).[9] In most jurisdictions, judges retain jurisdiction to revise their own sentences for a short period after they are imposed. In a handful of states, this power extends years into a prison term, and has been called "bench parole" (Klingele 2010, 24). Brand new sources of indeterminacy may also be on the horizon. Current proposals for a revised Model Penal Code include an innovative provision for sentence modification by a "judicial decision maker" that would activate at the 15-year point of a long prison sentence (American Law Institute 2011, § 305.6; Frase 2010).

There are also forms of wholesale indeterminacy. To address crises of prison overcrowding, states have often resorted to ad hoc early-release measures affecting large numbers of inmates.[10] The effect is to revise some prison sentences downward in ways unforeseeable at the initial sentencing (Archibold 2010; Austin 1986). Starting with Michigan in 1981, many parole boards have been ceded special statutory powers to respond to overcrowding emergencies. These laws vary in their specifics, but their main strategy is to loosen the ordinary eligibility and release rules that would otherwise apply (Rhine, Smith, and Jackson 1991, 84; Ga. Code § 42-9-60; Iowa Code § 906.5(2); Laws of R.I. § 42-26-13.3 Wis. Stat. § 304.02). In theory, this could serve as a safety valve for prison population growth, but little research has focused on these laws in operation. Existing studies, 20 years or more out of date, suggest that such mechanisms have not proven terribly important, and their use has largely dwindled out (Rhine 1986; Rhine, Smith, and Jackson 1991; Austin 1986; Finn 1984; Blumstein et al. 1983).[11]

Just as the particulars of indeterminacy vary from place to place, it is a mistake to think that there is a crystal-clear distinction between indeterminate and determinate systems. There is impressive diversity among determinate jurisdictions, too, and none is *absolutely* determinate. Pockets of indeterminacy always remain, such as good time, compassionate release, and the other non-parole mechanisms mentioned above. It is even conceivable that a putative determinate system may in fact have avenues for prison release—such as particularly generous good-time credits—that approximate the back-end discretion found in structures formally classified as indeterminate (American Law Institute 2011, 305.1; Chayet 1994, 525; Austin 1987, 22; Jacobs 1982).

Analysis of indeterminate (and other) sentencing systems is impoverished by a shortage of pertinent research—and by the absence of a language, as well as conceptual categories, that would make informed conversation possible. The very definition of indeterminacy is more slippery than commonly supposed—and quantifying the *degree* of indeterminacy in a particular system requires that we cumulate the effects of many discretionary actors and decision points. Merely understanding the differences among the many American systems, which is the necessary base for constructive policy debate, is largely beyond our present abilities.

WHAT INDETERMINACY IS TRYING TO ACCOMPLISH

For its policy foundation, the parole release system since late in the nineteenth century has most often been linked with rehabilitation theory. This view rests on expectations that prisoners are undergoing reformative change while incarcerated, yet it cannot be known in advance how long their individual journeys will take. The key function of the paroling authority is to review each prisoner's progress, and to use its expertise to identify those who have reached the goal (Winter 1893, 454; Wines 1910, 213; National Commission on Law Observance and Enforcement 1931, 142–143; American Law Institute 1985a, 122).

There has always been a puzzle about the true personality of the process, however. As a means of setting prison terms, the rehabilitative premise is unavoidably paired with a less compassionate incapacitative program. Every eligible inmate deemed unready for release is confined for an extended period on grounds of predicted reoffending. Both the progressive reformers of the early twentieth century and the drafters of the original Model Penal Code in the 1960s believed that some criminals were especially dangerous, and must be held for the full maximum term— or an extended term beyond the normal maximum sentence (Dawson 1966, 249; Rothman 1980, 193–194; Friedman 1993, 161; American Law Institute 1985a, 117, 119). From its origins, there has been a deep tension in underlying policies, and the potential for "soft" and "hard" treatment, within the indeterminate framework.

If anything, the riddle is more profound today than it has ever been. Because of the lack of transparency in parole release, and the thinness of pertinent research, we have no confident sense of the motivations that drive decisions. There is one large and accessible body of source materials that can be mined in every indeterminate jurisdiction, however. We can review the legal instructions that parole boards are given, as well as the formal statements of release criteria found in statutes, regulations, guidelines, manuals, and the like. These provide idealized statements of the purposes underlying the parole release function in each jurisdiction. It may be that parole boards do not faithfully execute the official plan. Still, if there is a sensible rationale behind the discretionary release system, one would hope to find it here.

A common thread that runs through the rhetoric of U.S. parole-release systems is that prisoners should not be freed if the board thinks they present an unacceptable risk to public safety. It is an accepted norm that years of confinement, dispensed by the most authoritative sentencer in prison cases, should turn on risk assessments (of questionable quality) together with the board's ultimate discretion to decide how much risk is too much in individual cases. The risk-incapacitative policy is often set out as an overarching principle of the parole board's function. The Colorado code, for example, says bluntly that "the primary consideration for any decision to grant parole shall be the public safety" (Colo. Rev. Stat. § 17–2–100.2). More obliquely, but to similar effect, the operative statutory language in Connecticut gives the parole board discretion to release only if "there is reasonable probability that such inmate will live and remain at liberty without violating the law and . . . such release is not incompatible with the welfare of society" (Conn. Gen. Stat. § 54–125). Similar provisions exist in many other parole-release states (e.g., Vt. Stat. § 502a(b)(2); S.D. Codified Laws § 24–15–8(2)). Specialized provisions on recidivism risk also exist in some states. For example, in Tennessee, "No person convicted of a sex crime shall be released on parole unless a psychiatrist or licensed psychologist . . . has evaluated the inmate and determined *to a reasonable medical or psychological certainty* that the inmate does not pose the likelihood of committing sexual assaults upon release from confinement" (Tenn. Code § 40–28–116(2)).

A majority of indeterminate jurisdictions now require that the board consult an actuarial risk assessment instrument of one kind or another before releasing any prisoner (Wolff 2008; Ratansi and Cox 2007, 10–11 and Appendix C). The composition of these tools suggests that incapacitation policy predominates over any inquiry into prisoners' progress toward rehabilitation. Although many different instruments are in use, they all rely most heavily or exclusively on *static* factors that a prisoner is unable to alter during a prison stay, such as prior criminal history (including the number, type, and recency of prior offenses), prior incarcerations, past failures on probation or parole, history of drug use, age, and pre-incarceration marital status and employment history. The development of validated *dynamic* predictive factors, having to do with an offender's rehabilitative progress while institutionalized, is still in its infancy (Wong and Gordon 2006, 279; Glover et al. 2002, 247; Gendreau, Little, and Goggin 1996, 588). In other words, parole boards are given almost no instructions about how to tell when an inmate has reached an acceptable point of rehabilitation.

Beyond the ubiquity of the incapacitative rationale, the statements of parole boards' intended functions, as contained in official sources, are muddled and perplexing. In most states, the board's mandate is so amorphous that it holds effective authority to reevaluate all aspects of the judge's original sentence, including how much time a prisoner *deserves* to spend in prison for his offense.[12] Considerations of retribution and proportionality in punishment are often—explicitly, or nearly so—made part of the decisional matrix. In New York and a number of other systems, for example, the parole board must be satisfied that the release date "will not so deprecate the seriousness of his crime as to undermine respect for law" (Cons. Laws of N.Y. § 259-i(2)(c)(A); Tenn. Rules and Regulations § 1100–01–01–.07(4)(b); Wis. Admin. Code § PAC 1.04; accord Laws of R.I., § 13–8–14(a)(2)). In other states, the board weighs the "sufficiency" of the amount of time that has been served by each prisoner, or is instructed to respond to the "severity" or "nature" of the offense for which the inmate is imprisoned (Alabama Board of Pardons and Parole 2009: 27; Ga. Code § 42–9–40(a); Iowa Admin. Code § 205–8.10(906); Tex. Gov. Code § 588.144(a)(2); Tex. Admin. Code § 145.2(b)(1)). Boards also commonly consider the prisoner's criminal record, anything contained in the original presentence report, and victim impact information (Tenn. Rules and Regulations § 1100–01–01–.07; Rev. Code Neb. § 83–192(1)(f)(v); N.H. Admin. Code Rules, Par. 301.03; Code of N.M. Rules, R. 22.510.3.8; N.D. Code § 12–59–05; R.I. Admin. Code, Rule 49–1–1:1).

Roberts (chapter 4 of this volume) reports that victims are often allowed to express their views on the gravity of the original crime as part of parole release proceedings, especially the degree of injury they have suffered. When parole boards respond to this kind of information, and Roberts finds that they do, they submerge themselves in a retributive evaluation of the prisoner's criminal act.

The absence of boundaries upon the proper remit of a parole board leads to some bizarre decisional criteria. Many of these would not withstand scrutiny if used by sentencing judges. Statutes in many states, for instance, forbid the release of a prisoner unless the board is satisfied that he will be "suitably employed" and will not become a "public charge" if released (Ala. Code § 15–22–28(d); Ga. Code § 42–9–42; Miss. Code § 47–7–17; S.D. Codified Laws § 24–15–8(3)). New Hampshire includes among its official reasons for denial of parole "[t]he existence of adverse public concern or notoriety" (N.H. Admin. Code Rules, Par. 302.01). Some state codes forbid release unless the prisoner has attained some minimal level of education (e.g., Tenn. Code § 40–28–115 (g)(1)). In Utah, it weighs against early release if the prisoner has brought "a claim that [any state of federal] court finds to be without merit and brought or asserted in bad faith" (Utah Code § 77–27–5.3(2)), a draconian way to discourage frivolous legal arguments. Perhaps most ominously of all, before releasing a prisoner, the New Mexico Parole Board is instructed by statute to consider "the inmate's culture, language, values, mores, judgments, communicative ability and other unique qualities" (Code of N.M. Rules, R. 22.510.3.8(C)(2)(s)).

If parole-release agencies make use of the free-ranging instructions they are given, we must face up to the fact that they are the primary sentencers in prison cases, with control over a majority share of the possible length of incarceration, authority to revisit any issue weighed by the sentencing judge, and full freedom to revise or ignore the judge's conclusions. Indeed, the range of considerations open to a parole board is effectively wider than those at work in judicial sentencings. Because the parole-release process has so little transparency, some spurious release requirements have been allowed to proliferate—requirements that judges in good conscience could not apply.

INDETERMINACY AND RISK ASSESSMENT

Many strenuously resist the idea that judicial sentencing should be oriented heavily toward risk of reoffending (e.g., Tonry 1999; Robinson 2001; Harcourt 2006; Netter 2007; Etienne 2009), yet this is precisely what the dominant sentencers in prison cases—the parole boards—have been doing for many decades.

The range of risk assessment instruments currently in use across the United States is dizzying. There is little apparent consensus on how these tools should be designed, which factors should be included, and how each factor should be weighted. Although comparative studies of all the varied instruments are not available—in many states, no evaluation of their own scale has been done—by all appearances there are dramatic differences in quality from place to place. Only a tiny number of states base their actuarial scales on research into offending patterns of ex-prisoners in their home jurisdiction. Some states use abbreviated forms with 8 or 10 factors, while others include relatively extensive worksheets and questionnaires. Some instruments use cut-and-dried objective considerations that are easily scored, but others require "soft" qualitative judgment calls about prisoners' attitudes and progress in treatment. These introduce slippery discretion into the scoring process itself. A number of states use research-based inventories such as the Salient Factor Score (developed by the U.S. Parole Board) or the LSI-R (developed by researchers in Canada), while many others use risk guidelines with no visible empirical grounding (Ratansi and Cox 2007, Appendix C; Missouri Department of Corrections 2009, Appendix B; Moffat 2010; Monahan and Walker 2006, 391–396).

Across the states, there is no uniformity in philosophy about the use or preclusion of potentially controversial risk factors. Most but not all risk scales incorporate age as a factor (with a large effect on the bottom-line score), a handful add gender (also a powerful factor where in use), and some include socioeconomic considerations like marital status and employment history. While all of the instruments include past criminality as an major predictor, there are wide differences in how this variable is measured. Some states include arrests in the mix, while most register only convictions or past incarcerations, and there are sharp differences of opinion on the use of juvenile records. No risk instrument explicitly uses race as a factor,[13] but there is danger that socioeconomic and criminal history factors correlate with race—and the use of arrest data threatens to incorporate racial profiling by law enforcement into prison policy.

A critical empirical question is how much predictive power the actuarial approach could realistically bring to bear if all parole-release systems were to adopt state-of-the-art measures. In the 1980s, there was consensus that even the best methodologies misfired more often than not when trying to identify high-risk offenders (Morris and Miller 1985). John Monahan's influential survey found that, even when dealing with previously violent and mentally ill offenders, "psychiatrists and psychologists are accurate in no more than one out of three predictions of violent behavior over a several year period" (1981, 48–49). In other words, for every three offenders classified as high risk for serious reoffending, two would turn out to be *false positives* (i.e., would never engage in the predicted behavior). Prison policies of selective incapacitation were seen as freighted with enormous human, ethical, and financial costs (Cohen 1983; Greenwood and Turner 1987).

The science of prediction has advanced considerably since the 1980s. Some of the new actuarial tools are reasonably good at predicting serious reoffending, although they still make significant numbers of errors. The better scales can yield correct classifications, measured against actual recidivism data, in up to 70 percent of all cases, although many instruments currently in use do not come up to this standard (Slobogin 2011; Gaes 2009, 5–6; Ratansi and Cox 2007, 6–7; Meredith et al. 2007, 15–17; Austin et al. 2003, 18).[14] One should not assume, of course, that the level of accuracy achieved in the hothouse of empirical research will automatically be replicated in the field. The same instrument does not necessarily get the same results across multiple studies. The success of the technology also depends heavily on the qualifications of the personnel making use of it. Inter-rater reliability is a recognized problem when filling out risk inventories (Austin et al. 2003). Also, where the tire meets the road, officials charged with interpreting the results often do not understand the limitations of probability scores (Moffat 2010, 12). Even so, current evidence suggests that actuarial risk tools can supply meaningful probabilistic information about future reoffending, much like the actuarial data used by insurance companies to set premiums, that these tools are getting better all the time, and that actuarial risk technologies are much superior to the intuitions of judges and parole boards, or even the trained clinical judgments of mental health professionals (Grove and Meehl 1996; Harris, Rice, and Cormier 2002). Just the same, there is no way to avoid the wrenching problem of false positives, with penalties of extended confinement visited upon those who would not reoffend as predicted—and no serious person believes that this difficulty will ever be eliminated, no matter how far our science advances.

If it is defensible to base the duration of prison terms on risk predictions, one of the core policy questions of indeterminate versus determinate sentencing is whether parole boards are the best agents of government to perform the function, or whether it ought to take place in open courtrooms (American Law Institute 2011, § 6B.09). Research has long shown that parole boards are no better at setting release dates based on risk than judges would have been on the day of sentencing (Wong and Gordon 2006, 279; Douglas and Skeem 2005, 347–358; Glover et al. 2002, 236, 247). So far, predictions about an inmate's future conduct are not improved by looking to "dynamic" factors concerning what he has done to improve himself while incarcerated. As one recent study concluded:

> [E]mpirical investigation of dynamic risk is virtually absent from the literature. . . .
> The field's next greatest challenge is to develop sound methods for assessing
> changeable aspects of violence risk. . . . To date, the scientific focus on dynamic
> risk and risk management has been more conceptual than empirical. . . . [I]t is
> unclear what the most promising dynamic risk factors are. (Douglas and Skeem
> 2005, 347, 349, 352, 358)

Norval Morris put it this way: "What it all comes down to is this: Prison behavior is not a predictor of community behavior" (Morris 1974, 16; Morris 2002, 186).

If little or nothing is gained in predictive accuracy in vesting discretion in parole boards, there are clear substantive and procedural implications in preferring boards over judges as responsible decision makers. On the substantive side, parole boards cannot use risk scales as prison diversion tools. In contrast, one state has pursued risk-based prison diversion as an express priority in judicial sentencing (Ostrom et al. 2002; Netter 2007), and several other jurisdictions supply judges with risk information prior to the "in-out" decision (Wolff 2008; Oregon Criminal Justice Commission 2011). Risk assessments by parole boards also unfold in a procedural context of little adversariness and few protections for prisoners (as discussed in a later section). Because defendants at judicial sentencing have lawyers, arguments may be raised in individual cases about possible errors in risk assessment calculations, and legal challenges assembled against the scheme as a whole (Marcus 2009a, 105–106; *Luttrell* 2004). When risk assessments are freely used at the parole release stage, however, with years of prison terms in the balance, no controversy ensues—and there are almost never defense lawyers to champion the interests of prisoners or otherwise stir up trouble.

Acknowledging that a risk-based prison policy is now in force in nearly every U.S. indeterminate jurisdiction, it is fair to ask what the societal benefits of that approach might be. The aggregate effects probably include reduced recidivism among those chosen for release. Assuming that a statistical instrument of fair quality is in use, and is followed with some degree of consistency by a parole board, then prisoners paroled before expiration of their maximum terms should on the whole reoffend at lower rates than those not discretionarily released, and less frequently than releasees in systems that do not use actuarial risk assessment tools either at judicial sentencing or for release determinations.

INDETERMINACY AND REHABILITATION

By the 1970s, after many decades of experience with indeterminate sentencing throughout the United States, expert opinion coalesced around the conclusion that indeterminacy was ineffective at—or even an impediment to—the successful rehabilitation of prisoners (American Friends Service Committee 1971, 93–96; Frankel 1973, 49, 96–97; Morris 1974, 50; Bagley 1979, 391–392). On this view, the prospect of early release coerced enrollment in rehabilitative programs, thus draining their effectiveness, or encouraged inauthentic participation—what Norval Morris called "play acting." The very project of in-prison rehabilitation was also called into question (Jacobs 1982, 264–265). In Hans Mattick's famous metaphor, "It is hard to train an aviator in a submarine; it is even harder to predict his flying capacity from observing his submarine behavior!" (quoted in Morris 1974, 16). Nor was discretionary release seen as beneficial for inmate morale, because prisoners did not believe that parole boards made their decisions in principled ways.

Today there are renewed hopes and claims that indeterminate sentences can be well-fitted to rehabilitation policy (National Institute of Corrections 2011; Campbell 2008; Burke and Tonry 2005; Stivers Ireland and Prause 2005; Petersilia 2003). Recidivism research has not produced consistent findings on the question, however. Recent studies have reached conclusions that are all over the map when comparing recidivism rates in determinate and discretionary release settings; results include the positive, negative, and null. (Bales et al. 2010; Zhang, Zhang, and Vaughn 2009; Bhati and Piquero 2008; Rosenfeld et al. 2005; Solomon et al. 2005). One study found that those released discretionarily fared better than those mandatorily released, but the results flipped if the single jurisdiction of California were removed from the data (Stivers Ireland and Prause 2005; American Law Institute 2011, App. B, 134–35). Measures of recidivism among prison releasees are much too unreliable, and inconsistently generated across jurisdictions, to permit confident conclusions (Rhine, chapter 26 of this volume; Zhang, Zhang, and Vaughn 2009, 7–9). And even if we knew there were lower recidivism rates among discretionarily released prisoners, it would be impossible to know if this were a genuine rehabilitation effect, or merely an artifact of the widespread use of risk scales (see previous section).

INDETERMINACY AND PROCEDURAL SHABBINESS

The procedural safeguards that have traditionally attended judicial sentencing are notoriously inadequate (Schulhofer 1980). Judge Gerard Lynch has dubbed sentencing a "second-string fact-finding process" (1997, 27). If this is a fair assessment, then the procedural accoutrements of parole release are of the *third-* or *fourth-*string variety.[15]

The release process is necessarily streamlined given small person-power and large caseloads. Parole boards could never marshal resources comparable to court systems when deliberating on individual cases; they are tiny agencies averaging a total of five or six members. The number of prisoners considered for release by the average state parole board in 2006 was 8,355—about 35 cases for each working day, and comprising only one part of a typical board's responsibilities (Kinnevy and Caplan 2008, 9). Davis reported that the well-resourced U.S. Parole Board, before abolition of parole in the federal system, heard roughly 50 cases per day (1971, 127). Studies of parole in its mid-twentieth-century heyday found decision-making times of only 3–20 minutes per case (Rothman 1980, 164–165; Dawson 1966, 301). With the explosion in correctional populations since then, it is unlikely that greater attention is given today.

Parole-release "hearings" are often no more than brief interviews of the prisoner, sometimes convened without notice. The prisoner's role at the hearing varies quite a bit among the states, but is often limited to responding to the board's questions. Sometimes there is no right for the prisoner to be present at all; the case is decided solely on the papers (Cohen 1999, vol. 1, 6–27; Fla. Stat. § 947.06; Vt. Stat. § 502(a); *Mahaney* 1992 (Me.)).

There is seldom a genuine adversarial process with the prisoner's interests effectively represented. Few prisoners are competent to raise the strongest legal and factual arguments on their own behalf. In court, defendants have or are provided lawyers, and sometimes expert witnesses, but such assistance is far from the norm in the parole milieu. Some states bar representation by counsel outright (Code of N.M. Rules, R. 22.510.2.8(A)(3); *Franciosi* 2000 (Mich.); *Holup* 1976 (Conn.)). Some permit only limited representation, such as allowing counsel to submit written statements—but even this assumes the prisoner has paid for the lawyer (Laws of R.I. § 13–8–26; Vt. Stat. § 502(d)). Only a tiny handful of states provide appointed counsel for indigent prisoners (Hawaii Rev. Stat. § 706–670(3)(c); Mont. Code § 46–23–202).

Often, there is no formal burden of proof that a parole board must apply for its factual determinations. For example, in Tennessee, release is permitted only when the board is "*of the opinion* that there is reasonable probability that the prisoner, if released, will live and remain at liberty without violating the law, and that the prisoner's release is not incompatible with the welfare of society" (Tenn. Code § 40–28–117(a) (emphasis supplied)). A minority of states define the applicable burden as the "preponderance of the evidence" standard (e.g., N.H. Admin. Code Rules, Par. 210.02). There is no requirement that the parole board's fact-finding be consistent with the facts established when the prisoner was convicted, or those found by the sentencing court. Real-offense sentencing (punishment for crimes for which there has been no conviction) is the norm in parole proceedings (Dawson 1966, 259; Tonry 1981; *Hemphill* 1991 (Ohio); Wis. Admin. Code § DOC 331.08).

The rules of evidence, and protections against the use of hearsay evidence, are inapplicable at parole hearings (*Davis* 2004 (D.C.); *Hubbard* 2004 (Kan.)). The lack of rigor in this regard should be considered in light of the usual contents of an inmate's dossier:

> Besides . . . hard data, the file may also contain "soft" information, such as observations of guards, counselors, and other corrections personnel. Even unsubstantiated rumors may appear. . . . [A]nything that an inmate may have done (and perhaps even some things that an inmate may not have done) in his or her life, but particularly while in prison, may be recorded in the file. (Cohen 1999, vol. 1, 6–31)

Basic rights of confrontation of witnesses against prisoners are often nonexistent. For example, a Vermont statute provides that "the inmate shall not be present when the victim testifies before the parole board" (Vt. Stat. § 507(b)). Indeed, the prisoner's ability to respond to adverse information of any kind can be severely limited. Some states refuse the prisoner access to the contents of his dossier (Ga. Code § 42–9–53; Ky. Rev. Stat. § 439.510; S.D. Codified Laws § 24–15–1), some routinely permit it (Ind. Code § 11–13–3–3(i)(2); Md. Code, Art. 41, § 4–505), while most give the board discretion to disclose some or all of the file on a case-by-case basis (Cohen 1999, vol. 1, 6–23, 6–32 to 6–33). Court challenges to rules barring access have generally failed (*Jennings* 1999 (E.D. Va.); *Ingrassia* 1993 (8th Cir.); *Counts* 1985 (Pa.)).

Fair process requires identifiable and enforceable decision rules. While some U.S. jurisdictions have adopted statutory presumptions or guidelines that must be applied by sentencing courts, there are no equivalent substantive directives for parole boards. Where statutory criteria or parole guidelines exist, they are merely advisory; where risk assessment instruments come into play, it is entirely up to the parole boards to decide whether they should be heeded or disregarded, and what level of risk should preclude release (Rhine, chapter 26 of this volume).

Decision standards also have little integrity without a meaningful review process. This is lacking in virtually all American parole systems (e.g., Utah Code § 77–27–5(3); Vt. Stat. § 454). In some systems, administrative review of parole denials is technically available, but almost never operates as a real check on the board's discretion (Tenn. Code § 40–28–105(11); Davis 1971: 130). Oversight of any kind is hindered by the fact that many states do not require a transcript or verbatim record of parole proceedings (Cohen 1999, vol. 1, 6–52), and the general absence of requirements of reasoned explanations for decisions (*Glover* 1999 (Mich.); *Freeman* 1991 (Idaho); *Georgia State Bd. of Pardons and Paroles* 1982).[16]

Shoddy process might, to some extent, be offset by highly qualified decision makers. One might imagine that parole board members should have expertise in corrections, criminology, and prediction science (see Campbell 2008, 5; American Law Institute 1985b, § 402.1). Instead, formal requirements for appointment to a state's parole board are often minimal or nonexistent (see Rev. Stat. N.H. § 651-A:3; Fla. Stat. § 947.02(2); Miss. Code § 47–7–5(2); Neb. Stat. § 83–189; Texas Government Code §§ 508.032(b) & 508.033; Mich. Laws § 791.231a(2); Utah Code § 77–27–29(1); Rev. Stat. Neb. § 83–189; N.M. Stat. § 31–21–24 (D)). Even in states that mandate a background in criminal justice, the prerequisites do not address the core function of risk prediction (see Colo. Rev. Stat. § 17–2–201(1)(a); Md. § 7–202(a)(3); N.D. Code § 19–59–0; Vt. Stat. § 451(a)). For instance, in Wisconsin, it is vaguely specified that: "Members shall have knowledge of or experience in corrections or criminal justice" (Wis. Stat. § 15.145(1)(a)).[17]

Political connections are often the main prerequisite for appointment (Rothman 1980, 162). Public recruitment of board members is virtually unknown in the United States; by and large, positions are doled out in a closed process controlled by the governor (Paparozzi and Caplan 2009, 411, 418). A member of the Arkansas parole board recently told the press, "We are not talking rocket science here. The board jobs are known to some degree [to be] political patronage, and they're not the most difficult jobs for the pay [$70,000 per year]" (Web Special 2005).

Fair process also requires a neutral decision maker—and one component of neutrality is the freedom to decide cases on the merits, without fear for one's job. Service on a parole board is usually a full-time commitment, and so a primary source of members' livelihoods. In nearly all states, the sole appointing authority is the governor (Kinnevy and Caplan 2008, 6–7), which includes reappointments at the expiration of members' terms. Also, in many states, members can be removed from parole boards relatively easily, often at the discretion or instigation of the governor (see Miss. Code § 47–7–5(1); Fla. Stat. § 947.03(3); Utah Code § 77–27–2(2)(c)). One board member expressed the "most obvious" reality of the situation: "If the governor likes you, you might get to keep your job" (Web Special 2005). Political pressure on a board to adopt new practices is remarkably successful. It is commonplace across the United States for parole release policy to change abruptly and radically in response to a single high-profile crime in the jurisdiction (Finucane 2011;

Paparozzi and Caplan 2009, 9; Meyer 2007; Fish 2005). Also, release rates have been shown to fall during election years, and vary markedly with different gubernatorial administrations, leading Jeremy Travis to charge that our prison policy is "determined by shifting political winds" (Travis 2002, 2).

The glaring weaknesses in American parole-release procedure stem, historically, from a naïve view of the benignity of government. The American Progressives who promoted indeterminate sentencing reforms saw the state as a force with considerable resources that could be turned for good, and did not reflexively distrust state officials ceded with free-ranging discretion (Rothman 1980, 70). In contrast, the failure of indeterminate sentencing to gain a strong foothold in England and the Continent is explained in part by a fear of giving the government too much unstructured power over individual liberty. As Michele Pifferi has argued, "[T]he hypothesis of a discretionary sentence immediately evoked the resurgence of the unlimited administrative arbitrament of the prerevolutionary era, as if the storming of the Bastille had been fruitless" (2011 forthcoming, ms. 39). In Pifferi's telling, Europeans' sensitivity to rule-of-law norms only intensified in reaction to the exuberant lawlessness of Nazi Germany (see Müller 1991; White 1998). In the United States, with its very different political culture, the horrendous shortfalls of the parole-release process have remained a blind spot for lawmakers, courts charged with constitutional review, and many academics. The stubborn belief that indeterminacy is at root a compassionate system still insulates it from attack.

INDETERMINACY AND LENITY

There is a romantic view of parole release that, no matter the defects of the process, it can at least be depended upon to work in the direction of lenity for many prisoners, and the reduction of incarceration rates overall (Berman 2009, 724; Rideau and Wikberg 1992: 136; American Law Institute 1985a, 22–23; Orland 1978, 49).[18] One often encounters theories that elimination of parole-release discretion was an important driver of the U.S. prison population explosion (Clear 2007, 51–53; Whitman 2003, 56–57; Garland 2002, 60–61; Mauer 1999: 49, 56–58; Rothman 1993, 34; Joyce 1992, 359–360; Zimring and Hawkins 1991, 169–171; Rhine, Smith, and Jackson 1991, 26; Bottomley 1990, 342; Blumstein 1988, 241).

The history of American prison growth over the last several decades calls this romantic view sharply into question. To begin with recent statistics, nine out of ten states with the highest standing imprisonment rates at year-end 2009 were indeterminate jurisdictions. The tenth state, Arizona, experienced most of its prison expansion prior to 1994, when it too was an indeterminate state.[19] If we ask which states have had the most per capita prison *growth* over time, the track record of indeterminate states is equally un-lenient. From 1980 to 2009, nine of the "top" ten prison-growth states were indeterminate jurisdictions (Bureau of Justice Statistics 2010, table 6.29.2009).

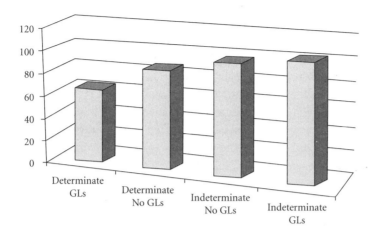

Figure 11.1. Average Per Capita State Prison Growth by Different Sentencing System
Types, 1995 to 2009

Source: Bureau of Justice Statistics 2010, table 6.29.2009.

Figure 11.1 shows per capita changes in prison rates from 1995 to 2009 among
states sorted into four basic system types. Determinate states have experienced less
prison buildup than their indeterminate counterparts, with the least occurring in
determinate states that have adopted sentencing guidelines. Substituting data all the
way back to 1980 yields the same rank ordering.[20]

Among social scientists, using a variety of statistical methodologies, there is an
emerging consensus that determinate sentencing reforms, presumptive sentencing
guidelines, and especially systems that combine the two, have been associated with
lower incarceration rates and less prison growth over the past three decades than
other sentencing system types (Stemen and Rengifo 2011, 190–194; American Law
Institute 2011, Appendix B; Zhang, Maxwell, and Vaughn 2009, 197; Spelman 2009;
Reitz 2006, 1798, 1800; Smith 2004, 933–935; Nicholson-Crotty 2004; Greenberg and
West 2001, 638; Jacobs and Carmichael 2001, 81; Marvell and Moody 1996, 120, 122;
Zimring and Hawkins 1991, 169–171). Such findings have been heralded as "a re-
freshing departure from the usual negative results when evaluating criminal justice
reforms" (Marvell 1995, 707; see Lucken and Blomberg, chapter 14 of this volume).
Indeed, this may be a rare instance of reform approximating intention. Proponents
have often advocated the adoption of guidelines, the abolition of parole release discretion, or both, based on a conclusion that their preexisting system was producing
ungovernable prison growth, and that a reformed system could bring it under control (Pryor 2005; Barkow and O'Neill 2006; Knapp 1993; Orland and Reitz 1993).

Determinate sentencing systems bear no special blame for the phenomenon
of mass incarceration in the United States—even though conventional wisdom
among criminal justice professionals has long held the opposite. Yet no sentencing system type—at least as classified in this article—can predestine high or
low prison growth over the long haul (Zimring and Hawkins 1991, 160–162). It
may be true that indeterminate systems have been disproportionately represented

among high-growth jurisdictions over the last three decades, and determinate-guidelines states have been disproportionately in the low-growth category, but there are counterexamples to each of these general statements. The federal sentencing system, designed on the determinate-guidelines model, has contributed to exceptional prison growth since its inception, even in recent years when state prison rates nationwide have begun to stabilize or drop. In contrast to the policy preferences in many states, this was the outcome desired by federal lawmakers (Simon 2011; Stith and Cabranes 1998; Tonry 1996). And some of the traditional indeterminate states, including Nebraska and Rhode Island, have experienced low increments of prison growth since 1980—comparable to the slowest-growth determinate-guidelines states: Minnesota, North Carolina, and Washington (Bureau of Justice Statistics, 2010, table 6.29.2009).

The outlier jurisdictions demonstrate the need to develop finer tools to describe and analyze the workings of individual systems. It would be of great policy significance, for instance, if we could identify the distinguishing characteristics of traditional systems that have experienced the smallest amounts of prison population growth. Perhaps there are specific practices that could be emulated by other states wishing to bring correctional expenditures under control—without undertaking wholesale sentencing reforms that include the creation of a sentencing commission and sentencing guidelines (see Weisberg, chapter 12 of this volume).

Conclusion

We know little about the quality of parole boards' release or denial decisions on the merits. Facing a void of information, outside observers are free to romanticize or demonize the substance of what boards do. That is a big problem. For instance, it is sometimes suggested that parole board decisions enhance sentence uniformity by ironing out idiosyncratic differences in judicial sentences (Tonry 1981; American Law Institute 1985a, 136; Bottomley 1990, 339), but the diametrically opposite claim is also made, that the boards' decisions themselves are inconsistent, inexplicable, or politically driven (Travis 2002; Frankel 1973, 92–95; Bagley 1979, 392). Overall assessments of indeterminate systems tend to be impressionistic and non-falsifiable. I am occasionally told, by people close to the federal system at the time, that the U.S. Parole Board of the 1960s is the best example of a well-run and successful parole-release agency in recent history (American Law Institute 2010), yet Kenneth Culp Davis's famous study concluded with searing condemnation: "The performance of the [U.S.] Parole Board seems on the whole about as low in quality as anything I have seen in the federal government" (1971, 133). Attitudes about parole release can easily reflect hopes, fears, and ideology because hard information is in short supply. In the abstract, it is just as easy to imagine parole boards as champions of rehabilitation-lenity, as to see them as agents of incapacitation-severity.

Compared with many other societies, Americans probably have higher expectations that their criminal justice systems will deliver utilitarian results. This is also a problem, if not tempered with hard-nosed realism. An uncritical belief in state-engineered solutions can be a font of optimism that shades into naïveté. It can also be a source of impatience, frustration, and overreaction when things do not go as planned. In the long history of indeterminate sentencing, all of these tendencies have been in evidence. Many of today's pathologies in U.S. sentencing and corrections are traceable to overconfidence in the rehabilitative ideal, followed by crashing disappointment (Cullen and Jonson 2011, 296; Ruth and Reitz 2003, 83–84). Indeterminate sentencing systems remain an important battleground for the warring priorities of rehabilitation and incapacitation, and will always pose questions of our ability to administer individualized prison policy with an acceptable level of fairness and restraint.

Despite the efforts of many sentencing "reformers," indeterminacy remains prominent on the American scene. It is still in place in half of the states, and may even be poised for resurgence (National Institute of Corrections 2011; O'Hear 2010; Bergstrom and Mistick 2010; Campbell 2008; Chanenson 2005; Petersilia 2003). Knowledge of the traditional "un-reformed" indeterminate systems, and how they compare to each another and to other system types, has never been more urgently needed. A new field of indeterminate sentencing studies could play the same formative role that the sentencing reform literature, since the 1970s, has enjoyed in national and international policy debates. Given how little we know, and how often the conventional wisdom of indeterminacy has proven spectacularly wrong, each new increment of knowledge will be an important contribution.

NOTES

   *   James Annenberg La Vea Professor of Law, University of Minnesota. I am grateful for extensive research assistance provided by David Morine. Many colleagues provided careful readings and comments, including Andrew Ashworth, Peggy Burke, Richard Frase, Nancy King, Kay Knapp, Nicola Padfield, Edward Rhine, Christopher Slobogin, and Michael Tonry.

   1.   These include Colorado, Connecticut, Georgia, Hawaii, Idaho, Iowa, Kentucky, Louisiana, Massachusetts, Mississippi (for nonviolent offenders), Montana, Nebraska, Nevada, New Hampshire, New Jersey, New Mexico, New York, North Dakota, Oklahoma, Rhode Island, South Carolina, South Dakota, Texas, Vermont, West Virginia, and Wyoming.

   2.   The last time there was a literature on the merits of indeterminate systems qua systems, in the 1960s and 1970s, it was scathingly critical, including Marvin Frankel's memorable charge that indeterminacy was "lawless" (e.g., Frankel 1973; American Friends Service Committee 1971; Davis 1971).

   3.   A robust field of indeterminate sentencing studies would include the growing body of research available from Commonwealth nations and Continental Europe, although

the prison systems in most other countries have far less back-end release discretion than found in the United States, and a more professionalized institutional framework for release decisions (e.g., Padfield, van Zyl Smit, Dünkel 2010; Hood and Shute 2002; Cole and Manson 1990).

4. For example, one often sees reference to "mandatory" sentencing guidelines, even though no such guidelines have ever existed in American law (Reitz 2005). Because mandatory minimum *statutory* penalty laws are widely—and understandably—held in strong disfavor (Tonry 2009; American Law Institute 2011, § 6.06, Comment *d*), the use of the same term to describe sentencing guidelines is not only inaccurate, but somewhat libelous.

5. The traditional approach has been described as *doubly* indeterminate because both judges and parole boards exercise broad and little-regulated sentencing discretion (Weisberg, chapter 12 of this volume; American Bar Association 1994).

6. Misleading because reservoirs of release discretion exist even in determinate systems, as explained above, and because the word "mandatory" raises immediate negative associations with mandatory minimum penalties. See note 4, above.

7. Sentencing guidelines, to be used by judges, are different from *parole guidelines*, addressed to parole boards when making release determinations. In contrast to sentencing guidelines, parole guidelines are not created by a sentencing commission or equivalent agency, are neither enforceable nor reviewable, tend to emphasize actuarial risk assessment over other considerations, and do not embody the full range of a jurisdiction's prison policies such as proportionality in sentence length, which offenders should receive nonprison sanctions, or the control of prison population growth (English 1990; Gottfredson et al. 1978; Kress 1980, 83–85).

8. Knapp (1993) observed that, in many states, only a small handful of people actually understand the combined operation of prison release mechanisms and rules in operation.

9. In the states, the executive pardon power was once used far more frequently than today and, functionally, was a precursor of or substitute for parole release in some jurisdictions. Partly because of its political costs, the pardon power fell into relative disuse in the late twentieth century (Barkow 2009; Rideau and Wikberg 1992, 124–147).

10. Occasionally, sentencing laws are softened by a legislature or sentencing commission. If the new, more lenient provisions are applied retroactively to prisoners serving sentences under prior law, this could be viewed as a kind of wholesale indeterminacy (Love 2009).

11. One important project for a new field of "indeterminate studies" would be a comparative evaluation of these emergency provisions across jurisdictions, with an eye toward how they might be strengthened.

12. Studies of parole boards in action have found that they weigh the offense of conviction (along with criminal history) most heavily of all, with institutional behavior secondary (Rhine, chapter 26 of this volume; see also Rhine et.al. 1991; Runda et.al. 1994; Rothman 1980, 166–168).

13. Amazingly, sentencing software used by some Oregon judges uses the defendant's race as a factor in generating sentencing and recidivism data meant to aid judges in arriving at their sentencing decisions (Marcus 2009b).

14. For some subpopulations, such as mentally ill offenders, the rate of correct predictions is even higher (Monahan 2006, 409–413).

15. As a matter of federal constitutional law, discretionary parole systems are not thought to create a "liberty interest" on the part of prisoners, so the Due Process Clause guarantees no minimum level of procedural regularity (e.g., *Saleem* 1995 (Ga.); *Dopp* 2004

(Idaho); *Quegan* 1996 (Mass.); *Morales* 2003 (Mich); *Vice* 1996 (Miss.); *Barna* 2001 (N.Y.); *Weaver* 1997 (Pa.)). A liberty interest does arise if state law requires release after a set period unless contrary findings are made by the parole board—but, even then, the safeguards mandated by the constitution are unimpressive (*Greenholtz* 1979).

16. Some jurisdictions require that reasons be given, but are not rigorous about the content of the explanations. Boilerplate, or a slight improvement on boilerplate, is often good enough (see *Walker* 1994 (N.Y.); *Goins* 1992 (Ill.); N.M. Stat. § 31–21–25(C)).

17. Nor do under-qualified appointees receive adequate training once they assume their posts (Paparozzi and Caplan 2009, 416, 418).

18. Of course, parole is sometimes *condemned* on the same empirical assumption, when it is characterized as releasing criminals prematurely and sacrificing public safety (Long 1995: 40; Rothman 1980, 159–161).

19. Arizona's prison rate grew more than sixfold from 1972 through 1994, when it still retained an indeterminate sentencing system (Bureau of Justice Statistics 2010, table 6.29.2009; 1991, 605 table 6.56). Arizona abolished parole-release discretion in 1994 (Petersilia 2003, 66–67). From 1994 through 2009, the state's prison rate has increased by only 26 percent (Bureau of Justice Statistics 2010, table 6.29.2009).

20. From 1980 to 2009, the per capita increment of prison population growth (per 100,000 general population) among indeterminate-guidelines states was 330; for traditional indeterminate states it was 301; for determinate-no-guidelines states it was 281; and for determinate-guidelines states it was 227. One problem with this crude measurement over the longer period is that so many states have changed their sentencing systems since 1980, so net prison growth for many states occurred under two or more different schemes. This difficulty is not nearly so great when going back to 1995. Other studies have addressed the issue of changing systems with more sophisticated methodologies (Stemen and Rengifo 2011; Reitz 2006), but their results lend credence to the gross observations reported here.

REFERENCES

Cases

Barna v. Travis, 239 F.3d 169 (2d Cir. 2001) (reviewing N.Y. parole procedures).

Counts v. Commonwealth, Pennsylvania Bd. of Probation and Parole, 487 A.2d 450 (Pa. Commw. 1985).

Davis v. Brown, 311 F. Supp. 2d 110 (D.D.C. 2004).

Dopp v. Idaho Commission of Pardons and Parole, 84 P.3d 593 (Idaho App. 2004).

Franciosi v. Mich. Parole Bd., 604 N.W.2d 675 (Mich. 2000).

Freeman v. State, Comm'n of Pardons and Paroles, 809 P.2d 1171 (Idaho App. 1991).

Georgia State Bd. of Pardons and Paroles v. Turner, 285 S.E.2d 731 (Ga. 1982).

Glover v. Michigan Parole Board, 596 N.W.2d 598 (Mich. 1999).

Goins v. Klincar, 588 N.E.2d 420 (Ill. App. 1992).

Greenholtz v. Inmates of Nebraska Penal and Correctional Complex, 442 U.S. 1 (1979)

Hemphill v. Ohio Adult Parole Authority, 575 N.E.2d 148 (Ohio 1991).

Holup v. Gates, 544 F.2d 82 (2d Cir. 1976) (reviewing Connecticut parole procedures).

Hubbard v. Simmons, 89 P.3d 662 (Kan. App. 2004).

Ingrassia v. Prukett, 985 F.2d 987 (8th Cir. 1993).

Jennings v. Parole Bd. of Virginia, 61 F. Supp. 2d 462 (E.D. Va. 1999).

Luttrell v. Commonwealth, 592 S.E.2d 752 (Va. App. 2004).

Mahaney v. State, 610 A.2d 738 (Me. 1992).

Morales v. Michigan Parole Bd., 676 N.W.2d 221 (Mich. App. 2003).

Shields v. Purkett, 878 S.W.2d 42 (Mo. 1994).

Quegan v. Mass. Parole Board, 673 N.E.2d 42 (Mass. 1996).

Saleem v. Snow, 460 S.E.2d 104 (Ga. 1995).

Vice v. State, 679 So.2d 205 (Miss. 1996).

Walker v. N.Y. State Div. of Parole, 610 N.Y.S.2d 397 (N.Y. App. Div. 1994),

Weaver v. Pa. Bd. of Probation and Parole, 688 A.2d 766 (Pa. Commw. Ct. 1997)

Other Sources

Alabama Board of Pardons and Parole Pardons and Parole. 2009. *Annual Report, Fiscal 2008–09*. Montgomery: Alabama Board of Pardons and Parole Pardons and Parole.

American Friends Service Committee. 1971. *Struggle for Justice: A Report on Crime and Punishment in America*. New York: Hill & Wang.

American Law Institute. 1985a. *Model Penal Code and Commentaries: Part I, §§ 6.01 to 7.09*. Philadelphia: American Law Institute.

American Law Institute. 1985b. *Model Penal Code: Complete Statutory Text*. Philadelphia: American Law Institute.

American Law Institute. 2003. *Model Penal Code: Sentencing, Report*. Philadelphia: American Law Institute.

American Law Institute. 2007. *Model Penal Code: Sentencing, Tentative Draft No 1* (approved May 16, 2007). Philadelphia: American Law Institute.

American Law Institute. 2010. *Annual Meeting, Transcript of Proceedings*. Philadelphia: American Law Institute.

American Law Institute. 2011. *Model Penal Code: Sentencing, Tentative Draft No. 2* (approved May 17, 2011). Philadelphia: American Law Institute.

Archibold, Randal C. 2010. "California, in Financial Crisis, Opens Prison Doors." *New York Times*, March 23, 2010.

Austin, James. 1986. "Using Early Release to Relieve Prison Overcrowding: A Dilemma in Public Policy." *Crime & Delinquency* 32: 404–502.

Austin, James. 1987. "The Use of Early Release and Sentencing Guidelines To Ease Prison Crowding: The Shifting Sands of Reform." In *Prison and Jail Crowding: Workshop Proceedings*, eds. Dale K Sechrest, Jonathan D. Caspar, and Jeffrey A. Roth. Washington, DC: National Research Council.

Austin, James, Dana Coleman, Johnette Peyton, and Kelly Dedel Johnson. 2003. *Reliability and Validity Study of the LSI-R Risk Assessment Instrument*. Washington, DC: The Institute on Crime, Justice, and Corrections.

Bagley, James J. 1979. "Why Illinois Adopted Determinate Sentencing." *Judicature* 62: 390–397.

Bales, William D., Gerry G. Gaes, Thomas G. Blomberg, and Kerensa N. Pate. 2010. "An Assessment of the Development and Outcome of Determinate Sentencing in Florida." *Justice Research and Policy* 12: 41–71.

Barkow, Rachel. 2009. "The Politics of Forgiveness: Reconceptualizing Clemency." *Federal Sentencing Reporter* 21: 153–159.

Barkow, Rachel and Kathleen M. O'Neill. 2006. "Delegating Punitive Power: The Political Economy of Sentencing Commission and Guideline Formation." *Columbia Law Review* 105: 1973–2019.

Bergstrom, Mark H. and Joseph Sabino Mistick. 2010. "Danger and Opportunity: Making Public Safety Job One in Pennsylvania's Indeterminate Sentencing System." *Justice Research and Policy* 12: 73–88.

Berman, Douglas A. 2009. "The Enduring (And Again Timely) Wisdom of the Original MPC Sentencing Provisions." *Florida Law Review* 61: 709–725.

Bhati, Avinash Singh and Piquero, Alex R. 2008. "Estimating the Impact of Incarceration on Subsequent Offending Trajectories: Deterrent, Criminogenic, or Null Effect?" *Journal of Criminal Law & Criminology* 98: 207–253.

Blumstein, Alfred. 1988. "Prison Populations: A System Out of Control?" In *Crime and Justice: An Annual Review of Research*, eds. Michael Tonry and Norval Morris, 10: 231–266. Chicago: University of Chicago Press.

Blumstein, Alfred, Jacqueline Cohen, Susan E. Martin, and Michael Tonry eds. 1983. Research on Sentencing: The Search for Reform. Washington, DC: National Academy Press.

Boerner, David, and Roxanne Lieb. 2001. "Sentencing Reform in the Other Washington." In *Crime and Justice: A Review of Research*, ed. Michael Tonry, 28: 71–136.

Bottomley, A. Keith. 1990. "Parole in Transition: A Comparative Study of Origins, Developments, and Prospects for the 1990s." In *Crime and Justice: An Annual Review of Research* eds. Michael Tonry and Norval Morris, 12: 319–374. Chicago: University of Chicago Press.

Bureau of Justice Statistics. 2010. *Sourcebook of Criminal Justice Statistics*. Washington, D.C.: U.S. Department of Justice. Available at: http://www.albany.edu/sourcebook/.

Bureau of Justice Statistics. 1991. *Sourcebook of Criminal Justice Statistics—1990*. Washington, DC: U.S. Department of Justice.

Burke, Peggy, and Michael Tonry. 2006. *Successful Transition and Reentry for Safer Communities: A Call to Action for Parole*. Silver Spring, MD: Center for Effective Public Policy.

Campbell, Nancy M. 2008. *Comprehensive Framework for Paroling Authorities in an Era of Evidence Based Practices*. Washington, D.C.: National Institute of Corrections.

Chanenson, Steven L. 2005. "The Next Era of Sentencing Reform." *Emory Law Journal* 54: 377–460.

Chappell, Richard A. 1965. Federal Parole. *37 F.R.D.* 207–214.

Chayet, Ellen F. 1994. "Correctional 'Good Time' as a Means of Early Release." *Criminal Justice Abstracts* 6: 521–538.

Clear, Todd R. 2007. *Imprisoning Communities: How Mass Incarceration Makes Disadvantaged Neighborhoods Worse*. New York and Oxford: Oxford University Press.

Cohen, Jacqueline. 1983. *Incapacitating Criminals: Recent Research Findings*. Washington, DC: U.S. Department of Justice, National Institute of Justice.

Cohen, Neil P. 1999. *The Law of Probation and Parole*, 2nd ed. Eagan, MN: West Group.

Cohen, Neil P. 2008. *The Law of Probation and Parole*, 2nd ed., *2008 Cumulative Supplement*. Eagan, MN: West Group.

Cole, David P., and Allan Manson. 1990. *Release from Imprisonment: The Law of Sentencing Parole and Judicial Review*. Toronto: Carswell.

Cullen, Francis T. and Cheryl Lero Jonson. 2011. "Rehabilitation and Treatment Programs." In *Crime and Public Policy*. eds. James Q. Wilson and Joan Petersilia, 293–344. New York: Oxford University Press.

Davis, Kenneth Culp. 1971. *Discretionary Justice: A Preliminary Inquiry*. Urbana: University of Illinois Press.

Dawson, Robert O. 1966. "The Decision to Grant or Deny Parole: A Study of Parole
    Criteria in Law and Practice." *Washington University Law Quarterly* 1966: 243–303.
Demleitner, Nora V. 2009. "Good Conduct Time: How Much and For Whom? The
    Unprincipled Approach of the Model Penal Code: Sentencing." *Florida Law Review* 61:
    777–796.
Douglas, Kevin S., and Jennifer L. Skeem. 2005. "Violence Risk Assessment: Getting
    Specific about Being Dynamic." *Psychology, Public Policy, and the Law* 11: 347–383.
English, Kim. 1990. *Colorado Parole Guidelines Handbook*. Denver: Colorado Division of
    Criminal Justice.
Etienne, Margareth. 2009. "Legal and Practical Implications of Evidence-Based Sentencing
    by Judges." *Chapman Journal of Criminal Justice* 1: 43–60.
Finn, Peter. 1984. "Prison Crowding: The Response of Probation and Parole." *Crime &
    Delinquency* 30: 141–153.
Finucane, Martin. 2011. "In Wake of Officer's Slaying, Mass. Gov. Shakes up Parole Board."
    Boston Globe, January 13, 2011.
Fish, Martin. 2005. "Killing Led to Tougher Parole System: Ten Years after 'Mudman,'
    Pennsylvania Convicts Still Serve Some of the Longest Terms." *Philadelphia Inquirer*,
    June 6, 2005.
Frankel, Marvin E. 1973. *Criminal Sentencing: Law Without Order*. New York: Hill & Wang.
Frase, Richard S. 2005. "State Sentencing Guidelines: Diversity, Consensus, and Unresolved
    Policy Issues." *Columbia Law Review* 105: 1190–1232.
Frase, Richard S. 2010. "Second Look Provisions in the Proposed Model Penal Code
    Revisions." *Federal Sentencing Reporter* 21: 194–202.
Friedman, Lawrence M. 1993. *Crime and Punishment in American History*. New York: Basic
    Books.
Gaes, Gerald G. 2009. *Review of CARAS: Colorado Actuarial Risk Assessment Scale*. Denver:
    Colorado Department of Public Safety.
Garland, David. 2002. *The Culture of Control: Crime and Social Order in Contemporary
    Society*. Chicago: University of Chicago Press.
Paul Gendreau, Tracy Little, and Claire Goggin. 1996. "A Meta-Analysis of the Predictors of
    Adult Offender Recidivism: What Works!" *Criminology* 34: 575–607.
Glover, Anthony J., Diane E. Nicholson, Toni Hemmati, Gary A. Bernfeld, and Vernon L.
    Quinsey. 2002. "A Comparison of Predictors of General and Violent Recidivism
    Among High-Risk Federal Offenders." *Criminal Justice and Behavior* 29: 235–249.
Gottfredson, Don M., Leslie T. Wilkins, and Peter B. Hoffman. 1978. *Guidelines for Parole
    and Sentencing*. Lexington, Mass.: Lexington Books.
Greenberg, David F. and Valerie West. 2001. State Prison Populations and Their Growth,
    1971-1991. *Criminology* 39: 615–653.
Greenwood, Peter W., and Susan Turner. 1987. *Selective Incapacitation Revisited: Why
    the High-Rate Offenders Are Hard to Predict*. Santa Monica, CA: The Rand
    Corporation.
Grove, William M., and Paul E. Meehl. 1996. "Comparative Efficiency of Informal (Subjec-
    tive, Impressionistic) and Formal (Mechanical, Algorithmic) Prediction." *Psychology,
    Public Policy and Law* 2: 293–323.
Harcourt, Bernard E. 2006. *Against Prediction: Profiling, Policing and Punishing in the
    Actuarial Age*. Chicago: University of Chicago Press.
Harris, Grant T., Marnie E. Rice, and Catherine A. Cormier. 2002. "Prospective Replication
    of the Violence Risk Appraisal Guide in Predicting Violent Recidivism among
    Forensic Patients." *Law & Human Behavior* 26: 377–394.

Harvard Law Review. 2006. "A Matter of Life and Death: The Effect of Life Without Parole Statutes on Capital Punishment." *Harvard Law Review* 119: 1838–1854.

Hood, Roger, and S. Shute. 2002. "The Changing Face of Parole in England and Wales: A Story of Some Well-Intentioned Reforms and Unintended Consequences." In *Festschrift für Klaus Lüderssen*, eds. C. Prittwitz, M. Baurmann, K. Günther, L. Kuhlen, R. Merkel, C. Nestler, and L. Schulz. Baden-Baden: Nomos Verlag.

Jacobs, James B. 1982. "Sentencing by Prison Personnel: Good Time." *U.C.L.A. Law Review* 30: 217–270.

Jacobs, David, and Jason T. Carmichael. 2001. "The Politics of Punishment across Time and Space: A Pooled Time-Series Analysis of Imprisonment Rates." *Social Forces* 80: 61–89.

Joyce, Nola M. 1992. "A View of the Future: The Effect of Policy on Prison Population Growth." *Crime and Delinquency* 38: 357–368.

Kinnevy, Susan C., and Joel M. Caplan. 2008. *Findings from the APAI International Survey of Releasing Authorities*. Philadelphia: Center for Research on Youth and Social Policy.

Klingele, Cecilia. 2010. "Changing the Sentence Without Hiding the Truth: Judicial Sentence Modification as a Promising Method of Early Release." *William and Mary Law Review* 52: 465–536.

Knapp, Kay A. 1993. "Allocation of Discretion and Accountability Within Sentencing Systems." *University of Colorado Law Review* 64: 679–705.

Kress, Jack M. 1980. *Prescription for Justice: The Theory and Practice of Sentencing Guidelines*. Cambridge, MA: Ballinger Publishing.

Lindsey, Edward. 1925. "Historical Sketch of the Indeterminate Sentencing and Parole System." *Journal of the American Institute of Criminal Law and Criminology* 16: 9–69.

Long, Robert Emmet. 1995. "Editor's Introduction." In Robert Emmet Long, *Criminal Sentencing*. New York: The H.W. Wilson Co.

Love, Margaret Colgate. 2009. "Sentence Reduction Mechanisms in a Determinate Sentencing System: Report of the Second Look Roundtable." *Federal Sentencing Reporter* 21: 211–225.

Lynch, Gerald E. 1997. "The Sentencing Guidelines as a Not-So-Model Penal Code." *Federal Sentencing Reporter* 10: 25–28.

Marcus, Michael. 2009a. "Conversations on Evidence-Based Sentencing." *Chapman Journal of Criminal Justice* 1: 61–126.

Marcus, Michael. 2009b. *Sentencing Support Tools: User Manual for Judges*. Available at: http://www.smartsentencing.info/2009%20judge%20instruction%20manual.pdf.

Marvell, Thomas B. 1995. "Sentencing Guidelines and Prison Population Growth." *Journal of Criminal Law and Criminology* 85: 696–709.

Marvell, Thomas B., and Carlisle E. Moody. 1996. "Determinate Sentencing and Abolishing Parole: The Long-Term Impacts on Prisons and Crime." *Criminology* 34: 107–128.

Mauer, Marc. 1999. *Race to Incarcerate*. New York: The New Press.

Meredith, Tammy, John C. Speir, and Sharon Johnson. 2007. "Developing and Implementing Automated Risk Assessments in Parole." *Justice Research and Policy* 9: 1–24.

Messinger, Sheldon L. and Philip E. Johnson. 1977. "California's Determinate Sentencing Statute: History and Issues." Reprinted in *The Criminal Justice System* (1980), eds. Franklin E. Zimring and Richard S. Frase, 950–987. Boston and Toronto: Little, Brown.

Meyer, Jeffrey A., and Linda Ross Meyer. 2007. "Abolish Parole." *New York Times*, October 28, 2007.

Missouri Department of Corrections. 2009. *Procedures Governing the Granting of Paroles and Conditional Releases*. Jefferson City: Missouri Board of Probation and Parole.

Moffat, Hannah. 2010. "Actuarial Sentencing: An 'Unsettled' Proposition." Paper presented at University of Albany Symposium on Sentencing, September 2010. Available at: http://www.albany.edu/scj/documents/Hannah-Moffatt_RiskAssessment_000.pdf.

Monahan, John. 1981. *The Clinical Prediction of Violent Behavior*. Rockville, Md.: U.S. Department of Health and Human Services, National Institute of Mental Health.

Monahan, John. 2006. "A Jurisprudence of Risk Assessment: Forecasting Harm Among Prisoners, Predators, and Patients." *Virginia Law Review* 92: 391–435.

Monahan, John, and Laurens Walker. 2006. *Social Science in Law: Cases and Materials*, 6th ed. New York: Foundation Press.

Morris, Norval. 1974. *The Future of Imprisonment*. Chicago: University of Chicago Press.

Morris, Norval. 2002. *Maconochie's Gentlemen: The Story of Norfolk Island and the Roots of Modern Prison Reform*. New York: Oxford University Press.

Morris, Norval, and Marc Miller. 1985. "Predictions of Dangerousness." In Michael Tonry, Michael, and Norval Morris, eds., *Crime and Justice: An Annual Review of Research* 6: 1–50. Chicago: University of Chicago Press.

Müller, Ingo. 1991. *Hitler's Justice: The Courts of the Third Reich*. Cambridge, MA: Harvard University Press.

National Commission on Law Observance and Enforcement. 1931. *Report on Penal Institutions: Probation and Parole*. Washington, DC: U.S. Government Printing Office.

National Institute of Corrections. 2011. *Evidence-Based Policy, Practice, and Decisionmaking: Implications for Paroling Authorities*. Washingtion, D.C.: National Institute of Corrections.

National Research Council. 2007. *Parole, Desistance from Crime, and Community Integration*. Washington, DC: National Academies Press.

Nellis, Ashley, and Ryan S. King. 2009. *No Exit: The Expanding Use of Life Sentences in America*. Washington, DC: The Sentencing Project.

Netter, Brian. 2007. "Using Group Statistics to Sentence Individual Criminals: An Ethical and Statistical Critique of the Virginia Risk Assessment Program." *Journal of Criminal Law and Criminology* 97: 699–729.

N.J. State Parole Board. 2010. *The Parole Book: A Handbook on Parole Procedures for Adult and Young Adult Inmates*, 4th ed. Trenton, NJ: New Jersey State Parole Board.

Nicholson-Crotty, Sean. 2004. "The Impact of Sentencing Guidelines on State-Level Sanctions: An Analysis over Time." *Crime and Delinquency* 50: 395–411.

O'Hear, Michael. 2010. "The Quiet Comeback of Early Release." *Life Sentences Blog*. Available at: http://www.lifesentencesblog.com/?p=327.

Oregon Criminal Justice Commission. 2011. *The Public Safety Checklist for Oregon*. Available at: http://risktool.ocjc.state.or.us/psc/.

Orland, Leonard. 1978. "Vengeance to Vengeance: Sentencing Reform and the Demise of Rehabilitation." *Hofstra Law Review* 7: 29–56.

Orland, Leonard, and Kevin R. Reitz. 1993. "Epilogue: A Gathering of State Sentencing Commissions." *University of Colorado Law Review* 64: 837–845.

Ostrom, Brian J., Matthew Kleiman, Fred Cheesman II, Randall M. Hansen, and Neal B. Kauder. 2002. *Offender Risk Assessment in Virginia: A Three-Stage Evaluation*. Williamsburg, VA: National Center for State Courts.

Padfield, Nicola, Dirk van Zyl Smit, and Frieder Dünkel. 2010. *Release from Prison: European Policy and Practice*. Devon and Portland, OR: Willan Publishing.

Paparozzi, Mario A., and Joel M. Caplan. 2009. "A Profile of Paroling Authorities in America: The Strange Bedfellows of Politics and Professionalism." *The Prison Journal* 89: 401–425.

Petersilia, Joan. 2003. *When Prisoners Come Home: Parole and Prisoner Reentry*. New York: Oxford University Press.

Pifferi, Michele. 2011. "Individualization of Punishment and the Rule of Law: Reshaping the Legality in the United States and Europe between the 19th and the 20th Century." Unpublished paper. Available at: http://works.bepress.com/michele_pifferi/1/.

Pryor, William H., Jr. 2005. "Lessons of a Sentencing Reformer from the Deep South." *Columbia Law Review* 105: 943–958.

Ratansi, Shamir, and Stephen M. Cox. 2007. *State of Connecticut, Assessment and Validation of Connecticut's Salient Factor Score*. New Britain: Central Connecticut State University.

Reitz, Kevin R. 2005. "The Enforceability of Sentencing Guidelines." *Stanford law Review* 58: 155–173.

Reitz, Kevin R. 2006. "Don't Blame Determinacy: U.S. Incarceration Growth Has Been Driven by Other Forces." *Texas Law Review* 84: 1787–1802.

Rhine, Edward E. 1986. *Prison Overcrowding Emergency Powers Acts: A Policy Quandary for Corrections. Proceedings of the 116th Congress of Correction*. College Park, MD: American Correctional Association.

Rhine, Edward E., William R. Smith, and Ronald W. Jackson. 1991. *Paroling Authorities: Recent History and Current Practice*. Laurel, MD: American Correctional Association.

Rideau, Wilbert, and Ron Wikberg. 1992. *Life Sentences: Rage and Survival Behind Bars*. New York: Times Books.

Robinson, Paul H. 2001. "Punishing Dangerousness: Cloaking Preventive Detention as Criminal Justice." *Harvard Law Review* 114: 1429–1456.

Rosenfeld, Richard, Joel Wallman, and Robert Fornango. 2005. "The Contribution of Ex-Prisoners to Crime Rates." In *Prisoner Reentry and Crime in America*, eds. Jeremy Travis and Christy Visher, 80–104. New York: Cambridge University Press.

Rothman, David J. 1980. *Conscience and Convenience: The Asylum and Its Alternatives in Progressive America*. Boston: Little, Brown.

Rothman, David J. 1993. "More of the Same: American Criminal Justice Policies in the 1990s." In *Punishment and Social Control: Essays in Honor of Sheldon L. Messinger*, eds. Thomas G. Blomberg and Stanley Cohen, 29–44. New York: Aldine de Gruyter.

Runda, John C., Edward E. Rhine, and Robert E. Wetter. 1994. *The Practice of Parole Boards*. Association of Paroling Authorities International. Council of State Governments. Lexington, KY.

Ruth, Henry, and Kevin R. Reitz. 2003. *The Challenge of Crime: Rethinking Our Response*. Cambridge, Mass.: Harvard University Press.

Schriro, Dora. 2009. "Is Good Time a Good Idea? A Practitioner's Perspective." *Federal Sentencing Reporter* 21: 179–181.

Schulhofer, Stephen. 1980. "Due Process of Sentencing," *University of Pennsylvania Law Review* 128: 733–828.

Smith, Kevin B. 2004. The Politics of Punishment: Evaluating Political Explanations of Incarceration Rates. *The Journal of Politics* 66: 925–938.

Solomon, Amy L., Kachnowski, Vera, and Bhati, Avinash. 2005. *Does Parole Work? Analyzing the Impact of Post Prison Supervision on Re-Arrest Outcomes*. Washington, DC: Urban Institute.

Speigel, Alix. 2004. "Researchers Contrast Statistics with Intuition." National Public Radio, *All Things Considered*, January 5, 2004.

Spelman, William. 2009. "Crime, Cash, and Limited Options: Explaining the Prison Boom." *Criminology & Public Policy* 8: 29–77.

Stemen, Don, and Andres F. Rengifo. 2011. "Policies and Imprisonment: The Impact of Structured Sentencing and Determinate Sentencing on State Incarceration Rates, 1978–2004." *Justice Quarterly* 28: 174–201.

Stith, Kate, and José A. Cabranes. 1998. *Fear of Judging: Sentencing Guidelines in the Federal Courts.* Chicago: University of Chicago Press.

Stivers Ireland, Connie, and JoAnn Prause. 2005. "Discretionary Parole Release: Length of Imprisonment, Percent of Sentence Served, and Recidivism." *Journal of Crime & Justice* 28: 27–49.

Tonry, Michael. 1981. "Real Offense Sentencing: The Model Sentencing and Corrections Act." *Journal of Criminal Law and Criminology* 72: 1550–1596.

Tonry, Michael. 1996. *Sentencing Matters.* New York: Oxford University Press.

von Hirsch, Andrew, and Kathleen J. Hanrahan. 1979. *The Question of Parole: Retention, Reform, or Abolition?* Cambridge, MA: Ballinger Publishing.

Tonry, Michael. 1999. "Rethinking Unthinkable Punishment Policies in America." *U.C.L.A. Law Review* 46: 1751–1791.

Travis, Jeremy. 2002. *Thoughts on the Future of Parole.* Washington, DC: Urban Institute Justice Policy Center.

Web Special. 2005. "Dumond Case Revisited—A Reminder of Huckabee's Role in His Freedom." *Arkansas Times*, September 1, 2005.

Weisburd, David, and Ellen S. Chayet. 1989. "Good Time: A Research Agenda." *Criminal Justice and Behavior* 16: 183–195.

Whitman, James Q. 2003. *Harsh Justice: Criminal Punishment and the Widening Divide Between America and Europe.* New York: Oxford University Press.

White, Ahmed A. 1998. "Victims' Rights, Rule of Law, and the Threat to Liberal Jurisprudence." *Kentucky Law Journal* 87: 357–415.

Wines, Frederick Howard. 1910. *Punishment and Reformation: A Study of the Penitentiary System, Revised Edition.* New York: Thomas Y. Crowell.

Winter, Alexander. 1893. "The Modern Spirit in Penology." *Political Science Quarterly* 8: 445–466.

Wolff, Michael A. 2008. "Evidence-Based Judicial Discretion: Promoting Public Safety Through State Sentencing Reform." *New York University Law Review* 83: 1389–1419.

Wong, Stephen C. P., and Audrey Gordon. 2006. "The Validity and Reliability of the Violence Risk Scale: A Treatment-Friendly Violence Risk Assessment Tool." *Psychology, Public Policy, and Law* 12: 279–309.

Wool, Jon, and Don Stemen. 2004. "Aggravated Sentencing: *Blakely v. Washington*: Practical Implications for State Sentencing Systems." New York: Vera Institute of Justice.

Zhang, Yan, Lening Zhang, and Michael S. Vaughn. 2009. "Indeterminate and Determinate Sentencing Models: A State-Specific Analysis of Their Effects on Recidivism." *Crime & Delinquency Online First* XX(X): 1–23.

Zhang, Yan, Christopher D. Maxwell, and Michael S. Vaughn. 2009. "The Impact of State Sentencing Policies on the U.S. Prison Population." *Journal of Criminal Justice* 37: 190–199.

Zimring, Franklin E., and Gordon Hawkins. 1991. *The Scale of Imprisonment.* Chicago: University of Chicago Press.

CHAPTER 12

....

THE SENTENCING COMMISSION MODEL, 1970s TO PRESENT

....

ROBERT WEISBERG

BY the mid-twentieth century, the idea of an administrative agency promulgating rules on delegation from the legislature was a staple of American government. A settled principle of American public law was that such an agency had great efficiency advantages in issuing the fine-tuned regulations, advantages not associated with the broader law-propounding competence of the legislature. But there was one great exception: aside from the common phenomenon of a parole board, an agency with quasi-adjudicative authority, along with the agencies that supervised probation or managed prisons and jails, there was little role for the modern administrative agency in criminal law. Perhaps there was always something about criminal law—the magisterial awe we feel before the power of the state to condemn and imprison—that set it apart from the economic and social regulation that became the regular subject matter of bureaucratic rules and decisions.[1] But the new idea of an agency for criminal law sentencing emerged in the 1970s.

To identify the founding moment in the history of sentencing commissions, we might turn to the great book by Judge Marvin Frankel (1973). The theme of Frankel's founding writings is clear: As sentencing evolved in the United States by mid-century, it came to take a doubly indeterminate form. First, in most prosecutions, judges were afforded broad, sometimes absolutely unrestricted discretion to choose a prison sentence from zero up to some high statutory maximum—all this after an essentially informal hearing. Second, even after the judge set a specific sentence, that sentence remained effectively indeterminate because ultimately a parole board would have considerable discretion to release the prisoner any time after a minimum time was served. Frankel denounced this system, mostly because it entailed that the legal system could provide no uniformity or equity in sentencing, and so the deprivation of liberty was subject to the views—or whims—of the judge (Frankel 1973; Frankel and Orland 1984; Lynch, 2009). But also, even the very conscientious judge seeking general philosophical guidance about which criteria to use in sentencing faced received no such guidance from the legislature or even the higher courts (Tonry 1987, 16–18). Thus, in a famously eloquent opinion which he took the unusual step of publishing, Judge Frankel, in sentencing the notorious nursing-home fraudster Bernard Bergman, assayed how the various purposes of punishment would apply to help determine the right sentence, and he then roughly averaged them all out (*U.S. v. Bergman* 1976).

In the background to Frankel's call for change was a historical story. To some extent, this broad discretion was simply in the venerable DNA of American criminal justice, whereby sentencing had always been an informal and rarely examined appendage to the heavily regulated criminal trial (King, chapter 13 of this volume; *Williams v. N.Y.* 1949). But to some extent, the prominence of all that double-discretion had to do with a particular goal of punishment that came to dominate public discourse by mid-century: rehabilitation. If the goals of a rehabilitation-based system were fully realized, the type of sanction or length of time it would take to turn an offender into a good citizen may have little necessarily to do with the nature of the crime of conviction, and so determinate rules correlated to the severity of the crime would disserve the professed goal. A guilty verdict simply meant that you entered into an administrative system whereby you would be released by the percipient parole board when, if ever, you were deemed sufficiently reformed. American criminal justice at mid-century was hardly so pure, but it did tilt in that direction (Allen 1981). And given the absence of scientific rigor or legal standards determining moral reformation, the system invited, even if it never intended, the inequitable and unpredictable outcomes that Frankel decried.

In a sense, Frankel might have been satisfied if the legislatures stepped in and wrote sentencing laws with much more purposive coherence and something closer to formulaic rules to ensure some degree of equity, uniformity, and predictability. But he was wise enough to recognize that in this regard criminal law may not be all that different from economic and social regulation: the legislature might not be well-suited to do the hard detail work of regulation, and so he advocated the then very novel idea of a sentencing commission.

Although Frankel was a federal judge mainly concerned with federal law, his *cri de coeur* resonated just as much within the state systems. As a result, the rise of state sentencing commissions followed this very historical trajectory. The commissions were at first associated with states using highly unstructured and indeterminate systems—and they arose precisely as a way of rendering those systems more structured and determinate. In one sense, the commission was the tail of the dog. The key thing was to have guidelines of some sort to constrain, cajole, or encourage judges to sentence according to more uniform criteria, and if it logically lay outside the competence of the legislature to create those guidelines, an agency was the obvious answer. The emphasis here will be on the nature and development of the American sentencing commission, and although legislatures themselves do sometimes refine their sentencing statutes into what we would call guidelines (Frase 2005b, 1197), any discussion of a commission is necessarily also about guidelines as the commission's most notable product.[2]

The basic assumption of a sentencing commission is that such an agency, relying on professional experts, representative public officials, and members of the general public, is an important tool for setting and continually evaluating sentencing policy (von Hirsch 1987a). More specifically, the notion of a commission assumes that some form of sentencing guidelines structure, whether mandatory or voluntary, is preferable to *either* a completely discretionary system *or* a system of statutorily prescribed mandatory punishments. Several common, if less than universal, predicates for sentencing commissions are: such agencies are especially adept at achieving certain specific worthy goals of sentencing policy, such as linking sentencing policy to correctional resources to address crowding and budgetary concerns; more transparent sentencing rules and practices, sometimes under the label of "truth in sentencing," are politically salutary and are disserved by excessive reliance on discretionary parole; commissions are excellent mechanisms for designing and evaluating alternatives to incarceration for nonviolent offenders, thereby helping to control incarceration rates without threatening public safety; and the entire sentencing system is enhanced by reliance on research-based data collection and analysis that commissions are well-conceived to perform (Weisberg 2007, 179–182; Dansky 2006, 6–7).

Identifying these premises and goals of sentencing commissions enables us to understand why the states that were pioneers in the sentencing commission movement exhibited several common features at the time they took steps toward the commission model: extremely unstructured sentencing rules; extremely unguided administrative parole schemes; and rising—or the rational fear of rising—prison populations and costs (which in turn bring threats of civil rights lawsuits (Dansky 2006, 2–3). Obviously, creation of a commission was easier where there was little political opposition to what might have seemed like a ceding of legislative power to an agency, but there is the risk of circular reasoning in identifying that as a key common factor. In fact, a few states, such as Alaska, managed to create commissions despite significant political division over the idea, or, as in Alabama and South Carolina, despite a vociferous objection from a judiciary that favored continued broad judicial discretion and had the political power to influence the debate (Dansky 2006, 3).

The most important commonality was the legal goal: the first commissions were given immediate mandates to devise the very criteria that would correct the perceived flaws of unstructured and indeterminate sentencing. The best example—and one that remains the gold standard for proponents of sentencing commissions—is that of Minnesota (American Law Institute 2003, 50–63; American Bar Association 1994, xxi; Tonry 1987, 18–20). Created in 1978, the significantly named Minnesota

Sentencing Guidelines Commission was composed of 11 members, including judges of all levels, public defense and prosecution lawyers, probation parole and police officials, and public members including a victim of a felony crime.

The first task of the Minnesota commission was to create a numerical grid of required sanctions that would guide trial judges in sentencing (von Hirsch 1987b). The vertical axis represented the presumptive score for the seriousness of the offense and certain aggravating or mitigating features of the conduct at issue; the horizontal axis was be the offender score, representing prior criminal record; and across these axes was the dispositional or in/out dividing line with incarceration sanctions above and lesser sanctions below.[3] Of course, other formats are possible, such as a sequential analysis (Frase 2005b, 1201), but Minnesota's epitomized the modern guidelines grid. Moreover, although in theory the prescribed sanctions can be ranges as narrow or broad as is desired, Minnesota also typifies the early commission states in making the ranges fairly narrow, and in permitting upward and downward departures out of the range in accordance with procedural rules for justifying them.

The overall goal of having a commission design, and trial judges then implement, a sentencing grid is clear: to enhance equity and uniformity and reduce disparity. But, of course, these are very abstract values, and it is only meaningful to say that like cases are treated alike if a jurisdiction can settle on the key factors that determine when indeed cases are alike. Thus, the key to understanding a system like Minnesota's is to see how it makes that judgment.

One would think that a first step in developing criteria for sentencing is to establish the operating purpose(s) of punishment among the ones conventionally posited by our jurisprudence. And what did Minnesota say or commit itself to on this core? The answer lies in the general approach that commission states have taken to explicit jurisprudence. The political discourse surrounding commissions suggests a rather mundane concern with "incapacitating" the most violent criminals, expressing "retributivist" goals by finding modest consensus on proportionate severity, but also taking a utilitarian tack by promoting "rehabilitation" through better drug treatment and vocational programs, just before or just after release, and, in some states, building in some provision for parole supervision (von Hirsch, 1987b, 84–93).

Notably, the discussion of general deterrence so ritualized in typical jurisprudential discussions of sentencing seems almost wholly absent from discourse on commission and guidelines, perhaps because of the perception that even revised legislated sentences are likely to remain so high that they are well past the point of diminishing returns in this regard (Webster and Doob, chapter 7 of this volume). Indeed, at most, proponents of the commission model tend to rely on fairly casual incantations of eclectic purposes, or to focus on public safety and economy with a nod toward the "limiting retributivism" associated with Norval Morris (1982, 182–187).[4] Indeed, more representative than any abstract discussion of punishment philosophy is eclectic discussion of the *functions* of a commission (Tonry 2005).[5]

Thus, in creating its commission, Minnesota eschewed any explicit commitment to any singular rationale, perhaps because any explicit philosophical commitment is itself either too abstract to be useful or too contestable to win consensus.

Nevertheless, one can infer from the dominant effect of the offense score on the sentence outcome in the Minnesota system that a retributivist rationale is at its heart, along with some accommodation of more utilitarian objectives. And that accommodation is limited and subtle. First, although general deterrence is the most oft-cited utilitarian objective, it cannot be really well addressed through a grid, as opposed to an adjustment to the offense score. Second, the emphasis on prior crimes on the offender score indicates that the commission, after reviewing the social science on risk prediction, concluded that criminal record was the only very reliable basis for measuring an individual's need for incapacitation or the time necessary for rehabilitation. Further, even that view overstates the commission's willingness to make utilitarian judgments, because even its cautious reliance on prior crimes may result chiefly from its descriptive review of pre-Commission sentencing patterns (von Hirsch 1987b, 92). The sentencing system does leave some flexibility for more contextually individual factors that might justify departures from the prescribed ranges, but here it was very parsimonious (von Hirsch 1987b, 93–94). As a procedural matter, it requires "substantial and compelling" reasons for departure, and as a substantive matter it forbids reliance on such factors as education or family or marital status. The parsimony may be due to the commission's lack of faith in the predictive power of these factors, or to its concern that, however useful they are in the hands of social scientists, the factors are so subject to interpretation or manipulation by judges that they would re-invite inequity, disparity, or even discrimination.

Of course, no two commissions were alike at this stage (nor are they now), and the new commissions states differed at least by degree from Minnesota on these dimensions. Nevertheless, the blend of substance and process reflected in Minnesota's system, the tilt in favor of offense or conduct-based measures as against more individualized factors as the dominant criteria, and the reliance on past actual sentencing consensus rather than new normative values—along these dimensions Minnesota is a decent rough proxy for the way in which the new commission states addressed their disparity concerns.

While the emphasis on guidelines production is important, commissions were conceived from the start to do other things as well. One other function is to address the problem of prison overcrowding and excessive cost, either by factoring population effects directly into guidelines scores or by providing population and cost "impact analyses" to the legislature whenever new laws are proposed to define new crimes or augment sentences. The Minnesota Commission built such "impact analysis" into its work from the start, using optimal housing ratios as a key determinant of the guidelines range-scores in the first place and then regularly subjecting its guidelines to re-analysis when the resource-to-population ration changed because of new legislation or other factors (Frase 2005c; von Hirsch 1987b, 93–95). This approach serves directly to avoid dangerous or illegal overcrowding, but also, more subtly, in its admonitory effect on the legislature it ensures that the social or political forces calling for particular sentences are intellectually honest in terms of choosing the putatively just punishment in light of society's willingness to bear the burdens as well as the benefits. The legislature can agree that no bill altering a criminal sentence or defining a new crime can be considered unless it contains a data analysis and projection done by the commission (Miller and Wright 2005).

Further, the very predicate for this impact analysis—the commission's capacity to perform empirical research—is an independent value as well. In myriad ways, criminal justice systems need as much information as possible about their institutional resources and the records and needs of the prisoners. Failure of "data sharing" and "data integration" are notorious flaws in state criminal justice systems. And although the flaws are sometimes ascribed to poor computer hardware, they really lie in the failure of "human software" to develop bureaucratic protocols for synthesizing and communicating the collective and individualized data that make incarceration safer and more efficient—and make parolee reentry more successful (Ball 2010).

Shortly after the Minnesota program was launched, it found imitators in other states (Tonry 1987, 20–26). Washington State quickly committed itself to a fully staffed commission that soon enacted guidelines. The guideline ranges were somewhat broader than Minnesota's, but Washington went beyond Minnesota in prescribing detailed standards for misdemeanors as well as felonies, in reallocating scarce prison space for violent offenders, and even taking the bold step of promulgating standards for prosecutorial charging and plea bargaining (Boerner and Lieb 2001). Pennsylvania took a still different route. In theory, sentencing rules propounded by the commission were to operate as law unless rejected by the legislative branch, but the 1982 commission rules turned out to be a very modest plan of triad ranges, not a Minnesota-style guidelines grid, and the commission did not even provide judges with guidance as to how to use the triads. Moreover, Pennsylvania retained discretionary parole. Nevertheless, the Pennsylvania commission became the gold standard for its other function—its collection and dissemination of criminal justice statistical data, especially inmate data that enhanced the regulation of parole decisions (Kramer and Ulmer 2008).

Some states, on the other hand, made only superficial efforts, because the political will to sustain a commission soon faltered in key branches of government in those jurisdictions. Thus, Maine's experiment collapsed when judges categorically resisted limitations on their discretion, and legislators never funded a commission staff. Connecticut experimented with a commission and guidelines but the guidelines, based just on a description of past patterns, were only exhortative, and the outcome of the state's experiment was a *legislative* set of determinate sentencing rules. New York's was perhaps the most superficial effort. In the 1980s the legislature created a large commission but invested no political capital or intellectual resources in it, and the agency disappeared, although a new, more modest version of it was created in 2007 with a charge to perform fiscal analyses of proposed legislation and promote ideas for alternatives to incarceration (Vinegrad and Bloom 2007, 1).

Michael Tonry's early assessment of this first wave of commission/guidelines systems was mildly, if ambivalently, positive (Tonry 1987, 26–29). He saw reasonably high compliance rates with presumptive and hortatory guidelines, and some evidence of reduction in disparity. He also noted some signs of increases in incarceration rates, although this is not necessarily a good or bad thing in light of the goals of commission systems. Further, Tonry observed some evidence of prosecutorial maneuvering to get around guidelines, but no increase in trial rates or appeals from sentences. Overall, even with just a few states to look at, his meta-conclusion was that the data are too unsettled and their meaning too ambiguous to warrant any major success-or-failure judgments.

Ironically, the great anomaly in the early history of sentencing commissions was the most visible one—the United States Sentencing Commission and its much-derided guidelines. The new federal system went into effect in 1987, and any study of sentencing commissions requires some explanation of why the federal system has been the target of such condemnation while many state systems have won praise and few have received severe criticism (Weisberg 2007, 186–188). The key source of difference lies in the legal context in which the federal system emerged. For one thing, federal criminal law is simply very different from state criminal law. State criminal law must address the most fundamental public safety concerns, and state prosecutors operate mainly under conventional ground-level criminal laws and considerable caseload pressure. Federal criminal law is more opportunistic: It has fewer unavoidable public safety crimes to deal with, and Congress legislates broadly and sometimes gratuitously, passing wide-ranging and often very vague and over-lapping criminal laws with exceptionally high sentences. Thus, federal prosecutors have both more freedom to choose their cases and more leverage because of the arsenal of statutes they can deploy. Moreover, Congress worries far less than state legislatures about the budgetary effect of high incarceration rates, because its crim-inal budget is a much smaller fraction of its overall budget than is true at the state level (Stuntz 2006, 802–805). As a result, even under pre-Guidelines sentencing, U.S. Attorneys enjoyed great power in their exercise of discretion, so that any shift toward more structured sentencing rules imposed on judges was bound to raise complaints of a magnified shift of power toward prosecutors.

And those complaints proved to be voluminous, especially because of the distinct nature of the federal guidelines. The guidelines manifested a hyper-mathematical complexity and rule-like rigidity that, in their mechanical effort to reduce disparity, broadly denied judges the power to consider most kinds of individualized offender criteria. Not just to judges but to most legal commentators, the guidelines seemed to actually disserve their professed goal of achieving rational uniformity across judges and districts (Stith and Cabranes 1998; Cassell 2006; Bowman 2005).

The reasons may lie in the motivation behind the whole initiative. By the 1970s, many states, encouraged by the Model Penal Code, had achieved a fair amount of organization and internal coherence in their major criminal laws. For these states, sentencing reform was not about the fundamental criminal law: it was truly about sentencing, a clean-up effort to resolve problems in the back end of criminal justice, often as a reaction to pressing financial or political problems.

Meanwhile, for decades Congress had fitfully but futilely tried to transform the mélange of federal criminal laws into a coherent code (Gainer 1998). Moreover, it was not significantly motivated by urgent practical concerns related to cost or prison overcrowding.[6] Thus, when Congress and the new Commission began their work, they were perhaps more ambitious than wise, creating an abstracted and distinctly *legislative* code. Indeed, within a few years the criminal law reporters were full of endless Circuit Court decisions construing the nuances of the guidelines, as if guidelines doctrine-parsing had become the new mode of statutory construction of elements of crimes.

The federal guidelines were threatened when the Supreme Court handed down *Blakely v. Washington* in 2004, holding that the Sixth Amendment required that key facts that raised the sentence beyond what was entailed by a jury verdict (or guilty plea) had to be tried to the jury, and that threat was realized in 2005 when, in *United States v. Booker*, the Supreme Court applied *Blakely* to the federal system and rendered the federal guidelines merely advisory. On the other hand, the U.S. Sentencing Commission itself is still alive and well; even under this advisory regime it is fine-tuning its guidelines, and most recently proposed adjusting them to create more individualized sentencing factors (U.S. Sentencing Commission 2010b).

A few decades later, the idea of a sentencing commission, tasked to generate sentencing guidelines, has gained great purchase in American law, especially through its approval by the American Bar Association and in the American Law Institute's new Model Penal Code of Sentencing (American Bar Association, 1994; American Law Institute 2007; Dansky 2010).[7] A significant fraction of the states, approaching half, have commissions, and an overlapping and almost equal number have operative or incipient guidelines. The numbers are uncertain because a number of states are in flux,[8] but there are very useful common denominators to observe. What might be called the "consensus" system involves a guided or structured discretionary system relying on sentencing guidelines, and these guidelines can be either "presumptive" or "voluntary" (Weisberg 2007, 193–196). Obviously, presumptive sentencing guidelines require judges to either hew to a presumptive sentence (or sentencing range) or to justify any deviation with reasons, often under a regime of appellate review of those reasons. Fully voluntary guidelines are merely hortatory, though in some systems—such as Virginia (described below)—voluntary compliance can be surprisingly high.

The consensus principle is that a commission is especially well adapted to generate guidelines that address aggravating and mitigating factors that cannot sensibly be captured in substantive criminal legislation.[9] The guidelines themselves can set very narrow ranges for the sentence calculated after the factors are taken into account. But beyond whatever range they allow the judge, they typically remain presumptive—the judge can, on some stated reason, depart from the range, but the departure must be based on on-the-record reasons, often subject to appellate review.[10] Judges also retain some of the traditional discretion to choose between concurrent and consecutive sentences but, again, they often have guidelines to help determine that choice (Frase 2005b, 1119–1200).[11]

For some jurisdictions, abolition of discretionary parole release by parole boards was a *sine qua non* of new structured guidelines systems, and it seems fairly consistent with the spirit of the change from indeterminate sentencing that motivated the commission model (Frase 2005b, 1199–1200; Frankel 1973). But that result is hardly universal, nor are the variations in retention of some form of post-prison supervised release serious divisions in the overall consensus (Frase 2005b, 1221–1223). A modest good-time reduction from that sentence, earned by passively good conduct while in prison and set by a formula, would be a fairly uncontroversial adjunct, and other variations are common.[12] Of course, the relevant question here is not so much the substantive principle of parole but the institutional question of whether the commission plays a distinct role in this area. Where parole is retained, *some* agency—whether or not called a parole board—has to assess whether the prisoner has indeed earned early release, and will also use risk assessment metrics at that point to evaluate the consequences of releasing the prisoner. In some versions of the commission model, the commission itself will guide release decisions with a kind of subset of presumptive guidelines that help determine whether, and under what conditions of supervision, a prisoner should be released (Chanenson 2005). Perhaps more significantly, some commissions are charged with the power to issue guidelines for parole revocation, since returns to prison for parole violations have proved a major problem for states trying to control the size and volatility of their prison populations (von Hirsch 1987b, 62, 74–75; Frase 2005b; Dansky 2006, 7–8).

Another variation among commissions concerns placement within or among the branches of government. Advocates of commissions have frequently disagreed on whether the commission should be treated as an executive branch or independent agency or a subset of the courts (Barkow and O'Neill 2006, 1989–1990). Such a decision might seem important—for example, could the executive remove commission members if the commission's work is viewed as a judicial function?—but the issue has proved to be more formalistic than consequential (Dansky 2010, 159).[13] More important than any division of views on placement within government has been the strong consensus among the states on the importance of the commission being permanent and reasonably independent of other parts of government (Dansky 2010, 158–159) and on the ideal membership of the commission—that is, that it be some combination of branch representation, professional representation, political representation, and expertise (Tonry 2005, 38–45).[14]

Two large Southern states typify these alternative schemes (Weisberg 2007)—and also illustrate the legal and political contexts that prove conducive to commission-building. North Carolina has won much attention and praise for its deep commitment to the commission model and presumptive guidelines (Wright 2002; Ross and Katznelson 1999). The impetus for a North Carolina commission came from a severe prison crowding problem and the lack of transparency in sentencing. The state had been relying on haphazard use of early release to alleviate crowding, thereby leading to a de facto indeterminate system whereby the percentage of the official sentence that prisoners actually served declined catastrophically. Notably, there developed bipartisan harmony on the need for a new regime, and also the good fortune of strong nonpartisan leadership in the first chair, a distinguished jurist. The newly mandated commission created a new guidelines system organized by categories of crime and criminal history severity,[15] relied on modern social science models to predict the effect of sentencing changes on prison population, and turned the state toward greater reliance on community corrections for nonviolent offenders. Under the state's grid scheme, the trial judge must determine whether to sentence the defendant within the presumptive, aggravated, or mitigated range, and then imposes a determinate sentence.

If North Carolina's effort rested on political harmony in the face of a practical crisis, Virginia's impetus came from public anger over the state's highly unstructured and indeterminate system, including largely unregulated parole release. In that sense, the goal was to impose constraints on judicial decision making (Fabelo, Naro, and Austin 2005). But when the legislature created the Virginia Criminal Sentencing Commission in 1994, the judiciary proved capable of strong resistance, and the interesting compromise was a system of "voluntary" guidelines. The commission rooted the guidelines in historical sentencing practices, while trimming away outliers, especially where the outliers were attributable to clearly improper factors such as geography or certain demographics. Under this compromise, the guidelines are fairly formalistic, replete with worksheets and explanations, but judges remain free to follow or not follow the guidelines as they choose.[16]

The pairing of North Carolina and Virginia may suggest that the typical modern sentencing commission represents an effort to react to and even to abolish highly unstructured and indeterminate systems. But in fact the commissions have proved useful in very different institutional contexts, and a survey of contemporary state systems illustrates the great versatility of the commission principle (Dansky 2006, 3–6). New Mexico, for example, had already adopted a strongly structured and determinate scheme by legislation in the 1980s, but it created a commission in 2003 to focus on collecting data and proffering ideas on sentencing policy to the legislature. Even without binding legal power, that commission has played an aggressive and influential role in monitoring how state's parole policies and new sentencing laws affect population flows and even critically analyzing the work of prosecutors and public defenders for their effect on prison populations.

Utah created a commission in 1996 after the legislature there had passed a number of mandatory sentencing laws, having found that the system had become too manipulable by prosecutorial charging. Thus, ironically, the state switched to a less structured system with broad sentencing ranges but with strong commission guidance for both judges and parole authorities. Utah seems quite confident about the value of hortatory guidelines, even proudly describing its scheme as a "discussion forum" between commission and judges and among judges.[17]

Missouri presents a somewhat mixed and changing picture. The Missouri Sentencing Advisory Commission, created in 1994, quickly issued advisory guidelines, but these were simply ignored by the judges, and the state remains explicitly and proudly committed to judicial discretion, which it describes as "the cornerstone of sentencing in Missouri." Nevertheless, the commission continues to conduct statistical research and is newly charged to advise the legislature on ideas for alternative sentences, work release, home-based incarceration, prison work programs, and probation and parole options. Moreover, the commission has renewed its effort at providing some guidance for judges, issuing a report that calls for a system of recommended sentences based on current practices, and including risk-assessment models for allocating some offenders to non-incarceration alternatives (Wolff 2008).

Michigan created its commission in 1994, after an era in which the state supreme court, confronting the flaws of a highly discretionary system, had itself done the work of promulgating proportionality guidelines through appellate review and administrative order. Thus, the court was a kind of de facto commission, relying mostly on consensus judicial practice to guide trial courts. The new commission itself then enacted guidelines that reflected the normative views of the legislature. The commission then fell into desuetude, and the legislature itself has taken on the task of evaluating and updating the guidelines. Given how ill-suited the legislature is to do the fine-tuning work of a commission, it appears that the commission/guidelines system in Michigan has mainly been undone by lack of political will and support (Dansky 2006, 6).

EVALUATING THE WORK OF COMMISSIONS

Although there is no method nor any authority for any official evaluation of the work of sentencing commissions, a consensus has emerged that at least the state systems have been highly successful (NASC 2010; American Law Institute 2007; American Bar Association 1994). First, even if we know what empirical questions to ask, given limited and uncertain data and wide variety in structures among systems, it is hard to come up with reliable numbers in the first place. And, of course, it is hard to establish what empirical questions to ask, because identifying the criteria for identifying success in a jurisdiction's system is a highly difficult and contestable affair. Of course, some fairly obvious potential criteria come to mind, such as reductions in prison population, redistribution of prison spaces toward more violent criminals, greater "transparency," reduction of costs, avoidance of judicial intervention, and at least no absolute or relative worsening of the crime rate (Weisberg 2007, 217–222).

As with any such evaluation, breadth and depth may need to be traded off. So if we eschew formal and rigorous comparisons across states, we may find some useful, if rough, evaluative insights by homing in on changes within a particular state. In that regard, the usefully paired states of North Carolina and Virginia again may supply good examples (Weisberg 2007, 212–213, 215–217).

In establishing its commission, North Carolina trumpeted "truth in sentencing" as a key justifying rationale, and although the usefulness of that concept is open to debate, under the new system prisoners were soon serving most or even all of the original official sentence. Further, the goal of reallocation has been substantially achieved: violent offenders are now serving longer sentences, and nonviolent offenders are serving shorter (and frequently noncustodial) sentences, with many more in rehabilitation or community supervision. Moreover, the prison population has tended to remain just at or above capacity, and there was a period between 1998 and 2000 when population fell below capacity, though it has turned somewhat upward of late. Most strikingly, North Carolina went from having the highest incarceration rate in the South in 1980 to now having the second lowest. And, finally, North Carolina has achieved one of the most impressive steady reductions or plateaus in incarceration rates in the country, while seeing its crime rate move down at least in synch with the average American crime drop that began in the early 1990s (Weisberg 2007, 213 n. 196).

As for Virginia, given its gamble on voluntary guidelines, the most striking success fact is the high degree of judicial compliance. One explanation may lie in a key aspect of the design of this voluntary system: The judges are not obligated to follow the guidelines, but they cannot merely ignore them: if they choose to depart, they must state their reasons for departure on the record. Further, although those reasons are not reviewable on appeal, the record and the reasons must be reported to the commission, which maintains this information and can use it if an accumulation or pattern of related departure reasons call for an actual change in the guidelines (Virginia Criminal Sentencing Commission 2010). Thus Virginia can claim some success for the subtle way in which it tweaked and calibrated the relationship among branches of government: it proved that "merely hortatory" guidelines can manifest considerable power of exhortation. Moreover, a substantial reallocation of prison space has occurred in the direction of more serious crimes, with higher-scoring offenders going to prison. At the same time, the overall incarceration rate has remained steady in Virginia, and thus in effect has decreased relative to national trends.

But still, evaluation of the success of the commission experiment still requires some intellectual consensus on the relevant criteria. Here are some candidates, and the problems they entail.

Reduction in crime: Perhaps lowering the crime rate should be the test of any change in criminal justice. But that test might put an unfair burden of proof on this one component of the system, since for over a century statisticians have debated the broader question whether meaningful relationships can be discerned between prison rates and crime rates (Zimring and Hawkins 1993). Moreover, answering the causation question would be extremely difficult, given the vigorous social science debate that has now arisen about how much the great increase in incarceration over the last three decades contributed to the dramatic decline in crime rates in the 1990s (King et al. 2005). So perhaps it would be better to simply ask the more modest question of whether the commission model is associated with a higher crime rate.

Lowering recidivism: Another criterion might be reduction just in recidivism, since that goal seems somewhat closer to the particular mission of prisons. But even defining recidivism, much less isolating comparable variables among jurisdictions, is a daunting challenge, especially when in many states there is a blurry line between true new crimes and parole violations (Petersilia 2006, 70–76).

Reducing incarceration: One plausible measure would be changes in the actual incarceration rate, because control of, if not reduction in, incarceration is a professed goal of many commission efforts, although on that score the current research is somewhat inconclusive.

The best we can say is that there is some tentative support for the inference that the adoption or maintenance of sentencing commissions/guidelines systems has a downward pressure effect on incarceration rates (Marvell 1995, 70; Nicholson-Crotty 2004, 396; Sorenesen and Stemen 2002, 469; Stemen, Rengifo, and Wilson 2005), and is associated with the few instances of actual reduction in a smattering of states in the late 1990s and a slowing of the rate of increase on others that had especially high growth rates (Reitz 2006, 1799–1800).

Reducing disparity: This criterion would seem especially central to the professed purposes of sentencing commissions and is also capable or being measured by conventional econometric techniques used to isolate such impermissible factors as race and ethnicity. Of course, that reduction in disparity requires very careful use of statistical regression methods, because an abstract commitment to equity in sentencing can sometimes be the enemy of reasonable individualization, and presumptively impermissible factors—especially gender—can sometimes mask or overlap with permissible individualized factors (Pfaff 2006, 281–282). Nevertheless, highly refined recent analyses do indicate that both presumptive and voluntary guidelines systems—most of which have been generated by commissions—have decreased disparity in terms of race and gender for many serious crimes (Pfaff 2006, 2007).

Efficiency: In general terms, the most neutral and incontestable criterion for any sentencing system is cost-efficiency. But defining the sub-criteria for efficiency is itself a very debatable matter. We might look to reducing cost per prisoner—but that is something more within the control of prison officials. Or we might look to what prison expenditures produce—but that framing of the question returns us to the question of whether sentencing systems can be meaningfully correlated with changes in the crime or recidivism rates and would also then require us to address the issue of measuring cost inputs. More modest measures would be some combination of reduced prison costs as a portion of the state budget, or the absence of any disturbing increase in the crime rate or recidivism rate.

Promoting evidence-based systems: In a broader and possibly more persuasive mode, the commission model might be just that—a model—representing a commitment to the general principle of cost-benefit rationality in criminal justice. Thus, it might indirectly lead to such beneficial effects as greater use of evidence-based risk-and-needs assessment at all relevant stages of criminal justice—including sentencing, probation, and parole, and any large-scale prisoner releases—even if those do not lie within the direct control of the commission (Warren 2007).

In sum, roughly half the states have created sentencing commissions, largely as a way of generating sentencing guidelines at a level of detail and with a grounding in research beyond the functional competency of the legislature itself. The motivations for creating them range from the need to address exigent financial necessity, to legal and constitutional problems of overcrowding, to social and political distress over problems in criminal justice generally. The commission structures differ widely, as do their guidelines, sorting themselves along a continuum from very binding to very largely hortatory. But the differences may be less important than the similarities in terms of overall state commitment to some negotiated political processes of cost-benefit analysis through a partially and flexibly structured sentencing metric.

Ironically, the mere survival of a commission is itself a proof of success, because it represents legislators' commitment to restrain their own tendencies to generate politically charged and often wasteful sentencing policies and instead to treat sentencing as a regulatory matter that warrants cost-benefit rationality in the first place.

NOTES

1. Ironically, a common criticism of the dominance of plea-bargaining in recent decades has been that it distorts our traditionally adversarial system into one of a regime of administrative law and practice run by a prosecutorial bureaucracy (Lynch 1998).

2. This is not to say that American sentencing commissions have invariably promulgated sentencing guidelines (see American Law Institute 2007: 54–55, counting 6 among 23 active commissions that had not done so).

3. For the grid itself in current form, see *Minnesota Sentencing Guidelines and Commentary*. Online. Available at: http://www.msgc.state.mn.us/msgc5/guidelines.htm.

4. The term refers to Morris's agnosticism on the possibility of social consensus on precise retributive price lists for offenses but the feasibility of identifying consensus boundaries, especially upper bounds.

5. Tonry pays only quick fealty to purposes-of-punishment jurisprudence and turns in elaborate detail to such "overt functions" of sentencing as distributive functions (consistency, evenhandedness, and fairness), preventive functions (crime, fear of crime, costs of crime, and consequences of victimization), and management functions (efficiency, cost-effectiveness, and resource management), as well as such "latent functions" as self-interest, ideological expression and partisan advantage (2005, 38–45).

6. Indeed, before long congressional leaders admitted or even proclaimed that their preferred solution to the disparity problem lay in part with a ratcheting up of actual sentences that was expected to increase the federal prison population in the name of rational parity (O'Hear 2006, 749–795).

7. *Blakely* affected some state commission/guidelines as well to varying degrees, but in no case as severely as it affected the federal system via *Booker*. So while some states have had to rework their guidelines and procedures somewhat to comply with the Sixth Amendment, *Blakely* has not been a major obstacle to the development of guideline systems (Frase 2005, 1191–1194).

8. Relatively up-to-date listings appear in legal commentary (Frase 2005, 1194–1204; Barkow and O'Neill 2006, 1994; Pfaff 2006, 241–245), but the most accurate listings appear as compiled on the web site of the National Association of State Sentencing Commissions (2010).

9. Chanenson calls this Indeterminate Structured Sentencing (ISS), whereby the guidelines set as a minimum some percentage of the statutory maximum sentence in order to allow for an adequate period of potential post-release supervision (2005, 433–442).

10. Appellate schemes vary, but a common one is most deferential to the trial judge for a sentencing in the presumptive range and then become less so for an above or below range departure. That is the current scheme that the Supreme Court has mandated for federal senescing (Chanenson 2005, 445).

11. The Supreme Court has held that the choice can be discretionary with the judge (*Oregon v. Ice* 2009).

12. One variation would provide some opportunity for "gain time" through positive good conduct, or, more specifically, constructive participation in pre-reentry programs, with ample opportunities for alternative, noncustodial forms of supervision

13. Virginia presents an interesting example of how placement within government might make a difference. As noted below, Virginia acquiesced to the demands of its judges that the guidelines remain chiefly voluntary. Perhaps for that reason, the Virginia Commission is part of the judicial branch, with a stated purpose to "assist the judiciary" in the imposition of sentences, and with a heavy allocation of seats on the commission to judges (Virginia Criminal Sentencing Commission 2010).

14. Tonry argues that to promote the best advantages of a commission, members should be only part-time, because full-time members may end up using their positions to proclaim large and ambitious policy changes that a commission should eschew, or, conversely, that full-time members might overly micro-manage the staff and its research. Thus, part-time status is itself an aspect of political insulation (Tonry 1991, 318–321).

15. It is worth noting that prior record is the *only* characteristic of the defendant that is factored into the guidelines calculation.

16. To help promote the symbolic value of "truth in sentencing," the commission relied on the time-served data, as opposed to sentence length. It thus ensured that the new recommended sentence ranges were based on the amount of time that offenders had actually been serving in prison, rather than the time that the judge had imposed (which was always understood to be essentially meaningless) (Ostrom et al. 1999, 10–11).

17. In addition, in 1997 Utah took the unusual step of promulgating juvenile sentencing guidelines. New Jersey actually resembles the more typical commission state, because it had a very discretionary and indeterminate system when the commission idea arose. But its original and temporary Commission to Review Criminal Sentencing actually recommended that the system remain that way. Instead, the commission's self-conceived role is to conduct research on sentencing policy (Dansky 2006, 10–11).

REFERENCES

Allen, Francis. 1981. *The Decline of the Rehabilitative Ideal: Penal Policy and Social Purpose.* New Haven: Yale University Press.

American Bar Association. 1994. *Standards for Criminal Justice: Sentencing*, 3rd ed. Washington, DC: ABA Press.

American Law Institute. 2003. *Model Penal Code Sentencing*, Report (April 11, 2003).

American Law Institute. 2007. *Model Penal Code Sentencing*, Tentative Draft No. 1 (April 9, 2007).

Ball, W. David. 2010. "E Pluribus Unum: Data and Operations Integration in the California Criminal Justice System." *Stanford Law and Policy Review* 21: 277–310.

Barkow, Rachel E., and Kathleen O'Neill. 2006. "Delegating Punitive Power: The Political Economy of Sentencing Commission and Guideline Formation." *Texas Law Review* 84: 1973–2022.

Blakely v. Washington, 542 U.S. 296 (2004).

Boerner, David, and Roxanne Lieb. 2001. "Sentencing Reform in the Other Washington." In *Crime and Justice: A Review of Research*, vol. 28, ed. Michael Tonry. Chicago: University of Chicago Press.

Bowman, Frank O. 2005. "The Failure of the Federal Sentencing Guidelines: A Structural Analysis." *Columbia Law Review* 105: 1315–1350.

Cassell, Paul G. 2006. Statement of Judge Paul G. Cassell, Chairman, Committee on Criminal Law, Judicial Conference of the United States, on "How Judges Are Properly Implementing the Supreme Court's Decision in *United States V. Booker*," before the Subcommittee on Crime, Terrorism, and Homeland Security Committee on the Judiciary, House of Representatives (March 16, 2006).

Chanenson, Steven. 2005. "The Next Era of Sentencing Reform." *Emory Law Journal* 54: 377–460.

Dansky, Kara. 2006. *Contemporary Sentencing Reform in California: A Report to the Little Hoover Commission*, 6–7. Online. Available at: http://sentencing.nj.gov/downloads/pdf/articles/2006/Sept2006/document02.pdf.

Dansky, Kara. 2010. "A Blueprint for a California Sentencing Commission." *Federal Sentencing Reporter* 22 (February): 158–163.

Fabelo, Tony, Wendy Naro, and James Austin. 2005. The JFA Institute. *Exploring the Diminishing Effects of More Incarceration: Virginia's Experiment*. Online. Available at: www.drugpolicvy.org/docUploads/JFAInstituteVirginia.pdf.

Frankel, Marvin, and Leonard Orland. 1984. "Sentencing Commissions and Guidelines." *Georgetown Law Journal* 73: 225–247.

Frankel, Marvin. 1973. *Criminal Sentences: Law Without Order*. New York: Hill & Wang.

Frase, Richard. 2005a. "Punishment Purposes." *Stanford Law Review* 58: 67–84.

Frase, Richard. 2005b. "State Sentencing Guidelines: Diversity, Consensus, and Unresolved Policy Issues." *Columbia Law Review* 105: 1190–1232.

Frase, Richard. 2005c. "Sentencing Guidelines in Minnesota, 1978–2003." In *Crime and Justice: A Review of Research*, vol. 32, ed. Michael Tonry. Chicago: University of Chicago Press.

Gainer, Ronald L. 1998. "Federal Criminal Code Reform: Past and Future." *Buffalo Criminal Law Review* 2: 45–160.

King, Ryan S., Marc Mauer, and Malcolm C. Young. 2005. *Incarceration and Crime: A Complex Relationship*. Washington, DC: The Sentencing Project.

Kramer, John H., and Jeffrey T. Ulmer. 2008. *Sentencing Guidelines: Lessons from Pennsylvania*. Boulder, CO: Lynne Rienner Publishers.

Lynch, Gerard. 1998. "Our Administrative System of Criminal Justice." *Fordham Law Review* 66: 2117–2152.

Lynch, Gerard." 2009. Marvin Frankel: A Reformer Reassessed." *Federal Sentencing Reporter* 21 (April): 235–241.

Marvell, Thomas B. 1995. "Sentencing Guidelines and Prison Population Growth." *Journal of Criminal law and Criminology* 85: 696–709.

Miller, Marc L., and Ronald F. Wright. 2005. "'The Wisdom We Have Lost': Sentencing Information and Its Uses." *Stanford Law Review* 58: 361–380.

Minnesota Sentencing Commission. *Minnesota Sentencing Guidelines and Commentary*. Online. Available at: http://www.msgc.state.mn.us/msgc5/guidelines.htm.

Morris, Norval. 1982. *Madness and the Criminal Law*. Chicago: University of Chicago Press.

National Association of State Sentencing Commissions. Online. Available at: http://www.ussc.gov/STATES.HTM.

Nicholson-Crotty, Sean. 2004. "The Impact of Sentencing Guidelines on State-Level Sanctions: An Analysis over Time." *Crime & Delinquency* 50: 395–411.

O'Hear, Michael. 2006. "The Original Intent of Uniformity in Federal Sentencing." *University of Cincinnati Law Review* 74: 749–817.

Oregon v. Ice, 555 U.S. 160 (2009).

Ostrom, Brian, et al. 1999. National Center for State Courts. *Truth-in Sentencing in Virginia: Evaluating the Process and Impact of Sentencing Reform.* Washington, DC: National Institute of Justice.

Petersilia, Joan. 2006. *Understanding California Corrections.* Berkeley: California Policy Research Center.

Pfaff, John F. 2006. "The Continued Vitality of Structured Sentencing Following *Blakely*: The Effectiveness of Voluntary Guidelines." *UCLA Law Review* 54: 235–308.

Pfaff, John F. 2007. "The Vitality of Voluntary Guidelines in the Wake of *Blakely v. Washington*." *Federal Sentencing Reporter* 19: 202–207.

Reitz, Kevin. 2006. "Don't Blame Determinacy: U.S. Incarceration Growth Has Been Driven by Other Forces." *Texas Law Review* 84: 1787–1802.

Ross, Thomas, and Susan Katznelson. 1999. "Crime and Punishment in North Carolina: Severity and Costs Under Structured Sentencing." *Federal Sentencing Reporter* 11: 207ff.

Sorensen, Jon, and Don Stemen. 2002. "The Effect of State Sentencing Policies on Incarceration Rates." *Crime & Delinquency* 48: 456–475.

Stemen, Don, Andres Rengifo, and James Wilson. 2005. *Of Fragmentation and Ferment: The Impact of State Sentencing Policies on Incarceration Rates, 1975–2002.* New York: Vera Institute of Justice.

Stith, Kate, and Jose A. Cabranes. 1998. *Fear of Judging: Sentencing Guidelines in the Federal Courts.* Chicago: University of Chicago Press.

Stuntz, William. 2006. "The Political Constitution of Criminal Justice." *Harvard Law Review* 119: 781–852.

Tonry, Michael. 1987. "Sentencing Guidelines and Their Effects." In *The Sentencing Commission and its Guidelines*, eds. Andrew Von Hirsch, Kay Knapp, and Michael Tonry, 16–46. Boston: Northeastern University Press.

Tonry, Michael. 1991. "The Politics and Processes of Sentencing Commissions." *Crime & Delinquency* 37: 307–366.

Tonry, Michael. 2005. "The Functions of Sentencing and Sentencing Reform." *Stanford Law Review* 58: 37–66.

United States Sentencing Commission. 2010a. *Amendments to the Guidelines.* (April 30, 2010). Online. Available at: http://www.ussc.gov/2010guid/finalamend10.pdf.

United States Sentencing Commission. 2010b. *News Release: U.S. Sentencing Commission Votes to Send to Congress Guideline Amendments Providing More Alternatives to Incarceration, Increasing Consideration of Certain Specific Offender Characteristics During the Sentencing Process.* (April 39, 2010). Online. Available at: http://ftp.ussc.gov/PRESS/rel20100419.htm.

U.S. v. Bergman, 416 F. Supp. 496 (SDNY 1976).

U.S. v. Booker, 543 U.S. 220 (2005).

Vinegrad, Alan, and Douglas Bloom, 2007. "New York's New Commission on Sentencing Reform." *New York Law Journal* 48, no. 87: 1–2.

Virginia Criminal Sentencing Commission. 2009. *Annual Report 2009.* Online. Available at: http://www.vcsc.state.va.us/2009AnnualReport.pdf.

von Hirsch, Andrew. 1987a. "The Sentencing Commission's Functions." In *The Sentencing Commission and its Guidelines*, eds. Andrew Von Hirsch, Kay Knapp, and Michael Tonry, 3–16. Boston: Northeastern University Press.

von Hirsch, Andrew. 1987b. "Structure and Rationale: Minnesota's Critical Choices." In *The Sentencing Commission and its Guidelines*, eds. Andrew Von Hirsch, Kay Knapp and Michael Tonry, 84–106. Boston: Northeastern University Press.

Warren, Roger. 2007. "Evidence-Based Practices and State Sentencing Policy: Ten Initiatives to Reduce Recidivism." *Indiana Law Journal* 82: 1307–1318.

Weisberg, Robert. 2007. "How Sentencing Commissions Turned Out to Be a Good Idea." *Berkeley Journal of Criminal Law* 12: 179–230.

Weisberg, Robert. 1995. "Guideline Sentencing, Traditional Defenses, and the Evolution of Substantive Criminal Law Doctrine." *Federal Sentencing Reporter* 7: 168.

Whitman, James Q. 2003. "A Plea Against Retributivism." *Buffalo Criminal Law Review* 7: 85.

Williams v. N.Y., 337 U.S. 241, 246 (1949).

Wolff, Michael A. 2008. "Evidence-Based Judicial Discretion: Promoting Public Safety Through State Sentencing Reform." *N.Y.U. Law Review* 83: 1389–1419.

Wright, Ronald F. 2002. "Counting the Cost of Sentencing in North Carolina, 1980–2000," in *Crime and Justice: A Review of Research*, vol. 29, ed. Michael Tonry. Chicago: University of Chicago Press.

Zimring, Franklin, and Gordon Hawkins. 1993. *The Scale of Imprisonment*. Chicago: University of Chicago Press.

CHAPTER 13

PROCEDURE AT SENTENCING

NANCY J. KING

PROCEDURAL requirements at sentencing serve competing goals. The sentencing process must allow courts to decide punishment efficiently with a reasonable degree of finality, but it must also ensure that sentences stay within legislated limits, appear fair, and rely on accurate information. For the determination of guilt, the Constitution provides a comprehensive set of procedural rules balancing similar concerns. But the Supreme Court has declined to apply many of these same rules to sentencing. Instead, it has left the sentencing process largely to legislatures. Contemporary procedure for the sentencing of adult, non-capital offenders is notable for the following features:

- Far fewer constitutional procedural protections apply at sentencing than apply at trial.
- The Supreme Court has drawn a bright line between the procedures that the Constitution requires for the selection of non-capital sentences and those it requires for the adjudication of guilt.
- Sentencing procedure is defined primarily by legislation and by court rule; it varies greatly among jurisdictions.
- Procedural rules for sentencing and the opportunity to enforce those rules are subject to negotiation by the parties.

I. Limited Constitutional Regulation

Compared to its comprehensive constitutional regulation of the trial process, the Supreme Court has preserved "enormous latitude" for legislatures in "constructing their arrangements for the imposition of criminal punishments" (Reitz 2003, 127). There are many possible explanations for the Court's relatively hands-off approach to sentencing. The Bill of Rights has little to say about sentencing, other than the Eighth Amendment's prohibition of "cruel and unusual punishments" and "excessive fines." In 1789, in prosecutions for serious offenses, there was no separate sentencing phase as we know it today. Judges at the time selected sentences for minor offenses, but felonies, for the most part, carried only one possible sentence—execution (Preyer 1982; King 2003). Consequently, not only constitutional text, but historical practice, has provided only limited guidance for the structuring of constitutional rules that govern selection among authorized punishments for serious crimes.

Nevertheless, the Court has recognized some constitutional constraints on sentencing (LaFave et al. 2007; Michaels 2003). These decisions generally have been rooted in specific guarantees in the Bill of Rights; the Court has yet to agree on whether or not a generic procedural due process standard should apply at sentencing, and if so, which one.[1] Adding to the uncertain application of the Constitution to the sentencing process in non-capital cases has been the Court's pattern of first establishing a constitutional requirement for sentencing procedure in the context of a capital case, then later declining to extend the rule to non-capital cases (Steiker and Steiker 1995; Douglass 2005; LaFave et al. 2007). A summary of the major constitutional requirements for sentencing procedure follows.

Who Sentences

The inclusion of the right to jury trial in both Article III and the Sixth Amendment reflects the Framers' "reluctance to entrust plenary powers over the life and liberty of the citizen" to judges (*Duncan*, 155). The Court, however, has concluded that these provisions guarantee only a jury determination of guilt or innocence based on the elements that define an offense. They do not create a right to a jury's choice of sentence from within the range of penalties authorized by law for that offense (*Spaziano*; *Ring*).

From the nation's beginning, sentencing authority has been shared between judge, jury, and the executive branch. In the late eighteenth century, when a jury's decision to convict a defendant of a serious offense meant a mandatory sentence of death, judges exercised sentencing authority by deciding whether to extend "benefit of clergy," sparing the condemned's life but branding him with the status of a convicted offender (Dalzell 1955; King 2003; Sawyer 1990; *Apprendi*). In addition, the executive actively exercised sentencing authority through clemency—commuting a significant proportion of sentences (Humbert 1941; Barkow 2008). This particular balance of sentencing authority was not uniform throughout the states. Nor did it last. In 1790, the first Congress abolished clergy for federal offenses and enacted several crimes carrying punishments of imprisonment up to a specified term of years (1 Stat. 112). After the nation's first prisons were constructed in the early 1800s and state legislatures expanded sentencing options for felonies to include terms of incarceration within designated ranges, the power of judges to select sentences for minor offenses was enlarged in many states to include the authority to select the appropriate term of imprisonment for convicted felons (King 2003). Over the nineteenth century, charging power migrated from the grand jury to the prosecutor and the new professional police (Steinberg 1989). Into the twentieth century, discretion to reduce incarceration terms through release became vested in parole boards and corrections officials who administered parole and good-time rules (Frankel 1972; Jacobs 1982; Reitz, chapter 11 of this volume). In many jurisdictions, substitutes for jury trials—namely bench trials and plea bargaining—undercut what little sentencing authority juries had retained (*Patton*; Fisher 2003). The eighteenth-century expectation that the jury's verdict would determine sentence gave way to the twentieth-century rule that jurors may not even be informed of sentencing consequences for fear that they would be distracted from a reliable determination of guilt (*Shannon*; Barkow 2003; Kemmitt 2006).

Distribution of sentencing discretion between jury, judge, and executive will continue to change with innovation in the institutions of criminal justice. In most American jurisdictions today, judges select sentences within statutory bounds, and corrections or parole officials determine actual sentence length (Reitz, chapter 11 of this volume; National Conference of States Legislatures). Executive clemency has withered (Kobil 2007; Heise 2003; Love 2006). Agencies as well as legislatures in many states now draft sentencing guidelines for the judiciary (Weisberg, chapter 12 of this volume). And as legislatures have increasingly assigned predictable punishment consequences to specific sentencing facts, prosecutors have gained even more ability to control the sentence through charge selection (Wright, chapter 10 of this volume). The future may include entirely new power arrangements, such as increased reliance on predictions of recidivism by researchers (Casey, et al. 2011), more deference to victims' preferences in setting the initial sentence, or more frequent post-sentence modification by agency-run innocence commissions.

Counsel, Timing, Hearing, Burden of Proof, Notice, and Evidence

The right to counsel, which may be the most important procedural guarantee of all, applies at sentencing as well as at trial (*Mempa*; *Glover*). An extraordinary delay of sentencing after conviction is probably unconstitutional, although there is some dispute over whether the Sixth Amendment right to a speedy trial or the Due Process Clause regulates the permissible period (*Pollard*; LaFave et al. 2007).

A defendant has throughout U.S. history been given the opportunity to make a statement to the sentencer before sentence is pronounced, but this statement can be restricted to a plea for mercy, or to assertions under oath. This limited entitlement to speak, known as allocution, dates from a time when defendants were often without counsel and had no right to take the stand themselves (Thomas 2007). Beyond giving the defendant this opportunity to weigh in before his sentence is announced, a formal sentencing hearing appears to be entirely optional, and is not required by the Constitution.

There are very few constitutional rules governing the information a sentencer may consider when selecting a sentence. A judge may not imprison an indigent probationer who fails to pay a monetary sanction until alternatives to incarceration are first considered (*Bearden*). A judge may not base a sentence upon "materially untrue" information (*Townsend*), but the Constitution provides surprisingly little protection against this. Unlike elements at trial, which the government must establish beyond a reasonable doubt, facts considered by the sentencer need only be proven more likely than not. The Court has upheld the use of this preponderance-of-the-evidence standard, even when the fact used to increase a sentence is another crime for which the defendant was never charged or was charged but acquitted (*Watts*). And the Constitution permits placing the burden of proof for mitigating facts on the defendant (*Booker; Marsh*).

There is no right to cross-examine government witnesses at sentencing as there is at trial; a judge may base a sentence entirely upon hearsay allegations about the offense or offender. The Court has yet to extend to sentencing the right to present evidence in one's defense or the right to subpoena defense witnesses. And many evidentiary rules, including the rule excluding evidence obtained in violation of the Fourth Amendment from trial, do not apply at sentencing (*Williams*; LaFave et al. 2007)

Moreover, the Court has yet to declare that a defendant in a non-capital case has a constitutional right to notice of the information that a judge considers at sentencing, much less advance notice (*Irizarry*; LaFave et al. 2007). Consequently, sentencing decisions may be based upon unsworn written assertions by probation officers, prosecutors, police, victims, and others in pre-sentence reports, sentencing worksheets, or other documents that are never made public and that the defendant and his counsel never see.

Justifications for Sentence

The Court has also placed very few restrictions on the permissible rationales for imposing one sentence or another. Inferences and arguments that would be considered improper as justifications for a finding of guilt are routinely made at sentencing (Hessick and Hessick 2011). A judge may increase an offender's sentence in order to send a message to others who might think they could get away with similar behavior, to incapacitate the defendant from committing future crimes, or to honor a victim's request for punishment. Higher sentences have been justified for defendants who testify falsely, or who decline to plead guilty (*Dunnigan; Bordenkircher*). Sentence reductions may even be contingent upon the amount of jail or prison space at a particular facility at a particular time (Guzman et al. 2008; Michigan Compiled Laws 801.57).

Only a handful of reasons for imposing a sentence are constitutionally off limits in a non-capital case. If a defendant was denied counsel altogether on a prior charge (now a rare occurrence), that charge may not be the basis for a recidivist sentence (*Tucker; Custis*). A judge may not select a sentence based on the race, gender, or national origin of a defendant or his victim, but the defendant must show purposeful discrimination in his case, a pattern of discrimination is not sufficient (*McClesky*). Nor may a judge resentence a defendant more severely as retaliation for a successful appeal of his initial sentence or conviction, except that an increased sentence after appeal for a non-retaliatory reason is permissible, as is a higher sentence for defendants who refuse to waive their right to appeal (*Smith*; King and O'Neill 2005). A defendant may not be forced to testify under oath at sentencing, nor may his refusal to confirm or deny an aggravating fact about the offense be the basis for concluding that the fact is true, though the same refusal may justify a higher sentence if it suggests to the judge that the defendant lacks remorse (*Estelle; Mitchell*). Because a judge is under no constitutional obligation to explain the reasons for a sentence, however, a defendant may never learn why he received one sentence rather than another.

Double Jeopardy and Appeal

The constitutional prohibition against being twice put in jeopardy has some application at sentencing, but the scope of protection depends largely upon legislative choice. A defendant convicted of two separate counts at the same trial may only be punished for one of those counts if the two counts punish the same offense, but the Constitution does not limit the legislature's ability to carve up a single course of conduct into multiple different offenses that can be punished cumulatively (*Dixon*). A defendant is not put in jeopardy twice for the same offense when the government sentences him for a crime then uses that same crime as a basis for increasing his sentence for a different crime (*Witte*). And even though the Double Jeopardy Clause bars the government from attempting to convict a defendant for the same crime after acquittal, it does not prevent a court from using conduct of which the defendant was acquitted as a reason for imposing a higher sentence for a different crime (*Watts*). Nor does a sentencer's rejection of factual allegations at sentencing bar the government from attempting to establish those facts a second time should resentencing be required, or prevent the government from seeking a higher sentence through appeal if the legislature chooses to permit the government to appeal sentencing errors (*Monge; DiFransesco*).

When a defendant is denied the limited procedural protections summarized above, he may have little recourse because appellate review of sentencing is not required by the Constitution (*Dorszynski; Rita*). States may restrict the grounds on which a defendant can challenge his sentence on appeal, or forbid sentencing appeals entirely, relegating the enforcement of constitutional rules regarding sentence to collateral or post-conviction review (e.g., *Johnson*).

II. TRIAL VERSUS SENTENCING PROCEDURE: THE COURT'S BRIGHT LINE

Maintaining this gulf between the procedure required for the determination of guilt and the procedure required for the selection of sentence depends upon some workable means of distinguishing guilt-finding from sentence selection. Without some constitutional concept of the difference between crime and punishment, a legislature could theoretically shrink crime definitions and trials to nominal showings and shift all of the fact-finding that matters most in calibrating punishment to sentencing.

1949—2000: A Functional Distinction

The Court first encountered this issue in 1949 in the case *Williams v. New York*. At the time, the Court was just beginning its "criminal procedure revolution" that redefined the "due process" that states must provide criminal defendants under the Fourteenth Amendment. Williams claimed that he was denied due process when his judge sentenced him based on a pre-sentence report that reported that Williams had committed dozens of other offenses, which had never been charged, that he "possessed 'a morbid sexuality,'" and that classified him as a "'menace to society,'" all allegations that he had no chance to rebut. In rejecting the invitation to import into the sentencing process the trial rights of notice, disclosure, and confrontation, the Court relied primarily on the functional difference between the guilt and the sentencing decisions.

Unlike the determination of guilt, the Court reasoned, sentencing is a decision about the *relative* individual culpability and rehabilitative potential of the defendant as compared to other defendants who commit the same offense. In order to distinguish among offenders, the sentencer needs information beyond that established by the conviction alone, such as information about what sentences similarly situated offenders receive, predictions about offender behavior, details about the commission of the offense and harm to victims, as well as information about the employment, financial, educational, family, and health status of the offender before and after the offense, his cooperation with the government in the prosecution of others, his own views about his culpability, and his prior criminal history. The Court explained that procedures for collecting and reviewing all of these facts are appropriately less formal and transparent than those used to test factual allegations at trial. Extending trial protections to sentencing information, the Court reasoned, would render that information "unavailable" and would make sentencing "totally impractical" (*Williams*, 250). Moreover, under the sentencing practices followed in both federal and state courts in the 1950s and 1960s, just which facts were considered or rejected at sentencing really did not matter anyway. Not only was the sentence subject to modification later by paroling authorities, it was unreviewable on appeal, and a judge could impose any sentence within the statutory range whether or not he believed the sentencing information provided.

For several decades, this functional justification for relaxed procedures at sentencing allowed the Court to continue expanding the constitutional rules governing trial in state courts while leaving state non-capital sentencing essentially unregulated. But in the 1970s and 1980s, legislatures concerned about abuses of sentencing discretion by judges began to direct that specific sentencing consequences follow from the presence or absence of specific designated facts determined at sentencing. Mandatory minimum sentencing statutes, such as "three strikes" laws, were enacted in every jurisdiction (Bureau of Justice Assistance 1996). These new statutes, along with legally enforceable sentencing guidelines and other presumptive sentencing schemes adopted in more than a dozen states, replaced the unbounded discretion that judges formerly enjoyed in assigning whatever weight they wished to whatever facts they chose to recognize. In some of these jurisdictions, appellate review was extended to allow reviewing courts to scrutinize judicial failures to sentence within the new, narrow sentence ranges, ranges that in turn were keyed to the presence or absence of specific facts. For the first time, fact-finding at sentencing carried predictable and legally enforceable consequences, much like fact-finding at trial. Critics argued that the reasons the Court gave for upholding informal procedure in *Williams* no longer applied in these new systems (Schulhofer 1980; Lear 1993; Reitz 1993).

Apprendi's "Maximum-Raising" Test

The Supreme Court's response to these developments was to redefine and strengthen the distinction between trial and sentencing rather than abandon it. It did this by formalizing the constitutional difference between an element, which must be established with trial protections, and a sentencing fact, which could be established using the traditionally less protective procedure outlined in Part I. The Court's approach, announced in *Apprendi v. New Jersey* (2000), has reduced but not eliminated the ability of lawmakers to shift fact-finding from trial to sentencing.

In *Apprendi*, a five-justice majority declared that any fact that increases the penalty for a crime beyond its prescribed "statutory maximum" must either be submitted to a jury and proved beyond a reasonable doubt, or be admitted by the defendant. Applying this maximum-raising standard for what must be treated as an offense element, the Court found that Apprendi's 12-year sentence could not stand. He had been convicted of a weapons offense carrying a statutory maximum penalty of 10 years' imprisonment, and the Court concluded that it was unconstitutional for the judge to have imposed a sentence that exceeded that maximum, even though a state statute authorized a judge to impose a higher sentence whenever the judge found at sentencing that the defendant had been motivated by racial bias. Essentially, the majority reasoned, the state had convicted Apprendi of one offense but had sentenced him for a more serious crime without proving the more serious crime to a jury beyond a reasonable doubt.

The Court soon invalidated state statutes that permitted a judge to determine facts legally required to be established before a defendant could be sentenced to death (*Ring*). Also struck down were sentencing systems that conditioned sentences greater than a presumptive range upon a judge's finding of aggravating facts. These systems included legally enforceable sentencing guidelines, like the complex federal sentencing guidelines, as well as simpler, tiered state systems in which a judge had only to find one or more aggravating facts in order to impose a sentence within a higher than average range (*Cunningham*). Washington State's sentencing law, for example, required an aggravating fact to be established before a judge could impose a sentence above the presumptive guideline range. The Court held in *Blakely v. Washington* that the Constitution prohibited the state's judges from imposing a sentence above the guideline range unless that aggravating fact was first proven to a jury beyond a reasonable doubt, or admitted by the defendant. As the Court later explained, the key question "is whether the law *forbids* a judge to increase a defendant's sentence *unless* the judge finds facts the jury did not find (and the offender did not concede)" (*Rita*). If it does, then the sentence cannot be increased unless those aggravating facts are first proven to a jury beyond a reasonable doubt or admitted, just like elements of a greater offense.

In the wake of these decisions, about a dozen states with presumptive sentencing systems opted to shift to the jury the determination of facts that state law required for sentences above the presumptive range (Bibas and Klein 2008). In most of these states, few cases actually require jury adjudication of maximum-raising facts (e.g., North Carolina Sentencing Commission 2009, 32). Prosecutors do not pursue aggravated sentences very often, and when they do, they usually secure a defendant's admission of the aggravating facts as part of the defendant's guilty plea, just as they would other elements of an offense. In cases that go to trial, prosecutors in these states either submit the aggravating fact to the jury along with the other elements of the offense, or submit the question separately to the jury after it decides guilt. The jury trial is identical to that of any other element, with the right to confrontation and proof beyond a reasonable doubt (Frase 2006; American Law Institute 2007, 298).

The status of these "*Apprendi* facts" as full-fledged elements remains uncertain. The Court has yet to pass on whether the notice that the defendant must receive about these facts must resemble the notice provided to the defendant about the other elements of an offense. States that have retained presumptive sentencing do not insist that aggravating factors be included in the initial indictment or information, but about half of these states require notice of the aggravating factor before trial (LaFave et al. 2007, § 19.3(a)). Nor has the Court addressed whether it is constitutionally permissible to retry one of these facts on its own should an enhanced sentence be overturned on appeal because of procedural error, or whether, instead, retrial must resemble that required whenever a greater offense is overturned, involving proof of all of the elements of the offense.

Maintaining Informal Procedure for Sentencing Facts

The Court's formula in *Apprendi* for distinguishing between sentencing factors and elements did limit legislatures' options somewhat, but it preserved plenty of leeway to maintain informal processes for finding facts that fell on the sentencing rather than the element side of the line. Most states have not attempted to structure judicial sentencing discretion through presumptive sentencing ranges or enforceable guidelines, so in these states fact-finding at sentencing is not affected by the *Apprendi/ Blakely* decisions. As the Court explained in its decision in *Booker v. United States*, sentencing ranges set by advisory guidelines are not functionally equivalent to statutory ceilings because judges have the discretion to exceed these recommended ranges without first finding particular facts. "We have never doubted the authority of a judge to exercise broad discretion in imposing a sentence within a statutory range," the *Booker* Court stated, citing its decision in *Williams* from more than 50 years earlier. Several states have changed their formerly presumptive guidelines to advisory guidelines in order to continue judicial application of their sentencing guidelines and to avoid new provisions for jury fact-finding (Reitz 2009; Bibas and Klein 2008).

Even for jurisdictions with presumptive sentencing systems, the Court has exempted the following sentencing facts from the *Apprendi* rule so that they need not be treated as elements:[3]

- *Prior convictions.* The Court has defended this exception to the *Apprendi* rule by referring to historical practice and also noting that, unlike any other type of fact, a prior conviction "must itself have been established through procedures satisfying the fair notice, reasonable doubt, and jury trial guarantees" (*Jones; Almendarez-Torres; Booker*). Given this rationale, it follows that any ancillary fact about a prior conviction that is specified as a condition for a higher recidivist sentence, such as a requirement that the prior offense be one that involved a firearm, must itself be proven to a jury beyond a reasonable doubt unless established by the elements of the prior offense or the defendant's admissions. Some lower courts also exclude from the exception for prior convictions juvenile adjudications, which lack jury and reasonable doubt protections.
- *Facts mandating a higher minimum sentence, as long as the higher sentence does not exceed the maximum sentence previously available to the judge.* Mandatory minimum sentencing statutes and binding sentencing guidelines that fix minimum sentences but do not regulate maximum sentences are untouched by the *Apprendi* rule (*McMillan; Harris*; Chanenson 2005).
- *Facts that mitigate sentences* need not be admitted or proven beyond a reasonable doubt to a jury, even when a lower sentence is conditioned upon such a finding (*Booker; Marsh*).
- *Facts that must be found in order for a judge to impose consecutive sentences, where a jurisdiction requires that judges otherwise run multiple sentences concurrently.* Most states leave to judges considerable discretion to decide

whether to order sentences for multiple convictions to be served concurrently or consecutively. But even in states that condition consecutive sentencing upon a specified finding of fact, that finding need not be made by admission or proof beyond a reasonable doubt to a jury (*Ice*).

The Future of the Guilt-Sentencing Distinction

There are many critics of the Court's closely divided decisions distinguishing between the facts that must be treated as elements and the facts that may be established by less formal procedures at sentencing. Some agree that there should be some distinction, but would prefer one based on the *type* of fact rather than its effect on the defendant's sentence. They would, for example, extend trial protections to facts that are related to the offense but not to facts related to the offender (Berman 2008; Huigens 2002). Others agree with the Court that the distinction should turn on the legal effect that a fact has on punishment, but argue that the Court's maximum-raising measure draws the line in the wrong place. Many have argued that trial protections should apply to prior convictions and facts triggering mandatory minimum penalties (e.g., Bowman 2010; *O'Brien*, Stevens and Thomas, J. J., concurring). Still others have argued that the Court's test should be consistent with those it has used to identify offense elements in other contexts, such as its test for determining when to treat as an element a fact designated as an affirmative defense, or its test for determining when to treat as separate elements two separate means of establishing a single element (King and Klein 2010).

Some critics have attacked the distinction itself, preferring a sliding scale of procedural protections for sentencing rather than an approach that provides some facts with "full-blown trial protections" and others "almost none" (Berman and Bibas 2006). The Court's apparent distaste for the application to sentencing of a rigorous test for procedural due process, however, and its recent failed experiment with a middle ground between full trial protection for criminal penalties and reduced procedural protection for civil penalties (*Hudson*),[2] both suggest that some form of binary distinction is here to stay.

III. Statutory Regulation of the Sentencing Process

Every jurisdiction provides additional regulation of the sentencing process above and beyond what the Court has held the Constitution requires. Procedures for felony sentencing typically are included in jurisdiction's rules of criminal procedure (LaFave et al. 2007). In most jurisdictions:

- Sentencing must take place within a "reasonable" or designated time after conviction.
- A pre-sentence report prepared by a probation officer is the primary source of sentencing information used by the judge to select a sentence. When the probation officer interviews a defendant to obtain information for the report, the defendant may choose to invoke his constitutional privilege against compelled self-incrimination, but most courts have rejected a constitutional right to counsel during the interview. Preparation of the report itself may be mandatory only for certain categories of cases, such as those carrying a potential sentence of probation or restitution, and un-common in others, such as those in which a guilty plea is contingent upon the judge imposing a stipulated sentence.
- The defendant or his attorney is entitled to review the pre-sentencing report before sentencing but several jurisdictions grant the judge discretion not to disclose certain sensitive portions of the report. Documents or other information used to compile the report generally are not discoverable by the defense.
- The defendant is given some opportunity to contest factual allegations in the pre-sentence report, although that opportunity may not include the right to present evidence, but may be limited to making a statement at the sen-tencing hearing.
- Crime victims are entitled to participate in sentencing by offering written or oral statements.
- Sentencing hearings are open to the public.
- Post-sentence procedures for reduction of sentence include some combina-tion of good time (decided by corrections officials), discretionary release on parole in most states (decided by paroling authorities), "compassionate release" based on advanced age or infirmity (decided by judges or paroling authorities), and clemency (decided by the governor and/or paroling authorities).
- Judicial review of compliance with sentencing statutes is available in the state's courts.

The sections below summarize a few notable statutory variations.

Structured Sentencing Jurisdictions

Jurisdictions that have attempted to structure the sentencing discretion of judges using sentencing guidelines tend to have additional procedural requirements for sentencing. Most guideline jurisdictions have created sentencing forms that the sentencing court must fill out or review. Most also require that the judge state on the record or in writing the reasons for the sentence, at least when departing from the recommended or presumptive range (Kauder and Ostrom 2008; American

Law Institute 2007, 290). A statement of reasons for sentence helps keep the sentencing process open and fair. It is also essential for appellate review of the sentence, which is provided in many guideline jurisdictions for the defendant and sometimes for the government (Frankel 1973; O'Hear 2010).

In these jurisdictions, sentence appeals are not the rare event that they were when judicial sentencing discretion was limited only by a broad statutory range and few rules. For example, in the federal courts in 2010 more than one in ten defendants sentenced under the guidelines appealed, and more than 60 percent of these appeals included a challenge to the sentence (USSC 2010). Sentence appeals in the state courts are common as well, although they are not as frequent as in federal court. Appellate review of sentencing typically is limited to compliance with sentencing procedure, whether the reasons stated for the sentence are permitted by law, and whether the sentence is within statutory limits. In a handful of jurisdictions, including the federal courts, sentences are also reviewed on their substantive merits, under a "reasonableness" or similar standard (Reitz 1997; Pfaff 2010; Scalia 2001; Shepard 2010; Kauder and Ostrom 2008). The vast majority of sentence appeals by defendants are unsuccessful.

Jury Sentencing

Although judges do most, if not all, of the sentencing in every American jurisdiction, juries are also used for death sentencing, and statutes in some states provide a limited right to a jury determination of non-capital sentences.[4]

In six states, jury sentencing is authorized for all felony cases, but in most of these states, the jury's authority to sentence is restricted to the small fraction of cases in which the defendant goes to trial before a jury and does not enter a guilty plea (King and Noble 2004; Iontcheva 2003). In at least three of these states, jury sentences tend to be consistently higher than judicial sentences. This may be because juries are given fewer options for leniency than the judge, and exercise those options with far less information than the judge is provided. A sentencing jury will be instructed to select a sentence within the minimum and maximum penalty permitted by statute, but will not receive a pre-sentence report. Nor will it be informed of the "going rate" or the guidelines-recommended sentence in states that employ judicial sentencing guidelines, for example. For indeterminate sentences, the jury will not receive any estimate of the proportion of the sentence that the defendant will serve before becoming eligible for parole. Sentencing juries lack the same authority that the judge has to select probation or suspend any portion of the minimum sentence. Moreover, judges are not inclined to reduce jury sentences to non-jury levels, although they are given this authority. Ironically, many attorneys and judges in these states regard jury sentencing as an effective deterrent to the exercise of the right to jury trial itself (King and Noble 2004, 2005; La Fave et al. 2007; Virginia Criminal Sentencing Commission 2009).

Some states authorize the jury to determine whether an offender is eligible for recidivist, habitual, or career offender penalties, using the standard of "beyond a reasonable doubt" as well as rules of evidence (Rottman and Strickland 2006; LaFave et al. 2007). The use of a jury for assessing recidivist penalties may date from the years before fingerprinting and photography, when determining whether the defendant was a prior offender was not a simple matter. Today, parties rarely contest whether a defendant committed a prior offense. Instead, disputes center around the existence of some feature related to the prior conviction that would bring it within the particular repeat-offender statute. Pre-trial notice of intent to seek recidivist penalties is mandated by statute in many of these jurisdictions, and some require that the notice of intent to seek recidivist penalties must be included in the indictment or information.

Modification of Sentence

Many jurisdictions authorize trial judges to modify sentences after sentencing (Braslow and Cheit 2011; Klingele 2010). For example, a federal judge may upon the government's motion reduce an offender's sentence to reward him for assisting the government in its investigation or prosecution of another. More than 2,000 federal prisoners, about 2.4 percent of defendants sentenced under the Guidelines in 2010, obtained such reductions in 2010 (USSC 2010). A handful of states allow judges to exercise discretion to modify a sentence long after sentencing, and this procedure is included in the model sentencing statutes under consideration by the American Law Institute (Frase 2009; American Law Institute 2009).

Misdemeanor Sentencing

Roughly two-thirds of criminal convictions are misdemeanors, but there is scant research concerning misdemeanor sentencing. As compared to felony cases, even fewer defendants go to trial and even more sentences are agreed upon or standardized. Only a small percentage of misdemeanor convictions result in any jail time, and sentencing often occurs at the same time as conviction in a single abbreviated proceeding (National Center for State Courts 2009; Feeley 1979). For example, in New York City in 2006, 45 percent of A misdemeanors, 67 percent of B misdemeanors, and 92 percent of lesser offenses were disposed of at arraignment, and less than 0.3 percentof misdemeanor and violation cases were tried, down from 2 percent in 1990 (Howell 2009). In Los Angeles in 2005, about two-thirds of misdemeanor dispositions occurred at arraignment (Kallman 2003). Many of the procedural rules for felony cases that are required by the Constitution or by statute do not apply in misdemeanor cases. A state need not provide counsel for a misdemeanor defendant who receives only monetary sanctions, and many jurisdictions do not require the preparation of pre-sentence reports for misdemeanor sentencing. Only a handful of states that use sentencing guidelines have adopted guidelines for misdemeanor sentencing (Frase 2005).

IV. Sentencing Procedure and Bargaining

One last inescapable feature of the sentencing process deserves mention: the procedural rules summarized above are often waived as part of an agreement between the defendant and the prosecution. All but a small percentage of criminal cases are settled by guilty plea, and, as Professor Wright has detailed in chapter 10 of this volume, plea agreements usually include some terms having to do with sentence. These terms typically involve the substance of the sentence itself, but plea agreements often address sentencing *procedure* as well. In return for a charge or sentence concession, a defendant may agree either to waive prospectively his right to challenge any violation of procedural rules at his upcoming sentencing, or to waive particular aspects of procedure at sentencing, say a statutory right to keep information in the pre-sentence report from the judge until after the guilty plea, or the opportunity to seek modification of sentence (King 2007). Courts have little incentive to veto such agreements. Indeed, in the federal courts, which have quite complex rules of procedure for sentencing, prospective waivers of the right to review procedural errors at sentencing are routine (King and O'Neill 2005).

In short, the rules of procedure for sentencing reviewed in this chapter, like many other rules of criminal procedure, are most consistently enforced in only the small percentage of cases that are not settled by negotiation. The freedom of the parties to bargain around procedural requirements for sentencing means that the sentencing process varies from county to county and from courtroom to courtroom, even when a jurisdiction's law appears to specify uniform rules.

NOTES

1. Two former justices have championed the all-purpose, multifactor test in *Matthews v. Eldridge* as appropriate for assessing the constitutionality of sentencing proceedings (*Burns*). Other justices have declared that a sentencing procedure should be consistent with due process "unless it offends some principle of justice so rooted in the traditions and conscience of our people as to be ranked as fundamental" (*Medina*).

2. In *Hudson v. United States*, 522 U.S. 93 (1997), the Court overturned its short-lived effort to apply double jeopardy protections to some combinations of civil and criminal sanctions for the same offense. Before the *Hudson* ruling, the civil sanctions that triggered these constitutional protections occupied a tenuous middle ground between civil and criminal sanctions (Steiker 1997).

3. Most lower courts have also rejected the application of *Apprendi* to facts that must be established before restitution can be ordered, before property can be forfeited, or a before a juvenile can be transferred to adult court. At least one court of appeals has even rejected the application of *Apprendi* to findings regarding the amount of loss caused by an offense when statute conditions a fine upon such findings (*Southern Union*).

4. Jury sentencing is also used in military courts-martial (Breen 2011).

REFERENCES

Cases

Almendarez-Torres v. United States, 523 U.S. 224 (1998).

Apprendi v. New Jersey 530 U.S. 466 (2000).

Bearden v. Georgia, 461 U.S. 660 (1983).

Blakely v. Washington, 542 U.S. 296 (2004).

Booker, United States v., 543 U.S. 279 (1987).

Bordenkircher v. Hayes, 434 U.S. 357 (1978).

Burns v. United States, 501 U.S. 129 (1991).

Custis v. United States, 511 U.S. 485 (1994).

Cunningham v. California, 549 U.S. 270 (2007).

DiFrancesco, United States v., 449 U.S. 117 (1980).

Dixon, United States v., 509 U.S. 688 (1993).

Dorszynski v. United States, 418 U.S. 424 (1974).

Duncan v. Louisiana, 391 U.S. 145 (1968).

Dunnigan, United States v., 507 U.S. 87 (1993).

Estelle v. Smith, 451 U.S. 454 (1981).

Glover v. United States, 531 U.S. 198 (2001).

Harris v. United States, 536 U.S. 545 (2002).

Hudson v. United States, 522 U.S. 93 (1997).

Ice, Oregon v., 555 U.S. 160 (2009).

Irizarry v. United States, 553 U.S. 708 (2008).

Johnson v. United States, 544 U.S. 295 (2005).

Jones v. United States, 526 U.S. 227 (1999).

Marsh, Kansas v., 548 U.S. 163 (2006).

Mathews v. Eldridge, 424 U.S. 319 (1976).

McCleskey v. Kemp, 481 U.S. 279 (1987).

McMillan v. Pennsylvania, 477 U.S. 79 (1986).

Medina v. California, 505 U.S. 437 (1992).

Mempa v. Rhay, 389 U.S. 128 (1967).

Mitchell v. United States, 526 U.S. 314 (1999).

Monge v. California, 524 U.S. 721 (1998).

O'Brien, United States v., 130 S.Ct. 2169 (2010).

Patton v. United States, 281 U.S. 276 (1930).

Pollard v. United States, 352 U.S. 354 (1957).

Ring v. Arizona, 536 U.S. 584 (2002).

Rita v. United States, 551 U.S. 338 (2007).

Shannon v. United States, 512 U.S. 573 (1994).

Smith, Alabama v., 490 U.S. 794 (1989).

Spaziano v. Florida, 468 U.S. 447 (1984).

Townsend v. Burke, 334 U.S. 736 (1948).

Watts, United States v., 519 U.S. 148 (1997).

Williams v. New York, 337 U.S. 241 (1949).

Witte, United States v., 515 U.S. 389 (1995).

Southern Union, United States v., 630 F.3d 17 (1st Cir.2010).

Other Sources

American Law Institute. 2007. *Model Penal Code: Sentencing, Tentative Draft No. 1* (approved May 16, 2007). Philadelphia: American Law Institute.

American Law Institute. 2009. *Model Penal Code: Sentencing, Discussion Draft No. 2.* Philadelphia: American Law Institute.

Barkow, Rachel E. 2003. "Recharging the Jury: The Criminal Jury's Constitutional Role in an Era of Mandatory Sentencing." *University of Pennsylvania Law Review* 152: 33–127.

Barkow, Rachel E. 2008. "The Ascent of the Administrative States and the Demise of Mercy." *Harvard Law Review* 121: 1332–1365.

Berman, Douglas A. 2008. "Conceptualizing *Booker.*" *Arizona State Law Journal* 38: 387–423.

Berman, Douglas A., and Stephanos Bibas. 2006. "Making Sentencing Sensible." *Ohio State Journal of Criminal Law* 4: 37–72.

Bibas, Stephanos, and Susan Klein. 2008. "The Sixth Amendment and Criminal Sentencing." *Cardozo Law Review* 30: 775–796.

Bowman, Frank O., III. 2010. "Debacle: How the Supreme Court Has Mangled American Sentencing Law and How It Might Yet Be Mended." *University of Chicago Law Review* 77: 367–476.

Braslow, Laura and Ross E. Cheit. 2011. "Judicial Discretion and (Un)equal Access: A Systematic Study of Motions to Reduce Criminal Sentences in Rhode Island Superior Court (1998–2003)." *Journal of Empirical Legal Studies* 8: 24–47.

Breen, Patricia D. 2011. "The Trial Penalty and Jury Sentencing: A Study of Air Force Courts-Martial." *Journal of Empirical Legal Studies* 8: 206–235.

Bureau of Justice Assistance. 1996. *National Assessment of Structured Sentencing*, at 20–23 and table 3–1.

Casey, Pamela M., Roger K. Warren and Jennifer K. Elek. 2011. *Using Offender Risk and Needs Assessment Information at Sentencing: Guidance for Courts from a National Working Group.* National Center for State Courts. Online. Available at: http://www.ncsconline.org/csi/analysis.html.

Chanenson, Steven L. 2005. "Guidance from Above and Beyond." *Stanford Law Review* 58: 175–194.

Dalzell, George W. 1955. *Benefit of Clergy in America and Related Matters.* Winston-Salem: J. F. Blair.

Douglass, John G. 2005. "Confronting Death: Sixth Amendment Rights at Capital Sentencing." *Columbia Law Review* 105: 1967–2028.

Feeley, Malcolm M. 1979. *The Process Is the Punishment.* New York: Russell Sage Foundation.

Fisher, George. 2003. *Plea Bargaining's Triumph: A History of Plea Bargaining in America.* Stanford: Stanford University Press.

Frankel, Marvin E. 1973. *Criminal Sentences: Law Without Order.* New York: Hill and Wang.

Frase, Richard S. 2005. "State Sentencing Guidelines: Diversity, Consensus, and Unresolved Policy Issues." *Columbia Law Review* 105: 1190–1228.

Frase, Richard S. 2006. "Blakely in Minnesota, Two Years Out: Guidelines Sentencing is Alive and Well." *Ohio State Journal of Criminal Law* 4: 73–94.

Frase, Richard S. 2009. "Second Look Provisions in the Proposed Model Penal Code Revisions." *Federal Sentencing Reporter* 21: 194–202.

Guzman, Carolina, Barry Krisberg, and Chris Tsukida. 2008. "Accelerated Release: A Literature Review." National Council on Crime and Delinquency. Available at: http://nccd-crc.issuelab.org/sd_clicks/download2/accelerated_release_a_literature_review_focus

Heise, Michael. 2003. "Mercy by the Numbers: An Empirical Analysis of Clemency and Its Structure." *Virginia Law Review* 89: 239–310.

Hessick, Carissa Byrne, and F. Andrew Hessick. 2011. "Recognizing Constitutional Rights at Sentencing." *California Law Review* 99: 47–94.

Howell, B. 2009. "Broken Lives from Broken Windows: The Hidden Costs of Aggressive Order Maintenance Policing." *New York University Review of Law and Social Change* 33: 271–326.

Huigens, Kyron. 2002. "Solving the Apprendi Puzzle." *Georgetown Law Journal* 90: 387–458.

Humbert, William Harrison. 1941. *The Pardoning Power of the President.* Washington, DC: American Council on Public Affairs.

Iontcheva, Jenia. 2003. "Jury Sentencing as Democratic Practice." *Virginia Law Review* 89: 311–383.

Jacobs, James B. 1982. "Sentencing by Prison Personnel: Good Time." *University of California, Los Angeles Law Review* 30: 217–270.

Kallman, Kenneth V. 2003. *A Comparative Analysis for Processing Misdemeanor Cases in the Criminal Justice Center of the Los Angeles Superior Court.* Online. Available at: http://contentdm.ncsconline.org/cgi-bin/showfile.exe?CISOROOT=/ctadmin&CISOPTR=473.

Kauder, Neal B., and Brian J. Ostrom. 2008. *State Sentencing Guidelines: Profiles and Continuum.* July 2008. Online. Available at: http://www.ncsconline.org/csi/PEW-Profiles-v12-online.pdf.

Kemmitt, Chris. 2006. "Function over Form: Reviving the Criminal Jury's Historical Role as a Sentencing Body." *University of Michigan Journal of Law Reform* 40: 93–148.

King, Nancy J. 2003. "The Origins of Felony Jury Sentencing in the United States." *Chicago Kent Law Review* 78: 937–993.

King, Nancy J. 2007. "Regulating Settlement: What Is Left of the Rule of Law in the Criminal Process?" *DePaul Law Review* 56: 389–399.

King, Nancy J., and Susan Klein. 2001. "Essential Elements." *Vanderbilt Law Review* 54: 1467–1553.

King, Nancy J., and Michael O'Neill. 2005. "Appeal Waivers and the Future of Sentencing Policy." *Duke Law Journal* 55: 209–261.

King, Nancy J., and Rosevelt R. Noble. 2004. "Jury Sentencing in Practice: A Three-State Study." *Vanderbilt Law Review* 57: 885–962.

King, Nancy J., and Rosevelt R. Noble. 2005. "Jury Sentencing in Non-Capital Cases: Comparing Severity and Variance with Judicial Sentences in Two States." *Journal of Empirical Legal Studies* 2: 331–367.

Klingele, Cecelia M. 2010. "Changing the Sentence Without Hiding the Truth: Judicial Sentence Modification as a Promising Method of Early Release." *William and Mary Law Review* 53: 465–536.

Kobil, Daniel T. 2007. "Should Mercy Have a Place in Clemency Decisions?" in *Forgiveness, Mercy and Clemency*, eds. Austin Sarat and Nasser Hussain.

LaFave, Wayne, Jerold H. Israel, Nancy J. King, and Orin S. Kerr. 2007. *Criminal Procedure*, vol. 6, chap. 26. Eagen: MN: Thomson/West.

Lear, Elizabeth. 1993. "Is Conviction Irrelevant?" *University California, Los Angeles Law Review* 40: 1179–1239.

Love, Margaret Colgate. 2006. *Relief from the Collateral Consequences of a Criminal Conviction: A State-by-State Resource Guide.* Buffalo: W. S. Hein.

Michaels, Alan. 2003. "Trial Rights at Sentencing." *North Carolina Law Review* 81: 1771–1863.

Michigan Compiled Laws § 801.57.

National Center for State Courts. 2009. *Examining the Work of State Courts: An Analysis of 2007 State Court Caseloads*. Online. Available at: http://contentdm.ncsconline.org/cgi-bin/showfile.exe?CISOROOT=/ctadmin&CISOPTR=1500.

National Conference of State Legislatures. 2009. *Cutting Corrections Costs: Earned Time Policies for State Prisoners*. July 2009. Online. Available at: http://www.ncsl.org/Portals/1/Documents/cj/Earned_time_report.pdf.

North Carolina Sentencing and Policy Advisory Commission. 2009. *FY 2008/09 Statistical Report Data*. Online. Available at: http://www.nccourts.org/Courts/CRS/Councils/spac/Documents/statisticalrpt_fy0809R.pdf.

O'Hear, Michael. 2010. "Appellate Review of Sentence Explanations: Learning from the Wisconsin and Federal Experiences." *Marquette Law Review* 93: 751–793.

Pfaff, John F. 2010. "The Future of Appellate Sentencing Review: Booker in the States." *Marquette University Law Review* 93: 683–715.

Preyer, Kathryn. 1982. "Penal Measures in the American Colonies: An Overview." *American Journal of Legal History* 26: 326.

Reitz, Kevin. 1993. "Sentencing Facts: Travesties of Real-Offense Sentencing." *Stanford Law Review* 45: 523–573.

Reitz, Kevin. 1997. "Sentencing Guideline Systems and Sentence Appeals: A Comparison of Federal and State Experiences." *Northwestern University Law Review* 91: 1441–1506.

Reitz, Kevin. 2003. *Model Penal Code: Sentencing, Report*. Philadelphia: American Law Institute.

Reitz, Kevin. 2005. "The New Sentencing Conundrum: Policy and Constitutional Law at Cross Purposes." *Columbia Law Review* 105: 1082–1123.

Reitz, Kevin. 2009. "Demographic Impact Statements, O'Connor's Warning, and the Mysteries of Prison Release: Topics from a Sentencing Reform Agenda." *Florida Law Review* 61: 683–707.

Rottman, David B., and Strickland, Shauna M. 2006. *State Court Organization 2004* (August 2006, NCJ 212351). Online. Available at: http://bjs.ojp.usdoj.gov/content/pub/pdf/sco04.pdf.

Sawyer, Jeffery K. 1990. "'Benefit of Clergy' in Maryland and Virginia." *American Journal of Legal History* 34: 49–68.

Scalia, John. 2001. *Federal Criminal Appeals, 1999 with Trends 1985–99*. April 2001. Online. Available at: http://bjs.ojp.usdoj.gov/content/pub/ascii/fca99.txt.

Schulhofer, Stephen. 1980. "Due Process of Sentencing." *University of Pennsylvania Law Review* 128: 733–764.

Shepard, Randall T. 2010. "Robust Appellate Review of Sentences: Just How British Is Indiana?" *Marquette University Law Review* 93: 671–681.

Steiker, Carol. 1997. "Foreword: Punishment and Procedure: Punishment Theory and the Criminal-Civil Procedural Divide." *Georgetown Law Journal* 85: 775–819.

Steinberg, Allen. 1989. *The Transformation of Criminal Justice: Philadelphia, 1800–1880*. Chapel Hill: University of North Carolina Press.

Steiker, Carol S., and Steiker, Jordan M. 1995. "Sober Second Thoughts: Reflections on Two Decades of Constitutional Regulation of Capital Punishment." *Harvard Law Review* 109: 355–438, 397.

Thomas, Kimberly A. 2007. "Beyond Mitigation: Towards a Theory of Allocution." *Fordham Law Review* 75: 2641–2683.

U. S. Congress. 1790. 1 Cong., Sess. II, ch. 9, Act of April 30, 1790, § 31, 1 Stat. 112.

United States Sentencing Commission (USSC). 2010. *Annual Report 2010—Chapter Five.*
    Online. Available at: http://www.ussc.gov/ANNRPT/2010/Chap5_09.pdf.

Virginia Criminal Sentencing Commission. 2009. *Annual Report 2009.* Online. Available
    at: http://www.vcsc.state.va.us/2009AnnualReport.pdf.

PART III

CORRECTIONS

Section A
The Correctional Context

CHAPTER 14

AMERICAN CORRECTIONS: REFORM WITHOUT CHANGE

KAROL LUCKEN AND THOMAS G. BLOMBERG[*]

THE major events shaping the history of American corrections have been reported before, with some analyses being quite focused and others being fairly general. This chapter provides an analysis that falls somewhere between in order to demonstrate more clearly the patterns emerging from two centuries of American corrections. By examining various social contexts and the ideas, practices and outcomes that have marked correctional history, several interrelated patterns can be observed. Recognition of these patterns is helpful to understanding the development of the correctional system or, as we argue, the too often adverse development characterized by "reform without change." The patterns that are revealed in this correctional development are summarized below.

- The pattern of social amnesia refers to the tendency to ignore history and to reinvent or repackage correctional practices formerly deemed ineffective. The expectation that these practices will yield more effective crime control another time around remains unbroken.
- Consistent with social amnesia, the patterns of oscillation and regression refer to the tendency of corrections to exhibit wide swings in ideology and practice and returns to less progressive or pre-modern means of crime control.
- The pattern of good intentions gone awry refers to the recurrent disparity between the stated goals and observed operations of correctional reform.

- The pattern of net-widening refers to the tendency of correctional reforms to extend control over more of the base population, which in the absence of the reform would have been treated less severely.

Leaving Colonial America: Modernity, Deterrence, and Penal Code Reform

At the turn of the eighteenth century, the pillars of modernity were firmly in place. In particular, an ethic of rationalism and egalitarianism was shaping the course of the new republic. However, the prospect of liberty still gave civic leaders cause for apprehension. Complaints of lawlessness were escalating, and increased liberty was often blamed for the increase in disorder (Kann 2005). Whereas colonial crime reports were dominated by fairly minor moral transgressions, post-colonial conviction reports indicated much higher rates of larceny, assault and battery, burglary, and other felonies (Hazards Register of Pennsylvania 1831).

Despite crime conditions that were disquieting, Enlightenment assumptions held out hope for wayward individuals. Reformers and other civic leaders expected that sound judgment and moral restraint would resume once the reason for the law and the obligation to comply with it was understood (Kann 2005). For example, Edward Livingston assumed that "When the true principles of legislation are impressed on the minds of the people, when they see the reasons for the laws by which they are governed, they will obey them with cheerfulness, if just, and know how to change them, if oppressive" (1822, quoted in Kann 2005, 58).

Guided by this democratic reasoning, reformers viewed colonial laws with a fair amount of disdain. Shaming, physical brutality, and public punishments were seen as overly severe, unrepublican, and ultimately counterproductive. Following the logic of Cesare Beccaria, reformers were persuaded that it was not the intensity of the sanction that had the greatest effect on human behavior, but its duration, certainty, and swiftness. These principles were incorporated into the penal codes of most states throughout the 1790s. Hence, public, corporal, and capital punishments were all but abolished, and incarceration was adopted as the primary form of sanctioning.

The Pennsylvania Act of 1791—which served as a model for the nation—abolished branding and the death penalty for those convicted of robbery, burglary, and sodomy (Barnes 1972). The act further stipulated imprisonment and hard labor for two years or less for any other non-capital offense that had been previously sanctioned by burning of the hand, cutting off ears, nailing the ears to the pillory, or whipping (ibid.). New York also repealed the death penalty, except for murder and first-degree arson, and by 1796 Virginia had limited the sanction of death to murder and certain offenses committed by slaves. This trend toward abolition continued into the 1850s, with some states opposing capital punishment altogether. Maine, Vermont, and Michigan, for example, presented evidence of a drop in murder rates upon the abolishment of capital punishment in their respective states ("Capital Punishment," 1846).

In repealing these practices, little thought was given to the replacement apparatus, namely the prison. Initially, states improvised by relying on makeshift facilities. Consequently, squalid conditions and prison overcrowding fast became a problem. In 1773, a Connecticut prison was fashioned out of an existing copper mine (Friedman 1993). By 1790, under the new name of Newgate, the prison was deemed little more than a dungeon, overwhelmed by "slippery stinking filth," fleas, lice, and vermin (Kann 2005). Between 1792 and 1822, 56 percent of the offenders admitted to New York's prison were released early due to overcrowding (Barnes 1972). In 1826, Robert Vaux lamented that overcrowding and the neglect of classification had kept prisoners of all ages, colors, and sexes in "one common herd" (Kann 2005, 111). The earliest institutions housed a mixture of offenders that included the young, old, men, women, feeble-minded, debtors, witnesses, pre-trial felons, and sentenced felons.[1]

Despite mounting criticism, the prison as a social necessity was not disputed. Even with its obvious defects, it was still viewed as an improvement over the archaic and theocratic practices of colonial America. Therefore, the prison was not abandoned; it was simply reinvented.

PERFECTING THE PRISON: MORAL REFORM IN A WELL-BUILT INSTITUTION

In the decades following 1830, America was far more populated, mobile, and commercial. However, as the new republic grew, racism intensified and communities became more stratified. Anxiety over immigration was so pronounced that one prominent Bostonian demanded that something be done "lest the sea of ignorance which lies around us, swollen by the wave of misery and vice which is pouring from revolutionized Europe upon our shores, should overflow the dikes of liberty and justice, and sweep away the most precious of our institutions" (Charles Elliott Norton, quoted in Vale 2000, 60).

For a nation aspiring to be, in many ways, different from Europe, the persistence of crime and vice was an unsettling reality. Alcoholism was viewed as one of the most prolific vices of the day, but psychic disorders and opium addictions generated their own share of alarm. Crimes of theft and burglary were unusually common (Friedman 1993) and violence perpetrated by street gangs was on the rise. It was reported that "from nearly all parts of the country accounts of horrible murders were pouring in" (*Prisoners Friend*, 1846).

The enlightenment assumption that people were rational and would therefore avoid the "certain" costs of illicit behavior now seemed dubious. Contemporary observers recognized that reason could be "dethroned" (Hood 1831), if not by intemperance then by idleness, ignorance, irreligion, and poverty. Some speculated that the lower classes were so accustomed to bad parenting, alcoholism, and ignorance that no amount of informal control would be effective (Kann 2005). The problem of crime, now being compared to a spreading moral disease, demanded a new social practice.

What followed was actually a perfected practice in the form of a well-built institution known as the penitentiary. Insulated from the vices of the community, the penitentiary was envisioned as a place that could reclaim lives and restore social order (Rothman 1977). Yet, it was also to be an edifice that would be sufficiently terrifying to both the public and the offender. Livingston, for instance, wanted to "wrap penitentiaries in a mantle of mystery" by closing them off to visitors (Kann 2005). Benjamin Rush similarly believed that the public and prisoners should be punished by their own imaginations, though the punishment should always appear worse than it actually was (ibid.).

By the 1830s, a more imposing and impressive institution indeed emerged, with the expectations of the institution being no less grandiose than its new-fangled design. One prison chaplain boasted that "could we all be put on prison fare for the space of two or three generations, the world ultimately would be the better for it" (quoted in Rotman 1995). The key to fulfilling this mission lay in the techniques of existing social institutions, including the factory (see Melossi and Pavarini 1981), monastery (see Skotnicki 2000), and military. Consequently, the new implements of reform would be routine, silence, labor, separation, surveillance, pure air, healthful labor, seasonable exercise, and adequate food and water. Though solitary confinement was promoted everywhere as an essential feature, many states held that time spent in isolation should only be partial, such as at night, or for a small percentage of the sentence (Kann 2005). However, Pennsylvanian reformers insisted that offenders should consistently live and work in silence and isolation for solitude was the "weightiest moral agent to make the thoughtless thoughtful" (Lieber 1838). They reasoned that "no two persons charged with or convicted of crime should be in each other's presence," as any gathering of inmates would only invite security threats and incite communication ("What Has Been Done and What Is to Do," 1856). After much trial and error, most states adopted New York's system of congregate labor, fearing too many offenders would go insane from prolonged solitude.

In the literature of the day, the penitentiary was touted as humane and philanthropic. Yet, what appeared to be true on paper was not always true in practice. Breaches of silence and other rules were met with oddly familiar and brutal measures, including whippings, iron gags, and the stretcher, which was similar in principle to the medieval rack. By 1852, several reports and commissions had questioned whether moral reform was attainable, even in a well-built institution. One critic charged, "Those whose business it is to restrain or punish him, do it in such a bungling way, that the attempt is quite as likely to fail, as to succeed; and in either event, the last state of the offender will probably be worse than the first" ("Of What Use Are Our Prisons?" 1857, 143).

Claims of ineffectiveness grew stronger amid evidence of more serious offenders being admitted to the penitentiary. For example, in Connecticut, of the 839 inmates admitted between 1828 and 1840, 343 were convicted of burglary and robbery, 78 for attempted murder, 42 for rape, and 45 for arson and escape. Demographic and other statistics revealed disturbing trends as well, such as an ever-increasing and dispropor-tionate number of immigrant inmates. By 1860, approximately 44 percent of the inmates at Auburn were foreign born. Additionally, 32 percent of New York jail inmates could not read, 72 percent were without trades, 49 percent admitted frequenting houses of ill-repute and gambling houses, and more than half were orphans (Bittenger 1870).

The rules of separation and isolation had also been long negated by overcrowd-ing. In Philadelphia, in 1861, 801 inmates occupied 489 cells (Kuntz 1988). In 1867, roughly one-third of all prisoners in New York were double celled, and prisoners in New Jersey lived as many as four to a cell that measured 7 feet by 12 feet or less (Friedman 1993). Early releases were so commonplace that many feared the "indis-criminate exercise of the pardoning power had deprived penal inflictions of half their terror" ("What Has Been Done and What Is to Do," 1856). In New York, it was not uncommon to see 5-year sentences reduced to 8 months or 10-year sentences reduced to 12 months ("Shower of Pardons," 1857).

Though the ideals of the penitentiary did not survive in practice, the will to reform the institution remained strong and resilient. With the flaws of the peniten-tiary in view, a different class of institution and community-based sanction was developed. An "altogether different prison procedure" (Towner 1886) would be founded in the reformatory, while probation and parole would initialize the use of community alternatives.

The Rehabilitative Ideal: Determinism, Knowledge, and Individualization

The progressive movement was well underway at the close of the nineteenth century. The movement confronted a number of social ills stemming from excessive urbani-zation, immigration, and industrialization. At the forefront of concern were the overcrowded slums and public health disasters that were consuming American cities. "Reservoirs of physical and moral death" was how one journalist of the day described the tenement districts of Boston (Benjamin Flower, 1893, quoted in Vale 2000).

To improve the quality of national life and the lives of the poor in particular, pro-gressive activists called for radical economic change and a stronger role for government in facilitating this change. This backdrop provided fertile ground for a developing soci-ology of crime and justice policy reform. Notions of anomie and social disorganization were no doubt advanced through the vivid accounts of settlement house activists:

When, in certain parts of Boston and New York, 1,200 people are crowded on an acre, it is difficult to individualize one's immediate neighbors sufficiently to be on human terms with any considerable portion of them. These non-individuated neighbors comprised a mass public of "nomadic factory hands who form no neighborhood ties, join no neighborhood associations, and involve themselves in no effort for community betterment." (quoted in Vale 2000, 73)

The idea that society was responsible for the conditions that caused crime was already gaining adherents in 1870. However, the correctional system—which comprised 2,200 prisons of different grades nationwide, collectively housing an average of 60,000 prisoners at any given time ("Prison Reform," 1872)—was not yet aligned with this latest ideology. The shift did take place when a new band of reformers proposed new system goals and methods of reform. The new goal of the correctional system was to produce a free and industrious citizen rather than an obedient prisoner. The new method, as Zebulon Brockway put it, was "to treat a prisoner as a patient, to study his symptoms and make the applications they require, to punish him for what demands punishment, to teach him, to reform him, to raise him, and to cure him— these are all parts of a system which has any promise of success" (ibid.). A central thesis to emerge from this reform era was that "more comprehension of the case leads to more comprehensive modes of managing it" ("Prison Reform," 1872, 380).

The system parts that would serve these rehabilitative ends included the reformatory, indeterminate sentence, parole, and probation. Reformatories were to function as "prison science" laboratories where new techniques of dealing with offenders could be devised and tested. In these laboratories, offenders would not be referred to as prisoners or convicts, but as "inmates," known by their name and not a number (Towner 1886). This change in status was meant to reflect and "build up the individuality and responsibility of the new character being formed" (ibid.).

New York's Elmira Reformatory, which became the national model, opened in 1876. In contrast to the penitentiary, the reformatory featured the indeterminate sentence, a mark/classification system, academic and vocational instruction, constructive labor, humane disciplinary methods, gain time, and eventually parole. In keeping with the dictum that "more comprehension of the case leads to more comprehensive modes of managing it," Elmira staff compiled all of the offender information that it was possible to gather in "great books as large as the ledgers of a counting-house" ("The Elmira Reformatory," 1885, 486). The most distinguishing feature was the mark/classification system, which was to measure inmate progress using three indicators: participation and performance in work (vocational) and in school (educational), and compliance with rules (Towner 1886).

The indeterminate sentence and parole were also unveiled at Elmira on the belief that the "entire discipline of the institution rested upon the indeterminate character of the sentence" ("The Elmira Reformatory," 1885). The indeterminate sentence was replicated throughout the nation, and by 1910 nearly every adult reformatory used an indeterminate sentence (Pisciotta 1994). By 1923, almost half of all offenders admitted to U.S. prisons were serving an indeterminate sentence (Rothman 1980). Parole developed independently, such that by 1900, every reformatory utilized parole. Twenty states also enacted parole laws for institutions outside the reformatory (U.S. Department of Justice 2003). By 1922, parole was authorized in 44 states and the indeterminate sentence in 37 states (ibid.).

Though probation was not operationally tied to the reformatory, parole, or the indeterminate sentence, its development was tied to a common rationale. The practice of probation, like the other reforms of the day, was motivated by the desire to individualize the treatment of offenders based on factors other than one's prior and current criminal record. Taking other life history variables into account, progressive-minded reformers and justice officials believed that offenders could be divided into two groups: those who required incarceration to be rehabilitated and those who did not (Rothman 1980). Massachusetts became the first state to implement the practice in 1891 (Friedman 1993). By 1930, the federal government and approximately 36 states and Washington, D.C., had authorized the use of probation (Rothman 1980).

The implementation of these reforms was equally ill-fated, however. Elected and appointed officials were openly condemned for their willful indifference to numerous complaints about reformatories:

> In the light of recent revelations regarding the management of reformatory
> institutions, the conclusion is logical that those in charge of them entertain
> contrary views and practice them in a manner which is a disgrace to civilization,
> to say nothing of the different states which tolerate the continuance of such a
> system. ("Prison Abuses," 1881, 2)

The integrity of parole and the indeterminate sentence suffered as well. Parole release served a host of administrative ends, such as gaining control over potentially unruly inmates and relieving prison overcrowding and inmate idleness. The original aims of parole release were further undermined by private sector contracts, the inmate leasing system, and hurried and unsystematic assessments of an inmate's progress. Speaking on the state of parole in 1930, Barnes (1972) claimed that parole " . . . neither provided supervision nor encouragement to reform" and that the only good to come from parole was that it got men out of prison sooner.

The practice of probation proved to be no exception in this succession of unmet expectations. Meaningful supervision of offenders was thwarted by excessively high caseloads (Rothman 1980) and probation defaulted on its most basic function as an alternative to prison. Because local jurisdictions were expected to assume the costs of supervising state-remanded offenders, probation was often used as an alternative to local jail sentences or nothing. Table 14.1 shows that, in 1940, every reporting state but Iowa, North Dakota, and Pennsylvania relied on a probation/suspended sentence more often than local jails/workhouses. However, of the total states reporting (27), only 10 relied on probation/suspended sentences and local jails/workhouses more than the prison and the reformatory. Of course, these figures do not indicate what percentage of sentenced defendants were felons or misdemeanants, but they do allude to the widening scope and diversification of the twentieth century correctional system.

Table 14.1 Defendants Sentenced by State and Type of Sentence, 1940

State	Defendants Sentenced	State Prisons and Reformatories		Probation and Suspended Sentences		Local Jails and Workhouses		All Other Sentences	
		Number	Percent	Number	Percent	Number	Percent	Number	Percent
California	4,987	1,524	30.6	1,689	33.9	1607	32.2	167	3.3
Colorado	1,054	628	59.6	371	35.2	39	3.7	16	1.5
Connecticut	780	230	29.5	250	32.1	265	34.0	35	4.5
D.C.	1,088	680	62.5	297	27.3	108	9.9	3	0.3
Idaho	473	246	52.0	132	27.9	83	17.5	12	2.5
Indiana	2,233	1,180	52.8	689	30.9	220	9.9	144	6.4
Iowa	1,697	698	41.1	303	17.9	585	34.5	111	6.5
Kansas	1,130	805	71.2	211	18.7	105	9.3	9	0.8
Massachusetts	2,647	1,429	54.0	735	27.8	–	–	483	18.2
Michigan	2,186	933	42.7	1,098	50.2	105	4.8	50	2.3
Minnesota	1,807	788	43.6	719	39.8	240	13.3	60	3.3
Montana	453	351	77.5	62	13.7	24	5.3	16	3.5
New Hampshire	381	104	27.3	202	53.0	66	17.3	9	2.4
New Jersey	5,519	1,960	35.5	2,098	38.0	1,053	19.1	408	7.4
New Mexico	685	360	52.6	237	34.6	47	6.9	41	6.0
New York	7,834	3,227	41.2	2,845	36.3	1,719	21.9	43	0.5
North Dakota	426	262	61.5	50	11.7	77	18.1	37	8.7
Ohio	4,453	2,090	46.9	1,880	42.2	295	6.6	188	4.2
Oregon	976	504	51.6	326	33.4	132	13.5	14	1.4
Pennsylvania	12,328	1,619	13.1	3,411	27.7	5,442	44.1	1,856	15.1
Rhode Island	571	116	20.3	423	74.1	27	4.7	5	0.9
South Dakota	416	246	59.1	95	22.8	60	14.4	15	3.6
Utah	320	153	47.8	122	38.1	33	10.3	12	3.8
Vermont	325	117	63.0	91	28.0	66	20.3	51	15.7
Washington	1,343	770	57.3	381	28.4	182	13.6	10	0.7
Wisconsin	2,664	917	34.4	1,052	39.5	364	13.7	331	12.4
Wyoming	250	147	58.8	78	31.2	8	3.2	17	6.8
TOTAL (26 states + D.C. = 27)	59,026	22,084	37.4	19,847	33.6	12,952	21.9	4143	7.0

Source: Cahalan, Margaret (1986). Historical Corrections Statistics in the United States, 1850–1984.

AWAY FROM THE STATE: LABELING AND A "LESS IS BETTER" CORRECTIONAL POLICY

Prior to the 1960s, serious challenges to the establishment were few. The social, political, and economic status quo did come under harsh attack, however, by an awakened "hippie" subculture and a growing constituency of young political activists. The systemic problems of race, gender, and class fueled contemporary debates and frequent protests against the actions and agents of the state.

Labeling theory emerged from this anti-establishment climate with a relatively radical message. In sharp contrast to the existing conventional wisdom, labeling theory posited that contact with the system could actually perpetuate criminal behavior. The time-honored premise of "more state intervention is better" became viewed as suspect. Experts portrayed prisons and mental hospitals as not only inimical to individual well-being, but seemingly immune to improvement. Consequently, rather than pursuing reform once again, many believed the institutions might as well be emptied (Scull 1977).

A tamer version of this position appeared in a federal report entitled *The Challenge of Crime in a Free Society* (U.S. President's Commission on Law Enforcement and Administration of Justice 1967). Here it was asserted that crime could not be overcome by merely expanding correctional services. It was believed that rehabilitative goals were unrealistic and were propelled by an overly sanguine assessment of crime's causes and what a well-equipped correctional system could accomplish. The report recommended that, because of the negative effects of labeling, clear alternatives to the criminal and juvenile justice systems ought to be developed.

The 1968 Safe Streets Act launched the implementation of alternative "pre-judicial dispositions" and other decentralization strategies. For the next decade, federal criminal justice funding was primarily devoted to diversion and deinstitutionalization-based initiatives. Diversion, as a policy and as a program, proposed a divorce from system involvement and a turning away from traditional criminal justice practice, be it arrest, adjudication, or incarceration. For example, juvenile diversion efforts were to narrow the jurisdiction of the courts to only those cases of "manifest danger." The bulk of delinquent youth were to be diverted into agencies that would provide individual, group, and whole-family counseling; placement in a group or foster home; and educational and vocational assistance.

Deinstitutionalization of status offenders and community treatment programs for juvenile and adult offenders also experienced major growth throughout the 1970s. Deinstitutionalization efforts were aimed at preventing confinement, or at least accelerating an offender's release from jail or prison custody. This could occur through such community-based programs as pre-trial release, work-release, or halfway houses. The Des Moines, Iowa, project exemplified this intent through graduated alternatives to jail for minor and nonviolent offenders. The project components included release on recognizance, supervised pre-trial release, intensive probation, and residential facility services (e.g., work release centers). The Des Moines project concept was replicated in other jurisdictions across the country. However, research found that the other sites were not fully committed to the "alternative" concept promoted by the Des Moines project (U.S. Department of Justice 1979).

Between 1968 and 1978, the federal government funded more than 1,200 community programs at an estimated cost of $112 million (Beckett 1997). Officially, these programs were to serve as alternatives to a potentially damaging and ineffectual correctional system. Yet, a series of empirical studies on diversion indicated that the most consistent program outcome was more system involvement (Austin and Krisberg 1981; Blomberg 1977; Hylton 1982; Klein 1979; Lemert 1981). This net-widening outcome is demonstrated in part by the fact that the total caseload for both incarcerated and community-supervised adults and juveniles was 1,281,801 or 661.3 per 100,000 in 1965, increasing to 1,981,229 or 921.4 per 100,000 in 1976. During this period of stable crime rates (Austin and Krisberg 1981), the prison population increased by 83,782, while the number of offenders on probation and parole increased by 190,557.

Given the findings that reduced system involvement and recidivism were uncertain, if not unlikely, diversion and rehabilitation lost adherents and funding. Robert Martinson's renowned 1974 study essentially concluded that, with few exceptions, rehabilitative programs have had little appreciable effect on crime. The "nothing works" translation of his findings combined with the questionable record of diversion ultimately led to the end of federal funding for decentralization in 1980. This "official" and documented failure would become a driving force behind the punitive policies that followed.

The Age of Conservatism: Tough and Tougher Punishment

The purported failure of rehabilitation was part of a string of defeats that marked the end of the 1970s. The Vietnam War, the Iran hostage affair, high unemployment, and other crises had deflated the national morale and weakened the stature of America abroad. Pledging to reverse this state of affairs, Ronald Reagan penned a "new day" agenda under a neo-conservative banner. The hallmarks of this agenda were not just smaller government and a strong national defense, but an ethos of individualism, self-sufficiency, and abstinence (i.e., from pre-marital and/or casual sex and drug use).

While crime in general was not publicly ranked as a top national priority (Dyer 2000), getting "tough on crime" became the focus of nearly every political move. Whether the crime problem truly warranted this level of attention or was merely accentuated for political gain has been the subject of much debate (see Beckett 1997). What is not controvertible, however, is the force with which the government responded to this alleged crisis.

The heavy-handed justice that developed was aided by a platform of individual responsibility. Reagan was wholehearted in rejecting the idea that crime could be reduced by reducing poverty (Beckett 1997). George H.W. Bush affirmed this ideology, stating that "we must raise our voices to correct an insidious tendency—the tendency to blame crime on society, rather than the criminal" (ibid.). The image of the offender as a purposeful, dangerous, and pervasive threat was further sealed by the stature of rational choice theories and media accounts of crime that were racially charged.

The image of the offender as a domestic enemy fueled perceptions of a system that was overly lenient and outright ineffective. Strategies to fix the system would include the abolition or reduction in the use of parole and the indeterminate sentence, war on drugs, mandatory minimums, habitual offender and "three strikes" statutes, intermediate punishment, "truth in sentencing," and the expansion of capital punishment. By 1982, 34 states had restricted their use of parole and 9 others had abolished it entirely (Clear 1994). The Federal Sentencing Reform Act of 1984 (FSRA) mandated the use of judicial guidelines and determinate sentencing for federal offenses. By 1990, this trend extended to 6 other states, with 14 more states abolishing discretionary parole release for all offenders (Ditton and Wilson 1999).[2]

Mandatory minimum statutes targeting drug and other offenses were especially popular among law and order advocates. By 1983, 43 states imposed mandatory prison terms for one or more violent crimes, and 29 states and the District of Columbia imposed mandatory terms for narcotics offenses (Gordon 1990). The FSRA also authorized mandatory minimum sentences for federal drug offenses and offenses involving a firearm (Schulhofer 1993). This legislation eventually led to 100 separate mandatory minimum provisions, located in 60 different statutes. In the decade following the enactment of federal drug laws, the number of people incarcerated for drug offenses increased by more than 400 percent, with first-time drug offenders serving an average of 68.4 months in federal prison.

As prison populations exceeded lawful capacities, intermediate punishments became the panacea of choice. Consistent with the get-tough environment, intermediate punishments offered a less costly sanction with a distinctly punitive edge. Yet, despite their widespread use, these community-based "alternatives" offered little if any relief to overpopulated correctional systems (Blomberg et al. 1993; Petersilia 1987; Lucken 1997). Due to net-widening and the "get-tough" mandate of punishing offender non-compliance, intermediate punishments often exacerbated the crowding that they were designed to alleviate. Nationwide, intermediate punishment programs were producing nearly twice the number of technical violations (and returns to prison) as routine supervision, though actual reoffending rates for both programs were largely equal (Petersilia and Turner 1993).

Despite this correctional crisis, elected officials enacted new, more costly, and even tougher "get-tough" measures. In 1982, only 21 states had life without parole (LWOP) provisions. This increased to 34 states by 1996. Currently, all states and the District of Columbia have LWOP legislation (Nellis and King 2009). Simultaneously, "three strikes" and "truth in sentencing" (TIS) laws were enacted to halt the lawful but early release of violent offenders. Though the terms of "three strikes" laws varied by state, the general intent was to keep habitual serious or violent offenders off the streets permanently. By 1997, 24 states and the federal government had enacted some version of "three strikes" legislation (Walker 1998). The first federal TIS law was passed in 1987 on the assumption that an inmate should serve at least 85 percent of the originally imposed maximum sentence. By 1995, 29 states had implemented 85 percent requirement TIS laws. Due to prohibitive costs, other states opted for a 50 percent requirement or a 100 percent of the minimum sentence requirement (Ditton and Wilson 1999).

The impact of these policies was foreseeable and unprecedented. Of the 850,566 inmates housed in state and federal facilities in 1992 (Bureau of Justice Statistics 1997), 13,937 were serving "natural life" sentences, with another 52,054 serving sentences of life without parole (LWOP). An added 125,995 inmates were serving sentences of 20 years or more, and 200,000 were serving "extremely long sentences" (Irwin and Austin 1997). Put differently, 46 percent of all inmates were serving sentences that, at a minimum, spanned a large majority of their adult lifetime. Overall, the number of people in jails and state and federal prisons increased from 493,815 in 1980 to 1,554,180 in 1994 (ibid.). In 1987, 8.6 million people were admitted to jails alone (Clear 1994). The number of state and federal probationers also increased dramatically. In 1980, 1.1 million offenders were on state and federal probation and 220,438 were on parole (ibid.). By 1998, the number of probationers reached 3.3 million and the number of parolees totaled 694,787 (McCarthy et al. 2001).

Though crime levels during this time were certainly higher than they were in the 1960s, crime rates were not increasing uniformly. Between 1980 and 1993, murder, robbery, and burglary rates nationwide were stable and, in some instances, declining (Blumstein 1995). Prison admission rates were also driven by returning parolees, especially in California. Yet, as with intermediate punishment, many of the parole returns were due to the commission of technical violations rather than new offenses. Between 1983 and 1993, state and federal prison admissions due to parole violations increased from 19.6 percent to 30.2 percent (Holt 1998). Moreover, in 1983, 48 percent of all state and federal parole returns were due to technical violations. This figure increased to 61 percent in 1987 and 56 percent in 1993 (ibid.).

Contemporary Corrections: Chaos, Contradiction, and Instability

An inventory of the correctional system today reveals a complex of strategies with miscellaneous roots. Several conflicting theories of crime, punishment philosophies, and correctional practices have become the indisputable norm. For even the expert observer, the assortment of options can be a dizzying sight to behold: fines, pre-trial intervention, arbitration, restitution, community service, teen courts, drug courts, community courts, mental health courts, victim-offender meeting programs, citizen panels, pre-trial release, work release, probation and restitution centers, halfway houses, probation, parole, day-reporting centers, intensive supervision probation, boot camps, home confinement, electronic monitoring, jail, prison, supermax prisons, sex offender civil commitment, registration and notification, the death penalty, and other variously named community residential facilities and reentry programs.

While previous reform eras were not entirely void of inconsistencies in ideology and practice, a prevailing narrative did exist whereupon deviations could be easily identified. Presently, the narrative is not only "volatile and contradictory"

(O'Malley 1999) but regressive more often than innovative. Four punishment trends illustrate this convoluted narrative: supermax prisons, sex offender statutes, death penalty, and offender reentry.

Supermax Prisons

As of 2004, 44 states operated supermax facilities. Collectively, they house approximately 25,000 inmates, all of whom are deemed "super" threats to institutional security (Mears 2006). Like the penitentiary of the 1830s, supermax prisons place inmates in perpetual solitude to minimize human contact. They are permitted one hour of recreation a day in a small typically private yard extending out from the cell, and meals, books, and correspondence are delivered to the inmate through a slot in the cell door. Video cameras positioned throughout the facility and cells, and computerized security doors also ensure a remote impersonal form of surveillance (Sheppard 1996). Isolated from staff and other prisoners, a rule of silence is effectively imposed.

In contrast to the nineteenth-century penitentiary, silence and isolation are intended to control rather than reform. This regulatory and punitive purpose has incited opposition from a variety of sources. Included in this group are correctional administrators and courts, as well as the United Nations, Amnesty International, American Civil Liberties Union, and Human Rights Watch (King 1999). A 2005 U.S. Supreme Court ruling, nevertheless, upheld their constitutionality. The Court ruled that the "atypical and significant hardship" posed by supermax custody only requires that inmates have a formal opportunity to contest their assignment to such a facility (Justice Kennedy, quoted in Kluger 2007). Interestingly, in 1890, the U.S. Supreme Court denounced the use of silence rules and isolation because of the "semi-fatuous condition" in which it left the inmates (Kluger 2007).

Sex Offender Registration and Notification, Civil Commitment, and Residency Restrictions

As the War on Drugs has become less of national priority, sex offenders have become a preferred target of lawmakers across the country. Since the 1990s, sex offenders alone have been subject to a series of laws such as notification/registration (NR), civil commitment (CC), and residency restrictions (RR). Reminiscent of colonial American shaming techniques, federal law requires that sex offenders register their whereabouts with law enforcement and that states develop sex offender registries or risk losing federal funding for state and local law enforcement (Terry 2006). The purpose of these registries is to provide citizens a means of knowing (or being notified) if and where a sex offender lives in their neighborhood.

Sex offender RRs, which have been implemented in 30 states, also signal a return to colonial-style control. Colonists used residency restrictions, or what was known as "warning out" (Vale 2000), to protect communities from undesirables, including individuals who were not in "good standing" elsewhere, were not economically self-sufficient, or shared a different set of values and beliefs. Sex offender RRs, whether statewide or jurisdictional, similarly prohibit undesirables (all sex offenders—not just pedophiles) from living within a specified distance of places inhabited by children, including schools, day care, parks, and bus stops.

Reviving the medical model of rehabilitation to its purist level, CC laws speak of "curing" a "mental abnormality" or "personality disorder" in a treatment facility. This treatment is to continue until the offender is no longer a risk or the "disease goes into remission" (Alexander 1995). Moreover, this confinement takes place after the prison sentence has already been served and upon a clinical finding of a "mental abnormality" that predisposes one to sexual offending. CC laws exist in 16 states, with approximately 2,700 sex offenders being civilly detained as of 2007.[3] This number is expected to rise, as some states (California, Florida, Minnesota, Nebraska, Virginia, Wisconsin) plan to increase their number of civil commitment beds (Terry 2006).

Many scholars have questioned the legality of these laws, CC and NR laws in particular, asserting that they violate a number of constitutional rights, namely those related to privacy, double jeopardy, cruel and unusual punishment, and/or retroactive application of a state action. Yet, the U.S. Supreme Court has ruled that both CC and NR laws are regulatory rather than punitive in nature and thus do not violate the constitutional rights of sex offenders. Controversy has continued, however, given the potential of NR and RR to increase vigilantism, ostracism, and sex offender absconding.

Death Penalty

Current trends in capital punishment seem to defy the get-tough and exclusionary trends reflected in supermax prisons and sex offender statutes. In 1999, the number of executions nationwide reached a high of 98. However, that number has declined every year since, with only 37 executions taking place in 2008. The number of death sentences imposed nationally has also dropped substantially and consistently from 326 in 1995, to 284 in 1999, to 111 in 2008, and to 106 in 2009 (Death Penalty Information Center 2009). Furthermore, states are beginning to question the legitimacy of capital punishment altogether. In 2005, Connecticut lost a close battle to abolish the death penalty, and an attempt to reinstitute the death penalty in New York failed. In 2007 and 2009, New Jersey and New Mexico, respectively, abolished the death penalty, bringing the total number of states without the death penalty to 15 (not including the District of Columbia). Additionally, in 2002, the U.S. Supreme Court (*Atkins v. Virginia*) held that it was unconstitutional to execute defendants with mental retardation. In 2005, they rendered the same decision with regard to juveniles (*Roper v. Simmons*) (Death Penalty Information Center 2009).

While it is not fully clear what accounts for this trend, publicity surrounding the discovery of several innocent death row inmates has been a significant factor. Between 2000 and 2007, nationally, there was an average of five exonerations per year (ibid.). In Florida alone, 22 death row inmates have been exonerated since 1973. Similarly, Illinois has granted 18 exonerations (ibid.).

Offender Reentry

The offender reentry movement represents one of the more profound examples of a clear policy reversal. The war-like rhetoric that recently dominated criminal justice policy has now been supplanted with the more conciliatory rhetoric of "redemption" (Lattimore 2006) and "second chances" (2004 Presidential State of the Union Address; State of Florida 2005). While the idea of offender reentry has been well received, it has not been well defined. Put simply, offender reentry is an umbrella term for anything associated with an inmate's release to and success in the community.

Given the broad spectrum and varying levels of offender need and risk, reentry programs and proposals are assuming any number of forms. Included in this mix are short-and long-term jail and prison pre-release programs, post-prison residential (e.g., work release) and non-residential programs, reentry courts, one-stop drop-in centers, educational, vocational, employment, housing, and/or substance abuse programs and assistance, and strategies to reverse or temper the regulatory and statutory measures that restrict or prohibit offender eligibility for civil rights, public housing, and numerous occupations (Lucken and Ponte 2008; Travis 2002).

This assortment of strategies is no doubt sorely needed, yet understanding of their impact on offenders and communities will be difficult to assess. There is a significant level of heterogeneity in program types as well as in the kinds of agencies and partnerships involved in service delivery.

CONCLUSION

The "what works" question has been a persistent force in criminological inquiry. For the past several decades, research has been exceptionally focused on correctional program effectiveness. Studies routinely examine the outcomes of various reforms, with the aim of directing policy makers toward the most humane, effective, and cost-efficient strategies.

Of late, correctional policymakers have expressed a heightened interest in this evaluation research. At the national, state, and local level of correctional administration, the need for evidence-based practice has become a dominant professional theme. This can be seen in the various practitioner training sessions on evidence-based practice, practitioner-targeted reports on evidence based practice (National Institute of Corrections 2004), U.S. Congressional testimony on best practices in youth correctional education, and the development of scientific advisory boards for the U.S. Department of Justice and the National Institute of Justice and Bureau of Justice Statistics more specifically.[4] Undoubtedly, this apparent interest in research reflects the fact that, when financial resources diminish, the demand for proven practice increases. Nonetheless, the traditional business as usual in correctional policy making appears to have reached a ceiling.

What is not apparent is how the scientific community will respond to the calls for more participation in public policy or what is being termed "public criminology." Some criminologists are resisting a "public criminology" role, claiming that too little is known to make measurable policy contributions. Others contend that criminology is an applied discipline and as such must seek a more meaningful role for science in, for example, correctional policy. Should this occur, the process will likely be incremental and will involve various scientific limitations and political impediments. But, as this chapter has documented, the alternative of social amnesia, net-widening, good intentions gone awry, and regressive policies is surely worse. Though calls for more science in correctional policy cannot fully eradicate the rash and short-sighted culture of political decision making, perhaps the time has arrived in which policy based on "illusions of knowledge" (Boorstin 1983) is on a permanent decline.

NOTES

*   The authors thank Julie Mestre for her editorial assistance.

1.   Throughout the 1800s, the separation of female and male inmates varied by state and type of institution. In state-run penitentiaries, women were typically housed in an adjoining wing or separate unit of a male institution ("Second Report of the Prison Association of New York," 1846; "Annual Reports of New York Prisons," 1853). In local jails or county prisons, however, women were often housed in the same room as men. The mingling and "promiscuous associations" between male and female inmates in Pennsylvanian jails were frequently denounced in the reports of the day ("County Prisons," 1848). Other charitable facilities solely for [wayward] women did exist, but they were not considered penitentiaries, prisons, or jails. At the turn of the twentieth century, reformatories for women only were developed, as was the first federal penitentiary for women in 1928.

2.   Discretionary parole was abolished entirely in Arizona, Delaware, Florida, Illinois, Indiana, Kansas, Maine, Minnesota, Mississippi, North Carolina, Ohio, Oregon, Washington, and Wisconsin.

3.   SOCC laws exist in Arizona, California, Florida, Illinois, Iowa, Kansas, Minnesota, New Jersey, North Dakota, South Carolina, Washington, District of Columbia, Missouri, Virginia, Massachusetts, Wisconsin, and Texas. In Texas, civil commitment operates on an outpatient basis.

4.   One of the authors has conducted correctional training sessions and the other has provided Congressional testimony.

REFERENCES

Alexander, Rudolph Jr., 1995. "Employing the Mental Health System to Control Sex Offenders after Penal Incarceration." *Law and Policy* 17: 111–115.

"Annual Reports of New York prisons." 1853. *Pennsylvania Journal of Prison Discipline and Philanthropy* 8(4): 180. Retrieved from American Periodicals Series Online database.

Austin, James, and Barry Krisberg. 1981. "Wider, Stronger and Different Nets: The Dialectics of Criminal Justice Reform." *Journal of Research in Crime and Delinquency* 78: 165–196.

Barnes, Harry E. 1972. *The Story of Punishment*. Montclair, NJ: Patterson Smith.

Beckett, Katherine. 1997. *Making Crime Pay: Law And Order in Contemporary American Politics*. New York: Oxford University Press.

Bittenger, D. 1870. "Sources of Crime." *New York Evangelist*, 8 December, 41(49). Retrieved from American Periodicals Series Online database.

Blomberg, Thomas G. 1977. "Diversion and Accelerated Control." *Journal of Criminal Law and Criminology* 68: 274–282.

Blomberg, Thomas G., William Bales, and Karen Reed. 1993. "Intermediate Punishment: Extending or Redistributing Social Control." *Crime, Law, and Social Change* 19: 197–201.

Blumstein, Alfred. 1995. "Stability of Punishment: What Happened and What Next?" In *Punishment and Social Control: Essays in Honor of Sheldon L. Messinger*, eds. Thomas G. Blomberg and Stanley Cohen, 259–274. Hawthorne, NY: Aldine de Gruyter.

Boorstin, Daniel. 1983. *The Discoverers: The History of Man's Search to Know His World and Himself*. New York: Random House.

Bureau of Justice Statistics. 1997. *Correctional Populations in the United States, 1997*. Washington, DC: U.S. Department of Justice.

Bureau of Justice Statistics. 2007. *Capital Punishment, 2007*. Washington, DC: U.S. Department of Justice.

"Capital Punishment." 1846. *Prisoner's Friend*, 4 November, 1(44). Retrieved from American Periodicals Series Online database.

Clear, Todd R. 1994. *Harm in American Penology*. Albany, NY: SUNY Press.

"County Prisons." 1848. *Pennsylvania Journal of Prison Discipline and Philanthropy* 3(3): 121. Retrieved from American Periodicals Series Online database.

Death Penalty Information Center. 2009. *Facts about the Death Penalty*. Available at: http://deathpenaltyinfo.org.

Ditton, Paula, and D. J. Wilson. 1999. *Truth in Sentencing in State Prisons*. Bureau of Justice Statistics Special Report, January 1999. Washington, DC: U.S. Department of Justice, Office of Justice Programs.

Dyer, J. 2000. *The Perpetual Prisoner Machine*. Boulder, CO: Westview Press.

"The Elmira Reformatory." 1885. *Christian Advocate*, 30 July, 60(31). Retrieved from American Periodicals Series Online database.

Florida Department of Corrections. 1994. *1993–1994 Annual Report*. Tallahassee, FL: Author.

Friedman, Lawrence. 1993. *Crime and Punishment in American History*. New York: Basic Books.

Gordon, Diana. 1990. *The Justice Juggernaut*. Newark, NJ: Rutgers University Press.

Hazard's Register of Pennsylvania 1831. *Statement of crimes*. 27 August, 1831 8 (9) Retrieved from American Periodical Series Online database.

Holt, Norman. 1998. "The Current State of Parole in America." In *Community Corrections*, ed. Joan Petersilia, 28–41. New York: Oxford University Press.

Hood, William M. 1831. "Temperance." *Hazard's Register of Pennsylvania*, 23 July, 8(4). Retrieved from American Periodical Series Online database.

Hylton, John. 1982. "Rhetoric and Reality: A Critical Appraisal of Community Correctional Programs." *Crime and Delinquency* 28: 341–373.

Irwin, John, and James Austin. 1997. *It's About Time: America's Imprisonment Binge*. 2nd ed. Belmont, CA: Wadsworth.

Kann, Mark E. 2005. *Punishment, Prisons, and Patriarchy: Liberty and Power in the Early American Republic*. New York: New York University Press.

King, Roy D. 1999. "The Rise and Rise of Supermax: An American Solution in Search of a Problem?" *Punishment and Society* 7: 163–186.

Klein, Matthew W. 1979. "Deinstitutionalization and Diversion of Juvenile Offenders: A Litany of Impediments." In *Crime and Justice: An Annual Review of Research*, eds. Norval Morris and Michael Tonry, 145–201. Chicago: University of Chicago Press.

Kluger, Jeffrey. 2007. "The Paradox of Supermax." *Time Magazine* 169(6): 52–53.

Kuntz, William F., II. 1988. *Criminal Sentencing in Three 19th Century Cities: Social History of Punishment in New York, Boston, and Philadelphia, 1830–1880*. New York: Garland.

Lattimore, Pamela. 2006. "Reentry, Reintegration, Rehabilitation, Recidivism, and Redemption." *The Criminologist* 31(3): 1–3.

Lemert, Edwin. 1981. "Diversion in Juvenile Justice: What Hath Been Wrought." *Journal of Research in Crime and Delinquency* 78: 34–46.

Lieber, Francis. 1838. "A Popular Essay on Subjects of Penal Law and on Uninterrupted Solitary Confinement." *The North American Review October*, XLVII. Retrieved from the ProQuest: American Periodical Series Online database.

Lucken, Karol. 1997. "Dynamics of Penal Reform." *Crime, Law, and Social Change* 26: 367–384.

Lucken, Karol, and Lucille Ponte. 2008. "A Just Measure of Forgiveness: Reforming Occupational Licensing Regulations for Ex-Offenders Using BFOQ Analysis." *Law & Policy* 30: 46–72.

Mears, Daniel. 2006. *Evaluating the Effectiveness of Supermax Prisons*. Washington, DC: The Urban Institute.

Melossi, Dario, and Massimo Pavarini. 1981. *The Prison and the Factory*. Totowa, NJ: Barnes and Noble Books.

McCarthy, Belinda R., Bernard J. McCarthy Jr., and Matthew Leone. 2001. *Community-Based Corrections*, 4th ed. Belmont, CA: Wadsworth.

National Institute of Corrections. 2004. *Implementing Evidence-Based Practice in Community Corrections: The Principles of Effective Intervention*. Department of Justice: National Institute of Corrections.

Nellis, Ashley, and Ryan S. King. 2009. *No Exit: The Expanding Use of Life Sentences in America*. Washington, DC: The Sentencing Project.

"Of What Use Are Our Prisons?" 1857. *Journal of Prison Discipline and Philanthropy*, 12(3): 136. Retrieved from American Periodicals Series Online database.

O'Malley, Pat 1999. "Volatile and Contradictory Punishment." *Theoretical Criminology* 3: 175–196.

Petersilia, Joan. 1987. "Georgia's Intensive Probation: Will the Model Work Elsewhere?" In *Intermediate Punishments: Intensive Supervision, Home Confinement, and Electronic Surveillance*, ed. Belinda R. McCarthy, 15–30. Monsey, NY: Criminal Justice Press.

Petersilia, Joan, and Susan Turner. 1993. "Intensive Probation and Parole." In *Crime and Justice: A Review of Research*, Vol. 17, ed. Michael Tonry. Chicago: University of Chicago Press.

Pisciotta, Alexander. 1994. *Benevolent Repression: Social Control and the American Reformatory Prison Movement*. New York: New York University Press.

"Prison Abuses." 1881. *National Police Gazette*, 15 January, 37(173). Retrieved from American Periodicals Series Online database.

"Prison Reform." 1872. *American Church Review*, 1 July. Retrieved from American Periodical Series Online database.

Rothman, David J. 1971. *The Discovery of the Asylum: Social Order and Disorder in the New Republic*. Boston: Little, Brown.

Rothman, David J. 1980. *Conscience and Convenience: The Asylum and Its Alternatives in Progressive America*. Boston: Little, Brown.

Rotman, Eduardo. 1995. "The Failure of Reform: United States, 1865–1965." In *The Oxford History of the Prison*, eds. Norval Morris and David J. Rothman, 169–197. New York: Oxford University Press.

Scull, Andrew. 1977. *Decarceration*. New Brunswick, NJ: Rutgers University Press.

Schulhofer, Stephen. 1993. "Rethinking Mandatory Minimums." *Wake Forest Law Review* 28: 199–222.

"Second Report of the Prison Association of New York." 1846. *Pennsylvania Journal of Prison Discipline and Philanthropy*, 2(3): 235. Retrieved from American Periodicals Series Online database.

Sheppard, Robert 1996. "Closed Maximum Security: The Illinois Supermax." *Corrections Today* 58: 84–88.

"Shower of Pardons." 1857. *Journal of Prison Discipline and Philanthropy* 12(1): 42. Retrieved from American Periodicals Series Online database

Skotnicki, Andrew. 2000. *Religion and the Development of the American Penal System*. Lanham, MD: University Press of America.

Terry, Karen. 2006. *Sexual Offenses and Offenders*. Belmont, CA: Thomson Wadsworth.

Towner, Ausburn. 1886. "The Treatment of Criminals, with Some Account of the Reformatory at Elmira, N.Y.—Its History and System." *The American Magazine* 22: 727–734.

Travis, Jeremy. 2002. "Invisible Punishments: An Instrument of Social Exclusion." In *The Collateral Consequences of Mass Imprisonment*, eds. Marc Mauer and Meda Chesney-Lind, 15–36. Washington, DC: New Press.

U.S. Department of Justice. 1979. *Evaluation of the Des Moines Community-Based Corrections Replication Programs: Summary Report*. Washington, DC: U.S. Government Printing Office.

U.S. Department of Justice. 2003. *History of the Federal Parole System*. Washington, DC: Author.

U.S. President's Commission on Law Enforcement and Administration of Justice. 1967. *The Challenge of Crime in a Free Society*. Washington, DC: U.S. Government Printing Office.

Vale, Lawrence J. 2000. *From the Puritans to the Projects: Public Housing and Public Neighbors*. Cambridge, MA: Harvard University Press.

Walker, Samuel 1998. *Sense and Nonsense about Crime and Drugs*. Belmont, CA: Wadsworth.

"What Has Been Done and What Is to Do." 1856. *Pennsylvania Journal of Prison Discipline and Philanthropy* October, 11(4). Retrieved from American Periodicals Series Online database.

Section B
Community Corrections and Intermediate Punishments

CHAPTER 15

PROBATION, INTERMEDIATE SANCTIONS, AND COMMUNITY-BASED CORRECTIONS

FAYE S. TAXMAN

PROBATION is a "lesser" punishment. It is lesser because the public perceives a sentence of probation to be "in lieu" of incarceration or a punishment that is provided as an alternative to incarceration. The key is for the offender to abide by the conditions of release in order to complete the requirements of probation. These conditions are established by the sentencing judge, although some correctional programs have set conditions that are part of the requirements. Probation is a form of conditional release where failure to comply with the mandated requirements can result in reinstatement of the original incarceration sentence.

Probation created the framework for the expansion of community-based sanctions through the concept of intermediate sanctions in which the liberty restrictions in the community provide for a "prison without walls." The movement and behaviors of the individual are monitored as part of the punishment, and treatment or program requirements are used to create or intensify the restrictions in such a manner that the individual learns more internal controls. Intermediate sanction policies and programs grew out of changes in technology that allowed for more constraints on the movement of individuals as well as public demand for stiffer sentences for offenders.

Today, over 4.3 million adults are on formal probation, in a myriad of community-based correctional supervision programs, or in specialized court programs; this is roughly twice the number of people in prison or jail. Probation and community corrections are largely untapped resources that have yet to be fully developed and integrated into sentencing systems. Fewer than 7 percent of the offenders in community supervision participate in intermediate sanctions or specialized court programs; the majority of offenders are involved in an array of "standard" probation oversight programs. Research in the contemporary environment is focused on testing different theoretical frameworks underlying probation and community correction programming. A largely unresolved research question is what role the probation officer should assume (e.g., resource broker, social worker, behavioral manager, or enforcer). The role of the officer has implications as to the purpose of the sentence, for example, whether the goal of community sanctioning is to alter behavior or punish the offender. A largely unresolved issue is the number and types of conditions required as part of the community sanction, and the degree to which these conditions affect outcomes during supervision (proximal outcomes) and post-supervision (distal outcomes). What can be said about probation and community supervision is:

- Criminal behavior is similar to other behaviors that require change in lifestyle factors to effect change; changes in human behavior that require alterations of lifestyle often require more than one "treatment" exposure. Overall probation results are similar to, or better than, outcomes from substance abuse treatment, medical care for chronic diseases (asthma, cardiac problems), and mental health treatment.
- The number of conditions attached to the probation sentence (or the intensity of the supervision contacts) does not affect the likelihood of completion of probation.
- Few resources are available in community-based correctional programming, therefore limiting the potential for this type of programming to achieve long-term offender change.
- Improving probation supervision and community correctional programming can best be achieved through the adoption of a set of well-defined (and research-based) practices; yet, few correctional agencies adopt such practices.
- Treatment for dynamic risk behaviors (e.g., substance abuse, criminal thinking) is infrequently available in the community, and this reduces the opportunities for long-term change.
- A long-term agenda is needed to understand the components of effective probation and parole services.

I. History of Community-Based Correctional Programs

Probation has its early roots in the prospects of providing a more humane and effective method of dealing with the problems of substance abusers (at the time, alcoholics) in society. John Augustus, the grandfather of contemporary probation in the

United States, was a boot maker who expressed concern that the incarceration of drunks was an ineffective method of effecting long-term reduction of alcohol use in Boston. As a merchant, John Augustus realized that too many men fell prey to drinking and that this resulted in them becoming unsuitable workers. He sought a better remedy than jail, which fostered an endless cycle of excessive alcohol consumption. He believed that providing support in the community could reduce the problems of alcoholism as well as serve as an alternative to jail. The Augustus model quickly spread across Massachusetts; within nearly 50 years, every court in the state had an allocated probation officer. Probation was born as a court service designed to reduce the use of jail sentences for first-time offenders. It was assigned to the judiciary and became part of the correctional system in 22 states by 1922, and was implemented in nearly all states by 1957.

The early era of probation was focused on alternatives to incarceration and assisting those with alcohol, mental health or social needs. For the first 150 years of probation services, the emphasis was a social work or resource broker model in which the goal was to assist individuals in stabilizing their lives. Probation officers were selected by the court and served judges in overseeing the safety and care of offenders in the community. In the 1970s, however, there was a fundamental shift in probation's emphasis away from reintegration in favor of oversight (law enforcement) and enforcement of conditions. Rehabilitation played a less prominent role as the movement toward retributive sentencing policies and incapacitation gained favor in the system (Garland 2001). The emphasis on enforcement of conditions of release (e.g., reporting, informing the officer of their whereabouts, and other emphasis on controls) has dominated probation services ever since.

The "War on Drugs" (mid-1980s) reignited an attempt to enlarge the role of probation to address the needs of drug offenders and to ensure that probation provided more oversight of offenders in the community. The average probation officer caseload size was approximately 1:100 offenders (DeMichele 2007). This created the impression that the probation system was merely a "slap on the wrist." The concepts of intensive supervision, drug treatment courts, and intermediate sanctions all unfolded in response to different overlapping but complementary public needs to enhance community-based correctional services and to tailor the conditions of probation services to better control the behavior of offenders. In 1991, Norval Morris and Michael Tonry wrote *Between Prison and Probation* to argue that sentencing systems should embrace a full range of community punishments. The underlying premise was that standard probation was insufficient to meet sentencing goals of punishment, deterrence, and incapacitation, and that new models of community punishments were needed.

The Morris-Tonry community correctional model embraced a full range of community sanctions that were used in other Western societies; the use of incarceration was to be preserved as a last resort. The model included: fines or monetary penalties, a cadre of liberty restrictions (e.g., more contacts with the probation officer, curfews, house arrest, day reporting centers), and programs that combined treatment with sanctions. The perspective was that the United States needed a full range of sanctions in the community to restrict the use of confinement for those offenders who offered the most risk to public safety.

II. The Community Correctional System Today

With over 4.3 million adults on some form of probation supervision, probation is the most frequently used sanction. Probation is no longer reserved for the first-time offender, as in the era of John Augustus. In fact, 48 percent of offenders have no criminal record, and new innovations in the field have expanded the range of diversion (pre-adjudication) sanctions that "first-time" offenders enjoy. We have no estimate of the number of offenders involved in formal diversion probation programs, but California has around 50,000 offenders involved in their drug diversion program alone (Proposition 36). Taxman, Perdoni, and Harrison (2007) estimate that there are over 1 million adults involved in community programming that is not part of a probation or parole agency, with many involved in drug treatment courts (about 50,000), diversion programs (about 300,000), and untold numbers in various other statuses, including pre-trial supervision and pre-adjudication programs that are used to affect sentencing outcomes.

What Are the Characteristics of Offenders on Supervision?

Very little is known about the probationer population in the United States, and the available information is dated. Recent Bureau of Justice Statistics (BJS) reports identify that 30 percent of probationers are drug offenders, 25 percent committed a property offense, and 19 percent a violent crime. Probationers are predominately male (76 percent). Racial backgrounds are: Caucasian (56 percent), African American (29 percent), and Hispanic or Latino (13 percent). Probationers are equally likely to have committed a felony or misdemeanor offense (see Glaze and Bonczar 2008).

In 1995, the BJS reviewed the records of nearly 2,618,132 sentenced probationers in the most comprehensive review ever undertaken (Mumola and Bonczar 1998). Based on these reviews, nearly 48 percent had a prior conviction. The age distribution of probationers was: 26 percent were 18–24 years old; 37 percent were 25–34; 8 percent were 45–54; and 3.2 percent were 55 years or older. Over 50 percent had never been married and 26 percent were married. Probationers were unlikely to have completed high school or obtained a GED (40 percent), with 7.5 percent having less than an 8th grade education and 40 percent with "some" high school (see Bonzcar 1997).

The BJS also interviewed over 2,000 probationers on active supervision to determine the needs for substance abuse treatment (see Mumola and Bonczar 1998). Nearly 40 percent of the probationers reported alcohol use and 14 percent reported drug use at the time of the offense. Offenders were more likely to have been treated for alcohol (32 percent) than drug use (17 percent). Probationers were frequent treatment clients; 41 percent had prior alcohol treatment and 22 percent had prior drug treatment services, although a considerable amount of this treatment included self-help groups. Nearly 70 percent of the probationers reported lifetime drug use, primarily involving marijuana/hashish (66 percent), cocaine/crack (31 percent), heroin/opiates (8 percent), and stimulants (25 percent). The interviews revealed that nearly two-thirds of the probationers were drug-involved, but only one-third of the males and half of the females were considered to have a substance abuse dependency. Recent evidence suggests that half of those with substance use disorders have co-occurring disorders (Sacks 2000). Given the extent of substance abuse among offender populations, it is surprising that the BJS survey has not been replicated; it was completed in 1995, and the field is still relying upon its findings, supplemented by scattered single-site studies.

How Are Probation Services Organized Today?

While probation in the first 150 years was primarily a judicial function, probation agencies have slowly become administered and funded by either executive agencies at the state or county level or are fragmented into multiple community correctional agencies in a jurisdiction. Currently, probation services are the responsibility of state probation, parole, and prison agencies that are centralized (29 states), decentralized (9 states), or partially centralized (12 states). The partially centralized states have varying levels of state and county authority for correctional agencies; in all 12, probation is offered at the county level by the county government (5 states) or judiciary (7 states) (Taxman 2007). The fragmented funding streams for correctional services—particularly probation—means that the responsibility for providing adequate supervision and treatment services is often left to coupling funding across various streams, rather than allocating the funding that includes all the needed services to manage probationers within one budget. In many states, different community correctional agencies exist, some having jurisdiction over misdemeanor offenders and some having jurisdiction over felony offenders.

The federal government also has a pre-trial and probation agency with 94 district offices. The federal agency has responsibility for front-end probation for slightly over 120,000 offenders with the majority being supervised after a period of confinement (around 98,000). (Note that with the abandonment of parole in the federal system, judges can place offenders on probation after prison.) The federal system operates separately from state and local probation and has a distinctive population of offenders, including white-collar offenders.

Beginning in the 1970s, when it became apparent that probation services needed to join forces with other agencies (e.g., substance abuse treatment and mental health) and that partnerships would be beneficial in providing services in the community, many states have enacted Community Corrections Act (CCA) legislation (Shilton and Weisfeld 2008). The purpose of the CCA is to expand correctional options through probation subsidy programs or community rehabilitation law. The CCA creates opportunities for funding streams that involve both state and local government agencies. CCA also is credited with promoting reforms to better "sort" those who should receive incarceration and those who merit community punishments. The CCA has resulted in some states creating separate agencies for standard probation and for community-based corrections.

Probation is now often used for post-incarceration offenders, either as part of the judge's sentence or as a tool to supervise release after a period of incarceration (as a replacement for parole). At the front end, 50 percent of offenders are required to spend time in jail for up to 12 months before their period of probation supervision (Mumola and Bonczar 1998). And, as many states have abolished the period of supervised parole (i.e., following discretionary release by a parole board), offenders have increasingly been placed on post-release probation supervision to provide oversight and monitoring during the volatile period of time after a lengthy period of incarceration. These changes in the nature of probation supervision have occurred over the last two decades, enforcing the perspective that probation is used as a sentence in lieu of incarceration and increasing the monitoring of offenders.

What Types of Correctional Programs Are Offered as Part of Probation/Community Corrections?

As originally conceived by John Augustus, probation services were to provide oversight in the community. This entailed face-to-face contacts between the probationer and the officer of the state. The goals of these meetings were to provide guidance, to review progress, and to make appropriate referrals as needed. This meeting model is still often used to define probation supervision today; the number of contacts between the offender and the probation officer varies widely, depending on the probation agencies. Agencies are known to have various levels of contacts: administrative (generally quarterly, may involve the use of kiosks or mailing in a postcard to indicate progress on jobs, treatment, etc.); standard (usually once a month); moderate (more than once a month); and intensive (more than standard). The number of offenders who are required to report regularly is around 70 percent, while the remainder are on some type of administrative reporting system (Glaze and Bonczar 2008). In some systems there are a variety of contacts, including: in-person contacts with the probation officer; collateral contact(s) with the employer, family, or other members of the person's support network; and home contacts, where the officer visits with the offender in his or her place of residence. Added to these contacts are various forms of oversight, including drug testing, electronically or geographical positioning monitoring, breathalyzers, interlock systems, and other technologies that intensify the oversight of the individual.

Morris and Tonry, in *Between Prison and Probation* (1991) offered a broad framework of a new system of sanctioning and programming in the community that could provide an alternative to *both* traditional probation and incarceration. Their model included a stair step approach to community sanctions based on the intensity of liberty restrictions. In table 15.1 the degree to which the intermediate sanctions—those that fall between standard probation and prison—are illustrated.

These data are from a 2005 survey of correctional agencies (see Taxman, Perdoni, and Harrison 2007 for a description of the National Criminal Justice Treatment Practices survey). The survey revealed that, on average, about 59 percent of correctional agencies have drug testing capabilities and that testing procedures vary considerably, with most agencies using a random approach. In random procedures, offenders were not drug tested on a regular basis, but rather it was ad hoc; most systems randomly select offenders for drug testing. One study that examined this practice found that only 7 percent of the offenders could be drug tested. The survey also revealed that less than 40,000 offenders were being electronically monitored; fewer than 1 percent of the agencies acknowledged the use of the interlock systems.

Table 15.1 illustrates that only a small number of agencies have a stair step of correctional programs, as recommended by Morris and Tonry, and even when the programs do exist, few offenders can participate in them for any significant period of time. The most prevalent programs are sex offender therapy (57.5 percent) and intensive supervision programs (41.9 percent); on any given day, only about 9 percent of the offenders in a given probation agency can actually participate in programs. Nearly 20 percent of the agencies participate in a drug treatment court, where slightly over 2 percent of the offenders participate. The last column reports on the percentage of programs that are at least 90 days in duration (the benchmark period of time for a program to have some positive effect); drug treatment courts tend to be longer in duration.

Interestingly, in 1995 the Bureau of Justice Assistance, after interviewing probationers, found the following participation rates in special programs or services: intensive supervision (10 percent), boot camp (.7 percent), electronic monitoring (3.5 percent), house arrest without any electronic monitoring (1.2 percent), community service (1.1 percent), drug testing (32.3 percent), sex offender therapy (2.5 percent), vocational education (2.5 percent), and day reporting (5 percent). Comparing offender reporting rates of required participation to the intermediate sanctions available in

Table 15.1. Correctional Programs in Community Correctional Agencies as Reported in the National Criminal Justice Treatment Practices Survey, 2005

Type of Program/ Service	% of Agencies with Program	% of Average Daily Population in Program (median)	Estimated Offenders in Program	% of programs > 90 days
Boot camp	<1	<1	2,136	46.1
Day reporting	13.4	3.8	140,463	48.6
Intensive supervision programs	41.9	9.3	320,931	65.2
Work release	7.4	3.9	34,150	45.3
Drug treatment court	20.2	2.3	39,718	94.9
Transitional housing	24.2	<1	27,355	19.5
Sex offender therapy	57.5	2	80,471	96.2
Vocational training	22.6	2.2	67,157	23

Source: Taxman, Perdoni, and Harrison (2007).

2005, the community corrections system has not increased in capacity, even when the probation population grew from 2.5 million in 1995 to 4.5 million in 2005.

What Are the Conditions of Release?

The last available national survey of the conditions of release for probation supervision was published in 1995 by the BJS. This special report on probation supervision found that half of probationers had a split sentence involving jail (37.3 percent) or prison (15.3 percent). Felony offenders were more likely to receive a split sentence (54 percent) compared to misdemeanor offenders (45 percent) (Mumola and Bonczar 1998). Bonczar (1997) also reported that 98.6 percent of the probationers had special conditions, including fines or fees (84.3 percent), drug testing (32.5 percent), drug or alcohol treatment (41 percent), employment (34.7 percent), and/or community services (25.7 percent). The average probationer is reported to have 13 conditions of release, including supervision fees that can range from $20 to $60 a month or a flat fee of up to $200, depending on the state.

What Type of Treatment Services Are Available Through Probation Agencies?

With nearly half of probationers required to obtain treatment or counseling services (particularly drug treatment, mental health, and sex offender programming), a major issue concerns the availability of these services for offenders. In traditional probation settings, services are determined by the sentencing judge, and probation is designed to fulfill those obligations, whereas in specialized programming models, the determination of services is based on assessments of individual offender's criminogenic needs. In either case, the style of the linkage or referral is important; 60 percent of the agencies use passive referrals (i.e., give the offender a list of appropriate places, recommend the probationer obtains an assessment), as compared to 36 percent that use an active referral strategy (Taxman, Perdoni, and Harrison 2007). With active referrals, probation officers make an appointment for the offender, the officer calls the treatment provider with the probationer, and the goal is to provide an immediate link between the offender and needed services. As shown in table 15.2, community correctional agencies are unlikely to offer treatment services directly or to have a working relationship with treatment agencies to provide services for offenders. Even more important, they are unlikely to have the capacity to thoroughly screen or assess probationers for service needs.

As discussed above, nearly half of probationers have orders for substance abuse treatment services. Yet, probation agencies are unlikely to offer direct substance abuse services from the probation officer or through connections to contractual or designated treatment placements. Table 15.3 provides the percentage of agencies that offer various services and the estimated number of probationers/parolees who can participate in these services. The average daily population (ADP) of probationers (median) illustrates the percentage of probationers in the average probation office. The

Table 15.2: Prevalence of Screening, Assessment, and Services as Reported in the National Criminal Justice Treatment Practices Survey, 2005

Program/Service	% Community Corrections Agencies
Criminal risk assessment	33.3
Substance abuse assessment	49.0
HIV/AIDS testing	11.9
HIV/AIDS counsel & treatment	12.9
TB screening	11.9
Hepatitis C screening	11.3
Physical health services	13.4
Assessment for mental health	19.2
Mental health counseling	18.3
Assessment for co-occurring disorder	19.6
Counseling for co-occurring disorders	17.9
Family therapy/counseling	12.8
Domestic violence intervention	19.4
Communication or social skills development	10.9
Life skills management	17.3
Anger or stress management	18.4
Cognitive skills development	17.5
Job placement/voc. counseling	19.2

Source: Taxman, Perdoni, and Harrison (2007).

majority of available treatment services are drug and alcohol education and group counseling, which are most appropriate for those with substance use disorders. They require more intensive services, such as intensive outpatient programs (26+ hours a week) and therapeutic communities (either specialized or not).

What Is the Success of Probation?

The BJS, in their most recent analysis of probation supervision, found that the current completion rate is slightly higher than in the last decade; 73 percent of probationers complete supervision, of which 82 percent fulfill conditions and 18 percent are unsuccessful in completing the conditions of release (Bonczar 2008). This means that with a probation population of 4.3 million, nearly 500,000 probationers are unsuccessful. Very little information is available about those who are unsuccessful, including whether they are misdemeanor or felony offenders. For those who are unsuccessful, 41 percent are revoked and reincarcerated for the existing charge, 29 percent are incarcerated for new charges, and the status of the remainder is unknown (Glaze and Bonczar 2008). In some instances, the offender is revoked from probation supervision and may be placed back on probation with slightly different conditions, depending on the sentencing judge. Offenders reincarcerated due to probation and parole revocations are about half of the new intakes to state prisons in any given year.

Even though 73 percent of offenders successfully complete the period of supervision, public concern is that probation is not effective enough. It is unclear whether success is related to the time under probation supervision or a post-supervision period.

Table 15.3. Substance Abuse Treatment Services in Community Supervision as Reported in the National Criminal Justice Treatment Practices Survey, 2005

Type of Services	% with Services	Estimated Offenders	% ADP (median)	% Programs > 90 days
Drug/alcohol education	53.1	190,906	8.6	56.9
Substance abuse group counseling	47.1	141,263	3.3	62.8
Intensive substance abuse group counseling	1.5	2,449	1.1	24.2
Therapeutic community- (segregated)	3.7	17,579	2.6	77.2
Therapeutic community (non-segregated)	3.4	9,815	6.6	86.8
Relapse prevention groups	34.3	43,740	1.3	57.4
Case management	7.1	93,088	18	88.4

The discipline is split on this question. Similar issues in understanding success and failure arise in other fields, both in terms of what is expected for the problem behavior (in this case offending) and what is feasible to achieve. Research outside the criminal justice arena has identified high failure rates for behavior changes that require alterations in one's daily lifestyle, such as medical management of asthma, diabetes, or cardiac problems, or psychological disorders such as depression, substance abuse, and bipolar disorders. Behavior, attitudes, or value changes are generally difficult to achieve (see McLellan et al. 2000) due to the habituated nature of the behavior, the extent to which individuals must vary their daily routines and regulate life factors, and the challenge of maintaining the changes, particularly in certain environments.

Consider substance abuse treatment, where the public concern about completion rates and tolerance for relapse is similar to that of probation. McLellan and colleagues (2000) examined the failure rate associated with substance abuse treatment, where the typical completion rate was around 40 percent. For those who are successfully discharged, nearly half do not use drugs in one year post-discharge, whereas another 15 to 30 percent have not fully relapsed into dependency. McLellan and colleagues (2000) note that "problems of low socioeconomic status, comorbid psychiatric status, and lack of family and social supports are among the most important predictors of low adherence" (p. 1693). Completion rates for substance abuse treatment are comparable to programs for asthma and hypertension (around 40 percent) and other disorders that require behavioral change (including diet, nutrition, and exercise). Post-involvement adherence to the regimes for behavioral-related disorders in treatment is around 30 percent, which means that 70 percent do not adhere. Adding to the parallel with substance abuse treatment, the percentage of patients with chronic physical disorders (e.g., asthma, diabetes, and hypertension) who need subsequent treatment is anywhere from 40 to 70 percent. Longitudinal studies on substance use disorders confirm disorders that require lifestyle changes frequently require multiple interventions (often referred to as a treatment career, see Hser et al. 1998) and that increased durations between relapses are signals of improvements. Criminal behavior, much of which is habitual and lifestyle oriented, is similar to disorders such as substance abuse. In the field of behavioral health, there is growing understanding of the complexities of behavioral change (see Prochaska, DiClemente, and Norcross 1992) and the need for reinforcements to support and maintain lifestyle changes. While the impression is that probation is not effective, a 27 percent failure rate is relatively low compared to analogous programming.

The general impression that probation has failed is sometimes based on the fact that over 50 percent of probationers have had a prior conviction (Glaze and Bonczar 2008). The fact that offenders are rearrested and resentenced to probation contributes to a belief that probation is an exercise in futility. The fact that many offenders sentenced to prison or jail have previously been successful on probation only adds to this perception. One should not judge probation too quickly by these standards, however. The same critique could be applied to incarceration or any punishment where repeat behavior is likely to occur. This raises the important question of whether probation reduces criminal behavior more or less than other sanctions that may be dispensed by the justice system.

The Impact of Probation on Crime Rates or Reoffending

A meta-analysis comparing the effects of prison (custodial or confinement in closed settings) and probation (community sanctions) identified a pool of 27 studies that measured the impact on reoffending. In the original studies, the reoffending rate was lower for community probation in 11 out of 13 comparisons where there are significant findings and in 14 out of the 27 comparisons that had non-significant findings. Only 2 of the 27 studies found differences that favored custodial sanctions. Among the 27, there were only five studies of high enough methodological quality to be included in the meta-analysis: four randomized experiments and one natural experiment. Grouping these data yielded positive findings in favor of non-custodial sanctions, but the effect sizes were small and not statistically significant. The authors concluded that they were "unable to say whether non-custodial sanctions are more effective to prevent re-offending than custodial sanctions." (Killias, Villettaz, and Zoder 2006, p. 43). This echoed the earlier conclusions of Smith, Goggin, and Gendreau (2002).

The original studies used in these meta-analyses are like comparative effectiveness studies that classify probation as the "treatment as usual" or standard protocol. This perspective assists in understanding the effectiveness of probation supervision overall—most studies that compare two feasible options (incarceration vs. sanctions) in probation supervision tend to have similar outcomes as other sanctions. That is, while the findings may be "null," they suggest that probation offers a sentencing option that might address other goals of reducing costs, providing a response that is proportionate to the offense as well as providing options that can be justified on other philosophical perspectives.

Table 15.4. Use of Evidence-Based Practices

Evidence-Based Practices (EBPs) **as reported in the National Criminal Justice Treatment Practices Survey, 2005**	% CC Agencies Implementing EBP
Use of a standardized substance abuse assessment tool (e.g., Addiction Severity Index, Substance Abuse Screening Inventory, etc.)	44%
Use of a standardized risk assessment tool (e.g., Level of Service Inventory-Revised, Wisconsin Risk and Need Assessment Tool)	34%
Employ techniques to engage the offender in treatment (e.g., motivational interviewing, motivational enhancements)	22%
Use of treatment orientations that are evidence-based (e.g., therapeutic communities, behavioral modification, cognitive-behavioral therapy)	12%
Use of comprehensive treatment methods that address the multiple needs of offenders	85%
Address co-occurring mental health and substance abuse disorders through integrated treatment models	25%
Involve family in the treatment process	10%
Use of treatment programs that are a minimum of 90 days or more	40%
Have policies and procedures that integrate with other agencies to provide services for drug-involved offenders (systems integration)	67%
Continuing care that provides for multiple stages of treatment, including aftercare	41%
Drug testing used frequently to monitor progress of the offender	59%
Use of a graduated sanctions schedule that ensures predictable, escalating reactions to negative offender behavior	37%
Use of an incentives schedule that ensures predictable reactions to positive offender behavior	53%
Mean Number of Evidence-Based Practices Implemented	**5.0**

IV. WHAT ARE THE ACTIVE INGREDIENTS OF PROBATION SUPERVISION?

Probation supervision is built on the premise that the contact between the officer and the offender helps suppress criminal behavior and improve compliance to conditions of release. The core component of supervision—contacts—has been empirically tested in a limited fashion. There have been no experiments or studies on whether being on probation (i.e., having contacts between the probation officer and offender) as opposed to having no oversight has any impact on offender behavior. This limits our ability to understand how probation can lead to more desirable outcomes.

A small body of literature has examined the impact of probation on per-person offending rates. Researchers tend to find a small effect of being on probation to reduce offending during the period of supervision. MacKenzie and Li (2002) found that, during the period of supervision, probationer's self-reported offending rates decreased slightly. They found that having more conditions of supervision or requirements did not impact offending rates or changes in offending behavior. While no significant body of work exists on the impact of probation on lambda (offending rates), it does appear that being on supervision has some impact but that the impact is not statistically significant. Absent experimental studies with a true control group (no supervision), it is difficult to know whether supervision has any impact. MacKenzie and Li's work clearly raises serious questions about the value of added conditions of release during supervision, given that the additional conditions do not appear to have a deterrent effect. And, given that increased conditions tend to result in more technical violations, the consequences of increased conditions is to offer more opportunities for more revocations or negative supervision findings.

The lack of research on the core efficacy of probation supervision limits the development of theories about how supervision can assist in improving offender outcomes. The main questions about supervision surround the concept of caseload size, such as: (1) What is the optimal size of the caseload a probation officer can manage to increase the success on probation? ; and, (2) What impact does increasing the contact between the probation officer and the probationer have on unwanted behaviors? The question about caseload size was addressed in several randomized trials to assess whether a caseload of 25 to 40 (depending on the study) had an impact on offending behavior as compared to large caseloads. The theory was that the assignment of too many probationers to a single officer will reduce the effectiveness of supervision (MacKenzie 2000; Taxman 2002). Most of the findings were null, meaning that the size of the caseload did not matter. However, it is difficult to interpret this literature since it did not address the full range of caseload sizes. That is, contemporary caseloads exceed 100:1, and there is not a research base to determine how caseloads greater than 40 perform compared to smaller caseloads. Since the concept of size of caseload was not associated with a particular theory of supervision, the studies did not contribute to a better understanding of what the probation officer should do as part of supervision.

Next, dosage studies (i.e., "frequency of contact") were conducted to determine how much contact is needed to improve offender outcomes. This set of studies was built on similar theoretical deficits in that they did not test different styles of supervision—only how often probation officers met with probationers. Petersilia and Turner (1993), in the largest multi-site randomized trial (13 sites for probation supervision and 2 for parole), found that intensive supervision services (the amount of required contacts varied by site) did increase the average contacts between the officer and probationer, increased the use of drug testing to detect drug use, increased detection of technical violations for those being observed more frequently, but had no impact on rearrest rates for criminal behavior. The increased contact model has been found to be ineffective in reducing criminal behavior and may actually increase technical violations (Aos, Miller, and Drake 2006; MacKenzie 2006).

Advancing the Theories of Probation Supervision

John Augustus's original concept of probation was to assist the offender to become attached to the social norms of society. His model was very much like the relationship-based model of supervision that has appeared in the contemporary literature. In this model, the offender must have a supportive, trusting relationship with the supervision staff in order to reduce offending behavior.

Theoretical Relationship-Based Models of Supervision

The question of which theoretical framework is best for probation supervision remains largely unanswered (Taxman 2002, 2008). For example, one theoretical dimension that remains untested is the different type of working alliance or trust between the probation officer and the probationer. While the Petersilia and Turner (1993) large-scale randomized experiment did not differentiate programs by the nature of the supervision, the study findings suggested that when the officer assumed a resource broker role (i.e., linkage with treatment and employment resources), offenders had fewer arrests and violations. This was confirmed in the recent meta-analyses that identified supervision combined with attendance at treatment (with the possibility that the probation officer is a resource broker, social worker, or behavioral manager) as effective in reducing recidivism (ES-=.07) (Aos et al. 2006). A number of quasi-and experimental studies have had similar findings (Paparozzi and Gendreau 2005; Petersilia and Turner 1993).

Byrne (2009) has proposed that supervision should be guided by three main principles: concentration on person, place, and time. The emphasis on person moves probation into more of a client-centered emphasis in which the goal is to tailor probation conditions and style of supervision to the individual. It draws heavily from the theoretical literature regarding reducing the risk of the individual by attending to dynamic criminogenic needs through specific case plans and responsive treatment programs. A major component of the model—besides the hard technology of using standardized tools for screening and assessment and placement in appropriate programming—is the emphasis on the "soft" technology of deportment or the relationship between officer and offender (Taxman 2002; Taxman, Shepardson, and Byrne 2004; Taxman 2008). This model draws upon the importance of probationers and officers having a working relationship to address the general factors that affect involvement in criminal conduct. Recent studies illustrate how improved working relationships (e.g., empathy, trust, care, voice) have a positive relationship with offender outcomes (Taxman and Ainsworth 2009). Probationers (with mental health conditions) who perceived their officer to be tough had more failures and higher numbers of violations than those who did not (Skeem et al. 2007). Studies have found that when offenders reported that they had a "voice" (i.e., the probation/probation officer allowed the offender to participate in deciding the type of sanctions for failure to comply with requirements), reductions occurred in both arrests and positive drug tests (Taxman and Thanner 2004). While recognizing the importance of the person-centered model in supervision, James Bonta and colleagues in Canada studied whether probation officers have the appropriate interpersonal skills, role modeling, and communication skills to work effectively with offenders in an evidence-based practices model of risk, needs, and responsivity. The general findings from their studies are that probation officers do not have these skills, and even if the officers have the skills, they do not use them (Bonta et al. 2008).

A few prospective studies have been conducted to test the efficacy of different person-centered models of supervision. The first study was a four-site randomized experiment that Taxman and colleagues implemented in 1998. This study involved placing a treatment counselor at a probation office to screen offenders for substance abuse disorders and then placing the offenders in appropriate treatment. The probation/parole officer's role was that of resource broker, working with the treatment counselor on treatment access, monitoring compliance with drug treatment, and responding to positive drug test results. The study resulted in increased access to treatment services and increased days in treatment, but the seamless intervention was more costly to deliver and did not result in reduced recidivism across all offenders (Alemi et al. 2006; Taxman, Thanner, and Weisburd 2006). The study did find that the seamless system process reduced arrests and opiate drug use for high-risk offenders (Thanner and Taxman 2003; Taxman and Thanner 2006). The lack of impact on rearrest or technical violations may be attributable to the study's failure to address the quality of treatment services offered to offenders. A continuing study is underway that focuses on improving the quality of treatment, an element that was lacking in the first study (Taxman, Wilson, and Trotman 2007).

Another study focused on the role of the probation/parole officer as a behavioral manager using a six-site trial. The Step 'n Out study required the officer and treatment provider to work together on a collaborative behavioral management (CBM) process of accessing treatment needs, reviewing treatment progress, and using a structured reward schedule to incentivize offenders for positive behavior (Friedmann et al. 2008). The project motto of "Catching People Doing Things Right" reflects the nature of the intervention, which creates the conditions to notice and reward offenders for achieving incremental pro-social steps as part of normal supervision (contingency management). CBM establishes a systematic, standardized, and progressive approach to reinforcement and sanctioning to ensure consistency and fairness. Study findings appear to indicate that improved outcomes occur when the officer has a working alliance with the offender (Friedmann, Rhodes, and Taxman 2009).

Finally, the Proactive Community Supervision (PCS) Study (Taxman 2008) tested a behavioral management style of probation supervision. This was a place-based design in which four probation/parole offices in Maryland implemented a behavioral manager supervision style that cast them as resource broker and counselor. The comparison group consisted of four similar offices that maintained their existing enforcement or hybrid style of supervision. When controlling for length of time on supervision and prior criminal history, logistic regression results found that offenders who were supervised in the behavioral management style were less likely to be rearrested (30 percent for the PCS and 42 percent of the non-PCS sample; $p < 0.01$) and less likely to have a warrant issued for technical violations, although this pattern is approaching significance (34.7 percent of the PCS group and 40 percent for the non-PCS group; $p < 0.10$). A recent replication of this study conducted in Travis County, Texas, used a pre-post model and found reductions in rearrest for felony offenders as well as reductions in recidivism for all three risk levels (Sprow 2009).

Theoretical-Based Models That Emphasize Place and Time (see Byrne 2009)

A movement toward temporal and spatially based supervision has evolved. The increasing awareness that offenders are concentrated in certain neighborhoods has spurred an interest in community-based probation models that focus on ameliorating the risks of the individual and the place. These models are based on the premise that the concentration of offenders into typically resource-deprived communities only serves to undermine supervision; the pressures of the community override the requirements of supervision. A few test models (referenced above) have been conducted using this concept of concentrated supervision (Maryland Proactive Community Supervision and Travis County, Texas) (Taxman 2008; Eisenberg et al. 2009) and also incorporated the general framework of the evidence-based supervision relying on risk-needs-responsivity (RNR). The Maryland PCS study found a positive impact comparing the PCS communities with the non-PCS offices, whereas the Travis County study did not explore this issue. More studies are needed, particularly to assess the role of the supervision officer and the type of relationships (with the offender, the community, the support system of the offender) on supervision outcomes.

Similarly, Byrne (2009) points out that targeting supervision at high-risk times—generally the early part of the supervision period—is a sound strategy for reducing recidivism. This emphasis on temporal factors is important since probationers' conduct during the early period of supervision affects successful outcomes (MacKenzie and Brame 2001; MacKenzie and Li 2002). During the early period of supervision, offenders are most likely to test the conditions of release and determine whether the probation officer pays attention to these conditions. Their judgment of "how serious" the probation system is tends to affect later behavior. If probation officers give lax attention to the conditions imposed, then the probationers are less likely to obey them. The research on temporally based supervision, however, lacks a test of the theoretical framework other than "tightening the noose" during the early periods of supervision.

V. Advancing the Field of Corrections

Over the last two decades, the "what works" movement from Canada has had a profound impact on the field of corrections, reframing the theories of how corrections overall can be a tool in offender change. The "what works" movement is accompanied by a set of core principles about effective interventions. As noted by Cullen (2005), these principles are based on four insights that have advanced the field: (1) the principles are based on theory and research; (2) identifying interventions or treatments that are changing dynamic factors; (3) specifying that interventions take into account individual differences such as anxiety, maturity levels, etc.; and, (4) targeting interventions for higher risk offenders. With a documented 30 percent reduction of recidivism when applying the works principles (Andrews and Bonta 1998), this approach challenged the conventional wisdom that supported only efforts aimed at punishment or deterrence.

The "what works" movement illustrates how community punishments are incapable of achieving the goals of deterrence, since behavior change is shaped by experiences and responses to behaviors that are the targets of change. Recently, Andrews and Bonta (2010, 42-43) noted that:

> To answer the question as to why the get tough criminal justice policy failed, one does not need to look far. The answer resides in the psychology of punishment. Psychologists have been studying punishment under well-controlled laboratory conditions with animals and humans for nearly a hundred years (e.g., Hoge & Stocking 1912). During the course of that century of research, much has been learned and a review of this body of knowledge would quickly demonstrate the folly of punishment as being the backbone of criminal justice policy.
>
> The effectiveness of punishment in suppressing behavior depends upon some very specific conditions. . . .

1. Punishment must be at maximum intensity. Lower levels of intensity may lead to tolerance and temporary effects. Applying very intense levels of punishment for a first offence is unlikely unless it is a very serious offence (e.g., murder). It would be hard to imagine, for example, a sentence of 10 years for an individual's first theft or first assault, as it offends our sense of justice and fairness.

2. Punishment must be immediate. A delay between the behavior and the punishment provides opportunities for other behaviors to be reinforced. An offender who commits a criminal act is likely not to be apprehended (thereby, creating opportunities for further criminal behavior that is rewarded) and, if caught, may be released until trial (once again, opportunities for further reinforced criminal behavior).

3. Punishment must be consistently applied. Related to #2, a failure to punish provides opportunities for undesirable behaviors to be rewarded. People are always behaving, and rewarding or punishing consequences follow. Unless the offender is punished for each and every criminal action, which is highly unlikely, criminal behavior will be rewarded.

4. Opportunities to escape or access alternative rewards must be blocked. Obviously, no one likes to be punished. When punished, one of two things may result: Escape behavior ensues that, if successful, serves to reinforce the escape behavior and maintain the early behavior that first led to punishment (e.g., the bank robber who escapes from prison only to rob again). Second, in order to avoid punishment the person may seek rewarding alternatives. When considering a specific criminal act that is likely to be punished, the alternative may be another form of criminal behavior that was successful in the past. For high-risk offenders with a large antisocial behavioral repertoire, punishing one antisocial type of behavior (e.g., assault) may only be replaced with another (e.g., stealing) unless the antisocial alternative is unavailable.

All of the above conditions consider only how punishment needs to be delivered to suppress behavior. They do not address characteristics of the person that may interact with the application of punishment. In situations where punishment is not delivered with immediacy and certainty, it may still be effective with certain types of people. For example, those who are future oriented and have good self-monitoring and regulation skills can make the connections between the problem behavior and the negative consequences that may occur days, weeks, or months later. However, many offenders are impulsive (Gottfredson and Hirschi 1990) and underestimate the chances of being punished (Piquero and Pogarsky 2002). There is even some evidence that punishment can lead to increased offending through operation of the "gambler's fallacy." That is, "if I was punished now then it is unlikely that I will get caught and be punished again" (Pogarsky and Piquero, 2003). In addition, applying "maximum" punishment can have undesired consequences ranging from learned helplessness (Seligman 1975) to retaliatory aggression (McCord 1997). The long and short of this is that one cannot possibly expect that a policy centered on punishment can reduce criminal behavior. (pp. 43-44)

Andrews and Bonta (2010) illustrate how the basic premise of punishment cannot be achieved through control-oriented sanctions, given the nature of justice and correctional processes. The challenge to the field of corrections overall, and probation and community corrections specifically, is to develop a punishment system that can be effective in changing behavior. The "what works" principles have been translated into a set of evidence-based practices that are recommended to implement a theory-driven process of offender change. The theory is based on responding to specific offender risk and needs in programming, services, and controls in such a manner to achieve better outcomes. Table 15.4 illustrates the accepted evidence-based practices that have been identified as they affect probation and community control programming in the United States as well as the percentage of probation agencies that indicate that they have the practice in place (see Friedmann, Taxman, and Henderson 2007). This information is from the National Criminal Justice Treatment Practices Survey (see above) using a nationally representative sample of probation agencies.

From this survey, the following appear to be the most salient features of a probation system that is effective in reducing recidivism:

1. *Manage risk levels: Target high-risk offenders.* Andrews and Bonta (1998) articulated the general policy that high-risk offenders should be triaged into more structured control and intensive treatment services than lower-risk individuals. The focus on high-risk offenders is to address their behavior that threatens public safety, as well as to ensure that probation agencies use limited resources to address their risk factors. The high-risk offenders are better suited to intermediate sanctions or other more intensive programs than other offenders. Medium-risk offenders with complex criminogenic needs should be targeted in a similar manner to reduce the odds of recidivism.

2. *Manage risk levels: Monitor with a "light touch" low-risk offenders.* Given that nearly half of the probationers are first-time offenders, many probation agencies are required to supervise offenders who have low probability of reinvolvement in the justice system. Lowenkamp, Latessa, and Hoslinger (2006), in a review of halfway houses in Ohio, found that high-risk offenders tended to have lower recidivism rates when the halfway house had a larger percentage of high-risk offenders, but low-risk offenders did not fare well in that environment. A recent study of strategies to supervise low-risk offenders, Barnes et al. (2010), found that reduced contacts (average of 2.5 per year) compared to traditional rates (average 4.5 per year) had similar recidivism results.

3. *Treat dynamic criminogenic needs* (i.e., substance abuse, impulsive behavior, criminal peers, and criminal thinking). As highlighted above, moving toward the use of treatment services for probationers who are moderate- to high-risk and targeting the interventions to specific criminogenic needs are key EBP principles. Treatment serves to provide structure in the community whereas cognitive behavioral therapy or therapeutic community builds the skills of the person to manage his or her own criminogenic needs. Similar to substance abusers, treatment provides a first step.

4. *Manage compliance.* In any behavioral disorder, initiating treatment or services is first step. But the more difficult process is one of retention or engaging in the treatment services. Probation agencies, through the use of various forms of "coerced treatment" (i.e., conditions, drug treatment court, etc.) have the advantage of assisting the offender to comply with treatment orders. Prior research on drug-involved offenders ordered to treatment services is that compliance is equal to or slightly greater than those who volunteer for services (Hubbard et al. 1997). Similarly, the use of incentives is an important component to retention in treatment. "Earned discharge" programs that allow offenders to earn abatement of supervision time (see Petersilia 2007 for a discussion for parolees) are examples of such an incentive process.

5. *Create an environment for offender change.* The punishment culture of probation can interfere with the building of a trusting relationship on supervision. As noted by Taxman and Ainsworth (2009), a supportive working relationship between the offender and the probation officer is an important component of the change process.

Overall, we know little about the ingredients of effective probation supervision. Research is clearly needed to advance practice in the field. From our present knowledge, following the five principles above provides the best foot forward to handle the community corrections population. As Morris and Tonry (1991) highlighted, a community corrections system is needed to balance mass incarceration policies. It is incumbent upon the field to move in this direction, but the efforts should be guided by caution in control-oriented policies. The gains from punishment are quite limited, whereas the gains from evidence-based community corrections systems have no fixed ceiling . Building our knowledge base about effective practices in this domain should guide us for the next decade.

REFERENCES

Alemi, F., F. Taxman, H. Baghi, J. Vang, M. Thanner, and V. *Doyon.* 2006. "Costs and Benefits of Combining Probation and Substance Abuse Treatment." *Journal of Mental Health Policy and Economics* 9(2): 57–70.

Andrews, D. A., and J. Bonta. 1998. *The Psychology of Criminal Conduct.* Cincinnati, OH: Anderson Publishing.

Andrews, D. A., and J. Bonta, 2010. "Rehabilitating Criminal Justice Policy and Practice." *Psychology, Public Policy, and Law* 16(1): 39–55.

Aos, S., M. Miller, and E. Drake. 2006. *Evidence-Based Adult Corrections Programs: What Works and What Does Not.* Olympia: Washington State Institute for Public Policy.

Barnes, G. C., L. Ahlman, C. Gill, L. W. Sherman, E. Kurtz, and R. Malvestuto. 2010. "Low-intensity Community Supervision for Low-Risk Offenders: A Randomized, Controlled Trial." *Journal of Experimental Criminology* 6(2): 159–189.

Bonczar, Thomas. 1997. *Characteristics of Adults on Probation, 1995.* Bureau of Justice Statistics Special Report. Rockville, MD: Bureau of Justice Statistics, U.S. Department of Justice.

Bonta, James, Tanya Rugge, Terri-Lynne Scott, Guy Bourgon, and Annie K. Yessine. 2008. "Exploring the Black Box of Community Supervision." *Journal of Offender Rehabilitation* 47(3): 248–270.

Bonczar, Thomas. 2008. *Characteristics of State Parole Supervising Agencies, 2006.* Washington, DC: Bureau of Justice Statistics.

Byrne, James. 2009. *A Review of the Evidence on the Effectiveness of Alternative Sanctions and an Assessment of the Likely Impact of Federal Sentencing Guideline Reform on Public Safety.* Written Testimony before the United States Sentencing Commission, July 10.

Cullen, F. 2005. "The Twelve People Who Saved Rehabilitation: How the Science of Criminology Made a Difference." *Criminology* 43(1): 1–42.

DeMichele, M. 2007. *Probation and Parole's Growing Caseloads and Workload Allocation: Strategies for Managerial Decision Making*. Kentucky: American Probation and Parole Association. Available at: http://www.appa-net.org/eweb/docs/appa/pubs/SMDM.pdf doiMay312010.

Eisenberg, M., Bryl, J., and Fabelo, T. 2009. *Travis County Community Impact Supervision Project: Analyzing Initial Outcomes*. New York: Justice Center, The Council of State Governments.

Friedmann, Peter D., Elizabeth C. Katz, Anne G. Rhodes, Faye S. Taxman, Daniel J. O'Connell, Linda K. Frisman, William M. Burdon, Bennett W. Fletcher, Mark D. Litt, Jennifer Clarke, and Steven S. Martin. 2008. "Collaborative Behavioral Management for Drug-Involved Parolees: Rationale and Design of the Step'n Out Study." *Journal of Offender Rehabilitation* 47(3): 290–318.

Friedmann, Peter, Anne Rhodes, and Faye Taxman. 2009. "Collaborative Behavioral Management: Integration and Intensification of Parole and Outpatient Addiction Treatment Services in the Step'n Out Study." *Journal of Experimental Criminology* 5(3): 227–243.

Friedmann, Peter, Faye Taxman, and Craig Henderson. 2007. "Evidence-based Treatment Practices for Drug-Involved Adults in the Criminal Justice System." *Journal of Substance Abuse Treatment* 32(3): 267–277.

Garland, David. 2001. *The Culture of Control: Crime and Social Order in Contemporary Society*. New York: Oxford University Press.

Gill, C. E. 2010. "The Effects of Sanction Intensity on Criminal Conduct: A Randomized Low-Intensity Probation Experiment." *Publicly Accessible Penn Dissertations*, Paper 121. Available at: http://repository.upenn.edu/edissertations/121.

Gill, C. E., J. Hyatt, and L. W. Sherman. 2009. "Probation Intensity Effects on Probationers' Criminal Conduct: Title Registration." *Campbell Systematic Reviews*. Available at: http://www.campbellcollaboration.org/lib/download/677/.

Glaze, L., and T. Bonczar. 2008. *Probation and Parole in the United States, 2007 Statistical Tables*. Washington DC: Bureau of Justice Statistics.

Gottfredson, Michael R., and Travis Hirschi. 1990. *A General Theory of Crime*. Stanford, CA: Stanford University Press.

Hoge, Mildred A., and Ruth J. Stocking. 1912. "A Note on the Relative Value of Punishment and Reward as Motives." *Journal of Animal Behavior* 2(1): 43–50.

Hser, Y., C. Grella, C. Chou, and M. D. Anglin. 1998. "Relationships Between Drug Treatment Careers and Outcomes: Findings From the National Drug Abuse Treatment Outcome Study." *Evaluation Review* 22(4): 496–519.

Hubbard, R. L., S. G. Craddock, P. M. Flynn, J. Anderson, and R. M. Etheridge. 1997. "Overview of 1-year Follow-up Outcomes in DATOS." *Psychology of Addictive Behavior* 11(4): 261–278.

Killias, M., P. Villettaz, and I. Zoder. 2006. *The Effects of Custodial vs. Non-custodial Sentences on Re-offending: A Systematic Review of the State of Knowledge*. Report to the Campbell Collaboration Crime and Justice Group, Institute of Criminology and Criminal Law, University of Lausanne, Switzerland.

Lowenkamp, C. T., E. Latessa, and A. Hoslinger. 2006. "The Risk Principle in Action: What Have We Learned from 13,676 Offenders and 97 Correctional Programs?" *Crime and Delinquency* 52(1): 77–93.

MacKenzie, Doris Layton. 2000. "Evidence-Based Corrections: Identifying What Works." *Crime and Delinquency* 46(4): 457–461.

MacKenzie, Doris Layton. 2006. *What Works in Corrections: Reducing the Criminal Activities of Offenders and Delinquents*. Cambridge: Cambridge University Press.

Mackenzie, Doris Layton, and Robert Brame. 2001. "Community Supervision, Prosocial Activities, and Recidivism." *Justice Quarterly* 18(2): 429–448.

MacKenzie, Doris Layton, and Spencer De Li. 2002. "The Impact of Formal and Informal Social Controls on the Criminal Activities of Probationers." *Journal of Research in Crime and Delinquency* 39(3): 243–276.

McCord, Joan. 1997. "Discipline and the Use of Sanctions." *Aggression and Violent Behavior* 2(4): 313–319.

McLellan, A. T., T. A. Hagan, M. Levine, F. Gould, K. Meyers, M. Bencivengo, and J. Durell. 1998. "Supplemental Social Services Improve Outcomes in Public Addiction Treatment." *Addiction* 93(10): 1489–1499.

McLellan, A. T., D. C. Lewis, C. P. O'Brien, and H. D. Kleber. 2000. "Drug Dependence, a Chronic Medical Illness: Implications for Treatment, Insurance, and Outcomes Evaluation." *JAMA* 284(13): 1689–1695.

Morris, Norval, and Michael Tonry. 1991. *Between Prison and Probation: Intermediate Punishments in a Rational Sentencing System.* New York: Oxford University Press.

Mumola, C. J., and T. P. Bonczar. 1998. *Substance Abuse and Treatment of Adults on Probation, 1995.* Rockville, MD: Bureau of Justice Statistics.

Paparozzi, Mario A., and Paul Gendreau. 2005. "An Intensive Supervision Program That Worked: Service Delivery, Professional Orientation, and Organizational Supportiveness." *The Prison Journal* 85(4): 445–466.

Petersilia, J. 2007. "Employ Behavioral Contracting for 'Earned Discharge' Parole." *Criminology and Public Policy* 6(4): 807–814.

Petersilia, J., and S. Turner. 1993. *Evaluating Intensive Supervision Probation/Parole: Results of a Nationwide Experiment.* Washington, DC: National Institute of Justice.

Piquero, Alex R., and Greg Pogarsky. 2002. "Beyond Stafford and Warr's Reconceptualization of Deterrence: Personal and Vicarious Experiences, Impulsivity, and Offending Behavior." *Journal of Research in Crime and Delinquency* 39(2): 153–186.

Pogarsky, Greg, and Alex R. Piquero. 2003. "Can Punishment Encourage Offending? Investigating The 'Resetting' Effect." *Journal of Research in Crime and Delinquency* 40(1): 95–120.

Prochaska, J. O., C. C. DiClemente, and J. C. Norcross. 1992. "In Search of How People Change: Applications to Addictive Behaviors." *American Psychologist* 47(9): 1102–1114.

Sacks, Stanley. 2000. "Co-occurring Mental and Substance Use Disorders: Promising Approaches and Research Issues." *Substance Use & Misuse* 35(12): 2061.

Seligman, Martin E. P. 2005. *Helplessness: On Depression, Development and Death.* San Francisco: W. H. Freeman.

Shilton, Mary, and Neil Weisfield. 2008. *Getting in Sync: State-Local Fiscal Partnerships for Public Safety.* Washington, DC: The Pew Charitable Trusts, July.

Skeem, Jennifer L., Jennifer Eno Louden, Devon Polaschek, and Jacqueline Camp. 2007. "Assessing Relationship Quality in Mandated Community Treatment: Blending Care with Control." *Psychological Assessment* 19(4): 397–410.

Smith, P., C. Goggin, and P. Gendreau. 2002. *The Effects of Prison Sentences and Intermediate Sanctions on Recidivism: General Effects and Individual Differences.* Ottawa, Canada: Solicitor General Canada.

Sprow, M. 2009. "The Probation Experiment." *County Magazine* 21(3): 24–28.

Taxman, F. 2002. "Supervision—Exploring the Dimensions of Effectiveness." *Federal Probation* 66(2): 14–27.

Taxman, F. S. 2007. *Probation Delivered in the U.S.* Washington, DC: Criminal Justice Drug Abuse Treatment Studies Meeting.

Taxman, F. S. 2008. "No Illusion, Offender and Organizational Change in Maryland's Proactive Community Supervision Model." *Criminology and Public Policy* 7(2): 275–302.

Taxman, F. S., and S. A. Ainsworth. 2009. "Correctional Milieu: The Key to Quality Outcomes." *Victims and Offenders* 4(4): 334–340.

Taxman, F. S, M. L Perdoni, and L. D. Harrison. 2007. "Drug Treatment Services for Adult Offenders: The State of the State." *Journal of Substance Abuse Treatment* 32(3): 239–254.

Taxman, F. S., E. Shepardson, and J. M. Byrne. 2004. *Tools of the Trade: A Guide to Implementing Science into Practice.* Washington, DC: National Institute of Corrections.

Taxman, F. S., and M. Thanner. 2004. "Probation from a Therapeutic Perspective: Results from the Field." *Contemporary Issues in Law* 7(1): 39–63.

Taxman, F. S., and M. Thanner. 2006. "Risk, Need, & Responsivity (RNR): It All Depends." *Crime and Delinquency* 52(1): 28–52.

Taxman, F. S., M. Thanner, D. Weisburd. 2006. *Comparison of Findings on the Seamless System Model.* Fairfax, VA: George Mason University.

Taxman, F. S., A. Trotman, and M. Wilson, 2007. *SOARING: A Supervision Treatment Manual.* Fairfax, VA: George Mason University.

Thanner, M., and F. Taxman. 2003. "Responsivity: The Value of Providing Intensive Services to High-Risk Offenders." *Journal of Substance Abuse Treatment* 24(2): 137–147.

Section C
Jails, Prisons, and Other Secure Facilities

CHAPTER 16

JAILS, PRE-TRIAL DETENTION, AND SHORT TERM CONFINEMENT

LIEUTENANT GARY F. CORNELIUS (RETIRED)

JAIL—THE word brings to the minds of most people visions of brick buildings with bars and heavy padlocks on the doors. Every jurisdiction in the United States—whether a city, county, or town—either operates a jail or has combined resources with other jurisdictions to have access to a jail. The local jail—whether a county jail, regional jail, or city jail—is the first stop on the incarceration highway for adult offenders and in some cases for juveniles. Jails in many ways are visible to the public through the Internet, news media, and so on. While some are located outside urban or dense population areas, some are located in the heart of cities and towns. Some modern jails do not look like correctional facilities; some resemble office buildings. Many are old, outdated facilities, built decades ago. The goal of this chapter is to give the reader an overview of the American jail, from its early beginnings in colonial America to the modern, efficient, well-staffed facilities of today.

To fully understand the jail, one must understand what it is not. There are three main correctional facilities in the United States: prisons, jails, and lockups. Jails are *not* prisons. A *prison* is defined as a correctional facility, administered by the federal government or a state government, that confines adult offenders who are sentenced to terms of confinement for more than one year. A *lockup* is a temporary holding facility, usually operated by the local police or sheriff's office, and is located in a station house, police station, a sheriff's substation, a municipal building, or a courthouse. Due to the vastness of the criminal justice system and the fact that some lockups are as small as one cell, the exact number of lockups cannot be ascertained. Lockups temporarily hold offenders until they are taken before a magistrate, a judge, are released on bail or personal recognizance, or are transported to a main jail facility. Lockups also hold inebriated offenders who are released when considered sober. Lockups also hold juvenile offenders, if permitted by statute, until such time that the juvenile courts place them in a juvenile detention facility, a jail if certified as an adult offender, or are released to parents or guardians.[1] Staffing and maintaining lockups require creativity. In some jurisdictions, the local sheriff's office supplies corrections deputies for lockups operated in local county police substations. If the offender does not make bond, bail, or is released on recognizance, he or she is transferred to the local jail.

A *jail* is a unique correctional facility. According to the Justice Policy Institute, the definition of jails is simple, but changing. Jails are defined as locally funded and operated correctional facilities that are centrally located in a community. While prisons hold long-term adjudicated offenders, jails hold pre-trial offenders and offenders sentenced to less than one year; many pre-trial offenders held are considered at risk to commit new crimes and are unlikely to return for a court date.[2] A recent trend is for jails to hold sentenced inmates awaiting transport to state departments of corrections. As the state correctional facilities become backed up and overcrowded, jails are forced to hold state-ready inmates, creating a backlog.

PHILOSOPHY AND FUNCTIONS OF JAILS

According to the American Correctional Association, there are 3,751 jails in the United States, divided into four categories based on size: mega jails (1,000 plus beds), large jails (250–999 beds), medium jails (50–249 beds), and small jails (1–49 beds). Most jails fall into the medium (1,487) and small (1,433) categories. There are 630 large jails in the United States and 201 mega jails.[3]

While the philosophy of jails has been to provide a place of incarceration in local communities for offenders awaiting trial or serving short periods of confinement, the functions of local jails have evolved from the simplistic view of "lock em' up" until court into a listing of multiple functions to assist various components of the criminal justice system and to lend support to community agencies.

Throughout U.S. history, jails have held offenders for short periods of time, and generally were not concerned with rehabilitation or programs. Rehabilitation of inmates is difficult inside jails due to short sentences, frequent court appearances, inmates being released on bond, and inmates finishing sentences and being transferred to other jurisdictions. By the time that inmates are classified, housed, and screened for participation in programs, many are gone. However, with a changing society come difficulties in the criminal justice system, and jails often must deal with them. Foremost is the overcrowding in U.S. correctional facilities. Jails hold offenders in cell space leased to state and federal governments and also can hold offenders for other jurisdictions. Jails also hold offenders who are awaiting transfer to federal facilities, state facilities, mental health facilities, and to the custody of Immigration and Customs Enforcement (ICE). Jails also provide secure housing for people found in contempt of court and in protective custody.[4]

Other functions of jails include the following, according to the U.S. Justice Department:[5]

- Receive and incarcerate offenders who are pending court arraignment, trial, and sentencing if convicted;
- Incarcerate violators of probation, parole, and bail/bond violators and absconders;
- Hold offenders who are mentally ill, pending transfer to treatment facilities or court actions;
- Release convicted offenders into the community per completion of sentence;
- Operate community-based programs (work release, community service, inmate labor, etc.) as alternatives to traditional incarceration;
- Hold offenders arrested on warrants from other jurisdictions (detainers) pending extradition.

Prison population growth and resulting overcrowding have affected jails by forcing them to hold more inmates for longer periods of time. Many jails incarcerate "state-ready" inmates—those inmates waiting transfer to departments of correction. Other inmates who are incarcerated longer have a variety of problems, including alcohol abuse, drug abuse, medical problems, and mental illness. According to the National Association of Counties (NACo), jails are providing programming and services in psychiatric, vocational, substance abuse, and educational areas, usually without any funding or compensation from the state.[6] Other programs in jail include library services, law library, and religious activities. The number of inmates who participate in programs varies from jail to jail, as not all jails offer the same number and type of programs. For example, in 2006 the Allegheny County Jail in Pittsburgh, Pennsylvania reported that 144 inmates earned their general equivalency diplomas (GED), the highest success rate to date.[7] The number of inmates who participate in jail programs varies among jails, as not all jails offer the same programs due to the physical plant and philosophy of the jail management. For example, a small rural jail may offer four or five programs—basics like Alcoholics Anonymous, Adult Basic Education, Sunday church, GED testing, and so on. A larger jail with classroom facilities may offer many more programs. Program availability for inmates primarily depends on how programs are viewed by agency heads. Some staff in jails consider programs a waste of time.

HISTORY AND DEVELOPMENT OF THE
AMERICAN JAIL

The American jail can trace its roots to the jails (originally called gaols; pronounced the same) of England. Gaols were locally operated, administered, and held the misfits of society, namely vagrants, drunkards, the poor, homeless, thieves, prostitutes, orphans, trespassers, children, debtors, murderers, and dissenters with the Church.[8] Each locality (shire) was responsible for the operation of the jail, a practice that has continued through today. The head public official, the *shire reeve* (now *sheriff*) could run the jail at his discretion and received reimbursements from taxes levied as fees on the wrongdoers in the jail. Corruption was rampant, as funds that were to be used for food, shelter, and so on, were pocketed. Conditions in jails soon became squalid; food was poor and jails became known for death, disease, and misery.[9]

The fee system had three negative aspects. First, jail keepers were allowed to charge inmates for admission, release, type of housing (such as open area or private cell), beds, mattresses, food, and so on. Second, the jailor could sell goods to inmates and use inmate forced labor to make a profit. Jailors were not obligated to maintain the jail, and their only responsibility was to prevent inmates from escaping. The lives of inmates were horrible. They were required to support themselves, meaning that they begged for help from family, friends, and anyone willing to help. Third, a system of extortion developed. Inmates had to pay the fees demanded upon them with whatever means they had; if they could not pay, punishments could be painful, resulting sometimes in death.[10]

The traditional practices of English jails continued in America. The earliest jail system is attributed to colony of Virginia, specifically the settlement of Jamestown Colony, later known as James City. By the seventeenth century, the Virginia colony pattern of jail construction in counties was followed by most colonies.[11] The fee system continued, and inmate labor developed from the concept of the English workhouse, resulting not in rehabilitation of inmates through work, but the pocketing of monies from such labor by corrupt jail officials. Regardless of age and gender, early American jails held orphans, prostitutes, thieves, robbers, murderers, and inebriates; all were placed in large rooms with hay and straw mattresses. Jails had no procedures for rehabilitation, treatment, or medical care. Punishment was the guiding philosophy.[12]

Jails at this time were typically small (15 feet by 10 feet), built of wood, needed constant upkeep, followed English traditions of imprisonment, and saw little progress.[13] William Penn, the Quaker governor of Pennsylvania, supported the enactment of laws requiring each county to build houses of corrections. Inmates would not be charged fees for food and lodging but would be required to perform useful work; stocks and pillories were no longer to be used. Bail was introduced. After Penn's death, these laws were repealed, but after independence was gained, a large part of these measures were restored.[14]

John Howard, the High Sheriff of Bedfordshire, England, published his recommendations for penal reform in the *State of Prisons* (1777) after being appalled at penal institutions in Europe. His far-reaching views, the forerunner of jail standards, influenced the correctional facilities of America today. According to Howard, prisons should be clean, with inmates who bathed daily and were separated by age, gender, and degree of criminal behavior. A system of inmate discipline was deemed necessary. Improved medical care, food, and laundry were recommended. Jailors should be persons of good character, sober and well paid. Random, unannounced inspections by magistrates should occur. Inspectors should hear inmate complaints and grievances and correct what is "manifestly wrong." Jailors should perform daily inspections and, with the chaplains, act as positive role models.[15]

The design and management styles of jails in American began to change, intermingling with the development of prisons. Due to the efforts of John Howard, William Penn, and Dr. Benjamin Rush (one of the signers of the Declaration of Independence), conditions in jails improved and different ideas were tried concerning how inmates were to be supervised and treated. Dr. Rush became the leader of the Philadelphia Society for Alleviating the Miseries of Public Prisons. In 1790, both the Society and Dr. Rush were instrumental in the opening of Philadelphia's Walnut Street Jail, following Penn's Quaker laws and John Howard's ideas. This jail was revolutionary—inmates were subjected to a regimen of hard work, reflection, and penance for their crimes.[16]

The Walnut Street Jail, while strict, established the early principle of prisoner classification. First constructed in 1773 as a city jail for Philadelphia, it had housed misdemeanants, debtors, and criminals who were awaiting trial or sentencing on serious charges. With the reform movement by Dr. Rush, a wing of the jail was used to house convicted felons separately from the inmate population. Some were housed in individual cells. Work programs allowed inmates to work on handicrafts, shoemaking, weaving, grinding plaster of paris, and cutting and polishing marble. As inmates hopefully were learning work skills and reflecting on their crimes, the Walnut Street Jail was termed the world's first penitentiary.[17]

The three eras of American penal development influenced how many jails were designed and operated from the 1820s through today. The *Pennsylvania system*, developed from the Walnut Street Jail, advocated keeping inmates in solitary confinement, reflecting on wrongdoing with little or no activity or work. Offenders were not to communicate or come into contact with each other. It gave way to the *Auburn system*, which housed inmates singly at night, but placed them in congregate daytime work groups. Silence and strict discipline were prevalent in the Pennsylvania and Auburn systems. In the late 1800s, the *Reformatory era* advocated education and vocational training for inmates, and indeterminate sentencing whereby inmates could earn an early release for good behavior and rehabilitative activities.[18]

While prisons in the United States made reforms that have resulted in the generally secure and humane facilities of today, jails were the "stepchild" of American corrections, described as a variety of buildings and practices, both lacking in uniformity. Michigan jails were described as having "no work, no instruction, no discipline, and no uniformity of structure" by penal reformer Enoch Wine in 1880. Jail inmates in Michigan were not classified and were just thrown together. Small rural Iowa jails were called "calabooses." The town of Grand Mound, Iowa, rented out jail beds to travelers.[19]

Jails varied by region. In the northern United States, jails were built of wood or stone, depending on the views of the authorities and costs. Many were built adjacent to the local courthouse and housed the jailor and his family. Stone gradually became the norm, but many jails built originally in the colonial era saw use for many years. Corrupt financial practices still existed. In a New York jail, inmates could get good food and bedding by paying the jailor a weekly sum. New York's Tombs had squalid conditions. In the Midwest, Hannibal, Missouri's jail was a one-room building. Council Bluffs, Iowa, boasted of its rotary jail, called a *squirrel cage jail*, which rotated the inmate housing area so staff could have access. Jails of the American West were "whatever works." Jails in frontier boom and mining towns ranged from brick to wood to basements and were so small and squalid that all the sheriff had to do was "hose it out." In the post–Civil War South, inmate labor was leased or contracted out to farms and businesses to replace slavery; inmates were transported to work sites in caged prison wagons.[20]

Through the twentieth century, conditions in jails improved but varied. For example, the Fairfax County (Virginia) Adult Detention Center underwent four major renovations from 1978 to 2000, resulting in being one of the few jails with single cell, linear, podular, and direct supervision housing. Communications equipment, security hardware, and medical services improved. But a "snapshot" of Virginia jails listed in *Who's Who in Jail Management* indicated that jails in that state range widely in age. The oldest listed was built in 1822; several others were built in 1900, 1937, 1951, and 1953.[21] In any discussion of the conditions of jails in the United States, mention must be made of the various ages of facilities. While closings and renovations of old jails and openings of new jails improve conditions for staff and inmates, the ability to effectively deal with old, substandard jails depends on the funding capability of the jurisdictions and their ability to convince taxpayers that improvements—including the building of new facilities—are desperately needed.

Though the Bureau of Justice Statistics (BJS) reports on jails are helpful to administrators, researchers, and trainers, the first jail statistics were compiled in 1880 by the U.S. Census Bureau, focusing on race, gender, age, and ethnicity. Statistics were compiled every 10 years. However, in 1923, federal jails inspector Joseph Fishman inspected 1,500 American jails and found conditions to be "horrible." In the decades after Fishman's observations, jails have varied in size and design. Organizations such as the American Correctional Association (ACA) and the National Commission on Correctional Health Care (NCCHC) have developed standards for jail operations, training, inmate management, and health care.[22] By 2005, most states had adopted some type of jail standards, subject to inspection for compliance by auditors experienced in corrections. Audit teams from the American Correctional Association comprise three highly experienced jail corrections professionals. Examples of clear and detailed jail standards include those of the states of Illinois

(29 sections that cover jail operations, including the detention of juveniles) and Tennessee, which categorizes three types of jails, depending on their functions, with applicable standards. Jails do not have to comply with ACA standards, but ACA has paved the way in creating effective jail standards with performance-based elements, designed with input from the National Sheriff's Association and the American Jail Association. Complying with well-written and researched jail standards, based on good correctional practices and case law, can protect jail staff from litigation and inmates from mismanagement.[23]

Some jail staff complain about jail standards, but in reality a well-written jail standard protects the jail. For example, a serious area of liability is the problem of fire, especially when the jail is old. A well-written mandatory ACA standard is 4-ALDF-1C-08, which reads: "The facility's fire prevention regulations and practices ensure the safety of staff, inmates and visitors. These include but are not limited to: an adequate fire protections service [and] availability of fire hoses or extinguishers at appropriate locations throughout the facility." Required by the jail to meet this standard are written policies, procedures, maintenance and testing records, facility logs, staff training records, incident reports dealing with fire emergencies, and staff interviews.[24]

Jail Architecture and Supervision

In today's jails, we see influences of the Pennsylvania, Auburn, and Reformatory era correctional intuitions in jail architecture and management. The Pennsylvania system institutions, such as Eastern State Penitentiary in Philadelphia, housed inmates individually in cells at right angles off a central corridor (commonly known as *linear supervision*); many jails, particularly older ones, continue to use this architectural style. Cell blocks are at right angles to a central corridor; each cell block has a main door for staff and inmate entry. Off a central dayroom there are 4 to 5 individual cells. Each dayroom has toilet and shower facilities, a table for eating, and a television hookup. While many jail staff favor this style as being secure, both communication and observation are limited to the correctional officer speaking to inmates through a food tray slot or Plexiglas window in the cell block door.

Throughout the 1970s and 1980s, a second generation of jail housing design was developed, called *podular*. Podular supervision has the correctional officer posted in a central control booth, monitoring the inmates in housing units around him or her. Based on the concept of the *panopticon*, developed by penal reformer Jeremy Bentham in 1791, the goal of this supervision is to observe the inmates as much as possible, though communication is limited to conversing by intercom.[25]

The Auburn system's main contribution to jail architecture was the *interior cell block*, or the construction of a cell block area within a building. Having a cell block and cells within it prevented inmates from having access to outside walls. Also, cell blocks were stacked in tiers, thereby saving space. This style has been used in jails, where each floor of a jail contains an interior cell block. Under certain guidelines, inmates in jails can earn time off their sentences for participation in rehabilitative programs, many staffed by personnel in the educational, vocational, substance abuse, and mental health areas. This concept of "good time" can be traced back to the Reformatory Era where inmates could earn early release by program participation.[26]

Period of Jail Improvements

A student of jails could view the period of 1980 to the present as a time of improvement. Not only did jail standards develop and continue to be refined, training and security procedures improved for jail staff. The architectures identified as linear and podular have been described as the first generation and second generation of jail design, respectively. The third generation, *direct supervision*, was devised as a more humane method to supervise inmates. Direct supervision requires the jail officer to constantly observe, supervise, and communicate with inmates in a housing unit without any physical barriers (such as windows or cell block doors). The purpose of such management is to be proactive and to defuse any tensions among inmates or between inmates and staff. Studies of direct supervision jails have indicated that control of inmates is better maintained, violence is at a lower level, and the overall climate of such units is safer.[27] The greatest contribution of direct supervision is arguably that staff is proactive rather than reactive. In the linear and podular styles, jail officers react to inmate misbehavior, while in direct supervision officers can walk up to inmates and investigate questionable behavior before it worsens. Also, direct supervision can serve to better classify inmates. The classification process assesses inmates' behavior, criminal history, and needs and assigns them to the best housing possible considering their needs and the security needs of the jail. Direct supervision can be used as a "carrot and stick" approach—inmates know that direct supervision is comfortable and more humane than linear or podular. They know and are frequently reminded that if they misbehave they can be segregated or placed into the older generations of housing; some jails have all three generations in one system.

Another development during this period was the pooling of funding and resources by jurisdictions to construct *regional jails*, or holding inmates from the several jurisdictions involved. Through the 1980s and 1990s the number of jails declined in the United States. Counties with small jails holding a few inmates began to find it economically unfeasible to fund, staff, maintain, and operate these facilities 24 hours a day, 365 days a year. As a result, several states, including Virginia and West Virginia, began moving to a regional jail system. Also, as smaller jails close and their inmates are absorbed into regional jails, responsibilities and operations change from sheriff's offices to regional jail authorities that hire staff and administrators and coordinate training.[28]

Conditions in American jails are for the most part humane, safe, and have procedures to meet the needs of the inmates as well as securely supervise them. Does that mean that jails have become a correctional utopia? No. It was not that long ago when jails in the United States subjected inmates to horrible conditions.

This was illustrated clearly in an August 1980 *Newsweek* report describing some jails as obsolete, unsanitary, and places where inmates are warehoused without any treatment or programs to address their needs. It also showed the variety of jail conditions. A jail in Colorado was described as having a humane atmosphere, compared to a jail in Alabama under court order to not feed inmates dead animals that had been scraped off the local highways. Many jails were old—a Mississippi jail described as having poor toilet facilities was built in 1845 and last renovated in 1980.[29] The nature of U.S. jails is that they vary by age, design, and conditions.

One indication of the state of jail conditions is the use of court orders. According to Dr. Richard P. Seiter, Saint Louis University, in 1999 the Bureau of Justice Statistics reported that 15 percent of jails surveyed reported that they were under directives of a consent decree or court order to reduce crowding and improve confinement conditions; 11 percent were court ordered to avoid overcrowding by lowering population. These rates are lower than were reported in 1993 due to the construction of new jails, renovation of older ones, successful inmate litigation, and compliance with jail standards.[30]

Court orders, especially when enacted through the Civil Rights of Institutionalized Persons Act (CRIPA) and letters of findings issued by the Department of Justice (DOJ), have some "teeth" to them. An example of this compliance is the Cook County Jail (CCJ) in Illinois, which has been under CRIPA and DOJ scrutiny, faced with a choice of compliance with federal recommendations or being subject to litigation. Conditions were described by correctional experts as egregious. Deficiencies were reported in staff supervision, training, and visibility of inmates in housing areas, grievance system, medical care, mental health care, and suicide prevention. One CCJ official conceded that a "culture of abuse" existed among staff.[31]

Another indication that jails are struggling is an examination of inmate litigation. While the frivolous nature of some inmate lawsuits has been curtailed by the Prison Reform Litigation Act (PRLA), some inmate lawsuits illustrate the mismanagement and faults found in some jails. For example, in September 2008, a jury awarded $900,000 to a man who, while at the Dallas (Texas) County Jail had been denied proper medical care, resulting in a paralyzing stroke. In 2007, the jail settled for nearly $1 million with the families of three mentally ill inmates who had been denied medication. In 2000, the DOJ, acting under CRIPA, issued a very negative report citing serious problems in the jail's medical and mental health care. As of late 2009, the jail was under federal court order to improve conditions.[32]

Excessive use of force, inadequate classification, and jail staff being criminally charged are other indicators that jails have continuing problems that need to be corrected. Corrections law expert William Collins cites several examples in which the courts have agreed to substantial settlements in cases alleging excessive force by jail officers—a violation of the Eighth Amendment to the U.S. Constitution. An Arizona jail agreed to an $8.5 million settlement after a jail inmate died as a result of being pushed into a restraint chair, gagged, and shot with a "stun" gun. A Utah jail inmate died after spending 16 hours restrained in a restraint chair; the primary cause of death was blood clots. A Florida court agreed to a $2.2 million settlement in a case involving an inmate who was beaten while in a restraint chair and subsequently died in the chair. Three jail officers were convicted of criminal charges in this case. While the misuse of restraint devices may not be viewed by some as problematic, Collins asks that the large amounts of settlements be considered as indicative of a larger problem of high liability.[33] One could ask: Are these negative (and expensive) occurrences, which have resulted in inmate injuries and deaths, due to a lack of professionalism in hiring, training, and supervision? Jails must undertake procedures and practices to address these deficiencies.

Another negative aspect of jail staff is sexual misconduct with inmates. With the passage of the Prison Rape Elimination Act (PREA) in 2003, the problems of inmate-on-inmate sexual assault and staff sexual misconduct were addressed. PREA established a zero tolerance policy for sexual misconduct in jails and mandated its prevention as a top priority. Corrections officials are held accountable through existing law and federal funding.[34] Inmate lawsuits alleging staff sexual misconduct can be embarrassing and costly. As a result of this legislation, staff sexual contact with inmates is improper and criminal, and jail officers have been prosecuted.

Some proactive jail professionals do not wait for litigious inmates or the courts to mandate action. In 2002, an interim warden commissioned his own study of a problem-ridden Pennsylvania county jail. An audit was also performed by a county corrections department supervisor in neighboring New Jersey. Previously, in 2001, reports criticizing the jail were issued from a county grand jury and state inspectors, resulting in a federal court-ordered task force. Among deficiencies cited were staff sexual misconduct with inmates, lack of teamwork, poorly structured management, inmates "baby sitting" mentally ill inmates, inadequate training, and a poor physical plant. The interim warden made improvements that resulted in praise from the county district attorney.[35]

Even though many jails are not new, many are clean, well managed, and safe, and offer programs and treatment for inmates. For example, the Bristol County (Massachusetts) Ash Street facility opened in 1826 and is still in operation today. The Norfolk County (Massachusetts) Correctional Center was constructed in a median of a major interstate highway and is a clean, modern facility. The county transitioned from a 175-year old linear jail to the "median strip" jail in 1992.[36]

A LOOK AT THE JAIL POPULATIONS

The offenders in our nation's jails are a mixture of serious felons, misdemeanants, some juveniles, the elderly, female, the undereducated, substance abusers, ethnic minorities, and the mentally ill. Jails were once viewed as holding the "dregs" of society; we now realize that many offenders in jail have serious problems and need specialized management from a well-trained staff. We know more about jail inmates now than at any time in the history of U.S. jails. The following is a statistical "snapshot" of the United States jail population:[37]

- At mid-year 2008, American jails held 785,556 inmates, with an average daily population of 776,573. The incarceration rate was 258 per 100,000 citizens.
- The rated capacity of American jails at mid-year 2008 was 828,413 with 94.8 per cent of capacity occupied.
- Statistically, 62.9 percent of jail inmates are unconvicted and 37.1 percent are convicted.
- In 2008, 87.3 percent of jail inmates were male and 12.7 percent were female.
- Juveniles can be held in adult jails awaiting trial and charged as adults or sentenced as adults (making up 0.8 percent of the jail population in 2008).
- At mid-year 2008, almost 48,000 non–U.S. citizens were held in adult jails; 20,785 persons were held in jails for Immigration and Customs Enforcement (ICE).
- To combat overcrowding, jails supervise offenders outside the jail facility. At mid-year 2008, 72,852 inmates were supervised in community corrections programs such as weekend confinement programs, electronic monitoring, work release, and day reporting. Statistically, 18,475 jail inmates were participating in community service programs.

Combating recidivism involves attempting to get inmates in jails to become sober, educated, to receive training in a marketable job and to think in a non-criminal way. According to the Bureau of Justice Statistics:

- Reported by BJS in 2002, almost 70 percent (68.7%) reported regular drug use; 33.4 percent used alcohol at the time of the offense. The most commonly used drug was marijuana or hashish, followed by cocaine or crack.[38]
- In 2002, approximately 77 percent of convicted jail inmates could be considered alcohol or drug involved.[39]
- Only 57.4 percent of jail inmates in 2002 were employed full-time.[40]
- Concerning education of jail inmates reported in 2003, 46.5 percent of jail inmates had some high school, 25.9 percent had a high school diploma, and 13.5 percent had some post-secondary education.[41]
- Jail inmates are not strangers to the criminal justice system: in 2002, 39 percent had served three or more sentences of incarceration or probation; 46 percent of inmates were on parole or probation status at the time of their arrest.[42]
- Approximately one-half of inmates held in jail in 2002 were incarcerated for a violent or drug offense.[43]
- In 2002, over one-third of inmates reported having a current medical problem; approximately 5 percent of females admitted to jail reported being pregnant.[44]
- Based on BJS statistics issued in 2006, the Justice Policy Institute reported in 2008 that 60 percent of the jail population suffers from a mental health problem, including major depressive disorders, mania disorders and psychotic disorders.[45]

- Concerning inmates held in jail in 2002, BJS reported that offenders were incarcerated in jail the longest for violent and drug offenses. The average maximum jail sentence length for all offenses was 24 months; for drug offenses it was 35 months, and for violent offenses it was 33 months.[46]

The problems of jail populations give rise to two things: programming for jail inmates on the positive side, and logistical problems on the negative side. Statistics aside, the various workers in the jail staff, from officers to counselors to medical personnel, see firsthand the dysfunctional lives that offenders lead. Those observations and dealings with substance abusing, sick, violent, and mentally ill inmates result in a stressful occupation. Jail populations are a mix of young and old offenders, substance abusers, mentally ill, violent, nonviolent, weak, predatory, mothers, fathers, unemployed, illiterate, undereducated—you name the type of offender and the jail population will have it.

There are distinct differences between prison and jail inmates. Lockups and the local jails represent the first experience of incarceration for many offenders and a return to custody by repeat offenders. By the time the prison receives the inmate, he or she has adjusted somewhat to being incarcerated; anxiety and fears have subsided, and the process of prisonization is well underway. By the time that the inmate is transferred to a prison, much information is known and documented about the offender, including criminal history, prior incarcerations, mental health status/ treatment, medical status, and institutional behavior. Conversely, when an offender is booked into the local jail, behavioral issues such as violent resistance to arrest and incarceration, substance abuse effects and withdrawals, and unmanaged mental illness are very prevalent and must be managed by the jail officer. As one veteran jail training instructor tells new recruits in basic training: "You never know who is going to come through the jail door; be ready for anything." Until the inmate is properly booked in, screened by medical and mental health personnel, interviewed, and classified appropriately into the jail population, various problems arise and must be dealt with. In that regard, some can argue that jails are more dangerous than prisons. The volume of admissions to jails is staggering. In the last week of June 2008, an estimated 260,075 were booked into local jails. Based on that, an estimated 13.5 million admissions occur annually. Also, an estimated 66.5 per cent of the local jail population turned over weekly in 2008.[47]

PROGRAMS

Programs in jails vary in number and size due differences in funding from rehabilitative agencies and the philosophy of the agency or staff that is heading the jail facility. Jail programs have one main goal: to work with the offender and address the problems that resulted in criminal behavior. In some jails, sheriffs and jail boards may encourage volunteers and community agencies to come into the jail and work with the inmates in such areas education/tutoring, substance abuse, vocational skills, life skills, parenting, and religious matters. It is becoming more evident to those who work inside jails that programs are an important safety valve. Inmates who participate in programs can get away from the boring, noisy, tense, and tedious climate of the cell block or housing unit. While it is hoped that inmates who attend programs receive the direction that they need to stay crime free, some will say that fights and arguments were avoided because they "got out of the [cell]block" for a while and calmed down. The benefits of jail programming are under fire from jails trimming budgets and trying to stay fiscally healthy. Examples of this are the Rehabilitation Substance Abuse Treatment (RSAT) and Staying in Touch programs at the Wicomico County Detention Center in Salisbury, Maryland. In May 2010, the Maryland Department of Corrections announced an estimated $660,000 budget cut for the following year, thereby ending the two programs where inmates could learn to stay drug free and to reconnect with their families.[48]

Due to the fluidity of the jail population and frequent releases of inmates while they are participating in a program, there is no set formula for jail programming. In the May 2008 Urban Institute report, *Life after Lockup*, data on jail program availability was published based on Bureau of Justice Statistics data collected in 1999 and released in 2001. Concerning educational programming, 60 percent of U.S. jails reported having education for inmates. Alcohol programs dealing with dependency, counseling, or education/awareness were offered in 62 percent of jails; drug programs were offered in 55 percent of jails. Inmates need personal development, and jails have progressed in that area. Religious programming is offered in 70 percent of jails. Life skills training and parenting training exists in 22 and 12 percent of jails, respectively.[49] It will be interesting to see in future jail studies whether programming trends continue to be positive. Chaplains from such organizations as the Good News Jail and Prison Ministry and rehabilitation staff and volunteers from agencies such as Offender Aid and Restoration (OAR) give inmates hope and a chance through programs and volunteers to begin crime-free lives. However, there are some jail officers who, though properly security minded, are of the opinion that the chances for rehabilitation of jail inmates are minimal and that programs are a waste of time.

A transition planning approach is taking root in jail programs, preparing inmates for life on the outside, using in-house jail programming and community corrections. Most jail inmates will be released eventually; the politically popular "lock em' up and throw away the key" does not make sense. According to the Urban Institute, approximately 34,000 jail inmates are released each day; an estimated 230,000 are released each week.[50] An example of this is provided by Auglaize County, Ohio, a rural county with a population of 46,000. Its jail is a 72-bed facility that holds pre-trial, pre–sentenced, and sentenced inmates up to a maximum of 18 months. The 11-year-old facility receives between 1,200 and 1,300 inmates annually. Over half are released within 72 hours. Approximately 600 inmates remain, and about one-third participate in programs offered by the jail every year. The county took a revolutionary approach in 2003 and formed the Auglaize County Transition Program (A.C.T.), which is a joint combination of the Auglaize County Sheriff's

Office and the Community Connection for Ohio Offenders, a nonprofit private organization that focuses on inmate reentry services throughout Ohio. Taking a case management approach, the program develops a reentry program that targets offender problem areas, develops reentry plans, and provides job placements.[51]

Inmates in the A.C.T. Program can participate in GED classes, drug and alcohol counseling, mental health counseling, religious programs, anger management, life skills, parenting, employment readiness, job placement, work release, school release, and an in-house inmate worker (trustee) program. It is the goal of the facility to have, at a minimum, one-third of jail inmates involved in some type of work program, such as trustee positions, community service workers, and work release. Upon release, offenders are eligible for continuing programming in the community under the supervision of a case manager, the municipal court probation department, and the Ohio Adult Parole Authority. The program has had noteworthy results; from 1999 to 2008, over $390,000 in room and board fees have been collected from work release inmates, and serious incidents in the jail have been reduced by 80 percent.[52] To combat the frustrating cycle of jail inmates going out and coming in over and over, this could be the approach of the future.

The effect of jail programs on inmates is being examined. Since 2001, inmates incarcerated at the Fairfax County Adult Detention Center in Fairfax, Virginia, have been studied by researcher Dr. June Tangney and staff from George Mason University (GMU). The GMU Inmate Project is a longitudinal multiphase study that examines selected inmates from the jail, focusing on factors that may reduce criminal recidivism, substance abuse relapse, HIV risk behavior, and may enhance crime-free behavior post-release. A critical part of the study was looking at short-term intervention—namely, inmate participation in jail programs. Researchers also focused on the effects of interventions on inmates' feelings of shame, guilt, and criminogenic beliefs. Dr. Tangney and staff believe that inmate participation in jail rehabilitative programs may cause inmates to adapt feelings of guilt and reduce their criminogenic beliefs. This ongoing study will examine post-release behavior of inmates in the study.[53]

Jail programs vary in intensity, depending on the curriculum, the training of the program staff, and the disciplinary policy of the jail. Some programs are court ordered, and staff is required to report the inmate's progress or lack of progress to the sentencing judge. Examples of programs with strict curriculum are substance abuse, education, and cognitive behavioral programs. Inmates are required (under threat of removal) to behave, actively participate, complete assignments, and follow a set of strict guidelines. If they do not, reports are sent to the sentencing judge and/or the probation/parole officer assigned to write the pre-sentence evaluation report.

Jail programs are primarily staffed by civilians. In some jails, civilians and volunteers have minimal training in jail security and interacting with inmates. In other jails, program staff and volunteers are required to undergo mandatory lengthy training sessions in which security, what to do in emergencies, and offender manipulation are discussed. Also important is the disciplinary policy and tolerance of the jail. Concerning programs, if inmates violate jail rules or prove to be management problems, they can be barred for a period of time or permanently from programs participation.

SENTENCES, PAROLE, AND OVERCROWDING

It is impossible to predict sentencing patterns that would apply to all of the jails in the United States. A jail could be located in a jurisdiction with a judiciary that is open to sentencing nonviolent offenders to community corrections programs such as community service, fine options, electronic monitoring, day reporting, and work release. Some judges, working with district and defense attorneys, may use probation, may be open to using electronic detention where the offender does time at home via electronic surveillance, or may sentence offenders to diversion. Any of these methods keeps offenders from doing time in the local jail. Also, some jail systems, such as the Northwestern Regional Adult Detention Center, Virginia, have a separate work-release facility apart from the main jail. That does not mean that the work release facility does not get overcrowded, but screened offenders who qualify to be released into the community to work do not take up housing space in the main jail.

Keeping offenders locked up in jail appeals to the public. Since 1980, the American public has become more supportive of tougher sentences, more fearful of crime and less tolerant of criminals. A Gallup poll conducted in 1989 indicated that 84 percent of Americans surveyed said that there was more crime than in the year before; crime rates, especially violent crime rates, increased during the 1980s. Since 1993, crime rates have decreased, but 44 percent of Americans surveyed in a 2008 Gallup poll believed that there was more crime than in the previous year. These beliefs have manifested themselves in public opinion: criminals should be sentenced for longer periods, and offenders should be accountable for their actions.[54]

The American public sees these views put into practice. In Maricopa County, Arizona, Sheriff Joe Arpaio prides himself for operating inmate chain gangs and a jail facility consisting of tents. Some jails have decreased the number of inmate programs and/or the number of volunteers conducting mentoring and programs. In state legislatures, laws are passed that fix determinate punishment for certain crimes (mandatory sentencing), removing discretion from judges. Other laws mandate a long prison term for the third felony conviction ("three strikes and you're out").

The average length of stay varies from jail to jail, depending on the volume of court activity, the nature of the crimes that inmates are charged with or convicted of, the ability of pre-trial inmates to make bail, and so on. Inmates charged with felonies will be held longer than inmates charged with misdemeanors. Complicating this view are inmates charged with both felonies and misdemeanors, or inmates held on charges from other jurisdictions (*detainers*). The differences in the average length of stay can be seen in almost every state. In Pennsylvania, for example, the average length of stay at the Columbia County Prison is 24 months; at the Philadelphia Prison System it is 88 days, and at the Centre County Correctional Facility it is 46 days.[55]

Issues concerning parole illustrate the increasingly conservative views about crime and punishment from the American public. In 1977, parole reached its zenith as over 70 percent of inmates were released on discretionary parole (parole granted by a parole authority or parole board based on an inmate's conduct, program participation, etc.). From 1977 to 1997, 15 states and the federal government ended the practices of discretionary parole and indeterminate sentencing. Inmates can continue to work toward earlier releases by earning good time for positive behavior and program involvement. Twenty other states placed strict limits on inmates who were eligible for parole; only 15 states still practice discretionary parole.[56]

Jail staffs must contend with inmate populations affected by these decisions. As state prison facilities become more overcrowded, the flow of inmates being transferred to them slows down. Simply put, new beds cannot be made available for incoming offenders from the street after arrest and from the courts. If inmates who are "state-ready" are languishing and waiting in the local jail to, as jail officers say, "go down the road," frustrations can build. Convicted inmates sentenced to prison time generally want to get on with their sentences. Jails are more restrictive than prisons. For example, in one Virginia jail, inmates in the general population are locked out in the cell block/unit dayroom from after morning inspection (9 A.M.) to after dinner (5 P.M.). This process means that inmates cannot have access to their individual cells and must bring all items (programs materials, legal material, hygiene items, etc.) necessary for the day with them. Exceptions to this policy would include inmates with medical problems who need bed rest and pregnant female inmates. There are several reasons for the lockout policy; most importantly, inmates can be more readily observed from the officer's post or from a corridor. Also, inmates can be pulled more easily for court, programs, recreation, medical sick call, visiting, and staff counseling. Inmates who have done time in prisons or have been transferred to a local jail from prison may find this policy constricting; prisons allow a higher freedom of movement and access to recreation. Due to the changing nature of the jail populations, the acute nature of inmates' problems, the fact that many inmates have not yet become adjusted to incarceration, and short staffing, jails restrict inmates' movements. Program and recreational activities are more restrictive and limited in jails than in prisons.

Overcrowding

With almost 95 percent of capacity occupied, according to BJS, many jail administrators are scrambling to find beds. In California, for example, jail overcrowding has reached a critical mass. Out of the state's 460 local jails, 12 percent are over 60 years old, and almost one-half are 30 years old or older. Not meeting state and federal standards and regulations have resulted in court-ordered population caps in 20 counties. Twelve counties, in order to escape litigation, have self-imposed population caps. The result is that for every inmate admitted to those jails, an inmate must be released. In 2005, 9,148 jail inmates in California were released every month due to pre-trial release; 9,323 were released per month per early release from their sentences, due to lack of jail bed space. In times of peak demand for jail space in 2005, the state was experiencing a shortfall of, at a minimum, 12,800 jail beds.[57]

As a jail fills up, the ability to classify inmates into the best housing assignments for staff supervision, inmate welfare, and rehabilitation becomes limited. Classification officers do the best that they can, but extremely limited bed space results in some inmates living together and sometimes not getting along. Jail staffs can "double bunk" inmates in cells originally designed for single occupation as long as inmates are afforded sanitation facilities, food, medical/dental care, recreation, hygiene items, and are safe from harassment and assault, including sexual assault. Areas such as gymnasiums can be converted into dormitories, such as in the Norfolk County facility in Massachusetts. Another problem is segregation. Several years ago, one mega jail did not have enough available bed space to house incoming females, as the female receiving unit was also used for female administrative segregation and disciplinary segregation. Classification staff took the time to talk to all females on administrative segregation about moving back to general population. Many moved back and readjusted to general population, under close staff monitoring. Jails may "farm out" or transfer inmates to other jails to reduce overcrowding, meaning that jail administrators or sheriffs agree to house inmates for each other. This is due usually to overcrowding, but "farmed out" inmates may include those who are security problems or are charged with infamous crimes such as killing a police or correctional officer. Accusations of revenge, mistreatment, and retribution can be avoided if such inmates are not held in the jurisdictions where they are charged.

Overcrowded jails can be tense powder kegs, where safety of staff and inmates can be in jeopardy. Violence in jails exists in large urban mega jail systems as well as smaller county jails, sometimes operated by private corrections corporations. Of utmost importance is training—training of the jail staff to recognize signs of inmate unrest and to defuse inmate tensions through quick intervention, good interpersonal communications, practicing of effective security procedures such as thorough searches, using the disciplinary and criminal codes, and monitoring security threat groups such as race supremacist groups and gangs. Jail officers realize that a calm jail climate can turn volatile in a second—they are packed facilities full of offenders who do not want to be there.

Violence and overcrowding can have tragic outcomes. In 2006, approximately 500 inmates rioted at the overcrowded Los Angeles (LA) County Pitchess Detention Center, one of five in the LA jail system. In five days of inmate violence involving over 1,000 inmates, one inmate was killed, at least 28 hospitalized, and 90 others injured. Officials suspected racial tension was a causative factor. The available beds in the LA system require most of the general population to live in dormitories, which left only about 1,000 cells available to be used to separate inmates and troublemakers. At the time, the LA jail system was estimated to hold 21,000 inmates.[58] Jail overcrowding puts a strain on the physical plant, staffing, and morale of the jail. To solve this problem, all of the "stakeholders" in jail operations and goals—the courts, probation, local governments, sheriffs, and correctional departments—must step up and offer their part of the solution. While the public might support a tough outlook and "lock em' up" view of criminals, solutions and safety valves, such as more use of electronic monitoring, probation, work release, suspended sentences, and so on, may be unpopular but necessary in keeping the jail population at lower, safer levels.

Special Populations

Jail inmates are not typified as a group that obeys the orders of officers and has no problems. Due to the acute nature of jail inmates and the fact that they are brought fresh from the "street" after arrest to the local jail, jail staffs have to contend with different groups, each with their own behaviors that present management problems for officers.

Security Threat Groups

The most realistic definition of a security threat group is a group that causes disruption of the orderly operations of the jail, due to its organization, views, and ability to recruit members to carry out illegal actions and activities. Security threat groups (STGs) can be criminal street gangs, such as the Bloods, the Crips, or MS-13 (Mara Salvatrucha-13), just to name a few. They also can be race supremacist groups, such as the Aryan Nation and Klu Klux Klan. While the exact number of jail inmates who belong to STGs is hard to predict, research by William Triplett published in 2004 in the *Congressional Quarterly Review* said that there were an estimated 21,500 gangs with a membership of 731,000 members in the United States.[59] As STGs engage in criminal activity, the members are arrested and incarcerated in local jails.

Jails are taking steps to combat the STG problem. If not closely monitored and securely managed, inmates in STGs engage in assault, homicide, extortion, prostitution, and drug smuggling inside the jail. Racial violence among inmates occurs; officers are caught in the midst of riots and disturbances. Two approaches that have taken hold in recent years are the *zero tolerance policy*, whereby criminal and unauthorized activities by STGs are not tolerated. Tools to enforce this are in-house inmate disciplinary procedures, use of administrative segregation, increasing custody levels, and criminal prosecution. The second method is the use of *gang intelligence units* consisting of specially trained correctional officers who work with local, state, and federal law enforcement agencies in identifying STG offenders, tracking their activities in the jail, enforcing the zero tolerance policy, and taking action based on law enforcement intelligence reports.[60]

Mentally Ill Offenders

To those who work in a local jail, it is no secret that jails have been described as the "biggest mental home in the community." One of the most stressful situations presented to jail staff is how to safely and humanely manage the wide variety of mentally ill offenders who are booked in—from personality disorders, bipolar offenders, to paranoid schizophrenics. According to BJS reports in 2005, 64 percent of jail inmates had a mental health problem. For the studies, BJS examined two criteria: a recent history or symptoms of a mental health problem. More than half of inmates in jail reported experiencing symptoms of mania; approximately 30 percent reported symptoms of major depression. Jail officers are aware of the fact that mentally ill inmates are unpredictable and dangerous. Almost half (49.4 percent) of inmates in the BJS study reported symptoms of persistent anger or irritability.[61] The majority of mentally ill jail inmates (73.5 percent) are incarcerated for property, drug, or public order offenses.[62] They may have a longer stay in the jail than other inmates; for example, 1990s studies of New York's Riker's Island jail indicated that the average stay for mentally ill inmates was 215 days, compared to just 42 days for non–mentally ill inmates.[63] Mentally ill inmates are sometime uncooperative with attorneys or have to be stabilized on medication so as to understand court proceedings.

Jails continue to struggle with this problem. While more training becomes available on dealing with mentally ill offenders, jails will continue to receive them, house them, and manage them. While the larger jail systems generally have support from community services boards who supply trained mental health staff, smaller jails must rely on mental health staff from local clinics and hospitals, many of whom have limited experience in jail security and operations. Courts are taking more of a protective role concerning mentally ill offenders, including revising procedures in disciplinary hearings, housing mentally ill inmates in special observation units with specially trained jail officers, and reaching decisions protecting mentally ill inmates from undue excessive force.

Most promising is the *mental health court*, defined as a specialized court docket for defendants with mental illness that affords opportunities for court-approved and supervised treatment, in conjunction with the judge, court personnel, and treatment providers. The case is resolved upon the offender successfully completing the treatment plan. According to the Bureau of Justice Assistance (BJA), there are more than 90 mental health courts in operation. In 2004, 37 mental health courts were funded by BJA, each ranging a participant load of 15 to 800. Results look promising; in Broward County, Florida, defendants are twice as likely to receive treatment for mental illness and are less likely to reoffend. Mental health court defendants in Broward County spend 75 per cent fewer days in jail, compared to non–mental health court defendants.[64]

Suicidal Inmates

Suicide is always on the mind of the jail officer as it is the second leading cause of death (32.3 percent) in jails, after illness (47.6 percent). Thanks to training and increased staff awareness, jail suicide rates have steadily declined since 1983. The Death in Custody Reporting Act of 2000 enabled the Bureau of Justice Statistics to study in-custody jail deaths.[65] More data is now known about suicidal methods, settings, and symptoms. Suicidal inmates are vulnerable to substance abuse, mental illness, shame/guilt over the offense, a fear of loss of loved ones, a job, or other stabilizing resource, or simply an inability to cope with the stress of being incarcerated, especially around violent and predatory inmates.

Jail staffs have a moral and legal duty to protect inmates from each other and from themselves. Suicides in jail can result from hanging, slashing, jumping from a high area (such as a stairwell or tier), or ingesting a substance such as drain cleaner. The possibility of litigation against the jail by the family or estate of a dead inmate is high, and staff must have regular, periodic training, and must follow procedures to prevent suicides. An example of this is taking place in the Orange County, California, jail system. Between 1993 and 2003, only five jail suicides occurred in a five-facility jail system that houses between 5,000 and 5,500 inmates daily. This resulted from collaborative efforts between mental health and custody staff, intense training, and improved screening procedures. For example, each custody deputy carries a card listing suicidal behaviors, high-risk factors, and symptoms of sudden custody death syndrome.[66]

JAIL COSTS

Jails are not inexpensive. According to the Justice Policy Institute, local governments had an increased spending rate on criminal justice spending of 347 percent between 1982 and 2003. Included in this period was a 517 percent increase in corrections spending. In 2004, local jurisdictions spent $97 billion on criminal justice; $19 billion was spent just on corrections, compared with $8.7 billion on libraries and $28 billion on higher education.[67]

To examine the cost effectiveness of jails, the costs of main jail incarceration versus community corrections must be compared. Based on data from the 2002 *Corrections Yearbook*, an inmate incarcerated in the nations' largest jail system averages approximately $68.58 per inmate per day; the national average for all U.S. jails is $58.64 per inmate per day. The average annual minimum cost per jail inmate for a one-year jail incarceration is $21,403. The average annual cost per offender in a community-based substance abuse treatment program is $2,198; intensive supervision using surveillance (such as electronic monitoring, etc.) ruins about $3,296 per offender per year.[68] Not every offender incarcerated inside a jail is eligible for such community-based programs, but efforts need to be made to place more low-risk offenders in such programs to reduce jail costs. Offenders in residential community corrections programs can be charged for room and board; offenders in electronic incarceration programs are charged a daily fee. A popular movement is to charge jail inmates a daily fee for their incarceration. Any fee charged to inmates will help to recoup the expenditures and costs of incarcerating them. One view is that a way to get offenders' attention and make them think about the consequences of the criminal lifestyle is to "hit them in the wallet."

There are collateral costs to the jail. If an inmate becomes seriously ill or is injured, the local jurisdiction operating the jail must pay for hospitalization, medicine, and so on. Some inmates receive the best medical care of their lives when they become incarcerated. One way to thwart malingerers and to cut costs is to charge jail inmates a fee for sick call visits. However, indigent jail inmates cannot be denied medical care.

Jails will continue to struggle in fluctuating economic times and will continue to fiercely compete for taxpayer dollars. Inmate services and safe confinement costs will increase as funding decreases. An example can be found in Harris County, Texas, a three-facility jail system that saw an average 2008 daily population of 10,000 inmates, *plus* 1,100 inmates transferred to northern Louisiana due to extreme overcrowding. Harris County has an annual $1.5 billion budget, and 25 percent of it is designated to law enforcement, including the jail. From 2006 to 2008, the jail population increased 21 percent. The annual jail expenditure of $200 million strains resources such as jail programs and services. Staff shortages force a payout of $35 million a year in overtime. The costs can be viewed in the medical service area, where jail physicians write $1 million monthly in prescriptions.[69]

THE FUTURE OF U.S. JAILS

Jails will continue to modernize as the corrections field moves through the twenty-first century. New security hardware, computerized booking systems, better audio and video surveillance systems, and online connections with local, state, and federal law enforcement will only continue to improve jail operations. Budget shortfalls and increased costs will affect the speed of that modernization. Jail agencies and the courts will have to be creative. In Georgia, for example, a pilot program in four courts utilized probation and parole to supervise offenders more and spend less time waiting for a judge. Jail time of offenders awaiting court appearance was reduced over 70 percent, with a two-year savings of $1.1 million.[70]

Training of jail officers has greatly improved in the last 30 years, thanks to several developments. One has been the development of jail standards from state departments of corrections and organizations such as the American Correctional Association and the National Commission on Correctional Health Care (NCCHC). In 2004, the American Correctional Association published its *Performance-Based Standards for Adult Local Detention Facilities* (4th edition), revolutionizing standards and accreditation for local jails. Jails seeking ACA accreditation must provide clear documentation that supports compliance with ACA's expected practices. To meet accreditation is not an easy task; there are a total of 384 expected practices, formerly called standards. In 2004 there were 62 mandatory and 322 expected practices.[71] The number of standards can change as corrections progresses. Jails benefit from specification of the training that all jail staff (sworn and civilian) are to receive, as well as recommended procedures. Jail administrators would be wise to follow ACA's lead. Expected practices are regularly reviewed and updated as necessary by experienced corrections professionals and experts. While some jail staff may feel that ACA jail accreditation is unnecessary and expensive, adherence to standards can enhance operations and provide an effective defense in inmate litigation. The development of standards is not confined to general jail operations. Standards have been and are being developed for ICE detainees and jails' adherences to the Prison Rape Elimination Act (PREA).

In many states, jail training is mandated by a state-level criminal justice agency, and officers must pass initial training to be certified and attend periodic in-service training to maintain that certification. Closely tied to this are the many aspects of the jail population, such as the mentally ill, the elderly, female offenders, juveniles held in local jails, offenders who belong to security threat groups, and sex offenders. Each group has its own characteristics and may pose security problems for the jail staff. Training also involves the latest in jail hardware and security systems.

To combat overcrowding, jails must concentrate on improving their community corrections programs where the least-risk offenders are turned away from being incarcerated in the jail, but no less placed under some type of correctional supervision. Work release, community service, fine options (performing community service instead of paying fines), electronic surveillance, and offender labor programs serve as correctional sanctions for offenders who are not behavioral problems and are convicted of public order offenses, nonviolent felonies, and misdemeanors. As a general rule, offenders placed in community corrections programs pose little or no risk to the public; sex offenders are usually excluded.

The new frontier for jails may be in the area of privatization. While the majority of American jails are operated by government entities—regional jail boards, cities, and counties—some jurisdictions have contracted with correctional firms in the private sector, such as the Corrections Corporation of America (CCA), to operate and staff the local jails. The debate continues whether private businesses can perform more efficiently than sheriffs' offices or local correctional departments. This is not a clear area. According to a General Accounting Office (GAO) report released in 1996 to Congress, there are several areas of contention. Local sheriffs and correctional departments are responsible for local jail operations by statute; questions arise as to how to turn over such authority to the private sector. Also, local correctional agencies have been responsible for screening, hiring, promoting, and retaining staff, as well as enforcing staff discipline. Professional organizations such as the American Jail Association (AJA) have gone on record opposing jail privatization.[72]

Some jail operations have been privatized due to cost-saving measures. Food, medical, commissary, and mental health services have been transferred to the private sector in many jails. However, the staff in those areas should undergo security training.

CONCLUSION

Jails in the United States have had an interesting evolution from their roots in colonial times. Though jails at that time were squalid, harsh, and corrupt, U.S. jails have evolved into modern, clean facilities staffed by professionally trained men and women. Jails are different in many respects from prisons. Jail populations are more fluid and the problems are acute and fresh off the street, adding to the dangers and difficult nature of offenders' problems that jail officers must face. Jails vary in size and function, but mainly serve to hold offenders in the short term—awaiting trial, sentenced to short periods of confinement, or awaiting transfer to a prison system.

More data have been and are being collected on the characteristics of jail offenders, from lack of vocational skills, low education levels, and substance abuse. This data, along with a look at the mentally ill jail offender, can provide treatment specialists with information to plan jail programs and court intervention strategies, such as mental health courts.

Recently, jails have come under more scrutiny as they have had to deal with security threat groups, such as gangs and racial supremacist groups, and arrests linked to terrorist activities. More jail officers must also undergo specialized training to handle mentally ill offenders and to prevent suicides. While three designs of jail housing have developed that improve staff/inmate contact, jails are offering more programs and administrators are realizing that community corrections programs can serve as an effective safety valve for jail overcrowding.

While there have been many improvements in jail conditions and staff operations, several problems continue to appear, namely inmate litigation in staff sexual misconduct, mistakes in medical care, excessive force by staff, and substandard jail conditions. These problems can be mitigated through the courts, but some proactive jail administrators are using standards compliance and audits to head them off.

Jails must offset costs and take steps to save taxpayer dollars as much as possible. Budget cuts are affecting rehabilitation programs for inmates. While inmate fees for incarceration, medical services, and community corrections participation help somewhat, it will be a large expansion of community corrections and community-based treatment programs that will keep the most offenders out of jail. This is a hard sell to a public citizenry who view incarceration as the most effective way to deal with lawbreakers.

NOTES

1. Gary Cornelius, *Jails in America: An Overview of Issues*, 2nd ed. (Lanham, MD: American Correctional Association, 1996), 2.

2. Amanda Petteruti and Nastassia Walsh, *Jailing Communities: The Impact of Jail Expansion and Effective Public Safety Strategies* (Justice Policy Institute, April, 2008), 5, http://www.justicepolicy.org/images/upload/08-04_REP_JailingCommunities_AC.pdf.

3. American Correctional Association, *2009–2010 National Jail and Adult Detention Directory* (Alexandria: American Correctional Association, 2009), 10.

4. Petteruti and Walsh, 5.

5. Doris J. James, *Profile of Jail Inmates, 2002*, Bureau of Justice Statistics Special Report, July 2004, 2.

6. Petteruti and Walsh, 5.

7. Allegheny County Jail, 2006 Annual Report, p. 21.

8. Dean J. Champion, *Corrections in the United States: A Contemporary Perspective*, 4th ed. (Upper Saddle River, NJ: Pearson Prentice Hall, 2005), 202.

9. Champion, 202.

10. Tod Kemble, "Jails in America," *Texas Journal of Corrections* (May-June 1996), 14.

11. Kemble, 14.

12. Champion, 203.

13. Kemble, 14.

14. John W. Roberts, *Reform and Retribution: An Illustrated History of American Prisons* (Lanham, MD: American Correctional Association, 1997), 14.

15. Gary F. Cornelius, *The American Jail: Cornerstone of Modern Corrections* (Upper Saddle River, NJ: Pearson Prentice Hall, 2008), 13–15.

16. Richard P. Seiter, *Corrections: An Introduction*, 3rd ed. (Upper Saddle River, NJ: Prentice Hall, 2011), 21.

17. Roberts, 26, 27.

18. Seiter, 22–24.

19. Cornelius, *The American Jail*, 23.

20. Cornelius, *The American Jail*, 23–31.

21. American Jail Association, *Who's Who in Jail Management*, 5th ed. (Hagerstown: American Jail Association, 2007), 413–422.

22. Cornelius, *Jails in America*, 4.

23. Cornelius, *The American Jail*, 378–383.

24. American Correctional Association, *Performance-Based Standards for Adult Local Detention Facilities*, 4th ed. (Lanham, MD: American Correctional Association, 2004), 12.

25. Cornelius, *The American Jail*, 15–16.

26. Cornelius, *The American Jail*, 24.

27. Seiter, 86–89.

28. Kenneth Kerle, *Exploring Jail Operations* (Hagerstown: American Jail Association, 2003), 276–277.

29. Aric Press, Jonathan Kirsch, Vern Smith, Michael Reese, and Eric Gelman, "The Scandalous U.S. Jails," *Newsweek*, August 18, 1980, 74–77A.

30. Seiter, 95–96.

31. "Cook County Jail Fails," *Correctional Mental Health Report* 10, no. 4 (November/December 2008), 49, 50, 56, 58, 60.

32. "Dallas County Jail: No Place to Be," *Correctional Mental Health Report* 11, no. 3 (September/October 2009), 48.

33. William Collins, Esq., *Jail and Prison Legal Issues: An Administrator's Guide* (Hagerstown: American Jail Association, 2004), chapter 3, p. 57.

34.   Captain Frank Leonbruno, "How to Reduce Inmate Sexual Assault and Coercion: Part 1: How Prevalent Is Sexual Assault Behind Bars?" *The Corrections Professional* 14(3) (August 2008): 1, 6.

35.   Peter Sigal, "Report Confirms Faulty Conditions at Prison," *The Philadelphia Inquirer*, June 14, 2002, http://www.philly.com/mld/inquirer/news/local/3468183. htm?template=contentModules/prin . . . (accessed July 23, 2002).

36.   Cornelius, *The American Jail*, 26, 42.

37.   Todd D. Minton and William J. Sabol, Ph.D., Bureau of Justice Statistics, *Jail Inmates at Midyear 2008 Statistical Tables*. Tables 1, 2, 7, 8,9,11.

38.   Doris J. James, U.S. Department of Justice, Bureau of Justice Statistics Special Report, *Profile of Jail Inmates, 2002*, revised 10/12/04, Washington, DC: GPO, 2004, p. 8.

39.   Ibid, 8.

40.   Ibid, 9.

41.   Caroline Wolf Harlow, U.S. Department of Justice, Bureau of Justice Statistics Special Report, *Education and Correctional Populations*, Washington, DC: GPO, 2003, 1.

42.   James, *Profile*, 1.

43.   James, *Profile*, 1.

44.   Laura M. Maruschak, U.S. Department of Justice, Bureau of Justice Statistics Special Report, *Medical Problems of Jail Inmates*, Washington, DC: GPO, 2006, 1.

45.   Petteruti and Walsh, 9.

46.   Petteruti and Walsh, 24.

47.   Minton and Sabol, *Jail Inmates at Midyear 2008*, Table 4.

48.   Greg Latshaw, "Jail's Substance Abuse Program Will Get Axed." *delmarvanow.com*, May 7, 2010, http://www.delmarvanow.com/fpcd/?1275060182765 (accessed May 28, 2010).

49.   Amy L. Solomon, Jenny W.L. Osbourne, Stefan F. LoBugliuo, Jeff Mallow, Debbie Mukamal, *Life after Lockup: Improving Reentry from Jail to the Community*, Urban Institute, 2008, 12 http://www.urban.org/url.cfm?ID=411660.

50.   Solomon et al., xv.

51.   Joseph P. Lynch and Charles "Mark" Fuerstenau, "The Auglaize County Transition Program," *American Jails*, November/December 2008, 25–26.

52.   Ibid., 26.

53.   June Price Tangney, Debra Mashek, and Jeffrey Steuwig, "Working at the Social-Clinical-Community-Criminology Interface: The George Mason University Inmate Study," *Journal of Social and Clinical Psychology* 26(1) (2007): 1, 2, 4, 5, 8, 13.

54.   Seiter, 143.

55.   American Correctional Association, *2009–2010 National Jail and Adult Detention Directory* (Alexandria: American Correctional Association, 2009), 426, 427, 432.

56.   Seiter, 176–177.

57.   California State Sheriffs' Association, "Do the Crime, Do the Time? Maybe Not in California," June 2006, http://www.calsheriffs.org (accessed May 29, 2010).

58.   David Pierson and Megan Garvey, "More Rioting Erupts at Jails," *Los Angeles Times*, February 9, 2009, http://articles.latimes.com/2006/feb/09/local/me-jails9.

59.   Cornelius, *The American Jail*, 109, 111.

60.   Cornelius, *The American Jail*, 110, 114.

61.   Doris J. James and Lauren E. Glaze, U.S. Department of Justice, Bureau of Justice Statistics Special Report, *Mental Health Problems of Prisons and Jail Inmates*, (Washington, DC: GPO, 2006), 1, 2.

62.   Petteruti and Walsh, 16.

63.   Ibid, 16.

64.   Domingo S. Herraiz, *Mental Health Courts Program*, U.S. Department of Justice, Bureau of Justice Assistance, Washington, DC: GPO, www.ojp.usdoj.gov/BJA/grant/ MentalHealthCtFs.pdf-2008–10–08 (accessed April 6, 2010).

65.   Christopher J. Mumola, U.S. Department of Justice, Bureau of Justice Statistics Special Report, *Suicide and Homicide in State Prison and Local Jails* (Washington, DC: GPO, 2005), 1.

66.   Erin Guidice, "Inmate Suicides at a Record Low for Orange County, California, Jail System," *American Jails*, January/February 2003, 69–71.

67.   Petteruti and Walsh, 18.

68.   Ibid, 18.

69.   Jesse Bogan, "America' Jail Crisis," *Forbes.com*, July 13, 2009, http://www.forbes.com (accessed December 15, 2009).

70.   Bogan, "America' Jail Crisis."

71.   American Correctional Association, *Performance-Based Standards for Adult Local Detention Facilities*, 4th ed. (Lanham, MD: American Correctional Association, 2004), xxviii, xxix.

72.   Cornelius, *The American Jail*, 45.

REFERENCES

Annual Report, Allegheny County Jail. Available at: www.alleghenycounty/acjail06.pdf (accessed May 26, 2010).

American Correctional Association. 2009. *2009–2010 National Jail and Adult Detention Directory*. Alexandria: American Correctional Association.

American Correctional Association. 2004. *Performance-Based Standards for Adult Local Detention Facilities*, 4th ed. Lanham, MD: American Correctional Association.

Bogan, Jesse. 2009. "America' Jail Crisis," *Forbes.com*, July 13, 2009. Available at: http://www.forbes.com (accessed December 15, 2009).

California State Sheriffs' Association. 2006. "Do the Crime, Do the Time? Maybe Not in California." June 2006. Available at: http://www.calsheriffs.org (accessed May 29, 2010).

Champion, Dean J. 2005. *Corrections in the United States: A Contemporary Perspective*, 4th ed. Upper Saddle River, NJ: Pearson Prentice Hall.

Collins, William. 2004. *Jail and Prison Legal Issues: An Administrator's Guide*. Hagerstown: American Jail Association.

"Cook County Jail Fails." 2008. *Correctional Mental Health Report* 10(4): 50, 56, 58, 60.

Cornelius, Gary F. 1996. *Jails in America: An Overview of Issues*, 2nd ed. Lanham, MD: American Correctional Association.

Cornelius, Gary F. 2008. *The American Jail: Cornerstone of Modern Corrections*. Upper Saddle River, NJ: Pearson Prentice Hall.

"Dallas County Jail: No Place to Be." 2009. *Correctional Mental Health Report* 11(3): 48.

Guidice, Erin. 2003. "Inmate Suicides at a Record Low for Orange County, California, Jail System." *American Jails* XVI(6) (January/February): 69–71.

Harlow, Caroline Wolf. 2003. *Education and Correctional Populations*. U.S. Department of Justice, Bureau of Justice Statistics Special Report. Washington, DC: GPO.

Herraiz, Domingo S. *Mental Health Courts Program*. U.S. Department of Justice, Bureau of Justice Assistance. Washington, DC: GPO (accessed April 6, 2010).

James, Doris J. 2004. *Profile of Jail Inmates, 2002.* U.S. Department of Justice. Bureau of Justice Statistics Special Report, Washington, DC: GPO.

James, Doris J., and Lauren E. Glaze. 2006. *Mental Health Problems of Prisons and Jail Inmates.* U.S. Department of Justice. Bureau of Justice Statistics Special Report. Washington, DC: GPO.

Kemble, Tod. 1996. "Jails in America." *Texas Journal of Corrections,* May-June 1996: 14–19.

Kerle, Kenneth. 2003. *Exploring Jail Operations.* Hagerstown: American Jail Association.

Latshaw, Greg. 2010. "Jail's Substance Abuse Program Will Get Axed." *delmarvanow.com,* May 7, 2010. Available at: http://www.delmarvanow.com/fpcd/?1275060182765 (accessed May 28, 2010).

Leonbruno, Frank, Captain. 2008. "How to Reduce Inmate Sexual Assault and Coercion: Part 1: How Prevalent Is Sexual Assault Behind Bars?" *The Corrections Professional* 14(3): 1, 6.

Lynch, Joseph P., and Charles "Mark" Fuerstenau. 2008. "The Auglaize County Transition Program." *American Jails* XXII(5) (November/December): 25–27.

Maruschak, Laura M. 2006. *Medical Problems of Jail Inmates,* U.S. Department of Justice, Bureau of Justice Statistics Special Report, Washington, DC: GPO.

Minton, Todd D., and William J. Sabol. 2009. *Jail Inmates at Midyear 2008 Statistical Tables.* Bureau of Justice Statistics. Washington, DC: Government Printing Office.

Mumola, Christopher J. 2005. *Suicide and Homicide in State Prison and Local Jails.* U.S. Department of Justice, Bureau of Justice Statistics Special Report. Washington, DC: GPO.

Petteruti, Amanda, and Nastassia Walsh. 2008. *Jailing Communities: The Impact of Jail Expansion and Effective Public Safety Strategies.* Washington, DC: Justice Policy Institute. Available at: http://www.justicepolicy.org/.

Press, Aric, Jonathan Kirsch, Vern Smith, Michael Reese, and Eric Gelman. 1980. "The Scandalous U.S. Jails." *Newsweek,* August 18, 1980, 74–77A.

Pierson, David, and Megan Garvey. 2009. "More Rioting Erupts at Jails." *Los Angeles Times,* February 9, 2009. Available at: http://articles.latimes.com/2006/feb/09/local/me-jails9.

Roberts, John W. 1997. *Reform and Retribution: An Illustrated History of American Prisons.* Lanham, MD: American Correctional Association.

Seiter, Richard P. 2011. *Corrections: An Introduction,* 3rd ed. Upper Saddle River: Prentice Hall.

Sigal, Peter. 2002. "Report Confirms Faulty Conditions at Prison," *The Philadelphia Inquirer,* June 14, 2002. Available at: http://www.philly.com/mld/inquirer/news/local/3468183.htm?template=contentModules/prin. . . (accessed July 23, 2002).

Solomon, Amy L., Jenny W. L. Osbourne, Stefan F. LoBugliuo, Jeff Mallow, and Debbie Mukamal. 2008. *Life after Lockup: Improving Reentry from Jail to the Community.* Washington, DC: Urban Institute. Available at: http://www.urban.org/url.cfm?ID=411660.

Tangney, June Price, Debra Mashek, and Jeffrey Steuwig. 2007. "Working at the Social-Clinical-Community-Criminology Interface: The George Mason University Inmate Study." *Journal of Social and Clinical Psychology* 26(1: 1–28.

Who's Who in Jail Management. 2007. Hagerstown: American Jail Association.

CHAPTER 17

PRISON GOVERNANCE: CORRECTIONAL LEADERSHIP IN THE CURRENT ERA

GEORGE M. CAMP AND BERT USEEM

CORRECTIONAL leadership—at the most senior agency-wide level—can be thought of in two ways. One is that it is directed *downward*, toward effective internal control over its agency, because that is the arena over which it can most easily exert control and affect change. Society, through its elected officials, establishes the goals of correctional agencies. The mission of correctional leadership is to ensure that these mandates are realized, while protecting the public purse and as stamped by the paramilitary aspects of prison culture. This is consistent with the traditional view of public management. Correctional leadership, in this conventional view, is responsible for the care and custody of its prisoners, the staff who implement that care and custody, and expending the funds provided by taxpayers to support these efforts. Traditional metrics of success include no riots, low rates of violence, no escapes, and a modicum of inmate programming. We call this Leadership-1.[1]

A second, less orthodox, approach is to view correctional leadership as managing *outward*, toward the creation of value beyond corrections' traditional mission, and upward, toward "educating" policy makers, or even the public, about the role that corrections can play to maximize its contribution to the public good. In this type of correctional leadership, leaders tend to view themselves and act in a more entrepreneurial manner. In this second view, correctional leadership can create value, beyond what might be obtained in the traditional approach to correctional leadership. It can nudge the public and the political establishment to rethink the goals of corrections, and to support new initiatives. Because strategic innovation is the goal, the metrics are perforce more open-ended. They may include, for example, "right-sizing" correctional populations, both in terms of the number of offenders behind bars, the types of offenders behind bars, and how long they remain incarcerated. We call this Leadership-2.

The first conception of correctional leadership, Leadership-1, remains persuasive in the public's mind and therefore is likely to be most visible, while Leadership-2 competes for and sometime achieves advantage. Democratic principles require that pubic agencies fulfill the mandate of citizens as they are expressed through and further formulated by their elected representatives. The risk of not giving Leadership-1 primacy is illegitimate bureaucratic power. Democratic accountability would be subverted. Moreover, the particular nature of corrections results in an inherent conservatism to the enterprise. Its first responsibility is the safety and security of people who are confined involuntarily and experience day-to-day deprivations like no other citizens. If mistakes are made, these involuntary participants cannot be trusted to wait out the bad time until the course is corrected. As a consequence, corrections is heavily path-dependent. The way things are done today depends in the first instance on the way they were done yesterday. Corrections *should* be conservative most of the time—but not all the time. The latter is an important qualification.

Leadership-2 is an occasional style of leadership. This may occur in periods of agency strain, when more traditional approaches appear insufficient to solve the problems at hand. Alternatively, Leadership-2 can arise when, through its own inventiveness, it identifies new opportunities to add value to society. Leadership-2 is unlikely to be dominant over time; but at certain historical junctures it may be indispensible.

Our central argument, then, is that correctional leadership may shift from one period to the next in the relative weight given to Leadership-1 and Leadership-2. Moreover, at any given time, the 51 correctional agencies (50 state agencies and the Federal Bureau of Prisons) may vary in their attention to the two types of leadership. Circumstances change, leaders change, and so do the demands on leadership. Our core points are threefold:

- Change-oriented leadership can be both risky and rewarding;
- Correctional leadership has transformed U.S. corrections toward greater stability and order through a change in its organizational culture; and
- The success of correctional leadership depends upon the support of the wider polity.

LEADERSHIP-1: CORRECTIONAL "SCISSORS"

Two facts dominated correctional history over the last three decades, with one more widely recognized than the other. The recognized fact is the very large increase in the number of prisoners. In 1980, there were 316,000 state and federal prisoners; by 2007, there were 1.5 million—a nearly fivefold increase. The conventional wisdom (at least among academic observers) is that the prisoner buildup would put pressure on the forces for prison order. Crowding due to a rapidly expanding population would cause prisons to boil over in riots, disturbances, and high rates of assaults and murders. The two trends, prisoner growth and increased violence, should, if the expert predictions were right, move in tandem.

But the data do not support this outcome. Rates of violence, both collective and individual, decreased as the number of prisoners increased. The two trends crossed, like a pair of scissors in 1986.[2] For example, there has been a steep drop in the number of prison riots between 1982 and 2005 (Useem and Piehl 2008, 94). Once frequent on the correctional landscape, they have almost disappeared, to just a few per year. What has disappeared almost entirely are large-scale disturbances lasting multiple days, encompassing entire facilities or at least large portions of them. Similarly, the rate of homicide has decreased significantly. In 1980, there were 54 homicides per 100,000 state inmates; in 2002, there were four homicides per 100,000 state inmates—a 94 percent decline, and it has not risen since then.

While the crossover pattern is fundamental to U.S. corrections, it has not been the focus of systematic data collection and analysis or, for that matter, much informed speculation. Our core argument is that Leadership-1, through effective action, restored order in U.S. corrections. This result was accomplished by state and federal correctional leaders through a series of deliberate initiatives, including the design and construction of prisons in which inmate movement was controlled and limited, application of inmate classification systems that better separated prisoners into smaller and more homogeneous groups, better trained staff, introduction of security electronic technologies, and the use of automated information systems that provided the leaders with the tools to make sound management decisions.[3] These processes did not occur naturally; they were achieved by purposive people seeking solutions to difficult problems. Only after the fact do they seem "inevitable."

LEADERSHIP AND ORGANIZATIONAL CULTURE

In his broad sweep on what makes some public agencies work better than others, James Q. Wilson (1989, 91) emphasizes a specific aspect of organizational culture. He defines organizational culture as "a persistent patterned way of thinking about

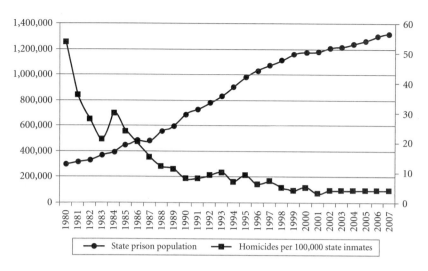

Figure 17.1. State Prison Population and Prison Homicides, 1980-2007.
Sources: Bureau of Justice Statistics; Corrections Yearbook.

the central tasks of human and human relationships within an organization. Culture is to organization what personality is to an individual." The specific aspect that Wilson emphasizes is organizational mission: what matters most is for an organization "to discover a rational definition of their core tasks and induce their members to share and act on this definition" (1989, 92). Our argument is that Corrections-1 led a cultural revolution within corrections, so as to infuse correctional agencies with a much stronger sense of mission, pride in work, and a feeling of special importance.

By way of background, during the 1960s, states began to bring together into single correctional agencies the operations of previously largely autonomous prisons (Camp and Camp 2004, 397). Wardens exercised considerable autonomy.[4] This power was shifted to the state agencies. As increasingly large numbers of state agencies achieved consolidation, their heads began to meet on an informal basis at national meetings. They shared their experiences, identified common problems, and discussed the viability of possible solutions. Many of the agency heads were former wardens, as well as others from the public and private sectors (Camp and Camp 2004, 397), who came to realize the distinctive problems and competence needs to lead large-scale correctional agencies. Seeing a need to formalize the informal networks, this group of agency heads established the Association of State Correctional Administrators (ASCA), first meeting in 1970 then securing formal incorporation in 1985.

In about the same period, the leadership of a much older organization, the American Correctional Association (ACA, the national association of corrections professionals) began to discuss the need to establish operational standards for correctional practitioners within facilities: what should be done, what must be done, and how (Keve 1995, 90–91). In 1968, the Ford Foundation and the Law Enforcement

Assistance Administration underwrote an ACA-directed project to develop standards, and a mechanism by which correctional agencies could be "accredited" for living up to those standards. The mechanism was formally established in 1974, under the name of the Commission on Accreditation for Corrections (CAC). Four years later, in 1978, the first facilities were awarded accreditation. Over the years, the standards have become more numerous, tightly specified, and reformulated with the goal of measuring what matters. As required by ACA bylaws, a Standard Committee regularly revises the standards based on experiences, new knowledge, and changing law. The CAC conducts on-site audits, and formal accreditation hearings, in which agencies are judged against those standards.

The ASCA and ACA/CAC have had an enormous impact on the *culture* of correctional institutions. In the first place, ASCA and ACA/CAC have developed correctional standards that reflect experienced judgment on the programs and operations that make for good corrections, that is, that are substantively right. Their scope is broad: staff training and on-the-job development; physical plant operations and sanitation; emergency operations and riot response; food services; rules for inmates and procedures for discipline. The standards help those who run facilities to diagnose problems and to come up with effective remedies.

Of equal, if not greater, importance has been the cultural impact. U.S. corrections came under heavy criticism in the 1970s, much of which has continued through today. Speaking generally, the peculiarity of prisons is that they entail the domination of some individuals (correctional staff) over other individuals (prisoners). Establishing the legitimacy of this domination is a core part of their mission, crucial to their safe and secure operation. This mission was under challenge. The prison riots of the 1970s and early 1980s hit corrections hard. Prisons appeared to be out of control, flawed institutions that could explode at moment's notice in unpredictable ways. Social criticisms of prisons was unrelenting, especially in academe. They were (and to some degree still are) described as unhelpful, at best, and instruments of economic and racial inequality at worst.

The major achievement of Leadership-1 in this period was the restoration of confidence in the mission of corrections: the belief that the time, emotional energy, and effort would bring about meaningful, positive results. This cultural shift was along the lines highlighted by Wilson, that is, establishing a clear sense of the mission within corrections, and one that it is achievable. This confidence, in turn, became a self-fulfilling belief.

As an example, field interviews in 2009 in New York State Department of Correctional Services suggest the importance of the cultural impact of accreditation (Useem 2010). For correctional employees in New York facilities, ACA/CAC accreditation represents a significant source of pride in their work. A senior administrator in one facility stated, "We work extremely hard to achieve ACA accreditation. Everyone here was thrilled when we got it." In another facility, a mid-level manager stated: "It's really a matter of engagement. We see how we measure up. And we do." A third official, from the central office with a long background of work in correctional facilities, emphasized the unifying effect that accreditation had on the agency as a whole. In an earlier period, he explained, superintendents managed their facilities relatively autonomously. Both staff and inmates alike would find it unsettling to be transferred from one facility to another, as new rules and procedures had to be learned. The official explained that ACA-accreditation has been an important element in overcoming facility provincialism. "Now everyone is marching to the beat of the same drummer. It creates unity for the agency."

RECONFIGURING CORRECTIONAL FACILITIES: INCREASING CONTROLS

A strategic change in corrections has been to increase the controls and regulation internal to maximum-security facilities. By way of establishing a point of contrast, Gresham Sykes (2007 [1958]) described the New Jersey State Prison as loosely run and weakly administered. The sanctions available to corrections officials were minimal and, besides, correctional officers were reluctant to enforce the full range of prison regulations. Many infractions were ignored (1958, 54). As a consequence, violence and inmate misconduct were commonplace occurrences rather than rare. "Far from being omnipotent rulers who have crushed all signs of rebellion against their regime, the custodians are engaged in a continuous struggle to maintain order—and it is a struggle in which the custodians frequently fail" (Sykes 1958, 442).

Our argument is that the correctional leadership has successfully reversed the conditions described by Sykes that caused the custodians to fail. Central to this reversal is the imposition of much tighter controls, at least, in high-security facilities. We have no quantitative measures of these tighter controls, although both our own observations and case studies offer palpable evidence along these lines. Upon entering a maximum-security facility, one immediately senses that Sykes's description no longer captures the dominant theme: there are very high levels of control.

Consider, for example, Marsha Clowers's (2001) compelling description of the Bedford Hills Correctional Facility, New York State's maximum-security prison for women. Clowers's overall picture is one of tight control and regulation.

> Every minute of every inmate's day is structured and under surveillance. The inmates are subject to four "counts" each day, plus an additional four counts if they participate in the educational program. . . . If the women are in school, a teacher and an officer each take attendance twice, both before and after the break. Additionally, correctional officers are posted at the entrances and exits of each the facility's buildings. There is no such thing as unaccounted for movement. Meals, mail, medication—everything is distributed at pre-specified times in pre-determined locations. . . . Nothing about life at Bedford is mysterious, ambiguous, or surprising. (2001, 25–26).

Moreover, in contrast to Sykes's portrayal, Clowers found that correctional staff did not ignore inmate violation of prison rules. To the contrary, "violence is not encouraged or unpunished" (2001, 26).

As a second example, 30 miles west of Philadelphia, the State Correctional Institution at Graterford has long been considered one of the toughest, most dangerous maximum-security prisons in the country. Built in 1929, the prison houses (in 2011) 3,000 inmates. Its architectural style—fortress-like exterior walls, little space for recreation and other inmate activities, each cell block housing 450 inmates—has long been superseded by smaller, more manageable designs. These architectural defects notwithstanding, in the last decade the prison has become safer, and in the firm control of prison authorities.

The turning point occurred in 1995, when senior agency officials initiated efforts to reduce violence through tightening controls. For example, inmates had been able to move through the prison relatively freely, but the new policy required them to have a pass with written origin and destination for each trip. Metal detectors were placed in hallways and other strategic locations, as were security cameras. Lines were painted on either side of the (often long) hallways, requiring passing inmates to keep a distance from each other. Uniforms replaced street clothes.

When we visited the facility in 2008, the prison order was restored and there was relatively little violence. One long-time Graterford inmate said, "Things are a lot different now than they were before 1995. It's a lot safer now, calmer." In his view, this was a mixed blessing. Before 1995, if two inmates had a grudge, they would fight it out, and correctional officers would stand to the side. Now "they swoop down on you." He complained that a "man now can't settle his own affairs." Another Graterford inmate stated, "Thirteen years ago, a lot of drugs, stabbings, rape. . . . That's now all changed. Much more safe." Another inmate stated, "You can't do nothing no more. They'll get you on those cameras."

Finally, an especially effective turn has occurred in the control of contraband. Writing about the Ohio Department of Rehabilitation and Corrections, former director Reginald Wilkinson observed, "In the past we frequently ignored or denied the influence of drugs . . . We [now] have a zero tolerance policy for drugs today in Ohio. We randomly test inmates and staff. We use urine testing, drug dogs, and phone monitoring. These weren't available in 1975" (Quoted in Riveland 1999, 186).

FROM LEADERSHIP-1 TO LEADERSHIP-2: MANAGING OUTWARD AND UPWARD

The mindset of Leadership-1 is to efficiently and effectively realize the goals mandated by the polity. The mindset of Leadership-2 is more entrepreneurial, focusing on how else the organization's resources can create additional value to society.

Leadership with this mindset looks for opportunities to use their organization to add value to society. With the success of Leadership-1 (controlling violence even while housing increasingly large numbers of offenders), Leadership-2 has space to develop. How has this evolved?

To help answer this, the Criminal Justice Institute conducted a survey, in March 2010, of the 51 directors of U.S. correctional agencies (50 state agencies and the Federal Bureau of Prisons). The core of the survey was two open-ended questions. One asked the respondents to look back: "Over the past two years, what have been your top three major accomplishments?" A second question asked respondents to look forward: "What do you see as the top three major challenges facing your agency over the next two years?" Table 17.1 reports the responses to these questions, coded into 16 categories (column 1). The second column reports the directors' self-identified major accomplishments; the third column reports major challenges ahead. The fourth column combines the second and third columns, representing, we believe, a broad overview of the directors' sense of the "issues and concerns" faced by directors, as they perceive them. The final column offers an assessment as to whether the accomplishments/challenges are *mainly* Leadership-1 or Leadership-2 type issues.

Turning to the bottom of the table, the central issues that have dominated corrections in the past appear to have lost salience. Significantly, improved safety and security receive only two mentions as major accomplishments, and are not mentioned as a major challenge looking to the years ahead. Prison riots are not mentioned. This is consistent with the "scissors" phenomenon described above. Establishing safety in prisons as a critical concern *requiring change* (safety will always be a core concern) appears to have been largely accomplished. This is a major achievement of corrections, and should be recognized as such. Another issue of the past, privatization, is a major concern of only one director, but no others.

Still another once-dominant concern, court intervention in prison operation, also has lost its salience. For reasons of parsimony, we combine this concern with that of responding to the Prison Rape Elimination Act (see a discussion of this act elsewhere in this volume). Two of the three mentions are to PREA. One director describes it as a "Well meaning but bad, one-size fits all decisions from Washington." Achieving accreditation from the American Correctional Association received two mentions by directors.

At the top of the table, unsurprisingly, budget concerns (dealing with them over the previous two years and major challenges ahead) are mentioned more frequently than any other. The recession, which hit state revenues hard beginning in 2008, is the crucial challenge. One director reported that he had to reduce the size of the agency "while population grew, thus cutting a $34.5 million from a $1 billion budget." Looking forward, he commented that he anticipated the budget crisis to continue for three to four years. Another director described his major accomplishment as "maintaining the operations of the correctional facilities in this down economy."

Table 17.1. Directors' Major Accomplishments and Future Challenges

Area of concern	Major accomplishments	Major challenges ahead	Total: Issues and concerns of the day	Leadership-1 [1] Leadership-2 [2]
1. Budget: shortfalls; fiscal constraints; maintain staffing levels; achieving cost savings	14	26	40	2
2. Reentry: programs, reducing recidivism	14	7	21	2
3. Capacity management: reduce crowding; restructuring for efficiency; population reduction; add beds	8	12	20	2
4. Staff culture: improve morale, enhance commitment; increased staff accountability	7	9	16	1
5. Leading up: inform legislators and public of agency mission/ options; restore legislative confidence; garner additional funding	8	6	14	2
6. Executive staff turnover and team building: training; retirements; mentoring	6	8	14	1

Table 17.1. (*continued*)

Area of concern	Major accomplishments	Major challenges ahead	Total: Issues and concerns of the day	Leadership-1 [1] Leadership-2 [2]
7. Staff development: enhance staff training; recruit new staff; mitigate stress on employees; new curriculum for staff training	4	8	12	1
8. Inmate programming: evidence-based practices; faith and character based programs; avoiding inmate idleness; improved case management; prison industry program	9	3	12	1
9. Policy and operational changes: eliminate tobacco; change in execution protocol; automate inmate records; reorganize supermax facilities; combat cell phones; manage medical costs; update policies	7	4	11	1
10. Interagency assistance: parole, probation, law enforcement; prison diversion programs	6	4	10	2

(*continued*)

Area of concern	Major accomplishments	Major challenges ahead	Total: Issues and concerns of the day	Leadership-1 [1] Leadership-2 [2]
11. Special population management: sex offenders; mentally impaired; drug offenders; gang members; youthful offenders	2	5	7	1
12. Upgrade physical plant: replacing antiquated facilities; open new facilities	4	2	6	1
13. Compliance with external mandates: court orders; PREA	2	1	3	2
14. ACA accreditation	2	0	2	2
15. Improved safety and security:	2	0	2	1
16. Privatization: managing pressure from privatization	0	1	1	2

Number of directors mentioning; maximum number is 36.

Just below in frequency of mentions, Leadership-2 type issues appear as frequent mentions. Increasing corrections' value to society, by addressing reentry concerns, is the second most mentioned issue. One director reported that he had "retained staff on reentry and converted three prisons to reentry centers." Another director described as one of his major accomplishments, "fostering new collaborative relationships with the judiciary, fellow Criminal Justice agencies and advocacy groups to enhance diversion and reentry efforts throughout the state." He added:

> The cornerstone of my administration is to concentrate major effort on diversion reentry. . . . Working with leaders of law enforcement, the judiciary, prosecutors,

the business community, advocacy groups and others are crucial to offender success. Corrections must take the lead in this education effort and fosters positive relationships among all these groups as the catalyst in achieving safer communities both within prison and in cities, towns and streets. All this must be achieved in a fiscal climate that is the poorest I have seen in my 37 years in the business. Fiscal issues do not absolve us in doing the very best we can to make the changes to improve offender success.

Another director reported that the major challenge ahead was to "keep the focus on reentry."

"Leading-up" issues (that is, helping to inform and guide senior state officials) are mentioned 14 times, when including both past accomplishment and future challenges. One director, for example, stated as a challenge ahead, "developing a collaborative approach to reprioritizing public safety resources that avoids the politics of 'soft-on-crime' allegations." Another commissioner reported as a major accomplishment helping to initiate the establishment of a state Sentencing Reform Commission. One director reported, as a major challenge ahead, "getting the legislature and critics to understand what corrections is really all about." In this same vein, another director stated, "Many underestimate the complexity of this business and also the gravity of how politics play into the future of corrections. Developing staff to lead as opposed to manag[e] is crucial."

Leadership outward, to the other criminal justice agencies, also received frequent mention. For example, one director reported that, as a major accomplishment, he had played a significant role in reducing homicides statewide through "parole initiative for violent offenders." Another director mentioned, as a major challenge ahead, "reinvestment in our community corrections."

Many Leadership Type-1 issues (naturally) are of high concern. Interestingly, a major concern is executive-level mentoring and staff turnover. One director reported that a major achievement of his was an "upper level staff-mentoring program." Another director reported that a concern for the future is "succession planning as many upper managers retire." Echoed by still another director was a major concern was the "transition to new leadership in many senior positions."

Other Leadership Type-1 issues remain important, either as accomplishments or future challenges. They include a number of policy and operational changes: disallowing tobacco; reforming the state's execution protocol; automating inmate records; reorganizing supermax facilities; combating cell phones; managing medical costs; and generally updating policies. Upgrading physical plants remains an important issue for a number of agencies.

Also of significance is that concern with traditional inmate programming remains a salient concern. This runs counter to the claim that corrections has lost its commitment to rehabilitation. One director mentioned, as one of his three major accomplishments, "implemented a[n] inmate skill program." Another mention as a major challenge for the future, "developing education, treatment, and vocational programs." Going a bit further, another director mentioned as one of his three major achievements, "getting colleges to provide college credit programs."

JAILS, PRISONS, AND OTHER SECURE FACILITIES

The last column in table 17.1 reports our classification of the areas of concern into the two types of leadership. The significant point is that 8 of the 16 areas of concern are primarily Leadership-2 issues. Moreover, they include the three most frequently cited types of concerns.

We also asked the directors in our survey how "important" in their approach to leadership are 11 leadership goals. The five-step scale ranged from "not important" to "crucial." As reported in Table 17.2, all received a majority, saying at least "important," although there was some variation in the degree of "importance," ranging from "important" to "very important" to "crucial." Consistent with responses to the open-ended questions, "balancing revenues" in the current economic period is identified as crucial by a large majority (83 percent) of the directors. Two other items are described by a majority of respondents as crucial: "improving staff culture" (60 percent) and "developing a vision for agency change" (51 percent). If "very important" and "crucial" are combined, all of the items receive that designation by a majority of the respondents. The items receiving the least support (combining "not important" and "somewhat important" are the "leading up" item (12 percent); ensuring front-line officers follow practices perfectly (11 percent); and measuring facility performance using quantitative measures (9 percent).

We asked the same set of questions to former commissioners, but do not code their responses in a standardized format because the dates of their tenure are too variable. (Some of the former commissioners have been out of office more than a decade.) Nevertheless, their comments are informative on a number of points. One is the complexity of management, having to lead both down (into the agency's administration) and up and out (to the broad polity and other criminal justice agencies). One former commissioner observed in broad terms:

> The challenge of any executive is to be balanced in their attention to the internal operations of their agency and the management of the relationships with the political entities that create policy (law) and allocate resources.

Consistently, this former director stated that his top three major accomplishments were: rewriting most of the agency's policies; collaboration with prosecutors, law enforcement, and victims and offenders' families; and "implementation of Legislation authorizing Risk Assessment as basis for allocation resources."

Another commissioner highlighted the importance of violence reduction, as well as reentry. He described his three major accomplishments as: "major reductions in inmate on inmate violence and improvement in safety;" "virtual elimination of suicides;" and the "implementation of reentry program." Another commissioner reported as his major accomplishments his successful efforts to "lower violence levels" and "right size the system."

The falsest of false dawns is an unwarranted confidence that Leadership-2 will inevitably give birth a new era of progress in corrections. Much will depend upon the priority given to corrections by the public. For example, absent adequate funding, reentry programs may promise much but deliver little. If they are seen as failures, reentry programs may suffer a severe backlash.

Table 17.2. Issue Importance to Agency Directors

How important is each of the following in your approach to Department of Corrections leadership?

Issue	Not important	Somewhat important	Important	Very important	Crucial	Leadership-1 [1] Leadership-2 [2]
Improving agency performance by mentoring key personnel.	0%	0%	17%	46%	37%	1
Developing a strong sense of loyalty and esprit de corps within the central office.	3%	3%	31%	37%	26%	1
Improving staff culture in facilities.	0%	3%	9%	29%	60%	1
Visiting facilities around the state to observe and manage.	0%	6%	29%	29%	37%	1
Measuring the performance of each facility using quantitative indicators.*	0%	9%	18%	41%	32%	1
Empowering frontline correctional officers to use their judgment.	0%	6%	29%	54%	11%	1
Ensuring frontline correctional officers follow policies exactly as written.	0%	11%	34%	46%	9%	2
Leading up: seeking to influence criminal justice policies regarding "who" is sent to prison and for how long.	3%	9%	23%	31%	34%	2

continued

How important is each of the following in your approach to Department of Corrections leadership?

Balancing resources in the current economic conditions of reduced revenues and budget cuts.	0%	0%	0%	17%	83%	2
Developing a vision for agency change.	0%	4%	23%	23%	51%	2
Developing new programs for inmate reentry.	0%	0%	20%	48%	34%	2

N= 35 *One respondent skipped this question (N=34).

CONCLUSION

Correctional agencies are created, staffed, and funded to make sure that prisons do their job. A key component of that job is securing the safety of staff and inmates. The evidence is that the taxpayers are getting their money's worth, more so now than in previous decades. Prisons have become safe. There was nothing inevitable about this outcome. A predominantly Leadership-1 style of leadership appears to have produced this result.

If correctional leadership has achieved one of its core goals, then other sorts of possibilities present themselves. The evidence is that correctional Leadership-2 has seized this opportunity to expand its mission outside its traditional limits. For example, corrections has always been committed to the rehabilitation of inmates. The concept of reentry, however, goes beyond the traditional concept of rehabilitation, to entail a genuine readiness to make a successful transition from prison to community. Correctional Leadership-2 has infused reentry concerns into the operation of prisons. Increasingly it will come to be seen as a routine part of correctional administration along side Leadership-1 values, but only if it works—and at this point it is still too soon to tell.

NOTES

1. This distinction (but not the term) is developed most fully by Mark Moore (1995).
2. The "scissors" metaphor is borrowed from James Q. Wilson, who referred to "Moynihan's Scissors"—the pattern observed by Daniel Patrick Moynihan that in the 1960s,

for the first time, a positive correlation between non-white male unemployment rate and the number of welfare cases opened turned negative (Moynihan 1996, 180).

3. No effort is made here to identify the full the set of factors that contributed to the decline in disorder. A full consideration would taken into account: changes in prison architecture toward smaller, more manageable and secure facilities; court intervention, mandating improved conditions and due process for inmates; political activism of correctional officer unions, demanding changes to improve safety; the rise and increased use of "supermax" facilities. For a discussion of these factors and their causal impact, see DiIulio (1987), Riveland (1999), and Useem and Piehl (2008). A full account of the causes of the restoration of order, backed by solid evidence, is yet to be developed.

4. Reginald Wilkinson, quoted in Riveland 1999, 173.

REFERENCES

Camp, Camille, and George Camp. 2004. "ASCA History." In *Correctional Best Practices, Directors' Perspectives*, ed. Reginald A. Wilkinson, 397–402. Middletown, CT: ASCA Publication.

Clowers, Marsha. 2001. "Dykes, Gangs, and Danger: Debunking Popular Myths about Maximum-Security Life." *Journal of Criminal Justice and Popular Culture* 9: 22–30.

DiIulio, John J. Jr. 1987. *Governing Prisons: A Comparative Study of Correctional Management*. New York: Free Press.

Keve, Paul. W. 1995. "From Principles To Standards To Accreditation." *Corrections Today* 57(5): 90–93.

Moore, Mark H. 1995. *Creating Public Value: Strategic Management in Government*. Cambridge, MA: Harvard University Press.

Moynihan, Daniel Patrick. 1996. *Miles to Go: A Personal History of Social Policy*. Cambridge, MA: Harvard University Press.

Riveland, Chase. 1999. "Prison Management Trends, 1975–2025." In *Prisons*, eds. Michael Tonry and Joan Petersilia, 163–203. Chicago: University of Chicago Press.

Sykes, Gresham M. 2007 [1958]. *The Society of Captives: A Study of a Maximum Security Prison*. Princeton: Princeton University Press.

Useem, Bert. 2010. "Right-Sizing Corrections in New York," *Justice Research and Policy* 12(1): 89 – 112.

Useem, Bert, and Anne Morrison Piehl. 2008. *Prison State: The Challenge of Mass Incarceration*. New York: Cambridge University Press.

Wilson, James Q. 1989. *Bureaucracy: What Government Agencies Do and Why They Do It*. New York: Basic Books.

CHAPTER 18

....

REGULATING PRISON CONDITIONS: SOME INTERNATIONAL COMPARISONS

....

RICHARD W. HARDING

INTRODUCTION: THE SCALE OF THE PROBLEM

....

In 2010 more than 9 million people were officially held in prisons around the world. In many countries, conditions are horrendous. For example, Vivien Stern has documented how, in some African states, prisons are places where human rights are abused and poverty and disease exacerbated. Forced labor is widespread in Chinese prisons (Stern 1998). Throughout much of Asia, competition among prisoners for sleeping and social space is fierce, and corruption is accordingly rife. In Israel, suspected terrorists are routinely held incommunicado, in oppressive conditions, and some of them are subjected to torture (Ginbar 2010). In Sri Lanka, Amnesty International estimated in 2009 that up to 12,000 persons suspected of membership in the Tamil Tigers were being held incommunicado or in secret detention (Amnesty International 2010, 301).

Moreover, the nature of closed institutions is such that even the best regimes are liable to have oppressive features. For example, both Sweden and Denmark still have isolation regimes for prisoners awaiting trial. In Canada, women prisoners have been required to undergo gynecological examinations in the presence of male officers and have also been strip-searched by male officers (Stern 1998, 150–153). In Western Australia, women have been shackled to their hospital bed while in childbirth labor (Office of the Inspector of Custodial Services 2002, 6). Prison conditions thus constitute a first order human rights issue. External regulation is crucial if decency is to be achieved and sustained.

Internationally, the focus of regulation has broadened to take in custodial conditions generally: police cells; immigration detention centers; psychiatric hospitals; juvenile detention institutions; secure welfare homes for juveniles and for the aged; military prisons; places of detention for enemy combatants; and the like. A discussion of the regulation of prison conditions should be seen in the context of the desirability of regulating custodial conditions across the board.

This article proceeds as follows:

- Section I briefly considers what is meant by "regulation," and what should be the substantive elements of regulation in relation to prison conditions.
- Section II describes some of the mechanisms for achieving regulation that are found around the world.
- Section III looks at the situation in the United States and poses the question of whether regulation that is primarily dependent for its efficacy on court orders and a voluntary prison accreditation system can reach and sustain acceptable standards.
- Section IV looks at the situation in the United Kingdom, where regulation is primarily achieved through the oversight of an autonomous inspection agency that has wide-ranging powers and reports publicly on its findings.
- Section V examines the European approach. This is based upon a regional Convention that sets out regulatory standards, provides for inspection by an autonomous regional agency, and is backed up by court decisions on substantive issues.
- Section VI assesses the future potential of the recently adopted UN Optional Protocol to the Convention Against Torture, which marries the notion of international inspection with that of standing national inspection agencies.
- Section VII evaluates the strengths and weaknesses of the various models, and concludes that autonomous inspection is a crucial mechanism in any regulatory package.

I. REGULATION

Regulation may be "hard" or "soft." In such areas as occupational safety or the prevention of anti-competitive conduct, the modern state typically mandates standards and establishes an independent or quasi-independent agency to enforce and further develop those standards. Once an enforcement order has been made, there must be compliance. Otherwise, sanctions will follow. This is "hard" regulation.

In the prison context, "regulation" is a collection of accountability arrangements—processes that enable the body politic and citizens to determine whether imprisonment is being done lawfully or unlawfully, well or badly, equitably or inequitably. "Regulation" thus refers to monitoring, recommending, exposing to public view, criticizing. This is "soft" regulation, characterized by the fact that the effects are indirect rather than mandated.

Nevertheless, the desired objectives are clear-cut. At the very least, prisoners should not be subjected to "torture or cruel, inhuman or degrading treatment or punishment"—a standard articulated in Article 5 of the Universal Declaration of Human Rights, adopted in 1945. The obverse is that they should positively be treated with "humanity and . . . respect for the inherent dignity of the human person," as mandated by the International Covenant on Civil and Political Rights, Article 10. That is the first step—the bare minimum which, if attained, would transform many national prison systems. This aspect of regulation can be characterized as "the avoidance of repression."

Beyond that, regulatory standards should ideally attempt to take account of the purposes of imprisonment, including rehabilitation, and the capacity of the particular regime to deliver good correctional outcomes. In the developed world, certainly, avoidance of oppressive conditions is not in itself good enough. Offender programs such as anger management, drug and alcohol dependency, cognitive skills, and sex offender treatment should be available. Likewise, basic education, some vocational training, and life skills guidance should be offered and physical and mental health needs addressed. The aim of an advanced prison regime should be that upon release the offender is measurably less likely to reoffend. This aspect can be characterized as the "attainment of the positive."

Regulation of prison conditions is thus subtle and multilayered, driven to some extent by whether it is simply trying to eliminate the repressive or also to foster the positive.

The institutional frameworks of oversight and enforcement are varied and complex. Very few nations have established a single dedicated agency with the authority and power to regulate across the whole system. Mostly, a patchwork of general jurisdiction state agencies and civil society organizations pick away at various aspects as they come to their attention. Regulation is not an integrated system.

It is difficult to differentiate the question of how imprisonment is done from that of who the prisoners are. There is hardly a prison system in the world whose population is not skewed in ways that reflect social, economic, educational, health, or ethnic disadvantage. Regulators can hardly be unaware of such factors. This complicates the regulatory task. To take the incarcerated population as a given is to ignore the fact that prison conditions are affected by the demographics and size of the prison population.

International comparisons are not always straightforward, for the complex layering of structures and the setting of substantive priorities reflects local culture, available human and financial resources, and political realities. In the abstract, regulatory expectations may be universal; on the ground, their attainment will inevitably be relative and should be assessed partly on that basis.

II. Existing Mechanisms for Achieving Regulation and Accountability of Prison Conditions

Around the world, numerous sources, agencies, and processes contribute to regulating prison conditions. The U.S. approach arises out of constitutional provisions and the role of professional associations. The European approach draws upon international and regional standards, whilst the British rely more upon autonomous inspection regimes. Globally, some or all of the following agencies and processes can be found in many countries:

- Autonomous inspection agencies created by the state specifically to deal with prison conditions: a prime example is the Chief Inspector of Prisons (HMCIP) operating in England and Wales;
- Autonomous inspection processes created by regional or international conventions: examples are the European Committee for the Prevention of Torture (CPT), and the structures that are progressively being activated pursuant to the Optional Protocol to the Convention Against Torture and other Cruel, Inhuman or Degrading Treatment or Punishment (OPCAT);
- Offices set up under the aegis of the United Nations to monitor state mistreatment of its citizens generally: examples are the Special Rapporteur on Torture and the UN Human Rights Committee;
- Autonomous investigatory agencies created by the state with generalized jurisdiction over official decision making: a prime example is the ombudsman model that is so embedded in public administration in Europe;
- Specialist ombudsman offices dealing with complaints by prisoners: examples are the Prisons and Probation Ombudsman in the United Kingdom and the Office of the Correctional Investigator in Canada;
- National human rights organizations: these are widespread in continents such as Africa and South America, whose nations have had to endure long periods of human rights abuses, as well as in Europe;
- Regional and international human rights organizations set up pursuant to treaties and whose remit goes much wider than prison conditions: examples are the Inter-American Human Rights Commission and the African Commission on Human and People's Rights;
- International NGOs such as the International Committee of the Red Cross, Amnesty International, Médecins sans Frontières, and Human Rights Watch;

- National NGOs and voluntary organizations paralleling the international ones;
- Special inquiries established by governments or legislatures in response to extreme incidents: examples include the New York State Special Commission on Attica (1972), the Argentine National Commission on the Disappeared (1986), the Woolf and Tumim Report on Prison Disturbances (1991), and the Senate Armed Services Committee Inquiry into the Treatment of Detainees in U.S. Custody (2008);
- Criminal prosecutions against persons who abuse their power within the prison system: this may be before a national court or the International Criminal Court, but in any case is highly exceptional;
- Judicial orders and determinations following litigation: this is particularly notable in the United States; and
- Systems for accrediting prisons as fit for purpose: the American Correctional Association (ACA) protocols are the prime example of this, though all autonomous inspection systems implicitly do so.

This list is not exhaustive. Most prison systems have some kind of internal quality control system. Such systems are sometimes tokenistic but can be useful and important. However, even the best lack the essential element of accountability, which is transparency. Almost inevitably, their standards tend to become self-referential. They stand inside the system; but the essence of good regulation is to stand outside the system.

Another element is media coverage, both in its own right and arising out of the activities of these agencies. An example of a media-driven accountability event was the establishment in Australia of the Royal Commission into the Deaths of Aboriginals in Custody (Johnston 1991). A Murdoch paper, *The Australian*, drove the agenda that led to the establishment of this significant inquiry. However, by and large the short attention span of the media has meant that, even in states that have a free press, accountability through media coverage is derivative rather than original.

International comparisons of the regulation of prison conditions involve identifying which of these tools are utilized in which country or region, the nature and content of the standards they seek to impose or enforce, and then trying to evaluate whether those tools have been effective. The broad measure of effectiveness is impact, both short-term and long-term. For example, the cessation of the torture and inhuman treatment carried out at Abu Ghraib prison testifies to the effectiveness of the scrutiny brought to bear by a variety of NGOs, the media, and finally the Senate Committee (Gourevitch and Morris 2008). In a more routine context, the various autonomous inspectorates such as HMCIP have developed measurement tools to assess implementation of recommendations that themselves are founded upon clear regulatory standards. In the broadest terms, the question "Is the prison system more humane and more respectful of prisoners' rights than it was before the regulatory phase began?" may sound rather imprecise. However, it is actually susceptible of a litmus test answer: yes or no. An experienced regulator working to clear criteria will almost always be able to respond in a way that does not fudge the answer.

Regulation of prison conditions is both a science and an art; and the question of effectiveness can both be measured and felt.

III. The United States of America

The United States has the largest prisoner population and the highest per capita incarceration rate in the world: 2.3 million adult prisoners and a rate of about 750 per 100,000 of the general population.[1] Minorities, particularly African Americans and Hispanics, comprise more than 55 percent of this figure (Bureau of Justice Statistics, 2009, table 15; 2010, table 13). Garland has characterized this as "mass imprisonment." The defining features, he states, are "a rate of imprisonment and a size of prison population that is markedly above the historical and comparative norm for societies of this type," added to the fact that it has ceased to be "the incarceration of individual offenders and [has become] the systematic imprisonment of whole groups of the population" (Garland 2001, 5). While conditions vary greatly across the thousands of prisons and jails in the United States, the Commission on Safety and Abuse in America's Prisons (Gibbons and Katzenbach 2006) reported problems of violent and sexual victimizations among prisoners in many U.S. institutions, serious shortfalls in the provision of health care and mental health care, the overuse of maximum security segregation, the diminishing supply of rehabilitative programming, and serious conditions of overcrowding in many jurisdictions. By any measure, the United States is a jurisdiction where prison conditions need to be regulated.

A threshold point is that the U.S. regulatory framework is almost entirely disconnected from international standards. Such instruments as the Standard Minimum Rules for the Treatment of Prisoners (SMR),[2] the International Covenant on Civil and Political Rights (ICCPR), the United Nations Convention Against Torture (UNCAT) and the OPCAT have not been absorbed into U.S. practice or law directly. The Convention on the Rights of the Child (CROC) has not even been ratified by the United States, nor have the UN Rules for the Protection of Juveniles Deprived of their Liberty (JDL). A corollary of this is that regular inspection of prisons by autonomous agencies—a key matter in the OPCAT, CROC, and JDL and one that has been on the agenda since the adoption of SMR by the UN in 1957—barely features in the United States.

Likewise, the Human Rights Commission model implemented so widely throughout Europe, South America, and Africa is underdeveloped in the United States. The U.S. Commission on Civil Rights has not displayed much interest in prison conditions, while very few individual states have autonomous human rights commissions set up under their own legislation.

The ombudsman model, which has been so crucial in Europe in mediating the relationship of the individual with the state, has never really taken hold in the

United States. Prisoners can raise complaints about treatment within the prison systems. However, this is far different from doing so with an autonomous external agency empowered to recommend reversal of administrative decisions of the prison authorities.

The U.S. approach thus draws upon its own specific sociopolitical culture. The main regulatory tools are judicial intervention on grounds of constitutional law, and prison accreditation by a private organization of corrections professionals.

Judicial Intervention

The Eighth Amendment to the U.S. Constitution prohibits the imposition of "cruel and unusual punishments." The reach of this provision has been fortified by the Fifth and Fourteenth Amendments, with their prohibition upon "the deprivation of life, liberty and property without due process of law." The Civil Rights Act of 1964 clarified that a remedy existed against state officials violating constitutional rights "under color of law" (42 U.S.C. § 1983). These provisions have been the peg from which litigation about prison conditions has hung for almost half a century.

Schlanger (2006, 558) has identified a 1962 Washington, D.C., case as the first in which court orders were made against correctional officials.[3] Bronstein and Gainsborough (2004, 812) point out that the "prisoner rebellion and its aftermath at Attica in 1971, in which forty three prisoners and guards lost their lives, served as an opening into the dark world of America's prisons and became the catalyst for the development of the modern prisoners' rights movement." Dinitz (1981, 5) argues that "the inaction of the States [in improving prison regimes] led to the intervention of the federal courts in rectifying the dreadful conditions prevalent throughout the country." Feeley and Swearingen (2004, 433–434) state that "by almost any measure it is clear that over the last thirty years [i.e., early 1970s until about 2004] litigation has had a dramatic impact on the nation's jails and prisons. New doctrine has become part of the established legal landscape. . . . Judicial intervention in prison conditions appears to be a distinct and singular success."

Initially, it was not easy to shake the "hands-off" judicial attitude, epitomized as late as 1974 by the statement that "the problems of prisons in America are complex and intractable and, more to the point, they are not readily susceptible of resolution by decree."[4] But once this barrier had been overcome, a rush of court orders triggered improvements to prison conditions. Feeley and Rubin (1999, 39–46) characterize the period up to 1986 as the reform movement "in full stride" in terms of its innovative reach and intensity.[5] The high water mark of judicial intervention was reached in 1995, with 15 states subject to system-wide court orders and 26 other jurisdictions, including Washington, D.C., the Virgin Islands, and Puerto Rico, under some form of court supervision or consent decree in relation to one or more facilities (Schlanger 2006, 577).[6]

The range of matters covered went to the heart of prison administration: racial discrimination; procedural safeguards for disciplinary hearings; conditions of solitary confinement; sanitation and hygiene arrangements; the provision of medical care; nutritious food; cell-sharing protocols to protect the weak from predators;

and, above all, dismantling of what Feeley and Swearingen (2004, 436–437) describe as "the Plantation model of Southern imprisonment."

Feeley and Swearingen (2004, 437) concede that "judicial intervention is admittedly an odd way to reform prisons." Its success derived from the willingness of the U.S. judiciary to become, in effect, policy makers and administrators. To European and, particularly, British eyes the spectacle of a trial judge appointing "special masters or monitors" to supervise the implementation of the often quite detailed court orders and reporting back to the court on progress was novel, arguably undermining the theoretical division of powers between the executive and the judiciary.[7] Yet U.S. prison conditions were such as to demand radical solutions.

In making orders, the judiciary did not pursue idiosyncratic theories about penal administration. They drew upon "the best of conventional thinking that had long been advocated by reform-minded prison officials" (Feeley and Swearingen 2004, 438). This approach was in turn anchored in the 1959 edition of the Manual of Correctional Standards published by the American Correctional Association (ACA).

Accreditation of Prisons

Mention of the ACA takes one to the prison accreditation process. The origins of the ACA go back to 1870, when the National Prison Association of correctional professionals was formed. After several metamorphoses, the organization was re-named as the ACA in 1954. Over the last half century it has been concerned to develop standards for prison and some other custodial settings. The 1959 Manual has been revised, but its paper commitment to what the United Kingdom calls the "decency agenda" has been consistent over time. The standards embraced in the Manual fed directly into the court order system (Rodriguez 2007, 109; Feeley and Swearingen 2004, 438–439).

These standards typically emphasize that "written policies" should govern all aspects of prison conditions. Feeley and Swearingen (2004, 444, 462) argue that the bureaucratization that follows from the requirement to develop written policies is a significant safeguard; it takes prison administration away from the "bumbling yokels" and "good ole boy" form of management that had been so oppressive, particularly in the South. Nevertheless, concentration on the absence or presence of "written policies" rather than what is actually happening on the ground is a weakness in the inspection and accreditation process (Feeley and Swearingen 2004, 470–474).

Accreditation is voluntary, not mandatory, for U.S. prisons. It proceeds on a fee-for-service basis. There is some suggestion that those jurisdictions whose prisons fall short of the required standards simply bypass the process. There is also a danger of "capture." This means that the ACA, as a paid service provider, comes to represent the interests of the institutions that it is supposed to regulate rather than those of the prisoners (Feeley and Swearingen 2004, 448). They state:

> Together, though not necessarily maliciously, prison officials and the ACA have engaged in a process that is both concerned with improving life behind prison walls and *creating the appearance* of improving life behind prison walls. Both seek to maximize their managerial goals through ostensible attention to prisoners' well being. (2004, 473; see also Keve 1996, 78–82).

Summary of the U.S. Regulatory Approaches

So how do these two principal means of regulating prison conditions measure up? In 1996—a year after the high watermark of judicial activity—Congress passed the Prison Litigation Reform Act.[8] The objective was avowedly to reduce the flow of future court orders and blunt the most important of the regulatory tools relating to prison conditions.

Schlanger (2006, 622) has shown that the faucet has still not been completely turned off, but that the subsequent litigation has been ever more resource-intensive in relation to increasingly narrow topics. She states that there are fewer American prisons with the repressive conditions that were originally the subject of court orders. However,

> In some ways our prisons are worse today—more idle, more dehumanizing—but Eighth Amendment law is extremely limited. It exempts from constitutional analysis many of the issues that matter most to prisoners, such as educational programming, work and other activities, and the custody level. So even though today's paradigmatic prison failings are deeply troubling, they do not violate our current understanding of the Constitution.

This is a crucial observation. The concerns of prisoners and the public interest agenda have each moved on, but the U.S. system has not kept up. In other words, what has been characterized above as the "positive" aspects of regulation are not within the scope of a litigation model that is primarily concerned to prevent only the most repressive or negative effects. Thus the U.S. regulatory regime cannot meet contemporary needs if it remains solely reliant on Constitution-based tools.[9]

A further limitation is that court orders are highly exceptional in relation to jails (Schlanger 2006, 622–623)—where at any given time about 750,000 prisoners are held. The National Institute of Corrections has led a project to develop Jail Standards and Inspection Programs (Martin 2007). However, it is non-mandatory; not all states have signed up; and for those that have done so, the most common reporting line is to the detention agency itself. This opaque and fragmented accountability tool does not compensate for the absence of vigorous judicial intervention.

These factors suggest that the dual-track regulatory tools applicable to U.S. prison conditions have become outmoded. The only reliable way to embed continuing good practice and sustain improvement to prison conditions is to create an autonomous standing inspection system, as in the UK and Europe and with the newly emerging OPCAT arrangements. This key factor is missing in the United States. Possessing the most complex and massive prison system in the world, the United States needs above all to bring this new element into its regulatory arrangements.

The Report of the Commission on Safety and Abuse in America's Prisons found that "oversight of America's prisons and jails is under-developed and uneven" (Gibbons and Katzenbach 2006, 78). The Commission argued that "there must be strong independent oversight of prisons and jails nationwide." Accordingly, "every state should create an independent agency to monitor prisons and jails" (Gibbons and Katzenbach 2006, 79). In recommending this, the Commission was mindful of the UK model, which will be described next.

The American Bar Association (ABA) has echoed this viewpoint. The Criminal Justice Section of the ABA resolved in April 2008 to urge "federal, state and territory governments to establish public entities that are independent of any correctional agency to regularly monitor and report publicly on the conditions in all prisons, jails and other adult and juvenile correctional and detention facilities operating within their jurisdiction."[10]

IV. The United Kingdom

Until 1988 the UK courts had "a powerful aversion to . . . becoming embroiled in the day-to-day decisions of prison life" (Livingstone, Owen and MacDonald 2008, 8). Accordingly, the notion of prisoners' rights is underdeveloped, and by U.S. standards court intervention had been minimal. Even after the 1988 breakthrough decision in Leech's case,[11] the willingness of the judiciary to become involved in these cases was still quite circumscribed. In a 2001 case, it was said:

> Any custodial order inevitably curtails the enjoyment, by the person confined, of rights enjoyed by other citizens. . . . But the order does not wholly deprive the person . . . of all rights enjoyed by other citizens. Some rights, perhaps in an attenuated or qualified form, survive the making of the order.[12]

That statement hardly presages imaginative or rigorous judicial activism. However, as will emerge, the European Court of Human Rights is starting to come in over the top of its conservative British colleagues, gradually engineering some change of approach.[13]

The United Kingdom has not been particularly tuned in to international instruments either, though it is not quite as deaf as the United States. The model for regulating prison conditions that has grown up is idiosyncratic, comprising two main components: autonomous inspection and a specialist ombudsman. These tools are only fully replicated in Western Australia (inspection)[14] and Canada (specialist ombudsman). However, as will be seen, the OPCAT also draws upon the UK inspection model.

Her Majesty's Chief Inspector of Prisons

In 1979 an independent inquiry recommended that an inspectorate of prisons should be established, autonomous from the Prison Service. It should report directly to the Home Secretary (the Minister politically responsible for prisons), and its reports should be published. There should be power to carry out unannounced inspections.

These recommendations reflected growing disquiet at the efficacy and objectivity of the in-house inspections hitherto carried out by the Prison Service. However, the new inspectorate's jurisdiction would be recommendatory only; there would be no enforcement powers (Morgan 1985).

Amendments to the Prisons Act in 1982[15] established the office of Her Majesty's Chief Inspector of Prisons (HMCIP). Its remit initially extended to prisons in England and Wales. A similar inspectorate model was subsequently created for Scotland, and administrative arrangements enabled HMCIP to carry out the inspection role in Northern Ireland.

The statutory provisions are surprisingly vague. The considerable powers of HMCIP ultimately depend on "custom and practice."[16] These powers include: free and unfettered access to any prison; requisition of documentation relating to the operation of that prison; the right to take equipment such as cameras or video-recorders into prisons; the right to speak with any prisoner, staff member, or management personnel; functional independence; and budgetary autonomy and control.[17]

The remit of HMCIP has been extended beyond prisons and now also covers: young offender institutions; secure training centers; immigration detention centers; prisoner and detainee transport arrangements; military prisons; police holding cells; and community offender management systems. These extensions to jurisdiction have come about as a result of Government administrative decisions, memoranda of understanding with various agencies, and in one case (immigration detention) by statute.

The inspectorate model is well-established across governmental activities generally in the United Kingdom. Recent legislation facilitates cooperative or joint inspections to be carried out by HMCIP and the other criminal justice inspectorates.[18]

In a typical year HMCIP carries out more than 80 inspections. Full prison inspections (announced or unannounced) involve a week on-site. Announced inspections will have been preceded by surveys of prisoners and staff. Short unannounced follow-up inspections involve three days on-site. The inspection team co-opts relevant specialists from other inspectorates or as consultants, for example, in the areas of education and health. Findings are triangulated from various sources: direct observation, documentation, prisoner interviews, staff interviews, survey material.

In addition, the continuous observations of independent monitoring boards, which are appointed for every prison, feed into the activities of HMCIP, both as an alert to emerging issues and as a possible element in triangulating findings.[19]

After the on-site phase, an inspection report is drafted. The draft is then sent to the Prison Service with an invitation to identify factual inaccuracies. There is a strict timetable; there was an earlier phase when the Prison Service would contrive a delay in the publication of a report by holding up their response to the draft.[20]

Publication is by release on the HMCIP website. Within two months of publication, formal responses must be made by the Prison Service. An action plan is then formulated. This will be sent to HMCIP. The Prison Service will self-report to HMCIP within 12 months as to progress in implementing that plan.[21]

The greatest value of these processes is that HMCIP can log two things: the rate of acceptance of recommendations and the extent of genuine implementation of accepted recommendations. Rejected recommendations can, if necessary, be revisited at subsequent inspections.[22] Likewise, actual implementation can be checked during short follow-up inspections. The implementation rate usually runs at around 65–70 percent of accepted recommendations (Her Majesty's Chief Inspector of Prisons 2008, 12). These tools enable the effectiveness of HMCIP inspections to be evaluated.

The Annual Report is tabled in Parliament. This gives the Chief Inspector the opportunity to highlight matters of broad policy concern. For example, in the 2008 Annual Report she strongly criticized government proposals to build "Titan" prisons housing up to 2,500 prisoners, on the basis that previous inspection experience demonstrated that large prisons are less safe for prisoners than small ones. This was one of the decisive factors in the Government's abandonment of the proposal (Her Majesty's Chief Inspector of Prisons 2008, 7).

Publication is a crucial element in accountability. A report may activate political reaction by Government or Opposition. It may also excite media interest, which in turn heightens accountability. Prisoner action groups and nongovernmental organizations (NGOs) can tailor the documented information to their own campaigns. In the absence of publication and the scrutiny that accompanies this process, the regulator and the government could do behind-the-scenes deals—the precursor to "capture" of the regulator.

The inspection criteria applied by HMCIP reflect both the "avoidance of repression" and the "striving for the positive" approaches, identified above. The "decency" agenda, mentioned previously, evolved gradually and was given sharper focus by the promulgation in 2001 of the "healthy prison" test. The Chief Inspector at the time, Lord David Ramsbotham, stated that, in future prison inspections, HMCIP would be evaluating four matters: (1) safety—that prisoners, even the most vulnerable, are held safely; (2) respect—that prisoners are treated with respect for their human dignity; (3) purposeful activity—that prisoners are able, and expected, to engage in activity that is likely to benefit them; and (4) resettlement—that prisoners are prepared for release into the community, and helped to reduce the likelihood of their reoffending (Ramsbotham 2003, 65–67).

Simultaneously, HMCIP was developing a code of standards, "Expectations: Criteria for assessing the conditions in prisons and the treatment of prisoners" (Her Majesty's Chief Inspector of Prisons 2006). This document sets out in specific detail what HMCIP expects in practically every aspect of prison administration. It also identifies the data sources on which it will rely in making its assessment. The standards are linked to the national, regional or international instruments that tie in with the particular expectation.[23] The latter point is important; it is the way that the United Kingdom, previously somewhat inured from regional and international influences, has established links to the increasingly important non-national sources.

"Expectations" is a dynamic document that evolves with changing perceptions of prison conditions.[24] It is a robust model of how autonomous inspection should proceed.[25] Applying these standards, HMCIP "marks" every prison on a scale of 1–4 on the four elements of a "healthy prison" (Her Majesty's Chief Inspector of Prisons 2009). This is not, strictly speaking, "accreditation," as in the U.S. model. But it has worked as a wake-up call to prisons that score below 3 on any criterion.

Two important contrasts should be made with the ACA accreditation process. First, "written policies" of the Prison Service are a starting point, not sufficient in themselves. The Chief Inspector has stated:

> There is no substitute for being there, or for the need to keep under regular and unpredictable review the institutions that have such a profound and direct effect on people's lives. In recent years, there has too readily been an assumption that inspection and regulation are always burdensome and sometimes unnecessary; that self-regulation and light touch inspection are preferable to rolling programs and specialist, detailed on-site investigation. (Her Majesty's Chief Inspector of Prisons 2008, 8)

Second, the standards applied to prisons are derived from the experience of an autonomous agency, rather than tied in by a fee-paying arrangement with inspected departments. Prison administrators would usually prefer to be inspected against standards that they themselves have developed or into which they have made a major input. Such standards inevitably tend toward being "self-referential. . . . with rules that are there because they have always been there or because they are convenient, rather than because they are necessary or right" (Owers 2003). Yet in a key area of human rights, they need to be dynamic.[26]

As well as on-site inspections, HMCIP examines the prison system thematically, identifying problems common to many or all prisons. Some examples include: "Extreme Custody" (2006) building upon a 2000 report; "Foreign National Prisoners" (2006), examining the particular problems confronting a prisoner cohort that had burgeoned in the previous decade; "Mental Health of Prisoners" (2007), following a 1996 report; and "Women in Prison" (2005), revisiting a 1997 report.[27]

Thematic reports do not trigger action plans. They are research-based and constitute a resource for the Prison Service to draw upon in formulating its policies, as well as a reference point for HMCIP in subsequent inspections and in the evolution of "Expectations."

HMCIP is now the unchallenged centerpiece for regulating prison conditions. Formally, its regulatory remit is "soft." However, its status and credibility, built up over three decades, are such that many of its findings reach into the interstices of prison administration in the United Kingdom.

The Prisons and Probation Ombudsman (PPO)

The Woolf Report found that a widespread sense of injustice among prisoners was one of the key underlying causes for the 1990 riots in English prisons. Prisoners should henceforth be given reasons for decisions that affected their conditions or lifestyle, such as transfer, mail censorship, and restrictions upon visits. These decisions should be reviewable (Woolf and Tumim 1991, 9.24 to 9.37).

In response, a special Prisons Ombudsman was appointed in 1994. The sense was that the general Ombudsman lacked the expertise and time to deal with prisoner complaints effectively. This new system was created administratively, not statutorily. Questions thus arose as to its autonomy from government and the bureaucracy (Harding 1997, 59).

Nevertheless, in the succeeding 16 years, the office has evolved into an active watchdog over prison administration. The remit was extended in 2001 to cover complaints by offenders under the supervision of the Probation Service, in 2004 to investigate deaths[28] in prison or immigration detention or prisoner transport, and in 2006 to immigration detention conditions generally.

Prisoner complaints that fall within the Ombudsman's remit are surprisingly few in number: only about 2,000 a year, in relation to 130 prisons and 85,000 prisoners. They are dealt with at two levels: first, by way of recommendation to the Prison Service in relation to each individual case; and second thematically, as illustrations of overall management practices that could be improved. The Annual Report typically contains sections on such matters as prisoner property, discipline and sanctions, sentence planning, and cell-sharing arrangements (Prisons and Probation Ombudsman 2009).

With regard to custodial deaths, in five years almost 1,000 files have been opened, 831 draft reports issued, and 762 final reports published. Prisoner deaths are subject to normal coronial inquiry processes, but these are held locally. The Prison Ombudsman's jurisdiction brings a national overview to death issues across the system. To date, more than 5,000 recommendations have been made. It has not been reported how many of these have been accepted and implemented (Prisons and Probation Ombudsman 2009).

The office still has no statutory basis. However, a Framework Document between the Ministry of Justice and the PPO was agreed and promulgated in 2009 (Prisons and Probation Ombudsman 2009). This seems to have moved the status and autonomy of the office to a somewhat clearer point. Nevertheless, continuing dependency on political goodwill is less than ideal if an agency is to be truly autonomous. This factor arguably bears upon the PPO's effectiveness.

In that respect, the office has not yet found an objective means to measure its own impact upon the system. "Plans to deliver a comprehensive management framework covering . . . organizational performance, have had to be bounced forward" (Prisons and Probation Ombudsman 2009, 6). At the very least, the PPO should mirror HMCIP, by reporting the percentage of recommendations nominally accepted and the implementation rate on the ground of those accepted recommendations.

In contrast, the Canadian Office of the Correctional Investigator (OCI) operates under statutory authority.[29] In 35 years it has received and dealt with 140,000 complaints—given the much smaller prisoner numbers, an apparently more active remit than that of the PPO. Its modus operandi is to visit all prisons at least four times a year. Its reporting style is thematic, focusing on the stated goals of Correctional Service Canada. These are: safe transition of eligible offenders into the community; safety and security for staff and offenders within institutions; effective interventions for indigenous prisoners; improved capacities to address mental health needs of offenders; and strengthened management practices, including service quality control and accountability. In accordance with the second stated goal, the OCI has also, like the PPO, made prisoner deaths a high priority for investigation.

The OCI, like the PPO, often expresses frustration at bureaucratic resistance to some of its recommendations. Nevertheless, it has made its mark in improving prison conditions. Its presence and activity ensure that there is a continuing dialogue in Canada about the nature of correctional regimes (Office of the Correctional Investigator 2007/2008).

Summary of the UK Position

HMCIP and PPO are the main players in the regulation of prison conditions. They are supported by Independent Monitoring Boards. The United Kingdom is also subject to the European inspection system involving the European Committee for the Prevention of Torture (CPT). The UK Government has also ratified the OPCAT.

Regulation of prison conditions is thus multilayered, and becoming more so. For the present, however, the HMCIP is the key agency.

V. European System

After World War II, Western Europe sought to embed safeguards against future abuse of human rights by governments. The early instruments reflected human rights preoccupations that were wide-ranging, rather than prison-specific. The 1950 European Convention on Human Rights (ECHR), which came into force in 1953, exemplified this, with its focus on broad-brush ideas such as the "inherent dignity of the human person." The regulation of prison conditions thus had to be fashioned with tools that were not created for that purpose. Van Zyl Smit and Snacken (2009, 1–12, 365) document how this held back the maturation of the regulatory system.[30]

The procedure under the ECHR required that individuals who believed that their human rights had been violated should first exhaust their domestic remedies— a procedural filter. Thereafter their complaint would go to the European Commission on Human Rights. This agency applied a substantive filter, namely the doctrine of "inherent limitations," which held that deprivation of liberty automatically entailed loss of other rights and freedoms. Only if a case survived this test would a complaint be sent through to the European Court of Human Rights. This self-created barrier was reminiscent of the approach of the UK judiciary.

In combination, these two filters meant that, in the first 30 years of its existence, the European Court heard only 15 cases relating to prison conditions and prisoners' rights (Van Zyl Smit and Snacken 2009, 10). Yet, during the same period, prisoner litigation in the United States was getting into "full stride." The contrast was epitomized by European Commission decisions in 1976 and 1977 that solitary confinement with no exercise or visits at all and punishment in the form of a reduced diet and a bed without a mattress did not amount to inhuman or degrading treatment under the ECHR.[31] These cases accordingly did not even reach the European Court for decision on the merits. The U.S. federal courts would have intervened in such cases.[32]

Subsequently, the European Court has become an active source for regulating prison conditions. To understand how this came about, it is necessary to break away from the litigation story and describe the development of the CPT (the European Committee for the Prevention of Torture and Inhuman or Degrading Treatment or Punishment).

Internationally, the United Nations Convention Against Torture and other Cruel, Inhuman and Degrading Treatment or Punishment (UNCAT) was being negotiated during the 1970s. To promote it beyond the level of exhortatory principles, some kind of inspection mechanism was needed. Nations were resistant to this. It became evident that international consensus would not be achieved at that time unless the inspection element were removed from the draft. This was done. The UNCAT was then passed in 1984, became operative in 1987, and has subsequently been ratified by 146 nations.

Abandonment of the inspection mechanism was frustrating to many European nations. Accordingly, within the Council of Europe[33] moves were made to agree upon a European Convention for the Prevention of Torture (ECPT). The substantive standards parallel those of UNCAT, specifically the prohibition of cruel, inhuman, or degrading treatment or punishment.[34] To give it some teeth, an inspection mechanism was created—the CPT. As from 1989, the CPT has been the engine-room for the development of standards for regulating prison conditions throughout Europe.

The significance of this should be seen in the context of the expansion of the Council of Europe. When the CPT commenced its role, there were 23 member nations, all Western European. Today there are 47 members.

The major expansion occurred following the break-up of the former Soviet Empire from 1989 onward. The new members comprised many Eastern European nations, including the Russian Federation, which has the second highest per capita rate of imprisonment in the world. The Council now also includes Turkey, which was regarded as having one of the most repressive prison systems. A non-negotiable pre-condition to being accepted into the Council is acceptance of the human rights standards encompassed by the various European instruments, *including submission to the inspection regime of the CPT.*

The CPT consists of one expert from each member state. Its modus operandi is to make announced or unannounced inspections of a sample of custodial institutions in each member state. Prisons are the prime example. However, in accordance with the philosophy that all involuntary detention authorized by the state bears the risk of human rights violations, other custodial institutions, particularly police cells and psychiatric wards, are targeted. The inspection team will not include the member from that state, and independent experts will be co-opted as required.

On-site the inspection team conducts itself very much as HMCIP—observations, prisoner interviews, staff interviews, and requisition of documents. Verbal feedback will be given to the management before departure, in the expectation that urgent matters will be addressed at once. However, the real thrust of the inspection is the formal report to the relevant government. Governments are given adequate time to respond to the report, both with written statements to the CPT and by changed practices. Unless the government objects, the report and the response will then be published. In practice only two governments have seriously objected—the Russian Federation and Turkey.[35] However, this phase has passed, and both states now permit publication.

The standards applied by the CPT link back to international and regional instruments prohibiting torture and inhuman and degrading treatment. These notions are anchored to empirical observations of practices in custodial settings. Over the years the CPT has built up a standards document covering every aspect of detention—health services, overcrowding, sanitation and hygiene, exercise and fresh air, productive activity, discipline and punishment, the needs of vulnerable prisoners, communication with the outside world, visits, issues for foreign nationals, and so on. The most recent standards document was consolidated in 2006 (Council for the Prevention of Torture 2006; Leidekker 2009).

The CPT now visits about 20 of the 47 states each year. Its inspection regime is far from comprehensive, therefore. Some states may not be visited more than every five years, though others may be visited annually or even more than once in a single year if they seem to require that degree of monitoring.[36] Each visit involves only a small sample of prisons and other custodial institutions, typically about eight.

These limitations are not insignificant. If sporadic sample inspections are to be effective, the central authorities must not only in good faith accept the broad implications of an inspection as requiring system-wide change (not just change in the inspected institution), but they must also have the capacity to enforce and sustain that change. Internal audits can only go so far; the nature of closed organizations is that they quite quickly take on their own idiosyncratic characteristics. As the former chair of the CPT has said: "Slippage is a common phenomenon in the human rights arena, and in the closed world of custody in particular" (Casale 2009, 10). The CPT model would be improved by national, comprehensive inspection systems. This is what the OPCAT contemplates.

To return to the litigation stream of regulating prison conditions, the development of standards by the CPT has fed into the approach of the European Court. This process was facilitated by the abolition of the European Commission in 1998, so that the Court could decide for itself whether to hear cases rather than their being filtered out by the Commission. From 2001 onward, a rich stream of case law, authoritative across the 47 states of the Council of Europe, has started to emerge.

The notion of "torture" necessarily involves intent, and this approach had previously colored the interpretation of "inhuman and degrading treatment or punishment," limiting its scope. A crucial decision was thus that the notion of "inhuman and degrading" did not require intent. In *Peers v. Greece*,[37] the European Court held that overcrowding of prisons could in principle contravene the ECPT, even though the prison authorities themselves did not endorse or deliberately engineer the overcrowding.[38] This decision potentially opened up to judicial oversight the whole field of imprisonment policy and prison administration.

In *Dickson v. United Kingdom*, the European Court emphasized that the "rehabilitative aim of imprisonment" possessed increasing importance in European prison policy.[39] Accordingly, this perspective would be taken into account as one of the factors in assessing what was inhuman or degrading. The Constitution-derived, Eighth Amendment approach to judicial intervention in the United States has not taken this factor into account in assessing cruel and unusual punishment.[40] In this respect, European Court-derived regulation, which lagged well behind the U.S. equivalent for many years, has now gone somewhat further.

At a day-to-day level, the European Court has adopted the approach of the CPT to such matters as: hygiene;[41] contact with the outside world;[42] shackling and handcuffing prisoners during transportation;[43] the procedures that must be observed in disciplinary proceedings;[44] and a wide range of other routine custodial matters (Van Zyl Smit and Snacken, *passim*).

The development of a code of European Prison Rules (EPR) has also fed into judicial activity providing as with CPT reports and standards, an interpretative context for European Court decisions about "inhuman and degrading" conditions. The current version of EPR was approved by the Council of Ministers in 2006. These replaced a 1987 version, which in turn replaced a 1973 version, which had more or less replicated the SMR.

In Europe, CPT inspection standards have given vitality to judicial intervention, and court decisions have in turn reinforced CPT reports and standards. The EPR, as the third main element in the regulation of prison conditions, have also provided reinforcement to, as well as drawing strength and validity from, the CPT and the European Court.

The missing element is regular and comprehensive on-site inspection at the national level by standing autonomous agencies. Judicial decisions, codes of standards, and sporadic sample inspections of prisons still do not tell the whole story of what is happening on the ground. No European nation had a standing inspectorate as clearly autonomous as the HMCIP to carry out that role. This is the hiatus that the OPCAT sought to fill.

VI. THE OPCAT

In 2002 the United Nations passed the OPCAT, thereby facilitating an inspection mechanism for UNCAT of the kind that had previously been rejected.[45] In June 2006, with the twentieth ratification, the OPCAT became operative and binding upon States Parties. By 2010, 50 states had ratified. To date, the States Parties mostly come from

Europe, South America, and, to a lesser extent, Africa.[46] Neither the United States nor the Russian Federation, the two nations globally with the greatest prisoner populations and highest imprisonment rates, has signed or ratified the OPCAT.

A Dual Track Regulatory System

There are two regulatory strands to the OPCAT. First, the Protocol establishes the Subcommittee for the Prevention of Torture (SPT). This is modeled upon the CPT. Its membership consists of experts from States Parties—10 when the Protocol became operative, 25 once the fiftieth State had ratified.

The remit of the SPT is to carry out visits-based inspections of "places of detention" in selected states. As with the CPT, the scope of places of detention takes in not just prisons but closed psychiatric wards, juvenile detention centers, immigration detention areas, police cells, and a range of other places where people are involuntarily detained. The modus operandi and the reporting arrangements likewise very much mirror those of the CPT. Ratification of OPCAT obliges States Parties under Article 20 to permit access and the untrammeled exercise of the required powers.

From a practical point of view, the SPT's capacity to influence whether a state's practices amount to "torture" or are "cruel, inhuman, or degrading" is very limited. Only a tiny sample of places of detention can be inspected. For example, Mexico has estimated that more than 5,000 places fall within the definition, yet the 2009 SPT inspection covered only 25 of them.[47] Also, the resources available to the SPT are sparse; it could well take a decade to conduct just a single sample inspection of all the States Parties.

The second regulatory strand is potentially the real driver of the OPCAT system. Under Article 17, States Parties are required to set up "national preventive mechanisms" (NPMs) under their own domestic laws. This is the "value added" aspect of the OPCAT, over and above the CPT approach (Tayler 2009).

In essence, the powers and modus operandi of these NPMs will mirror those of the England and Wales HMCIP, though taking account of local structures and arrangements. An important provision within Article 17 is that multiple agencies may be designated as NPMs. This takes into account political and legal complexities that may arise in federal or otherwise fragmented state governance arrangements.

Each NPM must have "functional independence," and States Parties "should make available necessary resources" ((Article 18). States Parties must grant the NPM power to "regularly examine the treatment of persons deprived of their liberty" (Article 19). The NPM shall be allowed access to all places of detention, shall be able to conduct private interviews with prisoners and others, and shall choose the places it wants to visit (Article 20). Implicit in this provision is that visits may be announced or unannounced.

Operational departments can be prone to intimidate or victimize detainees or staff for cooperating with inspectorates. Article 21 provides that "a State shall not order, permit or tolerate any sanction against any person or organization for communicating with the NPM." The same Article mandates that confidential information received by the NPM shall be privileged.

The standards to be applied will be developed further by NPMs in coordination with the SPT. To facilitate this, Article 20(f) specifically provides that "the NPM shall have the right to have contact with the SPT, to send it information and to meet with it." The starting point is the jurisprudence developed in the European Court and the standards promulgated by the CPT in the context of the European Convention's prohibition of "torture" and "inhuman and degrading treatment or punishment."

However, local factors must be incorporated if the NPM structures are to be effective. The first chair of the SPT, who was also the former chair of the CPT, has stated:

> At the universal level, the extent of diversity across regions and states is far greater, and therefore the need for an incremental approach to implementation of standards is all the more evident. The universal standards, such as the SMR, are in some respects vague and outdated. The SPT has therefore adopted a considered approach to the application of standards based on the *pro homine* principle. Thus within a region the SPT will refer to regional international standards, and even to national standards, to the extent that they confer greater protection of human rights. (Casale 2009, 9)

The OPCAT favors a "constructive dialogue" approach with States Parties. Neither the Reports of the SPT nor those of NPMs are intended to be instruments with which to bludgeon governments. The SPT will not publish its reports without agreement, though as with the CPT it may make a public statement pursuant to Article 16(2) if full publication is blocked. The expectation is that, as with the CPT, publication will become the norm. NPMs will be able to publish their annual reports, though under the OPCAT there is no requirement for the publication of individual reports. This is a point of departure from the HMCIP model, where publication occurs as a matter of course and is regarded as a core element of regulation.

The SPT's Jurisdiction So Far

In the period from October 2007 to December 2009, the SPT made eight country inspection visits. These related to Mauritius, the Maldives, Sweden, Benin, Mexico, Paraguay, Honduras and Cambodia. Three reports (Maldives, Sweden, and Honduras) and one country response (Sweden) have been made public.[48] In these early days of establishing procedures and relationships, the delay in publishing reports is longer than ideal.

The style of the reports would be familiar to readers of CPT reports. On-the-ground observations are quite robust, while the recommendatory tone is somewhat abstract. A report is a "part of the dialogue between the Subcommittee and the authorities aimed at preventing torture and other cruel, inhuman or degrading treatment or punishment" (Committee Against Torture 2008, 6). It is not a hard-nosed document against which to measure implementation. That contrasts with the approach in the United States, with its court orders, or with the HMCIP in its follow-up inspections.

The SPT also visits States Parties to consult and advise upon the development of their NPM structures. Autonomous national inspection systems for places of detention are, as we have seen, rare beasts globally. Governments are not always fully cognizant of what is expected of them once they have ratified the OPCAT. So the SPT has developed a set of guidelines designed to assist (Committee Against Torture 2008, 10–11).

Establishing NPMs

The OPCAT requires that an NPM structure be set up within 12 months of ratification (Article 17). In practice, this deadline has proved too demanding. Only 12 of the 31 States Parties that have so far designated their NPM managed to do so within that period.[49] Recognizing the logistical and internal political challenges that the creation of a new regulatory mechanism may involve, the OPCAT provides that States may upon ratification make a reservation postponing implementation by a period of up to three years (Article 24). However, only one State Party—Germany—has formally adopted this mechanism.

Three main paths have been taken in the creation of NPMs. These are: building a structure around an existing national human rights institution (NHRI); similarly, building around an ombudsman office; or creating an entirely new agency. Overlaid is the factor that multiple agencies may be designated as the NPM.

Mexico has designated its NHRI as the NPM. However, there are complexities in doing so. Constitutionally, the federal government lacks the power to impose the federal NHRI jurisdiction upon the 31 constituent states of the federation. Thus, some kind of collaborative arrangement with state NHRIs will need to be made. However, local exigencies are such that the central government is reluctant to confer NPM status upon the state NHRIs. There is something of an impasse, therefore, with the NPM structure still not fully comprehensive.

Another federal State, Argentina, has struggled to agree upon a model for the NPM. There are 23 state jurisdictions in addition to the federal district of Buenos Aires. Some of these states have drafted rival NPM proposals that do not accord with the federal proposals. An additional complication is that, in the light of the recent history of state terrorism, civil society still distrusts official agencies. In their view, these agencies are always potentially liable to become complicit in cover-ups of human rights abuses. Accordingly, they are determined to acquire some part of the NPM role and status. The debates continue. The consequence is that, although Argentina ratified the OPCAT in 2004, no NPM has yet been established.

Germany deposited its ratification subject to a three-year implementation period. This path was taken because of the complexity of the negotiations between the federal government and the 16 *Lander* (state governments). As of January 2010, agreement has been reached that there will be two new NPM agencies: one (the Federal Agency for the Prevention of Torture) to cover categories and places of detention under federal law, and the other (the Joint Commission of the *Lander* for the

Prevention of Torture) to cover the functionally and quantitatively far more signifi-cant categories and places of detention under *Lander* laws.

The United Kingdom has designated 18 agencies as NPMs. Though the United Kingdom is not a federal state, Scotland has autonomous jurisdiction over the mat-ters covered by the OPCAT, and Northern Ireland is partially autonomous. None of the agencies currently involved in inspection and regulation was prepared to be downgraded by exclusion from the NPM arrangements. The lead NPM agency—the one to deal with the SPT and lead the development of a national unifying ap-proach—will be HMCIP. This reflects its history and status as the iconic autonomous inspection agency in the United Kingdom.

New Zealand is a unitary state. There are no federal complications or com-peting jurisdictional claims. Nevertheless, it has been necessary to designate mul-tiple NPMs. The NHRI—the Human Rights Commission—has been designated the "Central NPM." Four other agencies—the Ombudsman, the Office of the Children's Commissioner, the Independent Police Conduct Authority, and the Registrar of Court Martials—have also been designated as NPMs. The Central NPM does not have any direct inspection responsibility. Its role is to coordinate the activities of the other NPMs, to identify priorities, to oversight inspection standards and practices, and to liaise both internationally with the SPT and nationally with government agencies (Harding and Morgan 2010, 107–114).

States Parties that have designated the ombudsman as the lead or exclusive NPM include: Costa Rica, Albania, the Czech Republic, Sweden, and Poland. The national NHRI has been designated in various countries including Mauritius, the Maldives, Mali, the Ukraine, and Armenia.

France ratified the OPCAT in November 2008. In the preceding 18 months both the Mediateur de la Republique (an ombudsman-like agency) and the Commission nationale consultative des droits de l'homme (the NHRI) staked their claims to be the lead NPM. However, the Ministry of Justice decided to create an entirely new mechanism, the Controleur général des lieux de privation de liberté (the General Inspector for Places of Deprivation of Liberty). This Inspector has been operational since July 2008.

A former French colony, Senegal, has replicated this model. New agencies have also been created in Liechtenstein and Switzerland, among others.

Civil society organizations have been layered into NPM arrangements in sev-eral countries, including the Republic of Moldova and Spain.

The Future of OPCAT

This brief conspectus confirms that the OPCAT can only be implemented in ways that fit with local value systems, bureaucratic structures, and political realities. If a uniform model were mandated by the OPCAT, it would be stillborn. The OPCAT's strength is the flexibility that it facilitates. This is also its weakness. Some NPM ar-rangements fall short of an ideal NPM model.

The prognosis must be that for most States Parties the OPCAT is at least a ten-year project, from the time of ratification. To acknowledge this is not as daunting and discouraging as it might seem. In the United Kingdom, HMCIP only reached its full maturity in about 1990—nine years after it first became operational. In Europe, the CPT likewise only became fully effective as more countries joined the Council of Europe—from the early 1990s, about ten years after its commencement. The regulation of prison and custodial conditions involves highly sensitive state priorities that will not be resolved rapidly.

Of course, internationally there are still far more states that have not ratified than those that have done so. Specifically, 96 UNCAT ratifying nations have not yet ratified OPCAT. A key aspect of assessing the future is thus whether more nations will ratify and at what rate.

The OPCAT is an unmistakably "Western" document. In that context, it can be expected that virtually all of the Council of Europe countries, most of Central and South America nations, several more African countries, and Canada and Australia will ratify within the foreseeable future. However, it is not surprising that Asian and Arab nations have to this point shown little enthusiasm for ratification. These nations have their own distinctive cultures, histories, and values that do not necessarily lead to the OPCAT being seen as high priority or even as particularly relevant to their longer term preoccupations (Harding and Morgan 2010, 99–106 and *passim*).

Nevertheless, it is possible to identify, particularly within Asia, some nations that may well lead the way. These include Korea, Japan, Malaysia, Thailand, and the Philippines. As one, and then perhaps the next, ratifies, the pace may pick up.

Another possibility is that regional regulatory arrangements may become more embedded. This has been the case with the European Convention Against Torture and the CPT. Possibly, some further development could occur within the ambit of the ASEAN Inter-Governmental Commission on Human Rights, just as has happened to some extent within the purview of the Inter-American Human Rights Commission and the African Commission on Human and People's Rights.

If this were to occur, the OPCAT anticipates complementarity of the systems, rather than exclusivity of OPCAT-derived arrangements:

> The provisions of the present Protocol shall not affect the obligations of States Parties under any regional convention instituting a system of visits to places of detention. The Subcommittee on Prevention and the bodies established under such regional conventions are encouraged to consult and cooperate with a view to avoiding duplication and promoting effectively the objectives of the present protocol. (Article 31)[50]

Nevertheless, further progress with the OPCAT is likely to be uneven and slow. It will never become a universal model. Some nations have insuperable ideological objections to the approach that it exemplifies. Moreover, as with other international conventions, the position of the United States is particularly significant. To this point, ratification does not seem to be an agenda item within the U.S. political establishment.

VII. Strengths and Weaknesses of the Various Models: The Need for Autonomous Inspection

The history of the regulation of prison conditions has been patchy and uneven. This is because the administration of a core state function—involuntary detention of citizens—has inevitably been dominated by national values, history, and culture. This will never completely change. However, regional and international values and standards have become increasingly significant both in themselves and also as they slowly become absorbed into national values and culture.

Globally, the aspect of regulation concerned to minimize repression is the highest priority. In many countries, prison and custodial conditions are still degrading. In these countries, regulatory standards and processes directed at optimizing the positive potential of the prison experience are hardly relevant.

Whichever aspect of regulation is being considered, however, international comparisons establish beyond dispute that autonomous visits-based inspections of prisons and other closed institutions comprise an essential tool in any package of mechanisms for regulating prison conditions. By themselves, court orders, accreditation systems, NGO and civil society interventions, international or regional standard-setting instruments, external complaints mechanisms, and political scrutiny will not provide the continuity and expertise that are crucial characteristics in effective regulation.

The OPCAT is a strong model, reflecting the experience of the most accountable regulatory regimes. This is what countries should ideally hope to achieve. However, in assessing global progress toward regulation, it is necessary to understand and accept that if we set the bar too high we simply guarantee that more countries will fall short. Relative progress is more important than none at all. The path would be smoothed if the two countries with the highest prisoner numbers and rates of imprisonment—the Russian Federation and the United States—showed leadership by committing to effective regulation of prison conditions.

NOTES

1.   The official figures distinguish between the prison population (c. 1,600,000) and the jail population (c. 750,000). This distinction has no significance for the purposes of this discussion.

2.   The SMR were first conceptualized in Europe in 1926, and that version was adopted by the League of Nations in 1934. After World War II, further development led to the formulation of the current version. This was adopted by the First UN Congress on the Prevention of Crime and the Treatment of Offenders in 1955 and approved by the UN's Economic and Social Council in 1957.

3.   *Fullwood v. Clemmer*, 206 F. Supp. 370 (D.D.C. 1962), relating to the right of Black Muslim prisoners to hold religious meetings.

4.   *Procunier v. Martinez*, 416 U.S. 396, 404 (1974).

5.   At pp. 51–143 the authors describe and analyze five key case studies: Arkansas (whole system); Texas (whole system); Colorado State Penitentiary; Santa Clara jail (California); and the federal maximum security prison at Marion, Illinois. In the latter case the government was successful.

6.   The high point numerically of court intervention came in 1990, when 44 states were subject to some kind of court order, of which 13 were system-wide.

7.   Feeley and Rubin (1999, 80–95) describe the detailed and "hands on" role of the Special Master appointed by the court to oversee the Texas Department of Corrections in the case of *Ruiz v. Estelle*.

8.   The Commission on Safety and Abuse in America's Prisons commented that "Congress conducted no studies and held only one substantive hearing to consider solutions before passing the PLRA as a rider to an Appropriations Bill" (Gibbons and Katzenbach 2006, 85).

9.   Nevertheless, in highly exceptional circumstances, the courts are still able to pick their way through the minefield of barriers set up by the Prisoner Litigation Reform Act. In *Brown v. Plata*, 131 S. Ct. 1910 (2011), the Supreme Court (5-4) upheld a US District Court decision requiring California to reduce overcrowding in the state prison system to the point where population only exceeded capacity by 37.5%. This would entail reducing the prison population by approximately 50,000. The state was ordered to formulate a compliance plan and submit it to the US District Court for approval. A 2-year deadline was set for relief.

10.   Criminal Justice Section Report to the House of Delegates, 29 April 2008.

11.   See *R. v. Deputy Governor of Parkhurst, ex parte Leech* [1988] 1 AC 533.

12.   *R. v. Home Secretary, ex parte Daly* [2001] 2 AC 532.

13.   See, e.g., the cases in footnotes 38 and 43, below.

14.   Other forms of autonomous inspection exist in various places such as South Africa and Norway. However, there are gaps in these examples. The Western Australian model is the only one that possesses the functional independence, powers, and reporting protocols of HMCIP. Indeed, in some ways that model exceeds the UK model: see Harding 2007, *passim*.

15.   See now § 5A of the Prisons Act 1952. The Chief Inspector's office had de facto been operating since January 1, 1981, and the 1982 legislation regularized its existence.

16.   Personal discussion between the author and the then Chief Inspector, Dame Anne Owers. Ms. Owers was Chief Inspector from 2001–2010.

17.   The most closely comparable inspection agency, the Western Australia Office of the Inspector of Custodial Services, has gone in the diametrically opposite direction. The *Inspector of Custodial Services Act 2003* explicitly spells out the wide-ranging powers of the Inspector.

18.   See § 28 of the Police and Justice Act 2006. There were five joint inspections in 2008–2009, principally with the Probation Inspectorate and the Chief Inspector of Constabulary. This aspect of jurisdiction is now on the increase.

19.   Independent monitoring boards consist of citizens from the local community. They encapsulate the values that prisons are community organisms and that civil society should be involved in regulating prison conditions.

20.   Author's conversations with Lord David Ramsbotham, Chief Inspector from 1995–2001. Ramsbotham (2003, 227–230) documents the worst case of Prison Service

blockage. This related to the publication of the key standards document, "Expectations," described below. The MOU between HMCIP and the National Offender Management Service now states that "HMCIP . . . is not responsible for chasing responses on factual accuracy. It is therefore important that responses are made to HMCIP by the stated deadline. If this does not happen, the report will be published according to the timetable set by HMCIP in any case. . . ."

21.   These matters are all spelled out in the MOU between HMCIP and the National Offender Management Service: www.justice.gov.uk/inspectorates/hmi-prisons.

22.   Operational agencies run a political risk in rejecting recommendations if they subsequently prove to have been crucially important. In Western Australia the bureaucracy and the government rejected a recommendation relating to security at a court holding complex, and nine prisoners subsequently escaped in circumstances that had been identified by the Inspector. Similarly, a prisoner died in the course of a long transport in circumstances previously identified as high risk by the Inspector. In each case the government of the day suffered significant political damage. In each case the identified deficiencies were belatedly rectified.

23.   An example is as follows. The safety criterion of the healthy prison test deals with intimidating behavior by prisoners toward other prisoners. One "expectation" (see p. 35 of the 2004 edition) requires that "allegations of bullying are treated fairly and consistently. They receive an immediate response, the incidents are fully investigated with outcomes recorded, and the prisoner who reported the bullying is kept fully informed." The evidence sources to be triangulated are: documentation held by the prison, questions to staff, interviews with prisoners, and answers to the survey questionnaires that will have been circulated to staff and prisoners in advance of the inspection. The sources for this expectation are identified as various clauses in the UN Standard Minimum Rules and the European Prison Rules.

24.   The first version appeared in 2004. The latest version is the third, published in 2006. See generally www.justice.gov.uk/inspectorates/hmi-prisons.

25.   As the remit of HMCIP has expanded, so tailor-made Expectations have been published for other custodial situations: e.g., Immigration Detention Expectations and Children and Young Offenders Expectations.

26.   In 2000 the UK Government commissioned Lord Laming to report on modernizing the management of the Prison Service. He recommended that the Prison Service and HMCIP agree upon standards and that henceforth HMCIP should carry out quality control audits against those agreed-upon standards. Apart from undermining the autonomy and status of HMCIP, this proposal would have guaranteed that inspection standards would be static or, at best, lose much of their forward momentum as changes would need to be negotiated. The operational agency would in effect have a power of veto over fresh expectations.

27.   Each of these reports can be found on the web site of the Chief Inspector: www. justice.gov.uk/inspectorates/hmi-prisons.

28.   "Near-deaths" are also investigated, i.e., incidents in which the person was saved from death by effective intervention of some kind. The rationale of this is that lessons to be learned about the management and health status of persons in custody will emerge equally from such incidents as from actual deaths.

29.   Corrections and Conditional Release Act 1992, §§ 157–195. The Office was established in 1973 and operated under administrative arrangements for 19 years.

30.   The author draws at various points in this section on this comprehensive treatise.

31.   *Eggs v. Switzerland* [E Com HR] 11 December 1976; *X v. Germany* [E Com HR] 11 July 1977.

32.   See, e.g., *Talley v. Stephens*, 247 F. Supp. 683 (D. Ark. 1965); *Jackson v. Bishop*, 404 F. 2d 571 (8th Cir. 1968); and *Ruiz v. Estelle*, 503 F. Supp. 1265 (D. Tex. 1980).

33.   The Council was established by the Treaty of London in 1949. The Council is the vehicle that has progressed all of the European Conventions under discussion. It is membership of the Council that attaches nations to these Conventions.

34.   However, the word "cruel" was omitted from the category of prohibited behavior. This seems to have made no tangible difference to the Convention's scope.

35.   Turkey objected to publication of Country Reports in 1992 and 1996, causing the CPT invoke its power to make a "Public Statement." Likewise, Public Statements were made in 2001, 2003, and 2007 with regard to the Chechen region of the Russian Federation. The CPT does not pull its punches. For example, the 2007 Statement relating to Chechen states that: "Resort to torture and other forms of ill treatment by members of law enforcement agencies and security forces continues, as does the practice of unlawful detentions": see CPT/Inf (2007) 17.

36.   The Chechen area of the Russian Federation has been visited seven times since 2000; Turkey twelve times since 2000. By contrast, Norway has only been visited once this century, and the Netherlands and Austria at five-year intervals.

37.   (2001) 33 EHRR 51.

38.   See also *Mamedova v. Russia*, 1 June 2006, where the overcrowding was due to maintenance work: "It is incumbent upon the Government to organize its penitentiary system in such a way as to ensure respect for the dignity of detainees, *regardless of financial or logistical difficulties*" [author's italics].

39.   18 April 2006, (2007) 44 EHRR 21. This case was decided by the Grand Chamber or Full Court of 17 Judges.

40.   A dictum in *Holt v. Sarver*, 309 F. Supp. 362, 382 (D. Ark. 1970) (Holt II), suggested that the courts could take absence of rehabilitation opportunities into account when assessing whether other deprivations amount to cruel and unusual punishment. However, this line of case law does not appear to have taken hold: see Schlanger (2006, 622).

41.   *Melnik v. Ukraine*, 28 March 2006.

42.   *Ilascu and others v. Moldova and Russia*, 8 July 2004, (2005) 40 EHRR 46.

43.   *Mouisel v. France*, 14 November 2002, (2004) 38 EHRR 34.

44.   *Ezeh and Connors v. United Kingdom*, 9 October 2003, (2004) 39 EHRR 1.

45.   The leading source on all matters relating to the OPCAT is the web site of the Geneva-based Association for the Prevention of Torture—www.apt.ch.

46.   Specifically, as of January 2010, 25 European nations, 12 South and Central American nations, 6 African nations, 5 nations from Central Asia, the Middle East, and the Indian Ocean, plus Cambodia and New Zealand, have ratified the OPCAT.

47.   The Report has not yet been released. Details of SPT visits can be found at http://www2.ohchr.org/English/bodies/cat/opcat/spt_visits.htm and go to CAT/OP/ SWE/1 at p. 39.

48.   Access to this information is via the web sites of either the Office of the UN High Commissioner for Human Rights (http://www2.ohchr.org) or of the Association for the Prevention of Torture (www.apt.ch).

49.   The source for most of the country-specific information contained in this Section is www.apt.ch—National Preventive Mechanisms—OPCAT Country Status, April 2010. Unless another reference is cited, it can be assumed that this is the source, therefore.

50.   The scope of this Article is already being explored in relation to CPT nations that have also ratified the OPCAT.

REFERENCES

Amnesty International. 2010. *Amnesty International Report 2010*. Online. Available at: http://report2010.amnesty.org/sites/default/files.AIR2010_AZ_EN.pdf.

Argentine National Commission on the Disappeared. 1986. *Nunca Mas (Never Again)*. New York: Farrar Strauss Giroux.

Association for the Prevention of Torture. Online. Available at: www.apt.ch.

Bureau of Justice Statistics. 2010. *Jail Inmates at Midyear 2009—Statistical Tables*. Washington, DC: Bureau of Justice Statistics.

Bureau of Justice Statistics. 2009. *Prisoners in 2008*. Washington, DC: Bureau of Justice Statistics.

Bronstein, Alvin J., and Jenni Gainsborough. 2003–2004. "The International Context of U.S. Prison Reform: Using International Human Rights Laws and Standards for U.S. Prison Reform." *Pace Law Review* 24: 811–824.

Casale, Silvia. 2009. "A System of Preventive Oversight." *Essex Human Rights Review* 6(1): 6–14.

Commission on Safety and Abuse in America's Prisons. 2006. *Confronting Confinement*. New York: Vera Institute of Justice.

Committee Against Torture. 2008. Online. Available at: http://www2.ohchr.org/English/bodies/cat/opcat/spt_visits.htm.

Council for the Prevention of Torture. 2006. *Inspection Standards*. Online. Available at: http://www.cpt.coe.int/en/standards.htm.

Dinitz, Simon. 2001. "Are Safe and Humane Prisons Possible?" *Australia and New Zealand Journal of Criminology* 14: 3–19.

Feeley, Malcolm, and Edward L. Rubin. 1999. *Judicial Policy Making and the Modern State: How the Courts Reformed America's Prisons*. Cambridge: Cambridge University Press.

Feeley, Malcolm, and Van Swearingen. 2004. "The Prison Conditions Cases and the Bureaucratization of American Corrections: Influences, Impacts and Implications." *Pace Law Review* 24: 433–475.

Garland, David. 2001. "The Meaning of Mass Imprisonment." *Punishment and Society* 3: 5–7.

Gibbons, J., and N. de B. Katzenbach. 2006. *Confronting Confinement: A Report of the Commission on Safety and Abuse in America's Prisons*. New York: Vera Institute of Justice.

Ginbar, Yuval. 2009. "'Celebrating' a Decade of Legalized Torture in Israel." *Essex Human Rights Review* 6(1): 169–187.

Gourevitch, Philip, and Errol Morris. 2008. *Standard Operating Procedure: A War Story*. New York: Picador Books.

Harding, Richard. 1997. *Private Prisons and Public Accountability*. Newark, NJ: Transaction Publishers.

Harding, Richard. 2007. "Inspecting Prisons." In *Handbook on Prisons*, ed. Yvonne Jewkes, 543–565. Portland, OR: Willan Publishing.

Harding, Richard, and Neil Morgan. 2010. "OPCAT in the Asia-Pacific and Australasia." *Essex Human Rights Review* 6(2): 99–124.

Her Majesty's Chief Inspector of Prisons. 2006. *Expectations: Criteria for assessing the conditions in prisons and the treatment of prisoners*. Online. Available at: www.justice.gov.uk/inspectorates/hmi-prisons.

Her Majesty's Chief Inspector of Prisons. 2008. *Annual Report 2007–2008*. Online. Available at: www.justice.gov.uk/inspectorates/hmi-prisons.

Her Majesty's Chief Inspector of Prisons. 2009. *The Prison Characteristics That Predict Prisons Being Assessed as Performing Well*. Online. Available at: www.justice.gov.uk/inspectorates/hmi-prisons.

Johnston, E. 1991. *Royal Commission into Aboriginal Deaths in Custody: National Report*. Canberra: Australian Government Publication Series.

Keve, Paul W. 1996. *Measuring Excellence: The History of Correctional Standards and Accreditation*. Lanham, MD: ACA Publications.

Leidekker, Marco. 2009. "Evolution of the CPT's Standards since 2001." *Essex Human Rights Review* 6(1): 98–105.

Livingstone, Stephen, Tim Owen, and Alison MacDonald. 2008. *Prison Law*, 4th ed. Oxford: Oxford University Press.

Martin, Mark D. 2007. *Jail Standards and Inspection Programs: Resource and Implementation Guide*. Washington, DC: National Institute of Justice, Accession Number 022180.

Morgan, Rod. 1985. "Her Majesty's Inspectorate of Prisons." In *Accountability and Prisons: Opening up a Closed World*, eds. Michael Maguire, Jon Vagg, and Rod Morgan, 106–123. London" Tavistock Publications.

New York State Special Commission on Attica. 1972. *Attica, the Official Report*. New York: Praeger Publishers.

Office of the Correctional Investigator. 2008. *Annual Report 2007/08: 35th Anniversary Office of the Correctional Investigator 1973–2008*. Online. Available at: http://www.oci-bec.gc.ca.

Office of the Inspector of Custodial Services. 2002. *Report of an Announced Inspection of Bandyup Women's Prison, June 2002*. Online. Available at: www.custodialinspector.wa.gov.au.

Owers, Anne. 2003. *Prison Inspection and the Protection of Human Rights*. London: British Institute of Human Rights.

Prisons and Probation Ombudsman. 2009. *Annual Report, 2009*. Online. Available at: www.ppo.gov.uk.

Ramsbotham, David. 2003. *Prisongate: The Shocking State of Britain's Prisons and the Need for Visionary Change*. London: Free Press.

Rodriguez, Sara A. 2007. "The Impotence of Being Earnest: Status of the United Nations Standard Minimum Rules for the Treatment of Prisoners in Europe and the United States." *Criminal and Civil Confinement* 33: 61–122.

Schlanger, Margo. 2006. "Civil Rights Injunctions over Time: A Case Study of Jail and Prison Court Orders." *New York University Law Review* 81: 550–630.

Senate Armed Services Committee Inquiry into the Treatment of Detainees in U.S. Custody. 2008. Online. Available at: http://levin.senate.gov. December 12, 2008.

Stern, Vivien. 1998. *A Sin Against the Future: Imprisonment in the World*. London: Penguin Books.

Tayler, Wilder. 2009. "What Is the Added Value of Prevention?" *Essex Human Rights Review* 6(1): 22–29.

Van Zyl Smit, Dirk, and Sonja Snacken. 2009. *Principles of European Prison Law and Policy: Penology and Human Rights*. Oxford: Oxford University Press.

Woolf, Harry K., and Stephen Tumim. 1991. *Prison Disturbances, April 1990: Report of an Inquiry*. London: Her Majesty's Stationery Office (Cm 1456).

Section D
What Works in
Correctional Treatment?

CHAPTER 19

UNDERSTANDING THE IMPACT OF DRUG TREATMENT IN CORRECTIONAL SETTINGS

STEVEN BELENKO, KIMBERLY A. HOUSER AND WAYNE WELSH

INTRODUCTION AND OVERVIEW

This chapter examines drug treatment in state prisons, including the need for and utilization of treatment, the effectiveness and economic benefits of drug treatment, challenges for implementing and expanding effective treatment, and the characteristics and principles of effective correctional treatment programs. We focus on inmates in state correctional facilities for several reasons. First, state correctional systems house about 60 percent of the nation's inmate population and 88 percent of the prison population (Sabol et al. 2009; Sabol and Minton 2008). Second, local jail and prison populations are similar in terms of drug and alcohol use patterns, while federal inmates have somewhat different profiles: fewer drug users, more non-using drug traffickers, and different demographic characteristics (Mumola and Karberg 2006). In addition, because jail inmates are either being held in pre-trial detention or sentenced for relatively short terms, the availability of drug treatment and the process for accessing treatment are much different from those for state prison inmates. Finally, focusing on one correctional system facilitates the presentation of data and discussion of the research on treatment effectiveness, which has primarily been conducted with state prison inmates. This chapter does not address alcohol abuse or the effectiveness of alcohol treatment for inmates, given the relative lack of research on these issues (although many drug treatment programs also address alcohol abuse).

The connections between the abuse of illegal drugs and crime have been well documented (Belenko and Peugh 2005; Chandler et al. 2009; Tonry and Wilson 1990). Histories of illegal drug use are common among inmates and other offenders, and more than 80 percent have indications of serious drug or alcohol involvement (Belenko and Peugh 2005). Within three years, about 95 percent of released state inmates with drug use histories return to drug use (Martin et al. 1999); 68 percent of drug offenders are rearrested (41 percent for a new drug offense), 47 percent are reconvicted, and 25 percent are sentenced to prison for a new crime (Langan and Levin 2002).

We analyzed the drug and alcohol use patterns, and drug treatment involvement, of state prison inmates using data from the 2004 Survey of Inmates of State Correctional Facilities. The survey was administered between October 2003 and May 2004 by the Bureau of the Census for the U.S. Bureau of Justice Statistics (BJS). The two-stage sampling procedure first selected 287 prisons (225 male, 62 female, including the 14 largest male and 7 largest female prisons, with the remainder stratified by region, security level, and size) from the universe of 1,585 operational state prisons, then inmates within those prisons (James and Glaze 2006). Second, inmates were randomly selected (approximately 1 in 85 males and 1 in 24 females) with 14,499 interviews completed (11,569 males, 2,930 females), and an overall response rate of 89.8 percent. Respondents were administered oral and written informed consent. The confidential audio computer-assisted interviews included items related to sociodemographic characteristics, current offense and sentence, criminal history, prior drug and alcohol use and treatment, prison activities and programs, and physical and mental health. Our analyses applied sample weighting factors calculated from the probabilities that the respondent was selected for the sample, adjusting for nonresponse rates across selection strata, inmate respondent characteristics, and offense types. See ICPSR (2004) for additional details on sampling and weighting procedures.

ILLEGAL DRUG USE AMONG STATE PRISON INMATES

Overall, 82 percent of state prison inmates reported any lifetime use of an illegal drug, more than two-thirds reported having ever used illegal drugs regularly (68 percent), and 55 percent were using in the month before the arrest that resulted in their incarceration (see table 19.1). In addition, 32 percent were under the influence of drugs at the time of the offense, and 16.5 percent reported committing their crime to get money to buy drugs. Although marijuana is the most commonly used illegal drug, substantial percentages of inmates also have used other illegal drugs: 42 percent have used cocaine, 25 percent crack, 19 percent heroin, 12 percent other opiates, 23 percent methamphetamine, and 18 percent LSD. All of these prevalence rates are far higher than observed in the general population (SAMHSA 2008). For nearly all these indicators, prevalence was higher among female inmates.

State prison inmates have very high rates of drug abuse and dependence. Based on DSM-IV criteria, 53.0 percent of male inmates and 60.2 percent of females meet the criteria for drug abuse or dependence (table 19.1), compared with an estimated 13.0 percent of males and 5.5 percent of females in the general population aged 18 or older (SAMHSA 2008). Drug abuse or dependence is common among inmates no matter what their offense: 46.7 percent of those incarcerated for violent crimes, 63.2 percent of property offenders, 63.1 percent of drug offenders, and 50.2 percent of public order offenders (Mumola and Karberg 2006).

Drug-Related Consequences

Inmates are highly likely to have experienced problems and consequences relating to their drug use (see table 19.2); such consequences raise the importance of delivering treatment to inmates, but also increase the challenges of implementing appropriate and effective treatment (Belenko and Peugh 2005; Chandler et al. 2009). More than

Table 19.1. Lifetime Illegal Drug Use among State Prison Inmates, 2004

	Male	Female	TOTAL
Ever used illegal drugs	82.3	81.8	82.3
Ever used illegal drugs regularly*	68.1	71.2	68.3
Used in month before incarceration	55.1	58.6	55.3
Under the influence of drugs at the time of offense	31.1	37.7	31.6
Committed crime to get money to buy drugs	15.9	24.5	16.5
Drug abuse or dependence	53.0	60.2	53.4
Ever used marijuana	78.1	70.0	77.6
Ever used cocaine	41.7	46.9	42.1
Ever used crack	23.7	40.8	24.8
Ever used heroin	18.5	21.7	18.7
Ever used other opiates	11.6	15.7	11.9
Ever used methamphetamines	22.8	32.4	23.4
Ever used amphetamines	17.5	20.1	17.6
Ever used LSD	24.1	22.1	23.9

*Ever used any illegal drug once a week or more for at least a month

Source: BJS Survey of Inmates in State Correctional Facilities (2004).

Table 19.2. Problems Associated with Illegal Drug Use among State Prison
Inmates, 2004

	Male	Female	TOTAL
Ever injected drugs	17.2	27.0	17.9
Shared a needle / used needle suspected someone else used	7.1	12.4	7.4
Driven any type of vehicle under the influence of drugs	55.0	54.1	54.9
Ever had an accident under the influence of drugs	8.8	9.1	8.8
Got into dangerous situations using or just after using drugs*	33.6	38.2	33.9
Have arguments with friends/family under the influence of drugs*	32.6	44.7	33.4
Lose a job because of drug use*	13.7	19.3	14.1
School or job troubles due to drug use*	17.8	23.8	18.3
Arrested or held by police for drug use*	22.5	28.3	22.9
Involved in physical fight under the influence of drugs*	24.6	27.6	24.9
DSM-IV criteria for abuse or dependence:			
Use larger amounts of drugs or for longer periods than expected*	30.9	42.7	31.7
Did you want to cut down on drug use, but was not able to do so*	31.0	44.2	31.9
Spent a lot of time getting drugs/using them/ getting over their effects*	28.4	41.1	29.3
Drug use kept them from important activities*	18.1	30.3	18.9
Gave up favorite activities for drugs*	25.2	38.8	26.1
Continued drug use despite emotional / psychological problems*	31.8	44.9	32.7
Continued drug use despite causing personal problems*	32.3	46.4	33.3
Continued drug use despite physical and medical problems*	27.4	40.0	28.3
Needed larger amount of drugs to get same effect*	32.4	42.9	33.1
Experienced withdrawal*	24.3	35.1	25.1
Keep using drugs to deal with bad aftereffects*	22.8	34.6	23.6
ANY OF THE ABOVE	66.6	69.4	66.8

*Year prior to admission to prison

Source: BJS Survey of Inmates at State Correctional Facilities (2004).

half (55 percent) of state prison inmates ever drove a motor vehicle while under the influence of drugs, and 34 percent were involved in dangerous situations while using drugs. One-quarter of inmates have gotten into a fight while under the influence of drugs, and 18 percent had ever injected drugs. With the exception of driving under the influence, female inmates had a higher lifetime prevalence of each drug-related consequence or problem than male inmates.

DRUG TREATMENT IN PRISONS

Several types of clinically based drug treatment are available in state prisons. Residential programs (most commonly using the therapeutic community [TC] model), provide long-term treatment lasting from 6 to 12 months in a separate housing unit or facility exclusively devoted to treatment. TCs provide an intensive, highly structured pro-social environment. They differ from other treatment approaches principally in their use of the community as the key agent of change, in which treatment staff and peers interact to influence attitudes, perceptions, and behaviors associated with drug use (De Leon 2000). Treatment stages move toward increased levels of individual and social responsibility. Peer influence, mediated through a variety of group processes, is used to help residents learn and assimilate social norms and develop more effective social skills. The therapeutic approach generally focuses on changing negative patterns of thinking and behavior through individual and group therapy, group sessions with peers, and participation in a therapeutic milieu with hierarchical roles, privileges, and responsibilities. Strict and explicit behavioral norms are emphasized and reinforced with specific contingencies directed toward developing self-control and responsibility. Prison TCs typically move inmates through three phases: orientation (3 months); main treatment phase (5–6 months); and preparation for reentry, including strengthening decision-making skills, relapse prevention training, and development of individual aftercare plans. Group counseling focuses on self-discipline, self-worth, self-awareness, respect for authority, and acceptance of guidance for problem areas.

Non-residential or outpatient treatment in correctional settings is less intensive and usually involves a combination of individual and group counseling, several times per week. Inmates in such programs remain in their regular housing units during treatment.

Medication-assisted treatment (MAT; e.g., methadone, buprenorphine) is effective for the treatment of opiate addiction and alcohol dependence (naltrexone) (Chandler et al. 2009; Comer et al. 2006; Gordon et al. 2008). Despite its well-established evidence base, MAT is rarely used in correctional settings: only 0.2 percent of state inmates reported receiving MAT since prison admission, reflecting concerns over potential diversion, the predominance of abstinence-only treatment models, medications costs, and institutional aversion to MAT. In a recent national survey of 12 state prison systems, most provide extremely limited access to methadone, mainly for detoxification or for pregnant women (Friedmann et al. 2011). Only two of the prison systems provide buprenorphine, and one provides naltrexone.

Two other types of non-clinical interventions are common in state correctional facilities. Drug education typically involves 1–2 weeks of didactic presentations about illegal drug use, addiction, and drug treatment. Although not clinical treatment, drug education is often viewed as an important step to motivate drug abusers to seek treatment. Self-help groups using the Alcoholics Anonymous or Narcotics

Anonymous 12-step models are offered in most correctional facilities, and inmates are free to participate. This participation is generally viewed as an important adjunct to more formal clinical treatment, but data on its effectiveness for inmates are not available.

Drug Treatment Utilization

Table 19.3 shows the percentage of state inmates who reported receiving treatment since their admission, among inmates reporting a history of illegal drug use. These data are based on self-reports and retrospective cross-sectional data, so only include treatment received between admission to prison and the interview. Actual treatment participation rates over the full incarceration term are likely to be somewhat higher. Overall, about two-thirds of state prison inmates with a history of drug use had ever received any type of treatment prior to their incarceration. However, only 33.1 percent reported receiving any type of drug treatment since admission (including non-clinical interventions such as self-help groups or drug education). At the time of their interview, only 12.4 percent reported receiving any clinically or medically based drug treatment since admission (i.e., excluding drug education or 12-step programs). The most common type of interventions received were self-help groups and drug education (22.2 percent and 14.3 percent, respectively). Only 7.4 percent of inmates with a history of drug use participated in residential treatment, and 4.9 percent received professional counseling on an outpatient basis (Belenko and Peugh 2005). In general, and for all specific types of intervention, female inmates were more likely to report receiving treatment or other interventions than males.

These treatment participation data indicate that only a small proportion of those in need of substance abuse treatment actually receive it. Belenko and Peugh

Table 19.3. Participation in Drug Treatment among State Prison Inmates, 2004 (%)*

	Male	Female	TOTAL
Ever in treatment **	64.0	69.5	64.4
In treatment since admission	32.6	39.9	33.1
Detoxification	.6	1.6	.6
Residential facility or unit	7.0	12.4	7.4
Outpatient counseling with a trained professional	4.7	7.4	4.9
Maintenance drug	.2	.6	.2
Other drug programs	1.0	1.4	1.1
ANY OF THE ABOVE	11.9	19.3	12.4
Self-help group/peer counseling	21.9	26.5	22.2
Education program	14.2	15.4	14.3

*Among inmates who have ever used illegal drugs

**Includes lifetime alcohol or drug treatment

Source: BJS Survey of Inmates of State Correctional Facilities (2004).

(2005) analyzed treatment needs among state prison inmates, using a framework based on American Society of Addiction Medicine (ASAM) patient placement criteria (Mee-lee et al. 2001) and incorporating dimensions of drug use frequency and intensity, as well as problems and consequences related to drug use. They estimated that 31.5 percent of male and 52.3 percent of female state prison inmates need long-term residential treatment, and an additional 18.7 percent of males and 16.2 percent of females need outpatient treatment. By comparison, among inmates with high intensity and frequency of drug use categories, only about one-fifth received any clinically based treatment services.

A recent national survey of correctional agencies confirmed that although most correctional facilities offer treatment, relatively few inmates access this treatment. For example, 26.9 percent of prisons offer TC treatment, but only an estimated 6.6 percent of inmates receive such treatment (Taxman et al. 2007). Similarly, about half of facilities offer outpatient counseling, but only about 3 percent of inmates receive such treatment. A number of factors may account for this lack of access, including lack of resources, stigma (Chandler et al. 2009), lack of incentives for inmate participation, and organizational factors (see below).

THE EFFECTIVENESS OF PRISON TREATMENT

Several decades of research have indicated that drug treatment can reduce relapse and improve health outcomes (Gerstein and Harwood 1990; McLellan and McKay 2002). Effective programs should incorporate evidence-based interventions such as skills-based cognitive behavioral therapies (emphasizing improvements in thinking patterns, recognition of triggers for drug use and relapse, and development of skills to resist drug use), motivational enhancement, and TCs (described above), and should use the leverage of the criminal justice system to enhance monitoring and accountability (Chandler et al. 2009; NIDA 2006). In addition, more than a decade of research has examined the impacts of prison-based treatment on post-release recidivism and relapse, primarily focused on evaluations and meta-analyses of several prison TCs and aftercare programs.

The Key-Crest program in Delaware provides a continuum of care from custody through release (Inciardi et al. 1997). In-prison treatment is delivered through the Key TC program, and following release, Key participants enter the Crest program, a TC-based work-release program for transitional aftercare (Inciardi et al. 1997; Nielsen et al. 1996). Finally, after release from residential aftercare, the clients receive supervised outpatient aftercare. Three years after release to the community, significantly more clients who completed Key and Crest remained arrest-free (55 percent) than an untreated comparison group (29 percent) (Martin et al. 1999). Those who also received outpatient aftercare following the Crest program had the best outcomes (69 percent arrest-free after 3 years). Results for relapse to drug use were similar, with 17 percent of those who completed only the in-prison therapeutic community, 27 percent who had the in-prison treatment and the transitional residential treatment, and 35 percent who also had outpatient aftercare remaining drug-free during the follow-up period, compared with only 5 percent of the untreated comparison group. Five-year outcomes were similar, with those who went through both Key and Crest or Crest alone having significantly lower recidivism rates. Participation *only* in the Key in-prison TC treatment did not significantly improve five-year outcomes, although it was associated with higher rates of aftercare retention (Inciardi et al. 2004).

Although one of the most-cited and best designed studies of prison TCs, the Delaware study also had some limitations. First, only a partial experimental research design was used, with random assignment occurring only for one cohort of inmates randomly assigned to Crest. No random assignment was used to assign subjects to the Key program or control group. Second, no pre-service assessment of need for drug treatment guided the creation of comparison groups (Martin et al. 1999, 300). Third, earlier analyses of outcomes (drug relapse, rearrest) relied upon inmate self-reports (Inciardi et al. 1997), although later analyses incorporated criminal records for part of the sample (Martin et al. 1999; Inciardi et al. 2004). Arrestees' self-reports may underestimate drug use detected by urinalysis (Taylor et al. 2001), as well as criminal behavior (e.g., Cantor and Lynch 2000; Thornberry and Krohn 2000).

In the Amity, California, prison TC study, Wexler et al. (1999) randomly assigned inmates who *volunteered* for treatment to either TC or a wait-listed, intent-to-treat comparison group. Volunteers were deemed eligible for TC if they had a drug problem and 9–14 months remaining prior to parole eligibility. Inmates remained in the TC-eligible pool until they had less than 9 months to serve, then were removed from the pool and assigned to the "no-treatment" control group. Inmates in that "no-treatment" group may have received some drug education, self-help, or outpatient services (Wexler et al. 1999, 325). Upon release, parolees could volunteer for aftercare in a 40-bed community-based TC; not all of those who received in-prison treatment also received aftercare. Three-year post-parole outcome data showed that only 27 percent of those who received both in-prison and aftercare treatment were reincarcerated during the follow-up interval, compared with 75 percent for the control group, 79 percent who completed only the in-prison treatment, and 82 percent for those who were in-prison treatment dropouts (Wexler et al. 1999). However, when the entire "treatment" group (i.e., before removing dropouts from TC or aftercare) was considered together in intent-to-treat analysis, the reincarceration rate for the treatment group increased to 69 percent, a difference that was no longer statistically significant.

Interestingly, the five-year outcome results for this sample suggested a "rebound" effect: the in-prison TC treatment group had a significantly lower reincarceration rate (76 percent) than the no-treatment control group (83.4 percent), although this difference was not large. It is difficult to interpret the stability of these findings, because "the unbiased assignment of randomization no longer operates,

and selection bias becomes a possible (although by no means exclusive) explanation for the findings" (Prendergast et al. 2004, 53).

Kyle New Vision is a 500-bed facility in Texas providing treatment during the
final nine months of incarceration (Eisenberg and Fabelo 1996). After release,
parolees are mandated to attend three months of residential aftercare in a transitional TC, followed by up to one year of supervised outpatient aftercare. The evaluation included a matched comparison sample based upon TC-eligible inmates who
were either rejected by the parole board or who had too little time remaining on
their sentence (Knight et al. 1999). TC-eligible parolees were rejected because the
parole board judged them either as unlikely to benefit from the program or inappropriate for the program (Knight et al. 1997, 82), introducing potential selection
bias into the research design. Researchers separated treatment admissions into
Aftercare Completers (TC + Aftercare) and Aftercare Dropouts (TC only). Three-
year outcome data showed that in-prison treatment followed by aftercare was most
effective for high-risk, high-need offenders (Griffith et al. 1999; Knight et al. 1999).
Aftercare completers had a three-year reincarceration rate of only 25 percent, significantly lower than the Comparison group (42 percent) or Aftercare Dropouts
(64 percent). Because the treatment and comparison groups differed significantly
on prior offense and problem severity (and perhaps other unmeasured characteristics), researchers further disaggregated the groups into low-risk and high-risk subgroups. Treatment effects were greatest for high-risk inmates completing both TC
and Aftercare (3-year rearrest rate of 26 percent) (Hiller et al. 1999).

A quasi-experimental study in Pennsylvania (Welsh 2007) examined multiple
post-release outcomes for 2,809 inmates who participated in TCs (n = 749) or comparison groups (n = 2,060) at five state prisons. The comparison group included
TC-eligible inmates participating in less intensive forms of treatment (e.g., short-
term drug education and outpatient treatment groups) and was constructed based
upon known predictors such as drug dependency, need for treatment, and criminal
history. Over post-release follow-up periods up to 26 months, TCs significantly
reduced reincarceration (30 percent vs. 41 percent for the comparison sample) and
rearrest (24 percent vs. 33 percent), but not drug relapse (35 percent vs. 39
percent).

Finally, a recent study analyzed recidivism outcomes (rearrest, reconviction,
reincarceration) among 1,852 inmates released from prisons in Minnesota in 2005
(Duwe 2010). Half received treatment (all in separate housing units and modeled
after TC concepts) and half did not; the retrospective quasi-experimental design
matched the untreated comparison sample with the treatment sample using propensity scores. Inmates received short-term (90 days), medium-term (180 days), or
long-term (365 days) treatment. Cox regression models indicated that participating
in any treatment reduced the hazard ratio of rearrest by 17 percent and reincarceration by 25 percent over the three- to four-year follow-up period. Interestingly, long-
term (one-year) treatment participation did not have a significant effect on
recidivism, while short- or medium-term treatment significantly reduced recidivism (with the larger effect for medium-term treatment).

Several systematic reviews and meta-analyses of research on prison drug treatment have also been conducted. Such reviews estimate mean treatment effects across studies, and examine the influence of factors that may increase or decrease the effects (e.g., sample characteristics, strength of the research design, and the intervention). Some have argued that the effectiveness of prison-based TC drug treatment has not been definitively established, due to methodological deficiencies including non-randomized or inadequate comparison groups, inadequate statistical controls, or selection bias (Gaes et al. 1999; Pelissier et al. 2007). Moreover, the effectiveness of other types of prison-based drug treatment (outpatient treatment, 12-step groups) remains largely unknown (Gaes et al. 1999; Mitchell et al. 2007; Pearson and Lipton 1999).

In a systematic review, Mitchell et al. (2007) examined published and unpublished studies of prison drug treatment in North America or Western Europe since 1979. Recidivism and drug-use outcomes for each study were calculated using the odds-ratio effect size (a standardized measure of the size of the treatment impact on the outcome variable). A total of 26 studies met the eligibility criteria, yielding 32 different effect sizes. To avoid confounding due to differential attrition, authors eliminated studies that used dropouts as a comparison group, or (where possible) combined dropouts into the total treatment admission sample. Seventeen outcomes were calculated from TC programs; ten from counseling or drug education programs (including 12-step programs); three from boot camp programs; and two from a jail-based methadone maintenance program. A four-point index of internal validity based upon the University of Maryland's Scientific Methods Scale (Sherman et al. 1997) assessed study quality. Only three studies (9 percent) were rated as having the highest quality (randomized experimental designs), and eight (25 percent) were rated in the second-highest quality category (rigorous quasi-experimental designs). Twenty-one studies (66 percent) used methods considered too weak to draw valid conclusions (i.e., no matching, inadequate statistical controls, inadequate comparison groups). Only eleven studies examined post-intervention drug use as an outcome variable.

Three-quarters of the studies had outcomes that favored the treatment group over the comparison group, with an overall mean odds ratio of 1.25 (roughly translated into a modest reduction in recidivism from 50 percent to 44.5 percent). TC programs produced the strongest overall effect (mean odds ratio = 1.47). As indicated above, these findings are tempered by the methodological weakness of the research (Mitchell et al. 2007). The meta-analysis was not able to indicate how the outcomes were related to client characteristics (age, gender, race, or offender type) or program characteristics (e.g., length of intervention, prison versus work-release, or inclusion of aftercare component), limiting the ability to make valid conclusions about the influence of such factors on program effects.

In a large meta-analysis of correctional treatment, Pearson and Lipton (1999) identified seven TC studies conducted between 1968 and 1996. Similar to the University of Maryland Scientific Methods Scale (Sherman et al. 1997), Pearson and Lipton (1999) concluded that TCs were effective in reducing recidivism (weighted mean effect size of .133); an effect size for drug/alcohol relapse (.17) could only be computed for one study (of fair methodological quality). None of the TC studies was rated as being of "excellent" quality; only one was rated as "good"; three were rated as "fair," and three were rated as "poor." Higher quality studies tended to show a slightly higher effect size, although the relationship between methodological quality and effect size did not reach statistical significance. The authors cautioned that methodological weaknesses have limited the conclusions that can be drawn from these studies.

Pearson and Lipton (1999) found only seven studies of prison-based outpatient or group counseling programs. Most of these studies only briefly described the actual interventions, providing little detail about program structure, content, theoretical basis, duration, or intensity (Pearson and Lipton 1999, 387–388). Although the paucity of studies and methodological weaknesses limit the conclusions that can be drawn, group substance abuse counseling programs were not effective in reducing recidivism (mean effect size = +.036, not statistically significant). The five studies of "fair" quality had a higher but still very small effect size (+.052). No group-counseling studies were rated as having "good" or "excellent" quality.

Gaes et al. (1999) reached similar conclusions in their review of adult correctional treatment. They particularly noted the threats to validity caused by subject selection and/or attrition bias. In many studies, inmates were allowed to self-select into treatment, were selected on criteria unrelated to their assessed level of need for treatment, or dropped out of treatment and were inappropriately analyzed as an independent comparison group. Although Gaes et al. (1999) found evidence of positive prison drug treatment effects, especially for prison TCs, they urged caution in interpreting these findings: (1) few studies provided detailed descriptions of the treatment delivered; (2) few studies monitored the quality or integrity of program implementation; (3) subject selection and attrition bias were persistent problems; and (4) few studies used "strong inference" designs (i.e., studies that not only detected a treatment effect, but also found a reduction in the client's needs or deficits that was statistically related to observed outcomes).

Finally, Pelissier et al. (2007) conducted a systematic review of research and practice in treatment aftercare in the criminal justice system. These authors concluded that existing research does not allow definitive conclusions about the effectiveness of aftercare, in part because aftercare is defined in many different ways and previous research had a number of methodological problems. Pelissier et al. (2007) concluded that more research, using stronger designs and controlling for selection bias, is needed on the types of and length of aftercare that are most effective for reducing relapse and recidivism. It should be noted that in a study of federal prison residential treatment, Pelissier et al. (2001) controlled for selection bias in the statistical analyses, and still found significant positive treatment effects over a six-month period after prison release. Prison treatment reduced post-release rearrest by 73 percent (3.1 percent of treated inmates rearrested, 16.7 percent of untreated inmates) and reduced use of drugs or alcohol by 44 percent (20.5 percent of treated inmates using drugs or alcohol, compared with 36.7 percent of untreated inmates).

In summary, studies of TC prison treatment consistently show positive impacts on recidivism and relapse when combined with aftercare in the community, but the effects are not always large, and caution is needed in drawing conclusions based on methodological shortcomings in many of the studies. In addition, there has been relatively little research on the impacts of other types of prison treatment. Nonetheless, the findings have been consistent across studies, and economic analyses of TC and other prison treatment, summarized in the next section, indicate that prison treatment can be cost effective.

ECONOMIC BENEFITS OF PRISON DRUG TREATMENT

The effectiveness of correctional drug treatment can be viewed through several different lenses. From a community or social perspective, effective treatment should reduce drug use and related criminal behavior, and thus improve both public safety and public health. From a correctional system perspective, effective prison treatment should facilitate prison management and classification, help prisons better manage scarce bed space, and improve inmate and staff conditions. Through the public policy lens, correctional treatment should not only improve public safety and public health, but also provide economic benefits. Substance abuse treatment in prison adds to already high correctional costs, and if these additional costs cannot be recouped through the beneficial effects of treatment, policy makers would be less willing to expand treatment. Determining the economic effects of treatment also facilitates policy decisions as to the appropriate level, length, and intensity of treatment. Other things being equal, policy makers would prefer to fund the least costly treatment that had the desired level of positive impacts on inmates.

Although there are many studies of the benefits and costs of community-based drug treatment (for reviews see Belenko et al. 2005; Cartwright 2000; Harwood et al. 2002; McCollister and French 2003), relatively few economic evaluations exist for prison drug treatment. Two studies examined the relative cost effectiveness of the Key-Crest (DE) and Amity (CA) TC and aftercare programs. McCollister et al. (2003a) found that the Key-Crest program was cost effective: the program costs were lower for each day of reduced incarceration due to the treatment, than the actual daily incarceration costs. The program was much more cost-effective when aftercare was added to the work release component. In a similar study, McCollister et al. (2003b) compared costs and outcomes for the Amity program compared with the control group. They also found that any treatment was cost-effective due to reduced reincarceration, but the program was more cost effective with aftercare treatment.

Griffith et al. (1999) conducted an economic evaluation of the Texas Kyle New Vision prison TC with outpatient aftercare. Calculating the cost per 1 percent reduction in reincarceration, they found that the TC was cost-effective only when aftercare was completed. In addition, the program was more cost-effective for high-risk inmates (those with a higher likelihood of drug abuse and recidivism): their incremental cost effectiveness was $165 per 1 percent reduction in reincarceration for aftercare completers versus comparisons, compared with $494 per 1 percent reduction in reincarceration for low-risk inmates.

In one of the only economic studies to include non-residential prison treatment, Daley et al. (2004) examined the costs and benefits of several types of prison treatment programs in Connecticut, for a sample of inmates released from prison. Inmates receiving any treatment prior to release were compared to a random sample of inmates screened as having a substance abuse problem but not receiving treatment. The four levels of treatment examined were: Tier 1—one week of drug education; Tier 2—three outpatient group counseling sessions per week for 10 weeks; Tier 3—intensive day treatment with four group sessions per week for four months; Tier 4—residential TC treatment for six months. Controlling for baseline differences, Daley et al. (2004) found significant reductions in rearrests one year after release for treatment participants overall (33 percent rearrested, compared with 46 percent for the no-treatment comparison sample). Assuming that each rearrest resulted in one-year reincarceration, Daley et al. (2004) found that the benefit-cost ratios (BCR) were 5.74 for Tier 2 (meaning that every dollar spent on treatment yielded $5.74 savings from reduced incarceration, 3.16 for Tier 3, and 1.79 for Tier 4 (Tier 1 drug education did not reduce rearrest). Thus, all three prison treatment programs yielded net economic benefits, with the largest BCR for the least intensive treatment. Although caution is needed in interpreting these results because inmates were not randomly assigned to the different treatment levels, low-intensity outpatient treatment appeared economically preferable to long-term residential treatment. It may be that the Tier 2 inmates were lower risk (although Daley et al. [2004] controlled for baseline factors, including risk score). These findings suggest the need for more research on the relative economic benefits and cost-effectiveness of outpatient prison programs of shorter duration, compared with long-term residential treatment, controlling for inmate risk.

PRINCIPLES OF EFFECTIVE PRISON DRUG TREATMENT

Improving correctional treatment requires that effective (i.e., evidence-based) treatment reach larger numbers of drug-involved inmates, and be implemented effectively. Despite the research and knowledge gaps outlined above, prior research and clinical practice have identified a number of evidence-based

treatment interventions, and a number of principles for designing and implementing more effective drug treatment, both in community and criminal justice
settings. At the heart of this issue are four key concepts. First, treatment interventions should use techniques and clinical practices that are research-based and
have been found to be effective with offender populations. Second, drug abuse
and dependence need to be viewed as chronic conditions in which relapse is likely,
with treatment needed in some form for a considerable period of time. Third,
inmates and other offenders have multiple risk factors for recidivism and relapse,
and multiple service needs, and in order for treatment to have a long-term, sustainable impact, these factors must be identified and services provided. Finally,
prison drug treatment should attend to the organizational, staff, and implementation issues that can undermine the delivery and effectiveness of evidence-based
treatment.

Another issue, beyond the scope of this chapter, is whether prison drug treatment (as well as aftercare) is more effective when it is mandated or legally coerced
rather than voluntary. Some research suggests that coercion keeps offenders in
treatment longer, which in turn improves outcomes (see below) (Farabee et al. 1998;
Hiller et al. 1998). However, the issue is complicated by the difficulty in defining
coercion; even if treatment is not explicitly mandated, inmates may feel that participating in treatment can improve the chances of parole or place them in a more desirable housing unit. Accordingly, it may not always be clear whether an inmate is
really "volunteering" for treatment or internally motivated to address his or her
drug problem (Wild et al. 1998). Research has suggested that what is important is
how offenders perceive and internalize coercion (Young and Belenko 2002). The
relative benefit of voluntary and mandated treatment for inmates and parolees is an
important issue that needs further research and conceptualization.

Incorporate Evidence-based Practices and Principles

Several decades of research have identified a number of treatment principles, practices, and models that should be incorporated to maximize the positive effects of
drug treatment. Professional organizations and federal agencies have been actively
promoting the identification and implementation of evidence-based practices (EBP)
in mental health, education, and substance abuse (NIH 2004). There are now several initiatives to synthesize scientific knowledge and disseminate scientific findings
about evidence-based interventions. Examples that include criminal justice-based
drug treatment include SAMHSA's National Registry of Evidence-based Programs
and Practices (http://nrepp.samhsa.gov/), and the Campbell Collaboration (http://
www.campbellcollaboration.org). These efforts have focused primarily on reviewing literature, establishing criteria for evidence-based treatments, identifying and
rating interventions, and producing summary papers that systemically review
research findings.

Two NIDA publications summarize principles of effective treatment for drug
abusers in community treatment in general (NIDA 1999) and for criminal justice

populations (NIDA 2006). Briefly, evidence-based principles and strategies for treatment, especially for offenders, include the following:

- Incorporation of skills building strategies that assess for and address dynamic risk factors for relapse and recidivism;
- Sufficient treatment length to move the inmate through stages of treatment engagement, motivation to change, and commitment to recovery;
- Monitoring and accountability of treatment progress, using systematic rewards and sanctions to manage behavior, especially after release from prison; use of contingency management techniques;
- Use of medication-assisted treatment (e.g., methadone, buprenorphine, naltrexone) where appropriate;
- Incorporation of cognitive behavioral therapy techniques to teach relapse prevention skills, ability to recognize relapse triggers, and correct errors in perception and cognition that foster drug use;
- Use of motivational interviewing and motivational enhancement techniques to increase readiness to engage in treatment and confront drug abuse or dependence problems;
- Family-focused interventions (especially for younger offenders), involvement of community supports such as community reinforcement and readiness models.

Chronic Care is Preferable to Acute Care

Drug abuse and dependence are considered by most addiction researchers to be a chronic, relapsing brain disease (Chandler et al. 2009; McKay 2009; McLellan et al. 2000; Volkow and Li 2005). As with other chronic diseases (e.g., hypertension, diabetes, asthma), drug dependence is often best managed under a chronic care model in which the patient may be initially treated with acute care, but then needs to be managed over time (NIDA 2006). For inmates and other offenders, this means that short-term or one-time treatment is unlikely to have any lasting effects on drug use or recidivism. Ongoing care in the form of aftercare treatment, continuing recovery monitoring (McKay 2009), relapse prevention counseling, self-help group participation, or other forms of recovery support are generally needed to maximize the chance of maintaining abstinence from drug use and desistance from criminal behavior.

Although prison TC treatment typically lasts between 6–12 months, the optimal length of treatment is unknown. National community-based evaluations suggest that longer treatment yields better outcomes with a minimum threshold of 90 days generally recommended (Simpson et al. 1997). Yet, at least two studies of prison treatment have found that some outcomes were worse when treatment lasted longer, with shorter stays associated with larger reductions in recidivism (Duwe 2010; Wexler et al. 1990). At a minimum, treatment must last long enough to produce behavioral and attitudinal changes that are stable (NIDA 2006), but additional research is needed on the optimal treatment length for specific types of offenders. Generally, the more extensive the client's problems and the longer the person has been involved with drugs, the longer and more intensive the treatment needs (Belenko and Peugh 2005; Mee-Lee et al. 2001). Clinical literature on patient placement in addiction treatment suggests that treatment length and intensity should be matched to the intensity and breadth of drug use, and the number of related health and social problems (Mee-Lee et al. 2001).

Inmates Have Multiple Risk Factors

Another key principle for inmates and other offenders is that treatment should assess for and target problems that are associated with the person's drug use and likelihood of recidivism (Belenko 2006; Taxman, Cropsey, et al. 2007). Many inmates exhibit criminal thinking patterns (errors in thinking), poor impulse control, uncontrolled anger, cognitive deficits, lack of empathy, and other psychological issues that are associated with criminal behavior. Addressing such criminogenic risk factors is necessary for long-term treatment success (Andrews and Bonta 2003; Taxman and Marlowe 2006; Taxman and Thanner 2006). There is evidence that clients with a higher severity of drug use and higher risk have better outcomes in more intensive or highly structured treatment, no matter what the modality (Melnick et al. 2000; Simpson et al. 1999; Thornton et al. 1998). Such treatment is better able to address their multiple needs and provide lengthier and closer supervision and monitoring.

Addiction-related problems (i.e., psychiatric, employment, family, social) can undermine treatment outcomes; the addition of health and/or social services to "standard" addiction treatment can significantly improve treatment outcomes (McLellan et al. 1993). Further, matching services to specific client needs (e.g., psychological services, housing, employment) improves treatment outcomes (Gastfriend and McLellan 1997; Hser et al. 1999; McLellan et al. 1993). This process is greatly facilitated through the use of validated and clinically appropriate assessment instruments.

Inmates have high rates of medical problems (Hammett et al. 2001; Marquart et al. 1997), including HIV and other infectious diseases (Belenko et al. 2004, 2005; Maruschak 2009); mental health disorders (Belenko et al. 2003; James and Glaze 2006, Lamb et al. 2004), including antisocial personality disorder and other psychopathy that have been linked to reoffending (Festinger et al. 2002; Gendreau, 1996); employment problems that can affect long-term recovery and complicate community transition (Laub and Sampson 2001; Leukefeld et al. 2004; Petersilia, 2001; Travis and Petersilia 2001; Western et al. 2001); low educational achievement (Batiuk et al. 2005); and peer networks with high rates of drug use and criminality (Friedman et al. 1999; Keenan et al. 1995). They also lack access to affordable, stable drug-free housing (Rossi 1989; Travis and Petersilia 2001). In particular, the high rates of co-occurring mental health and substance abuse problems among inmates greatly increase the complexity of treatment delivery, and few prison treatment programs provide the specialized, integrated approach that is needed for this subpopulation (Peters et al. 2004). Failure to address these factors adequately can undermine long-term recovery for released inmates and increase the likelihood of new arrests and technical violations and reincarceration (Belenko 2006).

Organizational and Implementation Issues

Improving the effectiveness of correctional drug treatment involves more than using evidence-based treatment practices and principles—that is necessary but not sufficient. Successfully implementing and sustaining effective treatment requires careful attention to the systems, organizational, and staff factors that affect implementation (Aarons and Sawitzky 2006; Fixsen et al. 2005; Liddle et al. 2002; Proctor et al. 2009; Simpson 2002; Taxman and Belenko 2011). Evidence-based drug treatment is slow to be disseminated (Kilbourne et al. 2007), and often poorly implemented (Bourgon and Armstrong 2005) or difficult to sustain (Brown and Flynn 2002; Miller et al. 2006). In general, the diffusion of innovation into regular clinical practice can be a slow, multistage process (Liddle et al. 2002; Roman and Johnson 2002; Simpson 2002).

There are particular challenges in introducing evidence-based treatment into CJ agencies (Farabee et al. 1999; Linhorst et al. 2001; Taxman and Belenko 2011). Significant system barriers relate to lack of exposure to research findings, vacillating funding or political support for offender programs, and a focus on security and punishment, not treatment. Current implementation practice in CJ drug treatment hinders effective implementation: target populations are inappropriate, non-performance-based staff evaluations are used, there is no organizational accountability for outcomes, high staff turnover, no reimbursement for implementation activities, and few incentives to enhance program effectiveness (Welsh and Harris 2008).

Recent research and theory development on the implementation of drug treatment and other behavioral health programs suggests several key external, organizational, and staff factors that are related to successful implementation (Taxman and Belenko 2011). External influences include political and central administrative support for rehabilitation, competing and overriding priorities of security and control, and funding (Fixsen et al. 2005). Organizational factors include the organizational culture for innovation and readiness to change (Liddle et al. 2002; Simpson 2002), administrative and leadership support, organizational resources, information technology (monitoring services and outcomes, information exchange, data management), and interagency communication and information sharing (Aarons and Sawitzky 2006; Fixsen et al. 2005). Staff can also either facilitate or undermine the implementation and sustainability of evidence-based treatment. Key factors include skills level and training needs; acceptability of treatment; line staff resistance to change (Miller et al. 2006; Simpson 2002); and overcoming the principal goal of security and supervision and lack of staff "buy-in."

Successful implementation and sustainability of effective treatment is facilitated by using organizational assessment, actively involving local stakeholders, using testable implementation and monitoring strategies, and improving organizational and systems collaborations to help drive CJ treatment services toward more sustainable and effective interventions. This is a challenging and complex process that is only recently attracting policy and research attention. Of key importance is the *effective implementation* of *effective programs*, encompassing both EBP and a systematic implementation process (Fixsen et al. 2005). Without both, positive client outcomes are unlikely to be achieved. Ineffective programs can be implemented well, and effective programs can be implemented poorly. Positive treatment outcomes are achieved only when both the intervention *and* implementation practices are effective.

Another important issue is that traditional dissemination, training, and implementation strategies (e.g., one-time training, dissemination of information only, implementation without changing staff roles, no assessment of organizational readiness) are often ineffective (Bero et al. 1998). Repeated or booster training, coaching, and performance monitoring and supervision are needed for sustained and effective implementation (Joyce and Showers 2002). Multistage training components that include coaching and consultation *in the practice setting* improve the implementation of evidence-based practices.

Recent experience in Delaware has demonstrated that providing organizational economic incentives for program retention and service delivery can dramatically reduce treatment dropout rates (McLellan et al. 2008). Focusing on key outcomes of critical interest to corrections and treatment agencies (e.g., recidivism reduction, reduced drug use, and increased employment) provides "buy-in." If appropriately incentivized, the system may move relatively rapidly toward effective strategies and interventions to achieve the performance goals. Incentives can be implemented at the organizational (McLellan et al. 2008) or staff level (Coiera 2003). Treatment programs may be wary of accepting criminal justice clients because of the extra paperwork burden, supervision requirements, or the perception that criminal justice clients are difficult to manage. Incentives for inmates successfully engaged in treatment (e.g., good time credits, early parole, reduced parole supervision requirements) are also needed.

Organizational culture and climate to support treatment and rehabilitation are important for increasing access to treatment and more effective implementation of such programs (Simpson et al. 2007; Taxman et al. 2009). Correctional facilities need to embrace a learning environment where staff are encouraged to become more knowledgeable about treatment and EBP, and in which agency and facility leadership and administrators support treatment, and organizational innovation and change. It can be a challenge to get correctional and addiction treatment organizations to adopt new practices or change existing practices (Taxman and Belenko 2011; Taxman et al. 2009). For example, as noted earlier, MAT has a strong evidence base but has not been widely adopted by correctional agencies (Chandler et al. 2009; Friedmann et al., 2011). With better coordination and systems integration, such organizational change becomes more achievable and is likely to improve access to treatment services for inmates

(Fletcher et al. 2009; Lehman et al. 2009). These factors can also vary widely across correctional facilities; fragmented and inconsistently implemented service delivery undermines a correctional system's ability to deliver effective treatment (Harrison and Martin 2003; Taxman et al. 2009; Welsh and Zajac 2004a).

Another key issue is the competing correctional and treatment (i.e., public health) missions, with the former focused on security and public safety (Taxman and Ressler 2009), and the latter on health services and health outcomes. Institutional and community correctional systems are not structured to deliver behavioral health services (Taxman and Belenko 2011; Taxman et al. 2009). Bridging this mission gap and achieving an appropriate balance between public safety and public health requires improved organizational relationships between public safety and public health agencies, regular information exchange, shared program goals, cross-training of staff, and other elements of systems integration (Fletcher et al. 2009; Lehman et al. 2009). With better alignment of rehabilitative goals, and increased support for rehabilitation by correctional agencies (Melnick et al. 2009), better systems integration can be achieved.

Finally, the treatment system in general has organizational, structural, and resource problems that can undermine its ability to support organizational change, or implement and sustain effective treatment using evidence-based practices (Kimberly and McLellan 2006; Taxman et al. 2009). Resource constraints and competing priorities can limit uptake of evidence-based practice (Simpson 2002), affect intervention fidelity, and make it difficult to hire and retain a skilled workforce.

THE FUTURE OF PRISON DRUG TREATMENT

Compared with non-offender populations, inmates have extremely high rates of problematic illegal drug use and drug abuse disorders. Moreover, this drug use is often associated with their criminal behavior and incarceration. Unless these problems are addressed through effective drug treatment, relapse to drug use and associated criminal behavior is highly likely following release from prison. Because effective models of corrections-based substance abuse treatment exist, implementing and expanding such treatment could have substantial impacts on crime, drug use, and correctional system costs.

Examination of the drug abuse patterns and treatment needs of prison inmates suggest that inmates need a range of treatment modalities, and that the existing delivery of correctional treatment, especially residential, is highly inadequate relative to need. By expanding the currently limited range of treatment levels and modalities offered to inmates, and conducting more comprehensive clinical assessments, correctional systems can meet their treatment needs in a more cost-effective manner. Given the declining resources available for correctional treatment, and the influence of behavioral managed care models that affect treatment length and other services in inmates (Godbole et al. 1998; Patterson 1998), matching need to treatment level is a key strategy for correctional systems. The higher levels of drug use and abuse/dependence, as well as drug-related consequences and associated health and social problems among women inmates (McClellan et al. 1997; Peugh and Belenko 1999; Prendergast et al. 1995) suggest a need to increase the attention to gender-specific treatment needs of female inmates, and to expand treatment capacity in women's correctional facilities.

Other issues present challenges for correctional treatment providers, policy makers, and researchers. Correctional systems need to implement expanded and improved multidomain assessment instruments, not only upon admission, but within a year of release (Belenko 2006; Hiller et al. 2011). Formal, standardized treatment placement criteria should be developed, implemented, and evaluated in state correctional systems. In addition to improved assessment, more effective inmate treatment placement decisions could be facilitated by expanding clinical evaluation of their readiness to change (De Leon, 2000; Prochaska and DiClemente 1986), treatment motivation (Joe et al. 2002; Shen et al. 2000), and criminogenic risks (Andrews and Bonta 2003; Gendreau et al. 1996). Finally, correctional treatment should focus on the identified health or social problems in addition to drug abuse or dependence, and should incorporate transitional planning for continuing care, addressing these multiple health and social needs following release from custody.

Given the importance of treatment retention and continuing care for maintaining abstinence and recovery, improved strategies are needed for engaging released inmates in aftercare, and retaining them in these programs. Ideally, aftercare should incorporate principles of adaptive care, with post-treatment recovery monitoring (McKay 2009), involvement of community and peer support networks, and use of graduated sanctions for technical violations.

Evidence indicating that prison treatment (especially TCs) reduces recidivism and relapse must be tempered with concerns about the methodological quality of much of the research: non-randomized research designs (recognizing that randomized designs can be difficult to implement in prison or parole settings); sampling, selection, or attrition bias; poor program implementation; and insufficient attention to interactions between treatment process and outcome (Gaes et al. 1999; Mitchell et al. 2007; Pearson and Lipton 1999; Pelissier et al. 2007). Few treatment outcome studies have incorporated the organizational, staff, or implementation measures that are important for understanding treatment effects.

Evidence about prison TC effectiveness is based on studies (some a decade old) from only four states, most of which received extensive federal technical assistance and program development funding (Melnick et al. 2004). Thus the generalizability of those studies for recently implemented TCs is not clear. Relationships among outcomes and inmate characteristics, treatment processes, and organizational and staff factors remain only partially understood (Farabee et al. 1999; Harrison 2001; Pearson and Lipton 1999; Welsh and Zajac 2004a, 2004b). Much also remains unknown about the mechanisms through which prison TCs and aftercare programs achieve their effects. The specific effects on post-release outcomes of their "active ingredients" (e.g., peer community, resocialization, hierarchical structure) have not been empirically tested (Welsh 2010)

Moreover, we know little about the efficacy of other, more common, forms of prison treatment. A number of other important questions about the effectiveness of prison drug treatment remain to be studied, including: (1) What is the optimal length of prison treatment and aftercare? (2) What are the effects of treatment on other outcomes such as employment, social functioning, and health? (3) What procedures or incentives are needed to increase parolee engagement in aftercare?

A central challenge for improving prison treatment is to apply the principles and practices of effective interventions to real world correctional settings. This in part requires emphasizing the concept of *fidelity*, or being faithful to a standard. Strict adherence to fidelity when conducting clinical trials is a basic requirement because the researcher must control experimental conditions to minimize threats to validity, so that the results can be confidently ascribed to the tested treatment protocol. When protocols are moved into practice, the field can exercise similar control over the implementation by devoting goals and resources to making sure that the standards are clear. Closely monitoring fidelity is important, but care must be taken to include allowances for some clinical flexibility, especially where target populations or local conditions may differ from those under which the evidence-based practice was developed and evaluated (Bell et al. 2007; Carroll et al. 2007; Welsh and Harris 2008).

Expanding and improving the effectiveness of correctional treatment will, in addition to ongoing research on program efficacy and effectiveness, require a more systems-oriented approach that emphasizes services integration, organizational and systems change, principles of effective implementation, and adoption of and support for evidence-based practice. Incorporating public health goals in the core mission of correctional agencies, even if secondary to their public safety and security missions, can lead to improvements in treatment integration and effectiveness. Given the level of drug and alcohol involvement of inmates, and the relative lack of access to coordinated treatment linked to chronic care in the community after release, this shift is crucial for achieving long-term reductions in recidivism and relapse.

REFERENCES

Aarons, G. and A. Sawitzky. 2006. "Organizational Culture and Climate and Mental Health Provider Attitudes Toward Evidence-Based Practice." *Psychological Services* 3: 61–72.
Andrews, D. A. and J. Bonta. 2003. *The Psychology of Criminal Conduct.* Cincinnati, OH: Anderson.

Batiuk, M., K. Lahm, M. McKeever, N. Wilcox, and P. Wilcox. 2005. "Disentangling the Effects Of Correctional Education: Are Current Policies Misguided? An Event History Analysis." *Criminal Justice* 5: 55–74.

Belenko, S. 2006. "Assessing Released Inmates for Substance-Abuse Related Service Needs." *Crime and Delinquency* 52: 94–113.

Belenko, S, M. Lang, and L. O'Connor. 2003. "Self-reported Psychiatric Treatment Needs among Felony Drug Offenders." *Journal of Contemporary Criminal Justice* 19(1): 9–29.

Belenko, S., S. Langley, S. Crimmins, and M. Chaple. 2004. "HIV Risk Behaviors, Knowledge, and Prevention among Offenders under Community Supervision: A Hidden Risk Group." *AIDS Education and Prevention* 16: 367–385.

Belenko, S., and J. Peugh. 2005. "Estimating Drug Treatment Needs among State Prison Inmates." *Drug and Alcohol Dependence* 77: 269–281.

Belenko, S., N. Patapis, and M. T. French. 2005. *Economic Benefits of Drug Treatment: A Critical Review of the Evidence for Policy Makers.* Philadelphia: Treatment Research Institute.

Belenko, S., M. Shedlin, and M. Chaple. 2005. "HIV Risk Behaviors, Knowledge, and Prevention Service Experiences among African American and Other Offenders." *Journal of Health Care for the Poor and Underserved* 16: 108–129.

Bell, S. G., S. F. Newcomer, C. Bachrach, E. Borawski, et al. 2007. "Challenges in Replicating Interventions." *Journal of Adolescent Health* 40: 514–520.

Bero, L. A., R. Grilli, J. M. Grimshaw, E. Harvey, A. D. Oxman, and M. A. Thomson. 1998. "Closing the Gap Between Research and Practice: An Overview of Systematic Reviews of Interventions to Promote the Implementation of Research Findings." *British Medical Journal* 317: 465–468.

Bourgon, G., and B. Armstrong. 2005. "Transferring the Principles of Effective Treatment into a 'Real World' Prison Setting." *Criminal Justice and Behavior* 32: 3–25.

Brown, B. S., and P. M. Flynn. 2002. "The Federal Role in Drug Abuse Technology Transfer: A History and Perspective." *Journal of Substance Abuse Treatment* 22: 245–257.

Cantor, D., and J. P. Lynch. 2000. "Self-report Surveys as Measures of Crime and Criminal Victimization." In *Criminal Justice 2000*, vol. 4, ed. D. Duffee, 85–138. Washington, DC: U.S. Department of Justice, Office of Justice Programs, National Institute of Justice (NCJ-182411).

Carroll, C., M. Patterson, S. Wood, A. Booth, J. Rick, and S. Balain. 2007. "A Conceptual Framework for Implementation Fidelity." *Implementation Science* 2: 40–47.

Cartwright, W. S. 2000. "Cost-benefit Analysis of Drug Treatment Services: Review of the Literature." *Journal of Mental Health Policy and Economics* 3: 11–26.

Chandler, R., B. Fletcher, and N. Volkow. 2009. "Treating Drug Abuse and Addiction in the Criminal Justice System: Improving Public Health and Safety." *Journal of the American Medical Association* 301: 183–190.

Coiera, E. 2003. "Disseminating and Applying Protocols." In *Guide to Health Informatics*, 2nd ed, ed. E. Coiera, 171–179. London: Arnold.

Comer, S., M. Sullivan, E. Yu, et al. 2006. "Injectable, Sustained-Release Naltrexone for the Treatment of Opioid Dependence: A Randomized, Placebo-Controlled Trial." *Archives of General Psychiatry* 63: 210–218.

Daley, M., C. T. Love, D. S. Shepard, C. B. Petersen, K. L. White, and F. B. Hall. 2004. "Cost Effectiveness of Connecticut's In-Prison Substance Abuse Treatment." *Journal of Offender Rehabilitation* 39: 69–92.

De Leon, George. 2000. *The Therapeutic Community: Theory, Model and Method*. New York: Springer-Verlag.

Duwe, G. 2010. "Prison-based Chemical Dependency Treatment in Minnesota: An Outcome Evaluation." *Journal of Experimental Criminology* 6: 57–81.

Eisenberg, M., and T. Fabelo. 1996. "Evaluation of the Texas Correctional Substance Abuse Treatment Initiative: The Impact of Policy Research." *Crime and Delinquency* 42: 296–308.

Farabee, D. M. Prendergast, and M. D. Anglin. 1998. "The Effectiveness of Coerced Treatment for Drug-Abusing Offenders." *Federal Probation* 62: 3–10.

Farabee, D. M. Prendergast, J. Cartier, et al. 1999. "Barriers to Implementing Effective Correctional Drug Treatment Programs." *Prison Journal* 79(2): 150–162.

Festinger, D. S., D. B. Marlowe, P. A. Lee, K. C. Kirby, G. Bovasso, and A. T. McLellanT. 2002. "Status Hearings in Drug Court: When More Is Less and Less Is More." *Drug and Alcohol Dependence* 68: 151–157.

Fixsen, D. L., S. F. Naoom, K. A. Blase, R. M. Friedman, and F. Wallace. 2005. *Implementation Research: A Synthesis of the Literature*. Tampa: University of South Florida, Louis de la Parte Florida Mental Health Institute, The National Implementation Research Network (FMHI Publication #231).

Fletcher, B. W., W. E. Lehman, H. K. Wexler, G. Melnick, F. S. Taxman, and D. W. Young. 2009. "Measuring Collaboration and Integration Activities in Criminal Justice and Drug Abuse Treatment Agencies." *Drug and Alcohol Dependence* 103 (Suppl. 1): S54–S64.

Friedman, S. R., R. Curtis, A. Neaigus, B. Jose, and D. C. Des Jarlais. 1999. *Social Networks, Drug Injectors' Lives, and HIV/AIDS*. New York: Kluwer Academic.

Friedmann, P., R. Hoskinson, Jr., M. Gordon, R. Schwartz, et al. In press, 2011. "Medication-assisted Treatment in Criminal Justice Agencies Affiliated with the Criminal Justice-Drug Abuse Treatment Studies (CJ-DATS): Availability, Barriers and Intentions." *Substance Abuse*.

Gaes, G. G., T. J. Flanagan, L. L. Motiuk, and L. Stewart. 1999. "Adult Correctional Treatment." In *Prisons. Crime and Justice, A Review of Research*, vol. 26, eds. M. Tonry and J. Petersilia, 361–426. Chicago: University of Chicago Press.

Gastfriend, D. R., and A. T. McLellan. 1997. "Treatment Matching: Theoretical Basis and Practical Implications." *Medical Clinics of North America* 81: 945–966.

Gendreau, P., T. Little, and C. Goggin. 1996. "Meta-analysis of the Predictors of Adult Offender Recidivism: What Works?" *Criminology* 34: 575–607.

Gerstein, D., and H. Harwood, eds. 1990. *Treating Drug Problems: A Study of the Evolution, Effectiveness, and Financing of Public and Private Drug Treatment Systems*, Vol. 1. Washington, DC: National Academy Press.

Godbole, A., T. Temkin, and C. Cradock. 1998. "Restructuring Public Mental Health and Substance Abuse Service Systems." *Journal of Health Care Financing* 24: 16–26.

Gordon, M., T. Kinlock, R. Schwartz, and K. O'Grady. 2008. "A Randomized Clinical Trial of Methadone Maintenance for Prisoners: Findings at 6 Months Post Release." *Addiction* 103: 1333–1342.

Griffith, J. D., M. L. Hiller, K. Knight, and D. D. Simpson. 1999. "A Cost-Effectiveness Analysis of In-Prison Therapeutic Community Treatment and Risk Classification." *The Prison Journal* 79(3): 352–368.

Hammett, T. M., C. Roberts, and S. Kennedy. 2001. "Health-related Issues in Prisoner Reentry." *Crime and Delinquency* 47: 390–409.

Harrison, L. 2001. "The Revolving Prison Door for Drug-Involved Offenders: Challenges and Opportunities." *Crime and Delinquency* 47: 462–485.

Harrison, L., and S. Martin. 2003. *Residential Substance Abuse Treatment for State Prisoners: Implementation Lessons Learned*. Washington, DC: Department of Justice, Office of Justice Programs, National Institute of Justice (Publication No.NCJ-195738).

Harwood, H. J., D. Malhotra, C. Villarivera, C. Liu, U. Chong, and J. Gilani. 2002. *Cost Effectiveness and Cost Benefit Analysis of Substance Abuse Treatment: A Literature Review*. Rockville, MD: Substance Abuse and Mental Health Services Administration.

Hiller, M., K. Knight, K. Broome, and D. Simpson. 1998. "Legal Pressure and Treatment Retention in a National Sample of Long-Term Residential Programs." *Criminal Justice and Behavior* 25: 463–481.

Hiller, M., K. Knight, and D. Simpson. 1999. "Risk Factors That Predict Dropout from Corrections Based Treatment for Drug Abuse." *The Prison Journal* 79: 411–430.

Hiller, M., S. Belenko, W. Welsh, G. Zajac, and R. Peters. 2011. "Screening and Assessment: An Evidence-Based Process for the Management and Care of Adult Drug-Involved Offenders." In *Handbook on Evidence Based Substance Abuse Treatment Practice in Criminal Justice Settings*, eds. C. Leukefeld, J. Gregrich, and T. Gulotta. New York: Springer.

Hser, Y.-I., M. L. Polinsky, M. Maglione, and M. D. Anglin. 1999. "Matching Clients' Needs with Drug Treatment Services." *Journal of Substance Abuse Treatment* 16: 299–305.

ICPSR. 2004. "Survey of Inmates in State and Federal Correctional Facilities, 2004." *Codebook: United States Department of Justice, Bureau of Justice Statistics*. Ann Arbor, MI: Inter-university Consortium for Political and Social Research, #4572.

Inciardi, J. A., S. S. Martin, and C. A. Butzin. 2004. "Five-year Outcomes of Therapeutic Community Treatment of Drug-Involved Offenders after Release From Prison." *Crime and Delinquency* 50: 88–107.

Inciardi, J., S. Martin, C. Butzin, R. Hooper, and L. Harrison. 1997. "An Effective Model of Prison Based Treatment for Drug-Involved Offenders." *Journal of Drug Issues* 27: 261–278.

James, D. J., and L. E. Glaze. 2006. *Mental Health Problems of Prison and Jail Inmates*. Washington, DC: Bureau of Justice Statistics.

Joe, G., K. Broome, G. Rowan-Szal, and D. Simpson. 2002. "Measuring Patient Attributes and Engagement in Treatment." *Journal of Substance Abuse Treatment* 22(4): 183–196.

Joyce, B., and B. Showers. 2002. *Student Achievement Through Staff Development*, 3rd ed. Alexandria, VA: Association for Supervision and Curriculum Development.

Keenan, K., R. Loeber, Q. Zhang, M. Stouthamer-Loeber, and W. Van Kammen. 1995. "The Influence of Deviant Peers on the Development of Boys' Disruptive and Delinquent Behavior: A Temporal Analysis." *Development and Psychopathology* 7: 715–726.

Kilbourne, A. M., M. S. Neumann, H. A. Pincus, M. S. Bauer, and R. Stall. 2007. "Implementing Evidence-Based Interventions in Health Care: Application of the Replicating Effective Programs Framework." *Implementation Science* 2: 42.

Kimberly, J., and A. T. McLellan. 2006. "The Business of Addiction Treatment: A Research Agenda." *Journal of Substance Abuse Treatment* 31: 213–219.

Knight, K., D. Simpson, L. Chatham, and L. Camacho. 1997. "An Assessment Of Prison-Based Drug Treatment: Texas' In-Prison Therapeutic Community Program." *Journal of Offender Rehabilitation* 24: 75–100.

Knight, K., D. Simpson, and M. Hiller. 1999. "Three-year Reincarceration Outcomes In-Prison Therapeutic Community Treatment in Texas." *The Prison Journal* 79: 321–333.

Lamb, H. R, L. E. Weinberger, and B. H. Gross. 2004. "Mentally Ill Persons in the Criminal Justice System: Some Perspective." *Psychiatric Quarterly* 75(2): 107–126.

Langan, P. A., and D. J. Levin. 2002. *Recidivism of Prisoners Released in 1994.* Washington, DC: Bureau of Justice Statistics, U.S. Department of Justice.

Laub, J. H., and R. J. Sampson. 2001. "Understanding Desistance from Crime." In *Crime and Justice,* ed. M. Tonry. 1–69. Chicago: University of Chicago Press.

Lehman, W. E., B. W. Fletcher, H. K. Wexler, G. Melnick. 2009. "Organizational Factors and Collaboration and Integration Activities in Criminal Justice and Drug Abuse Treatment Agencies." *Drug and Alcohol Dependence,* 103(Suppl. 1), S65–S72.

Leukefeld, C., H. S. McDonald, M. Staton, and A. Mateyoke-Scrivner. 2004. "Employment, Employment-Related Problems, and Drug Use at Drug Court Entry." *Substance Use and Misuse* 39: 2559–2579.

Liddle, H.A., C. L. Rowe, T. J. Quille, G. A. Dakof, D. S. Mills, et al. 2002. "Transporting a Research-Based Adolescent Drug Treatment into Practice." *Journal of Substance Abuse Treatment* 22: 231–243.

Linhorst, D. M., K. Knight, J. S. Johnston, et al. 2001. "Situational Influences on the Implementation of a Prison-Based Therapeutic Community." *Prison Journal* 81(4): 436–453.

Marquart, J., D. Merianos, J. Hebert, and L. Carroll. 1997. "Health Conditions and Prisoners: A Review of Research and Emerging Areas of Inquiry." *Prison Journal* 77(2): 184–208.

Martin, S. S., C. A. Butzin, C.A. Saum, and J. A. Inciardi. 1999. "Three-Year Outcomes of Therapeutic Community Treatment for Drug-Involved Offenders in Delaware: From Prison to Work Release to Aftercare." *Prison Journal* 79: 294–320.

Maruschak, L. 2009. *HIV in Prisons, 2007–08.* Washington, DC: U.S Department of Justice, Bureau of Justice Statistics, NCJ 228307.

McClellan, D. S., D. Farabee, and B. M. Crouch. 1997. "Early Victimization, Drug Use, and Criminality: A Comparison of Male and Female Prisoners." *Criminal Justice & Behavior* 24: 455–476.

McCollister, K. E., and M. T. French. 2003. "The Relative Contribution of Outcome Domains in the Total Economic Benefit of Addiction Interventions: A Review of First Findings." *Addiction* 89: 1647–1659.

McCollister, K. E., M. T. French, J. A. Inciardi, C. A. Butzin, S. S. Martin, and R .M. Hooper. 2003a. "Post-release Substance Abuse Treatment for Criminal Offenders: A Cost Effectiveness Analysis." *Journal of Quantitative Criminology* 19: 389–407.

McCollister, K. E., M. T. French, M. Prendergast, H. Wexler, S. Sacks, and E. Hall. 2003b. "Is In Prison Treatment Enough? A Cost-Effectiveness Analysis of Prison-Based Treatment and Aftercare Services for Substance-Abusing Offenders." *Law and Policy* 25: 63–82.

McKay, J. 2001. "Effectiveness of Continuing Care Interventions for Substance Abusers: Implications for the Study of Long-Term Treatment Effects." *Evaluation Review* 25: 211–232.

McKay, J. R. 2009. "Continuing Care Research: What We've Learned and Where We're Going." *Journal of Substance Abuse Treatment* 36: 131–145.

McLellan, A. T., I. O. Arndt, D. S. Metzger, and C. P. O'Brien. 1993. "The Effects of Psychosocial Services in Substance Abuse Treatment." *Journal of the American Medical Association* 269: 1953–1959.

McLellan, A. T., D. Lewis, C. P. O'Brien, H. G. Hoffmann, and H. D. Kleber. 2000. "Drug Addiction as Chronic Medical Illness: Implications for Treatment, Insurance and Evaluation." *Journal of the American Medical Association* 284: 1689–1695.

McLellan, A. T., and J. R. McKay. 2002. "Components of Successful Addiction Treatment: What Does the Research Say?" In *Principles of Addiction Medicine*, 3rd ed., eds. A. W. Graham and T. Schultz. Chicago: University of Chicago Press.

McLellan, A. T., J. Kemp, A. C. Brooks, and D. Carise. 2008. "Improving Public Addiction Treatment Through Performance Contracting: The Delaware Experiment." *Health Policy* 87: 296–308.

Mee-Lee, D., G. Shulman, M. Fishman, D. R. Gastfriend, and J. H. Griffith, eds. 2001. *ASAM Patient Placement Criteria for the Treatment of Substance-Related Disorders: Second Edition—Revised* (ASAM PPC-2R). Chevy Chase, MD: American Society of Addiction Medicine.

Melnick, G., G. De Leon, M. L. Hiller, and K. Knight. 2000. "Therapeutic Communities: Diversity in Treatment Elements." *Substance Use and Misuse* 35(12–14): 1819–1847.

Melnick, G., J. Hawke, and H. K. Wexler. 2004. "Client Perceptions of Prison-Based Therapeutic Community Drug Treatment Programs." *The Prison Journal* 84: 121–138.

Melnick, G., W, R, Ulaszek, H.-J. Lin, and H. K. Wexler. 2009. "When Goals Diverge: Staff Consensus and the Organizational Climate." *Drug and Alcohol Dependence* 103(Suppl. 1): S17–S22

Miller, W. R., J. L. Sorensen, J. A. Selzer, and G. S. Brigham. 2006. "Disseminating Evidence-Based Practices in Substance Abuse Treatment: A Review with Suggestions." *Journal of Substance Abuse Treatment* 31: 25–39.

Mitchell, O., D. B. Wilson, and D. L. MacKenzie. 2007. "Does Incarceration-Based Drug Treatment Reduce Recidivism? A Meta-Analytic Synthesis of the Research." *Journal of Experimental Criminology* 3: 353–375.

Mumola, C., and J. Karberg. 2006. *Drug Use and Dependence, State and Federal Prisoners, 2004.* Washington, DC: Bureau of Justice Statistics, NCJ 213530.

National Institute on Drug Abuse (NIDA). 1999. *Principles of Drug Addiction Treatment: A Research-Based Guide.* Washington, DC: National Institute of Health, National Institute on Drug Abuse, NIH-99–4180.

National Institute on Drug Abuse (NIDA). 2006. *Principles of Drug Addiction Treatment for Criminal Justice Populations: A Research Based Guide.* Washington, DC: National Institute of Health, National Institute on Drug Abuse, NIH-06–5316.

National Institutes of Health. 2004. *Report of the Blue Ribbon Task Force on Health Services Research at the National Institute on Drug Abuse.* Bethesda, MD. Available at: http://www.drugabuse.gov/about/organization/nacda/HSRReport.pdf.

Nielsen, A. L., F. R. Scarpitti, and J. A. Inciardi. 1996. "Integrating the Therapeutic Community and Work Release for Drug-Involved Offenders: The Crest Program." *Journal of Substance Abuse Treatment* 13: 349–358.

Patterson, R. F. 1998. "Managed Behavioral Healthcare in Correctional Settings." *Journal of the American Academy of Psychiatry and Law* 26: 467–473.

Pearson, F., and D. Lipton. 1999. "A Meta-Analytic Review of the Effectiveness of Corrections-Based Treatments for Drug Abuse." *The Prison Journal* 79: 384–410.

Pelissier, B., S. Wallace, J. A. O'Neil, G. G. Gaes, S. Camp, W. Rhodes, and W. G. Saylor. 2001. "Federal Prison Residential Drug Treatment Reduces Substance Use and Arrests after Release." *American Journal of Drug and Alcohol Abuse* 27(2): 315–337.

Pelissier, B., N. Jones, and T. Cadigan. 2007. "Drug Treatment Aftercare in the Criminal Justice System: A Systematic Review." *Journal of Substance Abuse Treatment* 32: 311–320.

Peters, R. H., M. E. LeVasseur, and R. K. Chandler. 2004. "Correctional Treatment for CO-OCG Disorders: Results of a National Survey." *Behavioral Science and the Law* 22: 563–584.

Petersilia, J. 2003. *When Prisoners Come Home: Parole and Prisoner Reentry*. New York: Oxford University Press.

Peugh, J., and S. Belenko. 1999. "Substance-involved Women Inmates: Challenges to Providing Effective Treatment." *The Prison Journal* 79: 23–44.

Prendergast, M. L., E. A. Hall, H. K. Wexler, G. Melnick, and Y. Cao. 2004. "Amity Prison-Based Therapeutic Community: 5-Year Outcomes." *The Prison Journal* 84: 36–60.

Prendergast, M. L., J. Wellisch, and G. P. Falkin. 1995. "Assessment of and Services for Substance-Abusing Women Offenders in Community and Correctional Settings." *The Prison Journal* 75: 240–256.

Prochaska, J., and C. DiClemente. 1986. "Toward a Comprehensive Model of Change." In *Treating Addictive Behaviors: Processes of Change*, eds. W. R. Miller and N. Heather. New York: Plenum Press.

Proctor, E., J. Landsverk, G. Aarons, D. Chambers, C. Glisson, and B. Mittman. 2009. "Implementation Research in Mental Health Services: An Emerging Science with Conceptual, Methodological, and Training Challenges." *Administration & Policy in Mental Health* 36: 24–34.

Roman, P. M., and J. A. Johnson. 2002. "Adoption and Implementation of New Technologies in Substance Abuse Treatment." *Journal of Substance Abuse Treatment* 22: 1–8.

Rossi, P. H. 1989. *Down and Out in America: Origins of Homelessness*. Chicago: University of Chicago Press.

Sabol, W. J., and T. D. Minton. 2008. *Jail Inmates at Midyear* 2007. Washington, DC: U.S. Department of Justice, Bureau of Justice Statistics, NCJ221945.

Sabol, W. J., H. C. West, and M. Cooper. 2009. *Prisoners in 2008*. Washington, DC: U.S. Department of Justice, Bureau of Justice Statistics, NCJ228417.

Shen, Q., A. T. McLellan, J. C. Merrill. 2000. "Clients" Perceived Need for Treatment and Its Impact on Outcomes." *Substance Abuse* 21: 179–192.

Sherman, L. W., D. C. Gottfredson, D. MacKenzie, J. Eck, P. Reuter, and S. Bushway, eds. 1997. *What Works, What Doesn't, What's Promising: A Report to the United States Congress* (NCJ 165366). Prepared For The National Institute of Justice [Online]. Available at: https://www.ncjrs.gov/works/ (accessed March 12, 2010).

Simpson, D. D. 2002. "A Conceptual Framework for Transferring Research to Practice." *Journal of Substance Abuse Treatment* 22: 171–182.

Simpson, D. D., G. W. Joe, and B. S. Brown. 1997. "Treatment Retention and Follow-Up Outcomes in the Drug Abuse Treatment Outcome Study (DATOS)." *Psychology of Addictive Behaviors* 11: 294–307.

Simpson, D. D., G. W. Joe, B. W. Fletcher, R. L. Hubbard, and M. D. Anglin. 1999. "A National Evaluation of Treatment Outcomes for Cocaine Dependence." *Archives of General Psychiatry* 56: 510–514.

Simpson, D. D., G. W. Joe, and G. A. Rowan-Szal. 2007. "Link the Elements of Change: Program and Client Responses to Innovation." *Journal of Substance Abuse Treatment* 33: 201–209.

Substance Abuse and Mental Health Services Administration (SAMHSA). 2008. *Results from the 2007 National Survey on Drug Use and Health: National Findings* (NSDUH Series H-34, DHHS Publication No. SMA 08–4343). Rockville, MD: U.S. Department of Health and Human Services, SAMHSA, Office of Applied Studies.

Taxman, F. S., and S. Belenko. 2011. *Implementing Evidence-Based Practices in Community Corrections and Addiction Treatment*. New York: Springer.

Taxman, F. S., K. L. Cropsey, D. Young, and H. Wexler. 2007. "Screening, Assessment, and Referral Practices in Adult Correctional Settings: A National Perspective." *Criminal Justice and Behavior* 34(9): 1216–1234.

Taxman, F. S., and D. M. Marlowe. 2006. "Risk, Needs, Responsivity: In Action or Inaction." *Crime and Delinquency* 52(1): 3–7.

Taxman, F., and L. Ressler. 2009. "Public Health Is Public Safety: Revamping the Correctional Mission. In *Contemporary Issues in Criminal Justice Policy: Policy Proposals from the American Society of Criminology Conference*, eds. Natasha A. Frost, Joshua D. Freilich, and Todd R. Clear. Belmont, CA: Cengage/Wadsworth.

Taxman, F. S., and M. Thanner, M. 2006. "Risk, Need, and Responsivity: It All Depends." *Crime and Delinquency* 52(1): 28–52.

Taxman, F., C. Henderson, and S. Belenko. 2009. "Organizational Context, Systems Change, and Adopting Treatment Delivery Systems in the Criminal Justice System." *Drug and Alcohol Dependence* 103S: S1–S6.

Taxman, F., M. Perdoni, and L. Harrison. 2007. "Drug Treatment Services for Adult Offenders: The State of the State." *Journal of Substance Abuse Treatment* 32: 239–254.

Taylor, B. G., N. Fitzgerald, D. Hunt, J. A. Reardon, and H. H. Brownstein. 2001. *ADAM Preliminary 2000 Findings on Drug Use and Drug Markets—Adult Male Arrestees*. Washington, DC: U.S. Department of Justice, National Institute of Justice, NCJ 189101.

Thornberry, T. and M. Krohn. 2000. "The Self-Report Method for Measuring Delinquency and Crime." In *Criminal Justice 2000*, vol. 4, ed. D. Duffee, 33–84. Washington, DC: U.S. Department of Justice, National Institute of Justice, NCJ-182411.

Thornton, C. C., E. Gottheil, S. P. Weinstein, and R. S. Kerachsky. 1998. "Patient-Treatment Matching in Substance Abuse: Drug Addiction Severity." *Journal of Substance Abuse Treatment* 15: 505–511.

Tonry, M. H., and J. Q. Wilson, eds. 1990. *Drugs and Crime*. Chicago: University of Chicago Press.

Travis, J., and J. Petersilia. 2001. "Reentry Reconsidered: A New Look at an Old Question." *Crime and Delinquency* 47: 291–313.

Volkow, N., and T. K. Li. 2005. "The Neuroscience of Addiction." *Nature Neuroscience* 8: 1429–1430.

Welsh, W. N. 2007. "A Multi-Site Evaluation of Prison-Based TC Drug Treatment." *Criminal Justice and Behavior* 34: 1481–1498.

Welsh, W. N. 2010. "Inmate Responses to Prison-Based Drug Treatment: A Repeated Measures Analysis." *Drug and Alcohol Dependence* 109: 37–44.

Welsh, W. N., and P. W. Harris. 2008. *Criminal Justice Policy and Planning*, 3rd ed. Cincinnati: LexisNexis, Anderson Publishing.

Welsh, W. N., and G. Zajac. 2004a. "Building an Effective Research Partnership Between a University and a State Correctional Agency: Assessment of Drug Treatment in Pennsylvania Prisons." *The Prison Journal* 84: 143–170.

Welsh, W. N., and G. Zajac. 2004b. "A Census of Prison-Based Drug Treatment Programs: Implications for Programming, Policy and Evaluation." *Crime and Delinquency* 50: 108–133.

Western, B., J. R. Kling, and D. F. Weiman. 2001. "The Labor Market Consequences of Incarceration." *Crime and Delinquency* 47: 410–427.

Wexler, H. K., G. P. Falkin, and D. S. Lipton. 1990. "Outcome Evaluation of a Prison
    Therapeutic Community for Substance Abuse Treatment." *Criminal Justice and
    Behavior* 17(1): 71–92.
Wexler, H., G. Melnick, L. Lowe, and J. Peters. 1999. "Three-Year Reincarceration Out-
    comes for Amity In-Prison Therapeutic Community and Aftercare in California." *The
    Prison Journal* 79: 321–333.
Wild, T., B. Newton-Taylor, and R. Aletto. 1998. "Perceived Coercion among Clients
    Entering Substance Abuse Treatment." *Addictive Behaviors* 23: 81–95.
Young, D., and S. Belenko. 2002. "Program Retention and Perceived Coercion in Three
    Models of Mandatory Drug Treatment." *Journal of Drug Issues* 32: 297–328.

CHAPTER 20

THE EFFECTIVENESS OF CORRECTIONS-BASED WORK AND ACADEMIC AND VOCATIONAL EDUCATION PROGRAMS

DORIS LAYTON MACKENZIE

I. Introduction

Correctional populations have, on average, less education and fewer marketable job skills compared to the general population (Andrews and Bonta 1994). Almost from the beginning of U.S. penitentiaries, and continuing today, education and work have been important components of daily life in correctional facilities. Recently there has been a concern about the large number of offenders who return to prison after only a short period in the community. In response, many jurisdictions are initiating reentry programs to increase opportunities for offenders to continue with rehabilitation activities during the transition from institutions to the community. Most reentry programs include some type of education and work programs (Brazzell, Crayton, Mukamal, Solomon, and Lindahl 2009). The question that this chapter addresses in whether there is research evidence indicating that these programs are effective in producing the desired outcomes of increased employment and reduced recidivism.

After reviewing the importance of education and work in corrections from a historical perspective, I give an overview of current education, vocational, and work programs, the desired goals of these programs, and theoretical explanations for why they may impact recidivism. The final sections of the chapter review the research on the effectiveness of these programs in reducing recidivism. I end with a theoretical proposal—effective programs are those that produce cognitive transformations, creating changes in the thought processes of delinquents and offenders so they are ready to take advantage of opportunities provided in the community. Administrators and designers of programs in facilities, during reentry and in the community, must consider how to create the cognitive changes that will assist participants in taking advantage of new opportunities in education and employment. Given the large number of education and work programs offered to delinquents and offenders, a surprisingly few strong research studies have been conducted to examine the effectiveness of the programs. More needs to be done to increase the number and quality of the research on evidence of what works, when and for whom in the area of education and work.

Work and academic and vocational education programs have been mainstays of rehabilitation since almost the start of penitentiaries. A large number of offenders and juveniles participate in these programs while they are in facilities or in the community. The public and policy makers generally believe education has benefits in its own right. Encouraging is the fact that:

- Education programs include many of the components of effective correctional treatment;
- Research demonstrates programs such as basic education, GED, postsecondary, and vocational training are effective in reducing later recidivism; and increasing future employment.

In contrast:

- Life skills and work programs have not been found to be effective in reducing recidivism; and
- Questions remain about the effect of these programs when they are embedded within multimodal or holistic programs.

Questions remain about educational programs. For example:

- Research fails to untangle the issues of what works for whom, when, why, and in what circumstances.
- Educators in facilities face tremendous difficulties in normalizing the experiences of student-inmates.
- Lockdowns, transfers between facilities, and restricted movement within facilities limits the time that students spend in classrooms.

Work programs face a different set of issues:

- Often the institutional goals of producing products and maintaining facilities conflict with rehabilitation goals for work programs.

Overall, considering the large number of vocational and academic education, prison industry, and work programs for juvenile delinquents and adult offenders,

- The research is disappointingly scarce; and
- It is severely limited in the scientific quality of the research methodology.

More rigorous research using randomized trials would greatly increase our knowledge of how to provide effective, evidence-based correctional education and work programs.

II. Education in Prisons and Reformatories: Historical Perspective

Educational programs for offenders originally focused on religious instruction, as this was supposed to help offenders achieve spiritual enlightenment (Gerber and Fritsch 1995; Teeters 1955). Consistent with the religious beliefs of those who were responsible for the early penitentiaries, offenders were thought to need time to reflect on their crimes and repent. They were kept in solitary confinement where they would realize the error of their sinful ways and become penitent. Religious instruction was expected to help them in reaching penitence.

The focus of education programs changed from religious instruction to basic literacy and communication skills when the reformation era began. Zebulon R. Brockway, credited with initiating the reformatory age, proposed his theory of rehabilitation in 1876 at the first conference of the American Prison Association (the forerunner of the current American Correctional Association). Since that time, academic education has been a cornerstone of correctional programming. As superintendent of the first reformatory in Elmira, New York, Brockway brought his revolutionary ideas into practice. In his opinion, the goal of the reformatory was to reform youth. With this goal in mind, reformatories were designed to provide physically and mentally healthy environments where youth would have access to academic education and extensive vocational training. Brockway believed that law-abiding behavior was attainable through legitimate industry and education (Reagan and Stoughton 1976). Elmira was used as a model for both adult prisons and juvenile reformatories throughout the United States.

The reformatory age led to an era of rehabilitation in corrections when the use of indeterminate sentencing became an important component of decision making. Offenders were released when there was evidence that they had been rehabilitated.

The goal of corrections was to "correct" through rehabilitation. Educational programs became a mainstay of correctional rehabilitation during this time. By 1930, academic and vocational educational programs were operating in most prisons, where they were considered to play a primary role in the process of rehabilitation. From the original basic literacy programs, the type and variety of educational programs grew to include opportunities for a high school or general equivalency diploma (GED), vocational education, life skills programs, postsecondary or college education, and educational release.

The focus on rehabilitation continued until the 1970s, when corrections in the United States turned away from a rehabilitation philosophy to just deserts and crime-control philosophies that emphasize retribution, deterrence, and incapacitation (MacKenzie 2006). Despite the "tough on crime" rhetoric of many decision makers and politicians, prisons continued to offer academic education. There appears to be a general belief that education has benefits in its own right and this may be, in part, the explanation for the continued interest in offering education programs in corrections (Applegate, Cullen, and Fisher 1997; Cullen, Skovron, and Scott 1990).

Another reason for the continuing emphasis on educational programs is the relatively low level of education among correctional populations. Convicted offenders are, on average, less educated and have fewer marketable job skills than the general population (Andrews and Bonta 2003; Harlow 2003). For example, 41 percent of the inmates in prisons or jails and 31 percent of probationers have not completed high school or its equivalent (Harlow 2003). In comparison, only 18 percent of the general public had not finished the 12th grade. Incarcerated adults also have high rates of illiteracy. In an assessment of adult literacy, a U.S. Department of Education study found prison inmates were lower in their ability to search, comprehend, and use information, to use documents, and to perform computations when compared to the general public (Greenberg, Duleavy, Kutner and White 2007). Ryan (1990) estimates that half of America's inmates are illiterate, if sixth grade achievement is used as a cutoff. According to several researchers, the average reading level of incarcerated offenders may be below the fifth grade level. More than one half of all prison inmates have not completed high school, and those who have are often two to three grade levels behind in actual skills (Tewksbury and Vito 1996).

Basic skills in reading, writing, and math are necessary for functioning in the modern world. Recognition of this, along with a belief that education will facilitate successful reentry, has led many jurisdictions to require prisoners to participate in educational programs, particularly if they test below a certain level. Twenty-two of the 50 states and the federal government have adopted legislation or implemented policies mandating education for prisoners (McClone 2002). In these jurisdictions, prisoners who test below a certain level are required to participate in education for a certain period of time.

III. WORK AND EMPLOYMENT PROGRAMS IN THE PENITENTIARY

Similar to educational programming, work and employment training have been impor-tant parts of the daily activities of inmates from almost the inception of the penitentiaries in America. Originally, the Pennsylvania prison system called for solitary confinement without work so that offenders would have time to reflect on their crimes and repent. Yet, the terrible psychological and physical effects of such isolation quickly became ap-parent, and decisions were made to incorporate moral and religious instruction and work into the daily schedule. Inmates were expected to work from 8 to 10 hours per day in isolation in their cells. Even for those convicted of serious crimes, William Penn's "Great Law" and the Quakers advocated hard labor in place of capital punishment.

Work was also the major component of the Auburn or "congregate" system; however, in contrast to the isolation of the Pennsylvania system, inmates in the Auburn system worked in groups. Inmates worked in shops during the day and at night they were separated into small cells. They were forced to walk in lockstep marching formations when they moved throughout the prison. Silence was enforced because it was believed that communication between prisoners would be contami-nating. Advocates argued for the Auburn system because the prisons were cheaper to construct, offered better vocational training, and produced more money for the state. The economic benefit of having inmates work was most likely one of the major reasons that the congregate system was adopted in almost all American prisons.

Since the time of the early penitentiaries, work has served many purposes in U.S. correctional systems (Flanagan 1989). It has been used to reduce costs, supply governments with needed goods, keep inmates busy, rehabilitate, maintain the insti-tution and as retribution. The primacy of these goals has waxed and waned over time. During the reformatory era, the goal was to change youth so that they would not return to crime after release. From this perspective, work and vocational training were considered important components in the process of reformation because these activities were expected to prepare youth for future employment, thus enabling them to live crime-free lives. Subsequently, these ideas were transferred to adult prisons.

IV. CORRECTIONAL ACADEMIC AND VOCATIONAL EDUCATION AND WORK PROGRAMS TODAY

Today, most correctional facilities offer educational programs. Academic education is legally mandated for juveniles and youthful adults. However, correctional admin-istrators do not limit the programs to only those for whom education is legally required. In a recent Bureau of Justice Statistics report, Harlow (2003) found over

90 percent (91.2 percent) of state prisons, all federal prisons, and almost 90 percent (87.6 percent) of private prisons offered educational programs. These facilities usually house offenders sentenced to a year or more; thus the inmates have sufficient time to achieve educational goals.

Many different types of programs fall under the rubric of education. The most commonly offered programs are basic education (including English as a second language, special education, and literacy classes), GED or high school, vocational education, and postsecondary education/college. Many facilities also offer life skills programs and vocational education. Life skills programs, also called social skills, are sometimes part of other curricula, such as basic adult education or vocational education.

At times, drug treatment and education, parenting, and cognitive skills programs are considered educational programs, but since many of these are not taught by academically trained educators they will not be included in this review of educational programs. Cognitive skills programs emphasize changes in thought processes such as errors in thinking, problem solving, coping skills, antisocial attitudes, and impulsivity. Sessions are usually taught by trained lay people, not educators. Parenting classes are also frequently led by people not trained as educators, and they use varied models for presenting the information. Similarly, drug treatment and education are usually provided by drug counselors, not educators. Furthermore, most studies examining the impact of drug treatment and education focus on a combination of treatment and education or treatment alone and not education alone.

Educational programs available to inmates differ somewhat by facility. Most state prisons offer basic adult education (80.4 percent) or secondary education (83.6 percent), and almost all of the federal prisons offer these programs (97.4 and 98.7 percent, respectively). Fewer private prisons offer basic adult education (61.6 percent) and secondary education (70.7 percent). Many of the state, federal, and private prisons provide college courses (26.7 percent, 80.5 percent and 27.3 percent, respectively) and vocational training (55.7 percent, 93.5 percent, and 44.2 percent, respectively).

In comparison to prisons, local jails hold people from arraignment through conviction and for short sentences. Despite the fact that inmates spend a relatively short time in these facilities, many jails (60.3 percent) provide educational programs (Harlow 2003).

Many inmates take advantage of the educational opportunities while they are incarcerated (Harlow 2003). Over 50 percent of the state (51.9 percent) and federal (56.4 percent) inmates reported participating in educational programs since their most recent incarceration. Fewer jail inmates participate (14.1 percent). Offenders on probation (22.9 percent) also reported participating in educational programs. While there may have been a decline in the percent of inmates who were able to take advantage of educational programs over time due to the great increase in the numbers of inmates in prison, a large percent still participate in educational programs.

Despite the encouraging statistics on the number of facilities offering educational programs and the large number of inmates who report that they have attended educational programs, this tells little about what actually occurs on the ground (Brazzell et al. 2009). Enormous variance occurs between programs and facilities in curricula and methods, staffing and quality of instruction, and participation and completion rates. While many inmates report exposure to educational programs, little information exists on dosage or the actual time spent in the classroom and achievements obtained. Institutional structural problems such as lockdowns, transfers, restricted movement, and short stays seriously limit classroom time, as do inconsistent funding streams and teacher vacancies. Security concerns limit materials to which students may have access, and most facilities prohibit use of the Internet. Volunteers and outside instructors may have trouble entering or exiting facilities in a timely manner. Little national data are available on classroom time, educational attainment, and staff training and qualifications, which would provide evidence that the needs of the inmates are being addressed adequately.

Another issue of concern for educational programs is the decline in programming. From 1997 until 2004 there was a slight decrease in the proportion of inmates in educational programs, particularly in vocational training and adult secondary education (Crayton and Neusteter 2008; Harlow 2003). With the severe budget problems and large prison populations in many states, there is reason to worry about what will happen in the future with correctional education.

Work, prison industries, and vocational education programs also permeate the U.S. correctional system. Ninety-four percent of all state and federal adult correctional systems offer work programs (Stephan 1997). Roughly a third of the facilities surveyed employed inmates in prison industry, approximately half provided vocational training, and almost two-thirds of the inmates participated in a work program while in prison. While many facilities offer work programs, these programs are not necessarily focused on rehabilitation of the inmates. And, with the budget crises going on in many states today, programs that are designed to assist inmates by giving them real world work experiences many be reduced or eliminated.

In contrast to education, work serves many different purposes in correctional facilities. While work has been considered an essential component of rehabilitation, it has also been viewed as important in alleviating the costs of incarceration, reducing management problems, providing social benefits or as retribution. For example, prison farms use inmate labor to help produce food for the inmates. In Texas inmates grow most of their own vegetables. Most institutions use inmates for maintenance tasks, thereby reducing the need for outside laborers and decreasing the operating costs of prisons. In prison factories and industries, inmates produce goods such as furniture or license plates that can be sold to other state agencies. In some systems, inmates are sentenced to "hard labor" as retribution for their crimes. Recently, work programs have been designed to have other social benefits, such as to provide payment of restitution to victims, reimburse the state for a portion of the costs of confinement, or to help support dependents. Work also reduces inmate idleness and its attendant problems, and gives structure to the daily activities. Work and employment skills are often important parts of reentry programs. Such programs are designed to help inmates make the transition from institutions to life in the community (Brazzell et al. 2009). In fact, some states have mandated that inmates participate in work or education 8 hours a day.

When the goal of inmate labor is to benefit society or the institution or as retribution, there is often little interest in whether such work has an impact on later criminal activities, and, often, these goals conflict. For example, an intensive vocational education program may remove inmates from maintenance jobs in the facilities. Using inmate earnings to pay victim restitution and dependent support may remove money that might otherwise be used by the inmate or the institution for other purposes.

In many situations, inmate labor is designed to benefit the inmate in some way. For example, work programs for offenders and delinquents are expected to help them develop good work habits and improve life management skills. Work in prison may also provide inmates with income to be used in the commissary while in prison or as "gate money" at release. Work may be considered rehabilitation when it gives the offender real world work experience, job skills, and vocation training.

V. THEORETICAL RATIONALE FOR EXPECTED IMPACT ON CRIMINAL ACTIVITIES

Conspicuously absent from the research literature in the area of education is a discussion of a theoretical explanation for the connection between education and post-release offending. Few correctional educators articulate the precise mechanism by which they expect the intervention to impact future offender behavior. There are many possible ways in which education may bring about changes that will reduce the future criminal activities of offenders.

Cognitive Theories

One mechanism by which education will theoretically affect recidivism is through improvement in inmate cognitive skills. The way individuals think influences whether they violate the law (Andrews and Bonta 2003; MacKenzie 2006). Deficiencies in social cognition (understanding other people and social interactions), problem-solving abilities, and the sense of self-efficacy are all cognitive deficits or "criminogenic needs" found to be associated with criminal activity (Foglia 2000; Andrews, Zinger, Hoge, Bonta, Gendreau, and Cullen 1990; MacKenzie 2006). Criminogenic needs are dynamic (or changeable) deficits or problems that are directly related to an individual's criminal behavior. Educational programs that increase offenders' social cognitions, ability to solve problems, and belief in their ability to control events in their lives may reduce their future offending.

Other research examining inmate cognitive skills demonstrates a connection between executive cognitive functioning (ECF) and antisocial behavior. ECF is defined as the cognitive functioning required in planning, initiation, and regulation of goal-directed behavior (Giancola 2000). It would include such abilities as attention control, strategic goal planning, abstract reasoning, cognitive flexibility, hypothesis generation, temporal response sequencing, and the ability to use information in working memory. From this perspective, education may be important in reducing crime because it improves the ability to use and process information.

Some researchers and educators argue that the importance of education and cognitive skills may be in its ability to increase individuals' maturity or moral development (Batiuk, Moke, and Rountree 1997; Duguid 1981; Gordon and Arbuthnot 1987). For example, academic instruction can help instill ideas about right and wrong, and these ideas may be associated with changes in attitudes and behaviors.

Education may also mitigate the harsh conditions of confinement or "pains of imprisonment" and reduce prisonization, the negative attitudes that are sometimes associated with incarceration. Deprivations of prison or imported criminogenic norms lead to a prisonized subculture with norms favoring attitudes hostile toward the institution and supportive of criminal activities. By providing safe niches and a more normalized environment, education may provide a basis for reconstruction of law-abiding lifestyles upon release from prison (Harer 1995). Educational opportunities may also mitigate suffering and lead to attitudes accepting the legitimacy of administrative rules and regulations (Tyler 1990; Bottoms and Hay 1996).

Economic Theories

In contrast to the perspective that educational programs will increase general problem solving, perspective taking, executive cognitive functioning, or stage of moral development, economic theories of crime hypothesize that educational programs are important in reducing offending more directly via increased skills and employability. Employability may increase for several reasons. One, the offenders may obtain necessary credentials, such as a high school diploma or GED, that make them eligible for jobs for which they previously would not have been considered. Second, the educational programs may provide them the skills needed for specific jobs. From this perspective, education would increase an offender's chances of getting and keeping legitimate employment after release, thereby eliminating the need to commit crimes for financial gain. There is some evidence that education in prison is associated with an increase in employment. In a review of the research, Gerber and Fritsch (1995) examined the impact of educational program participation on post-release employment and concluded that inmates who participated in or completed prison education programs were more likely to be employed after release.

Obviously, the academic curriculum will differ, depending upon the theoretical rationale for the relationship between education and offending. Although a general liberal arts curriculum might be crucial for increasing cognitive functioning, changing ones' antisocial beliefs, or increasing moral development, it might be less

apt to provide specific job skills. If gainful employment is the theoretical link to reducing crime, then education programs would focus more directly on teaching the
specific job skills that offenders will need in order to find work in the community.
Indeed, Duguid, Hawkey, and Pawson (1996) argue that evaluations should examine these theoretical differences in programs and intermediate outcomes to determine "what works for whom, when, why and in what circumstances." It is quite
possible that the needs of individuals differ and that the type of educational program successful in reducing recidivism for one person will not be the same for another individual.

The rationale for using work and employment as ways to reduce future criminal
activity is similar to that of education—research has consistently found an association
between crime and unemployment (Farrington 1986; Glueck and Glueck 1930; Sampson and Laub 1993; Wolfgang, Figlio, and Sellin 1972; MacKenzie, Browning, Skroban,
and Smith 1999). When offenders are compared to the general public, they are found
to be less educated, to have fewer marketable skills, and are more apt to be unemployed (Andrews and Bonta 2003). In comparison to those who desist, offenders
released from prison who continue to be involved with the criminal justice system
have lower earnings and lower employment rates (Needels 1996). During periods of
unemployment, adults are more criminally active than when they are employed
(Farrington, Gallagher, Morley, and St. Ledger, 1986; MacKenzie et al. 1999).

Theoretical explanations for the relationship between employment and crime
vary (Bushway and Reuter 1997; Fagan 1995; Uggen 2000). According to economic
choice theory, an individual makes a rational choice between legal and illegal work,
based in part on the relative economic attractiveness of the two options. If and when
legal work is more attractive (pay, hours, etc.) individuals will work in the legal
workforce. When illegal work becomes more attractive, people will turn to crime.
Those with low levels of education or job skills will turn to illegal activities because
these activities are more rewarding compared to the legal opportunities available.
From this perspective, correctional education may give people more gratifying
opportunities for legal work in the community.

Control theory provides another explanation for the relationship between
employment and crime. According to this theory, employment exerts social control
over people, and this reduces their desire to get involved in criminal activities. Employment is the main builder of social bonds, and these bonds, in turn, keep people
from engaging in criminal activity. Yet another theory used to explain the crime-
employment relationship is strain or anomie. From this perspective, frustrations
caused by inequalities will cause people to resort to crime. To the degree that education and work skills increase pay and status, frustrations may be reduced, resulting in less criminal activity.

In summary, almost from the beginning of the development of penitentiaries,
education, vocational education, and work have been major components of the
daily schedules of inmates. Education and vocational education were viewed as
important aspects of rehabilitation. Inmate labor and work has served many purposes within facilities but has also been considered important in rehabilitation.

In part, this support for education and work programs results from research demonstrating a strong relationship between both education and work skills and crime. In comparison to the general public, offenders are less educated, have fewer marketable job skills, and are more apt to be unemployed. A variety of theories are offered to explain these findings. A consistency across theories is the expectation that a change in offenders that increases educational levels, job skills, or employment would have an impact on reducing criminal activities. While there is theoretical and empirical evidence that academic underachievement and unemployment are related to criminal offending, evidence of the effectiveness of education, vocation, and work programs in reducing recidivism is less clear. The next section of this chapter reviews the literature on the impact of education, vocational education, and work programs on recidivism.

VI. EFFECTIVENESS OF ACADEMIC AND VOCATIONAL EDUCATION AND WORK PROGRAMS

Despite the fact that education and work are cornerstones of correctional interventions, the quantity and quality of the research examining the effectiveness of such programs in reducing recidivism and conversely increasing employment are extremely limited. In part, this stems from a belief that such opportunities should be offered to all inmates. Therefore, administrators and staff are hesitant to use experimental designs to randomly decide which offenders will be given the chance to participate. While this speaks to how important correctional officials believe these programs are, it severely limits our ability to determine how effective these programs are in producing the desired outcomes. That is, the internal validity of the studies is in question due to selection effects. Any significant outcomes could be due to previously existing differences between the treated (education, work) group and the comparison and may not result from the impact of the interventions.

Several early reviews of the education and vocation training for juveniles and adults called into question the effectiveness of these programs. For example, as he found with other correctional programs, Martinson (1974) concluded there was no clear evidence that these programs successfully reduced recidivism. A later review by Linden and Perry (1983) agreed with these conclusions. However, more recent reviews of the research found more positive results. Gerber and Fritsch (1995) in a review of education and vocational education programs and Taylor (1994) in a study of PSE programs concluded that there was sufficient evidence that these programs can successfully reduce recidivism.

My colleagues and I conducted systematic reviews and meta-analyses of evaluations of correctional education, vocational education, and work programs for adults (Wilson, Gallagher, Coggeshall, and MacKenzie 1999; Wilson, Gallagher, and MacKenzie 2000; MacKenzie 2006). We began with an intensive search for all published and unpublished evaluations that met our eligibility criteria. To be eligible to be in the review, the evaluation had to include a group who received one of these interventions and a comparison group who do not. The study had to report outcomes of either a return to criminal activities and/or employment after release.

In these meta-analyses we also attempted to code and analyze the characteristics of the different programs that may have made them more or less effective. For example, we wanted to ask questions like: Were programs with smaller class size more effective? How effective was tutoring by peers or volunteers? Were programs that incorporated transition or reentry programming more effective? Was obtaining a degree or certificate more effective than just participating? Did programs with drug treatment, parenting, cognitive skills, or life skills result in better outcomes? Disappointingly, based on the information given in the research manuscripts, it was not possible to identify these characteristics and relate them to outcomes. Many studies compared those who participated in education to those who did not. Education records did not give sufficient information for researchers to code achievement (Streurer, Smith and Tracy 2001).

We also attempted to examine characteristics of the participants and how these related to the effectiveness of the interventions. As with program characteristics, little information was given in the study reports about the characteristics of the participants. Most of the research participants in these studies were men; none of the studies had a sample of women only. While 19 (36 percent) of the programs studied included both men and women, there was insufficient information to determine the actual percentage of each. Women represented such a small proportion of the total that we do not believe that it is reasonable to generalize the findings to programs serving women.

Most evaluations studied offenders who participated in education during their incarceration (n = 50), only three studied probation programs. This probably reflects the limited number of programs offered to offenders in the community. However, in terms of the meta-analysis, it means that the results cannot be generalized to programs provided in the community. With the increased concern about and funding for reentry programs, most likely more programs, particularly work and employment, may be offered in the future.

It is important to note that significant results cannot be attributed with complete assurance to the effect of the intervention because the vast majority of the studies included in the meta-analyses used naturally occurring groups of participants compared to non-participants (Cecil, Drapkin, MacKenzie, and Hickman 2000; Bouffard, MacKenzie, and Hickman 2000; Gaes 2008; Wilson et al. 1999, 2000). Thus, the generally positive findings may result from differential characteristics of the offenders that existed prior to the program and not as a positive effect of program participation itself. That is, participating offenders may be more motivated to change and would have lower recidivism even if they did not have an opportunity to participate in a program. A few studies used random assignment, and some had stronger research designs by using propensity scores or comparing participants and non-participants in motivation levels (Streurer et al. 2001; Harer 1995).

VII. Impact on Recidivism

In total, we identified 53 program-comparison contrasts meeting our eligibility criteria: 6 Adult basic education (ABE); 3 general equivalency diploma (GED); 5 combined ABE and GED; 13 of PSE; 17 vocational education; 4 correctional industries; and 5 multicomponent or other work programs. Outcome data were measured mostly with reincarcerations (66 percent) and arrests (19 percent) with the remaining measuring convictions (11 percent) and parole revocations (4 percent). Since outcome data from many of the ABE and GED studies were combined in the studies, we combined these programs in the recidivism analyses. Overall, for the programs combined (work and education), there was a significant reduction in recidivism. If the comparison group's recidivism rate is set to 50 percent, the overall program group recidivism rate is estimated at 39 percent. The recidivism rate for comparison is arbitrarily set in order to provide a convenient benchmark for assessing the magnitude of the relationship reflected by the data analysis of effect size. Shown in figure 20.1 are the recidivism rates and significance levels for the separate analyses of program types.

Adult Basic Education (ABE) and General Equivalency Diploma (GED)

Participants in ABE, GED, and combined ABE or GED recidivated at a significantly lower rate than those in the comparison group. We estimated that program participants recidivated at a rate of 41 percent relative to a base recidivism rate of 50 percent for the comparison group.

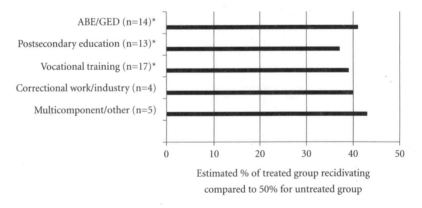

Estimated % of treated group recidivating
compared to 50% for untreated group

*= significant difference between treatment and comparison groups

Fig. 20.1.

Postsecondary Correctional Education (PSE)

Many people worried that loss of Pell Grant funding would have a long-term adverse impact on correctional education. This did happen immediately after the funding was abolished in 1994, but a recent survey of prisoners indicates that the level of college participation has returned to the percent participating during the Pell Grant period (Erisman and Contardo 2005). Erisman and Contardo (2005) found that approximately 5 percent of the total number of prisoners participated in PSE, a percentage similar to the time before the loss of the Pell Grants. However, wide differences existed among different jurisdictions. Forty-four of the 46 responding prison systems and the Federal Bureau of Prisons (FBOP) offered at least some PSE programs. However, 89 percent of the participants were in only 14 states and the FBOP. This means that the other state systems had very few participants.

What is interesting is that the type of PSE program has changed from the time of the Pell Grants until 2003–2004. In 2003–2004, prisoners were taking more vocational classes instead of purely academic courses. Almost two-thirds of the prisoners enrolled in PSE in 2003–2004 were enrolled in vocational certificate programs for college credit (Erisman and Contardo 2005). The other third were taking college classes for an associate's degree program. Thus, few prison inmates were earning college degrees, even at the associate's level. It is important to note that the research examining PSE treats the courses taken for college credit as PSE and not vocational education. Conversely, research on vocation education does not include PSE vocational education certificate programs as part of vocational education.

Most of the education programs for prisoners are provided by community colleges. Only approximately 16 percent of the providers were public four-year institutions and only 4 percent were for-profit institutions. Some inmates are enrolled in correspondence courses, but since they are not funded by public funds, correctional systems seldom have statistics about the type of college, courses, or characteristics of the inmate participants.

While it seems reasonable to use technology for prison education programs, few correctional facilities do so. Most use traditional instructional methods. In their survey, Erisman and Contardo (2005) found that almost all of the courses were provided by on-site instructors. Forty-five percent used some type of video or satellite instruction for at least some of their classes. Internet technology was least frequently used. Correctional educators cited security concerns as the reason that the Internet was not used more often. Of course, limitations on the use of the Internet to access information and library resources would be a severe disadvantage for prisoner students.

New Mexico was one jurisdiction using interactive distance education for college courses. Nine New Mexico correctional facilities were fitted with lab space, computers, and a secure, high-speed network connection to a computer server at Eastern New Mexico University-Roswell. This is an Internet-based program, but prisoners enrolled in the classes are not able to access the Internet to send e-mail or to view external web sites. Inmate students do not have direct contact with the instructors. Department of Corrections facilitators with college degrees monitor the classes and pass messages between faculty and students. One major benefit to this system is that the program exists in nine prisons; therefore when prisoners are transferred they may immediately enroll in the same course at the new facility.

One complication for PSE is that courses must be offered by degree-granting institutions if the students are to receive credit (Erisman and Contardo 2005). In many states, education programs at the ABE and GED levels are administered by in-house educators employed by the department of corrections. College courses require the involvement of external institutions. Some states with larger PSE programs have solved the problem of coordinating PSE and the institutions by centralizing the process (Erisman and Contardo 2005). For example, the Washington Department of Corrections contracts with the State Board for Community and Technical Colleges to provide for-credit vocational education certificate programs. North Carolina has a formal interagency partnership between the Department of Corrections and the community college system.

According to our meta-analyses, PSE programs significantly reduced the recidivism of participants. Compared to a base recidivism rate of 50 percent for the comparison, we estimate the participants would recidivate at a rate of 37 percent (Wilson et al. 1999). Insufficient information in the reports prohibited us from determining the type of classes (vocational, academic) given to participants, nor could we determine the type of inmate who most benefited from the courses.

In a more recent meta-analysis focusing on PSE, Chappell (2004) examined 15 experimental and quasi-experimental studies conducted between 1990 and 1999. According to Chappell, studies often failed to control for selection bias. She found that 22 percent of the PSE participants recidivated, compared to a rate of 41 percent for the comparisons, a relatively large reduction in recidivism. Chappell does not provide a list of the studies included in her analysis, so it is difficult to compare her results with other meta-analyses.

Life Skills

"Life skills" programs are a relatively new type of educational program. The rationale for these programs is that adult basic education programs, which focus on basic academic skills, may not address a number of other important deficiencies of offenders (Finn 1998). While inmates may have serious difficulties reading and writing, they may also have difficulty with other things, such as conducting job searches, balancing a checkbook, controlling anger, establishing healthy interpersonal relationships, and setting and meeting goals. Life skills programs are designed to address such skill deficiencies that may hinder the attempts of offenders to function successfully in everyday life. The actual components of life skills programs vary widely. Some common components include budgeting, building interpersonal relationships, conflict resolution, tax and credit management, job search skills, cultural diversity training, anger and stress management, decision making, and goal setting.

Life skills programs are often combined with other types of programs and may or may not be delivered by educators. At times the programs are delivered by laypeople and are similar to cognitive skills–type programs.

Some life skills programs are holistic and use a multimodal approach to life skills training (see, for instance, http:///wdp.doc.state.vt.us/programs.htm). In these programs, participants in facilities may live together in units separated from the general population. Programs have been designed for adults and juveniles and for those in facilities or in the community. They are given intensive treatment by trained personal.

Most life skills programs provide much more limited instruction and do not provide separate living units (see, for example, the description of San Diego County jail's Staying Out Successfully, SOS, by Melton and Pennell 1998 or the Delaware Life Skills Program described by Miller 1995, 1997). These programs may focus on communication, anger management, career planning, goal setting, time management, job skills, relationship building, personal budgeting, and drug use issues.

In my systematic review and meta-analysis, I did not find a significant difference between life skills programs and comparison groups (MacKenzie 2006). There are several problems in drawing conclusions about the effectiveness of these programs. First, there are relatively few studies that used strong research designs (MacKenzie 2006; Bouffard et.al, 2000). Second, the theoretical model for life skills varies greatly in implementation. At times it is more like a counseling program with a focus on adjustment, anger control, and changes in attitudes. At other times the life skills programs are delivered by educators and are more like a practical education program teaching people about skills needed to successfully live in U.S. society, such as balancing a checkbook, opening a checking account, or completing tax forms. Another reason that these programs may not be effective is that they do not focus on cognitive change. The skills emphasized in the program are very practical but may not bring about the type of cognitive transformation needed to change offender's criminal activities (MacKenzie 2006). A holistic program may be successful in changing offenders but we did not find any that demonstated the impact of a multimodal program on recidivism. Furthermore, in the more holistic programs it is often difficult to identify the specific components of the program that might have an impact, particularly if programs such as academic education or cognitive skills are offered as part of the life skills program.

The life skills programs that have been evaluated are those that are not part of a comprehensive program, and this makes it difficult to draw conclusions about the effectiveness of the programs that are embedded within larger, more comprehensive programs. For example, a multimodal program may be devoted to placing parolees in jobs after release from prison (Finn 1998). The programs provide job preparation services to inmates while they are still incarcerated in state prisons so that they have a head start in finding employment upon release. In-prison services include assessment and testing to evaluate the participant's skills and work history, assistance in gathering documentation needed for jobs (e.g., birth certificates, social security cards, school transcripts), job readiness training, and employability and life skills workbooks. The life skills program components offer information, education, and programs on things like: self concept/anger management; family relationships; civic and legal responsibilities; victim awareness; personal health and hygiene; and, job preparation. Upon release, these programs may help parolees find jobs and may match them with job openings. In such programs, life skills are offered in different ways—in prison working with an employment specialist, or in educational programs and out of prison during parole. This type of program that incorporates life skills within such a multimodal, holistic program is not the type of program examined in the meta-analyses we did. We do not know how important life skills programs may be when imbedded within a larger program.

Vocational Education

Vocational education is one of the most widely implemented educational programs in correctional systems because it addresses the high incidence of academic and employment failure of offenders. Over 50 percent of the state prisons, most federal prisons (93.5 percent), 44.2 percent of private prisons, and some jails (6.5 percent) offer vocational training. Over 30 percent of the inmates in state and federal prisons report participating in a vocational program while in the facility. Similar to life skills programs, vocational education programs vary greatly, and this makes it difficult to draw conclusions about their effectiveness. Programs include classroom-based education, job training, and apprenticeships in areas such as electricity and carpentry.

Some vocational education programs are holistic programs designed to address multiple deficiencies. For example, Lattimore et al. (1990) studied the Sandhills Vocational Delivery System (VDS) of the North Carolina Department of Corrections. The program was designed to improve the post-release employment prospects of youthful inmates using integrated training and employment services (Lattimore, Witte, and Baker 1990). A variety of state agencies provided services in a comprehensive program with the goal of improving the post-release employability and employment of the inmates. The protocol included individual work with inmates to identify vocational interests and aptitudes, individual plans of study, providing the needed vocational training as well as other services, and helping inmates to obtain post-release employment. Other services included such things as academic programs, self-improvement, and life enrichment activities.

Frequently vocational education programs begin with classroom instruction aimed at giving the inmates work-related knowledge, such as basic math skills needed for automotive mechanics or construction tasks. For example, in her study, Piehl (1995) reports on a program in the Wisconsin Department of Corrections that offered accreditation to offenders who complete vocational education programs, enabling them to obtain a necessary trade license. Other programs may offer more hands-on training in which juvenile delinquents and adult offenders have an opportunity to work on construction projects (Home Builders Institute, 1996). At times a partnership is formed between the correctional institutions and local tradespeople, so post-release employment possibilities are improved.

Systematic reviews and meta-analyses of vocational education programs indicate that these programs are successful in reducing the later criminal activities of participants (Wilson et al. 2000; Wilson et al. 1999; MacKenzie 2006). Wilson et al. (1999) estimate that if the comparison group's recidivism rate was 50 percent, the recidivism rate of those who participated in a vocational education program would be 38 percent. Vocational educational programs also increase the employment rate of offenders, and higher recidivism rates are associated with lower employment rates. One reason for the findings that vocational education has an impact on both recidivism and employment may be because many of the programs are very comprehensive, giving inmates classes and assistance while they are in the facilities but also assisting them in finding employment after release. This transitional help may be important in helping offenders adjust in the community. With the current emphasis on reentry services, more such transitional programs are being instituted in order to reduce the high reincarceration rates of those released from jails or prisons (Brazzell et. al. 2009). There is insufficient research and information to examine the effectiveness of different components of the vocational education programs.

Two difficulties arise if we try to conclude that vocational education participation leads to increases in employment and decreases in criminal activities. The first difficulty is ruling out alternative explanations for the results, due to the poor scientific quality of the research. For example, out of the 18 studies I examined, only two used experimental designs (MacKenzie 2006). Almost all of the studies use previously existing groups for the comparisons, so we can never be sure that the effects are due to the vocational program and not self-selection into the program. It may be that the groups differed prior to the program, and this is the reason for the differences in outcomes. It is highly likely that the participants are more motivated individuals who would be more apt to find employment and stop committing crimes even if they did not participate in the program. However, two studies (Lattimore et al. 1990; Saylor and Gaes 1996) used strong research designs, and the results of both demonstrated a significant reduction in recidivism, lending credence to the overall findings.

The second problem in drawing conclusions about the impact of the programs on later criminal behavior is that many of the studies combine vocational education with other services or institutional work. Participants receive vocational education but they may also be given a prison industry job or receive academic education and other services. Thus, we cannot rule out the possibility of a combination or multimodal aspect having the impact and not the vocational program alone. One reason for the success of vocational educational programs may be that they include an educational component along with environmental opportunities for work. The educational component may cognitively change participants so that they are ready to take advantage of the work opportunities.

Correctional Industries

The term "correctional industries" is used to describe a wide range of employment-related activities occurring during an offender's term of incarceration. Although some industrial facilities are located outside the prison, the workers are almost always serving time in some type of residential facility. The industries produce a number of different products and services, usually for government agencies but at times also for private-sector consumers. The industries may produce furniture, health technology, automobile parts, institutional and jail products, signs, printing products, textiles and apparel, traffic paint, and food. In general, inmates working in correctional industries are older, serving longer sentences, are less apt to be drug users/abusers and have better pre-prison employment records (Flanagan 1989). Most prison industries are not designed as rehabilitation mechanisms but rather serve other institutional goals, particularly reducing costs by the sale of the products and services.

Given the large number of correctional industries programs, it is surprising that in our search for evaluations we found only four studies examining correctional industries (MacKenzie 2006; Wilson et al. 1999, 2000). Most likely, this is because the industries are not considered treatment programs, and so there is little expectation or interest in the impact on future recidivism or employment. Of the four prison industry evaluations that we located, only two were judged to be methodologically sound. The other two studies were judged so low in scientific rigor that we did not use them to make decisions about effectiveness.

The two well-designed studies were conducted in New York (Maguire, Flanagan, and Thornberry 1988) and the Federal Bureau of Prisons (Saylor and Gaes 1992). In both studies, the participants had lower recidivism rates than the comparisons, but only in the Saylor and Gaes's (1992) study was the difference significant. However, both studies used preexisting groups that can be assumed to differ prior to the study. Most likely, those who volunteer and are accepted in the industry program would be different from others. Both studies attempted to control for these differences in multivariate analysis. Furthermore, the Saylor and Gaes evaluation had a large number of subjects and, thus, while the results were significant, the absolute differences in recidivism rates was relatively small (6.6 compared to 10.1).

Work and Multicomponent Programs

These are the type of programs that are becoming popular in reentry programs. The programs usually focus on assisting offenders in obtaining employment, acquiring job search skills, or other employment services. Participants may live in pre-release facilities in institutions, halfway houses, or other community residential facilities. In our meta-analyses, these programs were not significant in reducing recidivism. However, one difficulty that arises in drawing conclusions about these programs is the large differences in the programs studied. They varied in the types of employment services provided and whether the programs were provided in the community, prison, or both. There is little evidence from our examination of correctional work programs to suggest that they have been successful in reducing recidivism.

A recent systematic review by Visher and her colleagues for the Campbell Collaboration examining non-custodial employment programs for ex-offenders found similar results (Visher, Winterfield, and Coggeshall 2006). They examined employment services interventions for recently released prisoners and job training or job placement programs for people who had been arrested, convicted or incarcerated for a criminal charge. Their sample of eight eligible studies included only random assignment studies of programs for older youth and adults. The recidivism of offenders in these studies of employment interventions was not reduced, despite the fact that the random assignment studies included very heterogeneous programs in terms of both the type of program delivered and the individuals enrolled. However, they caution that employment-focused interventions for former prisoners have not been adequately evaluated for effectiveness. They identified only eight studies, and the majority of these were more than 10 years old.

VIII. Impact on Employment

In our meta-analysis, 16 studies measured employment status once offenders were in the community: educational programs (n = 4), vocational training (n = 8), correctional industries (n = 1) and multicomponent/others (n = 3). Overall, more were employed after release than the comparisons. The second question of interest was the relationship between recidivism and employment. If, as some theorists assert, employment causes a reduction in recidivism, we would expect the two to be correlated. Larger differences in the recidivism rates of program participants relative to non-participants were associated with larger differences in employment status at follow-up. That is, programs that have an impact on recidivism also have an impact on employment. These are the expected findings if there is a causal relationship between employment and recidivism; however, our study cannot rule out alternative explanations for the relationship.

IX. What Works in Corrections?

Cognitive changes that occur as a result of educational programs may be particularly important in changing offenders. After reviewing 284 research studies judged to be of sufficient scientific rigor and completing systematic reviews and meta-analyses, I conclude that the treatment and management strategies focusing on rehabilitating offenders were effective in reducing recidivism (MacKenzie 2006). In contrast to the more theoretical meta-analyses, I examined specific types of strategies, such as boot camp, intensive supervision, cognitive skills, and educational programs. Programs emphasizing punishment, deterrence, or control, such as boot camps, Scared Straight, or intensive supervision, were ineffective. Programs with poor or little theoretical basis or poorly implemented programs were also ineffective (e.g., psychosocial sex offender treatment; residential programs for juveniles; treatment for batterers). Similarly, programs that emphasized the formation of ties or bonds without first changing the individual's thought process were ineffectual. Examples of the latter programs are life skills education, correctional industries, and multi-component work programs.

Almost all the effective programs focused on individual-level change. In contrast, the ineffective programs frequently emphasize developing opportunities. For example, cognitive skills programs emphasize individual-level changes in thinking, reasoning, empathy, and problem solving. In contrast, life skills and work programs, examples of ineffective programs, often focus on giving the offenders opportunities in the community. Based on these observations, I proposed that effective programs must focus on changing the individual. This change is required before the person will be able to take advantage of opportunities in the environment. Giordano and her colleagues call this change a cognitive transformation (Giordano, Cernkovich, and Rudolph 2002). They propose that individual-level change must precede changes in ties or bonds to social institutions. The social environment may be conducive to the formation of ties, but the individual must change if the bond is to form. To get along with family, keep a job, support children, or form strong, positive ties with other institutions, the person must change in cognitive reasoning, attitude toward drug use, antisocial attitudes, reading level, or vocation skills. Such transformations are necessary before a person makes initial moves toward a different way of life. Only if a cognitive transformation occurs is the person able to sustain a new life. Thus, educational programs that bring about cognitive transformations would be expected to be effective in changing offenders.

Prison industries or other work programs may not be effective for correctional populations because the programs focus on giving opportunities for employment but do not emphasize individual change. The person may not have the individual abilities and/or attitudes to take advantage of the environmental opportunities, and thus a bond with the world of work is not formed. Education and vocational education programs may be effective because they focus on changing the thinking skills of the students. This, in turn, may increase an ex-offender's ability to find and keep employment. During the education process the individual changes and these changes make employment more likely, thereby increasing the chances that the person will form a tie or bond to the world of work.

These findings have direct implications for the development of effective re-entry programs. Programs would be expected to be most effective if they focus on individual transformations. There will be a temptation to focus on programs that increase opportunities for work, reunite families, and provide housing. Obviously, these are important needs of the reentering ex-prisoners. Such programs provide opportunities for the formation of ties or bonds to the community. However, the research on "what works" suggest that an emphasis on these opportunities for ties will not be effective if there is not also a focus on individual-level transformation, such as might occur with academic and vocation education programs. From this perspective, education programs are important in bringing about a change in thinking and cognitions, not just in their ability to directly impact the offender's ability to get employment. The individual learns to value employment and the associated benefits.

The Black Box of Correctional Education

The good news from research on correctional education is that ABE, GED, PSE, and vocational education appear to reduce the recidivism of offenders as well as increase employment. There is, however, serious concern about the quality of the research and whether these results will be upheld if more rigorous randomized trails that eliminate the self-selection problem are conducted. On the other hand, many education programs are consistent with the principles of effective programs, and they also would be expected to bring about the cognitive transformations associated with effective correctional programs.

There are still many unknowns about correctional education (MacKenzie 2008). Questions remain about the exact curriculum that is effective and what works for whom, when, why, and in what circumstances. Does the link between education and recidivism depend only on cognitive change, or some combination of cognitive change and increased opportunities for additional schooling or employment in the community?

We also know little about the exact curricula that may be most effective for different types of offenders. Strong arguments have been made about the importance of gender- and race/ethnicity-sensitive programming. However, we do not know if such "responsive" programming would increase academic progress, be more effective in reducing recidivism, or assist in employment success.

Given the importance of work and education to offenders and delinquents, the quality of the research examining the programs is, on the whole, acutely limited in both quantity and quality. Research designs use dropouts, people who did not volunteer or who for some other reason did not participate. Such designs have the internal validity problem of selection. The two groups are most likely very different before the educational or work program began; therefore, any differences found in outcomes cannot be attributed to the program. Those who volunteer to enter a educational program may be labeled the "motivated" group. The motivated group who volunteer for treatment would be expected to be more ready for treatment or more amenable to treatment. Comparing the educational group to the comparison group means that those who are the most ready, or most amenable to programming are being compared to a group that includes people who do not want to "waste" their time in educational programs. Thus, any differences in outcomes are most likely because the "good" candidates (the ready, amenable group) are being compared to a group that may include many who are "bad" treatment candidates. Any differences in later criminal activity can easily be attributed to differences between the groups that existed prior to the program and, therefore, little can be said about the impact of the educational program. While many correctional education administrators reject the idea of randomized research designs because they might deprive some individuals of educational experiences, they fail to see the large benefits that such research could provide. For example, more information is needed about the difference between education programs focusing on job-related skills versus those centering on problem solving and cognitive processes. Certainly, random assignment to these two programs would fairly give each group educational opportunities and at the same time provide relevant information about each type of program. This could be carried further to examine whether some types of individuals (genders, race/ethnic, past criminal history) benefited more from one or the other program. Well-planned, randomized trials would greatly add to our knowledge of what works for whom in vocational and educational programming.

Finally, there have been few studies examining educational programs that assist offenders in the process of reentry. Most research has examined programs that are provided in institutions, and some have examined programs provided in the community, but few have examined holistic, multimodal programs that take participants from institution to the community.

Some structural problems exist in facilities that greatly restrict the achievement obtained by student inmates. Lockdowns, transfers between institutions, and restricted movement in facilities limit classroom time. Concerns about security prohibit Internet use, thus greatly reducing the ability of offenders to obtain information and use library resources. Studies have examined education participation but not achievement. Nor do the studies examine the specific components of educational programs.

X. CONCLUSIONS

Certainly, more work needs to be done to examine vocational and academic education and work programs. With the current emphasis on reentry programs both educational and work-related, there will be an increased concern regarding how to design effective programs that help transition ex-offenders from facilities to the community. We need strong research designs that will tell us whether a combination of employment and education can be successful in reducing recidivism and increasing employment. It is possible to begin examining the theoretical issues to identify effective programs. While overall the evidence indicates that education is effective, more work needs to be done on the questions of whom, when, why, and what. Many of the studies of work and employment for offenders are poorly designed and were completed long in the past. The groups are so dissimilar that no one can tell whether differences in later criminal activity are the result of the program or because the groups are so different in characteristics. New studies need to be designed, particularly on the new reentry programs that are becoming so popular in many jurisdictions. With the increased interest in evidenced-based corrections, we can only hope that more emphasis will be placed on providing research evidence to support the use of educational and work programs (MacKenzie 2000, 2001, 2005).

REFERENCES

Andrews, D.A., and J. Bonta. 2003. *The Psychology of Criminal Conduct.* Cincinnati, OH: Anderson.

Andrews, D. A., I. Zinger, R. D. Hoge, J. Bonta, P. Gendreau, and F. T. Cullen. 1990. "Does Correctional Treatment Work? A Clinically Relevant and Psychologically Informed Meta-Analysis." *Criminology* 28: 369–397.

Applegate, B. K., F. T. Cullen, and B. S. Fisher. 1997. "Public Support for Correctional Treatment: The Continuing Appeal of the Rehabilitative Ideal." *The Prison Journal* 77: 237–258.

Batiuk, M. E., P. Moke, and P. W. Rountree. 1997. "Crime and Rehabilitation: Correctional Education as an Agent of Change." *Justice Quarterly* 14: 167–180.

Bottoms, A., and W. Hay. 1996. *Prisons and the Problem of Order.* Oxford: Clarendon Press.

Bouffard, J. A., D. L. MacKenzie, and L. Hickman. 2000. "Effectiveness of Vocational Education and Employment Programs for Adult Offenders: A Methodology-Based Analysis of the Literature." *Journal of Offender Rehabilitation* 31: 1–41.

Brazzell, D., A. Crayton, D. A. Mukamal, A. L. Solomon, and N. Lindahl. 2009. *From the Classroom to the Community: Exploring the Role of Education During Incarceration and Reentry.* Washington, DC: The Urban Institute Justice Policy Center.

Bushway, S., and P. Reuter. 1997. "Labor Markets and Crime Risk Factors." In *Preventing Crime: What Works, What Doesn't, What's Promising,* eds. L. W. Sherman, et al. Washington, DC: Office of Justice Programs, U.S. Department of Justice.

Chappell, C. A. 2004. "Post-Secondary Correctional Education and Recidivism: A Meta-Analysis of Research Conducted 1990–1999." *The Journal of Correctional Education* 55(2): 148–169.

Cecil, D. K., D. A. Drapkin, D. L. MacKenzie, and L. J. Hickman. 2000. "The Effectiveness of Adult Basic Education and Life-Skills Programs in Reducing Recidivism: A Review and Assessment of the Research." *Journal of Correctional Education* 51: 207–226.

Crayton, A., and S. R. Neusteter. 2008. "The Current State of Correctional Education." Paper presented at the Reentry Roundtable on Education, John Jay College of Criminal Justice, New York.

Cullen, F. T., S. E. Skovron, and J. E. Scott. 1990. "Public Support for Correctional Treatment: The Tenacity of Rehabilitative Ideology. Survey of Cincinnati and Columbus Residents." *Criminal Justice and Behavior* 17: 6–18.

Duguid, S. 1981. "Prison Education and Criminal Choice: The Context of Decision-Making." In *On Prison Education,* ed. L. Morin, 134–157. Ottawa: Canadian Government Publishing Center.

Duguid, S., C. Hawkey, and R. Pawson, R. 1996. "Using Recidivism to Evaluate Effectiveness in Prison Education Programs." *Journal of Correctional Education* 47: 74–85.

Erisman, W., and J. B. Contardo. 2005. *Learning to Reduce Recidivism: A 40-State Analysis of Postsecondary Correctional Education Policy.* Institute for Higher Education Policy.

Fagan, J. 1995. "Legal Work and Illegal Work: Crime, Work and Unemployment." In *Dealing with Urban Crisis: Linking Research to Action,* eds. B. Weisbrod and J. Worthy. Evanston, IL: Northwestern University Press.

Farrington, D., Gallagher, Morley, and St. Ledger. 1986. "Unemployment, School Leaving and Crime." *British Journal of Criminology* 26: 335–356.

Farrington, D. (1986. "Age and Crime." In *Crime and Justice,* Vol. 7, eds. M. Tonry and N. Morris, 189–250. Chicago: University of Chicago Press.

Flanagan, T. 1989. "Prison Labor and Industry." In *The American Prison*, eds. L. I. Goodstein and D. L. MacKenzie. New York: Plenum Press.

Finn, P. 1998. *The Delaware Department of Corrections Life Skills Program*. Washington, DC: National Institute of Justice. Office of Correctional Education, National Institute of Corrections.

Foglia, W. D. 2000. "Adding an Explicit Focus on Cognition to Criminological Theory." In *The Science, Treatment, and Prevention Of Antisocial Behaviors: Application to the Criminal Justice System*, ed. D. H. Fishbein. Kingston, NJ: Civic Research Institute.

Gaes, G. G. 2008. "The Impact of Prison Education Programs on Post-Release Outcomes." Paper presented at the Reentry Roundtable on Education, John Jay College of Criminal Justice, New York.

Gerber, J., and E. J. Fritsch. 1995. "Adult Academic and Vocational Correctional Education Programs: A Review of Recent Research." *Journal of Offender Rehabilitation* 22: 119–142.

Giancola, P. R. 2000. "Executive Functioning: A Conceptual Framework for Alcohol- Related Aggression." *Exp. Clin. Psychopharmacol.* 8: 576–597.

Giordano, P. C., S. A. Cernkovich, and J. L. Rudolph. 2002 "Gender, Crime, and Desistance: Toward a Theory of Cognitive Transformation." *American Journal of Sociology* 107(4): 990–1064.

Glueck, S., and E. Glueck. 1930. *500 Criminal Careers*. New York: A. A. Knopf.

Gordon, D. A., and J. Arbuthnot. 1987. "Individual, Group, and Family Interventions." In *Handbook of Juvenile Delinquency*, ed. H. C. Quay, 290–324. New York: Wiley.

Greenberg, E., E. Duleavy, M. Kutner, and S. White. 2007, May. "Literacy Behind Bars: Results from the 2003 National Assessment of Adult Literacy Prison Survey." Available at: http://nces.ed.gov/pubs2007/2007473.pdf. National Center for Educational Statistics, Institute of Educational Sciences, U.S. Department of Education.

Harer, M. D. 1995. "Recidivism among Federal Prisoners Released in 1987." *Journal of Correctional Education* 46: 98–127.

Harlow, C. W. 2003. *Education and Correctional Populations*. Bureau of Justice Special Report, Office of Justice Programs. Washington, DC: U.S. Department of Justice.

Lattimore, P. K., A. D. Witte, and J. R. Baker. 1990. "Experimental Assessment of the Effect of Vocational Training on Youthful Property Offenders." *Evaluation Review* 14: 115–133.

Linden, R., and L. Perry. 1983. "The Effectiveness of Prison Education Programs." *Journal of Offender Counseling, Services and Rehabilitation* 6: 43–57.

Martinson, R. 1974. "What Works? Questions and Answers about Prison Reform." *Public Interest* 10: 22–54.

MacKenzie, D. L. 2000. "Evidence-based Corrections: Identifying What Works." *Crime and Delinquency* 46(4): 457–471.

MacKenzie, D. L. 2001. "Corrections and Sentencing in the 21st Century: Evidence-based Corrections and Sentencing." *The Prison Journal* 81(3): 299–312.

MacKenzie, D. L. 2005. "The Importance of Using Scientific Evidence to Make Decisions about Correctional Programming." *Criminology & Public Policy* 4(2): 249–258.

MacKenzie, D. L. 2006. *What Works in Corrections? Reducing the Criminal Activities of Offenders and Delinquents*. Cambridge, UK: Cambridge Press.

MacKenzie, D. L. 2008. "Structure and Components of Successful Education Programs." Paper presented at the Reentry Roundtable on Education, John Jay College of Criminal Justice, New York.

MacKenzie, D. L., K. Browning, S. Skroban, and D. Smith. 1999. "The Impact of Probation on the Criminal Activities of Offenders." *Journal of Research in Crime and Delinquency* 36(4): 423–453.

Maguire, K. E. , T. J. Flanagan, and T. P. Thornberry. 1988. "Prison Labor and Recidivism." *Journal of Quantitative Criminology* 4:3–18.

McClone, J. 2002. *Status of Mandatory Education in State Correctional Institutions.* Washington, DC: U.S. Department of Education.

Melton, R., and S. Pennell. 1998. *Staying Out Successfully: An Evaluation of an In-Custody Life Skills Training Program.* San Diego, CA: San Diego Association of Governments.

Miller, M. 1995. "The Delaware Life Skills Program: Evaluation Report." *Cognitive-Behavioral-Treatment Review* 4: 1–4.

Miller, M. 1997. *Evaluation of the Life Skills Program.* Division of Correctional Education, Delaware State Department of Corrections.

Needels, K. 1996. "Go Directly to Jail and Do Not Collect? A Long-Term Study of Recidivism, Employment and Earnings Patterns among Prison Releasees." *Journal of Research on Crime and Delinquency* 33: 471–496.

Piehl, A. M. 1995. *Learning While Doing Time.* Unpublished manuscript, Harvard University, Cambridge, MA.

Reagan, M. V., and D .M. Stoughton. 1976. *A Descriptive Overview of Correctional Education in the American Prison System.* Metuchen, NJ: The Scarecrow Press.

Ryan, T. 1990. "Effects of Literacy Training on Reintegration of Offenders." Paper presented at Freedom to Read, International Conference on Literacy in Corrections, Ottawa, Ontario, Canada.

Sampson, R., and J. Laub. 1993. *Crime in the Making: Pathways and Turning Points Through Life.* Cambridge, MA: Harvard University Press.

Saylor, W. G., and G. G. Gaes. 1992. *PREP Study Links UNICOR Work Experience with Successful Post-Release Outcome.* Washington, DC: U.S. Federal Bureau of Prisons.

Saylor, W. G., and G. G. Gaes. 1996. *PREP: Training Inmates Through Industrial Work Participation and Vocational and Apprenticeship Instruction.* Washington, DC: U.S. Federal Bureau of Prisons.

Stephan, J. J. 1997. *Census of State and Federal Correctional Facilities, 1995.* Washington, DC: Bureau of Justice Statistics.

Steurer, S., L. Smith, and A. Tracy. 2001. *Three State Recidivism Study.* Report to the U.S. Department of Education Office of Correctional Education. Lanham, MD: Correctional Education Association.

Taylor, J. M. 1994. "Should Prisoners Have Access to Collegiate Education? A Policy Issue." *Educational Policy* 8: 315–338.

Tyler, T. 1990. *Why People Obey the Law.* New Haven, CT: Yale University Press.

Teeters, N. K. 1955. *The Cradle of the Penitentiary.* Philadelphia: Pennsylvania Prison Society.

Tewksbury, R. A., and G. F. Vito. 1996. "Improving the Educational Skills of Jail Inmates: Preliminary Program Findings." *Federal Probation* 58: 55–59.

Uggen, C. 2000. "Work as a Turning Point in the Life Course of Criminals: A Duration Model of Age, Employment, and Recidivism." *American Sociological Review* 65: 529–546.

Visher, C. A., L. Winterfield, M. B. Coggeshall. 2006. "Systematic Review of Non-Custodial Employment Programs: Impact on Recidivism Rates of Ex-Offenders." *Campbell Systematic Reviews* 2006:1. DOI: 10.4073/csr.2006.1

Wilson, D. B., C. A. Gallagher, M. B. Coggeshall, and D. L. MacKenzie. 1999. "A Quantita-
    tive Review and Description of Corrections Based Education, Vocation and Work
    Programs." *Corrections Management Quarterly* 3: 8–18.
Wilson, D. B., C. A. Gallagher, and D. L. Mackenzie. 2000. "A Meta-Analysis of Correc-
    tions-Based Education, Vocation, and Work Programs for Adult Offenders." *Journal of
    Research on Crime and Delinquency* 37: 347–368.
Wolfgang, M. E., R. M. Figlio, and T. Sellin. 1972. *Delinquency in a Birth Cohort*. Chicago:
    University of Chicago Press.

Section E
Managing a Changing Offender Population

CHAPTER 21

IDENTIFYING, TREATING, AND REDUCING RISK FOR OFFENDERS WITH MENTAL ILLNESS

JENNIFER L. SKEEM AND JILLIAN K. PETERSON

INDIVIDUALS with serious and often disabling mental illnesses like schizophrenia, bipolar disorder, and major depression are grossly overrepresented in the criminal justice system. Compared to the general population, the lifetime prevalence rate of these serious mental illnesses in the correctional population is twice as high for both men and women (Teplin 1990; Teplin, Abram, and McClelland 1996; see also Prins and Draper 2009). Of offenders with serious mental illness, nearly 3 of 4 have a co-occurring substance abuse disorder (Abram and Teplin 1991; Abram, Teplin, and McClelland 2003). These figures take on new meaning when considered in context. Currently, there are over 7.3 million people in the United States under correctional supervision (Bureau of Justice Statistics 2009). Roughly 1 in 7 of these men (15 percent) and 1 in 4 of these women (31 percent) suffer from a major mental illness (Steadman, Osher, Robbins, Case, and Samuels 2009; see also Fazel and Danesh 2002). Given the population's gender composition (Glaze and Bonczar 2009; West and Sabol 2009), over 1.3 million people with serious mental illness in the United States are on probation and parole or incarcerated in jail or prison. That is, nearly 1 in 5 people (18 percent) involved in our correctional system suffer from a major mental illness.

Offenders with mental illness are unusually likely to struggle in the correctional system, whether they are incarcerated or supervised in the community. Compared to their relatively healthy counterparts, these offenders are placed in "supermax" or solitary confinement more often (Lovell, Johnson, and Kane 2007; Toch and Adams 2002; for a review, see Fellner 2006). After they are released from prison on parole, they are two times more likely to be reincarcerated than offenders without mental illness (Eno Louden and Skeem, 2011; see also Cloyes, Wong, Latimer and Abarca 2010; Porporino and Motiuk 1995). Similarly, those who are placed on probation—which is, by far, the most common correctional disposition—are significantly more likely to have their community term suspended or revoked (Dauphinot 1996; Skeem, Manchak, Vidal, and Hart 2009).

These figures indicate that a large number of individuals with serious mental disorders enter the criminal justice system each year, and many plunge deeply into the correctional system over time. This problem has captured the attention of practitioners and policy makers in corrections (APPA 2003; BJA 2009; NIC 2009). Over recent years, the Council of State Governments Justice Center (CSG 2002, 2009) has been leading a national effort to bring together professionals in law enforcement, the courts, corrections, and mental health to identify programs that have been developed for offenders with mental illness, distill what is known about their nature and effectiveness, and provide technical assistance to help communities implement them. Reflecting the nature of virtually all programs that have been developed for offenders with mental illness, this laudable effort casts one factor as the linchpin to successful response: access to effective or evidence-based mental health services (e.g., CSG 2002, Policy Statement #1 and Chapter 7).

Contemporary policy largely assumes that mental illness is the direct cause of criminal behavior and that psychiatric treatment is the solution. In this chapter, we describe flawed assumptions that underpin this model and offer an alternative model that describes multiple pathways from mental illness to criminal behavior. We then summarize the limited effectiveness of current programs and outline hypotheses about *how* these programs work, when they do reduce recidivism. We conclude by summarizing implications of current research for smarter sentencing and correctional policies for this population, from assessment to problem solving over violations.

Evaluating the Current Policy Model: Mental Illness as Direct Cause

The model underpinning current programs is easily summarized. "People on the front lines every day believe too many people with mental illness become involved in the criminal justice system because the mental health system has somehow failed. They believe that if many of the people with mental illness received the services they needed, they would not end up under arrest, in jail, or facing charges in court" (CSG 2002, 26).

Perhaps instinctively, contemporary sentencing and correctional practices for offenders with mental illness respond to the offender's "master status" (Fisher, Silver, and Wolff 2006) with a demand for mental health services. Oftentimes, the court mandates mental health treatment as part of a sentence or suspended sentence agreement. For example, a probationer or parolee may be required to abide by a special condition to participate in treatment, in addition to the standard conditions typically imposed (e.g., maintain employment). According to the United States Code, "the court may provide, as further conditions of a sentence of probation . . . that the defendant . . . undergo available medical, psychiatric, or psychological treatment" (Title 18 §3563). Typically, judges' orders for psychiatric treatment are generic—they rarely specify a particular treatment, agency, or program (Skeem and Eno Louden 2008). Correctional practices tend to be similarly non-specific. In institutional settings, there is emphasis on psychotropic medication, suicide/crisis intervention, and psychotherapy designed to facilitate mental illness recovery (for a review, see Bewley and Morgan, 2011). In community settings, a variety of programs have been developed to enhance coordination between the criminal justice and mental health system and link offenders to community treatment services (Draine, Wilson, and Pogorzelski 2007), generating a "proliferation of case management services as the policy response" (p. 161) for this population.

ISSUE #1: MENTAL ILLNESS RARELY DIRECTLY CAUSES CRIMINAL BEHAVIOR

The fundamental problem with current problem-solving efforts is that there is little evidence that mental illness directly causes criminal behavior—or that psychiatric treatment will reduce it. With respect to the first issue, current evidence indicates that: (1) the availability of mental health services is unrelated to incarceration rates for people with mental illness; (2) police rarely arrest citizens with mental illness disproportionately or for inappropriate reasons; (3) psychosis (e.g., false beliefs, hallucinations) is rarely related to violence in offender populations; and (4) only a small proportion of offenders with mental illness have arrests or patterns of offenses that can be directly attributed to mental illness (for a review, see Skeem, Manchak, and Peterson, 2010).

The last point warrants emphasis. As one group of investigators concluded, "persons with serious mental illness may be overrepresented in jails and prisons, but we can offer little evidence . . . that it was their illness that got them there" (Junginger, Claypoole, Laygo, and Cristiani 2006, 881). Junginger et al. (2006) interviewed 113 arrestees with serious mental illness and co-occurring substance abuse disorders shortly after their booking into jail, and reviewed police records of the arrest. All arrestees had been deemed eligible for a jail diversion program. In the view of independent and reliable raters, psychiatric symptoms (ranging from delusions and hallucinations to depression and irritability) probably-to-definitely caused the arrest of only 8 percent of these offenders. Similarly, Peterson, Skeem, Hart, Vidal and Keith (2010) interviewed 112 parolees with serious mental illness who were enrolled in a special reentry program, as well as a matched sample of 109 parolees without mental illness. On the basis of interview data and parole records, reliable raters classified each parolee into one of five patterns of lifetime crime. They found that the modal pattern of offending for the vast majority of parolees—whether they were mentally ill or not—reflected hostility, impulsiveness, and reactivity. Only 5 percent of parolees with mental illness manifested a pattern that was attributable to hallucinations, delusions, and other symptoms of psychosis. Thus, although mental illness directly causes criminal behavior for a small but important minority of offenders with mental illness, it is not a direct causal risk factor or "criminogenic need" for the vast majority (for additional evidence, see Monahan and Steadman, in press).

Similarly, there is little evidence that the risk of incarceration has uniquely increased for those with mental illness over time. Frank and Glied (2006) examined changes in estimated living arrangements for people with serious and persistent mental illness (SPMI) in the United States from 1950 to 2000. During this period, the proportion of people with SPMI living in psychiatric institutions dropped 23 percent, whereas the proportion living in correctional institutions rose only 4 percent. The rise in incarceration rates for those with SPMI follows a predictable pattern, remaining at 1 percent from 1950–1970, but rising to 3 percent by 1990 and 5 percent by 2000. As a function of "get tough on crime" policies, incarceration rates for the entire population—most of whom do not have SPMI—grew sharply in the 1980s and 1990s (Bureau of Justice Statistics 2009). As Frank and Glied (2006) conclude, "it would be a mistake to attribute the increase in . . . incarceration among people with SPMI directly to the experience of deinstitutionalization" (p. 128); instead, the increase in this "undesirable circumstance" seems shared with the general population.

Indeed, it seems that most offenders with mental illness have the same criminogenic needs as offenders without mental illness (Bonta, Law, and Hanson 1998). What are these needs? According to one empirically supported model, there are eight main risk factors for crime: an established criminal history (especially with an early onset and diverse pattern), an antisocial personality pattern (stimulation seeking, low self-control, hostility-antagonism), antisocial cognition (attitudes, values, and thinking styles supportive of crime), antisocial associates, substance abuse, employment instability, family problems, and low engagement in pro-social leisure pursuits (Andrews, Bonta and Wormith 2006). These factors are assessed in a risk-needs tool called the Levels of Services Inventory/Case Management Inventory (LS/CMI; Andrews, Bonta, and Wormith 2004). Probationers and parolees with mental illness obtain significantly higher scores on the LS/CMI than those without mental illness (Girard and Wormith 2004; Skeem, Nicholson, and Kregg 2008), particularly on the antisocial pattern scale (Skeem et al. 2008). Similarly, offenders with mental illness obtain scores on a validated measure of antisocial cognition or "criminal thinking" that are similar to, or higher than, those obtained by offenders without mental illness (see Morgan, Fisher, and Wolff 2010).

Based on such evidence, Skeem, Manchak, and Peterson (2010) developed a policy-relevant theory about how mental illness relates to crime. Here, we elaborate that theory to suggest that those with serious mental illness follow one of three different pathways to criminal behavior. For a small subgroup (perhaps 1 in 10; Juninger et al., 2006; Peterson et al. 2010; Toch and Adams 1989), mental illness *directly* causes criminal behavior, including (1) violence motivated by delusions or hallucinations, and (2) arrests for minor crimes, such as public disturbance (e.g., "being psychotic in the wrong place at the wrong time"). This group may not engage in criminal behavior until later in life, *after* the onset of their symptoms (see Hodgins 2000). For this group, effective mental health services would reduce recidivism.

For the other two subgroups, effective mental health services would play a lesser role. For one of these subgroups, mental illness is incidental to or *independent* of criminal behavior. Here, conduct disorder and criminal behavior may begin at a young age (Hodgins and Carl-Gunner 2002), based on general causal factors that include a disinhibited temperament and/or poor parenting and supervision. For the other subgroup, mental illness causes criminal behavior *indirectly*, by exposing individuals to general risk factors for crime. For example, prodromal symptoms of psychosis can include impulsivity, aggression, and other conduct problems (Kim-Cohen, Caspi, Moffitt, Harrigonton, Milne, and Poulton 2003). When psychosis itself emerges during late adolescence, it may disrupt the development of pro-social identities, careers, and relationships (see Tessner, Mittal, and Walker 2011). This may cause some individuals to gravitate toward disadvantaged social and geographical environments that model, reinforce, and create opportunity for antisocial behavior. In short, mental illness could lead to crime indirectly through such risk factors as poverty (i.e., inability to hold a job), criminal peers (i.e., problems maintaining positive social bonds; exposure to other marginalized groups), or substance use (i.e., "self-medicating" symptoms; Walker, Kestler, Bollini, and Hochman 2004).

ISSUE #2: EVIDENCE-BASED PSYCHIATRIC TREATMENT AND SYMPTOM REDUCTION RARELY REDUCE CRIMINAL BEHAVIOR

If the theory above is correct, evidence-based treatment for general offenders that targets criminal thinking and attitudes may be necessary to reduce recidivism for the vast majority of offenders with mental illness. After all, even if mental illness is a distant cause of criminal behavior (as in the indirect group), it seems unlikely that mental health services will address the proximal factors that now maintain it (e.g., antisocial pattern, criminal peers).

Still, the "direct cause" model dominates contemporary policy. As testament to treating mental illness as the master status for this population, contemporary programs for offenders with mental illness focus on adapting existing evidence-based psychiatric services, including Assertive Community Treatment (ACT) and Integrated Dual Diagnosis Treatment (IDTT; for a list, see Monahan and Steadman, in press). These services have been shown to achieve important clinical outcomes such as reducing repeated hospitalization or improving psychosocial functioning.

So far, there is little compelling proof that evidence-based mental health services reduce recidivism for offenders with serious mental illness. By compelling proof, we mean evidence from studies that randomly assign offenders to the evidence-based services versus a comparison condition, given that experimental designs are the standard for drawing causal inferences about the effects of a program. "Pre-program, post-program" studies tend to inflate the apparent effects of a program (Weisburd, Lum, and Petrosino 2001; cf. Pearson, Lipton, Cleland and Yee 2002), as do studies that exclude individuals who drop out of the program (Lowenkamp, Latessa, and Holsinger 2006).

Three experiments are relevant. First, based on a sample of 223 patients with co-occurring disorders who were randomly assigned to Assertive Community Treatment (ACT) versus standard case management, Clark, Ricketts, and McHugo (1999) found no treatment-related difference in police contacts (80 percent) and arrests (44 percent) over a three-year period. In another randomized controlled trial for patients with co-occurring disorders, Calsyn, Yonker, Lemming, Morse, and Klinkenberg (2005) found no treatment-related difference in arrests and incarcerations between those assigned to ACT, Integrated Dual Diagnosis Treatment (IDDT), or treatment as usual. Similar results were obtained for a sample of offenders with co-occurring disorders who were randomly assigned to IDDT or treatment as usual (Chandler and Spicer 2006; see also Drake, Morrissey, and Mueser 2006). Given such results, scholars have cautioned that positive outcomes observed for evidence-based mental health services (e.g., reduced hospitalization, improved symptoms) will not necessarily extend to criminal behavior, and have called for "interventions that specifically target reduction of criminal behavior" (Casyln et al. 2005, 245; see also Drake et al. 2006; Morrisey, Meyer, and Cuddeback 2007).

An alternative way of evaluating the "direct cause" model underpinning current policy is to assess whether offenders who (for whatever reason) show marked symptom improvement during a program are less likely to recidivate than those whose symptoms remain unchanged or worsen. According to existing data, they do not. Using data on over 1,000 participants with mental illness in a multisite jail diversion study, Steadman et al. (2009) found that no relationship between symptom reduction and the number of re-arrests over time. Similarly, based on approximately 360 probationers with serious mental illness, Skeem et al. (2009) found that trajectories of symptom change bore no relation to the probability of arrest or revocation over a one-year period.

Synopsis of Current Programs and Effect on Recidivism

Thus far, we have cast doubt on the assumption that mental illness is the direct cause of criminal behavior and that evidence-based psychiatric treatment will reduce it. Although most contemporary programs for offenders with mental illness are based on this model, there is probably substantial diversity in how narrowly the model is implemented for this population, both within and across program types.

Skeem et al. (2010) summarized the main types of current programs for offenders with mental illness and evaluated their effectiveness. As shown in table 21.1 (from Skeem et al. 2010), most of these programs are derivatives of criminal justice models, including jail diversion programs, mental health courts (a frequently studied form of post-booking jail diversion), specialty probation or parole caseloads, and jail transition or prison reentry programs. Two programs adapt ACT, the most extensively studied mental health service (see above), to create "Forensic Assertive Community Treatment" (FACT) and "Forensic Intensive Case Management" (FICM). FACT or FICM may be used independently, or in conjunction with criminal-justice derived programs (e.g., a mental health court). These programs are united by their focus on linking offenders to community treatment services, but that goal does not wholly define all of them. Some programs include special court supervision, probation supervision, or both.

Skeem et al. (2010) drew three major conclusions about these programs. First, there is little evidence that recidivism is reduced by mental health–centric models that include FACT and FICM (see Morrissey et al. 2007, for a review) and jail diversion programs driven heavily by case management. Second, as suggested earlier, there is no evidence that recidivism reduction is achieved by linking individuals with psychiatric treatment or by reducing symptoms. Third, there is some evidence (if mixed) that criminal justice–based models that emphasize supervision by specialized courts or probation officers, or that include an emphasis on "criminal thinking" (Sacks, Sacks, McKendrick, Banks, and Stommel 2004) reduce recidivism.

What (Really) Works for Offenders with Mental Illness? Three Hypotheses

It is clear that contemporary programs for offenders with mental illness can "work." How they work, however, is an open and important question. It seems unlikely that they reduce recidivism for the reasons practitioners expect (i.e., because they link offenders with psychiatric treatment and control symptoms). Arguably, the most pressing challenge for this field it to isolate the active ingredients of programs that

Table 21.1. Contemporary Programs for Offenders with Mental Illness (from Skeem et al. 2010)

Program	Premise	Solution/Description	Exemplar or Prototype of Program	Focal Study	Reduced Recidivism in Study?	Reduced Symptoms in Study?
Criminal Justice Models Jail Diversion	Some PMIs are arrested when the more appropriate response to their behavior is treatment	Divert these PMIs from jail into treatment, either pre- or post-booking	Crisis Intervention Teams (Dupont and Cochran 2000)	Multisite Jail Diversion Study (Steadman and Naples 2005) —quasi-experimental, N = 617 diverted and 570 comparisons	No difference between groups in rearrests over one year; jail diversion associated with more time in community	No difference between groups in symptom change
Mental Health Courts	Traditional case processing allows some PMIs to cycle through the system repeatedly without addressing the problem that drives their criminal behavior	Consolidate these PMIs' cases and process them through a single judge who will enforce linkages with treatment	San Francisco Mental Health Court (McNiel and Binder 2007)	San Francisco Mental Health Court (McNiel and Binder 2007) — quasi-experimental, N = 170 MHC clients and 8,067 comparisons	Yes, probability of rearrest was 42% (MHC) vs. 57% (control) by 18 months	Not assessed
Specialty Mental Health Probation or Parole	PMIs have unique characteristics and pronounced needs that cannot be met via traditional community supervision	Assign these PMIs to officers who manage specialized, reduced size caseloads and work directly with treatment providers	Prototypic specialty probation model (Skeem et al. 2006)	Dallas specialty probation (Skeem, Manchak, et al. 2009) —quasi-experimental, N = 183 specialty vs. 176 traditional probationers	Specialty probationers modestly less likely to be arrested, and less likely to be revoked over one year	No difference between groups in symptom change

Program	Rationale	Approach	Study/reference	Study design and sample	Recidivism outcome	Other outcome
Jail Aftercare and Prison Reentry Programs	Discontinuation of treatment at release from incarceration leads some PMIs to decompensation and rearrest	Facilitate timely access to community treatment at the point of release for these PMIs	Prison reentry programs (Wilson and Draine 2006)	Therapeutic community in prison, with-vs.-without-aftercare at release (Sacks et al., 2004) experimental, N = 43 aftercare and 32 comparisons	Yes, aftercare group less likely to be reincarcerated over one year (5% vs. 16%)	Not assessed *Note: program targeted criminal thinking beyond symptoms
Mental Health Models Forensic Assertive Community Treatment (F-ACT)	ACT is an intensive, evidence-based mental health practice for patients with serious mental illness. With some adjustment, it should also reduce recidivism for offenders with serious mental illness.	Provide ACT to offenders, but with the explicit goal of preventing recidivism; include criminal justice professionals on the multidisciplinary treatment team of psychiatrists, nurses, and case managers	Core F-ACT elements (Lamberti, Weisman, and Faden 2004)	No published, controlled studies available; one unpublished report on a controlled study of 20 programs evaluated in California (Morrissey et al. 2007)—quasi-experimental, N unknown	"Small differences (3–4%) favoring the intervention groups" (p. 535) on re-convictions, jail bookings, and jail time	Unclear, but unspecified improvement in functioning for intervention groups
Forensic Intensive Case Management (FICM)	F-ACT is too costly; but a less resource-intensive variant should reduce recidivism for offenders with mental illness	Case managers provide assertive, community-based services, but without a multidisciplinary team, 24/7 capacity, or direct provision of psychiatric services (which are instead brokered).	FICM elements (Morrissey et al. 2007)	Most controlled studies overlap with Multisite Jail Diversion Study (see Table 2); one independent study compares FICM with FACT and usual care (Solomon and Draine 1995) — experimental, N = 60 ACT, 60 ICM, and 80 control	No difference in rearrests for FICM and controls (but FACT yielded *higher* rearrests than both comparisons)	No differences among groups in social or clinical changes over one year

are effective for this population. Why? Because understanding what is critical to treatment and how it operates will help develop fewer, more efficient, and more effective interventions for offenders with mental illness (see Kazdin 2007). If we pinpoint the mechanisms of change to define a coherent model of "what really works" for this population, this will help "exnovate" programs that are ineffective (see Frank and Glied 2006), disseminate clearly articulated programs that are effective, and protect active program ingredients in difficult economic times.

Based on the little evidence that is available, we formulated three hypotheses about how contemporary programs reduce recidivism, when they are able to do so. These programs may reduce recidivism (broadly construed) by (1) disproportionately targeting the small minority of offenders for whom the relation between mental illness and criminal behavior is direct to reduce new crimes; (2) targeting general criminogenic needs and improving core correctional practices to reduce new crimes; and (3) reducing stigma of mental illness and increasing tolerance for minor rule infractions to supervision "failure" in the absence of new crimes. Although these hypothesized mechanisms are not mutually exclusive (i.e., all may operate simultaneously) and have not been systematically tested, the last two seem likely to explain the lion's share of the variance of contemporary programs in improving criminal justice outcomes for offenders with mental illness. Each of these is discussed next.

Disproportionately Targeting the Small, "Direct" Subgroup

As suggested earlier, for a small minority of these offenders (perhaps 1 in 10), linkage with effective mental health services *will* reduce recidivism because their mental illness actually drives criminal behavior, that is, it is a criminogenic need. When this minority subgroup is disproportionately well-represented in a particular program or study, the effect of psychiatric treatment on criminal behavior would shine through. That is, the positive effect for this subgroup would not be completely swamped by the lack of effect in the group as a whole. One way of testing this hypothesis would be to determine whether subgroup membership moderates the effect of psychiatric treatment on new crimes. In contemporary mental health-oriented programs for this population, are offenders whose criminal behavior began *after* their symptoms less likely to be rearrested for a new crime than offenders whose criminal behavior began *before* their symptoms?

Targeting General Criminogenic Needs and Improving Core Correctional Practices

Symptoms of mental illness are not a criminogenic need for most offenders in this population. Instead, these offenders share the strongest criminogenic needs with their relatively healthy counterparts. For these reasons, we hypothesize that when contemporary programs for offenders with mental illness reduce new crimes, they do so for much the same reason as programs for general offenders.

Targeting Criminogenic Needs

Beyond mental illness, these programs may also (implicitly) target general criminogenic needs like antisocial cognition, substance abuse, or poor employment. A major principle of effective treatment for general offenders is the *need* principle: "the most effective programs for reducing recidivism are those that target needs closely related to criminality" (Bonta, Law, and Hanson 1998, 138; see also Andrews, Bonta, and Wormith 2006). That is, the effectiveness of programs is associated with the number of criminogenic needs they target (i.e., changeable risk factors for crime, like antisocial peers), relative to noncriminogenic needs (i.e., disturbances that impinge on functioning, like depression; Andrews et al. 1990). Second, cognitive behavioral treatment (CBT) programs that target a constellation of particularly strong criminogenic needs—antisocial cognition—are consistently ranked "in the top tier with regard to effects on recidivism" (Lipsey and Landenberger 2006, 57).

Formal CBT programs are rarely applied to offenders with mental illness in the United States, in both community and institutional settings (Skeem, Peterson, and Silver, in press; Bewley and Morgan, 2011). In fact, Skeem et al (2010) could locate only one small controlled outcome study for offenders with mental illness that focused on a program with any emphasis on "criminal thinking" (see Sacks et al. 2004, in table 1). Moreover, only one validated CBT program has been adapted for offenders with mental illness and systematically studied. Four small studies conducted on inpatient forensic wards in the United Kingdom and Germany provide preliminary evidence that this program, "Reasoning and Rehabilitation-2 for Mentally Disordered Offenders" (Young and Ross 2007) increases motivation to change, reduces criminal thinking and attitudes, and reduces disruptive behavior on inpatient units (see Antonowicz 2005; Young, Chick, and Gudjonsson 2010). Its effect on criminal behavior, however, is unknown. We hope that future research and practice will examine the extent to which evidence-based correctional treatments reduce new crimes for this population, compared to psychiatric "treatment as usual."

Despite the lack of formal focus on the criminogenic "need" principle, it sometimes seems to *informally* infiltrate contemporary programs for offenders with mental illness. When it does, it is likely to greatly improve their effectiveness in reducing criminal behavior. That is, to the extent that staff members in mental health courts or other programs go beyond their primary focus on mental health to target factors that actually get an offender in trouble (e.g., hanging out with her drug-dealing cousin), they are intuitively applying this important evidence-based correctional principle.

Although little data are available on this issue, Eno Louden et al. (2010) coded audiotapes of 83 interactions between specialty probation officers and supervisees with serious mental illness. They found that, although officers tended to focus heavily on general mental health issues (discussed in 66 percent of meetings), they also discussed supervisees' criminogenic needs, including attitudes supportive of crime (36 percent of meetings). In turn, the amount of time officers spend discussing criminogenic needs is inversely related to the risk of recidivism for general offenders

(Bonta, Rugge, Scott, Bourgon and Yessine 2008). Similarly, in a survey of correctional mental health providers in state facilities, psychologists and other clinically
trained respondents viewed traditional clinical issues (i.e., medication adherence,
mental illness awareness) as most essential to psychotherapy with offenders with
mental illness and spent the most time addressing those (Bewley and Morgan, 2011).
Still, a significant minority of respondents (16 percent) reported that they folded
correctional treatment principles into their work, including a focus on criminogenic
needs. In addition to better implementing formal CBT programs for offenders with
mental illness, we believe that the next step in research and policy for this population is to make informal or intuitive principles explicit, practice them consistently,
and evaluate their effect on new crimes.

Making Evidence-Based Correctional Principles Explicit

In addition to looking beyond mental illness to general criminogenic needs, some
contemporary programs may reduce new crimes because they improve core correctional practices (Dowden and Andrews 2004), which include establishing warm,
respectful, and "firm but fair" relationships with offender, and modeling and reinforcing pro-social behavior. Based on a study of approximately 360 offenders with
mental illness followed for over two years, Skeem, Manchak, et al. (2009) found
that specialty probation reduces risk of recidivism less because of mental health
service linkage or symptom reduction than because specialty officers are more
likely than traditional officers to establish high-quality "controlling but caring" relationships with offenders and to apply problem-solving strategies rather than
threats of incarceration. It will be crucial in the future for (1) practitioners who
work with this population to recognize the power of "core correctional practices,"
and (2) researchers who study this population to operationalize them and examine
their impact on criminal behavior.

Reducing Stigma and Increasing Tolerance

Recall that the vast majority of offenders are supervised in the community on probation and parole. As correctional practitioners know, offenders can "fail" community supervision without committing a new crime. Offenders with mental illness
may be particularly susceptible to such failures, given that mental illness is a heavily
stigmatized condition. Although more research is needed, some evidence reviewed
below suggests that officers and judges generally apply lower thresholds for revoking community supervision, as a function of mental illness. We suspect that
some contemporary programs may reduce recidivism not by preventing new crime,
but by increasing practitioners' tolerance for minor transgressions, using revocation as a "last resort" for true criminal behavior, thereby promoting greater success
in community supervision. This may be particularly true when programs involve
special judicial supervision (e.g., mental health courts) or special probation/parole
supervision (e.g., specialty caseloads).

Offenders with and without mental illness are about equally likely to be re-arrested for a new offense (Bonta et al. 1998; Gagliardi, Lovell, Peterson, and Jemelka 2004; cf. Baillargeon et al. 2009). However, those with mental illness are significantly more likely to commit technical violations (Baillargeon et al. 2009; Eno Louden and Skeem, 2011). This may be because those with mental illness: (1) have functional impairments that reduce their ability to adhere to such standard conditions of community release as maintaining employment or paying fines and fees (see Skeem and Eno Louden 2008); (2) are required to abide by *more* conditions of release (e.g., mandated treatment) than those without mental illness; and/or (3) are subject to increased monitoring and control, which increases the likelihood that minor infractions will be detected (Skeem, Eno Louden, et al., 2008). Regardless of the reason, those with mental illness are significantly more likely to commit technical violations and to have their community terms suspended or revoked than those without mental illness (Eno Louden and Skeem, 2011; Porporino and Motiuk 1995). This suggests that correctional officers and judges may have lower thresholds for revoking those with mental illness, compared to their relatively healthy counterparts.

These results are consistent with findings that correctional officers respond conservatively to offenders with mental illness, perhaps out of stigma-based fear or paternalism (Callahan 2004; Eno Louden 2009). Public conceptions of mental illness are "suffused with negative stereotypes, fear, and rejection" (Phelan et al. 2000, 189). Stigma of mental illness involves negative labels (e.g., "crazy"), a grossly exaggerated perception of the (weak) link between mental illness and violence, and willingness to use coercive strategies to achieve social control (e.g., Pescosolido et al. 2000). Based on an experiment conducted with 264 probation officers who read case vignettes, Eno Louden et al. (2009) found that mental illness (particularly schizophrenia) increased officers' perceptions of violence risk and promoted plans to keep the probationer under close surveillance and on a "short leash" (see also Callahan 2004). Lynch's (2000) ethnography suggests that reincarceration sometimes is inappropriately used for parolees in emotional crisis. In one case, a psychotic parolee who disclosed suicidal thoughts was arrested and "taken to the county jail for his safety" (p. 52). Skeem, Encandela, and Eno Louden (2003) found that probation officers perceive offenders with mental illness as atypical cases that create "problems to the system," in that their needs are perceived as non-routine and, therefore, time and resource consuming. Some adopt the strategy of watching these offenders closely until they have an opportunity to transfer or terminate the case (e.g. "If there's a nutso on my caseload and he's just taking up too much of my time . . . I'll transfer him").

Together, these findings are consistent with the notion that some supervision "failures" reflect minor infractions, fear, and paternalism, or both, rather than a new offense. To the extent that contemporary programs include practitioners who are more tolerant of minor infractions, are less affected by stigma, and are more likely to reserve revocation for new crimes, they will return fewer offenders with mental illness to custody than traditional programs.

Conclusion

More research is needed to determine *how* contemporary programs for offenders "work," when they actually reduce recidivism. It is not safe to assume that they work because they link offenders with psychiatric treatment, which controls their symptoms, thus preventing new offenses. To help develop more efficient and effective interventions for this population, we recommend that researchers and practitioners systematically test the three hypotheses offered here, that is, that (1) mandating and accessing psychiatric treatment reduces crime for the small subgroup of "direct relationship" offenders, (2) targeting general criminogenic needs and improving core correctional practices reduces crime for the larger group of "indirect" and "independent" relationship offenders, and (3) reducing the stigma of mental illness and increasing tolerance for minor rule infractions reduces supervision "failure" in the absence of new crimes.

To test these hypotheses, it will be necessary to: (1) differentiate between "recidivism" that does-and does not-occur with the commission of a new crime; (2) distinguish between offenders whose mental illness does, and does not, generally drive their criminal behavior; (3) articulate and systematically measure what practitioners are doing in a program (i.e., what explicit and implicit principles of evidence-based practice they are drawing from mental health or corrections); and (4) determine how particular aspects of what they are doing reduce recidivism, and for whom. These efforts will help us arrive at a coherent model of "what works" for offenders with mental illness. In the next section, we set these challenges aside to articulate principles of smarter sentencing and corrections for offenders with mental illness, given what we know now.

IMPLICATIONS FOR SENTENCING
AND CORRECTIONS

Although little data are available, it seems that offenders with mental illness typically are mandated to mental health treatment, as part of a sentence or suspended sentence agreement. Judge's orders tend to mandate offenders with mental illness to psychiatric treatment generically, without specifying any particular approach (Skeem and Eno Louden 2008). Although there is broad variation among contemporary programs for this population, most emphasize psychiatric service linkage.

Drawing from the literature on general offenders, there may be more effective sentencing and risk reduction alternatives to this "one size fits all," mental health-centric approach. That is, "smarter sentencing" could be applied to make better decisions about offenders with mental illness both at the point of entry to the system and at any point of trouble within the system (see Monahan and

Steadman, in press, for a "sequential intercept model" that articulates key stages of processing).

"Front End" Sentencing and Case Planning

For general offenders, Wolff (2008) recommends that judicial discretion be embraced as an opportunity to leverage evidence-based correctional principles to reduce reoffending. Specifically, he recommends using data to inform highly individualized decisions that (1) match the intensity of an offenders' supervision and services to his or her level of risk for reoffending (e.g., such that intensive supervision and services are reserved for medium-high risk offenders), and (2) specify particular types of programs or treatments that target his or her most prominent criminogenic *needs* (e.g., anger, antisocial cognition). The data used to make these decisions would be legally appropriate and could be based on validated "risk/needs" assessment tools used to help generate a probation officer's pre-sentence investigation report. Space in prison would be reserved "for the most dangerous and most likely to repeat" (Wolff 2008, 1394). Specific supervision and/or treatment programs would be mandated for offenders and evaluated routinely to assess their ability to meet individuals' criminogenic needs and reduce recidivism. Ostensibly, offenders would no longer be sentenced to programs that produced little evidence of effectiveness.

We believe that similar principles can be applied to offenders with mental illness to reduce recidivism. Below, we make practical recommendations for doing so.

Assess Offenders' Mental Illness and Risk-Needs

The first step toward effectively sentencing and supervising offenders with mental illness is identifying that population. Although a variety of screening tools for mental illness are available, we recommend the Brief Jail Mental Health Screen (BJMHS; Steadman et al. 2005); given that it is exceptionally short, it can be made part of any standard intake process, and has been shown to perform well in identifying both incarcerated and community offenders who qualify for a diagnosis of a serious mental illness (e.g., Steadman et al. 2005; Eno Louden, Skeem, and Blevins 2010). The relatively small proportion of offenders who "screen in" as potentially mentally ill can then be referred for a full psychological assessment to better characterize the severity and type of their disorder.

As is the case for all offenders, those with mental illness must be assessed for (1) their risk of recidivism and (2) the criminogenic needs that drive that risk. Many risk assessment tools are available, and the validated tools appear about equally effective in predicting recidivism (Kroner, Mills, and Reddon 2005). One of the best established tools is the Levels of Services Inventory (LSI; Andrews, Bonta, and Wormith 2004), which provides an indication of where the offender stands on each of eight robust risk factors for recidivism mentioned earlier (e.g., employment problems, criminal associates), and is equally predictive for offenders with and without mental illness (Girard and Wormith 2004; Skeem et al. 2008).

Tailor the Sentence to Target Risk and Be Responsive to Mental Illness

Judges can draw upon mental health and risk-needs assessments to inform an individualized approach that leverages evidence-based principles to reduce risk and maximize the possibility of safe community reentry. We have two recommendations for doing so:

- *Mandate psychiatric treatment judiciously.* When offenders have a serious mental illness, they need psychiatric treatment, even if they do not belong to the small subgroup whose symptoms actually drive criminal behavior. This is in accordance with the evidence-based correctional treatment principle of *responsivity*, that is, that services should be delivered in a manner that matches the abilities, styles, and needs of offenders (Andrews et al. 1990). For some offenders, psychiatric treatment may be necessary to control severe symptoms and organize their thinking enough that they can participate in evidence-based CBT programs that target criminal thinking and reduce recidivism. Provision of treatment is also consistent with the fact that correctional models that add treatment services ("care") to surveillance ("control") often are more effective in reducing recidivism than surveillance models alone (for a review, see Skeem and Manchak 2008). When offenders' clinical needs are particularly pronounced or unresponsive to traditional care, mental health programs like ACT or IDDT (see above) may be specifically mandated to achieve important clinical outcomes like reducing repeated hospitalization or improving psychosocial functioning.

- *Tailor services and supervision to recidivism risk and criminogenic needs.* Beyond individualizing psychiatric service linkage, assessment data can also be used to tailor the intensity and focus of supervision and services to reduce an individual's risk. Because symptoms are a criminogenic need for only a small minority of these offenders and even those with psychotic symptoms often are at relatively low risk for violence (for a review, see Skeem et al. 2010), an offenders' risk of recidivism (whether mentally ill or not) is best captured by a well-validated risk-needs tool. These tools can be applied to achieve two ends. First, intensive services can be reserved for higher risk offenders, given that correctional treatment programs for high-risk offenders are significantly more effective than those focused on low-risk offenders ($b = .27$; Lowenkamp et al. 2006). For a variety of reasons, placing low-risk offenders in intensive programs is not simply inefficient; it can increase their risk of recidivism (Andrews et al. 1990). Thus, the most intensive rehabilitation programs should be reserved for offenders who are at high risk of recidivating. Second, surveillance and treatment should focus on monitoring and reducing an individual offenders' most prominent criminogenic needs. For example, if an offenders' chief needs are criminal thinking and associates, he may be mandated to a CBT program that targets risky thinking and builds problem-solving skills and, during supervision, explicit efforts may be made to reduce his contact with friends who drink heavily, use drugs, or have a criminal history (see Andrews et al. 2006). As this example suggests, the offenders' psychiatric status or medication noncompliance should not automatically eclipse other risk factors that may relate much more strongly to risk of recidivism, like pro-criminal attitudes, an antisocial and/or impulsive-aggressive lifestyle, criminal companions, substance abuse, and poorly structured leisure time. To achieve maximum recidivism reduction, the judge and/or program staff should work toward treatment conditions and a case management plan that targets factors that have led an individual to criminal behavior in the past.

Require Programs to Demonstrate Effectiveness in Reducing Recidivism

Given the novelty and diversity of programs for offenders with mental illness, it seems crucial to evaluate in controlled studies whether local programs are effective in reducing recidivism. We learned, for example, that not all "specialty mental health probation" programs are created equal—some programs adopt the specialty label but have such large caseload sizes that they function no differently than traditional probation (Skeem et al. 2006). Wolff (2008) discusses how judges can be proactive in insisting that programs demonstrate—and maintain evidence of—their effectiveness in reducing recidivism. We add that stakeholders also should insist on knowing *why* the programs work because this will enable them to streamline programs while monitoring and protecting their most essential elements.

"Back End" Problem Solving

A variety of signs suggest that offenders with mental illness have difficulty adjusting to incarceration and community supervision. Here, we note three problem-solving points that may facilitate adjustment, prevent return to incarceration, and promote safe community re-entry.

Institutional Considerations

While incarcerated, offenders with serious mental illness are relatively prone to rule infractions, disciplinary misconducts, and suicide-related behavior (see Fellner 2006; Toch and Adams 1989). One way to prevent these adverse outcomes it to identify offenders early (with a screening tool like the BJMHS), assess whether symptoms are driving their behavior, and intervene appropriately.

Perhaps as a consequence of repeated infractions and misconducts, inmates with mental illness are nearly four times more likely than their relatively healthy counterparts to be placed on "special housing units" (SHU) or "the hole," which is marked by solitary confinement, intensive supervision during solo exercise, and lockdown during exposure to other persons (Lovell, Johnson, and Caine 2007). Offenders who "max out" and are released directly from SHUs are significantly more likely to return to custody than those who are released from less restrictive areas in prison (Lovell et al. 2007). At the same time, "step down" treatment programs for SHUs hold promise in reducing misconducts and violent behavior (Kupers et al. 2009). For that reason, we recommend that "step down" programs from SHUs be systematically implemented for offenders with serious mental illness prior to release to increase their likelihood of successful reentry.

An obvious prerequisite to reentering the community is being released from prison. Ideally, offenders would be released to parole, which might provide a period of "step down" supervision in the community. There are also problems at this stage of release decision-making, however. Offenders with mental illness are less likely than their relatively healthy counterparts to receive a term of parole and more likely to "max out," moving directly from full supervision in prison to no supervision in the community (see Matejkowski, Caplan and Cullen, 2010). Because it is difficult to believe that these offenders are at much greater risk for recidivism than their relatively healthy counterparts, it would seem wise for parole boards to guard against fear, paternalism, and other signs of stigma when determining whether an inmate with mental illness should be release.

Community Considerations

In many ways, evidence-based supervision of offenders with mental illness has been the focus of this chapter. As suggested earlier, it is crucial that offenders be linked with psychiatric services, be supervised by officers who can establish "firm but fair" relationships with them, and have their criminogenic needs targeted.

It is also clear, based on the data outlined above, that case managers, supervising officers, and judges should not apply lower thresholds for revoking community supervision for this population than they do with general offenders. That is, fear (that offenders will be violent) or paternalism (around treatment compliance) seem an inappropriate basis for using incarceration to achieve social control over these individuals when they are behaving no worse than offenders without mental illness. It is important to remain mindful of our tendency to watch offenders with mental illness more closely and to respond more forcefully to their behavior. Even if we isolate and perfectly implement the ingredients of sentencing and corrections that reduce criminal behavior, these individuals will continue to "fail" as long as we maintain an unusually high threshold for their success. We hope that the models and data reviewed here foster better assessment, management, and risk reduction for offenders with mental illness.

REFERENCES

Abram, K., and L. Teplin. 1991. "Co-occurring Disorders among Mentally Ill Jail Detainees: Implications for Public Policy." *American Psychologist* 46: 1036–1045.

Abram, K., L. Teplin, and G. McClelland. 2003. "Co-morbidity of Severe Psychiatric Disorders and Substance Use Disorders among Women in Jail." *American Journal of Psychiatry* 150: 1007–1010.

American Probation and Parole Association (APPA). 2003. *Resolution: Justice System's Response to Individuals with Mental Illness*. Retrieved on February 3, 2009, from http://www.appa-net.org/eweb/DynamicPage.aspx?Site=APPA_2&WebCode=IB_Resolutions.

Andrews, D. J., J. Bonta, and S. Wormith. 2004. *The Level of Service/Case Management Inventory (LS/CMI)*. Toronto: Multi-Health Systems.

Andrews, D., J. Bonta, and S. Wormith. 2006. "The Recent Past and Near Future of Risk and/or Need Assessment." *Crime and Delinquency* 52: 7–27.

Andrews, D., I. Zinger, R. Hoge, J. Bonta, P. Gendreau, and F. Cullen. 1990. "Does Correctional Treatment Work? A Clinically Relevant and Psychologically Informed Meta-Analysis." *Criminology* 28: 369–404.

Antonowicz, D. H. 2005. "The Reasoning and Rehabilitation Programme: Outcome Evaluations with Offenders." In *Social Problem Solving and Offending: Evidence, Evaluation and Evolution*, eds. M. McMurran and J. McGuire, 163–181. Chichester, UK: John, Wiley, and Sons.

Baillargeon, J., B. A. Williams, J. Mellow, A. J. Harzke, H. K. Hoge, G. Baillargeon, and R. B. Griefinger. 2009. "Parole Revocation among Prison Inmates with Psychiatric and Substance Use Disorders." *Psychiatric Services* 60: 1516–1521.

Bewley, M. T., and R. D. Morgan. 2011. "A National Survey of Mental Health Services Available to Offenders with Mental Illness: Who Is Doing What?" *Law & Human Behavior* 35: 351–363.

Bonta, J., M. Law, and C. Hanson. 1998. "The Prediction of Criminal and Violent Recidivism among Mentally Disordered Offenders: A Meta-Analysis." *Psychological Bulletin* 123: 123–142.

Bonta, J., T. Rugge, T. L. Scott, G. Bourgon, and A. K. Yessine. 2008. "Exploring the Black Box of Community Supervision." *Journal of Offender Rehabilitation* 47(3): 248–270.

Bureau of Justice Assistance. 2009. *Improving Responses to People with Mental Illness: The Essentials of a Mental Health Court*. Retrieved on February 3, 2009, from http://www.ojp.usdoj.gov/BJA/grant/mentalhealth.html.

Bureau of Justice Statistics. 2009. *Adult Correctional Populations, 1980–2007*. Retrieved on February 17, 2009, from http:www.ojp.usdoj.gov/bjs/glance/corr2.htm.

Callahan, L. (2004). "Correctional officer attitudes toward inmates with mental disorders." *International Journal of Forensic Mental Health* 3: 37–54.

Calsyn, R., R. Yonker, M. Lemming, G. Morse, and D. Klinkenberg. 2005. "Impact of Assertive Community Treatment and Client Characteristics on Criminal Justice Outcomes in Dual Disorder Homeless Individuals." *Criminal Behaviour and Mental Health* 15: 236–248.

Chandler, D., and G. Spicer. 2006. "Integrated Treatment for Jail Recidivists with Co-Occurring Psychiatric and Substance Use Disorders." *Community Mental Health Journal* 42: 405–425.

Clark, R., S. Ricketts, and G. McHugo. 1999. "Legal System Involvement and Costs for Persons in Treatment for Severe Mental Illness and Substance Use Disorders." *Psychiatric Services* 50: 641–647.

Cloyes, K. G., B. Wong, S. Latimer, and J. Abarca. 2010. "Time to Prison Return for Offenders with Serious Mental Illness Released from Prison: A Survival Analysis." *Criminal Justice and Behavior* 37: 175–187.

Council of State Governments. 2002. *Criminal Justice/Mental Health Consensus Project*. Retrieved on March 13, 2008, from http://www.consensusproject.org.

Council of State Governments. 2009. *Improving Outcomes for People with Mental Illness under Community Corrections Supervision: A Guide to Research-Informed Policy and Practice.* Washington, DC: U.S. Department of Justice, Office of Justice Programs.

Dauphinot, L. 1996. *The Efficacy of Community Correctional Supervision for Offenders with Severe Mental Illness.* Unpublished doctoral dissertation, Department of Psychology, University of Texas at Austin.

Dowden, C., and D. A. Andrews. 2004. "The Importance of Staff Practice in Delivering Effective Correctional Treatment: A Meta-Analytic Review of Core Correctional Practice." *International Journal of Offender Therapy and Comparative Criminology* 48: 203–214.

Draine, J., A. Wilson, and W. Pogorzelski. 2007. "Limitations and Potential in Current Research on Services for People with Mental Illness in the Criminal Justice System." *Journal of Offender Rehabilitation* 45: 159–177.

Drake, R., J. Morrissey, and K. Mueser. 2006. "The Challenge of Treating Forensic Dual Diagnostic Clients." *Community Mental Health Journal* 42: 427–432.

Dupont, R., and S. Cochran. 2000. "Police Response to Mental Health Emergencies: Barriers to Change." *Journal of the American Academy of Psychiatry and the Law* 28: 338–344.

Eno Louden, J. 2009. "Effect of Mental Disorder and Substance Abuse Stigma on Probation Officers' Case Management Decisions." Unpublished doctoral dissertation, University of California, Irvine.

Eno Louden, J., and J. Skeem. 2011. "Parolees with Mental Disorder: Toward Evidence-Based Practice." *Bulletin of the Center for Evidence-Based Corrections.*

Eno Louden, J., J. L. Skeem, and A. Blevins. 2010. "Identifying Probationers with Mental Disorder: Validation of a Mental Health Screening Questionnaire." Unpublished manuscript under review.

Eno Louden, J., J. L. Skeem, J. Camp, S. Vidal, and J. Peterson. 2010. "Supervision Practices in Specialty Mental Health Probation: What Happens in Officer-Probationer Meetings?" *Law and Human Behavior,* online first: 23 Dec 2010.

Fazel, S., and J. Danesh. 2002. "Serious Mental Disorder in 23,000 Prisoners: A Systematic Review of 62 Surveys." *Lancet* 359: 545–550.

Fellner, J. 2006. "A Corrections Quandary: Mental Illness and Prison Rules." *Harvard Civil Rights-Civil Liberties Law Review* 41: 391–412.

Fisher, W., E. Silver, and N. Wolff 2006. "Beyond Criminalization: Toward a Criminologically Informed Framework for Mental Health Policy and Services Research." *Administration and Policy in Mental Health* 33: 544–557.

Frank, R., and S. Glied. 2006. *Mental Health Policy in the United States since 1950: Better but Not Well.* Baltimore, MD: The Johns Hopkins University Press.

Gagliardi, G., D. Lovell, P. Peterson, and R. Jemelka. 2004. "Forecasting Recidivism in Mentally Ill Offenders Released from Prison." *Law and Human Behavior* 28: 133–155.

Girard, L., and J. Wormith. 2004. "The Predictive Validity of the Level of Service Inventory-Ontario Revision on General and Violent Recidivism among Various Offender Groups." *Criminal Justice and Behavior* 31: 150–181.

Glaze, L., and T. Bonczar. 2007. *Probation and Parole in the United States, 2006.* Washington, DC: U.S. Department of Justice, Bureau of Justice Statistics.

Hodgins, S. 2000. "The Etiology and Development of Offending among Persons with Major Mental Disorders." In *Violence among the Mentally Ill,* ed. S. Hodgins, 89–116. Dordrecht: Kluwer.

Hodgins, S., and J. Carl-Gunnar. 2002. *Criminality and Violence among the Mentally Disordered.* New York: Cambridge University Press.

Kazdin, A. E. 2007. "Mediators and Mechanisms of Change in Psychotherapy Research." *Annual Review in Clinical Psychology* 3: 1–27.

Kim-Cohen, J., A. Caspi, T. E. Moffitt, H, L. Harrigonton, B. S. Milne, and R. Poulton. 2003. "Prior Juvenile Diagnoses in Adults with Mental Disorder: Developmental Follow-Back of Prospective-Longitudinal Cohort." *Archives of General Psychiatry* 60: 709–717.

Kroner, D., J. Mills, and J. Reddon. 2005. "A Coffee Can, Factor Analysis, and Prediction of Antisocial Behavior: The Structure of Criminal Risk." *International Journal of Law and Psychiatry* 28(4): 360–374.

Kupers, T. A, T. Dronet, M. Winter, J. Austin, L. Kelly, W. Cartier, T. J. Morris, S. F. Hanlon, E. L. Sparkman, P. Kumar, L. C. Vincent, J. Noris, K. Nagle, and J. McBride. 2009. "Beyond Supermax Administrative Segregation: Mississippi's Experience Rethinking Prison Classification and Creating Alternative Mental Health Programs." *Criminal Justice and Behavior* 36: 1037–1050.

Junginger, J., K. Claypoole, R. Laygo, and A. Cristiani. 2006. "Effects of Serious Mental Illness and Substance Abuse on Criminal Offenses." *Psychiatric Services* 57: 879–882.

Lamberti, J., R. Weisman, and D. Faden. 2004. "Forensic Assertive Community Treatment: Preventing Incarceration of Adults with Severe Mental Illness." *Psychiatric Services* 55: 1285–1293.

Lipsey, M. W., and N. A. Landenberger. 2006. "Cognitive-behavioral Interventions." In *Preventing Crime: What Works for Children, Offenders, Victims, and Places*, eds. B. C. Welsh and D. P. Farrington, 57–71. Dordrecht, Netherlands: Springer.

Lovell, D. L., L. C. Johnson, and K. C. Kane. 2007. "Recidivism of Supermax Prisoners in Washington State." *Crime and Delinquency* 53: 633–656.

Lowenkamp, C., E. Latessa, and A. Holsinger. 2006. "The Risk Principle in Action: What Have We Learned from 13,676 Offenders and 97 Correctional Programs?" *Crime and Delinquency* 52: 77–93.

Lynch, M. (2000). "Rehabilitation as rhetoric: The reformable individual in contemporary parole discourse and practices." *Punishment and Society* 2: 40–65.

Matejkowski, J., J. Caplan, and S. Cullen. 2010. "The Impact of Severe Mental Illness on Parole Decisions: Considering Integration Within a Prison Setting." *Criminal Justice & Behavior* 37: 1005–1029.

McNeil, D., and R. Binder. 2007. "Effectiveness of a Mental Health Court in Reducing Criminal Recidivism and Violence." *American Journal of Psychiatry* 164: 1395–1403.

Monahan, J., and H. Steadman. In press. "Extending Violence Reduction Principles to Justice-Involved Persons with Mental Illness." In *Applying Social Science to Reduce Violent Offending*, eds. J. Dvoskin, J. Skeem, R. Novaco, and K. Douglas. New York: Oxford University Press.

Morgan, R. W. Fisher, and N. Wolff. 2010, April. "Criminal Thinking: Do People with Mental Illnesses Think Differently?" Policy Brief of the Center for Behavioral Health Services & Criminal Justice Research. Accessed June 15, 2010, at www.cbhs-cjr.rutgers.edu/pdfs/Policy_Brief_April_2010.pdf.

Morrissey, J., P. Meyer, and G. Cuddeback. 2007. "Extending Assertive Community Treatment to Criminal Justice Settings: Origins, Current Evidence, and Future Directions." *Community Mental Health Journal* 43: 527–544.

National Institute of Corrections (NIC). 2009. *Mentally Ill Persons in Corrections*. Retrieved February 7, 2009, from http://nicic.gov/MentalIllness.

Pearson, F., D. Lipton, C. Cleland, and D. Yee. 2002. "The Effects of Behavioral/Cognitive-Behavioral Programs on Recidivism." *Crime and Delinquency* 48: 476–496.

Peterson, J. K., J. L. Skeem, E. Hart, S. Vidal, and F. Keith. 2010. "Comparing the Offense Patterns of Offenders with and without Mental Disorder: Exploring the Criminalization Hypothesis." *Psychiatric Services* 61: 1217–1222.

Porporino, F., and L. Motiuk. 1995. "The Prison Careers of Mentally Disordered Offenders." *International Journal of Law and Psychiatry* 18: 29–44.

Prins, S. J., and L. Draper. 2008. *Improving Outcomes for People with Mental Illnesses under Community Corrections Supervision: A Guide to Research-Informed Policy and Practice.* New York: Council of State Governments Justice Center.

Sacks, S., J. Sacks, K. McKendrick, S. Banks, and J. Stommel. 2004. "Modified Therapeutic Community for MICA Offenders: Crime Outcomes." *Behavioral Sciences and the Law* 22: 477–501.

Skeem, J., J. Encandela, and J. Eno Louden. (2003). "Experiences of Mandated Mental Health Treatment in Traditional and Specialty Probation Programs." *Behavioral Sciences & the Law* 21: 429–458.

Skeem, J., and J. Eno Louden, J. 2008, March. "Mandated Treatment as a Condition of Probation: Coercion or Contract?" In *Understanding in Mandated Community Treatment,* A. Redlich (Chair), Symposium conducted at the annual meeting of the American Psychology-Law Society, Jacksonville, FL. Available at: https://webfiles.uci.edu:443/skeem/Downloads.html.

Skeem, J., and S. Manchak, S. 2008. "Back to the Future: From Klockars' Model of Effective Supervision to Evidence-Based Practice in Probation." *International Journal of Offender Rehabilitation* 47: 220–247.

Skeem, J. L., M. Manchack, and J. P. Peterson. 2010. "Correctional Policy for Offenders with Mental Illness: Creating a New Paradigm for Recidivism Reduction." *Law and Human Behavior* 35: 110–126.

Skeem, J., S. Manchak, S. Vidal, and E. Hart. 2009, March. "Probationers with Mental Disorder: What (Really) Works?" Paper presented at the American Psychology and Law Society (AP-LS) Annual Conference, San Antonio, TX. Available at: https://webfiles.uci.edu:443/skeem/Downloads.html.

Skeem, J., E. Nicholson, and C. Kregg. 2008, March. "Understanding Barriers To Re-Entry For Parolees With Mental Illness." In *Mentally Disordered Offenders: A Special Population Requiring Special Attention,* D. Kroner (Chair). Symposium conducted at the meeting of the American Psychology-Law Society, Jacksonville, FL.

Skeem, J., J. Peterson, and E. Silver. In press. "Toward Research-Informed Policy for High Risk Offenders with Serious Mental Illness." In *Managing High Risk Offenders: Policy and Practice,* eds. B. McSherrey and P. Keyser. New York: Routledge.

Skeem, J., C. Schubert, C. Odgers, E. Mulvey, W. Gardner, and C. Lidz. 2006. "Psychiatric Symptoms and Community Violence among High-Risk Patients: A Test of the Relationship at the Weekly Level." *Journal of Consulting and Clinical Psychology* 74: 967–979.

Solomon, P., and J. DraineJ. 1995. "One-year Outcomes of a Randomized Trial of Case Management with Seriously Mentally Ill Clients Leaving Jail." *Evaluation Review* 19: 256–273.

Steadman, H., and M. Naples. 2005. "Assessing the Effectiveness of Jail Diversion Programs for Persons with Serious Mental Illness and Co-Occurring Substance Use Disorders." *Behavioral Science and the Law* 23: 163–170.

Steadman, H., S. Dupius, and L. Morris. 2009, March. "For Whom Does Jail Diversion Work? Results of a Multi-Site Longitudinal Study." Paper presented at the annual conference of the American Psychology-Law Society, San Antonio, TX.

Steadman, H., J. Scott, F. Osher, T. Agnese, and P. Robbins. 2005. "Validation of the Brief Jail Mental Health Screen." *Psychiatric Services* 56: 816–822.

Steadman, H. J., F. C. Osher, P. C. Robbins, B. Case, and S. Samuels. 2009. "Prevalence of Serious Mental Illness among Jail Inmates." *Psychiatric Services* 60: 761–765.

Teplin, L. 1990. "The Prevalence of Severe Mental Disorder among Urban Male Jail Detainees: Comparison with the Epidemiologic Catchment Area Program." *American Journal of Public Health* 80: 663–669.

Teplin, L. A., K. M. Abram, and G. M. McClelland. 1996. "Prevalence of Psychiatric Disorders among Incarcerated Women: Pretrial Jail Detainees." *Archives of General Psychiatry* 53(6): 500–512.

Tessner, K. D., V. Mittal, and E. F. Walker. 2011. "Longitudinal Study of Stressful Life Events and Daily Stressors among Adolescents at High Risk for Psychotic Disorders." *Schizophrenia Bulletin* 37: 432–441.

Toch, H., and K. Adams. 1989. *The Disturbed Violent Offender.* New Haven, CT: Yale University press.

Toch, H., and K. Adams. 2002. *Acting Out: Maladaptive Behavior in Confinement.* Washington, DC: American Psychological Association.

Walker, E., L. Kestler, A. Bollini, and K. M. Hochman. 2004. "Schizophrenia: Etiology and Course." *Annual Review of Psychology* 55: 401–430.

Weisburd, D., C. Lum, and A. Petrosino. 2001. "Does Research Design Affect Study Outcomes in Criminal Justice?" *The Annals of the American Academy of Political and Social Sciences* 578: 50–70.

West, H., and W. Sabol. 2009. *Prison and Jail Inmates at Midyear 2008—Statistical Tables.* Washington, DC: U.S. Department of Justice, Bureau of Justice Statistics.

Wilson, A., and J. Draine. 2006. "Collaborations Between Criminal Justice and Mental Health Systems for Prisoner Reentry." *Psychiatric Services* 57: 875–878.

Wolff, M. 2008. "Evidence-Based Judicial Discretion: Promoting Public Safety through State Sentencing Reform." *New York University Law Review* 83: 1389–1419.

Young, S., K. Chick, and G. Godjonsson. 2010. "A Preliminary Evaluation of Reasoning and Rehabilitation 2 in Mentally Disordered Offenders (R&R2M) Across Two Secure Forensic Settings in the United Kingdom." *The Journal of Forensic Psychiatry* 21: 336–349.

Young, S. J., and R. R. Ross. 2007. *R&R2 for Youths and Adults with Mental Health Problems: A Prosocial Competence Training Program.* Ottawa: Cognitive Centre of Canada.

CHAPTER 22

SEX OFFENDER MANAGEMENT AND TREATMENT

ROXANNE LIEB

In the last two decades, legislative bodies in the United States have developed numerous innovations in legal efforts to protect society from sex offenders. These innovations have occurred at the federal, state, and local government levels. They have focused on matters as diverse as sentencing policy; civil commitment; registration and notification; controls on where sex offenders work, live, and travel; requirements to submit DNA material and take medications; and sentences of lifetime electronic monitoring. The adoption of special provisions for sex offenders has been more extensive than for any other class of criminals. This article will explore the history and purposes of these provisions, and will summarize what is known about their effectiveness as crime control measures.

HISTORICAL BACKGROUND: THREE ERAS OF SEX OFFENSE LAWS

As a starting point, it is helpful to review the three distinct periods of intense legislative and public attention regarding sex offenses in the United States. The practice of distinguishing sex offenders in the United States can be traced back almost 80 years (Freedman 1987, 83). From the 1930s to the 1950s, many states passed sexual psychopathy laws designed to offer treatment to this population in a hospital setting and release them when they were cured (Lieb, Quinsey, and Berliner 1998). The typical statute described the psychopath as someone "suffering from such conditions of emotional instability or impulsiveness of behavior, or lack of customary standards of good judgment, or failure to appreciate the consequences of his acts, or a combination of any such conditions, as to render him irresponsible for his conduct with respect to sexual matters and thereby dangerous to himself and to other persons" (Guttmacher and Weihofen 1952). The laws were promoted, in many cases by psychiatrists, as accomplishing two goals: separate the sex offender from society, and resolve the underlying mental condition (Brakel, Parry, and Weiner 1985). By the mid-1950s, critics from various perspectives began attacking the laws, arguing that the identified populations of sex offenders were not overly dangerous, that effective treatment was not known, that the duration of confinement was either too short or too long, and that some program graduates went on to commit horrific crimes (Lieb et al. 1998). Ultimately, the coalition supporting sexual psychopathy laws began to unravel and, by the early 1980s, states were repealing these laws or ending commitments to the treatment programs.

Starting in the 1970s, the feminist movement began asserting its voice in the public understanding of the range of sexual offenses and their consequential harm. Activists drew attention to the prevalence of sexual crimes committed by acquaintances and family members, including victimization of children, revealing a vast underground of unreported sexual crime (Janus 2006). The significant trauma to victims, both in the short as well as long term, was emphasized and later confirmed by an extensive body of research (Basile 2005). Social scientists began conducting surveys that revealed the prevalence of sex crimes outside the stereotypical definitions. Armed with new prevalence data and women willing to speak publicly about their sexual assault experiences, feminists promoted significant modifications to rape laws (Donat and D'Emilio 1992). These efforts were successful. Starting in 1974, state laws began expanding the range of conduct that was considered rape. Additionally, the behavior of the offender, rather than the conduct of the victim (e.g., degree of resistance), became the primary focus (Bernat 2002).

In the early 1990s, a third era of sex-crime focus emerged. The events and legislative responses in Washington State are frequently cited as the beginning of this era (LaFond 2005; Logan 2009; Petrunik 2005). Responding to a heinous crime against a young boy by a recidivist sex offender, a Blue Ribbon Task Force recommended a full slate of legislative remedies for "major flaws" in sanctions and controls over sex offenders (Governor's Task Force on Community Protection 1990, 1). The remedies included significant increases in sentence lengths, along with civil commitment for persons found to be "sexually violent predators." Registration laws that had become largely dormant were also revived, with a new concept called "community notification" established to warn communities about dangerous sex offenders released from jails and prisons (Petrunik 2005).

Over the next two decades, this community protection approach to sex offenses was adopted throughout the country. Sentences for sex offenders were increased, along with "two strikes" and "three strikes" laws. Between 1980 and 1996, incarceration for sexual assault grew approximately 300 percent, from 13 inmates per 100,000 adults to 52 per 100,000 (Blumstein and Beck 1999). Twenty states passed laws authorizing civil commitments for dangerous sex offenders (Deming 2008). Additional forms of social controls were enacted as well, including required DNA sample submission, electronic monitoring of released offenders, along with residency restrictions. Mandatory forms of castration were passed by several legislatures (Stinneford 2006).

CRIME TRENDS

What is known about the effectiveness of this third era of sex offense legislation? Before addressing this question, we need to explore the backdrop of crime trends in the United States. Calls for reform related to sex offenses have frequently emphasized a sudden acceleration of incidents—often referred to as a "sex-crime wave" (Freedman 1987, 83). While official statistics did show an increase in sex crimes through the 1980s, these rates stabilized in the 1990s, and, since then, the trend has been very different (see figure 22.1).

The 2007 violent crime rate was 43 percent lower than in 1998. Sexual assault has followed this trend, dropping by more than 60 percent in recent years. This change represents a reduction of over two and a half million victims (Rand 2009). When we look at the subcategory of sexual crimes against children, we see a similar pattern of decline. After about 15 years of steady increases, these crimes began to decline in the early 1990s. From 1990 through 2007, substantiated sexual abuse cases in the child welfare system decreased by 53 percent (Jones and Finkelhor 2007).

Explanations for the drop in violent crime typically focus on factors such as demographics (aging population), a stronger economy, increased incarceration,

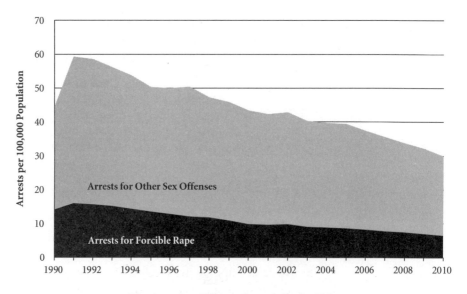

Fig. 22.1 Sex Offense Arrests in the U.S.
Source: FBI sex offense data

increased number of police, and decline in risky behaviors, among others (Blumstein and Wallman 2005; Mishra and Lalumiere 2009). Potential explanations for the drop in sex offenses against children have been examined in detail by Finkelhor and Jones. Their 2006 review concluded that multiple explanations are the most likely, including a combination of "economic prosperity, increasing agents of social intervention, and psychiatric pharmacology" (p. 707). Pharmacology is a potential explanation, because effective treatment of depression is theorized to lead to fewer individuals acting out aggressively and sexually.

During this period of a reduction in sex crimes, public concern has escalated. A 2005 national poll found that two out of three Americans described themselves as "very concerned" about sexual molestation of children, rating concerns about this crime higher than violent crime and acts of terrorism in their communities (Carroll 2005). A 2006–2007 telephone survey of American adults found that 92 percent expressed support for sex offender registries, and 76 percent said that such offenders should be restricted in where they live. The vast majority (94 percent) said that incarceration was the most appropriate response for sexual assault or rape of an adult. The authors concluded that public policy "appears broadly to converge with public opinion" (Mears, Mancini, Gertz, and Bratton 2008, 546).

As policy and public opinion have evolved in recent years, our research knowledge about sex offenders has evolved significantly as well. Key findings include the following:

- Sex offenders are not a homogenous population. For example, the motivation and patterns of offending are very dissimilar for men who rape adult women and those who target children. Sexual deviance is a strong predictor of further sexual offending, as is the presence of antisocial orientation/lifestyle instability (Hanson and Morton-Bourgon 2005).
- Systematic research using records of large populations of sex offenders has resulted in risk assessment instruments that reliably estimate the likelihood of reoffending by persons with certain characteristics and criminal histories. These instruments consistently surpass clinical prediction (Doren 2004; Quinsey, Harris, Rice, and Cormier 2006).
- Sexual offenders are more likely to recidivate with a non-sexual than a sexual offense. Social policies need to take account of sexual offenders' risk for violent as well as sexual reoffending (Quinsey et al. 2006).
- Juveniles and adolescents who commit sex offenses have low rates of sexual reoffending (Vandiver 2006).
- Treatment of sexual offenders shows mixed results; some reviews have concluded that psychological treatment works in reducing recidivism, whereas others have determined that the evidence overall shows that it is not effective (Hanson, Bourgon, Helmus, and Hodgson 2009). The study with the strongest research design (well-controlled random assignment) that relied on a credible treatment intervention (relapse prevention) was found not to affect the recidivism rates of prison participants (Marques, Wiederanders, Day, Nelson, and van Ommeren 2005).

- The brains of sex offenders who prefer children (pedophiles) have been found to be very different from other offenders, as well as those in the general population. Sexual attraction to children appears to have a biological basis, and there is no evidence that it can be changed through treatment (Cantor et al. 2008).
- Medical interventions with sex offenders target hormones or neurotransmitters underlying sexual drive, arousal, and behavior. The practices typically rely on cooperation from the patient, and there can be significant side effects (Seto 2007).

Sentencing Policies

Penalties for sex offenses are an infrequent topic for research, largely because of the difficulties in analyzing and comparing state sentencing practices. We do know that numerous states adopted harsher sentencing provisions for sex offenders in recent years, "often increasing prison time for offenses already subject to harsh terms" (King 2007, 2). Twenty-three states have "three strikes" laws requiring lifetime imprisonment for persistent offenders; the majority of these include rape and/or child sexual abuse as eligible offenses (Schiraldi, Colburn, and Lotke 2009). One state, Washington, with a determinate sentencing law, returned to an indeterminate sentencing system for many sex offenders as a means of allowing longer sentences and greater controls after release (Smith 2009).

The number and proportion of sex offenders under state control have increased significantly. In 2006, over 160,000 sex offenders were in state prisons, representing close to 13 percent of the total population (Sabol, West, and Cooper 2009). The figure in 1999 was 110,000 (Beck and Harrison 2001).

Treatment in the Community, Prison, and During Civil Commitment

The Safer Society surveyed sex offender treatment providers in the United States (McGrath, Cumming, Burchard, Zeoli, and Ellerby 2010) with responses from almost 1,400 treatment programs. During calendar year 2008, the responders reported that they provided services to close to 54,000 individuals who committed sexual offenses, primarily at the community level.

A 2008 survey of states examined prison-based sex offender treatment (Daly 2008). Thirty-one states reported that they had prison-based treatment, although the researchers found limited treatment capacity, particularly in comparison to community programs. California, for example, has the country's largest prison system and offers no treatment for sex offenders. For those states with sex offender programs, the percentage of sex offenders receiving treatment varied from 1 percent to 33 percent, with the duration of treatment lasting from 2 to 48 months. In terms of the type of treatment offered, most programs relied on cognitive-behavioral treatment and relapse prevention. The effectiveness of prison-based sex offender treatment has been studied by several researchers and the results are "inconclusive" (Daly 2008, 4). A cost-benefit analysis that took into account research through 2006 found that these programs, when combined with aftercare, did reduce recidivism to some extent, but because of the relatively high costs of the program, overall they resulted in increased costs to taxpayers by an average of $3,258 per participant (Aos, Miller, and Drake 2006, 9).

As mentioned earlier, 20 states have enacted civil commitment laws that authorize detention and offer treatment for sexual offenders found to be highly likely to reoffend (the individuals are typically called "sexually violent predators" or "sexually dangerous persons"). A 2006 survey found that over 4,500 persons had been committed under these laws (Gookin 2007). Although the legal structure was found constitutional by the U.S. Supreme Court, concerns persist about the unfairness of confining persons for their potential future danger to others (LaFond 2000). The process of identifying potential candidates for confinement under the program typically involves a screening process that includes evaluation by experts to determine if the person meets the legal criteria. In California, over 21,000 persons have been considered for commitment since 1996, with around 700 committed and 360 still under review in 2011 (California Department of Mental Health 2010). Since the vast majority of those committed are still confined, it is not possible to measure effectiveness by assessing recidivism after release. A 2007 study of persons recommended for the petition in Washington State but not committed found very high recidivism rates (50 percent new felony convictions with 23 percent felony sex offenses), suggesting that the selection process in that state focused on high-risk individuals (Milloy 2007).

Policy Focus: Controls after Release

In the last two decades, the United States has pursued a variety of social control measures that go into effect after release from incarceration. The next sections will summarize the evidence on the effectiveness of these post-release controls developed during this third wave of policy reforms. We will discuss civil commitment, lifetime supervision, registration and notification laws, electronic monitoring, post-conviction polygraphs, residency restrictions, and social media exclusions.

Sex offender registries, which identify individuals with prior sexual offense convictions, listed over 704,000 individuals in 2009 (National Center for Missing and Exploited Children 2009). Registries were first enacted in this country in the 1930s.

They focused on habitual violators of criminal laws. Their primary objective was to incarcerate or expel persons who were "undesirable," rather than to register them (University of Pennsylvania Law Review 1954). The first sex offender–specific state-wide law was enacted in California in 1947. Between 1951 and 1989, nine other states passed sex offender registration statutes. The early statutes, however, were "modest in scope" and typically not open to inspection by the public (Logan 2009, 31–32).

When Washington State revived sex offender registries as a public protection mechanism in the early 1990s, public dissemination of information about sex offenders was initially confined to those judged to pose high risks of reoffending (Lieb et al. 1998). However, as registries were adopted and implemented across the country, their reach was broadened considerably. As Logan (2009) notes, notification laws "drew the nation's attention to registration, and public sentiment and policy quickly awakened to the perceived benefits of empowering police with readily accessible information on criminally risky individuals" (p. 53). Early court decisions affirmed the constitutionality of registration and notification laws, finding that they are a reasonable exercise of regulatory power with any potential rights infringement outweighed by the contribution to public safety (Terry and Ackerman 2009).

The federal government entered this policy arena in 1994 with the Jacob Wetterling Act. States were required to make relevant information on released sex offenders public, or face a 10 percent reduction in criminal justice block grants. Congressional amendments broadening the Act were passed in 1997, 1998, 2000, and 2003. In 2006, the Wetterling Act was repealed and replaced by the far more comprehensive Adam Walsh Child Protection and Safety Act. As of early 2010, only one state and one Indian reservation had achieved substantial compliance with the law (U.S. Department of Justice 2009). Many state leaders expressed concerns that the measures will cost more to implement than their portion of federal block grant funds. Additionally, some organizations charged with developing sex offender policy have expressed disagreement with several policies reflected in the law (see: U.S. House of Representatives, Committee on the Judiciary, 2009; National Conference of State Legislatures 2010).

Because registration laws require the compliance of sex offenders, it is not surprising that they frequently have been found to be inaccurate (Benjamin 2007; thenewstribune.org 2007). In 2007, the National Center for Missing and Exploited Children estimated that 100,000 offenders were non-compliant with the laws (National Center for Missing and Exploited Children 2007). A USA Today analysis in 2007 determined that two-thirds of the states allow convicted sex offenders to register as homeless or to list a shelter or inexact location as long as they stay in touch with police. At least a dozen states list hundreds of sex offenders without specific addresses (Koch 2007). As of 2007, 22 states used some form of driver license–related process to encourage registration. Eventually, the Adam Walsh Act envisions a "real-time screening" for every driver license applicant to check against the sex offender registry. Such systems will undoubtedly lead to more accurate addresses (U.S. Government Accountability Office 2008). Courts have grappled with the constitutionality of both registration and notification laws, with most courts to date finding that these policies are a reasonable exercise of regulatory power, and that any potential rights infringement is outweighed by the contribution to public safety (Terry and Ackerman 2009).

In terms of the effect of these laws on crime, two studies analyzed multiple states and relied on aggregate-level data. Prescott and Rockoff (2008) analyzed National Incidence Based Reporting System data to examine the effects in 15 states, taking account of the timing and scope of state laws. The authors found evidence that registration reduces the frequency of sex offenses because law enforcement is knowledgeable about the location of registered offenders. Notification laws were found to deter first-time sex offenders, but to increase the recidivism rates of registered sex offenders. The authors speculate that this increase is caused by the "heavy social and financial costs associated with the public release of their information" (p. 34). Because registration has a greater effect than notification, the overall net effect is a 10 percent reduction. Shao and Li (2006) used Uniform Crime Report panel data for all 50 states from 1970 to 2002 and estimated that registration led to a 2 percent reduction in rapes reported to police.

Researchers have documented numerous other effects of registration/notification laws, including increased labor and equipment costs to law enforcement (Zevitz and Farkas 2000) and declines in property values for households close to registered offenders (Linden and Rockoff 2006; Pope 2008). At least five murders of sex offenders listed on public registries have been committed by persons who gained their knowledge of the individuals' sexual offense history through the registry (Logan 2009). The public strongly endorses the value of knowing about convicted sex offenders in their communities (Levenson, Brannon, Fortney, and Baker 2007; Mears et al. 2008), but the evidence regarding whether they use this information to prompt protective behavior is mixed (Anderson and Sample 2008; Lieb and Nunlist 2008; Beck and Travis 2006). Efforts to learn about sex offenders' experiences with registration and notification laws have been hampered by small sample sizes and consequential selection problems (e.g., Tewksbury (2006), with a 15 percent response rate; Tewksbury and Lees (2007), with a 12 percent response rate; and Mercado, Alvarez, and Levenson (2008), with a 9.5 percent response rate).

RESIDENCE RESTRICTIONS

With the implementation of community notification, citizens learned about convicted sex offenders living in their midst. This awareness launched numerous initiatives at the local and state levels that relied on zoning laws and other means to prohibit sex offenders from residing in certain locations. At present, 30 states have enacted laws restricting where convicted sex offenders can live in the community (Nieto and Jung 2006; Meloy, Miller, and Curtis 2008). Some laws also restricted where sex offenders could work. Often, the laws are referenced as child protection or exclusion zones and typically prohibit sex offenders from living within a prescribed number of feet from particular locations such as schools, churches, playgrounds, or other locations where children are likely to be present. Distances vary from 300 to 2,000 feet (National District Attorneys Association 2007).

Several studies have examined the consequences of such restrictions on allowable housing, frequently concluding that the restrictions severely limit sex offenders' options. A study of Orange County, Florida, in 2006 concluded that only 5 percent of potentially available parcels were outside the defined buffer zones (Zandbergen and Hart 2006).

Where, then, can sex offenders live? One consequence of residential restrictions has been increased homelessness among sex offenders. A 2008 study by the California Department of Corrections and Rehabilitation found that more sex offenders were reporting as homeless because of the law (California Sex Offender Management Board 2008). Among all registered sex offenders, the number registering as transient in that state increased from 2,050 in June 2007 to 3,267 in August 2008, an increase of 60 percent (California Sex Offender Management Board 2008).

The plight of sex offenders subject to these restrictions received national attention with news stories about Miami sex offenders living under a bridge. The news described them as "a large colony of convicted sex offenders, thrown into homelessness in recent years by draconian residency restrictions that leave them scant available or affordable housing. They live in tents and shacks built from cast-off supplies, clinging to pylons and embankments, with no running water" (Skipp 2010, 1).

The potential crime effects of residency restrictions have been studied. A Minnesota study collected information on over 3,000 sex offenders released from prison between 1990 and 2004 and examined those reincarcerated for a new sex offense before 2006. The researchers concluded that none of the 224 sex offenders likely would have been deterred by a residency restriction law (Duwe, Donnay, and Tewksbury 2008). The study revealed that the sex offender recidivists gained access to their victims through romantic relationships with adult women that were used to gain access to the women's children. A 2009 study of sex offenders in New Jersey concluded that a majority of sex offenders would be unable to live in their current homes if residence restrictions were in place, and that few options for housing exist outside of common buffer zones (Zgoba, Levenson, and McKee 2009). Concerns have been raised that residency restrictions will increase the social disorganization of particular neighborhoods, as sex offenders will move to areas outside protected zones (Tewksbury and Mustaine 2008).

Some expert bodies have gone on record opposing residency restrictions (e.g., Delson, Kokish, and Abbott 2008; Iowa County Attorneys Association 2006; Sex Offender Management Board of the New Mexico Sentencing Commission 2007). The Kansas Sex Offender Policy Board recommended that residency restrictions be set on "individually identified risk factors," with comprehensive education programs for children as an alternative means to prevent and respond to sexual abuse (2007, 31–32).

TECHNOLOGICAL INNOVATIONS IN SUPERVISION:
ELECTRONIC MONITORING AND POLYGRAPHS

In recent years, supervision of sex offenders has included use of technological equipment as a means of increasing controls over offenders. These practices include electronic monitoring of offenders' movements in the community, and the use of polygraph equipment to check up on offenders' risky or illegal behaviors. Both of these "techno-corrections" approaches rely on the premise that sex offenders will curtail their behaviors because they do not want to be caught.

Electronic monitoring has two principal forms: continuous signaling such as GPS, called "active" systems, and programmed contact or "passive" systems, in which a computer calls offenders to see if they are where they are supposed to be (Bonta, Wallace-Capretta, and Rooney 1999). The Bureau of Justice Statistics surveyed states in 2008 to determine the number of adults tracked by Global Positioning Systems: approximately 13,000 were on parole and, of these, close to 8,000 were sex offenders (Glaze and Bonczar 2009, 35, 55). A 2007 survey of states by the Interstate Commission for Adult Offender Supervision indicated that 34 states were using GPS monitoring systems for sex offenders. At least six states (California, Florida, Ohio, Missouri, Oklahoma, and Wisconsin) have enacted laws requiring lifetime electronic monitoring for certain sex offenders (Dunlap 2010). The ability to monitor a person's movements offers many potential benefits: helping the public feel safer, structuring offenders' time and movement toward productive activities, and helping investigations by pinpointing time and travel information (Renzema 2009).

The Kansas Sex Offender Policy Board outlined the limitations of the technology. First and foremost, it does not necessarily prevent crime; as they noted in their 2007 report, "the value of electronic monitoring depends on the individual's propensity to be compliant with the conditions of their release" (p. 10). A high-profile murder of a 13-year-old girl in Washington State was committed by a convicted sex offender on GPS monitoring (McLaughlin and Oppmann 2009). Other limitations include the fact that the equipment can be removed, GPS signals can be interrupted by geography and architectural features, and it is difficult for staff to avoid information overload and respond to all violations (p. 9). The Board concluded that electronic monitoring alone "will not change behavior and is not enough to provide security for the community"; they recommend that it be used "selectively on a specific population of sex offenders." The same conclusion was reached by Florida's Office of Program Policy Analysis and Government Accountability in 2005.

At present, there are no well-designed studies of electronic monitoring for sex offenders. A California study of a pilot program using GPS in San Diego will produce results by 2011 (Jannetta 2006; communication with Susan Turner, 2010). Research on the use of this technology for the general population of offenders has found that it saves taxpayers money because it is often a substitute for incarceration; however, electronic monitoring does not reduce recidivism (Aos et al. 2006).

Polygraphs are frequently used by sex offender treatment providers and supervision officers to verify treatment and supervision compliance. Surveys by the Safer Society found that 30 percent of adult sex offender treatment programs used polygraphy in 1996, 70 percent used it in 2002, and 79 percent did so in the 2009 survey (McGrath et al. 2010). A 2001 study reported that polygraphy was incorporated as part of sex offender supervision in 30 to 35 states (Consigli 2001). Polygraphy measures physiological arousal that is potentially associated with lying. Post-conviction questioning of sex offenders, either as part of treatment or supervision, often includes polygraph testing as a means of encouraging more truth telling (Meijer, Verschuere, Merckelbach, and Crombez 2008). Polygraphy is not accepted as valid evidence in U.S. courts; simply put, the guilty can pass a polygraph test and the innocent can fail (Committee to Review the Scientific Evidence on the Polygraph and National Research Council 2003).

One study has tested the specific contribution of polygraphy as a crime control measure for sex offenders. Comparing two similar groups of sex offenders, one subject to polygraphy and the other not, the 2007 study found no significant differences between the groups in charges for new sex offenses after a five-year follow-up (McGrath, Cumming, Hoke, and Bonn-Miller 2007). There was a significant reduction in new non-sexual violent offense. The participants receiving polygraphs knew that the testing would likely occur every six months; on average, however, they received only one exam every 22 months. As Grubin noted, this schedule dissipated the "likelihood that polygraphy would have an impact on behavior" (Grubin 2008, 185).

SOCIAL MEDIA AND COMPUTER RESTRICTIONS

When MySpace revealed that more than 90,000 registered sex offenders had been removed from their site in response to a subpoena, attention was drawn to the vulnerabilities of social media as an access point for sex offenders (Wortham 2009). Subsequently, states have passed legislation restricting convicted sex offenders' use of computers and other measures to restrict their access during periods of community supervision to particular sites. Community corrections' officers frequently monitor sex offenders' computer usage by retrieving Internet histories (Russo 2006; LaMagna and Berejka 2009).

WHAT ABOUT THE FUTURE?

Given the public support for increased controls and confinement terms for sex offenders, it is difficult to envision legislative bodies repealing current sex offender laws. The reduction in sexual victimization is likely to be linked in the public's mind to harsher laws; thus, repealing or limiting these laws will likely be labeled as back-sliding. The courts will continue to hear and decide a variety of challenges; however, with minor exceptions, they are likely to defer to legislative prerogative. If registration/notification laws are extended in "new or novel incarnations," William Logan believes that there is reason to think that the courts may be troubled. He also predicts that the possibility exists that other sub-populations could be drawn into registration/notification; some evidence exists for this trend already through proposed registries for animal abusers, child abusers, and those permitted to carry a concealed weapon (Logan 2009; Stateman 2010).

In recent years, state-level sex offender management groups have been created in 26 states (Lobanov-Rostovsky 2007). Interdisciplinary in membership, the groups commonly review policy topics and make recommendations to the executive and legislative branches. Some groups are time-limited and respond to particular issues, whereas others are ongoing. In some states, these entities have chosen to take on controversial topics and challenge the political status quo. For example, the Kansas Board declared that electronic monitoring "when used alone, will not change behavior and is not enough to provide security for the community" (Kansas Sex Offender Policy Board 2007, 2). The California Sex Offender Management Board studied the increase in homelessness among registered sex offenders following residency restriction laws (California Sex Offender Management Board 2008). The Iowa Sex Offender Research Council suggested that electronic monitoring should be risk-based rather than conviction-based, and recommended that the 2,000 foot residency restriction law be repealed (Iowa Sex Offender Research Council 2009). Whether these entities will have a long-term voice in sex offender management is still uncertain; there is always the risk that they may choose not to take political stands, or they may eventually be decommissioned by legislatures if their viewpoint is not welcome.

REFERENCE

Anderson, A. L., and L. L. Sample. 2008. "Public Awareness and Action Resulting from Sex Offender Community Notification Laws." *Criminal Justice Policy Review* 19: 371–396.

Aos, S., M. Miller, and E. Drake. 2006. *Evidence-Based Public Policy Options to Reduce Future Prison Construction, Criminal Justice Costs, and Crime Rates* (Rep. No. 06-10-1201). Olympia: Washington State Institute for Public Policy.

Basile, K. C. 2005. "Sexual Violence in the Lives of Girls and Women." In *Handbook of Women, Stress, and Trauma*, ed. Kathleen Kendall-Tacket, 101–122. New York: Brunner-Routledge.

Beck, A. J., and P. M. Harrison. 2001. *Prisoners in 2000* (Rep. No. NCJ 188207). Washington, DC: U.S. Dept. of Justice, Office of Justice Programs, Bureau of Justice Statistics.

Beck, V. S., and L. F. Travis. 2006. "Sex Offender Notification: An Exploratory Assessment of State Variation in Notification Processes." *Journal of Criminal Justice* 34: 51–55.

Benjamin, Elizabeth. 2007, March 8. "Flaws Cited in Sex Cases." Available at: http://Timesunion.com.

Bernat, F. P. 2002. "Rape Law Reform." In *Sexual Violence: Policies, Practices, and Challenges in the United States and Canada*, eds. J. Hodgson and D. Kelley, 85–99. Westport, CT: Greenwood Publishing Group.

Blumstein, A., and A. J. Beck. 1999. "Population Growth in U.S. Prisons, 1980–1996." *Crime and Justice* 26: 17–61.

Blumstein, A., and J. Wallman. 2005. *The Crime Drop in America*. 2nd ed. New York: Cambridge University Press.

Bonta, J., S. Wallace-Capretta, and J. Rooney. 1999. *Electronic Monitoring in Canada* (Rep. No. JS4-1/1999–01). Ottawa, ON: Public Works and Government Services Canada.

Brakel, S. J., J. Parry, and B. A. Weiner. 1985. *The Mentally Disabled and the Law*. 3rd ed. Chicago: American Bar Foundation.

California Department of Mental Health. 2011. "SOCP Statistical Data Summary Statistics Report 01/01/1996 Thru 06/30/2011" [Online]. Available at: http://www.dmh.ca.gov/services_and_programs/Forensic_Services/Sex_Offender_Commitment_Program/SummaryStatisticsReport.asp.

California Sex Offender Management Board. 2008. *Homelessness among Registered Sex Offenders in California: The Numbers, the Risks and the Response*. Sacramento: California Sex Offender Management Board.

Cantor, J. M., N. Kabani, B. K. Christensen, R. B. Zipursky, H. E. Barbaree, R. Dickey, et al. 2008. "Cerebral White Matter Deficiencies in Pedophilic Men." *Journal of Psychiatric Research* 42: 167–183.

Carroll, J. 2005. "Crystal Meth, Child Molestation Top Crime Concerns." Gallup, Inc. [Online]. Available at: http://www.gallup.com/poll/16123/crystal-meth-child-molestation-top-crime-concerns.aspx.

Committee to Review the Scientific Evidence on the Polygraph and National Research Council. 2003. *The Polygraph and Lie Detection*. Washington, DC: The National Academies Press.

Consigli, J. 2001. "Post-conviction Sex Offender Testing and the American Polygraph Association." In *Handbook of Polygraph Testing*, ed. Murray Kleiner, 237–250. New York: Academic Press.

Daly, R. 2008. *Treatment and Reentry Practices for Sex Offenders: An Overview of States*. New York: Vera Institute of Justice.

Delson, N., R. Kokish, and B. Abbott. 2008. *Position Paper on Sex Offender Residence Restrictions*. Orange: California Coalition on Sexual Offending.

Deming, A. 2008. "Sex Offender Civil Commitment Programs: Current Practices, Characteristics, and Resident Demographics." *Journal of Psychiatry & Law* 36: 439.

Donat, P. L. N., and J. D'Emilio. 1992. "Feminist Redefinition of Rape and Sexual Assault: Historical Foundations and Change." *Journal of Social Issues* 48: 9–22.

Doren, D. M. 2004. "Bibliography of Published Works Relative to Risk Assessment for Sexual Offenders." Association for the Treatment of Sexual Abusers [Online]. Available at: http://www.atsa.com/pdfs/riskAssessmentBiblio.pdf.

Dunlap, K. 2010. "Sex offenders after Prison: Lifetime GPS Monitoring?" Findlaw [Online]. Available at: http://blogs.findlaw.com/blotter/2010/02/sex-offenders-after-prison-lifetime-gps-monitoring.html.

Duwe, G., W. Donnay, and R. Tewksbury. 2008. "Does Residential Proximity Matter? A Geographic Analysis of Sex Offense Recidivism." *Criminal Justice and Behavior* 35: 484–504.

Finkelhor, D., and L. Jones. 2006. "Why Have Child Maltreatment and Child Victimization Declined?" *Journal of Social Issues* 62: 685–716.

Freedman, E. B. 1987. "'Uncontrolled Desires': The Response to the Sexual Psychopath, 1920–1960." *Journal of American History* 74: 83–106.

Glaze, L. E., and T. P. Bonczar. 2009. *Probation and Parole in the United States, 2008* (Rep. No. NCJ 228230). Washington, DC: U.S. Department of Justice, Office of Justice Programs, Bureau of Justice Statistics.

Gookin, K. 2007. *Comparison of State Laws Authorizing Involuntary Commitment of Sexually Violent Predators: 2006 Update, Revised* (Rep. No. 07-08-1101). Olympia: Washington State Institute for Public Policy.

Governor's Task Force on Community Protection. 1990. *Task Force on Community Protection: Final report.* Olympia: Washington State Department of Social and Health Services.

Grubin, D. 2008. "The Case for Polygraph Testing of Sex Offenders." *Legal and Criminological Psychology* 13: 177–189.

Guttmacher, M. S., and H. Weihofen. 1952. *Psychiatry and the Law.* 1st ed. New York: Norton.

Hanson, R. K., G. Bourgon, L. Helmus, and S. Hodgson. 2009. *A Meta-Analysis of the Effectiveness of Treatment for Sexual Offenders: Risk, Need and Responsivity.* Ottawa: Public Safety Canada.

Hanson, R. K., and K. E. Morton-Bourgon. 2005. "The Characteristics of Persistent Sexual Offenders: A Meta-Analysis of Recidivism Studies." *Journal of Consulting and Clinical Psychology* 73: 1154–1163.

Interstate Commission for Adult Offender Supervision. 2007. *Lifetime Supervision February 2007.* Lexington, KY: Interstate Commission for Adult Offender Supervision.

Iowa County Attorneys Association. 2006. *Statement On Sex Offender Residency Restrictions in Iowa.* Des Moines: Iowa County Attorneys Association.

Iowa Sex Offender Research Council. 2009. *Iowa Sex Offender Research Council Report to the Iowa General Assembly.* Iowa Sex Offender Research Council.

Jannetta, J. 2006. *GPS Monitoring of High-Risk Sex Offenders.* Irvine: Center for Evidence-Based Corrections, University of California, Irvine.

Janus, E. S. 2006. *Failure to Protect America's Sexual Predator Laws and the Rise of the Preventive State.* Ithaca, NY: Cornell University Press.

Jones, L., and D. Finkelhor. 2007. *Updated Trends in Child Maltreatment, 2007.* Durham: University of New Hampshire, Crimes Against Children Research Center.

Kansas Sex Offender Policy Board. 2007. *Kansas Sex Offender Policy Board, January 8, 2007 Report.* Kansas Sex Offender Policy Board.

King, R. S. 2007. *Changing Direction? State Sentencing Reforms, 2004–2006.* Washington, DC: The Sentencing Project.

Koch, Wendy. 2007, November 19. "Many Sex Offenders Are Often Homeless." *USA Today.*

LaFond, J. Q. 2000. "The Future of Involuntary Civil Commitment in the U.S.A. after *Kansas v. Hendricks.*" *Behavioral Sciences and the Law* 18: 153–167.

LaFond, J. Q. 2005. *Preventing Sexual Violence: How Society Should Cope with Sex Offenders.* Washington, DC: American Psychological Association.

LaMagna, R. C. and M. Berejka. 2009. "Remote Computer Monitoring: Managing Sex Offenders' Access to the Internet." *Journal of Offender Monitoring* 21: 11–24.

Levenson, J. S., Y. N. Brannon, T. Fortney, and J. Baker. 2007. "Public Perceptions about Sex Offenders and Community Protection Policies." *Analyses of Social Issues and Public Policy* 7: 1–25.

Lieb, R., and C. Nunlist. 2008. *Community Notification as Viewed by Washington's Citizens: A 10-Year Follow-Up* (Rep. No. 08-03-1101). Olympia: Washington State Institute for Public Policy.

Lieb, R., V. Quinsey, and L. Berliner. 1998. "Sexual Predators and Social Policy." In *Crime and Justice: A Review of Research*, ed. Michael Tonry, 43–114. Chicago: University of Chicago Press.

Linden, L. L., and J. E. Rockoff. 2006. "There Goes the neighborhood? Estimates of the Impact of Crime Risk on Property Values from Megan's Laws." National Bureau of Economic Research Working Paper Series, No. 12253.

Lobanov-Rostovsky, C. 2007. "Sex Offender Treatment/Management Policy Groups." ATSA Forum, XIX. Available at: http://www.csg.org/knowledgecenter/docs/SOMB-Chris.pdf.

Logan, W. A. 2009. *Knowledge as Power: Criminal Registration and Community Notification Laws in America*. Stanford, CA: Stanford Law Books.

Marques, J. K., M. Wiederanders, D. M. Day, C. Nelson, and A. van Ommeren. 2005. "Effects of a Relapse Prevention Program on Sexual Recidivism: Final Results from California's Sex Offender Treatment and Evaluation Project (SOTEP)." *Sexual Abuse: A Journal of Research and Treatment* 17: 79–107.

McGrath, R. J., G. F. Cumming, B. L. Burchard, S. Zeoli, and L. Ellerby. 2010. *Current Practices and Emerging Trends in Sexual Abuser Management*. Safer Society [Online]. Available at: http://www.safersociety.org/downloadables/WP141-Current_Practices_Emerging_Trends.pdf

McGrath, R. J., G. F. Cumming, S. E. Hoke, and M. O. Bonn-Miller. 2007. "Outcomes in a Community Sex Offender Treatment Program: A Comparison Between Polygraphed and Matched Non-Polygraphed Offenders." *Sexual Abuse: A Journal of Research and Treatment* 19: 381–393.

McLaughlin, Eliott, and Patrick Oppmann. 2009, March 12. Sex Offender Kills Teen while under GPS Monitoring, Police Say. Available at: http://CNN.com.

Mears, D. P., C. Mancini, M. Gertz, and J. Bratton. 2008. "Sex Crimes, Children, and Pornography: Public Views and Public Policy." *Crime & Delinquency* 54: 532–559.

Meijer, E., B. Verschuere, H. Merckelbach, and G. Crombez. 2008. "Sex Offender Management using the Polygraph: A Critical Review." *International Journal of Law and Psychiatry* 31: 423–429.

Meloy, M., S. Miller, and K. Curtis. 2008. "Making Sense Out of Nonsense: The Deconstruction of State-Level Sex Offender Residence Restrictions." *American Journal of Criminal Justice* 33: 209–222.

Mercado, C. C., S. Alvarez, and J. Levenson. 2008. "The Impact of Specialized Sex Offender Legislation on Community Reentry." *Sexual Abuse: A Journal of Research and Treatment* 20: 188–205.

Milloy, C. 2007. *Six-Year Follow-Up of 135 Released Sex Offenders Recommended for Commitment under Washington's Sexually Violent Predator Law, Where No Petition Was Filed* (Rep. No. 07-06-1101). Olympia: Washington State Institute for Public Policy.

Mishra, S., and M. Lalumiere. 2009. "Is the Crime Drop of the 1990s in Canada and the USA Associated with a General Decline in Risky and Health-Related Behavior?" *Social Science & Medicine* 68: 39–48.

National Center for Missing and Exploited Children. 2007. "National Center for Missing and Exploited Children Creates New Unit to Help Find 100,000 Missing Sex Offenders and Calls for States to Do Their Part." National Center for Missing and Exploited Children [Online]. Available at: http://www.missingkids.com/missingkids/servlet/NewsEventServlet?LanguageCountry=en_US&PageId=3081.

National Center for Missing and Exploited Children. 2009. "Map of Registered Sex Offenders in the United States per 100,000 Population." National Center for Missing and Exploited Children [Online]. Available at: http://www.missingkids.com/en_US/documents/sex-offender-map.pdf

National Conference of State Legislatures. 2010. *Cost-Benefit Analyses of SORNA Implementation.* Denver, CO: National Conference of State Legislatures.

National District Attorneys Association. 2007. *Residency Restrictions for Sexual Offenders.* Alexandria, VA: National District Attorneys Association.

Nieto, M., and D. Jung. 2006. *The Impact of Residency Restrictions on Sex Offenders and Correctional Management Practices: A Literature Review* (Rep. No. 06–008). Sacramento: California Research Bureau.

Office of Program Policy Analysis and Government Accountability. 2005. *Electronic Monitoring Should Be Better Targeted to the Most Dangerous Offenders* (Rep. No. 05–19). Tallahassee, FL: Office of Program Policy Analysis and Government Accountability.

Petrunik, M. 2005. "Dangerousness and Its Discontents: A Discourse on the Socio-politics Of Dangerousness." *Sociology of Crime, Law and Deviance* 6: 49–74.

Pope, J. C. 2008. "Fear of Crime and Housing Prices: Household Reactions to Sex Offender Registries. *Journal of Urban Economics* 64: 601–614.

Prescott, J. J., and J. E. Rockoff. 2008. "Do Sex Offender Registration and Notification Laws Affect Criminal Behavior?" National Bureau of Economic Research Working Paper Series, No. 13803.

Quinsey, V. L., G. T. Harris, M. E. Rice, and C. A. Cormier. 2006. *Violent Offenders: Appraising and Managing Risk.* 2nd ed. Washington, DC: American Psychological Association.

Rand, M. 2009. *Criminal Victimization, 2008* (Rep. No. NCJ 227777). Washington, DC: U.S. Department of Justice, Bureau of Justice Statistics.

Renzema, M. 2009. "Rationalizing the Use of Electronic Monitoring." *The Journal of Offender Monitoring* 22: 5. Civil Research Institute, New Jersey.

Russo, J. 2006. *Emerging Technologies for Community Corrections.* Alexandria, VA: Corrections Today, American Correctional Association.

Sabol, W. J., H. C. West, and M. Cooper. 2009. *Prisoners in 2008* (Rep. No. NCJ 228417). Washington, DC: U.S. Department of Justice, Office of Justice Programs, Bureau of Justice Statistics.

Schiraldi, V., J. Colburn, and E. Lotke. 2009. *Three Strikes and You're Out: An Examination of the Impact of Strikes Laws 10 Years after Their Enactment.* Washington, DC: Justice Policy Institute.

Seto, M. C. 2007. *Pedophilia and Sexual Offending Against Children: Theory, Assessment, and Intervention.* Washington, DC: American Psychological Association.

Sex Offender Management Board of the New Mexico Sentencing Commission. 2007. *Distance Restrictions on Sex Offender Residential Housing.* Albuquerque, NM: Sex Offender Management Board of the New Mexico Sentencing Commission.

Shao, L., and J. Li. 2006. "The Effect of Sex Offender Registration Laws on Rape Victimization." Unpublished manuscript.

Skipp, C. 2010. "A Law for the Sex Offenders under a Miami Bridge." Time.com [Online]. Available at: http://www.time.com/time/nation/article/0, 8599, 1957778,00.html.

Smith, R. P. 2009. *Determinate Plus/CCB Statistical Report.* Olympia, WA: Indeterminate Sentence Review Board.

Stateman, A. 2010. "Should There Be an Animal-Abuser Registry?" Time.com [Online]. Available at: http://www.time.com/time/nation/article/0, 8599, 1969346,00.html.

Stinneford, J. 2006. "Incapacitation Through Maiming: Chemical Castration, the Eighth Amendment, and the Denial of Human Dignity." *University of St. Thomas Law Journal.* University of St. Thomas Legal Studies Research Paper No. 06-25.

Terry, K., and A. Ackerman. 2009. "A Brief History of Major Sex Offender Laws." In *Sex Offender Laws: Failed Policies, New Directions,* ed. R.Wright, 65–98. New York: Springer Publishing Company.

Tewksbury, R. 2006. "Sex Offender Registries as a Tool for Public Safety: Views from Registered Offenders." *Western Criminology Review* 7: 1–8.

Tewksbury, R., and M. B. Lees. 2007. "Perceptions of Punishment: How Registered Sex Offenders View Registries." *Crime & Delinquency* 53: 380–407.

Tewksbury, R., and E. Mustaine. 2008. "Where Registered Sex Offenders Live: Community Characteristics and Proximity to Possible Victims." *Victims and Offenders* 3: 86–98.

U.S. Department of Justice. 2009. *Justice Department Announces First Two Jurisdictions to Implement Sex Offender Registration and Notification Act* (Rep. No. SMART09154). Washington, DC: U.S. Department of Justice.

U.S. Government Accountability Office. 2008. *Convicted Sex Offenders: Factors That Could Affect the Successful Implementation of Driver's License-Related Processes to Encourage Registration and Enhance Monitoring* (Rep. No. GAO-08–116). Washington, DC: GAO.

U.S. House of Representatives, Committee on the Judiciary. 2009 (3-10). *Sex Offender Notification and Registration Act (SORNA): Barriers to Timely Compliance by States.* Serial No. 111–21. Committee on the Judiciary House of Representatives, Crime, Terrorism, and Homeland Security.

University of Pennsylvania Law Review. 1954. "Criminal Registration Ordinances: Police Control over Potential Recidivists." *University of Pennsylvania Law Review* 103: 60–112.

Vandiver, D. M. 2006. "A Prospective Analysis of Juvenile Male Sex Offenders: Characteristics and Recidivism Rates as Adults." *Journal of Interpersonal Violence* 21: 673–688.

Wortham, Jenna. 2009, February 5. "MySpace Says It Banned 90,000 Sex Offenders." *International Herald Tribune.*

Zandbergen, P., and T. Hart. 2006. "Reducing Housing Options for Convicted Sex Offenders: Investigating The Impact of Residency Restriction Laws Using GIS." *Justice Research and Policy* 8: 1–24.

Zevitz, R. G., and M. A. Farkas. 2000. *Sex Offender Community Notification: Assessing theImpact in Wisconsin* (Rep. No. NCJ179992). Washington, DC: U.S. Department of Justice, Office of Justice Programs, National Institute of Justice.

Zgoba, K.M., J. Levenson, and T. McKee. 2009. "Examining the Impact of Sex Offender Residence Restrictions on Housing Availability." *Criminal Justice Policy Review* 20: 91–110.

CHAPTER 23

FEMALE OFFENDERS AND WOMEN IN PRISON

LATOSHA L. TRAYLOR AND BETH E. RICHIE

I. INTRODUCTION

Female offenders and women in prison are topics that traditionally receive little attention from criminology and criminal justice scholars. Despite the fact that for decades, a cadre of feminist criminologists has challenged the field of criminology to expand and reconstruct the narratives about the study of gender and crime, there continues to be a gender gap in the dominant literature on sentencing and corrections (Belknap 2001; Daly and Chesney-Lind 1988; Naffine 1987; Simpson 1989). This gap is manifested both in terms of the lack of research on women as offenders, inmates, and people returning to the community, as well as a gap in the theoretical work that understands gender roles and relationships as salient factors in the behavior and treatment of men and women who are involved in the criminal legal system. This essay is an attempt to bring those issues to the discussion of sentencing and corrections by presenting the empirical data about the extent and nature of women's involvement in illegal activity, by reviewing both the historical trends in imprisonment and contemporary issues affecting women in jails and prisons and, finally, by offering a set of recommendations about how things could be different for women who find themselves in conflict with the law.

At the outset, it is important to state the obvious: as in other spheres of social life, gender matters. Women who are involved in the criminal legal system are, quite simply, different from their male counterparts. First and perhaps most importantly, women are significantly less likely to be represented in the data on crime and punishment (Belknap 2001; Chesney-Lind and Paskow 2004; Young and Reviere 2006). They are less likely to be arrested, detained, adjudicated, charged, sentenced, confined to a correctional facility, and therefore released back to their community under correctional supervision. From some vantage points, the relative low rates of women's involvement in the criminal legal system justifies not including them in major research initiatives, which results in a significant empirical and theoretical oversight that this essay attempts to remedy. Second, in addition to the lower rates, it has been recognized that women's pathways to crime are different from men's. They commit different kinds of crimes and for different reasons. Intervention strategies aimed as desistance, treatment programs, and prevention initiatives must, therefore, be different if women are the targeted group. Finally, women who are involved in illegal activity experience a set of contradictory effects of society's gender arrangements. On the one hand, some women may be treated more leniently and at different historical moments than men; on the other hand, for a number of complicated reasons, others may be treated more harshly by the system than their male counterparts. In this chapter, we argue that in order to understand the different rates, patterns, and treatment of women, it is important to understand broader systemic patterns of gender inequality and the gendered dynamics of the U.S. criminal legal system.

II. Empirical Overview of Female Offenders and Inmates in the United States

This chapter focuses on sentencing rather than commission of crimes. While this is not a perfect proxy, sentencing patterns and conditions that lead to detention do illuminate important aspects of women's involvement in illegal activities more broadly. Over time, women have made up approximately 7 percent of the U.S. prison population, while men compose the other 93 percent (Sabol, West, and Cooper 2009). Most recently, there were 114,852 women under the jurisdiction of state or federal correctional institutions and local jails in the United States (West 2010). Despite lower rates relative to men, women's rates of incarceration have risen dramatically. Between the years 2000 and 2008, federal and state prisons have seen an 18.8 percent increase in the number of female inmates, whereas men accounted for a 13.2 percent increase (Sabol, West and Cooper 2009).

It is worth noting that black men and women are disproportionately represented within the correctional system, specifically. Blacks comprise approximately 12 percent of the total U.S. population, yet they are more likely to be incarcerated in comparison to their peers from other racial groups (West 2010). Black women are incarcerated at a rate of 333 per 100,000, while white and Hispanic women are at a much lower rate, 91 and 142, respectively (West 2010). Forty-six percent of the women incarcerated in the United States are white, while 32 percent are black, and 16 percent are Hispanic (West 2010). As such, black women have a disproportionate rate of incarceration in

comparison to their white and Hispanic counterparts in proportion to their representation within the general U.S. population.

Empirical data on rates of offending and subsequent incarceration for women
reveal that a majority of women are charged with nonviolent offenses, particularly
property and drug offenses (U.S. Department of Justice 2010). Table 23.1 shows the
aggregate number of arrests for men and women reported to the FBI by local criminal
justice agencies for 2009.[1] It is evident that male offenders comprise the majority of
arrests at 74.7 percent, while female offenders make up the other 25.3 percent. Women
are most prevalently arrested for offenses such as larceny-theft, forgery, fraud, embez-
zlement, prostitution and commercialized vice, drug abuse violations and driving
under the influence (U.S. Department of Justice 2010). The offense categories where
women significantly outnumber men are prostitution and commercialized vice and
runaways, with an arrest percentage of 69.6 and 55.2, respectively (U.S. Department
of Justice 2010). This suggests an influence of societal gender dynamics in that both of
these categories represent common "gendered" experiences for women involved with
the criminal legal system. Additionally, the prostitution and commercial vice offense
category suggests an area in which economic gain can be attained for women easily.
Estimated percentages on sentenced prisoners, as shown in table 23.2, reveal that
female offenders are most frequently incarcerated for nonviolent offenses (64.5 percent), such as property, public-order, and drug offenses (Sabol, West and Cooper
2009). Furthermore, female offenders comprise approximately one-third of all
inmates sentenced for violent crimes (Sabol, West and Cooper 2009).

When aggregating official statistical data on incarceration, the characteristics of
the typical female under correctional supervision can be summarized as unmarried, poor women of color (usually African American or Latino) with little education or job experience, between the ages of 20 and 44, and with at least one to two
children under the age of 18 (Greenfeld and Snell 1999; Morash and Schram 2002;
Sabol, West, and Cooper 2009). More than their male counterparts, women who are
arrested and subsequently incarcerated for property or drug offenses, such as larceny-theft or criminal possession of a controlled substance, are from the most disadvantaged groups in society. While this composite of female offenders provides a
general perspective on the population, the data do not distinguish between the specific characteristics and circumstances of incarcerated women.

III. Brief Overview of the Historical Development of Corrections for Women

A historical overview of the transformation of how, where, and why women who
commit crimes are incarcerated illuminate the contemporary issues that women
face with regard to sentencing and corrections.

Table 23.1: Arrests by Sex and Offense, 2009 [12,371 agencies; 2009 estimated population 239,839,971]

Offense charged	Number of persons arrested			Percent male	Percent female	Percent distribution[1]		
	Total	Male	Female			Total	Male	Female
TOTAL	10,741,157	8,026,796	2,714,361	74.7	25.3	100.0	100.0	100.0
Murder and non-negligent manslaughter	9,775	8,755	1,020	89.6	10.4	0.1	0.1	*
Forcible rape	16,442	16,234	208	98.7	1.3	0.2	0.2	*
Robbery	100,702	88,783	11,919	88.2	11.8	0.9	1.1	0.4
Aggravated assault	331,372	258,467	72,905	78.0	22.0	3.1	3.2	2.7
Burglary	235,226	200,117	35,109	85.1	14.9	2.2	2.5	1.3
Larceny-theft	1,060,754	597,246	463,508	56.3	43.7	9.9	7.4	17.1
Motor vehicle theft	64,169	52,761	11,408	82.2	17.8	0.6	0.7	0.4
Arson	9,509	7,892	1,617	83.0	17.0	0.1	0.1	0.1
Violent crime[2]	458,291	372,239	86,052	81.2	18.8	4.3	4.6	3.2
Property crime[2]	1,369,658	858,016	511,642	62.6	37.4	12.8	10.7	18.8
Other assaults	1,036,754	767,018	269,736	74.0	26.0	9.7	9.6	9.9
Forgery and counterfeiting	67,357	41,932	25,425	62.3	37.7	0.6	0.5	0.9
Fraud	162,243	92,850	69,393	57.2	42.8	1.5	1.2	2.6
Embezzlement	14,097	6,920	7,177	49.1	50.9	0.1	0.1	0.3
Stolen property; buying, receiving, possessing	82,944	65,644	17,300	79.1	20.9	0.8	0.8	0.6
Vandalism	212,981	174,477	38,504	81.9	18.1	2.0	2.2	1.4
Weapons; carrying, possessing, etc.	130,941	120,430	10,511	92.0	8.0	1.2	1.5	0.4

Prostitution and commercialized vice	56,640	17,203	39,437	30.4	69.6	0.5	0.2	1.5
Sex offenses (except forcible rape and prostitution)	60,422	55,085	5,337	91.2	8.8	0.6	0.7	0.2
Drug abuse violations	1,305,191	1,062,777	242,414	81.4	18.6	12.2	13.2	8.9
Gambling	8,067	7,163	904	88.8	11.2	0.1	0.1	*
Offenses against the family and children	87,889	65,557	22,332	74.6	25.4	0.8	0.8	0.8
Driving under the influence	1,112,384	860,689	251,695	77.4	22.6	10.4	10.7	9.3
Liquor laws	447,496	319,364	128,132	71.4	28.6	4.2	4.0	4.7
Drunkenness	471,727	393,586	78,141	83.4	16.6	4.4	4.9	2.9
Disorderly conduct	518,374	379,059	139,315	73.1	26.9	4.8	4.7	5.1
Vagrancy	26,380	20,725	5,655	78.6	21.4	0.2	0.3	0.2
All other offenses (except traffic)	2,946,277	2,249,656	696,621	76.4	23.6	27.4	28.0	25.7
Suspicion	1,517	1,093	424	72.1	27.9	*	*	*
Curfew and loitering law violations	89,733	62,229	27,504	69.3	30.7	0.8	0.8	1.0
Runaways	73,794	33,084	40,710	44.8	55.2	0.7	0.4	1.5

[1] Because of rounding, the percentages may not add to 100.0.

[2] Violent crimes are offenses of murder and non-negligent manslaughter, forcible rape, robbery, and aggravated assault. Property crimes are offenses of burglary, larceny-theft, motor vehicle theft, and arson.

* Less than one-tenth of 1 percent.

Table 23.2: Estimated percent of sentenced prisoners under state jurisdiction by offense and gender, year-end 2008

Offense		All inmates	Male	Female
	Total	100%	100%	100%
Violent		52.4%	53.8%	35.6%
	Murder [a]	12.9%	13%	11.8%
	Manslaughter	1%	1%	1.3%
	Rape	4.9%	5.3%	0.7%
	Other sexual assault	7.4%	7.8%	1.5%
	Robbery	13.6%	14%	8.7%
	Assault	9.9%	10.1%	8.5%
	Other violent	2.6%	2.6%	3.2%
Property		18.4%	17.7%	29%
	Burglary	9.1%	9.3%	6.6%
	Larceny	3.5%	3.2%	8.1%
	Motor vehicle theft	1.6%	1.6%	1.7%
	Fraud	2.4%	1.9%	10.2%
	Other property	1.8%	1.8%	2.3%
Drug		18.4%	17.8%	26.9%
Public-order [b]		9.2%	9.4%	7.2%
Other/unspecified [c]		1.3%	1.3%	1.4%

Note: Totals based on prisoners with a sentence of more than 1 year. Detail may not add to total due to rounding.

[a] Includes negligent manslaughter.

[b] Includes weapons, drunk driving, court offenses, commercialized vice, morals and decency offenses, liquor law violations, and other public-order offenses.

[c] Includes juvenile offenses and other unspecified offense categories.

Pre-reform

Early incarnations of the U.S. correctional system were focused almost exclusively on housing male offenders (Rafter 1985). Initially, women, men, and juveniles were housed together in these early prison facilities. Specifically, there was no separation by sex or age. This approach left women and juveniles, both girls and boys, vulnerable to violence at the hands of other inmates and prison officials (Young and Reviere 2006). These arrangements within the early prison system were seen as abysmal, especially concerning the influence that hardened male offenders would have on women and juveniles. It was argued that the prison system, as it existed, was no place for women and children (Young and Reviere 2006). Particularly for women, their presence within the mixed-sex prison facility was a threat to their perceived femininity that was far more threatening than the offenses they committed.

It was assumed that by separating women from male offenders, the women were more likely to be able to be reformed and thus their femininity restored. Thus, early prison activists began to implore officials within the correctional system and larger state governments to implement the relocation of female offenders from mixed-sex facilities to single-sex, women-only facilities (Young and Reviere 2006). After much debate, and in response to prison overcrowding, the first women-only prison facility in the United States opened in 1835 in New York State (Zedner 1995). Not only was this the first women-only prison facility, it became the first prison facility headed by a female matron when Eliza Farnham was put in charge of the facility. Under Farnham's leadership, the female prisoners in Mount Pleasant faced much better conditions than their male counterparts incarcerated at Sing-Sing. Unfortunately, Farnham's approach garnered much criticism, which led to her resignation and a swift deterioration in the conditions within Mount Pleasant, including increased overcrowding (Zedner 1995). Despite frequent rioting because of overcrowded conditions, Mount Pleasant Female Prison remained opened until 1865, when the state refused to authorize funds for its expansion (Young and Reviere 2006). Despite the closing of Mount Pleasant Female Prison, the reform efforts of early prison activists on "behalf" of female offenders were just beginning.

Reformatory Model

The failure of Mount Pleasant, due to lack of state funding, evidenced the need for a different approach to addressing the needs of female offenders, especially as they were perceived as women who had merely gone astray from their true role as "good" women. As such, Quaker reformers, led by Elizabeth Chase and others, campaigned for new methods to treat women prisoners (Young and Reviere 2006). Following the campaigning of these activists the first female reformatory for women offenders and girls opened in Indiana. The Indiana Reformatory for Women and Girls opened in 1873 and served as a model institution for rehabilitating female offenders and restoring them to the proper role within the patriarchal social arrangements of the United States. Further, this facility was unique in that it housed not only female adult offenders but also "wayward" girls, although, they were housed in separate wings of the prison (Young and Reviere 2006).

The central premise of the reformatory model of female correctional facilities was the restoration and rehabilitation of female offenders convicted of minor offenses (Rafter 1985; Young and Reviere 2006; Zedner 1995). Early reformers argued that female offenders were not "more depraved than men," as previously thought, but merely wayward (Zedner 1995). As such, these women not only violated the statutes of the jurisdictions from which they reside, but the tenets of womanhood on a societal level. Therefore, prison activists during this period of reform believed these women could be rehabilitated back to a life of feminine virtue through a regime of "feminine" activities such as sewing, cooking, and other household chores (Young and Reviere 2006).

Between the years 1870 and 1930, 20 reformatories were established for female offenders (Zedner 1995). These reformatories were organized using a number of cottages that formed a familial unit among the women living in them (Rafter, 1985; Young and Reviere 2006; Zedner 1995). These cottages reinforced the notion of women's lives within the domestic sphere. In a way, women in these early facilities were being retrained to a life of domesticity within a society organized around patriarchal control. In addition, some of the women were granted parole to work as domestic servants within homes; however, as Zedner states, if they did not perform adequately they were returned to the facility to finish their sentence (1995, 317).

The early reformatory model of prisons for women instituted a system of patriarchal control over women in very significant ways. Authorities within this system required that women conform to moral standards of femininity that (though the norm at the time) were rooted in gender oppression. As such, women were treated more harshly than men in that they were imprisoned for relatively minor offenses that were seen as a violation of the feminine mores of the time (Rafter 1985). Although the reform model had been replicated in many states across the United States, by the 1930s the reformatory approach to incarceration for women had died out (Rafter 1985; Young and Reviere 2006; Zedner 1995).

Custodial Institutional Model

As the Great Depression of the 1930s decimated the US economy, the reformatory model of imprisonment for women was fading away (Rafter 1985). State governments were ending funding for rehabilitation programs for women convicted of minor offenses and focused their efforts on housing women convicted of felonies. Previously, female offenders convicted of felonies were housed in separate wings in male prisons; but as prison authorities moved away from the reformatory model, female felons began to be transported to separate custodial institutions in the same facilities that were formerly used as reformatories (Rafter 1985). These former prison reformatories were transformed from private room, rehabilitation centers, to overcrowded cells within secure facilities set up to warehouse serious offenders. This model is still being utilized currently, although slightly altered, as more state and federal female prison facilities have opened across the United States.

The custodial institutional model of imprisonment for women represents a shift not only from the emphasis of reform for female offenders, but also the shift from the over-surveillance of femininity. Although patriarchal control over women is still present within the custodial institutional model, reformation through domestic activities is not the central approach used to "treat" female offenders.

IV. CONTEMPORARY INFLUENCES FOR FEMALE OFFENDERS AND INMATES

A review of the empirical data regarding gender differences in incarceration rates and the historical trends that have shifted over time in response to changes in the understanding of gender roles and crime brings us to a discussion of the contemporary issues that female inmates face.

The Influence of Patriarchal Control

Patriarchal control has been identified as a major construct that influences women's behavior and society's treatment of them. Defined as "a familiar-social, ideological, political system in which men—by force, direct pressure, or through ritual, tradition, law and language, customs, etiquette, education and the division of labor, determine what part women shall or shall not play, and in which the female is everywhere subsumed under the male" (Rich 1986). The notion of patriarchal control has particular relevance for understanding women's involvement in crime. There are several dimensions to this. At the most basic ideological level, women are expected to be obedient and compliant and to not violate social norms (Chodorow 1999; Rich 1986). Their involvement in law-breaking, more than any other norm-violating behavior, is therefore "out of order" in a patriarchal system that relies on rigidly defined gender roles. Men in power (and their representatives who occupy positions that monitor compliance with social norms, like police officers, religious leaders, social service workers) respond to women who violate the norms of obedience and compliance with a harshness that punishes *not only the violation* but the breach in ideological etiquette. This perspective helps to explain why women who commit crimes are treated more harshly than men who commit the same offenses. This harsh treatment can include excessive use of force during an arrest, being denied probation or having their charges elevated to include things like child endangerment, being sentenced to a facility that is far from their communities, or being housed in a correctional facility that does not include attention to the particular needs that incarcerated women face. Contrary to what might be expected, there is no evidence that the presence of more women in law enforcement and correctional institutions has helped this situation much. Indeed, scholars who study the gendered nature of policing, correctional policy, and judicial practices suggest that the issue is more one of policy and ideology that negatively affects women than of gendered employment patterns (Britton 2003; Price and Sokoloff 2003).

Patriarchal control can work in the other direction as well. Feminist scholars have argued that patriarchal social arrangements performs the function of ascribing gender roles to women that are based on virtues of piety, purity, submissiveness, and domesticity (Welter 1966). These roles are widely accepted and rigidly enforced, even though they sometimes manifest in subtle ways. In the case of women who are involved in illegal activity, research shows that gender expectations can lead to a kind of leniency toward women who commit crimes. This is especially the case for women who reflect identity characteristics that are consistent with the cult of womanhood (besides their illegal activity) (Steffensmeier, Kramer, and Streifel 1993; Williams 1999). This would mean that women who are passive when arrested, who commit crimes that could be understood to be related to caring for their children, or who appear more "like real women" are more likely to avoid the harsh treatment described above.

It bears mentioning that a considerable amount of research has been done to distinguish the factors that determine whether women evoke a more lenient or a harsher response from the criminal legal system. Much of the analysis seems to center on issues of race and class as key determinates, consistent with the theoretical paradigm of intersectionality. This theory points to the ways in which race, class, and gender have a compounding discriminatory effect on how women who commit crimes are treated by the criminal legal system (Crenshaw 1991). As such, poor communities of color, particularly black and Hispanic, have been dramatically impacted by the expansion of the criminal legal system and have been incarcerated in record amounts (Mauer 1999; Sudbury 2005; Western and Wildeman 2009).

Pathways to Incarceration for Female Offenders and Inmates

A second set of influences that deepen an understanding of the unique experiences of female offenders and inmates can be thought of as the pathways to incarceration that women take. A considerable body of feminist criminology has described the ways in which women's involvement in crime is related to patriarchal control through pathways (Britton 2003; Chesney-Lind and Pasko 2004; Faith 1993). This research points to three general patterns. First, as has been illustrated empirically, women are most likely to commit property and drug offenses, which subsequently lead to their incarceration. Second, female offenders are more likely to have a history of victimization, usually at the hands of a loved one, which has influenced her involvement in criminal activities. Lastly, women most frequently report having been using illicit drugs or alcohol at the time of arrest. These pathways do not line up precisely alongside the particular patterns of charges. Rather, this way of understanding the influences on women's patterns of crime is more nuanced, but still critical to the overall discussion of sentencing and corrections.

Property and drug offenses are the most prevalent reason that women are arrested and incarcerated in the United States; these offenses result in approximately two-thirds of all incarcerations for women (West and Sabol 2008). A closer look at the prevalence of women's involvement in the commission of property and drug offenses reveals an important relationship between drug addiction, economic marginalization, and what some researchers call "survival crimes" (Owen 1998).

The notion of property and drug crimes being linked to women's survival is predicated on the fact that women who have been arrested and subsequently incarcerated for property offenses are typically from the most economically marginalized communities in U.S. society (Chesney-Lind and Paskow 2004; Mauer 1999). Given the social and economic dislocation of the urban underclass and the vulnerable economic position of women from these communities, criminologists who articulate this argument have theorized that women turn to crime as a means to support themselves and their families with more frequency than men (Owen 1998). Indeed, the high concentration of property offenses among women reinforces the need for an understanding of the gender dynamics of how economic marginalization leads to crime—which must include attention to the structural arrangement that relegates women to a subordinated social status within the political economy of the United States.

With specific reference to drug crimes as a pathway, it must be noted that the increase in women arrested for and charged with drug offenses over the past three decades is related in part to the policy changes brought about by the War on Drugs (Parenti 2000). In particular, scholars point to several critical influences on the rising incarceration rate: the introduction of mandatory minimum sentences for sale, possession, and conspiracy; the powder cocaine versus crack cocaine sentencing disparities; and the severe limitations to judicial discretion (Dodge 2006; Young and Reviere 2006). Feminist criminologists have noted that the changes brought about by the War of Drugs impacted the lives of male and female offenders alike and the policies were framed as "gender-neutral"; however, women were disproportionately impacted by these changes, as they were more likely to be the low-level offenders who ended up caught up in drug-enforcement efforts aimed at arresting high-level drug manufacturers and suppliers. Sudbury (2002), Young and Reviere (2006), and Díaz-Cotto (2006) describe the experiences of women of color who have been arrested and convicted of drug offenses, not necessarily for their *own* drug usage, but being connected to intimate partners who were involved in the drug trade. Díaz-Cotto contends that the War on Drugs was an attempt to reestablish social order, but ended up targeting women and communities of color (2006). Through interviews with Latinas incarcerated in California, Díaz-Cotto demonstrates the effects of policies created out of the War on Drugs and "get-tough" rhetoric. The women in her study spoke of underlying themes of economic poverty and victimization, which seem to remain a common thread in the lives of women affected by incarceration, both inside and outside the criminal legal system. These researchers documented how policy changes implemented by the War on Drugs dramatically altered the criminal legal system's approach to dealing with drug offenses. Arguably, female drug offenders became an unintended casualty of these policies.

In sum, while the intent behind the War on Drugs was to punish and deter higher-level drug manufacturers and sellers, in reality, women were those who were most vulnerable to arrest policies and procedures (Young and Reviere 2006). Once caught, they faced charges of conspiracy and drug trafficking, in addition to possession, regardless of whether they were actively involved in sales. Women are more likely than their male counterparts to be unable (because they do not have any substantial information) or unwilling (due to the threat of violence) to provide any information to law enforcement authorities on the drug operation in exchange for a lighter sentence (Richie 1996; Young and Reviere 2006). As such, women caught up in the nation's War on Drugs are disproportionately more likely to end up serving a significantly longer sentence in U.S. correctional facilities than their male partners.

Another significant pathway to incarceration for women involves their history of victimization. Department of Justice researchers have documented that "over half of the women incarcerated in state prisons reported a history of physical and sexual abuse" (Greenfeld and Snell 1999). Criminology and feminist researchers are among the scholars who have shown a definitive link between women's incarceration and the history of victimization among female offenders and inmates (Chesney-Lind and Pasko 2004; DeHart 2008; Diaz-Cotto 2006; O'Brien 2001; Richie 1996, 2001).

The linkage between women's victimization and their pathways to incarceration can best be described as a culmination of a host of traumatic life events. When examining the life histories of female offenders and inmates, their incarceration has a seemingly inevitable quality.

Studies on the cumulative effects of victimization on female offenders and inmates reveals that victimization is not only a prevalent factor among the population, but the characteristics of their victimization vary tremendously across and among the women (DeHart 2008; Green, Miranda, Daroowalla, and Siddique 2005; McDaniels-Wilson and Belknap 2008; Richie 2000). In aggregate, these women's experiences with physical and sexual victimization reveals serious forms of sexual and physical abuse (those that can be legally defined as rape, sexual assault, and battery), usually beginning in childhood, committed by a loved one, and occurring in multiple forms at multiple times across the life course. In a recent study on the extent of sexual abuse among incarcerated women, over half of the participants reported some form of childhood sexual assault before their eighteenth birthday, usually committed by a family member. In addition, 70 percent of the women in this study reported abuse that can be classified as rape or serious forms of sexual assault. Most shockingly, many of these women had been victimized multiple times and by multiple offenders (McDaniels-Wilson and Belknap 2008).

An added layer to this discussion of the history of victimization of female offenders and inmates is that a woman's incarceration does not necessarily signal an end to her victimization. Feminist scholars have also pointed to the ways in which women have had to endure physical and sexual victimization within the correctional system (Davis 2003; Miller 1998; Morash and Schram 2002; Richie 1996). In an intense example of such behavior, Davis uses the narratives of female inmates to describe in detail how the everyday practices of strip searches and cavity searches constitute abuse for the women enduring the procedures. Davis contends that such practices "that verge on sexual assault" (2003, 63) are normalized within the interactions between prison officers and inmates.

Other instances of victimization of female offenders inside correctional facilities have been documented by organizations like Amnesty International (1999) and Human Rights Watch (1996). As these organizations have pointed out, in congruence with the contentions of other feminist scholars, women are particularly vulnerable to physical and sexual victimization while involved with the correctional system, and they are likely to be ignored or not taken seriously when attempting to access resources for help (Faith 1993). Although these examples may seem extreme or not the common experience of incarcerated women, the threat of victimization without recourse, combined with female offenders' extensive history of such occurrences, only furthers these women's vulnerability within correctional facilities and the criminal legal system as a whole.

The final aspect of the significant pathways to incarceration for female offenders involves their experiences with substance abuse and their subsequent addiction. A review of the literature suggests that the pattern of drug use for women is different from men (Dodge 2006; O'Brien 2001; Richie 1996, 2000; Young and Reviere 2006).

At the very basic level, there is research that indicates that there are biological mechanisms that make the effect of drugs and alcohol impact women differently, which is among the factors that are linked to women's faster progress toward dependence than men. While the onset of drug use is later for women than men, substance abuse appears to have a more rapid negative effect on women then men, including social isolation, family breakdown, and lack of ability to secure effective treatment. Drug use and excessive alcohol use for women are more likely to be used in response to victimization, when compared to reasons that men use mood-altering substances. Further, the rate of drug use occurring alongside mental health problems is higher for women. In particular, the occurrence of post-traumatic stress disorder (PTSD) and substance abuse is highly correlated for women.

The issue of drug use and its impact on women's involvement in illegal activity must also be discussed from the vantage point of patriarchal control of women insofar as social expectations seriously stigmatize women who are addicts. Both popular responses and policy initiatives take a harsh approach to women's substance abuse, most notably in the case of women who are pregnant and addicted to drugs or alcohol. For example, in *Killing the Black Body*, Roberts systematically illustrates harsh policy initiatives aimed at women who have given birth to opiate-exposed children (1997). These policies were disproportionately applied to incidences involving women of color and poor women. In particular, Roberts's work demonstrates the implications that arise when criminalizing women's addiction and legislating control over women's bodies in such a way that women are vulnerable to differential treatment by the criminal legal system and can be criminally prosecuted for a range of crimes that men cannot.

In sum, the pathways to incarceration for women are significantly influenced by factors that differ significantly from those of men, in part because of the patriarchal social arrangements described in the previous section. Women's economical marginalization, the changes in drug enforcement policies precipitated by the U.S. War on Drugs, women's history of victimization across the life course, and their experiences with the abuse of illegal and illicit substances must be understood in order to understand the factors that lead to women's incarceration. Any analysis of female offenders' pathways to incarceration is incomplete without the inclusion of these factors.

The Role of Relationships in the Lives of Female Offenders and Inmates

The third major issue that is pertinent to understanding the sentencing and corrections of incarcerated women is the role that relationships assume as influencing variables. Relationships—intimate and biological—play a significant role in the experiences of any person; however, for women who find themselves on one of the previously described pathways, there are particular relationship issues that emerge before, during, and after their arrest and incarceration that are salient.

Prior to women's arrest and subsequent incarceration, familial relationships have a paradoxical impact. Women feel drawn into illegal activity as a way to create intimacy (Richie 1996), as a way to provide material resources for her household (Owen 1998), as a way to protect other vulnerable family members from arrest (DeHart 2008), or as a way to avoid or minimize physical harm (DeHart 2008). Relationships may also provide a deterrent to involvement in illegal activity, as in the case of women who avoid or interrupt their illegal activity to protect their children (O'Brien 2001). In either case, relationships are described in the literature as having a profound effect on women's decision making regarding her involvement in illegal activity.

Considerable research has also been conducted that evaluates how relationships impact women while they are serving time in correctional facilities (Greer 2000; O'Brien 2001; Owen 1998). Here, it is important to consider relationships inside and outside the facility, those that are ruptured by arrest and detention and those that are created within the confines of a jail or prison. Inside prisons, the establishment of relationships is a central organizing features of an otherwise unstable and unpredictable life. Whether the relationships are platonic or intimate, ongoing or temporary, episodic or long term, women in prison describe the profound ways that forming close bonds with one another provides both material and emotional security (Owen 1998). Some limited research has also noted how these relationships can be manipulative, controlling, and dangerous, mirroring the volatility of relationships on the outside, where families and friends can either provide support or cause more chaos (Greer 2000). Complications like limitations on the nature and frequency of visits, distance between correctional facilities and home, and emotional and economic strain related to removal of an adult from a family unit are all important in shaping how relationships impact—positively and negatively—women who are in prison.

Although female offenders and inmates experience a range of relationships with individuals on the outside, one of the most significant relationships for an incarcerated woman is that with her children, especially during her imprisonment (Baunach 1988; Enos 2001). The relationships between incarcerated women and their children is a common theme throughout their interactions with the criminal legal system. Over 70 percent of the women incarcerated in the United States are mothers, and these women are more likely than male inmates to have lived with their children and to be the primary caregiver to their children prior to the incarceration (Glaze and Maruschak 2008). In fact, in the month prior to arrest and just before incarceration, 64.2 percent of women, compared to 47.9 percent of men, reported living with their children (Glaze and Maruschak 2008). These statistics illustrate another struggle that incarcerated women face in dealing with their lives behind bars. This struggles continues upon release, as formerly incarcerated women must deal with the task of reestablishing relationships with the family members they left behind at a much higher rate than men, who may not have played a central role in the care of their children.

While motherhood and, more specifically, the mothering of children distinguishes incarcerated mothers from the generic profile of incarcerated women *and* men, this relationship represents one of the most complicated for incarcerated women. Normative conceptualizations of motherhood involve a mother's continued presence within the lives of her children (Rich 1986). However, this is impossible for incarcerated women by virtue of their imprisonment. Normative conceptualizations of mothering solely do not involve the ability to biologically reproduce but involve taking a continual role in the lives of offspring, including the practices of caretaking, nurturing, and day-to-day work that go into child rearing. Family reunification, in particular reunification with *children*, is a central area of concern for many incarcerated women (Enos 2001; O'Brien 2001). Furthermore, scholars have illustrated the importance of maintaining mother-child contact during imprisonment as a way to facilitate the reunification process upon release (Snyder 2009). However, gendered expectations that women immediately will take up the role of mothering their children upon release are slightly impractical for incarcerated women. The mothering process has been disrupted, and this disruption sometimes lasts for years at a time.

In addition, reunification may not be in the best interest of the children or their mother, for numerous reasons. The reality of these women's lives prior to their incarceration further complicates their relationship with their children. As previously illustrated, the lives of incarcerated women are characterized by poverty, substance abuse, and victimization. These circumstances may serve as a barrier to their abilities to properly take care of their children, even prior to their incarceration. Upon their release, gendered expectations further complicate the relationship between incarcerated women and their children, given their disconnection from their children's lives during incarceration.

The relationships of women returning to the community following incarceration are best characterized as focused on the reestablishment of ties that may have been strained or severed during incarceration. Female offenders' need for connection and the maintenance of close relationships is a central theme in the lives of women transitioning from prison (O'Brien 2001). O'Brien characterizes women's reliance on relationships as both a source of empowerment, when nurturing growth, and one of abuse and exploitation (2001). For female offenders, relationships that nurture growth are those that not only are necessary to keep them from committing crimes, like the relationship with their family, but also relationships that provide social and emotional support, meeting their needs for connection and instilling a level of self-worth.

Reestablishing relationships following incarceration is an important but daunting task for women. Relationships have been complicated by activities prior to incarceration (including those that led to incarceration), which may have involved various levels of mistrust between female offenders, their loved ones, and even community members. Furthermore, many of the situations that placed them on the pathway to incarceration are still present for these women following incarceration. Their relationships prior to incarceration typically involved complex

levels of violence and illegal activities, especially in the interpersonal aspects of
their lives, and may remain as such following incarceration. In addition, formerly
incarcerated women are faced with the difficult task of navigating territory from
which they have been disconnected for at least months, but more likely years
(O'Brien 2001; Waterson 1996). All the while, these women are attempting to establish connections that may or may not have been positive and nourishing to their
well-being.

In sum, relationships serve an important role in the lives of female offenders
and inmates. These relationships are organized in a variety of roles prior, during,
and after incarceration. Relationships can function positively or negatively in the
lives of female offenders and inmates, especially in relation to fellow inmates, intimate partners, and their children. No matter the form their relationships take, one
thing is certain; relationships are a central aspect of the lives of female offenders
and inmates.

IV. The Necessity of Gender-Specificity in Addressing the Needs of Female Offenders and Inmates

Scholars, including criminal justice practitioners, have made numerous recommendations for addressing the needs of female offenders and inmates (Faith 1993; Green
et. al. 2005; O'Brien 2001; Richie and Freudenberg 2005; Young and Reviere 2006).
Despite the differences in approaches to their assessments of the needs of female
offenders and inmates and the recommendations brought forth from these assessments, the overall assertion is that an understanding of the gendered components
to women's experiences both inside and outside the correctional system must be
incorporated into any recommendations put forth. Female offenders and inmates
need programs and services that can address their unique needs, including (but not
limited to) physical and mental health (including substance abuse treatment), economic self-sufficiency, and the issues concerning their reentry and reintegration
into society following incarceration.

Physical and Mental Health

A vast majority of women entering correctional facilities suffer a variety of significant health issues that arise from poverty, substance abuse, and victimization (Acoca
1998; Belknap 2001; Young and Reviere 2006). Their needs differ from those of men
in very specific ways (Belknap 2001); they are more likely to enter the correctional
system with a host of mental and physical ailments, including (but not limited to)

depression, PTSD, and undiagnosed illnesses like breast cancer and reproductive health issues (Belknap 2001; Green et al. 2005; Shearer 2003).

Reproductive health needs are particularly salient. Incarcerated women who have a substance abuse problem are more likely to have engaged in high-risk behaviors, such as intravenous drug use, prostitution, and unprotected sex with multiple partners, prior to incarceration. These activities put them at risk for additional health problems, including sexually transmitted diseases. If left untreated—a common occurrence among this population—sexually transmitted diseases can develop into other serious health issues, such as pelvic inflammatory disease, cervical cancer, infertility, and HIV (Shearer 2003). Pregnancy is another significant physical health care issue that requires a gender-specific approach. National data suggests that as many as 25 percent of women are pregnant at the time of their arrest (Kubiak, Kasiborski, and Schmittel 2010). In some unusual instances, programs have been designed to respond to the particular needs that this population of women brings, including prison nurseries, extended family visits, and additional support for women who must turn their children over to the foster care system because of their incarceration. These are, by far, the exception. It is more common to see the wide range of policy and practical issues that are highly problematic for women, including shackling during pregnancy, improper prenatal and postnatal care, and lack of care for opiate-exposed infants, and so on. The implications of these practices are clear—correctional facilities need a better understanding of the unique health care needs of the women under their jurisdiction.

Mental health care and treatment of female offenders and inmates necessitate a gender-specific approach as well, especially in the areas of substance abuse, trauma, and victimization. Currently, many correctional facilities offer some form of substance abuse education or treatment and counseling programs to address the mental health needs of their inmates. However, these programs were based on meeting the needs of male offenders (Shearer 2003). These programs do not address the underlying issues of women's lives that lead to their substance abuse, which tend to be at the root of the problems. In particular, these programs are ill equipped to address the prevalence of trauma and physical, sexual, and emotional victimization among female inmates as they relate to women's usage of illegal and illicit substances (Green et al. 2005; Shearer 2003). To be most effective, correctional facilities must offer services that focus on the gendered experiences of their female inmates, especially in regard to their exposure to trauma and victimization.

Lastly, correctional facilities must utilize a gender-specific model in providing mental health care, specifically counseling, to address the concerns surrounding women's relationships. As previously noted, relationships are a central feature of women's lives both inside and outside the correctional facility. As such, the role that relationships play in women's lives, especially with intimate partners and their children, can positively and negatively affect the psychological well-being of female inmates. If women have been involved in relationships that are abusive, as is quite common among female inmates, it is imperative that mental health services are ready to address these needs using methods that are not designed for men, who are typically the perpetrators of the violence against women. When providing mental health services to female inmates, it is imperative that the correctional authorities understand the significance that women's relationships play in their lives, if they are serious about addressing these women's mental health needs.

Economic Self-sufficiency

Given the profile of incarcerated women and their pathways to crime, economic self-sufficiency is a vital component to success following incarceration[2] (Richie and Freudenberg 2005; Young and Reviere 2006). A gender-specific approach to economic self-sufficiency must comprehensively address the pressure to support one's family despite the lack of training and skills among female inmates, which inhibits their ability to obtain regular and full-time employment. In addition, gender-specific models to economic self-sufficiency must be used in addressing the unmet educational and housing needs of formerly incarcerated women (Richie and Freudenberg 2005), including an exploration of the connections between the stigmatization of incarceration and subsequent poverty among women. A gendered analysis of policy reform is also warranted. As Petersilia (2000) discussed, formerly incarcerated individuals are barred from specific types of jobs, ranging from such professions as law, dentistry, nursing, and real estate, to other types of employment, such as nail technicians, home attendants, and child care providers—positions that more typically match the skill level of formerly incarcerated women.

Lastly, numerous scholars, researchers, and practitioners have reiterated the importance of safe and adequate housing for women following incarceration (O'Brien 2001; Richie and Freudenberg 2005; Young and Reviere 2006). However, the process of finding and securing housing is complicated by policies that restrict offenders with certain types of convictions from residing there. For example, drug offenders are not eligible to live in federal low-income housing (Young and Reviere 2006). Policies such as these have tremendous impact on the lives of formerly incarcerated women in that this type of housing is usually all that is available to them following incarceration. Furthermore, these restrictions not only affect them, but also their children who may have been or are in the process of being returned to their care. A gender-specific model is necessary to counter policies that prohibit or restrict the availability and retention of housing to formerly incarcerated women, a majority of whom are mothers to minor children.

Prisoner Reentry and Reintegration

A related aspect to gender-specificity in addressing the needs of economic self-sufficiency for female offenders and inmates involves prisoner reentry and reintegration. Prisoner reentry and reintegration represent a growing area of research and innovation. It is imperative that gender-specific models be employed to address the needs of female offenders and inmates to decrease the chance of returning to prison. Feminist criminologists who call for gender-specific approaches to prisoner reentry illuminate the differential effects of gender oppression on women. Bloom, Owen, and Covington (2005) provide one of the most comprehensive models for "gender responsive" strategies for female offenders after prison. Bloom et al. define the term "gender responsive" as creating an environment in the criminal legal system that acknowledges the realities of women's lives, their pathways to offending, and the relationships that construct their lives. Numerous researchers have shown that women offenders' needs are different from those of men as a result of the disproportionate victimization that women experience, their history of substance abuse and trauma, their responsibilities for child rearing, and various health and well-being factors (Morash, Bynum, and Koons 1998; O'Brien 2001; Richie 2001; Shearer 2003). According to Bloom et al. (2005), women need a safe and nurturing treatment environment that reflects mutual respect, empathy, and compassion following incarceration. Given the prevalence of victimization and substance abuse, which is usually an extension of their involvement in illegal activities, the most effective reentry models incorporate comprehensive and holistic methods for dealing with these specific issues in women's lives.

Current prisoner reentry initiatives tend to focus on employment, housing, and health and well-being services for those returning to the community following incarceration, without attention to women's unique needs. Research has shown that a closer match between women's needs and the initiatives serving these purposes are vital to the reestablishment of community ties and reducing recidivism among formerly incarcerated women (O'Brien 2001; Travis and Waul 2003; Petersilia 2004).

V. Conclusion

Women's social location leaves them vulnerable to differential treatment inside and outside the correctional system because of societal influences of male privilege and patriarchal control in relation to their lives within U.S. society. Any analysis of female offenders and inmates is incomplete without an examination of the role that gender plays in women's involvement in crime. Attention must be paid to the differences in the pathways to incarceration for women, as well as the centrality of their relationships in their lives, in order to adequately address their needs, which differ significantly from those of men. In order for the correctional system to adequately address the needs of female offenders, they must utilize a gender-specific model that centralizes an understanding of women's involvement in criminal activities, the effects of such activities on their lives, and how reentry and reintegration for female offenders and inmates is experienced differentially by these women.

NOTES

1. This is the most recent data available at time of writing.
2. Other components of a gender-specific model of prisoner reentry and reintegration are discussed in the following section.

REFERENCES

Acker, J. 1990. "Hierarchies, Jobs, Bodies: A Theory of Gendered Organizations." *Gender and Society* 4(2): 139–158.

Acoca, L. 1998. "Defusing the Time Bomb: Understanding and Meeting the Growing Health Care Needs of Incarcerated Women in America." *Crime & Delinquency* 44(1): 49–69.

Adler, F. 1975. *Sisters in Crime: The Rise of the New Female Criminal.* New York: McGraw-Hill.

Amnesty International. 1999. *"Not Part of My Sentence": Violations of the Human Rights of Women in Custody.* London: Amnesty International Publications.

Baunach, P. J. 1988. *Mothers in Prison.* New Brunswick, NJ: Transaction.

Belknap, J. 2001. *The Invisible Woman: Gender, Crime, and Justice.* 2nd ed. Belmont, CA: Wadsworth.

Bloom, B., B. Owen, and S. Covington. 2005. *Gender Responsive Strategies for Women Offenders [Bulletin].* Washington, DC: National Institute of Corrections (NIC accession no. 020418).

Britton, D. M. 2000. "Feminism in Criminology: Engendering the Outlaw." *The Annals of the American Academy of Political and Social Science* 571: 57–76.

Britton, D. M. 2003. *At Work in the Iron Cage: The Prison as Gendered Organization.* New York: New York University Press.

Chesney-Lind, M. 1998. "The Forgotten Offender, Women in Prison: From Partial Justice to Vengeful Equity." *Corrections Today* 60(7): 66–73.

Chesney-Lind, M., and L. Pasko. 2004. *The Female Offender: Girls, Women, and Crime.* 2nd ed. Thousand Oaks, CA: Sage Publishers.

Chodorow, N. 1999. *The Reproduction of Mothering.* 2nd ed. Berkeley: University of California Press.

Crenshaw, K. 1991. "Mapping the Margins: Intersectionality, Identity Politics, and Violence Against Women of Color." *Stanford Law Review* 43(6): 1241–1299.

Daly, K., and M. Chesney-Lind. 1988. "Feminism and Criminology." *Justice Quarterly* 5(4): 497–538.

Davis, A.Y. 2003. *Are Prison's Obsolete?* New York: Seven Stories Press.

DeHart, D. D. 2008. "Pathways to Prison: Impact of Victimization in the Lives of Incarcerated Women." *Violence Against Women* 14(12): 1362–1381.

Díaz-Cotto, J. 2006. *Chicana Lives and Criminal Justice.* Austin: University of Texas Press.

Dodge, L. M. 2006. *Whores and Thieves of the Worst Kind: A Study of Women, Crime, and Prisons, 1835–2000.* DeKalb: Northern Illinois University Press.

Enos, S. 2001. *Mothering from the Inside: Parenting in a Women's Prison.* New York: State University of New York Press.

Faith, K. 1993. *Unruly Women: The Politics of Confinement and Resistance.* Vancouver: Press Gang Publishers.

Flavin, J. 2001. "Feminism for the Mainstream Criminologist: An Invitation." *Journal of Crime and Justice* 29: 271–285.

Glaze, L., and T. Bonczar. 2008. *Probation and Parole in the United States, 2007 Statistical Tables.* Washington, DC: Bureau of Justice Statistics.

Glaze, L., and L. Maruschak. 2008. *Parents in Prison and Their Minor Children.* Washington, DC: Bureau of Justice Statistics.

Green, B. L., J. Miranda, A. Daroowalla, and J. Siddique. 2005. "Trauma Exposure, Mental Health Functioning, and Program Needs of Women in Jail." *Crime & Delinquency* 51(1): 133–151.

Greenfeld, L., and T. Snell. 1999. *Women Offenders.* Washington, DC: Bureau of Justice Statistics.

Greer, K. R. 2000. "The Changing Nature of Interpersonal Relationships in a Women's Prison." *The Prison Journal* 80(4): 442–468.

Harding, S. 1980. "The Norms of Social Inquiry and Masculine Experience." *PSA: Proceedings of the Biennial Meeting of the Philosophy of Science Association*, Vol. 2: Symposia and Invited Papers, 305–324.

Hooks, b. 1984. *Feminist Theory: From Margin to Center.* Boston: South End Press.

Human Rights Watch Women's Rights Project. 1996. *All Too Familiar: Sexual Abuse of Women in U.S. State Prisons.* New York: Human Rights Watch.

Stephan, James J., and Jennifer C. Karberg. 2003. *Census of State and Federal Correctional Facilities, 2000.* U.S. Department of Justice: Bureau of Justice Statistics (NCJ 198272).

Kubiak, S. P., N. Kasiborski, and E. Schmittel. 2010. "Assessing Long-Term Outcomes of an Intervention Designed for Pregnant Incarcerated Women." *Research on Social Work Practice* 20(5): 528–535.

Mauer, M. 1999. *Race to Incarcerate.* New York: New Press.

Mauer, M., and M. Chesney-Lind, eds. 2002. *Invisible Punishment: The Collateral Consequences of Mass Imprisonment.* New York: New Press.

McDaniels-Wilson, C., and J. Belknap. 2008. "The Extensive Sexual Violation and Sexual Abuse Histories of Incarcerated Women." *Violence Against Women* 14(10): 1090–1127.

Miller, S. L., ed. 1998. *Crime Control and Women: Feminist Implications of Criminal Justice Policy.* Thousand Oaks, CA: Sage Publications.

Morash, M., T. Bynum, and B. Koons. 1998. *Women Offenders: Programming Needs and Promising Approaches.* Washington, DC: National Institute of Justice.

Morash, M., and P. Schram. 2002. *The Prison Experience: Special Issues of Women in Prison.* Prospect Heights, IL: Waveland Press.

Naffine, N. 1987. *Female Crime: The Construction of Women in Criminology.* Boston: Allen & Unwin.

O'Brien, P. 2001. *Making It in the "Free World": Women in Transition from Prison.* Albany: State University of New York Press.

Owen, B. 1998. *In the Mix: Struggle and Survival in a Women's Prison.* New York: State University of New York Press.

Parenti, C. 2000. *Lockdown America: Police and Prisons in the Age of Crisis.* New York: Verso.

Petersilia, J. 2000. "When Prisoners Return to the Community: Political, Economic, and Social Consequences." *Research in Brief: Issues for the Twenty-first Century.* Papers from the Executive Sessions on Sentencing and Corrections. Washington, DC: Office of Justice Programs, National Institute of Justice (NCJ 184253).

Petersilia, J. 2003 *When Prisoners Come Home: Parole and Prisoner Reentry*. New York: Oxford University Press.

Petersilia, J. 2004. "What Works in Prisoner Reentry? Reviewing and Questioning the Evidence." *Federal Probation* 68(2): 4–8.

Price, B. R., and N. Sokoloff, eds. 2003. *The Criminal Justice System and Women: Offenders, Prisoners, Victims, and Workers*. 3rd ed. New York: McGraw-Hill.

Rafter, N. H. 1985. "Gender, Prisons, and Prison History." *Social Science History* 9(3): 233–247.

Rich, A. 1986. *Of Woman Born: Motherhood as Experience and Institution*. New York: Norton.

Richie, B. E. 1996. *Compelled to Crime: The Gender Entrapment of Battered Black Women*. New York: Routledge.

Richie, B. E. 2000. "Exploring the Link Between Violence Against Women and Women's Involvement in Illegal Activity." Research on Women and Girls in The Justice System. NIJ Research Forum 3.

Richie, B. E. 2001. "Challenges Incarcerated Women Face as They Return to Their Communities: Findings from Life History Interviews." *Crime and Delinquency* 47(3): 368–389.

Richie, B. E., and N. Freudenberg. 2005. "Coming Home from Jail: The Social and Health Consequences of Reentry from Jail for Incarcerated Women and Male Adolescents, Their Families and Communities." *American Journal of Public Health* 95(10): 1725–1736.

Richie, B. E. 2007. "Women and Drug Use." *Women & Criminal Justice* 17(2): 137–143.

Roberts, D. E. 1995. "Motherhood and Crime." *Social Texts* 42: 99–123.

Roberts, D. E. 1997. *Killing the Black Body: Race, Reproduction, and the Meaning of Liberty*. New York: Pantheon Books.

Sabol, W., H. West, and M. Cooper. 2009. *Prisoners in 2008*. Washington, DC: Bureau of Justice Statistics.

Sabol, W., and H. West. 2010. *Prisoners in 2009*. Washington, DC: Bureau of Justice Statistics.

Shearer, R. 2003. "Identifying the Special Needs of Female Offenders." *Federal Probation* 67(1): 46–51.

Simon, R .J. 1975. *Women and Crime*. Lexington, MA: Lexington Books.

Simpson, S. S. 1989. "Feminist Theory, Crime, and Justice." *Criminology* 27(4): 605–631.

Snyder, Z. K. 2009. "Keeping Families Together: The Importance of Maintaining Mother-Child Contact for Incarcerated Women." *Women & Criminal Justice* 19(1): 37–59.

Steffensmeier, D., J. Kramer, and C. Streifel. 1993. "Gender and Imprisonment Decisions." *Criminology* 31: 411–443.

Sudbury, J. 2002. "Celling Black Bodies: Black Women in the Global Prison Industrial Complex." *Feminist Review* 70: 57–74.

Sudbury, J., ed. 2005. *Global Lockdown: Race, Gender, and the Prison-Industrial Complex*. New York: Routledge.

Travis, J. 2005. *But They All Come Back: Facing the Challenges of Prisoner Reentry*. Washington, DC: Urban Institute Press.

Travis, J. and M. Waul, eds. 2003. *Prisoners Once Removed: The Impact of Incarceration and Reentry on Children, Families, and Communities*. Washington, DC: Urban Institute Press.

U.S. Department of Justice. 2010. *Crime in the United States 2009: Uniform Crime Reports*. Washington, DC: Federal Bureau of Investigation, U.S. Government Printing Office.

Waterson, K. 1996. *Women in Prison: Inside the Concrete Womb*, rev. ed. Boston: Northeastern University Press.

Welter, B. 1966. "The Cult of True Womanhood: 1820–1860." *American Quarterly* 18(2): 151–174.

West, H. 2010. *Prison Inmates at Midyear 2009—Statistical Tables.* Washington, DC: Bureau of Justice Statistics.

West, H., and W. Sabol. 2008. *Prisoners in 2007.* Washington, DC: Bureau of Justice Statistics.

Western, B., and C. Wildeman. 2009. "The Black Family and Mass Incarceration." *The Annals of the American Academy of Political and Social Science* 621: 221–242.

Williams, M. R. 1999. "Gender and Sentencing: An Analysis of Indicators." *Criminal Justice Policy Review* 10(4): 471–490.

Young, V. D., and R. Reviere. 2006. *Women Behind Bars: Gender and Race in U.S. Prison.* Boulder, CO: Lynne Rienner Publishers.

Zedner, L. 1995. "Wayward Sisters: The Prison for Women." In *The Oxford History of The Prison: The Practice of Punishment in Western Society*, eds. N. Morris and D. J. Rothman. New York: Oxford University Press.

......

CHAPTER 24

THE PSYCHOLOGICAL
EFFECTS OF IMPRISONMENT

......

CRAIG HANEY

THIS chapter reviews the various psychological effects of imprisonment. At an individual level, prison effects can be broadly conceived as the multiple ways in which persons are changed or affected as a result of their incarceration. During the last half of the nineteenth century and most of the twentieth—a period widely regarded as the "age of rehabilitation"—many people believed that prisons could be structured to produce effects that were largely positive or "reformative" in nature. Indeed, imprisonment itself was justified during these years largely because of its supposed ability to reduce recidivism—in essence, to change prisoners in beneficial ways that would decrease their likelihood of committing crimes in the future.

Several developments led to a shift in this particular focus on prison effects. For one, systematic empirical research that addressed whether and how well rehabilitation programs actually reduced recidivism led to increased skepticism about their utility. Although the simplistic characterization that "nothing works" misrepresented the data on prison programming outcomes, the effectiveness of rehabilitation proved more complicated and mixed than many had thought. In addition, increased sociological and psychological sophistication about the effects of "total institutions" such as prisons on the human psyche led to a more critical analysis of the consequences of imprisonment. As a result, at least since the abandonment of rehabilitation as the primary goal of imprisonment in the mid-1970s, most scholarly attention has been focused on the negative or potentially harmful effects of prison confinement, rather than its expected benefits.

As such, prison effects can be conceptualized in two broad, inter-related ways. The first addresses the direct, hurtful, and potentially damaging effects of the pains of imprisonment—the ways in which the deprivations, indignities, and traumas of prison life produce adverse reactions and negative psychological consequences in the prisoners exposed to them. The second kind of prison effect includes the sometimes subtle psychological changes that prisoners undergo in order to adapt to (and survive) the rigors of prison life. This latter kind of prison effect represents a specialized form of socialization—psychological accommodations that occur when people strive to adhere to the formal and informal demands of the social structures and settings in which they live. Called "institutionalization" when it occurs in total institutional settings in general, it has been termed "prisonization" when it takes place in correctional institutions.

METHODOLOGICAL CAVEATS
CONCERNING PRISON EFFECTS

Several issues compromise the systematic, empirical study of prison effects. They are worth acknowledging at some length because they are often overlooked or given short shrift in prison research. The first issue is largely conceptual. Put simply, not all "prisons" are created equal. Notwithstanding the tendency among researchers to talk about prison as if it were some sort of Weberian ideal type, conditions of confinement vary widely along critical dimensions that can render one prison fundamentally different from—and more or less harmful than—another. One of the important lessons of the last several decades of research in social psychology is the extent to which specific aspects of a context or situation can significantly determine its impact or effect on the actors within it. This same insight applies to prisons. Thus, the effects of confinement in, say, a relatively well-run, program-oriented minimum security prison cannot automatically be generalized to those suffered in a dangerously overcrowded or brutally mismanaged maximum security prison. Scholars, researchers, and policy makers who refer to very different kinds of facilities—either to "overcrowded prisons," or "solitary confinement," or to "prisons" in general—as though the conditions that they denote are the same, when they are not, may blur critically important distinctions.[1] This may result in invalid generalizations about prison effects (or the lack thereof), and also may lead scholars to conclude that different research results or outcomes are somehow "inconsistent" when, in fact, they can be explained by the specific conditions to which they pertain.

The second caveat is that the interpersonal complexities of prison life frequently operate to compromise and limit the measurement of prison effects. For example, many prison researchers have observed that a number of "men in prison have a need to present themselves as 'super-masculine' and do not wish to portray themselves as having been vulnerable or potentially remaining so within the prison setting" (Goff et al. 2004, 156). Many prisoners have learned to be wary of persons asking probing, personal questions, are reluctant to share intimate and revealing information about themselves, and rarely have an incentive to publicly admit that they are suffering. Thus, developing rapport and interpersonal trust—especially between prisoners and professional outsiders—is difficult. The resulting lack of candor from prisoners about their personal vulnerabilities and reactions to the pains of imprisonment may lead to an underestimate of prison effects.

Third, the experience of "suffering" is inherently subjective, often psychologically complex, and difficult to precisely measure. Reliance on highly structured, quantitative indices of the pains of imprisonment may fail to capture the phenomenon. Commonly used measures of pain, harm, or impaired functioning that have been standardized in other contexts or with other populations may not be appropriate for prison, or for prisoners whose background and current experiences may be distinctive or unique. Thus:

> We still lack research instruments that can quantify the psychological effects of entering a world in which survival may depend on achieving total emotional control, constantly maintaining a high level of suspicion and hypervigilance, and striving for mastery over the intricacies of interpersonal deceit. Similarly, no standardized tests that I know can measure the precise consequences of being surrounded by models of aggressive domination, or calibrate the identity transformations that take place within many prisoners who are treated as categorically untrustworthy, worthless, and unpredictably and inexplicably violent. But that does not mean that these core aspects of the prison experience fail to produce pain or harm or significant psychological consequences that can be accurately described and thoughtfully analyzed. (Haney 2006a, 167)

In a related way, most indices of measurable harm or distress are dependent on self-report. Obviously, prisoners must be consciously pained or in distress over a symptom in order to complain about or report it; the greater their conscious awareness, the higher the likelihood that the frequency and extent of the negative effects will be accurately measured. However, in the course of adjusting and adapting to painful and distressing conditions of confinement, many prisoners necessarily strive to essentially "get used to it," adapting and accommodating in ways that they hope will make their day-to-day misery seem more manageable—what I will describe below as one aspect of the process of "prisonization." In any event, a lack of conscious awareness or the inability to verbally express the nature of the potentially harmful changes that are underway should not be mistaken for the absence of a prison effect.

Finally, precisely because many of the most powerful and potentially problematic prison effects include the adaptations that prisoners make to the extraordinary nature of prison itself, the full extent of the changes that they have undergone may not become completely apparent until *after* their release—that is, when they have left the environment to which they have more or less adjusted and subsequently try to reintegrate back into free society. Psychological changes and accommodations undertaken to reduce suffering or discomfort inside prison may not register as prison effects, especially for prisoners who appear to be otherwise well adjusted to their conditions of confinement. However, these changes may and often do become highly dysfunctional (even disabling) in the world outside prison. They surely represent prison effects, but they are difficult to measure during confinement.

THE DIRECT EFFECTS OF THE PAINS
OF IMPRISONMENT

The pains of imprisonment—including severe material deprivations, highly re-stricted movement and liberty, lack of meaningful activity, a nearly total absence of personal privacy, high levels of interpersonal uncertainty, danger, and fear—repre-sent powerful psychological stressors that can adversely impact a prisoner's emo-tional well-being. This is especially true if those stressors are experienced in extreme degrees over long periods of time. Indeed, as Hans Toch and Kenneth Adams have acknowledged, the "dictum that prisons are stressful cannot be overestimated," (Toch and Adams 2002, 230). They and others have written about patterns of "acting out" and other forms of "maladaptive" behavior engaged in by prisoners attempting to cope with the stress to which they are subjected (e.g., Haney, 2006a).

Early studies of the effects of exposure to extreme forms of environmental stress in general concluded that it "may result in permanent psychologic disability" and even that "subjection to prolonged, extreme stress results in the development of 'neurotic' symptoms in virtually every person exposed to it . . . " (Hocking 1970, 23). Although no one would argue that imprisonment is *uniformly* devastating or *inevi-tably* damaging, it is true that "particular vulnerabilities and inabilities to cope and adapt can come to the fore in the prison setting, [and] the behavior patterns and attitudes that emerge can take many forms, from deepening social and emotional withdrawal to extremes of aggression and violence" (Porporino 1990, 36). Indeed, even one review of prison effects that is often cited for the proposition that impris-onment is not necessarily as "cruel and unusual" as many scholars and researchers have contended (Bonta and Gendreau 1990) nonetheless reported a number of neg-ative prison effects. Thus, it cited empirical evidence of many of the measurable adverse consequences of incarceration, including symptoms of psychological dis-tress (such as elevated blood pressure, anxiety, depression, self-mutilation, and sui-cide), and a range of other problematic reactions (such as increased hostility, introversion, and other interpersonal problems).

In more recent research, Alison Liebling and her colleagues found that the mea-sured levels of distress in the prisons they studied were "extraordinarily high" (Liebling, et al. 2005, 216). In fact, in 11 of the 12 facilities they studied, the mean dis-tress score recorded among prisoners was above the threshold that ordinarily triggers an inquiry into whether a patient is suffering from a treatable emotional or psycho-logical illness. Furthermore, the levels of distress varied in predictable ways, in part as a function of the quality of life in the prison environment (or the prisoners' expe-rience of it). Thus, prisons whose "moral performance" was poor—ones rated low on social climate and other measures—also produced higher levels of distress among prisoners. Similar findings were reported by Claudia Kesterman (2005), in an analysis of the correlates of depressive symptoms among male prisoners in the correctional systems of several Baltic countries. Kesterman and her colleagues found that poor relations with staff and other prisoners (i.e., perceived rejection), the presence of environmental stress factors, the experience of victimization, the lack of respect by staff, and the absence of home and/or work release at the facility were all significant predictors of whether prisoners manifested depression.

Prison stress affects prisoners in different ways and at different stages of their prison careers. For some prisoners, experience the initial period of incarceration is the most difficult. This first stage of confinement can be so overwhelming that it precipitates acute psychiatric symptoms for the first time, or exacerbates preexisting disorders (e.g., Gibbs 1982). Other prisoners may move through the initial phases of incarceration relatively intact, only to find themselves worn down by the constant psychological assault and stress of confinement. These prisoners suffer a range of psychological problems in later stages of incarceration. Indeed, Taylor wrote that the long-term prisoner "shows a flatness of response which resembles slow, automatic behavior of a very limited kind, and he is humorless and lethargic" (Taylor 1961, 373). Jose-Kampfner has analogized the plight of long-term women prisoners to that of persons who are terminally ill, whose experience of this "existential death is unfeeling, being cut off from the outside . . . (and who) adopt this attitude because it helps them cope" (Jose-Kampfner 1990, 123; see also Rubenstein 1982).

Certain forms of prison stress can take a more immediate psychological toll. Post-traumatic stress disorder (PTSD) is a diagnosis that is applied to a set of inter-related, trauma-based symptoms, including depression, emotional numbing, anxiety, isolation, and hypervigilance.[2] Reviews of the literature on the prevalence of PTSD in prisoner populations suggest that it could occur as much as ten times more often than in the general population (Goff et al. 2004, 155). Another review reported that approximately 21 percent of male prisoners, 48 percent of female prisoners, and between 24–65 percent of male juvenile inmates suffered from the disorder, a much higher prevalence rate than in the population at large (Heckman, Cropsey, and Olds-Davis 2007, 47; see also Gibson et al. 1999 and Zlotnick 1997).

Psychiatrist Judith Herman has proposed an expanded diagnostic category that may more accurately describe the traumatic consequences of certain kinds of prison experiences. Thus, what she termed "complex PTSD" is brought about by "prolonged, repeated trauma or the profound deformations of personality that occur in captivity" (Herman 1992a, 118). Unlike classic PTSD—which arises from relatively circumscribed traumatic events—complex PTSD derives from a more chronic kind of exposure that is more closely analogous to the experience of imprisonment. Complex PTSD can result in protracted depression, apathy, and the development of a profound sense of hopelessness. It represents the long-term psychological cost of adapting to an oppressive situation from which there is no escape and little opportunity to resist: "The humiliated rage of the imprisoned person also adds to the depressive burden . . . During captivity, the prisoner can not express anger at the perpetrator; to do so would jeopardize survival" (Herman 1992b, 382).

Of course, the unique and potent stresses of imprisonment are likely to interact with and amplify whatever preexisting vulnerabilities prisoners may bring into the prison setting. I made the point at the outset of this chapter that not all prisons are equally painful, or capable of inflicting harm. Prisoners also vary in terms of their backgrounds and vulnerabilities, how they experience or cope with the same environments or events and, as a result, how harmful and disabling the same prison experience may be for them (e.g., Hemmens and Marquart 1999; Gullone et al. 2000). In fact, despite a common stereotype that "hardened" prisoners are especially resilient to stress and impervious to harsh treatment, there is reason to believe that the reverse may be true, at least for a significant percentage of them. Many prisoners come from social and economically marginalized groups and have experienced trauma and other adverse childhood and adolescent experiences that may have made them more rather than less vulnerable to psychological stressors, and less able than others (with less problematic backgrounds) to cope effectively with the chronic strains of prison life (e.g., Gibson et al. 1999; Greene, Haney, and Hurtado 2000; McClellan et al. 1997; Mullings et al. 2004; Zlotnick 1997).

Moreover, some of these pre-prison events—particularly, prior exposure to trauma and to violence—are related to higher rates of victimization inside prison in ways that can compound their effects over time. That is, prison victimization, in turn, can lead to higher levels of distress in prison and symptoms of post-traumatic stress disorder and depression following release. For example, one study of prison distress focused on the degree to which having been victimized in prison—specifically, been subjected to "theft, con games and scams, robbery, destruction of property, assault, and serious threats of bodily injury" (Hochstetler et al. 2004, 444)—led to depression and symptoms of post-traumatic stress. The researchers found that, indeed, "prison victimization contributes to the occurrence of depressive and [post-traumatic stress] symptoms" (448). However, they also found that a history of having been exposed to trauma and violence *prior* to coming to prison helped to explain the prisoners' level of prison distress. They concluded that the experience of being victimized in prison *added* to the pains of the preexisting events to which the prisoner had been exposed and—especially because of the potential for post-traumatic stress symptoms to prove disabling upon release—recommended that "[r]ehabilitative efforts should help inmates recover from trauma occurring inside and outside prison" (452).

In addition, especially over the last several decades, during which prisons have become the default placement for the mentally ill, higher percentages of prisoners appear to suffer from a range of serious, diagnosable psychological disorders, including clinical depression and psychosis as well as PTSD (e.g., Gunn 1978; Harding and Zimmerman 1989; Kupers 1999). The causal origins of these disorders cannot always be determined—some are undoubtedly preexisting conditions, some exacerbated by the pain and stress of incarceration, and others may originate in the psychological deprivation, turmoil, and trauma that the prison experience imposes. In any event, research conducted over the last several decades indicates that somewhere between 12–24 percent of prisoners in the United States now suffer from *serious* mental disorders (for a summary of these estimates, see Haney 2006a, 250; see also Fazel and Danesh 2002). Although this translates into literally hundreds of thousands of prisoners who should be receiving treatment for their psychological problems, no more than a fraction of that number are. Even fewer prisoners receive the kind of sustained and effective counseling and psychotherapy that they appear to need (e.g., Kupers 1996, 1999).

In extreme cases, some prisoners react to the psychic stresses of imprisonment by taking their own lives. Various studies have documented much higher rates of suicide among prisoners as compared to the general population (e.g., Bland, et al. 1990; Hayes 1989). Elevated rates of prison suicide appear to be the product both of the number of risk factors to which prisoners were exposed before incarceration and also to the harshness of the prison conditions they experience during their confinement (e.g., Liebling, 1995). For example, although Cooper and Berwick (2001) reported that there were individual factors and background characteristics that helped to predict suicide in different groups of incarcerated male prisoners, they also found that institutional factors—the severity of environmental stressors—played a significant role in the levels of anxiety, depression, and suicidality that the prisoners suffered. Most experts believe that psychotherapeutic and other kinds of interventions could have a significant effect in reducing suicide rates. Indeed, one noted that, despite causing the greatest number of prison fatalities, suicide also was "potentially the most preventable cause of death in prisons" (Salive, et al. 1989, 368). Here, too, the available therapeutic resources are not remotely commensurate with the magnitude of the prison-generated need.

Prisonization: Necessary Adaptations with Adverse Consequences

In the classic formulation of "prisonization," sociologist Donald Clemmer defined it as "the taking on in greater or less degree of the folkways, mores, customs, and general culture of the penitentiary" (Clemmer 1958, 299). In addition to the subcultural aspects to which Clemmer referred, there are broad psychological components to the process as well. These changes represent a form of "coping"; they are natural and normal adaptations made by prisoners in response to the unnatural and abnormal conditions of prison life. Of course, they vary somewhat from prisoner to prisoner, in part as a function of their pre-prison life and identity and the nature of the prison experiences to which they are exposed and must confront throughout their prison "careers" (e.g., MacKenzie and Goodstein 1995; Paterline and Petersen 1999; Walters 2003).

Here, too, the stage and duration of imprisonment matter as well. Thus, for example, as prison researcher Edward Zamble noted: "It would appear that the beginning of the term [of imprisonment] induces considerable psychological discomfort . . ." (Zamble 1992, 420). However, over time, prisoners come to accept the many aspects of prison life that they cannot change. Indeed, as Zamble noted, "the constancy of the prison environment leads to a slow and gradual amelioration" (420).

This amelioration may ease some of the pains of imprisonment and, because it appears to lead to a form of "prison adjustment," it can mask a number of prison effects. Precisely because many of these changes are functional in the prison setting but highly dysfunctional in the world outside, they are problematic and even disabling in the long run.

There are several important psychological dimensions to the process of prisonization. Like virtually all total institutions, prisons typically force people to give up most of the power to make their own choices and decisions. However, this seemingly reasonable practice is often taken to extreme lengths in prison: Prisoners must relinquish control over the most basic and mundane aspects of their daily existence; they generally have no choice over when they get up or turn their lights out; when, what, or where they eat; whether and for how long they shower or make a phone call. These and most of the other countless daily decisions that citizens in the free world make on a day-to-day basis and naturally take for granted are made for them in prison. Prisoners typically feel infantilized by this loss of control. However, over time, by "ameliorating" to the erosion of personal autonomy, the fact that others routinely decide these things begins to seem increasingly "natural."

As the process of prisonization continues, prisoners come to *depend* on institutional decision makers to make choices for them, and to rely on the structure and routines of the institution to organize their daily activities. Years spent having others make such decisions, depending on them to organize and direct one's own behavior, and otherwise submitting to the external control of the course of day-to-day life eventually accustoms prisoners to it. Indeed, the loss of autonomy and the corresponding dependency on prison structure may become so complete that some prisoners are troubled and even traumatized by the unstructured and unpredictable nature of the free world settings to which they return. In extreme cases, they may begin to lose the *capacity* to initiate activity, to use their own judgment to make effective decisions, or to engage in planful behavior of any kind.

As I indicated in the previous section, the threat of victimization is a persistent fact of prison life. As part of the process of prisonization, prisoners must develop strategies to cope with or adjust to it. Richard McCorkle's study of a maximum security Tennessee prison attempted to quantify the kinds of behavioral strategies that prisoners used to survive dangerous prison environments. He found that "[f]ear appeared to be shaping the life-styles of many of the men," that it had led over 40 percent of prisoners to avoid certain high-risk areas of the prison, and about an equal number of inmates reported spending additional time in their cells as a precaution against victimization. At the same time, almost three-quarters of the prisoners reported that they had been forced to "get tough" with another inmate to avoid victimization, and more than a quarter kept a "shank" or other weapon nearby with which to defend themselves. McCorkle found that age was the best predictor of the type of adaptation a prisoner took—younger prisoners were more likely to employ aggressive avoidance strategies than older ones.

Toch and Adams (2002) provided a different perspective, arguing that the threat of exploitation is "tangible" in prison because "fear is equated with 'weakness,' and weakness earns contempt and invites aggression" in prison (230). Many prisoners learn to target those who have already shown that they are susceptible to intimidation, a pattern that obviously worsens the plight of weaker prisoners. It follows, then, that prisoners will adapt to these contingencies by attempting to avoid appearing susceptible to intimidation at all costs. Of course, prisoners struggle to preserve their sense of self and to maintain self-respect in a larger context of pervasive and unavoidable subordination. For some, an exaggerated need to preserve one's "manhood" results, with prisoners trying to construct it in a prison environment where it is constantly undermined.

Some prisoners cope with the threat of victimization by promoting their own reputation for toughness, responding immediately to even seemingly insignificant insults, minor affronts, or slightest signs of disrespect, and doing so with decisive (sometimes deadly) force. As one prison observer put it, "The cultural rules for recouping manhood arise out of an environment of stress, loss, and deprivation" (Phillips 2001, 23). In these ways, the dangers and degradation of prison life contribute directly to prisoners adopting aggressive survival strategies in which they proactively victimize others.

The issue of sexual assault in prison is a tragic but instructive example of the way that the harsh context of prison helps to elicit extreme, hurtful forms of behavior from persons which, in turn, have severe, traumatic consequences for others. John Coggeshall (1991) described the general process by which this occurs: "In prison, inmates face antagonism from guards, violence from fellow inmates, deprivation from incarceration itself. One method by which inmates retaliate is to humiliate and assault their fellow inmates sexually" (84). Thus, the frustration of sexual deprivation combines with the daily degradations of self to produce a perverse dynamic in which prisoners may acquire some degree of status through the sexual victimization of others (e.g., Rideau and Sinclair 1998). As one researcher put it: "Men who have been deprived of most avenues of self-expression and who have lost status by the act of imprisonment may resort to the use of sexual and physical power to reassert their uncertain male credentials" (King 1992, 68–69).

Prisons also are characterized by elaborate *informal* rules and norms that are part of the unwritten but essential culture and "code" that prevail inside prison and among prisoners. Like the formal rules of the institution, these too must be abided; there are very real and often severe consequences when violations occur. Some prisoners, eager to defend themselves against what they perceive as the constant dangers and deprivations of the surrounding environment, fully embrace and internalize as many of these informal norms as possible (e.g., South and Wood 2006). The norms of the prisoner culture can be harsh, exploitative, and even predatory. In poorly run maximum security prisons, especially, where the informal prisoner culture may become especially strong, many prisoners—those who cannot manage the elusive task of somehow appearing and remaining aloof and uninvolved—perceive a stark choice between becoming a victim or victimizer (e.g., Haney, 2011).

Prisonization also leads many prisoners to fashion an emotional and behavioral "prison mask" that seems unrevealing and impenetrable. In so doing, however, they risk alienation from themselves and others. That is, they may develop an emotional flatness that becomes chronic and debilitating in social interactions and in their personal relationships. Some will find that they have created a permanent and unbridgeable distance between themselves and other people. Others find that the risks associated with open, genuine communication are too great; their prison experience leads them to withdraw from authentic social interactions altogether (e.g., Jose-Kampfer 1990; and Sapsford 1978). In this way, these prisoners seek safety in social invisibility. They become inconspicuous and unobtrusive by disconnecting from others. Some prisoners retreat deeply into themselves, trust virtually no one, and adjust to prison stress by leading isolated lives of quiet desperation (e.g., McCleary 1961).

The degraded conditions under which prisoners live serve as constant reminders of their compromised and stigmatized social status and role. A diminished sense of self-worth and personal value may result. In extreme cases of prisonization, the symbolic meaning that can be inferred from this externally imposed substandard treatment and these degraded circumstances are internalized. As Gresham Sykes expressed it, the prisoner's "picture of himself as a person of value"—that is, as a "morally acceptable" person with "some claim to merit . . . and inner strength" eventually "begins to waiver and grow dim" in a prison setting that refuses to acknowledge these characteristics or potentialities (1958, 79).

Of course, prisoners who truly internalize the broad set of habits, values, and perspectives that prisonization brings about are likely to encounter difficult transitions to free world norms. Indeed, the ability to successfully adapt to certain prison contexts may be *inversely* related to subsequent adjustment in the community. That is, as one study showed: "[I]nmates who adjusted most successfully to a prison environment actually encountered the most difficulty making the transition from institutional life to freedom" (Goodstein 1979, 265).

It is not difficult to understand why. A tough veneer that precludes seeking help for personal problems, the generalized mistrust that comes from the fear of exploitation, or a tendency to strike out in response to minimal provocations are highly functional in many prison contexts and problematic virtually everywhere else. Especially in interactions with persons who know nothing about the norms and psychological effects of the places from which they come, prisoners may be perceived as unfeeling, distant, or aloof, or cold, needlessly suspicious, or even paranoid, and capable of impulsive, dangerous overreactions. The lingering effects of prisonization function as psychological barriers that can impede post-prison adjustment.

COPING WITH THE EXTREMES
OF PRISON CONFINEMENT

Beyond the "routine" pains of imprisonment, and their attendant psychological effects, there are certain extremes of penal confinement that can produce even more adverse consequences for persons subjected to them. In particular, prison conditions that are on the end points of the continuum of social contact—far too much of it or far too little—have become increasingly common in certain prison systems. Their special and especially problematic prison effects they produce have been studied as well.

Because it touches virtually every aspect of a prisoner's day-to-day existence, *overcrowding* greatly amplifies the stressfulness of prison life. Not surprisingly, a large literature on overcrowding has documented a range of adverse effects that occur when prisons have been filled to near capacity and beyond. As a group of prison researchers concluded in the 1980s, as the scope of the problem was just becoming apparent, "crowding in prisons is a major source of administrative problems and adversely affects inmate health, behavior, and morale" (Cox et al. 1984, 1159; see also Gaes 1985 and Paulus et al. 1988) Two other early commentators concluded their review of the literature in much the same way, namely, that "[w]ith few exceptions, the empirical studies indicate that prison overcrowding has a number of serious negative consequences" (Thornberry and Call 1983, 351; see also Ruback and Carr 1984).

Overcrowding may directly affect prisoners' mental and physical health by increasing the level of uncertainty with which they regularly must cope. One useful psychological model of the negative effects of overcrowding emphasizes the way in which being confined in a space that is occupied by too many people increases the sheer number of social interactions persons have that involve "high levels of uncertainty, goal interference, and cognitive load. . . . " (Cox, et al. 1984, 1159). Indeed, crowded conditions heighten the level of cognitive strain that persons experience by introducing social complexity, turnover, and interpersonal instability into an already dangerous prison world in which interpersonal mistakes or errors in social judgments can be fatal. Of course, overcrowding also raises collective frustration levels inside prisons by generally decreasing the amount of resources that are available to the prisoners confined there. The sheer number of things that prisoners do or accomplish on a day-to-day basis is compromised by the number of people between them and their goals and destinations. Moreover, overcrowding has *systemic* effects on prison systems that struggle to provide prisoners with basic, necessary services. For example, as several commentators noted in the midst of the rapid increases in prisoner population throughout the United States that occurred during the last several decades, "the prospect of screening inmates for mental disorder and treating those in need of mental health services has become a daunting and nearly impossible task in the present explosion of prison growth" (DiCataldo, Greer and Profit 1995, 574). The United States Supreme Court has found that seriously overcrowded prison systems can become so dysfunctional that they are incapable of providing constitutionally adequate medical or mental health care (*Brown v. Plata*, 2011).

Despite an occasional study that yields an inconclusive finding (e.g., Bleich 1987),[3] it is widely understood that crowding can significantly worsen the quality of institutional life and increase the destructive potential of imprisonment. Among other things, we know from early research that prison overcrowding increases negative affect among prisoners (e.g., Paulus et al. 1975), elevates their blood pressure (e.g., D'Atri 1975), and leads to greater numbers of prisoner illness complaints (e.g., McCain et al. 1976). Exposure to "long-term, intense, inescapable crowding" of the sort that characterizes many prison environments results in high levels of stress that "can lead to physical and psychological impairment" (Paulus et al. 1978, 115; see also Ostfeld et al. 1987).

More recently, British researchers found that high levels of perceived crowding in prison were related to increased arousal and stress and decreased psychological well-being (Lawrence and Andrews 2004). Moreover, the prisoners in this study who experienced prison conditions as "crowded" were more likely to interpret the behavior of other prisoners as aggressive and violent. Other researchers have found that an individual-level factor—the degree of prior street drug use—interacted with the level of prison crowding to explain in-prison drug use. Specifically, "inmates who reported a history of using drugs on the streets prior to incarceration are especially likely to engage in drug abuse inside crowded prisons" (Gillespie 2005, 240). Studies also have shown that "overcrowding is a critical feature of prison environments that dramatically raises the risk of prison suicide" (Huey and McNulty 2005, 507). More specifically, "the reduced risk of suicide found in much prior research to be evident in minimum security facilities"—presumably because of the lower levels of deprivation there—"is in fact voided by the deleterious effects of high overcrowding" (507). Other researchers have found that overcrowding may lead to higher numbers of prison suicides because it decreases the level of "purposeful activity" in which prisoners are able to engage (e.g., Leese, Stuart, and Snow 2006, 359; Wooldredge 1999).

At the other end of the spectrum—and perhaps employed as a way of dealing with some of the dysfunctional systemic problems that overcrowding brings about—a number of prisons have resorted to the previously discredited practice of *long-term isolation*, implemented as a form of prisoner control and punishment. It, too, has a range of special, problematic psychological effects associated with it. There is an extensive empirical literature that establishes the painfulness of isolation or solitary confinement and its potential to inflict emotional damage. Empirical research on solitary-type confinement has consistently documented the psychological risks of living in these kinds of environments. Despite some methodological limitations that apply to some of the individual studies, the findings are robust. Evidence of these negative psychological effects comes from personal accounts, descriptive studies, and systematic research on solitary-type confinement, conducted over a period of four decades, by researchers from several different continents who had diverse backgrounds and a wide range of professional expertise. Even setting aside the corroborating data that come from studies of psychologically analogous settings—research on the harmful effects of acute sensory deprivation, the psychological distress and other problems that are created by the loss of social contact such as studies of the pains of isolated, restricted living in the free world, or the well-documented psychiatric problems that seclusion poses for mental patients—the psychological risks of solitary confinement are many and varied and empirically confirmed. (See Haney and Lynch 1997 and Haney 2003a for citations to the studies that document the specific symptoms and problematic patterns referred to in the paragraphs below.)

Specifically, in case studies and personal accounts provided by mental health and correctional staff who worked in prison isolation units, a range of similar adverse symptoms have been observed in prisoners, including appetite and sleep disturbances, anxiety, panic, rage, loss of control, paranoia, hallucinations, and self-mutilations. Moreover, direct studies of prison isolation have documented an extremely broad range of harmful psychological reactions. They include heightened levels of the following potentially damaging symptoms and problematic behaviors: negative attitudes and affect, insomnia, anxiety, panic, withdrawal, hypersensitivity, ruminations, cognitive dysfunction, hallucinations, loss of control, irritability, aggression, and rage, paranoia, hopelessness, depression, a sense of impending emotional breakdown, self-mutilation, and suicidal ideation and behavior.

In addition, there are correlational studies of the relationship between housing type and various incident reports that show that self-mutilation and suicide are more prevalent in isolated housing, as are deteriorating mental and physical health (beyond self-injury), other-directed violence, such as stabbings, attacks on staff, property destruction, and collective violence. The use of extreme forms of solitary confinement in so-called "brainwashing" and methods of torture also underscores its painfulness and damaging potential. In fact, many of the negative effects of solitary confinement are analogous to the acute reactions suffered by torture and trauma victims, including post-traumatic stress disorder (PTSD) and the kind of psychiatric sequelae that plague victims of what are called "deprivation and constraint" torture techniques.

Beyond these discrete, more measurable negative effects of isolation, a number of broader changes occur in many prisoners who have been placed in long-term solitary confinement. Although they are more difficult to measure, they may prove equally if not more problematic over the long term. These transformations come about because many prisoners find that surviving the rigors of penal isolation—accommodating to the absence of people and any semblance of normal social life—requires them change their patterns of thinking, acting, and feeling. Like prisonization in general, these changes have the potential to rigidify—to become deeply set ways of being that, in varying degrees for different people, more or less permanently alter who these prisoners are and, once they are released from solitary confinement, who they can become. Because they do not represent clinical syndromes per se, and because they constitute patterns of social behavior that are largely "functional" under conditions of extreme isolation—for the most part becoming increasingly dysfunctional only if they persist upon return to more normal social settings—I have termed them "social pathologies."

Among the various social pathologies that can develop in prisoners who struggle to adapt to the rigors of severe, long-term isolation are:

1. Adjusting to the unprecedented totality of control that prevails in solitary confinement units by becoming even more highly dependent on the institution to organize all aspects of their daily existence than in general prison settings. Because almost every aspect of the prisoner's day-to-day life is so carefully controlled in the typical solitary confinement unit, prisoners may lose the ability to set limits for themselves, or to control their own behavior through internal mechanisms.

2. Conversely, prisoners in highly controlled solitary confinement settings often report losing the ability to *initiate* behavior of any kind—to organize their own lives around activity and purpose. Living for the most part entirely within the confines of their cells, they have been stripped of any opportunity to do so for prolonged periods of time. Chronic apathy, lethargy, depression, and despair are often reported as a result.

3. Because they are denied regular, normal interpersonal contact within a meaningful social context, prisoners report feeling that they are at risk of losing their grasp on whether and how they are connected to a larger social world, to other people. As their social identities atrophy, some report losing a sense of who, in fact, they are. Some prisoners "act out" literally as a way of getting a reaction from their environment, proving to themselves that they are still alive and capable of eliciting a human response—however hostile—from other human beings.

4. The experience of total social isolation leads some prisoners to engage, paradoxically, in social withdrawal. That is, they move from initially being starved for social contact to eventually being disoriented and even frightened by it. As they become increasingly unfamiliar and uncomfortable with normal forms of social interaction, they are further alienated from others and made anxious in their presence. In extreme cases, another pattern emerges: their present environment is so painful, so bizarre and impossible to make sense of, so disconnected from more familiar social contexts that prisoners create their own reality—they live in a world of fantasy instead.

5. Finally, the deprivations, restrictions, the totality of control, and the prolonged absence of any real opportunity for happiness or joy fill many prisoners with intolerable levels of frustration that, for some, turns to anger, and then even to uncontrollable and sudden outbursts of rage. It leads others to ruminate over their mistreatment and commit themselves to fighting against the system and the people that surround, surveil, provoke, deny, thwart, and oppress them.

Obviously, these social pathologies—adopted in reaction to and in order to survive a pathological set of circumstances—are highly dysfunctional and potentially disabling if they persist in the highly social world to which prisoners are expected to adjust once they are released.

THE POST-PRISON CONSEQUENCES OF PRISON EFFECTS

Prisonization can combine with the high levels of distress and trauma experienced in harsh prison settings to produce lasting problems for ex-convicts (e.g., Haney 2003b). In fact, when Adrian Grounds and Ruth Jamieson (2003) conducted psychiatric assessments of a group on long-term prisoners who had been subsequently released, they found that the most serious psychological problems that many prisoners faced were only manifested *after* they reentered free society. Indeed, they uncovered a pattern of disabling symptoms and severe psychological problems that paralleled findings from the trauma literature in psychology and psychiatry. Grounds and Jamieson concluded that the "psychological consequences of imprisonment for these men and their families were complex and profound" (358).

Grounds conducted an additional study of persons who had been exonerated and subsequently released. He found that when these ex-prisoners attempted to reintegrate into society they experienced many of the same kinds of psychiatric problems and difficulties as they participants in his earlier study. Indeed, he concluded that the "extent of the suffering was profound" (Grounds 2005, 15). Grounds found "evidence of personality change and adjustment difficulties in this group similar to those described in clinical studies of others who have experienced chronic psychological trauma" (15), which included "marked features of estrangement, loss of capacity for intimacy, moodiness, inability to settle, loss of a sense of purpose and direction, [] a pervasive attitude of mistrust toward the world," being "withdrawn, unable to relate to the world," manifesting the diagnostic criteria for post-traumatic stress disorder, suffering depressive disorders, and encountering a whole range of serious problems with family contact, social adjustment, and employment (21–41).

The stress of prison confinement has medical as well as psychological consequences that may impair post-prison adjustment (e.g., Massoglia 2008a, b; Schnittker and Andrea 1997). In fact, some of the daunting medical and psychological challenges that ex-convicts face in the transition from prison to free society are reflected in their dramatically elevated mortality rates. For example, one study reported that within two years of their release, former prison inmates suffered mortality rates that were three and a half times that of the general population (Binswanger et al. 2007). Moreover, within the first two weeks immediately following their release, their mortality rates were over twelve times the rate in the population at large. Drug overdose, cardiovascular disease, homicide, and suicide were the leading causes of death.

In addition, the overcrowded conditions and lack of commitment to rehabilitation that characterized American corrections over the last several decades have increased the obstacles that ex-convicts must overcome following incarceration. Sociologist John Irwin (2005) summarized the state of mind of many long-term prisoners preparing to leave the medium-security California prison that he studied. These prisoners had endured many years "deprived of material conditions, living in crowded conditions, without privacy, with reduced options, arbitrary control, disrespect, and economic exploitation" (168). The mounting effects of these "excruciatingly frustrating and aggravating" experiences resulted in "[a]nger, frustration, and a burning sense of injustice" (168), which Irwin concluded was likely to significantly reduce their chances of successfully pursuing a conventional life after release. As Joan Petersilia (2003) has noted, in addition to the lack of rehabilitative services that the typical prisoner now receives, the sheer length of prison sentences in the era of harsh punishment insures that many of them will return home "more disconnected from family and friends, have a higher prevalence of substance abuse and mental illness, and be less educated and less employable than those in prior prison release cohorts" (53).

In addition to impeding successful reintegration generally, the negative psychological effects of imprisonment may also elevate recidivism rates. To be sure, the methodological challenges presented by attempts to determine how much crime a person *would have* engaged in *but for* his or her imprisonment are substantial (e.g., Bhati 2006). Not surprisingly, the estimates of the net effect of imprisonment on subsequent criminal trajectories vary somewhat. For example, Paul Gendreau and his colleagues have conducted a comprehensive meta-analytic study of the relationship between incarceration, length of confinement, and recidivism (Smith, Coggin, and Gendreau 2002). They concluded that doing time in prison actually had a "criminogenic"—crime-producing—effect. In fact, imprisonment not only appeared to have increased the chances of reoffending somewhat but also, the more time served, the more likely subsequent offending became. Although the overall effects were modest in size, Gendreau and his colleagues concluded that "the enormous costs accruing from the excessive use of prison may not be defensible" (20). Indeed, they noted that the long-term cost—in terms of increased amounts of crime produced by more people going to prison for longer amounts of time—was particularly problematic "given the high incarceration rates currently in vogue in North America."

Other research suggests that, in addition to the length of imprisonment, the severity of the conditions of confinement may have an adverse impact on the amount and nature of recidivism. Specifically, Chen and Shapiro (2007) concluded that incarceration under harsh conditions of confinement may increase the likelihood that persons will engage in criminal behavior following their release from prison, and that these effects "appear large enough to outweigh deterrence and drive a net increase in crime should prison conditions worsen" (23). They also concluded that the size of this effect may be stronger "for inmates housed for a longer period" (21).

Whether they reoffend or not, of course, many ex-convicts will reenter free society not only bearing the psychological burdens that years of prison distress and prisonization have created but also thwarted in their goals by a set of structural disadvantages and community-based obstacles that can impede their successful reintegration. As one researcher put it, "incarceration likely acts as a primary stressor, while characteristics of life after release—stigma, decreased earnings and employment prospects, and family problems—are a series of secondary stressors" (Massoglia 2008. 57), ones that many ex-convicts have been ill prepared to confront.

Conclusion

Prisons are powerful social settings that can produce a range of negative psychological effects on persons confined within them. In general, such prison effects include the ways in which prisoners are adversely affected by the severe stressors that characterize prison life (e.g., danger, deprivation, and degradation) and the many accommodations that they must make in order to adjust to and survive the psychological pressures they confront and the behavioral mandates with which they must comply. Prison conditions vary widely, and those variations influence and affect that nature of the changes that prisoners undergo in the course of their incarceration. Prisoners also vary in the degree to which they are affected by their conditions of confinement. However, the risk factors and various forms of trauma that we know predispose persons to a wide range of psychological problems (including substance abuse, criminality, and violence) are, not surprisingly, prevalent in the pre-prison lives of incarcerated men and women; these experiences may make them especially vulnerable to the prison stressors and process of prisonization to which incarceration subjects them. Many of these negative prison effects become fully apparent only after release, when the complete impact of the prison experience and its potentially disabling consequences in free society come to the fore.

NOTES

1. Most of what I have to say about the effects of imprisonment applies primarily to maximum and medium security prisons, where most prisoners are housed, rather than minimum security facilities, where a much smaller percentage are confined (Stephan and Karberg 2003). These prisons place a heavy emphasis on security and control, and generally house prisoners in cells. The facilities are typically surrounded by high walls or fences, with armed guards at the "security perimeters," and so on. Obviously, these, too, are gross categorizations, with countless variations in actual conditions of confinement occurring between seemingly similar prisons. My assertions about prison effects are all made with the continuing caveat that as prison conditions vary significantly from facility to facility so, too, do their effects.

2. Four criteria must be met in order for the diagnosis of PTSD to be applied. Specifically, a person must: (1) be exposed to a severe stressor resulting in intense fear or helplessness; (2) undergo psychic re-experiencing or re-enacting of the trauma; (3) engage in avoidance behavior or experience psychic numbing; and (4) experience increased arousal, typically in the presence of stimuli related to or reminiscent of the original trauma. *American Psychiatric Association, Diagnostic and Statistical Manual of Mental Disorders, IV T-R.* Washington, DC: American Psychiatric Association (2000). For additional discussions of the disorder, see Wilson and Raphael (1993).

3. The potential relationship between crowding and inmate disciplinary infractions and violence has been an especially elusive one, appearing in some studies but not in others (e.g., Steiner and Wooldredge 2009). This apparent inconsistency may be due in part to other facts of prison life that complicate research in this area, including the level of analysis at which crowding is measured and its effects assessed (e.g., "crowding" in an individual housing unit, institution, or system), and the extent to which prison practices actually change (and/or are perceived by prisoners to have changed) in response to crowding, altering things like classification and security procedures, the reporting of infractions and victimization, and so on, inside the prison or prison system. The point is

that prisons are complex environments, with many aspects and actors that respond in multiple ways to crowding-related pressures in order to adjust to and function within them. In this instance, we know that inmate violence levels themselves are affected by a complicated set of forces and factors (e.g., Steiner 2009). And we also know that prisoner behavior can be managed in part by a variety of techniques so that violence, even under crowded conditions, can be controlled through exceptional means, such as through an especially high concentration of staff (e.g., Tartino and Levy 2007). These and other complexities likely explain some of the complicated pattern of research results that have been reported on this issue.

REFERENCES

Bhati, A. 2006. *Studying the Effects of Incarceration on Offending Trajectories: An Information-Theoretic Approach.* Technical Report. Washington, DC: United States Department of Justice.

Binswanger, I., M. Stern, R. Deyo, P. Heagerty, A. Cheadle, J. Elmore, and T. Koepsell. 2007. "Release from Prison: A High Risk of Death for Former Inmates." *New England Journal of Medicine* 356: 157–165.

Bland, R., S. Newman, R. Dyck, and H. Orn. 1990. "Prevalence of Psychiatric Disorders and Suicide Attempts in a Prison Population." *Canadian Journal of Psychiatry* 35: 407–413.

Bleich, J. 1989. "The Politics of Prison Crowding." *California Law Review* 77: 1125–1180.

Bonta, J., and P. Gendreau. 1990. "Reexamining the Cruel and Unusual Punishment of Prison Life." *Law and Human Behavior* 14: 347–372.

Brown v. Plata, 131 S.Ct. 1910 (2011).

Chen, K., and J. Shapiro. 2007. "Do Harsher Prison Conditions Reduce Recidivism? A Discontinuity-Based Approach." *American Law & Economics Review* 9: 1–29.

Clemmer, D. 1958. *The Prison Community.* New York: Holt, Rinehart & Winston.

Coggeshall, J. 1991. "Those Who Surrender Are Female: Prisoner Gender Identities as Cultural Mirror." In *Transcending Boundaries: Multi-disciplinary Approaches to the Study of Gender,* eds. P. Frese and J. Coggeshall, 81–95. New York: Bergin & Garvey.

Cooper, C., and S. Berwick. 2001. "Factors Affecting Psychological Well-being of Three Groups of Suicide Prone Prisoners." *Current Psychology* 20: 169–182.

Cox, V., P. Paulus, and G. McCain. 1984. "Prison Crowding Research: The Relevance for Prison Housing Standards and a General Approach Regarding Crowding Phenomena." *American Psychologist* 39: 1148–1160.

D'Atri, D. 1975. "Psychophysiological Responses to Crowding." *Environment & Behavior* 7: 237–252.

DiCataldo, F., A. Greer, and W. Profit. 1995. "Screening Prison Inmates for Mental Disorder: An Examination of the Relationship Between Mental Disorder and Prison Adjustment." *Bulletin of the American Academy of Psychiatry and Law* 23: 573–585.

Fazel, S., and J. Danesh. 2002. "Serious Mental Disorders in 23,000 Prisoners: A Systematic Review of 62 Surveys." *Lancet* 359: 545–550.

Gaes, G. 1985. "The effects of overcrowding in prison." In *Crime and Justice: An Annual Review of Research,* Vol. 6, eds. N. Morris and M. Tonry, 95–146. Chicago:

Gibbs, J. 1982. "The First Cut Is the Deepest: Psychological Breakdown and Survival in the Detention Setting." In *The Pains of Imprisonment,* eds. R. Johnson and H. Toch. Beverley Hills, CA: Sage.

Gibson, L., J. Holt, K. Fondacaro, T. Tang, T. Powell, and E. Turbitt. 1999. "An Examination of Antecedent Traumas and Psychiatric Co-Morbidity among Male Inmates with PTSD." *Journal of Traumatic Stress* 12: 473–484.

Gillespie, W. 2005. "A Multilevel Model of Drug Abuse Inside Prison." *Prison Journal* 85: 223–246.

Goff, A., E. Rose, S. Rose, and D. Purves. 2007. "Does PTSD Occur in Sentenced Prison Populations? A Systematic Literature Review." *Criminal Behavior & Mental Health* 17: 152–162.

Goodstein, L. 1979. "Inmate Adjustment to Prison and the Transition to Community Life." *Journal of Research in Crime and Delinquency* 16: 246–272.

Greene, S., C. Haney, and A. Hurtado. 2000. "Cycles of Pain: Risk Factors in the Lives of Incarcerated Women and Their Children." *Prison Journal* 80: 3–23.

Grounds, A. 2005. "Understanding the Effects of Wrongful Imprisonment." *Crime & Justice: An Annual Review of Research* 32: 1–58.

Grounds, A., and R. Jamieson. 2003. "No Sense of an Ending: Researching the Experience of Imprisonment and Release among Republican Ex-prisoners." *Theoretical Criminology* 7: 347–362.

Gullone, E., T. Jones, and R. Cummins. 2000. "Coping Styles and Prison Experience as Predictors of Psychological Well-Being in Male Prisoners." *Psychiatry, Psychology and Law* 7: 170–181.

Gunn, J. 1978. "The Role of Psychiatry in Prisons and the Right to Punishment." In *Psychiatry, Human Rights and the Law,* eds. M. Roth and R. Bluglass, 138–147. Cambridge: Cambridge University Press.

Haney, C. 2003a. "Mental Health Issues in Long-Term Solitary and 'Supermax' Confinement." *Crime & Delinquency* 49: 124–156.

Haney, C. 2003b. "The Psychological Impact of Incarceration: Implications for Post-Prison Adjustment." In *Prisoners Once Removed: The Impact of Incarceration and Reentry on Children, Families, and Communities,* eds. J. Travis and M. Waul, 33–66. Washington, DC: Urban Institute Press.

Haney, C. 2006a. *Reforming Punishment: Psychological Limits to the Pains of Imprisonment,* Washington, DC: American Psychological Association Books.

Haney, C. 2006b. "The Wages of Prison Overcrowding: Harmful Psychological Consequences and Dysfunctional Correctional Reactions." *Washington University Journal of Law & Policy* 22: 265–293.

Haney, C. 2011. "The Perversions of Prison: On the Origins of Hypermasculinity and Sexual Violence in Confinement." *American Criminal Law Review* 44:121–141.

Haney, C., and M. Lynch. 1997. "Regulating Prisons of the Future: A Psychological Analysis of Supermax and Solitary Confinement." *New York University Review of Law and Social Change* 23: 477–570.

Harding, T. and E. Zimmerman. 1989. "Psychiatric Symptoms, Cognitive Stress and Vulnerability Factors: A Study in a Remand Prison." *British Journal of Psychiatry* 155: 36–43.

Hayes, L. 1989. "National Study of Jail Suicides: Seven Years Later." *Psychiatric Quarterly* 60: 7–29.

Heckman, C., K. Cropsey, and T. Olds-Davis. 2007. "Traumatic Stress Disorder Treatment in Correctional Settings: A Brief Review of the Empirical Literature and Suggestions for Future Research." *Psychotherapy: Theory, Research Practice, Training* 44: 46–53.

Hemmens, C., and J. Marquart. 1999. "Straight Time: Inmate's Perceptions of Violence and Victimization in the Prison Environment." *Journal of Offender Rehabilitation* 28: 1–21.

Herman, J. 1992a. "A New Diagnosis." In *Trauma and Recovery*, ed. J. Herman. New York: Basic Books.

Herman, J. 1992b. "Complex PTSD: A Syndrome in Survivors of Prolonged and Repeated Trauma." *Journal of Traumatic Stress* 5: 377–391.

Hochstetler, A., D. Murphy, and R. Simons. 2004. "Damaged Goods: Exploring Predictors of Distress in Prison Inmates." *Crime & Delinquency* 50: 436–457.

Hocking, F. 1970. "Extreme Environmental Stress and Its Significance for Psychopathology." *American Journal of Psychotherapy* 24: 4–26.

Huey, M., and T. McNulty. 2005. "Institutional Conditions and Prison Suicide: Conditional Effects of Deprivation and Overcrowding." *Prison Journal* 85: 490–514.

Irwin, J. 2005. *The Warehouse Prison: Disposal of the New Dangerous Class*. Los Angeles, CA: Roxbury.

Jose-Kampfner, C. 1990. "Coming to Terms with Existential Death: An Analysis of Women's Adaptation to Life in Prison." *Social Justice* 17: 110–124.

Kesterman, C. 2005. *Prison Life: Factors Affecting Health and Rehabilitation*. Paper presented at the European Conference on Psychology and Law, Vilnius, Lithuania, July.

King, M. 1992. "Male Rape in Institutional Settings." In *Male Victims of Sexual Assault*, eds. G. Mezey and M. King, 67–74. Oxford: Oxford University Press.

Kupers, T. 1996. "Trauma and Its Sequelae in Male Prisoners: Effects of Confinement, Overcrowding, and Diminished Services." *American Journal of Orthopsychiatry* 66: 189–196.

Kupers, T. 1999. *Prison Madness: The Mental Health Crisis Behind Bars and What We Must Do about It*. San Francisco, CA: Jossey-Bass.

Lawrence, C., and K. Andrews. 2004. "The Influence of Perceived Prison Crowding on Male Inmates' Perception of Aggressive Events." *Aggressive Behavior* 30: 273–283.

Leese, M., T. Stuart, and L. Snow. 2006. "An Ecological Study of Factors Associated with Rates of Self-Inflicted Death in Prisons in England and Wales." *International Journal of Law & Psychiatry* 29: 355–360.

Liebling, A. 1995. "Vulnerability and Prison Suicide." *British Journal of Criminology* 35: 173–187.

Liebling, A., L. Durie, A. van den Beukel, S. Tait, and J. Harvey. 2005. "Revisiting Prison Suicide: The Role of Fairness and Distress." In *The Effects of Imprisonment*, eds. A. Liebling and S. Maruna. Cullompton, UK: Willan Publishing.

MacKenzie, D., and L. Goodstein, L. 1995. "Long-term Incarceration Impacts and Characteristics of Long-Term Offenders." In *Long-Term Imprisonment: Policy, Science, and Correctional Practice*, ed. T. Flanagan, 64–74. Thousand Oaks, CA: Sage.

Massoglia, M. 2008a. "Incarceration as Exposure: The Prison, Infectious Disease, and Other Stress-Related Illnesses." *Journal of Health and Social Behavior* 40: 56–71.

Massoglia, M. 2008b. "Incarceration, Health, and Racial Disparities in Health." *Law & Society Review* 42: 275–306.

McCain, G., V. Cox, and P. Paulus. 1976. "The Relationship Between Illness Complaints and Degree of Crowding in a Prison Environment." *Environment and Behavior* 8: 283–290(1976).

McCleery, R. 1961. "Authoritarianism and the Belief System of Incorrigibles." In *Prison: Studies in Institutional Organization and Change,* ed. D. Cressey, 260–306. New York: Holt, Rinehart, and Winston.

McClellan, D., D. Farabee, and B. Crouch. 1997. "Early Victimization, Drug Use, and Criminality: A Comparison of Male and Female Prisoners." *Criminal Justice and Behavior* 24: 455–476.

Mullings, J., D. Hartley, and J. Marquart. 2004. "Exploring the Relationship Between Alcohol Use, Childhood Maltreatment, and Treatment Needs among Female Prisoners." *Substance Use & Misuse* 39: 277–305.

Ostfeld, A. 1987. *Stress, Crowding, and Blood Pressure in Prison*. Hillsdale, NJ: Erlbaum.

Paterline, B., and D. Petersen. 1999. "Structural and Social Psychological Determinants of Prisonization." *Journal of Criminal Justice* 27: 427–441.

Paulus, P., V. Cox, and G. McCain. 1988. *Prison Crowding: A Psychological Perspective*. New York: Springer-Verlag.

Paulus, P., V. Cox, G. McCain, and J. Chandler. 1975. "Some Effects of Crowding in a Prison Environment." *Journal of Applied Social Psychology* 5: 86–91.

Paulus, P., G. McCain, and V. Cox. 1978. "Death Rates, Psychiatric Commitments, Blood Pressure, and Perceived Crowding as a Function of Institutional Crowding." *Journal of Environmental Psychology & Nonverbal Behavior* 3: 107–116.

Petersilia, J. 2003. *When Prisoners Come Home: Parole and Prisoner Reentry*. New York: Oxford.

Phillips, J. 2001. "Cultural Construction of Manhood in Prison." *Psychology of Men & Masculinity* 2: 13–23.

Porporino, F. 1990. "Difference in Response to Long-Term Imprisonment: Implications for the Management Of Long-Term Offenders." *Prison Journal* 80: 35–45.

Rideau, W., and B. Sinclair. 1998. "Prison: The Sexual Jungle." In *Male Rape: A Casebook of Sexual Aggressions,* ed. A. Scacco, 3–29. New York: AMS Press.

Ruback, B., and T. Carr. 1984. "Crowding in a Woman's Prison: Attitudinal and Behavioral Effects." *Journal of Applied Social Psychology* 14: 57–68.

Rubenstein, D. 1982. "The Older Person in Prison." *Archives of Gerontology and Geriatrics* 3: 287–296.

Salive, M., G. Smith, and T. Brewer. 1989. "Suicide Mortality in the Maryland State Prison System, 1979 Through 1987." *Journal of the American Medical Association* 262: 365–369.

Sapsford, R. 1978. "Life Sentence Prisoners: Psychological Changes During Sentence." *British Journal of Criminology* 18: 128–145.

Schnittker, J., and A. John. 2007. "Enduring Stigma: The Long-Term Effects of Incarceration on Health." *Journal of Health and Social Behavior* 48: 115–130.

Smith, P., C. Goggin, and P. Gendreau. 2002. *The Effects of Prison Sentences and Intermediate Sanctions on Recidivism: General Effects and Individual Differences*. Solicitor General of Canada.

South, C., and J. Wood. 2006. "Bullying in Prisons: The Importance of Perceived Social Status, Prisonization and Moral Disengagement." *Aggressive Behavior* 32: 490–501.

Steiner, B. 2009. "Assessing Static and Dynamic Influences on Inmate Violence Levels." *Crime and Delinquency* 55: 134–161.

Steiner, B., and J. Wooldredge. 2009. "Rethinking the Link between Institutional Crowding and Inmate Misconduct." *Prison Journal* 89: 205–233.

Stephan, J., and J. Karberg. 2003, August. *Census of State and Federal Correctional Facilities, 2000*. Washington, DC: Bureau of Justice Statistics.

Tartino, C., and M. Levy. 2007. "Density, Inmate Assaults, and Direct Supervision Jails."
    Criminal Justice Policy Review 18: 395–417.

Taylor, A. 1961. "Social Isolation and Imprisonment." *Psychiatry* 24: 373–376.

Thornberry, T., and J. Call. 1983. "Constitutional Challenges to Prison Overcrowding: The
    Scientific Evidence of Harmful Effect." *Hastings Law Journal* 35: 313–351.

Toch, H., and K. Adams. 2002). *Acting Out: Maladaptive Behavior in Confinement.*
    Washington, DC: American Psychological Association.

Walters, G. 2003. "Changes in Criminal Thinking and Identity in Novice and Experienced
    Inmates." *Criminal Justice and Behavior* 30: 399–421.

Wilson, J., and B. Raphael, eds. 1993. *International Handbook of Traumatic Stress
    Syndromes.* New York: Plenum.

Wooldredge, J. 1999. "Inmate Experiences and Psychological Well-being." *Criminal Justice
    and Behavior* 26: 235–250.

Zamble, E. 1992. "Behavior and Adaptation in Longterm Prison Inmates: Descriptive
    Longitudinal Results." *Criminal Justice and Behavior* 19: 409–425.

Zlotnick, C. 1997. "Posttraumatic Stress Disorder (PTSD), PTSD Comorbidity, and
    Childhood Abuse among Incarcerated Women." *Journal of Nervous & Mental Disease*
    185: 761–763.

CHAPTER 25

....

LIVING LIFE BEHIND BARS IN AMERICA

....

MICHAEL G. SANTOS

In 1987, Drug Enforcement Administration (DEA) agents arrested me. A grand jury in Seattle had charged me with leading a Continuing Criminal Enterprise. That charge, commonly referred to as the *kingpin statute,* exposed me to a lengthy prison term. Prosecutors easily proved the essential elements of the crime: I had supervised five people in a conspiracy to distribute cocaine; the conspiracy had included three overt acts; and the conspiracy had involved significant amounts of money. Upon conviction, my judge imposed a 45-year prison term.

I was 23 years old when prison gates first locked behind me. I had not been previously exposed to confinement, nor did I have a history or proclivity for violence. I had never owned or used a gun. Nevertheless, the severity of my sentence, together with the Bureau of Prisons' classification procedures, necessitated that I begin serving my sentence in a penitentiary.

Although I had never been in prison before, the year that I spent locked inside a large county jail while awaiting the outcome of my judicial proceedings seasoned me somewhat to the abnormal world of confinement. While in the jail, I stepped over the first of many prisoners I would see oozing blood on tile or concrete. He had been a parolee who was returning to confinement. Instead of facing the system again, he chose to kill himself by lacerating his wrists. The easy exit of suicide was, to him, preferable to further incarceration.

I encountered this lifeless man before orderlies wheeled the breakfast cart to the jail's housing unit. In less than half an hour, nurses from the infirmary had wheeled the corpse away and orderlies had mopped up the blood, the pulse of the housing unit hardly disturbed by this death with the television blasting beats from music video channels, and gang members controlling card games or dominoes at every table. The loss of a prisoner's life did not seem to have any more significance than the swatting of an insect.

On the morning of my transfer from the county jail to prison, U.S. marshals confirmed that administrators had assigned me to a high-security penitentiary. Their transportation protocol was to lock my wrists in handcuffs that wove through chains wrapped around my waist. They cuffed steel manacles around my ankles and inspected me for contraband. Once secured, I shuffled as ordered onto buses and airplanes that transported me thousands of miles away from my family in Seattle.

That chained transport required more than 30 days, involving a series of layovers in federal prisons and detention centers across America. Whereas the county jail time had allowed me to interact with men on their way to state prison, that transport chain exposed me to thousands of men with experience in the federal system.

I hadn't fully accepted the consequences of my sentence and couldn't comprehend that my term would require that I live in prison for longer than I had yet been alive. From other prisoners I heard about "good time" and parole. Such concepts did not fully register with me. The nature of my conviction afforded me only a sliver of parole eligibility, and as the other prisoners explained good time to me, I realized that my term would require more than a quarter century of confinement, *if* I could earn the time.

As I lay on steel racks that served as beds in locked cages, thoughts about what it would mean to live apart from my family ate away at me. My parents and two sisters loved me dearly, despite the humiliation that my criminal convictions had heaped upon them. I knew that suicide would only cause my family additional grief; otherwise, it is likely that my blood might have congealed on the orderlies' mops at some point in those early days.

By the time that the judge imposed my sentence, I recognized that I had made every bad decision a defendant could make. Instead of accepting responsibility and expressing remorse, I had put my fate in the hands of an unscrupulous and dishonest defense attorney. Clinging to his counsel that "a huge difference existed between a criminal indictment and a conviction" and that with the right amount of money I could win, I made stupid decisions, revealing a hubris that angered prosecutors and the judge. In perjuring myself during the trial, I sealed my fate for a lengthy sentence.

Listening to other prisoners, I refused to believe what I had heard. They told me that prison terms were final. Once a court imposed sentence, nothing else mattered but the serving of time. The best strategy, they suggested, was to forget about the outside world. Let go. Learn to live in prison. Such an adjustment was the best strategy for surviving it.

Finally, more than a year after my initial arrest, my transport bus pulled into the circular drive of USP Atlanta. Through the bars that caged the bus's windows, I saw the 40-foot walls that surrounded the prison. Armed officers stood sentry and eyed the bus suspiciously from gun towers evenly spaced along the wall. More officers with assault rifles emerged to surround the bus before the doors opened. This dramatic unfolding convinced me that only bleakness awaited.

The penitentiary was large, confining more than 2,500 men when I began serving my sentence. The federal system was in transition. I was one of the last prisoners sentenced under what became known as the "old law," a system that provided administrators with the capacity to reduce sentences by up to 15 days a month for prisoners who avoided disciplinary infractions. Most old-law prisoners could also apply for relief from a parole board once they had served a portion of their terms.

Under the new law, or the Comprehensive Crime Control Act of 1984 (also known as the Sentencing Reform Act), which applies to prisoners convicted after November 1, 1987, prisoners are not eligible for parole. Furthermore, prison administrators cannot allow more good time than 54 days a year for prisoners who avoid disciplinary infractions. This extinguishes hope. Prisoners understand that they will serve more time in prison than those who came before them. Mechanisms are now removed that might have encouraged them to work toward advancing their release dates through merit.

As administrators processed me into the penitentiary, I remember a psychologist suggesting that I should allow my beard to grow, intimating that my clean-shaven face could lead to unwanted attention from prison predators. Such a look on young prisoners was referred to as "going naked," and by going naked, one was immediate prey.

A case manager who interviewed me asked why I left a blank on the intake form asking who should be notified in the event of my death. I told him that I was only 24 and that I wasn't going to die.

"No one walks into the penitentiary expecting to die," the case manager told me. "A few months ago we had a major disturbance where inmates took 90 hostages. No one expected that either. People die," he said, and he needed to know who to call if I were killed.

This interaction with the case manager shook me. Unable to remember any phone numbers or addresses, I gave him my sister's name. I promised to provide the numbers and address later.

As the case manager spoke, I sensed animosity, although the perception may have been rooted in my insecurities. His use of the word *inmate* sounded contemptuous. As he looked at me, I caught his sneer, as if he suspected that as a prisoner I may have been allied with those who had recently rocked the penitentiary with violence and mayhem. The tension and the hostility pervading this USP differed starkly from the relative peacefulness of the county jail and hum of the detention centers.

I felt enmity from all corners, as other prisoners with whom I had entered the penitentiary spewed invective. Forty of us transferred into USP Atlanta that day. Some had transferred in from other penitentiaries like Lewisburg or Leavenworth. Many were dealing with life sentences without the possibility of parole. Most accepted the penitentiary as the last stop on their life's journey.

Even though I am 5'10" and, after thousands of pushups in the county jail, physically fit, the prisoners around me looked sturdier. I didn't know if the skulls and demons tattooed on arms, necks, and faces clouded my judgment, but this prison population was highly intimidating.

In that penitentiary holding cage, I felt akin to a rabbit in a tank full of rattle-snakes. Despite my efforts at projecting a stony aloofness, I suspected that the predators had already caught the scent and perceived me as young, inexperienced, and untested.

My vulnerability wasn't just my personal perception. Within hours of my arrival, I was sidestepping puddles of blood. One madman had stabbed another in a dispute over drugs. A natural survival instinct guided my initial adjustment. Blend in. Be on full alert. Take purposeful, deliberate steps. Get through one hour at a time until I find safety. *Find safety.*

During those first months I learned the routines. Administrative rules required all prisoners to work. I sought employment in the library so that I could begin to educate myself. The library supervisor hired me, and a maze of bookshelves became my sanctuary, my hiding place, my respite from the chaos.

In meeting with my unit team I was introduced to my counselor, my case manager, and my unit manager. They confirmed my projected release date of 2013 with maximum good time. A quick mental calculation shoved 26 years in front of me. Disciplinary infractions could result in the loss of good time that would extend my confinement.

I asked for guidance on what I could achieve or how I could contribute to advance my standing. The unit manager's response was laced with ridicule. I had asked a stupid question, one that a prisoner who knew his place would not have humiliated himself by asking. That meeting was the first time a correctional officer gave me the standard derisive response every prisoner knows: "You've got nothin' comin.' "

The seemingly hopeless atmosphere of the penitentiary deflated me, sucking energy from my spirit. My convictions had resulted in more than the loss of my freedom. Thousands of miles separated me from family, and decades would pass before my return. The threat of extortion, rape, and murder always felt closer than a whisper. I struggled for a sense of meaning and lay awake night after night tormented by thoughts of how the penitentiary would shape my life.

Literature and, interestingly enough, the Bible, provided the only solace I could find. I had been a mediocre student through high school, accumulating just enough credits to graduate in 1982. After receiving my diploma, I did not pick up a single book for five years, until I was imprisoned. Through reading I discovered I could temporarily transport myself from my dismal existence. The Bible offered solace, and philosophy books showed me how little I knew about the world in which I lived. Together they opened up new worlds.

Through the Pell Grant program, Congress had appropriated funds to pay college tuition for people in prison. Learning that I could earn a university degree while serving my sentence gave me purpose, hope. I enrolled as a full-time student in correspondence courses through Ohio University and simultaneously participated in courses that professors from Mercer University taught inside the penitentiary.

With access to programs that could lead to authentic university credentials, I knew that I could build my own ladder out of this pit of psychological despair. Each completed assignment added another rung. Through the commitment that I made to accumulate credits leading to a degree, I no longer had to dwell on the frightening distance of my release date. Instead, I could set incremental goals against which I could measure progress.

The university program caused a seismic shift in my adjustment and attitude. I had no time to mope, deploring and reliving the predicament that my own actions had created. I could act—rectify. Working toward meaningful goals was empowering. Incremental progress motivated me to work harder and to become more vigilant in avoiding possibilities for conflict that could interrupt my progress. Education provided purpose, and purpose provided powerful and positive medicine for my damaged psyche.

Instead of serving my sentence by the hour, I was beginning to embrace a longer term perspective. Still, I never forgot—not for a moment—that every step in a prisoner's life in a U.S. penitentiary is one across the high wire. One false or careless move leads to peril, if not death.

That awareness, coupled with a burning eagerness to earn my degree, compelled me to discipline and structure each day. Although I had to live in the penitentiary, I discovered ways to minimize my exposure to its volatilities through education.

Many factors motivated this rather unusual track to prison adjustment. One was a need to prove worthy of the loving support my parents and sisters so generously gave. In spite of the pain and humiliation that my criminal choices had inflicted upon them, they stood by my side. They accepted my collect telephone calls. They sent money to ease my time inside. They chose harsh lights and demeaning searches and vending machine food in the prison's Visitation Center over beachfront vacations. I could not let them down again.

By my fourth month in the penitentiary, I transferred from the library job to a clerical position in the business office of the prison factory. Whereas the library job had required that I interact with every prisoner who wanted to check out the latest Louis L'Amour, Stephen King, or Danielle Steel, as a clerk, I sat in an office that isolated me from the prison population for eight hours a day.

My supervisor in that office, Ms. Lynn Stephens, treated me with dignity, as if I were human rather than "an inferior species." I sat at a desk and had access to a typewriter. Although institutional rules prohibit prisoners from reading or spending time on "personal work" while on an assigned work detail, Ms. Stephens exercised her own discretion. Once I had completed my duties for the day, she authorized me to work on my academic assignments.

I cherished the solitude I had in that office, the break from the rampant and constant penitentiary chaos: battle, contraband, hustling, drugs, gambling, predation, and other vices. The years passing began to lose importance as my vision of how I could emerge developed.

Creating more solitude or niches that would allow me to minimize interactions with other prisoners became an essential component of my adjustment strategy. My release date stretched too far into the future to concern myself with the possible loss of good time, but I couldn't afford disciplinary infractions. My absolute commitment to earn my undergraduate degree as quickly as possible was my motivation to avoid behavior that could lead to time in the segregated housing unit ("solitary") or a disciplinary transfer.

Besides the clerical job and the time I spent in classrooms, I sought further solitude by volunteering in health services as a suicide-watch companion. In a penitentiary population that exceeds 2,500 prisoners, many suffer from psychological disorders and meltdowns. Had I not found solace in reading and learning that brought meaning to my life, I know the pains of despondency could have placed me among them.

When staff members suspect prisoners of suicidal tendencies, the psychologists issue an order to detain the disturbed prisoner in a solitary cell on the suicide-watch wing. As a volunteer for the suicide-watch program, I sat in a chair outside the cell. Every 15 minutes I recorded the prisoner's activities in a logbook for the psychologist to review.

Although I would like to claim that my volunteering was driven by altruistic motivation, the truth was, it lacked such noble sentiment. This was for survival. Volunteering gave me another escape from the general population. I took advantage of every minute to isolate myself. While sitting in that chair on the suicide-watch wing, I prepared assignments that would boost the number of credits on my university transcript. I added another rung on my imaginary ladder with each.

The schedule I created kept me in my own world, despite my living in the midst of a penitentiary that the *New York Times* described as the most violent in America. When officers unlocked my cell at 6:00 A.M. each morning, I stood dressed and ready to leave. I walked straight to the gym for a morning workout with weights. Muscles would not stop the thrust of a knife, but a disciplined adjustment would lessen my exposure to potential conflict.

From the gym I reported to my clerical position. The wage I earned, together with financial support from my family, enabled me to purchase food from the commissary. I chose to avoid the chow hall, a highly volatile place in prison, where stabbings and other violence frequently erupt. I filled the rest of my time on the suicide-watch tier, totally absorbed in my schoolwork. By the time I returned to my assigned housing block, other prisoners were locked in for the night. Thus, I could shower alone. The officer on duty would then lock me in my cell so I could sleep until the next day. It was a routine I maintained for the first years of my sentence.

This daily structure and the goals I set kept me in a perpetual rush. *I had to finish.* I believed that to create the next opportunity, I first had to earn academic credentials that would distinguish me from the one million other souls locked up. An undergraduate degree gave me a start, one that would validate my commitment to a three-part adjustment I planned to follow to earn freedom.

To formulate that plan, I tried to understand the thinking of law-abiding citizens. What would they expect a nonviolent offender to achieve to earn their support? I wanted to build a record that would persuade others to consider me a fellow citizen, an American first rather than a felon first. I concluded that I would need to educate myself, contribute to society, and build a strong network of support that would assist my eventual transition into society.

An undergraduate degree marked the first hurdle I needed to clear, as Americans respect educational credentials. More than anything, I wanted to connect with these people, to reach beyond the walls and to interact with them. I longed for the world to see me as something more than a prisoner. Regardless of what I accomplished, I felt that the system would always see me as the young criminal who sold cocaine; I desperately ached to be seen differently—as a man, a fellow human being.

On occasion I would watch from a distance as the warden led tours through the prison. I didn't know the status of those on the tour. But to me they represented all that I missed, and I didn't know how to reach them. Officers and lieutenants flanked the tour groups and prohibited prisoners from approaching. I remember thinking "if only I could interact with those people, I know they would see me as something more than a prisoner." Freedom or liberty seemed too abstract. I only wanted to feel human, to build meaningful relationships with people I respected, to find a woman to love. I hurt inside, chronically.

In 1992, I received my undergraduate degree from Mercer University. That milestone brought the first permanent change to my sense of self.

I knew that neither the academic credential nor the commitment to earn it would change my status within the prison system. An undergraduate degree had the same relevance to classification procedures as participating in a recreational tournament—less, really, as the supervisor of recreation would reward those who won tournaments with cases of soda.

The degree may not have improved my status within the prison system, but I knew it would make a difference in the real world—eventually. Life in the penitentiary spawned a different code of values. Positive accomplishments yielded little in the way of recognition. If anything, they brought scorn from both staff and the general prison population. The culture of corrections expected a continuation of the prisoner stereotype. I was breaking it.

Prisoners who sought respect within the prison strove to lead gangs or build names as ruthless and violent criminals. To keep peace, administrators appeased gang leaders and killers with single cells and cushy job assignments—a "reward the naughty" philosophy. As a consequence of these twisted values, classrooms remained empty while gangs proliferated. During the time I served in the penitentiary, no other prisoner earned a university degree, despite the availability of Pell Grants.

Staying true to my tripartite plan, I leveraged the degree that Mercer awarded to create new opportunities. Because I had earned that credential, I found leaders in society more receptive to mentoring me. The dean at Hofstra University agreed to waive a residency requirement, allowing me to study toward a graduate degree from prison. Since imprisonment contextually defined my life, I studied prisons from the disciplines of sociology, cultural anthropology, and political science.

My deliberate adjustment had to continue if I were to succeed. By then I had totally embraced my penitentiary routines. Thousands of men served time there, yet I had only strategic interactions with them. From the moment my eyes opened until

I was in my cell at night, I lived with the singular purpose of reaching the next goal, building the next rung on my ladder.

Soon after Mercer awarded my undergraduate degree, Congress prohibited prisoner eligibility for Pell Grant funding (Petersilia 2009, 5). That change in public policy discontinued access to university degrees for most prisoners, further extinguishing hope for educational pursuits. In the penitentiary that confined me, few prisoners had been wholly devoted to educating themselves. I attributed their lack of commitment to intrinsic perceptions that prospects for a meaningful life did not exist, as well as to the prison's infrastructure that reinforced such perceptions. Since every indication they received affirmed that prisoners "had nothin' comin'," thousands adapted to the negative influences that kept the cycle of failure alive in the penitentiary. They were "prisonized" at taxpayers' expense. What a "gift" to society!

As public policy began to demand a more punitive prison system, I felt an urgency to complete my studies at Hofstra as quickly as possible. Although my family members sacrificed to meet my tuition payments (it cost the prison—and thus, the taxpayers—nothing), I worried that prison administrators could block my correspondence program at any time. They made their feelings clear to me. The regional supervisor of education told me point blank that he did not believe the penitentiary was the place for people to earn college degrees. If I wanted a college degree, he told me, I should have thought of that before I broke the law.

Regardless, I began writing to some of America's leading penologists, asking them to mentor me. When academic luminaries like Drs. Norval Morris, George Cole, Francis Cullen, and Marilyn McShane began to take note of and then support my work, I felt validated for my reclusive prison adjustment grounded in educational pursuits and knew that opportunities might exist to make a contribution to society. As a prisoner, I studied prisons. That unique perspective, I began to believe, might help influence consideration for prison reforms that would encourage more of my fellow prisoners to prepare for law-abiding lives.

Learning from those mentors and contributing to their work gave bright relief to my prison experience. I felt especially privileged when Dr. John DiIulio coordinated a field trip for a group of his students from Princeton to FCI McKean (where I had been transferred) and invited me to speak with them alongside Warden Dennis Luther. I felt a similar honor when Dr. Norval Morris invited me to review and comment on a manuscript he was preparing to profile Alexander Maconochie, a well-known prison reformer.

My adjustment to long-term imprisonment differed from my fellow prisoners. As a consequence of the incremental victories I earned, I was propelled forward, protecting the record that I had worked so hard to build. I always had something to gain and something to lose. The strategy protected me from the despair that afflicted so many who could find no purpose to their incarcerations. A prisoner who believes that nothing he does will matter in terms of the time he serves can easily turn deadly—or turn up dead.

For a brief moment, President Bill Clinton's election brought hope for a more liberal approach to corrections. I stood among those who cheered, clinging to the hope that we would see reforms influenced by the philosophy of John Locke. Instead, we received a heavier dose of Thomas Hobbes—such a disappointment. In part, I realized this was because Democrats were unwilling to be seen as soft on crime—but, if not them, *who* was going to insert humanity into this national insanity?

I read op-ed pieces in the *Wall Street Journal* by Dr. John DiIulio, calling for society to protect itself against super-predators. One of his articles came under the heading "Let 'em Rot," referring to the need for stricter conditions in prison.

Reading those articles by Dr. DiIulio spurred me to write him. I wanted him to know the reasons I felt convinced that encouraging the pursuit of education and vocational skills made far more sense than creating expensive policies that would increase already oppressive controls, breed an even deadlier prison population, and assure higher recidivism.

The letter I wrote prompted a correspondence with him that fulfilled me for years. Each envelope I received from Princeton was a quiet victory. I felt honored that a professor of his stature would consider my ideas worthy of his consideration, even though I disagreed with him. He enjoyed great influence with conservative legislators who demanded "tough on crime" policies. But I found those policies misguided. The British saying of "penny wise, pound foolish" seemed to describe his proposed policies.

Dr. DiIulio compared management techniques in three different state prison systems. His work suggested the need to minimize incentives for prisoners and maximize controls that foster the "us versus them" atmosphere through which I struggled.

Top-level administrators in prison establish the infrastructure and culture of confinement, as the principal of a high school sets the tone for his or her school. The more inmate autonomy that administrators eliminate, the more control they can wield over the institution. Yet, by eliminating opportunities for prisoners to distinguish themselves in positive ways, the "you've got nothin' comin'" culture ensues. And that breeds a dangerous environment—not just *in* prison, but also in the receiving society to which a prisoner is eventually released.

This type of management philosophy differs in remarkable ways from the manner in which successful American business leaders motivate excellence. Successful businesses encourage trust, responsibility, transparency, and encouragement for everyone to reach their highest potential. However, here I was communicating with an expert in criminal justice who was urging prison administrators to embrace a decidedly mean-spirited view of mankind. Those in prison are so recalcitrant, he concluded, that administrators should employ *more aggressive management techniques* to protect society. He called for more cages, believing that society is about to encounter a wave of super-predators. In his view, building and managing prisons with tighter controls represents society's best response.

Conservative legislators really embrace this philosophy. There was the No-Frills Prison Bill. U.S. House Speaker at the time, Newt Gingrich, even called for legislative changes that would have made my conviction a death-penalty offense! The only prison reform bill on the horizon during the 1990s promised to bring more punitive policies. Rehabilitation—the belief in and philosophy of—was abandoned. Society needed to punish—period.

The high-security prisoners in the penitentiary became more aggressive as the newer, more punitive policies took hold. By the mid-1990s, the possibility of parole lost its moderating effect. Old-law prisoner numbers dwarfed in comparison to the waves of new-law prisoners rolling in every week. These new-law men began serving long sentences that did not qualify for either parole or the possibility for much in the way of good conduct time. A prisoner with a 20-year sentence could expect to serve 17 years. For some, that release date stretched so far into the future that it might as well have been "life."

Prisoners made the penitentiary their home. Whereas I relied upon academic credentials to bring meaning to my life, others adjusted by expanding their power bases. They felt that they enhanced their value by forming alliances with others to gain an upper hand in the underground economy. And drugs drove the underground economy.

Prisoners strove to participate in the rackets both inside and outside prison boundaries. Inside, making connections became much easier, as every prisoner had felony convictions and a criminal history through which others could vouch for criminal worthiness. Because the new determinate sentencing scheme *decimated hope* for release, prisoners found empowerment in criminal associations and began creating new networks inside. Prisoners exploited relationships to build distribution networks and gangs. Such activities provided them with the power they needed to enhance their lives inside the penitentiary.

Ironically, legislators contributed to the virus of criminal subcultures spreading across America. The growing problem of gang proliferation across the United States manifested this unintended by-product of shortsighted determinate sentencing schemes. Prisoners accepted that they did not have anything coming, that they could never become a part of society. They adjusted accordingly.

Through the growing underground networks that result from long, immutable sentences, prisoners increase their incomes. The money that their schemes generate leads to more influence, which spreads corruption. Those with strong power bases become more effective at tempting guards with cash payments to mule drugs and other contraband. An entire criminal subculture is growing within the prison system, facilitating the availability of drugs, alcohol, and information that advances gang interests and power.

Levels of volatility increase. During this period, for example, I saw one prisoner knife another in the chest, killing him over a chess game. The victim had been an old-law prisoner who was scheduled for release within a few months, while the killer was beginning a long, new-law term. What did he have to lose?

Rather than aspiring to return to society, prisoners create subcultures of hatred with no compunctions about hiding them. Gangs recruit aggressively to expand their power bases. On a day when Dr. Kathy Hawk, the former director of the Bureau of Prisons, toured the penitentiary, a group of prisoners murdered someone who had been assigned to the cell adjacent to mine. A short time later, another prisoner slammed a hammer into the skull of a corrections officer, killing him instantly. Blood flows in that penitentiary every week.

Those higher levels of violence and volatility follow the changes to federal laws that abolish parole and change the manner by which administrators can compute good time. The literature I read while pursuing my education and the life I was leading and trying to protect in prison convinced me that, regardless of Dr. DiIulio's beliefs, this was bad public policy.

Dr. James Wilson suggests that the purpose of corrections is to isolate and punish (Wilson 1985, 193). Such ideas may appease an apparent desire for vengeance, but they aren't effective. When society pushes to isolate and punish, the horrific, negative consequence of prisoners abandoning hope is the result. Ultimately, it is just plain expensive.

Instead of preparing to build records that might warrant consideration from parole boards and the possibility for more fulfilling lives upon release, many of my fellow prisoners adjusted as if they would always live trapped in the criminal underclass. They accepted that they "didn't have anything coming" and thus there was no need to work to reconcile themselves with society. Instead, they hustled to make their lives easier in prison. They joined gangs. They ran rackets, plotted, and schemed against what they perceived as an oppressive system. That was the poisonous stew in which I spent my twenties.

Despite the protective niche I had created in this explosive atmosphere, I felt the pressure rising. Administrators responded with lockdowns. But when the cell doors eventually opened, that pressure-cooked hostility spilled out with unbelievable intensity. Without gang affiliation or ties to racial cliques, I knew I stood alone—independent and highly vulnerable. Recognizing the peril, I asked for a transfer to a medium-security prison as soon as my sentence warranted it.

The level of tension in the medium was nothing compared to that of the penitentiary, although it did not feel stable. Too many prisoners focused on adjusting in ways that would narcotize them to their estrangement from society. They were not interested in long-term efforts required for successful reentry to society. Instead, most adjusted in ways that would make their lives a little easier inside. For some, that meant a fanatical devotion to television and recreational activities; for others, it meant gambling and hustling.

In 1995, when I had lived through eight years of my sentence, Hofstra University awarded my Master of Arts degree. Hofstra sent the degree in a padded envelope that an officer delivered during the routine mail distribution to the housing unit. When I opened the flap, pulled out the heavy page, and read my name, I felt a sense of worthiness that had been absent long before the DEA agents locked me in handcuffs. In conferring that degree, Hofstra University authenticated me as a man, a human being. No matter how long I served in prison, this could not be taken away from me.

That same evening I mailed the degree home to my mother. My imprisonment had caused her such heartache. She was growing older without my being a part of her life. My two sisters had married and had children. During holidays, birthdays, and other family gatherings, my absence contributed only sadness. Life moved forward without me, and more decades would have to pass before I returned home. I could not change the consequences that my criminal actions had brought, but by sending my mother the degree, I hoped to show her the depths of my commitment to emerge as a better man.

With undergraduate and graduate degrees, along with eight years of imprisonment, I felt as ready for release as I ever would. At 31, I could have returned to society as a productive American ready to contribute to society. Through my studies I had come across and felt inspired by a speech that former Chief Justice Warren Burger had delivered to a graduating class at Pace University. In "Factories with Fences," Justice Burger called for prison reforms to encourage prisoners to work toward earning and learning their way to freedom. I had also read Dr. Norval Morris's works, in which he encouraged reforms that would recognize those who had earned their freedom.

Our society, however, had taken its prison system in a different direction from the enlightened concepts of Justice Burger and Dr. Morris. Instead of developing a system that would provide mechanisms through which offenders could work to reconcile with society and prepare for law-abiding lives, policy makers had gravitated to more punitive systems. Instead, they embraced the early findings of Robert Martinson, a New York criminologist who argued that society stood incapable of operating a system of true corrections. The only thing to do, writes Dr. Wilson, is to isolate and punish.

I received hard evidence of this commitment to isolate and punish on Christmas Eve in 1995. That was the day my case manager quelled any delusions I may have harbored about earning freedom. The U.S. pardon attorney had sent notice through my case manager that the office had rejected a petition I submitted for sentence commutation. No explanation, no reason given. I took the hit, steeling myself to face the fact that I had more rungs to build on my ladder, and that I would remain in prison.

Professor George Cole, from the University of Connecticut, had by then become a good friend and mentor. As the Dean at Hofstra had done, Dr. Cole made arrangements for me to continue the advancement of my education. Under his leadership, I began studying toward a Ph.D. However, prison administrators thought I had gone too far. Although I completed my first term at the University of Connecticut, the warden of my prison made a decision that my continuing pursuit of higher education—even though it cost the prison nothing—"threatened the security of the institution." His directive ended my formal education.

Appealing the warden's decision through administrative remedy procedures was not a viable option. As a prisoner, I did not have standing to question the warden's discretion of what constituted a "threat to the security of the institution." When the warden blocked the university library from sending books that I would need to complete my course work, limited my ability to keep paper files, and prohibited my use of typewriters for anything other than correspondence with the legal system, there was nothing I could do about it.

I was confined in a federal correctional institution, the misnomer being "corrections." One of my unit managers told me that the Bureau of Prisons (BOP) didn't care about my efforts to prepare for a law-abiding life upon release. All the BOP cared about, according to her, was protecting the security of each institution. Rather than achieving that end through encouraging personal growth and development, "corrections" officers were encouraged to isolate and punish and suppress the human spirit with ever-tightening controls. But as controls tighten, tension increases. This medium-security facility erupted in communal rage at the increasingly punitive measures raining down on its population. Prisoners' hostility grew as a new warden discontinued creative incentive programs on which the previous warden had relied to encourage positive adjustments. I woke one fall morning to fires burning in the housing unit and the sound of smashing furniture. The unit officer had abandoned his post as the prisoners seized control to wreak havoc inside. The lid was off the pot.

Prisoners had coordinated the riot, fires simultaneously burning in all the other housing units. I chose to remain in my cell, as I could tell that mob anger had taken on a life of its own. The destruction lasted for several hours before we saw groups of people in combat dress assembling in battle formation on the compound. By the looks of things, the warden had called in the National Guard, and the groups of soldiers had a strategy to reassert control of the prison. Administrators, apparently, had made preparations for such disturbances. When ready, the guards marched in, ordering an end to the violence.

Our prison remained on lockdown for several days. Administrators conducted their investigation, transferred the men they had determined played a role in the riot, and reopened the prison with more security and control mechanisms in place. The local newspaper reported that prisoners had caused damages to the prison that would require a million dollars to repair.

When I was within 18 years of my scheduled release date, I was transferred to a low-security federal correctional institution (FCI). As had happened when I was transferred from a penitentiary to a medium-security prison, I again felt a palpable change in tension levels. With nine years of my sentence under my belt, what had carried me through the first decade would not carry me through the second. It was time for a new adjustment strategy.

During the first decade of my sentence, I strove to merit distinction as a model prisoner. This meant that I worked every day to live within the spirit and the letter of every prison rule, while simultaneously preparing for the challenges I expected to face upon release. I had hoped that such an adjustment strategy would advance me as a candidate for relief. After more than nine years, however, I succumbed to the futility of such hopes. Regardless of what I achieved, this system would demand its pound of flesh. Relief would not be forthcoming, no matter what I did.

In accepting this, I began to reconcile with the likelihood of remaining in prison until my late forties, when a combination of days served and good time earned would result in the expiration of my sentence. In acknowledging this, I forced myself to change my focus. From now on, I would try to envision the obstacles I would encounter upon release and work to ameliorate them. I began to gather information from scores of prisoners who had been released from prison. What had they encountered?

In listening to my fellow prisoners, I came to expect that my quarter century in confinement would result in monumental resistance upon my release to society. Landlords might not want me as a tenant; employers would not want to hire me; lenders would not extend me credit. Despite my education and degrees, I would leave prison without clothes of my own, without financial resources, without a work history, insurance, a home, or prospects for success. If I did not make changes, I realized that I would leave prison as an ideal candidate for a life of failure.

I had to purge what I had concluded were ridiculous aspirations of living as a model inmate. I am convinced that *the longer society exposes a prisoner to "corrections," the more the system conditions him for failure upon release*. Thus, I thought about steps I could take to overcome the colossal struggles I expected to encounter when my prison term ended.

Experience, together with what I had learned from my studies, had convinced me that when prisoners were released to society without job prospects, financial resources, and/or frayed or nonexistent family ties, they returned to prison. I saw the trend and understood the quagmire. In all the years I had served, with very few exceptions, prison administrators resented my hunger for education. In many cases, they were threatened by it. And thus, finally, I was blocked from formal pursuits of higher education. The prison system had fully committed itself to isolate and punish; staff members, at the very least, expressed skepticism when encountering those aspiring to emerge as law-abiding citizens. Derision and low-level harassment were expected accompaniments to my efforts to plan for a positive future—and, from administrators and officers, scorn for those trying for positive improvement of their lives throughout America's penal system. The BOP mantra—*security of the institution*—gave politically sensitive, uncreative, and unimaginative wardens the mandate to kill meaningful rehabilitative programs.

So I began to focus on creating opportunities that would provide stability upon release. My disciplinary record had been as clean after a decade in prison as it was on the day my term began. Once I accepted that a record free of prison disciplinary reports would have less influence on my prospects for success upon release than money in the bank, I began conceptualizing steps that I could take to earn an income and pay taxes.

I decided to test the aphorism—that the pen is mightier than the sword—by developing writing skills. I believed that I could use those skills to build resources that would help me triumph over the obstacles that kept so many long-term prisoners on a treadmill of failure.

One of the rules in the prison disciplinary code prohibits inmates from conducting businesses. In writing for publication, I understood that I would expose myself to disciplinary sanctions. But those possible sanctions frightened me less than the failure that would likely accompany my release.

During the 17 remaining years I expected to serve, I aspired to build a financial cushion through writing that would ease my transition into society. I knew that I would need a place to live, clothing, a vehicle, and sufficient savings to last until I could count on a stable income. I set the goal of earning and saving enough during my remaining imprisonment to ensure that I could pay for my every expense through at least my first year, even if I could not find a job.

An awareness of my family's suffering drove those thoughts. My parents and sisters had stood by my side from the moment of my arrest. When administrators transferred me from one prison to the next, always in states far away from home, my family members did everything they could to ease my adjustment. They wrote letters, they paid my tuition costs, they visited, and they tried to include me in their lives as much as possible. In this regard, I felt blessed and grateful, for so many long-term prisoners struggle with family abandonment.

As the years turned into decades, the effective "isolation" aspect of confinement took its inevitable toll. My support from home never wavered, but I no longer felt as if I lived as an integral part of the family. My parents divorced. My mother married a man I did not know. My sisters married and started families. My father died from Alzheimer's disease, and I was not permitted to attend his funeral.

Without question, I felt that my family would accept me into their homes if I asked. Yet who needed such disruption in their lives? I did not want to further burden them upon release. I had caused enough havoc. No household needs the stress of accepting a penniless, forty-something stranger into their midst. This was my rationale. For although I was a son and a brother, in my mind, prison was making me a stranger. I needed to stand on my own, as a self-sustaining man rather than as a cipher, which was how I would envision myself if I were to further encroach upon my family.

I had time to contemplate the experience. My first decade of confinement convinced me that I could transcend the remaining years if I had a deliberate adjustment plan. I accepted my sentence, but it became crucial to create a deliberate strategy that would ensure I emerge unscathed, "unprisonized." Mine became a straight line of preparation for the life I wanted to live upon release, and every step had to advance the purpose.

There was a saying that I often pondered about living in prison but not being *of prison*. That described my life. Although I perceived that everyone else saw and judged me for the bad decisions of my early twenties, I aspired to live as something more and sought to emulate my role models. My mentors helped open opportunities to publish, and I seized them. Writing for academia, I believed, would distinguish me from other prisoners and bring a credibility that I hoped to leverage upon release.

As a pragmatist, I recognized that significant hurdles awaited me. I pursued every strategy I could conceive that would help me overcome them. Besides writing books and articles for academia, I sought to build a stronger network of support by writing for the Internet community.

As a consequence of my publishing for the Web, Carole found me. She and I had attended school together, although we had not seen or communicated with each other since high school graduation in 1982. Her Internet search for classmates led her to my work, and her discovery of my writing prompted her to send me a letter. That initial letter evolved into a correspondence, a romance, and years later, our marriage in a prison visiting room.

Carole did not commit a crime, but upon joining her life to mine she signed up to serve this sentence with me. We married in 2003, and in becoming my wife and partner, Carole became central to my adjustment. Together we crafted a carefully coordinated plan that would allow us to nurture our marriage while simultaneously preparing for my release.

Carole moved to New Jersey, where I was confined. When I was transferred without warning to Colorado, Carole moved again. She moved to California after administrators transferred me there, as she would not allow distances to interrupt our opportunities to visit. "I'm not going to live in one state when my husband lives in another," she would say. "We need to visit as much as the prison system will allow." We made our commitment to ensure that outside forces, including the complications of my imprisonment, would never destroy the beautiful blessing of our love.

We applied the earnings that my writings generated to fund Carole's living expenses and tuition through nursing school. We chose health care after careful consideration of numerous careers. As a nurse, Carole could earn a suitable income and still relocate whenever I was transferred. Further, as a registered nurse with national credentials, Carole could bring stability to our family while I built a career—at age 50.

The pursuit of educational credentials carried me through my first decade of confinement; an obsession with preparations for the obstacles I expected to encounter upon release carried me through my remaining years. By striving to improve my writing skills, I hoped to build a stronger network of support and to earn an income. In finding Carole, the woman to whom I pledged my life, I received much more.

I began serving this sentence at 23, and now, in 2011, I have more than 24 years of imprisonment behind me. I have taken nearly one of every two breaths on this earth inside prison. Soon I expect to return to society and join Carole, where we will learn to live with the very real conditions imposed by a parole officer who supervises my release, and the covert ones imposed by societal perceptions of reentering felons.

When DEA agents arrested me, the Sentence Reform Act that abolished parole eligibility for federal offenders had not yet taken effect. At that time, few prisoners served ten years without a review. That sentencing structure seemed to make sense. When imposing a sentence, judges would not have crystal balls with which to observe how offenders would respond to the prison experience.

Some offenders might require lengthy terms, perhaps life terms, to protect society. An enlightened system, however, should do more than isolate and punish. An effective system should also include a mechanism that periodically evaluates those who work to reconcile with society and establish positions as contributing citizens. In switching to determinate sentencing schemes, the predominant justification for incarceration is leverage. That creates dangerous environments where administrators can act with impunity, guards have more latitude to "go rogue," and everyone can hide behind *security of the institution*. How can anyone expect corrections to take place when no corrections are offered, or when the system does not provide a mechanism to encourage or distinguish prisoners striving to reconcile with society and prepare for law-abiding lives? Regardless of efforts to atone, all prisoners serve the determinate sentence imposed. Simplistically put: cage time equals justice. Except, it doesn't. This is *not* justice. Justice is *not* simple! Recidivism rates suggest that although determinate sentences may satisfy a primal, societal lust for revenge, they do not make sense from a public policy perspective. Not fiscally. Not even philosophically—if our greatest American jurisprudential minds are to be acknowledged!

In Dr. Joan Petersilia's book, *When Prisoners Come Home*, I learned that "research consistently shows an inverse relationship between recidivism and education. The higher the education level, the less likely the person is to be rearrested or reimprisoned" (Petersilia 2009, 32). Yet, rather than encourage and make available the opportunities for higher education in prison, legislators have abolished them. Compounding the problem, administrators are fostering a prison culture that discourages prisoners who work to educate themselves.

The Bureau of Justice Statistics published findings showing that *67.5 percent of all prisoners return to confinement within three years of release* (Petersilia 2009, 12). What an appalling statistic after all the money that is spent on "corrections." The 2008 Pew Report estimated that our massive prison system requires nearly $60 billion to operate each year. Finally, faced with these high recidivism rates and concomitant high costs, legislators are beginning to contemplate change. Senator James Webb published an article calling the criminal justice system "a national disgrace." He has proposed legislative remedy. But prison administrators I have known resist public outcry for prison reform. They cling to the familiar and simplistic notion that prisons should isolate and punish. I believe that America is greater than that—that not only economics, but also humanity, should guide and inform change.

In 2008, President George W. Bush signed the Second Chance Act of 2007, for the purpose of reducing recidivism. In proposing that legislation, Congress cited the Bureau of Prisons' own research indicating that, besides education, family and community support represent the best predictors for successful prisoner reentry. The legislation urged administrators to establish policies that would help prisoners facilitate and nurture community ties during confinement. Unfortunately, administrators have resisted implementing such policies.

During my extensive experience locked in American prisons of every security level, I have known of only three ways to maintain ties with society. Those include the telephone, visits, and correspondence. Rather than encouraging the use of these potential bridges to society, administrators have increasingly enforced policies—and have come up with new ones—that restrict and limit such access.

I am serving my final months in a minimum-security camp, yet national prison policies prohibit me from using the telephone for more than an average of 10 minutes a day. With little access to the telephone, the policies force me to choose between speaking with my wife, mentors, friends, or other family members. Carole represents the core of my reentry plans, thus I must reserve my daily 10 minutes for her. Consequently, the policies result in my not speaking with my mother, my sisters, or mentors from my network of support who could facilitate my reentry as a law-abiding citizen.

The same types of restrictions apply to visits. In this isolated camp, policies limit prisoners to two visits a month unless the visitor can visit on Fridays during work hours. Furthermore, policies throughout the federal prison system generally restrict inmates from visiting with anyone whom they did not know prior to their term. Visiting with Carole once each week required that I sacrifice visits with others who could assist my transition into society; that choice was necessary to strengthen my marriage, but it depletes my efforts to nurture other community ties.

Policies in the camp even restrict correspondence. Although typewriters sit empty in the law library, rules prohibit prisoners from using those typewriters for anything other than correspondence with the courts or legal system. Prisoners cannot use those typewriters to develop typing skills or to correspond with family, mentors, potential employers, or others who might assist them in preparing for reentry.

As a long-term prisoner, I worry that the isolationist tendencies of prison administrators mislead researchers who study prisons from the ivory towers of academia. Prisons post platitudes about a mission of preparing offenders for reentry, yet they enforce policies that obstruct those who strive to deepen connections to society.

There is an emphasis on recreational activities. Perhaps the thinking is that activity—no matter how mindless—numbs the population into acquiescence. But this does not encourage offenders to keep family ties strong, to learn valuable and marketable skills, or to prepare for positive futures.

I remain convinced that the types of programs available in the prisons where I have served time would not hold much sway in opening employment opportunities. Inmates can "earn certificates" in programs like walking, knitting, beginning guitar, and celebrity rehab. They can earn prizes for winning bingo, for playing on a softball team, and for participating in table-game tournaments. Administrators, in encouraging these certificates, despite their dubious value, expose their own shortsighted perspective on a huge national problem.

There is a cruel incongruity between what the system of corrections purports to support and the actual policies by which I had to live. Administrators can present researchers with data showing that inmates earn certificates by participating in programs like those I mention above. Those programs may reduce inmate idleness, but they don't make much difference in preparing offenders for the colossal struggles awaiting their release.

While administrators give high marks to inmates who quietly endure mind-numbing sentences by earning certificates in knitting and basket-weaving, they block me from earning a doctorate degree from the University of Connecticut *which costs them nothing*. When I began writing books, they admonished me. When the national media brought attention to my work, they locked me in segregation and transferred me to other prisons. Scholarship threatens them.

The purpose of this long term in confinement has made little sense to me, though I am convinced that it has not had much to do with *corrections*. Still, I have strived to serve it with dignity. Since 2003, I have been confined within the fenceless boundaries of minimum-security camps. I serve my final decade under the honor system. Sometimes I wonder about the point of it all, the irony of it, really, as I drive in prison vehicles at midnight on public roads for my prison job without staff supervision. Under such conditions, I do not understand the purpose of my continued incarceration.

Prisons are the only world I know. I may have been isolated. But the punishment aspect ceased to register with me. I have learned to live inside, among ruthless killers, sniveling whiners, and even men of honor. I expect that the preparations I have made will enable me to overcome the obstacles that I will encounter upon release, but I will be in a new world.

Knowing that I will be nearly 50 upon my release, I do not know whether I will return to academia or go into business or continue writing. Fortunately, thanks to my deliberate adjustments, my growing network of support, and the devotion of my exceptional wife, I will welcome the decompression and the choices, for they are a blessing that few long-term prisoners will enjoy. I remain optimistic that within my lifetime and with my help, America will ground itself in a humane, moral, and rehabilitative philosophy of incarceration.

REFERENCES

Associated Press. 1995. "Several Causes Are Cited for Prison Riot." *Reading Eagle/Reading Times*, November 8, Sec. B-7.

Burger, Warren. 1986. "Factories with Fences." In *Dilemmas of Punishment*, eds. Kenneth C. Haas and Geoffrey P. Alpert, 349–356, Prospect Heights, IL: Waveland Press.

DiIulio, John J., Jr. 1994. "Let `Em Rot." *Wall Street Journal*, January 26, p. A-14.

DiIulio, John J., Jr. 1991. *Governing Prisons*. New York: Free Press.

DiIulio, John J., Jr. 1991. *No Escape: The Future of American Corrections*. New York: Basic Books.

Martinson, Robert. 1974. "What Works? Questions and Answers about Prison Reform." *The Public Interest* (Spring): 22–54.

Morris, Norval. 2004. *The Future of Imprisonment*. New York: Oxford University Press

Petersilia, Joan. 2009. *When Prisoners Come Home: Parole and Prisoner Reentry*. New York: Oxford University Press

Pew Charitable Trust. 2008. "One in 100. Behind Bars in America 2008." http://www.pewtrusts.org/uploadedFiles/wwwpewtrustsorg/Reports/sentencing_and_corrections/one_in_100.pdf.

Wilson, James. 1975. *Thinking about Crime*. New York: Basic Books.

Section F
Prison Release and
Reentry Challenges

CHAPTER 26

THE PRESENT STATUS AND FUTURE PROSPECTS OF PAROLE BOARDS AND PAROLE SUPERVISION

EDWARD E. RHINE

INTRODUCTION

Parole has experienced significant change and continuing controversy during the past four decades. Paroling practices have evolved through different historical periods responding, often pragmatically, to the particular pressures and demands then resonating within the larger political and criminal justice arenas of the time (Rothman 1980; Bottomley 1990; Morris 2002; Travis 2005). For well over half of the twentieth century, parole was considered an integral part of a criminal justice system grounded in indeterminate sentencing and the rehabilitative ideal. Though subjected to frequent criticism, especially during its most formative years in the 1920s and 1930s, it was the application rather than the concept of parole that was challenged. Up to the President's Commission on Law Enforcement and Administration of Justice (1965–1967), the legitimacy of parole, as well as the indeterminate sentencing structure on which it rested, remained largely unquestioned. Every state relied on a system of parole.

Beginning in the 1970s and the ensuing decades, the ideological hegemony associated with indeterminate sentencing and faith in the capacity of corrections to effect offender change experienced a period of rapid disillusionment and a corrosive loss of confidence. The response in a sizable number of states was to introduce greater determinacy, or "truth in sentencing" in their criminal codes, and to abolish parole boards. Some jurisdictions engineered reforms producing a greater structuring of discretion under the rubric of sentencing guidelines retaining several elements of parole (Petersilia 2003; Reitz 2004).[1] Regardless, within a relatively brief period of time, parole suffered a significant diminution in credibility, in many states (and at the federal level) moving to the margins of criminal justice discourse and efforts at reform.

An understanding of the present status of parole must recognize the historicity of this evolution. It must also address the fact that the concept itself covers distinct areas of focus, targeting parole boards and parole supervision. In practice, these are separate, but functionally interdependent, organizations and responsibilities. Enormous state-by-state variation exists within the criminal justice system today relative to the influence, scale, and range of jurisdiction exhibited by paroling authorities and parole field services agencies.

This chapter describes parole developments in the United States, placing them within a larger context of sentencing goals and correctional trends—past, present, and future. It considers the functions and current status of paroling authorities *and* parole supervision. There has been a continuing and long-term trend toward the reduction of discretionary parole board decision-making. At the same time, the overall reliance on parole supervision has increased dramatically in a manner, however, that is often disconnected from the decision to release. Though the release authority of parole boards has been abolished or severely curtailed in many jurisdictions, they nonetheless serve as principal decision-makers relative to the parole violations process, exerting a disproportionate impact on states' rates of prison population growth. Despite the enormous and often unrecognized consequences that the dual components of parole exert relative to criminal justice system operations, their influence and future will be shaped by their capacity to clearly articulate a compelling narrative and set of practices firmly embedded within the emerging national conversation focusing on prisoner reentry and sentencing reforms accenting utilitarian goals.

KEY POINTS OF CHAPTER

- The evolution of parole reflects rapid growth in the early twentieth century. Despite ongoing controversy, until the 1960s it appeared that parole boards were essential players within correctional systems, albeit serving a multiplicity of purposes. Starting in the mid-1970s and extending through the 1990s, paroling authorities experienced a damaging diminution in the scope of their discretionary release decision-making as states embraced greater determinacy in their sentencing codes. They were abolished in a number of states, with sharp limits placed on their authority in others. This trend is most evident in the dramatic shift in the methods by which offenders are now released from prison.

- The rapidity of parole's early growth and the suddenness of its demise have pushed paroling authorities in many states to the margins of discussions relative to criminal justice reform, yet they remain important players within their newly configured roles and responsibilities. The reach of their decision-making remains substantial, especially relative to their size. Parole boards continue to exert a notable impact on the ebb and flow of most correctional systems' populations.

- The philosophy and practice of parole or post-release supervision also shifted during this time, alongside a sizable expansion in its population, and a corresponding increase in the impact of its decision-making. As a result of the dramatic growth of mass incarceration, historically unprecedented numbers of offenders now being released from prison are ill-prepared to make a successful reentry transition. Yet, they are placed under systems of parole or post-release supervision that emphasize strategies calling for monitoring, surveillance, and control. These strategies target risk management, undermine the prospects for successful reentry transitions, and reveal a lack of tolerance for violations of the conditions of supervision.

- Though the release authority of parole boards has been curtailed in many jurisdictions, they nonetheless remain the principal decision-makers relative to the parole violations process. Working in concert with parole field services agencies, they play a highly consequential role relative to the pronounced growth associated with mass incarceration in many states. Their willingness to trigger revocation remains substantial at a time when parole field services have adopted more enforcement-centered supervision policies.

- The growing impact of mass incarceration, combined with the unrelenting downturn in the nation's economy, has contributed to an emerging national conversation centering on prisoner reentry, and the need for a more utilitarian jurisprudence under the banner of sentencing and correctional reform. Paroling authorities in a number of states, and parole supervision agencies in most jurisdictions, remain uniquely positioned to contribute to this dialogue. There are sightings that suggest that in some places they are already beginning to do so.

THE SHIFTING HISTORICAL AND CONTEMPORARY CONTEXT OF PAROLE

The Evolution and Growth of Parole

The concept of parole, though not the term, may be traced to revolutionary innovations in prison management during the mid-nineteenth century in Australia and Ireland. These developments were widely discussed by prison reformers in the United

States receiving philosophical affirmation in the principles adopted in 1870 by the newly formed American Prison Association calling for a new and more humanitarian approach to prison reform. The core features of reform and the origin of parole came to fruition shortly thereafter with the appointment of Zebulon Brockway as superintendent of Elmira Reformatory in 1876, and the passage of legislation the next year providing for an indeterminate sentence, a system of marks, and the birth of parole.[2]

The practice of parole was seeded in the decades that were to follow. Initially, parole was introduced and often served functions unrelated to offender reform. In some states, parole legislation was enacted to relieve governors of the time and trouble associated with the review of petitions for executive clemency. In other states, it was used as a safety valve to reduce prison crowding, and thus avoid the expense of new prison construction. Often it was championed by prison managers who viewed it as an effective tool for maintaining order and control inside prison walls.

By 1900, 20 states had adopted a system of parole, though only 11 of these states also had indeterminate sentencing provisions (Lindsey 1925). The first several decades of the 1900s, which witnessed the ascendancy of Progressive Era ideology across the criminal justice system, also saw the rapid-fire passage of parole statutes in nearly every state and jurisdiction across the country. By 1922, 44 states had a parole system, along with the territory of Hawaii (Lindsey 1925). By 1942, every state and the federal government operated a parole system.

While the rapidity of this change is notable, what is even more striking is that state after state enacted parole legislation with a minimum of debate (Rothman 1980).[3] As the granting of parole became the primary means of releasing inmates from confinement, its expansion was given additional support, if not fueled, by the growing presence of the "rehabilitative ideal" within correctional institutions subsequent to World War II (Allen 1981). The rehabilitative ideal was to exercise an ideological hegemony over the field of corrections through the 1960s, incorporating several key features, including the indeterminate sentence, and discretionary parole release. In fact, indeterminacy in sentencing, linked to parole, acquired a newfound legitimacy under the rehabilitative ideal.[4]

Parole acquired significant and often unrecognized support at the national level.[5] Even more, the dominance of rehabilitative ideology was reaffirmed less than a decade later through the President's Commission on Law Enforcement and Administration of Justice (1965–1967). It is striking that the President's Commission endorsed the legitimacy of parole and the sentencing structure with which it was associated just as a groundswell of social and political changes were beginning to unfold, heralding a fundamental shift in criminal justice policy in the decades to follow (Conley 1994).

The Challenge to the Legitimacy of Discretionary Parole Release

A dramatic series of challenges emerged that engineered a long-term, unanticipated, but rapid-fire unraveling of the core assumptions embedded in the report of the President's commission. The challenges focused on the disparities associated with the indeterminate sentence resulting in unfair and arbitrary decision-making, the inefficacy of correctional programming, and the issue of unbridled coercion masquerading as treatment and concern for the welfare of the offender (American Friends Service Committee 1971; Martinson 1974; von Hirsch 1976). The philosophy and practice of parole was implicated at the very heart of these concerns.

The criticisms directed at parole were not new. From the Progressive Era through the late 1960s, numerous commissions and studies determined that the practice of parole (both release and supervision) was seriously flawed. During the 1970s, many of the same criticisms were made—albeit with a sharper edge. However, the demise of the rehabilitative ideal gave these criticisms new meaning. For the first time, the problems associated with parole were viewed as symptomatic not of a disparity between theory and practice, which could be addressed through reform, but of an inherently flawed concept that should be abolished altogether (Rhine et al. 1991).

At the start of the 1970s, every state and the federal system relied on indeterminate sentencing structures (Travis 2005). The decades since then have witnessed profound changes in sentencing philosophy and practice in many states, redirecting away from a reliance on a rehabilitative rationale that emphasized utilitarian goals and focused on the offender to a "just deserts" rationale that stresses retributive concerns and the nature of the offense. From the mid-1970s through the 1980s–1990s, all 50 states, the District of Columbia, and the federal government revised or considered replacing indeterminate with determinate sentencing codes (Tonry 1996, 1999; Reitz 2004; Stemen and Rengifo 2005). The changes that have been adopted reflect a fundamental shift to greater determinacy in sentencing codes, carrying enormous consequences for the jurisdiction and functioning of paroling authorities.

Though they display significant variation in structure, sentencing reforms have exerted a more far-reaching impact on parole than on any other component of the criminal justice system. With Maine in the forefront, five states either eliminated or severely limited discretionary parole release between 1976 and 1979: California, Illinois, Indiana, Maine, and New Mexico. Colorado abolished its parole board from 1979–1985, but later restored it. During the 1980s, four more states followed suit: Florida, Minnesota, Oregon, and Washington. Connecticut, which implemented determinate sentencing in 1981, eliminating the parole board's release authority, later rescinded the action and since 2004 has authorized the chair to grant release to offenders who are within 18 months of their eligibility. At the federal level, the Comprehensive Crime Control Act of 1984 was enacted, creating the U.S. Sentencing Commission. The legislation abolished the U.S. Parole Commission, though it assumed release jurisdiction in 1998 over cases from the District of Columbia.

The movement to abolish parole continued unabated through the 1990s, during which 12 additional states eliminated discretionary parole release for offenders who committed their crimes after a date designated in the legislation: Arizona, Arkansas, Delaware, Kansas, Mississippi, North Carolina, Ohio, Oklahoma, Oregon, South Dakota, Virginia, and Wisconsin. It may very well be that in those states that abolished the release authority of parole boards during the 1980s–1990s, especially those that moved to sentencing guidelines, the likelihood is low that they will reemerge as key decision-makers at the back end of the criminal justice system. As Reitz (2004) observes, there is a long-term trend in the direction of parole abrogation, most notably, in a majority of sentencing guidelines jurisdictions. It is important to note, however, that from 2000–2010, no parole board was abolished or lost a significant amount of authority relative to its discretionary release decision-making. In fact, at least one state (Mississippi) recently restored the parole granting function (JFA Institute 2010). Despite what appeared to be a sustained, long-term trend toward the abrogation of parole boards, there has been a decade long hiatus extending from 2000–2010.

A national survey reports that 24 states' parole boards operate with nearly full discretion, while in another 6 states they exercise such discretion, except when dealing with certain types of offenders (Association of Paroling Authorities International 2005). When considering determinate sentencing reform, the abolition of parole does not necessarily follow the adoption of presumptive sentencing structures (e.g., New Jersey), or a shift to presumptive sentencing guidelines (e.g., Pennsylvania). Nonetheless, most states, regardless of sentencing structure, have restricted the reach of discretionary parole by excluding certain types of crimes from eligibility, most often for violent offenses or multiple felonies.[6] It is evident that parole boards have experienced a pronounced contraction in their releasing authority. At the same time, they continue to exert sizable leverage over key areas of corrections.

THE RELEASE AUTHORITY OF PAROLE BOARDS: CONTRACTION AND LEVERAGE

In terms of contraction, even though nearly two-thirds of state parole boards retain statutory authority to grant release, discretionary release has receded significantly in accounting for the overall percentage of cases exiting from prison. There are several pathways to release from prison today. The first is through a discretionary action of the parole board. The second is via mandatory parole or supervised mandatory release, which occurs mainly in jurisdictions that rely on determinate sentencing statutes. Those exiting prison under supervised mandatory release do so automatically after serving a certain percentage of their original sentence, minus any good time credits earned during confinement. There is no screening for readiness or suitability for release. The final pathways include exiting prison due to the expiration of the statutory sentence, and other forms of conditional and unconditional release (e.g., shock probation, commutation of sentence). It is instructive to observe the extent to which discretionary release has fallen into relative disuse by comparing it to offenders returning under mandatory release.

In 1977, a high water mark was reached in which 72 percent of offenders released from prison exited via discretionary parole release. By 1980, just three years later, this figure had decreased to 54.8 percent, and by 1990, the percentage granted discretionary parole release had declined to 39.4 percent. The drop continued, registering 23.9 percent in 2000. A bottoming-out may have been reached, as 23 percent were granted discretionary parole release in 2008. Conversely, in 1980, mandatory releases accounted for just 18.6 percent of the total exiting prison. By 1990, that figure had grown to 28.8 percent, increasing further to a high of 41 percent by 1999. In 2000, the figure dropped slightly to 38.9 percent, dipping a bit further in 2008 to 37.6 percent. Since 1995, inmates leaving prison via mandatory release have exceeded the number exiting through a parole board decision. In 1980, 78,602 offenders left prison by state parole board action, while 26,735 exited as mandatory releases. In 2008, the comparable figures were 156,862, and 256,609, respectively. Presently, just under one-quarter of all releases from prison result from parole board decisions. In some states, the proportion is far smaller (Hughes, Wilson, and Beck 2001; Hughes and Wilson 2003).[7] Figure 26.1 highlights these trends.

This reduction has resulted mainly from wide-ranging statutory changes eliminating parole release for some or all prisoners. But it also reflects a palpable and growing reluctance on the part of parole boards to grant discretionary release prior to the expiration of an offender's maximum sentence (Burke and Tonry 2006; Paparozzi and Caplan 2009). Paroling authorities are part of the political process and are empowered by it, a distinction they share with all executive branch agencies (except for four states in which they are part of the judiciary). In contrast to most other executive branch agencies, in which only the head of the department is appointed by the governor, in a majority of states the governor nominates the entire membership of the parole board (Paparozzi and Caplan 2009). While this serves to increase the accountability of the parole board, it also exposes its decision-making to political and public pressure, especially following the commission of a heinous crime by a parolee. California, Connecticut, and Pennsylvania offer recent examples of tragic events that eventuated in actions affecting the parole process.

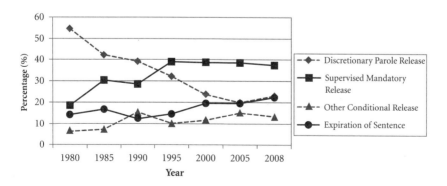

Figure 26.1. Trends in Method of Release from State Prison, 1980–2008.
Sources: Hughes, Wilson, and Beck 2001; Hughes and Wilson 2003; Sabol, West, and Cooper 2009.

Parole Board Decision-Making: Structure, Openness, and Residual Clout

In contrast to the other criminal justice system components, parole boards have always exercised the most visible display of discretion in their decision-making. It is often unrecognized that the contraction of discretionary parole release occurred alongside reform-oriented efforts made by parole boards to introduce greater structure, standardization, and consistency in decision-making, as well as a sustained commitment to create more openness and transparency in conducting parole reviews and hearings. In response to trenchant critiques regarding the arbitrary, closed, and abusive use of discretion, a majority of parole boards have since adopted risk assessment instruments or parole guidelines to bring greater structure to their release decision-making (Gottfredson et al. 1978; Burke et al. 1987; Rhine et al. 1991; Kinnevy and Caplan 2008; Caplan and Kinnevy 2010).[8]

When asked about the use of parole guidelines or risk assessment instruments in the release decision process, the most recent Association of Paroling Authorities' survey results illustrate that over 80 percent of 44 respondents claimed to use a parole decision-making instrument. More specifically, 32 of 37 (86.5 percent) of the same respondents indicated that the release authority relied on a risk assessment instrument. Though 18 respondents stated they used an instrument developed in-house, 12 said they relied on the Level of Service Inventory-Revised (Kinnevy and Caplan 2008). Figure 26.2 reflects those states indicating the use of a parole decision-making instrument (Caplan and Kinnevy 2010).[9]

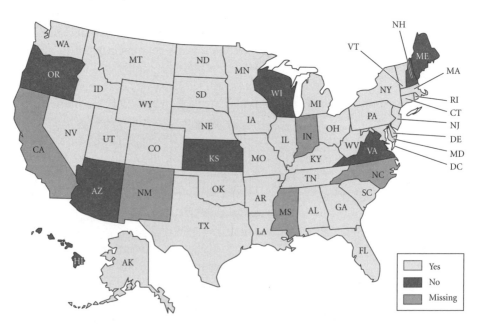

Figure 26.2. Majority of States Use Parole Decision-Making Instrument

Relatively few states actually employ formal parole guidelines for making release decisions (e.g., Georgia, Maryland, Pennsylvania). Even if a significant number of parole boards incorporate risk assessment instruments as a component of decision-making, the manner in which such assessments shape the decision to release is often unclear. In those states that have adopted the use of such tools as a matter of policy and practice, efforts to bring greater structure and fairness to decision-making function in considerable tension with the simultaneous commitment on the part of parole boards to open the hearing process by soliciting the input of victims, prosecutors, judges, and others.

Parole boards consider a host of factors when making a decision to release an offender from prison. Previous research on the ranking of such items revealed that most paroling authorities at the time embraced incapacitation and a modified just deserts philosophy when making release decisions. The single most important factor in the decision to grant or deny parole was the nature of the offender's current offense, though this was followed rather closely by any history of previous violence and prior felony convictions. In the middle range of such factors, program involvement, psychological reports, and the inmate's institutional disciplinary record were accorded importance (Rhine et al. 1991; Runda et al. 1994; Caplan 2007).

During the past several decades, many parole boards have "opened up" their decision-making process by granting victims, prosecutors, and judges the opportunity for input before a final parole decision is made. The Association of Paroling Authorities survey cited above noted that, in addition to official records on the offender and the crime, the top three sources of input considered by parole boards in their release decision process came from the victim, the offender's family, and the district attorney. Though tied to the nature of the instant offense, between 60–81 percent of paroling authorities are required to consider victim input when making release decisions. While all states responding considered victim input in release decision-making, the self-reported influence of the input reflected variation across jurisdictions (Kinnevy and Caplan 2008). Roberts (2009) observes that what limited research there is on impact statements at parole hearings suggests they may influence the outcome by making it less likely that an offender will be paroled. Caplan (2010), on the other hand, in a study of the New Jersey parole process, found that victim input was not significant as a predictor of parole release. His findings showed that the most influential predictors were measures of institutional history, crime severity, and criminal history—results consistent with the earlier research cited above.[10]

In addition to the release process, parole boards are authorized by statute to carry out a significant number of additional responsibilities, including rescinding established parole dates (e.g., for disciplinary violations), issuing subpoenas, setting the conditions of post-release supervision, granting final discharges for satisfactory performance on supervision, and, if violations occur during the period of supervision, deciding whether parole should be revoked. Reflecting their historical development, many paroling authorities still have statutory responsibility to either recommend or grant a pardon or commutation of sentence to the governor.

The range of matters over which parole boards have statutory jurisdiction remains substantial. Though parole boards have experienced a pronounced diminishment in their discretionary release authority, they still exercise residual, if not disproportionate, clout relative to their size and sphere of decision-making. Paparozzi and Caplan (2009), drawing from the Association of Paroling Authorities International national survey completed in 2008, report that roughly 347 individuals serve as full- or part-time members of state paroling authorities, with exclusive responsibility for determining the moment of parole release, as well as the conditions that govern their release. During 2008, such decisions affected 156,862 offenders (Sabol, West, and Cooper 2009).[11] What is less well known is that during the same year, these parole officials bore responsibility for setting the conditions of release for an additional 297,452 individuals exiting under mandatory supervised release or other forms of conditional release. They also oversaw compliance with conditions, and responded to petitions for revocation for the 824,365 individuals on parole or post-release control at the end of calendar year 2007 (Glaze and Bonczar 2008). Likewise, through 2008, they returned 248,317 individuals to confinement as a result of parole revocations, more than a third of all admissions to prison (Sabol, West, and Cooper 2009). This represents a great deal of power concentrated within the jurisdictional authority of a relatively small number of agencies and personnel. Even more, these figures affirm an all too often overlooked connectivity: the profound extent to which the actions of paroling authorities are still interdependent with and influence the operation of parole field services.

THE FUNCTIONS, CONDITIONS, AND CHANGING NARRATIVE OF POST-RELEASE SUPERVISION

Organization and Conditions of Parole Supervision

In most states, the actual function of parole or post-release supervision is carried out by parole field services agencies.[12] These agencies are usually housed under state departments of corrections. A 2006 census indicates that a total of 38 parole supervision agencies were so located, with responsibility for supervising 69 percent of the overall parolee population (Bonczar 2008). This reflects a long-term trend away from the parole board administering post-release supervision. At present, only 11 parole boards include this function within their operation supervising 25 percent of the adult parole population. A blend of agencies carries out supervision for the remaining 7 percent of parolees. It is notable that 35 of these agencies supervised caseloads of adult parolees and probationers, while 17 agencies supervised parolees only. Five state agencies (California, Texas, Illinois, New York, and Pennsylvania) provided supervision for over half of the total parole population nationwide. Though there is no consensus within the field regarding the "ideal" caseload size or standards, an issue that carries significant implications for agency staffing levels and effectiveness, for parolees under active supervision in 2006 the average caseload was rather modest, standing at 38 (Burrell 2007; Bonczar 2008).[13]

In a majority of states, in carrying out the supervision function, parole field services serves to enforce the decision goals framed in the conditions set by the parole board (Burke and Tonry 2006). Paroling authorities influence or play a key role in establishing the conditions governing the post-release supervision of offenders in 41 states (Bonzcar 2008). The period of community supervision that follows reflects an overriding emphasis on monitoring parolees' compliance with these conditions during the demanding and often problematic reentry transition from confinement to the community.[14] The conditions themselves display considerable variation in number and scope but, in essence, are intended to reduce the likelihood of new criminal behavior. Standard conditions continue to be imposed on every releasee within a given jurisdiction. Thus movement and travel are often limited, supervision fees imposed, association with known felons prohibited, submission to drug testing required, and the use of alcohol and drugs expressly forbidden. Special conditions are often added as well to individual cases either to deter certain behaviors, or to assist in the reintegration process (e.g., electronic monitoring or the completion of an outpatient drug-treatment program may be imposed).

It is difficult, given the absence of research, to discern the extent to which the actual number of parole conditions has increased in recent years. Offenders under supervision have long been expected to comply with exacting lists of rules and obligations that are often unrealistic and difficult to meet (Solomon et al. 2008). In most jurisdictions, the conditions do not differentiate the drivers of criminal behavior to guide the supervision process, nor assist offenders in prioritizing how best to attend to their reintegration needs (Taxman, Shepardson, and Byrne 2004).[15] Yet, it is also evident that for some categories (e.g., sex offenders) there has been a dramatic growth in supervision conditions, including notification and registration requirements. The increase in such conditions, alongside an already extensive listing of required conditions, carries important implications in view of the expansion of those subject to post-release supervision, and the shift toward a more surveillance-oriented approach to monitoring offenders' compliance with the rules.

The Expansive Growth of Parole Supervision

There has been a long-term expansion in the number of individuals under some form of parole or post-release supervision. As rates of incarceration have grown dramatically during the past 40 years, reaching record-setting levels, the number of persons being released from prison has likewise increased (Pew Center on the States 2008, 2009). At the close of 2007, a total of 824,365 persons were on parole. Of these, 92,673 were under federal jurisdiction, while 731,692 were supervised by state field services agencies. During 2007 alone, the parole population increased by 3.2 percent.

Even more, offenders under the jurisdiction of parole are at an all-time high, reflecting a fourfold increase in numbers since 1980 (Hughes, Wilson, and Beck 2001; Hughes and Wilson 2003; Glaze and Bonczar 2008).

Though the parole population has displayed a steady increase in both rates and total numbers, the growth in parole appears to have stabilized. In 1980, there were 196,786 adults on parole at the state level, reflecting a rate of 121 per 100,000 adult residents. The average annual rate of growth in parole from 1980 to 2000 was 6.2 percent. Twenty years later, in 2000, there were 652,199 adults on state parole. At year 2007, as mentioned above, the total under parole supervision at the state level was 731,692. This reflects a modest increase in the rate of parole from 312 in 2000 to 319 per 100,000 adult residents at the start of 2008. Though the growth continues, showing an overall increase of 10.8 percent during the past decade, the average annual increase presently stands at roughly 1 percent.

These trends conceal a significant distinction in the legal status of offenders coming home: Do they fall under conditional release supervision, or are they released unconditionally, that is, without any binding obligations? During the 1960s–1990s, the proportion of prisoners released conditionally was larger than in any of the preceding six decades (Travis and Lawrence 2002). The percentage of conditional releases started growing as states began introducing determinate sentencing codes, obtaining a high of 87 percent in 1990. Since then, there has been a slight decline to 78 percent of offenders in 2000 to 75 percent leaving under conditional release in 2008. Conversely, the share of unconditional releases has shown a steady, albeit incremental, growth upward, resulting in a total of 165,568 offenders exiting prison in 2008 without any requirements that they report to a parole officer (Sabol, West, and Cooper 2009).

Nonetheless, it remains that most offenders exit prison to supervision. In 2008, over 730,000 persons were released from federal and state facilities, the vast majority, nearly 500,000, moving from confinement to some form of supervised conditional release, namely, parole or post-release supervision (Sabol, West, and Cooper 2009). The reach of parole or post-release supervision continues to expand relative to the individuals subject to its terms and conditions. If the traditional function of parole was once designed to provide assistance targeting the reintegration of releasees, the philosophy and practice of supervision has shifted dramatically during the past several decades incorporating strategies accenting risk management, surveillance, and offender control.

The Shifting Narrative of Parole Supervision

It is evident that the mission, discourse, and practices associated with criminal justice have become more punitive during the past several decades (Garland 2001, Tonry 2008). The shift served to propel, as well as accompany, determinate sentencing reforms, mandatory minimum sentences, and a harsher tone toward offenders exerting a significant impact not just on paroling authorities, but on parole supervision as well. The "get tough" discourse directed at crime control became more retributive and more narrowly prescriptive in its directives to practitioners, eventually sparking a profound change in the mission and strategies embraced by parole (and probation) administrators.

It is possible to identify three eras of parole supervision, eras that Simon (1993) refers to as "disciplinary parole," "clinical parole," and "managerial parole." The first reflects a commitment on the part of parole officers to insert offenders into the community with and through the discipline of work and the labor market. Clinical parole focused more on the provision of assistance, and the social adjustment of offenders returning home from prison. Both of these eras were committed to brokering community resources and counseling (Petersilia 2003). The emphasis was on the normalization of the offender *in the community* by completing the rehabilitation process initiated in the prison setting.

The third era identified by Simon, managerial parole, offers a striking contrast. Across many states, since the mid-1980s, there has been a steady embrace of surveillance-oriented, control-based strategies of supervision. Parole supervision systems have adopted formal tools targeting the classification and management of offender risk. Their policies and, increasingly, their organizational culture place an overriding emphasis on monitoring and enforcing compliance with the conditions of supervision, and the detection of violations, often leading to offenders' arrest, revocation and return to custody. Offender needs assessments or requirements for assistance in the reentry transition become secondary to a heightened, if not singular, concern with risk management alone. Not surprisingly, many parole officers have come to view their role mainly as functioning in a law enforcement capacity within a culture that elevates detecting and catching violators. In essence, in these jurisdictions the focus of parole supervision has become almost exclusively that of crime control through more contacts, increased reliance on surveillance technology, aggressive enforcement, and more sanctioning of noncompliance (Rhine 1997; Seiter 2002; Caplan 2006; Petersilia 2003, 2008; American Bar Association 2007; Solomon et al. 2008).

The widespread adoption and continued use of formal risk assessment tools by parole agencies offers one indicator of this shift. Though these tools are often embedded in formal classification systems that incorporate an assessment of needs and a commitment to case planning, parole officers allocate most of their attention and resources away from casework to an overriding concern with enforcing parolee compliance with the conditions of supervision. Other indicators include the growing prominence of new surveillance technologies (e.g., GIS and electronic monitoring), frequent "rapid-results" drug testing of offenders, the spread of intensive supervision programs, and the creation of special fugitive units or warrants squads.[16]

The growing visibility of such indicators in both the discourse and practice of the field expresses an effort to market a more credible approach to supervision, one that is viewed as tough-minded and uncompromising relative to holding parolees accountable. The adoption of ever more aggressive strategies for supervision centering on the management and control of criminal offenders does not make any assumptions about reintegrating parolees back into the communities from which they came. In fact, it often betrays a deep cynicism about the prospects for positive offender change.

Within managerial parole, or what is elsewhere referred to as the language of the "new penology," there is a high expectation and a low tolerance for parolee failure (Simon and Feeley 1995). Left on its own, this narrative once constructed faces an intractable dilemma: as the perception and concerns about offender risk continue to escalate, legislators and the public alike become ever more convinced that the system of supervision is unable to manage such risk in a credible fashion. For evidence, they point to the very indicators that the surveillance-based, control-oriented model of supervision relies on as a benchmark of its success: the failure of those under post-release supervision, as revealed by high rates of revocation and the return to custody of growing numbers of parole violators.

THE VIOLATIONS AND REVOCATION PROCESS

The revocation of parole—the decision to return a parolee to prison for violating the terms of conditional release—is one of the major responsibilities of paroling authorities across the country. Parole officers are responsible for enforcing the conditions of parole—conditions that are most often established by the parole board. If the parolee commits a crime or violates other rules during supervision, the field services agency may initiate revocation proceedings. It must, however, refer the parolee to the board for a final determination.[17]

As prison populations have increased, it is becoming apparent that one key driver has been a dramatic jump in the number and percentage of parole violators returned to prison (Burke et al. 2007). The rise in parole violators subjected to reincarceration increased over ninefold from 1980 to 2008. In 1980, 27,000 parole violators were returned to state prisons. In 2000, 203,000 parole violators were returned to prison. In 1980, parole violators accounted for 17 percent of state prison admissions. In 2000, the comparable figure had risen to 36 percent of admissions to state prisons. Even more, nearly two-thirds of the parole violators were returned to prison for technical violations of the conditions of supervision, one-third for a new crime. The trend line since then has been remarkably stable. In 2008, 248,000 parole violators were returned to confinement. Though this represents a growth in numbers, parole violators accounted once again for just over one-third (36.6 percent) of overall admissions to prison (Hughes, Wilson, and Beck 2001; Travis and Lawrence 2002; Sabol, West, and Cooper 2010). Figure 26.3 illustrates the growth and stabilization in these trends.

It is reasonable to expect to find some rise in parole violations, especially given the pronounced growth associated with mass incarceration. However, the sheer increase in the numbers of such violations reflects that parole systems are investing

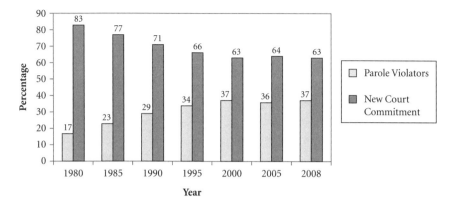

Figure 26.3. Growth and Stabilization in Parole Violators' Contributions to State Prison Admissions

substantial resources in detecting every instance of non-compliance with the conditions of supervision, and relying on revocation as the preferred sanction for responding (American Bar Association 2007). There is an accumulating body of evidence that suggests that this practice results in an expenditure of resources that does not improve public safety, only a costly cycle of repeatedly "catching and releasing" offenders in and out of prison (Solomon et al. 2005; Petersilia 2008; Grattet et al. 2009).

The response to violations is dependent, to some extent, on the behavior or conduct of parolees. It also reflects the fact that parole officers exercise significant discretion and leverage in addressing offenders who have violated the conditions of supervision. Ultimately, how parole officers respond is shaped by policy-based frameworks that vary state by state in their tolerance toward the frequency and range of violation behavior invariably presented by offenders. The variation is revealed in parole supervision systems' formal definitions of what constitutes a violation, the intensity of surveillance directed at parolees, the nature of the institutional culture driving parole field services operations, and the severity of sanctions most often imposed, given a determination that a violation(s) has occurred (Burke 2004; Reitz 2004; Piehl and LoBuglio 2005). As Reitz argues, "high or low revocation rates are more the result of the system's sensitivity to violations than any large difference in the post-release conduct of offenders from place to place" (2004, 217).

Excursus: The Risk Posed by Released Offenders

As a group, offenders released from prison represent a significant risk to reoffend, regardless of the method of release, or their placement under parole supervision.[18] Whether measured by rearrest for a new crime following release, reconviction, or return to prison, many prisoners fail—and fail rather quickly—to lead law-abiding lives subsequent to their return to the community (Travis 2005; Rosenfeld, Wallman, and Fornango 2005; National Research Council 2007; Pew Center on the States 2011). A sizable literature shows one thing very clearly: rates of recidivism for offenders released from prison have demonstrated a remarkable constancy, remaining persistently high for the past several decades (Glaser 1964; Beck and Shipley 1989; Langan and Levin 2002).

The most recent of two Bureau of Justice Statistics (BJS) cohort studies considered the outcomes of 272,111 prisoners subsequent to their release in 1994. During a follow-up period of three years, two-thirds (67.5 percent) of the individuals were rearrested for at least one crime involving a felony or serious misdemeanor. Just under one-half (46.9 percent) were reconvicted for a new crime, while one-quarter (25.4 percent) were re-sentenced to prison based on their convictions for such crimes. Even more, 51.8 percent were returned to prison either for new crimes or for technical violations of the conditions of their release.[19] The first year represents the period of greatest risk, accounting for nearly two-thirds of all the recidivism during the three-year period following release.

It is evident that the odds of making a successful reentry transition are highly problematic for a rather sizable percentage of ex-prisoners. As successive cohorts are released, they clearly present a significant risk of reoffending. Travis (2005), citing Raphael and Stoll (2004), states that recently released prisoners, when compared to the general population, are 20 to 50 times more likely to end up being arrested. The 1994 cohort alone accounted for 4.1 million arrest charges prior to their confinement, and close to three-quarters of a million charges within three years following their 1994 discharge.

These findings and others (Beck and Shipley 1989; Glaser 1964; Pew Center on the States 2011) suggest that the recurrence of high rates of reoffending by those returning from prison has not changed across the decades. The 1994 BJS cohort accounted for just under 5 percent of all arrests during the period 1994 to 1997. Another study of the same database determined that this cohort contributed between 13–16 percent of arrests (Rosenfeld, Wallman, and Fornango (2005). Petersilia (2003) points out that "persons being released from prison today are doing less well than their counterparts released a decade ago in successfully reintegrating into their communities. More of them are being rearrested; these arrests are occurring more quickly; and as a group, ex-convicts are accounting for a larger share of all serious crimes experienced in the United States." This trend, which contributes to and is a consequence of the growth in states' prison populations, carries significant implications for the future of parole.

MASS INCARCERATION AND RECASTING THE DISCOURSE ON PUNISHMENT

The past 30 to 40 years have witnessed unrelenting increases in federal and state prison populations in the United States. In 2008, for the first time, 1 in 100 adults were confined in prisons and jails across the land, while the incarcerated population stood at 2.3 million (Pew Center on the States 2008). Even more, 1 in 31 adults, or 3.2 percent of the adult population, were under some form of correctional control, including not just those confined behind bars, but another 5 million on probation or parole (Pew Center on the States 2009). Scholars have begun to take note of mass incarceration and its far-reaching implications for offenders, families, and communities (Alexander 2010; Barker 2009; Berman 2008; Bosworth 2010; Brown 2009; Clear 2007; Daedalus 2010; Gottschalk 2006; 2011; Jacobson 2005; Perkinson 2010; Thompson 2008; Useem and Piehl 2008; Western 2006).

The historically unprecedented growth associated with mass incarceration has begun to shows signs of abating (Sabol, West, and Cooper 2009; Pew Center for the States 2010). Though it is highly unlikely that rates of imprisonment will ever return to the level they were at in the early 1970s, before the growth began, the impact of the current economic downturn is for the first time producing cuts in corrections budgets (Scott-Hayward 2009). In many states, fiscal pressures are triggering calls for sentencing and correctional reforms that did not have a political foothold during the most active decades of the prison buildup (Useem and Piehl 2008). Within this context, the evolving ascendancy of the reentry movement in corrections offers opportunities for paroling authorities and parole services agencies to reshape practices that can coexist within the clashing narratives of punishment in the years ahead (Rhine and Thompson 2011).

As the field of corrections moves into the second decade of the twenty-first century, the boundaries for significant change are being recast in the complex interplay between what Garland (1990, 1995, 2001) refers to as "penological modernism" and retributive sanctioning. At any point in time, the response of the justice system to criminal offenders reflects the ongoing tension between the clashing narratives of penal modernism, with its utilitarian emphasis, and retributive sanctioning accenting expressive justice. While the former stresses utility in sentencing, and an enduring commitment to the rehabilitative ethos, the latter focuses on harsh and punitive penalties as ends in themselves. Both narratives are deeply embedded in the culture of punishment today.

The retributive narrative will continue to exert some impact, driving future legislation centering on crime control, but the discourse it offers will likely not prove as compelling or remain as effective in increasing the dosage of punishment as in past decades. This is due to the dissipation of budgetary support for further increases in prison capacity, as well as an emerging recognition that there are diminishing economic and social benefits attached to such an expansion (Austin and Fabelo 2004; Useem and Piehl 2008). In the near term, these shifts offer an important window of opportunity for experimentation and reform-oriented initiatives in corrections and parole. Numerous states are already pursuing innovations and legislative changes in sentencing and corrections, as well as downscaling their prison populations (Porter 2010; Greene and Mauer 2010; Mauer 2011). Additionally, the bipartisan commitment to prisoner reentry, culminating in the passage of the Second Chance Act in 2008, presents a timely and significant source of political and resource support. What these initiatives suggest is a growing receptivity to more "modernist" sentencing reforms and effective correctional strategies, but with the caveat that whatever is adopted must protect public safety, create utilitarian value, and cost less. It is within the shifting narratives of punishment and the growing focus on prisoner reentry that opportunities exist for parole to reemerge as a credible participant in criminal justice reforms.

PRISONER REENTRY AND PAROLE: THE NEED TO RE-ESTABLISH THE NEXUS

The past decade has experienced the rebirth of a remarkable concern with prisoner reentry across the field of corrections (Petersila 1999, 2003; Travis 2005; Travis and Visher 2005; Thompson 2008; Rhine and Thompson 2011). This interest has been kindled by the presence and impact of mass incarceration during the past four decades, especially the inevitability of what Travis (2005) refers to as the "iron law of imprisonment"—the fact that the vast majority of offenders "come back" following a period of confinement all too often ill-prepared to do so.[20] As the focus on prisoner reentry has evolved, it has become grounded in a commitment to public safety and the creation of sensible pathways to reintegration. Reentry is centered in a holistic paradigm calling for systemic changes in correctional systems—reforms that establish linkages supportive of offender transitions and community partnerships penetrating through and beyond prison walls.

The Question of Paroling Authorities

There is little doubt that parole boards have experienced a long-term, steady corrosion in their perceived place and value within the criminal justice system, leaving them in many jurisdictions marginalized and often unacknowledged in matters pertaining to criminal justice reform efforts (Campbell 2008). Voices from the academic community and national professional associations continue to present cogent arguments for the abolition of parole boards, including Travis's call for a "jurisprudence of reintegration" (2005), Reitz's (2004) questioning of the necessity or utility of back-end release decision-making, and the American Bar Association's formal recognition that judges should determine the time to be served in prison within a sentencing guidelines framework, bounded only by formulaic good-time reductions (American Bar Association 1994; Reitz 2004). The magnitude and implications of these challenges are mirrored not just in the number of paroling authorities abolished outright, but in the dramatic reversal in the methods by which offenders are released from a term of confinement.

Emerging on a separate track, the nascent reentry movement has encouraged some states to reconsider their sentencing and parole practices, in several instances adopting correctional reforms that represent a retooling of how prisoners are to be released, supervised, and/or returned from confinement (Lawrence 2009; Scott-Hayward 2009; Porter 2010). A recent example is found in Mississippi. In the mid-1990s, Mississippi implemented reforms under "truth in sentencing" laws requiring that all inmates, not just persons convicted of violent crimes, serve at least 85 percent of their sentence before release consideration. In response to dramatic prison population growth, and even a bit ahead of the state's economic slowdown, corrections officials, legislators and other stakeholders agreed to a dramatic statutory expansion of the parole board's discretionary authority. Specifically, the parole board was given authority to consider the release eligibility of all nonviolent offenders after they had served 25 percent of their sentence, subject to the adoption of a validated parole risk assessment (JFA 2010).[21] According to a former spokesperson for the governor at the time, "This legislation was more about re-entry than it was budget concerns. By focusing on inmates convicted of nonviolent crimes and having no violent crimes in their criminal history, we created a mechanism to transition—with parole board approval—a population of inmates back to society."[22]

Mississippi may prove to be the exception relative to discretionary parole release, but it reflects the imprint of penal modernism over purely just deserts and retributive concerns. It also demonstrates the extent to which paroling authorities might contribute as a "key pressure point in the system" to reducing the fragmentation that frequently hampers criminal justice system efforts (Burke and Tonry 2006). They are uniquely positioned in many states to look back and scan ahead in considering both an offender's time in prison and preparation for release. With their institutional and supervision counterparts, parole boards occupy a strategic niche through which to foster collaboration centering on effective reentry practices before and subsequent to an offender's release. The Transition from Prison to Community (TPC) initiative sponsored by the National Institute of Corrections since 2001 offers a promising example of how reentry has been integrated as part of the core mission in eight states routinely including parole boards and parole field services in implementing a holistic approach to returning offenders home (Burke 2008).

The interaction between paroling authorities and parole field services in managing the violations process offers another consequential area relative to reentry. Several noteworthy initiatives have been undertaken to develop progressive sanctions grids or their equivalent to better structure and guide violation decision-making. Burke (2004) reports on the experiences of four states in developing collaborative violation policies and strategies targeting higher risk offenders for return to prison, in tandem with efforts to engage in more problem-solving responses for identifying other moderate- to low-risk offenders. Three of these states (Georgia, Kansas, and New Jersey) were able to decrease admissions to prison as a result of technical parole violations by realigning their policies to encourage greater parolee success (Burke and Tonry 2006). Ohio, in 2005, adopted a progressive sanctioning policy and a violations grid designed to be responsive to offenders' risks and the seriousness of their non-compliance with parole conditions, aligned with the effective use of community-based treatment sanctions for responding, especially to early and chronic violations. The results have demonstrated the efficacy of such an approach in reducing unsuccessful discharges from parole, and in reinforcing the department's commitment to offender reentry (Martin and Van Dine 2008; Martin, Van Dine, and Fialkoff 2009).

The groundwork for addressing the issue of parole violations was seeded some time ago, well before the efforts discussed above (Carter 2001; Burke et al. 2007). The early efforts examined how resources were being deployed, and targeted responses in a manner that enhanced public safety and relied less on incapacitation. The steady evolution since then toward a policy-driven, more structured approach to violations of parole may, in fact, be viewed as a precursor to "justice reinvestment initiatives" (Council of State Governments 2009a), and programs and policies reflective of a commitment to evidence-based practices (National Institute of Corrections 2010), each of which carries significance for offender supervision.[23]

The Question of Parole Supervision

In terms of reentry, the reliance on post-release supervision remains the dominant approach to managing the risks that prisoners coming home present to returning to crime. The question of parole supervision must, of necessity, start with the recognition that in terms of reentry management, it is not possible to say "*definitively* that postprison supervision, as currently implemented, reduces crime" (Travis 2005, 108; National Research Council 2007; Taxman 2011). It is surprising, given its importance, that rigorous research studies on the efficacy of parole supervision are sorely lacking (see Solomon et al. 2005; Schlager and Robbins 2008).

Though the body of literature on the impact of the supervision process is relatively small, there are models of effective supervision practices that serve as useful exemplars given the mission of reentry. One such example is the Proactive Community Supervision model adopted in four probation and parole sites in Maryland (Taxman 2006, 2008). The results, comparing a behavioral management style of parole with an approach to parole focusing on monitoring and surveillance, showed the former to be more effective in reducing the likelihood of rearrest, and in decreasing the issuing of warrants for technical violations. The outcomes of this study have been replicated, albeit with more modest findings, in Travis County, Texas (Taxman 2011).

There are additional sightings in the field that suggest parole agencies are beginning to reconsider how they conduct supervision case management.[24] They appear to be more receptive to drawing on evidence-based practices to guide and enhance reentry outcomes. In 2008, the Urban Institute published a report recommending 13 strategies to improve parole supervision. Each of the strategies contained a summary of the available research, and highlighted specific sites that had adopted the changes under discussion.[25] The strategies were aimed at reducing the likelihood of future reoffending, which served as the overarching measure of performance and the first strategy in the report. The collective thinking illustrated how parole should work, if this outcome and viable linkages to offender reentry were to be consistently achieved (Solomon et al. 2008).

As an important next step in furthering the understanding of current practice, a survey was conducted under the auspices of the Urban Institute to determine the extent to which parole field services agencies embraced or had actually implemented the 13 strategies embedded in the report mentioned above (Jannetta et al. 2009). The authors acknowledged that they could not bore down to verify the extent or quality of implementation, and other methodological shortcomings. Drawing from its findings, the survey found a widespread and growing emphasis on the importance of using evidence-based practice. Perhaps not surprisingly, very few jurisdictions reported having implemented the 13 strategies in full.[26] The overall markers, according to the authors, point to movement in the direction of adopting research-informed supervision practices supportive of offenders' reentry transitions.

A cautious assessment of the survey suggests that a transition has begun, at least in some jurisdictions and in some field offices, away from a singular reliance upon monitoring, surveillance, and control toward a growing, albeit uneven, commitment to a greater balance incorporating research-based and effective principles for offender case management and supervision. Several studies have pointed out that line parole officers support a more balanced supervision style equipping them with effective case management strategies and support (Seiter 2002; Caplan 2006). An impressive literature illustrates that supervision in tandem with treatment is effective in reducing the likelihood that offenders released from prison will recidivate (Aos et al. 2006). In terms of a larger trend, it appears that the practice of parole supervision has entered a period of transition, and potentially, a more balanced realignment in its narrative.

Looking Ahead

There is a heightened appreciation, if not spreading recognition, by parole officials and others that they must rethink and retool their role in the criminal justice system (Paparozzi and DeMichele 2008; Papparozzi and Guy 2009). Doing so, however, must be tied closely to the creation of a compelling narrative that demonstrates how the work they do contributes tangibly to public safety and offender welfare. Whether a paroling authority or a field services agency, there are leading practitioners who understand the need to ground this narrative in the knowledge and principles reflected in the science of evidence-based practice and implementation. The recent launching of a National Parole Resource Center, and its nexus to the establishment of a Parole Academy, represent twin initiatives intended to serve as catalysts for moving the field of parole toward greater value and efficacy in the outcomes achieved.[27]

The place and future of paroling authorities and parole field services will be shaped by their willingness to embrace and create a strong and vibrant nexus to prisoner reentry within the larger context of sentencing and correctional reform. The prospects, especially for parole boards, for reacquiring credibility, if not legitimacy, within the boundaries of penal modernism will depend on their capacity to achieve a clear utility that both contributes to public safety and grounds the field's reawakening commitment to offender reintegration.

NOTES

1. Many states did not actually abolish parole boards; they abolished the exercise of certain forms of discretionary parole release. Often parole boards stayed in place to consider cases sentenced before the change or to make decisions on more specialized categories of crimes or types of cases, as well as to set conditions whenever release to supervision was mandatory, though conditional (Peggy Burke, personal correspondence, May 2010).

2. These innovations are credited to Alexander Maconochie, superintendent of the Norfolk Island Prison Colony from 1840–1844, and Sir Walter Crofton, who became chairman of the board of directors of the Irish prison system in 1854. The principles and practical methods they developed were influential in shaping the reformatory movement and eventually the birth of parole in the United States in the 1870s, emphasizing offender reformation over retribution, preparation for release through a system of graded classification, and successful performance while on a ticket-of-leave (Giardini 1959; Morris 2002). Bottomley (1990) cautions against overstating this linkage in an incisive historical and comparative review of the development of parole in the United States, Canada, and England.

3. Strong criticisms were highlighted in two major reports during this time. These reports, including the *National Commission on Law Enforcement and Observance* (1931) and the *Attorney General's Survey of Release Procedures* (Morse 1939), are notable, however, in that their criticisms of parole fully embraced the principles informing the Progressives' vision of criminal justice reform.

4. As the rehabilitative ideal acquired growing prominence in the vocabulary of American penologists, paroling authorities struggled to achieve its lofty goals in practice. In a majority of jurisdictions, its authority was decentralized, its membership part-time or ex-officio, statutory qualifications for appointment largely nonexistent, and the hearing process relatively unstructured and informal (Rubin 1949).

5. This is most clearly evidenced in the caliber of participants and the documents produced at the second National Conference on Parole held in Washington, D.C., in 1956. Convened by the attorney general, the conferees issued a reaffirmation of the 1939 Declaration of Principles (prepared during the first National Conference), and provided for the first time national standards for the practice of parole (National Probation and Parole Association 1957).

6. As Kinnevy and Caplan (2008) point out, 75 percent of parole boards in determinate sentencing jurisdictions say they have some authority to make release decisions prior to the completion of an offender's sentence. This illustrates that even determinate sentencing structures incorporate or retain varying degrees of discretionary release decision-making.

7. These figures, extending through the end of 2008, are drawn from the sources cited and from information furnished by William Sabol, Bureau of Justice Statistics, U.S.

Department of Justice. The data here and elsewhere serve to unpack Figure 4 and Table 4 in Sabol, West, and Cooper (2009).

8. There are normally three elements associated with parole guidelines, all of which factor into a release decision grid: time to be served, severity of presenting offense, and a risk assessment. The guidelines are intended to produce a presumptive period of time to be served based on a "parole prognosis" score (that is, the risk of reoffending) with a "seriousness" score that eventuates in a more rational and objective determination of a presumptive release date. The lower the crime severity level and parole prognosis (or risk level), the less the presumptive duration of confinement. Within states that rely on parole guidelines or risk tools to assist in decision-making, there are exceptions to setting release dates prescribed by the grid based on aggravating and mitigating factors. The guidelines do not bind the release decision.

9. The findings also showed that 17 states reported using the Static-99 for sex offenders only, while another 6 relied on the Salient Factor Score (Kinnevy and Caplan 2008).

10. It is difficult to rank order with precision what the major factors are governing parole board decision-making, that is, their actual versus self-reported impact on granting or denying parole. The variations in findings may reflect two very different sources of input. The first represents self-reporting in response to surveys by paroling authorities' chairs (or their designees). The results of the "APAI" surveys and an earlier American Correctional Association Parole Task Force survey (Rhine et al. 1991) offer examples. The second source reflects the empirical literature on parole release decision-making. See Caplan (2007) for a review of the latter.

11. Ibid, see 7.

12. As a result of sentencing reforms adopted during the past few decades, the term "parole" is no longer applied universally to refer to community supervision following release from prison (Solomon et al., 2008). This paper will use parole supervision, or post-release supervision, interchangeably, to refer to the period of supervision following release from prison.

13. Burrell (2007) observes that the issue of defining the ideal caseload size for probation and parole officers remains both contentious and difficult to resolve. His discussion demonstrates that while caseload size is important, and a necessary condition for effective supervision, manageable caseloads must be combined with effective strategies, drawing on the principles of evidence-based practice, if positive outcomes are to be achieved.

14. The usual period of supervision following release is for one to three years, but at least in some states it can last far longer (National Research Council 2007). Ohio requires a mandatory period of five years for sex offenders released from prison, while parole supervision in Texas may extend from 10–20 years. Other states show evidence that the average length of supervision is increasing. Between 2000–2007 the average period more than doubled in Wisconsin for post-release community supervision, rising from 23 to 54 months (Council of State Governments 2009b).

15. The Pennsylvania Board of Probation and Parole has developed procedures and special conditions that reflect a targeted assessment of offenders' risks and criminogenic needs, alongside guidance to support the supervision process (Solomon et al. 2008). The Parole Board in Ohio is engaged in a review of the conditions of supervision to ensure that they draw on evidence-based practices and are better tailored to support offender reintegration upon release.

16. As Burrell (2007) highlights, the spreading adoption of technological innovations has transformed the business of supervision, giving probation and parole officers a much

improved capacity to access information and monitor offenders. However, the use of technology has not altered what he refers to as the "core correctional practices that comprise case management" (38).

17. The parole revocation process continues to be governed by the requirements of *Morrissey v. Brewer*, 408 U.S. 471 *(1972)*, and *Gagnon v. Scarpelli*, 411 U.S. 778 (1973). Though they provide clear direction relative to the requisites of procedural due process, these provisions have not effectively constrained the growing percentage of offenders returned to prison as parole violators, especially for technical violations.

18. An often-cited BJS report (Hughes, Wilson, and Beck 2001) notes that the method of release impacts success rates. From 1990–1999, discretionary parole releasees exhibited higher rates of success (54 percent in 1999) than mandatory releasees (33 percent in 1999). As discussed shortly, these outcomes mask methodological issues and policy calculations pertaining to how "success rates" are shaped by state- and agency-level variations in responses to parole violations (Petersilia 2003; Reitz 2004; Paparozzi and Guy 2009).

19. Interestingly, there are substantial differences in those who are released after serving their first term in prison versus what happens in the aggregate to those released from confinement. As Tonry (2004, 171) observes, "[o]f those released from prison the first time, only about a third reoffend. Of all people released from prison, typically two-thirds reoffend." The distinction drawn by Tonry is salient to the extent that prevailing sensibilities about crime control have directed the focus toward the releasee population as a whole.

20. Reentry may be broadly defined as inclusive of the processes and experiences associated with offenders' release from prison, jail, or other forms of secure confinement. Reentry is not a program per se, nor is it equivalent to a term of community or post-release supervision. It is inclusive of the continuum that extends from an offender's admission to prison (arguably, it starts at sentencing) to the expiration of any period of community supervision that may follow.

21. The results of the 2008 national parole survey in Figure 26.2 on the use of parole decision-making instruments show Mississippi under the "missing" category. If the survey were to be done today, the state would be coded as a "yes," given its use of a risk assessment tool.

22. Though the findings are still preliminary, the projected growth was eliminated, the prison population has steadily declined, the rate of parole revocations has remained constant, and of 3,100 prisoners released, 121 (or 4 percent) had been returned to custody. Of the latter, "all but five were returned for technical parole violations." The policy changes governing release were not tied to parole supervision, a linkage the state intends to address (JFA 2010).

23. I am indebted to Peggy Burke for sharing this insight in personal correspondence (May 2010). The recent experiences in several states (e.g., Michigan, Kansas) participating in the Justice Reinvestment Initiative have shown impressive reductions in the percentage of parole revocations (Council for State Governments 2009a).

24. The Georgia Board of Pardons and Parole has implemented automated, evidence-based supervision case management practices that target and reinforce the linkages that are essential to offenders' successful reentry transitions subsequent to imprisonment (see: http://www.pap.state.ga.us/opencms/opencms/; National Institute of Corrections 2010).

25. The strategies included tailoring the conditions of supervision, drawing on risk-needs assessments, front-loading supervision services, implementing earned discharge and place-based supervision strategies, engaging other agency and community partners, balancing surveillance and treatment in supervision case plans, engaging informal social

controls, incorporating incentives and rewards into the supervision process, and relying on graduated problem-solving responses in a swift and timely manner in response to violations.

26. There appears to be considerable uncertainty over what the concept of evidence-based practices really means, with parole administrators stating that they do not receive the support they need to actually implement such practices.

27. Funding has been provided by the Bureau of Justice Assistance, supporting a partnership between the Center for Effective Public Policy, the Association of Paroling Authorities International, and the Urban Institute to establish a National Parole Resource Center (NPRC). Its overriding mission is to help shape the evolving role and future of parole as an increasingly effective stakeholder within criminal justice systems across the country. The NPRC is jointly managed by the Bureau of Justice Assistance and the National Institute of Corrections and collaborates with the Urban Institute's - Parole Academy. The latter provides technical assistance to sites selected to implement the 13 parole supervision strategies highlighted in the *Putting Public Safety First* report by Solomon et al. (2008).

REFERENCES

Alexander, Michelle. 2010. *The New Jim Crow: Mass Incarceration in the Age of Colorblindness.* New York: The New Press.

Allen, Francis A. 1981. *The Decline of the Rehabilitative Ideal: Penal Policy and Social Purpose.* New Haven, CT: Yale University Press.

American Bar Association. 1994. *Standards for Criminal Justice: Sentencing,* 3rd ed. Chicago: American Bar Association Press.

American Bar Association. 2007. *Report to the House of Delegates on Improvements in Probation and Parole Supervision.* Midyear Meeting. Commission on Effective Criminal Sanctions.

American Friends Service Committee. 1971. *Struggle for Justice: A Report on Crime and Punishment in America.* New York: Hill and Wang.

Aos, Steve, Marna Miller, and Elizabeth Drake. 2006. *Evidence-Based Adult Correctional Programs: What Works and What Does Not.* January. Washington State Institute for Public Policy.

Association of Paroling Authorities International (APAI). 2005. Paroling Authorities Survey. Available at: apaitl.org.

Austin, James and Tony Fabelo. 2004. *The Diminishing Returns of Increased Incarceration: A Blueprint to Improve Public Safety and Reduce Costs.* Washington, DC: JFA Institute.

Barker, Vanessa. 2009. *The Politics of Imprisonment: How the Democratic Process Shapes the Way America Punishes Offenders.* New York: Oxford University Press.

Beck, Allen J., and Bernard E. Shipley. 1989. *Recidivism of Prisoners Released in 1983.* Washington, DC: U.S. Department of Justice. Bureau of Justice Statistics.

Berman, Douglas A. 2008. "Reorienting Progressive Perspectives for Twenty-first Century Punishment Realities." *Harvard Law and Policy Review* 3: http://www.hlpronline.com/Berman_HLPR_120808.pdf.

Bonczar, Thomas P. 2008. *Characteristics of State Parole Supervising Agencies, 2006.* Washington, DC: U.S. Department of Justice. Bureau of Justice Statistics.

Bosworth, Mary. 2010. *Explaining U.S. Imprisonment.* Thousand Oaks, CA: Sage.

Bottomley, Keith A. 1990. "Parole in Transition: A Comparative Study of Origins, Developments, and Prospects for the 1990s." In *Crime and Justice: A Review of Research*, eds. Michael Tonry and Norval Morris, 319–374. Chicago: University of Chicago Press.

Brown, Michelle. 2009. *The Culture of Punishment: Prison, Society, and Spectacle*. New York: New York University Press.

Burke, Peggy, Linda Adams, Gerald Kaufman, and Becki Ney. 1987. *Structuring Parole Decisionmaking: Understanding the Past; Shaping the Future*. Washington, DC: National Institute of Corrections. U.S. Department of Justice.

Burke, Peggy. 2004. *Parole Violations Revisited: A Handbook on Strengthening Parole Practices for Public Safety and Successful Transition to the Community*. Washington, DC: U.S. Department of Justice, National Institute of Corrections.

Burke, Peggy and Michael Tonry. 2006. *Successful Transition and Reentry for Safer Communities: A Call to Action for Parole*. Silver Springs, MD: Center for Effective Public Policy.

Burke, Peggy, Adam Gelb, and Jake Horowitz. 2007. *When Offenders Break the Rules: Smart Responses to Probation and Parole Violations*. Public Safety Policy Brief. Washington, DC: The Pew Charitable Trusts.

Burke, Peggy. 2008. *TPC Reentry Handbook: Implementing the NIC Transition from Prison to the Community Model*. Washington, DC: National Institute of Corrections. U.S. Department of Justice.

Burrell, William D. 2007. "Issue Paper on Caseload Standards for Probation and Parole." *Perspectives* 31(2): 37–41. Lexington, KY: American Probation and Parole Association.

Campbell, Nancy. 2008. *Comprehensive Framework for Paroling Authorities in an Era of Evidence-based Practice*. Washington, DC: U.S. Department of Justice, National Institute of Corrections.

Caplan, Joel M. 2006. "Parole System Anomie: Conflicting Models of Casework and Surveillance." *Federal Probation* 70(3): 32–26.

Caplan, Joel M. 2007. "What Factors Affect Parole? A Review of Empirical Research." *Federal Probation* 71(1): 16–19.

Caplan, Joel M. 2010. "Parole Release Decisions: Impact of Positive and Negative Victim and Nonvictim Input on a Representative Sample of Parole-Eligible Inmates." *Violence and Victims* 25(2). Springer Publishing.

Caplan, Joel M., and Susan C. Kinnevy. 2010. "National Surveys of State Paroling Authorities: Models of Service Delivery." *Federal Probation* 74(1): 34–42.

Carter, Madeline M., ed. 2001. *Responding to Parole and Probation Violations: A Handbook to Guide Local Policy Development*. Washington, DC: National Institute of Justice. U.S. Department of Justice.

Conley, John A., ed. 1994. *The 1967 President's Crime Commission Report: Its Impact 25 Years Later*. Cincinnati, OH: Anderson Publishing.

Clear, Todd R. 2007. *Imprisoning Communities: How Mass Incarceration Makes Disadvantaged Neighborhoods Worse*. New York: Oxford University Press.

Council of State Governments. 2009(a). *Justice Reinvestment Initiatives*. Available at: http://www.justicerinvestment.org/.

Council of State Governments. 2009(b). *Justice Reinvestment in Wisconsin: Analyses and Policy Options to Reduce Spending on Corrections and Increase Public Safety*. New York: Council of State Governments Justice Center.

Daedalus. 2010. "Special Topic: Mass Incarceration." Summer. *Journal of the American Academy of Arts & Sciences*. Cambridge, MA.

Garland, David. 1990. *Punishment and Modern Society.* Chicago: University of Chicago Press.

Garland, David. 1995. "Penal Modernism and Postmodernism." In *Punishment and Social Control,* eds. Thomas G. Blomberg and Stanley Cohen. New York: Aldine De Gruyter.

Garland, David. 2001. *The Culture of Control: Crime and Social Order in Contemporary Society.* Chicago: University of Chicago Press.

Giardini, Giovanni I. 1959. *The Parole Process.* Springfield, IL: Thomas.

Glaser, Daniel. 1964. *The Effectiveness of a Prison and Parole System.* New York: Bobbs Merrill.

Glaze, Lauren E., and Thomas P. Bonczar. 2008. *Probation and Parole in the United States, 2007 Statistical Tables.* Washington, DC: U.S. Department of Justice. Bureau of Justice Statistics.

Gottschalk, Marie. 2006. *The Prison and the Gallows: The Politics of Mass Incarceration in America.* New York: Cambridge University Press.

Gottschalk, Marie. 2011. "The Past, Present, and Future of Mass Incarceration in the United States." *Criminology and Public Policy* 10(3): 483–504.

Gottfredson, Don M., Leslie T. Wilkins, and Peter B. Hoffman. 1978. *Guidelines for Parole and Sentencing.* Lexington, MA: Heath/Lexington.

Grattet, Ryken, Joan Petersilia, Jeffry Lin, and Marlene Beckman. 2009. "Parole Violations and Revocations in California: Analysis and Suggestions for Action." *Federal Probation* 73(1): 2–11.

Greene, Judith, and Marc Mauer. 2010. *Downscaling Prisons: Lessons from Four States.* The Sentencing Project. Washington, DC.

Hughes, Timothy, and Dorris J. Wilson. 2003. *Reentry Trends in the United States.* Washington, DC: U.S. Department of Justice. Bureau of Justice Statistics.

Hughes, Timothy A., Doris J. Wilson, and Allen J. Beck. 2001. *Trends in State Parole, 1990–2000.* Washington, DC: U.S. Department of Justice. Bureau of Justice Statistics.

JFA Institute. 2010. *Reforming Mississippi's Prison System.* Public Safety Performance Project. Washington, DC: The Pew Charitable Trusts.

Jacobson, Michael. 2005. *Downsizing Prisons: How to Reduce Crime and End Mass Incarceration.* New York: New York University Press.

Jannetta, Jesse, Brian Elderbroom, Amy Solomon, Meagan Cahill, Barbara Parthasarathy, and William D. Burrell. 2009. *An Evolving Field: Findings from the 2008 Parole Practices Survey.* Washington, DC: The Urban Institute.

Kinnevy, Susan C. and Joel M. Caplan. 2008. *Findings from the APAI International Survey of Releasing Authorities.* Philadelphia: Center for Research on Youth and Social Policy. University of Pennsylvania.

Langan, Patrick A., and David Levin. 2002. *Recidivism of Prisoners Released in 1994.* Washington, DC: U.S. Department of Justice. Bureau of Justice Statistics.

Lawrence, Alison. 2009. *Cutting Corrections Costs: Earned Time Policies for State Prisoners.* Washington, DC: National Conference on State Legislatures.

Lindsey, Edward. 1925. Historical Sketch of the Indeterminate Sentence and Parole System. *Journal of the American Institute of Criminal Law and Criminology* 16: 9–126.

Martin, Brian, and Steve Van Dine. 2008. *Examining the Impact of Ohio's Progressive Sanction Grid: Final Report.* Grant # 2005-IJ-CX-0038. Washington, DC: U.S. Department of Justice. National Institute of Corrections.

Martin, Brian, Steve Van Dine, and David Fialkoff. 2009. "Ohio's Progressive Sanction Grid: Promising Findings on the Benefits of Structure Responses." *Perspectives* 33(2): 22–29. American Probation and Parole Association. Lexington, Kentucky.

Martinson, Robert. 1974. "What Works? Questions and Answers About Prison Reform." *Public Interest* 35: 22–54.

Mauer, Marc. 2011. "Sentencing Reform: Amid Mass Incarceration-Guarded Optimism." *Criminal Justice* 26(1).

Morris, Norval. 2002. *Maconochie's Gentlemen: The Story of Norfolk Island and the Roots of Modern Prison Reform*. New York: Oxford University Press.

Morse, Wayne, ed. 1939. *Attorney General's Survey of Release Procedures*. Washington, DC.: U.S. Department of Justice.

National Commission on Law Observance and Enforcement. 1931. *Penal Institutions, Probation, and Parole*. Washington, DC: U.S. Government Printing Office.

National Institute of Corrections. 2010. *A Framework for Evidence-Based Practices in Local Criminal Justice Systems*. 3rd ed. Available at: http://www.cepp.com/documents/EBDM%20Framework.pdf.

National Probation and Parole Association. 1957. *Parole in Principle and Practice: A Manual and Report*. New York: National Parole and Probation Association.

National Research Council. 2007. *Parole, Desistance from Crime and Community Integration*. Washington, DC: National Academies Press.

Paparozzi, Mario, and Matthew Demichele. 2008. "Probation and Parole: Overworked, Misunderstood, and Under-Appreciated: But Why?" *The Howard Journal* 47(3): 275–296.

Papparozzi, Mario A., and Joel M. Caplan. 2009. "A Profile of Paroling Authorities in America: The Strange Bedfellows of Politics and Professionalism." *The Prison Journal* 89(4): 401–425.

Papparozzi, Mario A., and Roger Guy. 2009. "The Giant That Never Woke: Parole Authorities as the Lynchpin to Evidence-based Practices and Prisoner Reentry." *Journal of Contemporary Criminal Justice* 25(4): 397–411.

Perkinson, Robert. 2010. *Texas Tough: The Rise of America's Prison Empire*. New York: Metropolitan Books.

Petersilia, Joan. 1999. "Parole and Prisoner Reentry in the United States." In *Prisons*. eds. Michael Tonry and Joan Petersilia. Chicago: University of Chicago Press.

Petersilia, Joan. 2003. *When Prisoners Come Home: Parole and Prisoner Reentry*. New York: Oxford University Press.

Petersilia, Joan. 2008. "California's Correctional Paradox of Excess and Deprivation." In *Crime and Justice: A Review of Research*, ed. Michael Tonry, Chicago: University of Chicago Press.

Pew Center on the States. 2008. *One in 100: Behind Bars in America*. Public Safety Performance Project. Washington, DC: The Pew Charitable Trusts.

Pew Center on the States. 2009. *One in 31: The Long-Reach of American Corrections*. Public Safety Performance Project. Washington, DC: The Pew Charitable Trusts.

Pew Center on the States. 2010. *Prison Count 2010: State Population Declines for the First Time in 38 Years*. Public Safety Performance Project. Washington, DC: The Pew Charitable Trusts.

Pew Center on the States. 2011. *State of Recidivism: The Revolving Door of America's Prisons*. Public Safety Performance Project. Washington, DC: The Pew Charitable Trusts.

Piehl, Anne M., and Stefan F. LoBuglio. 2005. "Does Supervision Matter?" In *Prisoner Reentry and Crime in America*, eds. Jeremy Travis and Christy Visher. New York. Cambridge University Press.

Porter, Nicole D. 2010. *The State of Sentencing 2009: Developments in Policy and Practice*. Washington, DC: The Sentencing Project.

President's Commission on Law Enforcement and Administration of Justice. 1967. *Task Force Report: Corrections*. Washington, DC: Government Printing Office.

Raphael, Steven, and Michael A. Stoll. 2004. "The Effect of Prison Releases on Regional Crime Rates." In *The Brookings-Wharton Papers on Urban Affairs 2004*, eds. William G. Gale and Janet R. Pack. Washington, DC: Brookings Institution Press.

Reitz, Kevin. 2004. "Questioning the Conventional Wisdom of Parole Release Authority." In *The Future of Imprisonment*, ed. Michael Tonry. New York: Oxford University Press.

Rhine, Edward E., William R. Smith, Ronald W. Jackson, Peggy B. Burke, and Roger Labelle. 1991. *Paroling Authorities: Recent History and Current Practice*. Laurel, MD: American Correctional Association.

Rhine, Edward E. 1997. "Probation and Parole Supervision: In Need of a New Narrative." *Correctional Quarterly* 1(2): 71–75.

Rhine, Edward E., and Anthony C. Thompson. 2011. "The Reentry Movement in Corrections: Resiliency, Fragility, and Prospects." *Criminal Law Bulletin* 47(2): 177–209.

Roberts, Julian V. 2009. "Listening to the Crime Victim: Evaluating Victim Input at Sentencing and Parole." In *Crime and Justice: A Review of Research*, ed. Michael Tonry. Chicago: University of Chicago Press.

Rosenfeld, Richard, Joel Wallman, and Robert Fornango. 2005. "The Contributions of Ex-Prisoners to Crime Rates." In *Prisoner Reentry and Crime in America*, eds. Jeremy Travis and Christy Visher, 80–104. New York: Cambridge University Press.

Rothman, David J. 1980. *Conscience and Convenience: The Asylum and Its Alternatives*. Boston: Little, Brown and Company.

Rubin, Sol. 1949. *Adult Parole Systems in the United States*. New York: National Council on Crime and Delinquency.

Runda, John C., Edward E. Rhine, and Robert E. Wetter. 1994. *The Practice of Parole Boards*. Association of Paroling Authorities International. Lexington, KY: Council of State Governments.

Sabol, William J., Heather C. West, and Matthew Cooper. 2009. *Prisoners in 2008*. Washington, DC: U.S. Department of Justice. Bureau of Justice Statistics.

Schlager, Melinda and Kelly Robbins. 2008. "Does Parole Work? Revisited: Reframing the Discussion of the Impact of Postprison Supervision on Offender Outcome." *The Prison Journal* 88(2): 234–251.

Scott-Hayward, Christine S. 2009. *The Fiscal Crisis in Corrections: Rethinking Policies and Practices*. New York: Vera Institute of Justice.

Seiter, Richard. 2002. "Prisoner Reentry and the Role of Parole Officers." *Federal Probation* 66(3): 50–54.

Simon, Jonathan. 1993. *Poor Discipline: Parole and the Social Control of the Underclass, 1890–1990*. Chicago: University of Chicago Press.

Simon, Jonathan, and Malcolm M. Feeley. 1995. "True Crime: The New Penology and Public Discourse on Crime." In *Punishment and Social Control*, eds. Thomas G. Blomberg and Stanley Cohen. Hawthorne, NY: Aldine De Gruyter.

Solomon, Amy L., Jenny W.L. Osborne, Laura Winterfield, Brian Elderbroom, Peggy Burke, Richard P. Stroker, Edward E. Rhine, and William D. Burrell. 2008. *Putting Public Safety First: 13 Parole Supervision Strategies to Enhance Reentry Outcomes*. Washington, DC: The Urban Institute.

Solomon, Amy L. Avinash Bhati, and Vera Kachnowski. 2005. *Does Parole Work? Analyzing the Impact of Post-Prison Supervision and Recidivism*. Washington, DC: The Urban Institute.

Stemen, Don, and Andres Rengifo. 2005. "The Impact of State Sentencing Reforms on Prison Populations." *Research in Progress Seminar Series.* Washington, DC: National Institute of Justice. U.S. Department of Justice. March.

Taxman, Faye S., Eric S. Shepardson, and James M. Byrne. 2004. *Tools of the Trade: A Guide to Incorporating Science into Practice.* Washington, DC: National Institute of Corrections. Available at: http://www.nicic.org/Library/020095.

Taxman, Faye S. 2006. "What Should We Expect from Parole (and Probation) under a Behavioral Management Approach?" *Perspectives.* 30(2): 46–53.

Taxman, Faye S. 2008. "No Illusions: Offender and Organizational Change in Maryland's Proactive Community Supervision Efforts." *Criminology & Public Policy.* 7(2): 275–302.

Taxman, Faye S. 2011. "Parole: 'What Works' Is Still Under Construction." In Handbook of Evidence-Based Substance Abuse Treatment in Criminal Justice Settings, eds. Carl Leukefeld, Thomas P. Gullotta, and John Gregich. New York: Springer.

Thompson, Anthony C. 2008. *Releasing Prisoners, Redeeming Communities: Reentry, Race, and Politics.* New York: New York University Press.

Tonry, Michael. 1996. *Sentencing Matters.* New York. Oxford University Press.

Tonry, Michael. 1999. "The Fragmentation of Sentencing and Corrections in America." *Sentencing and Corrections: Issues for the 21st Century.* Washington, DC: U.S. Department of Justice. National Institute of Justice.

Tonry, Michael. 2004. *Thinking about Crime: Sense and Sensibility in American Penal Culture.* New York: Oxford University Press.

Tonry, Michael. 2008. "Crime and Human Rights: How Political Paranoia, Protestant Fundamentalism, and Constitutional Obsolescence Combined to Devastate Black America." American Society of Criminology 2007 Presidential Address. *Criminology* 46(1): 1–33.

Travis, Jeremy. 2005. *But They All Come Back: Facing the Challenges of Prisoner Reentry.* Washington, DC: Urban Institute Press.

Travis, Jeremy, and Christy Visher, eds. 2005. *Prisoner Reentry and Crime in America.* New York. Cambridge University Press.

Travis, Jeremy, and Sarah Lawrence. 2002. *Beyond the Prison Gates: The State of Parole in America.* Washington, DC: The Urban Institute.

Useem, Bert, and Anne Piehl. 2008. *Prison State: The Challenge of Mass Incarceration.* New York: Cambridge University Press.

Von Hirsch, Andrew. 1976. *Doing Justice: The Choice of Punishments.* New York: Hill and Wang.

Western, Bruce. 2006. *Punishment and Inequality in America.* New York: Russell Sage Foundation.

CHAPTER 27

LIFE ON THE OUTSIDE: TRANSITIONING FROM PRISON TO THE COMMUNITY

THOMAS P. LEBEL AND
SHADD MARUNA

INTRODUCTION

There are 1.6 million men and women incarcerated in state and federal prisons (Sabol, West, and Cooper 2009). A major consequence of the prison-building strategy over the last three decades is that more prisoners are let out and returned to society than ever before. In fact, close to 700,000 prisoners will be released each year for the foreseeable future (Sabol et al. 2009). Consequently, prisoner reentry has become a major concern for states and the federal government (e.g., Re-Entry Policy Council 2005), as well as a topic of great academic interest to criminal justice researchers (e.g., Maruna 2001; Petersilia 2003; Travis 2005).

It is a well-known fact that many returning prisoners will recidivate. A study of prisoners released in 15 states in 1994 found that 67.5 percent were arrested and just over one-half (52 percent) were returned to prison within three years (Langan and Levin 2002). Due to these high failure rates, the subject of "what works" in prisoner reentry has become among the most pressing issues in criminology (see e.g., Visher and Travis, chapter 28 of this volume; Maruna and Immarigeon 2004; Morgan and Owers 2001; Petersilia 2003; Seiter and Kadela

2003; Travis, Solomon, and Waul 2001). Reentry researchers are particularly interested in determining the pre- and post-prison factors most closely related to success or failure (see e.g., La Vigne, Shollenberger, and Debus 2009; LeBel et al. 2008; Social Exclusion Unit 2002; Visher and Courtney 2007; Yahner and Visher 2008).

Austin (2001, 314; see also Maruna and LeBel 2002) argues that "reentry" has become "the new buzzword in correctional reform." Jeremy Travis (2005, xxi) defines reentry as "the process of leaving prison and returning to society." He argues that:

> Reentry is not a form of supervision, like parole. Reentry is not a goal, like rehabilitation or reintegration. Reentry is not an option. Reentry reflects the iron law of imprisonment, they all come back.

Expanding upon this definition, Maruna, Immarigeon, and LeBel (2004; see also Taxman, Young and Byrne 2002; Visher and Travis 2003) state that:

> Reintegration is both an event and a process. Narrowly speaking, re-entry comes the day a prisoner is released from confinement. . . . More broadly, re-entry is also a long-term process, one that actually starts prior to release and continues well afterwards. (5)

Under this broader definition, prisoner reentry includes many processes that begin before the individual is released from prison, experiences at the moment of release and during the first month out, and during the (perhaps equally difficult to define) reintegration process of the first few years in the community (Irwin 1970; Visher and Travis 2003). This chapter focuses on this more inclusive definition of prisoner reentry.

We have clustered the key themes emerging from this qualitative and quantitative field research with formerly incarcerated persons into seven main sections dealing with each of the following key research areas:

- The initial release from prison;
- The major obstacles to reintegration;
- The importance of family;
- The stigma of the ex-convict label;
- Socio-cognitive factors and reintegration;
- The function of parole supervision;
- The role of mutual aid in reintegration.

Although we divide our discussion into these various sections for convenience of presentation, in the lived experiences of ex-prisoners all of these factors intersect, and indeed there is overlap from section to section in our chapter.

In each section, we focus on giving voice to the concerns of prisoners and formerly incarcerated people. Gonnerman (2004, 10) argues that public (and academic) discussions surrounding prisoner reintegration "usually leave out the voices of former prisoners, relying instead on statistics." Yet, she argues that "the true story of America's exodus of ex-cons cannot be told only with numbers." To address this gap, this chapter primarily examines the transition from prison to the community from the perspective of individuals in prison and formerly incarcerated persons. Our discussion draws almost exclusively on the experiences and perspectives of adults returning from state and federal prisons, although many of the topics are also relevant to juveniles and persons reentering communities from local jails. Qualitative and quantitative research on the lives of former prisoners underscores the need to understand the *subjective changes* (e.g., in motivation, self-efficacy, or identity) as well as the *social changes* (e.g., in marital or employment status) that may help sustain abstinence from criminal offending. As such it is important to understand the reintegration process from the perspective of the person reentering society him- or herself. Appropriately, then, we conclude our chapter with a brief discussion of a variety of initiatives, nationwide, led by ex-prisoners and their supporters, themselves, to influence the public debate around reentry policy.

Reentry Shock

Irwin (2005, n.3, 202) asserts that in his 50 years of contact with prisoners and former prisoners he has been "consistently reassured that *most* persons passing through the prison make up their mind to attempt to live a noncriminal life and stay out of prison." This observation has been consistently supported in field research: at the point of release, most offenders express a strong desire and willingness to "go straight" (Burnett 1992; Lin 2000; Visher and Courtney 2007; Visher et al. 2004). Petersilia (2003, 14) argues that "if we fail to take advantage of this mindset, we miss one of the few potential turning points to successfully intervene in offender's lives."

Most are optimistic about their chances as well. Research from the Urban Institute's *Returning Home* study consistently finds that prior to release, about three-fourths of respondents expected it to be "pretty easy" or "very easy" to stay out of prison following release (see e.g., Visher and Courtney 2007; Visher et al. 2004). For some, this is clearly over-confidence or naïveté. Yet, importantly, research studies have typically found that prisoners who think it will be easy to stay out of prison are in fact less likely to be reincarcerated after release (LeBel et al. 2008; Visher and Courtney 2007). Prisoners often report that to be successful they must have willpower, but also need to ask for help and support (Coalition for Women Prisoners 2008; Howerton et al. 2008). "It's pretty tough, but if you've got any kind of will power and intestinal fortitude, you can make it. It's all up to the individual. There's help out there" (Erickson et al. 1973, 43). Research also indicates that most prisoners and former prisoners have essentially the same goals and aspirations as the law-abiding public (Burnett 1992; Erickson et al. 1973; Helfgott 1997; Irwin 1970; Petersilia 2003). For example, Helfgott (1997) found in her study in Seattle, Washington, that former prisoners' most common long-term goals were to own a home, to establish a career, to be self-employed and to own a business, to obtain an educational degree, to be able to help their children financially through college, and to have a "normal life" (16). However, research suggests that for most returning prisoners, these expectations for "conventional" success are unrealistic (Bucklen and Zajac 2009; Erickson et al. 1973; Glaser 1969; Irwin 1970) and perhaps need to be scaled back (Lin 2000). Gonnerman (2004) points out that "Nobody in prison fantasizes about returning home to a low-wage job, a three-train commute, a pile of unpaid bills, . . . a 9:00 P.M. curfew, an empty refrigerator" (338). The reality of reentry, then, is often quite different from the "land of milk and honey" often imagined from behind bars: "Being in the penitentiary, you sit up there and you dream about what's going to happen when you get out. You expect everything to fall in place when you get out, but yet it don't fall in place like you want it to" (Erickson et al. 1973, 60). According to Irwin (2005, 174) "Most prisoners step into the outside world with a small bundle of stuff under their arm, a little bit of money, perhaps their $200 'gate' money, and that's all." In fact, in some states, the situation could be even worse. Indeed, a recent study of prisoners released in Houston, Texas found that many were released with $50 in gate money, about three-fourths had only one set of street clothing, and fewer than two in five (37 percent) had non-prison issue photo identification (La Vigne et al. 2009b).

Many recently released prisoners report negative experiences the first few days out, due to being a "stranger in a strange land" (Irwin 2009, 130). "As for what I call the Rip Van Winkle syndrome, it's like coming awake after 100 years, suddenly you're pushed out . . . not pushed out, released, and you have to become a passenger, neighbor, pedestrian, customer, all the things I listed, and nobody prepares you for it" (Howerton et al. 2009, 450). Another released prisoner notes that "The first day of release is the scariest day. I was shook up. There was too much temptation. I didn't know what was up" (Festen and Fischer 2002, 1). The shock of reentry causes many returning prisoners to feel confused, lost, depressed, nervous, anxious, frightened, lonesome, or paranoid (see, e.g., Erickson et al. 1973; Martin and Sussman 1993; Richards and Jones 2004).

KEY HURDLES TO REINTEGRATION

Before release, prisoners report that obtaining employment, finding a place to live, and abstaining from substance use will be the most important factors keeping them from returning to prison (Visher and Courtney 2007). Each of these substantial hurdles (employment, housing, and substance abuse) will be treated separately below. However, it is important to keep in mind that these issues are all interrelated in the lives of ex-prisoners (see Burnett 1992). One recently released prisoner described the sorts of catch-22 situations that prisoners often face in regard to multiple needs: "I think one of my biggest problems was no transportation and no immediate job. I was hassled because I couldn't find work without transportation, and I can't get transportation without work, so it was one of those things" (Erickson et al. 1973, 24).

Get a Job

> "I gotta survive. No ifs, ands, or buts about it and that's the cold hard reality of it.
> I ain't gonna starve too long for nobody. Not for Jesus Christ if he came down
> here and told me, 'don't sell drugs.' Damn, you ain't in my shoes" (Male, 47, served
> 6 months, homeless). (Festen and Fischer 2002, 6)

Perhaps the best-documented roadblock faced by persons with criminal records concerns employment (e.g., Solomon et al. 2006; Western et al. 2001). Laws frequently bar employers from hiring released prisoners (i.e., convicted felons) in growing sectors of the economy, including jobs involving child care, elder care, health care, and financial services (Love 2006). Gonnerman (2004) reports that in New York State, formerly incarcerated persons are also barred from becoming barbers, check cashiers, real estate brokers, sanitation workers, and taxi drivers. Research indicates that former prisoners face considerable discrimination in competing for jobs, leading to dim prospects for even low-wage employment (see Holzer, Raphael, and Stoll 2004; Pager 2007). Of course, many returning prisoners have poor employment skills and limited work experience to begin with (Petersilia 2003), leaving them doubly disadvantaged (Festen and Fischer 2002). The majority (71 percent) of male formerly incarcerated persons felt that their criminal record had negatively affected their job search (Visher, Debus, and Yahner 2008). For example:

> I tried to get a job and they wouldn't even hire me at Burger King. That's like the
> easiest place to get a job now. . . . It's because of your record. They don't tell you
> that, but they just blow you off totally. It's like they took your [application] and
> threw it in the trash. (La Vigne, Wolf, and Jannetta 2004, 49)

When prisoners and parolees are asked to express their needs, employment and job training are typically at, or near, the top of the list (Erickson et al. 1973; La Vigne, Brooks, and Shollenberger 2007; Nelson et al. 1999; Visher and Lattimore 2007). The related needs of lack of money and lack of education are also perceived as major obstacles that must be addressed in order to succeed (Erickson et al. 1973; Visher and Lattmore 2007). After release, men consistently report struggling most with finding a job (70 percent at one month, 65 percent at one year) and making enough money to support themselves (66 percent, 56 percent) (Visher and Courtney 2007; Visher et al. 2004). As one released prisoner exclaimed, "I need job leads. Everything else they talk about is useless" (Nelson et al. 1999, 29). Formerly incarcerated persons also note that job training was the most useful program since release (Visher et al. 2008), and a significant percentage also express a need for more job training in prison and in the community (Brooks et al. 2008; La Vigne et al. 2009b; Visher and Lattimore 2007). In a comprehensive report of employment outcomes for released prisoners in three states, Visher and colleagues (2008) report that only 45 percent were currently employed at eight months. Many released prisoners who find jobs do so through family and friends or by being rehired by a former employer (Nelson et al. 1999; Visher et al. 2008). Women appear to be less likely than men to find full- or part-time employment in the first year after release (La Vigne, Brooks, and Shollenberger 2009a). This may be due to women having a higher unemployment rate prior to admission to prison (Greenfeld and Snell 1999), having fewer job skills (Messina, Burdon, and Prendergast 2001), having more extensive histories of substance use, and being much less likely to have received job training while in prison (La Vigne et al. 2009a). The former prisoners who are most likely to find jobs and maintain employment after release are those who have worked before incarceration and participated in employment programs in prison and in the community soon after release (Nelson et al. 1999; Visher et al. 2008). Conversely, the use of drugs in the first 2 to 4 months after release was the strongest predictor of the percentage of time (not) employed at 8 to 10 months post-release (La Vigne et al. 2009b).

Finding and maintaining employment after release has been shown to reduce recidivism (La Vigne, Visher, and Castro 2004; La Vigne et al. 2007; Rossman and Roman 2003; Visher and Courtney 2007; Visher et al. 2008; Yahner and Visher 2008). For example, Visher and colleagues (2008) note that the likelihood of reincarceration during the first year out is lower for individuals employed at two months compared to those who were unemployed. The reduction in recidivism was especially strong (23 percent) for those earning $10 or more per hour compared with those who were unemployed. The positive effect of in-prison work experience on post-release employment has also been noted (e.g., Aos et al. 2006; La Vigne et al. 2007; Saylor and Gaes 1996). Expanding transitional employment opportunities for recently released prisoners could have positive effects on employment outcomes and recidivism after incarceration (Buck 2000; Finn 1998; Redcross et al. 2009; Rossman and Roman 2003). Redcross and colleagues (2009), in a rigorous evaluation of the Center for Employment Opportunities (CEO) in New York City, found that returning prisoners who received transitional jobs and post-employment support services were significantly less likely than a control group to be convicted of a crime (30.5 percent vs. 38.3 percent) over a two-year follow-up period.

A decent job can be a source of non-criminal contacts and also reinforce "legitimate" goals and values that promote the adoption of a law-abiding lifestyle. Sampson and Laub (1993), however, argue that employment "by itself" does not support desistance, rather, "employment coupled with job stability, commitment to work, and mutual ties binding workers and employers reduces criminality" (146). In a similar vein, Uggen (1999) stresses that not just any job will do, but that job quality is critical for desistance from crime. Moreover, Irwin (2009) argues that "doing good involves having a job with a 'living wage,' security, and job satisfaction" (132). Finally, formerly incarcerated persons (like many other groups) often express a preference for jobs that enable them to exercise some intelligence, creativity, and autonomy (Shover 1996).

Many returning prisoners appear to be frustrated because they have few options besides "McJobs" (i.e., low-paying and "dead end" jobs):

> I can't live on $5 or $7 an hour. Considering my background, that is all I am worth in the eye of the public. Just because I'm a convict with a history of drugs, I [still] think I should get [a job] I'm qualified for. (Festen and Fischer 2002, 10)

Visher and colleagues (2008) report that about half of released prisoners who do find work are unhappy with their pay. A recent study found that released prisoners who made more than $10 an hour were half as likely to return to prison as those making less than $7 an hour (Visher et al. 2008). Pezzin (1995) also found that higher current legal earnings increase the chance for offenders to terminate criminal careers. In addition, one's attitude toward work appears to play a role in whether a parolee is successful. Bucklen and Zajac (2009) report that parole violators had negative attitudes toward employment and unrealistic job expectations, and did not want to accept lower end jobs. Overcoming the barriers to employment facing convicted felons, then, represents an important challenge for policies aimed at effective prisoner reentry.

No Place Like Home?

> "I was dropped back into the same environment I came out of. Bottom line, most of us are. If you go back to the same environment, eventually you are going to get pulled back into that same lifestyle. It doesn't matter how strong you say you are" (Male, 47, served 6 months, homeless). (Festen and Fischer 2002, 6)

Prior to release, prisoners rank having a place to live (14 percent) as the second most important thing needed to stay out of prison (La Vigne et al. 2007). Recent studies indicate that about three-fourths of former prisoners reside, at least initially, with family members after release (La Vigne et al. 2004; Nelson et al. 1999; Solomon et al. 2006). Returning prisoners have difficulty affording reasonable housing on their own (Lewis et al. 2003; Roman and Travis 2004), and often find themselves excluded from apartments in the public and private market (La Vigne et al. 2009b; LeBel, forthcoming; Thacher 2008). As a result, many exhibit a high degree of residential mobility in the first year in the community (see e.g., Visher and Courtney 2007). Austin and Irwin (2000, 156) estimate that more than 25 percent of released prisoners "eventually end up on the streets, where they live out a short life of dereliction, alcoholism, and drug abuse." Obtaining a safe place to live is important, as researchers consistently find that released prisoners without stable housing are more likely to return to prison (Metraux and Culhane, 2004; Roman and Travis, 2004; Thompson, 2008; Visher and Courtney, 2007). In particular, the ability to find stable housing in the first month following release is one of the strongest inhibitors of reincarceration (Visher and Courtney 2007). Released prisoners who live in a home of their own at two months also are much less likely (12 percent vs. 37 percent) than those who do not to be reincarcerated 16 months out (Yahner and Visher 2008).

The reality of reentry is that at least half of released prisoners return to their old neighborhood (Brooks et al. 2008; La Vigne et al. 2009b; Yahner and Visher 2008), often a disadvantaged urban neighborhood with high rates of crime and relatively few services and support systems to promote successful reintegration (see e.g., Clear 2007; Lynch and Sabol 2001; Travis 2005; Solomon et al. 2006). This phenomenon is referred to as the "geographic concentration" of returning prisoners (Lynch and Sabol 2001). Prisoners who return to more disadvantaged and disorganized neighborhoods recidivate at a greater rate (Kubrin and Stewart 2006; Yahner and Visher 2008). Yahner and Visher (2008), for example, found that respondents living in more disorganized communities were more likely to return to prison in the first 16 months out (38 percent vs. 26 percent).

Kubrin and Stewart (2006, 189) argue that "by ignoring community context, we are likely setting up ex-inmates for failure." Released prisoners themselves certainly appear to recognize that their chances of success are diminished by returning to the old neighborhood:

> Whatever was there has not changed. It's like you're putting new seed in old soil—no nutrients to support new growth. (O'Brien 2006, 109)

Returning to these neighborhoods makes it especially difficult to avoid the people, places, and things partly responsible for going to prison in the first place (Maruna and Roy 2007). A significant portion of formerly incarcerated persons report that drug dealing is a major problem, that it is difficult to avoid crime, and that their neighborhood is not a good place to find a job (see e.g., Brooks et al. 2008; La Vigne et al. 2009b; Visher and Courtney 2007). Released prisoners who are able to reenter in a different neighborhood most often report doing so to stay out of trouble or to live with family (Brooks et al. 2008; Yahner and Visher 2008). Rose and Clear (2003) note that former prisoners often move to a new neighborhood in an attempt to "start over." Importantly, prisoners returning to a new neighborhood were much less likely (42 percent vs. 69 percent) to be reincarcerated three years out (Yahner and Visher 2008). Moreover, Kirk (2009) found that parolees in New Orleans who moved to a new neighborhood (or parish) due to the destruction caused by Hurricane Katrina were significantly less likely to be reincarcerated within one year of prison release.

Getting Clean

"And, as soon as I got out the first thing on me mind was smack (heroin). I had, like, I took some money off a couple of the lads, getting out, I had like £300 (approx. $500) in me pocket, I had another £200 waiting for me on the way home. . . . I bought a bottle of whiskey, 4 tins of lager and just got bevvied up (drunk) on the train going home. As soon as I got home, it was just smack, rocks (crack cocaine), smack, rocks" (British male ex-prisoner, 27 years old, quoted in Maruna, 2001, 78).

An analysis of the *Survey of Inmates in State and Federal Correctional Facilities in 2004*, a nationally representative survey of the incarcerated population, found that 53 percent of state and 45 percent of federal prisoners met the DSM-IV criteria for drug dependence or abuse in the 12 months prior to their admission to prison (Mumola and Karberg 2006). Prisoners returning home recognize their drug use as a primary factor in many of their legal and social problems (La Vigne et al. 2004; Visher et al. 2004), and those who recidivate are more likely to have used drugs before incarceration and soon after release (La Vigne et al. 2004; Visher et al. 2004; La Vigne et al. 2007). One year removed from prison, women are more likely than men to engage in drug use and to have problems due to their drug use (La Vigne et al. 2009a).

When released prisoners fail, the greatest percentage recognize that drug use caused them to return to prison (Visher and Courtney 2007). For example, in a study of former prisoners at the time of their rearrest, the highest percentage (28 percent) reported that drugs or alcohol was their biggest problem (Brooks et al. 2008). In fact, 67 percent of released prisoners reincarcerated in a Massachusetts study reported drunkenness or illegal drug use in the month before reincarceration, and more than a third reported daily substance use (Brooks et al. 2008). Prisoners who participate in substance abuse programs while incarcerated and immediately after release are less likely to return to prison (La Vigne et al. 2009b) and report less frequent drug use (La Vigne et al. 2007; Visher and Courtney 2007; Visher et al. 2004).

In their review of prisoner reentry programs, Seiter and Kadela (2003) found that drug rehabilitation interventions have been studied most frequently and have the most positive results (i.e., program-completers were less likely than non-completers to have been arrested, continue drug use, or have a parole violation). In particular, the continuum of drug treatment model—with an in-prison therapeutic community (TC), a transitional TC as part of a work-release program, and an aftercare component—has been most successful in reducing recidivism and drug use (Inciardi, Martin, and Butzin 2004; Prendergast, Hall, Wexler, Melnick, and Cao 2004). Inciardi and colleagues (2004) report that those who completed treatment and attended aftercare were much more likely than those not receiving treatment to be drug free (26 percent vs. 5 percent) and arrest free (48 percent vs. 23 percent) at 60 months. Unfortunately, after returning to the community, few released prisoners continue to receive appropriate substance abuse treatment (Winterfield and Castro 2005).

FAMILY VALUES

Strong social bonds to conventional society are thought to be important for successful prisoner reintegration (see, e.g., Wolff and Draine 2004) and for the desistance from crime more generally (e.g., Laub, Nagin, and Sampson 1998; Sampson and Laub 1993), and the strength of one's family relationships are typically seen as being of central importance (Braman 2004). Recent reentry studies have found that married men are less likely to self-report committing a new crime (Visher et al. 2009); women who were married and/or have minor children were less likely to be reincarcerated (La Vigne et al. 2009a); and being married or living as married and higher quality relationships with partners reduces self-reported drug use (Visher et al. 2009).

Indeed, Petersilia (2003) asserts that "*Every* known study that has been able to directly examine the relationship between a prisoner's legitimate community ties and recidivism has found that feelings of being welcome at home and the strength of interpersonal ties outside prison help predict postprison adjustment" (245–246, italics in original).

Family members often provide both material (housing, food, money, clothing) and emotional (encouragement, acceptance, a person to talk to, etc.) support (see e.g., Nelson et al. 1999). Tromanhauser (2003, 93) argues "By far, the greatest need is emotional and psychological support. Parolees need a 'significant other,' a believer, . . . someone to turn to when things seem hopeless." Returning prisoners consistently report receiving high levels of each form of support from their families, often exceeding their pre-release expectations (La Vigne et al. 2009b). After release, the vast majority of released prisoners felt that family support had been an important factor in avoiding a return to prison (La Vigne et al. 2004; Visher et al. 2004). In fact, Visher and Courtney (2007) report that over the first year after release, the largest percentage of returning prisoners identified family support as the *most important thing* that had kept them out of prison.

Returning prisoners who maintained better family connections while incarcerated (e.g., through letters, phone calls, and visits), and those who report more positive family relationships more generally, have been found to be less likely to recidivate (Hairston 1988, 2003; La Vigne et al. 2004; La Vigne et al. 2009b; Nelson et al. 1999; Sullivan et al. 2002; Visher and Courtney 2007). For example, La Vigne et al. (2009a) found that women who felt that their families were more helpful to them were less likely to be reincarcerated at one year, while men who received greater tangible support from their families were less likely to use drugs frequently 8–10 months after release (La Vigne et al. 2009b). Of course, some of this may be explained by selection effects (those who have greater family supports may have other advantages going for them as well).

However, as social beings, all humans need others and may also have a "need to be needed" in life as well. Maruna (2001) has argued that "generative commitments"—defined as "the concern for and commitment to promoting the next generation" (McAdams and de St. Aubin 1998)—seem to fill a particular void in the lives of former offenders, providing a sense of purpose and meaning, allowing them to redeem themselves from their past mistakes, and legitimizing the person's claim to having changed. For the individual engaged in generative concerns, criminal behavior either seems pointless (its role in establishing one's masculinity or toughness no longer needed) or else too risky in the sense that it could jeopardize the person's new self-identity.

Evidence is accumulating in support of the benefits of these sorts of generative family relationships. For instance, about 10 percent of released prisoners report that seeing their children is the most important thing keeping them from returning to prison (La Vigne et al. 2009b; Visher and Courtney 2007). Sampson and Laub (1993) found that former offenders who assume the responsibility of providing for their spouses and children are significantly more likely to successfully desist from crime than those who make no such social commitments. Interestingly, they also found that desistance from crime is correlated with assuming social and financial responsibility for one's aging parents or one's siblings in need as well (219–220). LeBel et al. (2008) found that self-characterization as a "family man" (i.e., a "good partner," a "good father," and/or a "good provider") contributes positively to the desistance process of formerly incarcerated persons by reducing the likelihood of experiencing social problems 4–6 months after release and of being reimprisoned in the next 10 years. Bucklen and Zajac (2009) found that successful parolees (as compared to violators) were more likely to report being in stable supportive relationships and to describe their identity as that of a "family man." Finally, research suggests that both having minor children at home (La Vigne et al. 2009b) and reporting a stronger attachment to children reduces the likelihood of drug use (Visher and Courtney 2007).

Of course, many prisoners are highly isolated, with no family ties, and others may have "burned such bridges" when they became consumed with crime and drugs. Only around 17 percent of state prisoners self-report as being married (Petersilia 2003), and about half of one sample of returning prisoners said they did not have someone who could meet them at the gate at the time of their release (La Vigne et al. 2009b). As such, attempts to re-develop pro-social bonds and social capital appear to be critical for successful reintegration (Cullen 1994; Travis 2005; Wolff and Draine 2004). Unfortunately, creating pro-social bonds is not a task that correctional agencies tend to do well (see, e.g., MacKenzie and Brame 2001). Although arranging "good" marriages for returning prisoners is probably only an intervention fit for reality television, developing natural support systems to reconnect prisoners with their families (Hairston 2003; Lanier 2003; Shapiro and Schwartz 2001) appears to be a realistic and workable intervention.

Finally, returning to live with family members is not always a positive factor. Unfortunately, a substantial number of released prisoners report living with someone who has a problem with drinking or drug use and/or has served time in prison or jail (Brooks et al. 2008; Visher and Courtney 2007). Released prisoners with these sorts of family influences are more likely to use drugs frequently in the first year out (Visher and Courtney 2007). In addition, Yahner and Visher (2008) report that released prisoners who experienced family violence or conflict before prison were twice as likely to return to prison in the first 16 months after release. Formerly incarcerated persons face challenges in reestablishing family ties (Hairston 2003; Lanier 2003; Richie 2001). Several studies indicate that providing services to strengthen the family network of recently released prisoners results in positive outcomes for both the returning prisoner (i.e., lower rates of recidivism and drug use) and the individual family members (see Shapiro and Schwartz 2001; Sullivan et al. 2002). For example, in the La Bodega de la Familia program there was a significantly greater reduction in drug use at 6 months for the program group compared to the comparison group. Moreover, although La Bodega did not include a specific goal of reducing recidivism of the drug users whose families used its services, these drug users were about half as likely as a comparison group to be arrested or convicted of a new offense both during the study period and in the following 6 months (Sullivan et al. 2002).

THE STIGMA OF THE "EX-CON" LABEL

It is almost a truism in criminology that "a criminal conviction—no matter how trivial or how long ago it occurred—scars one for life" (Petersilia 2003, 19). Garland (2001, 180) argues that "the assumption today is that there is no such thing as an 'ex-offender'—only offenders who have been caught before and will strike again." Johnson (2002) argues,

> Released prisoners find themselves "in" but not "of" the larger society. Like lepers, we keep ex-prisoners at a distance and avoid them entirely when we can. Even under the best of conditions, ex-offenders face formidable obstacles to reassimilation in the community. (319)

It is well documented that former prisoners suffer from many "civil disabilities" such as statutory restrictions placed on public and private employment, voting, eligibility for public assistance and public housing, financial aid to attend college, firearm ownership, criminal registration, and the like (e.g., Legal Action Center 2004; Mauer and Chesney-Lind 2002; Travis 2002). Travis (2002) refers to these restrictions as "invisible punishments."

A select few researchers have assessed perceptions of "ex-con" stigma from the perspective of formerly incarcerated persons themselves (see e.g., Irwin 1970; La Vigne et al. 2004; LeBel, forthcoming; Taxman et al. 2002; Winnick and Bodkin 2008, 2009; Ewald and Uggen, chapter 3 of this volume). LeBel (2012a) found that nearly two-thirds (65 percent) of his sample of formerly incarcerated persons believe they have been discriminated against because of their status as former prisoners.

> I know I did bad things but I paid the price for five years by being in these walls. I want to go back and start over but how do I do that. They won't let me forget and they have my picture around. I am a changed man but they won't let me be changed. (Taxman et al. 2002, 17)

Moreover, approximately half of the sample reported instances of encountering stigmatization in the crucial life domains of employment and housing (LeBel 2012b). Such findings have been reinforced in considerable qualitative research with ex-prisoners: "No matter how much time we do, everyone always thinks it's like once a criminal always a criminal and that is how people see me and it's very hard to deal with" (Dodge and Pogrebin 2001, 49). Another former prisoner stated:

You are labeled as a felon, and you're always gonna be assumed and known to have contact with that criminal activity and them ethics. And even when I get off parole, I'm still gonna have an "F" on my record. (Uggen, Manza, and Behrens 2004, 283)

Importantly, LeBel and colleagues (2008) found that such perceptions have real consequences. How prisoners respond to a question of whether "social prejudice against ex-convicts will make it difficult for them to go straight" was a strong predictor of recidivism in a study of British ex-prisoners. In the study, those who reported feeling stigmatized and excluded in a prison-based interview were more likely to be reconvicted and reimprisoned in a 10-year follow-up study, even after controlling for the number of social problems an individual experienced after release. In the sample, only 2 out of the 40 (5 percent) participants who felt stigmatized were not reconvicted of a crime, versus 24 percent (21/86) of participants who did not perceive stigma against them.

Many former prisoners, of course, seek to conceal their criminal pasts, "never telling anyone but their closest friends that they were once locked up" (Gonnerman 2004, 349). However, with the proliferation of criminal registries and the increased use of background checks (see Bushway 2004; Holzer et al. 2004; Petersilia 2003), it is becoming much harder today for former prisoners to keep their past hidden in our information-driven society. Former prisoners face a catch-22 situation of sorts. "If parolees are truthful about their backgrounds, many employers will not hire them. If they are not truthful, they can be fired for lying if the employer learns about their conviction" (Petersilia 2003, 120). McCall (1994) states that:

Every time I filled out an application and ran across that section about felony convictions, it made me feel sick inside. I felt like getting up and walking out on the spot. What was the use? I knew what they were going to do. (234)

Researchers have noted that many prisoners and former prisoners attempt to conceal their criminal past, and that perceptions of stigma are related to the use of secrecy as a coping strategy (LeBel 2006; Winnick and Bodkin 2009). Participants in one study were asked, "Have you avoided indicating on written applications (for jobs, licenses, housing, etc.) that you have a felony conviction for fear that information will be used against you?" More than one-third (36.7 percent) reported that they had often or very often avoided disclosure of their criminal history on applications, and thus may be able to avoid potential discrimination and rejection in certain social contexts (LeBel 2006). Importantly, the use of concealment or secrecy by former prisoners is related to lower self-esteem and being less satisfied with life as a whole (LeBel 2006).

Finally, several researchers have pointed out that formerly incarcerated persons have multiple stigmatized identities and suffer from double or triple stigma as a former prisoner and because of their race (Pager 2007), past substance use (van Olphen et al. 2009), or a mental disorder (Hartwell 2004; Visher and Mallik-Kane 2007). Pager (2007, 101), for example, found that "while being black or having a criminal record each represent a strike against the [job] applicant, *with two strikes, you're out.*" One formerly incarcerated person summarizes this bluntly: "I am an outcast four times over. . . . Ex-con, ex-junkie, black, and HIV-positive. I'd be lyin' if I told you I had any dreams" (Wynn 2001, 17).

LeBel's (forthcoming2) quantitative research suggests that discrimination due to one's status as a former prisoner is only one of the obstacles that men and women face upon reentry to the community. Nearly half (47 percent) of the formerly incarcerated persons in his sample reported feeling discriminated against for three or more reasons. One respondent commented after completing the questionnaire, "If one doesn't get you another one will." More respondents reported discrimination due to being a former prisoner (65.3 percent) than any other reason. However, discrimination due to race/ethnicity was the second most frequently reported reason (48.0 percent), followed closely by past drug/alcohol use (47.5 percent) and lack of money or being poor (35.3 percent). Women in the study were found to perceive more reasons for discrimination than their male counterparts, supporting the assertion that women returning home from prison may have to overcome more challenges than their male counterparts (see e.g., Bloom, Owen, and Covington 2003; O'Brien 2001; Richie 2001; van Olphen et al. 2009). These subjective perceptions regarding the multifaceted stigmata that many ex-prisoners face have been strongly supported in systematic, experimental research on employment discrimination for ex-prisoners by Pager (2007) and others (see also Holzer et al. 2004). Such findings are crucial because formerly incarcerated persons who face multiple barriers to full participation for reasons as varied as their race, substance use history, social class, and mental health issues may also be more likely to recidivate (Hartwell 2004; LeBel et al. 2008; Messina, Burdon, Hagopian, and Prendergast 2004).

ABANDON HOPE?

Maruna (2001, 55) argues that "the situation facing recidivist offenders is something like a brick wall. It is surmountable but is enough of an obstacle to make most turn around and 'head back.'" Socio-cognitive research with former prisoners suggests that long-term, persistent offenders tend to lack feelings of agency, experiencing their lives as being largely determined for them in a fatalistic mindset that Maruna (2001) refers to as being "doomed to deviance." The negative impact of this belief system also gains credibility from Maruna's finding that:

> The active offenders . . . seemed fairly accurate in their assessments of their
> situation (dire), their chances of achieving success in the "straight" world
> (minimal), and their place in mainstream society ("need not apply"). (2001, 9)

Parole violators have been found to have "tunnel vision, seeing no alternatives" (Bucklen and Zajac 2009, 258), and attributing negative life outcomes to "external, stable, and uncontrollable factors" in a fatalistic mindset (Maruna 2004): "I expect I've got another big sentence in me yet, if I'm honest, be it through selling drugs or fighting. I'll do me best not to, but . . . it's quite hard" (Howerton et al. 2009, 453). Moreover, many parolees who fail tend to "crash and burn," as about three-fourths indicated some sort of negative emotion in the last 48 hours before they violated their parole (i.e., frustrated, worried, depressed, angry, stressed, etc.) (Bucklen and Zajac 2009).

Laub and Sampson emphasize that "personal agency looms large" in persistence and desistance trajectories (2003, 280). Many researchers note that the belief in one's ability to "go straight," or one's sense of self-efficacy, self-confidence, optimism, or hope may be a necessary, if not sufficient condition for an individual to be able to desist from crime (see e.g., LeBel et al. 2008; Maruna 2001; Nelson et al. 1999; O'Brien 2001). Snyder et al. (1991, 570) define hope as "the perception of successful agency related to goals" and "the perceived availability of successful pathways related to goals." Having hope, then, is different from just wishing that something would happen. Hope requires both the "will and the ways," the desire for a particular outcome, and also the perceived ability and means of achieving the outcome (Burnett and Maruna 2004; LeBel et al. 2008).

Research suggests that hope and self-efficacy may even condition the experience of social problems after prison. Hope can impact a person's likelihood of selecting into and taking advantage of positive social opportunities, like employment or marital attachment; it can also help a person weather life's disappointments or inevitable setbacks in such areas (LeBel et al. 2008; O'Brien 2001). This potential for self-concept to overcome obstacles is, of course, applicable more generally, away from the field of criminology. Bandura writes:

> There is a growing body of evidence that human attainments and positive well-being require an optimistic sense of personal efficacy. This is because ordinary social realities are strewn with difficulties. They are full of impediments, failures, adversities, setbacks, frustrations and inequities. People must have a robust sense of personal efficacy to sustain the perseverant effort needed to succeed. (1989, 1176)

It is not surprising, then, that a considerable amount of prison-based treatment focuses on cognitive restructuring and the development of new patterns of thinking and making decisions (Andrews and Bonta 2006; McGuire 2002).

CAN PAROLE SUPERVISION BE JUSTIFIED?

About 80 percent of all released prisoners will be required to report to local parole authorities and begin the process of community supervision (Glaze and Bonczar 2007). Failure rates on supervision are high, with less than half (44 percent) of parolees successfully completing parole without violating a condition of release, absconding, or committing a new crime (Glaze and Bonczar 2007). Based on the low success rate, Solomon (2006, 28; see also Piehl and LoBuglio 2005) asks:

> How can the criminal justice community focus so much attention on prisoner
> reentry and NOT demand to know if post-prison supervision—the biggest
> reentry intervention there is—is contributing to public safety?

Parole supervision is associated with increased employment and reduced drug use
or intoxication at 8 months, compared to those not on parole (La Vigne et al. 2009b;
Yahner et al. 2008). However, prisoners released to parole supervision do not seem
to fare any better than similar prisoners released without supervision in terms of
rearrest and reconviction outcomes (see Solomon, 2006; Yahner et al. 2008). It is
important to note that Solomon's (2006) study used data from 1994 and did not
control for type of supervision or for program participation. What is clear, however,
is that released prisoners on parole are more likely to be returned to prison than
those not on parole due to technical violations and other factors. Yahner and colleagues (2008), for instance, found that 23 percent of parolees were reincarcerated
during their first year out of prison, compared to 9 percent of their non-supervised
counterparts.

Despite high failure rates, most parolees report that their parole officers were
"helpful" with their transition to the street (see e.g., La Vigne et al. 2009b; Yahner et
al. 2008): "I need the supervision. It keeps me intimidated, keeps me walking a
straight line. I'm grateful for it" (Nelson et al. 1999, 26). Another parolee remarked
that "I wanted to have supervision, 'cause it's a leash that is tied around my neck
automatically. A leash around the neck lets a person feel that he needs to be careful,
you see, he knows that he has a red light . . . " (Gideon 2009, 51). However, most
parolees state that this helpfulness mainly involves moral support (i.e., encouragement and understanding) as opposed to tangible assistance (i.e., help in finding a
job, housing, or a drug treatment program) (see Nelson et al. 1999; Yahner et al.
2008). At two months out, the majority of men and women on parole report that
being under supervision is a good thing in regard to staying out of prison, not committing crime, and remaining drug free (La Vigne et al. 2009b; Yahner et al. 2008).

However, the perceived benefit of being under supervision appears to wear off
fairly quickly; by 8 months out, these numbers drop to 50 percent or below (La Vigne
et al. 2009b; Yahner et al. 2008). In fact, close to one-third of parolees in one sample
stated that their parole officer had done nothing to help them succeed (Yahner et al.
2008). One well-known former prisoner states: "I resented the whole notion of being
on parole. I felt I'd paid my debt to society—or whoever the hell felt they were
owed—and that the slate should be squeaky clean" (McCall 1994, 232). Far from en-
dorsing a "seamless" transition from prison control to community control, "convict
criminologists" Alan Mobley and Chuck Terry (2002) write, "No one wants the separation of prison and parole more urgently than do prisoners. When people 'get out,'
they want to *be out*. Any compromise or half-measure, any 'hoops' or hassles placed
in their path, breeds resentment." Parole conditions that include prohibitions against
associating with fellow formerly incarcerated persons or entering drinking estab-
lishments (both of which are nearly impossible to enforce) often undermine the perceived legitimacy of the entire parole process. Another source of aggravation and
frustration for parolees is the frequent handing-off of supervision responsibility

from one parole officer to another, with each having a unique supervision style, and enforcement of conditions (Austin and Irwin 2000, Gonnerman 2004).

Petersilia (2007) argues for the implementation of an "earned discharge" parole system that allows parolees who complete pro-social activities believed to reduce the probability of recidivism (e.g., substance abuse treatment or employment for a specified period of time) to be released from supervision early—in as little as 6 months. It is thought that this incentive will increase motivation and promote positive behavioral change in parolees. Petersilia's (2007) proposal also calls for parole authorities and administrators to front-load scarce resources on those parolees who need more services and supervision in the first days and weeks after release from prison (see also National Research Council 2007). Each of these proposals, if enacted, would likely receive enthusiastic support from parolees (as well as the authors).

Mutual Aid

For many prisoners and former prisoners, mutual-help is viewed as a more important component of "going straight" than professional supervision (e.g., Erickson et al. 1973; Hamm 1997; LeBel 2007; McAnany and Tromanhauser 1977). Many released prisoners express a desire to receive mentoring from formerly incarcerated persons who are "making it" in conventional society (see e.g., Erickson et al. 1973; Festen and Fischer 2002; Irwin 2005; LeBel 2007; McAnany, Tromanhauser and Sullivan 1974; Richie 2001; Sowards, O'Boyle, and Weissman 2006; Uggen et al. 2004):

> The real role model to me is the guy who has been in prison for 20 years. . . . I couldn't think of anyone more I could look up to today. Because he's a man who walked in my shoes and he can tell me today, you don't have to live like that. (*Glidepath to Recovery* 1999)

Describing the prisoner reentry process for women, Richie (2001) writes:

> Most services that are successful in helping women reintegrate into the community have hired (or are otherwise influenced by) women who have been similarly situated. The extent to which women have a peer and/or mentoring relationship with someone whom they perceive is 'like them' is critical. (385)

Successful formerly incarcerated persons can provide newly released prisoners with an introduction to life in the community and help them to deal with problems related to reentry and reintegration. Persons who have made the transition can prepare returning prisoners to resist peer pressure and environmental influences that promote offending, help to negotiate the hazards of being a former prisoner in a "high risk" neighborhood, provide information about the best places to find employment, introduce individuals with substance use histories to support groups (e.g., AA/NA), and provide guidance about being under parole supervision.

Maruna (2001) found that many former prisoners assumed the role of wounded healer or professional "ex-." In fact, he argues that "the desisting self-narrative frequently involves reworking a delinquent history into a source of wisdom to be drawn from while acting as a drug counselor, youth worker, community volunteer, or mutual-help group member" (117). There "may be a natural tendency to help and serve others that characterizes a significant portion of the incarcerated population" (Bazemore and Karp 2004, 29; Irwin 2005; Maruna 2001). Formerly incarcerated persons often describe a newfound ability to find satisfaction in altruistic, other-centered behavior—quite diametrically opposed to the types of behavior that led the person to prison in the first place (see LeBel 2007; Maruna, LeBel and Lanier 2003; O'Brien 2001; Uggen et al. 2004).

However, due to risk considerations (see Burnett and Maruna 2006), former prisoners are frequently barred from going back inside prisons, even as counselors, and can often be prohibited from working with young people or other at-risk groups. Indeed, one of the restrictions most parolees face is a prohibition against talking to other former prisoners (Petersilia 2003), which can make mutual support rather difficult. As one ex-prisoner points out:"The only ex-cons I'm not supposed to hang out with are the ones who could do me some good—the people I might talk to on the phone in the course of earning a legitimate living; also, old friends who have found a way to stay straight and are eager to help me remain out here" (Martin and Sussman 1993, 323). Such restrictions are highly difficult to enforce outside of mutual aid situations, so appear to do more harm than good.

LAST WORDS: REENTRY AS A SOCIAL MOVEMENT

The wider conversation about the reentry of large numbers of individuals from prison to society tends to focus on the risks that this process entails and the multiple needs that people in that situation have. Importantly, this chapter has sought to address these factors from the perspective of formerly incarcerated persons themselves, who are, after all, the experts on their own situation.

Williams and Strean (2002) have argued that reentry interventions should be based on the "most important things" identified by each individual returning from prison. Such an approach—beginning "where the released prisoner is"—can at the very least increase the prisoner's motivation and engagement in the reintegration process (Ward and Maruna 2007).

Others have gone further, suggesting that the perspective of formerly incarcerated persons should be at the forefront of not just individual interventions, but indeed the wider policy debate regarding reentry. Indeed, formerly incarcerated persons are increasingly speaking out, as a group (LeBel 2009), and becoming politically active (see esp. Maruna and LeBel 2009). For example, in May 2008, nearly 100 formerly incarcerated persons traveled from New York City to the state capital in Albany to lobby lawmakers to reform sentencing laws and to adopt legislation to protect their employment and voting rights (Virtanen 2008). The group "All of Us or None"—a national organizing initiative of formerly incarcerated persons and persons in prison—argues that, "It's OUR responsibility to stop the discrimination, and to change the public policies that discriminate against us, our families, and our communities" (see http://www.allofusornone.org). On its publicity materials, the organization states that, "Advocates have spoken for us, but now is the time for us to speak for ourselves. We clearly have the ability to be more than the helpless victims of the system."

Similar organizations like The Center for NuLeadership on Urban Solutions and the Women's Prison Association (WPA) seek to develop "a group of leaders equipped to craft solutions to the problems facing incarcerated and formerly incarcerated persons" (http://www.wpaonline.org/institute/wahtm). These grassroots organizations provide a voice to formerly incarcerated persons and give them the opportunity to be engaged in attempts to change public policy. Within academia, a similar movement called "Convict Criminology," largely consisting of ex-prisoner academics, has made important strides in changing the way in which crime and justice are taught and studied at the university level (see Jones et al. 2009). Even life-sentenced prisoners, who will never be released from prison, have joined this growing conversation around reentry. The "Lifers" group at Graterford prison in Pennsylvania argue that "one ensures change by assisting in the efforts to change others" (60), and that "society should begin to use the experience, knowledge, insight, and expertise of transformed ex-offenders to do the work that members of the community and those in positions of authority are not equipped to do" (Lifers Public Safety Steering Committee 2004, 65).

By providing a supportive community and a network of individuals with shared experiences, these sorts of initiatives can be interpreted as transforming reentry from an ostensibly individual process into a social movement of sorts (Hamm 1997). As difficult a process as reentry clearly is—by all the available research evidence reviewed here—this appears to be a most welcome development. The returning prisoner, after all, needs all of the support that he or she can get.

REFERENCES

Andrews, Donald A., and James Bonta. 2006. *The Psychology of Criminal Conduct,* 4th ed. Cincinnati, OH: Anderson/LexiNexis.

Aos, Steve, Marna Miller, and Elizabeth Drake. 2006. *Evidence-based Adult Corrections Programs: What Works and What Does Not.* Olympia: Washington State Institute for Public Policy.

Austin, James. 2001. "Prisoner Reentry: Current Trends, Practices, and Issues." *Crime & Delinquency* 47: 314–334.

Austin, James, and John Irwin. 2000. *It's about Time: America's Imprisonment Binge,* 3rd ed. Belmont, CA: Wadsworth.

Bandura, Albert. 1989. "Human Agency in Social Cognitive Theory." *American Psychologist* 44: 1175–1184.

Bazemore, Gordon, and David R. Karp. 2004. "A Civic Justice Corps: Community Service as a Means of Reintegration." *Justice Policy Journal* 1(3): 1–37.

Bloom, Barbara, Barbara Owen, and Stephanie Covington. 2003. *Gender-responsive Strategies: Research, Practice, and Guiding Principles for Women Offenders.* Washington, DC: National Institute of Corrections.

Braman, Donald. 2004. *Doing Time on the Outside: Incarceration and Family Life in Urban America.* Ann Arbor: Michigan.

Brooks, Lisa E., Amy L. Solomon, Rhiana Kohl, Jenny W.L. Osborne, Jay Reid, Susan M. McDonald, and Hollie Matthews Hoover. 2008. *Reincarcerated: The Experiences of Men Returning to Massachusetts Prisons.* Washington, DC: Urban Institute.

Buck, Maria L. 2000. *"Getting Back to Work: Employment Programs for Ex-offenders." Field Report Series.* Philadelphia, PA: Public/Private Ventures.

Bucklen, Kristofer Bret, and Gary Zajac. 2009. "But Some of Them Don't Come Back (to Prison!): Resource Deprivation and Thinking Errors as Determinants of Parole Success and Failure." *The Prison Journal* 89(3): 239–264.

Burnett, Ros. 1992. *The Dynamics of Recidivism: Summary Report.* Oxford: University of Oxford, Centre for Criminological Research.

Burnett, Ros, and Shadd Maruna. 2004. "So 'Prison Works'—Does It? The Criminal Careers of 130 Men Released from Prison under Home Secretary Michael Howard." *Howard Journal of Criminal Justice* 43: 390–404.

Burnett, Ros, and Shadd Maruna. 2006, "The Kindness of Prisoners: Strength-Based Resettlement in Theory and in Action." *Criminology and Criminal Justice* 6: 83–106.

Bushway, Shawn D. 2004. "Labor Market Effects of Permitting Employer Access to Criminal History Records." *Journal of Contemporary Criminal Justice* 20(3): 276–291.

Clear, Todd R. 2007. *Imprisoning Communities: How Mass Incarceration Makes Disadvantaged Neighborhoods Worse.* New York: Oxford University Press.

Coalition for Women Prisoners. 2008. *My Sister's Keeper: A Book for Women Returning Home from Prison or Jail.* New York: Correctional Association of New York.

Cullen, Francis T. 1994. "Social Support as a Concept for Criminology: Presidential Address to the Academy of Criminal Justice Sciences." *Justice Quarterly* 11: 527–559.

Dodge, Mary, and Mark R. Pogrebin. 2001. "Collateral Consequences of Imprisonment for Women: Complications of Reintegration." *The Prison Journal* 81: 42–54.

Erickson, Rosemary J., Wayman J. Crow, Louis A. Zurcher, and Archie V. Connett. 1973. *Paroled but Not Free: Ex-offenders Look at What They Need to Make It Outside.* New York: Behavioral Publications.

Festen, Marcia K., and Sunny Fischer. 2002. *Navigating Reentry: The Experiences and Perceptions of Ex-offenders Seeking Employment.* Prepared on behalf of The Chicago Urban League.

Finn, Peter. 1998. "Job Placement for Offenders in Relation to Recidivism." *Journal of Offender Rehabilitation* 28(1–2): 89–106.

Garland, David. 2001. *The Culture of Control: Crime and Social Order in Contemporary Society.* Chicago: University of Chicago Press.

Gideon, Lior. 2009. "What Shall I Do Now? Released Offenders' Expectations for Supervision upon Release." *International Journal of Offender Therapy and Comparative Criminology* 53(1): 43–56.

Glaser, Daniel. 1969. *The Effectiveness of a Prison and Parole System.* Indianapolis, IN: Bobbs-Merrill.

Glaze, Lauren E., and Thomas P. Bonczar. 2007. *Probation and Parole in the United States, 2006.* Washington, DC: U.S. Department of Justice, Bureau of Justice Statistics (NCJ 220218).

Glidepath to Recovery. 1999. Family Theater Productions, a Division of Holy Cross Family Ministries. Available at http://www.familytheater.org/en/TelevisionandFilm/Glide-pathtoRecovery.aspx.

Gonnerman, Jennifer. 2004. *Life on the Outside: The Prison Odyssey of Elaine Bartlett.* New York: Farrar, Straus, & Giroux.

Greenfeld, Lawrence A., and Tracy L. Snell. 1999. *Women Offenders.* Washington, DC: U.S. Department of Justice, Bureau of Justice Statistics (NCJ 175688).

Hairston, Creasie F. 1988. "Family Ties During Imprisonment: Do They Influence Future Criminal Activity?" *Federal Probation* 52(1): 48–52.

Hairston, Creasie F. 2003. "Prisoners and Their Families: Parenting Issues During Incarcer-ation." In *Prisoners Once Removed: The Impact of Incarceration and Reentry on Children, Families, and Communities,* eds. Jeremy Travis and Michelle Waul, 259–282. Washington, DC: The Urban Institute Press.

Hamm, Mark S. 1997. "The Offender Self-help Movement as Correctional Treatment." In *Correctional Counseling and Rehabilitation,* 4th ed., eds. Patricia Van Voorhis, Michael Braswell, and David Lester, 211–224. Cincinnati, OH: Anderson Publishing.

Hartwell, Stephanie W. 2004. "Comparison of Offenders with Mental Illness Only and Offenders with Dual Diagnoses." *Psychiatric Services* 55: 145–150.

Helfgott, Jacqueline. 1997. "Ex-offender Needs Versus Community Opportunity in Seattle, Washington." *Federal Probation* 61: 12–24.

Holzer, Harry J., Steven Raphael, and Michael Stoll. 2004. "Will Employers Hire Ex-offend-ers? Employer Preferences, Background Checks, and Their Determinants." In *Impris-oning America: The Social Effects of Mass Incarceration,* eds. Mary Patillo, David F. Weiman, and Bruce Western, 205–246. New York: Russell Sage Foundation.

Howerton, Amanda, Ros Burnett, Richard Byng, and John Campbell. 2009. "The Consola-tions of Going Back to Prison: What 'Revolving Door' Prisoners Think of Their Prospects." *Journal of Offender Rehabilitation* 48: 439–461.

Inciardi, James A., Steven S. Martin, and Clifford A. Butzin. 2004. "Five-year Outcomes of Therapeutic Community Treatment of Drug-involved Offenders after Release from Prison." *Crime & Delinquency* 50(1): 88–107.

Irwin, John. 1970. *The Felon.* Englewood Cliffs, NJ: Prentice Hall.

Irwin, John. 2005. *The Warehouse Prison: Disposal of the New Dangerous Class.* Los Angeles: Roxbury Publishing.

Irwin, John. 2009. *Lifers: Seeking Redemption in Prison.* New York: Routledge.

Johnson, Robert. 2002. *Hard Time,* 3rd ed. Belmont, CA: Wadsworth.

Jones, Richard S., Jeffrey I. Ross, Stephen C. Richards, and Daniel S. Murphy. 2009. "The First Dime: A Decade of Convict Criminology." *The Prison Journal* 89: 151–171.

Kirk, David S. 2009. "A Natural Experiment on Residential Change and Recidivism: Lessons from Hurricane Katrina." *American Sociological Review* 74: 484–505.

Kubrin, Charis E., and Eric A. Stewart. 2006. "Predicting Who Reoffends: The Neglected Role of Neighborhood Context in Recidivism Studies." *Criminology* 44(1): 165–195.

Langan, Patrick A., and David J. Levin. 2002. *Recidivism of Prisoners Released in 1994.* Washington, DC: U.S. Department of Justice, Bureau of Justice Statistics (NCJ 193427).

Lanier, Charles S. 2003. "'Who's Doing the Time Here, Me or My Children?' Addressing the Issues Implicated by Mounting Numbers of Fathers in Prison." In *Convict Criminology*, eds. Jeffrey I. Ross and Stephen C. Richards, 170–190. Belmont, CA: Wadsworth.

Laub, John H., Daniel S. Nagin, and Robert J. Sampson. 1998. "Trajectories of Change in Criminal Offending: Good Marriages and the Desistance Process." *American Sociological Review* 63: 225–238.

Laub, John H., and Robert J. Sampson. 2003. *Shared Beginnings, Divergent Lives: Delinquent Boys to Age 70*. Cambridge, MA: Harvard University Press.

La Vigne, Nancy G., Lisa E. Brooks, and Tracey L. Shollenberger. 2007. *Returning Home: Exploring the Challenges and Successes of Recently Released Texas Prisoners*. Washington, DC: The Urban Institute.

La Vigne, Nancy G., Lisa E. Brooks, and Tracey L. Shollenberger. 2009a. *Women on the Outside: Understanding the Experiences of Female Prisoners Returning to Houston, Texas*. Washington, DC: The Urban Institute.

La Vigne, Nancy G., Tracey L. Shollenberger, and Sara A. Debus. 2009b. *One Year Out: Tracking the Experiences of Male Prisoners Returning to Houston, Texas*. Washington, DC: The Urban Institute.

La Vigne, Nancy G., Christy Visher, and Jennifer Castro. 2004. *Chicago Prisoners' Experiences Returning Home*. Washington, DC: The Urban Institute.

La Vigne, Nancy G., Samuel J. Wolf, and Jesse Jannetta. 2004. *Voices of Experience: Focus Group Findings on Prisoner Reentry in the State of Rhode Island*. Washington, DC: The Urban Institute.

LeBel, Thomas P. 2006. "To Tell or Not to Tell? Coping with the Stigma of Incarceration." Presented at the Annual Meeting of the American Society of Criminology, Los Angeles, California (November).

LeBel, Thomas P. 2007. "An Examination of the Impact of Formerly Incarcerated Persons Helping Others." *Journal of Offender Rehabilitation* 46(1–2): 1–24.

LeBel, Thomas P. 2009. "Formerly Incarcerated Persons' Use of Advocacy/Activism as a Coping Orientation in the Reintegration Process." In *How Offenders Transform Their Lives*, eds. Bonnie M. Veysey, Johnna Christian, and Damien J. Martinez, 165–187. Cullompton, UK: Willan.

LeBel, Thomas P. 2012a. "Invisible Stripes? Formerly Incarcerated Persons' Perceptions of Stigma." Under review at *Deviant Behavior*.

LeBel, Thomas P. 2012b. "'If One Doesn't Get You Another One Will': Formerly Incarcerated Persons' Perceptions of Discrimination." Under review at *The Prison Journal*.

LeBel, Thomas P., Ros Burnett, Shadd Maruna, and Shawn Bushway. 2008. "The 'Chicken and Egg' of Subjective and Social Factors in Desistance from Crime." *European Journal of Criminology* 5(2): 130–158.

Legal Action Center. 2004. *After Prison: Roadblocks to Reentry: A Report on State Legal Barriers Facing People with Criminal Records*. New York: Legal Action Center.

Lewis, Sam, Mike Maguire, Peter Raynor, Maurice Vanstone, and Julie Vennard. 2003. *The Resettlement of Short-term Prisoners: An Evaluation of Seven Pathfinders*. RDS Occasional Paper, No. 83. London: Home Office.

Lifers Public Safety Steering Committee of the State Correctional Institution at Graterford, Pennsylvania. 2004. "Ending the Culture of Street Crime." *The Prison Journal* 84(Suppl. 4): 48–68.

Lin, Ann Chih. 2000. *Reform in the Making: The Implementation of Social Policy in Prison*. Princeton, NJ: Princeton University Press.

Lynch, James P., and William J. Sabol. 2001. *Prisoner Reentry in Perspective*. Washington, DC: The Urban Institute.

Love, Margaret C. 2006. *Relief from the Collateral Consequences of Conviction: A State by State Resources Guide*. Buffalo, NY: William S. Hein.

MacKenzie, Doris L., and Robert Brame. 2001. "Community Supervision, Prosocial Activities, and Recidivism." *Justice Quarterly* 18(2): 429–448.

Martin, Dannie M., and Peter Y. Sussman. 1993. *Committing Journalism: The Prison Writings of Red Hog*. New York: W.W. Norton.

Maruna, Shadd. 2001. *Making Good: How Ex-convicts Reform and Rebuild their Lives*. Washington, DC: American Psychological Association.

Maruna, Shadd. 2004. "Desistance from Crime and Explanatory Style: A New Direction in the Psychology of Reform." *Journal of Contemporary Criminal Justice* 20(2): 184–200.

Maruna, Shadd, and Russ Immarigeon, eds. 2004. *After Crime and Punishment: Pathways to Offender Reintegration*. Cullompton, UK: Willan.

Maruna, Shadd, Russ Immarigeon, and Thomas P. LeBel. 2004. "Ex-offender Reintegration: Theory and Practice." In *After Crime and Punishment: Pathways to Offender Reintegration*, eds. Shadd Maruna and Russ Immarigeon, 3–26. Cullompton, UK: Willan.

Maruna, Shadd, and Thomas P. LeBel. 2002. "Revisiting Ex-prisoner Re-entry: A New Buzzword in Search of a Narrative." In *Reform and Punishment: The Future of Sentencing*, eds. Michael Tonry and Sue Rex, 158–180. Cullompton, UK: Willan.

Maruna, Shadd, and Thomas P. LeBel. 2009. "Strengths-Based Approaches to Reentry: Extra Mileage Toward Reintegration and Destigmatization." *Japanese Journal of Sociological Criminology* 34: 59–80.

Maruna, Shadd, Thomas P. LeBel, and Charles Lanier. 2003. "Generativity Behind Bars: Some 'Redemptive Truth' about Prison Society." In *The Generative Society: Caring for Future Generations*, eds. Ed de St. Aubin, Dan P. McAdams, and Tae-Chang Kim, 131–151. Washington, DC: American Psychological Association.

Maruna, Shadd, and Kevin Roy. 2007. "Amputation or Reconstruction: Notes on 'Knifing Off' and Desistance from Crime." *Journal of Contemporary Criminal Justice* 23: 104–124.

Mauer, Marc, and Meda Chesney-Lind, eds. 2002. *Invisible Punishment: The Collateral Consequences of Mass Imprisonment*. New York: The New Press.

McAdams, Dan P., and Ed de St. Aubin. 1998. "Introduction." *Generativity and Adult Development: How and Why We Care for the Next Generation*, eds. Dan P. McAdams and Ed de St. Aubin, xix–xxiv. Washington, DC: American Psychological Association.

McAnany, Patrick. D., and Edward Tromanhauser. 1977. "Organizing the Convicted: Self-help for Prisoners and Ex-prisoners." *Crime & Delinquency* 23(1): 68–74.

McAnany, Patrick D., Edward Tromanhauser, and Dennis Sullivan. 1974. *The Identification and Description of Ex-offender Groups in the Chicago Area*. Chicago: University of Illinois.

McCall, Nathan. 1994. *Makes Me Wanna Holler: A Young Black Man in America*. New York: Vintage Books.

McGuire, James, ed. 2002. *Offender Rehabilitation and Treatment: Effective Programs and Policies to Reduce Re-offending*. New York: John Wiley & Sons.

Messina, Nena, William Burdon, Garo Hagopian, and Michael Prendergast. 2004. "One Year Return to Custody Rates among Co-disordered Offenders." *Behavioral Sciences and the Law* 22: 503–518.

Messina, Nena, William Burdon, and Michael Prendergast. 2001. *A Profile of Women in Prison-Based Therapeutic Communities*. Draft. Los Angeles, CA: UCLA Integrated Substance Abuse Program, Drug Abuse Research Center.

Metraux, Stephen, and Dennis P. Culhane. 2004. "Homeless Shelter Use and Reincarceration Following Prison Release: Assessing the Risk." *Criminology & Public Policy* 3: 201–222.

Mobley, Alan, and Charles Terry. 2002. "Dignity, Resistance and Re-entry: A Convict Perspective." Unpublished paper.

Morgan, Rod, and Anne Owers, 2001. *Through the Prison Gate: A Joint Thematic Review by HM Inspectorates of Prisons and Probation*. London: HM Inspectorate of Prisons.

Mumola, Christopher J., and Jennifer C. Karberg. 2006. *Drug Use and Dependence, State and Federal Prisoners, 2004*. Washington, DC: U.S. Department of Justice, Bureau of Justice Statistics (NCJ 213530).

National Research Council. 2007. *Parole, Desistance from Crime, and Community Integration*. Committee on Community Supervision and Desistance from Crime, Committee on Law and Justice, Division of Behavioral and Social Sciences and Education. Washington, DC: The National Academies Press.

Nelson, Marta, Perry Deess, and Charlotte Allen. 1999. *The First Month Out: Post-incarceration Experiences in New York City*. New York: Vera Institute of Justice.

O'Brien, Patricia. 2001. "'Just Like Baking a Cake': Women Describe the Necessary Ingredients for Successful Reentry after Incarceration." *Families in Society* 82(3): 287–295.

O'Brien, Patricia. 2006. "Maximizing Success for Drug-affected Women after Release from Prison: Examining Access to and Use of Social Services During Reentry." *Women & Criminal Justice* 17(2–3): 95–113.

Pager, Devah. 2007. *Marked: Race, Crime, and Finding Work in an Era of Mass Incarceration*. Chicago: The University of Chicago Press.

Petersilia, Joan. 2003. *When Prisoners Come Home: Parole and Prisoner Reentry*. New York: Oxford University Press.

Petersilia, Joan. 2007. "Employ Behavioral Contracting for 'Earned Discharge' Parole." *Criminology & Public Policy* 6(4): 807–814.

Pezzin, Liliana E. 1995. "Earning Prospects, Matching Effects, and the Decision to Terminate a Criminal Career. *Journal of Quantitative Criminology* 11: 29–50.

Prendergast, Michael L., Elizabeth A. Hall, Harry K. Wexler, Gerald Melnick, and Yan Cao. 2004. "Amity Prison-based Therapeutic Community: 5-Year Outcomes." *The Prison Journal* 84(1): 36–60.

Redcross, Cindy, Dan Bloom, Gilda Azurdia, Janine Zweig, and Nancy Pindus. 2009. *Transitional Jobs for Ex-Prisoners: Implementation, Two-Year Impacts, and Costs of the Center for Employment Opportunities (CEO) Prisoner Reentry Program*. A Report from MDRC-Building Knowledge to Improve Social Policy. Retrieved May 7, 2010, from http://www.urban.org/UploadedPDF/1001362_transitional_jobs.pdf.

Re-Entry Policy Council. 2005. *Report of the Re-entry Policy Council: Charting the Safe and Successful Return of Prisoners to the Community*. New York: Council of State Governments.

Richards, Stephen C., and Richard S. Jones. 2004. "Beating the Perpetual Incarceration Machine: Overcoming Structural Impediments to Re-entry." In *After Crime and Punishment: Pathways to Offender Reintegration*, eds. Shadd Maruna and Russ Immarigeon, 201–232. Cullompton, UK: Willan.

Richie, Beth. 2001. "Challenges Incarcerated Women Face as They Return to Their Communities: Findings from Life History Interviews." *Crime & Delinquency* 47: 368–389.

Roman, Caterina G., and Jeremy Travis. 2004. *Taking Stock: Housing, Homelessness, and Prisoner Reentry*. Washington, DC: The Urban Institute.

Rose, Dina R., and Todd R. Clear. 2003. "Incarceration, Reentry, and Social Capital: Social Networks in the Balance." In *Prisoners Once Removed: The Impact of Incarceration and Reentry on Children, Families, and Communities*, eds. Jeremy Travis and Michelle Waul, 313–341. Washington, DC: The Urban Institute Press.

Rossman, Shelli B., and Caterina G. Roman. 2003. "Case Managed Reentry and Employment: Lessons from the Opportunity to Succeed Program." *Justice Research and Policy* 5(2): 75–100.

Sabol, William J., Heather C. West, and Matthew Cooper. 2009. *Prisoners in 2008*. Bureau of Justice Statistics Bulletin. Washington, DC: U.S. Department of Justice, Office of Justice Programs, Bureau of Justice Statistics (NCJ 228417).

Sampson, Robert J., and John H. Laub. 1993. *Crime in the Making: Pathways and Turning Points Throughout Life*. Cambridge, MA: Harvard University Press.

Saylor, William, and Gerald Gaes. 1996. *PREP: Training Inmates Through Industrial Work Preparation and Vocational and Apprenticeship Instruction*. Washington, DC: Federal Bureau of Prisons.

Seiter, Richard P., and Karen R. Kadela. 2003. "Prisoner Reentry: What Works, What Does Not, and What Is Promising." *Crime & Delinquency* 49(3): 360–388.

Shapiro, Carol, and Meryl Schwartz. 2001. "Coming Home: Building on Family Connections." *Corrections Management Quarterly* 5(3): 52–62.

Shover, Neal. 1996. *Great Pretenders: Pursuits and Careers of Persistent Thieves*. Boulder, CO: Westview.

Snyder, C. R., Cheri Harris, John R. Anderson, Sharon A. Holleran, Lori M. Irving, Sandra T. Sigmon, Lauren Yoshinobu, June Gibb, Charyle Langelle, and Pat Harney. 1991. "The Will and the Ways: Development and Validation of an Individual-Differences Measure of Hope." *Journal of Personality and Social Psychology* 60: 570–585.

Social Exclusion Unit. 2002. *Reducing Re-offending by Ex-prisoners*. London, UK: Social Exclusion Unit.

Solomon, Amy L. 2006. "Does Parole Supervision Work? Research Findings and Policy Opportunities." *Perspectives* 30(2): 26–37.

Solomon, Amy, Christy Visher, Nancy La Vigne, and Jenny Osbourne. 2006. *Understanding the Challenges of Prisoner Reentry: Research Findings from the Urban Institute's Prisoner Reentry Portfolio*. Washington, DC: The Urban Institute.

Sowards, Kathryn A., Kathleen O'Boyle, and Marsha Weissman. 2006. "Inspiring Hope, Envisioning Alternatives: The Importance of Peer Role Models in a Mandated Treatment Program for Women." *Journal of Social Work Practice in the Addictions* 6(4): 55–70.

Sullivan, Eileen, Milton Mino, Katherine Nelson, and Jill Pope. 2002. *Families as a Resource in Recovery from Drug Abuse: An Evaluation of La Bodega de la Familia*. Vera Institute of Justice Research Report. New York: Vera Institute of Justice.

Taxman, Faye S., Douglas Young, and James M. Byrne. 2002. *Offender's Views of Reentry: Implications for Processes, Programs, and Services*. College Park: University of Maryland, Bureau of Government Research.

Thacher, David. 2008. "The Rise of Criminal Background Screening in Rental Housing." *Law & Social Inquiry* 33: 5–30.

Thompson, Anthony C. 2008. *Releasing Prisoners, Redeeming Communities: Reentry, Race, and Politics*. New York: New York University Press.

Travis, Jeremy. 2002. "Invisible Punishment: An Instrument of Social Exclusion." In *Invisible Punishment: The Collateral Consequences of Mass Imprisonment*, eds. Marc Mauer and Meda Chesney-Lind, 15–36. New York: The New Press.

Travis, Jeremy. 2005. *But They All Come Back: Facing the Challenges of Prisoner Reentry*. Washington, DC: The Urban Institute Press.

Travis, Jeremy, Amy L. Solomon, and Michelle Waul. 2001. *From Prison to Home: The Dimensions and Consequences of Prisoner Reentry*. Washington, DC: The Urban Institute.

Tromanhauser, Edward. 2003. "Comments and Reflections on Forty Years in the Criminal Justice System." In *Convict Criminology*, eds. Jeffrey I. Ross and Stephen C. Richards, 81–94. Belmont, CA: Wadsworth.

Uggen, Christopher. 1999. "Ex-offenders and the Conformist Alternative: A Job Quality Model of Work and Crime." *Social Problems* 46(1): 127–151.

Uggen, Christopher, Jeff Manza, and Angela Behrens. 2004. "'Less Than the Average Citizen': Stigma, Role Transition, and the Civic Reintegration of Convicted Felons." In *After Crime and Punishment: Pathways to Offender Reintegration*, eds. Shadd Maruna and Russ Immarigeon, 261–293. Cullompton, UK: Willan.

van Olphen, Juliana, Michele J. Eliason, Nicholas Freudenberg, and Marilyn Barnes. 2009. "Nowhere to Go: How Stigma Limits the Options of Female Drug Users after Release from Jail." *Substance Abuse Treatment, Prevention, & Policy* 4: 1–10. Retrieved September 14, 2009, from http://www.substanceabusepolicy.com/content/pdf/1747-597X-4-10.pdf.

Virtanen, Michael. 2008. "Ex-convicts Join Ranks of Lobbyists in Albany." *The Albany Timesunion*, May 20. Retrieved May 22, 2008 from http://www.timesunion.com.

Visher, Christy A., and Shannon M. E. Courtney. 2007. *One Year Out: Experiences of Prisoners Returning to Cleveland*. Washington, DC: The Urban Institute.

Visher, Christy, Sara Debus, and Jennifer Yahner. 2008. *Employment after Prison: A Longitudinal Study of Releasees in Three States*. Washington, DC: The Urban Institute.

Visher, Christy, Vera Kachnowski, Nancy La Vigne, and Jeremy Travis. 2004. *Baltimore Prisoners' Experiences Returning Home*. Washington, DC: The Urban Institute.

Visher, Christy A., Carly R. Knight, Aaron Chalfin, and John K. Roman. 2009. *The Impact of Marital and Relationship Status on Social Outcomes for Returning Prisoners*. Washington, DC: The Urban Institute.

Visher, Christy A., and Pamela K. Lattimore. 2007. "Major Study Examines Prisoners and their Reentry Needs" (NCJ 219609). *NIJ Journal* 258: 30–33.

Visher, Christy A., and Mallik-Kane, Kamala 2007. "Reentry Experiences of Men with Health Problems." In *Public Health Behind Bars: From Prisons to Communities*, ed. Robert B. Greifinger, 434–460. New York: Springer.

Visher, Christy A., and Jeremy Travis. 2003. "Transitions from Prison to Community: Understanding Individual Pathways." *Annual Review of Sociology* 29: 89–113.

Ward, Tony, and Shadd Maruna. 2007. *Rehabilitation: Beyond the Risk Paradigm*. London: Routledge.

Western, Bruce, Jeffrey R. Kling, and David F. Weiman. 2001. "The Labor Market Consequences of Incarceration." *Crime & Delinquency* 47(3): 410–427.

Williams, D. J., and William B. Strean. 2002. "Quality of Life Promotion: The Foundation of Offender Rehabilitation." *Forum on Corrections Research* 14(2): 43–45.

Winnick, Terri A., and Mark Bodkin. 2009. "Stigma, Secrecy and Race: An Empirical
    Examination of Black and White Incarcerated Men." *American Journal of Criminal
    Justice* 34(1–2): 131–150.
Winnick, Terri A., and Mark Bodkin. 2008. "Anticipated Stigma and Stigma Management
    among those to be Labeled 'Ex-con.'" *Deviant Behavior* 29: 295–333.
Winterfield, Laura, and Jennifer Castro. 2005. *Returning Home Illinois Policy Brief:
    Treatment Matching*. Washington, DC: The Urban Institute.
Wolff, Nancy, and Jeffrey Draine. 2004. "The Dynamics of Social Capital of Prisoners and
    Community Reentry: Ties that Bind?" *Journal of Correctional Health Care* 10(3):
    457–490.
Wynn, Jennifer. 2001. *Inside Rikers: Stories from the World's Largest Penal Colony*. New
    York: St. Martin's Press.
Yahner, Jennifer, and Christy Visher. 2008. *Illinois Prisoners' Reentry Success Three Years
    after Release*. Washington, DC: The Urban Institute.
Yahner, Jennifer, Christy Visher, and Amy Solomon. 2008. *Returning Home to Parole:
    Former Prisoners' Experiences in Illinois, Ohio, and Texas*. Washington, DC: The Urban
    Institute.

CHAPTER 28

THE CHARACTERISTICS OF PRISONERS RETURNING HOME AND EFFECTIVE REENTRY PROGRAMS AND POLICIES

CHRISTY A. VISHER AND
JEREMY TRAVIS

INTRODUCTION

In the last decade, "prisoner reentry" has emerged as a critical issue affecting families, communities, state and local governments, and social service providers. Of course, ever since prisons were first built, people incarcerated in prisons have returned home when their sentences were completed. But today, more people than ever before are making this journey home. According to the Bureau of Justice Statistics, during calendar year 2008 in the United States, state and federal correctional authorities admitted 733,009 prisoners and released only slightly fewer, 698,459 (Sabol and Couture 2009). Thirty years ago, fewer than 200,000 made this journey home. Why has the prisoner reentry population increased? There is a simple explanation: more people are coming home because more people are sent to prison. Over the past generation, the rate of incarceration in America has more than quadrupled (see Figure 28.1), and the state and federal prison population at mid-year 2008 was

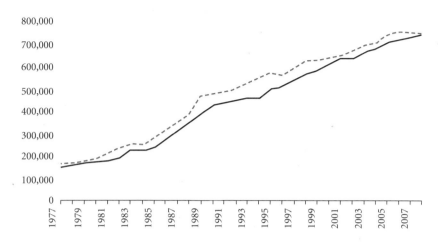

Figure 28.1. Sentenced Prisoners Admitted and Released from Federal and State Prison, 1977–2008.
Source: The Urban Institute, 2010. Based on data from the Bureau of Justice Statistics, National Prisoner Statistics series.

1.6 million people. There is a very simple and immutable "iron law of imprisonment" (Travis 2005): except for those who die in prison, everyone who goes to prison ultimately returns home (Petersilia 2003).

The net effect of these realities is profound: a large number of individuals, 90 percent of them men, are every year removed from their families and communities, held in prisons and jails, and then returned home facing substantial barriers to reintegration. In the United States, a majority of these individuals come from a small number of urban communities. These communities, already struggling with poor schools, poor health care, and weak labor markets, are now shouldering the burden of reintegrating record numbers of former prisoners. Not surprisingly, men and women reentering society from prison have difficulty finding a job, a place to live, reliable transportation, and affordable health care. Many of these exiting prisoners need transitional and supportive services such as job training, substance abuse treatment, and mental health counseling that are unavailable in the disadvantaged communities to which many of them return (Visher and Travis 2003).

Given the magnitude of the prisoner reentry phenomenon, it has become a salient local, state, and federal policy concern for several reasons. First and foremost is the public safety dimension. Nearly two-thirds of released prisoners will be rearrested, and over half will be reincarcerated within three years of release. The recidivism rate has remained virtually unchanged for the last decade or more (Langan and Levin 2002). More parolees are returning to prison than ever before: one-third of all prison admissions nationwide are parole violators who are being returned to prison for new crimes or technical violations (Blumstein and Beck 2005). Such high recidivism rates translate into thousands of new instances of victimization each year. It is estimated that former prisoners account for 15 to 20 percent of all arrests among adults (Rosenfeld et al. 2005).

The magnitude of the prisoner reentry phenomenon also profoundly affects other aspects of communities, including public health, homelessness, declines in civic participation, and lost connections among families and within communities. Finally, there are fiscal implications. Significant portions of state budgets are now invested in the criminal justice system. Expenditures on corrections alone increased from $11 billion in 1982 to $65 billion in 2005 (U.S. Bureau of Justice Statistics 2005), and these figures do not include the cost of the arrest and sentencing processes, nor do they take into account the cost to victims of crimes committed by released prisoners.

The fiscal and social consequences of former prisoners returning to urban areas in record numbers have resulted in unprecedented political and policy attention in the United States. In 2001, the Council of State Governments passed a resolution focused on prisoner reentry. The resolution described the concern of state government officials about prisoner reentry, their desire to inform state policy making around this issue, and their efforts to ensure that the federal government facilitates reentry initiatives that recognize the uniqueness of each jurisdiction. The resolution established a national Re-Entry Policy Council charged with developing a comprehensive, bipartisan set of recommendations for policy makers to use to improve the likelihood that adults released from prison or jail will avoid crime and become productive members of families and communities. That effort resulted in a comprehensive report that has received national media attention and has inspired legislative activity on both state and federal levels (Re-Entry Policy Council 2005). The Re-Entry Policy Council is continuing to facilitate coordination and information sharing among elected officials and other policy makers to help organizations develop and implement effective public policy and programs concerning prisoner reentry.

The bipartisan attention that prisoner reentry has received in the last several years is also striking. Mayors, county councils, and governors have created special prisoner reentry coordinators in their offices. Federal support for prisoner reentry began in the Clinton administration and has continued under Presidents George W. Bush and Barack Obama in the form of several initiatives that provide grants to states for developing and enhancing efforts to ease the transition of prisons back to the community. Both the Serious and Violent Offender Reentry Initiative (SVORI) and the Prisoner Reentry Initiative (PRI) have helped to galvanize state correctional agencies and communities into focusing on the prisoner reentry phenomenon. The latest reentry initiative, the Second Chance Act, is a bipartisan congressional effort to send additional federal resources to states to help improve the reintegration of former prisoners into civilian life. Some of the strategies that are incorporated into these reentry initiatives—education, job training, and work release—have been the focus of offender rehabilitation efforts for the better part of the past century. However, attention to the problem of prisoner reentry in this decade has not just focused on the individual offender, but has taken a broader organizational approach in conceptualizing the problem and devising solutions. These new solutions seek to mobilize resources from a variety of social service sectors, to focus on community organizations, and to test new models to support successful reentry.

This chapter presents a snapshot of what we have learned in the last decade about exiting prisoners and summarizes the research on what works to improve the chances of former prisoners being successful. It includes findings from the first multi-site study in the United States undertaken to gather information about the men and women who are released from prison and their experiences as they return to their families and communities. It also presents results from multi-site evaluations of reentry initiatives. In these studies, multiple in-depth interviews with former prisoners during their first year out of prison have yielded rich insight into these individuals, and important policy lessons are beginning to emerge from these studies.

SUMMARY POINTS

- Men and women returning home from prison face formidable and simultaneous challenges, including finding a job and a place to live, locating health services and substance abuse treatment, arranging transportation, rejoining their families, and developing pro-social relationships.
- Most prisoners in reentry programs receive a low-to-moderate level of services to meet their needs before release from prison, but the services available in the community are rarely adequate to meet the needs of these individuals in the high-risk period after release.
- State responses to prisoner reentry have expanded in the last decade and are embracing promising strategies that create coalitions of community organizations to support returning prisoners.
- Reentry programs that are evidence-based and well-implemented have the potential to reduce recidivism rates, at levels as high as 15 to 20 percent; greater reductions may be possible with targeted, community-based strategies.

CHARACTERISTICS AND NEEDS
OF PRISONERS RETURNING HOME

As recently as 2000, there were no national data describing the characteristics of former prisoners, what they did in the first few weeks and months after their release from prison, and how they confront the transition from prison to the community. The U.S. justice statistics agency, the Bureau of Justice Statistics, regularly surveys inmates in state prisons and jails, and collects other statistics on state prison admissions and releases. However, those who are released from prison are not necessarily a representative group of those who are currently in prison. For example, on any given day, those who are released are typically serving shorter sentences than those who remain in prison, and they are likely to differ on other characteristics as well.

Other data on former prisoners were from studies of unrepresentative samples (e.g., women with children), or journalistic accounts of the experiences of former prisoners. In the 1960s, a longitudinal study of men released from prison was carried out in Canada (Waller 1964), but the results of that project were based on a time and place that were quite different from the contemporary reentry experiences of U.S. men and women. A study of the experiences of 50 individuals during their first month after release in New York in 1999 was circulated among researchers but was not formally released because the findings were considered controversial at the time (Nelson et al. 1999). Other studies have restricted their samples to those who were not successful after release and were returned to prison (Zamble and Quinsey 1997), probably because of the complexity (and expense) of locating individuals once they left prison.

To fill this knowledge gap and gather data on former prisoners, their return to the community, and their reintegration experiences, in 2001, a team of researchers at the Urban Institute designed a multi-state longitudinal study that interviewed men and women prior to their release and several times in the year after their release (Visher 2007; Visher, La Vigne, and Castro 2003). The *Returning Home* project explored experiences of prisoner reentry in four states, including a pilot study in Maryland and full research studies in Illinois, Ohio, and Texas. *Returning Home* was not intended as an outcome evaluation of a particular programmatic effort or an evaluation of a specific policy. It was a longitudinal study of the multiple and often complex challenges that prisoners face upon release and as they reintegrate into society.

The perspective on the experience of reentry from this project is both distinctive, because it is richer than official data, and representative, because it tells the story of all prisoners returning to free society, rather than just those who avail themselves of social services or who are rearrested. In each state, soon-to-be released prisoners within 30 to 60 days of release and returning to specific communities (Baltimore, MD; Chicago, IL; Cleveland, OH; and Houston, TX) were identified. The goal was to ensure that samples reflected the population of released prisoners returning to the identified communities and would be large enough to support multivariate analyses and tests of significance.

Another important source of available data on the characteristics of prisoners returning home is the recently completed *Multi-Site Evaluation of the Serious and Violent Offender Reentry Initiative* (SVORI). SVORI, discussed in detail later in this chapter, was an unprecedented federal initiative to provide states with funds to develop, enhance, or expand programs to facilitate the reentry of adults and juveniles to communities from prisons or juvenile detention facilities. As part of the evaluation of the Initiative, men and women enrolled in SVORI and a comparison group were interviewed prior to release and at 3, 9, and 15 months after release, using a similar methodology and protocol as that used in the *Returning Home* project (Lattimore and Visher 2009). These interviews gathered detailed information on the self-reported needs of individuals as they left prison and returned to the cities and neighborhoods they had left years earlier.

UNDERSTANDING THE CHALLENGES
OF RETURNING HOME

Until recently, answering the question "Who is returning home?" produced a wide range of answers. Partly this was the result of a lack of data, as described earlier, but in addition, the experience of reentry was often told through the eyes of service providers or parole officers. Utilizing data from self-reports of prisoners reveals that prisoners' perspectives of the reentry experience differ in important respects from the assumptions shared by many researchers, practitioners, and policy makers. It is also likely that some commonly held views of prisoners are shaped by the experience of working with certain sub-populations rather than with all those who return to society. For example, former prisoners who appear at shelters, soup kitchens, or community mental health clinics are likely to have different needs and characteristics than ex-prisoners who do not need shelters, donated food, or mental health treatment.

In addition, former prisoners are not a homogeneous group and they do not have identical experiences in their transition from prison to the community. Although the majority have extensive criminal careers, about one in five are serving their first prison term and one-third of those released are not reincarcerated (Piehl and LoBuglio 2005; Petersilia 2005). One in five has served a sentence of five years or more, although the average prisoner in the United States serves about 28 months (Lynch and Sabol 2001). The average age of men leaving state prison is about 35 years, older than many realize, and those in their thirties will likely have different needs from those in their twenties (Visher et al. 2010; Petersilia 2005).

Nonetheless, numerous social and economic disadvantages characterize the vast majority of individuals who are released from prison, including poor educational attainment and employment histories, poor physical and mental health, and alcohol and other drug misuse. Prior to incarceration, almost half of former prisoners (48 percent) had not completed high school or obtained a GED (Visher et al. 2008; Petersilia 2005). A small group of prisoners are able to obtain a GED while incarcerated, but such opportunities depend on the availability of education programs and inmate eligibility for those programs. Although about two-thirds of prisoners nationwide had worked before incarceration (Petersilia 2005), among *Returning Home* respondents, only half had ever held a permanent job and 32 percent were unemployed in the six months before incarceration (Visher et al. 2008).

It is well-known that a majority of prisoners have extensive substance use histories. Two-thirds (64 percent) of *Returning Home* respondents reported frequent (more than weekly) drug use or alcohol intoxication prior to prison (Visher et al. 2010). For example, in the six months before entering prison, 41 percent of Maryland respondents reported daily heroin use, and 57 percent of Texas respondents reported daily cocaine use (Solomon et al. 2006). Given high rates of substance use, it is not surprising that exiting prisoners are also likely to suffer from health problems and mental illness (see Greifinger et al., 2007; Petersilia 2005). The majority of men exiting prison (54 percent) reported having a chronic physical or mental health condition, with the most commonly reported conditions including depression, asthma, hepatitis, and high blood pressure (Visher and Mallik-Kane 2007).

Family members provide critical support to men and women after their release from prison. Research has found that strengthening the family network and maintaining supportive family contact can improve outcomes after prisoners are released (Sullivan et al. 2002; Shapiro and Schwartz 2001). Most prisoners (88 percent) in the *Returning Home* study reported that they have at least one close family member, and 45 percent reported that they have four or more close family members (Visher 2007). Moreover, the majority of returning prisoners live with family members and/or intimate partners immediately after release (Visher et al. 2010). Two months after release, 85 percent of *Returning Home* respondents were living with a family member, typically their mother or sister (50–60 percent) or intimate partner (20–23 percent). However, many of these living arrangements are only temporary. Seven months after release, 35 percent of former prisoners had lived at more than one address, and 52 percent believed that their housing situation was temporary or that they would not be staying in their current neighborhood for long (Visher et al. 2010).

This portrait of former prisoners reveals the formidable challenges in their personal lives as they leave prison and return to the community. Not surprisingly, the self-reported needs of exiting prisoners mirror these challenges. As revealed in interviews as part of the evaluation of the Serious and Violent Offender Reentry Initiative, the needs of former prisoners ranged from general needs such as more education to specific needs such as photo identification or driver's license (Lattimore, Visher, and Steffey 2008).

In interviews conducted about 30 days before release, respondents were asked to identify the extent to which they needed 28 different types of services in five broad categories: services to help with the transition from prison to the community; health care services (including substance abuse and mental health); employment, education, and skills services; domestic violence–related services; and child-related services (Lattimore, Visher, and Steffey 2008). Among men, the levels of expressed need are highest for education, job training, and employment, followed by the need for a variety of transitional services and health-related services (see Figure 28.2). Almost all soon-to-be-released prisoners report needing more education (94 percent), job training (82 percent), and a job (80 percent); and the need for a driver's license (83

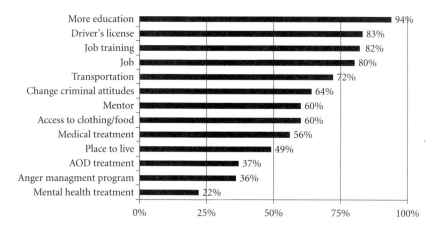

Figure 28.2. Self-Reported Need for Specific Services among Soon-to-be-Released Male Prisoners.
Source: Compiled from data on male respondents (n = 1,697) presented in Lattimore, Visher, and Steffey 2008.

percent) ranked higher than the need for employment. Substantial proportions of exiting prisoners report needing basic transitional services such as housing (49 percent), access to clothing and food (60 percent), and transportation (72 percent). More than half of prisoners report needing medical treatment (56 percent). Treatment for substance use and mental health issues is also a significant need for up to one-third of prisoners who are close to release. Exiting prisoners also recognize a need for services that will help them change their past behavior patterns as they return to the community, such as mentoring (60 percent), services to help change criminal attitudes (64 percent), and anger management classes (36 percent). Finally, men with children report needing a variety of child-related services, including parenting skills (60 percent), help with child support payments (45 percent), and even child care assistance after release (39 percent).

Female prisoners report higher expressed need for services than men (Lattimore and Visher 2009; Lindquist et al. 2009). Women had significantly higher needs than men for 19 of 28 identified services. In comparison with the men, women most commonly report needing education (95 percent), employment (83 percent), a mentor (83 percent), a driver's license (82 percent), and access to clothing and food (77 percent) (see Figure 28.3). Moreover, women report needing more health services than men, with 55 percent needing mental health treatment and about two-thirds needing substance use treatment. About one-third requested access to support groups for abuse victims. Not surprisingly, need for child-related services among exiting female prisoners is high, with 90 percent of women with children reporting needing some type of child-related service. More mothers than fathers report needing to learn parenting skills (70 percent), but otherwise women and men appear to have similar levels of need for child-related services.

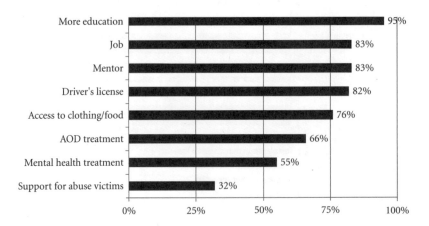

Figure 28.3. Self-Reported Need for Specific Services among Soon-to-be-Released
Female Prisoners.
Source: Compiled from data on female respondents (n = 357) presented in Lindquist et al. 2009.

The SVORI evaluation also questioned men and women in the study about their need for a variety of services during the months after their release from prison. The researchers report that women continued to have higher self-reported needs than men, particularly for health and family-related services. Other gender differences decreased over time in other service areas. In the later interviews at 9 and 15 months, men reported higher levels of need for employment and education than the women (Lattimore and Visher 2009; Lindquist et al. 2009). On average, the men reported needing about 40–45 percent of all the service items up to 15 months after release, compared to 54 percent of items just prior to release; women reported needing about 45–50 percent of all the service items after release, compared with 64 percent of items prior to release (Lattimore and Visher 2009). The highest continued needs for both men and women were more education, financial assistance, and health care insurance.

Thus, men and women returning to the community are a population with extremely high needs, which remain high up to 15 months after release from prison. In addition to these recognized needs for assistance and support, former prisoners may experience collateral effects of the prison experience and a criminal record, which both create additional obstacles to a successful transition from prison back to the community. These collateral effects (sometimes called "invisible punishments") may include exclusions from certain professions (e.g., realtor or health care), access to public benefits (e.g., student loans, public housing, or food stamps), as well as loss of parental rights (Petersilia 2003; Hagan and Dinovitzer 1999; Travis 2002). These realities, in conjunction with conditions imposed upon their release (e.g., employment, in-person reporting, payment of restitution, fees, and fines), and the need for state-approved identification and transportation, make the first few weeks and months after release especially difficult.

State Responses to the Challenges
of Prisoner Reentry

The complexity of the disadvantages and the depths of the needs confronting men and women being released from prison means that the reentry "problem" cannot be addressed with a single generic program or intervention. Reentry experts are encouraging a broader focus on comprehensive reentry *strategies*, not programs (Lattimore 2007; Travis 2005). Such strategies usually involve multiple levels of government, coordination of efforts across agencies, and involvement of organizations that are traditionally not part of the reentry discussion (e.g., public health department, the business community, local community colleges).

States are beginning to realize that reducing recidivism and improving the chances that former prisoners do not return requires a coordinated, sustained response—at both the state and local levels. In 2003, the National Governors Association launched the Prisoner Reentry State Policy Academy to help state governors and other state policy makers develop and implement prisoner reentry strategies to reduce recidivism rates. Many states have created task forces to identify major barriers for former prisoners in their states, such as housing regulations and employment prohibitions, which can be modified to reduce obstacles to successful reintegration. Other states are establishing State Reentry Policy Councils to develop policies, coordinate programming across state agencies, and make recommendations to redesign the reentry process. These Councils can also work with community-level reentry task forces and organizations to develop a continuum of care that organizes services in the prison and the community.

In addition to the state's role, local governments can play important roles in developing reentry policies that foster successful reintegration. Many cities have established local reentry task forces or created a position within the mayor's office to coordinate local reentry efforts. The Re-Entry Policy Council report suggests that cities with high populations of returning prisoners consider co-locating programs in a single location—a "reentry one-stop." In response to this idea, the Department of Labor's Prisoner Reentry Initiative is providing funds to local communities to coordinate employment and other reentry services in existing one-stop centers. The "Ban the Box" initiative, in which some U.S. cities have eliminated any requirement that prior felony convictions be disclosed on employment applications for publicly funded jobs, is an example of a locally driven policy change that could have a significant impact on the lives of former prisoners.

Perhaps most important, the new reentry conversation is spurring significant changes in the operations of the components of the criminal justice system most directly involved in influencing reentry outcomes. Practitioners in the corrections field have embraced the challenge of rethinking their core functions through a reentry lens. Prior to 2000, many correctional professionals explicitly stated that prison administrators could not be held responsible for the behavior of prisoners once they left the prison walls. Now, a number of state corrections systems, led by the Ohio Department of Corrections and Rehabilitation, have expanded their institutional mission statements to include responsibility for successful reentry and reintegration. Others, even without amending their mission statements, are engaged in strategic coalitions with community service providers to improve reentry outcomes.

This coordinated state and local attention to prisoner reentry is leading to new legislative proposals and requests to realign resources. In Michigan, for example, Governor Jennifer Granholm made prisoner reentry a major plank in her first campaign for election, appointed a reform-minded staff to oversee the effort, and launched a coordinated effort with foundation support and local government buy-in to improve reentry services and reduce prison populations. To help states make informed choices, the "justice reinvestment" initiative led by the Re-Entry Policy Council is using technical assistance and state data to help legislators and other policy makers develop data-driven, policy options that will generate savings and increase public safety (http://justicereinvestment.org/states/). By reallocating resources and implementing new policies, states may be able to substantially reduce recidivism within existing budgets and create healthier communities with former prisoners who can become productive citizens.

Around the country, there are a number of demonstration projects that are testing a very new reentry model: a community-based approach to reentry. Recognizing that some communities are experiencing very high rates of incarceration and reentry, these projects approach reentry as a community phenomenon. These programs create coalitions of community organizations to interact with every person returning home from prison. They attempt to create a different climate in the neighborhood, one promoting successful reintegration, and they devote community resources to supporting returning prisoners. One example of this approach is the Offender Notification Forum.

As part of its Project Safe Neighborhood (PSN) initiative in designated neighborhoods in Chicago, individuals recently assigned to parole or probation with a history of gun violence and gang participation were requested to attend a forum hosted by the PSN team. In these Offender Notification Forums, the offenders would sit for an hour or more with representatives from state and local law enforcement agencies and community service providers. The first part of the meeting focused on the consequences of gun crimes, both for the individual and for the neighborhood. The second segment featured a talk by a former prisoner who had turned his life around; he stressed the impact of violence on the community, the problems of intra-racial violence, and the seriousness of the PSN initiative. The third segment focused on community services that are available, including job training, education programs, drug treatment, temporary shelter, and counseling. According to a recently published evaluation of the PSN initiative in Chicago, the intervention has been "remarkably effective in reducing neighborhood crime rates" (Meares et al. 2009). There was a 37 percent reduction in homicide rates in the target neighborhood after the program began, compared to the previous three years.

Other community-based reentry efforts are being developed and implemented across the country (Travis 2009). These demonstration efforts represent a new frontier in reentry innovation. They do not focus exclusively on individual-level interventions. Rather, they create a coalition of support for individuals returning from prisons and jails, bring together law enforcement and community leaders, often provide a role for coalitions of formerly incarcerated individuals, communicate clearly about the consequences of illegal behavior, and provide a clear pathway out of a life of antisocial conduct.

The "reentry court" is another new model for coordinating services and realigning government resources. First proposed by National Institute of Justice Director Jeremy Travis in a paper developed for the Executive Session on Sentencing and Corrections (Travis 2000), the concept of a reentry court, in many critical respects, builds on the idea of "drug courts" and other "problem-solving courts." In addition to resolving the criminal case, these latter courts address the underlying conditions giving rise to a criminal offense, such as addiction or family stress. In problem-solving courts, judges marshal resources and services, create direct personal connections with defendants and their families, apply modest sanctions in response to misconduct or failure to adhere to agreements, and celebrate the defendant's program completion, or "graduation" (Berman and Feinblatt 2005).

There are important differences, however, between reentry courts and these other innovations. Whereas most problem-solving courts serve as pre-trial diversion interventions, or alternatives to incarceration, reentry courts operate at the back end of the criminal justice system, following an individual's release from prison. Because there is little precedent for judicial involvement at this stage of the process, and the oversight of released prisoners is traditionally the province of an executive branch agency (the parole department), reentry courts are breaking new ground by positing a realignment of governmental responsibilities for successful reentry (Travis 2005; Petersilia 2004). Placement at the back end also allows formerly incarcerated individuals to create personal narratives of redemption and thereby facilitate the restoration of citizenship status (Maruna and LeBel 2003).

Attorney General Janet Reno announced the selection of the first nine pilot reentry courts in February 2000 (U.S. Department of Justice 2000). By December 2007, according to one count, a total of 28 reentry courts had been launched in United States criminal justice systems (Huddleston, Marlowe and Casebolt 2008). Whether this innovation reaches its promise is yet to be determined (Lindquist et al. 2004). In quasi-experimental evaluations, reentry courts have been associated with lower rates of arrest and conviction, although the tighter supervision practices associated with reentry courts have also led to higher rates of parole revocation and return to prison (Hamilton 2010; Farole Jr. 2007). With federal funding now available for demonstration projects under the Second Chance Act, this new model for prisoner reentry should be subjected to rigorous testing to examine its potential as an effective reentry strategy.

EFFECTIVE REENTRY PROGRAMS AND POLICIES

Given the explosion of new federal, state, and local policy and practice related to prisoner reentry, it is not surprising that existing research on effective reentry programs and policies has not captured these recent innovations (Petersilia 2004). Moreover, numerous challenges characterize the extant research assessing the effectiveness of programs for formerly incarcerated individuals, whether focused on reentry or general rehabilitation. Foremost among the challenges is the lack of theoretical models that articulate behavior change among former prisoners. Within any particular substantive area, there are also problems of fidelity in that a particular service approach may manifest itself in different ways under different programs and circumstances. As a result, it is often difficult to generalize research findings from one program to others, and substantial variability exists among the outcome variables examined (e.g., employment, homelessness, substance use). The numerous combinations of program types unique to each study also render comparisons difficult. Finally, there are problems related to the research itself, as rigorous experimental designs—including the use of comparison groups (randomly assigned or otherwise)—are rare in this research literature (National Research Council 2007).

Nonetheless, researchers have developed an impressive body of studies that underscore the modest effectiveness of a variety of interventions. Recent reviews and meta-analyses of evaluations of rehabilitative programming (Aos et al. 2006; Gaes et al. 1999; Lipsey and Cullen 2007; MacKenzie 2006; Petersilia 2004; Seiter and Kadela 2003) indicate that a variety of programs can reduce recidivism by up to 10 percent, depending on program design and implementation integrity, including in-prison and jail drug treatment (i.e., therapeutic communities), especially with a community component; cognitive behavioral therapy, vocational education and training programs; employment training and job assistance; and adult basic education. Approaches with the largest impact on recidivism, possibly 20 percent or greater, are likely to require a combination of intensive supervision in the community with mandatory treatment programs tailored to individual needs (MacKenzie 2006; Aos et al. 2006; Petersilia 2004; Gaes et al. 1999).

MacKenzie (2006) has summarized the "what works" literature in corrections, with specific chapters on various programs (e.g., life skills, cognitive behavioral therapy, education, drug treatment, and intensive supervision) for treatment of individuals under criminal justice supervision in the community. She concluded that human service–oriented programs were much more effective than those based on a control or deterrent philosophy. In particular, there is growing consensus that practices focusing on individual-level change, including cognitive change, education, and drug treatment, are likely to be more effective than other strategies, such as programs that increase opportunities for work, reunite families, and provide housing (see also Andrews and Bonta, 2006).

All of the strategies that MacKenzie identified as effective share several traits: they focus on dynamic criminogenic factors, are skill-oriented, are based on cognitive/

behavioral models, and treat multiple offender deficits simultaneously. These conclusions are based on another line of research that has produced a set of guidelines for effective rehabilitation strategies, including having strong program integrity, identifying criminogenic factors, employing a multi-modal treatment approach, using an actuarial risk classification, and ensuring responsivity between an offender's learning style and mode of program delivery (Andrews and Bonta 2006; Cullen and Gendreau 2000; Gendreau et al. 1996). Applying these principles to practice, programs should be designed that: (1) focus on behavioral outcomes, targeting criminogenic needs and using positive reinforcements; (2) target high-risk offenders; (3) use risk assessment instruments; (4) begin treatment in prison and provide continuity in the community; and (5) provide intensive interventions for at least six months (Solomon et al. 2008).

Evaluations also point to what interventions do *not* work. The evidence has been very consistent in establishing that contact-driven supervision, surveillance, and enforcement of supervision conditions have a limited ability to change offender behavior or to reduce the likelihood of recidivism (Aos et al. 2006; MacKenzie 2006). Individuals placed on parole supervision after prison are no less likely to be rearrested than individuals released with no supervision (Solomon et al. 2005). Other programs that have no impact on recidivism include boot camps, some types of sex offender treatment, electronic monitoring, and life skills education (MacKenzie 2006).

Adding to this body of literature on rehabilitation and reentry programs for reducing recidivism are the results of recent prisoner reentry demonstration projects, such as the Serious and Violent Offender Reentry Initiative (SVORI) and the Prisoner Reentry Initiative (PRI). The emerging consensus of the need for integrated, needs-based reentry programming for adult and juvenile offenders to reduce recidivism and promote public safety provided the context for SVORI. In 2003, the U.S. Departments of Justice, Labor, Education, Housing and Urban Development, and Health and Human Services provided more than $100 million to states to develop, enhance, or expand programs to facilitate the reentry of adult and juvenile offenders to communities from prisons or juvenile detention facilities (Lattimore and Visher 2009). Sixty-nine agencies received federal funds ($500 thousand to $2 million over 3 years) to develop 89 programs to improve criminal justice, employment, education, health, and housing outcomes for exiting prisoners. Grantees were to use their SVORI funding to create a three-phase continuum of services that began during the period of incarceration, intensified just before release and during the early months after release, and continued for several years as former inmates took on more productive and independent roles in the community.

Each SVORI program was locally designed along a variety of dimensions, including the types of services offered, the focus on pre-release and post-release components, and the types of individuals to be served. Programs varied in terms of what was being provided, when, and to whom. Thus, the SVORI grants provided an opportunity to evaluate the impact of a diversity of reentry programming efforts across the nation. The multi-site SVORI evaluation conducted by RTI International and the Urban Institute was the largest examination of prisoner reentry programs ever conducted in the United States. The evaluation collected data on subject character-istics and needs, service receipt, and outcomes with a sample of 2,391 adult and juvenile males and adult females from 12 programs in 14 sites. Follow-up interviews were conducted at 3, 9, and 15 months post-release (Lattimore and Visher 2009).

The results of the SVORI evaluation are complex and raise a number of issues for reentry researchers, policy makers, and practitioners. First, in all sites, adults participating in SVORI programs received more services and programming, in-cluding programs to prepare for release, meeting with a case manager, and receiving a needs assessment than non-SVORI comparisons. However, similar to other studies of reentry programs, SVORI participants experienced considerable "treat-ment dilution." Adult SVORI participants reported levels of service receipt that were far short of 100 percent, were substantially lower than their levels of expressed need, and declined substantially after release (Lattimore et al. 2009). For example, having a reentry plan could be considered a core requirement for successful reinte-gration and a necessary component of any reentry program. At the first interview, conducted 30 days prior to release, 57 percent of the adult male SVORI program participants reported having developed a reentry plan—in comparison to 24 per-cent of the non-SVORI respondents. Similarly, 73 percent of adult females in SVORI programs reported having a reentry plan, in comparison to 19 percent of those who were not in a SVORI program (Lattimore, Visher, and Steffey 2010). The discrep-ancies in service delivery between what was intended and what was actually pro-vided at the program level, and what was needed and what was actually received at the individual level, suggests that programs were not "fully implemented," insofar as implementation required the provision of intended and needed services. Moreover, service receipt for both SVORI and non-SVORI respondents was highest during incarceration, despite growing knowledge that exiting prisoners are at highest risk for recidivism immediately after release and could benefit from intensive services during that period (Solomon et al. 2008; National Research Council 2007).

Second, despite less than full implementation, modest increases in services among SVORI respondents, compared to "business as usual," were associated with modest improvements in outcomes (Lattimore, Steffey, and Visher 2009). SVORI respondents did better than non-SVORI comparisons on self-reported criminal behavior, employment, substance use, and housing. For example, at 15 months, 71 percent of SVORI participants were supporting themselves with a job, compared to 60 percent of the comparison respondents. Levels of drug use (using a combined measure of self-report and drug test) were quite high overall, but at 15 months, drug use was slightly lower among SVORI participants (54 percent) than comparison respondents (57 percent).

Finally, recidivism outcomes (based on official measures) were not significantly improved for adult male SVORI participants in the evaluation. Rearrest rates were high for both SVORI participants and comparison respondents: at 12 months after release, half of both groups had been rearrested (49 percent of SVORI, 51 percent of comparisons). And, at 12 months, 25 percent of both groups had been reincarcer-ated (Lattimore, Steffey, and Visher 2009). The SVORI evaluators acknowledge that the official recidivism results are at odds with improvements in services received and the intermediate outcomes that would be expected to reduce recidivism (Lattimore and Visher 2009). Among the possible explanations is that the low levels of services delivered to the SVORI participants were insufficient, given levels of need.

The SVORI evaluation results suggest that a properly and fully implemented program may generate improvements in intermediate outcomes, but the impacts on recidivism may be minimal. Other reentry experts have expressed similar views that poor implementation may explain why criminal justice interventions often fail to produce positive impacts on recidivism (Andrews 2006; Lowenkamp et al. 2006; Rhine et al. 2006; White 2007; Wilson and Davis 2006). Some of the most common implementation problems include ineffective delivery of services, poor matching of individual needs to program content, and failure to incorporate established principles for effective rehabilitative programming. The timing of service delivery may also be important (National Research Council 2007). Thus, greater reductions in recidivism from prisoner reentry programs may only be achieved through attention to implementation issues.

CONCLUSION

We should view this emerging body of research very positively. We know far more than we ever did before about the experience of leaving prison—the attitudes of returning prisoners, their needs and expectations, the role of family and communal networks in providing support or posing obstacles to their successful reintegration. Research has documented the particular challenges experienced during the first weeks and months following release, and the unstable, often chaotic, lives of returning prisoners as they move from home to home, sometimes community to community, as they seek stability. These experiences of the individuals who leave our prisons, now well-documented in the *Returning Home* study, should inform our approaches to the development of interventions designed to improve reentry outcomes.

We also know far more than we did a few decades ago about program effectiveness. Recognizing that the literature is still characterized by methodologically weak evaluations, and many promising interventions have not yet been evaluated, we can now begin to move toward policies supporting evidence-based programming, so that all prison- and community-based programs can be assessed to determine whether they comport to research-based principles of program effectiveness. We expect that this shift toward evidence-based policies will be facilitated and accelerated by the creation of the Reentry Resource Center as envisioned by the Second Chance Act (see http://www.nationalreentryresourcecenter.org/).

These improvements in the state of knowledge and the emerging commitment to evidence-based practices set the stage for a new era of accountability in which the entities involved in reentry management—public and private agencies alike—can and should be held to standards of recidivism reduction. According to best estimates of the research community, if we could implement effective programs for all returning prisoners with all the resources needed, we could expect recidivism reductions on the order of 15 to 20 percent. We can also state with confidence that these programs would be cost-effective—they would pay for themselves by reducing future criminal justice and corrections costs. Finally, the emergence of new models of community-based reentry interventions, which mobilize the resources of family, community, and positive networks of formerly incarcerated individuals, in addition to traditional service delivery systems and criminal justice agencies, hold the promise for even greater reductions in new crimes. The organizational challenge in implementing this accountability agenda is daunting, as the public and its elected officials must hold coalitions of public and private agencies responsible for increasing the odds of successful reentry.

These advances in research knowledge present enormous challenges to the nation. We can now state with considerable confidence that we can intervene in the lives of former prisoners and reduce their failure rates, particularly their rearrest rates. Seen from one perspective, the potential for improvement is modest—perhaps on the order of 20 percent reductions in recidivism in the cohort leaving prison. But this improvement would represent the prevention of hundreds of thousands of crimes each year. More important, progress on this agenda would help restore to full and productive citizenship hundreds of thousands of men and women who return home to live in free society after paying their debt to society for the crimes they have committed. In a powerful sense, this progress would represent a fuller realization of the ideals of justice.

REFERENCES

Andrews, Donald Arthur. 2006. "Enhancing Adherence to Risk-Need-Responsivity: Making Quality a Matter of Policy." *Criminology and Public Policy* 5 (Sept.): 595–602.

Andrews, Donald Arthur, and Bonta, James. 2006. *The Psychology of Criminal Conduct*. 4th ed. NJ: Lexis/Nexis/Matthew Bender.

Aos, Steve, Marna Miller, and Elizabeth Drake. 2006. *Evidence-Based Adult Corrections Programs: What Works and What Does Not*. Olympia: Washington State Institute for Public Policy.

Berman, Gordon, and John Feinblatt. 2005. *Good Courts: The Case for Problem-Solving Justice*. New York: New Press.

Blumstein, Alfred, and Allen Beck. 2005. "Reentry as a Transient State Between Liberty and Recommitment." In *Prisoner Reentry and Public Safety in America*, eds. Jeremy Travis and Christy Visher, 50–79. New York: Cambridge University Press.

Cullen, Francis T., and Paul Gendreau. 2000. "Assessing Correctional Rehabilitation: Policy, Practice, and Prospects." In *Criminal Justice 2000: Policies, Processes, and*

Decisions of the Criminal Justice System, ed. J. Horney, 109–175. Washington, DC: National Institute of Justice.

Farole, D. J., Jr. 2007. "The Harlem Parole Reentry Court: Implementation and Preliminary Impacts." In *Documenting Results: Research on Problem-Solving Justice*, eds. G. Berman, M. Rempel, and R. V. Wolf, 319–328. New York: Center for Court Innovation.

Gaes, Gerald G., Timothy J. Flanagan, Laurence L. Motiuk, and Lynn Stewart. 1999. "Adult Correctional Treatment." *Crime and Justice* 26: 361–426.

Gendreau, Paul, Tracy Little, and Claire Goggin. 1996. "A Meta-Analysis of Adult Offender Recidivism: What Works!" *Criminology* 34: 575–607.

Greifinger, Robert B., Joseph A. Bick, and Joe Goldenson, eds.2007. *Public Health Behind Bars: From Prisons to Communities*. Dobbs Ferry, NY: Springer-Verlag.

Hagan, J., and R. Dinovitzer. 1999. "Collateral Consequences of Imprisonment for Children, Communities, and Prisoners." In *Prisons*, eds. Joan Petersilia and Michael Tonry, 121–162. Chicago: University of Chicago Press.

Hamilton, Z. 2010. *Do Reentry Courts Reduce Recidivism? Results from the Harlem Parole Reentry Court*. New York: The Center for Court Innovation. Available at: http://www.courtinnovation.org/_uploads/documents/Reentry_Evaluation.pdf.

Huddleston, C. W. III, D. B. Marlowe, and R. Casebolt. 2008. *Painting the Current Picture: A National Report Card on Drug Courts and Other Problem-Solving Court Programs in the United States* 2, no. 1. Alexandria, VA: National Drug Court Institute. Available at: http://www.ndci.org/publications/publication-resources/painting-current-picture.

Langan, Patrick A., and David J. Levin. 2002. *Recidivism of Prisoners Released in 1994*. Washington, DC: U.S. Bureau of Justice Statistics (NCJ 193427).

Lattimore, Pamela K. 2007. "The Challenges of Reentry." *Corrections Today, 2007*. Alexandria, VA: American Correctional Association.

Lattimore, Pamela K., Danielle M. Steffey, and Christy A. Visher. 2009. *Prison Reentry Experiences of Adult Males: Characteristics, Service Receipt, and Outcomes of Participants in the SVORI Multi-Site Evaluation*. Research Triangle Park, NC: RTI International.

Lattimore, Pamela K., and Christy A. Visher. 2009. *Multi-Site Evaluation of SVORI: Summary and Synthesis*. Raleigh, NC: RTI International.

Lattimore, Pamela K., Christy A. Visher, and Danielle M. Steffey. 2008. *Pre-Release Characteristics and Service Receipt among Adult Male Participants in the SVORI Multi-Site Evaluation*. Raleigh, NC: RTI International.

Lattimore, Pamela K., Christy A. Visher, and Danielle M. Steffey. 2010. "Prisoner Reentry in the First Decade of the 21st Century." *Journal of Victims and Offenders* 5: 253–267.

Lindquist, C. H., K. Barrick, P. K. Lattimore, and C. A. Visher. 2009. *Prison Reentry Experiences of Adult Females: Characteristics, Service Receipt, and Outcomes of Participants in the SVORI Multi-site Evaluation*. Research Triangle Park, NC: RTI International.

Lindquist, C., J. Hardison, and P. Lattimore. 2004. "The Reentry Court Initiative: Court-based Strategies for Managing Released Prisoners." *Justice Research and Policy* 6: 97–118.

Lipsey, Mark W., and Francis T. Cullen. 2007. "The Effectiveness of Correctional Rehabilitation: A Review of Systematic Reviews." *Annual Review of Law and Social Science* 3: 297–320.

Lowenkamp, Christopher T., Edward J. Latessa, and Paula Smith. 2006. "Does Correctional Program Quality Really Matter? The Impact of Adhering to the Principles of Effective Intervention." *Criminology and Public Policy* 5: 575–594.

Lynch, James P., and William Sabol. 2001. *Prisoner Reentry in Perspective*. Washington, DC: Urban Institute, 2001.

MacKenzie, Doris L. 2006. *What Works in Corrections: Reducing the Criminal Activities of Offenders and Delinquents*. New York: Cambridge University Press.

Maruna, Shadd, and Thomas P. LeBel. 2003. "Welcome Home? Examining the "Reentry Court" Concept from a Strengths-Based Perspective. " *Western Criminology Review* 4: 91–107.

Meares, Tracey, Andrew W. Papachristos, and Jeffrey Fagan. 2009. *Homicide and Gun Violence in Chicago: Evaluation and Summary of the Project Safe Neighborhood Program*. Available at: http://www.psnchicago.org/PDFs/2009-PSN-Research-Brief_v2.pdf.

National Research Council. 2007. *Parole, Desistance from Crime, and Community Integration*. Washington, DC: National Academy Press.

Nelson, Marta, Perry Deess, and Charlotte Allen. 1999. *The First Month Out: Post-Incarceration Experiences in New York City*. New York: Vera Institute of Justice.

Petersilia, Joan. 2003. *When Prisoners Come Home: Parole and Prisoner Reentry*. New York: Oxford University Press.

Petersilia, Joan. 2004. "What Works in Prisoner Reentry? Reviewing and Questioning the Evidence." *Federal Probation* 68: 4–8.

Petersilia, Joan. 2005. "From Cell to Society: Who is Returning Home?" In *Prisoner Reentry and Crime in America*, eds. Jeremy Travis and Christy Visher, 15–49. Cambridge: Cambridge University Press.

Piehl, Anne, and Stephan LoBuglio. 2005. "Does Supervision Matter?" In *Prisoner Reentry and Crime in America*, eds. Jeremy Travis and Christy Visher, 105–138. Cambridge: Cambridge University Press.

Re-Entry Policy Council. 2005. *Report of the Re-Entry Policy Council: Charting the Safe and Successful Return of Prisoners to the Community*. New York: Council of State Governments.

Rhine, Edward, Tina Mawhorr, and Evalyn C. Parks. 2006. "Implementation: The Bane of Effective Correctional Programs." *Criminology and Public Policy* 5: 347–358.

Rosenfeld, Richard, Joel Wallman, and Robert J. Fornango. 2005. "The Contribution of Ex-Prisoners to Crime Rates." In *Prisoner Reentry and Public Safety in America*, eds. Jeremy Travis and Christy Visher, 80–104. New York: Cambridge University Press.

Sabol, William J., and Heather Couture. 2009. *Prison Inmates at Midyear 2008*. Washington, DC: U.S. Bureau of Justice Statistics.

Seiter, Richard P., and Karen R. Kadela. 2003. "Prisoner Reentry: What Works, What Does Not, and What Is Promising." *Crime & Delinquency* 49: 360–388.

Solomon, Amy L., Jesse Jannetta, Brian Elderbroom, Laura Winterfield, Jenny Osborne, Peggy Burke, Richard P. Stroker, Edward E. Rhine, and William D. Burrell. 2008. *Putting Public Safety First: 13 Strategies for Successful Supervision and Reentry*. Washington, DC: The Urban Institute, Justice Policy Center.

Solomon, Amy L., Vera Kachnowski, and Avi Bhati. 2005. *Does Parole Work?: Analyzing the Impact of Postprison Supervision on Rearrest Outcomes*. Washington, DC: The Urban Institute, Justice Policy Center.

Solomon, Amy L., Christy Visher, Nancy G. La Vigne, and Jenny Osborne. 2006. *Understanding the Challenges of Prisoner Reentry: Research Findings from the Urban Institute's Prisoner Reentry Portfolio*. Washington, DC: The Urban Institute, Justice Policy Center.

Shapiro, Carol, and Martin Schwartz. 2001. "Coming Home: Building on Family Connections." *Corrections Management Quarterly* 5: 52–51.

Sullivan, Eileen, Milton Mino, Katherine Nelson, and Jill Pope. 2002. *Families as a Resource in Recovery from Drug Abuse: An Evaluation of La Bodega de la Familia*. New York: Vera Institute of Justice.

Travis, Jeremy. 2000. "But they all come back: Rethinking prisoner reentry." *Sentencing and Corrections Bulletin*, No. 7. Washington, DC: National Institute of Justice.

Travis, Jeremy. 2002. "Invisible Punishment: An Instrument of Social Exclusion." In *Invisible Punishment: The Collateral Consequences of Mass Imprisonment*, eds. Marc Mauer and Meda Chesney-Lind, 15–36. New York: New Press.

Travis, Jeremy. 2005. *But They All Come Back: Facing the Challenges of Prisoner Reentry*. Washington, DC: Urban Institute Press.

Travis, Jeremy. 2009. "What Works" for Successful Prisoner Reentry. Testimony before the U.S. House of Representatives, Committee on Appropriations, Subcommittee on Commerce, Justice, Science, and Related Agencies, March 12, 2009.

Travis, Jeremy, and Christy Visher. 2005. *Prisoner Reentry and Crime in America*. Cambridge: Cambridge University Press.

U.S. Bureau of Justice Statistics. 2005. Direct expenditures by criminal justice function, 1982–2006. Retrieved March 24, 2010 from http://bjs.ojp.usdoj.gov/content/glance/tables/exptyptab.cfm.

U.S. Department of Justice. 2000. *Attorney General Reno to Announce Reentry Court Initiative; Nine Pilot Sites Chosen from Around the Country* (2000 OJP Press Release). Retrieved from the Office of Justice Programs web site on April 2, 2010 http://www.ojp.usdoj.gov/archives/pressreleases/2000/op0053.htm.

Visher, Christy. 2007. "Returning Home: Emerging Findings and Policy Lessons about Prisoner Reentry." *Federal Sentencing Reporter* 20: 93–102.

Visher, Christy, Sara Debus, and Jennifer Yahner. 2008. *Employment After Prison: A Longitudinal Study of Releasees in Three States*. Washington, DC: Urban Institute.

Visher, Christy, Nancy LaVigne, and Jennifer Castro. 2003. "Returning Home: Preliminary Findings from a Pilot Study of Soon-to-be-Released Inmates in Maryland". *Justice Research and Policy* 5: 55–74.

Visher, Christy, and Kamala Mallik-Kane. 2007. "Reentry Experiences of Men with Health Problems." In *Public Health Is Public Safety: Improving Public Health through Correctional Health Care*, ed. Robert Greifinger, 432–447. London: Springer-Verlag.

Visher, Christy A., and Jeremy Travis. 2003. "Transitions from Prison to Community: Understanding Individual Pathways." *Annual Review of Sociology* 29: 89–113.

Visher, Christy, Jennifer Yahner, and Nancy G. LaVigne. 2010. "Life after Prison: Tracking the Experiences of Male Prisoners Returning to Chicago, Cleveland, and Houston." Washington, DC: The Urban Institute, Justice Policy Center.

Waller, Irwin. 1964. *Men Released from Prison*. Toronto: University of Toronto Press.

White, Thomas F. 2007. "Creating Leadership to Facilitate Implementation of Evidence-Based Practice." *Journal of Community Corrections* 17: 13–28.

Wilson, James. A., and Robert C. Davis. 2006. "Good Intentions Meet Hard Realities: An Evaluation of the Project Greenlight Reentry Program." *Criminology and Public Policy* 5: 303–338.

Zamble, Edward, and Vernon L. Quinsey. 1997. *The Criminal Recidivism Process*. Cambridge: Cambridge University Press.

Section G
The Death Penalty

BROKEN AND BEYOND REPAIR: THE AMERICAN DEATH PENALTY AND THE INSUPERABLE OBSTACLES TO REFORM

CAROL S. STEIKER AND JORDAN M. STEIKER

INTRODUCTION

The most distinctive characteristic of the contemporary American death penalty is its complex overlay of federal constitutional regulation. Forty years ago, states' systems of capital punishment were largely free from federal constraint. But concerns about the arbitrary and inequitable imposition of the death penalty, as well as more general concerns about whether the punishment should be retained at all, culminated in the development of an extensive body of constitutional doctrines governing the administration of capital punishment. These doctrines ushered in the modern era of American capital punishment. Extensive constitutional regulation, however, has not produced a rational, equitable, or reliable death penalty system.

Some of the present difficulties stem from the inadequacies of the regulatory doctrinal framework; other difficulties reflect deeply entrenched structural obstacles to a workable system that would likely undermine any regulatory path.[1]

I. The Inadequacies of Constitutional Regulation

The Supreme Court's constitutional regulation of capital punishment, which commenced in earnest with the Court's temporary invalidation of capital punishment in *Furman v. Georgia* in 1972 (408 U.S. 238) and its reauthorization of capital punishment in *Gregg v. Georgia* in 1976 (428 U.S. 153), produced some significant advances, both substantively and procedurally, in the administration of the death penalty. For example, most states reformed their capital statutes to attempt to guide sentencing discretion through consideration of "aggravating" and "mitigating" factors, in response to the *Furman* Court's rejection of "standardless" capital sentencing discretion and the *Gregg* Court's approval of "guided discretion." These new statutes represented an advance from the pre-*Furman* practice of instructing juries merely that the sentencing decision was to be made according to their conscience, or in their sole discretion, without any further elaboration. By invalidating the death penalty for rape in 1977 (*Coker v. Georgia*, 433 U.S. 584) and later extending that invalidation to other non-homicidal crimes (see *Kennedy v. Louisiana*, 554 U.S. 407), the Supreme Court has essentially limited the death penalty for ordinary criminal offenses to the crime of murder, in contrast to the pre-*Furman* world in which death sentences for rape, armed robbery, burglary, and kidnapping were authorized and more than occasionally imposed. The Court has also categorically excluded juveniles and offenders with mental retardation from execution (*Roper v. Simmons*, 543 U.S. 551; *Atkins v. Virginia*, 536 U.S. 304). Although the Court has never held that bifurcated proceedings (separate guilt and sentencing phases) are constitutionally required, post-*Furman* statutes have made bifurcation the norm, and it would likely be held to be a constitutional essential today.

Despite these improvements to the administration of capital punishment, constitutional regulation has proven inadequate to address the concerns about arbitrariness, discrimination, and error in the capital justice process that led to the Court's intervention in the first place. At its worst, constitutional regulation is part of the problem. When the Court requires irreconcilable procedures, its own conflicting doctrines doom its efforts to failure. Such conflicts have led several Justices to reject the Court's regulatory efforts as unsustainable. In many more instances, the Court's doctrine, though it may recognize serious threats to fairness in the process or may establish important rights, fails to provide adequate mechanisms to address the threats or vindicate the rights. Finally, the existence of an extensive web of constitutional regulation with minimal regulatory effect stands in the way of *non*-constitutional legislative reform of the administration of capital punishment— not only because such reform is generally extremely unpopular politically, but also because political actors and the general public assume that constitutional oversight by the federal courts is the proper locus for ensuring the fairness in capital sentencing and that the lengthy appeals process in capital cases demonstrates that the courts are doing their job (indeed, maybe even *over*-doing their job, considering how long cases take to get through the entire review process). What follows is a discussion of the four most serious inadequacies in the constitutional regulation of capital punishment.

1. The Central Tension Between Guided Discretion and Individualized Sentencing

The two central pillars of the Court's Eighth Amendment regulation of capital punishment are the twin requirements that capital sentencers be afforded sufficient guidance in the exercise of their discretion and that sentencers at the same time not be restricted in any way in their consideration of potentially mitigating evidence. The first requirement led the Court to reject aggravating factors that failed to furnish sufficient guidance to sentencers, such as the factor asking whether the murder was "especially heinous, atrocious or cruel, manifesting exceptional depravity." The Court rejected such vague factors as insufficient either to narrow the class of those eligible for capital punishment or to channel the exercise of sentencing discretion (*Godfrey v. Georgia*, 446 U.S. 420). The second requirement led the Court to reject statutory schemes that limited sentencers' consideration of any potentially mitigating evidence, either by restricting mitigating circumstances to a statutory list (*Lockett v. Ohio*, 438 U.S. 586), or by excluding full consideration of some potentially relevant mitigating evidence (*Penry v. Lynaugh*, 492 U.S. 303).

From the start, the tension between the demands of consistency and individualization were apparent. As early as a year prior to *Furman*, the lawyers who litigated *Furman* and *Gregg* argued that unregulated mercy was essentially equivalent to unregulated selection: "'Kill him if you want' and 'Kill him, but you may spare him if you want' mean the same thing in any man's language" (Brief Amicus Curiae in *McGautha v. California* 1971). After more than a decade of attempting to administer both requirements, several members of the Court with widely divergent perspectives came to see the incoherence of the foundations of their Eighth Amendment doctrine. In 1990, Justice Scalia argued that the second doctrine—or "counterdoctrine"—of individualized sentencing "exploded whatever coherence the notion of 'guided discretion' once had." (*Walton v. Arizona*, 497 U.S. 639, 661). Justice Scalia rejected the view that the two doctrines were merely in tension rather than flatly contradictory: "To acknowledge that 'there perhaps is an inherent tension' [between the two doctrines] is rather like saying that there was perhaps an inherent tension between the Allies and the Axis Powers in World

War II. And to refer to the two lines as pursuing 'twin objectives' is rather like referring to the twin objectives of good and evil. They cannot be reconciled" (*Walton* at 664). As a result, Justice Scalia (later joined by Justice Thomas) has chosen between the two commands and rejected the requirement of individualized sentencing as without constitutional pedigree.

Four years later, Justice Blackmun came to the same recognition of the essential conflict between the doctrines, but reached a different conclusion. Justice Blackmun found himself at a loss to imagine any sort of reform that could mediate between the two conflicting commands:

> Any statute or procedure that could effectively eliminate arbitrariness from the administration of death would also restrict the sentencer's discretion to such an extent that the sentencer would be unable to give full consideration to the unique characteristics of each defendant and the circumstances of the offense. By the same token, any statute or procedure that would provide the sentencer with sufficient discretion to consider fully and act upon the unique circumstances of each defendant would 'thro[w] open the back door to arbitrary and irrational sentencing' (*Callins v. Collins*, 510 U.S. 1141, 1155).

Unlike Justices Scalia and Thomas, however, Justice Blackmun did not resolve to jettison either constitutional command—not merely because of the demands of *stare decisis*, but "because there is a heightened need for both in the administration of death" (*Callins* at 1155). Consequently, Justice Blackmun concluded that "the proper course when faced with irreconcilable constitutional commands is not to ignore one or the other, nor to pretend that the dilemma does not exist, but to admit the futility of the effort to harmonize them. This means accepting the fact that the death penalty cannot be administered in accord with our Constitution" (*Callins* at 1157).

Another Justice's response to the conflict between the need for guidance and the need for individualization was to call for limiting eligibility for capital punishment to a very small group of the worst of the worst—"the tip of the pyramid" of all murderers, in the words of Justice Stevens (*Walton* at 716–718). If unguided mercy reprieves some from this group, there will still be arbitrariness in choosing among the death eligible, but it will operate on a much smaller scale, and with greater assurance that those who make it to the "tip" belong in the group of the death eligible. However, even if it were agreed that limiting arbitrariness to a smaller arena is sufficient to mediate the conflict between guidance and discretion, this solution is neither constitutionally prescribed nor politically feasible. The Court's "narrowing" requirement is formal rather than quantitative; there is no requirement that any state restrict the ambit of the death penalty to a group of any particular size or with any particular aggravating attributes. And in the absence of a constitutional command, the scope of most capital statutes remains extraordinarily broad. The widespread authorization of the death penalty for felony murder, murder for pecuniary gain, and murders that could be described as "cold-blooded," "pitiless," and the like have ensured a wide scope of death eligibility, and capital statutes have tended to grow rather than shrink over time.

The conflict between guidance and individualization thus has been resolved by the Court not by Justice Stevens's suggestion of strict narrowing, but rather by reducing the requirement of guidance to a mere formality. States must craft statutes that narrow the class of the death eligible to some subset—however large and however defined—of the entire class of those convicted of the crime of murder. In contrast, the Court has enforced the requirement of individualization with greater zeal. Consequently, the structure of capital sentencing today is surprisingly similar to the pre-*Furman* structure (bifurcation aside). The sentencer must determine whether the defendant is death eligible—today not merely by conviction of a capital offense but also by the additional finding of an aggravating factor. These factors can be numerous, broad in scope, and still quite vague; indeed, the Court has held that the aggravator can duplicate an element of the offense of capital murder (in which case the aggravator adds nothing to the conviction) (*Lowenfield v. Phelps*, 484 U.S. 231). After this fairly undemanding finding, the inquiry opens up into pre-*Furman* sentencing according to conscience: the sentencer is asked whether any mitigating circumstances of any type, statutory or non-statutory, call for a sentence less than death. This sentencing structure, which dominates the post-*Furman* world, is not accidental, nor is it the product of deliberate undermining of constitutional norms by states; rather, it is the *product* of constitutional regulation and thus fairly impervious to all but constitutional reform. In the absence of a constitutional solution, states (and Congress) will continue to operate capital sentencing schemes that fail to adequately address the concerns about arbitrariness and discrimination that led to constitutional intervention in the first instance.

2. Racial Disparities and Constitutional Remedies

The failure of constitutionally mandated guided discretion to offer much in the way of guidance might be less worrisome if there were other constitutional avenues to address discriminatory outcomes. After all, the challenge to standardless capital sentencing that led to the constitutional requirement of guided discretion was premised in large part on the concern that the absence of guidance gave too much play to racial discrimination. The NAACP Legal Defense Fund, the organization that spearheaded the constitutional litigation challenging the death penalty that culminated in *Furman* and *Gregg*, was also involved in litigation under the Equal Protection clause directly challenging racial disparities in the distribution of death sentences. For the first few decades of constitutional regulation of capital punishment, however, the Court avoided this issue, deciding cases that raised it on entirely non-racial grounds. Finally, in 1987, the Court took up the issue directly in *McCleskey v. Kemp* (481 U.S. 279).

McCleskey involved a constitutional challenge to the imposition of the death penalty based on an empirical study conducted by Professor David Baldus and his associates (the Baldus study) using multiple regression statistical analysis to study the effect of the race of defendants and the race of victims in capital sentencing

proceedings in Georgia. The study examined over 2,000 murder cases that occurred in Georgia during the 1970s. The researchers used a number of different
models that took account of numerous variables that could have explained the
apparent racial disparities on non-racial grounds. The study found a very strong
race-of-the-victim effect and a weaker race-of-the-defendant effect: after controlling for the non-racial variables, the study concluded that defendants
charged with killing white victims were 4.3 times as likely to receive a death
sentence as defendants charged with killing blacks, and that black defendants
who killed white victims had the greatest likelihood of receiving the death
penalty.

The Court rejected McCleskey's challenge to his death sentence on both Equal
Protection and Eighth Amendment grounds. The Court assumed for the sake of
argument the validity of the Baldus study's statistical findings, but held that proof of
racial disparities in the distribution of capital sentencing outcomes in a geographic
area in the past was insufficient to prove racial discrimination in a later case. Proof
of unconstitutional discrimination, held the Court, requires proof of discriminatory *purpose* on the part of the decision makers in a particular case. Moreover, in
light of the importance of discretion in the administration of criminal justice, proof
of such purpose must be "exceptionally clear" (*McCleskey* at 297) In light of this
heavy burden, the Court found the Baldus study's results "clearly insufficient" to
prove discriminatory purpose under the Equal Protection clause (*McCleskey* at
297). As for the Eighth Amendment challenge, the Court held that the "discrepancy
indicated by the Baldus study is a far cry from the major systemic defects identified
in *Furman*" (*McCleskey* at 313). The Court concluded that the "risk of racial bias"
demonstrated by the Baldus study was not "constitutionally significant" (*McCleskey*
at 313).

In part, the Court's rejection of McCleskey's claim was informed by its concern
that there might be no plausible constitutional remedy short of abolition: "McCleskey's claim . . . would extend to all capital cases in Georgia, at least where the victim
was white and the defendant is black"(*McCleskey* at 293). But the Court's requirement of exceptionally clear proof of discriminatory purpose on the part of a particular sentencer makes constitutional challenges to intentional discrimination
essentially impossible to mount. Not surprisingly, there have been no successful
constitutional challenges to racial disparities in capital sentencing in the more than
two decades since *McCleskey*, despite continued findings by many researchers in
many different jurisdictions of strong racial effects (Baldus and Woodworth 2003).
By rendering racial disparities in sentencing outcomes constitutionally irrelevant
in the absence of more direct proof of discrimination, the Court has dispatched the
problem of racial discrimination in capital sentencing from the constitutional
sphere to the legislative one, where it has not produced much reform. Notably,
Justice Powell, the author of the 5–4 majority opinion in *McCleskey*, repudiated his
own vote only a few years later, when a biographer asked him upon his retirement
if there was any vote that he would change, and he replied, "Yes, *McCleskey
v. Kemp*" (Jeffries 1994, 451).

3. Innocence

Just as *McCleskey* effectively precludes challenges to racial discrimination in capital sentencing (at least challenges based on patterns of outcomes over time), the Court's doctrine also makes virtually no place for constitutional consideration of claims of innocence. In *Herrera v. Collins* (506 U.S. 390), the Court rejected petitioner's claim of actual innocence as a cognizable constitutional claim in federal habeas review. The Court held that while claims of actual innocence may in some circumstances open federal habeas review to other constitutional claims that would otherwise be barred from consideration, the innocence claims themselves are not generally cognizable on habeas. The Court assumed—without deciding— that a "truly persuasive" showing of innocence would constitute a constitutional claim and warrant habeas relief *if* no state forum were available to process such a claim (*Herrera* at 417). But, the Court found that Herrera's claim failed to meet this standard. More recently, the Court has suggested just how high a threshold its (still hypothetical) requirement of a "truly persuasive" showing of innocence is. In *House v. Bell* (547 U.S. 518), the petitioner sought federal review with substantial new evidence challenging the accuracy of his murder conviction, including DNA evidence conclusively establishing that semen recovered from the victim's body that had been portrayed at trial as "consistent" with the defendant actually came from the victim's husband, as well as evidence of a confession to the murder by the husband and evidence of a history of spousal abuse. The Court held that this strong showing of actual innocence was the rare case sufficient to obtain federal habeas review for petitioner's *other* constitutional claims that would otherwise have been barred, because no reasonable juror viewing the record as a whole would lack reasonable doubt. But even this high showing was inadequate, concluded the Court, to meet the "extraordinarily high" standard of proof hypothetically posited in *Herrera*.

This daunting standard of proof suggests that even if the Court does eventually hold that some innocence claims may be cognizable on habeas, such review will be extraordinarily rare. Thus, the problem of dealing with the possibility of wrongful convictions in the capital context (like the problem of dealing with patterns of racial disparity) has been placed in the legislative rather than the constitutional arena. The reliance on the political realm to deal with the issue of wrongful convictions is less troubling than such reliance on the issue of racial disparities, because there is far more public outcry about the former rather than the latter issue. But the problem of wrongful convictions in the capital context has proven to be larger and more intractable than might have been predicted. The large numbers of exonerations in capital cases may be due in part to the fact that many of the systemic failures that lead to wrongful convictions are likely to be more common in capital than other cases (Gross 1996). Moreover, courts have been resistant both to providing convicted defendants with plausible claims of innocence the resources (including access to DNA evidence) necessary to make out their innocence claims, and to granting relief even when strong cases have been made (Garrett 2008).

4. Counsel

Unlike innocence, the problem of inadequate counsel has been squarely held to undermine the constitutional validity of a conviction. Despite the fact that "effective assistance of counsel" is a recognized constitutional right, the scope of the right and the nature of the remedy have precluded the courts from being able to ensure the adequacy of representation in capital cases. Perhaps in response to repeated accounts of extraordinarily poor lawyering in capital cases, the Court recently has granted review and ordered relief in a series of capital cases raising ineffectiveness of counsel claims regarding defense attorneys' failure to investigate and present mitigating evidence with sufficient thoroughness (*Williams v. Taylor*, 529 U.S. 362; *Wiggins v. Smith*, 539 U.S. 510; *Rompilla v. Beard*, 545 U.S. 374). This development appears to raise the constitutional bar for attorney performance, at least in the sentencing phase of capital trials. Nonetheless, constitutional review and reversal remain an inadequate means of ensuring adequate representation, both because the constitutional standard for ineffectiveness remains too difficult to establish in most cases, and because the remedy of reversal is too limited to induce the systemic changes that are necessary to raise the level of defense services.

One of the hurdles to regulating attorney competence through constitutional review is the legal standard for ineffective assistance of counsel. In crafting the governing standard in *Strickland v. Washington* (466 U.S. 668), the Court maintained that "the purpose of the effective assistance guarantee of the Sixth Amendment is not to improve the quality of legal representation, although that is a goal of considerable importance to the legal system" (*Strickland* at 689). In light of the Sixth Amendment's more modest goal of ensuring that the outcome of a particular legal proceeding crosses the constitutional threshold of reliability, the Court established a strong presumption in favor of finding attorney conduct reasonable under the Sixth Amendment, in order to prevent a flood of frivolous litigation, to protect against the distorting effects of hindsight, and to preserve the defense bar's creativity and autonomy. This general deference was amplified for "strategic choices," which the *Strickland* Court described as "virtually unchallengeable" (*Strickland* at 690). Moreover, the Court declined to enumerate in any but the most general way the duties of defense counsel, instead deferring to general professional norms. Finally, the requirement that a defendant also prove "prejudice" from attorney error (a reasonable probability that the outcome of the trial would be different) necessarily immunizes many incompetent legal performances from reversal.

The difficulty of winning a reversal, even in cases of manifestly incompetent counsel, is amplified by the procedural context in which such claims are made. Although there is often no legal bar to raising claims of ineffective assistance on direct appeal (when indigent defendants still have a constitutional right to appointed counsel), appellate review is appropriate only for record claims, where the basis for asserting ineffective assistance is a trial error evident from the transcript. Claims of ineffective assistance, however, routinely involve the presentation of factual evidence beyond the record, such as evidence about information that the defense attorney failed to discover or to introduce at trial. Such evidence must be developed in collateral proceedings, where the constitutional right to counsel runs out. Although almost all states formally provide for counsel for indigent defendants in capital post-conviction proceedings, there is virtually no monitoring of the performance of such counsel (McConville 2003). Moreover, should post-conviction counsel fail to perform adequately, *their* ineffectiveness does not preserve the claims that they are seeking to raise from state procedural bars, because there is no constitutional right to counsel in such proceedings. The inadequacy of post-conviction representation is compounded by the deferential review of state court decisions under the 1996 Anti-Terrorism and Effective Death Penalty Act (AEDPA), which seeks to ensure that state post-conviction proceedings are the primary venue for the litigation of non-record claims. The decline in the number of federal habeas grants of relief in the post-AEDPA era demonstrates the impact that AEDPA has had—an impact necessarily greatest on claims, like those of ineffective counsel, that will rarely see direct review (King 2007).

The constitutional review and reversal of individual capital convictions is by its nature an inadequate tool for achieving the institutional changes that are necessary in the provision of indigent defense services in capital cases. On the same day that the Court announced the constitutional standard in *Strickland*, it decided a companion case, *United States v. Cronic* (466 U.S. 648), which rejected a claim of ineffectiveness based on the circumstances faced by the defense attorney in litigating the case (lack of time to prepare, inexperience, etc.). The Court insisted that a defendant must identify particular prejudicial errors made by counsel, rather than merely identify circumstances that suggest that errors would likely be made. *Cronic* has widely been held by courts to preclude Sixth Amendment challenges to the institutional arrangements (fee structures, caseloads, availability of investigative or expert services, lack of training and experience, etc.) that lead to incompetent representation, except in the most extraordinary of circumstances (Klein 1999). Without any ability to directly control fees, caseloads, resources, or training, courts conducting Sixth Amendment review of convictions can reverse individual convictions only on the basis of individual errors.

II. THE POLITICIZATION OF CAPITAL PUNISHMENT

Perhaps the most important feature of the landscape of capital punishment administration that imperils the success of any regulatory scheme is the intense politicization of the death penalty. Capital punishment (like the rest of criminal justice in the United States) is politicized *institutionally*, in that some or all of the most important actors in the administration of capital punishment are elected (with the exception of lay jurors). At the same time, capital punishment is politicized *symbolically*, in that it looms much larger than it plausibly should in public discourse because of its power as a focus for fears of violent crime and as political shorthand for support for "law and order" policies generally. These two aspects of politicization ensure that the institutional actors responsible for the administration of the capital justice process are routinely subject to intense pressures, which in turn contribute to the array of problems that we review below—for example, inadequate representation, wrongful convictions, and disparate racial impact. There is little hope of successfully addressing these problems in the absence of profound change on the politicization front, which would require fundamental reorganization of the American political system.

The vast majority of death penalty jurisdictions within the United States have elected rather than appointed prosecutors, and these prosecutors are usually autonomous decision makers in their own small locales (counties). Rarely is there any state or regional review of local decision making or coordination of capital prosecutions. These simple facts of institutional organization generate enormous geographic disparities within most death penalty jurisdictions. In Texas, for example, Dallas County (Dallas) and Harris County (Houston), two counties with similar demographics and crime rates, have had very different death sentencing rates, as have Allegheny County (Pittsburgh) and Philadelphia County (Philadelphia) in Pennsylvania (Steiker 2002, 106). Large geographic variations exist within many other states that are similarly uncorrelated with differences in homicide rates (Liebman 2000). These geographic disparities are troubling in themselves because they suggest that state death penalty legislation is unable to standardize the considerations that are brought to bear in capital prosecutions so as to limit major fluctuations in its application across the state. But these geographic disparities are also troubling because they may be one of the sources of the persistent racial disparities in the administration of capital punishment in many states.

In addition, the symbolic politics of capital punishment is very much at play in the election of local prosecutors. Candidates for local district attorney and state attorney general in a wide variety of jurisdictions have run campaigns touting their capital conviction records, even going so far as listing individual defendants sentenced to death (Bresler 1994). As a practical matter, an elected prosecutor's capital conviction record should be a relatively small part of any prosecutor's portfolio, given the limited number of capital cases that any prosecutorial office will handle— a small fraction of all homicide cases, and an even smaller fraction of all serious crimes. Clearly, many prosecutorial candidates perceive that the voting public has a special interest in capital cases, both because of the fear generated by the underlying crimes that give rise to capital prosecution and because a prosecutor's support for capital punishment represents in powerful shorthand a prosecutor's "toughness" on crime. These general incentives are troubling in themselves, because they suggest that political incentives may exist to bring capital charges and to win death verdicts, quite apart from the underlying merits of the cases. Even more troubling are the incentives that may exist to favor those in a position to provide campaign contributions or votes. The racial disparities in capital charging decisions favoring cases with white victims mirror the racial disparities in political influence in many mixed-race communities (Bright 1995, 453–454).

Judges as well as prosecutors must face the intense politicization that surrounds the administration of capital punishment. Almost 90 percent of state judges face some kind of popular election (Streb 2007). Politicization of capital punishment in judicial elections has famously ousted Chief Justice Rose Bird and colleagues Cruz Reynoso and Joseph Grodin from the California Supreme Court, as well as Justice Penny White from the Tennessee Supreme Court. These high-profile examples are only the tip of the iceberg of political pressure, as no judge facing election could be unaware of the high salience of capital punishment in the minds of voters, especially in times of rising crime rates or especially high-profile murders. The UN Special Rapporteur on extrajudicial, summary, or arbitrary executions, after an official visit to the United States, reported that many of those with whom he spoke in Alabama and Texas, which both have partisan judicial elections, suggested that "judges in both states consider themselves to be under popular pressure to impose and uphold death sentences whenever possible and that decisions to the contrary would lead to electoral defeat" (Alston 2008).

Of course, most judges will conscientiously endeavor to resist such pressures and decide cases without regard to political influences. Nonetheless, several statistical studies suggest that, in the aggregate, judicial behavior in criminal cases generally and capital cases in particular appears to be influenced by election cycles (Brace and Boyea 2008; Hall 1992; Huber and Gordon 2004; but compare Blume and Eisenberg 1999). Moreover, in many jurisdictions, judges not only preside over and review capital trials, they also appoint lawyers, approve legal fees, and approve funding for mitigation and other expert services. These decisions, which are crucial to the capital justice process, are less visible but no less likely to be subject to political pressures. Finally, in a few capital jurisdictions, elected judges actually impose sentences in capital cases through their power to override jury verdicts, and a comparison among these states strongly suggests that the degree of electoral accountability influences the direction of such overrides (Bright and Keenan 1995).

Governors, too, are influenced by the intense politicization of capital punishment. Like prosecutors and judges, governors have often campaigned on their support for the death penalty, emphasizing their willingness to sign death warrants. While governors are less implicated in the day-to-day workings of the capital justice process than prosecutors and judges, they play a crucial role in the exercise of clemency powers, which the Supreme Court has recognized as an important defense against conviction and execution of the innocent. Some governors, like George Ryan of Illinois, have not been afraid to use the clemency power to respond to concerns about wrongful conviction. However, the use of the clemency power in capital cases trended sharply downward in the decades immediately following the reinstatement of capital punishment in 1976, at the same time that the trend in death sentencing and executions was sharply upward (Rappaport 2003). The persistent high political salience of capital punishment, as reflected by its prominence at all levels of political discourse, has no doubt affected the willingness of governors to set aside death sentences.

Finally, the politicization of the issue of capital punishment in the legislative sphere limits the capacity of legislatures to promote and maintain statutory reform. The kind of statutory reform that many regard as the most promising for ameliorating arbitrariness and discrimination in the application of the death penalty is strict narrowing of the category of those eligible for capital crimes. The Baldus study reported that racial disparities were not evident in the distribution of death sentences for the category of the most aggravated murders, because death sentences were so common in this category (Baldus et al. 1990). However, most states have been unwilling to restrict the scope of the death penalty, and the continued inclusion of broad aggravators like felony murder, pecuniary gain, future dangerousness, and heinousness (or its equivalent) preclude the strict narrowing approach in most jurisdictions.

Moreover, even if a jurisdiction were able to pass a truly narrow death penalty, the pressure to expand the ambit of the death penalty over time will likely prove politically irresistible. The tendency of existing statutes, even already broad ones, to expand over time through the addition of new aggravating factors has been well documented (Simon and Spaulding 1999). When former Governor Mitt Romney introduced legislation drafted by a blue-ribbon commission to reinstitute capital punishment in Massachusetts, supporters of the draft emphasized the very narrow ambit of the proposed statute. However, a symposium of experts organized to discuss the proposed statute noted the problem of what one called "aggravator creep" (an analogy to "mission creep" referred to in military contexts), in which "[a] statute is passed with a list of aggravating factors, and then structural impulses often push that list to become longer and longer as new aggravators are added" (*Symposium: Toward a Model Death Penalty Code* 2005 at 35). The most eloquent case for the inevitability of "aggravator creep" has been made by lawyer and novelist Scott Turow. Turow, a former federal prosecutor who supported the death penalty for most of his life, wrote a book describing how his later pro bono work on the capital appeal of a wrongfully convicted man and his service on the Illinois Governor's Commission to reform the death penalty convinced him to vote as a Commission member for abolition rather than reform. As a moral matter, Turow remains persuaded that a narrow death penalty is both morally permissible and desirable. But he has come to see that expansion is inevitable, with the arbitrariness and potential for error that expansive capital statutes necessarily entail:

> The furious heat of grief and rage the worst cases inspire will inevitably short-circuit our judgment and always be a snare for the innocent. And the fundamental equality of each survivor's loss, and the manner in which the wayward imaginations of criminals continue to surprise us, will inevitably cause the categories for death eligibility to expand, a slippery slope of what-about-hims (Turow 2003, 114).

III. RACE DISCRIMINATION

Race discrimination has cast a long shadow over the history of the American death penalty. During the antebellum period, race discrimination was not merely a matter of practice but a matter of law, as many Southern jurisdictions made the availability of the death penalty turn on the race of the defendant or victim. After the Civil War, the discriminatory Black Codes were largely abandoned, but discrimination in the administration of capital punishment persisted. Discrimination permeated both the selection of those to die as well as the selection of those who could participate in the criminal justice process. African Americans were more frequently executed for non-homicidal crimes, were more likely to be executed without appeals, and were more likely to be executed at young age (Bowers 1984). Discrimination was most pronounced in Southern jurisdictions. The most obvious discrimination occurred in capital rape prosecutions, as such prosecutions almost uniformly targeted minority offenders alleged to have assaulted white victims, and the numerous executions for rape post-1930 (455) were entirely confined to Southern jurisdictions, border states, and the District of Columbia (Wolfgang 1974). Until the early 1960s, the differential treatment of both African American offenders and African American victims was attributable in part to the exclusion of African Americans from jury service, again largely (although not exclusively) concentrated in Southern and border-state jurisdictions.

When the Supreme Court first signaled its interest in constitutionally regulating capital punishment in the early 1960s, several Justices issued a dissent from denial of certiorari indicating their willingness to address whether the death penalty is disproportionate for the crime of rape (*Rudolph v. Alabama*, 375 U.S. 889). Although these Justices did not mention race in their brief statement, they were undoubtedly aware of the racially skewed use of the death penalty to punish rape. The NAACP Legal Defense Fund thereafter sought to document empirically race discrimination in capital race prosecutions with an eye toward challenging such discrimination in particular cases. The first significant study, produced by Professor Marvin Wolfgang and others at the University of Pennsylvania, found both race-of-the-defendant and race-of-the-victim discrimination in the administration of the death penalty for rape (after controlling for non-racial variables); African American defendants convicted of raping white females faced a greater than one-third chance of receiving a death sentence, whereas all other racial combinations yielded death sentences in about 2 percent of cases (Wolfgang 1974).

The Wolfgang study did not ultimately lead to success in litigation, and the Eighth Circuit's rejection of the study as a basis for constitutional relief, authored by then-Judge Blackmun—foreshadowed the Supreme Court's subsequent denial of relief in *McCleskey*, discussed above. But the Wolfgang study did contribute to the accurate perception that the prevailing administration of the death penalty was both arbitrary and discriminatory, and thus contributed to *Furman*'s invalidation of existing statutes and the "unguided" discretion they entailed.

The central question today is whether efforts to guide sentencer discretion successfully combat the sort of discrimination reflected in the Wolfgang study. The current empirical assessment is "no"—that race discrimination still plagues the administration of the death penalty, though the evidence suggests that race-of-the-victim discrimination is of a much greater magnitude than race-of-the-defendant discrimination. The more difficult question is whether the persistent role of race in capital decision making can be significantly reduced or eradicated, whether through statutory efforts to narrow the reach of the death penalty or other means.

The Baldus study, described above, found that defendants charged in white-victim cases, on average, faced odds of receiving a death sentence that were 4.3 times higher than the odds faced by similarly situated defendants in black-victim cases. Other studies have similarly pointed to a robust relationship between the race of the victim and the decision to seek death and to obtain death sentences (also controlling for non-racial variables). Leigh Bienen produced a study of the New Jersey death penalty that reflected greater prosecutorial willingness to seek death in white victim cases (Bienen 1988). Baldus, et al, studied capital sentences in Philadelphia and found both race-of-the-victim and race-of-the-defendant discrimination (Baldus 1998). Given the remarkably different histories and demographics of Philadelphia and Georgia, it is surprising that the Philadelphia study found a magnitude of race-of-the-victim effects quite similar to the magnitude found in the Georgia study addressed in *McCleskey*. A federal report issued in 1990, which summarized the then-available empirical work on the effects of race in capital sentencing (28 studies), likewise found consistent race-of-the-victim effects (in 82 percent of the studies reviewed), particularly in prosecutorial charging decisions (U.S. General Accounting Office 1990).

Apart from these statistical studies, a broad scholarly literature often highlights American racial discord as an important explanatory variable of American exceptionalism with respect to capital punishment—the fact that the United States is alone among Western democracies in retaining and actively implementing the death penalty. Such works point to the fact that executions are overwhelmingly confined to the South (and states bordering the South), the very same jurisdictions that were last to abandon slavery and segregation, and that were most resistant to the federal enforcement of civil rights norms.

Professor Frank Zimring, in his recent broad assessment of the American death penalty, argued that the regional persistence of "vigilante values" is strongly correlated with state execution rates (Zimring 2003). Many scholars have speculated that contemporary state-imposed executions might serve a role similar to extralegal executions of a previous era, and a recent article in the *American Sociological Review* presents empirical data supporting the claim that current death sentences might be linked to such vigilante values (Jacobs et al. 2005).

Supporters of the death penalty would certainly resist the claim that the death penalty remains in place *because of* underlying conscious or unconscious racial prejudice. Moreover, the high level of executions in Southern jurisdictions correlates not only with racial factors (such as past race discrimination and contemporary racial tensions) but also with other potential explanatory factors such as high rates of violent crime and the prevalence of fundamentalist religious beliefs. Some empirical literature, though, modestly supports the claim that racially discriminatory attitudes may account for some of the contemporary support for the death penalty (Barkan and Cohn 1994; Young 1991).

The most significant efforts to reduce the effect of race in capital proceedings have focused on narrowing the class of death-eligible offenses and guiding sentencer discretion at the punishment phase of capital trials. The first solution—restricting the death penalty to the most aggravated cases—appears promising, because the Baldus study found that race effects essentially disappear in such cases given the very high frequency of death sentences in that range.

The problem, though, played out over the past 30 years, is that no state has successfully confined the death penalty to a narrow band of the most aggravated cases. Death eligibility in prevailing statutes remains breathtakingly broad, as aggravating factors or their functional equivalent often cover the spectrum of many if not most murders. The failure to achieve genuine narrowing is partly a matter of political will in light of the constant political pressure to expand rather than restrict death eligibility in response to high-profile offenses (consider the expansion of the death penalty for the crime of the rape of a child). But the failure also stems from the deeper problem identified by Justice Harlan (discussed above), that it remains an elusive task to specify the "worst of the worst" murders in advance. Any rule-like approach to narrowing death eligibility will require jettisoning factors such as the "especially heinous" provision of the Model Penal Code; but those factors often capture prevailing moral commitments—some offenses are appropriately regarded as among the very worst by virtue of their atrociousness, cruelty, or exceptional depravity. At the same time, many objective factors taken in isolation seem appropriately narrow (such as the commission of an additional murder at the time of the offense), but collectively these factors establish a broad net of death eligibility. The breadth of death eligibility in turn invites and requires substantial discretion, particularly in prosecutorial charging decisions, which permits racial considerations to infect the process.

The prospect of a meaningful legislative remedy to address race discrimination seems quite remote. After *McCleskey*, legislative energies were directed toward fashioning a response to the discrimination reflected in the Baldus study. At the federal level, the Racial Justice Act, which would have permitted courts to consider statistical data as evidence in support of a claim of race discrimination within a particular jurisdiction, failed to find support in the U.S. Senate (Bright 1995). Many state legislatures have considered similar legislation (including Georgia and Illinois), but to date only Kentucky and North Carolina have enacted such a provision (Vito 2010).

Apart from its lack of political appeal, racial justice legislation seems inadequately suited to address the problems reflected in the empirical data. On a practical level, the numerous variables involved in particular cases make it difficult to demonstrate racial motivation or bias at the individual level, even if such discrimination is evident in the jurisdiction as a whole. Introducing evidence of system-wide bias might cause a court to look more closely at the facts surrounding a particular prosecution, but the sheer "thickness" of the facts in a particular prosecution will likely permit courts to find inadequate proof of bias in case after case. Indeed, racial justice legislation risks legitimating capital systems that are demonstrably discriminatory by ostensibly providing a remedy when in fact none is forthcoming. More broadly, the litigation focus of racial justice acts fails to address the underlying problems. Many of the most troublesome cases in which race influenced prosecutorial or jury decision making are those in which no death sentence was sought or obtained because of the minority status of the victim. Courts are (appropriately) powerless to compel decision makers to produce death sentences in such cases, and the troubling differential treatment is irremediable. Notwithstanding their increased political participation generally, minorities remain significantly underrepresented in the two roles that might make a difference: as capital jurors (Bowers et al. 2001) and as elected district attorneys (Pokorak 1998). The combined influences of discretion, underrepresentation, historical practice, and conscious or unconscious bias make it extraordinarily difficult to disentangle race from the administration of the American death penalty.

IV. Jury Confusion

Another significant post-*Furman* effort to solve the problem of arbitrariness and discrimination has been to impose structure and order on the ultimate life-death decision. The universal adoption of bifurcated proceedings—with a punishment phase focused solely on whether the defendant deserves to die—was embraced in hopes of producing reasoned moral decisions rather than impulsive, arbitrary, or discriminatory ones. In this respect, the post-*Furman* experiment has been focused on rationalizing the death sentencing process through a combination of statutory precision and focused jury instructions. Such provisions precisely enumerate relevant aggravating and mitigating factors and carefully explain burdens of proof, the role of mitigation, inappropriate bases for decision (e.g., "mere sympathy"), and the process for reaching a final decision.

As noted above, the *constitutional* requirements respecting states' efforts to channel sentencer discretion are quite minimal. Indeed, once states have ostensibly "narrowed" the class of death-eligible defendants via aggravating circumstances, states need not provide any additional guidance to sentencers as they make their life-or-death decision (*Zant v. Stephens*, 462 U.S. 862). The central question as a matter of policy and practice is whether the post-*Furman* experiment with guided discretion has resulted in improved and more principled decision making. The available empirical evidence—largely developed by the Capital Jury Project (CJP)— is discouraging along these lines.

Over the past 18 years, the CJP has collected data from over a thousand jurors who served in capital cases with the goal of understanding the decision-making process in capital cases. CJP interviewers spent hours with individual jurors exploring the factors contributing to their decisions and their comprehension of the capital instructions in their cases. The CJP designed its questions to determine whether the intricate state capital schemes adopted post-*Furman* actually reduce arbitrariness in capital sentencing by controlling sentence discretion. Dozens of scholarly articles have been published based on the CJP data, and much of the research has documented the failure of jurors to understand the guidance embodied in the sentencing instructions and verdict forms they receive. By collecting data from numerous jurisdictions (14 states), the CJP project has been able to identify not only idiosyncratic defects in particular state statutes but endemic flaws in jury decision making, such as the propensity of jurors to decide punishment during the guilt-innocence phase of the trial (Bowers 1995), their frequent misapprehension of the standards governing their consideration of mitigating evidence (Bentele and Bowers 2001), and their general moral disengagement from the death penalty decision (Haney 1997). Jurors tend to misunderstand the consequences of a life-without-possibility-of-parole verdict, and, in jurisdictions that permit the alternative of a life-with-parole verdict, jurors consistently underestimate the length of time a defendant will remain in prison if not sentenced to death (Blume 2003). A significant number of jurors serve in capital cases notwithstanding their unwillingness to consider a life verdict, and many jurors who have served on capital trials simply are unable to grasp the concept of mitigating evidence (Haney 1995). Other findings of the CJP point to the skewing of capital juries through death-qualification (Sandys and McClelland 2003), the significance of the racial composition of the jury in capital decision making (Bowers et al. 2001), and the particular problems posed in jurisdictions (such as Florida and Alabama) where juries and judges share responsibility for capital verdicts (Foglia and Bowers 2006).

The empirical findings of the CJP are disheartening because they reflect widespread, fundamental misunderstanding on the part of capital jurors. Perhaps some of the findings can be discounted by the fact that the jurors' explanations of their role and the governing law were offered well after their actual jury service (and perhaps the jurors' understanding of their sentencing instructions at the time of interviews did not correspond perfectly to their understanding of the instructions at the time of their deliberations). But even a superficial review of instructions given in capital cases today reveals the unnecessary technical complexity of prevailing practice. Jurors are told about the role of aggravating factors, their ability (in many jurisdictions) to consider non-statutory aggravators, the role of mitigation, and so on. They are then asked to weigh or balance aggravation against mitigation or to decide whether mitigating factors are sufficiently substantial to call for a sentence less than death.

These sorts of efforts to tame the death penalty decision do not necessarily ensure more principled or less arbitrary decision making. Casting the decision in terms of "aggravation" and "mitigation" and requiring jurors to "balance" or "weigh"

these considerations might falsely convey to the jurors that their decision is a mechanical or mathematical one, rather than one requiring moral judgment.

More fundamentally, the problem identified by Justice Harlan in *McGautha*
casts a shadow over any effort to rationalize the decision whether to impose death.
In many jurisdictions, jurors are permitted to consider both statutory and non-
statutory aggravating factors (including victim impact evidence), making the
grounds for their ultimate decision virtually limitless. At the same time, every jurisdiction—responding to the Supreme Court's direction—currently permits unbridled consideration of mitigating factors, which likewise undercuts any effort to
structure the death penalty decision. In the 35 or so years of constitutional regulation since *Furman*, states have reproduced the open-ended discretion of the pre-
Furman era, but have packaged it in the guise of structure and guidance. In the
absence of *substantive* limits on sentencer discretion, the complicated and confusing
procedural means of implementing that discretion cannot reduce arbitrary or discriminatory decision making. It can only obscure the jury's current responsibility
for deciding, essentially on any criteria, whether a defendant should live or die. In
this respect, reform of contemporary capital statutes should focus on reducing complexity and communicating clearly the sentencer's awesome obligation to make an
irreducible moral judgment about the defendant's fate. The states' failure to make
such reforms is largely attributable to their misguided belief that the complicated
overlay of instructions is somehow constitutionally compelled. It is also partly
attributable to the fact that such reform efforts—and the return to the pre-*Furman*
world that they would represent—would amount to a concession that Justice Harlan
was right: that statutory efforts are likely unable to reduce the arbitrary imposition
of the death penalty.

V. The Inadequacy of Resources, Especially Defense Counsel Services, in Capital Cases

Capital prosecutions are expensive. A number of studies have tried to ascertain the
relative expense of capital prosecutions vis-a-vis non-capital prosecutions, using a
variety of methodologies (e.g., Urban Institute 2008; Connecticut Commission on
the Death Penalty 2003; Williams Institute 2001). What emerges from these studies
is a consensus that capital prosecutions generate higher costs at every stage of the
proceedings, and that the total costs of processing capital cases are considerably
greater than those of processing non-capital cases that result in sentences of life
imprisonment, even when the costs of incarceration are included. Although the
data are often incomplete or difficult to disaggregate, it appears that the lion's share
of additional expenses occur during the trial phase of capital litigation, as a result of

a longer pre-trial period, a longer and more intensive voir dire process, longer trials, more time spent by more attorneys preparing cases, more investigative and expert services, and an expensive penalty phase trial that does not occur at all in non–death penalty cases. Appellate and especially post-conviction costs are also considerably greater than in non-capital cases, though they tend to make up a smaller share of the total expense of capital litigation.

Despite the very large costs that are currently incurred in the administration of capital punishment, there is also good reason to believe that the capital process remains substantially underfunded, especially in the area of defense counsel services. The best reference point for what constitutes minimally adequate defense counsel services in capital cases has been provided by the American Bar Association (ABA). The ABA's *Guidelines for the Appointment and Performance of Defense Counsel in Death Penalty Cases*, originally adopted in 1989 and revised in 2003, offer specific guidance on such matters as the number and qualifications of counsel necessary in capital cases, the nature of investigative and mitigation services necessary to the defense team, and the performance standards to which the defense team should be held. The *Guidelines* also instruct about the need for a "responsible agency" (such as a Public Defender organization or its equivalent) to recruit, certify, train, and monitor capital defense counsel. In addition, there are separate Guidelines regarding the appropriate training for capital counsel, the need to control capital defense caseloads, and the need to ensure compensation at a level "commensurate with the provision of high quality legal representation."

Nonetheless, it is obvious that the vast majority of states do not comply with the ABA *Guidelines*, and many do not even come close. In response to concerns about the lack of fairness and accuracy in the capital justice process, the ABA called in 1997 for a nationwide moratorium on executions until serious flaws in the system are identified and eliminated. In 2001, the ABA created the Death Penalty Moratorium Implementation Project, which in 2003 decided to examine several states' death penalty systems to determine the extent to which they achieve fairness and provide due process. Among other things, the Project specifically investigated the extent to which the states were in compliance with the ABA *Guidelines* for capital defense counsel services. The first set of assessments were published near the end of 2007, and the record of compliance with the ABA *Guidelines* was extremely low: of the eight states studied, not a single state was found to be fully "in compliance" with any aspect of the ABA *Guidelines* studied. For the five guidelines that were studied over the eight states, there were 15 findings of complete noncompliance and 23 findings of only partial compliance (in two cases, there was insufficient information to make an assessment). The eight states studied were Alabama, Arizona, Florida, Georgia, Indiana, Ohio, Pennsylvania, and Tennessee. The full assessment is available at http://abanet.org/moratorium/.

For example, the assessment described Alabama's indigent defense system as "failing" due to the lack of a statewide indigent defense commission, the lack of qualifications and training of capital defense counsel, the failure to ensure the case staffing required by the Guidelines, the failure to provide death-sentenced inmates with appointed counsel in state post-conviction proceedings, and the very low caps on compensation for defense services. While Alabama had the worst record of compliance among the states studied, Indiana had the best record. Nonetheless, the Project found that Indiana, too, "falls far short of the requirements set out in the ABA *Guidelines.*" In particular, the report pointed to inadequate attorney qualification and monitoring procedures, unacceptable workloads, insufficient case staffing, and lack of an independent appointing authority (such as a Public Defender office). Indiana is not alone in this latter failing, as fewer than one-third of the 34 states that currently retain the death penalty have statewide capital defense systems as called for by the ABA.

The 2003 revisions to the ABA *Guidelines* insist that the Guidelines are not "aspirational" but rather are the minimum necessary conditions for the operation of the capital justice process in a fashion that adequately guarantees fairness and due process. Unfortunately, the record of compliance with the Guidelines, even among the states most committed to providing adequate defense services, remains poor. New York, which provided for generous levels of capital defense funding when it reinstated capital punishment in 1995, slashed that allocation by almost one-third three years later, and then maintained funding at the reduced rate until its capital statute was judicially invalidated in 2004. The record of state compliance with the *Guidelines* overall suggests that the states agree with the ABA that the *Guidelines* are not aspirational—not because the states believe that they are required, but rather because they simply do not aspire to meet them.

Failure to meet (or even to aspire to meet) the ABA *Guidelines* should not necessarily be written off as simple intransigence. The costs involved in providing the resources necessary for a minimally fair capital justice process can be staggering. Instructive in this regard is the Brian Nichols prosecution in Atlanta. Nichols was charged in an infamous courthouse shooting and escape that killed a judge, a court reporter, a sheriff's deputy, and a federal agent. In the investigative stage of the case, Nichols's appointed counsel quickly generated costs totaling $1.2 million, wiping out Georgia's entire indigent defense budget and requiring the postponement of the trial. Note that this price tag covered only the early investigative costs and did not include the costs of Nichols's trial or the years of appellate and post-conviction costs that would have followed had a death sentence been imposed (Nichols was sentenced to life imprisonment). The provision of the resources necessary for fair capital trials and appeals may simply not be possible, or at least not possible without substantial diversion of public funds from other sources—something state legislatures have shown themselves again and again unwilling to do in the context of providing indigent defense services. Moreover, when excellent defense services are provided to capital defendants at every stage of the criminal process, the process may become endlessly protracted. As Frank Zimring has most aptly observed, "A nation can have full and fair criminal procedures, or it can have [a] regularly functioning process of executing prisoners; but the evidence suggests it cannot have both" (Zimring 2003, 228).

VI. Erroneous Conviction of the Innocent

Although there is debate about what constitutes a full "exoneration," it is beyond question that public confidence in the death penalty has been shaken in recent years by the number of people who have been released from death row with evidence of their innocence. The Death Penalty Information Center (2011) keeps a list of exonerated capital defendants that now totals 138 for the years since 1973. While it is difficult to extrapolate from the number of known exonerations to the "real" rate of wrongful convictions in capital cases (for the same reason that it is difficult to extrapolate from the number of professional athletes who test positive for steroids to the rate of steroid use among athletes), reasonable estimates range from 2.3 percent to 5 percent (Gross and O'Brien 2008; Risinger 2007).

Because exonerations of death-sentenced prisoners are such dramatic events, they have generated extensive study of the causes of wrongful convictions, in capital cases and more generally. There is widespread consensus about the primary contributors to wrongful convictions: eyewitness misidentification; false confessions; perjured testimony by jailhouse informants; unreliable scientific evidence; suppression of exculpatory evidence; and inadequate lawyering by the defense. Professor Samuel Gross of Michigan has studied wrongful convictions in both capital and non-capital cases, and he has made a convincing case that erroneous convictions occur disproportionately in capital cases because of special circumstances that affect the investigation and prosecution of capital murder. These circumstances include pressure on the police to clear homicides, the absence of live witnesses in homicide cases, greater incentives for the real killers and others to offer perjured testimony, greater use of coercive or manipulative interrogation techniques, greater publicity and public outrage around capital trials, the "death qualification" of capital juries which makes such juries more likely to convict, greater willingness by defense counsel to compromise the guilt phase to avoid death during the sentencing phase, and the lessening of the perceived burden of proof because of the heinousness of the offense (Gross 1996).

In light of the well-known causes of wrongful convictions and the great public concern that exonerations generate, especially in capital cases, one might expect that this would be an area in which remedies should be relatively easy to formulate and achieve without much resistance in the judicial or legislative arenas. In fact, remedies have proven remarkably elusive, despite the clarity of the issues and degree of public sympathy. First, it did not prove easy for those who were eventually exonerated by DNA to get access to DNA evidence or to get relief even *after* the DNA evidence excluded them as the perpetrators of the crimes for which they were convicted. A recent study of the first 200 people exonerated by post-conviction DNA testing revealed that approximately half of them were refused access to DNA testing by law enforcement, often necessitating a court order. After being exonerated by DNA evidence, 41 of the 200 required a pardon, usually because they lacked any judicial forum for relief, and at least 12 who made it into a judicial forum were denied relief from the courts despite their favorable DNA evidence (Garrett 2008).

Second, these early difficulties cannot be written off as preliminary kinks that have been worked out of the system. While the vast majority of states have now passed legislation requiring greater preservation of and access to DNA evidence, the ABA Moratorium Implementation Project's recent assessment of eight death penalty states included an assessment of how well these states were complying with the ABA's recommendations regarding preservation of and access to biological evidence, and the provision of written procedures, training, and disciplinary procedures for investigative personnel. As in the context of the provision of defense counsel services, findings of complete non-compliance or only partial compliance with the ABA's recommendations were commonplace, while full compliance was rare. Similar resistance can be found to implementing reforms aimed at preventing some of the most common causes of wrongful conviction, such as videotaping police interrogations to prevent false confessions, changing photo identification procedures to avoid misidentification, subjecting jailhouse snitch testimony to greater pre-trial scrutiny, and performing external independent audits of crime labs. Resistance to providing adequate funding for capital defense services has already been documented above, and the failure of defense lawyers to challenge misidentifications, false confessions, and unreliable scientific evidence has been an important element in the generation of wrongful convictions.

This resistance has a variety of causes. Some law enforcement groups resist changes in investigative procedures with which they have been comfortable, such as interrogations and identification procedures. Moreover, they may oppose proposals for greater monitoring and disciplining of investigative personnel because they fear that misunderstandings may lead to misuse of such procedures. Some reforms are expensive, such as investing in the infrastructure for reliable preservation of biological material, while others promise to be too open-ended in the resources that they might require, such as improving defense counsel services.

Once again, as in the provision of adequate defense counsel services, there is not very much question about the general types of improvements that would be helpful in reducing wrongful convictions; rather, there appears to be an absence of political will to implement them (or to do so in an expeditious fashion). Moreover, a number of the factors that render capital prosecutions more prone to error are simply inherent in the nature of capital crimes and not obviously subject to amelioration by changing the capital justice process.

VII. Inadequate Enforcement of Federal Rights

The preceding sections discuss the limits of constitutional regulation of the death penalty to counter many of the institutional and structural challenges of the American death penalty. Some of the challenges are simply beyond the reach of courts and "law," such as the difficulties described above in guiding sentencer discretion and combating the influence of race in discretionary decision making; other institutional problems, such as the inadequate level of resources at capital trials and the failure to safeguard against wrongful convictions, require the involvement and leadership of political branches. The constitutional edifice that remains secures only limited benefits, and, regrettably, those limited benefits are frequently undermined by inadequate enforcement mechanisms, particularly the stringent limitations on the availability of federal habeas review of state capital convictions.

Over the past three decades, coinciding with the Court's inauguration of constitutional regulation of the death penalty, the availability of federal habeas review has been sharply curtailed. The initial limitations were Court-crafted, but they were followed by the most significant statutory revision of federal habeas in American history, the adoption in 1996 of the Anti-Terrorism and Effective Death Penalty Act (AEDPA). The net effect of these judicial and statutory refinements has been to dilute the limited constitutional protections that the Court has developed.

The case for strong federal habeas review of state criminal convictions is rooted in experience. During the early part of the twentieth century, state trial courts, especially in the South, often made little pretense of ensuring basic fairness, and state appellate courts appeared more than willing to ratify those truncated proceedings. After the infamous denial of habeas relief to Leo Frank (*Frank v. Mangum*, 237 U.S. 309), whose mob-dominated murder trial led to his death sentence despite his likely innocence, the Court granted habeas relief to five African Americans who had been convicted of murder and sentenced to death following a race riot in Arkansas (*Moore v. Dempsey*, 261 U.S. 86). The Arkansas case illustrated the potential for state hostility to federal rights: the five defendants were represented by a single lawyer who never consulted with them, and the 45-minute trial before an all-white jury, in front of an angry white mob, included no defense motions, witnesses, or defendant testimony. As the Court extended most of the constitutional criminal protections in the Bill of Rights to state criminal defendants in the 1950s and 1960s, the Court adjusted the scope of federal habeas as well. Perceived state court hostility to federal constitutional protections, especially those rights newly recognized and extended to state proceedings, led the Court to expand the federal habeas forum and to relax procedural barriers to federal review of federal claims.

Beginning in the 1970s, though, the availability of federal habeas review was significantly limited. Most importantly, the Court tightened the federal enforcement of defaults imposed in state court, so that the failure of state inmates to preserve federal claims within state court forecloses later consideration of those claims in federal court as well—with extremely narrow exceptions (*Wainwright v. Sykes*, 433 U.S. 72). Strict enforcement of state procedural default rules has significantly limited the effectiveness of the federal forum. Indeed, some courts have even applied stringent default rules against fundamental claims of excessive punishment—including the prohibition against executing persons with mental retardation. The enforcement of procedural defaults in this context means, as a practical matter, that the execution of all persons with mental retardation is not constitutionally prohibited; the prohibition extends only to those persons with mental retardation who have successfully navigated state procedural rules and preserved their claim for state or federal review. In this respect, limitations on the availability of federal habeas review promote misconceptions about prevailing capital practices; the public is likely to believe that the Court's decisions announcing absolute prohibitions—such as the *Atkins* exemption—effectively end the challenged executions, whereas the reality is more qualified and complicated.

The near-blanket prohibition against litigating claims defaulted in state proceedings encourages state courts to resolve claims on procedural grounds, and state courts have occasionally imposed defaults opportunistically to deny enforcement of the federal right. Moreover, strict enforcement of defaults in federal courts is particularly troublesome in cases involving claims defaulted on state post-conviction review (typically claims alleging ineffective assistance of counsel at trial or prosecutorial misconduct). As noted above, because state inmates have no constitutional right to counsel on state habeas, they have no right to *effective* assistance of counsel in that forum. Ordinarily, in cases involving attorney error at trial, the one avenue for reviving a procedural defaulted claim is for the inmate to demonstrate that he had been denied constitutionally adequate representation; but if the attorney error occurs on state habeas, the inmate is held to his attorney's mistakes and cannot seek relief under the Sixth Amendment. Given the inadequate resources and monitoring of state post-conviction counsel, it is not uncommon for death-sentenced inmates to forfeit substantial claims on state habeas, and the current regime of federal habeas review permanently forecloses consideration of such claims. The strict enforcement of procedural defaults ensures that many death-sentenced inmates will be executed, notwithstanding constitutional error in their cases.

The Court has also crafted limitations on the ability of inmates to benefit from "new" law on federal habeas (*Teague v. Lane*, 489 U.S. 288). The Court's non-retroactivity doctrine is ostensibly designed to prevent excessive dislocation whenever the Court identifies a new constitutional rule; its roots are traceable to the Warren Court era, when the Court's vast expansion of constitutional criminal procedure threatened to throw open the jailhouse doors. But in its more recent incarnation, the non-retroactivity doctrine has blocked retroactive application of many decisions far less dramatic or path-breaking than the Warren Court rulings that had given rise to the doctrine. The Supreme Court, as well as lower federal courts, have rejected as impermissibly "novel" claims that are barely distinguishable from previously decided cases. Apart from generating extraordinarily time-consuming and complex litigation, the non-retroactivity doctrine has thwarted the development and evolution of constitutional principles surrounding the administration of capital punishment. Federal habeas courts are discouraged from modestly extending or refining established precedents, so all constitutional realignment must come from the Supreme Court itself (on direct review of state criminal convictions). This institutional arrangement is a built-in headwind against adaptation to changing circumstances, and given the Eighth Amendment's focus on "evolving standards of decency," the non-retroactivity doctrine is at cross-purposes with the underlying substantive law of the death penalty.

The most significant reform of federal habeas is embodied in AEDPA's unprecedented limitations on the availability and scope of federal review. AEDPA imposes a strict statute of limitations for filing in federal court, stringent limitations on successive petitions, and restrictions on the availability of evidentiary hearings to develop facts relating to an inmate's underlying claims. These procedural barriers have proven formidable, and many inmates have lost their opportunity for federal review of their federal claims on these grounds. The most far-reaching of AEDPA's provisions, though, has been the elimination of de novo review for federal claims addressed on their merits in state court. In its place, AEDPA requires, as a condition for relief, that the state court adjudication "resulted in a decision that was contrary to, or involved an unreasonable application of, clearly established Federal law, as determined by the Supreme Court of the United States." (28 U.S.C. § 2254(d)(1). This statutory revision essentially requires federal courts to defer to wrong but "reasonable" decisions by state courts. It insulates from review all decisions but those that demonstrably flout established rules. In many areas of constitutional doctrine, this "reasonableness" standard of review amounts to "double deference" on federal habeas. Numerous constitutional doctrines, including the Court's standards for reviewing the effectiveness of counsel or a prosecutor's alleged discriminatory use of peremptory challenges, already require deferential review of the underlying conduct; state courts are not expected to grant relief unless trial counsel's performance wildly departed from established norms or a prosecutor's race-neutral explanation defies belief. When these cases get to federal habeas, AEDPA imposes an *additional* level of deference. For Sixth Amendment claims concerning the right to effective counsel, the question is not whether trial counsel's performance was unreasonably deficient—it is whether the state court's determination of reasonableness was *itself* unreasonable. This relaxation of federal review of state decision making essentially insulates all but the most egregious denials of rights in state court.

AEDPA's significance in curtailing federal enforcement of federal rights is reflected in the substantial decline in habeas relief since AEDPA's enactment (King 2007). It is also reflected in numerous federal habeas decisions that explicitly recognize that relief might be required under de novo review. For example, the Fifth Circuit Court of Appeals recently reversed a District Court grant of relief on a claim of impermissible judicial bias (*Buntion v. Quarterman*, 524 F.3d 664). The state court judge, at petitioner's capital trial, had indicated in open court that he was "doing God's work to see that [Petitioner] gets executed"; the judge also taped a postcard to the bench depicting the infamous "hanging judge" Roy Bean, altering it to include his own name and self-bestowed moniker, "The Law West of the Pedernales"; and the judge engaged in extensive ex parte contacts with the prosecution, threatened to remove petitioner's attorneys, and laughed out loud during the defense presentation of mitigating evidence at the punishment phase. The panel opinion recognized that such conduct might require relief under de novo review, but reversed the District Court because it could not find the state court's rejection of the bias claim unreasonable. AEDPA's mandated deference, which ratifies unconstitutionally obtained death sentences absent gross negligence on the part of the state court, removes the strongest incentive for state courts to toe the constitutional mark and allows executions to go forward despite acknowledged constitutional error.

Unlike several of the institutional and structural obstacles to the fair and accurate implementation of the death penalty described above, the scope of federal habeas is subject to legislative and judicial revision. But it seems unlikely that meaningful reform or restoration of federal habeas will be forthcoming. The politicization of criminal justice issues makes it extraordinarily difficult to expand review, and all of the pressures run in the other direction. In the absence of reform, though, the Court's minimalist constitutional regulation becomes virtually irrelevant; though enormous resources are expended in federal habeas, and the litigation results in delayed executions, most of the energies are directed toward overcoming procedural barriers rather than enforcing the underlying substantive rights of death-sentenced inmates (Steiker 1998). Despite the articulation of many constitutional protections, the enforcement is relegated to state courts, and at least some of those courts, particularly in active executing states, are notably unsympathetic to the Court's regulatory efforts.

The inadequacy of federal habeas review to enforce federal rights is lamentable in itself; but it also generates the same legitimation problem described above. Despite the Court's seeming regulation of the American death penalty via its declaration of substantive rights, the procedural mechanisms currently in place under-enforce those protections. Casual observers of the death penalty will likely regard the death sentences and executions that emerge from the current process to be the product of careful, extensive review by many courts. The reality, though, is much different. States have essentially the first and last opportunity to focus on the constitutional merits of inmates' claims. After that review, the many years of legal wrangling are primarily spent navigating the procedural maze and deferential forum that federal habeas has become. Thus, even if increased constitutional regulation of the death penalty could solve many of the deficiencies of the prevailing system, which appears unlikely, the inadequate mechanisms for enforcing that regulation would in any case undermine the effort.

CONCLUSION

The foregoing review of the unsuccessful efforts to constitutionally regulate the death penalty, the difficulties that continue to undermine its administration, and the structural and institutional obstacles to curing those ills presents a portrait of an ailing American death penalty, without much hope of a cure. The basic preconditions for an adequately administered regime of capital punishment do not currently exist in the United States and cannot reasonably be expected to be achieved. Recognition of this reality should strike a cautionary note for hopeful reformers, policy makers, and the citizenry at large.

NOTES

1. The following account of the prevailing system was produced as a report to the American Law Institute (ALI) as it considered whether to revisit the death penalty provisions of its influential Model Penal Code. We have condensed our report, in particular by removing passages tailored specifically to the ALI audience concerning the history and role of the Model Penal Code death penalty provisions, though the full report is available both on the ALI's web site and as a recently published special feature in the *Texas Law Review* (Steiker and Steiker 2010). We have also removed the last section of the report to the ALI focusing on the impact of prevailing death penalty practice on the much larger non-capital criminal justice system, as this topic is the focus of chapter 30, by Franklin Zimring and David Johnson, in this volume.

REFERENCES

Alston, Philip, 2008. Press Statement: United Nations Human Rights Council Special Rapporteur on Extrajudicial, Summary or Arbitrary Executions. June 30, 2008. Online. Available at: http://detentionwatchnetwork.org/node/2233.

Atkins v. Virginia, 536 U.S. 304 (2002).

Baldus, David C., et al. 1990. *Equal Justice and the Death Penalty: A Legal and Empirical Analysis.* Boston: Northeastern University Press.

Baldus, David, et al. 1998. "Race Discrimination and the Death Penalty in the Post-Furman Era: An Empirical and Legal Overview, with Recent Finding from Philadelphia." *Cornell Law Review* 83 (September): 1638–1770.

Baldus, David C., and George Woodworth. 2003. "Race Discrimination in the Administration of the Death Penalty: An Overview of the Empirical Evidence with Special Emphasis on the Post-1990 Research." *Criminal Law Bulletin* 39: 194–226.

Barkan, Steven E., and Steven F. Cohn. 1994. "Racial Prejudice and Support for the Death Penalty by Whites." *Journal of Research in Crime & Delinquency* 31: 202–209.

Bentele, Ursula, and William J. Bowers. 2001. "How Jurors Decide on Death: Guilt is Overwhelming: Aggravation Requires Death; and Mitigation is No Excuse." *Brooklyn Law Review* 66: 1011–1080.

Bienen, Leigh, et al. 1988. "The Reimposition of Capital Punishment in New Jersey: The Role of Prosecutorial Discretion." *Rutgers Law Review* 41: 27–372.

Blume, John, and Theodore Eisenberg. 1999. "Judicial Politics, Death Penalty Appeals, and Case Selection: An Empirical Study." *Southern California Law Review* 72 (January/ March): 465–503.

Blume, John H., et al. 2003. "Lessons from the Capital Jury Project." In *Beyond Repair? America's Death Penalty*, ed. Stephen Garvey, 167–. Durham: Duke University Press.

Bowers, William J. 1984. *Legal Homicide: Death as Punishment in America, 1864–1982.* Boston: Northeastern University Press.

Bowers, William J. 1995. "The Capital Jury Project: Rationale, Design, and Preview of Early Findings." *Indiana Law Journal* 70: 1043–1102.

Bowers, William J., et al. 2001. "Death Sentencing in Black and White: An Empirical
    Analysis of the Role of Jurors' Race and Jury Racial Composition." *University of
    Pennsylvania Journal of Constitutional Law* 3 (February): 171–275.
Brace, Paul, and Brent D. Boyea. 2008. "State Public Opinion, the Death Penalty, and the
    Practice of Electing Judges." *American Journal of Political Science* 52: 360–.
Bresler, Kenneth. 1994. "Seeking Justice, Seeking, Election, and Seeking the Death Penalty:
    The Ethics of Prosecutorial Candidates' Campaigning on Capital Convictions." *George-
    town Journal of Legal Ethics* 7: 941–958.
Brief Amicus Curiae of the NAACP Legal Defense and Education Fund, Inc., and the
    National Office for the Rights of the Indigent at 69, *McGautha v. California*, 402 U.S.
    183 (1971) (No. 71–203).
Bright, Stephen B. 1995. "Death and Denial: The Tolerance of Racial Discrimination in
    Infliction of the Death Penalty." *Santa Clara Law Review* 35: 433–484.
Bright, Stephen B., and Patrick J. Keenan. 1995. "Judges and the Politics of Death: Deciding
    Between the Bill of Rights and the Next Election in Capital Cases." *Boston University
    Law Review* 75 (May): 759–835.
Buntion v. Quarterman, 524 F.3d 664 (5th Cir. 2008).
Callins v. Collins, 510 U.S. 1141 (1994) (Blackmun, J., dissenting from denial of certiorari).
Coker v. Georgia, 433 U.S. 584 (1977).
Connecticut Commission on the Death Penalty, Study of the Imposition of the Death
    Penalty in Connecticut. 2003. Online. Available at: http://www.ct.gov/redcjs/lib/
    redcjs/documents/commission_on_the_death_penalty_final_report_2003.pdf.
Foglia, Wanda D., and William J. Bowers. 2006. "Shared Sentencing Responsibility: How
    Hybrid Statutes Exacerbate the Shortcomings of Capital Jury Decision-Making."
    Criminal Law Bulletin 42: 663–686.
Frank v. Magnum, 237 U.S. 309 (1915).
Furman v. Georgia, 408 U.S. 238 (1972).
Garrett, Brandon L. 2008. "Judging Innocence." *Columbia Law Review* 108 (January):
    55–141.
Godfrey v. Georgia, 446 U.S. 420 (1980).
Gregg v. Georgia, 428 U.S. 153 (1976).
Gross, Samuel R. 1996. "The Risks of Death: Why Erroneous Convictions Are Common in
    Capital Cases." *Buffalo Law Review* 44: 469–500.
Gross, Samuel R., and Barbara O'Brien. 2008. "Frequency and Predictors of False Convic-
    tion: Why We Know So Little, and New Data on Capital Cases." *Journal of Empirical
    Legal Studies* 5: 927–962.
Hall, Melinda Gann. 1992. "Electoral Politics and Strategic Voting in State Supreme
    Courts." *The Journal of Politics* 54: 427–446.
Haney, Craig. 1995. "Taking Capital Jurors Seriously." *Indiana Law Journal* 70: 1223–1232.
Haney, Craig. 1997. "Violence and the Capital Jury: Mechanisms of Moral Disengagement
    and the Impulse to Condemn to Death." *Stanford Law Review* 49 (July): 1447–1486.
Herrera v. Collins, 506 U.S. 390 (1993).
House v. Bell, 547 U.S. 518 (2006).
Huber, Gregory A., and Sanford C. Gordon. 2004. "Accountability and Coercion: Is Justice
    Blind When It Runs for Office?" *American Journal of Political Science* 48: 247–263.
Jacobs, David, et al. 2005. "Vigilantism, Current Racial Threat, and Death Sentences."
    American Sociological Review 70: 656–677.
Jeffries, John C., Jr. 1994. *Justice Lewis F. Powell, Jr.: A Biography*. Riverside, NJ: Scribner's.

King, Nancy, et al. 2007. *Habeas Litigation in U.S. District Courts*. Online. Available at: http://www.ncjrs.gov/pdffiles1/nij/grants/219558.pdf.

Klein, Richard. 1999. "The Constitutionalization of Ineffective Assistance of Counsel." *Maryland Law Review* 58: 1433–1479.

Liebman, James S., et al. 2000. "A Broken System: Error Rates in Capital Cases, 1973–95." Online. Available at: http://www2.law.columbia.edu/instructionalservices/liebman/.

Liebman, James S., et al. 2002. "A Broken System, Part II: Why There is So Much Error in Capital Cases and What Can Be Done about It." Online. Available at: http://www2.law.columbia.edu/brokensystem2/index2.html.

Lockett v. Ohio, 438 U.S. 586 (1978).

McCleskey v. Kemp, 481 U.S. 279 (1987).

McConville, Celestine Richards. 2003. "The Right to Effective Assistance of Capital Postconviction Counsel: Constitutional Implications of Statutory Grants of Capital Counsel." *Wisconsin Law Review* 2003: 31–113.

Moore v. Dempsey, 261 U.S. 86 (1923).

Penry v. Lynaugh, 492 U.S. 303 (1989).

Pokorak, Jeffrey. 1998. "Probing the Capital Prosecutor's Perspective: Race and Gender of the Discretionary Actors." *Cornell Law Review* 83 (September): 1811–1820.

Rapaport, Elizabeth. 2003. "Straight is the Gate: Capital Clemency in the United States from *Gregg* to *Atkins*." *New Mexico Law Review* 33: 349–379.

Risinger, Michael. 2007. "Innocents Convicted: An Empirically Justified Factual Wrongful Conviction Rate." *Journal of Criminal Law and Criminology* 97: 761–806.

Rompilla v. Beard, 545 U.S. 374 (2005).

Roper v. Simmons, 543 U.S. 551 (2005).

Rudolph v. Alabama, 375 U.S. 889 (1963).

Sandys, Marla, and Scott McClelland. 2003. "Stacking the Deck for Guilt and Death: The Failure of Death Qualification to Ensure Impartiality." In *America's Experiment with Capital Punishment*, 2nd ed., eds. James Acker et al. Durham: Carolina Academic Press.

Simon, Jonathan, and Christina Spaulding. 1999. "Tokens of Our Esteem: Aggravating Factors in the Era of Deregulated Death Penalties." In *The Killing State: Capital Punishment in Law, Politics, and Culture*, ed. Austin Sarat, 81–113. Oxford: Oxford University Press.

Steiker, Carol S. 2002. "Capital Punishment and American Exceptionalism." *Oregon Law Review* 81: 97–130.

Steiker, Carol S., and Jordan M. Steiker. 2010. "Special Feature: Part II: Report to the ALI Concerning Capital Punishment—Prepared at the Request of ALI Director Lance Liebman by Professor Carol S. Steiker and Jordan M. Steiker." *Texas Law Review* 89: 367–421.

Steiker, Carol S., and Jordan M. Steiker. 2010. "Special Feature: No More Tinkering: The American Law Institute and the Death Penalty Provisions of the Model Penal Code." *Texas Law Review* 89: 353–365.

Steiker, Jordan. 1998. "Restructuring Post-Conviction Review of Federal Constitutional Claims Raised by State Prisoners: Confronting the New Face of Excessive Proceduralism." *University of Chicago Legal Forum* 1998: 315–347.

Streb, Matthew, ed. 2007. *Running for Judge: The Rising Political, Financial and Legal Stakes of Judicial Elections*. New York: New York University Press.

Strickland v. Washington, 466 U.S. 668 (1984).

"Symposium: Toward a Model Death Penalty Code: The Massachusetts Governor's Council Report. Panel One—The Capital Crime." *Indiana Law Journal* 80: 35–46.

Teague v. Lane, 489 U.S. 288 (1989).

Turow, Scott. 2003. *Ultimate Punishment: A Lawyer's Reflections on Dealing with the Death Penalty*. New York: Farrar, Straus & Giroux.

U.S. General Accounting Office, Death Penalty Sentencing (February 1990).

United States v. Cronic, 466 U.S. 648 (1984).

Urban Institute. 2008. *The Cost of the Death Penalty in Maryland*. Online. Available at: http://www.urban.org/publications/411625.html.

Vito, Gennaro F. 2010. "The Racial Justice Act in Kentucky." *Northern Kentucky Law Review* 37: 273–285.

Wainwright v. Sykes, 433 U.S. 72 (1977).

Walton v. Arizona, 497 U.S. 639 (1990).

Wiggins v. Smith, 539 U.S. 510 (2003).

Williams Institute. 2001. "Case Study on State and County Costs Associated with Capital Adjudication in Arizona." Online. Available at: http://www.azag.gov/CCC/Attachment%20D%20-%20Data%20Set%20III.pdf

Williams v. Taylor, 529 U.S. 362 (2000).

Wolfgang, Marvin E. 1974. "Race Discrimination in the Death Sentence for Rape." In *Executions in America*, ed. William J. Bowers, 109–120. Lexington: Lexington Books.

Young, Robert L. 1991. "Race, Conceptions of Crime and Justice, and Support for the Death Penalty." *Social Psychology Quarterly* 54: 67–75.

Zimring, Franklin E. 2003. "Postscript: The Peculiar Present of American Capital Punishment." In *Beyond Repair? America's Death Penalty*, ed. Stephen P. Garvey, 212–230. Durham: Duke University Press.

Zimring, Franklin E. 2003. *The Contradictions of American Capital Punishment*. Oxford: Oxford University Press.

CHAPTER 30

THE DARK AT THE TOP OF THE STAIRS: FOUR DESTRUCTIVE INFLUENCES OF CAPITAL PUNISHMENT ON AMERICAN CRIMINAL JUSTICE

FRANKLIN E. ZIMRING AND DAVID T. JOHNSON

STATE execution is a tiny part of the nation's practice of criminal punishment but casts a long shadow over the principles and practice of criminal justice generally. At no time in the last century has the number of executions in the United States exceeded 4 percent of its criminal homicides, and the 98 persons executed in 1999 (the highest number in the last 60 years) were less than 1/100th of one percent of the persons in prison at the end of that year (BJS 2000, 2000a). In 2009, there were more than 14,000 homicides in the United States but only 106 death sentences, making the chance of any particular killer being caught, convicted, and sentenced to death "vanishingly small" (Garland 2010). Execution is not a major element of America's system of crime control, and yet this drastic punishment for a very few has not only generated huge attention and concern but has also (1) had a powerful negative influence on the substantive criminal law; (2) promoted the practice of using extreme penal sanctions as status rewards to crime victims and their families;

(3) provided moral camouflage for a penalty of life imprisonment without possibility of parole, which is almost as brutal as state killing; and (4) diverted legal and judicial resources from the scrutiny of other punishments and governmental practices in an era of mass imprisonment.

This chapter discusses these four latent impacts of attempts to revive and rationalize the death penalty in the United States. We focus on these effects not because we aim to move the debate about state killing away from its central and most visible harms. Indeed, in some ways the phenomena we discuss here are peripheral to the main political and human issues at the center of the campaign against capital punishment. But at the same time, our focus on the top end of the penalty scale—a frame that includes both death sentences and life without parole—enables us to explore how these most severe sanctions affect each other and also the penalties below them. This focus generates fresh insights about how the death penalty's ripple effects extend to tens or even hundreds of thousands of offenders beyond those formally charged with capital crimes.

I. The Hyperextension of Substantive Criminal Law

When first-year law students begin to sort through the doctrinal complexities of the criminal law of homicide—the mysterious differences between first degree and second degree murder, the zigs and zags that distinguish murder from various forms of voluntary manslaughter—they are visiting the results of a series of attempts of the substantive criminal law to avoid mandatory capital punishment. The division of murder into a first and second degree in Pennsylvania in 1794 was in order to create with the second degree offense a non-capital category. While the premeditation concept lacked both clarity and moral authority as a life and death legal distinction, the reason for the problematic substantive distinction between the first and second degrees could be justified as the avoidance of executions. The same motive can be found in the origins of manslaughter as a crime encompassing actions intended to cause death or great bodily harm (Kadish, Schulhofer, and Steiker 2007).

But the price of these avenues of mercy was a series of murky distinctions that lacked moral authority and intellectual rigor. The better reform proposals of the Model Penal Code called for the unification of murder into a single grade of crime (with an indeterminate prison sentence as its penalty). Manslaughter, too, was to be restricted to clearly defined emotional mitigations or unreasonable but genuine claims of self-defense (American Law Institute 1962). Whatever the benefits had been in avoiding execution, the lesson by the mid-twentieth century was that subdivisions of murder did not do a good job of bearing the enormous weight of a life versus death distinction. By the time that *McGautha v. California* and *Furman v. Georgia* were decided (in 1971 and 1972, respectively), there was no grade of homicide for which a death sentence was mandatory; instead, juries were free to choose between imprisonment and a death sentence for those convicted of first degree murder with unguided discretion. In *McGautha v. California* (402 U.S. 183), the Supreme Court's majority opinion approved jury discretion without standards because:

> To identify before the fact those characteristics of criminal homicides and their perpetrators which call for the death penalty, and to express these characteristics in language which can be fairly understood and applied by the sentencing authority, appear to be tasks which are beyond present human ability. (*McGautha v. California*)

As an appendix to the Court's opinion, Justice John Marshall Harlan inserted the Model Penal Code's death penalty provision, which proposed a framework of "aggravating circumstances," any one of which could support a death sentence if not offset by "mitigating circumstances" (American Law Institute 1962, § 210.6). The reference was not meant as a compliment, for Justice Harlan presumably saw the provision as evidence of the futility of efforts to produce rational standards that were beyond "human ability."

Only one year later, the Court reversed course.[1] By a 5–4 vote, the Justices struck down the model of unguided discretion for life-versus-death decisions in *Furman v. Georgia* (408 U.S. 238), effectively invalidating every capital punishment law in the country. This left the states with the need to create new legal standards for death eligibility that would survive constitutional review. What followed was a series of hasty legislative attempts in dozens of states to meet the new requirements, where the legislative goal was not really to distinguish levels of culpability for murder but, rather, to create a formula that would obtain the Supreme Court's approval for some form of death penalty.

By 1976, the Court gave its seal of approval in *Gregg v. Georgia* (428 U.S. 153) and *Proffitt v. Florida* (428 U.S. 242) to the same Model Penal Code framework of aggravating and mitigating circumstances that Justice Harlan had disapproved five years earlier,[2] as well as to a more mechanical and arbitrary legislative formula from Texas (*Jurek v. Texas,* 428 U.S. 262). A majority of seven of the nine Justices were now satisfied that the constitutional difficulty of unregulated discretion had been solved.

What the Court had demanded in *Furman v. Georgia* in 1972 was a set of principled penal standards to separate cases potentially deserving death from general run-of-the-mill murder cases, in essence a jurisprudence of capital desert. What the *Gregg, Jurek,* and *Proffitt* majorities settled for in 1976 was a list of aggravating and mitigating circumstances without any detailed justification. The formulas accepted from the states were a political success (because they gained the Court's approval) but a jurisprudential muddle. The single "aggravating factor" in these new statutes that generated more executions than all the others combined was that the killing took place during the commission of a forcible felony such as robbery, rape, or burglary (Turow 2004). But what is it about a killing during a robbery that makes the killer more blameworthy than an attacker who stabs or shoots his victim with the intent to kill but doesn't wish to take his wallet? The Model Penal Code commentary spends a single sentence on this, the rationale for the majority of modern executions, and gets it wrong. It alleges:

[Felony murder] concerns murder committed in connection with designated felonies, each of which involves the prospects of violence to the person. (ALI Comments on 210.6, 137)

The problem is that non-robbery aggravated assaults lead to victim deaths more than ten times as frequently per thousand acts as robberies, and the death rate from assaults is more than a thousand times higher than the Mode Penal Code's own studies found for burglary (Zimring 2005, 1404). So why not make malicious assault an aggravating violent intention that makes murder death eligible?

But at least the Model Penal Code provided a single sentence of justification for selecting this critical aggravating factor. The state legislative process usually manufactures or copies a list of aggravating factors with no justification or analysis. *Furman* requires juries to be guided by rules, but the rules that select candidates for state killings are not subject to any detailed scrutiny in the peculiar jurisprudence of the Eighth Amendment.

The result is an assortment of categorical aggravations—some dealing with the characteristics of the crime (e.g., felony, contract killing, or killing for monetary gain), some dealing with the number or types of victims (e.g., children, law enforcement officers, multiple victims), and some dealing with the status of the offender (killing by prisoner, or by a person previously convicted of murder). Detailed consideration of these factors is almost never evident in the legislative process, nor do constitutional courts question the rationality or moral content of most aggravations, and little legal scholarship has scrutinized the jurisprudence of aggravation.

One consequence of this hasty process has been that several characteristics of homicides do double or triple duty in the grading and punishment of killings. Some legal literature refers to what is called "the felony murder rule," usually describing a common law doctrine that allows the intention to commit a felony like robbery or burglary to substitute for the intention to seriously injure called "malice," which is the mental state at common law for murder. This constructive common law shortcut is notoriously unpopular with legal analysts (see ALI 1963; Wechsler and Michael 1938), but it is only the tip of the iceberg in modern death penalty states. In the typical state of California, there are currently *three* separate penal upgrades using felony status to escalate penal consequences. The common law rule makes the intent to rob or burgle the equivalent of malice. Then the "first degree" statutory felony murder rule makes all killings committed during a listed felony into the first degree crime (Cal. Pen. Code §189). And then the *capital* statute makes killing during listed felonies eligible for a death sentence (Cal. Pen. Code §190.2). Does this mean that a robber with no intent to injure his victim could be sentenced to death if an accident or a co-felon causes death? Probably. Did the California legislature (or those of 35 other states) consider or discuss this kind of issue?

What happened instead is that state legislative bodies searched around for lists of the usual categories for upgrading the penal stakes in homicide and thought nothing of using them redundantly. Just as the attempt to provide for mercy cluttered up the substantive law of homicide with concepts like premeditation and intentional but non-malicious killing, when the U.S. Supreme Court required standards for discriminating between death-eligible and other killings, it put more weight on the substantive criminal capacities of those who drafted penal codes in the United States.

The results are redundant, unexamined, and arbitrary. And the Byzantine complexity of all the ascending categories of homicide (manslaughter to murder to first-degree murder to capital murder) is almost a satire on the incoherence of formal legal conceptions of human fault. But the humor is muted by the fact that this apparatus has been the legal boundary between execution and imprisonment for a generation in the United States.

The metaphor we use for the distortive pressure put on the substantive law of homicide by the need to separate killings into capital and normal penal categories is the hyperextension of the criminal law. If you demand from a methodology of classification more than it is capable of producing, the resultant efforts will always be a failure and will frequently appear ludicrous. Asking the criminal law to coherently sort between killings that justify execution and those where protracted imprisonment will suffice is an impossible task in the twenty-first century.

Moreover, pushing the criminal law beyond its capacity may have a destructive impact on domains far removed from the capital section of the modern penal code. When judges encounter obviously vulnerable structures of distinguishing criminal offenses, one tempting alternative to the briar patch of continued judicial scrutiny is to construct doctrines of judicial non-involvement, to assume legislative competence precisely because one's suspicions are that most penal grading is arbitrary. In that way, the flimsiness of the substantive law separating capital from imprisonable murder may have helped create a broader immunity for distinctions of severity in criminal law to continue unchallenged. Once a presumption of non-scrutiny surrounds the rationale of capital statutes, why not extend it to other legislative penalty gradings?

This leaves only Eighth Amendment cruelty as a legal restriction on capital sentencing, and little or nothing in the law to scrutinize penal judgments about prison sentences. In this way, the notoriety of the hyperextended criminal law of capital punishment may have helped maintain a hands-off doctrine on legislative grading practices much broader than the death penalty.

There has been little in the way of scholarly or professional analysis of the standards for choosing between prison and death. The two state government commissions that reviewed current death penalty systems both thought the standards for death eligibility in all operating systems were grossly over-broad, and both commissions urged that a much smaller proportion of murders should be death eligible. Both commissions rejected involvement in a forcible felony as a foundation for a death sentence (Illinois Commission 2002; Massachusetts Commission 2004). But neither of them did a good job of constructing a positive theory of when the commission of a murder might justify or require execution as its criminal punishment.

So the major question looming over the practice of execution—when and why is it necessary?—is a blank page in the otherwise extensive discourse about the death penalty in the United States. And if the most extreme punishment in the system is not justified or scrutinized, then this failure at the very top of the penal enterprise impeaches the legitimacy of the entire system.

II. THE SYMBOLIC TRANSFORMATION TO HARSH PUNISHMENT AS A PRIVATE REWARD

In discussing the shifts in image and justification for capital punishment in the United States after 1979, Zimring has argued that:

> The major change in the announced purpose of capital punishment in the U.S. . . . was the transformation of capital trials and of executions into processes that were thought to serve the personal interests of those closely related to the victims of capital murder. The penalty phase of capital trials has become in many states an occasion for telling the jury its choice of sanction is a measure of the value (to the community) of the homicide victim's life. Years after the trial is completed, the execution becomes an occasion to seek psychological 'closure' for the family and friends of the victims . . . The novelty of the emphasis on these aspects of the death penalty after 1977 would be difficult to overstate. The radical degovernmentalization of the death penalty was without important precedent in American history. (Zimring 2003, 52)

The image of state killing as private closure served a number of public relations functions for capital punishment, including reducing the discomfort of citizens worried about the destructive power of the state. If killing is for the benefit of victims, it might seem less worrisome.

The structure of the rhetorical transformation of punishment into a personal benefit can be seen in the facts of the death penalty trial in *Payne v. Tennessee,* where the prosecutor suggested to the jury that a death penalty rather than a life sentence would help the young child of the murder victim when he grows up. "There is something you can do for Nicholas . . . He is going to want to know what happened. With your verdict, you will provide the answer" (*Payne v. Tennessee,* 501 U.S. at 815).[3]

This sort of status competition between offenders and victims is far from the concept of retribution or just deserts. It asks for punishment to vindicate the value of particular victims, and in doing so assumes that the more punishment that is administered, the better for the victims. There is no obvious limit or excess, no stopping point at which the jury may say "that's more vindication through punishment than little Nicholas will deserve when he grows up." So the search for punitive symbols as a status reward for victims leads ever upward; it is a one-way penal escalator (Simon and Spaulding 1999).

There is a further strategic advantage to justifying punitive measures as a status reward to victims—the extra harm to the offender need not be based on any other positive impact to the community. As long as the offender's additional suffering confers extra status on Nicholas and serves as evidence that his mother's loss saddened the community, who needs extra deterrence, incapacitation, or reform? The open-ended symbolic reward can be construed as all the reason the system needs for a wide variety of penal measures.

The legacy of this symbolic transformation is extensive in American criminal justice. In the past 15 years, there have been a number of settings in which non-capital penal measures have been reimagined as symbolic reaffirmations of the value of victims. First is the use of penal laws as personal memorials or commemorations. Since 1993, 50 states have enacted what they call Megan's Laws, which the federal government has followed up with the Jacob Wetterling Act and the Adam Walsh Act. The part of the Adam Walsh legislation dealing with juvenile offenders has been dedicated as "Amy's Law" in honor of a living victim and punishment advocate. California voters enacted "Jessica's Law" in 2006, providing compulsory geo-tracking of released sex offenders with no apparent supervisory rationale. But, of course, if anything that hurts offenders should make crime victims feel better, who needs more utilitarian justification?

When punishments are used as symbolic rewards, there are two separate effects. One is inflation in the quantity of punishment. If 5 years is good, 10 years must be better, and 15 years would be better still. As long as punishment is a primarily symbolic currency, not even the sky is the limit. That is the central difference between a status competition between victim and offender—with no upward limits—and conventional retribution where penal proportionality is a limiting principle. Twenty-five years to life for a petty theft "third strike" almost certainly offends requirements of proportional justice, but if the point of "third strike" sentences is to make the families of crime victims feel better, then there is no such upper limit to symbolic affirmation.

A second consequence of penal measures having primarily hierarchical and symbolic meanings is that punishments tend to proliferate in kind. Penal confinement certainly remains a mainstay of American punishment, but both the variety of prison terms and the proliferation of penal add-ons are major developments in crime policy after 1990. If every distinction is a new status reward, why not create special forms of imprisonment—"two strikes" sentences, "three strikes" sentences, life without possibility of parole—where each new rung on the penal ladder creates another distinction that is a status reward? Similarly, the registration, residence prohibitions, public notices of address, and drugs called "chemical castration" provide steps up the punishment ladder that are independent of imprisonment for sex offenders and can function as status rewards for sex crime victims imagined as beneficiaries. Thus, the multiplication of forms of punishment can be seen as another by-product of making penal measures into status rewards.

Cause or Consequence?

Are all of these Amy's Laws and "three strikes" constructions really the bastard off-spring of victim impact statements in the capital punishment system that grew in the 1970s and 1980s? One alternative possibility is that the proliferation of punishments as status rewards (à la "three strikes" and Megan's Laws) *and* the degovernmentalization of state killings were both produced by a changing politics of punishment, so that the death penalty experience did not encourage the non-lethal proliferation of symbolic punishments (see Zimring, Hawkins, and Kamin 2001, 151–180). This view would regard the degovernmentalized death penalty and the Adam Walsh Act as siblings rather than as parent and child.

The question is a close one. The invention of victim impact focus and closure in the death penalty did precede most of the other penal proliferations, but not by much, and it is certainly possible that both are effects of an unspecified prior cause. But another argument for seeing other penal forms as the legacy of the death penalty is that the concentration of these new personal and symbolic measures in the United States is much greater than elsewhere. This is circumstantial evidence that this country's adventure with the symbolic transformation of the death penalty played a causal role in the proliferation of other victim status rewards. But here again, perhaps the same cultural forces that relaunched and transformed the American death penalty would have produced Megan's Laws as well, even without the peculiar developments in capital punishment. The ambiguity as to the ancestry of this species of American exceptionalism cannot be conclusively resolved.

Regarding some aspects of American penal developments, however, the causal responsibility of capital punishment for non-capital penal innovations is beyond controversy, and one of those, the metastasis of life without the possibility of parole, is the subject of the next section.

III. The Problematics of Life Without Parole (LWOP)

The inclusion of life terms of imprisonment without possibility of parole in the previous section's list of penal innovations may at first glance seem like a logical error. Imprisonment has been a part of punishment for centuries, and life terms are also a long-standing feature of imprisonment for crimes of the highest seriousness. To the extent that parole release became widespread in the United States, one might regard that as the innovation and a Life Without Parole (LWOP) system (where adopted) as merely a return to previous practice. But even then, the life term can always be modified by pardon, commutation, or clemency from the executive branch of government.

While there is technical merit in some of the legal points in the last paragraph, it is a dreadfully inaccurate portrait of the recent history of life without parole. Life without possibility of parole as a distinctive sentencing frame found in legislation was a product of the 1970s. In states that were forced to create a separate category of murder by the Supreme Court's death penalty discussions in 1976, the alternative to a death sentence that also had to be part of the scheme was usually defined as Life Without Possibility of Parole (see e.g., Georgia, Alabama, and California). In all but four states and the federal system, the life-without-parole sentence was a new subcategory of life terms, which did not replace the old life terms but rather was what the previous section called an "add-on" to conventional life terms, a step up the penal ladder from ordinary life terms. What are the motivations for creating this new step? In some jurisdictions, LWOP sanctions were welcomed or encouraged by death penalty abolitionists who sought an alternative to the capital sentence that might be attractive to juries at the sentencing stage of capital trials (Liptak 2005; Hood and Hoyle 2008). And in all cases, LWOP provides a symbolically distinct status for victim families, a step up the punishment ladder from ordinary life terms that will certify the importance of the victim's loss. LWOP also reassures those who distrust government actors and fear that parole will be granted later in a prison sentence. Finally, the LWOP innovation in the 1980s and 1990s provided an enhanced penalty for the symbolic sweepstakes that was of particular importance in murder trials.

Life without possibility of parole becomes a consolation prize in many death penalty states when a capital defendant is convicted of the top grade of the murder offense but does not receive a death sentence (Cal. Pen. Code §190.2). In some states without a death penalty, the special version of life known as LWOP provides a distinct kind of life term to establish the special severity of the crime. This is the evident purpose in states such as Massachusetts, Rhode Island, Maine, Michigan, and Iowa.

Putting aside distrust of government, there is no penal theory to distinguish life without parole from life with parole chances in the 37 states of the United States that have both kinds of life sentence in effect. It certainly is not based on individual predictions of dangerousness, because LWOP is usually mandatory if the defendant has been convicted of the top grade of murder. As discussed in the first section of this chapter, the singling out of felony or multiple killings for retributive reasons is also not an easy matter.

What is clear is that the death penalty is the dominant partner in all places where LWOP became an add-on punishment rather than a new version of all life terms. In non–death penalty states, it is the red meat to symbolize the victim's special status in the most serious murders. Where capital murder charges do not produce death sentences, the LWOP outcome is frequently the mandatory minimum sentence available if the defendant pleads guilty to the charges or is convicted at trial.

Mercy or Penal Inflation?

While the separate LWOP sentence might have originally been considered an alternative to death sentences, the LWOP population in the United States now far outnumbers those under sentence of death, and is growing swiftly. A 2009 report shows an expansion of LWOP prisoners from 12,453 in 1993 to 41,095 in 2008, for an increase of 230 percent (Nellis and King 2009, 10). Table 30.1 presents estimates from an earlier Sentencing Project report (2004) of the number and rate per 100,000 population of LWOP sentences as of 2004 for the seven states with the highest number of LWOPs.

The first finding from table 30.1 is that the large number of LWOP sentences in the United States does not result from non–death penalty states adopting this innovation. Six of the top seven users in 2004 were states with capital punishment, including Louisiana, the runaway leader in LWOPs per 100,000 population, with a rate 2.5 times that of the next highest state (Florida). The second feature of table 30.1 is the tremendous variation in rates of usage. Louisiana (with a death penalty) has an LWOP rate ten times that of retentionist California and eight times higher than abolitionist Michigan. One reason that states like Louisiana and Pennsylvania have such large LWOP populations is that they entirely displaced the standard life with parole structure. But even states that retained standard life terms, like Florida and Alabama, have high LWOP rates, 50 times or more their cumulative execution rates. And California, which restricts LWOP to capital murder convicts who are not sentenced to death, has an LWOP total that is five times its death row population.

So, in the great majority of cases, the LWOP sentence is an expansion of punishment rather than a reduction or an alternative to some standard life term. The LWOP sentence is frequently provided for top grades of murder in non–death penalty states and was thought to be necessary in New Jersey when the legislature abolished the death penalty in 2007. Some analysts contend that an LWOP alternative reduces the rate of death verdicts when states provide both options (Hood and Hoyle 2008, 390), but there is little evidence that the large number of LWOP sentences in death states like Louisiana and Alabama has produced fewer death sentences in either location. While there may be cases in which a jury selects LWOP as a parole-free alternative when they might have rejected a standard life term in favor

Table 30.1. Top American States in Number of LWOP Prisoners and Rate of LWOP Prisoners per 100,000 population in 2004.

	Number of LWOP	Rate per 100,000 population in 2004
Florida	4,478	35
Pennsylvania	3,865	32
Louisiana	3,822	88
California	2,984	8.2
Michigan	2,629	26
Alabama	1,334	29
Illinois	1,291	10.3

Sources: LWOP estimates are from The Sentencing Project's The Meaning of "Life": Long Prison Sentences in Context (2004); population figures are from the U.S. Bureau of the Census, American Community Survey, three-year average population estimates for 2005–2006 and 2007.

of a death sentence, there is no evidence of systematic decline in death sentencing rates in LWOP states (*Harvard Law Review* 2006; Appleton and Grover 2007; Hood and Hoyle 2008, 391). A more direct approach to the problem of jury mistrust of parole would be judicial instructions that address the tendency of jurors to underestimate the amount of time that offenders will serve if they are not sentenced to death (Sundby 2005, 184).

One setting where LWOP seems like shipping coals to Newcastle is California, where voter-passed initiatives and politically sensitive governors make the release through parole of *any* first-degree murderer a very rare and visible event. There were nevertheless 3,000 LWOP terms in place by 2004 (see table 30.1). The demand for LWOP in this environment strongly suggests that the symbolic distinctiveness of the penalty remains attractive even when its practical impact in delaying release from prison is near zero.

There are few penal measures in modern history in which the gap between public perception and actual impact is as great as for LWOP. Here is a mandatory minimum punishment that lasts a lifetime but carries a reputation as an act of mercy. Used now in tens of thousands of cases, it has seldom been subject to serious scrutiny in academic literature or to skepticism in legislative discourse. Nothing combines high fiscal expense with low preventive potential quite as much as a 79-year-old inmate with limited physical mobility and high medical bills who cannot be paroled. So why is the law that leads to this outcome immune from criticism?

It is capital punishment that provides LWOP with moral camouflage as the lesser of evils in American criminal justice. Death penalty opponents delight when survey research shows the public closely divided between the death penalty and LWOP, and they think that this capacity to compete with capital punishment reflects the operational significance of LWOP in legislation and in the judicial system. But only a tiny fraction of the many thousand LWOPs are really death penalty substitutes. And while life without parole is sometimes useful as a rhetorical substitute for death in efforts to legislate abolition (as it was in New Jersey in 2007 and the Philippines in 2006), it should be used carefully (Johnson and Zimring 2009, 103). It is essential that any use of LWOP be restricted to the most serious punishment available for the highest grade of murder and never as the only punishment available for any grade of crime.

The causes of the proliferation of LWOP and its remedy deserve far more attention from legal scholars and social scientists than they have received. Any cluster of penal sanctions that includes state killing will divert attention from everything in the cluster except execution, and that is why so little attention has been focused on LWOP. Executions provide moral camouflage for the next most severe sanction—an emotional innocuousness and innocence by comparison—because state killing makes everything else appear merciful and mild. This insight also raises the question of whether the American focus on capital punishment has desensitized public concern about the huge growth of imprisonment in the generation after 1975, a question that some scholars answer in the affirmative (Gottschalk 2006).

The big gap between how most people think life without parole works and its actual operation suggests one reasonable strategy for law reform. The best approach may be to propose changes in law and practice that would make LWOP in practice conform to its image as a sanction for only the most extreme cases. The tactic would be to replace 120 death sentences a year in the United States with 160 or 200 LWOPs, rather than with 3000! This would require routine administrative review of most long and life sentences, a sharply restricted category of LWOP cases for the most culpably guilty of the highest grade of murder, where any prospect of release would denigrate the seriousness of the crime committed. But the distance between such a system and a current jurisprudence in which the LWOP sanction takes out the garbage left in the legal and administrative death penalty process must be measured in light years.

In the best of all possible American legal systems, there would be no LWOP or any need for it. In the near term, however, the best we can expect is to rationalize and reduce the scope of the penalty by making it live up to its advertised image.

There is one other reason that the death penalty has diverted attention from extreme penal measures like LWOP. The amount of resources and attention that can be devoted to preserving liberty and limiting the exercise of state power is limited. The need to spend time, care, and effort on limiting the use of capital punishment diverts these scarce resources from being used to examine other governmental threats. In this way, the need to struggle against the death penalty has limited the capacity to scrutinize and protect against other abuses of state power, in many more arenas than life without possibility of parole (Hood and Hoyle 2008, 383). The impact of the revival of the death penalty on the priorities and limits of the guardians of justice is the final effect that we consider.

IV. Diversion of Legal and Judicial Resources from the Scrutiny of other Uses of State Power

The legal and material resources devoted to maintaining the death penalty in the United States play a prominent role in discussions of the economic cost of capital punishment, as they should. Capital punishment systems in the United States are always more expensive than punishment systems without death as a sanction because "super due process" is required in the former but not in the latter and because lawyers are a lot more expensive than prison guards (Bohm 2003, 592).

But the *opportunity costs* of the legal concentration on capital cases may be more important than the monetary expenditures. In any developed nation, there are only a limited number of lawyers with the political values and special skills required to defend against governmental excess in the prohibition of conduct and the punishment of crime. The death penalty is, and should be, a magnet for those attorneys concerned with excessive governmental power of this type. But when most of these fine lawyers are concentrating on the 3,500 capital defendants on death row in the United States, the result is a shortage of resources to monitor state authority in a nation with more than 2 million persons behind bars. In the generation since the death penalty was reintroduced in the United States, imprisonment has expanded more than sevenfold and the jail population has tripled. The opportunity costs of putting so many resources into the death penalty system for human rights and procedural justice in the rest of the criminal justice system are uncounted but no doubt substantial (Steiker and Steiker 2006).

There may also be a drain on judicial and administrative actors who become preoccupied with due process in the death penalty system (Dickson 2006; Gillette 2006; Goldberger 2006; Hawkins 2006; Hintze 2006; Leyte-Vidal and Silverman 2006; Walker 2006; Kozinski 2004). Since the number of resources devoted to quality control in criminal justice is limited, the opportunity cost of super due process in the capital system is less scrutiny on other parts of the criminal justice system. The docket of the U.S. Supreme Court reflects the diversionary impact of the death penalty. From 1976 to 1996, death penalty cases flooded the Court from the state systems, but only the tiniest trickle of cases dealt with the rules and discretion that generated explosive growth in American imprisonment.

In order to investigate this phenomenon, we counted criminal cases granted full review by the Supreme Court in 1995 and 2005. In 1995, the Court heard 12 criminal cases (out of 82 granted full review), and 5 of the 12 were capital. In 2005, the Court heard 9 criminal cases, and 4 were capital.[4] So nearly half of all criminal cases (9 of 21) reviewed by the Supreme Court during this period have been death penalty matters, while the ratio of imprisonment to execution in the United States is more than 15,000 to 1, and the ratio of imprisonment to death sentence is more than 500 to 1. There is an acute shortage of resources and concern to scrutinize the vast expansion of state punishment in the United States.

The opportunity costs of capital punishment are also evident at the state level. In California, home of the largest death row in America,[5] the safeguards in place to protect the wrongly convicted are especially small for prisoners with long or life sentences. Defendants facing a death sentence get two court-appointed trial lawyers in addition to funds for investigators and expert witnesses. If they are convicted, the state pays for multiple appeals in the California Supreme Court and in the federal courts. Lifers, by contrast, are entitled to a single lawyer at trial and another one for a state court appeal, with almost no chance of review by the state Supreme Court. After that, they are on their own. The state also pays to reinvestigate cases that result in a death sentence, but not botched cases that lead to life imprisonment. So capital cases get a decade or more of appellate scrutiny, while lifer cases get only a year or two. And according to the U.S. Supreme Court, "actual innocence" is reason to reverse a conviction only if someone is on death row—not if the sentence is life. Thus, an innocent Californian convicted of murder may be better off being sentenced to death than to life, for a miscarried capital case will at least get a long look.

Lawyers find death cases more appealing, too. Jeff Adachi, San Francisco's public defender, once tried to arrange pro bono legal assistance for a prisoner named John Tennison. Several large law firms initially expressed interest, but when they learned that Tennison was only a lifer, they refused to get involved (Martin 2004).

It is difficult to measure the aggregate damage inflicted on the institutions and objects of American criminal justice because the best human resources in the legal profession were diverted to the struggle against capital punishment. But missing protections against governmental excess may be the most enduring legacy of the American resurgence of capital punishment, a burden that could continue long after the executioner has been retired.

NOTES

1. Technically the cases presented different constitutional claims. The challenge in *McGautha* was based on the Due Process Clause, while *Furman* was premised on the Cruel and Unusual Punishment Clause.
2. Justice Harlan retired in 1971, and was replaced by Justice William Rehnquist. Also new to the Court after the *Furman* decision were Justices Louis Powell and John Paul Stevens.
3. In its *Payne* decision of 1991, the Supreme Court held that the Eighth Amendment does not bar the admission of victim impact evidence during the penalty phase of a capital trial.
4. Search conducted by Christopher Felker at Boalt Hall School of Law.
5. As of May 2009, more than 20 percent of America's death row convicts (678 out of 3297) were incarcerated in California (Death Penalty Information Center 2009).

REFERENCES

American Law Institute. 1962. *Model Penal Code, Complete Statutory Text*. Philadelphia, PA: American Law Institute.

American Law Institute. 1980. *Model Penal Code and Commentaries (Parts I and II)*. Philadelphia, PA: American Law Institute.

Appleton, Catherine, and Bent Grover. 2007. "The Pros and Cons of Life Without Parole." *British Journal of Criminology* 47: 597–615.

Bureau of Justice Statistics. 2000. *Capital Punishment 1999* (NCJ 184795). December, pp. 1–16.

Bohm, Robert M. 2003. "The Economic Costs of Capital Punishment: Past, Present, and Future." In *America's Experiment with Capital Punishment: Reflections on the Past, Present, and Future of the Ultimate Penal Sanction*, eds. James R. Acker, Robert M. Bohm, and Charles S. Lanier, 573–594. Durham, NC: Carolina Academic Press.

Death Penalty Information Center. 2009. Available at: www.deathpenaltyinfo.org.

Dickson, Brent E. 2006. "Effects of Capital Punishment on the Justice System: Reflections of a State Supreme Court Justice." *Judicature* 89(5): 278–281.

Furman v. Georgia, 408 U.S. 238.

Garland, David. 2010. "Five Myths about the Death Penalty." *The Washington Post*. July 18.

Gillette, Dane R. 2006. "Defending Death Penalty Judgments." *Judicature* 89(5): 262–265.

Goldberger, Benjamin A. 2006. "The Impacts of Capital Cases on a Federal Trial Court." *Judicature* 89(5): 274–277.

Gottschalk, Marie. 2006. *The Prison and the Gallows: The Politics of Mass Incarceration in America*. New York: Cambridge University Press.

Gregg v. Georgia, 428 U.S. 153.

Harvard Law Review. 2006. "A Matter of Life and Death: The Effect of Life-Without-Parole on Capital Punishment." *Harvard Law Review* 119: 1838–1854.

Hawkins, Bill. 2006. "Capital Punishment and the Administration of Justice: A Trial Prosecutor's Perspective." *Judicature* 89(5): 258–261.

Hintze, Michael. 2006. "Tinkering with the Machinery of Death: Capital Punishment's Toll on the American Judiciary." *Judicature* 89(5): 254–257.

Hood, Roger, and Carolyn Hoyle. 2008. *The Death Penalty: A Worldwide Perspective*. New York: Oxford University Press.

Illinois Governor's Commission Report on Capital Punishment. 2002. Available at: http://www.idoc.state.il.us/ccp/index.html (accessed May 13, 2009).

Johnson, David T., and Franklin E. Zimring. 2009. *The Next Frontier: National Development, Political Change, and the Death Penalty in Asia*. New York: Oxford University Press.

Jurek v. Texas, 428 U.S. 262.

Kadish, Sanford H., Stephen J. Schulhofer, and Carol S. Steiker. 2007. *Criminal Law and Its Processes*. 7th ed. New York: Aspen Publishers.

Kozinski, Alex. 2004. "Tinkering with Death." In *Debating the Death Penalty: Should America Have Capital Punishment? The Experts on Both Sides Make Their Best Case*, eds. Hugo Bedau and Paul Cassell, 1–14. New York: Oxford University Press.

Leyte-Vidal, Henry, and Scott J. Silverman. 2006. "Living with the Death Penalty." *Judicature* 89(5): 270–273.

Liptak, Adam. 2005, October 2. "To More Inmates, Life Term Means Dying Behind Bars." *New York Times*.

Martin, Nina. 2004. "Innocence Lost." *San Francisco Magazine*. November. Available at: http://www.deathpenalty.org/downloads/SFMag.pdf (accessed May 27, 2009).

Massachusetts Governor's Council on Capital Punishment. 2004. Available at: http://www.lawlib.state.ma.us/docs/5-3-04Governorsreportcapitalpunishment.pdf (accessed May 13, 2009).

McGautha v. California, 402 U.S. 183.

Model Penal Code. Guide to Model Penal Code Records. Available at: http://www.law.upenn.edu/bll/archives/ali/collections/ali.04.005.html (accessed on May 13, 2009).

Nellis, Ashley, and Ryan S. King. 2009. *No Exit: The Expanding Use of Life Sentences in America*. Washington, DC: The Sentencing Project.

Payne v. Tennessee, 501 U.S. 808.

Proffitt v. Florida, 428 U.S. 242.

Sentencing Project, The. 2004. "The Meaning of 'Life': Long Prison Sentences in Context." Marc Mauer, Ryan S. King, and Malcolm C. Young. May: 1–37. Available at: http://www.sentencingproject.org/Admin%5CDocuments%5Cpublications%5Cinc_meaningoflife.pdf (accessed May 13, 2009).

Simon, Jonathan, and Christina Spaulding. 1999. "Tokens of Our Esteem: Aggravating Factors in the Era of Deregulated Death Penalties." In *The Killing State: Capital Punishment in Law, Politics, and Culture,* ed. Austin Sarat, 81–113. New York: Oxford University Press.

Steiker, Carol, and Jordan Steiker. 2006. "The Shadow of Death: The Effect of Capital Punishment on American Criminal Law and Policy." *Judicature* 89(5): 250–253.

Sundby, Scott E. 2005. *A Life and Death Decision: A Jury Weighs the Death Penalty.* New York: Palgrave Macmillan.

Turow, Scott. 2004. *Ultimate Punishment: A Lawyer's Reflections on Dealing with the Death Penalty.* New York: Picador.

U.S. Bureau of the Census, American Community Survey, 2005–2006 and 2007. Available at: http://www.census.gov/acs/www.

Walker, R. Neal. 2006. "How the Malfunctioning Death Penalty Challenges the Criminal Justice System." *Judicature* 89(5): 265–268.

Wechsler, Herbert, and Jerome Michael. 1938. "A Rationale of the Law of Homicide." *Columbia Law Review* 37: 701, 1261.

Zimring, Franklin E. 2003. *The Contradictions of American Capital Punishment.* New York: Oxford University Press.

Zimring, Franklin E. 2005. "The Unexamined Death Penalty: Capital Punishment and the Reform of the Model Penal Code." *Columbia Law Review* 105(4): 1396–1415.

Zimring, Franklin E., Gordon Hawkins, and Sam Kamin. 2001. *Punishment and Democracy: Three Strikes and You're Out in California.* New York: Oxford University Press.

INDEX

10-20-Life Law (Florida), 184–185
100-to-1 law, 57, 59, 66, 79n4
18-to-1 rule, 66, 79n4

academic and vocational programs: adult-based education (ABE) and, 504; cognitive theories and, 499–500; distance learning and, 505–506; economic theories and, 500–502; education level among incarcerated population and, 493, 495, 502; effectiveness of, 493, 502–504; executive cognitive functioning (ECF) and, 500; general equivalency diploma (GED), 496, 504; history of, 494–495; impact on employment and, 500–501; implementation challenges and, 498; life skills and, 497, 506–508; mitigation of prison conditions and, 500; Pell Grants and, 505; postsecondary education (PSE) and, 505–506; recidivism and, 502, 504–506, 513; rehabilitation, 494–495; research challenges and, 513–514; variations in, 497–498; vocational education and, 508–509
Adachi, Jeff, 750
Adam Walsh Child Protection, 88, 550, 743, 744
Adoption and Safe Families Act, 88
Africa, 218–219, 432, 435, 454
African Commission on Human and People's Rights, 435, 454
African-Americans: arrest rates and, 55–56, 58–59, 64, 66–69, 71–72, 77; conviction rates and, 72–73; drug enforcement and, 9, 56–58, 63–68, 71–73, 77; drug trafficking and, 69–72, 74; drug usage rates and, 58, 67–69; incarceration rates and, 5–6, 28, 53–55, 57–62, 64, 67, 72, 74–76, 85, 88–89, 93; racial profiling and, 9, 56–58, 63, 66–67, 72–74, 76–77; racialized animus against, 39; sentencing and, 55–58, 61–63, 65–66, 73–74; violent crime and, 55, 58–59, 64, 65. *See also* racial disparities in punishment
Alabama, 118, 301, 397, 717, 723, 725–726, 745–746
Alaska, 264, 301
Alito, Samuel, 86
"All of Us or None," 675
Almendarez-Torres v. United States, 325
American Bar Association (ABA), 83–84, 86, 95, 141, 157, 306, 441, 725–726, 728, 735
American Correctional Association (ACA), 394–395, 409–410, 419–421, 436, 439, 444
American Jail Association (AJA), 395, 410

Amity (California) Therapeutic Community prison study, 470, 474
Amy's Law, 743–744
Andrews, Donald, 379–381
Anti-Terrorism and Effective Death Penalty Act (AEDPA), 715, 729, 731
Apprendi v. New Jersey, 203–204, 323–325, 330n3
Argentina, 436, 452
Arizona, 31, 45, 46n4, 47n7, 286, 291n19, 356nn2–3, 397, 403, 631, 725
Arkansas, 114, 118, 285, 631, 729
Arpaio, Joe, 403
ASEAN Inter-Governmental Commission on Human Rights, 454
Assertive Community Treatment (ACT), 526–527, 529
Association of State Correctional Administrators (ASCA), 419–420
Atkins v. Virginia, 171n54, 354, 708, 730
Attica prison rebellion, 436, 438
Auburn system, 393, 395, 496
Auglaize County (Ohio) Transition Program (A.C.T.), 401–402
Augustus, John, 364–365, 368
Australia: incarceration rates in, 41; parole and, 629; prison conditions in, 433; problem-solving courts in, 150, 155–156, 158–160, 164; restorative justice and: 220, 227, 229–231, 233–234, 238–239; victim impact statements and, 104, 110–113

Baldus study, 711–712, 718, 720–721
Barefoot v. Estelle, 201, 206
Barker, Vanessa, 30–31
Bauder v. Department of Corrections, 86
Bearden v. Georgia, 320
Beccaria, Cesare, 139, 141, 220, 342
Becker, Gary, 26
Bedford Hills Correctional Facility (New York), 421
Belgium, 33, 34, 37
Bentham, Jeremy, 139, 141, 395
Between Prison and Probation, 365, 368
Bird, Rose, 717
Blackmun, Harry, 17, 710, 719
Blackstone, William, 139, 141
Blakely v. Washington, 306, 312n7, 324, 325
Bonta, James, 377, 379–381
Bordenkircher v. Hayes, 320
Brady v. Maryland, 256
Brennan, William, 17